D1732924

WITHDRAWN
UTSA Libraries

Dictionary of

ATHEISM, SKEPTICISM, & HUMANISM

"With over 1,600 entries—everything from Atheists in Foxholes to the Anthropic Principle, from Blik to Brights, from Chaos to Children of God—Bill Cooke's *Dictionary of Atheism, Skepticism, and Humanism* is an indispensable research tool for all nonbelievers and scholars in the field of religion. . . .Writing in the tradition of Voltaire's *Philosophical Dictionary* and Ambrose Bierce's *Devil's Dictionary*, Cooke displays an impressive grasp of the field."

Michael Martin
Professor of Philosophy Emeritus, Boston University;
Author of *Atheism: A Philosophical Justification* (1990)

"This book will be a very valuable addition to the literature dealing with atheism, skepticism, and humanism. . . . There is hardly any doubt that it will give readers a new and very useful tool for studying these issues. . . .Bill Cooke is a man of great learning, and he has studied a great number of subjects. As opposed to most learned people, he is able to write in an easily accessible style. Everyone who finds time to read and study this book will increase her own knowledge and enhance her own perspective. Cooke's book promises to be a unique source book written by a true freethinker in the best sense of the word."

Finngeir Hiorth
Lecturer of Philosophy Emeritus,
University of Oslo (Norway)

Dictionary of

ATHEISM, SKEPTICISM, & HUMANISM

BILL COOKE

Prometheus Books

59 John Glenn Drive
Amherst, New York 14228–2197

Published 2006 by Prometheus Books

Dictionary of Atheism, Skepticism, and Humanism. Copyright © 2006 by Bill Cooke. All rights reserved. No part of this publication may be reproduced, stored in a retrieval system, or transmitted in any form or by any means, digital, electronic, mechanical, photocopying, recording, or otherwise, or conveyed via the Internet or a Web site without prior written permission of the publisher, except in the case of brief quotations embodied in critical articles and reviews.

Inquiries should be addressed to
Prometheus Books
59 John Glenn Drive
Amherst, New York 14228–2197
VOICE: 716–691–0133, ext. 207
FAX: 716–564–2711
WWW.PROMETHEUSBOOKS.COM

09 08 07 06 05   5 4 3 2 1

Library of Congress Cataloging-in-Publication Data

Cooke, Bill, 1956–
     Dictionary of atheism, skepticism, and humanism / Bill Cooke.
        p. cm.
     ISBN 1–59102–299–1 (hardcover : alk. paper)
     1. Free thought—Dictionaries. I. Title.
BL2705.C66 2005
211'.8'03—dc22

                                                            2005006910

Printed in the United States of America on acid-free paper

for Bobbie

CONTENTS

AUTHOR'S NOTE

Bill Cooke is Senior Lecturer at the School of Visual Arts, University of Auckland at Manukau (New Zealand). He is also Visiting Assistant Professor of Philosophy at the University of Buffalo, a Fellow of the Committee for the Scientific Examination of Religion, and International Director of the Center for Inquiry–*Transnational*.

His previous works include *Heathen in Godzone: Seventy Years of Rationalism in New Zealand* (NZARH, 1998), *A Rebel to His Last Breath: Joseph McCabe and Rationalism* (Prometheus, 2001), and *The Gathering of Infidels: A Hundred Years of the Rationalist Press Association* (Prometheus, 2004). His email is bcooke@centerforinquiry.net.

ACKNOWLEDGMENTS

The original idea for this book came from a chance comment in 2001 by the veteran British atheist campaigner Barbara Smoker, who praised Joseph McCabe's *Rationalist Encyclopedia* as a very useful work and added that it was a shame it had never been updated. I owe the opportunity of beginning this project to a recommendation from the Norwegian philosopher Finngeir Hiorth. Professor Hiorth's many works of popular atheism and humanism have provided a model for how this work should be approached.

I am also grateful for the superb library at the Center for Inquiry, based in Amherst, New York. Several people have assisted me with various entries. The only entry I did not write was supplied by Ben Radford, who wrote the entry on **humanism in films**. Joe Nickell alerted my attention to **expectant attention**, and Kevin Christopher alerted me to, and lent me material on, the splendid Epicurean idea of the **Four-Part Cure**. Norm Allen put me on to some important African American humanist thinkers, and Ibn Warraq looked over most of the entries related to Islam.

But by far the most important person to acknowledge is my wife, Bobbie Douglas Cooke, who has been a source of inspiration in all conceivable capacities. Anybody who has written a book knows that the debt they owe their partner is too great to repay.

PREFACE

Why This Book?

If the twentieth century taught us anything, it taught us to be wary of anyone bearing absolutes. But, as the twenty-first century begins, so many people in the Western world have taken this distrust of absolutes to heart and have become skeptical of any sort of truth-claim, leaving the door open for nihilism. Postmodernist scholars have done their best to encourage this development by delighting in problematizing everything into a confusing tangle. Among those hungry for some sort of program by which they can live their lives, many have turned to the available array of ethnic rivalries or religious fundamentalisms. These have the advantage of offering easy solutions and catchy slogans, but at the high price of renouncing intellectual honesty and empathy for other points of view.

So where does this leave the rest of us? There are millions of conscientious people around the world who are suspicious of absolutisms and labels, and wary of slogans, but who are uncertain how to proceed from there. This book is for them, for the people who are curious about the world, and who feel that it is important to live decently but don't have the time to read all the academic journals or books they see in bookshops.

The title notwithstanding, this book is not only for atheists, skeptics, and humanists. It is quite likely that the era of labels is drawing to a close. This book is for freethinkers in the broadest sense of the word; people who like to think for themselves, and not according to preplanned routes set by others. And by no means are all atheists, skeptics, and humanists freethinkers in this broad sense.

This dictionary is not designed to be a handbook against religion. I have deliberately refrained from a large number of entries about religion. This book is not about the falsity of religion—it is about the possibility of a morally engaged, intellectually full, and laughter-filled life without it. Just as it is possible to be religious and be a good person, so is it also possible to be without any religious belief and be a good person. It is not the intention of this dictionary to "convert" people to atheism, skepticism, or humanism. Rather, the goal is to give strength and sustenance to the millions of morally responsible people who are bemused by the moral vacuum of the so-called postmodern and globalized world we live in.

Another important goal of this work is to make the case for real dialogue between people who are religious and those who are not. As this book attempts to show, freethinkers of every persuasion have valuable things to say about morality, society, politics, and a host of other issues. They have a long and honorable history, and it is no longer justifiable that they be excluded from the public discourse, as has happened for so long. It is a central contention of this work that, though religious and nonreligious people differ on many subjects, they also have many points of common interest and future dialogue can revolve around these points.

This work is in the tradition of Voltaire's *Philosophical Dictionary*. Voltaire's masterpiece was a vehicle for his breadth of vision over a wide range of subjects. Another book that influenced this one is Joseph McCabe's *Rationalist Encyclopedia*, which was published in 1948. Less directly influential, but no less admired, is Ambrose Bierce's *Devil's Dictionary* (1911) and John Ralston Saul's *Doubter's Companion* (1994). Saul's work is subtitled "A Dictionary of Aggressive Common Sense," which strikes me as an admirable idea.

HOW THE DICTIONARY IS ORGANIZED

Don't expect to find everything imaginable in this work. As the product of one person's curiosity, it is bound to be limited in some ways, many of which I am probably unaware. This dictionary is intended to act as a complement to the forthcoming *New Encyclopedia of Unbelief*, edited by Tom Flynn, and the *Encyclopedia of the Paranormal* (1996), edited by Gordon Stein. These two works, as well as the original *Encyclopedia of Unbelief* (1985), also edited by Gordon Stein, are the most authoritative sources of in-depth articles regarding the world of atheism, skepticism, and humanism.

This dictionary is the product of thirty years of eclectic reading. What I have tried to do is to bring much of that reading together to provide a quick thumbnail sketch on some phrase, idea, topic, or person. When relevant there will be a suggested title for further reading at the end of an entry. In virtually all cases the entry will not have come exclusively from the work cited as further reading, and in some cases the suggestion for further reading may say something different than my entry. And in the interests of keeping things simple, I have dropped the usual references of publisher, place of publication, and, in most cases, the date, as these details differ from country to country—I only list the core details of the author's name and book title.

I have also tried to weave cross-references through each entry. Each word highlighted in **bold** alerts you to another entry that is relevant to the one you are reading. In the interests of readability some entries might be slightly altered, for instance, **social scientists** might be in bold, but the actual title is **social sciences**.

This dictionary features these broad types of entries:

Ideas and concepts: they are included because they give some extra dimension to understanding our world in a naturalistic way. Some might be well-known notions like **God**, while others might be more obscure ideas like **Disseminated Primatemaia**. The scientific ideas are included on the basis of being the indispensable minimum for an educated view of the world. Ideas we already know about will focus more on the atheist/skeptical/humanist understanding of them. Ideas that may well be new to us will be explained more straightforwardly.

People: there are a myriad of reference works about people, so why bother even attempting yet another who's who? First, I have tried to include freethinkers from a broader range of cultures than has usually been the case in reference works of this sort. It is wrong to see freethought as a solely Western phenomenon. And the other reason is that so many reference books make no mention of a person's beliefs *unless* they happen to be religious beliefs. And not infrequently, religious beliefs are ascribed or implied to people who were in fact quite irreligious. This is an insult, assuming as it does that one cannot be good *and* nonreligious. Like many religious people, I believe that our beliefs have an important role in our lives. It is no coincidence that the people mentioned in this book are brave, intelligent, passionate, or distinguished in some way while also being nonreligious or highly unorthodox in their religious beliefs. The people included here are only a tiny selection of those who have led distinguished lives and who have been freethinking in some way or other. But the point is made: you can be good, brave, honest, and sincere without being religious. It shouldn't need to be said, but there you are.

Events and organizations: as with the rationale for including people, the events and organizations included here by no means exhaust the potential candidates. The ones included are those that I have come across in my reading or travels, or have been ignored elsewhere. And they all have some relevance to the broad community of freethinkers around the world.

Buzzwords: these are interesting illustrations of the never-ending evolution in our language. Examples include words like **metrosexual** and **quote whore**. Once again, the buzzwords included here by no means exhaust the range. They have been chosen because they have some bearing on the atheist/skeptical/humanist worldview.

For those who want the short version, there are a few key entries which you shouldn't go past. These entries serve as a foundation upon which most of the other entries rest, and so I would encourage readers to acquaint themselves with them.

With respect to **atheism**, the key entries would include **anthropocentric conceit**; **atheism, ethical implications of**; **cosmic modesty**; and **transcendental temptation**. For **skepticism**, the key entries are **critical common-sensism**; **critical receptiveness**; **fallibilism**; **inquiry, tools of**; **reliabilism**; and **skepticism, core principles of**. And for **humanism**, the key entries are **agathonism**; **cosmic perspective**; **eupraxsophy**; **good life, the**; **humanism, foundations of**; **humanist virtues**; **moral truisms shared by us all**; **paideia**; **value meaning**; and **wide reflective equilibrium**.

A

'ABDUH, MUHAMMAD (1849–1905).
Egyptian scholar who founded an influential
school of thought within Islam. After
spending 1883 to 1889 in exile, 'Abduh
became more influential, lecturing at Al-
Azhar University in Cairo and, after 1899,
serving as Grand Mufti of Egypt.

'Abduh was concerned with encouraging the
reform and revitalization of Islam, and he sought
to do this by applying a freer approach to
reading and interpreting Muslim sources. Rather
than strict rote learning of secondary texts,
'Abduh favored the more open-minded strands
of Muslim thinking: the *qiyas* (or argument by
analogy), the *istihsan* (the principle of desir-
ability), and the *al-masalih al-mursala* (the general interests of the community). Muhammad
'Abduh was a disciple of **Jamal al-Din al-
Afghani**. 'Abduh was subjected to bitter criticism from traditionalists, who accused him of
straying from the path of orthodoxy. However,
his legacy will be important in the future for the
development of an Islamic reformation.

**ABOLITIONISTS AND SUBSTITU-
TIONISTS**. A distinction among humanists
pointed out by the English sociologist Colin
Campbell. The two types are distinguished
largely by their attitudes toward **religion**.

Abolitionists are more generally hostile
toward religion and regard it as a false system
of thought and behavior which needs to be
combated. Their priority for the humanist
movement, therefore, is to expose the errors
of religion by scriptural criticism, historical
and philosophical analysis, and to juxtapose
supernaturalist thinking with naturalist
thought. As a general rule, abolitionists have
been brought up in religious families or were
themselves religious before realizing the
error of their ways.

Substitutionists have a more sanguine attitude toward religion, seeing it as something
endemic in **human nature** or, at the very
least, something that will not be abolished by
reason. They are less hostile to religion as an
idea, and prefer the idea of peaceful coexistence. Indeed, they are often keen to build in
the humanist movement some sort of substi-
tute for the religious tradition they have left
behind. With this in mind, substitutionists
often prefer to develop a ritual or rite-of-pas-
sage element into the movement. They are
also more inclinded to develop social ties
within the movement, sensing that these are
the drawcards for many religious people,
rather than the beliefs.

It has been a long-standing challenge for
the humanist movement to accommodate
these two quite different approaches to how it
should operate and what its priorities should
be. The most successful humanist organizations have been those that have found room
for both tendencies to work together.

Further reading: Colin Campbell, *Toward
a Sociology of Irreligion.*

ABORTION. The medical process whereby a
woman procures a miscarriage of her fetus.
The decision to have an abortion is never an
easy one and is usually made because the pregnancy is the product of a rape or will endanger
the life of the woman, the fetus is carrying
debilitating deformities, or the mother is in no
position to give the child an adequate
upbringing. It is the choice of the woman carrying the child to have an abortion. Medical
professionals can offer relevant advice, but the
decision remains with the woman.

The best way to reduce the number of
abortions is to ensure that people, especially
teenagers on the threshold of becoming sexually active, are provided intelligent, balanced
sex education and are familiar with various
forms of available contraception. The preference of religious conservatives for **abstinence** *and* a ban on abortion is completely

unrealistic. It suggests an underlying hostility to sexual freedom, particularly for women.

ABRAHAM. Legendary figure who is claimed by each of the **monotheist** religions as their own. "Abraham" is variously translated as "father of many peoples" or "father of a multitude." To the extent that Abraham has any genuine historicity, he is probably a dramatization of a **pagan** tribal patriarch who led his people from Mesopotamia toward the Mediterranean around the end of the third millennium BCE. Abraham's likely god was the Canaanite deity El. He is identified in the **Hebrew scriptures** as one of the "gods of our fathers," further attesting to the pagan and polytheist origins of the Hebrew people before they adopted **Yahweh** and united him with their existing deities.

Abraham is described in different ways by different creators of the Hebrew scriptures, according to the needs of the author. "The Yahwist," or "J," whose works were designed to strengthen the claims of Judaea as the legitimate successor of the Solomonic kingdom, writes of Abraham as the "father of all nations." "J" tells the story of Abraham being visited by Yahweh and two angels. The "Elohist," or "E," by contrast, alters the emphasis by portraying Abraham as a model of faith. "E" represents the relationship between Abraham and **God** as more formal, less cozy, and less anthropomorphic. This had the effect of undermining "J's" claims of Judaea enjoying a straight line of legitimacy running back to Abraham. Later again, the "Priest," or "P," who was writing in a context of exile, stressed Abraham's role as guarantor of Israel's survival.

Abraham also has a significant role in Islam, being credited, among other things, with the reconstruction of the Kaaba in Mecca. Part of the ritual the pilgrim to Mecca must undertake is to visit the Maqam Ibrahim, where Abraham is believed to have prayed to the **Kaaba**. Latterly, Abraham is used as an exemplar of **faith** in God, by virtue of his barren wife giving birth to their son, Isaac, and Abraham's later willingness to gratify God's command to slaughter Isaac as a test of his faith.

Robin Lane Fox summarized the situation. "Historians no longer believe the stories of Abraham as if they were history: like Aeneas or Heracles, Abraham is a figure of legend."

Further reading: Werner Schmidt, *The Faith of the Old Testament*; and Robin Lane Fox, *The Unauthorized Version: Truth and Fiction in the Bible*.

ABSOLUTISM. The belief that all things have one, and only one, answer—usually one's own. Absolutism works from the notion of an absolute, which is not a coherent idea. The American philosopher John Ryder defines an absolute as that which is unrelated and unconditional to anything at all. In this sense, "absolute" should not be confused with "objective." See the entry on **Objectivity**.

In politics, absolutism requires a dictatorship led by a *führer* or an ayatollah. In philosophy, the absolute is satisfied with simply being given a capital letter. In moral debate, absolutism favors **command moralities** and almost always requires those who disagree to be seen not merely as *wrong* but as *wicked*. This is because absolutism does not have any way to admit that those who disagree can do so in good faith. By definition, **monotheist** religions have an absolutist strain in them. See the entries on **demonizing the opposition** and **theopathic condition**.

ABSTINENCE. The word currently fashionable among religious conservatives for celibacy, and usually applied to teenagers or those not yet married. If teenagers genuinely want to remain sexually abstemious prior to marriage, best of luck to them. But when abstinence becomes a pervading morality with social penalties attached to ending this condition, then it becomes dangerous and liable to encourage hypocrisy. What is more, abstinence is often preached more than it is practiced. A study by the US National Institutes of Health surveyed 15,000 teenagers between twelve and eighteen and found that fully 88 percent of those who took abstinence pledges did in fact have **sex** before **marriage**. And these teenagers were less likely to use a condom than sexually active teenagers who had not taken an abstinence pledge. A smaller survey by the University of Northern Kentucky found that 61 percent of its college undergraduates who had taken abstinence pledges had broken them, and 55 percent of those who had claimed to have kept the pledge had engaged in oral sex, following the lead of President Clinton in considering this not to be a sexual act.

Abstinence is certainly effective as a means to avoiding sexually transmitted diseases, but safe sex—that is, sex while using contraceptives (condoms in particular)—works just as well. Like it or not, *Homo sapiens* are highly sexed creatures. We have evolved with highly charged sex drives. The more sensible approach, and the approach most in keeping with our actual biological makeup, is to ensure teenagers are educated about sex and can make sensible and safe decisions. Wrapping the whole subject up in a mysterious cocoon is of no help to anybody. There is no evidence that abstinence has any other positive function. See the entry on **abortion**.

ABSURDITY. In the aftermath of giving up the **anthropocentric conceit** of seeing the universe as programmed for our pleasure, it is understandable to see an element of absurdity in all things. In the absence of some easy-fit divine plan, we are made fully aware of the essential contingency of things. Some of the best writings on this theme were from the French-Algerian playwright and author **Albert Camus**, in particular, *The Myth of Sisyphus* (1942) and *The Rebel* (1951).

The Swedish secularist philosopher **Ingemar Hedenius** developed his philosophy of absurdism. For Hedenius, absurdism had two factors:

- in the world of humans, anything can happen, without regard to its awfulness, meanness of spirit, or downright stupidity; and

- absurd things happen all the time, and always have.

Everything from the rise of National Socialism to petty academic intrigues tended to confirm Hedenius's conviction in the ubiquity of the absurd. It also underscored his essentially melancholic view of life.

Jean-Paul Sartre's character Roquentin in *Nausea* (1938) also explores the grimmer side of absurdity. But recognizing the absurdity of human pretensions is also a source of **humor** as it is of pessimism or austere philosophy. Then the absurdity of life has been given humorous interpretations by comedians like Spike Milligan, **Richard Adams**, and **Monty Python's Flying Circus**. In fact it is the ability of absurdity to express itself in the form of humor that saves it from lapsing into despair or nihilism.

Further reading: Finngeir Hiorth, *Secularism in Sweden*.

ACADEMY. School of higher learning established by the philosopher **Plato** in about 387 BCE, and which serves as a prototype of the modern university. It was called the Academy in honor of Academus, a Greek hero. Plato bought some land at a spot sacred to Academus and established the Academy there. Significantly, there was an altar to **Prometheus** in the groves of the Academy and a sculpture of Prometheus and Hephaestus, another deity connected to fire, nearby.

The Academy was designed to train the sons of the wealthy in the ways of sound government and philosophy. It offered a wide curriculum, but was particularly strong in the areas of **mathematics** and astronomy, reflecting the influence **Pythagoras** had on Plato's thought. Inscribed above the gates to the Academy was the sign "No one ignorant of geometry admitted here." The Academy seemed to have discussed rather than lectured, although they may have given occasional lectures for the general public.

Among its more famous students included Zeno of Citium (333–262 BCE), the founder of **Stoicism**. In line with Greek thinking about women, Plato thought women even less capable of rational thought than men, but there was no absolute ban on women studying at the Academy. We know of **Axiothea** and Lasthenia who studied there, for instance.

Inevitably, the Academy underwent changes after Plato's death. Plato chose his follower, and nephew, Speusippis to succeed him. For the rest of its long career, the Academy swung between emphasizing either Plato's more dogmatic doctrines or his more questioning approach that often comes through in his dialogues. Notable leaders of this approach were Arcesilaus (315–240 BCE, approx.) who ended the period of recycling Platonist dogma by returning to an open approach to questioning more in keeping with **Socrates**. Arcesilaus led a potent critique of the **Stoics**, whose arguments improved as a result of this pressure. Overall, Arcesilaus shaped the preferences of the Academy for the next two hundred years.

Arcesilaus's most notable successor was **Carneades**, who continued and improved on Arcesilaus's brand of **skepticism**. Carneades's successor was Philo of Larissa (160–83 BCE, approx.), who was Cicero's teacher. One of Carneades's most brilliant pupils was Clitomachus, who wrote a large amount, although none of his writings have survived. Cicero also heard Antiochus of Ascalon, head of the Academy between 86 and 68 BCE, try to proclaim the essential commonality between Platonism, the teachings of **Aristotle**, and the Stoics.

The last two centuries of the Academy were undistinguished in terms of academic achievement, it being dominated by **Neoplatonism**. But if its academic standing declined, the Academy grew wealthy by endowments and bequests, and enjoyed enormous prestige across the ancient world. It had long ceased to determine intellectual developments but continued to keep alive the pre-Christian philosophy of Greece. This was not good enough for Justinian however, who enforced a general ban on non-Christians holding public teaching appointments. "It is right," Justinian wrote, "that those who do not worship God correctly should be deprived of worldly advantages too." As part of this ban, the Academy was closed in 529 CE and its property seized by the government. The head of the Academy, Damascius, a Plato scholar, fled to Persia. The career of the Academy, which had lasted almost 900 years, had come to an end. Many scholars see the closing of the Academy as an appropriate symbolic date of when the **Dark Ages** began. See the entry on **Intolerance, Principle of**.

But the memory of the Academy did not die. During the **Renaissance** a series of Academies were set up in conscious imitation of Plato's original. The most important of them was set up by Cosimo de Medici (1389–1464) in Florence. These Academies were important centers of heterodox thinking and of reacquainting people with the glories of the ancient world.

ACCUMULATION OF DESIGN, PRINCIPLE OF THE. A principle coined by **Daniel C. Dennett**, which helps explain the existence of design in organisms that evolve. **Chaos** is best characterized as the absence of any design. **Evolution** is the slow accumulation by trial and error of designs that help the organism survive and reproduce. The design of any particular organism is a copy and, in some cases, an improvement of earlier designs. This, of course, in no way postulates that there must be a grand designer at the beginning of the process. See the entry on **design, argument to**.

Further reading: Daniel C. Dennett, *Darwin's Dangerous Idea*.

ACTION PAINTING. An idea conceived by the American art critic Harold Rosenberg (1906–1978) which envisaged the work of art not so much as a finished representation but as an act of expression. Rosenberg's notion of action painting came from his experience of the works of his lifelong friend Willem de Kooning (1904–1997), and Jackson Pollock

(1912–1956) whose works were strongly gestural. De Kooning was influenced by the **existentialism** of **Jean-Paul Sartre**, and wanted his art to be expressions of his **authentic** personality as an artist. In this way, the finished result was less important than the process of doing the painting, and the painting becomes a biographical record of the painter.

Less helpfully, Action Painting is sometimes used as the term for the entire genre of Abstract Expressionist painting, of which De Kooning and Pollock were prominent members. This tends to confuse the issue, as some of the other painters in this movement were not action painters in the sense understood here.

ACTIVIST FRAME. Term coined by **Paul Kurtz** to denote his preferred mode of living, and which he contrasted favorably with the various ideals of passivity or quiescence as a manner of living. Kurtz envisaged the activist frame as that where individuals are responsible for shaping their own future, rather than having it shaped for them. Overcoming odds, perseverance, and determination are the values Kurtz has in mind as central to the activist frame. See the entry on **eupraxsophy**.

Further reading: Paul Kurtz, *Exuberance: A Philosophy of Happiness*.

ADAMICS. A term coined by the English novelist and critic **Marghanita Laski** and articulated in her Conway Memorial Lecture to the **South Place Ethical Society** in 1967 and again in her book *Everyday Ecstasy* (1980).

Adamics, in Laski's terms, relates to the felt need among many people to romanticize an earlier way of life and wish to return to it. The drive to join communes is an adamic drive. Adamic society would be characterized as "composed of simple people linked together in brotherly love, void of all forms of competitive striving. Laws, institutions, boundaries of property have been abrogated; the state has withered away." In short, a utopia.

The adamic drive may have a religious or secular, left- or right-wing orientation. Whatever the orientation, these sorts of attempts to put the ideals of the past into daily practice are bound to fail, Laski argued. Indeed, Laski said that it is the duty of secularists to beware of the adamic temptation. This wariness is what she meant by the secular responsibility.

Further reading: Marghanita Laski, *The Secular Responsibility* (the Conway Memorial Lecture for 1967).

ADAMS, DOUGLAS (1952–2001). Brilliant and witty writer and thinker. Born in Cambridge and educated in Essex, Adams studied English at St. John's College, Cambridge. Adams became widely known after his *Hitchhiker's Guide to the Galaxy*, which began life as a radio comedy series in 1978, was published the following year. The instant success of the book was described by Adams as like having an orgasm without the foreplay. A few years later the book was televised by the BBC. Adams had a long association with the BBC, being highly valued as a producer of radio comedy.

The *Hitchhiker's Guide to the Galaxy* was published in 1979 and sold more than 14 million copies worldwide. Other books followed, notwithstanding a notorious problem with writers' block. Later books included *The Restaurant at the End of the Universe* (1982); *Life, the Universe and Everything* (1982); *So Long and Thanks For All the Fish* (1984); and *The Long, Dark Tea-time of the Soul* (1988).

Adams moved to the United States in 1999, so as to facilitate the production of a film version of *Hitchhiker's Guide to the Galaxy*, which he was still involved with when he died of a heart attack at forty-nine at his gym in Santa Barbara in 2001.

An accomplished guitarist, Adams occasionally played alongside his friends in **Pink Floyd**. Adams was also highly valued for his sophisticated understanding of **science**, evidence of which abounds throughout his books. Adams described himself as a radical atheist. See the entries on **humor** and **Monty Python's Flying Circus**.

AD HOMINEM ARGUMENT. A very common and completely unacceptable form of argument which involves criticizing one's opponent rather than the argument one's opponent is putting forward. Strictly speaking, the character of the person has no bearing on the quality of the argument being put forward. See the entry on **demonizing the opposition**.

ADVERSE CONSEQUENCES, ARGUMENT FROM. Fallacious method of argument. It works along the lines of "things will get worse if you don't agree with me." The dishonest subtext of this argument is "people who disagree with me are in favor of the adverse consequences I am outlining." **Plato** was among the best known exponents of this practice.

AESCHYLUS. See **GREEK PLAYWRIGHTS**.

AESTHETICS. A branch of philosophy concerned with theorizing about art and why art matters. In this sense aesthetics is not art criticism, nor is it art history. The word was first used in the 1750s by Alexander Baumgarten (1714–1762) in an unfinished treatise called *Aesthetica*. However, the study of beauty goes back to the ancient philosophers **Plato** and **Aristotle**. As an academic discipline within formal philosophy, aesthetics began with **Immanuel Kant**.

Aesthetics has fallen into disfavor among many proponents of the **visual arts** (as opposed to fine arts) by virtue of its longstanding association with beauty and aesthetic value. As has frequently been observed, a **piece of art** may have tremendous value and merit while not being beautiful. Aesthetics has had this difficult career because there are no known objective standards by which aesthetic qualities can be judged or compared. It is now generally acknowledged that trying to construct an objective methodology of aesthetics, supposedly unrelated to one's preferences, training and **life-stance**, is futile. But in no way does

this mean that the appreciation of, and discussion about, art is not worthwhile.

Further reading: David Novitz, *The Boundaries of Art*.

AFFIRMATION OF HUMANISM FOR KIDS. This is a variation of the **Affirmation of Humanism** which was recast by Lynne H. Schultz, with specific reference to children. The Affirmation of Humanism for Kids originally came in a bulky sixteen-point program. Later it was reduced to this shorter, more concise, nine-point program. The Affirmation of Humanism for Kids goes like this:

(1) Be the best person you can be.
(2) Hurting people is wrong, and helping people is good.
(3) Be nice and fair to everyone, including people who are different from you.
(4) Be kind and careful with animals.
(5) Take care of the Earth.
(6) The arts are important for sharing how we feel and for developing talents.
(7) Get all the facts. Test claims against reality, don't let others tell you what is true, and don't jump to conclusions.
(8) Science is the best way to find out about stuff and it makes our world better.
(9) Everything that exists follows natural laws and is not magical.

See also the entry on **humanist family values**.

Further reading: "Affirmation of Humanism for Kids," *Secular Humanist Bulletin* 17, no. 1 (Spring 2001): 5.

AFFLUENZA. A term defined as "a painful, contagious, socially transmitted condition of overload, debt, anxiety, and waste resulting from the dogged pursuit of more." The term was taken up by John de Graaf, David Wann, and Thomas Naylor for an influential documentary series which ran on American public television in 1997, and which became a book in 2001. Needless to say, this is a condition confined to the wealthy societies of the West and to the United States in particular. No other country on the planet is as geared to consumerism as is the United States. Consumer spending accounts for two-thirds of all American economic activity. However, the contagion is spreading like wildfire through India and China, and many environmentalists warn that the planet simply couldn't cope with American levels of waste and consumerism being extended to those countries as well.

The idea of affluenza is new, but warnings of the dangers of **narcissistic** and self-defeating consumerism are not. John Kenneth Galbraith wrote *The Affluent Society* in 1958 and the popular writer Vance Packard wrote *The Waste Makers* and *The Hidden Persuaders* in the 1960s. But not enough notice has been taken of these earlier warnings, and no harm is done by repeating the message.

The religious right is in the paradoxical position of decrying the baleful effects of consumerism, while being staunch advocates of limited government and the private enterprise system that relies on the continuance of the affliction. See the entry on **satisficers and maximizers**. And neither does recognition of the dangers of affluenza mean one has to retreat into **fundamentalism** or **New Age** flummery. See the entries on **voluntary simplicity** and **genuine progress indicator**.

Further reading: John de Graaf, David Wann, and Thomas Naylor, *Affluenza: The All-Consuming Epidemic*.

AFGHANI, JAMAL AL-DIN AL- (1838/9–1897). Muslim scholar, possibly of Persian origin, who was active in Egypt and Turkey. He studied in Teheran, then at Najaf in Iraq. Afghani revived the tradition within Islamic scholarship of independent reasoning and interpretation (*ijtihad*) as opposed to ritualistic rote learning of commentaries. Afghani also supported the **Mu'tazilite** doctrine of freedom over the current orthodoxy of fatalism. A sincerely religious man, al-Afghani was concerned to unite Islam once

more and to modernize it in the face of the Western challenge.

Al-Afghani's modernism met with a lot of criticism from traditionalists, some of whom questioned his ethnic origin and religious affiliation. Nevertheless, al-Afghani was very influential among the intelligentsia of his day. His most important follower was **Muhammad 'Abduh**. If there is going to be the much hoped-for Muslim Reformation, then al-Afghani is going to be an important figure. Muslim scholars will be able to look back on his work and use it as a springboard for more work on the liberalization of Islam.

AFRICAN AMERICANS FOR HUMANISM. An organization formed on August 31, 1989, to provide assistance for African Americans seeking liberation from religion. African Americans for Humanism (AAH) has been led by Norm Allen Jr. since its inception. The goals of AAH were outlined in the African American Humanist Declaration, which first appeared in the Spring 1990 issue of *Free Inquiry* magazine. The goals were to:

- fight all forms of racism;
- incorporate an Afrocentric outlook into the broader world perspective;
- obtain redress in imbalance in historical studies that overlook the contribution of Africans to world history;
- develop **Eupraxsophy** among African American communities;
- improve the lot of African Americans through education and self-reliance; and
- build up self-help groups in the African American community.

Since 1991 AAH has produced the *AAH Examiner*. Over the years, interest in its activities has broadened to include the continent of Africa. While international humanism largely ignored Africa, AAH kept up contacts there and supplied resources to new humanist groups. These have taken the form of titles from **Prometheus Books**, copies of *Free Inquiry*, *Skeptical Inquirer*, and the *AAH*

Examiner, financial assistance for locally run welfare programs, and speakers for conferences. AAH was also instrumental in founding the African Humanist Alliance (AHAL), which serves as a liaison body for African humanist groups. AAH now has contacts with forty-five **freethought** groups in Africa. The most successful has been in Nigeria, where in 2001 the **Nigerian Humanist Movement** formed the **Center for Inquiry**—*Nigeria*. In 2004 another center was established in Uganda.

Allen has edited two works relevant to African and African American humanism. They are *African American Humanism: An Anthology* (1991) and *The Black Humanist Experience* (2003). These are essential resources for the understanding of African and African American humanism.

AFTER-MAN. A variation of **Friedrich Nietzsche**'s notion of the **Overman** which was developed by the prolific and vastly influential writer **H. G. Wells**. In his late work *The Conquest of Time* (1942), Wells posited the After-Man, which he described as our "bodily and mental offspring." However, Wells is more conventionally humanist when he insists that it would be due to education that "the new world of the After-Man dawns upon the face of the waters. The dissolution of the old bigotries and intolerances, that seemed invincibly rigid a score of years ago, goes on more and more conspicuously."

AGATHONISM. A system of humanistic ethics, devised by Mario Bunge, which balances **rights** and **responsibilities** and centers around what is good. It is an improvement on the **golden rule**. Agathon (450–400 BCE, approx.) was an Athenian tragedian, and *agathon* is the Greek word for "good." Despite being the common property of every system of belief, some philosophers have detected logical problems with the golden rule. For instance, is it right for a masochist to inflict pain on others because he might want pain inflicted on him? Bunge has devised the

notion of agathonism as a reliable method for determining humanist ethics. The two base postulates of Agathonism are as follows:

(1) Whatever contributes to the welfare of an individual without jeopardizing the basic rights of any others, is both good and right.
(2) Everyone has the right to enjoy life and the duty to help others enjoy life.

Agathonism can be simplified to the maxim "Enjoy life and help live an enjoyable life." Agathonism is specifically realist and materialist and thus can be employed in the real world. It is also grounded in **science**; see the entry on **reciprocal altruism**. Agathonism balances selfishness and altruism and places a premium on the moral equality of people and on the principle of fairness. In addition, its simplicity makes it accessible to everyone. Agathonism has the intellectual clarity and humanitarian simplicity to become the foundation for any humanist ethics.

Further reading: Mario Bunge, *Philosophy in Crisis: The Need for Reconstruction*.

AGE OF REASON. A book written in two parts by **Thomas Paine** that was enormously influential. Contrary to common belief, none of the *Age of Reason* was written while he was in jail in France. Paine finished the first part of *Age of Reason* in 1793, just before he was arrested in France. On the way to prison, Paine slipped the manuscript to his friend Joel Barlow to have it published. Part 1 came out in February 1794 and part 2 was written after his release from jail eleven months later and published in early 1795. It was written in the home of James Monroe (1758–1831), who was the American ambassador to France.

Age of Reason cost Paine very dearly both during his life and after it even though most of its main conclusions had been aired in earlier writings that had met with general approval. A century after his death Theodore Roosevelt (1858–1919), one of America's most devoutly Christian presidents, felt moved to label Paine a "filthy little atheist," with the *Age of Reason* in mind. In fact Paine was not an atheist, and indeed, *Age of Reason* was written with a view to countering what he saw as the harmful tendencies of **atheism**. Paine wrote as a **deist** and with the intention of vindicating what he saw as true religion. The *Age of Reason* was a critique of the Bible, and of the claim made by its apologists that it represents the infallible word of **God**. Paine outlined what have since become relatively uncontroversial criticisms of the inconsistencies and moral failings of the Bible. Paine rejected the divinity of **Jesus Christ** and the efficacy of revelation. If *Age of Reason* has not impeded the advance of Christianity, as many apologists have triumphantly declared, it should be added, wrote **Moncure Conway**, Paine's biographer, that this "has been largely due to modifications rendered necessary by that work."

Age of Reason was read and reread, often at risk of fines or imprisonment, by ordinary people for at least a century after it was written. Paine's arguments for deism were generally overlooked but the criticisms of the Bible and revelation took hold. *Age of Reason* was one of the most influential books among the growing ranks of radicals in the nineteenth century.

Further reading: Moncure Conway, *The Life of Thomas Paine*; John Keane, *Tom Paine: A Political Life*; and Susan Jacoby, *Freethinkers: A History of American Secularism*.

AGEQUAKE. Term for the aging of the world's population, the consequences of which are starting to be felt in the first years of the twenty-first century, as the first round of **baby boomers** start to retire. It is projected that by 2050 the number of elderly people will exceed the number of young for the first time in the history of the species. For the near future, this phenomenon will be limited mainly to the more prosperous nations, but may well roll on to the developing nations later in the century. The rise in the number of elderly people will be the most significant demographic trend of the twenty-first century.

The consequences of this shift in the age structure of the species will be enormous. People are living longer because of improvements in science, technology, medicine, and hygiene. But this has imposed on a declining population of taxpayers potentially crippling costs of supporting older citizens with pensions, accommodation, subsidized medical care, and other age-related provisions.

The repercussions for the **welfare state** are significant. In the United States, millions of people are without health insurance and as those people reach old age their chance for the level of health care enjoyed by their wealthier neighbors will reduce dramatically. In many other countries being elderly and poor is an even more unpleasant scenario. See the entry on **overpopulation**.

AGNOSTICISM. A word coined in 1869 by **T. H. Huxley** when he realized he was not comfortable with any of the standard labels on offer at the time. The word means "without definite knowledge" (*a-gnosis*). Huxley, and those who followed him in using the word, argued that both theism and **atheism** required a degree of certainty, even **dogmatism**, which he felt uncomfortable with. While the word is relatively recent, the idea behind it is ancient. The **Sophist** thinker **Protagoras** was one of the first to expound an agnostic position when he said, "As the gods, I have no means of knowing either that they exist or that they do not exist."

After Huxley some very influential thinkers took up and developed the idea of agnosticism. Especially important was **Sir Leslie Stephen** who, in *An Agnostic's Apology* (1893) did a great deal to popularize the concept. Stephen began his essay with the simple claim that agnostics assert what nobody would deny; that there are limits to the sphere of **human knowledge**. Agnosticism allowed people to reject the rigid certainties of theism without having to embrace what was feared to be the equally rigid certainties of **atheism**. For upward of a century, agnosticism was the label of choice for people keen to appear reasonable. Some prominent atheists, like **G. W. Foote**, **Chapman Cohen**, and **Joseph McCabe** accused agnosticism of being little more than atheism in a silk hat.

Huxley's reasons for coining the word are similar to the people who, one hundred and fifty years later, coined the word **brights**. And interestingly, agnosticism suffers from some of the same problems that the notion of brights suffers from. The unwillingess to use the word "atheist" has social as well as philosophical grounds. And since the 1960s, the philosophical weaknesses of agnosticism have become more apparent, as atheist philosophy has clarified its position.

Agnosticism is fundamentally unphilosophical because it declares that the question of God's existence is unanswerable. This assertion is therefore just as dogmatic as the positions they were originally setting out to avoid. What is more, agnosticism accepted some of the standard religious **prejudices against atheists**. Atheism does not, and never has, declare dogmatically that there is no **God**, although agnosticism worked from that premise. Agnosticism also tacitly accepts the theistic retort that atheists **can't prove a negative**. What is more, agnosticism has now been superseded by negative atheism, which is the view that there are no coherent accounts of God or gods, which makes faith in such an entity unjustified on the basis of the available evidence.

AIDS. One of the scariest pandemics of the early twenty-first century. "AIDS" stands for "Acquired Immunodeficiency Syndrome" and is the result of the spread of the Human Immunodeficiency Virus (HIV), which attacks the body's immune system and leaves the body fatally vulnerable to any new infection. AIDS is the final stage of HIV, which is spread when bodily fluids are transferred from an infected person to an uninfected person.

A **United Nations** report in 2003 painted a gloomy picture of the spread of the disease. At that time more than forty-six million people were thought to be infected, more than two-thirds of them in sub-Saharan Africa. That figure was expected to grow in 2003 by about five million people, and to take the lives of at least three million. The **World Bank** estimates that fourteen thousand people are infected each day. The worst hit country is Botswana, with more than 40 percent of the entire population infected. Rates are growing quickly in China, Russia, and India. In these parts of the world, about 55 percent of people infected with AIDS are women, whereas in the United States that figure drops to 20 percent.

Only in prosperous Western countries are the rates of infection being contained. This is largely due to greater ability to pay for expensive medicines, more comprehensive public education programs encouraging the use of condoms, and warning addicts against sharing needles.

Some countries are making progress, in particular Uganda, Cambodia, and Thailand, all of which have encouraged public campaigns on condom use. Some campaigns such as these in Africa have run up against opposition from Evangelical and Catholic churchmen, who have forbidden their followers to use condoms. There have also been delays getting generic medicines to those suffering from AIDS in poorer countries because of opposition from major pharmaceutical firms. See the entry on the **global gag rule**.

AITKENHEAD, THOMAS (1679–1697). The last person to be executed for blasphemy in the United Kingdom. Thomas Aitkenhead was only eighteen when he was indicted for blasphemy by order of the Privy Council for calling the Old Testament "Ezra's Fables," and for maintaining that God and nature were the same. Aitkenhead was found guilty on Christmas Eve 1696 and hanged on January 7, 1697, two months before his twenty-first birthday.

Further reading: Michael Hunter, "'Aitkenhead the Atheist': The Context and Consequences of Articulate Irreligion in the

Late Seventeenth Century," in Michael Hunter and David Wootton, eds., *Atheism from the Reformation to the Enlightenment*.

AJIVIKAS. An early movement of Indian **skepticism**, now known only through its detractors. The Ajivikas flourished between the sixth and third centuries BCE, and their influence can be traced for more than fifteen hundred years. Eventually the Ajivikas were absorbed into **Jainism** and Saivism. Like some early Jains and Buddhists, the Ajivikas went about naked, to indicate their contempt for worldly goods. In the main, they upheld a principle of nonaction, denying that merit accrued from virtuous activity or that demerit from wicked activity. Coupled with this was a thoroughgoing **determinism** and skepticism regarding **karma** and any sort of afterlife. As Ajita Kesakambali, an Ajivika thinker put it: "Man is formed of the four elements; when he dies earth returns to the aggregate of earth, water to water, fire to fire, and air to air, while the senses vanish into space."

One of the Ajivika thinkers, Pakudha Kaccayana, was an early theorist of **atomism**. The determinism of the Ajivikas found expression in the concept of *niyati*, or destiny, which governed the entire cosmos and was completely inflexible. *Niyati* did not reject karma so much as deny it had any moral force. It also had the effect of undermining any active program of ethics. The slogan of the Ajivikas was "Human effort is ineffectual." The Ajivika's emphasis on determinism in their philosophy marked them off from the Jains, Buddhists, and even the **Carvakas**. Characteristic of Ajivika's skepticism was a story about an Ajivika monk called Upaka, who was said to have met the Buddha soon after his enlightenment. When told of his enlightenment, Upaka reportedly said, "It may be so, sir!" and went on his way.

The Ajivika whose influence was the greatest was Makkhali Gosala, whose dates are uncertain, but who was roughly contemporaneous with Mahavira and the Buddha. Gosala features in early Jain texts, where he is regularly worsted in debate with Mahavira, and in early Buddhist texts, where is he portrayed as eccentric and irascible. Gosala's thought was characterized by a thoroughgoing determinism, an atomism similar to **Democritus**, and a skepticism regarding karma. This apparent hostility notwithstanding, the Ajivikas were patronized by Bindusara, and by his son, **Ashoka**, the greatest of the Maurya kings.

Further reading: Dale Riepe, *The Naturalistic Tradition in Indian Thought*.

AL QAEDA. Fundamentalist Muslim terrorist organization. Al Qaeda was formed in about 1988 from the coalition of the supporters of Osama bin Laden, who had been active in resisting the Soviet forces occupying Afghanistan, and two Egyptian organizations, the Egyptian Islamic Jihad, led by Ayman al-Zawahiri, and the Islamic Group. Al-Zawahiri is thought to be bin Laden's second-in-command and ideological advisor. The two Egyptian groupings had emerged out of the Egyptian-based **Muslim Brotherhood**, whose leading theoretician was **Sayyid Qutb**.

Al Qaeda is thought to share the priorities of Sayyid Qutb in seeing the total reform of the Arab leadership as its primary aim. The Arab leadership is thought to be fatally compromised by its collaboration with the West. Al Qaeda looks to a reformed, passionately Islamic leadership of a united Muslim world, which will be strong enough to withstand the encroachments of the West. They also seek the reinstatement of the **Khalifat** and **jihad** against the infidels, just as the Qur'an commands. It is important to stress that al Qaeda is first and foremost, motivated by religious **faith**. Its political and social goals are all secondary to, and informed by, its theology, which in turn rests on an extreme reading of **Wahhabi Islam**. It follows from this that **secularism** and the **toleration** it promotes is an important weapon against al Qaeda.

Al Qaeda was thought to have operated out of Sudan from 1991 until 1996 and then from Afghanistan until 2001. Since the US-led invasion of Afghanistan, al Qaeda has operated from wild areas on the Afghan-Pakistani border and at a more decentralized level. It is thought to have about a hundred cells in countries around the world. And since the collapse of Saddam Hussein, al Qaeda or al Qaeda–related organizations have been able to take advantage of the chaos in Iraq and operate there to great effect.

Among the attacks credited to al Qaeda include the September 11 attacks on the World Trade Center and the Pentagon, the attack on a Jewish-owned hotel and rocket assault on an El-Al plane taking off from Mombasa airport in Kenya in November 2002, and the attacks on the compounds in Riyadh, Saudi Arabia, in May 2003. Al Qaeda is the principal target of the **war on terror**.

An interesting fact about many of the terrorists, and not simply those from al Qaeda, is that they are from the upper echelons of Muslim society, with greater access to job opportunities and privileges than the vast majority of their coreligionists. This poses a problem for conventional wisdom that terrorism is the offspring of poverty.

ALBERTI, LEON BATTISTA (1404–1472). A prime example of what we now call a **Renaissance humanist**, Alberti was a brilliant architect and is credited as the founder of art theory. Leon Alberti was born in Genoa, the bastard son of a prominent Florentine family during the Renaissance. The family was down on its luck, having been on the losing side in one of Florence's perennial factional struggles. Alberti nevertheless rose on his merits, gaining distinction as a mathematician, scientist, musician, architect, and writer on art theory and art history.

From 1428, Alberti worked in Florence as an architect, designing the Santa Maria Novella Church in Florence, among others. His ten-volume *De Re Aedificatoria*, which was not published until 1485, was important in reigniting interest in Roman architecture and classical design. It also examined the social role of architecture. *Della Pictura*

(1436) developed current ideas on perspective in painting and was very influential among Renaissance artists. Alberti argued that painting was a noble activity, with the same status as a liberal art as rhetoric or poetry. Less helpful, in retrospect, was Alberti's differentiation between artist and craftsman, a distinction that has bedevilled art history and art theory ever since.

ALEXANDRIAN LIBRARY. One of the most significant centers of learning in the ancient world. Founded in the later stages in the reign of the Ptolemy I (Soter) whose reign spanned from 323–287 BCE. The library lasted six hundred years before being destroyed by Christian, and later Muslim, mobs. It had about half a million scrolls, an observatory, a zoo, and a botanical garden. In its prime there were about a hundred scholars, paid by the king. Many of the brightest men of the age worked at Alexandria, attracted by the financial support given to academics by the Ptolemies. Euclid and **Archimedes** both studied there.

The heyday of the library was in its first two hundred years, after which its intellectual rigor hardened somewhat, and it suffered various persecutions. Ptolemy IX Euergetes (146–117 BCE), while a supporter of learning, was hostile to the Greek scholars and subjected them to mistreatment. This had the effect of scattering them around the Roman world and helping with the profusion of Greek knowledge. The first damage to the library's stocks (though not to the library itself) was during Caesar's siege of Alexandria in 48–47 BCE, but Mark Antony later replaced most of the destroyed works with 200,000 volumes from the library of Pergamus.

The library, along with the temple of **Serapis**, was destroyed by a Christian mob in 391 CE, in response to a command from the emperor **Theodosius I** to destroy all vestiges of **paganism**. The Christians were led by Theophilus, Patriarch of Alexandria from 385 to 412 CE. The campaign to destroy paganism was tied up with internecine rivalries between Christian factions. The unrest culminated in 415 with the murder of **Hypatia**, during which more of the library was destroyed. What was left was probably destroyed in 640 by the Muslim leader Omar. But most of the stories of this come from Christian sources three hundred years after the event and are not reliable. The destructions perpetrated by the Christians between ̶ ̶ ̶ ̶ ̶ ̶ ̶ ̶ ̶ sible for the most

Due Wednesday

UTSA Library (Item Charged)
Patron Group: Undergraduate Student
Due Date: 11 2 2011 11 59 PM
Title: Dictionary of atheism skepticism
                 & humanism Bill Cooke
Author: Cooke Bill 195(
Call Number: BL 2705 Coo 2006
Enumeration:
Chronology:
Copy: 1
Barcode: *C 10337203*

ison with angels or the ....
As with angels, aliens are usually possessed of greater powers than are humans. Even more important, they come in "goody" or "baddy" flavors. Like angels, aliens are the intermediaries between the mundane and variously conceived extramundane worlds among gullible or vulnerable people.

It comes as no surprise that interest in aliens can be measured in proportion to exposure to the idea in the mass media. There were virtually no reports of UFOs before 1947 and no reports of alien abductions before 1975, when a television program featured the story of a family who claimed to have been abducted by aliens in 1961. Since then aliens have shown a prodigious interest in abducting credulous or sensation-hungry Americans.

It is no coincidence that one of the earliest descriptions of aliens comes from Johannes Kepler (1571–1630), the founder of the science of astrophysics. In his book *Somnium* (*The Dream*), Kepler tells of the varieties of life on the moon. They are mostly reptilian but some

are held to exercise a degree of intelligence.

ALLEN, ETHAN (1738–1789). American pioneer, soldier, and publicist of **deism**. After a distinguished record fighting for America's independence, Allen settled in Salisbury, Connecticut, where he came under the influence of ideas of the main **Enlightenment** thinkers. Allen was opposed to the joyless Calvinism so prominent in the New England ̶ ̶ ̶ 's youth. He was also suspicious of the ̶ ̶ l denigration of **reason** popular among ̶ ̶ ̶ tant clerics. In 1778 or 1779, Allen ̶ ̶ ̶ in possession of a manuscript from his ̶ ̶ ly deceased friend, Thomas Young. ̶ ̶ ̶ reworked parts of it and published it as ̶ ̶ *on the Only Oracle of Man* (1785). This ̶ ̶ , though unstructured and carelessly ̶ ̶ ght through, is generally thought of as ̶ ̶ irst formal criticism of Christianity pub- ̶ ̶ ̶ d in America.

̶ ̶ Allen's work never achieved the popu- ̶ ̶ y or influence as that of **Thomas Paine's**, ̶ ̶ his earthy writing style showed how deep ̶ ̶ roots of **skepticism** had gone in prerevo- lutionary America. Allen was also an early campaigner for statehood for Vermont, as well as the subject of deathbed conversion stories. See the entry on **infidel deathbeds**.

Further reading: Susan Jacoby, *Freethinkers: A History of American Secularism*.

ALLEN, STEVE (1921 2000). American broadcaster, author, poet, and humorist. Allen was best known as the creator and first host of NBC's *Tonight Show*, an influential American television program. He was also involved in a series called the *Meeting of Minds*, which ran on American public television. *Meeting of Minds* won Peabody and Emmy awards. Allen was also a gifted jazz pianist who recorded forty albums and composed more than 8,500 songs, the best known being *This Could Be the Start of Something Big* and the *Gravy Waltz*, for which he won a Grammy award.

Allen was raised a Catholic but was excommunicated when he remarried in his early thirties. He remained a theist but of a liberal persuasion. Allen only took any serious interest in religion after his son joined a religious cult in the 1970s. He wrote a moving book about the process, called *Beloved Son: A Story of the Jesus Cults* (1982).

Allen was also an outspoken critic of the **dumbing down** of society. One of his better-selling of his fifty-four books was called *Dumbth*, which included eighty-one ways for people to think at a higher standard, which in later editions was increased to become 101 ways. There is, after all, no limit to how we can improve our thinking. Allen was married for forty-six years to Jayne Meadows, an actress. The couple had four children.

ALTERNATIVE MEDICINE. Those branches of medical practice or **pseudoscientific** practice pertaining to health issues that lie outside current bounds of conventional medicine. It is important to note that not all alternative medicine is bad, wrong, or harmful. It may not yield the semi-miraculous results its more zealous partisans claim, but alternative medicine works on a key insight into the power of the human mind, which is that our attitude to an illness plays a critical part of the success we will have in overcoming it. See the entry on **placebo**.

This was taken to ridiculous extremes by Mary Baker Eddy (1821–1910) and many of her successors, who believed that actual physical illness didn't exist. While this is clearly not true, it *is* true that a positive attitude plus correct diet and exercise can sometimes have incredible curative powers. **Meditation** is also very useful as a vehicle by which we can relax, de-stress ourselves and achieve some **peace of mind**, without having to accept the spiritual explanations that often go with the practice of meditation.

The correct approach to alternative medicine is to:

- apply one's skeptical skills very closely;
- seek a variety of opinions, from conventional and alternative sources; and
- read up on the alternative medicine you

are attracted to, using your **tools of inquiry**, and make an honest **judgment** as to the validity of the practice and practitioner.

In the tradition of Aristotle's **Doctrine of the Mean**, it is wise to seek the right balance between conventional and alternative medicine that is appropriate for your complaint and for your current state of mind. The many skeptical magazines around the world (*Skeptical Inquirer*, in particular) are invaluable sources of reliable information about alternative medicine. For more academically oriented studies of alternative medicine, there are the publications of the **Commission for Scientific Medicine and Mental Health**.

ALTRUISM. Described by the American philosopher Marvin Kohl as "impersonal self-enlargement, benevolent love for mankind, and dedication toward achieving the well-being and **happiness** of people and society. . . ." The goal of **humanism** is the welfare of humanity, which means understanding humanity's role in a broad, interdependent planetary ecosystem. The word was coined by Auguste Comte (1798–1857), the founder of **Positivism**, and is derived from the Latin word *alter*, or "other."

Recently, the concept of altruism has come under criticism from **libertarians** and supporters of **Ayn Rand**, who see altruism as an authoritarian means by which rational self-interest, which would include some measure of concern for others as appropriate, is undermined and devalued. Rand, in particular, saw altruism in a particularly dim light, seeing it as the polar opposite of rational self-interest. This is too simplistic, however. It is not a simple black-and-white choice between altruism or egoism. See the entry on **either black or white, fallacy of**. Following **Aristotle's Doctrine of the Mean**, we each need to work out the appropriate boundary for altruism and self-interest for ourselves. *Homo sapiens* have developed a sophisticated mechanism by which we interact successfully with other people. See the entry on **reciprocal altruism**. To deny all traces of altruism, quite apart from the dire moral consequences, is to run against our evolutionary heritage.

AMBEDKAR, DR. BHIMRAO (1891–1956). Born the fourteenth child of a **dalit** (otherwise known as untouchables) family in Madhya Pradesh. As a dalit child, he suffered continuous petty humiliation from higher caste children and adults. Despite this, his intelligence was quickly recognized and Ambedkar was given access to education. In 1912 he graduated from Bombay University in Politics and Economics, and in the early 1920s, was awarded a PhD from Columbia University for his dissertation on British provincial finance in India and a DSc from London on "The Problem of the Rupee." From his return to India in 1923, Ambedkar immersed himself in the rights of untouchables. That year he established the Bahishkrit Hitkarini Sabha, or Outcastes Welfare Organization.

Dr. Ambedkar's first two public struggles involved winning for untouchables the right to draw water from the same tanks and enter the same temples everybody else used. Ambedkar also encouraged untouchables to look to changing their religion, as the main restrictions against them were specific to Hindu beliefs. Ambedkar said he had been born a Hindu but was not going to die one. Ambedkar's public protests were notably nonviolent, often in the face of considerable violence from orthodox Hindus and the authorities.

When India became independent in 1947, **Jawaharlal Nehru** asked Ambedkar to play an important role in devising the new state's constitution. Ambedkar was elected chairman of the drafting committee, and the emphasis in the constitution on equality before the law and a secular state were marks of his influence.

But it is one thing to enshrine changes in a constitution and quite another to have those changes actually implemented. Ongoing frustration with the slow pace of change in the conditions of untouchables led Dr. Ambedkar

to renounce Hinduism in the last year of his life and embrace Buddhism. Inspired by his example 800,000 untouchables also renounced Hinduism and embraced Buddhism. This is thought to be the biggest single movement in history of people from one system of belief to another. Dr. Ambedkar issued twenty-two vows that underlined the extent of his departure from Hinduism. The fourth vow included renouncing any belief in an incarnate god. In 1990 Dr. Ambedkar was bestowed the honor of Bharat Ratna and the 1990–1991 year was declared the year of social justice in his memory. See the entry on **secularism**.

AMERICAN ASSOCIATION FOR THE ADVANCEMENT OF ATHEISM. Short-lived organization devoted to popular **atheism**. Known as "the Four A's." The group was formed in 1925 by Charles Lee Smith (1887–1964) and a friend, Freeman Hopwood. The group had a great deal of difficulty being incorporated. New York State tried to refuse its incorporation on the grounds that the Four A's stated goal of being "purely destructive" was not in the public interest. Only on its second attempt was the group successfully incorporated, toward the end of 1926.

For a few years the Four A's had a noisy career, but there was little substance to it. The Four A's mounted a series of legal challenges to instances of religious privilege but usually lacked the money to see the battles through to any sort of conclusion. More constructive, though less popular, was the Ingersoll Forum, which was a series of lectures on scientific and philosophical themes.

The Four A's was quite successful at generating press attention, not the least reason being the stories it put out about the growth of its branches on university campuses and in secondary schools. The Four A's became a victim of the Great Depression, ceasing any effective activity in 1933. The Four A's is a cautionary tale of the limitations of atheism. Unless atheism is accompanied by a positive message of what will replace it (see **Gora's** vision of **positive atheism** for an example), it can only have a limited appeal. **American atheists** found this out later on in American history. See the entry on **atheism, insufficiency of**.

AMERICAN ATHEISTS. Organization founded by **Madalyn Murray O'Hair**. Originally founded as the Maryland Committee for Church-State Separation on July 1, 1963, as a vehicle to help O'Hair finance her Supreme Court struggle to take prayer out of state schools.

With support from Gustav Broukal, a German-Austrian emigrant then living in Iowa, O'Hair founded the *American Atheist* magazine and a small publishing house that produced atheist books and pamphlets. American Atheists also built up the Charles E. Stevens library, a significant collection of **freethought** works.

For many years American Atheists kept busy with a series of legal battles defending the rights of atheists or restricting the encroachments of religion across the wall of separation of church and state. Some of these battles were worthwhile, while others were simply expensive and even counterproductive. In many respects, American Atheists is best understood as the successor to the **American Association for the Advancement of Atheism**, sharing with its predecessor most of the same shortcomings. See the entry on **atheism, insufficiency of**.

American Atheists struggled for its life after the death of O'Hair, her son Jon, and her adopted daughter Robyn, but under the leadership of Ellen Johnson, the organization has relocated to New Jersey and maintains the *American Atheist* magazine and other services.

AMERICAN CIVIL LIBERTIES UNION. One of the most significant defenders of the freedoms Americans take for granted. The ACLU was founded on January 20, 1920, by Roger Nash Baldwin (1884–1981), scion of an old American family that could trace its line directly to the *Mayflower*. This is ironic

as the ACLU is frequently charged with being "un-American" by its opponents. It was under the influence of the charismatic atheist and anarchist campaigner Emma Goldman (1869–1940) that Baldwin took up the cause of defending the Bill of Rights for all Americans. Nash served as the ACLU's first director-general, serving until 1948. For resisting the draft during World War I, Nash served a spell in prison under the Espionage Act of 1917. The ACLU's first national committee, while mainly coming from the left of the political spectrum, did in fact represent most shades of political opinion. **Helen Keller** was also part of the establishment of the ACLU.

Since its inception, the ACLU has defended any persecuted minority, without regard to their religious or political affiliation. Despite this, some religious conservatives have sought to portray the ACLU as being secularist or even antireligious. In the 1930s it found itself defending women's rights against an increasingly aggressive Catholic Church. Since then it has defended the civil liberties of people of all persuasions. It was the ACLU that defended many victims of persecution of McCarthyism during the **Great Fear**. In 1973 the ACLU was the first significant national organization to call for the impeachment of Richard Nixon during the Watergate scandal.

AMERICAN DREAM. See **PARADISE SPELL**.

AMERICAN HUMANIST ASSOCIATION. Founded in 1941, the AHA is the foremost organization representing the **religious humanist** point of view in the United States. Its first president was Raymond B. Bragg (1902–1979), a graduate of Meadville Theological School, minister in the **Unitarian** Church, and signatory of the *Humanist Manifesto I*. Another signatory of the *Humanist Manifesto I*, Edwin Wilson (1899–1993), ran the association and edited its journal *The Humanist*, for many years. The AHA arose out of the journal, which was called the *New Humanist* and was sponsored by the Humanist Press Association, which was established in 1935. In 1941 the Humanist Press Association changed its name to the American Humanist Association and the journal became *The Humanist*. Wilson eventually left the AHA and founded the Fellowship of Religious Humanists and a journal, *Religious Humanism*. Another conflict arose between the AHA and **Priscilla Smith Robertson**, the editor of *The Humanist* between 1956 and 1959. Robertson resigned in 1959, citing censorship from AHA officials, and her entire staff agreed and resigned in support.

From 1967 until 1978 *The Humanist* was edited by **Paul Kurtz**. During this time, Kurtz drafted the *Humanist Manifesto II*, which attracted very broad support and generated a great deal of media comment. Kurtz's period as editor was probably the high-water mark for the influence of the AHA, both in the United States and internationally.

Since 1990, the AHA has been classified as an educational, nonprofit organization. It operates chapters around the United States. The current editor of *The Humanist* is Fred Edwords (1948–), a longtime member and officeholder of the AHA. One of the AHA's most recent initiatives is the *Humanist Manifesto III*. Throughout life **Corliss Lamont** was a generous benefactor of the AHA. Even on his death, Lamont bequeathed his mansion to the AHA for the use of its library.

AMERICAN RATIONALIST. Longstanding American journal devoted to **rationalism** and **freethought**. The *American Rationalist* began publication in May 1956 and was part of a coming together of several freethought and rationalist organizations around the United States. Strongly represented were some German and central European freethought and anticlerical groups. The magazine was funded by those who served as its staff and with donations of $120 from a few Life Members. The first editor was Arthur B. Hewson (c. 1900–1978) who set what he hoped would be the tone of the journal: "We must get away from mere anti-ism directed medieval nonsense if we are to make our philosophy intellectually respectable. We must formulate a dynamic forthright positive program which fire eager acceptance among great masses of bewildered people." If the *American Rationalist* didn't entirely succeed in that goal, it hasn't been alone. In fact, the *American Rationalist* has shared the interests of the earlier publications of the **Rationalist Press Association**, with biblical criticism and the history of freethought being prominent subjects.

Hewson retired from the editorship in 1958 and nobody succeeded in keeping that position for very long. Lowell Coate (1890–1973), an Ohio-born educator with a long record of work with freethought magazines around the United States held the post for two years, followed by Edd Doerr (who went on to have a distinguished career in the **American Humanist Association**), but it was **Walter Hoops** and Victor Cejka who were the key figures in the *American Rationalist*. The next significant figure to come along was **Gordon Stein**, who became editor in 1978, retaining the position until his death in 1996. He was replaced by Kaz Dziamka. In 2000 the publication of the *American Rationalist* was taken over by the **Center for Inquiry**. This has given the magazine a new lease on life.

AMOR FATI. A term used by **Friedrich Nietzsche** that means love of necessity. Nietzsche described *amor fati* as his formula for greatness in a human being. *Amor fati* means not just putting up with what one has and what one is and what one will be; it means not just enduring what happens to us, but loving what happens to us, so much so that we could live our lives over again, in an **eternal recurrence**.

While Nietzsche gave this idea its name, the idea is old. The **Stoic** thinker **Epictetus** said, "Demand not that events should happen as you wish; but wish them to happen as they do happen, and you will go on well."

AMSTERDAM DECLARATION. A restatement of the fundamental principles of humanism, and declared at the **International Humanist and Ethical Union**'s 2002 conference in Amsterdam, the Netherlands. The original Amsterdam Declaration was issued at the IHEU's inaugural congress in August 1952. It says:

Humanism is ethical. It affirms the worth, dignity, and autonomy of the individual and the right of every human being to the greatest possible freedom compatible with the rights of others. Humanists have a duty of care to all of humanity including future generations. Humanists believe that morality is an intrinsic part of human nature based on understanding and a concern for others, needing no external sanction.

Humanism is rational. It seeks to use science creatively, not destructively. Humanists believe that the solutions to the world's problems lie in human thought and action rather than divine intervention. Humanism advocates the application of the methods of science and free inquiry to the problems of human welfare. But Humanists also believe that the application of science and technology must be tempered by human values. Science gives us the means but human values must propose the ends.

Humanism supports democracy and human rights. Humanism aims at the fullest possible development of every human being. It holds that **democracy** and human development are matters of **right**. The principles of democracy and human rights can be applied to many human relationships and are not restricted to methods of government.

Humanism insists that personal liberty must be combined with social responsibility. Humanism ventures to build a world on the idea of the free person responsible to society, and recognizes our dependence on and responsibility for the natural world. Humanism is un-dogmatic, imposing no creed upon its adherents. It is thus committed to education free from indoctrination.

Humanism is a response to the widespread demand for an alternative to dogmatic religion. The world's major religions claim to be based on revelations fixed for all time, and many seek to impose their world views on all of humanity. Humanism recognizes that reliable knowledge of the world and ourselves arises through a continuing process of **evolution**, evaluation, and revision.

Humanism values artistic creativity and imagination and recognizes the transforming power of art. Humanism affirms the importance of literature, music, and the visual and performing arts for personal development and fulfillment.

Humanism is a life stance aiming at the maximum possible fulfillment through the cultivation of ethical and creative living and offers an ethical and rational means of addressing the challenges of our times. Humanism can be a way of life for everyone.

Further reading: http://www.iheu.org; and David Tribe, *100 Years of Freethought*.

ANALYSIS. The core intellectual activity of the freethinker. With characteristic irony, **Bertrand Russell** described analysis as his strongest prejudice in regards to methods of philosophical investigation. He also said it produced knowledge not otherwise obtainable. Almost by definition, analysis is a method rather than a finished set of beliefs.

The German novelist and thinker **Thomas Mann** gave one of the most succinct summaries of the value of analysis in his great novel *The Magic Mountain* (1924). Analysis, Mann concluded, is good for:

- shattering absurd convictions;
- acting as a solvent against prejudices; and
- undermining authority.

That is, analysis "sets free, refines, humanizes, makes slaves ripe for freedom."

However, analysis is less helpful when:

- it stands in the way of action; or

• stultifies spontaneity.

That is, analysis is "a very unappetizing affair." It was with this in mind that **Paul Kurtz** conceived the idea of **eupraxsophy**, which combines analysis with compassion and action.

ANAXAGORAS (500–428 BCE). Philosopher, born in Clazomenae in Ionia, and brought to Athens by **Pericles**. Anaxagoras was part of the **Pre-Socratic** tradition of philosophy begun by **Thales**. Anaxagoras was a **naturalist** thinker and was opposed to **superstition**. He taught that the planets were not gods but were made of rock and were a great distance away. The universe consisted of an infinite complexity of matter of which "mind" was the unifying core. But "mind" was not some opposing principle, mind was a species of matter. From a study of physiology, Anaxagoras derived a theory of **complexity** when he asked how first principles work if things are continually breaking down into new constituents.

Anaxagoras fell foul of Athenian political rivalries and religious reaction. As an ally of Pericles, his enemies thought it was safer to attack him indirectly by persecuting Anaxagoras. As happened to **Socrates** later on, Anaxagoras was accused of **atheism**. Unlike Socrates, Anaxagoras escaped and spent his exile in Lampsacus on the Turkish coast along the Dardanelles.

ANAXIMANDER (610–546 BCE, approx.). The next prominent **Pre-Socratic** philosopher after **Thales**. It is not known whether Anaximander was a pupil of Thales, but he was widely regarded as his successor. Anaximander wrote a work called *On Nature*, of which less than one sentence survives, but was a general speculation on the nature of the universe. Contrary to Thales who posited water as the fundamental element of the universe, Anaximander spoke of "the indefinite," by which he meant the vast, interdependent web of nature. It was not so much one element, but many elements, in permanent contention. The universe was spherical, although the planets are actually circles of fire, and the Earth lies at the center of the universe, supported by equilibrium or symmetry. Anaximander's notion of equilibrium was one of the first systematic attempts to understand the universe in mathematical and scientific terms. See the entry on **geocentric universe**.

Anaximander is sometimes credited with anticipating a theory of **evolution**, but this isn't quite correct. Anaximander thought that humans emerged from another species—in his case, fish. He was also thought to have produced the first map of the world.

ANCIENT GREECE AND ROME, LEGACY OF. It is difficult to overestimate the legacy of the ancient world. We are often told of the great debt owed to Christianity. But this is to overlook the incalculable debt Christianity itself owes to the Greek and Roman pagans and naturalists. Neither the **Renaissance** nor the **Enlightenment** would have been possible without the example of the ancient world to act as an inspiration against the deadening effect of Christian orthodoxy and oppression. Ancient Greece and Rome provided us with the framework through which we think of civilization: words like "**democracy**," "**philosophy**," "geography," "politics," all come from there. **Homer**'s two masterpieces, the *Iliad* and the *Odyssey*, on their own, are achievements of unsurpassed imagination, beauty, and power. The poet **Shelley** captured the mood when he said, "We are all Greeks. Our laws, our literature, our religion, our arts, have their root in Greece."

A. C. Grayling gave a general assessment of the debt we owe ancient Greece when he praised its appreciation of beauty, its respect of reason and the life of reason, its freedom of thought and feeling, and its absence of **mysticism** and false sentimentality. Taken together, Grayling credits that ancient Greece taught us about "living nobly and richly in spirit as the aim of life." What is now known as the ideal of the **Renaissance man** is in fact an ideal inspired by Cicero (106–43 BCE). George Novack made similar points when he listed the four main achievements of Greek and Roman **naturalism**:

- In *physics*: the universe is explained as an independently existing reality in constant change, operating to its own laws and with an atomic structure of matter.
- In *logic*: sensation is regarded as the primary factor in acquiring acquaintance with the external world. Reasoning that leads to scientific knowledge depends upon materials provided in the first place by sensory experience.
- In *sociology*: history is seen as man imitating nature, using it to satisfy material needs and then developing civilization by improvement of one's own skills.
- In *ethics*: it is seen as a secular and humanistic conception of moral conduct and its changing standards.

It is worth adding that some of the perennial themes of human ethics were stated first by the Greeks: justice, honor, **free inquiry**, the **good life**, and the life well spent. The American historian Marvin Perry wrote: "Reason, freedom, humanism—these constitute the enduring legacy of Greece."

Further reading: A. C. Grayling, *What is Good? The Search for the Best Way to Live*; George Novack, *The Origins of Materialism*; Charles Freeman, *The Greek Achievement*; and Marvin Perry, "The Enduring Humanist Legacy of Greece," *Free Inquiry* 3, no. 4 (Fall 1983): 28–32.

ANDERSON, JOHN (1893–1962). Scottish-born Australian philosopher, radical, mentor, and **smiter of humbug**. John Anderson was born in Stonehouse, Lanarkshire, to a freethinking family. His father, a socialist and rationalist, had a profound influence on him. He was educated at the Hamilton Academy, then at Glasgow University. In 1922, the year he was appointed to Edinburgh University, he married Janet Baillie. They had one child, Alexander.

In 1927 Anderson was appointed the Challis Chair of Philosophy at the University of Sydney, a position he held until his retirement in 1958. During his tenure at Sydney, Anderson ruffled many feathers. He was censured by the university's Senate in 1931 for criticizing the role of war memorials in glorifying war. And in 1943 the parliament of New South Wales censured Anderson for arguing that religion has no place in schools. The university, although incensed by Anderson's views, narrowly decided to take no action. These censures had little effect on Anderson.

Soon after arriving in Australia in 1927, Anderson joined the Communist Party, although he left in 1932, disillusioned with the advance of **Stalinism**. After World War II, Anderson became more stridently anticommunist. However, he remained a consistent freethinker. He actively opposed the federal government's ban on certain publications by circulating a copy of **James Joyce**'s banned novel *Ulysses* with a cover on which he wrote "The Book of Common Prayer." And long after he had left the Communist Party, he opposed moves to outlaw the party.

Anderson founded the Sydney University Freethought Society in 1931, which had an influential role in university life for twenty years. Anderson has been described as Australia's most original philosopher, as well as an inspiration to younger generations. He was an inspiring teacher and a strong influence on some of Australia's greatest twentieth-century philosophers, like J. L. Mackie (1917–1982) and **John Passmore**. A collection of his writings were published as *Studies in Empirical Philosophy* (1962). Other studies, including a biography, have appeared since then, and there is an excellent Web site on Anderson maintained by Sydney University.

Further reading: http://setis.library.usyd .edu.au/oztexts/anderson.html.

ANTHONY, SUSAN B[ROWNELL] (1820–1906). American pioneer for women's suffrage. Anthony began her active life as an abolitionist, but, with her friend **Elizabeth Cady Stanton**, devoted her long life to women's suffrage. Anthony's gift was as an organizer and foil for the many, often difficult, personalities among her political allies. An **agnostic** and **freethinker**, Anthony was more politically pragmatic than her friend, and was able, even willing, to work with a broad spectrum of political and religious interests in order to achieve her principal aim: women's suffrage.

In 1869 Anthony was involved in forming the National Woman's Suffrage Association (NWSA). As well as her excellent abilities as an organizer and peacemaker, Anthony also had a shrewder political sense than her friend Stanton. After the formation of the politically and religiously conservative Women's Christian Temperance Union in 1874, Anthony realized that women's rights, and even women's suffrage, would not progress until mainstream religious opinion could be brought onside. Anthony was able to forge a working relationship between the NWSA, the WCTU, and another conservative suffrage organization, the American Woman Suffrage Association (AWSA). The US Senate's defeat of a suffrage proposal in 1887 illustrated the problem. Anthony's patience was rewarded in 1890 when, thanks largely to her efforts, the NWSA and AWSA merged to form the National American Woman Suffrage Association. Stanton became the president but the real power lay with Anthony, the vice president.

Like Stanton and **Matilda Joslyn Gage**, Anthony has not received her due recognition since her death. This can be put down almost entirely to her agnosticism.

ANTHROPIC PRINCIPLE. A set of speculations advanced in the 1980s regarding the universe and our role in it. The term was coined in the 1960s by the physicist Robert Dickie and brought to wider attention in 1973 at a conference of physicists by Brandon Carter.

There is a weak version and a strong version, which have quite different consequences. The Weak Anthropic Principle says that humans are entitled to infer facts about and laws of the universe simply because humans are here and able to infer them. This is a reasonable enough observation, and not particularly controversial. And it makes no reference to supernatural agencies. Stephen Hawking advanced the weak anthropic principle in *A Brief History of Time* (1988).

By contrast, the Strong Anthropic Principle (SAP), in its strongest form, argues that the basic physical constants of the universe are so inherently improbable that to factor in intelligent human life demands that those improbable physical constants be there. Put more simply, the universe exists as a backdrop for human purpose. Even stronger versions of the SAP have come along since then. John Barrow and Frank Tipler have postulated both the Participatory Anthropic Principle and the Final Anthropic Principle. Both have been at pains to distance their various Anthropic Principles from an **argument to design**, but religious apologists have been quick to make that connection.

The SAP and its stronger variants have received little support and a great deal of criticism from the scientific community. **Daniel Dennett** observed that, while it is true the universe has to exist as it does for human beings to exist, it might not have, and if it hadn't, human beings would not exist, and so couldn't get upset on its own behalf. **Lucretius** made a very similar point two thousand years ago. Others have noted that the Strong Anthropic Principle is incapable of **falsification** and is little more than a stop-gap to fill in holes in scientific thinking. A still stronger criticism likens it to little more than **anthropocentric conceit**. Martin Gardner summed up the criticisms when he postulated the Completely Ridiculous Anthropic Principle (CRAP).

ANTHROPOCENTRIC CONCEIT. The presumption of according to oneself a place in the scheme of things that one does not deserve. *Homo sapiens* have traditionally done this through devices such as the **great chain of being**, the **transcendental tempta-**

tion, and **speciesism**. **Friedrich Nietzsche** put it best when he said that Christianity—although this applies to all **monotheist** religions—has given humans an absolute value, which undermines the truth about our "smallness and accidental occurrence in the flux of becoming and passing away."

The rejection of anthropocentric conceit is the first move in the construction of any morally sound **life stance**. **Heraclitus** called conceit "the sacred disease." Anthropocentric conceit is a specific form of **anthropomorphism**. The danger of anthropocentric conceit was well understood by **George Jacob Holyoake**, who said, "Were I to pray, I should pray **God** to spare me from the presumption of expecting to meet him, and from the vanity and conceit of thinking that the God of the universe will take the opportunity of meeting me." But anthropocentric conceit does not only come in religious forms. The evolutionist **Julian Huxley** argued that *Homo sapiens* were sufficiently special to justify its very own classification; what he called the Psychozoan. This idea was not taken up and the motive behind it has been criticized. Recently, the cosmologist Steven Weinberg warned that "our species has had to learn in growing up that we are not playing the starring role in any sort of grand cosmic drama." See the entry on **geocentric universe**.

The rejection of anthropocentric conceit implies a full understanding that, while humans matter to other humans, we do not matter in the least to the universe, which can get along very well without us. The logical corollary of the rejection of anthropocentric conceit is **atheism**. In this way, atheism is a guarantor of a properly humble **cosmic perspective**. See the entries on **heliocentric universe**, **evolution, consequences of**, and **astonishing hypothesis**.

Further reading: Bill Cooke, "Religion's Anthropocentric Conceit," *Free Inquiry* 24, no. 2 (Dec. 2003/Jan. 2004).

ANTHROPODICY. A stratagem employed by theologians to reconcile the irreconcilable contradiction between the existence of an all-powerful, loving **God**, and the existence of **evil** and suffering in the world. In an attempt to absolve God from the blame, theologians attribute the blame for the existence of evil on humanity. By virtue of being given **free will** to make choices, humanity chose evil, or at least permitted evil to enter the world. In this way God is not responsible for the ubiquity of suffering. See the entries on **theodicy** and **evil, problem of**.

ANTHROPOMORPHISM. The tendency in human beings to credit nonhuman objects as having human qualities, or to invent supernatural entities that have human qualities. Anthropomorphism is endemic among human beings, and in our primitive past, was an advantage. The person who confused a boulder for a bear ran the risk of running away unnecessarily or appearing a fool in front of others, but the person who confused a bear for a boulder ran the risk of being lunch for a bear.

In the twenty-first century, however, anthropomorphism is a dangerous delusion that lessens the chance of us as a species learning to interact with other living and nonliving beings on the planet in a spirit of interdependence and mutual respect. More than any other factor, **religion** thrives on anthropomorphism because of its insistence that a supernatural realm exists that has some significance for human beings. **Science**, by contrast, is the most effective tool to combat the arrogance implicit in anthropomorphism.

Further reading: Stewart Guthrie, *Faces in the Clouds: A New Theory of Religion*.

ANTHROPOSOPHY. A movement founded in February 1913 by Rudolf Steiner (1861–1925) as a breakaway from the Theosophical movement to which he had hitherto belonged. Steiner was a lifelong admirer of **Goethe**. Steiner believed, like the Theosophists, that there was a spiritual reality independent of ourselves that could be understood only by pure thought and study. He believed we were once privy to this knowledge, but have slowly lost it because of the deadening influence of materialism. Steiner's movement was much closer to the tradition of western **mysticism** than the orientalizing **Theosophy**.

ANTICLERICALISM. The suspicion of the power and pretensions of priests and other visible agents of power in the established church. Anticlericalism in this formal sense is usually confined to countries with a Catholic majority and is to be distinguished from simple anti-Catholicism as exhibited by many Protestants. While opposition to the pretensions of the Catholic Church is laudable, anticlericalism is hardly a comprehensive view of the world. Some of the weaknesses of atheism apply to it. See the entry on **atheism, insufficiency of**.

ANTINATURALISM. According to the philosopher Peter Manicas, antinaturalism is the view that, because there are differences in the way we see the domains of nature and culture, there must also be a wholly different (i.e., nonnaturalist) methodology of exploring these ideas. See also the entry on the **passes-for fallacy**. In fact, nature and culture do not require different methodologies. Both can be studied, with no necessary danger of **reductionism**, by philosophical **naturalism**.

Further reading: Peter Manicas, "Nature and Culture" in *American Philosophic Naturalism in the Twentieth Century*, ed. John Ryder.

ANTI-SEMITISM. One of the most bitter legacies of Christianity and Islam, the two **monotheist** religions that followed in the footsteps of Judaism. And as the Catholic historian James Carroll shows with respect to his religion, this legacy is by no means an incidental one but a hatred that goes to the heart of Christianity. The term "anti-Semitism" was coined only in 1880 by the German racialist Wilhelm Marr (1819–1904) as a "modern" alternative to the older term *Judenhass* (Jew-hatred). But the phenomenon of

anti-Semitism has been around since the rise of Christianity, which arose as a heretical sect of Judaism. In order to establish an identity separate from Judaism, Christians came to emphasize the role of the Jews in the death of Jesus. Indeed, this became a dominant theme in the New Testament, which was brought together first by **Marcion** with specifically anti-Jewish motives. Alongside this was the doctrine of **supersessionism**, in which Christianity claimed to have superseded the earlier and less full revelation of Judaism.

The message of anti-Semitism in the New Testament was quickly taken up. The first known incident of a prominent Christian blaming the Jews for the death of Christ was as early as the second century CE by bishop Melito of Sardis. One of the earliest recorded incidents of a synagogue being burned by Christians was in 388 at Callinicum on the Euphrates. When the emperor Theodosius wanted to punish the criminals and compensate the victims, he was taken to task by the powerful bishop Ambrose, who criticized the very idea of helping those who denied Christ.

This was not an isolated incident, particularly once Christian emperors took over the Roman empire. St. Jerome (342–420) said of the Jewish synagogue, "If you call it a brothel, a den of vice, the Devil's refuge, Satan's fortress, a place to deprave the soul, an abyss of every conceivable disaster or whatever else you will, you are saying less than it deserves." St. John Chrysostom (347–407) was similarly rabid. In a series of sermons in Antioch in 387 he castigated the Jews as carnal, lascivious, avaricious, accursed, and demonic. Chrysostom repeated the calumny of Jews as the Christ killers. Most Christian leaders wrote a tract called *Against the Jews* at some point in their careers, something the historian Charles Freeman described as "almost a ritual which had to be gone through to claim credentials as a Christian theologian."

After this, anti-Semitism settled down as a permanent condition of Christian Europe. During each time of social anxiety or economic hardship, the Jews became an easy target to focus generalized fears upon. In the Middle Ages, anti-Jewish legislation was first called for by the Fourth Lateran Council of the Roman Catholic Church in 1215. This call was heeded at the Council of Arles in 1253, which required Jews to wear a round yellow patch, four fingers in circumference, over their heart. Over the next century Jews were subjected to discrimination and frequent pogroms over much of Europe. Pope John XXII (1316–1334) oppressed Jews and ordered the burning of the Talmud. In 1555 Paul IV (1555–1559) passed *Cum Nimis Absurdum*, which created the ghetto in Rome and instituted a series of discriminatory measures against the Jews. Pius V (1566–1572) expelled the Jews from the Papal States, excepting only the city of Rome and the region around Ancona.

Sporadic persecution continued right into the twentieth century, when anti-Semitism took on even more brutal forms. The Nazis in Germany, though primarily pagan or non-Christian in outlook, took over the old Christian hatred of Jews and placed that hatred at center stage of their worldview. See the entry on **Adolf Hitler**.

The legacy is no less awful with respect to Islam, although until recently its record of treatment of Jews was less inhumane than the Christian record. However, the Qur'an gives readers plenty of ammunition to mount a campaign of hate against Jews. The Qur'an distinguishes between Christians, who have simply gone astray, from Jews, who have incurred God's wrath. One passage likens Jews to apes and swine who serve the devil and who have incurred the displeasure of Allah (5:60). Jews in Muslim societies have been subjected to many of the same humiliations they faced in Europe: wearing distinctive clothing and a star of David; passing Muslims with eyes averted and only on their left, and so on. Contemporary anti-Semitism among Muslims is complicated by resentment at the state of Israel. Much of the recent rise in anti-Semitism in Europe has been attributed to Muslims.

Since World War II, the more extreme anti-Semites have often become, or have supported, **Holocaust deniers**. In the face of these extremes, and in partial recognition of its own role in the history of anti-Semitism, the papacy began to reform after the death of **Pius XII** in 1958. The papacy did not officially renounce its own anti-Semitism until October 1965 when Paul VI issued *Nostra Aetate*, which absolved the Jews of responsibility for the killing of Jesus. Even here, however, an element of **supersessionism** was retained when it insisted that the Catholic Church remains "the new people of God." *Nostra Aetete* also skirted the issue of guilt by declaring that anti-Semitism involves a misreading of **scripture**. The ambivalent nature of Catholic recognition of anti-Semitism is built in to its structure. See the entry on **structures of deceit**.

In fact, the anti-Semitism of the New Testament is all too clear, and too often repeated to be explained away. Not least because of the ambivalence of this declaration, anti-Semitism remains strong today. The French novelist **Anatole France** put it most succinctly when he said, "The Christian God was once a Jew. Now he is an Anti-Semite." And neither is it a coincidence that the first country to return to the Jews their rights as citizens was the French Republic, on September 27, 1791. Without the historical baggage of the Christians, the French revolutionaries extended civil rights to all its peoples. As nations have become more secular, so has the malevolence and extent of anti-Semitism been mitigated.

Further reading: James Carroll, *Constantine's Sword: The Church and the Jews*; and Micheline Ishay, *A History of Human Rights*.

ANTITHEISM. The condition of basing one's worldview on a dislike of theism. Antitheism is not the same as **atheism**, which is the conviction that **God** or gods don't exist. Atheism requires no element of hostility to theism. It is, in fact, absurd to be hostile to something one believes not to exist.

It is more understandable to harbor some hostility to the religious system that supports such notions. This is relevant to **anticlericalism**, for instance. However, in the end, all forms of antitheism are self-defeating. The rejection of notions of God or gods is a crucial first step in a humanist view of the world, but it must be followed by a positive account of how the world actually works. Antitheism is, by definition, too limiting. Atheism is different than antitheism, although it is also insufficient as a stand-alone worldview. See the entries on **religion, criticism of** and **atheism, insufficiency of**.

APATHEIA. The idea of moral courage in the face of adversity as advocated by the **Stoics**. The Stoics taught that we should cultivate indifference to the many varieties of suffering we endure during our life. While it is certainly important to keep control of our feelings during times of stress, many have thought the Stoics went a bit far in cultivating indifference to suffering, not least because it can result in indifference to the suffering of others. A logical extension of apatheia is the Christian notion of being "dead to the world," which involves cultivating an indifference to all worldly things. Quite apart from being practically impossible, this is a profoundly self-centered attitude.

APOLLONIUS OF TYANA (first century CE). Wandering healer and miracle worker. Little is known about Apollonius's life or beliefs, but he is thought to have lived at much the same time as **Rabbi Yeshua**. Apollonius's beliefs were an assortment of neo-Pythagoreanism and popular superstition.

What is interesting about Apollonius is the parallel tales told about him as were told about Yeshua/Jesus. Stories of Apollonius of Tyana credit him with performing miracles, raising the dead, exorcizing demons. He even rose from his own death, and appeared to his disciples, and ascended to heaven.

Apollonius's life was written about by Philostratus circa 220 CE. The interesting point is that the range of signs and wonders attributed to Jesus Christ were the common property at the time of anyone wanting to establish credibility for the messiah figure one was writing about. See the entry on **dying and resurrected gods**.

APOSTATE. The word derives from *Apikoras*, the Greek spelling of **Epicurus**; a sign of the extent of Christian fear of him and his subversive message. Technically, an apostate is not the same as a **heretic**. An apostate is one who once believed but who came to turn his back on the **faith**, and as such is now a heretic. In Islam, the Arabic word for apostate is *mortad*. Apostasy from Islam is seen as an especially wicked offense and is punishable by death, even should the apostate revert to the original faith. The Qur'an carries some gruesome punishments for apostates (3:86–91).

Apostasy is a phenomenon peculiar to **monotheistic** religions, which have great difficulty in ascribing honest motives to apostates. See the entries on **command morality**, the **Principle of Intolerance**, and **demonizing the opposition**.

APOTHEOSIS OF UNCERTAINTY. It was recognized in 1913 by the underappreciated author **Adam Gowans Whyte** that for those nursed in the belief of a consoling afterlife, the life of a humanist would seem little more than the apotheosis of uncertainty. The same idea was expressed by A. E. Heath (1887–1961), an English philosopher, when in 1947 he wrote that rationalism "cannot give us the glittering prizes of final certitude which resplendent dogmatisms hold out for our attraction." Those who don't believe in **God** and **immortality**, where goodies are rewarded and baddies punished, must get used to a level of uncertainty in their lives. It's part of being a responsible adult.

Decades later, **postmodernist** critics have made careers out of extolling the messiness and uncertainty of life, as if they had discovered the idea, and not infrequently criticizing rationalists of assuming too hard a level of certainty.

APPEAL TO IGNORANCE. A very popular method of defending supernatural or **pseudoscientific** claims. It works along the lines of "you can't prove I'm wrong," with the unstated subtext being "therefore I'm right." It is often true that supernatural or pseudoscientific claims can't be *proved* wrong, but that in no way means that they have therefore been proven right. And neither does it mean that there is no evidence against the claim. The appeal to ignorance works on the known difficulty of proving a negative. It can't be proved, for instance, that **souls** don't exist or that world isn't flat, but that is to ignore the significant, high quality evidence against either of these claims.

APPROPRIATION. Problematic term in the **visual arts**, which came to prominence in the 1980s. It refers to the growing practice among artists to copy an image used by another artist and use it, usually in a slightly altered form, in one's own work. The new context of the appropriated image, whether or not it has been altered, requires the viewer to reconsider issues of authenticity of creation. See the entries on **ready made** and **modern art**.

ARCHIMEDES (287–212 BCE). Brilliant Greek mathematician. Born in Syracuse, Sicily, Archimedes is thought of as one of the finest mathematicians in all history, although his own debt to Euclid, who was active around 300 BCE, was great. Archimedes is best known for the story of him leaving his bath and running naked through the town shouting "Eureka" when he discovered the principle of upthrust on a floating body.

Archimedes is credited with founding the science of hydrostatics, which looks at how objects float. As part of determining volume, Archimedes determined the value of *pi*, one of the most basic forms of mathematical measurement to this day. He also anticipated very significant aspects of calculus and approaches to understanding concepts such as infinity. One of his most important works, *The Method*, was lost for centuries, only being rediscovered in the twentieth century. His manuscript had been erased and written over by some tenth-century monk.

Archimedes was killed during the Roman assault on Syracuse in 212 BCE. The story goes that Archimedes was quite unaware of the battle going on outside, and when a Roman soldier burst into his house, he didn't look up from his work until it was too late.

AREOPAGETICA. The title of a book by the English poet John Milton (1608–1674) that was an impassioned plea for freedom of the press. In 1643 the puritan parliament passed legislation arrogating to itself the power to approve any proposed publication before it went to press. Milton responded with the *Areopagetica* in 1644, which disputed parliament's right to do this. Reason was a gift from **God**, Milton argued, and killing a good book was tantamount to killing reason, and thus doing an injury to God. Milton was one of the first people to point out that truth is often the first casualty of censorship in the name of some truth or other. Truth, wrote Milton, "needs no policies, nor stratagems nor licensings to make her victorious; those are the shifts and the defenses that error uses against her power." The *Areopagetica* had little influence at the time, but went on to have a great influence after Milton's death. It was constantly referred to during the American and French revolutions.

Milton, though a deeply religious man, had already established a reputation as a **freethinker** with his advocacy of divorce. In this, he was three hundred years too early. And, of course, Milton also wrote *Paradise Lost* (1667), considered by many historians to be second only to **William Shakespeare** in importance to the history of English literature.

ARISTARCHUS OF SAMOS (310–230 BCE, approx.). The first person to propose the **heliocentric universe**. Aristarchus was a pupil of **Strato the physicist**. His astronomical works are now lost, but **Archimedes** credits Aristarchus with arguing that the sun remains unmoved and the Earth revolves around the sun in the circumference of a circle. Aristarchus's theory was so shocking to religious sensibilities of the time that few people publicly advocated it, and it died from lack of support and development. Aristarchus is also credited with an improved design for sundials. Most importantly, it was to Aristarchus's idea that Copernicus returned when he constructed his heliocentric model of the universe.

ARISTOSCIENCE. A word coined by the philosopher **John Passmore**, and by which he meant the ethereal, theoretical science that all the rest of us are quite unable to understand. For example, aristoscience would include theoretical astrophysics and mathematics, quantum physics, and other subjects which lay the foundations for practical science, but which are a closed door to the vast majority of humanity. Every day we rely on gadgets made possible by the breakthroughs of aristoscience, but how they work is a complete mystery to most of us.

It is this alienation from the foundation principles that aristoscience has uncovered, that gives rise to some of the more eccentric applications of these finds, or in an antiscientific reaction. These reactions are another manifestation of **anthropocentric conceit**, because they are reacting against the **cosmic perspective** which aristoscience habitually employs. The inevitable complexity of aristoscience makes the work of popularizers of science all the more valuable, so as to demystify the principles it has unearthed, and helps prevent the spread of junk science as a more easily absorbed rival. See the entries on **science, suspicion of** and **physics-envy**.

Further reading: John Passmore, *Science and Its Critics*.

ARISTOTLE (384–322 BCE). One of the most brilliant thinkers of all time. Born in the remote village of Stagira, the son of a court physician attached to the royal house of Macedon, the country on the periphery of the Greek world, far from the intellectual center of Athens. In 367 Aristotle went to Athens and quickly ended up at Plato's **Academy**, where he soon made a name for himself as an industrious student. In 347, the year **Plato** died, Aristotle left Athens, possibly due to a rise of anti-Macedonian feeling in the city. For several years he lived at Atarneus, where the ruler, Hermias, provided sanctuary and support. Aristotle worked here with **Theophrastus**, who later succeeded him as head of the Lyceum, on a series of biological and zoological works which stood as foundational works in those sciences for more than two thousand years.

In 343, Aristotle was summoned back to Macedonia where he may have served as tutor to Alexander the Great. In 335 Aristotle felt able to return to Athens and here he set up his school, the Lyceum (the site of which was discovered in 1997). It was probably during the next ten years that most of Aristotle's works were composed, serving originally as lecture notes for his students. When news reached Aristotle in 323 that Alexander had died in Babylon, Aristotle once again left Athens. He settled in Chalcis on the island of Euboea, where he died the following year.

Probably only a quarter of Aristotle's large corpus of writing has survived, although it still amounts to a sizable quantity of works, far more than all the **Pre-Socratic** philosophers put together. None of Aristotle's dialogues has survived, and yet his lecture notes did, in contrast with Plato, none of whose lecture notes survived, while his dialogues did.

Aristotle's achievements are extraordinary in their range. He is credited with the invention of logic as a form of determining what is valid, as opposed to what is true. And in what he called First Philosophy, Aristotle's **four causes** set new standards for clear thinking. In the sciences, many of Aristotle's observations on the physiology of plants and animals remained of serious scientific value until relatively recently. In cosmology, Aristotle spoke of an **unmoved mover**, but it would be a mistake to equate this notion with

God. In ethics, Aristotle advanced, at least for most of his career, a formula later known as the **Doctrine of the Mean**. The goal of life was **eudaimonia**. With regard to gender issues, Aristotle's legacy was less helpful. See the entry on **Axiothea**.

ARISTOTELIANISM. A medieval body of thought that claimed to have derived from the teachings of **Aristotle**. There was, in fact, relatively little in common between what Aristotle taught and the dogma of Aristotelianism. Aristotle had a scientific turn of mind and did not want his philosophy to harden into a dogma. Even less would he have countenanced a set of ideas opposed to his views being touted in his name. Aristotle's main ideas on the **unmoved mover** and the universe were quite different from those of the Aristotelian theologians. For instance Aristotle believed that the universe had always existed, but Christian theologians taught that **God** had created the universe. The same happened for theories about the **soul** and matter.

To begin with, medieval theologians recognized these problems, and were hostile to Aristotle's teachings. But a remarkable turnaround happened in the thirteenth century. In 1277 the Bishop of Paris condemned 219 propositions about the universe that were thought to be Aristotelian ideas. But at the Council of Lyons in 1274 the work of Thomas Aquinas (1225–1274), who claimed to have reconciled these divergences in his work, was upheld. The reconciliation of Aristotelianism and Christianity eventually became known as Thomism and became the only permissible way to look at things. As late as 1879, in a papal encyclical called *Aeterni Patris*, the Catholic Church entrenched Thomism as the only acceptable slant on Christian theology. This resulted in some of the Church's best scholars being declared heretics. The most prominent example was Alfred Loisy (1857–1940), a biblical scholar, who was excommunicated in 1908. Outside of the Catholic Church, Aristotelianism had ceased to have any genuine explanatory power after the seventeenth century.

Further reading: Anthony Gottlieb, *The Dream of Reason*.

ARMS TRADE. A truly massive multinational trade commodity. As of 2003, this trade is dominated by the United States, which in that year alone signed arms deals worth more than $14.5 billion. In 2003, 56.7 percent of all arms agreements were undertaken by the United States. Russia ranked a distant second with $4.3 billion and Germany third with $1.4 billion worth of sales. Also worrisome is the trade in arms by **rogue states** like North Korea, which have no compunctions to trade to unstable regimes or even to groups and individuals. The biggest single purchaser of arms between 2000 and 2003 was China, which bought more than $9.3 billion worth of arms. Other major purchasers of arms are Egypt, Israel, Saudi Arabia, India, South Korea, and Malaysia.

While several countries have legislation dealing with arms trade, efforts to construct a transnational code of conduct for arms sales have foundered. This code would not be an outright ban on arms sales, more a code of practice as to how the arms trade should proceed. Most national codes (the United States passed its in 1999) include themes like:

- not selling to nondemocratic regimes;
- not selling in situations of internal or external conflict; and
- not selling in situations that could undermine development and increase poverty.

Even if such a transnational code is adopted, it is hard to be optimistic that it would achieve a great deal. The money is too high, the loopholes are too big and too many, and **corruption** is too endemic.

Then there is the murky world of private entrepreneurs who make a handsome living trading in weapons. As of 2003, there were six major private arms dealers. They are mostly of Central Asian or Russian origin, and they have access to planes and ships for the passage of arms. Among the best known are Victor Bout and Alexander Islamov, both Russians; Leonid Minin, a Ukrainian; and Sarkis Soghanahian, an Armenian American. These dealers are vital to the continuation of low-level bloodletting around the world. They take advantage of surprisingly lax international laws regarding the arms trade, and the need of the great powers to have them as conduits for sales that are politically sensitive. The United States manufactures more arms than all other countries combined and has a special interest in the private arms dealers staying in business. See the entry on **cascading**.

Most arms dealers have a varied portfolio, also trading in illegal gems, drugs, and prostitution. The problems of private arms dealing, and all the misery that is caused by it, will be very difficult to tackle, let alone solve, without serious commitment to transnational authority with coercive powers.

The only remotely good news in all of this is that the volume of world trade in arms is falling. In 2000, the total value of world arms deals was $41 billion, but in 2003 that figure had declined to $25.6 billion. This decline has been variously put down to the spiraling cost of weapons, the end of the **cold war**, and the change in emphasis to a war against terrorism, which requires different forms of expenditure.

ARROGANTISM. A word coined by the popular Japanese cartoonist Yoshinori Kobayashi to describe the new sense of national pride he wants his fellow Japanese to adopt. Kobayashi wants Japan to stop feeling apologetic for its past. For instance, he has opposed the move by the Japanese government to compensate the "comfort women" who were coerced into prostitution for the Japanese troops during World War II.

Arrogantism, in its English translation, is an extremely unfortunate word for a sense of national pride. Other translations render the word as "Haughtiness-ism." The word comes from his book *Gomanizumu Genzen*, or *The Arrogantism [or Haughtiness-ism] Manifesto*

(1997). Kobayashi is right that we all need to feel proud of our national identity. However, the challenge is to be able to develop a pride in the various factors that have determined one's personality and values—national background is only one of them—*without* the need for arrogance and haughtiness.

ART FOR ART'S SAKE. Phrase variously attributed to the French Romantic novelist Théophile Gautier (1811–1872) in his novel *Mademoiselle de Maupin* (1834), or the English essayist and critic Walter Pater (1839–1894). Art for art's sake was said in the context of the disgust many young **Romantics** felt at the philistinism of nineteenth-century society. To be a writer or novelist was, by definition, to set oneself against the values of the bourgeois. It meant to hold fast to nonmaterial values for their own sake, rather than for the sake of profit or prestige, which were thought to be the principal bourgeois values. The idea of art for art's sake is deeply imbued with the Romantic idea that the artist is a vehicle for a special intensity of feeling and perhaps even truth that is denied to the average run of people.

ARTIFICIAL INTELLIGENCE. Thought by many to be *the* area of twenty-first-century research. The field was begun by the work of **Alan Turing** in the 1940s and has major implications in fields as varied as computer design, medicine, **philosophy**, and science fiction. Computers, for example, have become incomparably more powerful over the past half century. They can process huge quantities of information more efficiently and quickly than human brains can. They can also perform many functions that involve learning from experience, the best known example being the ability to play chess. But computers can also arrive at completely new ideas and in areas such as mathematics, arrive at conclusions that are close to the limits of what the human brain can compute.

This said, there are still some major obstacles to be overcome. The sheer unpredictable flexibility of the human brain is almost impossible to simulate. The original benchmark, established by Turing, was whether a person interacting with another person and with a computer ends up unable to determine which is which. No computer has passed the Turing test, and this despite the fact that computers are tremendously more powerful and sophisticated than those available to Turing. **John Searle** has argued convincingly that a computer is not able to think. It can produce output in response to what has been put in, and it can do this very rapidly and efficiently, but it cannot think. The relationship between the brain and **consciousness**, Searle argues, is causation, whereas the relationship between computer hardware and software is implementation. This argument is known as the Chinese Room Argument.

Largely because of difficulties arising over the Chinese Room Argument, artificial intelligence is less about preprogrammed output and more about creating the conditions for open-ended behavior, based on evolutionary models. Some of the more enthusiastic supporters of artificial intelligence have gathered under the label **transhumanism**.

ASHOKA (third century BCE). One of India's most renowned rulers. Ashoka was the son of Bindusara, who was the son of Chandragupta, the founder of the Maurya dynasty of Indian kings. It is not known when Ashoka was born, but we can date his reign fairly reliably to 268–233 BCE. He died in 231 BCE.

Tradition has it that after being converted to Buddhism by the monk Nigrodha, Ashoka became a monk. This is not now thought to be the case. And the whole idea of conversion to Buddhism rather misunderstands how the **Asian traditions** work. Ashoka's many inscriptions never mention the Buddha, nor does he show any awareness of some core Buddhist ideas like the Eightfold Path that leads to no desire. However, it is still fair to claim that Ashoka tired of the bloodthirsty military career of his younger days and devoted the bulk of his long reign to pro-moting the cultivation of moral virtues. This was to be done by realizing one's *dhamma*. Ashoka's notion of *dhamma* was an amalgamation of several contrasting understandings of the concept, from the brahmins, the **Jains**, the **Ajivikas**, and the Buddhists. It is also true that what is now called the Third Buddhist Council was convened by Ashoka in about 247 BCE and dealt with 218 points of doctrine and practice.

Ashoka devoted his time to the peaceful development of the large areas of India under his control. His lands were placed under efficient central control, run through provincial administrations. In one edict Ashoka entreated his subjects to treat each other's beliefs with respect and to refrain from disparaging them, noting that "by thus acting, a man exalts his own sect, and at the same time does service to the sects of other people." Visiting diplomats spoke enthusiastically of the tree-lined road network Ashoka encouraged. Taxes, weights, and measures were standardized and the reign of Ashoka was generally recognized as a golden age for India. The example set by Ashoka of appealing to all people, regardless of belief and caste, was a powerful one, and was an inspiration to reformers for centuries to come.

Further reading: John Keay, *India: A History*.

ASIAN TRADITIONS. The name frequently given by religious studies scholars to the great traditions of Asia: Hinduism, Buddhism, Confucianism, and Taoism. It has been observed by many scholars that to call these traditions **religions** is to misunderstand their *modus operandi*. Generally speaking, Hindus, Buddhists, Confucianists, and Taoists are as likely to describe their systems as ways of life or as philosophies than as religions.

The great Asian traditions are predominantly concerned with ethical behavior, in the context of subsuming the ego to a wider universal reality. Western religions are **monotheistic**, and are focused on an image of **God**, as revealed in written scriptures and exemplified (particularly in Christianity and Islam) by the words and deeds of a founder. It is important to western religions that people accord to the tenets of the religion, and people who do not are judged to be in fundamental error. Buddhism is the Asian tradition with the strongest tradition of a founder, but it is significant that the Buddha exhorted people to follow their own paths and not to follow his thoughts simply because they were his. See the entry on **Siddhartha Gautama**. Asian traditions are less concerned with what one believes, but how one behaves. For western religions how one behaves is supposed to be dependent on what one believes, with the result that hypocrisy is a widely observed behavior.

Neither are Asian traditions concerned with personal **immortality**, as monotheistic religions are. Such a concern is perceived by the Asian traditions to be misguided as it prevents the individual from working toward the extinction of egoism, which is such an important goal among Asian traditions.

As a general rule, it is unwise to describe Hinduism and Buddhism, Confucianism, or Taoism as religions, as it runs counter to how practitioners describe themselves, and involves a great number of assumptions, values, and methods that are foreign to an accurate understanding of Asian traditions. This also means that **atheism** has little to argue with against the Asian traditions, while **humanism** has a great deal in common with them.

ASIAN VALUES. A concept that arose in East Asia, most notably Malaysia and Singapore, in the 1970s and 1980s, and which sought to combat what was seen as foreign and hegemonic notions of value. Generally, those who speak in terms of Asian values highlight the Asian stress on duty, as opposed to the western stress on rights. Emphasis on rights, it is held, leads to confrontational societies whereas emphasis on duties leads to stable and harmonious societies. The values that produce stability and harmony are thought to be invaluable to the economic suc-

cess of the Asian economies. Furthermore, emphasis on duties is more conducive to preserving the collectivist nature of most Asian societies, in contrast to the individualism of the West. Other values often described as Asian include reliance on family and other close networks, delaying immediate gratification by taking a long-term view, and saving for the future. **Kongfuzi** is usually held up as the quintessential exponent of Asian values, but this does him a disservice. Kongfuzi did stress the qualities the proponents of Asian values admire but not to the exclusion of opposing tyranny.

Talk of Asian values was most prominent during the years of rapid economic growth, up until the late 1990s. Among its more extreme advocates there arose a note of triumphalism, not dissimilar to the talk of the superiority of Western values that accompanied the Western economies during their period of domination early in the twentieth century.

Models of economic development based on Asian values have been quite influential in other non-Western parts of the world, particularly Latin America. Critics have observed that the concept of Asian values is very likely to prove attractive to those in control of regimes with poor human rights records. The concept of Asian values also ignores those Asian countries that value human **rights** and the Western countries that do not. The attractiveness of Asian values declined after the severe economic downturn many Asian economies suffered in the late 1990s. See the entry on the **Lee Thesis**.

Further reading: Lucien W. Pye, "'Asian Values'—from Dynamos to Dominoes?" in Lawrence E. Harrison and Samuel P. Huntington, eds., *Culture Matters: How Values Shape Human Progress*, and Finngeir Hiorth, *Values*.

ASIMOV, ISAAC (1920–1992). Novelist, science prophet, and encyclopedic thinker. Born in Russia but brought to the United States when only three years old, he earned a PhD in chemistry at Columbia University and went on to have a distinguished career as a biochemist.

But it is as a popular author that Asimov is best known. He began contributing to popular science fiction magazines in 1939, and through his life made outstanding contributions to this genre. His trilogy *Foundation* (1951), *Foundation and Empire* (1952), and *Second Foundation* (1953) remains a landmark of science fiction, as do his short stories which came together as *I Robot* (1950). *The Road to Infinity* (1979) is an authoritative anthology of his fantasy and science fiction writings.

Asimov later became one of the most prolific popularizers of all time, following in the tradition pioneered by **Joseph McCabe**. For example, the *Intelligent Man's Guide to Science* (1960) is a systematic effort to provide a coherent overview of the physical and biological sciences for the nonspecialist. This work went through many editions and changes of title and was very influential in making the world of science approachable to the nonspecialist reader. *The Roving Mind* (1983) is a good collection of his essays.

Asimov was an outspoken atheist and humanist and was one of the inaugural laureates of the **International Academy of Humanism**, being elected in 1983. Shortly before his death, Asimov wrote, "Fortunately, I believe neither in heaven nor hell, so death holds no terror for me. I have had a long and happy life and I have no complaints about the ending thereof."

Further reading: Isaac Asimov, *It's Been a Good Life*.

ASPASIA (480–410 BCE, approx.). Powerful Greek woman who played an important role during the golden decades of Athens's rule. Aspasia was born in the Ionian city of Miletus and was not a citizen of Athens. From 445 BCE until his death, Aspasia was the mistress of **Pericles**, the most important statesman in Athens. Their son, also called Pericles, became a respected soldier and eventually became a citizen of Athens.

Aspasia was the butt of malicious gossip and accusations from the opponents of Pericles. She was accused of fomenting war and impiety. As well as Pericles, Aspasia was known to and respected by **Anaxagoras**, Euripides (484–406 BCE), Hippocrates (460–377 BCE, approx.), and **Socrates**.

ASSERTION. A simple declaration that something is so. And as such, assertions are not to be confused with propositions for which **evidence** is produced. To simply declare that **God** exists (or doesn't exist) or that some **pseudoscience** works (or doesn't work) is not the same as providing evidence, no matter how passionate the declaration.

ASSUMPTION OF MARY. The only incident where a pope has exercised the power given to him by the First Vatican Council (1869–1870) to make a pronouncement on faith and morals that is held to be infallible Catholic doctrine. Pope **Pius XII** declared 1950 a Holy Year and as a central celebration of that year, declared as Infallible Doctrine the Immaculate Assumption of Mary to heaven, without having gone through the agony and indignity of death. The announcement was made on November 1 to a crowd at St. Peter's Square and was published three days later as *Munificentissmus deus* (God the Most Generous). The Assumption of Mary is the logical continuation from Pius IX's declaration in 1858 of the **Dogma of the Immaculate Conception**.

This has important repercussions for the Roman Catholic conceptions of womanhood and **gender** equality. The only truly successful woman, according to this infallible doctrine, is the only woman who managed to be both virgin and mother. It has established forever a strict **dualism** between sexual gratification and the normal course of parenthood on the one hand and true faith, born of obedience and chastity, on the other. See the entry on **virgin-whore dichotomy**.

ASTONISHING HYPOTHESIS, THE. Name given to the contention of Nobel Prize–

winning scientist Francis Crick (1916–2004) that, contrary to common supposition, everything that happens in the brain is due to the activities of nerve cells. There is no **mind** which operates over and beyond the activities of the brain, and neither is there a **soul**, **psyche**, or any other sort of form of **consciousness** that determines or regulates brain activity. Crick's hypothesis correlates with that of **Daniel C. Dennett**, who argues that there is no single center in the brain to act as coordinator. Dennett called it the Cartesian theater. See the entry on **cranes and skyhooks**.

The findings of leading scientists like Crick and leading philosophers like Dennett should make all existing ideas of the brain obsolete, but we know enough about the resilience of non- and even antiscientific notions not to be unduly optimistic. And that is partly why Crick felt moved to call his idea the *astonishing* hypothesis. Nevertheless this exciting work on the brain is one of the last assaults on our **anthropocentric conceit**, whereby we can imagine some special status or destiny for ourselves by virtue of possessing an immortal soul or some such appurtenance.

Further reading: Francis Crick, *The Astonishing Hypothesis*.

ASTRAL TRAVEL. One of the more eccentric forms of **New Age pseudoscience**. For some it means stepping out of the physical body and moving around like a ghost. For others it means leaving not only the physical body but traveling to a different world or dimension altogether. For yet others, astral travel is a form of visionary experience, a form of which we can all experience when we dream.

As with a lot of New Age thinking, there is a core of actual experience, which is then puffed up with lots of flummery. But the explanations given to this by New Agers are not remotely real or credible. Some reasons to reject and some questions to ask about astral travel include:

- The differing stories about whether astral bodies wear clothes, not to mention how something astral *could* wear clothes. Why do most accounts of astral bodies that do wear clothes, wear clothes of the period?
- How does an astral body remember impressions of an event, and then transfer them to the physical body upon return?
- Do astral bodies also age and die as physical bodies do?
- If my astral body commits murder, am I responsible?
- If astral bodies are exact replicas of the physical bodies, as is usually claimed, then they must die with the physical body, and so we are no further ahead with regard to an afterlife.

Further reading: Paul Edwards, *Reincarnation: A Critical Examination*.

ATHEISM. An attitude of **skepticism** toward claims of the existence of any sort of **God** or gods. Atheism is as old as theism and comes in almost as many shapes and sizes. The claims frequently made by religious apologists that atheism involves the denial of **God** and/or the certain knowledge that there is no God are little more than caricatures that can only be made by ignoring what atheist thinkers have actually said. The philosophy of atheism was helped enormously when **Antony Flew** made the distinction between negative and positive atheism. This has done a lot to clear up very old misconceptions about what atheism is really saying. And incidentally, the distinction between negative and positive atheism has also brought to an end the usefulness of **agnosticism** as an idea. Flew has also made enormous contributions with his ideas on the **burden of proof** and the **presumption of atheism**.

Negative atheism is the weaker variant of atheism, which says that faith in God or gods is not justified. This approach stresses the improbability, rather than the impossibility, of God. One of the classic expressions of negative atheism comes from **Charles Brad-**

laugh, who wrote in *A Plea for Atheism* (1864): "The atheist does not say 'There is no God,' but he says: 'I know not what you mean by God; I am without idea of God; the word 'God' is to me a sound conveying no clear or distinct affirmation. I do not deny God, because I cannot deny that of which, by its affirmer, is so imperfect that he is unable to define it to me.'" In his classic study of atheism, **Michael Martin** concludes that negative atheism is justified because the sentence "God exists" is neither true nor false, but meaningless.

Positive atheism is the stronger variant of atheism, which says that it is justified not to believe in God or gods. This approach argues for the impossibility of God, not simply God's improbability. Michael Martin argues that positive atheism is justified if all the available evidence supporting belief in God can be shown to be inadequate and that there are no acceptable beneficial reasons to believe that God exists. Martin demonstrates that these conditions exist and that positive atheism is a philosophically sound position. See the entry on **positive atheism, justification for**. This understanding of positive atheism is not to be confused with the **positive atheism** as articulated by the Indian atheist thinker **Gora**.

Atheism involves the questioning of the belief in God or gods on three grounds:

- because it is very probably false that such a God exists;
- because the concept of God is meaningless, contradictory, or incoherent; and
- because the concept of God being proposed is so empty of real substance that it is little more than atheism in disguise.

The first approach is most telling against the crudest anthropomorphic notions of God. The second approach is most telling against the mainstream God of the Christian tradition, and the third approach is most telling against some of the abstractions put forward by Paul Tillich (1886–1965), **John Dewey**, or A. N. Whitehead (1861–1947).

Joseph McCabe, a pioneer of twentieth-century atheism, wrote that the roots of a conscious atheism lie in "a sufficient study of **science** to realize that no spiritual or supernatural powers can be discerned at work in nature, an extensive study of history and comparative religion, and a frank consideration of those evils and stupidities of contemporary life which discredit the idea of a vigilant and sympathetic deity."

The most important argument for atheism, however, is the moral argument. Atheism is the surest corrective against **anthropocentric conceit** and for a **cosmic perspective**. Atheism is the most humble of worldviews because it provides its adherents with no compensating presumptions about being of central importance to the cosmos. Atheists believe they are a species of bipeds on one planet in one galaxy in one corner of what may well be multiple universes. Given our cosmic irrelevance, it behooves us to act responsibly toward the planet that provides us with sustenance for our brief period on it.

Further reading: Michael Martin, *Atheism: A Philosophical Justification*; and Kai Nielsen, *Naturalism and Religion*.

ATHEISM, BOOKS ABOUT. There is an ever growing range of high quality literature on **atheism**. The best introductions to atheism for the general reader are *Atheism: A Very Short Introduction* (2003) by Julian Baggini; *What is Atheism? A Short Introduction* (1998) by Douglas E. Krueger; *Why Atheism?* (2000) by George H. Smith; and *Introduction to Atheism* (1995) by **Finngeir Hiorth**. Slightly more complicated is *An Intelligent Person's Guide to Atheism* (2001) by Daniel Harbour. An attempt to give the basic arguments of atheism in fictional form can be found in *The Big Domino in the Sky* (1996) by **Michael Martin**.

The two best collections of arguments for atheism are *Critiques of God* (1997) edited by Peter Angeles and *The Impossibility of God* (2003) edited by Michael Martin and

Ricki Monnier. The best defenses of atheism by a single author include *The Existence of God* (1965) by Wallace Matson; *God and Philosophy* (1966) by **Antony Flew**; *The Miracle of Theism* (1982) by J. L. Mackie; *Atheism: A Philosophical Justification* (1990) by Michael Martin; *Nonbelief and Evil: Two Arguments for the Nonexistence of God* (1998) by Theodore M. Drange; and *Atheism, Morality, and Meaning* (2002) by Michael Martin. None of these are easy reading but all are worth the effort. The most comprehensive work is *Atheism: A Philosophical Justification*, and the most influential, and easiest to read, is *The Miracle of Theism*.

There are also a few debates in book form between theists and atheists, but these are an acquired taste. But the best are *Does God Exist?* (1991) by Terry Miethe and Antony Flew; and *Atheism and Theism* (1996), by J. J. C. Smart and J. J. Haldane. There have been some attempts to outline the ethical and political consequences of atheism: from the left comes *An Atheist's Values* (1964) by **Richard Robinson**, and from the right comes *Atheism: The Case Against God* (1989) by George H. Smith.

The history of atheism has still not been explored as fully as is necessary. The best general introduction remains *Western Atheism: A Short History* (1999, this being a reprint of *A Short History of Western Atheism*, 1971) and *The Alternative Tradition: A Study of Unbelief in Ancient World* (1980), both by James Thrower. More specialized is *Atheism from the Reformation to the Enlightenment* (1992) edited by Michael Hunter and David Wootton, and *A History of Atheism in Britain* (1988) by David Berman. Much harder to find is *Indian Atheism* (1991 [1969]) by Debiprasad Chattopadhyaya. S. T. Joshi has done a good job bringing together the best defenses of atheism from earlier times in *Atheism: A Reader* (2000). Other valuable material can be found in *Varieties of Unbelief: From Epicurus to Sartre* (1989) edited by J. C. A. Gaskin, and two anthologies edited by **Gordon Stein**, *An Anthology of Atheism and Rationalism* (1980) and *A Second Anthology of Atheism and Rationalism* (1987). The best encyclopedia of atheism is *The New Encyclopedia of Unbelief*, edited by **Tom Flynn** (2005). This is the successor volume to *The Encyclopedia of Unbelief*, 1985.

ATHEISM, ETHICAL IMPLICATIONS OF. Atheism is nothing more than the conviction that the evidence for the existence of **God** is poor and the evidence against the existence of God is solid. But a universe without God has important moral implications. Chief among these are:

- the responsibility to work out a valid way to live for oneself;
- the recognition that one's thoughts are always going to carry the possibility of error, with the resulting requirement for toleration;
- the inference that if this form of **anthropocentric conceit** is invalid, then other ones could well be invalid as well; and
- recognition of the brevity of life and the desire to enjoy it and help others enjoy it too.

It is important to note that these are only *implications* of atheism. How one actually addresses these implications is another matter. This is an issue of the **insufficiency of atheism**. Having established the incoherence of notions of God, the job of atheism is done. We need then to turn to whatever philosophy of life we adopt that will be consistent with the ethical implications of atheism.

ATHEISM, INSUFFICIENCY OF. The intellectual ascendancy of **atheism** is beyond any serious challenge. However, all that means is that traditional claims about **God**, gods, and supernatural entities are without warrant. This still leaves unanswered the question of how we live our lives given the nonexistence of any God or gods. Atheism is invaluable as a corrective against **anthro-**

pocentric conceit, but it is unable to provide a program for living. That is where freethought comes in, whether conceived as rationalism, skepticism, or humanism. Rationalism and skepticism provide the tools for learning and determining quality information from bogus claims. And humanism can provide the actual program of beliefs that can sustain a happy and fulfilled life.

Atheism is only about what we *don't* believe, rationalism and skepticism are about *how* we believe, and humanism is about what we *do* believe. Unless each of these three pillars of **freethought** is in place, the structure is incomplete. See the entry on **antitheism**.

ATHEISM, MORAL ARGUMENT FOR. It is an old argument that one needs to oppose notions of **God** for the sake of morality. While the traditional philosophical proofs of the nonexistence of God are compelling, they are dry. This argument, and the consequences thereof, are far more important.

A recent version of the argument has been put forward by the New Zealand philosopher Raymond Bradley, who argues that if there are objective moral truths, then God does not exist. When Bradley speaks of "God," he means the all-powerful and all-loving God of popular imagination; the holy God who reveals himself in **scriptures**. What Bradley does is to postulate some objective moral truths (see the entry on **objective morality**):

- It is morally wrong to deliberately kill people innocent of any serious wrong-doing.
- It is morally wrong to provide one's troops with young women for the purpose of being used as sex slaves.
- It is morally wrong to make people cannibalize their friends and family.
- It is morally wrong to practice human sacrifice, in whatever form.
- It is morally wrong to torture people endlessly for their beliefs.

Bradley then goes on to show how each of these maxims of objective morality are broken in the Bible. In order, each maxim is broken in Genesis 7:23 or 2 Samuel 24:1–15; Numbers 31:17–18; Leviticus 26:29 or Deuteronomy 28:53–58 among others; Judges 11:30–39; and Revelation 14:10–11. More examples of each can be found, but the point is made. The existence of these violations of objective morality in the Bible makes it impossible to hold without contradiction the views that the Bible is God's inerrant word, that God is good, that there are objective truths while also recognizing that God violated those truths in the scriptures ascribed to him. This leads us to the question of having to reject some other of the blood-curdling commands of the Bible in the very name of morality.

So, take the command "go and strike Amalek and utterly destroy all that he has, and do not spare him: but put to death both man and woman, child and infant . . ." (1 Samuel 15:3). If God asked you to perform these against some new menace, would you obey? By this argument, the person who says "Yes" may well be godly, but is also morally abhorrent. And by contrast, the person who says "No" may well be godless, but is clearly the more moral of the two.

Further reading: Raymond Bradley, "A Moral Argument for Atheism," in *The Impossibility of God*, ed. Michael Martin and Rikki Monier.

ATHEISM VERSUS RELIGION: DOES IT MATTER? Many people are uninterested in the question of God's existence or nonexistence. Does it really matter? There are good arguments either way. The answer really depends on what importance ideas have for you. Here are some contrasting answers to the question:

- *Yes it does*, because what we believe is important, and has a bearing on how we live our lives.
- *No it doesn't*, because there are good people and bad people from all opin-

ions, whether religious or not.

- *Yes it does*, because the trend in philosophical and scientific argument over the past four centuries is inexorably against any sort of supernatural dimension or God, which makes it important that our beliefs reflect this basic reality.
- *No it doesn't*, because it can't be proven one way or another, and is therefore a waste of our time.

- *Yes it does*, because the outcome of this question would determine how I would live my life.
- *No it doesn't*, because there are many far more pressing problems in the world than whether God exists or not.

Two less helpful arguments go like this:

- *Yes it does*, because I know I'm right and have a duty to share my knowledge with others.
- *No it doesn't*, because I know what I believe and have no interest in talking to other people about it.

Each of these arguments is a mirror of each other. Whether you see the question of atheism versus theism as important will depend on where you stand on these issues. See the entry on **indifferentism**.

ATHEIST CENTRE, THE. One of the premier institutions devoted to **atheism** in the world. The Atheist Centre was founded by **Gora** in August 1940 in the remote village of Mudunur, Andhra Pradesh. A refugee from teaching posts from which he was regularly fired because of his atheism, Gora established the Atheist Centre to focus on adult education and the eradication of superstition. In 1941, he organized a local conference on atheism at which 300 people attended over three days. From 1940 to 1947, Gora worked toward the improvement of sanitation, elimination of untouchability, and adult education in Mudunur

and the neighboring villages. Mudunur came to be known as the godless village. In 1947 the Atheist Centre moved to Vijayawada in Andhra Pradesh. In 1949 it began a Telugu weekly paper called *Sangham* (Society) and in 1954 renamed *Arthik Samata* (Economic Equality). In 1969 an English-language monthly called *The Atheist* was included.

Central among the Atheist Centre's work over its career has been the promotion of intercaste marriages, criminal rehabilitation, assistance to untouchables, and education. Among its subsidiary organizations is the Arthik Samata Mandal, or Association for Economic Equality, which was founded in 1951. The Arthik Samata Mandal operates in 150 villages around Andhra Pradesh in the fields of health, education, sanitation, and poverty relief. The Vasaya Mahila Mandali, founded in 1969 focuses more on the needs of women and children. This runs a small hospital and operates in 50 villages. The most recent is Samskar, founded by Lavanam and his wife, Hemalata, and is devoted to the rehabilitation of ex-convicts. It is ironic that, while Mother Teresa was praised around the world for what in fact were negligible acts of charity, the Atheist Centre, which has an impeccable record of achievement, is unknown outside India.

The Atheist Centre also sponsors periodic **world atheist conferences** that explore various aspects of **positive atheism**

ATHEIST SOCIETY OF INDIA. Founded on February 13, 1972, by Jaya Gopal (1942–). Gopal edits the society's Telugu-speaking monthly, the *Nastika Yugam*. He has written twenty-one books in Telugu and English, including *Hindu Fascism* (1994) and *ABC of Atheism*. The Society manages a cultural troupe called Nastika Kalamandali, which tours the country educating people through songs and dances. The Atheist Society of India campaigns for secular marriages and against the caste system and religious superstition.

ATHEISTS IN FOXHOLES. Among the more malevolent **prejudices against atheists**, none can compare to the commonly repeated sneer that there are no atheists in foxholes. To cite but one instance, **George Macdonald**, whose two sons were serving in the United States forces in World War I, quoted a Catholic priest who told his listeners "Atheists will be the first to be shot in the back when forced to go to war by conscription." The specific barb that there are no atheists in foxholes was first made by an American army chaplain, William Thomas Cummings, to troops fighting the Japanese in the Philippines in 1942.

This accusation is in the worst possible taste for three reasons. First, it is not true. Second, not only is it not true, but it devalues the contribution atheists have made in the armed services, usually in the face of persecution and ridicule. And third, it judges a whole group of people according to a miserable standard.

The slightest acquaintance with the humanist movement will quickly reveal how many people actually *became* atheists in a foxhole. Many are mentioned in this book. The incongruity—to say the least of it—of a loving god while lying face down in the ground evading bombs and bullets, probably from armies as replete with pious chaplains as one's own, quickly becomes apparent. The sneer that there are no atheists in foxholes also mocks and undervalues the courage of the atheist soldier who, while being no less scared than his religious comrade, is less prepared to petition for his own safety.

ATHEISTS, PREJUDICES AGAINST. Truly atheists are the last minority. There is no other group that can be vilified, sneered at, and misrepresented with impunity more than atheists. It is an important point that this attitude only exists in **monotheist** societies, that is, societies where the majority religion is either Judaism, Christianity, or Islam. Hatred and fear of atheists hardly exists in Hindu, Buddhist, or Confucian societies.

Atheists have traditionally been seen as not merely intellectually mistaken but morally flawed. Nowhere has this been more true than in Islam, where denying Allah is often seen as self-evidently immoral and wicked. In Christian societies, atheists have been portrayed as needing to avoid the reality of God in order to live immoral and criminal lives. Even today, many religious conservatives are content to accuse atheists of being maladjusted outcasts. See the entry on **God, denial of**. Philosophers as different as **Plato** and **John Locke** both opposed extending **toleration** to atheists. Neither thinker thought that atheists could be trusted.

There is also the "village atheist" stereotype; strident, unbalanced, and worthy of contempt. More recently, atheists are portrayed as emanating from the effete, superficial urban centers, people without roots and depth. **Fundamentalists** will cheerfully recite the passage from Proverbs that says "the fool in his heart says there is no god," apparently oblivious to the level of simple abuse this passage relies on. Religious liberals rely more on condescension than abuse, preferring to observe that we are all *Homo religiosus* with the unsaid inference that atheists are not fully human. Other popular slanders include those about **infidel deathbeds** and **atheists in foxholes**. People wishing to clothe their prejudice in philosophical garb employ the **can't prove a negative** argument.

The facts, of course, tell a different story. Atheists are usually among the best educated citizens and constitute a minute proportion of prison populations around the world. Atheists are rarely as prejudiced as their religious neighbors and overwhelmingly live conspicuously moral and productive lives. What is more, they do so with no thought of supernatural reward. Many of the people whose lives are outlined in this book are atheists: philosophers, scientists, philanthropists, playwrights, authors: people who have contributed positively to the **social intelligence**. See the entry on **religion, criticism of**.

ATHEOLOGY. A term originally coined by British thinker Ralph Cudworth (1617–

1688), whose life work involved defending the reality of a divine intelligence. Atheology was then taken to mean the tendency of atheist thinkers who, no less than theist thinkers, ground their thinking on the assumed moral attributes of divinity, only in their case to build an atheistic worldview.

More recently, the word has taken on a less pejorative flavor, meaning the project of constructing a valid worldview without recourse to **God** or the supernatural.

ATOMISM. An ancient variety of **naturalist** philosophy and the one which, in general terms, most closely approximates the way we understand the world today. The best-known proponent of atomism is **Democritus** of Abdera, but Pakudha Kaccayana, an Indian thinker, preceded him by more than a century, though he did not argue to the same degree of sophistication. Pakudha, an **Ajivika** thinker, theorized seven elements: earth, fire, air, water, joy, sorrow, and life. Atoms are neither created nor destroyed, neither could they divide, grow, expand, or in any way change their basic organization. Atoms could only be seen when aggregated into molecules, and the element of life consisted in perceiving the other elements operating interdependently. There was also a strand of early Buddhists known as the Sautrantikas who were atomists.

Like Pakudha and the Sautrantikas, the Greek atomists were intent on explaining the world without resorting to grandiose notions of cosmic purpose or final cause. Greek atomism had no concept of a deity or any sort of life after death. The universe is infinite and all things are composed of countless tiny atoms which, when they collide, produce everything we know. The atoms themselves are indivisible and are the foundation matter of the universe. The main tenets of Greek atomism were:

- all things, including **souls**, are composed of atoms, which can neither be created nor destroyed;
- all things are governed by mechanical laws;

- thought is a physical process; and
- there is no purpose in the universe, beyond what we make for ourselves.

Greek atomism was best expressed by **Lucretius** in his timeless work, *On the Nature of Things.* Lucretius wrote:

Bear this well in mind, and you will immediately perceive that nature is free and uncontrolled by proud masters and runs the universe without the aid of gods. For who—by the sacred hearts of the gods who pass their unruffled lives, their placid aeon, in calm and peace!—who can rule the sum of the measureless?

Atomism was vastly influential in the development of modern **science**. Pierre Gassendi (1592–1655) devoted his career to reconciling atomism with Christianity, which earned for him the reputation of **heresy**. The rediscovery of atomism was instrumental in developing the notion of the **heliocentric universe**, particularly by thinkers such as **Giordano Bruno** and **Galileo**.

Further reading: Richard C. Vitzhum, *Materialism: An Affirmative History and Definition.*

ATTATÜRK. See **KEMAL, MUSTAPHA.**

ATWOOD, MARGARET (1939–). Canadian novelist and critic. She was born on November 18, 1939, in Ottawa. Her family moved to Toronto when she was seven, and she has lived most of her life there since. She is married to Graeme Gibson, a writer. Atwood was a published poet before turning to fiction writing. *The Circle Game* (1966) received the Governor General's Award, Canada's highest literary award.

Atwood's first novel was *The Edible Woman* (1969). Her best-known novel is *The Handmaid's Tale* (1985), a grim tale set in the future about a fundamentalist dictatorship after some sort of nuclear catastrophe. Fertile women are at a premium in this state, and simple biological needs mix with religious misogyny to make a fearsome place for women. The book was made into a film by Volker Schlondorff in 1990. *The Handmaid's Tale* also won the Governor General's Award.

Other important Atwood novels are *Surfacing* (1972), *Alias Grace* (1996), *The Blind Assassin* (2000), which won the 2000 Booker Prize and was made into a film in 2002, and *Oryx and Crake* (2003), the story of the world, already rendered nightmarish by societal and environmental decay, brought to its knees by a malevolent virus.

Atwood's novels are often pessimistic, even grim, but as the English literary critic **Jim Herrick** notes, her work "shows a humanist belief in the power of survival of the deepest feelings." This comment, made about *The Handmaid's Tale*, is appropriate for all her work. And while her books are often about the blighted lives many women find themselves leading, Atwood does not see herself as a feminist author. There is a Margaret Atwood Society that sponsors discussions and conference papers on Atwood's books and produces its own newsletter. See the entry on **humanist-themed novels**.

AURELIUS ANTONINUS, MARCUS (121–180 CE). That rare combination, an emperor who is also a wise person. Marcus Aurelius was the last of the Antonine emperors of Rome who ruled during the empire's greatest years. He was also the last of the great **Stoic** thinkers. Marcus Aurelius studied under another famous Stoic thinker, the former slave **Epictetus**, whose genial influence was apparent in his willingness to share power, work collegially with others, and oversee some of the most progressive legislation the empire ever enacted. The rights of women and slaves improved considerably during his reign. He was also active in the empire's defense. While campaigning in the north against barbarian invasions, Marcus Aurelius wrote notes to himself on how to live and think better. They are published in Eng-

lish as *Meditations*, and are easily available.

Marcus Aurelius's philosophy featured most of the pillars of Stoicism: the universe is an interdependent organic unity in which human beings are but one small part. Aurelius specifically warned against **anthropocentric conceit**. And just as we are part of a dynamic and interdependent cosmos, so are we also part of a community of people, and we cannot flourish as individuals unless our community flourishes, and this requires some effort on our behalf, though it should be undertaken without thought of reward and honors. But when engaged in public activity, we should always be mindful of what is within our power and what is not. Awareness of those limitations will lead to **peace of mind**. All of this constitutes living according with nature.

Marcus Aurelius's philosophy of life was wise and humble in equal measure. He died in Vienna while campaigning. The tragedy was that Marcus Aurelius could not instill his noble worldview on his degenerate son, Commodus (161–192 CE) whose reign can be seen as the beginning of the decline and fall of the Roman Empire.

Further reading: C. Clayton Dove, *Marcus Aurelius Antoninus: His Life and Times*.

AUTHENTICITY. A word arising out of **existentialist** philosophy and which came to mean the requirement each of us has to realize our unique individuality. Settling for less than that will involve us in **bad faith**, a form of self-deceit. Authentic individuals accord their own priorities and values by their own standards, and not according to the expectations of **society**, the dictates of **command moralities**, or the prejudices of one's class or nation. Our authentic selves are not derived from outside sources (advertising, peer pressure, craving for approval, and so on) but from our own sense of who we are and what we are about. But along with this independence comes a total responsibility for the consequences of our decisions.

While the concept of authenticity is best known from its use by existentialist philosophers, it has a wider appeal and applicability. Authenticity was an important concept for **humanistic psychology**, not least in providing the model for the notion of self-actualization.

AUTHENTICITY, CRITERIA OF. The problem among biblical scholars of how to determine which statements attributed to **Jesus Christ** are authentic has become a serious one. The German theologian **Gerd Lüdemann** has devised these five criteria to determine the authenticity of the statements attributed to Jesus in the New Testament:

- *offensiveness*: statements or acts by Jesus that offend current sensibilities, and which, if not genuine, we could expect to see dropped from later accounts;
- *difference*: sayings that cannot be found in later communities or which are consistent with the thoughts and priorities of the time of Jesus;
- *growth*: if sayings have layers of later additions, the core may well be authentic;
- *rarity*: sayings or actions which have few or no other parallels; and
- *coherence*: sayings or actions that cohere with authentic Jewish sayings and actions at the time.

By these means, Lüdemann has come up with a sound core of what, in all probability, are authentic sayings of Jesus. This has serious consequences for conventional Christianity, because it does not support the traditional theology of the Christian Jesus, but confirms the general trend in scholarship that portrays a Jewish rabbi who had no intention of forming a new religion, much less one as anti-Semitic as Christianity.

Further reading: Gerd Lüdemann, *The Great Deception, and What Jesus Really Said and Did*.

AUTHORITY, ARGUMENT FROM. One of the oldest forms of fallacious argument. The argument from authority rests on the fallacy that the opinions of a person in a position of authority are superior to those not in such a position *solely by virtue of his position of authority*. The classic example of the argument from authority is from St. Augustine (354–430 CE) who wrote "I would not have believed the Gospels, except on the authority of the Catholic Church."

The method of operation of the argument from authority is to intimidate one's opponent by asking how they could presume to challenge the view of such an impeccable source, be it priest, judge, mayor, or "expert." It ignores the fact that people in authority are just as prone to error as anyone else and, if anything, more susceptible to the temptation to prefer arguments that suit one's current position of privilege.

This does not mean that we should reject all opinions of those in authority. It simply means that people in authority can also be wrong, and that if we find their opinion acceptable, we find it so because it is a convincing argument, not because it comes from someone in authority.

AVAILABILITY HEURISTIC. A term used by psychologists that refers to our frequently mistaken belief that something happens more often than is the case simply because we have seen more instances of it. The classic example is murders. In the United States the suicide rate is nearly twice as high as the murder rate, and yet people repeatedly say they believe the murder rate is higher. This is largely because people see evidence of murders on television considerably more frequently than they do of suicides. In other words, there is a greater availability heuristic for the belief in the greater incidence of murders than of suicides.

This is further evidence of the tricks our minds can play on us, and the constant need we have to be skeptical of things, even—perhaps especially—of things we believe to be true.

AVANT-GARDE. A much talked-over concept that usually refers to the idea of a small vanguard of artists who are producing art that is derided and undervalued in its own day, but when the general population finally gets the point, is praised and its true value is recognized. The *avant-garde* idea thought of the artist in terms of being a cultural and intellectual pioneer, in whose inner conflicts and subsequent artistic renderings would serve as a direction-pointer for the rest of us, who were not so endowed.

The idea owes a great deal to the **Romantic** movement of the nineteenth century. The expanding bourgeois no longer sought legitimacy or a program of belief from the churches, but from secular sources. The talk of the salons enabled the leaders to provide new forms of thought and ways of understanding the world. But there was a love-hate relationship between the avant-garde and the bourgeois who sustained them. Until well into the 1930s, the avant-garde took their role seriously enough to write earnest and passionate manifestos, calling for change in society, principally in the form of a renewal of values. But this idealist zeal depended on the visual arts having a central role in the education of the masses that it no longer enjoyed. The idea of the avant-garde had collapsed by the 1970s.

AWE. A word in danger of becoming drearily overused. Most works outlining a cosmic worldview speak at some point of awe before the beauty of a sunset, the complexity of nature, or the grandeur of **God**, according to the taste of the author. The motive behind the overuse of what **Richard Dawkins** called the "awe-factor" is simple: we all want to avoid **anthropocentric conceit** and to reaffirm our smallness in the scheme of things. And without doubt, many of the facts of nature are staggeringly complicated and conducive to producing awe. However, it would be healthy to declare a moratorium on awe for the time being. Unless one can write like Dawkins, most people's description of the awe they feel (or try to feel) at appropriate moments ends up as a patch of forgettable purple prose.

I prefer the term **cosmic modesty** to awe.

Cosmic modesty suggests having gone a step further than simple, passive awe. Cosmic modesty suggests that one has specifically rejected anthropocentric conceit and adopted a **cosmic perspective**. See the entry on **spirituality**.

AXIAL AGE. A term coined by German **existentialist** thinker and theologian Karl Jaspers (1883–1969) to denote the period circa 800–200 BCE, when many major religious and philosophical traditions first emerged. Jaspers claimed that the defining new element of this age is the newfound awareness humanity has both of itself and of its limits. And from this new awareness came a drive for liberation and redemption, and the hope, which has dominated much religious thinking ever since, of serenity in a world beyond the world we live in. Other commentators have spoken of the Axial Age as having come to the realization that human effort unaided by divine support was vain.

The whole concept of an axial age has been criticized since Jaspers's death. Any idea of an age being defined in some way according to the standards of another age run into problems. Furthermore, Jaspers did not make enough distinction between religions and the **Asian traditions**, which differ from the **monotheist** religions in significant ways.

AXIOTHEA (fourth century BCE). The name of a female philosopher in Plato's **Academy**. We know nothing about her life or philosophy. Her name is mentioned, along with a Lasthenia, as women who attended the Academy. Although Plato had a very low opinion of women, he went against the grain of Greek society when he said that women were just as able to participate in public duties as men. With that in mind, women were occasionally permitted, however grudgingly, to study at the Academy. Inevitably, Axiothea paid a high price for her intellectual curiosity. Diogenes Laertius reports she attended lectures dressed in men's clothing.

This is also one of the few areas where **Aristotle** represents, from the contemporary standpoint, a step backward from Plato. Aristotle believed that women were naturally inferior to men. See the entry on **Aspasia**.

AYER, ALFRED JULES (1910–1989). Described by **Ted Honderich**, a prominent English philosopher, as a hussar against nonsense. Ayer was a lifelong **atheist**, **rationalist**, and **humanist**. His reputation was made with his first book, *Language, Truth and Logic* (1936), which argued boldly for the elimination of many philosophical problems simply by seeing them as meaningless. In a long career in academic philosophy, Ayer held prestigious chairs such as the Grote professorship in philosophy at University College (1946–1959), London, and the Wykeham professorship in philosophy at New College, Oxford (1959–1977).

Ayer believed that philosophy could not solve problems by asking large, metaphysical questions. He rejected very firmly all the wordy formulae of **mysticism** and philosophical idealism. Some of Ayer's finest works, and most accessible to the nonspecialist reader, were written late in his life. *Russell* (1971) and *Hume* (1980) remain two of the best short introductions to these philosophers, and Ayer is very much in their philosophical tradition. *Voltaire* (1986) and *Thomas Paine* (1988) are excellent studies of these men and their legacy to the modern world. *The Central Questions of Philosophy* (1973) is more difficult but worth the effort. It provides a valuable introduction to some of philosophy's main problems.

Ayer was active in the humanist movement for much of his life. An honorary associate of the **Rationalist Press Association** from 1947, Ayer also served as vice president and president of the **British Humanist Association**. Ayer was technically dead for four minutes in May 1988 but was revived. He lived for another year, during which time he reiterated his atheism.

Further reading: John Foster, *A. J. Ayer*, on his philosophy; and Ben Rogers, *A. J. Ayer: A Life*, on his life.

AYODHYA. The Jerusalem of India, Ayodhya has become a flashpoint for rival fundamentalists clothed in religious garb. Ayodhya is a city in the Indian state of Uttar Pradesh, which is holy both for Hindus and Muslims, and, as with belief systems the world over, they find it impossible to share the city in peace. Hindus claim that Ayodhya is the birthplace of the Hindu god Rama, a claim repeated in many other cities in India. Meanwhile Muslims also claim Ayodhya as a holy city by virtue of the four-hundred-year-old Babri Mosque built there by the Mughal emperor Zahir al-Din Muhammad (1483–1530), known as Babar the Conqueror.

Inflamed by a growing **Hindutva** intolerance, Hindu extremists declared that the mosque must come down and be replaced by a temple in honor of Lord Rama. In 1992 the mosque was utterly destroyed by Hindu extremists, an act which precipitated widespread rioting that cost the lives of several thousand people. Since then India has had a dangerous stalemate on its hands, with the government unable to assuage either side.

AZAD, HUMAYUN (1947–2004). Prolific Bangladeshi scholar, humanist, secularist, poet, and professor of Bengali at Dhaka University. Dr. Azad has long been a critic of the lack of democracy in Muslim societies and is a strong supporter of the separation of mosque and state. Among his seventy books include ten novels, seven works on linguistics, and many volumes of poetry. He was the recipient of the Bangla Academy Award and Shishu Academy Award, both prestigious literary awards.

In February 2004, Dr. Azad was stabbed by religious bigots armed with butchers' knives. He had already received several death threats following the publication of a work outlining his nonbelief in Islam and a novel *Pak Sar Zamin Saad Baad* (the first words in the Pakistani national anthem), which discussed the collaboration between religious groups and the Pakistani army during Bangladesh's war of independence in 1971. Azad spent months in the hospital fighting for his life. He then went to Germany, where he died in mysterious circumstances.

The brutality of the attack on Dr. Azad provoked a widespread reaction among students, teachers, and union groups. The Bangladesh government, to its credit, ensured that Azad received the best possible medical attention. It was widely recognized that the attack on him represented an attack on the **open society**. Only four days before the attack, Dr. Kamal Hossein, a prominent human rights lawyer and campaigner, was attacked in Chittagong.

B

BABY BOOMERS. A term given to the generation born in the Western world in the decade or so after World War II: 1945–1955. What made this generation different from all other ones, before or since, was its unprecedented size and the unparalleled quantity of resources diverted toward its education and prosperity. As this generation grew up, it received the best of the health facilities the expanding postwar Western economies could provide, and when it came time to leave school there were more spaces at universities available for them than in the history of civilization. Entire tertiary facilities were created in an unprecedented expansion of this sector. In the United States, this development was done for reasons of national security as much as for the disinterested education of its citizens, the country having had a nasty shock at its technological inferiority to the Soviet Union, which had launched Sputnik into space in 1957.

Ironically, it was this generation that led the protests against the norms and values of the society that had provided them with such unprecedented levels of opportunity. Protests against the Vietnam War, the oppression of women, racism, cultural conformity, and consumerism, were all led by baby boomers. And while this generation believed many different things, one thing it rejected pretty comprehensively was the conventional religion of its predecessors. While Christianity was in decline before the 1960s, it was not until that decade that religious adherence around the Western world began to decline precipitously. Even in the United States, where peculiar factors have slowed the rate of that decline, the same noticeable change can be pinpointed to the 1960s. It has become fashionable to criticize the **narcissism** of the baby-boomer generation, but these criticisms overlook the unparalleled stresses this generation experienced, in particular the very real threat of nuclear war that hung over those years, which are now looked back on as golden years of innocence. The baby boomers cannot be blamed for rejecting the values that had come within an inch of destroying the entire planet.

The baby boomers' next major effect on Western societies will come when they begin to retire in the first decade of the twenty-first century. The prospect of this massive draining of funds into pension schemes for this cohort is placing enormous pressure on our notions of the **welfare state**. The stresses on already stretched pension and healthcare facilities are raising fears that some people call an **agequake**.

And while the Western baby boomers enter into retirement, another generation of baby boomers are just coming of age. Across the Muslim world a huge youth bulge of people born in the 1980s is putting pressure on those countries' more fragile infrastructures. In many Muslim countries, more than half the population is under twenty-five. In Yemen that percentage is 68. See the entry on **overpopulation**. There is a great deal of apprehension that the rising expectations of these young people cannot be met by their corrupt governments, and that the appeal of various brands of **Islamism** will increase as a result.

BAD FAITH. A term invented by the existentialist thinker **Jean-Paul Sartre** in his best-known philosophical work *Being and Nothingness* (1943). Bad faith is one of the most useful ideas to come out of **existentialism**. Hypocrisy and shallowness are not new, of course, but Sartre's analysis did cast fresh light on old problems. Bad faith is the self-deceit we frequently practice when we are trying to evade our burden of responsibility. By shaping our personality to conform to the **command moralities** of religion or ideology, we are indulging in bad faith. When we behave as we think we should behave, given our station in life, we are indulging in bad faith. Bad faith is when we pretend to ourselves that we are less free than in fact we are. Bad faith is the opposite of **authenticity**.

Further reading: Jean-Paul Sartre, *Being and Nothingness*.

BALANCED INTELLECTUAL PERSONALITY. A notion conceived by the American philosopher James Montmarquet, who has challenged the idea that trying to arrive at the truth is necessarily a virtuous way to proceed. This would leave no valid way to criticize fanatics and dogmatists who are quite convinced that they have sought out, and indeed already arrived at, the truth.

Instead Montmarquet proposes the balanced intellectual personality whose virtues would consist not so much in arriving at the truth as developing a sound mechanism for further questioning and study. This would revolve around the two virtues of impartiality and intellectual courage. Impartiality involves openness to the view of others and recognition of the **fallibility** of one's own views. Intellectual courage involves the willingness to question popular beliefs and perseverance in the face of opposition, and continual openness to question one's own beliefs.

These two virtues are complementary in that impartiality is outwardly focused, in that it is directed toward sustaining a worthwhile intellectual community, while intellectual courage is inwardly focused, because it is directed toward maintaining one's own intellectual integrity.

BALLANCE, JOHN (1839–1893). Free-thinking pioneer and prime minister of New Zealand. John Ballance was born the son of an evangelically inclined Primitive Methodist farmer and his Quaker wife at Ballypitmave, County Antrim, Northern Ireland. He was apprenticed to an ironmonger at the age of eighteen in Birmingham, where he was influenced by **Robert Owen** and the Secularist movement. He emigrated to Australia, then New Zealand in 1865, settling in Wanganui, where he cofounded the local newspaper, which still operates. Ballance also formed the Wanganui Cavalry in 1868 and adopted a policy of militant opposition to Maori interests, for which he ran into trouble with his cavalry unit.

Ballance helped form the Wanganui Freethought Association and wrote articles for the freethought press in the country. When the NZ Freethought Association was formed in 1884, he became its vice president. In 1875 Ballance was elected MP for the district around his home town of Wanganui, and he kept the seat until 1881. It is symptomatic of how his views had changed that part of the reason for his defeat was his sympathy for Maori interests. In 1884 he was reelected MP for Wanganui, holding the seat until his death in 1893.

In January 1891, Ballance became Premier. His administration lasted only little more than two years, but it anticipated later Liberal administrations by initiating progressive legislation, including votes for women. Even Ballance's opponents acknowledged his integrity and honesty.

Further reading: Timothy McIvor, *The Rainmaker: A Biography of John Ballance*.

BANDISTE, D. D. (1923–). Prominent Indian rationalist campaigner and intellectual. Bandiste grew up a fervent Hindu nationalist. So deep was his involvement in Hindu nationalism that he was imprisoned for five years after the assassination of Mohandas Gandhi (1869–1948). Upon his release in 1953 he enrolled at Banares Hindu University where he embarked on a study of the philosophies and religions of the world. From this study he became an atheist and rationalist. His PhD dissertation, from the University of Saugar, was on the ethics of **Bertrand Russell**. Until his retirement in 1981, Bandiste taught in Indian universities retiring from the Government Arts and Commerce College in Indore, Madhya Pradesh.

For the past fifty years, Bandiste has been a prominent critic of religious extremism and an exponent of **atheism**, **rationalism**, and **humanism**. Among his many books include studies of the thought of **M. N. Roy** and **Gora**; *The Ethics of Bertrand Russell* (1984); *Humanist Values: A Source Book, Creative Rationalism*, and *Humanist Thought in Contemporary India* (all 1999); and *Beyond God and Religion* (2000).

BAYES' THEOREM. In its strictest application, a theorem of the calculus of probabilities, with important uses in statistics, but which is often used in a broader sense. The theorem is named after a brilliant mathematician and nonconformist minister Thomas Bayes (1702–1761).

The current understanding of Bayes' Theorem does not stress knowledge itself, but emphasizes the role of rational belief. The strength which one believes an idea must be in accord with the probability calculus. In this way, we can consider several alternative ideas at the same time, judging each one according to the quality and quantity of information that can be brought to their defense. The strength of the Bayesian approach is that final **certainty** can be reached on not single theory, but this has the related disadvantage that no theory, no matter how discredited, can be rejected entirely either.

BAYLE, PIERRE (1647–1706). French philosopher and encyclopedist. Son of a Protestant minister, though trained at a Jesuit college. Appointed professor of philosophy at a Protestant school in Sedan. When the school was suppressed by Catholic forces in 1681, Bayle moved to Rotterdam and taught

there. In 1684 he founded a **freethought** journal called *News from the Republic of Letters*, which quickly became very influential. The journal lasted about three years before Bayle's health broke down due to overwork. Even the tolerant Dutch felt moved to revoke his teaching license in 1693 after Bayle advocated that universal **toleration** should include atheists. Bayle's own views have been a matter of considerable speculation. In all probability he was a sincere believer in the minimal variety of Calvinism he adhered to for much of his adult life.

Bayle is best known for his *Dictionnaire Historique et Critique*, which was published in 1697. Once again, Bayle worked incredible hours to make this work a success, putting in fourteen hours a day for four years. His effort was rewarded because the dictionary was an instant success. Bayle followed the dictionary in 1702 with a larger, four-volume edition. Here he praised classical civilization and made as many criticisms of the bigotry and small-mindedness of orthodox Christianity as he thought he could get away with. He was particularly severe with those who presumed to have a **monopoly of truth**. Bayle contrasted the immoral lives of many Old Testament figures with the outstanding lives of many known **unbelievers**, such as **Diogenes** and **Spinoza**.

Bayle's achievement was to demonstrate that there was no essential link between **God** and reason, which most thinkers had assumed to be the case. And neither was there any essential link between belief in God and a stable society, as was also widely believed— and still is in some quarters. Bayle was enormously influential on the thinkers of the **Enlightenment**. His dictionary was the model for **Diderot's Encyclopedia** and was used extensively by most leading Enlightenment thinkers.

BECKWITH, PHILO D. (1825–1889). American entrepreneur and **freethinker**. In 1854 Beckwith moved to the unprepossessing town of Dowagiac in southwestern Michigan.

There he put down roots and made a seminal contribution to the civic life of the town.

Beckwith owned the Round Oak Company, which made stoves and furnaces and was the largest employer in the town. He ran his firm in the spirit of **Robert Owen**, providing generous rates of pay and even sick days for his workers. As a result, he avoided the labor troubles that plagued America at the time. Beckwith extended his philanthropy to build the town's first public library and the Beckwith Memorial Theater on the main street of Dowagiac. The theater included busts of all Beckwith's heroes, including **Robert Ingersoll**, **Voltaire**, **Ludwig van Beethoven**, **Susan B. Anthony**, **George Eliot**, and **Thomas Paine**. The theater opened on January 25, 1893, with Ingersoll in attendance. It became known as the finest theater outside the large cities, and attracted a high caliber of show. The building was demolished in 1968 and the bust of Robert Ingersoll is now in the Ingersoll Museum in Dresden, New York.

In his speech at the opening of the theater, Ingersoll praised Beckwith as a person "who tried to make a heaven here and who believed in the blessed gospel of cheerfulness and love—of happiness and hope."

BEETHOVEN, LUDWIG VAN (1770–1827). Thought by many to be the greatest composer of all time, Beethoven was born in Bonn, where his father was a tenor working for the Elector of Cologne. Beethoven's father was a hard-drinking, ambitious man, determined to transform his son into a musical prodigy. Under this pressure, many people would have caved in, but Beethoven rose to the fearsome challenge set by his father, producing his first piece of music at the age of eight. In 1792 Beethoven was in Vienna, being taught by Franz Joseph Haydn (1732–1809).

Musical experts divide Beethoven's career into three phases, with each of them being greater than the last. His own personal life was always turbulent and filled with quarrels and discord as he battled depression

and other anxieties, not to mention the deafness which overcame him.

Beethoven's musical repertoire consists of nine symphonies, five piano concertos, thirty-two piano sonatas, and sixteen string quartets. His Ninth Symphony took on a new life when it was used in Stanley Kubrick's chilling film *A Clockwork Orange* (1971). This violent movie is not entirely inappropriate to the tempestuous and quarrelsome Beethoven. His personal life notwithstanding, Beethoven quickly became the darling of Vienna, which was enraptured by his ferocious and brilliant music.

Beethoven was not a churchgoer and was suspicious of any sort of orthodoxy, religious or secular. He composed very little religious music, in the narrower sense of the term. His most ostensibly religious piece was *Missa Solemnis*, which was first completed in 1824 and played in St. Petersburg soon after. The *Missa Solemnis* is a hymn to **Deism**, and evokes the ideal not of humanity managing to qualify for entrance into a distant heaven above, but, in the words of Paul Griffiths, of a "sovereign humanity in ultimate concord here on earth."

Beethoven's life became an archetype for the **Romantic** ideal of the tortured artist as hero. His heroic status was confirmed by the ten thousand people who turned up at his funeral.

BELIEF. A state of mind, according to **Bertrand Russell**, in which an animal acts in accordance with something not immediately present. In more recent language, they are propositional attitudes, or the means by which we arrive at some understanding of the world, which in turn determines our actions. Given this understanding of belief, it is beholden on *Homo sapiens*, in their capacity as animals that can **reason**, to hold their beliefs in a responsible way. This means subjecting them to scrutiny, changing them when the bulk of the evidence suggests they are faulty, and holding them with confidence but not with **certainty**.

One of the beliefs that atheists have in common with religious believers is that what one believes is important. See the entry on **what atheists and religious believers have in common**. People's actions are determined by their beliefs, so public debate over the quality of beliefs is a positive act, even—especially—when those beliefs are religious beliefs. It also follows that if beliefs are important, then they have a public dimension to them, and if they have a public dimension to them, they need to be exposed to the same public scrutiny and criticism any other public act is. See the entries on **rational beliefs**, **testing our beliefs**, and **critical receptiveness**.

Further reading: Bertrand Russell, *Human Knowledge: Its Scope and Limits*; and Sam Harris, *The End of Faith*.

BELIEVE IN NOTHING. One of the more common **prejudices against atheists** is that, because they don't believe in **God**, atheists believe nothing. This prejudice is preposterous. Freethinkers of any persuasion are identified by what they believe. What is more, many of the things they believe are the same things religious people believe. The importance of civic virtues, personal responsibility, compassion for those who suffer, the facts of science, the beauty of nature . . . the list goes on.

This prejudice depends on the confusion that not believing one particular thing is the same as not believing anything at all. The notion that the only alternative to belief in God is belief in nothing is absurd and verging on meaningless. It is absurd because it contrives an arbitrary either/or between belief in God and every other sort and style of belief. See the entry on **either black or white, fallacy of**. There is also an element of confusion in this prejudice between believing nothing and believing *in* nothing. The idea of believing *in* nothing is meaningless, as it is impossible to direct a belief toward nothing.

It is not that atheists and humanists believe nothing, let alone believe in nothing. It is simply that they see no need to contrive some supernatural explanation for the things in which they believe. Rather than some unprovable supernatural contrivance, atheists, skeptics, and humanists demand some degree of **evidence** for their beliefs, and their beliefs are held in strict proportion to the evidence that is available in each case. Resisting the **transcendental temptation** also has a moral dimension by virtue of its recognition that we are not of central importance in some cosmic drama.

BENDA, JULIEN (1867–1956). French novelist, critic, and **smiter of humbug**. Benda is best known outside France for *The Treason of the Intellectuals* (1927, tr. 1928), which attacked prominent thinkers of the day for abandoning the program of the **Enlightenment**. By shrugging off or sneering at the search for **truth** and universal human values in favor of **totalitarian** ideologies or romantic nonsense, Benda accused intellectuals of reneging their responsibilities to the people. A particular target of Benda was the French philosopher Henri Bergson (1859–1941). While Bergson did not himself subscribe to the uses his philosophy was sometimes put, it is true that some extreme Catholic rightists and even some fascists have taken on elements of his thought.

Later in his life, Benda wrote *The Crisis of Rationalism* (1949?), a fiery attack on some of the more extravagant brands of **rationalism**. Dialectical Materialism was subjected to some withering scorn, mainly on account of its **teleological** mysticism. Some French thinkers of the day, now largely forgotten, were also criticized. Benda was a thoroughgoing rationalist and humanist, who wanted to defend rationalism from some of the caricatures its opponents subjected it to. He was defending a more modest reason, without the pompous capital letters that Marxists, Platonists, and some mystics had wanted to confer on it. Benda was a defender of the **Enlightenment**.

BENEFFECTANCE. Word coined in 1980 by the psychologist Anthony Greenwald, bringing together the words "beneficial" and "effective." Greenwald and others have shown that humans tend to portray themselves as having optimum amounts of these two qualities. By bringing the two words together as beneffectance, the two most significant developments of recent **evolutionary psychology** are combined. **Reciprocal altruism** tends to stress our benevolence to others, while our consciousness of status hierarchies tends to emphasize our effectiveness. Presenting ourselves in these lights involves a degree of deception of others and even of ourselves, not least because the qualities of benevolence often run contrary to the qualities of effectiveness. Beneffectance is the sum total of our ability to fuse these contradictions in ourselves and convince others of our successful application of them.

Further reading: Robert Wright, *The Moral Animal*.

BENNETT, ARNOLD (1867–1931). Prolific English novelist, critic, and humanist. Bennett was born and raised in the pottery towns of Staffordshire, and his early experiences of joyless puritanism provided material for a great deal of his later writing. The moment he was free of parental authority, Bennett abandoned religion. After some study at London University, Bennett entered a solicitor's office in London, where, in normal circumstances, he may have spent the rest of his working life. In 1893 he took up journalism and from 1896 until 1900 was editor of *Woman* magazine.

Bennett always wanted to earn a living by writing. His first novel, *A Man From the North* (1898) opened up this possibility. From 1900–1908 he lived in France, where he immersed himself deeply in the naturalism of writers like Flaubert and **Zola**. Under their influence, Bennett wrote his greatest novels, which include *The Old Wives' Tale* (1908), *Clayhanger* (1910), *Riceyman Steps* (1923), and *Lord Raingo* (1926). Bennett was also a respected playwright and critic. By nature a gentle man, Bennett's reviews were kind and he was quick to encourage and praise.

Under the influence of **Herbert Spencer**, Bennett became an **agnostic**. He became an honorary associate of the **Rationalist Press Association** in 1916. That same year he made his thoughts on religion plain, admitting to never having prayed "without a sharp sense of the ridiculous." "I have no supernatural religion," he wrote, "and I never had one. I do not feel the need of a supernatural religion, and I have never felt such a need."

Further reading: Margaret Drabble, *Arnold Bennett*.

BENNETT, DE ROBIGNE MORTIMER (1818–1882). American **freethought** pioneer and martyr. Bennett was founder and editor of the long-running New York paper, the ***Truth Seeker***. Bennett was born in modest circumstances in Springfield, New York. While still only fifteen, he joined the stern sect known as the Shakers, remaining with them for fifteen years before leaving in order to marry a fellow Shaker, Mary Hicks. The couple then spent many years moving around the country as Bennett made money and lost it just as quickly. During this time, mainly as a result of reading **Thomas Paine**, Bennett became a freethinker.

In 1873, Bennett resolved to set up his own newspaper after a journal refused to print his letters disputing a local clergyman. The *Truth Seeker* began publication in September 1873 in Paris, Illinois, moved to New York early the next year, and became a weekly in January 1876. As soon as the *Truth Seeker* arrived in New York, it began to attract the hostile attention of Anthony Comstock (1844–1915), after whom the notorious Comstock Laws were named. See the entry on **Comstockery**. Bennett was arrested on three separate occasions for distributing blasphemous material through the post. On the third arrest, for his involvement in the distribution of a pamphlet *An Open Letter to Jesus Christ*, Bennett went to prison in 1879 for thirteen months. A petition signed by 200,000 people was unsuccessful in persuading President

Hayes to ensure his release, allegedly because of the opposition from the president's staunchly Methodist wife. For much of his incarceration Bennett made shoes and was forbidden access to papers and books. After the restrictions were lifted he wrote a two-volume work called *The Gods and Religions of Ancient and Modern Times.* Bennett's writing style was prolix, but he was an imaginative thinker. In his last years Bennett turned more to spiritualism in 1875, and he ended his life a member of the Theosophical Society.

Further reading: G. E. Macdonald, *Fifty Years of Freethought.*

BENTHAM, JEREMY (1748–1832). English liberal thinker and reformer. Born and brought up in London, Bentham was a precocious child. He entered Queen's College, Oxford, when he was twelve and was admitted to Lincoln's Inn at fifteen.

Bentham is best known for devising the philosophy of utilitarianism. He was appalled by the state of hospitals and prisons in England, and the unalloyed misery they, and the beliefs which sustained them, engendered. Among Bentham's various plans included new layouts for schools and prisons. Bentham also helped establish the *Westminster Review* in 1823, which went on to become very influential. It was run for a while by **George Eliot**. Bentham also helped found University College, London, and he supported **Robert Owen**'s visionary social experiment at New Lanark.

In *Introduction to the Principles of Morals and Legislation* (1789), Bentham said that the standard by which legislation should be judged is the degree to which **happiness** is maximized for the greatest number of sentient creatures, in which he specifically included nonhuman animals. To this end, he devised the **Principle of Utility** to give measure to happiness in each instance. While it is easy to find fault with many of Bentham's ideas, he deserves credit for this simple and yet easily forgotten ideal. Certainly, his reforms and ideas were enormously influential.

Bentham was a convinced atheist, referring to Christianity as "Jug[gernaut]." Along with the historian George Grote (1794–1871), Bentham wrote *Analysis of the Influence of Natural Religion on the Temporal Happiness of Mankind* (1822). Anticipating **evolutionary psychology** a century and a half later, Bentham and Grote outlined the irrational nature of religion, and showed that it can be explained entirely in naturalistic terms. They went even further by arguing that **religion** is damaging to society.

BERNHARD, THOMAS (1931–1989). A wide-ranging and gritty Austrian writer. Best known among English-speaking audiences for his novels, he also wrote poetry, plays, short stories, and three volumes of autobiography. His autobiography relates in brutal detail the stifling hypocrisy of the anti-Semitic Catholicism of Salzburg, where he grew up after the war. Bernhard received, among other awards, the Bremen Prize and the Austrian National Prize.

Like many brilliant writers, Bernhard spent much of his life battling ill-health, in his case tuberculosis. He was not expected to live long and, at the age of nineteen he began writing in an Austrian hospital. His illness had already brought a promising musical career to a premature close. The parallels between Bernhard's life and the fictional character Hans Castorp in **Thomas Mann**'s great novel, *The Magic Mountain* (1924) are remarkable.

Bernhard's definitive character is a thinker whose life's work is being given a new perspective through some imminent crisis, such as death. And his definitive theme is failing to go under, despite the many good reasons we might have to do so.

Among his novels include *Correction, Concrete, The Loser, Old Masters, Cutting Timber, The Cheap-Eaters,* and *Wittgenstein's Nephew.*

Further reading: Stephen Mitchelmore, "Failing to Go Under," www.spikemagazine.com.

BESANT, ANNIE (1847–1933). Gifted and complex woman who devoted her considerable energies to a variety of causes. Brought up a devout Anglican, Annie Wood married Frank Besant, a dour and brutish clergyman, in 1867. Religious doubts soon crept into Annie's life, partly from the behavior of her husband, partly from the suffering her infant daughter endured during an illness. By the time she secured a separation from her husband in 1873, Besant was a convinced **free-thinker**. From 1875, she was an active writer and speaker for the **freethought** movement, and became increasingly valued and trusted by **Charles Bradlaugh**. In 1877, Besant became coeditor of Bradlaugh's paper, the *National Reformer*.

During her campaign alongside Bradlaugh to allow him to take his seat in parliament, Besant was subjected to several demeaning persecutions. She was refused leave to use the garden of the Royal Botanic Society, the reason given that the daughters of the Curator used it. And in 1883 Besant was refused admittance to the Practical Botany Classes at University College on grounds of her immorality. During her atheist period, Besant wrote some works that have remained classic polemics, in particular, *The Gospel of Atheism* (1877). A collection of essays from this period was published as *My Path to Atheism* (1877).

In 1889, while still an atheist, Besant was given a copy of *The Secret Doctrine* to review by George Bernard Shaw (1856–1950), although other accounts say it was the journalist W. T. Stead (1849–1912), only to surprise everyone by being converted. In February 1890, Besant resigned as vice president of the National Secular Society and by 1896 was a major leader of the Theosophical movement, and remained so for the rest of her life. She led the move to deemphasize the supernatural elements in **Theosophy**. But she also gave close support to **Charles Leadbetter**, whose sexual exploitation of boys in his care was provoking outrage among other Theosophists. Besant claimed fifty earlier reincarnations, from mineral to vegetable and then from a variety of primal beings to **Hypatia** and **Giordano Bruno**. Her extensive writings became increasingly eccentric, and as she got older, coming to resemble a brand of esoteric Christianity. The longest-lasting contribution from this part of her career was her consistent advocacy of Indian independence.

Significant books include *My Path to Atheism* (1877), *An Autobiography* (1893), *The Ancient Wisdom* (1897), *Esoteric Christianity* (1898), and *The Changing World* (1909).

BEST OF CAUSES, THE. A phrase originally used by the **agnostic** abolitionist James Russell Lowell (1819–1891) with regard to the campaign against **slavery** but the phrase stuck when the novelist George Meredith (1828–1909) applied it to **freethought** in a letter to his friend **G. W. Foote**. And who's to say he's wrong? The best of the freethinkers are less bothered by what people believe than by how they acquire their beliefs. This is because if someone believes such-and-such as a result of **free inquiry**, open research, and an honest attitude to inconvenient **evidence**, then they are more likely to extend to others the right to undertake the same process, even if they come to different conclusions. Freethought in this way is inherently tolerant. Supporters of **command moralities**, by contrast, are less comfortable with genuine freethought, because they have a greater investment in everyone arriving at the same conclusions as themselves.

Sometimes the pursuit of freethought comes by way of **smiting humbug**. Other times it comes by way of positive affirmation of one's own views in the hope they will find acceptance in an open market of ideas. Both are valuable approaches, and it often boils down to a simple question of personality and style as to which method is most suitable. There is usually room for both approaches, to varying degrees. See the entry on **rationalism** for the quotation by **Joseph McCabe**, which best sums up the freethought position.

BEYOND. A very popular word among those who want to avoid the trouble of justifying their thoughts or beliefs. We frequently hear people declare that they are now "beyond" seeing things in terms of black and white, or that this mystical insight is "beyond" mere rationality, or that my religion's truths are so sublime as to be "beyond" the reach of your earth-based criticisms. See the entry on **mereymustification**.

What this means is that we want to skirt around these obstacles without the bother of providing reasons for doing this. It is a principle of **philosophy** that preference should go to the simpler of the solutions being offered, and that the **burden of proof** lies with those advancing the more outlandish claim. To say one is beyond something is nothing more than a rhetorical assertion. The moral of the story is to beware anyone who claims to have gone beyond this or that. Too often, the word "beyond" is a fig leaf for intellectual sloppiness or laziness.

BEYOND HUMAN UNDERSTANDING. It is a favorite gambit of religious believers and **mystics** of various persuasions to declare that **God** is **beyond** human understanding. It has also been a popular approach to take when doctrinal strife threatens to destroy the unity of the Church. The Christian thinker Gregory of Nazianzus (329–390 CE) was an early proponent of this argument as a response to the vicious doctrinal disputes of his day. The claim usually made is that God is incomprehensible or ineffable to mortal minds, except for a few spiritually blessed people. For Gregory, only those "pure in heart" and those with prior theological training—people like Gregory—might hope to contemplate the mystery of the divine.

The claim that God is beyond human understanding is often made in the context of rebuking supposedly arrogant human rationality claiming to know God and subject it to criticism. And yet the **anthropocentric conceit** of claiming to know, and speak on behalf of, something that is beyond human under-

standing, is rarely challenged. The argument also runs into the problem of what to do with all the details about God that are revealed in the **scripture** of the religion in question. See the entry on **divine hiddenness**.

BIERCE, AMBROSE (1842–1914). American humorist and journalist. Bierce saw distinguished service for the North in the American Civil War before becoming a journalist in San Francisco. Between 1872 and 1875 he worked in London, where, under the pseudonym "Dod Grile," he wrote a very popular column for the journal *Fun*. After returning to America, Bierce wrote columns for a succession of journals and under a series of pseudonyms. He also wrote a series of satirical novels of which *Cobwebs From an Empty Skull* (1874) was the first.

While editor of a minor journal called *Wasp*, Bierce began compiling a series of biting apothegms on a wide range of subjects. Twenty-five years later, Bierce brought as many of them as he could find together and published them as *The Cynics Word Book* (1906). Bierce was working for William Randolph Hearst (1863–1951) at the time and it was felt the weak title was required so as not to offend religious sensibilities. In 1911 the book was rereleased in expanded form under Bierce's preferred title, *The Devil's Dictionary*. After his death the scholar Ernest Jerome Hopkins went through Bierce's entire corpus of writing and recovered many more apothegms. They have been included in what is now called *The Enlarged Devil's Dictionary*, and is a classic of its type.

Legend has it that Bierce died in mysterious circumstances on a trip to Mexico. In the late 1970s **Joe Nickell**, one of the most important sham-busters in the United States, proved that Bierce shot himself in a canyon beside the Colorado River with a German revolver.

BIG BANG. The name given to the cataclysmic event many scientists believe created the universe. The idea was first mooted in

1947 by the Russian-born American physicist George Gamow (1904–1968), but the title, "big bang" was first used in a derogatory sense by **Fred Hoyle**, an opponent of the theory. But the name caught on. Hoyle was a supporter of the steady state theory, which was overthrown by the big bang theory.

The big bang refers to the beginning of time and space about fifteen billion years ago. The big bang is the beginning of space-time. There was no time, no causality, no physical law before the big bang.

The big bang idea gained far greater credibility following the discovery in 1964 by Arno Penzias (1933–) and Robert Wilson (1936–) of the rapid expansion of radiation throughout the universe, leading to notions of the expanding universe. The notion of the steady state was unable to account for the new data in the way the big bang theory could. This discovery won Penzias and Wilson the Nobel Prize for physics in 1978.

Some **theologians** have contrived to find **God** in the big bang. Superficially, the big bang talks of a beginning, and a beginning requires a cause, at least to theologians. In fact, the big bang is not an event in time that requires some causal explanation. It is, therefore, meaningless to ask what happened before the big bang, or to ascribe the big bang to God. The big bang is the test case for the **theory of everything**, which scientists are trying to accomplish.

Further reading: Steven Weinberg, *The First Three Minutes*.

BIG CRUNCH. Term coined, in tongue-in-cheek imitation of the **big bang** by the physicist John Wheeler (1911–), who also gave black holes their name. Whereas the big bang refers to the beginning of the universe, the big crunch is the term given to speculation as to how the universe might end. The big crunch postulates the universe expanding, about 50 billion years from now, to the point at which it can no longer sustain itself, leading to an implosion back to the big bang.

Not wanting to be left out, others have speculated on the big rip, which is where **dark energy** strengthens, leading not to an implosion, but an explosion which shatters the universe.

BILDUNG. German word which can be translated as the full development of the individual. This was the ideal of some of the most significant German humanists of the late eighteenth and early nineteenth centuries; men like **Johann Wolfgang Goethe** and Karl Wilhelm Humboldt (1767–1835) whose profession of Christianity was nominal at best, and Johann Cristoph Friedrich von Schiller (1759–1805), who was an avowed pagan. The less helpful element in *Bildung* thought was the cultivation of the individual by withdrawing oneself from active participation in the public affairs of the community. This can lead to complacency and a decline in public spiritedness. **Thomas Mann** was an early exponent of the narrower form of *Bildung*, but came around to a more expansive understanding of the term, although too late to prevent the Nazis from taking over.

Bildung can best be associated with what English speakers call "Renaissance man," which means a cultured person, well versed in the arts and sciences, who is active in civic affairs and who has a full family life. This was what **Friedrich Immanuel Niethammer** had in mind when he coined the word **humanism** and what **Paul Kurtz** had in mind when he coined the world **eupraxsophy**.

BILL OF RIGHTS FOR UNBELIEVERS. A charter of freedoms devised in the spirit of the separation of church and state, drawn up by the Campus Freethought Alliance, the forerunner to the **Center for Inquiry—On Campus** on July 12, 1998. The charter was signed by a wide range of American academics.

Unbelievers shall have the right to:

(1) Think freely and autonomously, express their views forthrightly, and debate or criticize any and all ideas,

without fear of censure, recrimination, or public ostracism.

(2) Be free from discrimination and persecution in the workplace, business transactions, and public accommodations.

(3) Exercise freedom of conscience in any situation where the same right would be extended to believers on religious grounds alone.

(4) Hold any public office, in accordance with the constitutional principle that there shall be no religious test for such office.

(5) Abstain from religious oaths and pledges, including pledges of allegiance, oaths of office, and oaths administered in a court of law, until such time as these are secularized or replaced by nondiscriminatory affirmations.

(6) Empower members of their community to perform legally binding ceremonies, such as marriage.

(7) Raise and nurture their children in a secular environment, and not be disadvantaged in adoption or custody proceedings because of their unbelief.

(8) Conduct business and commerce on any day of their choosing, without interference from laws or regulations recognizing religious days of prayer, rest, or celebration.

(9) Enjoy freedom from taxation supporting government employment of clergy and access to secular counseling equivalent to that provided by chaplains.

(10) Declare conscientious objection to serving in the armed forces under any circumstances in which the religious may do so.

(11) Live as citizens in a democracy free from religious language and imagery in currency, public schools and buildings, and government documents and businesses.

It is testimony to the increasing marginalization of and discrimination against freethinkers in many societies that a charter such as this needs to be written. While written with the United States in mind, it has relevance in many other societies.

While the need for a charter such as this is sadly evident, some of the clauses here overreach themselves. Items six, eight, nine, and eleven all go a step too far in the advocacy of equal rights for freethinkers. They presuppose a society geared toward secularist principles in the same unbalanced way that it currently favors religions. It is not that these are undesirable outcomes, rather it is unreasonable to expect them to occur.

Further reading: "Bill of Rights for Unbelievers," *Free Inquiry* 18, no. 4 (Fall 1998): 13.

BILLIONS AND BILLIONS. Term associated with **Carl Sagan** although Sagan, a famous popularizer of **science** didn't actually use the term. "Billions and billions" was made popular by Johnny Carson, who used it while lampooning Sagan on television. Although he disliked the term, Sagan eventually took the phrase up. His final work of popular science, published after his death, was called *Billions and Billions* (1997), and the first article was a brief discussion of the term and what it actually means.

BIODIVERSITY. See **DIVERSITY**.

BIOETHICS. In all likelihood, the most important branch of **philosophy** today. As science makes ever greater advances in understanding the genetic makeup of living beings, the question of the boundaries of permissible research is bound to be raised. Should rich families be able to select for designer babies? Should parents be allowed to reject their child upon learning it is female? Should experimental work be permitted on stem cells? Should cloning of human beings be attempted? Each of these is a bioethical question in that each one involves questions of biology and of ethics.

Bioethics is a new field. The International Association of Bioethics and the academic journal *Bioethics* are both recent formations. The range of issues bioethics can cover has expanded exponentially since the completion of the **Human Genome Project** in 2003. Much of the credit for pioneering this discipline has been given to Joseph Fletcher (1905–1991), who was called by Richard Taylor (1919–2004) "the father of biomedical ethics."

A characteristic argument in the field of bioethics is that of stem cell research. In the United Kingdom it is legal to experiment with human embryos up to fourteen days for fertility purposes. In the United States, however, the religious right engineered a comprehensive, though not total, ban on stem cell research early in the administration of George W. Bush. This prompted a petition by forty-eight Nobel Laureates in 2004 to have the ban lifted on the grounds that it was hurting American science.

Another hot bioethics topic is cloning. A great deal of the more dogmatic opposition to stem cell research and cloning is informed by the same prescientific idea of people having **souls** that somehow carry their essence—and any sort of tampering with the soul is a crime against it. But as it is clear that there is no such thing as a soul, this argument collapses under its own weight.

Bioethics is another example of a topic that can best be managed on a transnational basis. The Universal Declaration on the Human Genome and Human Rights, which was adopted by UNESCO in 1997 and the **United Nations** the following year, is the only transnational agreement on bioethics. The declaration set the ground rules for research in the area of the human genome while respecting our genetic heritage and diversity. See the entry on **neuroethics**.

BIOLOGICAL REALITY. A term coined by the French scientist François Jacob (1920–) that refers to the fundamental categories through which any species perceives the world. *Homo sapiens*, for instance, are closely attuned to distinctions between living and not living, newborn and dying, intelligent and unintelligent. Any absolutes that a species may conceive, therefore, are direct consequences of that species' biological reality. It is with concepts like biological reality in mind that philosophers speak of biology needing to be the starting point of philosophy. See the entry on **biophilia**.

Jacob received the Nobel Prize in Medicine in 1965. His two corecipients were Jacques Monod (1910–1976) and Andre Lwoff (1902–1994), who was also a Laureate of the **International Academy of Humanism**.

BIOPHILIA. A term coined by **E. O. Wilson**, which is summed up in his statement, "Treat this world as if there is none other." Biophilia encapsulates important elements of Wilson's growing interest in and explication of naturalistic ethics. As humanity lives in intimate association with its wider physical environment, it follows that developing an empathy with one's environment and with the other species we share our environment with makes good sense. Biophilia, in this context, means "love of life." Wilson extended his thinking on biophilia in 1993 when he coedited with Stephen Kellert of Yale University *The Biophilia Hypothesis*.

Further reading: E. O. Wilson, *Biophilia* (1984) and *The Diversity of Life* (1992); and E. O. Wilson and Stephen Kellert, *The Biophilia Hypothesis* (1993).

BIRX, H. JAMES (1941–). American scholar, and one of the most prominent exponents of evolution. Born in Canandaigua, in western New York state, Birx took an MA in anthropology and PhD in philosophy from the State University of New York at Buffalo (SUNY). He has taught at Canisius College in Buffalo since 1969 and is presently Distinguished Research Scholar in the Department of Anthropology at SUNY Geneseo. Birx is on the editorial board of *Free Inquiry* magazine and is a research fellow at the **Center for Inquiry**.

Birx's main books include *Theories of Evolution* (1984), *Human Evolution* (1988), and *Interpreting Evolution* (1991). In 2003 he took on the editorship of a major, five-volume *Encyclopedia of Anthropology*. As well as scholarship on the life of **Charles Darwin**, Birx has been an enthusiastic promoter of the memory of **Ernst Haeckel**, Pierre Teilhard de Chardin (1881–1955), and **Marvin Farber**, who supervised his PhD. He has a string of academic honors, including being a Visiting Scholar at Harvard University on two occasions, and recipient of the 2003 Professional Achievement Award from SUNY Geneseo. Among the terms Birx has coined to extend understanding of evolution include **exoevolution** and **dynamic integrity**.

BIZET, ALEXANDRE CÉSAR LÉOPOLD

(1838–1875). French composer of precocious talent. Entered the Paris Conservatoire when he was only nine, and during his ten years there won almost every prize on offer. After further education in Italy, Bizet returned to France where he wrote a series of operas, but none of them won much esteem.

Then in 1875 he produced *Carmen*, which soon after Bizet's death was recognized as the classic of comic opera that it is. The original reaction, though, was hostile. Religious conservatives condemned the obscene libretto, and other critics scorned the work. Disappointed by the reception to his work, Bizet had two heart attacks and died. Soon after his death, opinion about *Carmen* changed, and it has remained a staple of popular opera ever since. Religious opinion was right to worry about Bizet's orthodoxy. In his letters he was bitingly critical of the aridity of Christianity, which he described as replete with "system, egoism, intolerance, and a complete lack of artistic taste."

Bizet's widow, Genevieve, a capable and intelligent woman, married again and went on to run the most influential salon in Paris.

BLACKHAM, HAROLD (1903–). One of

the leading figures in twentieth-century Eng-

lish humanism. Harold Blackham was born near Birmingham, the son of a lay preacher. After education at King Edward Grammar School, Blackham left school at sixteen and worked on a farm, so he could work with horses, which he loved. Blackham's political baptism of fire came during the general strike in 1926, when he volunteered to join a militia to help suppress the coal miners. After this, he decided he needed more of an education, so he enrolled in university to train as a teacher. Blackham loved the university study, but not the teaching in Doncaster, so he left after two years. After some time spent drifting, Blackham answered an advertisement from **Stanton Coit** to work in the Ethical Church in London. As Coit and the older generation of the Ethical Church moved on, Blackham found himself pretty well in charge of the movement in the middle of the 1930s. He quickly altered the direction of the Church, turning it to a more secular and humanist direction.

This provided the *leitmotif* for the rest of Blackham's career. For the rest of his active career, Blackham did what he could to promote the concept of **humanism** as a positive ethical alternative to traditional religion. Blackham was less interested in the criticism of religion that had been the staple of the **Rationalist Press Association**, and more in the promotion of ethical alternatives to religion. Blackham was a central figure behind the creation of the **International Humanist and Ethical Union** and the **British Humanist Association**. Blackham edited the Ethical Union's journal, *Plain View* from 1944 until 1965.

Blackham has written several books. The most influential of which was *Six Existentialist Thinkers* (1952), which has gone through many editions and is still in print. It is a sympathetic account, and contrasts well with the more critical *The Feast of Unreason* (1952), which Blackham's contemporary **Hector Hawton** from the Rationalist Press Association wrote. Blackham's other important work is *Humanism* (1968), a book designed to popularize humanism to a wide reading audience. Unfortunately, Blackham's pedestrian writing style worked against that, and disguised the book's real value. Blackham's other main works include *Political Discipline in a Free Society* (1961), *Religion in a Modern Society* (1966), and *The Future of Our Past* (1994).

BLASPHEMY. Widely considered by the ancients to be the most heinous crime. As late as 1736 the bishop and philosopher George Berkeley (1685–1736) demanded that blasphemy be treated like high treason. Blasphemy is generally thought of as offensive speech against **God** or **religion**. The problem is that reasoned criticism of religion can easily be deemed "offensive" by believers unwilling to have their faith challenged. It was blasphemy to deny the **Trinity** in Britain until 1813. The **Hebrew scriptures** is clear that blasphemy merits death by stoning. "Whoever blasphemes the Name shall certainly be put to death. The whole congregation shall stone him, the stranger as well as the native, in case he blaspheme the Name" (Leviticus 24:16). In the New Testament, the gospel of Mark has **Rabbi Yeshua** being accused by the Jewish scribes of blasphemy for claiming divine status. This is yet another example of the gospels' **anti-Semitism**, given Rabbi Yeshua's total identification with Jewish interests and concerns.

As western societies have become more secular, blasphemy looked likely to disappear as a crime altogether. It is, after all, another "crime" without victims. The battle to push back the boundaries of blasphemy was led by a succession of **freethought** leaders in the nineteenth and early twentieth centuries (see **Carlile**, **Foote**, etc.). Blasphemy remained a peculiar survival of bygone times on the statute books until the orchestrated outrage following the publication of Salman Rushdie's *The Satanic Verses* in September 1988. With western societies now becoming more multicultural and multifaith, it looks less likely that blasphemy laws will disappear, although they are slowly being altered to include blasphemy toward any religion. Elsewhere, the battle against blasphemy laws has hardly begun. See the entry on **Younas Sheikh**.

Further reading: Nicolas Walter, *Blasphemy: Ancient and Modern*.

BLIK. Word coined by philosopher R. M. Hare (1919–2002) to name what he considered the uniquely biased perspective each person brings to the world. Thus, atheists and religionists have totally different worldviews, but both are ultimate worldviews. This makes any conflict between the worldviews irrelevant because judging one person's worldview by the standards of another is unjustified. Hare's blik argument is a brand of **fideism**. See the entry on **social worlds**.

This sounds all very well, until one realizes that this would result in total **relativism**. No worldview, even one palpably insane could be exposed to legitimate criticism, according to this view. It also ignores the claim of **science** that its knowledge does apply to all, without regard to their opinions about it. Hare, a devout Christian, must also have realized that the notion of bliks undermined the moral imperative of Christianity to claim it had the whole truth. Bliks, like Stephen Jay Gould's later notion of **nonoverlapping magisteria**, was an attempt to insulate **religion** from secular criticism, but it did so at too great a price. See the entry on **external realism**.

BONCH-BRUEVICH, VLADIMIR (1873–1955). One of the more prominent Communist Party members who went on to have an important role in official Soviet atheism. Vladimir Bonch-Bruevich was a friend of Lenin (1870–1924) and was actively involved in the October Revolution that established the Soviet regime. He played an important role in preparing the *Decree on Separation of Church and State and School and Church*, which took effect on January 23, 1918, before taking over the management of the Life and Knowledge Publishing House.

Bonch-Bruevich survived the purges of the 1930s, despite being an Old Bolshevik, and despite his daughter being married into the circle of supporters of NKVD chief Genrikh Yagoda (1891–1938), who was liquidated to make way for Lavrenti Beria (1899–1953). Needless to say, this was done by repeated and public affirmations of undying support for Stalin. From 1946 Bonch-Bruevich was in charge of the Museum of the History of Religion and Atheism in Leningrad (now St. Petersburg), and from 1947 he ran the History of Religion and Atheism Department of the History Institute, which was part of the USSR Academy of Sciences.

Bonch-Bruevich wrote on Russian sectarianism and religiously inclined social movements in Russia. A *Selected Works* was published in 1959 as well as a shorter collection, *Selected Atheist Writings* (1973). The moral of the story with respect to Bonch-Bruevich is that **atheism**, when tied to an authoritarian system like Soviet communism, is no less dangerous to individual freedoms than religiously inspired theocracies. Atheism is worth little without **humanism**. See the entry on **atheism, insufficiency of**.

BONFIRE OF THE VANITIES. Name given to the fires set in Florence in the 1490s at the urging of the fanatical Catholic priest Girolamo Savonarola (1452–1498). Savonarola's splenetic sermons fueled a puritanical backlash against the high culture and social permissiveness of Florence under the Medici family, who had attracted some of the best artists in Italy to the city. Savonarola unleashed gangs of disciples, known as *piagnone* or "snivelers," who acted as religious vigilantes, in a manner not unlike the militias who enforced strict religious codes under the Taliban in Afghanistan. Jewels, books, clothing, paintings by Botticelli (1445–1510), and other items were all consigned to the flames.

The flames acquired the label "bonfire of the vanities," although it is not difficult to see a vanity of equal proportion underlying Savonarola's celibate paranoia. Savonarola's puritanical revolt did not last long. In 1498 he was burned at the stake.

Savonarola's campaign can be seen as an early example of a **culture war**. One of the many ironies of all this is that today's religious conservatives frequently cite the **Renaissance** as an example of Christian culture that compares favorably to the secular vulgarity of today.

BONNER, HYPATIA BRADLAUGH (1858–1935). English **freethought** activist and writer. Hypatia Bradlaugh was the second daughter of the great atheist and liberal, **Charles Bradlaugh**. Hypatia's life was defined by her father. Bradlaugh's wife had been incapacitated by drink and his eldest daughter, Alice, had died in 1888. From then on Hypatia became Bradlaugh's secretary, confidant, and constant companion. She made her first public speech in 1877, during her father's struggle over the *Fruits of Philosophy* pamphlet. That same year, the forces of reaction had their revenge. Protests were made about her attending classes at the City of London College, and after only one term Hypatia was excluded. So frightened were the powers-that-be that the college stopped enrolling any women.

Hypatia Bradlaugh married Arthur Bonner (1861–1939) in 1885. Around 1891 they formed the publishing firm A. and H. B. Bonner, but it soon proved unable to compete with Watts and Co., the publishing arm of the **Rationalist Press Association**. And in 1897 Bradlaugh Bonner tried to revive her father's paper, now called *The Reformer*. It lasted until 1904. And along with Bradlaugh's disciple, **J. M. Robertson**, Bradlaugh Bonner cowrote *Charles Bradlaugh: A Record of His Life and Work* (1895). While not managing to create a critical distance from their subject, this book is nevertheless an indispensable guide to Bradlaugh's life.

Bradlaugh Bonner's other books included *Penalties Upon Opinion* (1912), a survey of official persecution of freethought in nineteenth-century Britain; *The Christian Hell* (1913), a critique of some of the more lurid representations of the awful abode; *Christianity and Conduct* (1919), a record of some less-than-saintly preachers; and *Christianizing the Heathen* (1922), a critique of missionaries. A biography of Hypatia Bradlaugh Bonner was begun by her husband, and, after his death, by their son, Charles Bradlaugh Bonner (1890–1966), whose life was also devoted to freethought.

Further reading: Arthur Bonner and Charles Bradlaugh Bonner, *Hypatia Bradlaugh Bonner*.

BOUDJEDRA, RACHID (1941–). Algerian journalist, playwright, and novelist. An atheist and communist, Boudjedra has been courageous in his public criticisms of **sharia** law and reactionary Islamic politics in the Muslim world. His best known work is *La répudiation* (1969, translated 1995). Boudjedra had a **fatwa** pronounced against him in 1983, but has continued to criticize Islam and Islamic practices when necessary. For instance, in 1992 Boudjedra criticized the Algerian Islamist party, the FIS, as being undemocratic and extremist.

BRADLAUGH, CHARLES (1833–1891). Tireless campaigner for birth control, republicanism, the alleviation of **poverty**, **secularism**, and **atheism**. George Bernard Shaw (1856–1950), not a man given to hero worship of others, described Bradlaugh as "a hero, a giant who dwarfed everything around him, a terrific personality."

Bradlaugh was brought up a pious believer. At the age of fifteen he was already a Sunday school teacher. Shortly before his confirmation ceremony, Bradlaugh brought some theological concerns to his pastor. Instead of having them patiently explained to him, the pastor suspended the lad for "atheistical tendencies." While under this ban, Bradlaugh went to the fields where freethinking lecturers debated, and he earned their respect for his courageous defense of Christianity. But the

ideas he was exposed to in these encounters soon corroded his rigid belief, and he became a Deist. Bradlaugh entrusted this change to his pastor, who handled the situation with characteristic insensitivity. Under the pastor's blandishments, the young Bradlaugh was thrown out of the house by his father.

By now a confirmed atheist, Bradlaugh joined the **freethought** lecturers, and lived as precariously as they did. In order to pay mounting debts, Bradlaugh joined the army in 1851. His mother, having received a small legacy, was able to buy him out two years later. Bradlaugh returned to London and gained employment as an errand boy in a lawyer's office. For the next several years Bradlaugh studied law and became one of London's most talented and courageous freethought lecturers. In 1855 Bradlaugh stood his ground against a baton charge by police, who were trying to break up the gathering of working people on a Sunday at Hyde Park.

Contrary to critics, who claimed he pandered to popular opinion, Bradlaugh was a consistent campaigner for republicanism, at a time when support for the monarchy under Victoria was growing. His most significant work on this theme was *Impeachment of the House of Brunswick*, published originally in 1871 and in many subsequent editions. Bradlaugh's main arguments were that the money spent on the monarchy would be better spent alleviating poverty, that the monarchy encouraged the growth of unearned privilege, and that monarchy was synonymous with political incompetence.

Bradlaugh's role in the development of the British freethought movement was absolutely central. He founded the **National Secular Society** in 1866, the *National Reformer* in 1860, and the Freethought Publishing Company with **Annie Besant** in 1877. Bradlaugh came to national attention in 1877 over a protracted dispute over the publication of a controversial work on birth control called *The Fruits of Philosophy*. This battle cost Bradlaugh the support of **Charles Watts** but saw the arrival into public life of his daughter,

Hypatia. See the entry on **Hypatia Bradlaugh Bonner**.

After several attempts Bradlaugh narrowly won the seat of Northampton at the 1880 General Election. Upon arriving at Parliament, he asked to be allowed to make an affirmation of allegiance (as had previously been made available for Jews and Quakers) instead of being sworn in by a religious oath taken on the Bible. The House appointed a committee to consider the request and duly turned it down. Bradlaugh then told them he was content then to proceed with the oath, but the committee then declared that, as an unbeliever, he could not swear the oath. Newly reelected prime minister William Gladstone (1809–1898) engineered a change in Standing Orders allowing Bradlaugh to take his seat on the affirmation but at his own legal risk. After the first vote following his affirmation, Bradlaugh was handed a writ of penalty by his enemies for voting without having taken an oath. Bradlaugh's seat was declared vacant.

The next six years involved a complex legal and political struggle between Bradlaugh and a determined group of establishment figures who were determined an atheist would not sit in the House of Commons. Cardinal Manning (1808–1892) declared that the English people would not endure an unbeliever to sit in Parliament. In 1881, having been reelected by the electors of Northampton, Bradlaugh was forcibly ejected from the House, and it took four messengers and ten policemen to subdue him. Bradlaugh was reelected five times between 1880 and 1886, and it was the election of a new government under the Marquis of Salisbury (1830–1903) that turned the tide. In that year, the new speaker, Mr. Peel, permitted Bradlaugh to take the oath. In 1888 Bradlaugh had the satisfaction of seeing his Affirmation Bill become law, thus enshrining an important post-Christian freedom. The bill passed despite a petition signed by 13,000 clergymen who objected to this extension of liberty.

The battle to take his seat left Bradlaugh heavily in debt and exhausted, although he still had energy to advance the cause of India, visiting that country to attend the Fifth Indian National Congress in 1889–1890. Thinking it a rebuke, his opponents called Bradlaugh "the Member for India." Bradlaugh died at age fifty-seven of overwork and the accumulated effects of Bright's Disease. His pen name was "Iconoclast" and his motto was "Thorough."

Further reading: David Tribe, *President Charles Bradlaugh MP*.

BREAD AND CIRCUSES. Modern phrase which refers to the practice of Roman rulers to supply the poorer population of Rome with regular portions of bread and periodic entertainments as a means to ensure peace in the city and distract them from more serious pursuits. This practice, which was continued in Constantinople, was done in full knowledge of how unruly and prone to rioting these populations were. The policies were designed to buy them off.

Nowadays the phrase is used to refer to the less direct methods governments and ruling elites employ to divert people from scrutinizing their activities too thoroughly. Endless media coverage of sports and celebrities has the effect of numbing people and diverting their attention from the more important business of government.

The philosophy of bread and circuses was expressed most openly in the Chinese classic of **Taoist** thought, the *Laozi*, otherwise known as the *Tao te Ching*, from about the third century BCE. "The people all have something to occupy their eyes and ears, and the sage treats them all like children." See the entry on **manufactured consent**.

BREAREY, PETER (1939–1998). English **freethought** journalist. Born into a Methodist family in West Yorkshire, Brearey ran away from home at fourteen when his father destroyed his collection of books. From then on he was an atheist and freethinker.

At sixteen Brearey founded his own newspaper, the *Dewsbury Sentinel*, and much of his adult life was spent with provincial papers in the north of England. And in partnership with his wife, Pamela, he created a series of National Health Service periodicals. Brearey also wrote *Never Say Scoop* (1981), an introduction to journalism from one who had learned the trade from the bottom up.

Brearey was also active politically, serving as chairman of the Wakefield branch of the National Union of Journalists. His political life began in the Young Communist League, then the Communist Party, but when he became disillusioned with communism, he moved on to the Socialist Party of Great Britain with an interest in anarchism.

Since a teenager, it had been Brearey's ambition to edit *The Freethinker*, Britain's longest-standing freethought journal. His chance came in 1993. Until his untimely death from cancer at 58, Brearey brought color and life to the journal.

BRIGHTS. A term suggested in 2003 by Paul Geisert and Mynga Futrell as a general noun to include all varieties of freethinkers: atheists, naturalists, skeptics, agnostics, and so on. Homosexuals have cornered the word "gay" as an umbrella term, and Geisert and Futrell thought this would be a good idea for religious nonbelievers. The idea won some early support from **Daniel C. Dennett** and **Richard Dawkins**. But critics of the idea have accused it of giving the impression of arrogance, as the opposite of "bright" is "dim."

Further reading: www.the-brights.net.

BRITISH COMMONWEALTH. See **COMMONWEALTH OF NATIONS**.

BRITISH HUMANIST ASSOCIATION. Formed after a great deal of preparation on May 17, 1963, when two hundred people gathered at the House of Commons as the guests of Laurie Pavitt MP. Sir **Julian Huxley** became president and **A. J. Ayer** vice president. It had been intended that the BHA would supersede and encompass all the existing freethought and rationalist organizations, in particular the Eth-

ical Union, the **Rationalist Press Association**, and the **National Secular Society**. This was never that likely to happen, as each organization had different emphases and was run by people who did not always find cooperation as easy as would have been ideal.

While the BHA has not become *the* single humanist organization in Britain, it has gone on to provide many valuable services to its members. The BHA provides positive ethical alternatives to religion, most notably the secular celebrants service it offers. The popularity of humanist weddings, baby namings, and funerals has grown consistently as Britain has become post-Christian. It also hosts conferences that consider various questions of religion and the state and ethical issues. The BHA also provides support to the dozens of local humanist groups and fellowships throughout Britain.

The BHA's other focus is on education. The association has long campaigned for a broadening of scope in religious education in British schools to include humanism. Though not a religion, it is a comprehensive worldview that deserves to be considered alongside religions. Accordingly, it does not oppose religious education as such, it simply wants its focus to expand to reflect the real contours of belief in British society. The BHA has produced some highly regarded resources for teachers who want to deal with social or ethical issues. The BHA sponsors the Humanist Philosophers' Group, which publishes occasional pamphlets on topical issues.

BRODIE, FAWN McKAY (1915–1981). Scholar convicted of heresy for writing the truth about Mormon founder Joseph Smith. Brodie's book, *No Man Knows My History: The Life of Joseph Smith* (1945) denied the church's claim that Smith was divinely inspired, showing instead that Smith was a fraudster who conjured up a miscellany of ideas from other ideas that were current at the time.

Fawn McKay was brought up in Utah by her devout Mormon father and a mother who held quietly heretical views. McKay showed signs of exceptional intelligence, too much to be comfortable for the normal role expected of Mormon women. University education completed an unraveling of McKay's Mormonism. By 1936 her departure from Mormonism was complete and was made more so by her marriage that year to Bernard Brodie, of Latvian-Jewish extraction. Bernard Brodie went on to have a successful career as a scholar of international relations.

Ten years of research went into *No Man Knows My History*, and it was generally recognized as a first-class work of scholarship. Brodie was excommunicated from the Mormon Church in June 1946. Brodie went on to criticize the then practice of the Mormons of excluding Blacks from the church's priesthood—a practice not stopped until 1978. Fawn Brodie also wrote successful biographies of Thaddeus Stevens (1959), Richard Burton (1967), Thomas Jefferson (1974), and Richard Nixon (1981).

BRONOWSKI, JACOB (1908–1974). Scientist, humanist, and popularizer of **science**. Jacob Bronowski was born in Lodz, then part of Russian Poland, the son of an observant Jewish father and an atheist, communist mother. The family fled their home town at the beginning of World War I and lived in Germany until 1920, when they migrated to Britain. Bronowski studied mathematics at Cambridge and lectured at University College in Hull from 1934 to 1942, when he went into wartime military research. Bronowski spent part of 1945 in Nagasaki, monitoring the effects of the plutonium bomb that had been dropped on that city on August 9. In 1964, he moved to the United States, where he worked at the Salk Institute for Biological Studies in California.

Bronowski is best remembered as a brilliant popularizer of science. His early work *Science and Human Values* (1958) brought together a series of articles written for the *New York Times* about nuclear science and the morality of nuclear weapons. *The Identity of Man* (1965) sought to find a viable humanist account of

what it is to be human in an era of mechanization. Bronowski also cowrote with the American historian Bruce Mazlish *The Western Intellectual Tradition* (1960), a magisterial intellectual history of thought from the Renaissance to the nineteenth century. Bronowski is best known for the thirteen-part BBC television documentary *The Ascent of Man*, which was issued as a book in 1973. Bronowski was an outspoken rationalist and humanist, and was an honorary associate of the **Rationalist Press Association** from 1958 until his death.

BROPHY, BRIGID (1929–1995). English author, activist, **feminist**, and hell-raiser. Born in London to John Brophy, a novelist, and Charis Grundy, the American daughter of an eccentric sect leader. Educated at St. Paul's Girls School in London, she went on to St. Hugh's College, Oxford, though she was sent down in her second year. The reason is unknown, but rumors spoke of drunkenness at chapel and lesbianism.

Brophy's first novel, *Hackenfeller's Ape* (1953), which explored aspects of animal rights, won critical attention. Much of her writing explored questions of bisexuality, hedonism, and issues around marriage. In 1954, Brophy married the prominent art historian Sir Michael Levey. The marriage was an open one, with Brophy carrying on extramarital lesbian affairs, most notably with her friend, novelist and philosopher **Iris Murdoch**. In 1965 Brophy was asked by the *Sunday Times* to write an article on the state of marriage. Her article was called "The Immorality of Marriage" and argued that marriage is an intrinsically exploitative institution. Not surprisingly, the article caused a media furor. Brophy was denounced by religious apologists of the time as the high priestess of British humanism.

Other important novels include *In Transit* (1969) and *A Palace Without Chairs* (1978). Brophy also wrote some biographies, most notably one on the outrageous late Victorian artist Aubrey Beardsley (1872–1898). Brophy's main contribution to the welfare of writers came when she campaigned throughout the 1970s for a law change that would have payments sent to authors in proportion to their rate of being lent out by libraries. This law was enacted in 1979 and was a considerable assistance to struggling writers.

Brophy was, in her own words, a "proselytizing atheist" and was an honorary associate of the **Rationalist Press Association** from 1984 until her death, and of the **National Secular Society** until she left that organization for not supporting her campaign to have Amnesty International include animals in its purview. Brophy died in 1995 of multiple sclerosis after a long illness.

BRUNO, GIORDANO (1548–1600). Brilliant if erratic scholar, **smiter of humbug**, and martyr to **freethought**. Bruno was born at Nola, near Naples, the son of a soldier. At fourteen he began studying in Naples before entering a Dominican convent in 1572. Bruno's brilliance soon landed him in trouble with religious authorities. On one occasion he was caught reading **Erasmus** on the toilet. Erasmus had been excommunicated after his death and all his works put on the **Index of Forbidden Books**. So as to avoid trouble, Bruno went to Genoa, known as a more tolerant society, where he lived as a teacher. From there he wandered around much of western Europe. During his time in England, he may well have been involved in a spying network. Bruno's truculent personality was a dangerous mix in a Europe embroiled in the **wars of religion**. He described himself as "a wakener of minds, a tamer of presumptuous and obstinate ignorance . . . whom only propagators of folly and hypocrites detest, whom the honorable and studious love, whom noble minds applaud."

Bruno wrote on a wide range of subjects from ancient Egyptian religions, to cosmology, magic, and the occult. Influenced in part by **Lucretius** and the **atomists**, Bruno took seriously the ideas of the **heliocentric universe** as outlined by Copernicus (1473–1543). But where Copernicus thought the sun was at or near the center of the universe, Bruno argued that the universe had no center. He argued for an infinity of worlds, which was a standing challenge to the **anthropocentric conceit** of Christian theology. Bruno was not a Christian, rather he embraced an idiosyncratic form of **pantheism**. He rejected any notion of personal **immortality**. Bruno revived the atomist idea of atoms as minute spheres of matter that float endlessly in fluid ether.

In 1590 Bruno was invited by Zuane Mocenigo, a wealthy gentleman to come to Venice to teach. When Bruno decided to leave Venice in 1592, Mocenigo, who had links to the **Inquisition**, had him arrested. Early in 1593 Bruno was handed over to the Papal Inquisition and incarcerated for seven years. On February 19, 1600, Bruno was burned at the stake for being a heretic. Most dates say February 17, but it appears this is incorrect. In 1889, a bronze statue of Bruno, sculpted by Ettori Ferrari, was unveiled in Rome, within sight of the Vatican, to act as a permanent warning against bigotry. Bruno's courage lived on as a model for freethought and his views served as an inspiration for **Galileo Galilei**.

Further reading: Michael White, *The Pope and the Heretic*.

BÜCHNER, FRIEDRICH KARL CHRISTIAN LUDWIG (1824–1899). German scientist and author, and proponent of **materialism**. It has become received wisdom to pronounce Büchner's version of materialism entirely superseded by the developments of twentieth-century physics. This is not entirely true, however. While most of Büchner's explanations have been superseded, the basic assumptions of contemporary **science** are much the same as those of Büchner. Neither has Büchner received the credit he deserves for expressing his theories with appropriate tentativeness.

Büchner's most important work was *Force and Matter* (1855, with expanded editions after 1884) for which he was deprived of his chair at Tübingen. But the widespread appeal of the book gave him an influence he would never have achieved as an academic. Büchner practiced as a physician in his home town of Darmstadt until his death. He was responsible for a series of publications: *Nature and Spirit* (1857); *Man in the Past, Present, and Future* (1869); *Materialism: Its History and Influence on Society* (1873); *The Idea of God* (1874); *Mind in Animals* (1880); and *Light and Life* (1882). After his death a series of essays were brought together under the title *Last Words on Materialism* (1901).

Further reading: Richard C. Vitzhum, *Materialism: An Affirmative History and Definition*.

BUDDHA, THE. See **GAUTAMA, SIDDHARTHA.**

BUFFON, GEORGES-LOUIS LECLERC (1707–1788). French naturalist who came under pressure from religious authorities for his scientific work. Buffon's huge work *Histoire naturelle* (1749) went over forty-four volumes, thirty-six of which appeared in his lifetime.

An important feature of Buffon's system was that the animal and plant worlds were ever-changing. This put him against the Swedish naturalist **Carolus Linnaeus**, who at that time Buffon was active, was constructing his ambitious system of classification of the plant and animal kingdoms, based on their fixity. Buffon advocated a pre-Darwinian model of evolution, arguing that the Earth is 74,832 years old. It is possible he actually thought the Earth was considerably older than that, but chose not to publicize his preferred date. Not surprisingly, *Histoire naturelle* was condemned by the theologians of the University of Paris, and under mounting pressure, Buffon was forced to recant all his points.

BURDEN OF PROOF. Refers to the question of who has the prime responsibility to justify their claims. In a crime in the United States, the burden of proof rests with those wanting to prove someone guilty of the crime. But in **religion** or with respect to **paranatural** claims, it is generally agreed that the burden of proof rests with the person making the claim. The reason for this is simple: the theist or the paranormalist is making the larger claim. Whether claiming that the universe was created by **God** or that so-and-so can bend spoons by sheer willpower, both require our understanding of the way things work to be revised. In both cases, a simpler explanation can be given that is consistent with the principles of natural science and philosophy. See the entries on **Ockham's Razor** and the **Principle of Parsimony**. And so the burden of proof lies with those who claim the simpler explanation is flawed and that we need instead to accept this more convoluted explanation. To do this they need to do at least these three things:

- describe what it is that they are claiming to exist;
- demonstrate how this thing exists; and
- demonstrate why it exists.

The failure to achieve any of these things destroys their case. With respect to the debate between theism and **atheism**, the failure to achieve any of these three things justifies atheism by default. **Antony Flew** has provided similar arguments with the **presumption of atheism** and the **stratonician presumption**. Also, see the entries on **Newton, Sir Isaac** and **science, presumption of**.

Further reading: Antony Flew, *An Introduction to Western Philosophy* and *God, Freedom, and Immortality*.

BURNING OF THE BOOKS. One of the most remarkable attempts at creating a completely totalitarian society, which took place in China in 213 BCE. On the recommendation of the first minister, Li Ssu, the Ch'in emperor, Shi Huang ti, instructed that all historical records apart from those of the Ch'in dynasty, all literature, and all philosophy should be turned over to the authorities and destroyed. The aim of this exercise was to expunge all historical memory of the tyes of government and society that had preceded the Ch'in dynasty. The only exceptions were certain works on medicine, divination, and agriculture, which were to be kept by an elite of seventy officials (called Erudites). The only school of philosophy exempted from the ban was the Legalists, under whose influence the Ch'in emperor was.

The burning of the books was about the last straw for a deeply discontented population. They had already put up with bureaucratic centralization of administration, standardization of weights and measures, and the creation of a national road network, and work was begun on the Great Wall to keep out the barbarian Huns from the north. Four years after the death of Shi Huang ti in 210 BCE, the Ch'in dynasty was ovethrown in a popular revolt.

Although the Ch'in dynasty was the shortest in Chinese history, it was one of the most influential, if not *the* most influential, in setting the tone for Chinese history. The name China is derived from the Ch'in dynasty. The Han dynasty, which followed the Ch'in, retained many of their centralizing initiatives and ways of government. But the burning of the books irrevocably destroyed the reputation of the Legalists and restored the reputation of Confucianism. Mengzi (371–289 BCE), in particular, had argued for the right of the people to rebel against leaders whose leadership was not in harmony with the needs of the people. Confucianists were by no means anarchists or rebels; they favored strong government, but they also demanded a standard of behavior from the ruler that would justify his leadership.

BUYER'S REMORSE. The widely observed phenomenon of consumers regretting a purchase they have made once they get it back home. Features of this remorse include:

- disappointment at having broken a pledge to save money;
- self-loathing for falling for some advertising patter; and

- recognition that the purchased item is not as necessary or amusing as it was thought to be prior to the purchase.

Often this remorse results in a complete refusal to use the purchased item, as well as a sense of failure to return it each time it is remembered or seen. Buyer's remorse takes place within a broader context of awareness of the pressures consumer societies put on people to spend simply for the sake of spending. See the entry on **affluenza**. The remorse is the knowledge of having caved in to that relentless pressure. Maximizers are more likely to experience buyer's remorse than satisficers. See the entry on **satisficers and maximizers**.

C

CAFETERIA CATHOLICS. The term given to the growing trend of people calling themselves Roman Catholics while observing few if any of the dogmatic requirements emanating from the Vatican. It is an open secret, for instance, that in France and Italy, the Vatican's proscriptions against contraception are almost universally ignored. And in the United States, 55 percent of Catholics support a woman's right to an abortion. Polls often reveal a deep skepticism among Catholics about claims of papal infallibility. There is also a far more widespread practice of **New Age** beliefs and cooperation with other denominations than is approved of by the Vatican. See the entry on **theological correctness**.

CALIPHATE. See **KHALIFAT**.

CAMBRIAN EXPLOSION. The term given to a period about 530 million years ago when the Earth underwent a dramatic growth in the range and **complexity** of life. Over the period of a few million years, life on earth multiplied exponentially from relatively simple cellular life (see the entry on **cells**). Among the proliferating forms of new life during this epoch was the tiny wormlike *amphioxus*, the ancestor of all vertebrates, including *Homo sapiens*. The most likely explanation for this explosion of new life-forms over a relatively short period of time is the changing levels of oxygen in the atmosphere. As the amount of oxygen rose, so did the number of life-forms nourished by it.

Creationists and other opponents of **evolution** often cite the Cambrian explosion as evidence of the flaws in evolutionary theory. If this explosion of new life-forms happened over a short period of time, geologically speaking, where does this leave the theory of **natural selection**, which speaks of gradual change? This argument is specious because it confuses **Darwinism** with evolution. It is true that the gradualism of natural selection has had to be modified in light of the Cambrian finds, but this in no way weakens the general evolutionary account. The Cambrian explosion strengthens evolutionary thinking by eliminating what is now seen as an error in the assumptions underlying natural selection, which remains the principal mechanism by which evolution takes place.

Further reading: Richard Leakey and Roger Lewin, *The Sixth Extinction*.

CAMUS, ALBERT (1913–1960). Brilliant novelist and playwright. Albert Camus was born in Mondovia, a small town in Algeria, then a part of France. His family was poor, especially after his father's death in 1914. Camus worked in Algeria as a journalist before moving to France shortly before World War II. During the war he worked with the French Resistance. Camus won the Nobel Prize for Literature in 1957. He died as a passenger in a car accident in Algeria in 1960.

Camus met and befriended **Jean-Paul Sartre** in 1943, a friendship that ended in 1952 in a violent disagreement that became a *cause célèbre*. Sartre and Camus had radically different views on the Soviet Union.

Sartre became more dogmatically supportive of the Soviet Union and of **Marxism**, while Camus was strongly anticommunist. Camus was, we can see now, more consistent in his defense of freedom than Sartre, who juggled his views on freedom with belligerent apologetics for Marxism. And Camus' writing has stood the test of time in the way most of Sartre's has not.

Camus' genius was to understand and articulate the ethical consequences of the fact that there is no **God**. In a series of novels; *The Stranger* (1942), *The Plague* (1947), and *The Fall* (1956), as well as his best-known nonfiction works **The Rebel** (1951) and *The Myth of Sisyphus* (1942), Camus explored ideas of freedom, responsibility, and tragedy in the modern world. Camus became known for his notion of **absurdity**, which he discussed most thoroughly in *The Rebel* and *The Myth of Sisyphus*. Camus took his **atheism** seriously and wrote about the tragic freedom which wells up once one realizes that there is no God to hold one's hand.

CAN'T PROVE A NEGATIVE. One of the oldest **prejudices against atheists** is that they are trying to prove a negative, which is impossible. The argument goes that atheists would need total access to the entire universe to show that **God** is not there before their claim could be vindicated. Given that this is impossible, proving a negative is a vain exercise and **atheism** stands condemned.

The main problem with this prejudice is that no atheist has ever defended atheism in this way. As with many other prejudices against atheists, the "can't prove a negative" only retains whatever credibility it has if it ignores what atheists have actually said. The argument attacks a straw man.

What atheists actually say is quite different. Some atheists, following **Charles Bradlaugh**, speak of atheism as being *without* a conception of God that isn't simply some assertion from a human being. Person *a* says God is like this, but person *b* says that God is not like that at all, but is like this.

Person *c* dismisses both those claims and insists that God is in fact like this. What Bradlaugh said was that until he hears an account of God that is more than just rival assertions, he is without a conception of God that is truly objective. This is known as negative atheism.

Then there is positive atheism, which philosophers like **Michael Martin** have argued for so effectively. Positive atheism says that the **evidence** for God is so weak while the evidence against God is so strong that a belief that God does not exist is the most philosophically sound position to hold.

No reputable atheist has argued against the existence of God in a way that would be defeated by the "can't prove a negative" argument. It is really not an argument at all, just another form of insult.

CARLILE, RICHARD (1790–1843). English **freethought** pioneer and martyr for freedom of expression. Known principally for his courageous struggle for a free press in England. His battle began in 1817 when the Habeas Corpus Act was suspended. Between 1817 and 1835, Carlile spent more than nine years in prison for publishing freethought material. In 1819 the Society for the Suppression of Vice led a prosecution against Carlile for republishing **Thomas Paine**'s classic book *Age of Reason*. Carlile insisted on reading the entire book to the court, so that they may know what he was being prosecuted for publishing. He was fined £1,500 and sentenced to three years' imprisonment. The fine was impossibly steep and as Carlile had no hope of paying it, his term in prison was extended to six years. Carlile had another work he published in 1819 dedicated to the Society for the Suppression of Vice.

While Carlile was incarcerated, his colleagues and employees (male and female) continued to publish heretical works, and were in turn imprisoned. By 1824, eight of them were serving prison terms. One such person, Susannah Wright, was imprisoned for eighteen months and fined £100. While conducting her defense she was continually interrupted by the prosecution and the judge. Carlile's persecution attracted the attention of Julian Hibbert (1801–1834) a wealthy liberal freethinker, who provided generous financial assistance for Carlile's publishing ventures. It is said that Carlile did not use the money from Hibbert to pay his fine and thus secure release, because he found imprisonment preferable to living with his wife. In Carlile's decline, he lapsed into a theistic **mysticism** and was given an Anglican burial, notwithstanding the objections of his sons.

Freethinkers of all persuasions owe Carlile a huge debt. After he and his colleagues, it is no longer possible to contrive a successful charge of **blasphemy** against someone who denied the truth claims of Christianity. From then on the anti-Christian item had to be specifically abusive or offensive before it could be deemed blasphemous. Carlile should also be remembered as a brave pioneer for the freedom of the press against religious authoritarianism.

CARNEADES (219–129 BCE). Born in Cyrene, Carneades rose to become head of Plato's **Academy**, the so-called New Academy, which had been revived by Arcesilaus. Very little is known about his life. Like **Socrates**, Carneades wrote nothing himself. Rather, all material attributed to his name was compiled by his students. Carneades survived into old age, becoming blind in his last years. Most of what is attributed to Carneades is actually found in the writings of Cicero and Sextus Empiricus (third century CE).

Carneades was an opponent of the **Stoics**, having more in common with the **skeptics**. Though Carneades argued we cannot have knowledge, he did not think, unlike most of his fellow skeptics, that we must simply suspend judgment. Instead, Carneades postulated the theory of probability, by which he meant plausible reasoning rather than probable in the contemporary statistical sense. The arguments of Carneades have remained influential in the philosophy of **atheism** to this day.

CARTESIAN METHOD. The great philosopher **René Descartes** proposed a four-part method of inquiry built upon an active **skepticism**:

- never accept anything that has not presented itself so clearly and distinctly that you might have no occasion to doubt it;
- divide difficulties into many different segments to solve it;
- work from the simpler problems to the more complex; and
- make complete enumerations and general reviews so that nothing is omitted.

Descartes said his method will work because, among other reasons, "there is only one truth of each thing. . . ." That may or may not be true, and philosophers have criticized each of Descartes' four rules of **skepticism**, but nevertheless each one is an effective tool of learning, and all four constitute a formidable array of research methods. See the entries on **inquiry, tools of** and the **ten tropes of judgment**.

Further reading, René Descartes, *Discourse on Method*.

CARVAKA. The **materialist** school of thought (*darshana*) in India and one of the oldest **naturalist** traditions in the world. Carvaka is thought to be the name of the founder of the school, but nothing is known of him beyond his name, and even his historicity is uncertain. Tradition has Carvaka as the moral accuser of Yudisthira, a leading figure in the Hindu epic, the *Mahabharata*. Alternatively, Carvaka also means "sweet-tongued," or "pleasant words," which may refer to the general perception of Carvaka philosophy as hedonist.

As is common with naturalist movements from the ancient world, the main work representing Carvaka philosophy, the *Carvaka Sutra* (600 BCE, approx.), is lost and is only known through the works of its detractors. The traditional author of these sutras is given as Brihaspati, son of Loka.

Carvaka doctrines rose in response to the growing dogmatism and formalism of Vedic philosophy. Carvaka philosophy regards the universe as interdependent and subject to perpetual evolution. Central tenets of the Carvaka school include: sacred literature should be regarded as false; there is no deity or supernatural; there is no immortal soul or afterlife; karma is inoperative and illusory; matter is the fundamental element; only direct perception, and not religious injunctions or sacerdotal classes, can give us true knowledge. The aim in life is to get the maximum amount of pleasure from it. This had various interpretations, from unalloyed hedonism to an altruistic service of others on the principle that this will maximize one's own happiness as well as that of others.

Carvaka materialists are generally considered to be *nastika* (unorthodox) in that they reject or question the authority of the **Veda**. This does not mean, however, that materialists cannot be Hindus. It simply means that they are unorthodox Hindus. Most authorities acknowledge that the Carvaka tradition has saved Hinduism from lapsing into **dogmatism** or ritualism and has operated as an important irritant to majority patterns of thought. See the entry on **Lokayata**.

Further reading: Dale Riepe, *The Naturalistic Tradition in Indian Thought*, and Debriprasad Chattopadhyaya, ed., *Carvaka/ Lokayata*.

CASCADING. The process of selling on, or even giving, aging military equipment to allied countries rather than scrapping it. Sometimes the cascading is done through private arms dealers. It is very costly to decommission obsolete military equipment, so it is cheaper to pass it on to some other country. What use they make of it is their business. See the entry on **arms trade**.

CATALOG OF SUPERNATURAL TEMPLATES. Phrase coined by the American religious studies scholar Pascal Boyer to refer to the limited number of templates *Homo sapiens* have from which the huge number of supernatural concepts emerge. **Religion** is a human construct, so it follows that there is a limit to the number of basic religious styles that have emerged from the human mind. Those limited number of templates are then reworked to adapt to local conditions, and in this way a great variety emerges.

Further reading: Pascal Boyer, *Religion Explained*.

CATEGORICAL IMPERATIVE. Absolute ethical maxim devised in 1785 by **Immanuel Kant**. Kant distinguished this categorical imperative from a series of hypothetical imperatives, which could be implemented in the event of having a particular aim to follow. The categorical imperative, by contrast, was intended as a primal source of moral principles, something that is objectively true. It says act only in a manner that you would wish to become a universal law. In Kant's own words: "Act so as to use humanity, whether in your own person or in the person of another, always as an end, never as merely a means."

The categorical imperative has several major problems attached to it. To begin with, it assumes that all true moral thinking happens within oneself, and not as a social discourse with other people. Neither can it tell us *which* moral principles to adopt; it can only operate as a way to test the principles we have already got. And this leads to the next problem of the categorical imperative being unable to acknowledge the need for compromise on occasions. As critics have noted, if a murderer burst in to our house and asked the whereabouts of our loved ones, under the categorical imperative we would be obliged to tell him, whereas a more flexible situational ethics would permit us to lie to the murderer. The categorical imperative is an example of **idealism** in philosophy.

Several humanist philosophers have attempted variations on the categorical imperative, but without the pretensions to being writ somehow across the cosmos. For instance, Karl Marx (1818–1883) spoke of "the categorical imperative to overthrow all relations in which man is debased, enslaved, abandoned, despicable essence." Needless to say, Marx had **religion** in mind. See the entries on the **golden rule** and **supreme moral rule**.

CATEGORY MISTAKE. An idea invented by Gilbert Ryle (1900–1976) in his most important work, *The Concept of Mind* (1949). It involves representing the facts from one category of thinking as if they belonged to another. For instance, were we to act on the recommendation of a circus fortune teller we would be making a category mistake. Because the facts of the fortune teller belong to the category of entertainment, whereas making decisions about our lives require facts from an entirely different category.

Further reading: Gilbert Ryle, *The Concept of Mind*.

CATHOLIC CHURCH'S BIBLE PROBLEM. The term coined by Daniel Jonah Goldhagen for the central issue underlying the continuing inability of the Catholic Church to come to grips with **anti-Semitism**. The foundational text of Christianity, the New Testament, is massively anti-Semitic in tone, with more than four hundred fifty anti-Semitic passages in Mark, Matthew, Luke, John, and Acts alone. Admitting any of this, let alone expunging the offending texts, would tear the heart out of the New Testament, and with it, the claims to authority of the Catholic Church. Given this, it is easier for the Church to evade responsibility for making any serious restitution for its long history of anti-Semitism.

Further reading: Daniel Jonah Goldhagen, *A Moral Reckoning*.

CECCO D'ASCOLI (1269?–1327). Italian mathematician and astrologer burned at the stake by the Roman Catholic church. His principal work was *L'acerba*, a wide-ranging allegorical poem. D'Ascoli attracted negative attention when he criticized Dante for the attacks on astrology in the *Divine Comedy*. D'Ascoli's astrology got him into even more danger when he wrote that **Jesus** lived a sluggard's life and that his death by crucifixion was no more than his stars predicted would happen. This was too close to free speech for the ecclesiastical authorities, and on September 16, 1327, d'Ascoli was burned at the stake as a **heretic**.

CELL, THE. The universal unit of living matter. The oldest living matter found on earth are single-celled organisms fossilized into rocks dated as being 3.75 billion years old. For two billion years, life on the planet was defined exclusively by the simplest cells called prokaryotes; cells without nuclei. And for another billion years after that, the more complex eukaryotic cells were what set the pace. Eukaryotic cells have nuclei, which can store genetic information. It was only 530 million years ago when complex multicellular organisms began to take off. This is known as the Cambrian explosion.

Each human cell is made of forty-six chromosomes, which are composed of eighty-million base pairs of genetic code. The genetic code goes on to determine which proteins it shall create. Different proteins are responsible for different functions.

The slow development of cell theory was the crucial development of biology, and of the passage of that discipline from a soft to a hard science. It was only in 1838 that the German chemists Schleiden and Schwann discovered that all living things were made up of myriads of cells. The German biologist Rudolf Virchow (1821–1902) brought together a variety of different theories to establish the cell as the basic biological unit. His motto was "All cells arise from other cells."

It is redundant now to speak of outdated notions like the **soul**. There is no such thing. But there are cells and proteins, the story of which is incomparably more intriguing and inspiring than prescientific notions of souls.

CELSUS (second century CE). **Pagan** philosopher and critic of Christianity. Very little is known of Celsus's life. He may have been a Roman citizen, but equally, he may well have come from the Eastern Mediterranean. Most of his known writings date from about 175– 180 CE. Celsus was a friend of **Lucian of Samosata**.

Celsus became known for his book *The True Word* (178 CE), which was a strong attack on Christianity. He criticized Christian claims to having a **monopoly on the truth** and pointed out the problems in the claims surrounding the divinity of Christ. As happened to so many writers critical of Christianity, his words survive only in fragments. What we know of Celsus's thought comes from the Christian theologian Origen (185–254 CE), who wrote *Contra Celsus* (248 CE) to refute the pagan's damaging criticisms. After Christianity became the official religion of the Roman Empire, copies of *The True Word* were destroyed.

CENSORSHIP. The practice of limiting public access to written or other material deemed offensive. The problem with censorship has always been how to determine what constitutes "offensive." It is no coincidence that Mainz, the city of Gutenberg, was also the first city to experience censorship. At the request of the archbishop-elector of Mainz, the first censorship office in Europe was established in Frankfurt-am-Main in 1486. The first edict issued by the Frankfurt office was against vernacular translations of the Bible.

Censorship can easily slip into the prohibition of free expression, so it is best that the criteria for censorship be transparent and simple. It is reasonable to censor material that is exploitative of people unable to make an informed choice (children in particular) or of animals. However, it is unreasonable to censor nonexploitative material that simply offends one group of people. Censorship is one of the frontline issues for the **open society**. One of the first denunciations of censorship was the *Areopagetica* (1644), written by John Milton (1608–1674).

CENTER FOR INQUIRY. Conceived by

Paul Kurtz in 1990 as an umbrella organization, to include his two hitherto independent organizations; **CSICOP** (commonly known as the Skeptics), which publishes the *Skeptical Inquirer*, and the **Council for Secular Humanism**, which publishes *Free Inquiry*. Increasingly, the broader notion of the Center for Inquiry is overtaking the hitherto autonomous CSICOP and Council for Secular Humanism.

The stated goal of the Center for Inquiry (CFI) is "to promote and defend science, reason, and free inquiry in all aspects of human endeavor." With that goal in mind, the center sees its purpose as contributing to the public understanding of science and reason, with particular reference to their applications to human conduct, ethics, and society. The Center for Inquiry wants to move on from engaging solely in the criticism of religion. See the entry on **religion, criticism of**. What is of paramount need today is to promote positive ethical alternatives to outmoded **command moralities**, and this is the main focus of CFI activities. The first activity conducted by the Center was a radio announcement featuring prominent media personality **Steve Allen** on the importance of **critical thinking**.

The principal Center for Inquiry is located in Amherst, New York, adjacent to the State University of New York at Buffalo's north campus. This is known as the Center for Inquiry—Transnational. The Amherst Center is a complex of four buildings that include the largest library of skeptical, humanist, and rationalist material in the world, and sophisticated seminar, conference, and media facilities. It operates as a resource facility for inquirers who seek objective information on fringe science, claims of the paranormal, and supernatural claims. The center maintains the Council for Media Integrity, which acts as a rapid response unit when unbalanced or irresponsible material on **science**, the **paranormal**, or **religion** appears in the media. The center also runs the Center for Inquiry Institute, which promotes understanding of the skeptical attitude and trains spokespeople who

can act as leaders in their local community. And, since 1990, it has sponsored **African Americans for Humanism**, and since 1996, the **Center for Inquiry—On Campus**.

The Amherst Center for Inquiry was opened on its present site in 1995, and in 2004, an expansion into a fourth building with ten new offices and a large conference center was begun. Following the example of the Amherst center, other Centers for Inquiry have been opened in Los Angeles (CFI—West), New York (CFI—Metro New York), and St. Petersburg, Florida (CFI—Florida), as well as branch offices in Russia, Germany, France, Nigeria, India, Peru, Poland, Egypt, Spain, Uganda, and Nepal. Its official newsletter is the *CFI Report*.

CENTER FOR INQUIRY—ON CAMPUS. The largest campus organization devoted to the promotion of **free inquiry** in the world. The campus outreach program formed on August 9, 1996, under the name Campus Freethought Alliance (CFA), changing its name to Center for Inquiry—On Campus in 2004. The group's sponsor is the **Center for Inquiry**, led by **Paul Kurtz**, and its director is D. J. Grothe, a former Evangelical Christian. On its formation, the CFA released the Declaration of Necessity, which lamented the rising tide of obscurantism on campuses and what it called the "caustic environment" to free inquiry generally. The declaration noted the existence of organizations catering to the welfare of people of every major religious tradition, but that freethinkers remained unrepresented. It then mentioned the necessity of reversing this inequity.

Within a year, forty campus groups were established and in 2004 the figure had risen to about one hundred fifty, with thirty outside the United States. Many groups have come and gone in the intervening years, as it is in the nature of campus groups to have a rapidly rotating membership. With a staff of three, Center for Inquiry—On Campus is fully stretched trying to keep up with the demand for some **freethought** presence on their campus. Activities include providing speakers for talks, debates, and panels; organizing conferences and seminars; and maintaining informal ties between freethinkers on different campuses. CFI—On Campus has an *Affiliate Group Organizing Guide* and other free materials to help people establish groups on their campus.

Further reading: www.campusinquirer .org.

CERTAINTY. The god that fails, everytime. Certainty is the sure conviction that something is true, beyond any reasonable **doubt**. The only problem with this is that we can hold no item of **knowledge** with certainty. **Bertrand Russell** gave as a first principle of philosophy the maxim: "Do not feel absolutely certain of anything." The histories of all societies are replete with the detritus of the failed certainties of the past. Some items of knowledge are held up as certain truths by entire cultures, with penalties against those who would demur. But in all cases, the certainty proves, sooner or later, to be false, or at least highly questionable. And the tragedy is that, until that time happens, those who don't share that certainty are likely to face persecution.

Freethinkers of all persuasions, whether humanist, skeptic, or atheist, hold only one belief as certainly true: there is no such thing as certain truth. Lovers of paradox can do with this what they will. Everything we believe may be false, and we should hold our beliefs with degrees of certainty in direct proportion to the quantity and quality of **evidence** we can bring to bear. See the entry on **W. K. Clifford**. The quest for certainty is doomed to fail, as **John Dewey** noted many decades ago. But neither does this mean, as many opponents of humanism allege, that we must therefore wallow in moral **relativism**. The trick, observed the British philosopher Bernard Williams (1929–2003), is to have *confidence* in one's values, as opposed to *certainty* in them.

The absence of credible certainty presents us with many dangers. On the one hand, we can try to contrive certainty by subscribing to some **command morality** or **fundamentalism**. Or on the other hand, we can lapse into **nihilism**. The German philosopher **Jürgen Habermas** identified this as the choice of **Scylla and Charybdis**. It is the task of freethinkers to chart a course between the Scylla of fundamentalism and the Charybdis of nihilism. It is a difficult, though worthwhile, passage. See the entries on **fallibilism**, **reliabilism**, and **theopathic condition**.

Further reading: Bertrand Russell, *Human Knowledge: Its Scope and Limits*.

CHANCE. According to some **fundamentalist** apologists, the only explanation offered by **freethinkers** to account for the creation of the universe. Against chance (sometimes "blind chance") apologists offer their variations on the **argument to design**.

However, it is not true that freethinkers attribute the creation of the universe to blind chance. Each element that has gone into the universe operates according to some rule or another, and can in most cases be expressed in mathematical terms. The universe operates according to a seemingly infinite array of interdependent relations, which, for want of a better term, can be called the laws of nature.

Freethinkers consider that understanding the interrelationship of these laws of nature constitutes a sufficient understanding of the creation of the universe as our limited perspective can hope to realize. They do not see the universe being the result of chance, but neither do they presume to credit some anthropomorphic projection for it. The simple reduction into an either/or, chance/design binary hardly does credit to such a massive question as the creation of the universe. See the entry **either black or white, fallacy of**. And to presume it can be answered so neatly is another example of **anthropocentric conceit**.

What freethinkers mean when they speak of chance is an absence of cause, in particular, supernatural cause. For instance, chance does become a viable explanation on the level of random mutation. Here it is scientifically respectable to speak of these important instances of evolutionary change as chance developments. Chance also operates at the quantum level, as the **Uncertainty Principle** demonstrates. And paleontologists have noted that the survival of *Homo sapiens* through the many extinctions that have visited the planet is attributable as much to luck as to any superior skills we possess.

CHANDRASEKHAR, SUBRAHMANY-AN (1910–1995). Pioneering Indian physicist. Born in Lahore, now part of Pakistan, to a very prestigious Hindu family. His uncle, Sir C.V. Raman, was the first Indian to receive a Nobel Prize (physics, 1930). It was clear early on that Chandrasekhar was similarly gifted, and while still in his teens, he sailed to England to further his education.

Chandrasekhar was a Fellow of Trinity College, Cambridge, from 1936–1937, during which time he developed some major new insights into what later become known as black holes. Unhappily for Chandrasekhar, his ideas ran counter to the religious prejudices of his teacher and mentor, Sir Arthur Eddington (1882–1944), who mounted a campaign against his young protégé that sent him out of England and away, at least for a while, from his chosen field. Chandrasekhar returned to physics during his time as professor of physics at the University of Chicago, from 1944–1946. See the entry on **Clarke's Three Laws**.

Chandrasekhar's unique contribution was to propose what has since become known as the Chandrasekhar Limit. If a star has a mass less than the Chandrasekhar Limit (1.44 times the mass of the sun), new forces, driven by **quantum mechanics**, arise to stop its contraction, making it stable. But stars with a mass more than three times that of the sun will at some point turn into black holes, if they don't simply explode.

Chandrasekhar went on to have a very important career in physics. He was a fellow of the Royal Society and a member of the American Academy of Arts and Sciences. His best-known work, the *The Mathematical*

Theory of Black Holes (1983) remains a standard work in the field. In the same year Chandrasekhar followed in his uncle's footsteps and received a Nobel Prize in Physics.

Shortly before his death, Chandrasekhar outlined his religious beliefs. "I am a Hindu atheist," he said, "with no belief in God but following a rational way of life." The idea of being a Hindu atheist is not contradictory to the **Asian traditions** as it is with **monotheistic** religions. Chandrasekhar became an honorary associate of the **Rationalist Press Association** in 1968.

CHAOS. The name given to the recognition of high levels of unpredictability existing within many systems. This high level of unpredictability is the result of a high level of sensitivity to local conditions, which in turn results in the difficulty of establishing a secure baseline of information from which to plot any sort of progression. Provided one can begin with exact information, the results can be calculated with equal precision, even within so-called chaotic systems.

Contrary to chaos theory's more excitable advocates, chaos does not refute **classical physics** or **determinism**. While the path of any molecule is virtually impossible to predict, it remains nonetheless bound by the general rules of physics. It is predictability that is the problem, not determinism.

CHARACTER. The notion of being a person of substance, although what constitutes a person of substance has changed a great deal over the centuries. **Aristotle** spoke of the **virtues** of character and the virtues of intellect. This was no simplistic split between reason and emotion, however. The virtues of the intellect directly employed reason while virtues of character were linked crucially to **reason**. And Aristotle's **Doctrine of the Mean** rested upon a mature character to be able to chart life's challenges without recourse to **command moralities**. For **Kongfuzi** (Confucius), character was the mark of the superior man. Before Kongfuzi, character was something you were born with, but it was his genius to recognize that anyone can be a superior man. This was his single greatest contribution to Chinese thought.

Progressives have tended to shy away from the notion of character. They have reacted against the more conservative variations of character that were popular in the nineteenth century: "soundness" often meant conformism and reliability, which in turn often meant nonintellectual pliability. But conservatives do not have a monopoly on the notion of character.

Character is a blend of nature and nurture. A child born to a malnourished or alcoholic mother is less likely to be able to develop a mature and balanced depth of character than someone born healthy and in a stable, financially independent household. The brutal fact is that nature is grossly unfair in its handing out of talents and health. But, the development of character is only possible because of this gross unfairness. In a land where all are equal by decree, character is unnecessary, and possibly even a hindrance. For humanists, the surest test of character is the ability to resist the **transcendental temptation** and to be able to say to oneself that one is not of great significance to the cosmos, but that our lives have a significance in the way we live them and by the people whose lives we have touched.

CHARLES SOUTHWELL AWARD.

Annual award given by the New Zealand Association of Rationalists and Humanists to honor outstanding defenders of the **open society** in that country. **Charles Southwell** was the first known **freethinker** on New Zealand soil. The award was inaugurated in 1998, and has gone to Dame Cheryll Sotheran in her capacity as Director of Te Papa, the country's national art museum. Sotheran had come under intense criticism from fundamentalists to withdraw a piece of art that offended them. Sotheran refused, and the exhibition continued.

Two prominent journalists with reputations as **smiters of humbug** have received

the award; Brian Rudman in 1999 and Michael Laws (a practicing Anglican) in 2003. In 2000 the award went to a pioneering campaigner for abortion rights and other issues of women's health, Dr. Zoë During. In 2001 the award went to the prominent Australian pioneer for voluntary euthanasia, Dr. **Philip Nitschke**.

CHEAP REPRINTS. A series of inexpensive reprints of important works of nonfiction published by the **Rationalist Press Association** (RPA) between 1902 and 1912. Until the Cheap Reprints, nobody believed that working people would want to buy those types of books. The only cheap reprints before 1902 had been of middle- and low-brow fiction. But **Charles Albert Watts**, the founder of the RPA, believed that working people *did* want to read serious nonfiction. Other publishers thought he would go bankrupt, and some religious publishers were slow to cooperate with him.

Watts had to borrow money for the series to go ahead, and it is testimony to his character that his friends put their money into such an apparently risky venture. The first Cheap Reprint was a collection of lectures and essays by **T. H. Huxley**, a hero of Watts's. Against all expectations, the Cheap Reprints sold very well. The first impression of *Lectures and Essays* sold more than thirty thousand copies and the five titles released in 1902 combined sold more than 155,000 copies. Hardcovers sold for a shilling, and paperbacks at what Watts called the "wastepaper price" of sixpence. The series went on for ten years (with one title added as an afterthought in 1918) and sold more than four million copies. In the process, the RPA had rewritten the rules about publishing. Other publishers now saw that inexpensive nonfiction was economically viable. The road was open for the paperback and for works of popular science geared toward the general reader.

Established religion was horrified at the development. A flurry of pamphlets and articles came out lamenting the poisoning of the working class mind with all this **atheism** and **unbelief**. They didn't mind the books coming out, but until then they had been at a price the poor couldn't afford. The Cheap Reprints series was gradually starved into submission after a protracted campaign by churchmen to prevent titles being sold at railway stalls or being stocked in libraries. But by then the damage had been done.

The success of the Cheap Reprints had two important consequences:

- publishers realized there was a market for popular science among the general public; and
- publishers also realized that paperbacks had more of a future than simply reprinting light fiction.

The development of paperback nonfiction and popular science both owe a debt of gratitude to the pioneering experiment of the Rationalist Press Association.

Further reading: Bill Cooke, *The Gathering of Infidels: A Hundred Years of the Rationalist Press Association.*

CHILDREN OF GOD. A cult founded in 1968 by David Berg (1919–1994), a one-time Methodist preacher. Berg preached an apocalyptic message of doom and declared himself the Endtime Prophet, and renamed himself Moses David. The Children of God originally preached celibacy and poverty (for members, not for David Berg) as a means of avoiding the inevitable demise of the United States as it pays the price for untrammeled materialism and imperialism. The popularity of the cult among young women and Berg's growing messianism saw a radical change in the sexual ethics of the movement. Within a few years, virtually all forms of sexual behavior and deviance were permitted, including pedophilia and pornography, which was called the Love of God. Berg also began the "Hookers for Jesus"—women who would prostitute themselves in order to entice young men into the movement. This process was known as "Flirty Fishing."

Under pressure from authorities, Berg relocated in 1972 to Britain. In 1987, under further pressure from authorities, Berg renamed the organization, the Family of Love. But the saintly new name could not hide the goings-on within the movement. Many of the ever-growing number of offspring of the Hookers for Jesus became victims of pedophilia within the movement. Berg is thought to have died in 1994 and the movement, by now known as the Family, was taken over by his widow, who claimed to receive her authority from the spirit of her departed husband, and from Marilyn Monroe and Elvis Presley, among others. The Family is predicting the end of the world in 2006 or 2007.

CHINA RESEARCH INSTITUTE FOR SCIENCE POPULARIZATION. An organization set up in China in 1980 for the propagation of **science** against the rising tide of **pseudoscience**. CRISP's purpose is to "enlighten scientific spirit, defend science wisdom, refute superstition, and counteract pseudoscience." The idea for an institute of this kind came from the prominent scholar Gao Shiqi, who also served as CRISP's first chairman.

CRISP, which has branches throughout the country, is one of twenty-two nonprofit organizations that are part of the China Association of Science and Technology (CAST). CRISP has a range of scholars who maintain a close watch on foreign and domestic science popularization research. It also produces popular science writing and material directed toward young people. It maintains contacts with universities and schools throughout the country and publishes a range of journals, including the bimonthly *Science Popularization Research* and the annual *Report on Survey of Public Literacy in China*. It also publishes *Science and Atheism* and a range of stand-alone works. CRISP's Web site claims a million readers. CRISP maintains close links with the **Committee for the Scientific Investigation of Claims of the Paranormal** and, more recently, the **Center for Inquiry**.

CHINESE ROOM ARGUMENT. See **ARTIFICIAL INTELLIGENCE.**

CHRISTIAN ATHEISM. See **DEATH OF GOD, THE.**

CHRISTIAN ETHICS, IRRELEVANCE OF. It has been argued that Christian ethics are now so outmoded as to be irrelevant to contemporary living. Modern globalized societies value individual autonomy, the ability to earn a living, to provide for one's family, and to get along with a very broad range of people. Contemporary societies emphasize that women are in all respects the equal of men and that **slavery** is forbidden.

In contrast to all this, Christian ethics, which began life as a temporary fill-in before the imminently expected Second Coming of Christ, told people not to worry about tomorrow, make no provision for the future, and give everything away to the poor. The **Hebrew scriptures**, otherwise known as the Old Testament, goes even further with some arcane rules about the treatment of slaves, working on Sundays, using cloth with different materials, and slaughtering neighboring tribes.

In many areas of modern living, the Bible is entirely unable to provide any guidance, unless one is prepared to interpret passages in highly eccentric ways. Just as problematic is that the dogmatic exclusivism of **command moralities** is inimical to the dialogue-based methods of proceeding with ethical debate in **open societies**.

Over the last century and a half, Christian moralists have sought to overcome this problem by taking over the humanist approaches to ethics and calling them their own. After supporting, or at least not opposing, **slavery**, for example, Christian moralists are now eloquent in their denunciation of slavery. The church is going through similar processes with regard to **anti-Semitism**, the ordination of women, and gay priests. Insofar as Christianity remains relevant as a moral player, it is because it has quietly abandoned the specifically Christian teachings and taken on instead a generalized altruism. See the entry on **moral truisms shared by us all**.

Further reading: A. C. Grayling, *What is Good? The Search for the Best Way to Live*, and Richard Holloway, *Godless Morality*.

CHRISTIANITY, BOOKS ABOUT. This list is a basic minimum of reliable books on Christianity which are critical and scholarly, and yet accessible to the nonspecialist reader. It is really important to have a sound grasp of how Christianity emerged out of Judaism. For early Christianity, it is well worth reading *Pagans and Christians* (1986) and *The Unauthorized Version: Truth and Fiction in the Bible* (1991) both by Robin Lane Fox; *The Closing of the Western Mind* (2002) by Charles Freeman; *Christian Origins* (1985) by Christopher Rowland; *Liberating the Gospels: Reading the Bible with Jewish Eyes* (1996) by John Shelby Spong; and *Who Wrote the New Testament?* (1995) by Burton L. Mack. Also, see the entries on **Satan** and **Jesus Christ, books about** for recommendations in those areas.

For the papacy, read *Saints and Sinners: A History of the Popes* (1997) by Eamon Duffy; *Hitler's Pope* (1999) by John Cornwell; and *Papal Sin* (2000) by Garry Wills. *Eastern Christendom* (1961) by Nicolas Zernov gives a thorough account of the Orthodox Church, a branch of Christianity that is usually ignored by Western readers. For the contemporary situation, *The Hallelujah Revolution* (1996) by Ian Cotton is very good. And *Fundamentalism* (1986) by James Barr is worth wading through.

Good single-volume criticisms of Christianity include *The Misery of Christianity* (1968) by **Joachim Kahl** and *The Dark Side of Christian History* (1995) by Helen Ellerbe. *The Case Against Christianity* (1991) by **Michael Martin** is longer than these two and more scholarly. Older criticisms still well worth reading include *The Testament of Christian Civilization* (1946) by **Joseph McCabe**; *The Pathetic Fallacy* (1930) by Llewelyn Powys; and *The Twilight of the Idols/The Anti-Christ* (1888) by **Friedrich Nietzsche**.

CIVIL SOCIETY. An idea that goes back to ancient Greece, though was first articulated in detail during the **Enlightenment**, as a means to distinguish the needs of the people as distinct from the needs of the state. **Thomas Paine** spoke of the civil society in these terms as part of his justification for the American War of Independence. More recently, civil society was taken up by **Ernest Gellner** to provide a theoretical basis for a liberal polity. He defined civil society as "the idea of institutional and ideological **pluralism**, which prevents the establishment of monopoly of power and truth, and counterbalances those central institutions which, though necessary, might otherwise acquire such monopoly."

Gellner was concerned about providing the basis for a society that permitted individual liberty without collapsing into **relativism**. Each institution should be strong enough to prevent tyranny, but open enough that people may leave them without undue social disadvantage or, as in primitive societies, undergoing some awesome ritual. There should be regular rotation of the leadership and managers of civil society, and those positions should bring relatively low rewards for the holders. It is an essential precondition of the civil society that it be **secular**, or in his words that the circle between **faith**, **power**, and society be broken. Societies that prohibit some topics of debate, whether through state coercion or unstated conformism, are not civil societies in the full sense of the term. See the entries on **open society** and **democracy**.

Further reading: Ernest Gellner, *Conditions of Liberty*.

CLARKE, ARTHUR C[HARLES]. (1917–). Prodigious talent. Novelist, journalist, and prophet of the Space Age. Clarke was born in Minehead, England. His early education was in the sciences. During World War II, Clarke served in the RAF, working as a radar instructor. As a result of this work, he wrote an article in 1945, which spoke for the first time about the communications satellite.

After the war he studied at King's College, London. His first love during these years was science fiction and the possibility of interplanetary travel. Clarke served as president of the British Interplanetary Society between 1946–1947 and 1950–1953.

In 1956 Clarke emigrated to Sri Lanka, and from there he wrote a series of very influential science fiction books and short stories, as well as reviews, articles, and radio and television appearances. His most important books are *Prelude to Space* (1951), *Rendezvous with Rama* (1973), and *The Fountains of Paradise* (1979). But Clarke's best-known venture was the film project with Stanley Kubrick (1928–1999), *2001: A Space Odyssey* (1968), for which he and Kubrick were nominated for an Oscar. Reversing the usual order, Clarke's book of this title came after the film. Very influential and often cited as one of the best films ever made, *2001* spawned three sequels and many imitations. Clarke is in many ways a continuation of **H. G. Wells**, in the sense of being a prodigious talent and having a thirst to explain science to nonspecialists.

Clarke is an atheist and a humanist, and was elected a member of the **International Academy of Humanism** in 1994. On several occasions he has applied himself to book and television projects which have given scientific explanations to some of the so-called mysteries beloved by peddlers of the **paranormal**. Like **Carl Sagan**, Clarke had little patience with **pseudoscience**, but, also like Sagan, he was fully aware of the sense of wonder that pseudosciences exploit. In *Profiles of the Future* (1982), a work of popular science, Clarke postulated what he calls **Clarke's Three Laws**.

Clarke's list of honors is lengthy. He was awarded the **Kalinga Prize** in 1961. In 1982 he was awarded the Marconi International Fellowship for his invention of the communications satellite. And he was knighted in 1998, although a squalid campaign of innuendo regarding Clarke's sexual orientation delayed it being conferred until 2000.

CLARKE'S THREE LAWS. A set of "universal laws" coined, only half tongue-in-cheek, by **Arthur C. Clarke**. The laws go as follows:

- *First Law*: "When a distinguished but elderly scientist states that something is possible he is almost certainly right. When he states that something is impossible, he is very probably wrong";
- *Second Law*: "The only way of discovering the limits of the possible is to venture a little way past them into the impossible";
- *Third Law*: "Any sufficiently advanced technology is indistinguishable from magic."

With regard to the first law, Clarke added that "elderly" in the context of mathematics and physics means over thirty. There are many examples of Clarke's First Law in operation, but the case of Sir Arthur Eddington (1882–1944) and **Subrabrahmanyan Chandrasekhar** is as good as any. The young Chandrasekhar's theory of black holes was scorned by the elderly and highly honored Eddington, to the point where Chandrasekhar abandoned the whole area of inquiry for many years. But of course Chandrasekhar was proved to be right. Eddington, a religious man, was upset by the theological implications of black holes. Clarke's Second Law follows on from the First.

Clarke's Third Law is a timely reminder to skeptics that many items of technology today taken for granted have been authoritatively dismissed as impossible by reputable scientists. So while **skepticism** is clearly the most sensible response to extraordinary claims, we need to be skeptical even about our skepticism. **Richard Dawkins** has pointed out that Clarke's Third Law does not work in reverse, so it does not follow that any magical claim made today is indistinguishable from tomorrow's technological advance.

Further reading: Arthur C. Clarke, *Profiles of the Future* and Richard Dawkins, *Unweaving the Rainbow*.

CLASH OF CIVILIZATIONS. A term commonly associated with the American scholar Samuel P. Huntington, although it was actually coined by Bernard Lewis, a prominent scholar of the Middle East. The clash of civilizations refers to the new condition of the world after the **cold war** where global conflict has become multipolar. The cold war conflict was essentially bipolar, between the so-called free world and the communist world, but since then the world has fractured into these multipolar conflicts, which are organized not around ideology so much as culture and religion.

Huntington argued that so many conflicts around the world are on the borders between the Muslim world and its various neighbors. **Islam**, Huntington wrote, has bloody borders. And following the downfall of the Soviet Union as a rival source of world authority, it was inevitable that these conflicts would involve the United States. While many people have made many points critical of the clash of civilizations thesis, this core observation has been shown to be valid.

Like most grand theories, the clash of civilizations theory tends to paint with a broad brush, and some of its generalizations are questionable. For instance, it has understated the differences *within* civilizations. The culture wars of the United States would be difficult to understand in the context of the clash of civilizations theory. However, it has made a very useful contribution toward providing a general theory of the post–cold war world. Without question, the clash of civilizations theory has been shown more useful and more accurate than its main rival, the **end of history** theory.

Further reading: Samuel P. Huntington, *The Clash of Civilizations and the Remaking of World Order*.

CLASSICAL MUSIC. Something most of us like the thought of while knowing very little about. Classical music is frequently understood as music played by orchestras enjoyed by older people or those affecting airs and graces. It has the same forbidding feel to many people as **modern art** has. However, this stereotype is generally giving way, as people are increasingly exposed to music that is not pop or rock music in musicals, film scores, and even advertisements. Classical music is an umbrella term that can apply to these main musical traditions:

- *symphony music*, usually ranging from Johann Sebastian Bach (1685–1750) to Igor Stravinsky (1882–1971);
- *opera*, with special reference to the golden age of opera between 1780 and 1925; and
- *chamber music*, ranging from arrangements by Franz Joseph Haydn (1732–1809) to Bela Bartok (1881–1945).

There are lots of good introductions to classical music. But the best way to become familiar with it is simply to experiment and buy some that you have heard. Like appreciating wine or art, the best way to learn to appreciate classical music is to immerse yourself in it and trust your **judgment**. Buy or borrow some CDs, and listen to them. Then listen to more of the music you enjoyed. It's as simple as that.

Further reading: Michael Walsh, *Who's Afraid of Classical Music?*

CLEAR AND PRESENT DANGER. A legal formula used in the United States as a means to act against individuals or organizations held to pose a serious threat to the safety of the country. The clear and present danger formula was first used in a series of cases after World War I when some socialist and anarchist politicians and pamphleteers were prosecuted under the 1917 Espionage Act. The most prominent example was Eugene Debs (1855–1926), leader of the Socialist Party and five-time presidential candidate. Debs was prosecuted for a talk called "Socialism is the Answer" given in Ohio in 1918. He was sentenced to ten years, imprisonment. The manifest injustice of these convictions came from the fact that the authori-

ties had failed to prove anything resembling a constitutional crisis had been provoked by the words of the defendants. Debs was pardoned in 1921.

Subsequent American leaderships have invoked the phrase to justify their decisions. For instance, John F. Kennedy spoke of a clear and present danger to the United States during the Cuban Missile Crisis in 1962 at the height of the **cold war**. Forty years later, and much less plausibly, George W. Bush spoke of Saddam Hussein's regime as posing a clear and present danger to the United States.

The phrase entered popular parlance in 1994 with the Tom Clancy film *Clear and Present Danger*, starring Harrison Ford.

CLIFFORD, WILLIAM KINGDON (1845–1879). English mathematician, freethinker, and **smiter of humbug**. He was born in Exeter, the son of a bookseller. His mother had a delicate constitution and died when William was only nine years old. It was soon apparent that the boy was a genius. In 1863 he was sent to Trinity College, Cambridge, where he broke new ground in geometry. While still a teenager, Clifford lost his religious belief, but unlike many of his Victorian contemporaries, he found the experience liberating, and foresaw great things to come from the demise of organized **religion**. Ironically, for someone who died so young, Clifford was an enthusiastic athlete. He once climbed a church spire and hung by his toes from the weathercock.

As well as excelling in mathematics, Clifford mastered French, German, Spanish, Arabic, Greek, and Sanskrit. Indeed, his knowledge of other languages helped him keep abreast of overseas developments better than his colleagues. In 1871 Clifford was professor of applied mathematics at University College, London. In 1874 he was elected a fellow of the Royal Society.

As well as his busy work schedule, Clifford was active in **freethought** circles. After his death, his main freethought works were brought together in a two-volume *Lectures* *and Essays* (1879). The best known of his freethought works was *The Ethics of Belief*, originally given as a lecture to the Metaphysical Society in 1876 and published in the *Contemporary Review* in January the following year. *The Ethics of Belief* gave rise to the passage Clifford is remembered by to this day:

It is wrong, always, everywhere, and for anyone, to believe anything upon insufficient evidence. If a man, holding a belief which he was taught in childhood or persuaded afterwards, keeps down and pushes away doubts which arise about it in his mind, purposely avoids the reading of books and the company of men that call in question or discuss it, or regards as impious those questions which cannot easily be asked without disturbing it—the life of that man is one long sin against mankind.

That remains as true today as it was in 1876. Clifford also wrote an amusing children's book called *The Little People* (1874). His last years were overshadowed by the onset of tuberculosis, which killed him, at 33, on March 3, 1879. He was survived by his wife Lucy Clifford (1853–1929) who went on to have a successful career as a writer and dramatist. Among her best books were *Mrs. Keith's Crime* (1885) and *Aunt Anne* (1893).

Further reading: Timothy Madigan, ed., *The Ethics of Belief and Other Essays*.

CLODD, EDWARD (1840–1930). British rationalist and popularizer. Clodd was born in Aldeburgh, Suffolk, the son of a seaman and devout Baptist of puritan slant. Clodd's childhood was steeped in the Bible. While still in his teens he left Aldeburgh to become a clerk in London. His career was successful; he rose to become secretary of the London Joint Stock Bank in 1872, a post he held until his retirement in 1915. Much of Clodd's success can be put down to his genial personality. He was a member of several London clubs and helped found the Omar Khayyam Club.

During his years in London, Clodd was exposed to the great controversies of the day, and slowly lost his religious belief. He served as chairman of the **Rationalist Press Association** between 1906 and 1913, and was an honorary associate from 1899 to his death in 1930. Clodd was a **reverent agnostic** and an ardent disciple of **Herbert Spencer** and **T. H. Huxley**.

He was a successful popularizer of knowledge. Among his many works include *The Childhood of the World* (1872) an account of human prehistory, vaguely theistic in orientation; and *Jesus of Nazareth* (1879), an account of the life of Jesus, putting him in his Jewish context. This book went through several editions, appearing in 1905 as an RPA **Cheap Reprint**. Two of Clodd's most successful works were his popular accounts of evolution: *The Story of Creation* (1888, later abridged and rereleased in 1895 under the title *A Primer of Evolution*) and *The Pioneers of Evolution: From Thales to Huxley* (1897), an account of the development of evolutionary thought before Darwin. Incidentally, this work counts as evidence against the frequently repeated accusation of rationalists as being Darwin worshipers, or not recognizing evolution was an idea with a long past. If Clodd worshiped anyone, it was T. H. Huxley, as shown in his hagiographic biography *Thomas Henry Huxley* (1902). Clodd also wrote a criticism of **spiritualism** and a book of memoirs, which recounted his many friends, including Grant Allen (1848–1899), **W. K. Clifford**, **Thomas Hardy**, George Meredith (1828–1909), and others. He died in Aldeburgh in 1930.

Further reading: Joseph McCabe, *Edward Clodd: A Memoir*.

CLOSED MIND. Something that the other person suffers from. It is a common ploy to declare that the person we disagree with has a closed mind. This may well be unfair because it assumes that disagreement with oneself is the same thing as having a closed mind. But making a presumption like that is itself suggestive of a closed mind. The fact is that people can disagree with us in good faith and with an open mind. And vice versa. People have closed minds when they:

- cannot see any possibility that they might be in error;
- cannot see any possibility that the other person might be correct; and
- refuse to accord honorable intentions to their opponent.

Having said this, maintaining an open mind is no easy matter, and it involves constant vigilance on our part. **Skepticism** is an essential ingredient of an open mind. **Adam Gowans Whyte** wrote a very good book called *The Religion of the Open Mind*, which expanded on these things.

But we can't be expected to examine **evidence** thrust under our nose on every occasion. Life is too short to examine every outlandish claim we come across. We may have seen similar evidence before and found it wanting, or it may be palpably absurd according to established and publicly accessible standards of knowledge. But all inquirers have a duty to remember that every now and then a claim that appears outlandish turns out to be correct. Perhaps the prime example from the twentieth century was Alfred Wegener's (1880–1930) theory of plate tectonics (otherwise known as continental drift). Plate tectonics was derided by almost everybody, but it was Wegener who proved to be correct. See the entry on **certainty**.

COGNITIVE DISSONANCE. A phrase coined by the psychologist Leon Festinger (1919–1989) that refers to the tension between what someone believes and the contrasting way the world actually behaves. The easiest example of cognitive dissonance is the millenarian cult that expects the end of the word on a particular day. When the day comes and goes, the resulting need to adjust one's beliefs in the face of new evidence is what Festinger called cognitive dissonance. Festinger proposed that the psychological

tension of the irreconcilable ideas can, under favorable conditions, lead to the adjustment of one's beliefs to conform to the new **reality**. However, in less favorable conditions, people can protect their erroneous beliefs from the new conditions by a partial reconfiguring of their beliefs, or, even more drastically, reconfigure the outside reality to conform to one's unchanged beliefs.

While most of us are delusional to some extent about our beliefs and perceptions, it is beholden on each of us to keep these delusions to a minimum, and to subject them to as thorough a scrutiny as we can genuinely manage. An excellent first step in this process is to recognize that one's beliefs are **fallible** and open to error.

COHEN, CHAPMAN (1868–1954). Atheist journalist and campaigner. Born to a Jewish family in Leicester, largely self-educated. Cohen came to freethought in 1889 after hearing a Christian Evidence Society speaker bullying and deriding an aged secularist. Cohen immediately took the old man's side in the dispute, inquired into his beliefs, and soon joined the **National Secular Society**. Cohen became a prominent speaker for the NSS, and remained a popular speaker for half a century.

Cohen had read many of the classic works of philosophy by the time he was seventeen, with particular emphasis on **Spinoza** and **Herbert Spencer**. He began lecturing for the secular movement in 1889 and first elected vice president of the National Secular Society in 1895. After the death of **G. W. Foote** in 1915, Cohen became editor of *The Freethinker*, a position he retained until 1951. Old age wasn't kind to Cohen, and his last years at the *Freethinker* were not helpful to his memory. His retirement as president of the NSS in 1949 was very much against his wishes.

One of Cohen's most important contributions was his fearless and consistent advocacy of **atheism** rather than **agnosticism**. Cohen's pamphlets on atheism were among the clearest expositions of popular atheism in the first half of the twentieth century. Many of Cohen's articles were later used in his books. The best of Cohen's books are *The Grammar of Freethought* (1921) and *Almost an Autobiography* (1941).

COIT, STANTON (1857–1944). American English ethicist and **religious humanist**. Stanton Coit was educated at Amherst College, Columbia University, and the University of Berlin. In his teenage years, he counted himself a disciple of Ralph Waldo Emerson (1803–1882). In 1881 he heard about Felix Adler's **Ethical Culture** Movement, which had begun only five years previously. He was convinced by its message and trained to become an Ethical Lecturer. Soon afterward, he traveled to London, where he was impressed by the social work undertaken by religious radicals at Toynbee Hall in London. He returned to New York, where he worked in the slums. During this time, Coit was instrumental in establishing the Neighborhood Guild, the predecessor of the University Settlement, the first settlement house in the United States.

Back in England in 1887, he took up the invitation of the **South Place Ethical Society** to become its lecturer in 1888, following the departure of **Moncure Conway** to the United States. In 1890 he again returned to the United States, but in 1894 was back in London as the leader of the West London Ethical Society. Coit worked untiringly for the West London Ethical Society for many years, and was instrumental in creating the Union of Ethical Societies (1896), which later became the Ethical Union (1920). He had toyed with the idea of taking up the new word "humanist," but decided not to in the end because of the several ways the word was being used at the time.

When Coit retired in the early 1930s, his Ethical Church was in noticeable decline. Sources hostile to Coit also spoke of a scandal involving an indecent assault charge, which, though acquitted, nevertheless did his reputation no good. He lived out his last years in retirement in Eastbourne, Sussex. Coit's successor as leader of the Ethical Movement was **Harold Blackham**, who quickly took the movement away from the quasi-religious tone set by Coit.

Coit wrote widely; his most important books being *The Message of Man* (1902), *National Idealism* (1908), and *The Soul of America* (1914). One of Coit's unacknowledged services was his translation in 1931 and 1932 of Nicolai Hartmann's *Ethics*. Hartmann (1882–1950) is an important German philosopher, although underappreciated in English-speaking countries. Even Coit's friends admitted he was a difficult man, not easy to get along with. They often resorted to describing their friend as "complex." Coit was an odd, though not unusual, combination of an intolerant tyrant who devoted his life to the message of tolerance and democracy.

COLD WAR. The period from 1945 until 1991 that was characterized by a struggle between the United States and its allies and the Soviet Union and its allies. It was given the title "cold" war because the struggle between the two superpowers was conducted largely in sideshow struggles rather than by direct combat. This was because, for the first time in human history, the technology existed which, if used, would have assured the destruction of everyone, making the concept of "victor" and "vanquished" meaningless. The cold war took shape following the **Yalta Conference**, which met to help shape the postwar world.

The cold war had many ironies. Among the most prominent is that the West lost (or at least failed to win) most of the battles— Korea, Suez, Vietnam—but won the war. And not only did the West win the cold war, it won it more comprehensively than almost any conventional "hot" war. Despite this, the world came close to nuclear annihilation at least twice: during the 1962 Cuban Missile Crisis and again in 1983, for no particular reason apart from growing Soviet alarm at the militarist bluster of President Reagan.

The real legacy of the cold war was the creation of the Western economy, which since the end of the cold war has become the global economy. One of the sadder legacies of it was the rigidification of the international system of **global governance**; the **United Nations**, the **World Bank**, and the **International Monetary Fund** in particular, into conflict mode between great powers. Now, in our multipolar and multicivilizational age, we need more responsive and more accountable international institutions.

Further reading: Martin Walker, *The Cold War*.

COLENSO, JOHN WILLIAM (1814–1883). English clergyman, appointed Bishop of Natal in 1853. The conscientious churchman learned Zulu, so he could translate religious works into that language. When asked by a Zulu convert whether the story of the flood was literally true, Colenso found himself at a loss to answer truthfully. Colenso then wrote a book called *The Pentateuch and the Book of Joshua Critically Examined* (1862), where he denied the Mosaic authorship of the Pentateuch and pointed out many other historical absurdities in the Old Testament. Colenso's book was published during the height of the *Essays and Reviews* dispute, and a fraught Church of England was alarmed to face a similar challenge, this time from a bishop. Even saintly religious liberals like Frederick Denison Maurice (1805–1872) were moved to castigate what they saw as the historical and religious untruths of the work.

Colenso was subjected to a great deal of harassment and rancor as a result of his book. All but three English bishops took part in a letter demanding that Colenso resign his office, which he refused to do. While he was defending himself in England, an Episcopal synod in South Africa condemned Colenso in his absence. In November 1863 Colenso was charged with denial of the divinity of Christ, the atonement, endless punishment in hell, and literal inspiration of scripture. Colenso appealed to the council, as the *Essays and Reviews* writers had done shortly before. And as with the earlier case, the council found in favor of Colenso and declared the South African decision null and void. Fanatical opposition, led by the Bishop Gray of Cape Town, was not to be put off. Gray publicly excommunicated Colenso in 1864 and continued his campaign until 1869 when Colenso was successfully deposed.

The level of hostility to Colenso was motivated, in part, by racism. After all, Colenso had taken seriously the question of his Zulu convert. He also had an honorable record championing the rights of Africans.

COLLINS, ANTHONY (1676–1729). English freethinker. Born in Heston, near Hounslow in London and educated at Eton, Cambridge, and the Temple. He lived as an independently wealthy country gentleman, serving as Justice of the Peace and Treasurer for the County of Essex. A genial personality, Collins was very popular for his open-use policy of his extensive library. The crucial influence in Collins's life was his friend, the philosopher, **John Locke**. It is usually said that Collins made it his task to develop Locke's thought with regard to **Deism**, although the historian David Berman asserts that nowhere does Collins actually mount a systematic defense of deism. It is Berman's opinion that Collins was, for all practical purposes, an atheist.

Collins wrote quite widely, ranging through history and philosophy. His main titles include *Essay Concerning the Use of Reason* (1707), *Discourse of the Grounds and Reasons of the Christian Religion* (1724), and *A Discourse on Liberty and Necessity* (1729). But his best-known book was *Discourse of Freethinking* (1713), which sought to bring the criticism of religion into respectable society. In line with current thinking, Collins denounced **superstition** and "enthusiasm," the phrase used then to mean irrational, emotional **fundamentalism**. Collins criticized the various contradictions of contemporary theologians and followed his friend Locke in advocating religious **toleration**. What excited the furious reaction to this book was Collins's claim that all belief must be based on **free inquiry** and that the use of **reason** necessarily involves the abandonment of supernaturalism. Elsewhere, in the *Grounds and Reasons of the Christian Religion*, Collins exposed the double standard of apologists who claimed that theological doctrines command the authority as scientific statements but without having to meet the same standards scientific statements need in order to acquire that authority.

Further reading: David Berman, *A History of Atheism: From Hobbes to Russell*.

COLLINS, WILLIAM WHITEHOUSE (1853–1923). One of the most lovable of the nineteenth-century rationalists. William Whitehouse Collins was born in Harborne, Staffordshire, on September 4, 1853, the son of Joseph Collins, a die-sinker, and Eleanor Collins (nee Whitehouse). His grandfather was John Collins, a prominent Chartist. William was educated at Mason College, Birmingham, and became a Sunday School teacher. While training for the ministry, he became dissatisfied with the lifeless religious training he was receiving. From this he moved on to a study of science, and in so doing, lost his religious **faith** entirely. In about 1878 he joined the **National Secular Society**. In 1884 he became an appointed lecturer for the NSS and traveled England extensively, giving lectures and taking part in debates.

In 1885, at the request of the Australian Secular Association, Collins left England. For the next five years, he became an influential and respected **freethought** lecturer. His greatest victory during this period was his successful appeal in 1888 of a conviction for distributing **Annie Besant**'s pamphlet *The Law of Population* (1877). The decision was a landmark of liberal thought in Australian history.

In 1890 Collins moved to New Zealand, where he took up residence in Christchurch. There he became the secretary of the Canterbury Freethought Association (CFA), which went on to become the New Zealand Rationalist Association (NZRA), the forerunner of today's **New Zealand Association of Rationalists and Humanists**. Collins went on to become the best-known and most-respected freethinker in the country. He was twice elected to parliament, from 1893 to 1896 and again from 1899 to 1902. During this time he was a consistent advocate of progressive issues. For example, his private member's bill in 1896 to abolish the death penalty was narrowly defeated. New Zealand abolished the death penalty in 1941, but the new conservative government reinstated it in 1950, and it was finally taken off the statute books for all cases except treason in 1961.

Collins founded *The Examiner* in 1907, which was the country's only freethought paper for all its ten years of existence. In April 1911, it became the official organ of the NZRA and in 1914, Collins took over presidency of NZRA. At the end of 1918 Collins returned to Sydney, where he lived until his death on December 4, 1923. Collins was universally admired for his breadth of knowledge and good manners. He became New Zealand's first honorary associate of the **Rationalist Press Association** in 1911.

Further reading: Harry Hastings Pearce and Nigel Sinnott, "W. W. Collins, 1853–1923," *NZ Rationalist and Humanist* (December 1985): 13–14.

COMMAND MORALITIES. The term given to moral systems that emphasize the top-down nature path of moral instruction. Religious fundamentalisms are the classic example. Fundamentalists claim our moral system comes from **God**, not infrequently in the form of commandments from an inerrant **scripture**, about what we should and should not do. The individual has little positive role in such a system but to obey. Command moralities usually employ the **principle of universalism**. Also, see the entry on **absolutism**.

There are many reasons command moralities do not work. When faced with a new moral situation, the individual who is used to a command morality is in a dilemma. Because no commands exist to deal with the situation and the free exercise of **judgment** is frowned upon, the individual is left in the dark with no skills to turn on the light. Into this void have stepped priests and others who presume to speak on behalf of the command system. See the entry on **Hadith**. Before long the individual is obeying other humans who claim special authority, rather than the special authority itself. As the moral philosopher James Gouinlock has said, "[d]ivine command does not relieve us of choice."

Another problem with command moralities is that they tend to get stuck in one period of time, and do not adjust well to changing circumstances. Good examples are the Christian proscriptions against homosexuality, women priests, and birth control, all of which are now widely ignored by many people who also claim to be sincere Christians. This has meant religious liberals have had to divest themselves slowly of the whole command morality structure, although they are uncertain where to draw the line (see the entry on **fatal flaw in religious liberalism, the**). Command moralities are best suited to those who crave **certainty** in their life, or who want a simple formula for making ethical decisions. For the rest of us, we need to be satisfied with a moral understanding that requires constant reworking and refiguring. See the entries on **objective morality**, **wide reflective equilibrium**, **theopathic condition**, and **limitless communication**.

COMMISSION FOR SCIENTIFIC MEDICINE AND MENTAL HEALTH. A commission established in 2003 to oversee the publication of two peer-reviewed journals on medicine and on mental-health care. Among its more prominent fellows include Francis Crick (1916–2004), Baruj Benacerraf, Leon Lederman (all Nobel Laureates), Elizabeth Loftus, Sergei Kapitza, Steven Pinker, Martin Gardner, Susan Blackmore, Adolph Grünbaum, Richard Wiseman, and many others. The commission's executive director is Andrew Skolnick, formerly an associate editor of the *Journal of the American Medical Association* (JAMA).

The commission publishes two flagship publications. One is *The Scientific Review of Alternative Medicine* (SRAM) edited by Dr. Wallace Sampson. This journal was founded in 1997 and examines **alternative medicine** from a strictly scientific basis. In SRAM's founding statement, the journal notes the rise of alternative medicine and laments the lack of reliable information on these various practices. While the many skeptical magazines around the world have done an excellent job in **debunking** much of the nonsense, there remained a need for a peer-reviewed journal that could help separate **fact** from fiction in alternative medicine.

The other journal of the commission is *The Scientific Review of Mental Health Practice* (SRMHP), which was founded in 2002 and investigates controversial and unorthodox claims in the fields of clinical psychology, psychiatry, and social work. SRMHP is edited by Dr. Scott Lilienfeld of Emory University in Atlanta, Georgia. SRMHP's foundation statement is similar to SRAM's when it notes the widening gap between researchers and practitioners in the field of mental health, into which all manner of unsubstantiated and potentially dangerous remedies and theories have rushed. Most people's views of mental health are shaped by self-help books, radio psychologists, and quacks, with little media space given to the scientific validity of the cures being peddled. SRMHP is designed to bridge that huge gap.

COMMITTEE FOR THE SCIENTIFIC EXAMINATION OF RELIGION. A nonprofit educational organization working to promote the academic study of **religion** without reference to the dictates of theology. The group, originally known as the Religion and Biblical Criticism Research Project, began in 1982 and was formally established in 1983 at the National Press Club in Washington, DC, during a conference on the subject of "Religion in American Politics." It reformed in April 1985 under the current name. It was established under the auspices of the Council for Democratic and Secular Humanism, now known as the **Council for Secular Humanism** (CSH). The committee was chaired by the respected biblical scholar Gerald Larue and included a large number of influential religious studies scholars.

From these beginnings, the committee's focus broadened to include a range of topics, including biblical studies, comparative religion, and religious and social ethics. When the committee met in 1984 it examined the topic of the "Armageddon and Biblical Apocalyptic." In 1985 the topic was "Jesus in History and Myth." This conference, and the book which came from it are acknowledged as having been a significant incentive in the revival of Jesus scholarship in the 1980s, and to the **Jesus Seminar**, which grew out of that scholarship.

A series of important books was produced as a result of the meetings hosted by the committee, most notably R. Joseph Hoffmann's own work, *Jesus Outside the Gospels* (1984), his edited anthology called *The Origins of Christianity* (1985), and *Jesus in History and Myth* (1986), which he coedited with Gerald Larue.

The committee was less active through the 1990s and was revived once more in 2003 when R. Joseph Hoffmann returned to the country after a long time teaching outside the United States. The revived committee includes some well-respected religious studies scholars, like John Dominic Crossan, Karen Armstrong, **Gerd Lüdemann**, James M. Robinson, and **Ibn Warraq**. In November 2004, CSER hosted a major conference at Cornell University on the theme, "Just War and Jihad: Violence in Christianity, Islam, and Judaism."

COMMITTEE FOR THE SCIENTIFIC INVESTIGATION OF CLAIMS OF THE PARANORMAL (CSICOP). The most important skeptical organization in the world. CSICOP was founded on May 1, 1976, and was led by **Paul Kurtz**, then professor of philosophy at the State University of New York at Buffalo, and Marcello Truzzi (1935–2003), a sociologist from Eastern Michigan University. After Truzzi's departure, CSICOP has been led by Kurtz and, since 1989, managed by Barry Karr. The not-for-profit committee is one of the principal wings of the **Center for Inquiry**, alongside the **Council for Secular Humanism**. Commonly known as the Skeptics, CSICOP is based at the Center for Inquiry—Transnational headquarters in Amherst, New York. When CSICOP was founded, it also began a journal, called *The Zetetic*, which means "skeptical seeker" and related back to **Pyrrhonism**. In 1978 the journal was renamed *Skeptical Inquirer*, and has grown to become the largest-circulation journal of its type in the world. In 1978 *Skeptical Inquirer* went from semiannual to quarterly and in 1995, it became bimonthly. CSICOP members also receive the newsletter, *Skeptical Briefs*.

As well as the journal, CSICOP has hosted a succession of international conferences. The first was in 1983 on the subject of "Science, Skepticism, and the Paranormal," held at the SUNY—Buffalo campus in New York State. Since then, conferences have been held in most years and in many different parts of the world. CSICOP has also attracted a very impressive range of fellows, including Martin Gardner, **Richard Dawkins**, Susan Haack, Lin Zixin, **E. O. Wilson**, Jill Tarter, and Eugenie Scott, among others.

Over the years, CSICOP has sponsored investigations into a bewildering range of allegedly **paranormal** claims. None so far have been found convincing. CSICOP's activities have attracted a series of lawsuits. The most dangerous came from the self-styled psychic Uri Geller, who launched a series of suits against the Skeptics. In June 1992, the District Court in Washington, DC, threw out Geller's case and imposed sanctions amounting to $120,000 for a "frivolous complaint."

One of CSICOP's most noteworthy ventures was the *Critical Eye*, a television series it coproduced with the Science Channel (formerly Discovery Science Channel). The series hosted by William B. Davis, of *X-Files* fame, and is devoted to presenting responsible science and exposing **pseudoscience** for nonspecialist audiences. Another CSICOP initiative is the Skeptiseum, an online museum of the paranormal. All the items featured have been acquired by CSICOP senior research fellow **Joe Nickell** during a lifetime of investigating paranormal claims.

CSICOP insists it is not simply a matter of **debunking** claims of the paranormal, but, as its opening statement made clear, to "examine them openly, completely, objectively, and carefully." Since CSICOP was formed it can take the credit for seeing off all major paranormal claims that have come to its attention. So much so that interest in things like UFOs has fallen away considerably in the past two decades. Since 1987 CSICOP has been slowly changing its focus away from the investigations of monsters, hauntings, and weeping icons, and more onto the larger questions of science education, the role of science in society, and the relationship between **science** and **religion**. It has also been the principal source of support for the growth of Skeptics' organizations around the world.

COMMON MORAL DECENCIES. Phrase used by **Paul Kurtz** to denote the ethical principles that can be affirmed as objectively true, despite the lack of a **God** or gods to do the affirming. The common moral decencies, Kurtz argues, are objectively true by virtue of being fundamental to human intercourse.

- *Integrity* as manifested in truthfulness, promise-keeping, sincerity, and honesty;
- *Trustworthiness* as manifested in fidelity, and dependability;
- *Benevolence* as manifested in good will, nonmalfeasance toward others and toward private and public property, sexual consent, and beneficence; and
- *Fairness* as manifested in gratitude, accountability, justice, tolerance, and cooperation.

Kurtz acknowledges that these common moral decencies are practiced differently in various societies around the world, but the points themselves are common to all human beings. Kurtz even sums up the common moral decencies with his version of the **Golden Rule**: "The general rule of moral decency is to cooperate as best we can, to tolerate the differing views of others, and to negotiate."

Further Reading: Paul Kurtz, *Forbidden Fruit: The Ethics of Humanism*.

COMMONWEALTH OF NATIONS. The successor grouping to the British Empire, where the bonds between the member nations are based on historical ties and grouped informally around a common allegiance to the British crown. The Commonwealth of Nations is the second largest international grouping of nations after the **United Nations**.

The commonwealth was first aired openly at the Imperial Conference, held in October and November 1926, and given formal standing in December 1931 when the British parliament passed the Statute of Westminster which brought Australia, Canada, Ireland, New Zealand, and South Africa as equal nations in a free association. The commonwealth was given a rather more tangible status in 1932, when a system of tariffs, known as Commonwealth Preferences was enacted, in contravention of the hitherto strongly held opinion in favor of free trade among many British and commonwealth politicians. This system worked well for almost forty years, and was only dismantled after Britain joined the European Union in 1973.

Even after this change, the commonwealth has remained a viable association of nations. Membership has become sufficiently advantageous that some countries with tenuous or even no historical links to the British Empire or royal family, like Cameroon and Mozambique, gained membership in 1995. The commonwealth now includes fifty-four countries and about 30 percent of the world's population.

Today, the activities of the commonwealth are set by the Singapore Declaration of Commonwealth Principles (1971) and the Harare Commonwealth Declaration (1991). These principles declare support for the United Nations; opposition to all forms of racial and other forms of discrimination; and equitable trade, and disinterested support for developing nations. Significant among the additions to the Harare Commonwealth Declaration is a commitment to the equality of women, to environmentally sustainable development, and to combat against drug traffic. Leaders of member countries meet every other year at a Commonwealth Heads of Government Meeting (CHOGM).

COMMUNISM, REJECTION OF. There are so many good reasons why humanists rejected communism, but the clearest were given by **Bertrand Russell**, first in his prophetic book, *The Practice and Theory of Bolshevism* (1920), written after a visit to the Soviet Union, and in an essay that appeared in *In Praise of Idleness* (1935). Russell rejected or objected to:

- The presumption that communism will inevitably succeed because the laws of history say it will succeed. There is no evidence that progress leads to communism;
- The theories of value and surplus value that underlie Marxist economics. These theories are simply incorrect;
- The notion that any one man is incapable of error, as was being said both of Marx and Lenin;
- The antidemocratic nature of communist politics, noting that the "dictatorship of the proletariat" means the dictatorship of a small elite;
- The restrictions on freedoms, particularly intellectual freedom;
- The denigration of intellectual labor in favor of manual labor;
- The preaching of stratified class; and
- The sheer quantity of hate communism generates.

Part of his rejection was based on rejecting the communist view of the world. For instance, he rejected the **historicism** inherent in communism, whereby its success was bound in the laws of history. It is never inevitable that something should happen, as communists believed in the inevitable victory of their faith. Also, the economic theory of **Marxism** was soon shown to be basically incorrect. As an analysis of nineteenth-century conditions, Marx made many salient points, but as a scientifically inescapable understanding of how the future would unravel, it was dangerous nonsense. Plenty of people came along later and wrote fuller critiques of communism, but they all followed the trail set by Bertrand Russell.

Russell was also one of the first people to note the striking parallels between communism and the Christian religion. He outlined these parallels first in *The Practice and Theory of Bolshevism*, a work which Alan Ryan described as being at least thirty years ahead of its time. Much later on, the historian Arnold Toynbee (1889–1975) recognized the same similarities when he described communism as a "page torn out of the New Testament." And many commentators have noted the cultic aspects of the veneration of Lenin after his tomb, not the least factor being the mummification of his body for posterity, and the refrain "we vow to thee, comrade Lenin" used by Stalin in his capacity as high priest. It follows from this that many of the objections to religions as **command moralities** also apply to communism.

Further reading: Bertrand Russell, "Scylla and Charybdis, or Communism and Fascism," from *In Praise of Idleness* and *The Practice and Theory of Bolshevism*.

COMMUNITY. A fashionable term at the moment, but one which is surprisingly elusive of a clear definition. Its normal understanding is of a series of formal and informal relationships that help bind together those within it. In this sense a community is a positive good, as it fosters cooperation, loyalty, and steadfastness. It is this understanding of community that people have in mind in our age of **globalization**, mutually uncomprehending **social**

worlds, and fractured **moralnets**. The less positive understanding of community, which looks instead at the **groupishness** and tendency toward coercive narrowmindedness is overlooked.

Philosophers like **John Rawls** have recognized this less helpful tendency in the notion of community, and with that in mind, have distinguished the potentially authoritarian notions of a **community**, which involves all citizens sharing the same religious and political views, with the more inclusive notion of the **well-ordered society**. See the entry on **general will**.

COMPLEXITY THEORY. An idea, associated mainly with Stuart Kauffman, which looks for mathematical principles behind all complex systems, from **cells** to galaxies. Complexity theory has been misused by some with a pseudo- or antiscientific bias to declare Darwinian **natural selection** to be anachronistic. Kauffman and other complexity theorists have distanced themselves from these extreme interpretations. A more telling criticism of complexity theory has come from **E. O. Wilson**, who mentioned the insufficiency of **facts** to back the theory up at this stage, reducing its conclusions to be little more than metaphors.

COMSTOCKERY. A word coined by George Bernard Shaw (1856–1950) in 1905, which means the fevered urge to censor all forms of nudity, sexual explicitness, or "lewdness" in art or literature. The word derives from Anthony Comstock (1844– 1915), an American **virtuecrat** and longtime secretary of the New York Society for the Suppression of Vice. Comstock achieved a remarkable level of influence among politicians and decision makers, and conducted a series of campaigns against individuals and organizations he deemed obscene. Late in his life Comstock boasted that he had sent enough people to prison to fill a long passenger train.

One of Comstock's many victims was **D. M. Bennett**, founder and founding editor of the **Truth Seeker**, who went to prison for thirteen months from 1879 to 1880 for publishing a tract called *An Open Letter to Jesus Christ*. A petition to President Hayes with 200,000 signatures failed to secure his release. A later victim of Comstock was **Ida Craddock**, who was driven to suicide at the hands of his persecution. Other subjects of Comstock's persecution included **Mark Twain**, **Walt Whitman**, and Theodore Dreiser (1871–1945). Shaw coined the word "comstockery" after Comstock had dismissed him as an "Irish smut dealer." See the entry on **Intolerance, Principle of**.

CONCEPTUAL ART. An art movement that arose in the later 1960s and was influential for several years. Conceptual art is distinctive because it is the idea that underlies the work of art that is of central importance rather than the work itself. It might even transpire that the idea does not resolve itself into an actual art object at all, and yet still be a successful piece of conceptual art. An important feature of a piece of conceptual art is that the planning and decisions made before the piece is created are the crucial elements of the work, and the execution of the work itself is of little importance.

Conceptual art was also a protest against the art industry and the hierarchy among art galleries. By making works of little or no aesthetic appeal, conceptual artists hoped to undermine or at least bypass the gallery system. In this, they were largely unsuccessful, as galleries and the art-buying public showed themselves more adaptable than they were given credit for. Another weakness of it is that the art work is entirely unsuccessful if the idea that sustains it is a poor idea. While many conceptual artists have been quite clever, others have been content to wallow in paradoxes or dally with mediocre ideas. Influential conceptual artists include Joseph Kosuth, On Kawara, Bruce Nauman, Jenny Holzer, Sol LeWitt, Victor Burgin, and Hanne Darboven.

Further reading: Tony Godfrey, *Conceptual Art*.

CONDORCET, MARIE JEAN ANTOINE NICOLAS DE CARITAT (1743–1794). Brilliant mathematician and **Enlightenment** thinker. He was born in Ribemont in Picardy and educated by the Jesuits at the Collège de Navarre. Condorcet made his name at only twenty-one when he presented a paper on integral calculus to the French Academy of Sciences. He was promptly admitted to the academy (in 1769) and served from 1777 as perpetual secretary. He contributed extensively to the **Encyclopedia**, edited by **Denis Diderot**. Condorcet was a strong opponent of slavery and an advocate of a broad range of progressive reforms, notably pluralism and the emancipation of women. He was, in fact, tremendously optimistic about the future and the promise of **progress**. This has made him something of a fall guy for **postmodernists** and others who sneer at the notion of progress. In fact, Condorcet also sounded an early warning on **overpopulation**, anticipating the works of **Thomas Malthus**. Condorcet's atheistic views on religion were made known in *Letters to a Theologian* (1774). The attacks on religion were so caustic that many thought the work by **Voltaire**.

Condorcet accepted the French Revolution and became a member of the Legislative Assembly in 1791 and became its president the following year. But he fell foul of the regime when he opposed the excesses of the Terror. Like **Thomas Paine**, Condorcet opposed the death penalty for the deposed Louis XVI. Condorcet was arrested and committed suicide in prison. He was survived by his wife, no less brilliant than him. Marquise Sophie de Condorcet (1764–1822) continued his work, translating **Adam Smith**'s *Theory of the Moral Sentiments* into French, and editing and publishing her late husband's works, in particular the *Sketch for a Historical Picture of the Progress of the Human Mind* (1795). Condorcet was an inspiration for the feminist radical **Olympe de Gouge** to compile the *Declaration of the Rights of Woman* (1791).

Further reading: Edward Goodell, *The Noble Philosopher: Condorcet and the Enlightenment.*

CONFLICT BETWEEN SCIENCE AND RELIGION. An important and controversial concept, which first became popular in the 1860s and 1870s as a result of the disputes then raging between supporters of **Darwinism** who were, in most cases, secularists or **freethinkers**, and opponents who, in most cases, were adherents of traditional Christianity. The idea of the conflict came to public attention with the publication of the *History of the Conflict between Science and Religion* (1873) by J. W. Draper (1811–1882), although *History of the Warfare of Science with Theology* (1876) by **Andrew Dickson White**, was by far the better book. More recent scholarship has discerned three main models for looking at the relationship between science and religion:

- conflict;
- compartments; and
- complementarity.

The *complementarity* model argues that science and religion are not essentially at odds. Many advocates of this model point to the large number of theistically inclined scientists as evidence of there being no irrevocable conflict. Some have argued for complementarity by arguing that science and religion have a common ancestor in magic. Others have said that science was born out of religion. Still others have argued that it is meaningless to oppose "science" and "religion" (complete with **scare quotes**) as if they were specific objects. The complementarity thesis has been defended mainly by religious apologists who work from the premise of the spiritual authority of religion, by which they usually mean their own religion.

The *compartments* model has had some influential advocates, most notably, Stephen Jay Gould (1941–2002), who argued that science and religion are **nonoverlapping magisteria**. This argument is often preferred by liberal religious apologists and theistically inclined scientists. It is the weakest of the three theses.

The *conflict* model is advanced mainly by

spokespeople for the hard sciences and non-religious philosophers. The conflict model has several grades. Some are content to clarify the basic differences in approach between science and religion, without necessarily postulating that this inevitably means the two shall conflict. Others are more willing to take that next step. The bottom line, however, is that science and religion are different projects. The philosopher of science Susan Haack has itemized the essential differences between science and religion as:

- their conception of the nature of the universe and our place in it;
- their explanatory accounts of how this came about; and
- what their beliefs are and how they are held.

Given these significant differences, it is hardly surprising that there have been periodic clashes between institutions largely made up of people with a religious outlook and those whose approach is more scientific in nature. Others have taken Haack's point to make the stronger claim that religion has not simply been wrong on certain facets of science, but that religion is flawed *in principle*. The very foundations of religion are flawed, not just the truth-claims they make.

A neglected point is that the conflict model is notable for taking religious truth-claims seriously. If religious truth-claims are merely allegories, then it is true that there is no real conflict. But if religions make claims, drawn from supernaturalism or revelation, about the world, and which we are required to assent to, then there is room for conflict with the scientific understanding of the world. And it is an essential feature of religion that such claims should be made. Certainly, Pope Alexander III was taking science seriously in 1163 when he forbade the study of physics or the laws of the world to all clerics.

If the conflict between science and religion was fought over the question of evolution in the last century and a half, the front line will almost certainly shift in the twenty-first century to the area of genetics, cloning, and **transhumanism**.

Further reading: Tad S. Clements, *Science and Religion*; and Susan Haack, *Defending Science—Within Reason*.

CONFLICTING THEORIES, ARGUMENT FROM. An argument devised by **Michael Martin** which calls into question some of the more prominent Christian claims for the necessity of religious belief as a foundation for morality. The argument goes like this: In order to lead a meaningful life in a Christian worldview, we would need to know which path leads to salvation. What is more, in order to know which path leads to salvation, there can't be inconsistent accounts of salvation. But there *are* inconsistent accounts of salvation, therefore, one can't lead a meaningful life in a Christian worldview.

Martin shows that we can't achieve total certainty about which of the many competing accounts of salvation is true, which means that whichever account we choose is going to be to some extent arbitrary, and a choice made on such terms can't provide the basis for a meaningful life.

Further reading: Michael Martin, *Atheism, Morality, and Meaning*.

CONFUCIUS. See **KONGFUZI**.

CONJECTURES AND REFUTATIONS. The process, according to **Karl Popper**, by which progress in science is made. Popper argued that a theory that has no means by which it can be refuted is not a theory because if it cannot even in principle be refuted, then presumably it explains absolutely everything, which is to say, it explains nothing. This is very true, but his other points about how science works, are a long way from being generally accepted. See the entries on **falsifiability** and **scientific method**.

Further reading: Karl Popper, *Conjectures and Refutations*.

CONSCIOUSNESS. One of the most elusive of concepts. For many centuries it was theologians who appeared to say the most useful things about consciousness, but gradually the mantle was passed on to philosophers. But it has become apparent that so much of the philosophical debate about qualities and boundaries of **mind** and matter amounted to little more than playing with words. Even less useful was the apologetic attempts to preserve some place for the idea of an immortal **soul**. The idea of **neutral monism**, discussed most intelligently by **Bertrand Russell** was a constructive advance, but even neutral monism soon foundered. Consciousness is now best seen as an idea only the sciences, along with scientifically minded philosophers, can do useful work on. To the extent that consciousness is a useful concept at all, is to the degree it can shed light on the interface between neural activity and the development of concepts.

John Searle described consciousness as the processes and states of sentience in our brain. Consciousness is a biological phenomenon. The neurophilosopher Patricia Churchland describes the characteristics of consciousness as including:

- utilizing short-term memory;
- independence of sensory inputs, which allows us to do things like imagining unreal things;
- displaying steerable attention;
- having the capacity for varying interpretations of complex data;
- the reappearance of consciousness while dreaming; and
- the ability to hold several brands of experience within the context of a single unified experience.

This said, some philosophers are still asking relevant questions about consciousness. There still remains the question of why each of these characteristics Churchland outlines is accompanied by experience. See the entry on the **astonishing hypothesis**.

Some strands of the great **Asian traditions** have avoided much of the Western debate on consciousness, largely because they were more willing to jettison notions of immortal souls. For the Buddha, consciousness is the embodiment of the five aggregates (the others being feeling, perception, disposition, and the body) and has no mysterious self apart from the body. And neither is consciousness permanent.

Further reading: Daniel C. Dennett, *Consciousness Explained* and William H. Calvin, *How Brains Think: Evolving Intelligence, Then and Now*.

CONSEQUENTIALIST ETHICS. See **NORMATIVE ETHICS**.

CONSILIENCE. A term popularized by **E. O. Wilson** in an effort to speculate scientifically about the unity of all phenomena. The word was coined originally in 1840 by the American scholar William Whewell (1794–1866) and means "jumping together."

The central idea of consilience is that all tangible phenomena are ultimately reducible to the laws of physics. This has exposed Wilson to charges of **reductionism**, which he has happily pled guilty to. Whether dealing with a problem of the physical world, or a question of sociology, the frontiers of knowledge are closer together than we suppose. Wilson concedes that consilience is still a metaphysical theory and is not a science.

Further reading: E. O. Wilson, *Consilience: The Unity of Knowledge*.

CONSPIRACY THEORIES. The view that underlying truths about events can be discerned only when the people with an interest in the events at issue are known publicly. And these interested parties usually prefer to remain anonymous, which only adds fuel to the conspiracy theorists's original suspicion.

Karl Popper saw conspiracy theories as the secularization of a religious **superstition**. Where earlier religious thinking (still manifested among many fundamentalists) saw the hidden hand of the devil behind all deeds beyond immediate comprehension, contemporary conspiracy theorists have switched **Satan**'s role to some newer bogey, be it Zionists, "the Americans," communists, capitalists, or **secular humanists**.

It is not that conspiracies don't happen, it is that we must be wary of viewing society in such a way. Popper noted that conspiracies are most likely to occur in societies where people who believe in conspiracy theories are in power. Half a century after Popper wrote this, the truth of it can be seen when examining Middle Eastern culture and politics, where conspiracy theories abound.

CONSTANTINE (272/4?–337 CE). The Roman emperor credited with being the first Christian emperor and the man who made Christianity the official religion of the empire. In fact neither of these is true. Nevertheless, the significance of Constantine for the triumph of Christianity is difficult to exaggerate. Eusebius, Constantine's biographer, describes him as "God's Commander in Chief." The Christianizing of the Roman Empire also had long-term implications in the development of **anti-Semitism**.

Constantine was said to have become a Christian in 312, the night before he defeated Maxentius, his rival for the throne at Milvian Bridge, on the outskirts of Rome. Constantine's biographers claimed he saw a cross in the sky with the words "Conquer by this." However, the story of a simple conversion is not credible. For most of his reign, Constantine balanced his **paganism** with Christianity. Images of Sol Invictus, the Unconquerable Sun, remained on his coins until 321, and it was only after 324, when he defeated Licinius, his last rival for the throne, that Constantine was unequivocally and publicly Christian. Constantine's intention seems to have been to unite the empire by including the Christian community within it, rather than resorting to the periodic persecutions of his predecessors.

In 315 Constantine and Licinius jointly issued what is known as the Edict of Milan, which extended official toleration to Christianity within the context of general freedom of worship. In the century to come, this edict was ignored as Christianity took hold of the instruments of power and unleashed a systematic persecution of paganism. See the entry on **Theodosius**.

One factor Constantine hadn't taken into account in his plan to embrace Christianity as a means to unify the empire was that Christianity was itself rent with divisions. In 325 he brought his errant bishops together at what has become known as the Council of Nicaea, and pushed through a formula designed to bring peace to the quarreling factions. Over the next century, the Nicene creed hardened into the basic principles of Christian orthodoxy. It was here that the doctrine of the **Trinity** was first articulated.

Constantine's role in Nicaea as the most important Christian of the empire did not prevent him from overseeing the murder of his son, Crispus, and his second wife, Fausta, in 326. These events shocked pagans and Christians alike. And in 330, Constantine dedicated his new city, Constantinople, and ensured both pagan and Christian sensibilities were catered to. Only on his deathbed in April 337 was Constantine baptized.

Further reading: Charles Freeman, *The Closing of the Western Mind*.

CONSUMERISM. See **AFFLUENZA**.

CONTRARIAN. A person with the reputation of adopting a view precisely because it is contrary to that held by most people. The contrarian's position is quite popular among some journalists and public intellectuals who are keen to make a name for themselves. The contrarian's viewpoint can be worthwhile as a challenge to the conformism of majority opinion, but it can also become a tiresome and egotistical display if pursued for its own sake.

One of the best known contrarian journalists active today is Christopher Hitchens. His work *The Missionary Position* (1995), which exposed the less well known and more disreputable aspects of Mother Teresa's career, was a classic example of contrarian journalism at its best. His views shocked majority opinion, but were valid and needed to be expressed. Such work is important for the continuation of democracy built on a well-informed citizenry.

CONTRARY MIRACLES ARGUMENT. An argument from **David Hume**'s famous essay *Of Miracles*. The contrary miracles argument says that if miracles are used to confirm religion *A*, then the evidence for those miracles is tarnished, not only by the force of everyday experience, but by whatever evidence can be produced for miracles on behalf of religion *B*. So if the Christian claims a miracle as proof of the validity of his religion, how will he deal with the Muslim who argues that the same miracle is proof of *his* religion?

Further reading: J. C. A. Gaskin, *Hume's Philosophy of Religion*.

CONWAY, MONCURE DANIEL (1832–1907). Author, organizer, ethicist. Brought up in the rural Virginia Methodist squirearchy, Conway was bright and received an MA at Dickinson College, Pennsylvania, at the age of seventeen. His Methodism was soon shattered on exposure to a group of Quakers, who lived an exemplary life without any knowledge of their innate sinfulness and certainty of damnation. Conway went to Harvard Theological College and emerged a Unitarian and abolitionist, much to the horror of his family and friends. His family fought for the Confederacy during the Civil War while Conway actively supported freed slaves to begin a new life, including the slaves who had fled his own family's estate.

While on a trip to London in 1864 a vacancy at the **South Place Ethical Society** came to his notice. This coincided with the premature death of his son, Emerson, after which Conway abandoned the last vestiges of theism he had retained. Conway created an immediate impression and South Place embarked on its golden age. Conway became

intimate with an impressive list of eminent people on both sides of the Atlantic, including William Morris (1834–1896), Dante Gabriel Rossetti (1828–1882), **W. K. Clifford**, Charles Dickens (1812–1870), Robert Browning (1812–1889), George Meredith (1828–1909), **George Eliot**, and Thomas Carlyle (1795–1881).

In the ten years after 1882 Conway spent much of his time in the United States, arranging **Stanton Coit** to work as his successor. After another spell in London between 1892 and 1897, Conway left once more, this time for good. He died in Paris in 1907. Conway was a prolific journalist, contributing to a range of influential periodicals of his day, as well as helping struggling ones. His most impressive written achievement was his *Life of Thomas Paine* (1892), which remains an invaluable source to this day. In 1929 the South Place Ethical Society moved to a new building in Red Lion Square in London which it named Conway Hall in his honor.

COOKE, BILL (1956–). Humanist thinker, writer, and activist. Charles William Newton Cooke was born in Kenya, and educated there, as well as in Britain and New Zealand. Cooke returned to higher education in his early thirties and earned a PhD in religious studies from Victoria University of Wellington in 1998. He became an active atheist and humanist in 1984 after a fundamentalist sect intervened in his relationship with one of its members by questioning the quality of an unbeliever's love.

He joined the NZ Rationalist Association in 1986 and served as president from 1993 to 1997 and as editor of its journal, the *Open Society* (formerly the *NZ Rationalist and Humanist*) since 1992. From 1996 until 2002 and again from 2005 he was a senior lecturer at the School of Visual Arts, University of Auckland at Manukau (New Zealand). Between 2002 and 2004 he worked in the United States as the director of transnational programs for the **Center for Inquiry**. In 2003 he was appointed senior editor of *Free*

Inquiry magazine and visiting associate professor of philosophy, University of Buffalo, 2003–2006. He is a Fellow of the **Committee for the Scientific Examination of Religion**.

As well as this dictionary, Cooke is the author of *Heathen in Godzone: Seventy Years of Rationalism in New Zealand* (1998), *A Rebel to His Last Breath: Joseph McCabe and Rationalism* (2001), and *The Blasphemy Depot: A Hundred Years of the Rationalist Press Association* (2003, and published by Prometheus under the title *The Gathering of the Infidels*). Cooke is married to Bobbie Douglas Cooke, an artist.

CORE VIRTUES FOR THE MORAL LIFE. The American moral philosopher James Gouinlock has identified three core **virtues** for leading a moral life. They are:

- *rationality;*
- *courage; and*
- *respect for persons.*

These core virtues are tightly interdependent dispositions on how to behave virtuously. By rationality, Gouinlock simply means the sincere attempt to seek the **truth** in any given situation. By courage he means the willingness to question our own **beliefs** and change them when they are found wanting. And by respect for persons, Gouinlock means acknowledging that everyone else is in the same boat you are and so should be included in whatever you regard as fair. Gouinlock is happy to keep these understandings open to question, because rigidly defined controlled **command moralities** run the risk of undermining these very virtues in favor of blind obedience to the definition.

With each individual possessed of these virtues and confident in using them and applying them to the varying situations we find ourselves in, the individual can play a responsible part in contributing to the **social intelligence**. The conscientious application of the core virtues for the moral life won't produce utopia, but neither will the **command moralities** which promise such a thing. The core virtues for the moral life are not a set of principles to be accepted and obeyed; they are a *way of life*. See the entries on **humanist principles**, **humanist values**, and **humanist virtues**.

Further reading: James Gouinlock, *Rediscovering the Moral Life*.

CORRUPTION. Thought by many to be one of the most endemic problems of the twenty-first century. Corruption has a powerful corrosive effect on the fragile civic virtues that are essential to an **open society**. Corruption is also a powerful disincentive for investors. It is the dishonest and unlawful abuse of a responsible position for one's personal gain, or for the gain of one's family and friends, to the detriment of the responsibilities of one's position, and of society as a whole. And yet the problem is hardly a new one. In the ninth century BCE, Hesiod, the Greek poet and contemporary of **Homer**, lamented corrupt judges, and in the 1540s, the retired grand vizier of the Ottoman Empire, Lufti Pasha, cried in despair, "Bribes to officials are an incurable disease. Oh God, save us from bribes!"

Transparency International is a nongovernmental organization devoted to monitoring levels of corruption around the world. It releases a Corruption Perceptions Index, which lists perception among businesspeople, analysts, academics, and others of corruption levels in countries.

The 2002 list rated (out of 10) these countries among the least corrupt: Finland (9.7), Denmark and New Zealand (9.5), Iceland (9.4), Singapore and Sweden (9.3), and Canada, Luxembourg, and the Netherlands (9.0). By contrast the most corrupt countries were Bangladesh (1.2), Nigeria (1.6), Paraguay, Madagascar, and Angola (1.7), and Kenya and Indonesia (1.9). It is a worthwhile point to note that the least corrupt societies are also among the most secular societies on earth.

Perhaps the most egregious form of corruption is the systematic ransacking of a country's resources by its leader. The most notorious example is T. N. J. Suharto, Indonesia's leader between 1967 and 1998 who is thought to have embezzled between US$15 and $35 *billion* from the country he ruled. Other big-time embezzlers of their own people include:

Ferdinand Marcos (Philippines, 1972–1986) $5–10 billion;

Mobutu Sese Seko (Zaire, 1965–1997) $5 billion;

Sani Abacha (Nigeria, 1993–1998) $2–5 billion;

Slobodan Milosevic (Yugoslavia, 1989–2000) $1 billion;

Jean-Claude Duvalier (Haiti, 1971–1986) $300–800 million;

Alberto Fujimori (Peru 1990–2000) $600 million;

Pavlo Lazarenko (Ukraine, 1996–1997) $114–200 million;

Arnoldo Aleman (Nicaragua, 1997–2000) $100 million; and

Joseph Estrada (Philippines, 1998–2001) $78–80 million.

While their people struggle and starve, these people and/or their families live in luxury in the West.

Corruption has become such an important issue that the **World Bank** has increased the value it places on anticorruption efforts as a criterion for lending to countries. It has also improved the range of responses it can provide to countries asking for assistance in fighting corruption. Through its Department of Institutional Integrity, the bank monitors corrupt institutions and individuals, and keeps a public register of those who have breached its guidelines and policies regarding transparency. See the entry on **Singapore issues**.

Further reading: www.transparency.org.

COSMIC MODESTY. The ability to accept and integrate fully into one's life the fact that one's existence is entirely irrelevant to the cosmos, while retaining a healthy love of life. This involves rejecting the **transcendental** temptation and all other forms of **anthropocentric conceit**. Cosmic modesty is the logical conclusion to accepting the Copernican revolution fully. See the entry on the **heliocentric universe**.

One well-known atheist—ironically one who is often accused of arrogance—is **Baron d'Holbach**, who wrote, "It is not given to man to know everything; he cannot know of his origin; he cannot penetrate unto the essence of things, nor can he ascend to first principles." D'Holbach's **atheism** was predicated on this cosmic modesty. His system was built not on what he thought he could prove, but was a moral argument about how suffering could be alleviated and how we could live in proper relation to nature. In the twentieth century **Bertrand Russell** was the greatest exponent of cosmic modesty. Russell wrote that the Copernican revolution will not have done its work "until it has taught men more modesty than is to be found among those who think man sufficient evidence of Cosmic Purpose." See the entry on **awe**. Cosmic modesty works best alongside a sturdy atheism and **naturalism**.

Further reading: Bertrand Russell, *Religion and Science* and "The Theologian's Nightmare," in *Fact and Fiction*.

COSMIC PERSPECTIVE. The position urged by many physicists, such as Victor Stenger, to overcome our incipient **anthropocentric conceit**. So as not to vainly imagine our planet, our species, or ourselves from occupying some central place in the great cosmic scheme, as **supernaturalist** worldviews tend to do, we need to take the cosmic perspective.

The cosmic perspective involves us recognizing the staggering unimportance of our galaxy, our planet, our species, and ourselves in the wider scheme of things. With that firmly in our mind, we can avoid accepting fanciful religious or **pseudoscientific** ideas that presume to anoint us with portentous cosmic significance. **Baruch Spinoza** spoke in these terms when he extolled the virtue of *sub specie aeternitatis*, or "under the aspect of eternity." Bertrand Russell had the same thing in mind in a 1941 article called "On Keeping a Wide Horizon," where he wrote, "To me it is very consoling to sit and look at a mountain range, which took thousands of ages in the building, and to go home reflecting that it is not after all so bad that the human race has achieved so little in the paltry six thousand years or so of civilization. We are only at the beginning." See the entry on **cosmic modesty**.

The cosmic perspective is poetically uplifting while also being grounded solidly in **naturalism**. It is also strongly suggestive of **atheism**, with its humble recognition of our unimportance in the scheme of things. The cosmic perspective is one way of appreciating the symbolism of the **winged anchor**. The most coherent contemporary articulation of the cosmic perspective is **planetary humanism**. See also the entries on *sapere aude*, **command moralities**, **egoistic ethics**, **the astonishing hypothesis**, and **mortalism**.

The cosmic perspective is also liberating, as it provides the framework for us to take an active interest in the world around us and the lives of other people. See the entry on **activist frame**. Freed from a narrow perspective that focuses on ourselves as the sole legitimate item of interest, we soon notice that the wider interest we take in things around us is infinitely more rewarding than the self-centered approach. And finally, the cosmic perspective is far more conducive to **humor** and **fun** than is commonly supposed. The cosmic perspective is rich with the sort of self-deprecating **humor** that is apparent, for instance, in **Monty Python's Flying Circus**.

COSMOLOGICAL ARGUMENT. An old argument for the existence of **God**, which was comprehensively demolished by **David Hume** and **Immanuel Kant**. Various attempts have been made to breathe new life into it, none of them successful. The most recent attempt to restate the cosmological argument came from the American apologist William Lane Craig. The core of the argument is that everything that begins to exist has a cause of its existence. The universe began to exist, therefore the universe has a cause of its existence, and that cause is God.

There are many objections to this argument. First comes the obvious one, that is that if all things which exist require a cause, then this must apply to God as well. The attempts to get around this fatal objection amount to little more than special pleading and hand waving. Everything needs a cause, the answer goes, *except God*. This can only ever be an arbitrary declaration. And it leaves no sound objection to the atheist who then retorts that maybe the universe doesn't need a cause. See the entry on the **Stratonician presumption**. The reverse side of this coin is Craig's insistence that an eternal universe is impossible but an eternal God is possible. Why this should be so is never satisfactorily explained.

If we ignore this basic objection, the Kalam Cosmological Argument (as Craig calls it) then runs into the equally basic problem that maybe the universe doesn't actually need a cause after all. Certainly, the whole direction of physics, cosmology, and **quantum mechanics** over the last century have rendered traditional notions of cause redundant. The cosmological argument also misunderstands the **big bang** and relies on a hopelessly outdated theory of **science**.

COSMOLOGICAL CONSTANT. First devised by **Albert Einstein** in 1917 as a method of theorizing cosmic stability, but abandoned when it was discovered that the universe was not stable but expanding. But more recently the idea of a cosmological constant has been revived as a way of explaining precisely that continuous expansion. See the entry on the **big bang**.

COSMOPOLIS. The idea of the universal **community** where all people can live in harmony. The word was first used by the **Stoics**, who spoke in terms of **reason** uniting while **faith** divides. *Cosmopolite* means "citizen of the world." Just as there is only one order of the universe, and there is only one life, so is there only one order of people. All people are common compatriots across the world. Such was the message of people like **Thomas Paine** and **H. G. Wells**.

Cosmopolis was also used by the prophets of despair. Advocates of **degeneration** theory often spoke of cosmopolis as the place where healthy, rural values were diminished in a whirl of smoke, noise, and transitory encounters.

Globalization, at its best, offers us the best vision of cosmopolis yet available. The vision of cosmopolis is not a disguised **globalism**, or at least it doesn't have to be. The two main dangers to this vision of cosmopolis are environmental degradation and the rising tide of **fundamentalism**. Cosmopolis is the vision of **planetary humanism**.

Further reading: Stephen Toulmin, *Cosmopolis*.

COSMOPOLITAN. A Greek word that means "citizen of the universe." Diogenes the Cynic (400–325 BCE) has been credited with coining the word. Diogenes was asked where he came from, and, ever the **debunker** of national or religious pomposity, he answered that he was cosmopolitan. Cosmopolitanism has sought to extend and enrich cultures by opening them up to the practices of other cultures. Its preference is for the most civilized customs, regardless of where they are from.

The claim to being cosmopolitan has always been liable to misunderstanding, even danger. Not infrequently, it excites fears among nationalists that the cosmopolitan is insufficiently patriotic or in some other crucial way does not share his values. But these are backward-looking fears. Today, in the age of **globalization**, the planet has become more cosmopolitan than previous generations would have thought possible. **Planetary humanism** is the end result of cosmopolitanism. See the entry on **cosmopolis**.

COUNCIL FOR SECULAR HUMANISM. Created by **Paul Kurtz** in 1980, the not-for-profit CSH is one of the principal wings of the **Center for Inquiry**, alongside **CSICOP**, the Committee for the Scientific Investigation of Claims of the Paranormal, commonly known as the Skeptics. Based at the Center for Inquiry headquarters in Amherst, New York, the council is the leading organization for nonreligious people in North America. Its chief publication is *Free Inquiry*, a bimonthly founded in 1980, although members also receive the *Secular Humanist Bulletin*. The council sees its role as giving a lead in promoting reason, secular values, and the good life. Until June 1996 the CSH was known as CODESH, or the Council for Democratic and Secular Humanism. This was to distinguish itself from the marxist humanism championed by the communist bloc. After the fall of communism, this distinction was no longer thought necessary.

Several other organizations and publications are sponsored by the Council for Secular Humanism. The **International Academy of Humanism** is a who's who of distinguished thinkers from around the world. The Secular Family Network gives advice and provides resources for nonreligious families, and is responsible for the quarterly newsletter, *Family Matters*. The Campus Freethought Alliance was launched in 1995 and is active on campuses throughout North America. **African Americans for Humanism** directs its program to the black community and publishes the *AAH Examiner*. **Secular Organizations for Sobriety** directs its work to people recovering from alcohol or substance abuse but for whom the religious treatments are inappropriate; and *Philo*, which began in 1998, is a biannual refereed academic periodical which explores the philosophical issues around **naturalism**, **humanism**, and **atheism**.

COUNCIL OF AUSTRALIAN HUMANIST SOCIETIES. A general council consisting of representatives of the major humanist societies in Australia, with all states represented except Tasmania. CAHS was formed in 1965 at a meeting in Sydney. It publishes a quarterly journal, the *Australian Humanist*, and sponsors the Australian Humanist of the Year Award. This award has been given to some of Australia's most prominent citizens, most notably Gareth Evans, former Australian foreign minister; Phillip Adams, an important journalist; and **Fred Hollows** and **Philip Nitschke**. Policy is decided upon at an annual conference and implemented by an executive committee. The council also seeks to promote humanist ethics to a broader public and make submissions on social and ethical issues to government bodies.

COUNTERENLIGHTENMENT THOUGHT, MAIN ELEMENTS OF. The British physician and thinker Raymond Tallis has determined several major elements that are common to counterenlightenment thinking, ranging from the Romantics in the middle of the nineteenth century to **postmodernists** in the later twentieth century:

- there is an intrinsic wisdom in myths that goes beyond the wisdom of **rationalism** and **science**;
- science and **technology** are no more advanced than primitive **magic**;
- we need to recover our sense of the sacred in this disenchanted world; and
- there is something called wisdom that we have lost and which has been replaced by mere cleverness.

These strands of thinking can be detected in people as diverse as Miguel de Unamuno (1864–1936), **C. G. Jung**, **Adolf Hitler**, **Martin Heidegger**, and Joseph Campbell (1904–1987). These strands of thinking can also be detected in most strains of fascism.

Many counterenlightenment thinkers have been deeply worried about the cruelty and brutality of the modern world, and have sought to lay the blame for this on the doorstep of the **Enlightenment**. Tallis notes, however, that there has scarcely been an element of counterenlightenment thought that has not bred monsters even more dangerous than those alleged to have been spawned by the Enlightenment.

Further reading: Raymond Tallis, *Enemies of Hope: A Critique of Contemporary Pessimism.*

COUNTERMISERY, PRINCIPLE OF. A version of humanist **ethics** posited by the English classical scholar and atheist **Richard Robinson**. Robinson notes, correctly, that positive principles are more restricting than negative ones and with that in mind, expressing principles in the negative runs a lesser risk of being an unintended source of further restrictions. Robinson's principle of countermisery are:

- Any kind of thing is bad if it, to the pursuit of it, increases the misery of living things upon the whole;
- No kind of act may be forbidden unless its discontinuance would lessen the misery upon the whole;
- Anything is good if the pursuit of it pleases somebody and does not increase misery.

For Robinson, the purpose of life is simple (and yet not so simple)—enjoy being alive. See the entry on **agathonism**.

Further reading: Richard Robinson, *An Atheist's Values.*

COVENTRATE. A word coined by Nazi propagandists during World War II to refer to the systematic destruction of a city. The word comes from the English city of Coventry, which was extensively damaged on the night of November 14–15, 1940, by five hundred German bombers. The word was used by British authorities as a justification for its own, even more systematic destruction of German cities later in the war. Hiroshima and Nagasaki were then coventrated even more comprehensively.

At the beginning of the twenty-first century we can see plenty of cities that have been coventrated: Grozny, Kabul, and other towns throughout Afghanistan, as well as Iraq, Liberia, former Yugoslavia, Eritrea, Sudan, and elsewhere.

CRADDOCK, IDA (1857–1902). Pioneer for the liberation of women through the understanding of contraception. After her father died when she was two, Ida's mother turned away from **spiritualism** and esoterica to a punishingly puritanical **fundamentalism**. Ida was very intelligent and campaigned unsuccessfully to be allowed into the University of Pennsylvania. Instead she studied at Giraud College in Philadelphia.

In 1887 Craddock became interested in esoteric **religion**, mainly under the influence of the then fashionable **Theosophy** movement. She also became interested in sexuality and free love. She wrote on these topics in *Lunar and Sex Worship* (1902) and became a very popular speaker on the public-lecture circuit. Craddock began to attract the attention of more puritanical minds who were suspicious as to how an unmarried woman could be so knowledgeable about **sex**. In 1894, Ida's mother joined an organized action to have Ida committed to an asylum. In 1898 Ida was actually committed to the Pennsylvania Hospital for the Insane, but was released three months later when it was quite apparent that she was not insane.

In a series of pamphlets such as *The Wedding Night* and *Right Marital Living*, Craddock provided women with plain-spoken information about sex and contraception. Craddock insisted that unconsensual sex is tantamount to rape, even within marriage—an idea that is still controversial today. She also taught that sex should last at least half an hour so that the woman could also have an orgasm.

For her pains, Craddock was persecuted unmercifully. This persecution was led by Anthony Comstock (1844–1915), the founder and secretary of the New York Society for the Suppression of Vice, using the generous police powers the United States government had granted him. On March 5, 1902, Comstock had Craddock arrested for violating obscenity laws by sending copies of *The Wedding Night* through the post. The judge refused even to let the jury see copies of the pamphlet, describing it as "indescribably obscene." Without having seen the evidence, the jury convicted Craddock to three months in the city workhouse, during which time she was subjected to harsh conditions and mistreatment. Immediately upon release, Craddock was rearrested and was offered the option of declaring herself insane. Craddock refused. On the morning she was to be sentenced, October 16, 1902, Craddock committed suicide. See the entry on **Comstockery**.

Comstock's religious bigotry had unintended consequences for his cause. Public support for Craddock grew during her incarceration. Indeed, Craddock's suicide proved to be the turn of the tide for Comstock. Public opinion was so incensed by circumstances of Craddock's death that support for the Society for the Suppression of Vice fell off and his influence declined. In a final letter to her mother, Craddock wrote: "I maintain my right to die as I have lived, a free woman, not cowed into silence by any other human being."

Further reading: Vere Chappell, "Ida Craddock: Sexual Mystic and Martyr for Freedom," http//:idacraddock.org/intro.html.

CRANES AND SKYHOOKS. Idea from **Daniel C. Dennett** to help us distinguish ideas solidly grounded in empirical facts—cranes—from fanciful notions that can't possibly be proved or disproved—skyhooks. Most religious ideas like **God** or the **soul** are skyhooks, because there is no **evidence** that they exist and a great deal of evidence that they don't. See the entries on **naturalism**, **materialism**, and **astonishing hypothesis**.

Further reading: Daniel C. Dennett, *Darwin's Dangerous Idea*.

CRAPSEY, ALGERNON SIDNEY (1847–1927). Rector of St. Andrew's Protestant Episcopalian Church in Rochester, New York, who became a rationalist after reading the works of Karl Marx and Ernest Renan.

Crapsey was a successful pastor, who refused to charge pew rentals, helped found an industrial school, and supported work with African Americans. He was always more interested in social activities than theology.

Crapsey first clashed with church authorities in 1895 when he disobeyed instructions not to work cooperatively with other churches. In 1905 he got into trouble for a work called *Religion and Politics*, which denied a special destiny for Jesus Christ, seeing him more as a symbol of humanity. For this he was charged with heresy. The trial began on April 17, 1906. He was found guilty on May 15, and the verdict was upheld on appeal on November 20 of the same year.

During his trial Crapsey claimed, truthfully, that his views were shared by many of his fellow clergy. It is probable that the Episcopalian leadership singled Crapsey out as an example to the others. Crapsey was the ideal scapegoat because he refused to couch his language in the evasions and circumlocutions his colleagues preferred. After his dismissal, Crapsey left the church and spent the rest of his life as a state parole officer and peace campaigner. He wrote *The Re-birth of Religion* (1907) and an autobiography, *The Last of the Heretics* (1924).

CREATIONISM. An antiscientific creed used as a weapon against the teachings of evolution. Creationism holds that **evolution** is wrong and that the account of creation and development of the world given in the Bible is accurate. Thus, creationists usually claim that the world was created by **God** 6,000 years ago, that Noah's flood is a real historical event, and that all fossils are either younger than 6,000 years or some trick. Some even insist that fossils were put there by God to give the appearance of great age. Why he should want to do this is not usually made clear.

Creationism is the preserve of a particular strand of American Protestantism, although the financial clout of that group is allowing it to export the problem around the world. Many Muslims also maintain creationist views.

Most mainstream Christian churches accept evolution, even if they reserve for God some role in setting the whole process in motion. Given this, creationism versus evolution is not a straightforward example of the **conflict between science and religion**. Most Christians accept the reality of evolution and acknowledge that creationism is not a science.

Creationism is not just an attack on evolution, but on all **science**, because no sciences could function on the terms set out by creationists. Creationism violates most principles of science and **philosophy** by relying on **arguments from authority**, namely the Bible. Creationist claims are also unable to be **falsified**. Wherever inconvenient **facts** intrude into the creationist account, the usual answer is to declare this to be the will of God. Resorting to a tactic like this makes it impossible to falsify the creationist claims, even in principle. When examined against the **plausibility criteria of science**, creationism fails on every count. Creationism is not relevant, testable, compatible with established scientific data, able to make predictions or hypotheses, or logically simple.

The focus of creationism has been on Darwinian evolution because creationists have seen, correctly, that **Darwinism** renders nonsensical the theistic claim of a moral or created universe operating to a design from a benign, personal god. Since the later 1990s, even many fundamentalists have abandoned creationism, moving instead to a marginally less specious variation, known as **intelligent design**.

CREDULITY. There are, according to mathematician Norman Levitt, two kinds of credulity. There is *petty credulity*, which is harmless and which most of us indulge in at some point in our lives, reading our horoscopes in the newspaper, playing fantasy games, or reading Harry Potter. But then there is *grand credulity*, which is a more serious matter because it involves a systematic narrowness. A feature of grand credulity is the existence of in-group **jargon**, which helps create the illusion of profound knowledge, available only to the fine minds of the in-group. This applies to cults of course, but Levitt added that postmodernism and various **pseudoscience** fads like the Roswell case are also good examples of grand credulity.

Further reading: Norman Levitt, *Prometheus Bedevilled: Science and the Contradictions of Contemporary Culture.*

CRIMINE SOLICITATIONIES. The Latin title of a Vatican document, which was to have been kept strictly confidential, dealing with procedures for deception and concealment of incidents of clerical sexual abuse. The document, sixty-nine pages long and signed by Pope John XXIII in 1962, was sent to every bishop in the world and threatened excommunication to anyone who breaks the secrecy with which the document was to be treated. *Crimine solicitationies* instructed the bishops to urge each victim to take an oath of secrecy while making their complaint against the church officials. Under no circumstances was anyone to speak of the matter outside the church.

Crimine solicitationies was not discovered until 2003, when an American lawyer, Daniel Shea uncovered it as part of research for a case against the church on behalf of sexual-abuse victims. It was later admitted to be genuine by the church hierarchy of England and Wales. As late as May 2001, *Crimine solicitationies* was stated to be still in operation in a letter signed by Cardinal Ratzinger, the second most powerful man in John Paul II's pontificate. *Crimine solicitationies* is evidence of a culture, derived from the highest reaches of the Vatican, of secrecy and deception regarding crimes committed in its name, rather than taking open responsibility for them and seeking to make amends and change the conditions that fostered them. It is evidence of what Garry Wills has called the **structures of deceit** of the Vatican. *Crimine solicitationies* is not available on the Vatican's otherwise comprehensive Web site.

CRITICAL COMMON-SENSISM. A program for understanding how **science** works devised by the British-born American philosopher-scientist Susan Haack. Critical common-sensism is designed to forge a middle ground between uncritical **scientism** and the overly critical antiscience strands of **postmodernism** and the **Strong Program** of sociology, which Haack calls the **New Cynicism**. The main features of critical common-sensism are that:

- there are objective standards of better and worse **evidence**, though the standards are more flexible than proponents of scientism claim;
- observation and theory are interdependent, as opponents of science say, but these aren't obstacles to understanding the successes of science;
- the core standards of good evidence are not peculiar to the sciences;
- while the sciences aren't epistemologically *privileged*, they are epistemologically *distinguished*, in that their success rate is unparalleled;
- the determinants of evidential quality are objective, even when the judgments of them are perspectival or context dependent;
- there is no **scientific method** that is exclusive to the sciences, but holds true for all thinking;
- scientific theories are either true or false;
- there is no built-in guarantee that scientists are more disinterested or objective than anyone else; and
- **critical thinking** and institutional frustrations and controls have their place in scientific development.

Critical common-sensism has a lot in common with **critical realism**.

Further reading: Susan Haack, *Defending Science—Within Reason.*

CRITICAL RATIONALISM. A term coined by **Karl Popper** to distinguish true from pseudorationalism. Popper described critical rationalism as an attitude of readiness to listen to critical arguments and to acknowledge that one may be wrong and that one's opponent may be right, and that with a spirit of cooperation, we can all work together toward something like objectivity.

The critical rationalist considers an argument on its merits, without judging the person making the argument. The critical rationalist needs to be aware at all times of his or her limitations, and of the limitations of **reason** itself. In this way, anyone can be a source of worthwhile argument and **knowledge**. Popper described this as "the rational unity of mankind." He saw **Socrates** as the exemplar of critical rationalism. See the entry on **critical receptiveness**.

Further reading: Karl Popper, *The Open Society and Its Enemies.*

CRITICAL REALISM. The philosophy that maintains we can gain reliable **knowledge** about the world, although always with the proviso that we must not be overly confident or naive about the quality of the information we bring in. See the entry on **certainty**. Critical realism as an identifiable term arose in the United States as an answer both to **idealism** and to earlier rejections of idealism. Critical realism was first identified and articulated as a coherent philosophy by the American philosophical naturalist Roy Wood Sellars (1880–1973) in his book *Critical Realism*, published in 1916. The idea was expanded in *Essays in Critical Realism* (1920), which included contributions from several prominent American thinkers, or people who went on to become prominent thinkers. As well as Sellars, contributors included **George Santayana**, Arthur O. Lovejoy (1873–1962), and Durant Drake (1878–1933).

The critical realists agreed with the **pragmatists**, for instance, that **evidence** for the existence of the external world was overwhelming, primarily because the evidence "worked." But they were suspicious of the monists' quest for too certain a link between the external world and our knowledge of it.

The critical realists were naturalists without being reductive materialists. As Sellars put it: "Physical things are the objects of knowledge, though they can be known only in terms of the data which they control within us."

But if the critical realists knew what they were against, they were less clear about what they were for. The contributors to *Essays in Critical Realism* straddled a variety of opinions across the metaphysical, social, and political divide. And during the 1930s, the focus shifted away from the epistemological questions of the *Essays* toward social and political questions. And after World War II, the intellectual trends moved further away from critical realism when philosophy took the so-called linguistic turn. An important voice for critical realism, without using the term, was the American philosopher **Marvin Farber**, the latter part of whose philosophical career was spent criticizing some of the more extravagant implications of **phenomenology**. In the United Kingdom, critical realism has been championed by the philosopher Roy Bhaskar (1944–) who was also instrumental in the establishment of the International Association for Critical Realism in 1997. The IACR seeks to further the aims of critical realism and facilitate contact between critical realists around the world.

The foundation of the IACR is one manifestation of the reemergence in the 1990s of critical realism as an important philosophy. Once again, it has emerged largely as a reaction to the excesses of earlier trends. Today's critical realists are reacting to the perceived follies and excesses of **postmodernism**. A worthwhile example of the recent styles of critical realism can be found in a collection of essays edited by José López and Garry Potter. Heavily influenced by Bhaskar, the critical realism as outlined by López and Potter claims that we can have good, rational grounds for believing one theory rather than another. It is not simply an arbitrary choice, as postmodernists argue. Furthermore, we can have these grounds because some theories give better accounts of **reality** than others do.

Critical realists accept that knowledge is constructed in society, that it is built up with language, and that all these construction methods are **fallible**. But it refuses to then leap to the conclusion that no objective knowledge or truth is possible. And notwithstanding all the objections that could be made about the ways science gathers its knowledge, the fact remains that it does have the best track record of producing reliable knowledge about the world and that we ignore this at our peril. See the entries on **critical commonsensism** and **external realism**.

Further reading: Drake et al., *Essays in Critical Realism*; and José López and Garry Potter, eds., *After Postmodernism: An Introduction to Critical Realism*.

CRITICAL RECEPTIVENESS. A variation of **skepticism** advanced by **Bertrand Russell**. Russell was opposed to what he called lazy skepticism and dogmatic doubt. Instead, Russell argued for two dispositions he thought captured the heart of the inquiring spirit:

- a welcoming attitude toward new and controversial ideas; and
- an unwillingness to accept any of these ideas before they have been examined fully.

No less unhelpful than lazy skepticism in Russell's mind was the demand for intellectual certainty, because down that road lies **dogmatism** and **anthropocentric conceit**. Critical receptiveness understands the paradox at the heart of genuine intellectual inquiry. While being open to new ideas, we must also treat them with caution. Critical receptiveness is a variety of **fallibilism**. "Critical receptiveness" is actually William Hare's title for this disposition. Russell spoke of "critical undogmatic receptiveness." See the entry on **critical rationalism**.

Further reading: William Hare, "Bertrand Russell and the Ideal of Critical Receptiveness" *Skeptical Inquirer* (May/June 2001): 40–43.

CRITICAL THINKING. One of the most valuable, and underused, human resources. The American thinker Garret Hardin (1915–2003) has argued that critical thinking requires three filters:

- *literacy*, because for any idea to be accessible it needs to be effectively communicated;
- *numeracy*, in order that claims can be tested against one another within well-defined limits; and
- *ecolacy*, which is the recognition that all definitions and formulas conceived under the first two criteria are themselves limited and prone to yielding unforeseen consequences. This has been characterized as the "wow, oops" phenomenon.

In this way, thinking that deserves the title *critical* is clearly expressed, free from jargon, testable and repeatable, and flexible enough to survive the transition from perfect plan on paper to workable (and reversible) method in the field. The clearest example of a polar opposite of critical thinking would be the Muslim doctrine of **Taqlid**.

Further reading: Garret Hardin, *Filters Against Folly* (1985).

CUBISM. A hugely radical innovation in art-making inspired by the unprecedented rate of technological change in Europe through the 1890s and 1900s. Cubism as a distinct movement has been dated to around 1907. Leading Cubist artists like Pablo Picasso (1881–1973), Georges Braque (1882–1963), and Léger painted in a way that frustrated the desire of the viewer to read any coherent view of life from the works. The viewer might make out flowers or a still-life composition, but they were always dominated by the man-made element in the works.

Picasso spearheaded the ground for Cubism with paintings like *Les Demoiselles d' Avignon* (1907), but his friend and rival Braque did the most to develop the new style.

Drawing heavily on his mentor Paul Cezanne (1839–1906), Braque's work came to challenge traditional thoughts on the value of perspective. The two artists developed in unison, and by 1911 had arrived at abstraction, with works ostensibly of a subject, but in which reality had broken down almost completely.

These artists also make widespread use of African artifacts; not simply painting them, but imitating their style. This was not done through any anthropological interest in African culture or the artifacts, but simply from an enjoyment of the designs. See the entry on **modern art**.

CULTS. Inward-looking groups of people, usually brought together by some item of dogma and led by a charismatic individual. The American psychologist Robert Lifton has identified five characteristics of a cult:

(1) *Totalism*: us-against-them language to separate people from their own past and the community.
(2) *Environmental control*: control of all elements in recruits' daily life and actions.
(3) *Loading the language*: **jargon** and catchphrases which have special meaning for cultists and encourage isolationism.
(4) *Demand for purity*: as defined by the cult leader.
(5) *Mystical leadership*: which the cult leader bestows upon himself and to which the cult members pay homage.

Cult members need not be unintelligent, in fact they are often more intelligent than average. But they do need to seek a program for living which comes in a total package. A cult is an unhealthy way of living, pretty much by definition, whereas a commune or other form of close society can be very rewarding. The two should not be confused.

Further reading: Robert Lifton, *Thought Reform and the Psychology of Totalism*.

CULTURE OF CONTENTMENT. A condition first noted by the American economist John Kenneth Galbraith (1908–) that denotes the large section of better-off people in Western democracies (particularly the United States) who dominate the voting population. This group has effectively taken over much of the political discourse in society and has become the only real group political parties are careful to appeal to. This group is the self-regarding section of society which looks to lower taxes, toughen up on welfare, stiffen penalties, and generally disenfranchise those sections of society who pose a threat to their complacency and comfort. See the entry on **affluenza**.

Further reading: J. K. Galbraith, *The Culture of Contentment*.

CULTURE WARS. A phenomenon as old as civilization, but which, in its present incarnation, began in the United States during the civil rights movement and sexual revolution in the 1960s. The culture wars then intensified in the wake of *Roe v. Wade*, the Supreme Court decision to legalize abortion in 1973. Since then some other English-speaking countries (Australia, New Zealand, and Great Britain) have experienced cultural skirmishes, but nothing on the scale of the American confrontations. The culture wars are political/religious/social conflicts over divisive issues such as the **separation of church and state**, **abortion**, homosexuality, **gender**, **modern art**, education curricula, and other issues of this sort. Culture wars usually involve two broad groups against each other. On the one hand there are people with religious worldviews and/or social conservatives. On the other hand there are social progressives, people whose religious worldviews are more liberal, and people whose worldview is secular. And in the middle are the **indifferentists**, who care little either way. On the one hand the indifferentists generally sympathize with the conservatives in their suspicion of modern art, but on the other hand they usually agree with the progressives that freedom of expression should not be unnecessarily curtailed. How this huge middle group reacts usually decides the outcome in each particular skirmish in the culture wars.

The social conservatives are anxious to preserve some benchmark of morality, usually in accordance with a **command morality**. The progressives, by contrast, are more motivated by issues of equality, **pluralism**, and **toleration**. An interesting aspect of culture conflicts is that compromise is usually very difficult, if not impossible. The conservatives often use apocalyptic language about the imminent threat to society's moral fabric if the current issue ends in a victory for the liberals (see the entry on **adverse consequences, argument from**). And the liberals often couch their arguments in terms of the dire threat to individual liberty if the conservatives should win.

The term "culture war" was first used in August 1992 by Pat Buchanan, a conservative Catholic, in a speech to the Republican National Convention. Culture wars tend to flare up over an issue, only to settle down until the next issue flares up. The level of stridency from each group is often determined by who was perceived to have won the previous engagement.

An earlier example of what could be seen as a culture war was the campaign against the Renaissance led by the puritanical monk Savonarola (1452–1498). See the entry on the **bonfire of the vanities**.

CURTIN, JOHN JOSEPH (1885–1945). Australian prime minister and rationalist. John Curtin was born in Creswick, Victoria, the son of a policeman of Irish Catholic background. Curtin's education was brief, ending when he was only thirteen. He quickly became deeply involved in Melbourne working-class politics, being an active socialist and trade unionist. In 1916 Curtin moved to Perth in Western Australia where he became editor of the *Westralian Worker*. Curtin opposed conscription and was arrested for sedition. As did **Michael Joseph Savage** in New Zealand, Curtin turned to a more evolutionary brand of politics when he joined the Labor Party.

Curtin was elected to parliament in 1928, only to be defeated three years later. Then, only a year after reelection to parliament in 1934, Curtin became leader of the Labor Party. In October 1941, one of the most dangerous times in Australia's history, he became Australia's eighteenth prime minister. He quickly recognized that conscription for this war was necessary, and he worked tirelessly toward implementing it, as well as other necessary wartime measures. Curtin was said to have wept after securing the support of the cabinet for conscription. Most important, Curtin saw that Australia needed the support of the United States to help protect it against Japan. Accordingly, he changed his policies to one of favoring the United States over Great Britain. Curtin invited Douglas MacArthur to help prepare a joint Australian-American force to resist the Japanese advance. And, against the opposition of Winston Churchill, Curtin oversaw the withdrawal of Australian forces from the North African theater of war and back to Australia. He also oversaw significant welfare-state legislation, in particular an extension of unemployment and sickness benefits.

Curtin's health was destroyed by the strain of his wartime work, and he died in office on July 5, 1945. He was survived by Louise Curtin (nee Needham) his wife of twenty-eight years, and their two children. Shortly before his death, his Labor Party predecessor James Scullin (1876–1953), a practicing Catholic who had earlier kept Curtin out of his cabinet, came to Curtin and begged him to make peace with his maker. Curtin replied "I've seen it through like this so far, and I am not going to change now."

Further reading: Ray Dahlitz, *Secular Who's Who*.

CUTNER, HERBERT (1881–1969). English commercial artist and **freethought**

activist. Cutner earned his living as an illustrator. Among his many assignments, he did book covers for Watts and Co., the publisher linked to the **Rationalist Press Association**. He wrote *Teach Yourself Etching* (1947) and *Teach Yourself Commercial Art* (1949) for the influential *Teach Yourself* series.

In 1920 he also started writing for the ***Freethinker***, which continued until his old age. As well as contributing a regular item called "Acid Drops," Cutner wrote many articles under his own name. He was especially interested in the **myth theory of Jesus Christ**, which he supported, and **spiritualism**, which he opposed. His freethought publications included *Jesus: God, Man or Myth?* (1950) and three pamphlets, *Pagan Elements in Christianity* (1936), *What is the Sabbath Day?* (1951), and *A Short History of Sex Worship* (1940).

CYBERSPACE. A term coined in 1984 in William Gibson's novel *Neuromancer*, which means the wider world of the Internet. The Internet was first developed by the Advanced Research Projects Agency of the United States Department of Defense in 1969. At the end of that year it had a grand total of four sites. By August 1972 there were twenty-nine sites, mainly in high profile academic and research sites. In 1980 the National Science Foundation sponsored a network to cater to civilian users. Through the eighties a series of new networks developed, and toward the end of the eighties an Internet Protocol was drawn up to manage what was a fast-growing trend.

In 1985 the National Science Foundation increased its investment in the whole business by building a national network to work as the skeleton for a series of regional networks. This greatly expanded the availability of the Internet. From then on access to the Net by ordinary people around the world has grown exponentially. By the end of 1998 it was thought that 100 million people were using it. Just as significant is the growth of e-commerce. If the commercial use of the Internet has experienced its booms and busts, general Internet usage continues to grow exponentially.

Many people predicted that cyberspace would spell the end of the printed word. While there are many signs that the reading of books is in decline, particularly among young people, book purchases have actually risen since the Internet has become a major force. It is now possible to find out about works, and to order them, in a way that was inconceivable only a few years ago.

One area that rose and fell as quickly as some early hopes about e-commerce was the industry of theorizing about cyberspace. A great deal of extravagant claims were made about cyberspace as a new type of space, free from the traditional restrictions of gender, age, race, or creed. This was never true and cyberspace is spoken about now in more sober terms. Cyberspace is a reality in our lives, but it is not going to transform them.

Further reading: Margaret Wertheim, *The Pearly Gates of Cyberspace*.

CYNICISM. The Greek school of thought arising out of, though not accurately representing, the thought of **Socrates**. Antisthenes (445–360 BCE, approx.) had been present when Socrates died and is usually credited as founding this strand of Greek thought. Antisthenes was inspired by Socrates' indifference to worldly wealth as a source of **happiness**. Antisthenes then took Socrates' unconcern about material possessions and turned it into a positive move against material possessions.

The best-known Cynic was not Antisthenes but Diogenes of Sinope (400–325 BCE, approx.). Diogenes has gone down in history as the man who lived in a barrel and who wandered around town with a lit lamp in broad daylight looking for an honest man. It was the ambition of Diogenes to live like a dog. The Greek word for dog is *kyon*, hence the name dog-men, of which the word "cynic" is a fair translation. When Alexander the Great came to visit Diogenes, Alexander asked him to name whatever he wanted and it would be given to him. Diogenes is reported to have asked Alexander simply to stand aside so as not to block the sunlight.

Alexander replied, "Were I not Alexander, I would be Diogenes."

Diogenes was also a critic of **religion**, seeing it as a barrier to his version of **peace of mind**. Religion's morbid fear of **death**, enslavement to **superstition**, and support for moral conventions and priestcraft all served as impediments to peace of mind. He wanted to show that virtue can only be achieved through renunciation of any but the most basic of worldly goods. While the Cynics made some valid points about the hypocrisy of established society, their own protests against it have little to offer beyond a protest designed to shock. The most lasting legacy of the cynics was the preference for plain-speaking and distrust of long-winded word games and **jargon**.

There is an interesting, though controversial, theory that **Rabbi Yeshua** (later known as Jesus Christ) was influenced by Cynicism. Even provincial backwaters like Galilee were infused with Greek thought like Cynicism. Theologians such as John Dominic Crossan portray Rabbi Yeshua as a blend of backwoods Jewish religion and popular Cynicism. This would explain, they say, Joshua's criticism of power and privilege as impediments to genuine spiritual integrity.

Further reading: Anthony Gottlieb, *The Dream of Reason*, and John Dominic Crossan, *The Historical Jesus*.

D

DA COSTA, URIEL (1585–1640). Freethinker brought to ruin by religious intolerance. Gabriel da Costa was born in Oporto, Portugal, to a prosperous family. His father was a devout Catholic but his mother had recently converted from Judaism. In 1614, after the death of the father, Gabriel persuaded his family to move to the Netherlands,

in whose more tolerant society they would be able to revert to their Jewish faith without danger. However, once in Amsterdam, Uriel da Costa, as he had renamed himself, found the Judaism practiced there to be as closed and repressive as the Catholicism of his childhood. In *Eleven Theses* (1616) da Costa criticized aspects of rabbinical Judaism. The Jewish community ordered him to recant, which he refused to do, and in 1623 he was arrested and excommunicated. In 1624 da Costa followed this up with *On the Mortality of the Human Soul*, which extended his earlier criticisms. After this he was totally ostracized by the Jewish community. Even his brothers refused to have anything to do with him. Only his aging mother stood by him.

In 1633, after the death of his mother and his first wife, and feeling completely isolated, da Costa arranged to recant his views so as to regain admittance into Jewish society, although his views had not changed. That soon became apparent and he was excommunicated for the second time. He endured the isolation for another seven years before recanting once more. This time he was subjected to public humiliation. He was given thirty-nine lashes and had to lie at the door of the synagogue so that congregants could walk across his body as they left. Unable to endure his situation, he committed suicide. He left behind an autobiography that criticized Christianity and Judaism alike. *A Specimen of Human Life* was published in 1687 and was translated into English in 1695. Da Costa believed religion was contrary to natural law and that it bred fanaticism and superstition. He advocated a natural religion more akin to natural law. Uriel da Costa is thought to have been an inspiration to **Baruch Spinoza**, who was a child when these events took place. Certainly his life is a reminder of the overriding importance of **free inquiry** and an **open society**.

DAI ZHEN (1724–1777). The most important philosopher of the Ch'ing dynasty. Dai Zhen (Tai Chen in old spelling) was born on January 19, 1724, in Hsui-ning, Anwhei, to poor parents. His only education was from the books he could borrow. As nearly all bright young men did, or wanted to do, Dai Zhen took the civil service examinations to enter the civil service. He passed the first level but failed six times to pass the crucial *chin-shih* exam. This says more about the esoteric exam criteria than about Dai Zhen, who was an expert in **mathematics**, ancient geography, phonetics, and textual criticism, as well as Chinese **philosophy**. Two years before his death the emperor awarded the exam to him in recognition of his valuable work in the Imperial Manuscript Library.

Dai Zhen wrote or edited fifty works, which covered most of his major areas of interest. Most of his main philosophical ideas were expressed in a commentary on Mengzi (371–289 BCE). See the entry on **Four Beginnings, The**. With respect to philosophy, Dai criticized the dualism of his Neo-Confucian predecessors by demonstrating that Neo-Confucianists were reinterpreting their traditions through Buddhist eyes. Dai Zhen's major target was the influential Neo-Confucianist thinker Xuzi (1130–1200, Chu Hsi in old spelling). Dai Zhen criticized Xuzi for his elevation of the notion of principle (*li*) into a transcendental one. Xuzi spoke of principle as if it were a thing, Dai Zhen noted. Rather, principle is no more than a word to describe the order of things, to be understood in day-to-day terms. And given that principle was in the world, then the methods of critical analysis, experimentation, and research were the ways to understand it, not abstract speculation. Dai Zhen also criticized the way the Ch'ing emperor Yung-cheng (who ruled from 1723 to 1735) abused philosophical ideas to justify oppression. Dai Zhen expressed a simple **humanism** when he said, "When a person fulfills his life and by extension helps all others to fulfill their lives, that is humanity." See the entry on **agathonism**.

Dai Zhen played an important role in rescuing Confucianism from becoming overburdened with transcendental, even mystical, notions that would undermine the down-to-earth **rationalism** and humanism in **Kongfuzi**'s own works. Dai Zhen was lucky to have the followers that he did. Late in his life Duan Yucai (1735–1815, Tuan Yü-tsai in old spelling), an important etymologist, became a devoted follower. After Dai's death, Duan wrote a biography of him and edited his collected works. For an interesting parallel in Japanese Confucianism, see the entry on **Miura Baien**.

Further reading: Wing-tsit Chan, ed., *A Source Book in Chinese Philosophy*.

DALITS. The lowest section of Indian society, often known as the Untouchables. The caste system is supposed to have come from Brahma, one of the most important deities in the Hindu pantheon. The highest caste is the Brahmins, said to have come from Brahma's mouth. Then there are the Kshatriyas, who come from Brahma's arms. After them come the Vaisyas, who emanate from Brahma's thighs, and the Sudras, who are from Brahma's feet. Then come the dalits, who are technically not a caste at all, but are true **outsiders**, in all senses of the word. By virtue of not having emanated from Brahma, dalits are not considered part of society at all. They are outcasts, fit only for the most menial and degrading jobs. If a Brahmin is touched by even a dalit's shadow, he is considered unclean until he has undergone cleansing rituals. Nobody knows how many dalits there are. Figures range from about 160 to 250 million, about a quarter of the country's population.

It is widely believed that the condition of dalits who convert to Islam or Christianity improves because their lowly status is overlooked. But the evidence for this is not at all clear. More than three-quarters of Catholics in India are dalits, although they make up less than 5 percent of the priesthood. The vast majority of responsible positions are held by higher-caste Indians. Islam has also adapted to Indian conditions by reflecting caste divisions.

After India gained independence, legislation was passed easing most of the restrictions on dalits, but these have been imperfectly enforced. Abuses and even violence against them have been on the rise in India recently. The **Hindutva** fundamentalists have shown little interest in tampering with the caste system, which after all is a core foundation of Hinduism. The best champion the dalits ever had was **Dr. Bhimrao Ambedkar**. Several prominent organizations now follow Dr. Ambedkar's lead and campaign for the relief of discrimination and violence against dalits. Chief among them is the National Campaign on Dalit Human Rights. Indian **freethought** organizations also have an honorable history in campaigning for the relief of dalits. **Dravidar Khazagam** and the **Atheist Centre** have both been active in promoting full social equality and publicizing intercaste marriages.

DAO. See **TAO**.

DARA SHIKOH (1615–1659). Eldest son of the Moghul emperor Shah Jahan, the creator of the Taj Mahal (1592–1666). The Moghuls were Muslim, but Dara Shikoh's Islam was of a distinctly freethinking variety. He translated the Upanishads into Persian and argued for an essential identity between Hinduism and Islam. He was attracted by the syncretic sect led by Baba Lal, and the conversation between them in 1649 is the only extant source of knowledge about Baba Lal's thought. Bringing together Hindu, Muslim, and Sufi thinking, Baba Lal taught that the human **soul** is but a particle of the supreme soul and that only forgetfulness of **God** is an unacceptable form of worldliness. Dara Shikoh brought his thoughts together in *Majma'ul Bahrayn* (*Mingling of the Two Oceans*), which was a serious attempt to bring Hinduism and Islam together. He also learned from the Sufi mystic Miyan Mir.

These heresies attracted the deep hostility of the conservative Muslim *ulema*, or religious scholars of Delhi, the Moghul capital. Even more tragically for Dara Shikoh, being a scholar was not enough because circumstances also required him to be a soldier. He was defeated in 1658 during a dynastic struggle for power with his younger brother, the sternly puritanical Aurangzeb (1635–

1707). Dara fled the battle but was caught and handed over to Aurangzeb, who had him dragged through the streets in chains, then cut to pieces, which were then once more dragged in chains around the city.

Following Dara's death Aurangzeb reversed the Moghul policy of religious tolerance toward non-Muslims. He imposed a tax on unbelievers, revoked permission for revenues from temples to stay in Hindu hands, prohibited Hindus from taking government employment, destroyed large numbers of Hindu temples, and forbade new ones to be built. Varanasi, in many senses the intellectual heart of Hinduism, was particularly hard hit. Aurangzeb's rule did much to poison relations between Hindus and Muslims and push the newly emerging Sikhs into a more militant stance. While Aurangzeb's policies and constant campaigning took the Moghul empire to its greatest territorial extent, he also fatally weakened the internal ties that bound the empire together. Dara Shikoh may not have extended the boundaries of the empire so far, but he may well have preserved the culture of toleration that had served it so well until then.

DARK AGES. The name given to the centuries between circa 500 and 800 CE, during which the ancient civilizations of Greece and Rome were destroyed by wars over **religion**, leaving Europe economically and intellectually impoverished. The symbolic opening of the Dark Ages was the emperor Justinian's persecution of non-Christians and heretics, culminating in the closure of the **Academy** in 529 CE. Justinian (who reigned 527–565 CE) was determined to destroy the last vestiges of **pagan** learning, and he was successful. Pope Gregory the Great (who reigned 590–604 CE) carried on Justinian's work by proscribing the writings of the Greek and Roman thinkers, and even going so far as to discourage any form of imitation of their writing style. See the entries on the **Alexandrian Library**, **Theodosius**, and the **Theodosian Code**.

In Italy, the Dark Ages can be said to have

been brought on by the generation of warfare between the Romans and the Goths for the control of the country. The fortunes of this war ebbed and flowed throughout the decades between 530 and 560 CE, leaving Italy devastated, underpopulated, and impoverished. Rome, once a sizable city even by modern standards, had by 560 CE been reduced to around twenty thousand cowering and traumatized people.

The Dark Ages deserve the title because of the lamentable state of learning through those centuries. They were ages of uncritical **faith** and **superstition** coupled with an active persecution of **free inquiry**.

Further reading: Charles Freeman, *The Closing of the Western Mind*.

DARK MATTER AND DARK ENERGY.

Probably the most intriguing problem set for twenty-first-century astrophysics. Dark matter was originally discovered by Fritz Zwicky (1898–1974), the brilliant Swiss American astronomer and physicist. Dark energy was not postulated until late in the 1990s.

Only a tiny percentage, possibly around 4 percent, of all matter in the universe is visible, but this does not mean that what is not visible does not exist. Dark matter probably comprises another 25 percent of the universe. But the rest of the universe, probably 70 percent, is made up of dark energy. What is more, dark energy is thought to be the motor behind the expansion of the universe. However, it is thought that dark energy is not unlimited, which means there may well come a time when the universe stops expanding, leading to the **big crunch**.

It may well transpire that the whole dark matter and dark energy thesis is unsound. By definition, we know nothing about dark matter and dark energy from themselves, but only from studying the effects on what we can see and inferring from there. This should not dissuade us, of course, as much of our knowledge of quantum mechanics is derived in this way.

Further reading: www.space.com.

DARROW, CLARENCE (1857–1938).

American lawyer and campaigner for civil liberties. Born in Kinsman, Ohio, the son of a convinced freethinker, Darrow was inspired as a youth by **Thomas Paine**'s classic *The Age of Reason*. Darrow was admitted to the bar in 1878 and worked as a lawyer in Ohio until moving to Chicago in 1887. He went on to have a long and illustrious career defending unpopular men and causes, often forgoing fees from impoverished clients. Darrow was a lifelong opponent of the death penalty. His first marriage to Jessie Ohl in 1880 ended in divorce in 1897, and in 1903 he married Ruby Hammerstrom. He had one son, Paul, by his first marriage.

Darrow was a political ally of William Jennings Bryan (1860–1925), three-time Democratic presidential candidate, but their friendship soured as Bryan became increasingly rigid in his **fundamentalism** and refused to distance himself from the Ku Klux Klan. In the end, the two men met head on at the famous Scopes Trial, held in Dayton, Tennessee, in 1925 over the question of the legality of teaching **evolution** in that state. Darrow tied his old ally up in knots over his biblical literalism. Though he lost the case on the narrow point of its illegality in Tennessee law, Darrow won the more important battle for hearts and minds.

Darrow's support for the underdog extended to those whose political and religious views differed from his own. For instance, he became a vocal defender of Al Smith (1873–1944), the Democratic candidate for the presidency in 1928. Smith, a Catholic, faced a storm of religiously inspired abuse and death threats throughout his campaign. Darrow spoke publicly in his defense.

Darrow was a warm-hearted humanitarian whose philosophy of life was a stern, agnostic **determinism** derived largely from **Arthur Schopenhauer**. He was the author of *Crime: Its Causes and Treatment* (1922) and *The Story of My Life* (1932).

DARWIN AWARDS. A satirical Web site and series of publications that honor those

who improve the gene pool by removing themselves from it. Stories include acts of almost unbelievable stupidity by people, like the man who phoned for help for his car which had broken down over railroad tracks. The driver stood on the tracks, with a cellphone on one ear and blocking the noise by putting his hand over his other ear. Unfortunately the noise he was blocking out was the approaching train. . . .

Further reading: www.darwinawards.com.

DARWIN, CHARLES (1809–1882). The man who gave **evolution** its working mechanism, and so changed the world. From childhood Darwin enjoyed wandering through the country and examining what he found. An average student, Darwin attended the Edinburgh medical school, largely at his father's behest, but found himself unable to countenance the sight of blood. Instead, Darwin studied **theology** at Cambridge, where he earned a BA in theology, Euclid, and the Classics. His childhood interest in nature never left him, and in December 1831, Darwin was chosen to sail with the *Beagle*, which was to undertake a scientific fact-finding trip.

The most important part of this five-year trip was spent along the coast of Patagonia in Argentina, and on the Galapagos Islands, now part of Ecuador. Darwin spent the trip collecting specimens and examining new forms of flora and fauna. His discoveries led Darwin to lose his Christian **faith**, with all its beliefs in the fixity of species. This led to fierce quarrels with the captain of the *Beagle*, Robert Fitzroy (1805–1865), a passionate Christian given to violent mood swings. Fitzroy was also a strong defender of **slavery**.

It was at the Galapagos Islands that Darwin was confronted most clearly with the bewildering range of species on each island, each of which had evolved along slightly different paths in response to the slightly different biological niche they found themselves in. He noticed this in particular with the various species of finches on the islands.

Once back in England, Darwin had no doubt that species underwent change, both within themselves and into new species. What still eluded him was how this process happened. The breakthrough happened in October 1838 when he read *An Essay on the Principle of Population* by **Thomas Robert Malthus**. Malthus proposed a law of population growth that will tend to grow exponentially unless checked, either by war, disease, or sexual **abstinence**.

Darwin now saw clearly that the central fact behind the species change he had observed was the struggle for existence that he had read about in Malthus. Darwin now saw that nature provides the backdrop in which species struggle for existence. Those with habits or tendencies that work to their disadvantage will be less likely to survive long enough to reach the age whereby they can reproduce. In effect, nature is selecting the winners and losers of the struggle for survival. Hence, Darwin called the process **natural selection**.

He spent the rest of his life perfecting his theory of evolution by natural selection, slowly accumulating evidence for his theory, and presenting papers before scientific audiences. When in 1858 Darwin received a letter from Alfred Russel Wallace (1823–1913) who had arrived at a similar conclusion from his researches in Borneo, Darwin was provoked into speeding up publication of his findings. So, on November 24, 1859, the fruit of Darwin's researches, called *The Origin of Species*, was published. *Origin* became an almost instant sensation. The extent of Darwin's researches, the quality of the proofs he offered, and the simplicity of the theory being expounded, guaranteed the book's influence. In 1871 Darwin followed up *Origin* with *The Descent of Man*, which extended to mankind the same conclusions he had made regarding plants and animals in *Origin*.

The work of Charles Darwin was the next great revolution against the **anthropocentric conceit** of *Homo sapiens*. The earlier check to our cosmic pretensions came in the form of the **heliocentric universe** in the seventeenth century. The Darwinian revolution then destroyed the **great chain of being**, the vertical theory of order in the universe that had been dominant since ancient Greece. See the entry on **evolution, consequences of**.

Further reading: Peter Bowler, *Charles Darwin: The Man and His Influence*.

DARWIN MEDAL. An award created by the Royal Society to honor scientists working in the field that **Charles Darwin** had done so much to revolutionize. The award is given every two years. It was first awarded in 1890 to Alfred Russel Wallace (1823–1913), the codiscoverer of natural selection, but who then took a wrong turn when he embraced **spiritualism**.

Other prominent awardees include **T. H. Huxley**, **Ernst Haeckel**, August Weismann (1834–1914), William Bateson (1861–1926), R. A. Fisher (1890–1962), George Gaylord Simpson (1902–1984), **Julian Huxley**, Ernst Mayr (1904–2005), and John Maynard Smith (1920–2004). On two occasions the Darwin Medal has been given to husband and wife teams. For instance, in 2002, the medal went to professors Peter Grant and Rosemary Grant (fellows of the Royal Society), for their work breeding and conserving Darwin's finches on the Galapagos Islands.

DARWINIAN ETHICS. Contrary to many fears that Darwinian ethics must involve a primeval survival of the fittest, Darwinian ethics in fact speak of cooperation. In 2003 the American scholar Gerald Larue summed up the main conclusion of Darwinian ethics as:

- we are one family;
- all life-forms have had to learn to adapt;
- we have a common world ecology; and
- we have not yet learned how to replace our native aggressiveness with aggressiveness for research, learning, etc.

These conclusions mesh well with the main findings of **evolutionary psychology**, in particular, the idea of **tit for tat** and **reciprocal altruism**.

DARWINISM. The body of thought about **evolution** that claims **Charles Darwin** as its founder. It is important to remember that evolution and Darwinism are not indistinguishable. Darwin's brilliant insight was to propose, and then provide ample evidence for, the mechanism of **natural selection** as the means by which we evolve. Darwinism is the body of thought that has built up since *The Origin of Species*, the book published in 1859 that outlined Darwin's views. Darwin converted people to the fact of evolution, but was not so successful in convincing them that his own solution of natural selection is the mechanism by which we evolve. The early proponents of Darwinism were **Thomas Henry Huxley** in England and **Ernst Haeckel** in Germany. But neither were strict Darwinians as we would now understand the term. Haeckel and Huxley retained significant amounts of pre-Darwinian evolutionary thought, principally from **Jean-Baptiste Lamarck** about the inheritance of acquired characteristics and **Herbert Spencer** about progress in evolution.

Darwin did not fully dislodge the prevailing belief that the study of embryological growth was a key to understanding evolution. This belief was given prominence by Haeckel, whose slogan "ontogeny recapitulates phylogeny" symbolized this viewpoint. The triumph of Darwinism did not happen until the 1930s when the apparent conflict with the Mendelians was resolved. Mendelians were non-Darwinian evolutionists who considered genetic mutationism to hold the key to understanding evolution. This approach had originally been discovered by Gregor Mendel (1822–1884) in the 1860s but did not become widely known, even within the scientific community, until the 1900s.

After a period of ferocious competition, Darwinians and Mendelians came to the realization that their views were complementary rather than mutually exclusive. The **neo-Darwinian synthesis** was pioneered by R. A. Fisher (1890–1962), in his appropriately titled book, *Genetics and the Origin of Species*

(1930). In this way, modern Darwinism is almost equally in the debt of genetic research as it is of the principle of natural selection. It was only now that Darwinism became the most favored explanation for evolution.

Since then, Darwinism has been criticized for relying too much on its gradualist view of history. The growing awareness of mass **extinctions** has called the idea of slow and steady evolutionary change into question. But a modification of Darwinian gradualism poses no threat to the core of Darwinism, let alone to the wider fact of evolution.

Further Reading: Peter J. Bowler, *The Non-Darwinian Revolution.*

DA VINCI, LEONARDO (1452–1519). Described by the English art historian Kenneth Clark (1903–1983) as the most relentlessly curious man in history. Leonardo comes closer than anyone else to embodying the richness of **Renaissance humanism**, and what we now call **Renaissance man**, meaning someone well versed in a wide variety of arts and sciences. Born the illegitimate son of a Florentine official, Leonardo was fortunate to enter the studio of Andrea del Verrocchio. In 1482 Leonardo settled in Milan where he was taken up by the famous Sforza family. Leonardo's early masterpiece, the *Last Supper* (1498) was commissioned by Ludovico Sforza and the monastery where the work was painted. After the fall of Ludovico Sforza in 1500, Leonardo moved to Florence where he worked for Cesare Borgia (1475–1507), the bloodthirsty son of Pope Alexander VI. In 1504 Leonardo completed the *Mona Lisa*, the work he is best known for.

Leonardo saw no conflict between the arts and the sciences. He searched for a mathematical theory of human proportions, in the manner of **Pythagoras**. As **Alberti** did in architecture, Leonardo wrote studies of perspective and human proportions, believing that this was a mathematical and artistic quest and even a search for the divine. He was both an anatomist and an artist. He encouraged artists to learn about the world they were seeking to represent.

In philosophy, Leonardo anticipated **Giordano Bruno** eighty years later, with his criticisms of **Aristotelianism**. He kept his **heresy** to himself, and his thoughts did not become known for more than two hundred years after his death. And Leonardo had a more discerning eye than many of his contemporaries with respect to **pseudosciences**, which were then very popular. He was scathing of astrology for instance.

DAVISON, EMILY WILDING (1872–1913). English Suffragette, radical, and martyr. An intelligent women, born into relatively privileged background, Davison gained a BA at London University and took further study at Oxford. She was deeply frustrated at the lack of real opportunities for women in Britain outside of marriage and motherhood. Davison joined the Suffragettes in 1906, and quickly became a leading radical in the movement, being imprisoned on seven occasions for acts of radical protest. During one imprisonment, Davison barricaded herself into her cell to avoid the force-feeding she was being subjected to. Authorities sprayed freezing water into the cell to immobilize her while the door was broken down.

In 1913, frustrated by the slow progress her cause was making, Davison resolved to transform the situation with a radical gesture. On June 4 she ran into the king's horse, Anmer, who was racing at the Derby at the Epsom Racing Course. Bystanders heard her call "Votes for Women" as she ran into the horse. Davison sustained very severe injuries, and died four days later. In the short run, Davison's death set the Suffragette movement back, as moderate opinion was shocked by what had happened. But in the long run, her sacrifice was instrumental in persuading people of the justice of her cause.

DAWKINS, RICHARD (1941–). Scientist, writer, and **smiter of humbug**. Dawkins is best known for his brilliant works of popular science. Born and raised in Kenya, Dawkins was educated at Oundle School and Balliol

College, Oxford. He taught for a while at the University of California at Berkeley before returning to Oxford, where he has taught since 1970. He was a lecturer in Animal Behavior and a fellow of New College before becoming the first holder of the newly endowed Charles Simonyi Chair of Public Understanding of Science in 1995.

Dawkins became widely known after his first book *The Selfish Gene* (1976) attracted a great deal of—frequently misinformed—criticism. Part of the book's attraction was Dawkins's superb writing style, which made the topics he wrote about approachable to the nonspecialist. One reviewer of his books observed perceptively that Dawkins makes the reader feel like a genius. Dawkins followed that work up with *The Extended Phenotype* (1982), which, though not a bestseller, was widely hailed as an important work in its own right. *The Selfish Gene* went into a second, revised edition in 1989. Among the more contentious of the many ideas raised in *The Selfish Gene* was the idea of **memes**.

Dawkins' next three works were a return to popular science and helped turn him into an international celebrity. They were *The Blind Watchmaker* (1986), *River Out of Eden* (1995), and *Climbing Mount Improbable* (1996). Each of these was brilliantly written, impatient of **pseudoscience** and religious apologetics. A constant feature of Dawkins's work has been to try to convey the beauty and grandeur of the scientific understanding of the world, free from the pretensions of **anthropocentric conceit**. Dawkins's followed these books up with *Unweaving the Rainbow* (1998) which, while still being well worth reading, lacked the sparkle of his earlier books. He returned to his best form with *The Ancestor's Tale: A Pilgrimage to the Dawn of Evolution* (2004).

Dawkins has been loaded with honors. In 1993 he was elected to the **International Academy of Humanism**. He has been an honorary associate of the **Rationalist Press Association** since 1989. In 1997 he became a fellow of the Royal Society of Literature. In the same year he was awarded the International Cosmos Prize.

DE BEAUVOIR, SIMONE (1908–1986). French novelist, feminist, and humanist. Born in Paris, it was clear from an early age that de Beauvoir was brilliant. She studied at the Ecole Normale Supérieure, coming second in the philosophy class of 1929 after **Jean-Paul Sartre**, with whom de Beauvoir went on to have a lifelong relationship. The examiners admitted later it had been hard to choose between de Beauvoir and Sartre. In the end it may simply have been because she was female that she was placed second.

In 1945 de Beauvoir and Sartre founded *Les Temps modernes*, which became a very influential left-wing magazine. But de Beauvoir's most important achievement was *The Second Sex* (1949, translated 1953), one of the most important feminist books ever written. Here, de Beauvoir argued that women are not able to be complete in their own right, but achieve some simulacra of completeness only by virtue of their relationships with men. But men can achieve autonomy as individuals in their own right. De Beauvoir did not describe herself as a feminist until she was sixty years old. Consistent with her **existentialism**, de Beauvoir argued that women are largely responsible for their own oppression. She has been widely criticized by later generations of feminists, but most have acknowledged that they nevertheless walk in her footsteps.

De Beauvoir wrote extensively in other areas, including the novel *The Mandarins* (1954) which won the prestigious Prix Goncourt, and several volumes of autobiography. And, like **Betty Friedan**, de Beauvoir wrote about aging, because the process of understanding older women has important implications for how women are portrayed. Too often, the only women in the public eye are younger women whose sexual attractiveness becomes their sole feature.

Further reading: Deirdre Bair, *Simone de Beauvoir: A Biography*.

DEATH. The absence of life. All living creatures, so far as we know, live only a set term, and the condition on either side of that set term is death. **Richard Dawkins** wrote that we are all going to die, "and that makes us the lucky ones." What Dawkins means is that death goes with the territory: death is the necessary price we pay for the privilege of having lived. All reasonable, healthy people want to delay their own death and most people don't like the thought of being dead. But like it or not, we will all die, and we need to come to terms with that fact. Succumbing to the **transcendental temptation** is no way to come to terms with death.

Monotheist systems of belief pander to our **anthropocentric conceit** by promising us that, should we observe a set of doctrines and commands, we will escape the finality of death by living for all time. How this is done has been forever disputed, but it revolves around the survival of an incorporeal **soul**, which goes to somewhere called heaven. **Asian traditions** have a different understanding of death. The core of the Hindu and Buddhist systems is that we need to step off the endless wheel of life and achieve an extinction of our selves by merging into the universal reality.

Humanist systems, like Confucianism, **Taoism**, and Western humanism, reject ideas of personal immortality and see that the value of life is in the living of it. Death is the final extinction of every aspect of the individual excepting memories in other people and whatever changes the departed has effected in the world. The humanist attitude to death was put best by **H. G. Wells**, who wrote: "The life to which I belong uses me and will pass beyond me, and I am content."

DEATH OF GOD, THE. A trend in Christian **theology** that was influential in the 1960s, and which attempted to find a coherent place for Christian belief in a post-Christian age. The death-of-God idea was never really popular enough to warrant being called a movement. It was really the idea of a few of the more radical American theologians who were trying to come to terms with the **secularization** of society. But for a few years, particularly between 1961 and 1969 or so, it was influential. The high point in terms of popular recognition came in October 1965 when *Time* magazine ran a cover that asked the question "Is God Dead?"

Several books ushered in death-of-God theology, in particular, Gabriel Vahanian's (1927–) *The Death of God* (1961), Paul van Buren's *The Secular Meaning of the Gospel* (1963), and Thomas Altizer's *The Gospel of Christian Atheism* (1966). Altizer (1927–) is generally recognized as the principal spokesman for the death-of-God theology.

But the idea was not new to these thinkers. The first major thinker to speak specifically about the death of God was G. W. F. Hegel (1770–1831), but it was **Friedrich Nietzsche**, who in *The Gay Science* (1882) wrote one of the more memorable passages of Western philosophy when a madman declared that God is dead, and we have killed him. By "we," Nietzsche meant Western civilization. Nietzsche wasn't lamenting the death of God so much as our lack of awareness of the magnitude of what was happening.

The death-of-God theologians were following on from Hegel and Nietzsche, and wanted to give some voice to the reality of **faith** in a post-Christian age. When they spoke of the death of God, most of these theologians meant the end of any serious meaning to a transcendental God in contemporary society. What had died, they argued, was the cultural significance and relevance of God in people's lives. The more conservative death-of-God theologians like Vahanian still believed that God was alive and real, while the more radical thinkers like Thomas Altizer, William Hamilton, and Paul van Buren (1924–1998) spoke in terms of a "real loss of real transcendence."

The death-of-God movement paralleled the attempt by Marxist philosophers to find some *modus vivendi* for Marxism in the 1960s, in the wake of its increasingly obvious failures to usher in the New Age of plenty.

For example the Czech philosopher Vitězslav Gardavsky wrote an influential book, which was translated into English as *God Is Not Yet Dead*. While remaining an atheist, Gardavsky wanted to effect some reconciliation between Christianity and Marxism. See also the entry on **socialist humanism**.

It has become customary to speak slightingly of the death-of-God movement in the wake of the fundamentalist resurgence that has taken place since then. It was always foolish, the argument goes, to speak of the death of God when God still has such power to inspire millions of people. This may be the case, but the fact remains that the Western world is moving into a post-Christian age, and the death-of-God theologians were trying to find a place for faith in such an environment. A more telling criticism of this movement was its inability to draw the line at a reduced and yet still credible and emotionally satisfying religious belief. See the entry on the **fatal flaw at the heart of liberal religion**. Groups like the **Sea of Faith** could be seen as successor movements to the death-of-God theologians.

DEBUNKING. The process of uncovering fallacious arguments and nonsensical claims. The important point here is that the investigator must not begin the debunking project with the preset notion that the claim to be investigated will automatically be nonsense. To enter into the controversy with this mindset is contrary to the spirit of genuine **skepticism**, which demands we begin each new investigation with as open a mind as we are capable of achieving. The investigator may well end up debunking the claim, after genuine and thorough research has revealed the claim to be nonsense. But that will have happened in the right order:

- full and open-minded investigation of the facts behind a claim;
- in the light of that investigation, establish that the facts are unsound; and then
- debunk the claim.

An investigation conducted in this order is debunking at its best. See the entry on **Joe Nickell**. There are so many outrageous, exploitative, and downright stupid claims being made that the role of the debunker is a very positive one, although this positive role is rarely acknowledged. Debunkers should be seen as unpaid quality-control inspectors in the realm of ideas. See the entry on **smiters of humbug**.

Debunking has become associated with what skeptics do, and they have been criticized as being mean-spirited killjoys for doing it. But what is good for skeptics should apply to all systems of belief. The Hebrew prophets spared no invective in debunking the claims of the peoples they found occupying Palestine before them. And their claims were in turn debunked by Christians, whose were then debunked by Muslims. Buddhists have debunked Hindu claims. It would be very one-sided for skeptics to be the only debunkers while religious apologists who do the same thing are seen in a more positive light.

DEBUSSY, CLAUDE ARCHILLE (1862–1918). French composer and the man credited with being the father of modern music. Born in relatively modest circumstances and enjoying indifferent health, Debussy was educated at home by his mother. His parents' declining circumstances meant that Debussy was farmed out to a wealthy aunt. Here the clear signs of his musical talent were noticed, and he was able to receive a musical education at the Paris Conservatoire between 1873 and 1884.

His early work was greatly influenced by Wagner, but he soon developed a more individual style, influenced more by the symbolist poets of the time. His first major work *Prélude à l'après-midi d'un faune* was inspired by a poem of that title by Stephané Mallarmé (1842–1898). This enjoyed great success, and Debussy was famous from then on. He then set the play by Maurice Maeterlinck (1862–1949) *Pelléas et Mélisande* to opera, and wrote some brilliantly novel works for piano, *Images* and

Préludes. Later in his career, he wrote a great deal of chamber music, much of which featured the flute and harp.

Under the influence of a close friend, the pianist Erik Satie, Debussy experimented with some of the pagan esoterica of the time. In 1911 he ran into trouble from religious bigots when he put to music the five-part mystery play *La Martyre de saint Sebastian*, written by the Italian poet Gabrielle d'Annunzio (1863–1938). The archbishop of Paris was outraged at the license he thought was being taken, put the play on the **Index of Forbidden Books**, and forbade Catholics to see or even speak about the play. The play went ahead but was not as successful as it might have been. This did nothing to alter Debussy's already poor opinion of organized religion. He could best be described as an anticlerical pantheist. In 1909 Debussy was diagnosed with stomach cancer, and his last years were spent in a great deal of pain and misery.

Further reading: Peter Hansen, "Claude Debussy: The Pagan Perfectionist," *New Zealand Rationalist and Humanist*, Autumn 1999.

DECLARATION OF INTERDEPEN-DENCE: A NEW GLOBAL ETHICS. Declaration drafted by **Paul Kurtz** and endorsed at the Tenth World Congress of the **International Humanist and Ethical Union**, held in Buffalo, New York, in August 1988. The declaration was signed by some very prominent humanist scholars like **E. O. Wilson**, **Isaac Asimov**, Jean-Claude Pecker, Gerald Larue, Mario Bunge, Bonnie Bullough (1927–1996), and Adolf Grünbaum, all laureates of the **International Academy of Humanism**. The declaration called for the creation of a world community built upon shared transnational values.

The declaration began with the recognition that we need a new global consensus, the core of which was the understanding of our common humanity and of the **moral truisms shared by us all**. "It is time that we clearly enunciate these ethical principles so that they may be extended toward all members of the human family living on this planet." The declaration then itemized a range of rights and responsibilities that are common to us all. And it ended with a set of observations on the ethics of a global community:

- The basic imperative faced by humankind is the need to develop a worldwide ethical awareness of our mutual interdependence and a willingness to modify time-hardened attitudes that prevent such a consensus;
- We face a common challenge to develop scientific education on a global scale and an appreciation for critical intelligence and reason as a way to solve human problems and enhance human welfare;
- It is necessary to create on a global scale new democratic and pluralistic institutions that protect the rights and freedoms of all people;
- A new global economic system based on economic cooperation and international solidarity needs to emerge;
- We need to firmly defend the ideals of political democracy on a worldwide basis, and to encourage the further extensions of democracy.
- We urgently need to enlarge our common ground. We should encourage the intermingling of peoples in every way we can;
- We urge the establishment of an international environmental monitoring agency and recommend the development of appropriate standards for the disposal of industrial waste and the control of toxic emissions; and
- We have a clear duty to future generations to curtail excessive population growth, to maintain a healthy environment, and to preserve the earth's precious resources.

The *Declaration of Interdependence* can clearly be seen as a predecessor to the *Humanist Manifesto 2000*, which pursued many of the same themes. Five years after the declaration, a remarkably similar document was issued by the Catholic theologian **Hans Küng**, and endorsed by the Parliament of World Religions in Chicago in 1993.

Further reading: Paul Kurtz, "A Declaration of Interdependence: A New Global Ethics," *Free Inquiry* 8, no. 4 (Fall 1988): 4–7.

DECLARATION OF THE RIGHTS OF MAN AND OF THE CITIZEN. One of the landmarks in the development of humanity's conception of human **rights**. The declaration has seventeen articles and was endorsed by the French National Assembly on August 20 and 26, 1789, little more than a month after the start of the French Revolution. In 1793 the declaration was incorporated into the French constitution.

The declaration stated that all men are born free and with equal rights. The basic rights were life, liberty, the possession of property, and freedom from oppression. Freedom of **religion** was specified, as was freedom of speech. The Declaration of the Rights of Man and of the Citizen drew inspiration from many different sources: **Montesquieu**, **Thomas Jefferson**, the *Encyclopedia*, **John Locke**, **Voltaire**, and **Jean-Jacques Rousseau** being the main sources. Article 4 of the declaration states that liberty "consists of the power to do whatever is not injurious to others; thus the enjoyment of the natural rights of every man has for its limits only those that assure other members of society the enjoyment of same rights; such limits may be determined only by law." Thus, the balance of rights and **responsibilities** was struck perfectly. It is important that revolutionary France was the first country to grant civic emancipation to Jews. See the entry on **anti-Semitism**.

The Declaration of the Rights of Man and of the Citizen has been criticized from many angles. Reactionaries accused it of destabilizing the natural order of things, which included **inequality**. Conservatives saw it as a major step in the **slippery slope** to the Terror. Communists accused it of favoring the middle classes. Liberals noted the groups which remained disenfranchised by it. Theorists of various persuasions have criticized the concept of the rights of man. Postmodernists accused it of being part of a **logocentric** discourse and of being a major step in the slippery slope to **totalitarianism**. Some of these criticisms are at least partially valid, but the fact remains that the declaration remains a milestone in the development of the idea of human rights.

The less helpful elements of the declaration, we can now see in hindsight, were the ideas of sovereignty and the **general will** borrowed from **Jean-Jacques Rousseau**. These ideas allowed for an irrationalist interpretation of the people's will that is pregnant with totalitarian implications. The collapse of the French Revolution into Terror and dictatorship says more about the difficulty of imposing revolutionary change while also being challenged from without than about the declaration. The inspiring message of the declaration was not lost on the framers of the **Universal Declaration of Human Rights** in 1948.

DE CLEYRE, VOLTAIRINE (1866–1912). American atheist activist. As her first name would suggest, she was born into a radical family. Voltairine De Claire grew up in the small town of St. Johns, Michigan, where she showed signs of her precocious intelligence and independence. Her family was desperately poor and broke up when she was young. Only twelve, she went to live with her father, Hector, who sent her off to a convent at Sarnia, Ontario, of unusual severity and harshness. At seventeen she left the convent and returned to St. Johns, where small-town life soon palled. She moved to Grand Rapids, where she found herself editing the *Progressive Age*. At this point Voltairine took the surname de Cleyne as a pseudonym.

After a group of anarchists were executed in 1887 for an incident at Haymarket, in Chicago, de Cleyne had found the cause that motivated her for the rest of her life. She rose to become one of the best anarchist speakers in the country, and was deeply admired by Emma Goldman (1869–1940). For the rest of her life, de Cleyne lived in the slum districts of Philadelphia, New York, and Chicago, earning her keep between lectures by teaching French. As well as being an excellent speaker and capable writer, de Cleyne was also an accomplished poet.

De Cleyne's last years were sad. In 1902 she narrowly escaped death at the hands of a deranged young anarchist who shot her four times. She refused to press chares. A succession of unhappy romances darkened her life. Her first love, a Scottish former preacher, left her in the lurch. Her second love, a man much older than herself, died from drink, and her third relationship was with James B. Elliott, who was also a lot older than she. They had a son, but the relationship was a difficult one, not least because of Voltairine's horror of being "owned" by a man. Her last years were clouded with depression, illness, and grinding poverty. She was on the edge of starvation for much of her adult life, a fact which helped cause her early death at the age of 46.

Further reading: Paul Avrich, *An American Anarchist: The Life of Voltairine De Cleyne*.

DECONSTRUCTION. A term introduced by Jacques Derrida (1930–2004) in the late 1960s and which enjoyed a vogue in literary criticism in the 1980s and 1990s. Deconstruction is an extreme form of **hermeneutics**. Attempts to arrive at a definition of deconstruction fail almost at once, not least because Derrida himself has insisted that it is neither an analytical tool nor a method by which we can understand a body of text. It is, he says, resistant to definition and translation. This notwithstanding, the most sensible attempt at a definition came from **Iris Murdoch**, who defined deconstruction as a technique in literary criticism that subjects texts to minute scrutiny in an attempt to reveal deep meanings of which even the author may not be aware. In this way, the deconstruc-

tionist can choose a body of text—any body —with no requirement to justify the choice, and subject that text to close study.

Derrida's evasion of any coherent understanding of deconstruction has exposed it to some stern criticism. For instance, it has been observed that deconstruction is parasitic because its apparent close scrutiny of the text is not based on any principles which can themselves be subjected to critical scrutiny. It is therefore self-referential in an unsuccessful way. Deconstruction, in this way, is simply a variety of **nihilism**, one which reduces academic work to a game where the rules are anything but clear. For a more constructive approach to language, see the entry on **semantic holism**.

Further reading: Newton Garver and Seung-Chong Lee, *Derrida and Wittgenstein*.

DEDUCTION AND INDUCTION. Two very important methods of reasoning. The first person to write specifically about deduction was **Aristotle**. Deduction begins works from two premises to a conclusion. If the premises are valid, then the conclusion will definitely also be valid. An example of deduction is something like:

- Only gods can arrange a virgin birth;
- Jesus had a virgin birth;
- Therefore, the gods arranged Jesus's birth.

As this example shows, the logic of deduction is flawless, but it does depend on the initial premises being valid. If the premises are valid, then you can guarantee the conclusion will also be valid. In this case, however, they are not, and so doubt can safely be cast on the conclusion. Incidentally, this example also shows the difference between a valid argument and a true one. This argument is *valid*, in that the conclusion does follow reasonably from the premises. However, it is not *true*, because the premises are faulty. See the entry on **truth**.

With the growth of **science**, it became clear that deduction couldn't be used in an exploratory way, in cases where definitely true premises cannot be provided. So there arose a need for a different way to reason to a conclusion. Induction as a method of reasoning was first proposed by the English thinker Francis Bacon (1561–1626). The simple understanding of induction is that it proceeds from specific cases on to a general conclusion. However, there are other forms of induction to this basic model. Here is an example of induction:

- All kangaroos in Australia carry their young in pouches;
- All animals that carry their young in pouches are marsupials;
- Therefore, all kangaroos are marsupials.

Induction as a method of reasoning has run into a minefield of problems, some of which seem unanswerable. The first person to raise serious questions about what has become known as the problem of induction was **David Hume**. In the twentieth century **Karl Popper** carried on the criticism of induction as a critical method. While many of the issues raised by Hume, Popper, and others are formidable, the fact remains that we can't do without induction as a tool of reasoning.

Further reading: Julian Baggini and Peter Fosl, *The Philosopher's Toolkit*; and A. C. Grayling, ed., *Philosophy: A Guide through the Subject*.

DEGENERATE ART. A term used originally by the Hungarian author Max Nordau (1849–1923) as an example in a wide-ranging work called *Degeneration* (1892). Nordau spoke of the moral degeneracy of contemporary artists and thinkers, in particular Impressionist painters such as Georges Seurat (1859–1891) and Claude Monet (1840–1926). But the term has become notorious by its use in an attempt by Nazi Germany to create a new art aesthetic. In July 1937 the Nazis staged in Munich the Great German Art Exhibition, which was divided into two exhibitions, being held side-by-side. Visitors could view the exhibition of degen-

erate art and then refresh themselves with the exhibition of authentically Germanic art.

The degenerate art was held to be fatally imbued with Jewish, African, and Marxist elements and, therefore, corrosive of German values. Expressionism, **Cubism**, and any sort of abstract painting was thought to break up coherent representations of the world and of the human body, which led inexorably to disorientation and cultural decay. Included in the exhibition was a line-up of distinguished artists: Otto Dix (1891–1969), Ernst Kirchner (1880–1938), Emil Nolde (1867–1956), Oskar Schlemmer (1888–1943), and Georg Grosz (1893–1959). Kirchner committed suicide in Switzerland the following year, having become deeply depressed at the treatment of his work.

Not surprisingly, the degenerate art exhibition was a great success, attracting more than two million visitors, three times the number the favored Germanic art exhibition attracted. The authentic German art was a mixture of heroic sculpture and sentimental landscapes. However, most historians agree that the campaign against degenerate art was generally popular among Germans. Neither is the story of degenerate art merely a historical curiosity. There is an alarming similarity between the Nazi objections to degenerate art and contemporary polemics against **modern art** by American fundamentalists.

Further reading: Robert S. Wistrich, *Weekend in Munich: Art, Propaganda and Terror in the Third Reich*.

DEGENERATIONISM. An old idea, although the term only arose in the nineteenth century. Examples can be found in the mythologies of Egypt, India, Greece, and Rome of the idea that we are degenerate survivors from a long-lost golden age. They all postulate a theory of history which sees it in terms of inevitable decline.

In the nineteenth century the idea of degeneration gained new strength. The Swiss historian Jacob Burckhardt (1818–1897) popularized the idea that most of the ideas of modern civilization were harbingers of a nascent barbarism. **Friedrich Nietzsche** also played with the degeneration idea, blaming Christianity in large part.

In the 1870s, degenerationism took on a new form in response to the theories of **evolution** then being discussed. In strictly scientific terms, the idea was not entirely unsound. Some scientists noted that not all organisms progress from the simple to the more complex, as was generally assumed. Some move in the opposite direction. The problem came when others leapt to **social Darwinist** conclusions that some peoples have also shown this trend toward degeneration. The Italian criminologist Cesare Lombroso (1836–1909) and the German biologist Anton Dohrn (1840–1909) both argued variations of this theme. The most prominent attempt at a theory of degeneration in England came from Phillip Gosse (1810–1888) in his book *Omphalos* (1857).

Degenerationism also became popular among some missionaries as a means to explain the "savagery" of the "heathen." Not only were the "savages" degenerate by virtue of being descended from the sin of Adam, as all humans were thought to be because of **original sin**, but they shared an extra helping of degeneracy by virtue of their very savagery. Unlike the Christians, savages had degenerated still further into devil worship, cannibalism, and all the other horrors that confronted the missionaries. Classified in this way, the missionaries were able to see their role as entirely beneficent and kindly.

Degenerationism lost whatever validity it had as a scientific theory very quickly, but has lingered on in literature, particularly among those anxious to bewail the decline in morals. This said, degenerationism could well take on a new lease on life in the twenty-first century as experimentation with the genetic stock of humanity provokes a new sense of irrevocable decline.

Further reading: Arthur Herman, *The Idea of Decline in Western History*; and G. W. Stocking, *After Tylor: British Social Anthropology 1888–1951.*

DE GOUGE, OLYMPE (1748–1793). Pioneering feminist radical who died for her beliefs. Marie Gouze was born in Montauban, in the south of France, the daughter of a butcher. Her mother was also gainfully employed, selling quality goods. In 1865 Gouze married Louis Aubry, but, when still only eighteen, fled the marriage and went to Paris. There she changed her name to Olympe de Gouge.

De Gouge's learning began from scratch, as she had not even been taught to write. She overcame these obstacles and became a prominent essayist and playwright. She wrote *Negro Slavery*, a play critical of **slavery** in 1774, but it was not performed until 1789, after the revolution. De Gouge's most radical ideas were with respect to **gender** issues and sexual relations. She advocated equal treatment of illegitimate children and the right to sex outside **marriage**.

For someone of such radical views, it was not surprising that de Gouge was happy about the French Revolution. But she soon came to see that the emancipation was going to benefit men disproportionately. Nevertheless, in the spirit of the **Declaration of the Rights of Man and of the Citizen**, de Gouge wrote the *Declaration of the Rights of Woman and the Female Citizen* in 1791. It began:

> Woman, wake up; the tocsin of reason is being heard throughout the whole universe; discover your rights. The powerful empire of nature is no longer surrounded by prejudice, fanaticism, superstition, and lies. The flame of truth has dispersed all the clouds of folly and usurpation. Enslaved man has multiplied his strength and needs recourse to yours to break his chains. Having become free, he has become unjust to his companion. Oh, women, women! When will you cease to be blind?

De Gouge also drew up a marriage contract, which was predicated on full gender equality.

De Gouge was part of a radical salon called the *Cercle Social*, led by Sophie de Condorcet (1764–1822), the highly intelligent wife of the **Marquis de Condorcet**. But tragically for de Gouge and the cause of women's rights, the French Revolution was animated by the spirit of **Jean-Jacques Rousseau**, whose misogyny fueled the negative reaction to her and the *Declaration of the Rights of Woman*. Reacting to the hostility to her conception of women's rights, de Gouge wrote a satirical work criticizing the revolution, which led to a charge of treason in July 1793, for which, on November 3 that year, she was executed by the guillotine.

DEISM. A new vision of the universe which rose to prominence in the seventeenth century in the wake of the progress of science, particularly the cosmological changes wrought by Copernicus through to **Isaac Newton**. Most of the influential leaders of the **Enlightenment** were Deists. The word was first used in the middle of the sixteenth century in France.

Deism rejected all of the mystical and revealed elements of Christianity such as **miracles**, original sin, the virgin birth, and the **Trinity**. In its place, deism advocated a natural religion, one of mathematical laws and natural harmony as uncovered by Newton. Deists advocated religious **toleration**, arguing that all religions were, to some extent at least, a representation of the divine truth in the universe. Deists tended to believe in a creator but, in most cases denied that the creator took any part in the day-to-day running of the universe or was partial to miracles. God was implicit in the universe but had no part in running it or in overseeing the moral lives of humans.

Deism was first articulated clearly in Lord Herbert of Cherbury's *De Veritate* (1624), but its most powerful voices were Alexander Pope's poem *Essay on Man* (1733–34) and John Toland's *Christianity Not Mysterious* (1696), which tried to reconcile reason and religion.

Deism reached its apogee with the publication in 1730 by Matthew Tindal of *Christianity as Old as Creation*. **Anthony Collins** is usually considered a deist, but some recent scholarship has argued he should be thought of as an atheist. See the entry on **parallel theology**.

Deism was seen by the established churches as a significant threat. The first major attempt at a refutation came from Bishop Stillingfleet in 1677 in *Letter to a Deist*. Indeed, Stillingfleet's letter marks something of a turning point in the history of Christianity, in that it was the first occasion when an established Christian authority figure was required to treat a rival theory seriously and not simply respond with physical coercion. From the middle of the eighteenth century Deism began to attract some powerful attacks from orthodox Christians. But Deism declined not because of its inherent flaws but because of its inability to reach the general population, who still yearned for the **transcendental temptation**. Nowadays Deism is seen to be faulty not because of the Christian counterattacks of the eighteenth century, but because Deism's assumption of the importance of a first cause and a lawgiver are no longer valid. Nevertheless, Deism made a positive contribution to the progress of humanity, not least for its important role in securing the repeal of laws relating to **witchcraft** and campaigns against **slavery**.

DELIUS, FREDERICK (1862–1934). English composer. Of German, Dutch, and Swedish descent, Delius was born and brought up in Bradford, England. Early on he displayed musical gifts but his parents wanted him to enter business. With that in mind Delius was sent to Florida to manage an orange orchard. He quickly showed himself to be incompetent in this, but immersed himself in the musical life of the state. After teaching music in various parts of the United States, Delius returned to Europe, when in 1886 he entered the Leipzig Conservatory. There he befriended the Norwegian composer Edvard Grieg (1843–1907). In 1890

Delius moved to France, where he lived for most of the remainder of his life.

Delius wrote operas such as *Koanga* (1897) which was influenced by the songs he heard African American plantation workers sing in Florida, *A Village Romeo and Juliet* (1901), and a wide range of concertos for violin, cello, and piano as well as larger orchestral works like *Appalachia* and *Sea Drift*. Even late in his life and in the face of paralysis and blindness after 1924, Delius, with the help of Eric Fenby, wrote a series of works, including the choral work *Songs of Farewell*. Fenby was able to interpret Delius's gestures and whispers and transcribe them to music.

Delius was an atheist. In 1905 he transcribed some of the writings of **Friedrich Nietzsche** into songs, and his *Mass of Life* was constructed on Nietzsche's *Thus Spake Zarathustra*. While Delius had a reputation as a difficult man, he inspired deep affection in his few real friends and his patient wife Jelka Rosen. They recognized in Delius a passionate love of nature.

DEMOCRACY. Described by Winston Churchill (1874–1965) as the worst form of government—except all the others. More specifically, Joseph Schumpeter (1883–1950) described democracy as a particular method of electing, rejecting, and influencing government officials. It is the method that allows the general population a greater say in these things than any other governmental system. Several political philosophers have noted that the key to the difference of democracy is the mechanism it provides to eject unpopular governments. **Karl Popper** was specific on this. Any system can provide a means by which a government can be installed, but systems are at their most vulnerable when it is time to eject unpopular governments. Only in democracies is this process handled peacefully and with a minimum of disruption. We underappreciate that strength at our peril.

Following on from this, Amartya Sen, the Indian Nobel Prize–winning economist, has noted that no famine has ever occurred in a working democracy, whether it be a wealthy democracy like the United States or Great Britain, or a democracy of more modest means like Botswana. This is because democratic governments have a powerful incentive (reelection) to ensure their people remain properly fed. In authoritarian regimes, however, this incentive is not as direct. The twenty-first century may put pressure on this record, but so far at least, democracies can make this claim.

Democracy is an invention of the Greeks. **Solon** laid the groundwork for democracy in Athens, which Cleisthenes (570–508 BCE) later built upon. See also the entry on **ancient Greece, legacy of**. From the decline of classical Greece until the **Enlightenment**, democracy was little more than a memory. It took the rebirth of the memory of these ancient ideals, and the ability to oppose the authoritarian preferences of the Christian church, before ideas of democracy could assert themselves once more. A democracy is by definition an **open society**.

Among the many objections to democracy is that it encourages short-term thinking. The politician who promises all the cake now is likely to beat the one who says we should keep some of it for a rainy day. In questions like **sustainable development** and **global governance**, these shortcomings are of more than academic concern. There is also the problem that majorities can push through illiberal, even discriminatory measures against minorities. There is also strong evidence that Michels's pessimistic **iron law of oligarchy** can be applied to democracy without undue danger of error. And see the entry on **culture of contentment**.

The threat to democracy during the **cold war**, so we were told, was the external menace of communism. Now, the dangers are internal ones as well as external. A major internal threat is **corruption** while a growing external threat comes from **terrorism**. And in the United States there are the dangers of **incrementalism** and **dominionism**.

But for all these weaknesses and dangers, the idea of democracy is growing around the world. In 1950 only 14 percent of the nations of the world were democratic, but fifty years later that figure had risen to 62 percent. Democracy is the system of government most conducive to **humanism**, and in return, humanist thinkers over the centuries have made seminal contributions to the development of democracy. If the **war on terror** is to be won, then the merits of democracy must be paramount among the arguments employed against the terrorists.

DEMOCRITUS OF ABDERA (460–357 BCE, approx.). Very significant philosopher from ancient Greece. Democritus was a student of Leucippus (460–390 BCE, approx.), who had moved to Abdera from Miletus. Abdera was considered a backwater of Greek intellectual culture, and Democritus was often mocked for his origins and accent. Between them, their **philosophy** of **atomism** revolutionized world thought.

Like all **Pre-Socratic** philosophers, we know relatively little about Democritus's life. He is thought to have traveled very widely and to have written about fifty works; more than most other Pre-Socratic thinkers put together. Like most of his contemporaries, relatively little of his work survives, although there is enough to piece together an outline of his thought. Democritus has become known as "the laughing philosopher" for his habit of being thoroughly amused by the absurdities people are prone to. For Democritus, cheerfulness was the goal in life.

Democritus rejected **religion** and embraced a thoroughgoing **naturalism**. Among the many speculations of Democritus was the atomic theory of matter, in which all things are composed of tiny, indivisible particles. He believed that not just matter, but also time and space, were divided into discontinuous sections. Everything was held together by **necessity**, by which he meant what we would call the laws of the universe. The existence of atoms was not proved conclusively until the

twentieth century. In **ethics**, Democritus counseled moderation and equanimity. See the entry on **Doctrine of the Mean**. Being consumed by wants and desires only disturbs the atoms that make us up, and this can lead to ill-health. He understood the interdependence between mental and physical health.

Aristotle said of him, "He has thought about everything." Sadly for the progress of **science**, Aristotle was opposed to Democritus's atomism. Democritus's views were widely reviled by **Plato** and survived only in the form of **Lucretius**'s poem *De rerum natura*, which itself only survived by the skin of its teeth through the **Dark Ages**.

DEMONIZING THE OPPOSITION. One of the few current buzzwords, which carries a useful idea. Demonizing the opposition is more than simply disagreeing with someone. It is to ascribe base motives to their disagreement with your position. To demonize the opposition, they are not simply *wrong*, they are *wicked*. Sadly, religions are most prone to this failing, because of their claim to possessing a **monopoly on truth** that comes from ascribing absolute authority to one's own set of **scriptures**. The precedent was set with the infamous passage in Psalm 14:1 which says that the fool in his heart knows there is no god. Paul followed this up when he said that the existence of **God** is so obvious that those who "refuse to honor" him have no excuse (Romans 1:10–21). The Qur'an follows in the same vein when the Jews are disparaged as swine and apes who serve the devil (5:60). From these passages, many religious conservatives and **fundamentalists** find it beyond belief that people could question the validity of their scriptures in good **faith**. The alternative is that the scriptures are unconvincing to some people, which for certain types of fundamentalists is an unthinkable conclusion. See the entry on **monotheism**.

Atheists have long been the targets of choice to demonize. Rather than criticizing what atheists have actually said, their supposedly underlying motives are exposed and attacked. Their "real" motives have varied over the centuries from satanic possession, sexual licentiousness, general moral corruption, communism or at least want of sufficient patriotism, intellectual laziness, **dogmatism**, or simple lunacy. However, demonizing the opposition is not peculiar to fundamentalists. Communists used to do it to their opponents, who were simply relabeled "kulaks," "bourgeois," "reactionary," or some other label. Once recategorized in this way, the opponents could be portrayed as being irrevocably opposed to the Soviet system by virtue of their social station, rather than their convictions. The Religious Right today has accomplished the same thing with the word *liberal*, which has become an all-purpose term of abuse.

The advantage of demonizing the opposition means one doesn't have to take their arguments seriously. Instead one can play to the crowd by raising the specter of any of the follies just listed. **Humanism** is well suited to avoiding the dangers of demonizing the opposition, not because humanists are intrinsically superior to other people, but because there is a presumption of **fallibilism** in the humanist outlook. See the entries on *ad hominem* **argument** and **hermeneutics of suspicion**; **religion, criticism of**; and **talking past one another**.

DEMOTHEOLOGY. A word coined in 1970 by the American scholar of religion, Robert Tapp, and which refers to what he called "the religion on the ground." Tapp makes the important point that religious beliefs are largely determined by the people who practice that **religion** at any one time. This means that the study of **scripture** and **theology** will not provide a comprehensive view of that religion.

Theologians are only one group who determine the evolution of religious belief. The rabbis, clergy, or mullahs are more important still, because it is they who distill the thoughts of those theologians to the religious population. But in the end, the religious pop-

ulation make their own theology, and this is what Tapp refers to as demotheology. The current reduction of American evangelicalism to what is called the "pelvic preoccupation" of **abortion** and gay marriage is a good example of demotheology at work.

DENNETT,   DANIEL   C[LEMENT] (1942–). American philosopher and one of the most intellectually significant thinkers of the time. Dennett has been described as "our best   current   philosopher ... the   next **Bertrand Russell**." He studied at Harvard, where he was taught by **W. V. O. Quine**, and took his doctorate at Oxford University, where he studied under Gilbert Ryle (1900–1976). Dennett is a distinguished arts and sciences professor, professor of philosophy, and director of the Center for Cognitive Studies at Tufts University.

Dennett became known outside the academic community with his book *Consciousness Explained* (1991). Here Dennett argued for a materialistic notion of the brain based on what he called the "learning algorithm." He challenged the traditional notion that the mind has a single clearing house, what he called the Cartesian Theater. Dennett expanded his reach in *Darwin's Dangerous Idea* (1995), which was a powerful restatement of the **neo-Darwinian synthesis** with respect to **human nature**. This is a wonderfully creative work, with a lot of useful ideas. See the entry on **cranes and skyhooks**. *Darwin's Dangerous Idea* is one of the more comprehensive attempts to incorporate the Darwinian revolution into philosophy. Dennett is a strong supporter of the computational theory of **consciousness**, which is opposed by the equally respected philosopher, **John Searle**. See the entry on **artificial intelligence**. Dennett's most recent book is *Freedom Evolves* (2003). A sign of Dennett's importance is the growing number of books devoted to his thought.

His other books include *Brainstorms* (1978), *The Intentional Stance* (1987) and, with Douglas Hofstadter, *The Mind's I* (1981).

Dennett was elected to the American Academy of Arts and Sciences and, in 2001, to the **International Academy of Humanism**.

DEPENDENT ARISING. A notion of central importance to Buddhism, and arrived at by the Buddha as a middle ground between the overly metaphysical notion of the self (*atman*) of the Hindu brahmins, and the **atomist** notion of nature advanced by the **Carvakas** and **Ajivikas**. The Buddha had little time for metaphysical speculation, regarding it as a process of overstating, and each of the rival ideas seemed to him overly metaphysical. The Buddha also said that, "He who sees dependent arising perceives the doctrine."

Instead of the rival understandings, the Buddha proposed the notion of dependent arising (sometimes called dependent origination). The Buddha explained that dependent upon ignorance arise dispositions, from which in turn arise consciousness, personality, our senses. Dependent upon our senses arise feeling, craving, and grasping, upon which hang the whole cycle of birth, **death**, and suffering. Conversely, the fading away of ignorance arises the fading away of dispositions and so on. The links from ignorance to birth, death, and suffering are known as Nidanas. So there is no mystical substance or inner meaning to all this. It boils down to the simple understanding that ignorance leads on to desire, which leads on to suffering and death, whereas the cessation of ignorance leads to the end of desire and thus to the end of suffering. What the Buddha then offered was a way out of ignorance. And his program is essentially humanistic, in that it eschewed the **transcendental temptation**, **mysticism**, and wordy metaphysics. See the entry on **Gautama, Siddhartha**.

Further reading: David Kalupahana, *A History of Buddhist Philosophy*.

DEPRESSION. Thought by many to be the fastest-growing illness in the developed world. There is depression, which we all suffer from at various times, and clinical depression, which usually comes in three main varieties:

- *bipolar disorder*, which involves mood swings between the extremes of mania and depression;
- *seasonal affective disorder*, where a person becomes severely depressed in autumn and winter, when the hours of darkness are longer; and
- *dysthymia*, where a person's feeling of depression is less severe but can be felt for years on end.

Clinical depression involves feelings of great sadness, worthlessness, hopelessness, and despair. These are felt with sufficient strength to impair a person's ability to function normally, either at work or in domestic situations.

In the United States, rates of clinical depression tripled among the last two generations raised in the twentieth century. In most developed countries, the suicide rate is growing, and increasing fastest among young people. What seems to be happening is that the blandness, vacuity, and pointlessness of contemporary **affluenza** has become too obvious to ignore. And as the twenty-first century begins, there are few ideologies or religions that still have any power to inspire or even console while remaining honest. All that's left is a black hole of mindless consumption. And as many people are stuck in positions where the pay is relatively modest, even access to that short-term palliative is circumscribed. In these conditions, it is not surprising that for many people the **transcendental temptation** is too much to resist. But for those who do resist the transcendental temptation (and for many who don't) depression remains an ongoing burden.

Barry Schwartz, an American psychologist, has observed that the widespread choice so symptomatic of affluenza, often decreases satisfaction. When faced with a choice, the consumer is required to gather information about the competing products, with the unsaid subtext of "let the buyer beware" should that choice be the wrong one, in which case a dose of **buyer's remorse** is inevitable. See the entry on **satisficers and maximizers**.

Despite all this, some of the greatest people in history suffered from severe depression and yet went on to achieve great things: Winston Churchill (1874–1965) and **Abraham Lincoln**, to name but two. Churchill called depression his "black dog."

DESCARTES, RENÉ (1596–1650). Mathematical genius and (along with **Plato**) by far the most influential philosopher whose main conclusions were almost all wrong. Born near Tours in France, Descartes was educated at a Jesuit college at La Flèche until 1614. He went on to study law at Poitiers, graduating in 1616. While on military service in Germany in 1619, Descartes is said to have had the inspiration to remodel **philosophy** into a unified system that would permit no **doubt**. He traveled widely through western Europe until 1628, when he settled in Holland. During his twenty years there he wrote a series of books which reshaped philosophy forever. Indeed, Descartes is thought, rightly, to be the founder of modern philosophy. His main books were the *Discourse on Method* (1637), the *Meditations* (1641), and the *Principles of Philosophy* (1644).

Descartes' brilliance lay not so much in his conclusions, but in his method. See the entry on **Cartesian Method**. Descartes set out to shed himself of everything he had been told and everything he knew that was based on the testimony of others or of authority. The only exception he made to this rule (publicly at least) was his belief in **God** and the truths of the Catholic faith. Despite his intellectual sympathy with Copernicus and **Galileo**, Descartes was reluctant to state his sympathy openly. Debates have raged ever since as to the extent to which he was expressing a genuinely held belief or simply that he was cowed by the repressive policies of the church. Either way, with the exception of religion, Descartes shed all his beliefs down to what for him was the core, self-evident foundation; his famous "I think, therefore, I am," thought to be the best-known phrase in the history of philosophy. Any other belief could be wrong, or the creation of an evil genius. But not this one. This has to be true. And from that foundation, Descartes rebuilt a comprehensive philosophy.

Much of this philosophy has been shown to be wrong, especially his strict **dualism** between a body and **soul** and his related belief that animals, because they can't be Christians, cannot have souls or experience pain of any sort. But his method of doubt, of applying **skepticism** to all current knowledge, was an invaluable contribution to philosophy. And others, in times freer from clerical oppression, have been able to apply Descartes' method to religion as well, with devastating results for religious orthodoxy. It is also true that the *Discourse* and the *Meditations* are delightfully written and remain a pleasure to read to this day.

Despite his caution with regard to religion, Descartes attracted the suspicion of theologians, to the extent that in 1649 he accepted an offer from Queen Christiana of Sweden to move there and become her tutor. The cold and the 5 AM starts after a lifetime of long, slow mornings killed Descartes within months of arriving in Stockholm. Incredibly, the Roman Catholic Church placed the *Meditations* on the **Index of Forbidden Books**—in 1948.

DESERT, PRINCIPLE OF. A principle coined by **Ted Honderich**, which he has argued is the foundational principle of political conservatism. It revolves around the idea of getting one's just deserts. For Honderich, the conservative ideal is of an organic, naturally balanced and harmonious society, the balance and harmony of which derives from the hierarchy and order of the society. This order and hierarchy is preserved by the foundational principle that everyone has his or her place in society in accordance with their deserts. For some conservatives the order is religiously conceived, for others economically conceived, and for still others, a mixture of the two. Honderich argues that Liberalism is partly motivated by the Principle of Desert, but that the political left is, with some niggling qualifications, motivated by the **Principle of Equality**.

Other philosophers like **John Rawls** have written about the notion of getting our deserts, though not in reference to Honderich. Rawls more or less accepts Honderich's reading, and argues that nobody can claim to deserve the deserts they are born with. Nobody, in effect, gets *just* deserts. These are nothing more than accidents of natural endowment. It is on this basis that Rawls posits the **Difference Principle**. Critics of Honderich have portrayed his view of conservatism as little more than a caricature.

DESIGN, ARGUMENT TO. An argument that purports to explain the existence of **God** by virtue of the complexity and interdependence of nature. While being no more successful than the other traditional arguments for the existence of God, the design argument is the most popular and resilient of them. Usually known as the argument *from* design, the English philosopher **Antony Flew** has noted that the argument is more accurately called the argument *to* design, because it is the purpose of the argument to establish a designer who created the design. An argument *from* design begins by assuming that the design is there.

The argument to design can be traced back to Diogenes of Appolonia in the fifth century BCE, and then in his contemporary Xenophon's work *Memorabilia*. The argument resurfaced periodically for the next two thousand years, but it only began to take its modern shape in the 1690s, in the wake of the scientific revolution which tended to see the universe as a gigantic mechanism operating according to natural laws, and which required, so it was thought, a lawmaker. The classic formulations of the argument to design from this time come from John Ray's *The Wisdom of God Manifested in the Works of the Creation*

(1691) and Richard Bentley's 1692 Boyle Lectures, *A Confutation of Atheism*.

The argument enjoyed widespread support for a century and a half, notwithstanding problems it was never able to resolve. The argument to design has never been able to show that a single god, let alone the Christian god, is responsible for the design. For a long time, this was not considered a serious problem, because it was simply assumed that proving a god meant proving the Christian god. Broader perspectives and greater appreciation of systems of belief other than Christianity have made this supposition untenable to all but fundamentalists. Just as damaging in the long run was that the argument to design limited their notion of God to what was understandable in terms of the science of the day. As science that needed a watchmaker to set it all in motion has been replaced, so has the watchmaker god of the design argument become redundant.

Most of these arguments came originally from **David Hume** in *Dialogues Concerning Natural Religion* (1777). Together they amount to a comprehensive demolition of the design argument, although it took a while before the force of Hume's arguments were truly felt. And Antony Flew has continued Hume's critique when he asked why would a Creator bother to design something, when he could simply create it?

Despite the bankruptcy of the design argument as a serious proof of God's existence, it is still resurrected every now and then and flogged back into service. Most recently, **intelligent design** enthusiasts have argued that there is evidence of divine fine-tuning of the universe to support life. This is also a version of the **Anthropic Principle**.

Further reading: Antony Flew, *Atheistic Humanism*; Daniel C. Dennett, *Darwin's Dangerous Idea*; and Taner Edis, *The Ghost in the Universe*.

DETERMINISM. The view that the way things are now has a significant bearing on how things will turn out in the future. Put differently, determinism is the doctrine that our choices and actions are the effect of a succession of causal sequences. It does not mean that our actions were written in some cosmic logbook before we were born. It means that each of our actions is an effect of a series of actions or properties, which themselves are an effect. Even an apparently random action is made within a range of options limited to the individual exercising them. In this way, we are quite capable of free actions, it is just that no action is completely free, in the same way that no action is completely determined. Every free action has an element of causation behind it. See the entry on **free will**.

Determinism has a long history. It found an early voice in the Indian **Ajivikas**, who argued for the existence of *niyati*. And in Greece, determinism was articulated in various ways by the **atomists** and **Stoics**. Until the twentieth century, and in particular the work of **Ted Honderich**, most versions of determinism made stronger claims about our current actions being effects of previous actions or forces than is now the case. Most contemporary determinists are wary of that claim.

Further reading: Ted Honderich, *How Free Are You?*

DEUBLER, KONRAD (1814–1884). Dubbed the "peasant-philosopher," Deubler matured from a conventional orthodoxy to materialism and rationalism via the thorough study of most of the eminent scholars of his day, in particular **Ludwig Feuerbach, David Strauss**, and **Ernst Haeckel**.

Born in humble circumstances in the village of Goisern in Upper Austria, Deubler worked his way from a laborer to burgermeister of the village and an amateur naturalist and correspondent to a wide range of thinkers in the German-speaking world. Deubler was self-taught to the point of never having actually been taught to write. It was not Deubler's scholarship that endeared him to everyone, but his genial personality and genuine love of learning. Carl Vogt (1817–1895), the prominent Swiss scientist, told

Deubler that knowing him meant more to him than ten diplomas of learned societies. These traits resulted in problems with the Roman Catholic authorities of the Austrian empire, and between 1853 and 1857, Deubler was imprisoned for **blasphemy**.

Deubler served as a rallying point in a country which at the time had no organized **freethought** movement. Austria now has the Freidenkenbund, which organizes occasional Konrad Deubler symposia to discuss important issues of the day.

DEV SAMAJ. A society founded in India in February 1887 for the purpose of moral regeneration. Dev Samaj can be translated to mean "Divine Society" or "Society of Excellence." Dev Samaj was founded by Satya Nand Agnihotri (1850–1929), who was born near Kanpur in Uttar Pradesh. While studying in Lahore, Agnihotri joined the Brahmo Samoj, an influential movement seeking the reform of Hinduism. Under the influence of this organization, Agnihotri formed the Dev Samaj, but by 1895, having read the works of **Herbert Spencer**, Spencer's American popularizer John Fiske (1842–1901), and Henry Drummond, Agnihotri gave up theism altogether.

Now an atheist organization, Dev Samaj set for itself the task of developing character by the disinterested service through secular moral education, concentrating its work in the villages. Agnihotri was subjected to ostracism, harassment, and violence for his views and soon stopped speaking in public. This role was taken up by his son Har Narayan Agnihotri (1871–1926), who also edited its journal, called *Science-Grounded Religion* from its foundation in 1905 until 1923. This magazine, the oldest atheistic journal in India, is still in print. There are four other journals, one each in Hindi, Urdu, Punjabi, and Sindhi. Dev Samaj has also published a very large amount of literature, again in a variety of languages. Satya Nand Agnihotri has gone through a process of deification since his death, with more recent Dev Samaj thinkers arguing that the Devatma

(Agnihotri's honorific title) is the embodiment of truth and goodness and can be meditated upon, even worshiped.

Among its other activities, Dev Samaj runs twenty-seven educational institutions in Punjab, Haryana, and Delhi, catering for more than twenty-two thousand students. Dev Samaj emphasizes its role in the education of females. It teaches a humanistic morality of self-reliance, abstinence from any stimulants or narcotics, and altruistic work for others.

Further reading: Finngeir Hiorth, *Atheism in India*.

DEWEY, JOHN (1859–1952). American philosopher, educationist, and humanist. Born in Burlington, Vermont, Dewey began his adult life as a secondary school teacher before securing university positions. During his long career Dewey worked at Johns Hopkins, Michigan, Chicago, and finally Columbia, where he was professor of philosophy from 1904 until his retirement in 1930.

Dewey was heavily influenced by **William James** and Charles Peirce (1839–1914) and continued on in the tradition of **pragmatism** they had pioneered. Dewey is credited with synthesizing the pragmatism of his predecessors into a coherent whole, especially in *Reconstruction in Philosophy* (1920). In *Experience and Nature* (1929) Dewey sought to reconcile **naturalism** and **science** with our most "cherished values, provided they are critically clarified and reinforced." He argued that experience is the only way we can discover and understand nature.

Dewey's legacy is mixed. He was wrong in arguing that **human nature** is as plastic as he thought it to be. He underestimated the role of genetic hardwiring, attributing almost all variations in human nature to nurture over nature. But while Dewey was a consistent critic of **idealism**, he retained a debt to G. W. F. Hegel (1770–1831), which was seen in his conception of **evolution**. He was also content, in *A Common Faith* (1934) to resort to speaking of **humanism** in religious language, which was a serious mistake. Dewey was too complacent in seeing the old religious forms dying out and waiting simply to be given new meaning. But **religion** has not died out. On the contrary, religion is far stronger (though in a brittle sort of way) than it was in Dewey's day. Dewey's successor, **Paul Kurtz**, has clarified this confusion by taking humanism in a secular direction.

A more helpful legacy was Dewey's enthusiasm for **democracy**, which he spoke of in terms of **social intelligence**. The two best books on this theme are *Democracy and Education* (1916) and *Freedom and Culture* (1939). The notion of social intelligence has been described as Dewey's most important contribution to philosophy. Dewey also had an appreciation of the tragic sense of life, and the artificiality of many distinctions others see as set in concrete. Dewey has been tremendously influential in the United States, but is not as highly regarded outside that country.

Further reading: Alan Ryan, *John Dewey and the High Tide of American Liberalism*.

DHARMA. Probably the central notion of the two **Asian Traditions** known as Hinduism and Buddhism. The Sanskrit spelling used by Hindus is *dharma*, while the Pali spelling preferred by Buddhists renders the word *dhamma*. Hindu and Buddhist philosophers have argued over the nature of dharma for many centuries. The concept is used in different ways in the **Veda**, which changes once again in later Hindu writings.

Perhaps the least inaccurate way to understand dharma is as the norm, the way things are, and around which our duty should be directed toward. Other ideas that encapsulate important parts of dharma are the moral law, or principle. Dharma is about **free will** and **determinism** at the same time. Dharma is about choice as much as it's about performing the duties destiny has determined we must do.

DHIMMITUDE. A recently coined word that refers to the discriminatory attitude among majority Muslims to the treatment of non-Muslims in their midst. The word derives from *ahlu 'z-Zimmah*, a non-Muslim subject in a Muslim society. The *ahlu 'z-Zimmah* were in most cases Jews, Christians, Zoroastrians, and Sabeans. In many respects Islam has a much better record of dealing with minority religions than Christianity—although both have a dreadful record with respect to people who are not religious. Their incomprehension of a nonreligious way of life leads to a drastic need to persecute.

The word was coined in 1983 by an Egyptian-born journalist and writer who works under the pseudonym Bat Ye'or. In 1957 Ye'or arrived in Britain a stateless refugee, having had her Egyptian citizenship revoked by the Nasser regime. From exile, Ye'or has kept up a steady stream of writing with the overall purpose of reversing the growing trend toward **fundamentalism** and intolerance among Muslims.

Further reading: Bat Ye'or, *Islam and Dhimmitude*.

DIAGORAS OF MELOS (fifth century BCE). **Pre-Socratic** Greek poet and thinker, a disciple of **Democritus**, and an atheist. Originally an exceptionally pious man, Diagoras was shocked into **unbelief** when he was deceived by a man who had violated a sworn oath and who had suffered no divine punishment as a result. He was later persecuted by the authorities for his **atheism**. Diagoras outraged pious opinion when he broke up a wooden idol of Herakles and used it for firewood, declaring that Herakles' thirteenth labor would be to cook his turnips. He was also accused of divulging the Eleusinian mysteries. A reward of a silver talent was offered for Diagoras' corpse and two talents for taking him alive. Despite these inducements, Diagoras escaped capture and became one of the proverbial atheists of the ancient world. None of his works survive.

DIALOGUE. The process whereby spokespeople from different or even opposing belief systems come together to gain a better understanding of each other's position. The aim, in principle at any rate, is not to convert each other, but simply to understand. Dialogue is a popular idea among various systems of belief. So far, freethinkers have largely been excluded from this process. See the entry on **talking past one another**.

DIDEROT, DENIS (1713–1784). French essayist, critic, encyclopedist, and atheist. Denis Diderot was born into a Catholic family but his early attempts at piety were quickly dispelled by the intellectual clumsiness of the Catholic priests who educated him. Diderot called Christianity "the Great Prejudice."

The overriding fact about Diderot is his obvious and infectious joy to be alive. His eclectic mind was stimulated by a wide range of things. He wrote widely on **philosophy**, literature, art, history, and fiction, although one of his first books was an outrageously salacious novel called *Indiscreet Jewels* (1748). Even here, as well as in his sense of **fun**, Diderot is making some serious points about religious hypocrisy regarding **sex**. Among the better known of his works include *Rameau's Nephew* (1761, with later additions) *d'Alembert's Dream* (1769), *Jacques the Fatalist* (1792), and fiction like *The Nun* (1796). All of these titles are available in modern translations.

But Diderot's principal intellectual achievement was to see through to completion the seventeen-volume *Encyclopedia*, often in the face of serious church and political opposition. Diderot's legacy has been taken up by the Diderot Project, a philanthropic organization in Europe looking to extend communications between schoolchildren in Denmark, Italy, and Britain. Diderot is the subject of Malcolm Bradbury's wonderful novel *To The Hermitage* (2000). See the entry on *sapere aude*.

Further reading: P. N. Furbank, *Diderot*.

DIFFÉRANCE. A word popular among postmodernists and psychoanalysts, although its meaning remains unclear. According to

Elizabeth Grosz, one of its more prominent proponents, différance "is *both* as well as *neither* identity and difference.... The term thus refers to a difference within difference itself, a difference which distinguishes difference from distinction, a different difference from that which opposes identity." Well, that's cleared up! See the entries on **glossogonous word-salad** and the **Incontinence Principle of Continental Philosophy**.

DIFFERENCE PRINCIPLE, THE. Principle coined by **John Rawls** which states that inequalities of income and wealth should be worked out in such a way as to:

- be to the greatest advantage of the least advantaged; and
- ensure genuine equality of opportunity to occupy public offices and positions.

The difference principle accepts only those inequalities that work in favor of the least advantaged members of society. This principle is fundamental to his conception of **justice as fairness**.

The difference principle has a large number of critics, and not exclusively from the political right. For example, some progressives have argued that it would only set into concrete a large class of dependents and that it would serve as a drag on the economy and thus work against the interests of the least advantaged. More predictably, Rawls's opponents on the right have responded by complaining of the stifling of freedom by a **nanny state**.

Further reading: John Rawls, *Political Liberalism*.

DIFFERENTIAL ASSOCIATION. A general theory of criminal behavior devised by the American sociologist Edwin Sutherland (1883–1950) in the 1930s, and developed over the rest of his career. The main principles of differential association are:

(1) Criminal behavior is learned by interaction with others; it is not an inborn disposition;
(2) Learning takes place within intimate personal groups;
(3) One engages in crime because of an excess of understandings favorable to lawbreaking over those unfavorable to lawbreaking. This is the process of differential association;
(4) Differential association varies in place, intensity, and regularity; and
(5) While criminal behavior is an expression of general needs and values, it is not explained by those needs and values, because noncriminal behavior also emanates from those same needs and values.

What this means is that people engage in criminal activity because the cultural environment they are in feeds them more understandings favorable to crime than unfavorable. Differential association helps us understand the essentially similar motives and mechanics of blue- and **white-collar crime**.

Critics of differential association argue that this method works well as a model for understanding criminal subcultures (be they motorcycle gangs or corporate boardrooms) but doesn't explain the motivations of isolated crimes such as homicide. And moral conservatives are critical of the liberal implications in differential association, preferring to cast the criminal as evil and an aberration, fit for society's vengeance. The first criticism is partially valid, but the second one only reveals a preference for a punitive mentality.

Further reading: a fuller version of the principles of differential association can be found at http://www.indiana.edu/~theory/Kip/Edwin.htm.

DIONYSIANISM. The ecstatic state of instinctual reality as outlined by **Friedrich Nietzsche**. Dionysianism is named after Dionysus, the Greek god of wine. The Roman name for Dionysus is Bacchus, from which comes the word "bacchanalian," as in bacchanalian revels. This refers to the ecstatic and orgiastic rituals common in many primitive religions. See the entry on **dying and resurrected gods**.

From this heritage, Nietzsche took up Dionysianism and employed it in a slightly different way. He contrasted Dionysianism with Apollonianism, a more rational principle, which looks at things as they are, like sculpture. Dionysianism, by contrast, is about our most basic instincts. For Nietzsche, music is the ultimate form of Dionysianism. The Dionysian act is authentic, spontaneous, and involves overcoming any formality and reserve. It is the effective antidote to the dreaded **herd instinct**.

Nietzsche wrote about Dionysianism in his early work *The Birth of Tragedy* (1872), but spoke less in these terms when he devised the notion of the **Overman**, which in turn was superseded by his idea of the **will to power**. Nietzsche's concept of Dionysianism was very influential among twentieth-century artists, notably the Abstract Expressionists in America in the 1940s. A rock concert is often given as a prime example of a dionysian event, in contrast, say, to visiting an art gallery. For a more sober version of this distinction, see the entry on **modes of religious transmission**.

One of the most telling comments against Dionysianism came from **Bertrand Russell**, who said that while tigers are more beautiful than sheep, we nonetheless prefer them behind bars.

Further reading: Friedrich Nietzsche, *The Birth of Tragedy*; and Bertrand Russell, *A History of Western Philosophy*.

DIONYSUS THE AREOPAGITE. The name, mentioned in Acts 17:34, of someone who was apparently converted by St. Paul in Athens. Absolutely nothing is known about him other than his name. More interesting is the posthumous career "Dionysus the Areopagite" has enjoyed. Several cases of **pious fraud** have been attached to his name, the most significant of which was a fifth or sixth century CE series of theological works that

were attributed to him. In fact, these works were written by someone very familiar with the pagan theologian Proclus (410–485 CE), whose work they closely resemble.

The fraudulent attribution of these pagan-inspired works to Dionysus gave them a great deal of authority they would not otherwise have enjoyed. They were translated by John Scotus Erigena (810–877 CE, approx.), closely studied by St. Thomas Aquinas (1225–1274), and used by Dante (1265–1321) and Milton (1608–1674) in their various works. All this important Christian thought and theology, all derived from a pagan! Since the forgery has been exposed, the theological works are described as being the work of "Pseudo-Dionysus." One of the first people to challenge the attribution of the works to the original Dionysus the Areopagite was **Erasmus**, the great humanist of the Northern Renaissance.

DISAGREEABILITY PRINCIPLE, THE. A principle noted first by the American philosopher Matthew Stewart. The Disagreeability Principle states that a philosopher will remain prominent so long as he can be plausibly disagreed with. **Plato** and **Descartes** would perhaps be clearest examples of the truth of this maxim. This ubiquitous law has particular application to philosophy, but applies to other disciplines as well.

Further reading: Matthew Stewart, *The Truth About Everything*.

DISINTERESTEDNESS. An undervalued quality. Being disinterested is not the same as being uninterested, which means being unconcerned about the outcome of something. Being disinterested, however, implies having a commitment to honest study and an acceptance of the **truth**, without regard to one's own views, no matter how strongly held they might be. In this way, the disinterested scholar will search assiduously for all relevant information on the issue at question, including—*especially*—the information known to hold conclusions contrary to one's own. Disinterestedness lies at the heart of the **scientific method**.

Some **postmodernist** scholars have sneered at the notion of disinterestedness, saying that it is impossible. But it is a long step from acknowledging that something is difficult to dismissing it as worthless. Being disinterested does not mean not caring what the outcome of one's study is. It means being able to put aside one's preferences in the interests of gaining the most **objective** knowledge possible. Disinterestedness is an important component of the **cosmic perspective**.

For the nonspecialist looking for reliable information among all the "experts," one of the surest litmus tests they can apply is how disinterested they prove to be. Has the expert sought information from a wide variety of sources, including the unfriendly ones? Has the expert summarized the views of opponents reasonably, or are they a caricature? Are inconvenient facts genuinely repudiated or are they simply explained away? These are **judgment** calls the nonspecialist can make when choosing which expert to consult.

DISSEMINATED PRIMATEMAIA. A term used by the scientist James Lovelock, inventor of the **Gaia theory**, which means literally a plague of people. This plague of people poses a unique level of environmental stress on the entire planet. Lovelock outlines four possible outcomes of the disseminated primatemaia:

- destruction of invading species;
- chronic infection of all species;
- destruction of the host ecosystems; or
- mutually beneficial relationship between host and invading species.

The last outcome is by far the least likely on the strength of the current **evidence**, where many species are being destroyed each year. The most likely outcome is the first one: destruction of the invading species—*Homo sapiens*. While the planet can survive without *Homo sapiens*, the opposite is not the case.

While not using the term, the issues of disseminated primatemaia are discussed in **Margaret Atwood**'s powerful novel *Oryx and Crake* (2003).

DIVERSITY. A highly valuable condition, at all levels. On one level, we speak of biodiversity, which refers to the abundant range of plants and animals that the planet Earth has been home to. There are three different types of diversity:

- *Alpha diversity*, or the number of species in any ecosystem;
- *Beta diversity*, or the range of species in contrasting **ecoregions**; and
- *Gamma diversity*, or the range of species in similar though separate ecoregions.

Biodiversity is essential for so many reasons, but the most important is the interdependence of all species in the complex fabric of life on our planet. The **extinction** of any one species threatens an ever-widening circle of related species. Indifference to the extinction of species apparently unrelated to us is the worst form of **anthropocentric conceit**.

Some ecoregions are home to particularly abundant biodiversity—tropical rainforests in particular. More than half the known species on the planet live in tropical rain forests, so destruction of those ecoregions has a disproportionate impact on planetary biodiversity. This is but one more reason why we can no longer think on anything less than a planetary scale, and that solutions on anything less than a planetary scale are almost bound to fail.

When speaking sociologically, the value of diversity is no less. Being exposed to people from different cultures with different values and outlooks on the world to ourselves can only be a learning experience. It doesn't mean we have to blandly accept everything so as not to appear "prejudiced." But it does mean that we need to articulate our position more clearly and adapt it to take on those new views or outlooks we consider beneficial.

Every culture has its strong and weak points, so the broader our exposure to them, the broader our own experience will be. In the long run, cultural diversity can mean we learn to appreciate the culture of others while also confirming the value of our own.

DIVINE COMMAND THEORY. A venerable piece of religious apologetic, which holds that moral laws derive from the divine commands of **God**, because goodness is an essential property of God. This theory is only relevant to **monotheist** religions, where a central god figure requires our obedience.

The most obvious flaw in the Divine Command Theory is the existence of extensive and intellectually credible evidence against the existence of the God that is supposed to issue these divine commands. There is also the problem of different monotheist religions issuing different and inconsistent divine commands. A less well-understood objection is that Divine Command Theory leads to a complete collapse of any objective morality (see **seeds of moral skepticism in Christian ethics**). There is also the problem, going all the way back to **Plato**'s *Euthyphro*, of the Divine Command Theory having morally outrageous consequences. Is killing innocent people right because God commands it, as is claimed by some contemporary terrorists? Or does God condemn terrorism against the innocent because it is wrong? If the latter is true, then terrorism is wrong independently of God's commands, so we're no further ahead.

The assumption behind the theory is that for universal moral standards to be possible, then we must have a God. In fact, this is not necessary at all. See the entries on **moral truisms shared by us all**, **objective morality**, and **Euthyphro dilemma**.

DIVINE HIDDENNESS. An argument for **atheism** put forward most recently by the philosopher J. L. Schellenberg. For centuries people have wondered why, if there is a **God**, he should remain so hidden from us. The main answer offered by apologists is that God is hidden from us for some sort of reason, usually so that we may have **free will**, or that it develops **character**. Others simply resort to abuse, saying that God is available to those with "open hearts." Schellenberg is particularly scornful of this *ad hominen* argument. There are many people of good faith and intellectual honesty who have found no evidence for any sort of God. So the problem is not so much with the people, but with the idea of God.

Schellenberg argues that for God to remain so obstinately hidden is incompatible with being all good and loving. Would it not have been more loving of God, for example, to intervene during the Holocaust, or the Black Death, rather than remain distant and apparently impervious to all that suffering? The more reasonable answer for the hiddenness of God is that there is no God and that his so-called hiddenness is actually evidence for atheism. The divine hiddenness argument is closely related to the **problem of evil**. Also, see the entries on **nonbelief, argument from**, and **beyond human understanding**.

Further reading: J. L. Schellenberg, *Divine Hiddenness and Human Reason.*

DNA. Stands for deoxyribonucleic acid and is, with RNA, the most important nucleic acid which constitutes the fundamental building blocks of life. These acids are constructed in an orderly array of blocks that constitute DNA. Deoxyribose is the core acid of the DNA range, which is composed of four nucleotides: adenine (A), thymine (T), guanine (G), and cytosine (C). The order in which these nucleotides are arranged determines the genetic makeup of the individual. DNA duplicates itself by unzipping its double helix structure, leaving two halves, which are then renewed, creating two exactly replicated chains of genetic information.

DNA was discovered in 1869 by the Swiss biochemist Friedrich Miescher (1844–1895), although no particular significance was accorded to it until 1944 when the Canadian bacteriologist Oswald Avery

(1877–1955) discovered that DNA was the vehicle by which genetic information is carried. It then became very important to learn more about DNA, particularly how it was structured. The race to discover the structure of DNA was won by James Watson and Francis Crick (1916–2004), although **Rosalind Franklin** had a central role in the work leading to the discovery. See the entry on the **Human Genome Project**.

DOCTRINE OF THE MEAN (ARIS-TOTLE). A very influential theory of ethics conceived by **Aristotle**, which advocated seeking, through self-knowledge, the mean point between extremes of behavior. In the pursuit of pleasure, for instance, Aristotle counseled temperance as the mean point between licentiousness and asceticism. The Doctrine of the Mean does not insist on unthinkingly taking the middle ground between too much and too little. Rather, it counsels taking the right amount for you, hence the self-knowledge. This relativizes the doctrine, as what is the right amount for one person will not be so for another. That middle ground between the opposite vices was what Aristotle called *sophrosyne*.

In advancing the Doctrine of the Mean, Aristotle was reacting against **command moralities**, in particular the prescriptive moralizing of **Plato**. It's not simply a question of looking up which command applies to the situation, but applying sound judgments, using reason, and showing **character**. The term "golden mean" was not Aristotle's own, but was employed by later Aristotelian publicists.

The doctrine has relevance for us today when we want to determine priorities for ourselves. For instance, the **Epicureans** counseled retreating to the garden and taking little part in public affairs. Others, like the **Stoics** and Confucians had a higher opinion of being actively involved in society. It is for each of us to determine the right balance for ourselves between civic duty and private peace of mind. **Democritus** actually anticipated Aristotle when he said the aim of life was to achieve equanimity, by which he meant a state of balance where all of our desires and pleasures are had only to the degree they are beneficial, and no more. And recently, the Canadian humanist thinker John Ralston Saul has written a book called *Equilibrium*, which can be put in the same broad tradition.

Further reading: Aristotle, *Ethics*.

DOCTRINE OF THE MEAN (KONG-FUZI). Translation of a central tenet of Confucian ethics. The ideal person will live in a way that conforms with the way of heaven. But this is emphatically not some **command morality**. Heaven, as in **Taoism** and Chinese Buddhism, has no **dualist** implications of being some place apart from humankind. In modern parlance, the **New Age** notions of cosmic harmony come closest to portraying what is meant.

The ideal person will cultivate goodness in the manner outlined in *The Great Learning*, and in doing so, will realize his own best nature, which is the same as realizing the inseparability of heaven and man. The Doctrine of the Mean boils down to the idea of doing things "just right," and "just right" is understood as being in harmony with the **Tao**.

DOGMA OF THE GHOST IN THE MACHINE. A term coined by British philosopher Gilbert Ryle (1900–1976) in his major work, *The Concept of Mind* (1949). The main purpose of the dogma of the ghost in the machine, Ryle argued, was to buttress the "polar opposition" between the **mind** and the body. This was not just a mistake, but a **category mistake**. The dogma of the ghost in the machine goes at least back to **René Descartes'** notion that mind and matter are substantially different entities, obeying different laws, but being held together by the pineal gland. Scientific advances have shown Ryle to be correct.

More recently, Antonio Damasio has referred to the same problem, using the term *Descartes' error*, also the title of a well-received book. There is not an independent entity called "mind," rather, "mind" is just a convenient term for our brain and its productions. And more recently still, Taner Edis wrote a book called *The Ghost in the Universe* (2002), which took Ryle's concept and applied it to notions of **God**. If the polar opposition between mind and body is a category mistake, Edis shows, then so is the polar opposition between natural and supernatural. *The Ghost in the Universe* was awarded the **Morris D. Forkosh Book Award** in 2003.

Further reading: Gilbert Ryle, *The Concept of Mind*; and Taner Edis, *The Ghost in the Universe*.

DOGMATISM. The state whereby a person holds a view without regard to valid **evidence** against it, and who insists nonetheless that his views are superior to any others. Dogmatism is the opposite of **fallibilism**. The fallibilist is prepared to recognize that one's views could be incomplete or even wrong. The dogmatist, by contrast, has no such **doubts**, and is certain that one's views are absolutely correct. Dogmatism is found among all types of people and all strands of belief, but it is most liable to be found among people who ascribe to absolutist beliefs and **command moralities**. See the entry on **certainty**.

DOMINIONISM. A term given to the fundamentalist program in the United States since the early 1980s. The word is taken from the Bible and reapplied in a loose sense to suggest that **God** gave man dominion over the earth, but it has now been lost though all the liberal legislation that inhibits our freedoms. It also refers to the need fundamentalists feel to take back control over the political machine from the wicked **secular humanists**.

The dominionist program is to reverse the secular and liberal trends in the United States that have taken place since the New Deal of the 1930s, in particular the *Roe v. Wade* decision in 1973 that legalized **abortion**. Other important items on the dominionist agenda include dismantling the **welfare state**, particularly with regard to public schools where

evolution is taught, and reversing liberal legislation on a variety of issues, such as **marriage** and homosexuality. See the entry on **incrementalism**.

DONATION OF CONSTANTINE, THE. One of the more audacious **pious frauds** ever perpetrated. The donation purported to be a gift from Roman emperor **Constantine** to Pope Sylvester I (314–335 CE) and his successors in perpetuity of the city of Rome, the papal states, and indeed all of Western Europe. The document even has Constantine offering Sylvester the crown of the Western Empire, which the pious Sylvester refuses, although he agrees to the transfer of imperial government from Rome to Constantinople, which effectively left the church as the most powerful body still standing in the west.

The donation was in fact forged in the eighth century by a papacy under severe pressure from the Lombards and in desperate need of military assistance against them. The donation was shown by Hadrian I (reigned 772–795 CE) to the Frankish emperor Charlemagne in an attempt to preserve the papacy's independence from and dominance over, secular authorities. In the fifteenth century the humanist scholar **Lorenzo Valla** exposed the donation of Constantine as a forgery.

DOUBLE EFFECT, PRINCIPLE OF. Supporters of **command moralities** have long had a major difficulty with the consequences of obliquely intended actions. To give a simple example, there is the commandment, "Thou shalt not kill." But what is the status of commandments such as this when confronted with a mass murderer who one is able to kill in order to save the lives of many innocent people? Here, the individual is faced between the moral charge to defend the lives of innocent people and the moral proscription against killing. This is the Principle of Double Effect. Two absolutist commandments, both laudable on their own, present a lethal moral dilemma when brought up against each other, as in the situation outlined here.

With the Principle of Double Effect, religious apologists have tried to accommodate situations such as this while retaining the absolute authority of the commandments. Thomas Aquinas (1225–1274) made a serious attempt to allow for unusual situations while preserving the absolute commandments. He would allow for the motive of rescuing the innocent to trump, as it were, the cost of doing so, namely killing a person. Various popes employed variations of the Principle of Double Effect when preaching Crusades against the Muslims. Yes, killing is wrong, they would concede, but this is killing heathens in the name of Christ, and therefore permissible.

What the Principle of Double Effect actually does is to expose the fundamental weakness of command moralities. However satisfying it may be to have absolutist commandments, there will always be valid exceptions to them, where good people end up committing supposedly irretrievably wicked actions. Religious apologists like to scoff at situation ethics, claiming they lack the moral force of command moralities. But situation ethics recognizes the complexity and conflicts of interest which many moral decisions involve, and which the simplistic nature of command moralities can make no sensible provision for. The fact remains that the Principle of Double Effect is nothing more than an attempt to provide command moralities with a fig leaf of respectability. And, paradoxically, that fig leaf is derived from the unlikely source of situation ethics.

Further reading: J. L. Mackie, *Ethics: Inventing Right and Wrong*.

DOUBT. One of the important faultlines between religious believers and **freethinkers**. For people without **religion**, doubt is a positive quality, signifying a refusal to succumb to **dogmatism**. It means not holding one's beliefs with unhelpful **certainty**, but with an appropriate level of tentativeness. Healthy doses of doubt also act as stimulants to further learning. **Giordano Bruno** said, "He who desires to philosophize must first of all doubt all things." **René Descartes** carried this insight on and made it the foundation stone of his philosophy. The American lawyer **Clarence Darrow** went one step further when he said, "I have always felt that doubt was the beginning of wisdom, and fear of **God** was the end of wisdom."

Attitudes toward doubt among **monotheistic** religions, however, are often less positive. This hostility was clearly expressed by St. Augustine (354–430 CE), who argued that now that we have the **knowledge** of the Savior, there is no need for doubt. Indeed, doubt becomes a **sin** in the face of this precious knowledge. This attitude is seen clearly among many fundamentalists who say they *know* they are right. The danger of this attitude is that those who disagree with them can be seen not simply as *wrong* but as *wicked*. Once that link has been made, intolerance and even persecution quickly become a religious duty. **Winwood Reade** understood this when he said, "Without doubt there can be no tolerance, and the history of tolerance is the history of doubt."

Further reading: Jennifer Michael Hecht, *Doubt: A History*.

DRAVIDAR KAZHAGAM. The South Indian reform movement that was founded on August 27, 1944, in Tamil Nadu out of the ruins of the Justice Party. "Dravidar Kazhagam" simply means Dravidian Association, Dravidians being the aboriginal people of South India. The Dravidar Kazhagam was more anti-British than the Justice Party. In fact, **Periyar**, the founder and chief inspiration of the movement, was, at heart, a separatist. The organization saw itself as a small atheist and rationalist organization in a large, superstitious world. Its focus has been to engender self-respect among Dravidian people, who are so often at the bottom of the social and cultural ladder in India. Periyar was opposed to Brahminism, and this opposition often took on the look of being opposed to Brahmins. Atheism and rationalism are valued as means by which non-Brahmins,

Dravidians in particular, can have self-respect in the face of the immovable caste barriers. The Dravidar Kazhagam deeply admires the work of **Dr. Ambedkar**. See the entry on **dalits**.

Periyar led the Dravidar Kazhagam until his death in 1973. He was succeeded by his second wife, Maniyammai. On her death in 1978, she was succeeded by Thiru K. Veeramani (1933–), a lawyer from the town of Cuddalore. Veeramani gave up a promising legal career to work voluntarily for the Dravidar Kazhagam, and has been imprisoned on several occasions as a result of various campaigns the organization has run.

The Dravidar Kazhagam runs many educational and social institutions. Most of these have been developed under the leadership of Veeramani. Unlike religious organizations, the Dravidar Kazhagam's institutions are almost entirely self-funded. The Dravidar Kazhagam also runs its own daily newspaper, *Viduthalai* (Freedom), and a semimonthly magazine called *Ummai* (Truth) and even an English language journal, *The Modern Rationalist*. All three publications are edited by Veeramani.

A significant feature of the Dravidar Kazhagam is the promotion of self-respect marriages. The marriages are performed without the presence of a priest, can be intercaste, and assume the equality of male and female. These have been legal marriages since 1967 and about fifty thousand such marriages are carried out each year. Going back to Periyar's time, the Dravidar Kazhagam has condemned the exploitation of women.

In 1949 C. N. Annadurai, a longtime follower of Periyar, broke away from the Dravidar Kazhagam and founded the Dravida Munnetra Kazhagam (DMK). Annadurai complained that Periyar ran the organization too dictatorially and that his anti-Brahminism was too negatively charged. The DMK embarked on the long task of making itself electable, during which time it slowly abandoned its explicit support for atheism. The DMK has gone on to have an interesting career in the politics of Tamil Nadu.

Further reading: Finngeir Hiorth, *Atheism in India*.

DRUYAN, ANN (1949–). American popularizer of science, novelist, and activist. Born in Queens, New York, and attended New York University between 1967 and 1971, but left without completing her degree to pursue a career as a novelist. A novel duly appeared: *A Famous Broken Heart* (1977) a modern-day reworking of a theme similar to *Alice's Adventures in Wonderland*. The year before, Druyan married **Carl Sagan**, becoming his third wife.

Druyan has been a political activist and an insider. As a young woman, she was active in protesting the American nuclear program in Nevada and monitored underground testing. In 1988 she began a ten-year stint as secretary of the Federation of American Scientists. Druyan also worked as creative director of NASA's Voyager Interstellar Message Project. She is also a director of the Children's Health Fund, which provides mobile pediatric care to underprivileged American children.

Druyan worked beside her husband on several very important projects. Most significantly, she cowrote with him the successful television series *Cosmos*, which is thought to have had 400 million viewers in sixty countries. Druyan also cowrote with him *Comet* (1985), *Shadows of Forgotten Ancestors* (1992), and was instrumental in creating the Warner Brothers film *Contact*, based on Sagan's novel of that title. Druyan wrote the epilogue for Sagan's last book ***Billions and Billions***, which was published posthumously in 1997.

Druyan is the founder-president of the Carl Sagan Foundation and chief executive officer of Cosmos Studios, which produces science-based entertainment for all media.

DUALISM. An ancient, and entirely incorrect, theory of **human nature** which posits a **soul**, or spirit, of life essence that can be separated from the body that houses it and yet retain its essential characteristics. Indeed, most varieties of dualism require that the essential nature of the soul, spirit, or life essence can only manifest itself when it is apart from the body. How this is done forms the basis of dualistic thought. Dualism has three components:

- the nature of the soul or spirit;
- the nature of the union between the body and soul or spirit; and
- the nature of the causal connections between the body and soul or spirit.

The second and third problems follow from the first problem. The tragedy of the dualistic view of the world is that it expresses a preference for a nonmaterial fantasy at the expense of the understanding how the world, and people, actually work. The denigration of the body and of material objects in general led to a sidelining of **science** and naturalistic inquiry, which in turn gave birth to the conditions of **superstition** and ignorance prevalent in the **Dark Ages** and other periods of intellectual poverty and oppression.

DUMBING DOWN. The controversial idea that society is getting progressively more stupid with each passing generation. There is a great deal of anecdotal evidence to support this thesis. Reading seems to be on the decline around the world as more people sit in front of the television. And universities around the Western world have noted the deterioration in writing skills among students over the past thirty years. And it seems that each generation is becoming more monosyllabic than the last.

But changing patterns of language use do not necessarily imply lower intellect. And while the decline in reading is a painful fact for those brought up with books, it does not inevitably mean that people are becoming more stupid. It may mean that they are seeking their information from other sources, most notably of course, the Internet.

It is also true that each generation has lamented the grave stupidity of those younger

than themselves. The current generation doing the lamenting would be the laughing stock of the Elizabethans of **Shakespeare**'s generation, whose standards of spoken English were far superior to all but the most erudite person today. And Victorian audiences had attention spans at public events that few today could hope to emulate.

It is also true that young people today have vastly expanded access to knowledge that even the wealthiest could only have dreamt of a few centuries ago. A person of mediocre ability today has a range of skills and knowledge inconceivable to the average youth of previous centuries.

But it would be a mistake to be complacent. Lack of curiosity and the readiness to accept **command moralities** or **pseudoscientific** explanations for complex events must always be challenged. And the temptation to accept easy slogans over hard thinking, or conspiracy theories over recognition of life's complexity, must be avoided. Most claims to **certainty** on an issue can usually be taken as evidence of serious dumbing down. On the other hand, contributing constructively to the **social intelligence** is a worthwhile activity. You never know when someone will pick up on something you have said, and transform her life as a result.

DUMBTH. A term coined in 1989 by American broadcaster and humorist **Steve Allen** to bring attention to the decline he perceived in the general knowledge of the average American. Allen went on to advocate eighty-one (later expanded to one hundred one) ways people could arrest their own **dumbing down**. The first five were as follows:

- decide that in future you will reason more effectively;
- do some casual studying about the brain, the **mind**, memory, the whole field of psychology;
- beware of rushing to **judgment**;
- beware of falling in love with your first answer; and

- beware of the erroneous assumption.

Even taking these to heart would make an amazing difference! Allen saw dumbth as a combination of ignorance, stupidity, and incompetence. Since then, this phenomenon has been observed around the world.

Further reading: Steve Allen, *"Dumbth."*

DUTY OF THE WELL-INFORMED CITIZEN. The Canadian sociologist John O'Neill described this as:

- considering oneself perfectly qualified to decide who is a competent expert; and
- making up one's mind after having heard opinions from opposing experts.

O'Neill had in mind the imperative of muddying the otherwise clear distinction between **science** and common sense, both as a way of checking the pretensions of science, and to close the gap between the general citizen's common-sense views and those of specialists and experts.

The implications for the citizen are clear too—in particular the unstated emphasis on being well informed. There can be no doubt, though, that well-informed citizens are citizens least likely to put up with attacks on their liberties and other unjustified encroachments by coercive authorities. O'Neill suggested these duties as part of a systematic rebuke of **postmodernists** and others who sneer at the possibility of individual citizens being able to take charge of their lives in this way. There are alternatives to **nihilism**, and well-informed citizens are less likely to succumb to nihilism's bleak charm. See the entries on **rights** and **responsibilities**.

Further reading: John O'Neill, *The Poverty of Postmodernism.*

DYING AND RESURRECTED GODS. One of the oldest and most widespread of all mythological motifs. Across the various cultures, the cults of resurrected gods usually had these features:

- ecstatic experience whereby communion with the deity was established;
- a sacramental meal to symbolize this communion; and
- a drama which tells the story of the death and resurrection.

In many cases the ecstatic part of the ritual was taken literally, with drug-induced dancing and orgies. See the entry on **Dionysianism**. The theme of dying and resurrected gods had its symbolic power in agrarian societies, where life or death depended on successful growing seasons for the crops. The dying **god** was a scapegoat for human transgressions and often acted as a stand-in for human sacrifice.

The theme of dying and resurrected gods is widespread. To take just a few examples, Krishna met his death by crucifixion. He is represented in Hindu temples with his arms extended, hanging on a cross, with nail marks on his hands and feet and a spear wound at his side. At his death the sun darkened. After a descent into hell, Krishna rose on the third day and ascended into heaven.

And in Egypt, the god Osiris had many features of a dying and resurrected god. Osiris had been shut up in a coffer, encased in a tree and dismembered by his wicked brother Set. But Isis, Osiris's wife (and sister) searched for him, and brought the dismembered pieces together, which, through the divine intervention of Re, the sun god, brought about the resurrection of Osiris. In the death and resurrection of Osiris, the Egyptians saw the pledge of eternal life after death for themselves. In religious rituals they reenacted the resurrection of Osiris as an act of faith that they should also achieve eternal life.

The religion of Mithraism, a derivation of **Zoroastrianism**, spread throughout the Mediterranean in the first centuries of the common era. Mithras was born from rock on December 25 and slew the sacred bull and took it back to the cave that he had been born in. Mithras's birth was supposed to take the **sin** away from the world. After many signs and wonders, Mithras held a farewell banquet, which his followers celebrated as a solemn sacramental meal. Mithras was portrayed in heaven with a halo, enjoying a heavenly banquet. Like Horus, Mithras was known as the Good Shepherd. Each year Mithraists mourned before a statue of their god, during which the priests would intone, "Rejoice followers of the saved god, because there is for you relief from your grief."

The early Christian fathers, then, were more than familiar with this theme. Despite their initial reluctance to incorporate pagan themes into the growing religion, many of these dying and resurrection motifs were included in the Christian story. For example, St. Jerome (342–420 CE) admitted that the place that Christians claimed was the birthplace of Jesus had formerly been where the death and resurrection of Adonis or Tammuz had been celebrated.

Further reading: Homer W. Smith, *Man and His Gods*.

DYNAMIC INTEGRITY. A term coined by **H. James Birx** to denote the attitude of mind and approach to life people will need to employ when faced with the enormity of this universe and the brevity of our own time as part of it. Dynamic integrity involves building a coherent understanding of the universe, and using that coherent knowledge in order to act in a morally unified and integral way. It is not the *content* of the understanding of the universe that matters so much as the attitude. Dynamic integrity is an interdisciplinary attitude that "fosters a holistic character that is amenable to social change, critical dialogue, and pervasive investigation."

Birx talks of the integrity being dynamic rather than passive, because integrity in times of change takes effort and resolution. It resembles **Bertrand Russell**'s idea of **taking the wide horizon** and Paul Kurtz's notion of **eupraxsophy**. See also the entry on **cosmic modesty** and **anthropocentric conceit**.

E

E=MC². The equation that sums up **Albert Einstein**'s special theory of **relativity**, devised in 1905. E=mc² means the energy of an object equals its mass times the speed of light squared. The mc^2 refers to the amount of energy locked up in mass m. The c stands for celeritas, the Italian word for swiftness. Essentially, Einstein was saying that mass and energy are the same thing.

Further reading: David Bodanis, $E=mc^2$: *A Biography of the World's Most Famous Equation*.

EASTERN PHILOSOPHY. Generic and potentially highly misleading term to denote all philosophy emanating from Asia, in particular China and India. These two countries are home to the most influential **Asian traditions**, namely, Hinduism, Buddhism, Confucianism, and **Taoism**. It is important to note that Chinese and Indian thought are in some respects further apart than philosophy from those countries is from European thought. It is also important not to conflate Eastern philosophy with Eastern religion.

With these qualifications in place, some generalizations can be made. All Eastern traditions are concerned, in one way or another, with subsuming the ego to a wider reality. They try to do this not by contriving a **command morality** which must be believed, but by focusing on the way we behave. Indian systems are concerned with **dharma**, or the way things are. So one's behavior is judged according to how one has lived in accordance to one's station in life, which is one's **dharma**. Chinese systems focus more on the concept of *Tao* (also spelt *Dao*), which can loosely be seen as living in harmony with the universe and doing what is right. Eastern thought is ethical without being religious in the Western sense of the word, which is one reason it is problematic to think of Asian traditions as religions.

The **monotheistic** religions, by contrast, work not to subsume the ego to a wider reality, but to inflame the ego by pandering to the **transcendental temptation**. By emphasizing personal **immortality, prayer**, and an eternal **soul**, Western religions accentuate the importance of self over the cosmos. This is in direct contrast with the Eastern approach. Eastern philosophy has more in common with **humanism** than with the monotheistic religions.

Another feature of Eastern philosophy is that the goal, whether defined in Hindu terms as *moksha*, in Buddhist terms as *nirvana*, or in Chinese terms as union with or absorption by the *Tao*, is at least in principle open to everyone. This is in contrast with monotheism, which divides humanity into those who believe and who are therefore saved, and those who do not believe and who therefore are damned. In Eastern philosophy, everyone can find their own path to enlightenment, however variously that enlightenment might be conceived.

And following on from the emphasis on finding one's own way, Eastern philosophy does not concern itself with **scriptures** as the monotheistic religions have done. One can criticize or ignore the **Veda**, the classical Buddhist texts, the *Analects* of **Kongfuzi** or the *Tao Te Ching* without anyone questioning that person's beliefs or integrity.

Further reading: Ray Billington, *Understanding Eastern Philosophy*.

ECOHUMANISM. An important new concept, bringing together **ecology** and **humanism**. It has become a telling criticism against humanism that it is **speciesist**, in other words, that it arrogantly puts the interests of the human species ahead of all others on our planet. This charge is incorrect because it ignores the significance of the rejection of **anthropocentric conceit**, which is central to humanism. However, the accusation has a wide circulation and ecohumanism is a credible attempt to address this issue.

Ecohumanism is an attempt to embed the rejection of anthropocentric conceit into the heart of humanism. It takes seriously the interconnectedness of any species, including *Homo sapiens* with other species and the wider environment in which we all live. No decision made on behalf of *Homo sapiens* alone is justified if it fails to take the broader interconnectedness into account.

Further reading: Robert B. Tapp, ed., *Ecohumanism*.

ECOLOGICAL FOOTPRINT. A term used to refer to the quantity of land and resources each of us consumes. The average American, for instance, is going to have a far larger ecological footprint than the average inhabitant of Chad. Environmentalists have totaled up the productive land on the planet and divided it between each human being. By this method there are 5.5 acres for each human being. But the bad news is that the average human being uses seven acres of land. Put another way, humanity as a whole is consuming more than one-third of the resources than nature can regenerate. And this makes no provision for the needs of any other species on the planet.

Clearly, *Homo sapiens* are using far more than their share of the world's resources. It is apparent that the people of the West, whose ecological footprint is by far the largest, are going to need to consume less. Many people already recognize this and are looking for ways to adopt **ecological values** such as **voluntary simplicity** in their lives. At the planetary level, it is imperative to take on board the principles of **sustainable development** if we are to survive. See the entry on **Millennium Ecosystem Assessment**.

ECOLOGICAL VALUES. A system of values that places as the central idea the need for humans to live harmoniously with the rest of the natural world. Tim Hayward, a leading proponent in this area, has itemized the core ecological values as:

• live in harmony with nature;

- overcome **anthropocentric conceit**; and
- recognize intrinsic value in nonhuman beings.

Unlike many of his more excitable colleagues, Hayward sees this program as observing the values of the **Enlightenment**. The English sociologist Ronald Fletcher (1921–1992) dealt with this issue when he said that **humanist values** are human centered without being human confined. It makes no sense to value all things human if we place no value on the planet that sustains the species. A lot of religious values are sanguine about the damage being done to the world's environment due to a misplaced confidence that God won't let them die out. This is an extreme form of anthropocentric conceit. See the entry on **speciesism**.

Further reading, Tim Hayward, *Ecological Thought: An Introduction.*

ECOLOGY. The science of detecting patterns of interdependence in nature. The word comes from the Greek word *oikos*, meaning "a home." Ecology developed into a serious science after World War II and in particular once it was paired up with evolutionary biology.

The word was coined in 1866 by the German zoologist **Ernst Haeckel**, who was advocating a new field of study—the study of the immediate environment living organisms occupy. Along with **T. H. Huxley**, Haeckel was **Charles Darwin**'s most prolific and successful defender and popularizer. He was also an uncompromising rationalist. Haeckel believed that nature constituted a single substance, within which all its extraordinary variety lived. Haeckel wanted a closer relationship between humanity and the environment that sustained it. He believed Christianity had broken this relationship by replacing nature as an object of worship with **God**, a human creation. Haeckel was an early critic of humanity's **anthropocentric conceit**. More recently, the word has taken on a broader meaning of general environment conservation.

ECOREGION. A coherent regional ecosystem which has its own environmental needs and problems. For instance, the Danube river has a catchment that covers at least eleven countries. This basic truth means that thinking about the Danube cannot take place in any rational form unless it takes place on an ecoregional scale. Other examples include the Black Sea, Lake Victoria, and the Himalayas. For any of these ecoregions, programs based on national interest are of little long-term value and are indeed likely to be part of the problem.

Even when an ecoregion, such as the Yangtze River valley occurs almost entirely within one country, decisions made about it should take into account its impact on neighboring ecoregions. The basic truth is that transnational solutions to **sustainable development** are needed, and national governments are poorly suited to providing them. See the entry on **global governance**.

ECOTAGE. A variation on the word "sabotage," but with an ecological slant. For instance, kidnapping animals from laboratories, attacking scientists who work on animals, or destroying genetically modified crop experiments count as ecotage. Several of the more radical environmentalist groups have justified the use of ecotage as a means to advance their aims.

Ecotage is in the same tradition as the Luddites in nineteenth-century Britain who destroyed manufacturing equipment on the premise that it was endangering their jobs. And, even more disturbing, ecotage is related to the harassment and murder of medical professionals at **abortion** clinics in the name of being "pro-life." Ecotage automatically undermines its own cause.

ECOTOURISM. A form of niche tourism designed in part to reconcile the needs of tourism with the needs of conservation. There is a growing market for catering to environmentally aware tourists who are anxious to minimize the destruction or ruination of the regions they visit by the distorting effect of their money. For example, the trade in exotic animals and plants is so lucrative that many of them are endangered in their native habitats. Part of the rationale of ecotourism is that Western tourists will prefer to see the plants or animals in their native habitat, thus boosting the economy of local communities in underdeveloped countries. It is hoped that ecotourists will help make conservation a more lucrative option for locals than poaching or despoliation.

Partly with these issues in mind, the World Tourism Organization (WTO) introduced in 1999 a Global Code of Ethics for tourism, which was endorsed by the United Nations General Assembly. The WTO has also appointed a special advisor whose job is to promote sustainable tourism. The problems facing tourism around the world is yet another illustration that global problems need global solutions.

EGOISTIC ETHICS. The English philosopher Bernard Williams (1929–2003) wrote of egoistic ethics including the cruder forms of religious ethics which involve **command moralities**, or the submission to a set of commandments on the ground that to do so is to conform to the will of **God**. Such a method stifles creative thinking and undermines personal responsibility. Williams argued that if ethical understanding is going to develop, and if **religion** is going to understand its own development in relation to that growth in ethical understanding, then religion must come to understand that it itself is a human creation. But once religion makes that realization, Williams noted, it must in the end collapse.

Further reading: Bernard Williams, *Ethics and the Limits of Philosophy*.

EINSTEIN, ALBERT (1879–1955). The creator of the twenty-first century. Einstein was born in Ulm, in southern Germany. While at school, he was exposed to the then widespread **anti-Semitism**. So alienated was he from the country of his birth that he renounced his German citizenship when only sixteen. At the same time he renounced any formal commitment to the Jewish religion he was brought up in. While he rejected the claims of **monotheism**, Einstein remained deeply committed to the cultural and philosophical traditions of the Jewish people.

When based in Switzerland, Einstein studied mathematics and physics with a view to becoming a teacher. His marks were average and he was unsuccessful in securing an academic position. So between 1902 and 1909, he worked at the now famous patent office in Bern, the capital of Switzerland. In his spare time he worked on papers which were to change the face not just of physics, but of the world. In 1905 he wrote a series of papers on electromagnetism, statistical mechanics, and the special theory of **relativity**. When Einstein won the Nobel Prize for physics in 1921, it was his work on electromagnetism that was cited, and indeed that would have been enough of an achievement for anyone.

In 1909 Einstein was able to leave the patent office and begin a career in the universities. After teaching in Prague and Switzerland, he taught at the Prussian Academy of Sciences and the University of Berlin. It was while he was at Berlin that Einstein developed the General Theory of Relativity. When relativity was confirmed in 1919 by an expedition of scientists observing an eclipse, Einstein became a household name.

He spent the rest of his life searching for a unified **theory of everything**. In this he was unsuccessful, but the jury is still out on whether he was wrong. He also opposed the developments of **quantum mechanics**, mainly because he was disturbed by its implications on a unified theory of everything. In 1932 he left Germany for the United States. He was incensed by the rise of the Nazis, who in turn, were glad to see him go and hoped to see the end of "Jewish science." He lived in Princeton, New Jersey, for the rest of his life. Shortly before his death, Einstein cosigned the famous Russell-Einstein Manifesto calling on all countries to abandon nuclear weapons.

Most systems of belief have tried to claim Einstein as one of their own. What can clearly be said is that Einstein did not believe in any sort of personal **God** and rejected any form of **transcendental temptation**. In a letter to the *New York Times* in 1930, Einstein wrote:

> I cannot imagine a God who rewards and punishes the objects of his creation, whose purposes are modeled after our own—a God, in short, who is but a reflection of human frailty. Neither can I believe that the individual survives the death of his body, although feeble souls harbor such thoughts through fear or ridiculous egoism.

Einstein's conception of God closely resembled the pantheism as articulated by **Baruch Spinoza**. It is also relevant that Einstein became an honorary associate of the **Rationalist Press Association** in 1934. He endorsed some of the RPA's books and read their magazine. The famous photograph of Einstein's desk at the time of his death shows the latest copy of the RPA's journal, the *Literary Guide* (now the *New Humanist*) uppermost on his pile of papers.

EITHER BLACK OR WHITE, FALLACY OF.

A fallacy detected by the English philosopher **L. Susan Stebbing** that confuses a *clear* distinction with a *sharp* distinction. The fallacy of either black or white requires us, in the name of logical thinking, to draw some supposedly determinative line in what is an infinite set of gradations from black to white. This line is said to mark the point where black officially becomes white.

Supporters of this fallacy equate the ability to draw this line with clear thinking and even with greater courage than those who see only the ever-changing shades of gray. It doesn't allow for complexity in an issue. As a classic example, we now know that light has the qualities of a wave and a particle, and attempting to determine a sharp either-or would not merely confuse the issue but would also lead to misunderstanding. The moral of the story is that one can be thinking clearly without having to draw sharp distinctions on issues.

Further reading: L. Susan Stebbing, *Thinking to Some Purpose*.

ELIOT, GEORGE

(1819–1880). Pseudonym for Mary Ann, or Marian Evans, a brilliant English novelist, translator, and editor. Brought up a fervent Evangelical, Evans moved on to **rationalism** with leanings to **positivism** after reading Charles Hennell's *Inquiry Concerning the Origin of Christianity* (1838). Familiar with Greek, Italian, Latin, and German, Evans translated **David Friedrich Strauss**'s *Life of Jesus* (1844–46) and **Ludwig Feuerbach**'s *Essence of Christianity* (1854). Strauss concluded that Christianity was a pious fiction, much as Hennell had done. Unusually, Evans translated Feuerbach's work under her own name, the only time she did that. She assumed her pseudonym when she took up writing for the prominent journal the *Westminster Review* in 1850. It was feared that readers would not take contributions from a woman seriously. However, her talent quickly became apparent, and the following year she became the journal's assistant editor. Her *Westminster Review* articles, many of which were subsequently anthologized, revealed Eliot's intelligence, broad reading, and transnational outlook.

After entering a relationship with the prominent thinker George Lewes (1817–1878) in 1854, Eliot took to writing novels. After some short stories, later published as *Scenes from Clerical Life*, she wrote *Adam Bede* (1859), which quickly established her as a major talent. Her other main novels were *The Mill on the Floss* (1860), *Silas Marner* (1861), *Romola* (1863), *Felix Holt* (1863), *Middlemarch* (1871–72), and *Daniel Deronda* (1876). It is generally agreed that Eliot's novels remain among the best in the history of English literature. Most of them have been televised.

In a letter to a friend, Eliot wrote in 1859 that opinions are a poor cement between human souls, and "the only effect I ardently long to produce by my writings is that those who read them should be better able to imagine and to feel the pains and the joys of those who differ from them in everything but the broad fact of being struggling, erring, human creatures."

Further reading: Ina Taylor, *George Eliot: Woman of Contradictions.*

EMERGING CHURCHES, also known as postmodern churches and thought by some scholars as the next major manifestation of **religion** in America. Emerging churches involve people mainly in their twenties and thirties and are generally eclectic in their **theology** and practices. Emerging churches meet in various locations as few of them have buildings of their own. In fact, they are often reacting against the **dogmatism** and well-oiled showmanship of the vast Evangelical megachurches.

Emerging churches often mix Evangelical preferences for direct experience with God with mystical and even New Age ideas. And they are opposed to the political activism of the older Evangelical churches that rose to prominence in the 1980s and 1990s. In true postmodern fashion, the emerging churches are picking and choosing bits from various traditions in ways that suit them, with little thought to the coherence of the overall package. Their priority is more about personal transcendence and less about judging the "unchurched."

EMPIRICISM. The approach in **philosophy** which rejects all forms of Platonism, **idealism**, and philosophical **rationalism**, each of which argued for a body of **knowledge** existing in the world and which humans can reach through abstract reasoning. Against these claims, empiricists argue that knowl-

edge is based on experience. The word "empiricism" is derived from the Greek *empeirein*, "to experience." It is with this in mind that the American philosopher **John Dewey** noted that the central question of empiricism is our relation to the external world.

Empiricism began, writes Anthony Gottlieb, as a reaction among medical men to the doldrums medicine had gotten itself into in the ancient world. There were so many conflicting theories of medicine, each one accompanied by a lengthy philosophy of life to back it up, that things were stuck. What some medical men started to do, then, was to simply circumvent all the dogmas, and return to examining for themselves what they thought the problem was and, on the strength of their experience, suggest a remedy. This was an important step forward for **science** and philosophy, and empiricism has had a close relationship with science ever since.

By virtue of its rejection of grand metaphysical schemes, empiricism is well suited to embracing **fallibilism** and **reliabilism**. Put differently, because our knowledge ultimately comes from experience, and because we know our experience is limited and prone to error, the empirical method is best suited to suitable levels of **cosmic modesty**. Nowhere was this better put than by **Bertrand Russell** at the end of his scandalously undervalued book ***Human Knowledge: Its Scope and Limits*** (1948). Russell wrote:

Indeed, such inadequacies as we seemed to find in empiricism have been discovered by strict adherence to a doctrine by which empiricist philosophy has been inspired: that all human knowledge is uncertain, inexact, and partial. To this doctrine we have not found any limitation whatever.

Further reading: Anthony Gottlieb, *The Dream of Reason* and Bertrand Russell, *Human Knowledge: Its Scope and Limits.*

ENCYCLOPEDIA. The word made up from

the Greek prefix *en* (in), and the nouns *kyklos* (circle) and ***paideia*** (instruction, science, knowledge). As described by **Denis Diderot** the word *encyclopedia* means "interrelation of all **knowledge**," and its purpose was to "collect the knowledge dispersed on the surface of the earth and to unfold its general system."

In Europe before the **Enlightenment**, the most authoritative compendium of knowledge was held to be the Bible, and the basis of its authority was the perception that it was **God**'s word. This understanding became harder to justify once it became apparent that significant parts of the Bible were unreliable and inaccurate. By the time of the Enlightenment, the failure of the Bible as a general guide had become apparent to most intelligent people, and it was the idea of Diderot to rectify this situation by compiling the most comprehensive compendium of useful knowledge then known. It was the aim of the *Encyclopedia* to bridge the gap between **science** and technology.

The encyclopedia project led by Diderot did not arise out of thin air. It was heavily influenced by the *Dictionnaire Historique et Critique* (1697) compiled by **Pierre Bayle**. And even before then, **Pliny the Elder**'s *Natural History* was an early encyclopedia, complete with table of contents and citations of works referred to.

The project began when Denis Diderot and Jean d'Alembert (1717–1783), the two editors, began collecting material from the finest minds in Europe at the time. The full title of the work was *Encyclopédie, ou Dictionnaire Raisonné des Sciences, des Arts and des Métiers*. The first volume, which came out in 1751, acknowledged its debt to Francis Bacon (1561–1626), **Newton**, **Locke**, and Bayle. It created a sensation and became very influential, and very unpopular indeed with church and reactionary elements, who were offended by the naturalistic tone the works took. As each volume came out the opposition grew more vocal, and in 1758 d'Alembert succumbed to the criticism and left the pro-

ject. His departure was brought on by the banning of the work by the Council of State, after the seventh volume. And on September 3, 1759, Pope Clement XIII instructed Catholics to hand their copies in to church authorities for destruction. Another important contributor, the **Marquis Marie Jean Condorcet**, continued to contribute to the encyclopedia.

Diderot was unperturbed, and continued until the last volume came out in 1773, twenty-five years after it had started. The completed work had seventy-two thousand articles by one hundred forty authors. Volumes 8–17 were all produced against this opposition, thanks in no small way to the support of Madame La Pompadour. The attempts at persecution having failed, the *Encyclopedia* helped to change the intellectual climate of Europe. It also spawned an industry for reference books that continues unabated to this day. The *Encyclopedia Britannica*, for example, is a direct descendent of the *Encyclopédie*.

END OF HISTORY. An idea made popular by the right-wing thinker Francis Fukuyama in his book *The End of History and the Last Man* (1992). By end of history, Fukuyama is taking an idea from the German philosopher G. W. F. Hegel (1770–1831), who argued for a directional history (see the entry on **historicism**) that ended up in an absolute realization of spirit and a worldwide apotheosis of the Prussian state, which, in Hegel's mind, was the ideal that time had been slowly working its way toward. Fukuyama saw the collapse of the Soviet Union and the triumph of liberal **democracy** as the same thing and made the case, following Hegel, that directional history had in effect come to an end in the wake of this victory.

By history coming to an end, Fukuyama meant that the great themes of history had finally worked themselves out in the triumph of liberal democracy and that events from now on would merely be tinkering with the mechanics of this now universally successful political system.

Events since *The End of History* was published have shown Fukuyama to be wrong. The collapse of communism is not the same as the triumph of capitalism. And the new struggle with **Islamism** is not understandable in the terms of Fukuyama's theory. Samuel P. Huntington's **clash of civilizations** theory has done a better job of explaining the post–cold war world.

Further reading: Francis Fukuyama, *The End of History and the Last Man*.

ENLIGHTENMENT, BOOKS ON THE. Here are some of the better books on the Enlightenment. Some excellent single-volume books are *Ingenious Pursuits* (1999) by Lisa Jardine and *In Search of Humanity* (1960) by Alfred Cobban. And *The Enlightenment* (2000) by Thomas Munck is an interesting social history of the time. *The Enlightenment* (1968) by Norman Hampson is still an excellent short survey. The Enlightenment is discussed intelligently in *What is Good? The Search for the Way to Live* (2003) by A. C. Grayling. A brilliant attempt to restate some important insights relevant to the Enlightenment was made in story form by Steven Lukes; *The Curious Enlightenment of Professor Caritat* (1995) is a delightful tale told in the tradition of Jonathan Swift.

The Portable Enlightenment Reader (1995) edited by Isaac Kramnick, is a useful compendium of thoughts from prominent thinkers of the era. *The Age of Enlightenment* (two volumes, 1979) edited by Simon Eliot and Beverley Stern does the same in more detail.

A good way to read about the Enlightenment is to read biographies of the main protagonists. Highly recommended are *Hume* (1980), *Voltaire* (1986), and *Thomas Paine* (1988), all by **A. J. Ayer**. Also recommended are *Diderot: A Critical Biography* (1992) by P. N. Furbank and *Tom Paine: A Political Life* (1995) by John Keane. *Founding Brothers: The Revolutionary Generation* (2002) by Joseph Ellis deals with the American leaders during the Enlightenment very well.

Still the most authoritative account is *The Enlightenment: An Interpretation* (1970) by Peter Gay. Despite going over two volumes, these books are a joy to read.

ENLIGHTENMENT, LEGACY OF. The intellectual historian Alfred Cobban (1901–1968) summarized the legacy of the **Enlightenment** in these terms:

- progress of scientific knowledge and technological innovation;
- religious toleration;
- freedom of thought and expression;
- liberal political ideas; and
- autonomy and primacy of ethics.

Cobban saw the Enlightenment as a greater age than ours because it made an effort to create a better society, an ambition that has largely been abandoned. Even in light of the dreadful state of the world today, that is probably too pessimistic a conclusion. But his summary of the legacy of the Enlightenment is valid. More recently, Micheline Ishay has acknowledged that the Enlightenment "supersedes other influences" with respect to our contemporary understanding of **human rights**. The wave of reformers in the nineteenth century who fought for the eight-hour day, the abolition of slavery, care for the poor, and extension of the franchise, all saw their battles as the practical application of the ideas generated in the eighteenth century. We sneer at these achievements at our peril.

This is not to say the Enlightenment was without fault, or that it was some mythical golden age. That is obviously not the case. But as the case of **Thomas Jefferson** illustrates so clearly, the Enlightenment's legacy had considerably more positive attributes than negative ones.

Further reading: Alfred Cobban, *In Search of Humanity*; and Micheline Ishay, *A History of Human Rights*.

ENLIGHTENMENT, METHODOLOGY OF. Described by **Ernest Gellner** in these terms:

- there are no absolute substantive truths;
- all facts and all observers are equal;
- there are no privileged sources or affirmations above inquiry; and
- all facts and features are separable; no linkages escape scrutiny.

Each of these methods of learning had been around before the Enlightenment, and were particularly noticeable among the **Pre-Socratics**, but during the Enlightenment they were brought together with renewed power and eloquence.

Further reading: Ernest Gellner, *Postmodernism, Reason and Religion.*

ENLIGHTENMENT, THE. Title given to the period of European history between about 1700 and 1780, although it is a mistake to think the Enlightenment was confined to Europe. What gives the Enlightenment special interest is the lessons thinkers of the time learned from the great scientific revolution of the seventeenth century, exemplified in particular by **Isaac Newton** in physics, **Galileo Galilei** in astronomy, and **John Locke** in philosophy. The Renaissance had made great gains by rediscovering the wisdom of the ancient world, but the thinkers of the Enlightenment were able to go several steps further thanks to their greater understanding of the sciences. The Enlightenment was also fueled by widespread disgust with the religious hatreds that had fueled the **wars of religion**, culminating in the ruinous Thirty Years' War (1618–1648).

The American intellectual historian Peter Gay wrote the most authoritative history of the Enlightenment. Gay saw the Enlightenment program as a vastly ambitious one of "secularism, humanity, cosmopolitanism, and freedom, above all, freedom in its many forms," which Gay itemized as "freedom from arbitrary power, freedom of speech, freedom of trade, freedom to realize one's own talents, freedom to aesthetic response, freedom, in a word, of moral man to make his own way in the world." The program was

undertaken in the name of a wide range of principles, which the Argentinian-born philosopher Mario Bunge outlined as:

- trust in **reason**
- rejection of **myth**, superstition, and groundless belief or dogma;
- **free inquiry** and **secularism**, plus encouragement to nontheistic systems;
- **naturalism** over supernaturalism, especially materialism;
- adoption of scientific approach to the study of society and nature;
- utilitarianism;
- respect for craftsmanship, industry, and the machine;
- modernism and progressivism, contempt for the past (except Classical Age), criticism of present, and trust in the future;
- **individualism** plus **libertarianism** and egalitarianism; and
- universalism and **cosmopolitanism**, as well as **human rights**.

Some of the most important thinkers of the time were **Voltaire**; **Diderot**; **David Hume**; Edward Gibbon (1737–1794), author of the magisterial *Decline and Fall of the Roman Empire*; **Thomas Jefferson**; and **Thomas Paine**. The most important figures in the Japanese Enlightenment were Hiraga Gennai (1728–1779), Sugita Genpaku (1733–1817), and Shiba Kokan (1738–1818).

The eighteenth century only slowly became known as the Enlightenment. The word was first used in this context by **Immanuel Kant** in his essay *Answer to the Question: What Is Enlightenment?* (1784). Kant was not declaring his own age to be enlightened. But he did, he argued, live in an age of enlightenment.

In the 1980s and 1990s, when **postmodernism** was still the intellectual fashion, the Enlightenment became known as "the Enlightenment Project." This caricature involved a relentless drive toward some indefinite perfectibility without tolerating dissent along the way. Ironically, the thinker of the period whose work lent most credence to caricatures of this sort is **Jean-Jacques Rousseau**, whose works were bitterly critical of his Enlightenment contemporaries. See the entry on **Nakamoto Tominaga**.

Further reading: Peter Gay, *The Enlightenment*, and Mario Bunge, "Counter-Enlightenment in Contemporary Social Studies," in Paul Kurtz and Timothy Madigan, eds., *Challenges to the Enlightenment*.

ENLIGHTENMENT, VALUES OF THE. Have been outlined by Peter Gay as:

- the supremacy of **philosophy** and the autonomy of humanity;
- the superiority of eclecticism over dogma;
- the superiority of intelligent ignorance over grandiose rationalism; and
- the preference for practical moral reflection over theoretical speculation.

As with the principles and methodology of the Enlightenment, the values we attribute to it have all been aired at various times in history before, most notably in Ancient Greece. But they were brought together, alongside the dramatic increase in reliable scientific knowledge of the seventeenth century, to acquire new meaning and relevance during the Enlightenment. The "grandiose rationalism" Gay was referring to is the philosophical rationalism of **Plato**, **Descartes**, and Gottfried Leibniz (1646– 1716). See the entry on **rationalism**.

Further reading, Peter Gay, *The Enlightenment*.

ENTERTAINMENT EDUCATION. The term given to a new trend in the dissemination of public information. Public-health organizations are recognizing that traditional methods of distributing information: pamphlets, articles, lectures, and so on are becoming less and less effective because few people read this material. Accordingly, the strategy is slowly changing toward securing

the inclusion of one's message in popular soap operas, sitcoms, and infomercials. The power of entertainment education was made apparent in the 1970s when an episode of *Happy Days* had the character Fonzie going to the library to meet girls. In the months that followed, demand for library cards increased 500 percent. No conventional campaign could have dreamed of achieving such a result. Since then campaigns to eradicate drunk driving, smoking, unprotected teenage sex, teen violence, and other issues have been waged by being inserted as subplots in television programs.

By the late 1990s, poll data in the United States was showing very significant proportions of people were getting health information from television, and frequently from prime-time shows and soap operas.

This trend is not without its dangers, of course. If prime-time entertainment can be used to promote public-health information, they can also be used to promote controversial political or social programs. To some extent the need to preserve high ratings will foil the more unpopular ideas from breaking through to the prime-time programs. It is also evidence of the long-term decline in the habit of reading, which can be used as evidence in favor of the widely held fear that contemporary society is dumbing down. The trend to entertainment education is also evidence of the power of images. See the entry on **imagology**. Partly in order to allay these fears, the growing entertainment-education community drafted the Entertainment Education Declaration 2000, a responsible seven-point program which focused on valuing **diversity**, inclusiveness, sustainability, and all the rest of it.

ENTROPY. A term coined by the German physicist Rudolf Clausius (1822–1888) in 1865. Entropy is bound up with disorder. It is thought that until the **big bang**, a condition of maximum entropy existed, because the universe was nothing more than a black hole. Once it exploded, however, the universe became an expanding gas with less than its maximum entropy. As the universe continues to expand, it is thought that entropy continues without end, eventually resulting in a state once again of maximum disorder, known as the **big crunch**. Some have speculated that this would find itself in a cosmically large black hole. In such a condition all life would be impossible.

Entropy has been pressed into service for a large number of pseudoscientific causes. For example, **creationists** have used entropy as a weapon against **evolution**. This is obviously false, not least because of the different scales involved. The universe is more than big enough for some element of entropy to decrease on earth, or any single location, while it increases throughout the universe as a whole.

EPICTETUS (55–135 CE, approx.). Stoic philosopher who, more than many great thinkers, lived as he taught. Epictetus was born in Hierapolis in Phrygia, in what is now northwestern Turkey. He was the slave of Epaphroditus, a senior official in Nero's administration. From a young age Epictetus showed intellectual promise, so his kindly owner sent him to Rome to study under the great **Stoic** teacher, Gaius Musonius Rufus. Epictetus thrived under Rufus's tolerant and democratic influence, and became his star pupil.

Epictetus taught in Rome until 94 CE, when he was banished from there by the emperor Domitian, as part of a general action against intellectuals. By now a free man, Epictetus spent the rest of his life teaching in the small coastal town of Nicopolis in Epirus (northwestern Greece). Among his most distinguished students was **Marcus Aurelius Antoninus**, the future emperor of Rome. Epictetus left behind a short series of *Meditations*, and another pupil, the historian Arrian, brought together a work that came to be known as the *Enchiridion* (*Manual*). Epictetus taught a benign and civilized form of Stoicism, centered around living the **good life**. Drawing on his personal experience, Epictetus concluded that none of us is free unless we are in control of our passions and desires and have ceased to fear **death**. Reason played a central role in achieving this happy result.

EPICUREANISM. A humanistic worldview developed in ancient Greece and Rome named after its founder, **Epicurus**. Unlike most other Greek and Roman schools of thought which were urban, Epicureanism centered around a garden. This garden became the center for Epicurean thinkers and functioned not unlike a modern commune. It was still in existence 450 years later. The Epicureans preferred withdrawing from active life and living in communities of like-minded people. In a dramatic departure from the practice of the ancient world, men and women, freemen and slaves, were all treated equally.

A central notion of Epicureanism was "live unnoticed." They preferred to stay in their garden and discuss philosophy. The four issues they thought important to get clear on were **god**, **death**, pleasure, and suffering. This is because each of these notions harbors the fears and desires which haunt us and can reduce us to a life of misery. Epicureanism values **happiness** and **peace of mind** in this world. It is frankly agnostic and naturalistic. Worrying about death or yearning for **immortality** merely made one unhappy and fretful and wasted our precious time, the Epicureans taught. The Epicurean philosophy is most succinctly outlined in the **four-part cure**.

Epicureans were attacked, often bitterly, by Christians and other pagans, as being hedonists. This was never true. In fact Epicureans lived a relatively ascetic existence. But the slander stuck and the very word **apostate** derives from the Greek spelling of Epicurus's name.

Most of the writings of the Epicureans have been destroyed by enemies or lost. The most complete account of Epicureanism comes in the form of a poem, *De rerum natura* (*On the Nature of Things*), by **Lucretius**. This is a beautiful poem and is freely available in paperback. When Epicurean works were rediscovered in the sixteenth century, it became a significant influence in the development of modern **humanism**. The rediscovery of Epicurus also meant the rediscovery of **atomism**, which was a very important stimulus to physics. **Galileo** was deeply influenced by atomism and Epicureanism, as told by Lucretius.

EPICURUS (341–271 BCE). One of the most influential figures of the ancient world. Epicurus was born on the island of Samos. Like most intelligent men, he moved to Athens, where, about 306 BCE, he established what we would now call a commune very near the **Academy**, the school set up by **Plato**. The commune was notable for its asceticism and purity. Food and comfort were supposed to be unadorned and without fuss. **Sex** was generally not encouraged, although there may not have been a formal ban. The philosophy known as **Epicureanism** is based loosely on the thoughts of Epicurus.

Most of his own writings have been lost, although papyri found at Herculaneum, which was destroyed in 79 CE along with Pompeii, have revealed the complete works. The papyri were scorched and compressed, and the method of unraveling safely has yet to be developed. When this is managed we could well experience a golden age of Epicurean thought.

EPISTEMOLOGY. A branch of philosophy that is concerned not so much with what we know, but how we know it. While questions about how we know such-and-such are very ancient, epistemology only came into its own relatively recently, following the work of **Immanuel Kant**. Epistemology may focus on articulating how we can acquire reliable **knowledge**, and how we can determine what is reliable and what is not. It is very important to get these issues straight before rushing off and building imposing theories about the world.

EQUALITY, PRINCIPLE OF. A principle coined by **Ted Honderich** and thought by him to be the **supreme moral principle**. The highest purpose would be to help make well-off those who are badly off. This could be done by implementation of variations on the following policies: (1) expanding the provision of well-being to cover as many people as possible, (2) transferring means from the better-off to those less well-off in a way that does not adversely affect the well-being of the better-off, (3) transferring means which may well affect the well-being of the better-off, but not so far as to actually increase the number of those badly off, and (4) broadening the way those whose contributions to the means of well-being can be rewarded.

Honderich argues that the Principle of Equality is, by and large, the foundational principle of the political left, in contrast to the **Principle of Desert**, which guides the direction of political conservatism.

EQUANIMITY. See **DOCTRINE OF THE MEAN**.

ERASMUS, DESIDERIUS (1466–1536). Dutch humanist thinker of the Northern Renaissance. Erasmus was the illegitimate son of a physician's daughter, who died when he was still young. Erasmus was brought up by a sect known as the Brethren for the Common Life, which sought to turn away from abstract **theology** and **mysticism** to devotion to living in the world as Christ was thought to have lived in it. This upbringing, plus the influence of the ancient **Pyrrhonists**, encouraged Erasmus to criticize the pretentious dogmas of theologians. Erasmus worked in the cause of a less-rigid Christianity, and to this end he devoted his life to the scholarly work of editing the documents of the early church and translating the Bible, with the idea that this would help strip away later impurities and allow the reader to see the purity of the original texts, and deepen their own religious commitment on the strength of this reliable knowledge. He was also an important figure in the Renaissance drive to reconcile the works of the **Neopla-**

tonists with Christianity.

Erasmus was a humanist in the sense of valuing human effort and study, and being of the opinion that this approach was important in determining how one lived one's life. He was a devout Christian all his life, although he was sharply critical of the hypocrisy of the Catholic Church and its many corrupt practices. This was given brilliant expression in *Praise of Folly* (1509), a work which underscored his debt to the pagan **Lucian of Samosata**. *Praise of Folly* was wildly popular and was quickly translated into a dozen languages. In the *Colloquia familiaria* (1519), Erasmus criticized the abuses of the Roman Catholic Church. His humanism involved seeing religion as no less prone to folly and abuses than any other human institution. Later he extended his criticisms to the Protestants when he saw them behaving with just the same degree of intolerance. And true to seeing that ideas of value could come from a variety of sources, he also produced his own scholarly translation of the works of **Aristotle** in 1531. Also, see the entry on **Dionysus the Areopagite**.

The civilized attitude of **Erasmus** was soon overwhelmed by the widening religious differences between Catholics and reformers, who were becoming known as Protestants. It was no longer possible to adopt his refined position. The harshness of religious exclusivism demanded that everyone must be one thing, clearly and simply defined, or another. In 1544 Pope Paul IV excommunicated Erasmus posthumously and placed all his writings on the **Index of Forbidden Books**.

ERDINE. Formerly Adrianople, a city in Turkey with the dubious honor of being the site of more battles than any other on earth. Thirteen significant battles were fought at Adrianople between 323 CE and 1913. The first battle of Adrianople was between the Roman emperor Constantine and his challenger Licinius, in which Constantine was the clear victor. The second battle, on August 9, 378 CE, was the most important. It was when the Goths overwhelmed the Roman army and killed the emperor Valens. This fatally weakened the western part of the Roman empire and strengthened the place of the barbarian tribes settling within its borders.

Other battles of Adrianople were in 718 between Bulgars and Muslims seeking to take Constantinople. On this occasion the Bulgars saved Constantinople from attack, but the next three battles at Adrianople, in 813, 914, and 1003, were between Byzantines and Bulgars, who on these occasions were trying to seize the city. The seventh battle was in 1094 between the Byzantine emperor and a challenger to the throne. The battle in 1205 was between Bulgars and Crusaders who, the year previously, had treacherously attacked Christian Constantinople rather than attack the Muslims as all previous crusades had done. Nineteen years later, in 1224, there was a confused, three-way struggle for Adrianople as part of the wider contest between the Byzantines and Crusaders. The tenth battle in 1255 was an internal struggle between rival Byzantine contenders for the throne. It was won by Theodore II Lascaris of Nicaea, who laid the groundwork for the eventual victory of his family over the Crusaders, and the last extended period of Byzantine rule. Exactly a century later in 1355 the Byzantines defeated the Serbs, but only ten years after that, in 1365, the Ottoman Turks defeated the Byzantines and Murad I made Adrianople the capital of his Ottoman nation.

The next battle was not until 1829, when invading Russians briefly took the city from the Turks. The Turkish defeat at Adrianople resulted in them having to grant autonomy to Serbia, as well as Wallachia and Moldovia, which later became Romania. The last time Adrianople was fought over was in 1913 when the Turks lost and then recaptured the city from the Serbs and Bulgarians. This victory ensured the Turks retained Adrianople (now renamed Erdine) as their westernmost point on the continent of Europe.

Why should Erdine have been so heavily

fought over? A quick look at an atlas will show it is in a pivotal position on the approaches to Constantinople, in all cases the real prize being fought over. Standing at the confluence of three rivers, and thus able to provide water for large numbers of soldiers and horses, Erdine has been an obvious place to defend Constantinople, and an equally obvious place to launch an attack against it.

Further reading: John Keegan, *A History of Warfare*; and R. Ernest and Trevor Dupuy, *The Encyclopedia of Military History*.

ESSAYS AND REVIEWS. A work of biblical criticism published in 1860 that rocked the religious foundations of England and rivaled the publication of ***Origin of Species*** in terms of the controversy generated. The seven contributors, Frederick Temple (1821–1902), Rowland Williams (1817–1870), Baden Powell (1796–1860), Henry Bristow Wilson (1803–1888), C. W. Goodwin (the only layman among them), Mark Pattison (1813–1884) and Benjamin Jowett (1817–1893), were all educated and responsible members of the Church of England. The essays returned to the ground covered by the deists and rationalists the previous century by extolling conscience over dogma and reason over blind **faith**, and were critical of **miracles**. None of the articles were prepared to accept **scripture** unquestioningly.

Within a year *Essays and Reviews* had passed through nine editions. The contributors were faced with an unprecedented level of criticism, being denounced as, among other things, "parrots" and the "Seven against Scripture." Two of the contributors were summoned to the Court of Arches, but of the thirty-two charges only five were upheld. On the strength of those five charges, however, the two accused (Dr. Williams and Mr. Wilson) were found to be in breach of the thirty-nine articles pertaining to inspiration, atonement, and justification, and were suspended for one year. This amounted to a moral victory for Williams and Wilson, but they decided to appeal to the Privy Council,

which found in their favor, with even two archbishops giving ground.

Following the successful appeal, a notorious conservative, Dr. Pusey, led eleven thousand clergymen in a solemn declaration of their continued belief in eternal punishments and divine inspiration of the Bible. The debate over *Essays and Reviews*, along with that surrounding **Charles Darwin**'s *Origin of Species* contributed significantly to the making of a post-Christian Britain.

ESSENTIALISM. The idea that objects can have an essence, or an ultimate explanation. This essence is usually held to be of more account than a simple scientific definition. Very often the essence of something is held to reflect its "proper" ranking and place in a larger cosmology. A lot of discussion about the **soul** is couched in this language. It also encourages mystical obfuscation.

Karl Popper and **Marvin Farber** are two philosophers who have observed that the seeking after essences often encourages obscurantism. If one understands the essence of something, there is little need to examine it any further, indeed, the temptation becomes to defend with varying degrees of rigidity that essence against rival interpretations. For example, a great deal of misogynist writing about the "essence of woman" has served only to hinder progress in **gender** relations. More recently, "essentialist" has become a catch-all term of abuse for all manner of things one doesn't like.

ETERNAL RECURRENCE. An old idea, discussed by Zeno of Citium (333–262 BCE), the founder of **Stoicism**, among others. But without doubt, the doctrine of eternal recurrence was articulated most tellingly by **Friedrich Nietzsche**, who described it as "the highest formula of affirmation that can possibly be attained."

In a haunting passage of *The Gay Science* (1882) Nietzsche challenges the reader to imagine a demon asking you how you would reply to him when he says you will live every second of your life again and again, without the slightest change of detail. Would such a thought drive you mad or has there been some moment, even if only one, that makes all the rest of your life worthwhile going through again and again, forever?

Nietzsche didn't intend people to believe in the eternal recurrence as something that actually happened. He posited the idea as a device to bring out the **Overman** in us. If you can say yes to the demon, then you have achieved the true self-overcoming necessary for the Overman. You have also reached the state of *amor fati*, or love of necessity. The most important consequence of the eternal recurrence is the realization that there is not and cannot be any kind of final goal or cosmic purpose for humanity. The eternal recurrence is best seen as a poetic symbol, an illusion that can sustain our ability to live. In this way, it can also serve as a **supreme moral rule**.

Further reading: Friedrich Nietzsche, *The Gay Science*.

ETHICAL CULTURE. A brand of **religious humanism** founded in 1876 by Felix Adler (1851–1933), a reformed Rabbi. Adler recognized that nineteenth-century biblical criticism and scientific developments had destroyed the old theological orthodoxies, but he wanted to preserve the social aspects of **religion**. Adler opposed the idea, advanced by John Dewey and others, that **naturalism** could provide any serious basis for **ethics**. He toyed instead with notions of transcendentalism and the "supersensible." Though not an atheist himself, Adler welcomed atheists as well as theists into the ethical-culture movement, because he reckoned that behavior was a more important guide to a person's moral worth than what they believed. In this, Adler came to what the **Asian traditions** had long thought to be the proper priority. With this in mind, ethical culture had no rituals or creeds. But it did have practical services like kindergartens, emergency housing, and schools. Ethical culture described itself as religious only in the sense that it involved "passionate devotion to a supreme cause." The details of the cause were left to the individual.

The ethical culture idea spread quickly, with new groups starting in Chicago in 1882 and Philadelphia in 1885. Before long the movement spread to Europe, gaining strong footholds in Britain, Germany, and Switzerland, in particular. In 1896 the Union of Ethical Societies was formed at a congress in Zurich. In 1920 the British ethical-culture movement renamed itself the Ethical Union, which in 1963 became the **British Humanist Association**. For many years the Ethical Church in Britain was led by **Stanton Coit**. His successor, **Harold Blackham**, moved the movement in a more secular direction. The Ethical Culture movement was also an important force in the creation of the **International Humanist and Ethical Union** in 1952.

In the United States, ethical culture enjoyed a minor resurgence in the 1950s and 1960s, with cooperation extended to the **American Humanist Association**. This didn't last long, however, as tensions between a secular and more overtly religious understanding of the movement remained unresolved. There is still a very small ethical-culture movement in the United States, but the **Unitarian** Church is now the largest organization sympathetic to religious humanism in that country. See the entry on **Howard Radest**.

ETHICAL EXCELLENCES. A phrase used by **Paul Kurtz** to indicate the **common moral decencies** actually incorporated into one's life. Reaching and maintaining as wide a range of ethical excellences as possible can help the individual achieve what Kurtz called Excelsior, which is the fullest sense of creative fulfillment we can attain. The ethical excellences have two main strands:

(1) *Excellence Primarily in Regard to Oneself*, manifested in autonomy, intelligence, self-discipline, self-respect, creativity, motivation, affir-

mation, health, *joie de vive*, and aesthetic appreciation.

(2) *Excellence as Related to Others*, manifested in integrity, trustworthiness, benevolence, and fairness.

Further reading: Paul Kurtz, *Forbidden Fruit: The Ethics of Humanism.*

ETHICS. The branch of philosophy that examines the principles of what distinguishes right from wrong, and why. For the purposes of this dictionary, the various topics of ethics have been broken up into some of their component parts, like **metaethics**, which are the larger questions about ethics, and **normative ethics**, which look at providing and evaluating the guidelines by which we would wish to act. The first person to attempt a comprehensive exploration of ethics was **Aristotle**.

EUDAIMONIA. Greek word which is often translated as "happiness" or "fulfillment," but the British philosopher A. C. Grayling has spoken of it as a flourishing of the soul. **Aristotle** spoke of eudaimonia in terms of the end goal of life. By this he did not confuse happiness with an endless succession of pleasures. Neither was happiness to be the specific aim of everything we do. Rather, eudaimonia is best understood as living a life in which one has fulfilled oneself. More specifically, eudaimonia can be seen as self-fulfillment through personal excellence and the use of reason. This can be summed up as the contemplative life. In this way, the person who has employed all his senses and abilities to produce something worthwhile is a person who can be said to be fulfilled.

Aristotle's concept of eudaimonia has some contemporary successors in the form of the concept of **eupraxsophy** and the **ethical excellences**, both devised by **Paul Kurtz**. Eupraxsophy tends to stress not so much the contemplative life as the life of public service and activity measured and punctuated with contemplation and private repose. There is also a fascinating parallel with the theory of **flow**.

Further reading: A. C. Grayling, *What is Good? The Search for the Best Way to Live*; and Richard Taylor, "Aristotle's Analysis of Love and Friendship," in *Promethean Love: Paul Kurtz and the Humanistic Perspective on Love.*

EUGENICS. A **pseudoscience** that distorted evolutionary thinking in the service of what was thought of as social improvement. The word was coined in 1883 by the British scientist Francis Galton (1822–1911) who was referring to a science of breeding children with superior qualities. It was feared that too many lower-class children, with inferior mental and social characteristics, were being bred. The eugenics movement purported to advance a scientific solution to the problem of the decline of the race. Among more extremist advocates of eugenics, superior characteristics were allotted to the various races, with dark skinned people being seen as inherently inferior. See the entry on **Lothrop Stoddard**.

The eugenics derived from Galton's theories can justifiably be labeled as a pseudoscience because it rested on the **Lamarckian** notion of the inheritance of acquired characteristics. Opponents of **evolution** (which they insist on calling Darwinism) often cite eugenics as a prime example of the moral deficiencies of Darwinism. In fact, by resting on the Lamarckian notion of the inheritance of acquired characteristics, eugenics was specifically non-Darwinian. What is more, once the Darwinian understanding of evolution rose to prominence, eugenics suffered a corresponding decline in support. What little scientific credibility eugenics had was destroyed forever by the **neo-Darwinian synthesis** of the 1930s.

EUHEMERISM. The belief that gods are deified men who lived long ago. The word is named after Euhemerus, about whom we know little, except that he was a Sicilian Greek who wrote a book called *Sacred History*, where he first outlined his theory that is now known as Euhemerism. He lived in Macedonia at the court of Cassander, son of one of Alexander the Great's generals, between 319 and 296 BCE. He was thought by his contemporaries to be an atheist.

EUMEMICS. A term coined by **Daniel C. Dennett** to parody the fashion of political correctness. Eumemics conjures notions both of **eugenics** and **memes**. Political correctness is designed, Dennett argues, to close down *in advance* unusual avenues in thought. As with eugenics, eumemics is designed to impose "myopically derived standards of safety and goodness on the bounty of nature." But where eugenics does so in the genetic field, eumemics works in the memetic field.

EUPRAXSOPHY. A term coined by **Paul Kurtz** in the late 1980s in an attempt to condense into one word the **humanist** ethic. Kurtz recognized the **insufficiency of atheism**; in particular its inability to create a positive humanist ethic in the wake of the discredited theologies and **command moralities**. But Kurtz did not want to make **John Dewey**'s mistake of speaking of humanism using the religious vocabulary of the past. Kurtz has gone to great lengths to demonstrate that humanist ethics are independent of theistic ethics. One can be awed by the beauty of the universe, love life to distraction, find fulfillment in other people, and live openly and actively without being religious, and it is the intention of eupraxsophy to encapsulate that.

Eupraxsophy owes an intellectual debt to **Aristotle**'s concept of **eudaimonia**, and yet it goes further in one crucial sense. Aristotle sees the final goal as the contemplative life, whereas Eupraxsophy seeks a dynamic fusion of contemplation and action. The nub of the question, Kurtz wrote, is not just to love wisdom, but the *practice* of it. Eupraxsophy is an amalgam of *eu* (good, well), *praxis* (conduct, practice), and *sophia* (scientific and philosophic wisdom). Brought together, eupraxsophy stands for "a set of convictions and practices offering a cosmic outlook and an ethical guide to life." See the entry on **phronesis**.

The word was initially spelled "eupraxophy," but after some confusion about how the word should be pronounced, an *s* was added after the *x*. It is unlikely that doing this has helped. See the entry on **Xu Fuguan**.

Further reading: Paul Kurtz, *Eupraxophy: Living Without Religion*.

EURIPIDES. See **GREEK PLAYWRIGHTS**.

EUROPEAN HUMANIST FEDERATION. Founded in Prague in July 1991, but registered in Belgium. The EHF is a federation of humanist societies from fifteen European countries. It represents its member organizations and through them the broader humanist movement at numerous European and international bodies and institutions, including the Council of Europe, the European Commission, the European Parliament, the European Economic and Social Committee, and several other bodies.

The EHF sponsors a series of conferences which address significant themes of interest to **humanism**, **pluralism**, and the **open society**.

EUROSCLEROSIS. A term coined in the late 1970s by the German economist Herbert Giersch (1921–) to describe the features he saw constricting economic progress in Europe, particularly Germany, at the time. The problems were overregulation and a **welfare state** system that was more generous than the economy could really sustain, and which, Giersch maintained, would hinder job creation and governmental efficiency. Eurosclerosis is also exacerbated by the large deficits many European nations run.

In 1998 Giersch established the Herbert Giersch Foundation, which finances an annual conference on various elements of economic policy. See the entry on **Third Way, The**.

EUTHYPHRO DILEMMA, THE. The name given to a very old dilemma about the relationship of **God** to acts of goodness.

Euthyphro is the name given to one of **Plato's** earlier works, which features a dialogue between Socrates and Euthyphro. The dilemma revolves around the question posed by Socrates: "Is what is pious loved by the gods because it is pious, or is it pious because it is loved?" In other words (and speaking of God rather than gods), does God love what is good because it is good, or is it good because God commands it?

Neither option is conducive to religious claims that God is an essential bulwark for morality. If we say that it is good because God commands it, we end up saying that God is good because good is God, a circular and unhelpful assertion. It also raises the problem that doing something wicked like killing innocent people may have to be called "good" if it can be demonstrated that God commands it. Many religious thinkers have opted for the first option, but this comes at the equally serious cost of admitting that morality does not depend on God, who is reduced to the role of mere messenger. And, of course, it means that ethics can be discussed without reference to religious dictates.

Further reading: Plato, *Euthyphro*; and J. L. Mackie, *Ethics: Inventing Right and Wrong*.

EVIDENCE. A datum of **knowledge** that, by virtue of being true, can serve to corroborate another item of knowledge. However, evidence might support a claim that is nonetheless untrue. This is why our faculty of **judgment** is so important; it enables us to rank the various items of evidence we have so as to accord an appropriate level of confidence to our belief. See also the entry on **reliabilism**.

A theory is valid and can enjoy the confidence of people in direct proportion to the range and quality of evidence cited in its defense. See the entry on **W. K. Clifford**. An assertion without evidence is not a theory. As the journalist Christopher Hitchens said, "What can be asserted without evidence can also be dismissed without evidence." See the entry on **burden of proof**.

EVIL. A term which can only be used appropriately in an **absolutist** sense, or in the context of **command moralities**. Evil is more than just bad. Evil is an absolute and willing rejection of what is good.

It has become fashionable to speak of criminals, terrorists, and tyrants as evil. This is understandable, as the word gives emotional expression to our sense of outrage. Neither was it an accident that President George W. Bush spoke in 2002 of Iran, Iraq, and North Korea as an axis of evil. He wanted his condemnation to have a moral, even religious, tone, rather than merely a political one.

But for the idea of evil to work, there has to be a religious idea of a universe, complete with moral proscriptions writ across the cosmos. As the universe does not work in these terms, the word "evil" is redundant.

EVIL, ARGUMENT FROM. An argument for **atheism** first formulated by **Epicurus** and paraphrased here by **Michael Martin**: "God is by definition all-powerful, all-knowing, and all-good. If God is all-powerful, He can prevent evil. If God is all-knowing and can prevent evil, He knows how to prevent it. If God is all-good, He wants to prevent evil. But since there is evil, God cannot exist." The argument from evil is frequently recognized by theologians as the most intractable problem for anyone wishing to defend the existence of God.

Carl Lofmark (1936–1991) a distinguished linguist, spoke of the argument from evil on a BBC World Service talk only days before dying of cancer. He described the idea of a God who was all-powerful and all-loving as a "contradiction in terms, because if he were good and had the power to impose his good, the world would be good and I wouldn't be dying here of cancer. The greatest minds in the world for the past two thousand years have been trying to explain how it is possible that there could be evil in a world created by a good God and after two thousand years they have still not found an answer to that question. I suggest there is not an answer." See the entries on **theodicy** and **anthropodicy**.

EVIL, PROBLEM OF. One of the most intractable dilemmas facing religious thinkers. The classic formulation of the problem of evil is that the existence of evil in the world calls into question the existence of a **god** who is both all-loving and all-powerful. If this god were all-loving, it would want to prevent evil, and if it were all-powerful, it would be able to prevent evil, and yet we find that evil persists. One of the earliest systematic accounts of this dilemma was posed by **Epicurus**.

Many attempts have been made to overcome or outflank the problem of evil, but none of them are successful. See the entry on **theodicy**. The traditional argument in the West was that evil was the preserve of **Satan**, but this argument requires Satan to exist, which few people admit to nowadays. It also leaves unanswered why an all-powerful and all-loving god should permit someone like Satan to operate. The response from Hinduism and Buddhism to the problem of evil is found in the doctrine of **karma**.

Some have tried to argue that evil is necessary in the world so that we may appreciate what is good, but this argument doesn't explain why there has to be so much evil; couldn't a lesser amount have the same effect? More recently, attempts have been made to argue that evil is not real, or not for God anyway, but this seems to run counter to the lived experience of evil in people's lives. See the entry on **anthropodicy**.

Among humanists, the problem does not even arise, as evil is a theological concept which has no place in a naturalistic framework. There is much suffering, and many people do wicked things, but evil as a supernatural entity or essence is an irrelevant idea. Rather than abstract theorizing about the nature of evil, humanists focus more on eradicating suffering from the world.

EVOLUTION. The body of **knowledge** centered around the development of life on earth from single-celled organisms, living in water, to the array of life-forms today, all of which are descended from them. The main features of evolutionary thinking are:

- a drastic expansion of the time scale from nonscientific explanations;
- the concept of a changing universe;
- the abandonment of theories of design; and
- the inclusion of humanity within nature.

Evolution is not the same as **Darwinism**. In the wake of the **neo-Darwinian synthesis**, evolution has become a mixture of the Darwinian theory of **natural selection** and the science of genetics, pioneered by Gregor Mendel (1822–1884). This means that evolution now has two, intertwined mechanisms: natural selection and mutation. See the entry on the **cell**. There is no serious doubt *that* evolution takes place, but there is still plenty of room to investigate *how* evolution takes place.

Further reading: Ernst Mayr, *What Evolution Is.*

EVOLUTION, CONSEQUENCES OF. Following the Copernican revolution that ushered in the idea of the **heliocentric universe**, evolution provided the second great assault on **anthropocentric conceit**. The heliocentric universe means that humans can no longer presume themselves to be at the center of the universe or be the reason for its existence. But with **evolution**, human beings must extend their newfound **cosmic modesty** to the animal kingdom. No longer are we qualitatively superior to animals by virtue of having **souls**. Evolution means that human beings are now one more animal in a mutually dependent planetary ecosystem.

The vast majority of religious people have come to terms with the truth of evolution. However, some (admittedly large) sections of Christianity and Islam have yet to make this transition. Religious conservatives from these traditions are correct when they suspect that evolution poses a fundamental threat to their worldview. It does. Evolution eliminates the need for a **God** to create and manage the universe. Evolution puts the universe, and human beings, in a naturalist setting and turns us into accidents. Ernst Mayr lists the four beliefs basic to Christian dogma that are overthrown by evolutionary thinking:

- belief in a constant world;
- belief in a created world;
- belief in a world created by a wise and benign creator; and
- belief in the unique position of humanity in that creation.

Each of these is quite fundamental to the traditional understanding of the **monotheistic religions**. Mayr also notes that secular beliefs, albeit ones with a religious flavor, have also been challenged by evolutionary thinking. Those included a belief in **essentialism** and **teleology**.

Another important casualty of the Darwinian revolution was what is called the **great chain of being**, and the particular form of anthropocentric conceit that went with it. Instead of a hierarchical view of the universe, we now have a naturalistic view, where human beings play a more modest role than they have been used to while thinking religiously. The difficulty many religious conservatives have had with evolution is powerful evidence for the **conflict between science and religion**.

Further reading: Ernst Mayr, *One Long Argument;* and John Haught, *God After Darwin.*

EVOLUTIONARY PSYCHOLOGY. A discipline that brings together the dramatic progress of the 1950s in explaining the mechanics of the brain and developments in evolutionary biology made during the 1960s. These two disciplines enabled a better explanation of not simply what sort of brain we have, but why we have it. Evolutionary psychology is the successor discipline to socio-

biology, which was pioneered by **E. O. Wilson** in his book of that title in 1975. Evolutionary psychology has played a very important role in **philosophy** at the turn of the twenty-first century.

Robert Wright summarized the working hypothesis of evolutionary psychology in terms of the reality of **human nature** and the ways in which human nature interacts with the world. Evolutionary psychology stands in opposition to what is known as the Standard Social Science Model, which sees human beings as uniquely free of biological constraints, and bound only by cultural constraints. Evolutionary psychology is the attempt to extrapolate philosophically from our biological roots.

Critics argue that evolutionary psychology is stuck with some serious methodological problems, and has yet to determine the exact role **genes** play in human behavior. They add that evolutionary psychology risks becoming dogmatic by underplaying the influence of environment. However, contrary to its detractors, evolutionary psychology does not simply assert that "it's all in the genes," rather that our biological constitution plays a role in our psychology.

It has been widely observed that the greatest success of evolutionary psychology has been to banish once and for all the fallacy of the **social Darwinist** notion that evolution is solely about the survival of the fittest. While we are programmed to compete, we are programmed to cooperate. See the entry on **reciprocal altruism**.

Further reading: Robert Wright, *The Moral Animal.*

EXISTENTIALISM. A trend in philosophy that became enormously influential in the decade after World War II. The main historical antecedents of existentialism were the German philosopher **Friedrich Nietzsche** and the Danish religious thinker Søren Kierkegaard (1813–1855). The most influential voice of twentieth-century existentialism was **Jean-Paul Sartre**. Its longest-lasting voice, along with Nietzsche, may well end up being **Simone de Beauvoir**. **Martin Heidegger** is often described as an existentialist, although he rejected the term.

Existentialism had its origins in the general pessimism experienced by European thinkers after World War II. Not surprisingly, existentialists were ambivalent about humanity, and rejected any set theories of **human nature**. It was felt that modern industrial society was dehumanizing humanity. For some existentialists, this then meant that our real selves were being overwhelmed by a vast tide of conformity and mediocrity. But other existentialists concluded that we don't have a real self at all, but that this real self must be constructed by us during the course of our lives. Life, it was argued, is absurd, and we create our selves in the context of that essential fact. Other important existentialist concepts include **authenticity** and **bad faith**, both vehicles for creating our selves in the face of **absurdity**. The positive aspect to all this was the emphasis on personal responsibility for our actions in the absence of some **transcendental temptation**. A less helpful consequence of existentialism was its tendency toward self-absorption.

The existentialism of Nietzsche, Sartre, and de Beauvoir was explicitly atheist, and equally explicitly irrationalist. Religious existentialism, in the wake of Kierkegaard was no less irrationalist, only in the service of a variation of theism. Existentialism had largely petered out by the end of the 1960s, although some elements of its program were taken up by **postmodernism**. It was also influential in **humanistic psychology**.

Further reading: H. J. Blackham, *Six Existentialist Thinkers*; Robert C. Solomon, *From Rationalism to Existentialism*; and Hector Hawton, *The Feast of Unreason*.

EXOBIOLOGY. The newly developed discipline of learning about and exploring for the origins of life in the universe. Exobiology is the study of biology, not just on Earth, but wherever biological entities can be found.

Early speculations in exobiology can be found in **Anaxagoras**, **Lucretius**, and **Giordano Bruno**. It is still a discipline-in-waiting, as no empirical evidence for the existence of life on other planets has yet been found. However, as astronomers and astrobiologists are searching, there are a large number of planets with sufficient conditions to sustain life-forms of some sort, so exobiology is unlikely to remain dormant for ever. **Carl Sagan** was closely associated with exobiology, being known as the poet of it. See the entries on **panspermia** and **exoevolution**.

EXOEVOLUTION. A term coined by **H. James Birx** to complement the notion of **exobiology**, which is the search for the existence of life elsewhere in the universe. Birx argues that exobiology infers exoevolution. "As on this planet," he writes, "life-forms elsewhere would have evolved to meet the challenges of their dynamic habitats." Birx foresees the rise of the discipline of comparative exoevolution. An important consequence of exoevolution is that all residual forms of **anthropocentric conceit** become redundant. The moment any sort of life-form is found on another planet is the moment when *Homo sapiens* will finally have to relinquish any claims to special significance in the cosmos. Exoevolution will become an integral part of taking a **cosmic perspective**. See the entry on **dynamic integrity**.

Further reading: H. James Birx, "The Challenge of Exoevolution," *Free Inquiry* 15, no. 1 (Winter 1994/95): 32–34, and *Interpreting Evolution: Darwin and Teilhard de Chardin*.

EXPECTANT ATTENTION. A phrase originally used by the English sleuth Rupert T. Gould (1890–1948), who explored unsolved mysteries, sometimes, but not exclusively from a skeptical point of view. Writing in the context of the Loch Ness Monster, Gould attributed many sightings to expectant attention, which means going out to look for something that we want to be able to describe as the Loch Ness Monster. The notion of expectant attention helps explain the phenomenon of multiple sightings of something unusual after a publicized original sighting.

A famous example was in the Netherlands, when a panda escaped from a zoo and was sighted in dozens of places across the country once its escape had been made public. As it turned out, not one of the sightings were genuine because the panda had been flattened on a railway track. But people had ventured out with the thought of seeing something unusual, so many did. Expectant attention helps explain much about apparent sightings of UFOs and other psychic phenomena. See the entry on **pseudoscience**.

EXTERNAL REALISM. Defined by **John Searle** as the view that there is a way that things are logically dependent on all human representations. And unlike other philosophical maxims, external realism is a necessary presupposition for most of our other presuppositions, and indeed for language or thought itself. External realism functions as a component of the taken-for-granted part of our surroundings. Searle argues that the very first step in combating **irrationalism** is to defend the notion of external realism and refute arguments against it. The external realism of Searle has much in common with **critical realism**, to the point where the two labels are describing the same philosophy. See the entries on **reality**, **pragmatism**, and **relativism**.

Further reading: John Searle, *The Construction of Social Reality*.

EXTINCTION. As **death** is an inevitable part of the life of a single living creature, so is extinction an inevitable part of the life of a species. It is thought that 99.9 percent of all species which have existed are now extinct. Estimates vary as to how many different species this might involve, but many paleontologists suggest there have been upwards of thirty billion in the history of planet Earth. The rate of extinctions has increased dramatically since the **Cambrian explosion**, when the number and range of life-forms grew so exponentially. There have been five major extinctions since the Cambrian explosion:

- the end-Ordovician, 440 million years ago;
- the late Devonian, 365 million years ago;
- the end-Permian, 225 million years ago;
- the end-Triassic, 210 million years ago; and
- the end-Cretaceous, 65 million years ago.

To qualify as a mass extinction, at least 65 percent of species need to have perished, and for the losses to be among land and sea animals. The Permian extinction is thought to have eliminated 95 percent of species then living. And the latest was when the dinosaurs became extinct, brought on, in all probability, by climate change associated with an asteroid hitting the Earth.

The first evolutionist to notice the fact of mass extinctions was Georges Cuvier (1769–1832) who determined that mammoth bones were not from elephants, but from a different species altogether, which no longer exists.

Extinctions are brought on by modifications in the physical environment that adversely effect a species' ability to eat and reproduce. A species can easily become extinct through no fault of its own, or in the language of **natural selection**, with no reference to any lessening in its ability to adapt.

Many scientists are drawing attention to the sixth major extinction, which is taking place right now. But unlike all previous extinctions, this one is being helped along by *Homo sapiens*, whose relentless spread throughout the world is destroying the habitat of countless other species. There are few clearer instances of **anthropocentric conceit** than our treatment of other species. And, equally, there are few means more effective for seeing things with a **cosmic perspective** than to appreciate the reality of periodic mass extinctions.

Further reading: Richard Leakey and Roger Lewin, *The Sixth Extinction*.

EXTREMISM. Defined by Roger Scruton as the tendency to take an idea to its limits, without regard to unfortunate implications or impracticalities, and with the intention not merely to confront, but to eliminate opposition. Extremism is characterized by intolerance to any view but one's own. The American political scientist Laird Wilcox has itemized a comprehensive list of characteristics of extremism:

- character assassination, and reliance on *ad hominem* arguments;
- irresponsible and sweeping generalizations for which little or no proof is offered;
- unwillingness to concede that those who differ do so in good faith;
- simplistic black-and-white, us-and-them worldview;
- willingess to advocate **censorship** or repression of critics;
- willingness to argue in an intimidating manner;
- the use of slogans, buzzwords, and clichés;
- assumption of moral superiority over one's opponents;
- belief that the ends justify the means;
- preference for emotional responses over reasoning and logical analysis;
- use of supernatural or teleological rationale for beliefs and actions; and
- tendency toward **groupishness**.

Wilcox noted that extremists tend to see "the system" as being no good unless they win. If public opinion is against them, that is because people have been brainwashed or otherwise hoodwinked, not infrequently as part of some conspiracy. See the entry on **conspiracy theories**. As with the entry on **sects**, few groups will conform to every one of these criteria, although the ones that do spell real trouble.

Further reading: Laird Wilcox, "What Is 'Political Extremism,'" *Free Inquiry* 10, no. 4 (Fall 1990): 13–16.

F

FACTS. An actual state of affairs. The American philosopher **John Searle** maintains that there are two types of facts: institutional facts and brute facts.

Institutional facts are things like money or **marriage**. They are facts, but only because human beings make them so. Brute facts, however, are facts, whether we like them or not—things like **death** or gravity. It follows from this that brute facts have logical priority over institutional facts. This distinction is very important, because it helps us determine the degree of confidence with which we should hold particular beliefs. For instance, we can be more confident that our pen will fall to the floor when it slips from our hands than we can be about the state of marriage.

Searle goes on to say that making distinctions between facts is an important way to understand social **reality**. He distinguishes an intrinsic fact from an observer-related fact. The intrinsic fact is that the object on my desk is a stone. The observer-related fact is that the object on my desk is an attractive paperweight. In this way, the intrinsic fact is an objective fact while the observer-related fact is a subjective fact. Searle's understanding of facts dissolves the **relativism** of the **social worlds** theory.

Further reading: John Searle, *The Construction of Social Reality*.

FAILED STATE. The condition where the government and infrastructure of a once-stable country has been so completely destroyed that no effective central control remains. States fail in this way most commonly from the effects of civil war, often fueled by bitter ethnic and/or religious conflicts, or from endemic corruption from self-serving government officials. And into the vacuum step regional warlords, or tribal or religious leaders, who maintain private armies and live by banditry.

In earlier times a country so weakened would have been invaded and incorporated into a more powerful neighbor, but in the contemporary world, with so many fragile nations operating within artificial boundaries, this option is too destabilizing for world peace. So now, the failed state occupies the same extent of territory on the map, but there is no authority in effective control of it. The collapse of governmental authority provides ideal conditions for terrorists to find sanctuary, launder funds, acquire weapons of mass destruction, and recruit new members.

The most graphic cases of failed states include Somalia, Afghanistan, Liberia, and Sierra Leone. The process of restoring civil society is very expensive and requires long-term commitment from the international community, but such work is in the world's interest, as failed states constitute both human tragedy on a massive scale and a serious threat to world peace.

FAITH. The willingness to believe what one cannot demonstrate rationally as being true. The New Testament calls faith an assurance of what is hoped for, a conviction of unseen realities (Hebrews 11:1), and claims that faith can allow one to handle venomous snakes or drink deadly poison unharmed (Mark 16:18). Faith is therefore intimately bound up with belief in supernatural realities as revealed by **God** or gods. It makes no sense to speak of faith without the belief that God has revealed the object of faith. It was in the sense of faith leading to **certainty** that the English philosophers Anthony Kenny and **Richard Robinson** both describe Christian faith as a vice, and as such, something to be condemned.

Faith is the opposite of **rational belief**, which is belief based on information from reliable sources and in proportion to the available evidence. A rational belief is a belief that justifies being accepted because it can be demonstrated, even if only in principle. But faith has a built-in hostility to this method. The Danish philosopher Søren

Kierkegaard (1813–1855) was adamant that faith is an act of will to believe something despite the lack of evidence for it, or even because there is so little evidence for it. This is what he meant by the leap of faith—it is a leap across a chasm of unknowing.

Some attempts have been made to see science as built essentially on faith, but they depend on peculiar or very broad understandings of faith. The rationalist philosopher **L. Susan Stebbing** spoke of the faith of a scientist as the basic acceptance of the laws of nature and our ability to discover those laws. And some theologians, like the Canadian Wilfred Cantwell Smith (1916–2001) have argued that faith is not necessarily tied to belief. By this reasoning all people not irretrievably alienated are people of faith, by virtue of their everyday life and practice. See the entry on *Homo religiosus*.

However, these attempts have not generally been convincing, and neither have they been accepted by the majority of religious believers. Faith, if the word means anything at all, and in the sense it is generally understood, means religious faith, usually with respect to one's own chances of cheating death. It would be best for freethinkers not to use the word faith, as it gives rise to these sorts of misunderstandings.

Further reading: Anthony Kenny, *What is Faith?* and Sam Harris, *The End of Faith: Religion, Terror and the Future of Reason.*

FALLIBILISM. An ancient idea, although the word was coined by Charles Sanders Peirce (1839–1914), American philosopher and founder of the school of **pragmatism**. For an ancient account of fallibilism, see the entry on the **ten tropes of judgment**. Fallibilism requires the individual to accept that one's opinions are always prone to error, and therefore fallible. It also stresses that new knowledge can arrive at any time which renders one's most cherished beliefs invalid. Fallibilism was later discussed at length, and outside the strictly pragmatist angle, by **Karl Popper**. It has become an essential feature of what was later called the **scientific method**. See the entry on **metacognition**.

Fallibilism also has some significant ethical implications. In particular, the need to renounce any **dogmatism** and the openness to further study and new ideas. For fallibilism's polar opposite, see the entry on **Intolerance, Principle of**. But if fallibilism has no truck with dogmatism, neither does it go as far as **nihilism** and **postmodernism** in abandoning any claim to truth. The trick, as the English philosopher Bernard Williams (1929–2003) said, is to hold our views with confidence, but not with **certainty**.

FALL, THE. The item of Christian dogma which holds that as a result of the **sin** whereby Eve picked the apple from the tree of knowledge of the difference between good and evil against the specific wishes of **God**, she and Adam were expelled from the paradise of Eden. This explains in Christian terms, why we are all so irretrievably wicked. St. Augustine (354–430 CE) later developed the dogma of **original sin** from the Fall. The fundamental sinfulness of humanity is essential to the whole Christian schema because without the dogma of the Fall, there is little point in the entire story of **Jesus Christ** being sent by God his father to redeem sinful humanity in an act of loving sacrifice.

This also then provides the basic Christian division of humanity into those who have faith that Christ is who he said he was and are therefore saved by virtue of that faith, and those who don't believe that, and are therefore damned to hell. The most important problem with the notion of the Fall is that it isn't true. There was no such historical event, and the theory of **human nature** it assumes is not supported by any evidence. It is a mythological account which, because it is not true, can only be accepted on **faith**.

FALSIFIABILITY. A notion introduced by **Karl Popper** as a means by which a claim or system of claims can be determined as scientific and which he saw as an improvement on the **Verification Principle**. The demarcation point between science and **pseudoscience**, Popper argued, is whether it is possible in principle to refute a theory. Put simply, a scientific theory can in principle be refuted whereas a pseudoscientific theory cannot be. The scientist is the person who posits a theory which is at least capable of being criticized and then actively seeks possible ways to falsify the theory.

Popper criticized notions of justifying a scientific hypothesis on the grounds of it explaining everything, or having a high probability, or merely one that can be confirmed. Popper argued that a highly probable hypothesis is by no means a highly useful one. It is more probable that the sick person is unwell rather than having one specific malady, but this probability is of little use. The highly probable hypothesis commits us to nothing. The business of **scientific method** is to work on a series of hypotheses by subjecting them to repeated tests to weed out the inaccurate ones. If a hypothesis has survived this grueling process, it reaches the status of having been corroborated. Popper devoted much effort to showing that his "corroboration" was different than "a high degree of probability," which has not convinced many critics of the falsification thesis.

Taking examples of transcendental metaphysics, astrology, **psychoanalysis**, and the Marxist philosophy of history, Popper showed that these systems are all **pseudosciences** precisely because they cannot, even in principle, be falsified. Popper went on to say that this does not mean that these systems are incorrect, only that they are not scientific. **Faith** has also shown itself to be unfalsifiable. Faith is so resilient that some explanation can always be found to explain away **God**'s latest failure to deliver. However, it is a small and quite reasonable step to object to the truth-claims of any system that cannot, even in principle, be shown to be false.

Popper's falsification thesis has been heavily criticized by philosophers and scientists. It has been observed, for instance, that science has not, in fact, progressed in the way Popper recommends. Neither does falsification rely on the deductive methods of reasoning as totally as Popper claims. Another relevant point here is that being able to determine whether a theory can in principle be falsified is not the same thing as demonstrating that it is valid. To do that, some real evidence that supports the theory is needed as well. Nevertheless, his falsifiability thesis remains a very useful test by which pseudosciences can be discovered and uprooted.

Further reading: Karl Popper, *The Logic of Scientific Discovery.*

FALSIFICATION CHALLENGE. A philosophical challenge devised by **Antony Flew** that asks what would have to happen to show that your statement is false. This derives from a famous essay by Flew called "Theology and Falsification." Here Flew posits a scenario where two people come across a garden which has some attractive flowers in it. One of them postulates that a gardener must tend the plot, but when no gardener turns up, he changes his story by saying the gardener must be invisible. When they find an electric fence but still find no sign of a gardener, invisible or otherwise, the man says he is invisible and immune to electric shocks. At each point the other man asks: "What remains of the original assertion that a gardener tends the flowers?" As the first person has been prepared to alter his account of the features the gardener must have each time, his earlier claim is shown to be faulty, and it becomes impossible to disprove the claim at all.

The applicability of this problem to claims about **God** is clear. Theists have continually changed their claims about God as each new bit of **evidence** that questions or disproves the hypothesis arises. The suspicion is that religious believers hold their views about God with little or no real interest in whether the claim is coherent or not.

Further reading: "Theology and Falsification" in Antony Flew and Alasdair MacIntyre, eds., *New Essays in Philosophical Theology.*

FAMILY VALUES. Against all reason, a controversial subject. Protecting and nurturing the family shouldn't be in the slightest bit problematic. The family unit is an ancient social grouping, with clear evolutionary advantages. Families existed because of the advantages they gave people in a **state of nature.** Families are very important for the provision of a safe psychological foundation for children, as well as for many forms of instruction. Families play a major role in bringing people up to be loving, responsible, and socially active adults. So when families are dysfunctional, for whatever reason, the chances increase that children from these families will grow up to become emotionally unstable. It follows, then, that a major role for any civilized society is to ensure conditions are conducive to healthy families.

The problem arises when we try to define what we mean by a family. Religious conservatives are united in preferring a narrow conception of what a family should be. In almost all cases, they insist a family is defined as something only heterosexuals can be part of. Religious conservatives are also united in insisting that a family should be bound by some solemn marriage contract, preferably sanctioned by their own **religion**. And more often than not, the male is deemed the head of the household, with the woman required to play a subservient role. The **scriptures** of all three **monotheist** religions give strong encouragement on these points. The **Asian traditions** also have strongly misogynist tendencies, but such attitudes are not bound up in scripture, which makes them easier to challenge and discard.

And it has long been known by **social scientists** that the conception of the ideal family preferred by religious conservatives has never been as universal as we have been led to believe. In the United States, only about a quarter of the people live in the supposedly traditional family unit of father, mother, and children. There are as many single-parent homes and people living alone as there are "traditional" families. And who is to say that only the "traditional" form of organization can produce happy, healthy people?

It is to the enormous credit of freethinkers that they have traditionally supported a broader, more inclusive conception of a family group. Any group of adults in a loving relationship can be a family. There is no reason why people should be formally married to have a meaningful, long-term relationship, where healthy, balanced children are raised. Monogamous relationships have generally been found to work the best, although there have been—and still are—stable societies that favor other family structures. Heterosexual families are obviously better at producing children, and have a long tradition of raising them, but families need not be heterosexual. Families are no less valuable when family members elect, for whatever reason, not to have children. **Love** and mutual consent are the key family values, not official licenses, gender hierarchies, or pat formulas memorized from **command moralities**. See the entry on **humanist family values**.

FAN CHENG (450–515 CE, approx.). Confucian scholar and critic of the supernaturalism of Chinese Buddhism. In *Shen-mieh lun (On the Mortality of the Soul)*, written about 500 CE, Fan attacked Buddhist notions then current about the immortality of the **soul** and life after death. Fan struck a humanist note when he rejected notions of **immortality** and stressed the importance of working in the here-and-now, during life on Earth.

FARBER, MARVIN (1901–1980). Courageous American philosopher. Marvin Farber was born in Buffalo, New York, and received a PhD in philosophy at Harvard in 1925. He also studied in Germany, where, under the influence of Edmund Husserl (1859–1938) he developed an expertise in **phenomenology**. Upon his return to the United States, Farber became one of that country's leading exponents of phenomenology. His academic life was at the State University of New York at Buffalo. He founded the academic journal *Philosophy and Phenomenological Research*, which quickly became the most influential journal in the field.

Through the second half of his career Farber became more critical of phenomenology. He became an early critic of Martin Heidegger. His mature thought on the subject was put to brilliant effect in his book *Naturalism and Subjectivism* (1959).

Outside of academic work, Farber was a courageous opponent of Senator McCarthy's House Un-American Activities Committee's attempts to persecute people suspected of communism during the time now known as the **Great Fear**.

FARMER, JAMES (1920–1999). African-American activist and humanist. The son of a preacher, James Farmer was born in Marshall, Texas. After a rapid promotion, he went to Wiley College in Marshall before going off to Howard University's School of Religion, from which he graduated in 1941. After graduation, he refused to become a Methodist minister because he opposed that denomination's practice of segregating congregants. Instead he joined the Quaker Fellowship for Reconciliation. And in 1942, he helped found the Congress of Racial Equality (CORE), a civil-rights organization intent on nonviolent protest against segregation and inequality. Under Farmer's leadership, CORE organized the "Freedom Rides" throughout the South as a protest against segregation in buses.

These and other activities led Farmer to be seen as one of the four most prominent black civil-rights leaders of the 1960s, known as the "Big Four." The other three were Martin Luther King (1929–1968), Whitney Young (1921–1971), and Roy Wilkins (1901–1981). Farmer was also instrumental in recruiting **Michael Schwerner** and his two friends, who were murdered by white supremacists in 1964. Farmer left CORE in the late 1960s when it began to move away from its nonviolent roots. From 1968 until 1971, he had a political career as a Republican, serving in the Nixon administration as assistant secretary of Health, Education, and Welfare. In 1998, President Clinton awarded Farmer the Presidential Medal of Freedom. Farmer wrote an autobiography, *Lay Bare the Heart* (1985).

As happens so often, Farmer's **humanism** is ignored in the obituaries and accounts of his life. The fact is that James Farmer was a signatory to the *Humanist Manifesto 2000* and was on the advisory board of **African Americans for Humanism**.

FATAL FLAW AT THE HEART OF RELIGIOUS LIBERALISM. An idea propounded by the American **religious humanist** and environmentalist Duncan Howlett (1906–2003). After a career in the **Unitarian** church, Howlett came to recognize the fatal flaw, as he put it, in the liberal religious position. There always comes a point, he wrote in 1995, when religious liberals have to stop asking questions and taking on new ideas. Too many questions and the religious believer will end up nonreligious. So at some point, the religious liberal, in order to remain in any way religious, has to stop asking questions and rely unthinkingly on old dogmas. Where this point is at which the questioning ends will depend on the individual. But this gives an arbitrary feeling to religious liberalism. This demilitarized zone inside each religious liberal between what is open to question and what is not results in a weak worldview and constitutes the fatal flaw in the heart of religious liberalism.

This brilliant analysis has not, to my knowledge, been answered. The consequences of Howlett's idea are dramatic. It leaves religious liberals without any defensible justification for whatever position they end up taking. Deuteronomy 13:1, for example, commands that "whatever I am now commanding you, you must keep and observe, adding nothing to it, taking nothing away." This would seem to disallow any attempt to render the barbarous passages of the Bible as merely "symbolic." And neither can one say that Jesus Christ got beyond those barbarities, because Matthew 5:17–19 has Jesus insisting he has come to uphold every jot and tittle of the law. It leaves the fundamentalist on surer ground than the religious liberal, because, while their worldview is narrow, irrationalist, and exclusionary, it is, by this standard at least, not inconsistent. See the entries on **fundamentalism** and **certainty**.

Further reading: Duncan Howlett, *The Fatal Flaw at the Heart of Religious Liberalism*.

FATWA. A nonbinding legal opinion concerning Islamic law issued by a mufti to settle a question where Islamic jurisprudence is unclear. As with any statement by Christian church leaders, a fatwa can be about any topic, and its significance will depend largely on the level of authority ascribed to the author of the fatwa.

The notion of a fatwa only became widely known in the West after the death sentence Iran's Ayatollah Khomeini issued on February 14, 1989, calling for the novelist Salman Rushdie (1947–) to suffer death for **blaspheming** against Islam in his book *The Satanic Verses*, which was published in 1988. There are legitimate doubts about the status of Khomeini's judgment. Some scholars of Islam contend that his statement was not technically a fatwa because he went further than simply condemning Rushdie's acts by also pronouncing a sentence of death against him.

FAUSTIAN BARGAIN, THE. A term given to a person's willingness to fatally compromise one's principles in order to secure career or social advancement. The name comes from the sixteenth-century story which was retold most famously by **Goethe**. Here, Faust sells his soul to the devil in return for special wisdom. The tragedy, of course, is that the price paid for that wisdom is so high that the wisdom turns to ashes in one's hands. The Faustian bargain is often such that the victim was willing to enter into the fatal relationship for often very lofty and unselfish grounds. Many principled people cooperated with the Nazis, for instance, and sometimes for quite commendable reasons, but found themselves sucked into the vortex of evil in the process.

The Buddha understood this dilemma when he stipulated right livelihood as one of the steps in the eight-fold path that leads to no desire. See the entry on the **Four Noble Truths**. To take a simple example, how can someone engaged in filming child porn be able to maintain a consistent ethical position on any other issue? A young filmmaker may do this sort of work for a while, with laudable goals of using the money earned from it to do good works later on, but the Faustian bargain will already have compromised the person and his goals. On a practical level this means that the means by which one earns one's living has moral consequences on one's whole life. And more generally, the Faustian bargain serves as a reminder that good intentions aren't enough to negate the moral consequences of the dishonorable methods those good intentions may be brought about by.

FEAR MORALITY AND HOPE MORALITY. A distinction drawn by **Bertrand Russell** in his book *New Hopes for a Changing World* (1951). Fear morality is pessimistic and seeks to avoid disaster. With this in mind, fear morality has been instrumental in creating moral codes and commandments on the assumption that it is impossible to prevent or overcome sinful, violent, or otherwise harmful impulses in human beings. Fear morality seeks to crush these natural impulses to evil by constructing systems which evoke an even greater fear. The clearest example of this is the doctrine of **hell**. Parallels can also be drawn between fear morality and **command morality**.

Hope morality, by contrast, is the simpler, and yet vastly more difficult approach of seeking to create things that are good and delightful.

Further reading: Bertrand Russell, *New Hopes for a Changing World*.

FEMINISM. In its simplest sense, feminism is the belief, as the American writer Marilyn French (1929–) put it, that women are of equal worth to men. Themes central to feminism include the importance of women's experiences and a critique of men's theories about women. The word is usually attributed to the French socialist Charles Fourier (1772–1837) and first appeared in English in the 1890s. But, as is also the case with the word "**humanism**," there were feminists before there was feminism; **Olympe de Gouge** and **Mary Wollstonecraft** are prime examples.

Feminism has gone through several stages of development. Very broadly, feminism was concerned originally with the acquisition of **rights** that had traditionally been denied to women. This is still very much part of the struggle in developing countries and countries with strong religious traditions. In the West, the emphasis has swung to a broader concern with women as agents of change in their own right, rather than as recipients of change granted from above. One of the most important books to articulate this message was *The Second Sex* (1949, English translation 1953) by **Simone de Beauvoir**.

A problem that has dogged feminism is the degree to which the holding of particular ideologies is integral to it. Feminism has been presented in Marxist, psychoanalytic, postmodernist, liberal, and humanist forms, to mention only the most prominent. In *The Skeptical Feminist* (1980), Janet Radcliffe Richards argued that attachment to any one outlook was not necessary. What was integral to feminism, Radcliffe Richards argued, was the belief that women are subjected to discrimination, and that the subjection arising from this discrimination is unjust.

Another problem that has dogged feminism has been the difficulty in identifying issues and solutions common to all women, across cultural, religious, and class divides. One point seems clear: traditional **religion** and feminism are incompatible without a radical reassessment of religious beliefs and practices. In the same way that there is a fundamental **conflict between science and religion**, so there is also a basic conflict between traditional religious and feminist conceptions of the rights and roles of women.

Feminism has suffered an increasingly bad press, caused in part by the irrationalist, antiscience nonsense many of the more extreme feminists produced in the 1970s and 1980s. Now, many young women, who take for granted the liberties that their predecessors won for them, feel able to dismiss feminism as a relic of the past that involves man-hating. This is unfortunate, and could end up working to their disadvantage as many of their liberties are slowly rolled back.

FERRER, FRANCISCO (1859–1909). Spanish educator and martyr to **freethought**. As a young man, Ferrer was involved in revolutionary activity against the corrupt and brutal Spanish regime. He fled to France in 1886 and lived in Paris for a number of years. In Paris, Ferrer renounced violence as a method of securing permanent change and turned his attention to education.

Upon his return to Spain, Ferrer opened a school, which broke with tradition by admitting girls and children of the poor. Religion was not taught and a comprehensive scientific education was provided instead. The powerful Catholic Church in Spain declared his school to be godless (which was true) and an agent of Satan (which was not). His school became popular, and within a few years he had forty of them around Catalonia. When King Alfonso XIII was the target of an assassination attempt in 1906, Ferrer was arrested and his schools closed down. Ferrer was acquitted of any involvement in the attack, but the church was determined to shut him down. He was kept under police surveillance. He later established the International League of Rational Education, which did nothing to mend relations with the church.

During renewed unrest in 1909, there was serious rioting in what became known as the Tragic Week, and Ferrer's enemies saw an opportunity to saddle him with the blame. Ferrer was charged with fomenting the riots and after a travesty of a trial was shot on October 13, 1909. Ferrer's death brought the downfall of the conservative Spanish government and a storm of international criticism. Oblivious of this, Pope Pius X sent the military prosecutor responsible for Ferrer's death an engraved, gold-handled sword as reward.

Further reading: Joseph McCabe, *The Martyrdom of Ferrer*.

FEUERBACH, LUDWIG (1804–1872). German philosopher and radical. Born in Landshut, Bavaria, the son of an important jurist and thinker Paul Feuerbach (1775–1833). While Marxism was a living philosophy, appreciation of Feuerbach was limited to his role as a stepping stone to Marxism. Now liberated from this shackle, appreciation of Feuerbach's bold thinking can take on broader forms.

Feuerbach is best known for his two books, *Essence of Christianity* (1841) and *Essence of Religion* (1851), which provided important new understandings of **religion**. Feuerbach's influence was broadened by the English translation of *Essence of Christianity* by **George Eliot** in 1854. Feuerbach had already lost any chances of a professorship with his *Thoughts on Death and Immortality* (1830), which denied a personal **God** and **immortality**.

He was greatly influenced by G. W. F. Hegel (1770–1831) and took his mentor one step further by arguing that religion is humanity projecting itself onto nature. Hegel had argued that the Absolute slowly objectifies itself in the world and comes to complete self-consciousness through the growing self-consciousness of humanity. Feuerbach was not denying divinity so much as he was redefining divinity as a human quality. In his later books, he moved away from his earlier Hegelianism and argued that we become alienated from ourselves by worshiping a creation of our own imagination. Our desire for immortality and willingness to petition the Lord of all creation for one's own petty little ambitions isolate us from nature as it really is. The later Feuerbach thus became a powerful voice against the **anthropocentric conceit** implicit in religion. In *The Essence of Religion*, he wrote:

> My only wish is . . . to transform friends of God into friends of man, believers into thinkers, devotees of prayer into devotees of work, candidates for the hereafter into students of the world, Christians who, by their own admission, are *"half animal, half angel"* into *persons*, into *whole persons*.

Now emerging from the shadow of the Marxist criticism of him, Feuerbach is returning to a position of great influence.

FIDEISM. A brand of religious apologetics that claims that essential religious dogmas are **beyond** rationality. They exist, and can be accepted only by nonrational ways such as **faith**. In this way, any philosophical demolition of the existence of God, for example, is irrelevant to true belief. This option of religious thinking is relatively recent; the word "fideism" was coined only in the nineteenth century. As the natural world has moved ever more clearly away from supernaturalist explanations, those wanting to defend supernaturalism have had to retreat to areas where rationality is thought unable to follow.

FINE ARTS. See **VISUAL ARTS**

FIRTH, RAYMOND (1901–2002). One of the most significant anthropologists of the twentieth century. Raymond Firth was born in New Zealand and raised in an undogmatic Christian family. By the time Firth moved to Britain in 1924 his religious faith had eroded away entirely. After beginning his study at Auckland University College, he continued

his education at the London School of Economics (LSE), where he took his PhD. After a short stint at the University of Sydney, Firth returned to the LSE, where he became professor of anthropology in 1944. During his spell in Sydney, he met **John Anderson** and was vice president of the Freethought Society.

Firth wrote a series of influential works on the peoples of the South Pacific, in particular *Primitive Economics of the New Zealand Maori* (1929) and *We the Tikopia* (1936). *Elements of Social Organization* (1951) was the result of the Josiah Mason Lectures, which were sponsored by the **Rationalist Press Association**. Firth had the honor of giving the first in this series of lectures, in 1946–47. As his study of anthropology deepened, it became more apparent to Firth that religion is a human construct. Firth was by nature skeptical of religion, rather than actively opposed to it. Firth was still writing well into his nineties. His last book was *Religion: A Humanist Interpretation* (1996). In it, he wrote, "Assertions about revelation, and relations with transcendental beings or powers can be clearly seen as imaginative invention, often corresponding to vested interests of a social, economic or political order."

Firth became an honorary associate of the Rationalist Press Association in 1943, and retained that honor for 59 years until his death. He was knighted in 1973, and in 1983 he was elected a laureate of the **International Academy of Humanism**.

Further reading: Kenneth Maddock, "Anthropology and the Falsity of Religions," *Open Society* 76, no. 1 (Autumn 2003): 2–6.

FIVE PRINCIPLES OF COEXISTENCE. Five principles arrived at by a major conference of twenty-nine nonaligned nations at Bandung, Indonesia, in April 1955. As the **cold war** was gathering pace, the United States and its allies on the one hand, and the Soviet Union and its allies on the other, were seeking firm commitments from the countries of the world for their cause. But most countries in Africa, Asia, and Latin America preferred to remain at arms length from both blocs. Some stuck to this stance as a matter of principle, others as a way to increase their bargaining position from the two camps. Either way, the Bandung conference was instrumental in creating the concept of the third world, as a separate entity from the first world (the so-called free world) and the second world (the communist bloc).

The five principles of coexistence decided at the Bandung conference were:

- respect for each country's territorial integrity;
- noninterference in each other's internal affairs;
- nonaggression;
- equal and mutual benefits in economic relations; and
- peaceful coexistence.

Each of these principles were betrayed at some point or another by the signatories and by later members of the third world, but the principle of the third world as a separate entity, with its own interests and needs, was an important milestone in international politics. The next step in this growing awareness was the formation of the **Group of 77**, which stressed the shared economic interests of the third world.

FLEW, ANTONY (1923–). One of the most distinguished English philosophers since World War II. His engaging writing style and formidable breadth of knowledge have been put to good use in a succession of fine books. His earliest contributions were in the form of editing or coediting some influential studies, in particular *Logic and Language* (First Series in 1951 and Second Series in 1953) and, coedited with Alasdair MacIntyre, *New Essays in Philosophical Theology* (1955). His first full-length book was a sympathetic study of psychic phenomena. He was encouraged to write the book by **Hector Hawton** at the **Rationalist Press Association**.

Flew is known for his close support of

David Hume. He has written short introductions to Hume as well as more scholarly studies of his work, in particular *Hume's Philosophy of Belief* (1961). His *An Introduction to Western Philosophy* (1971, revised edition 1989) has proved to be a massively successful thematic introduction to Western philosophy. Flew has also written successful primers on thinking philosophically which have gone through many editions.

Flew has not been afraid to advance controversial or unpopular ideas, such as his conservative political position. Even more controversial, he has been one of the most consistent and influential philosophers of **atheism** of the twentieth century. An early foray in this field was the short essay "Theology and Falsification," which was originally written in 1944 and 1945 for a long-defunct student paper. "Theology and Falsification" quickly established itself as a classic and has appeared regularly in anthologies on the philosophy of religion ever since. Flew's first book-length study was *God and Philosophy* (1966). This was followed by *The Presumption of Atheism* (1976), which was later published in the United States as *God, Freedom and Immortality* (1984), and *Atheistic Humanism* (1993), which was the first of the influential **Prometheus Lectures**. In these books, Flew developed his theme of the **presumption of atheism** and the related **Stratonician Presumption**. Flew has also taken part in several important debates with religious believers, most of which have been published.

Flew has also written extensively for nonspecialist readers. This can be seen especially in the journals of the Rationalist Press Association in Britain. Flew has been an honorary associate of the RPA since 1976 and served as vice president from 1973 until 1988.

FLOW. The name given to a theory by the psychologist Mihaly Csikszentmihalyi, which refers to the ability some people have to lose themselves in their work. Flow is essentially about human creativity. Csikszentmihalyi studied creative people and found some common features of their person-alities, without regard to how their creativity was manifested. Whether among moun-taineers, chess players, musicians, or scholars —anyone deeply passionate about what they do—creative people have these things in common:

- knowing clearly what it is they have to do;
- getting feedback on what they are doing; and
- having the ability to match their skills with the level of difficulty of the project at hand.

When these common features are present, the creative individual is able to concentrate at the level required to excel. And that is when they seem to lose themselves, or as Csik-szentmihalyi puts it, have the "flow experi-ence." Flow is not the same as happiness, because the person is too busy with the task at hand. But *afterward*, they often say these times are the happiest of their lives. Flow is the psychologist's version of the concept of **eudaimonia**.

Further reading: Mihaly Csikszentmi-halyi, *Finding Flow: The Psychology of Everyday Experience*.

FLYNN, THOMAS W[ILLIAM] (1955–). One of the leading secular humanists in the United States. Tom Flynn was born in Erie, Pennsylvania, into a Catholic family but by the time he had graduated in 1977 from Xavier University in Cincinnati, he was well along the way to abandoning his religious beliefs, a process completed by 1980.

In 1989, after a career in advertising and video production, Flynn joined the staff of the **Council for Secular Humanism**. He had been working there on a voluntary basis since 1985, when he cofounded the *Secular Humanist Bulletin*, which he then coedited for twelve years. In 1995, he was appointed senior editor of *Free Inquiry* magazine, and

in 2000 he became the editor. He is a strong supporter of the *secular* in **secular humanism**, which his pamphlet, *Secular Humanism Defined* (2002), made clear. Flynn has been a central figure in the creation of the Ingersoll Museum at Dresden, New York, the house where **Robert Ingersoll** was born. This museum opened in 1993 and is the only museum dedicated to **freethought** in the United States. He was an inaugural director of the **Center for Inquiry** from its founda-tion in 1990.

The first of Flynn's three books was *The Trouble with Christmas* (1993), an exposé of the Christmas story and a plea for humanists not to celebrate it. He has also written two science fiction novels: *Galactic Rapture* (2000), a black comedy with some caustic observations on the religious mind; and *Nothing Sacred* (2004), its sequel. Flynn is editor of the *New Encyclopedia of Unbelief* (2006).

FOLK PSYCHOLOGY. Term originally coined by **Daniel C. Dennett** in 1978 but best known now for the use given to it by the neurophilosophers Paul and Patricia Church-land, who describe it as an integrated body of nonscientific lore about internal states, our relations with the world, and laws thought to guide these things. Folk psychology favors **dualistic** notions of mind, and anachronistic notions about how we think and perceive. It is the contention of the Churchlands that folk psychology is radically false and should be abandoned in favor of understandings based on genuinely scientific study.

FOOTE, GEORGE WILLIAM (1850–1915). Atheist pioneer and journalist. Born and raised in Plymouth, Foote had become a convinced freethinker while still a teenager, before his move to London in 1868. For a short while Foote associated himself with opponents of **Charles Bradlaugh**. In 1876, Foote challenged Bradlaugh for the leadership of the secular movement but was decisively defeated. The same year, Foote established the *Secularist*, with **George Jacob Holyoake**, becoming editor after a few issues. This magazine had a short life, however, and in 1881 Foote established the *Freethinker*, which, against all odds, has been constantly in print since then; easily the longest-running freethought journal in the world.

Foote was soon reconciled with Bradlaugh, becoming vice president of the **National Secular Society** in 1882 and succeeding him as president after his death in January 1891. Foote defended Bradlaugh's memory stoutly for the remainder of his life. Foote achieved nationwide notoriety in 1883 when he was sentenced to twelve months' hard labor in Holloway prison for blasphemy. It also did the *Freethinker*'s circulation no harm at all. The charge involved a series of comic sketches of various Bible passages. His comment from the dock ranks as one of the most memorable sentences in freethought history. When told of his sentence Foote said, "Thank you, my Lord, the sentence is worthy of your creed." Despite a petition in defense of free speech, signed by **T. H. Huxley, Herbert Spencer**, and others, Foote served his full sentence. After his release, he resumed, even enlarged, the comic sketches which had provoked his sentence, but was not prosecuted again. Foote had effectively defanged the **blasphemy** issue.

Shortly before his death, Bradlaugh conferred the leadership of the **National Secular Society** to Foote, a position he held until his own death. Foote's next instance of notoriety was less fortunate. Sensing a fabrication, Foote publicly called the Rev. Hugh Price Hughes a liar for telling the story of an atheist shoemaker who had converted on his deathbed. Unfortunately for Foote, the story was in fact true, but Foote's refusal to retract the charge did his public standing little good.

It is a scandal that this intelligent and interesting man has not been the subject of a biography.

FORCE, APPEAL TO. Probably the most fallacious style of argument. In Latin it is known as the *argumentum ad baculum*. It consists of "agree with me because I have the power to apply force against you if you don't." It should go without saying that a threat of coercion is not a logical ground for accepting an argument. It may, however, be a good practical argument for accepting it. People being what they are, the fallacious nature of this argument has not been an impediment to its very widespread use. Every act of coercion, overt or covert, by thought police, inquisitors, vigilantes, or others has been done on the back of the appeal to force.

FORETHOUGHT. See **PROMETHEUS**.

FORMER PREACHERS. The freethought movement has long been filled with former preachers, sincere people who came to see that their faith in religion was misguided. In the nineteenth century there were people like **Robert Taylor** and **Sir Leslie Stephen**, and in the twentieth, **Joseph McCabe**, who went on to have a very significant career as a popularizer of science and speaker on all forms of freethought. McCabe wrote a powerful account of his odyssey, *Twelve Years in a Monastery* (1897).

Among the many other former preachers there were people like Dennis Hird (1850–1920), a prominent Anglican churchman, one-time secretary of the Church of England Temperance Society and the London Police Court Missionary. Hird lost his faith trying to reconcile **evolution** with his religious beliefs. He compiled *An Easy Outline of Evolution* (1903), which went on to have a long career, first as a **Cheap Reprint** of the **Rationalist Press Association**, then as an illustrated guide to evolution.

G. Vincent Runyon (1898–1978), a Methodist priest for twelve years, left the church and wrote *Why I Left the Ministry and Became an Atheist* (1959). Runyon was shocked to find that he liked the atheists he met, and he found them warmer and more full of life than his parishioners. Runyon wrote, "You can put a purpose into your life. You can go about doing good. Do something that needs to be done. Without a god there is plenty to do. The world needs you. Have a goal. Have a philosophy. No religion or church has a monopoly on morals or ethics despite what the clergy say."

Then there was Emmett McLaughlin (1906–1970), who left the Catholic Church in 1948 and continued his life's work of helping the poor of Phoenix, Arizona, where he lived. McLaughlin was known as the People's Padre, and wrote a book by that title.

More recently, Skipp Porteous (1944–) was an American Evangelical preacher who lost his faith and became a humanist. In 1966, Porteous entered the Lighthouse of International Foursquare Evangelism in Los Angeles. He had recently been converted to Evangelical Christianity and was fired with zeal for the Last Days, which were imminent. His Bible College dealt with each of the traditional problems with the Bible, and every time the Bible was shown to be right. He later became director of the Institute for First Amendment Studies. Porteous is author of *Jesus Doesn't Live Here Anymore: From Fundamentalist to Freedom Writer* (1991) and many articles on contemporary religion and **humanism**.

Another important example is Charles Templeton, for two decades one of North America's most successful preachers, and a man known as the Billy Graham of Canada. Templeton was director of Evangelism for the Presbyterian Church USA and later for the National Council of Christian Churches. But he came to see that the foundations of his Christian belief were unsound, and he lost his faith. He wrote about his path to humanism in *Farewell to God: My Reasons for Rejecting the Christian Faith* (1996).

To take one more important example, Robert M. Price is a lecturer in philosophy and religion at Johnston Community College in North Carolina. For many years, Price was a fervent Evangelical. After he left he wrote *Beyond Born Again: Towards Evangelical Maturity* (1993) and more recently two books

on Jesus: *Deconstructing Jesus* (2000) and *The Incredible Shrinking Son of Man* (2004). Price is a fellow of the **Jesus Seminar** and the **Committee for the Scientific Examination of Religion**.

These prominent individuals are the tip of the iceberg. Huge numbers of people around the world are moving away from fervent religious belief to a more intellectually credible and tolerant form of liberal religion, or to **Unitarianism**, or to **humanism**. These various **life-stances** have the advantage of being strengthened by developments in science and philosophy, rather than weakened by them, as **monotheist** religions are—this is the most common reason so many former preachers can no longer remain in the church in good conscience. This moral earnestness is one of the things that humanism and religions have in common, and which separates humanism from **indifferentism**. See the entry on **Enyeribe Onuoha**.

Further reading: Edward T. Babinski, ed., *Leaving the Fold: Testimonies of Former Fundamentalists* and the Web site *Ex-Christian Webring*.

FORSTER, E[DWARD] M[ORGAN]

(1879–1970). Novelist and humanist. Born in London and educated at Tonbridge School and King's College, Cambridge. There he came under the influence of leading thinkers known later as the Bloomsbury Circle. Forster wrote some of Britain's most important twentieth century novels: *Where Angels Fear to Tread* (1905), *A Room with a View* (1908), *Howards End* (1910), and *A Passage to India* (1924). Most of these works have been adapted to television. He also wrote a novel on the subject of homosexuality, called *Maurice*, but it was not published until after his death. He wrote some memorable essays as well, most notably *Two Cheers for Democracy* (1951). He was responsible for one of the more poetic encapsulations of the core of humanism ever written. See the entry on **only connect**.

Forster renounced Christianity while at Cambridge and became active in the humanist movement later in his life. He insisted that if his rejection of religion is not vehement, people should not suppose that it is not tenacious. He was president of the Cambridge Humanists from 1955 and an honorary associate of the **Rationalist Press Association** from 1959. In a tribute to Forster after his death, R. C. Churchill said that if **Bertrand Russell** is the head of the movement, E. M. Forster was its heart.

FOUNDAMENTALISM. A word coined by the Muslim dissident Irshad Manji, which refers to the backward-looking tendency among many Muslims to fixate on the founding moment of Islam and to want to measure everything by that standard. Foundamentalism is intrinsically anti-innovation and anti**freethought**, because its standards are strictly backward-looking. Foundamentalism threatens any intellectual, moral, or social advances unless some correlation with the wishes of the founder can be contrived. And, of course, foundamentalism favors the clerics whose job it is to interpret the words and thoughts of the founder for general consumption. In this way, foundamentalism favors **theocracy**. **Wahhabi Islam** conforms closely to Manji's understanding of foundamentalism, although parallels in fundamentalist Christianity would not be difficult to find.

Another problem with foundamentalism that Manji did not mention is that it encourages the preservation of views of the founder long after they have been discredited by scholarly inquiry. In the case of **Jesus Christ**, for example, strict foundamentalism finds it next to impossible to accommodate the findings of the **quest for the historical Jesus**, which now recognizes the Jewishness of **Rabbi Yeshua**, and the absence of any plans to create a new religion outside Judaism. This research has only just begun with regard to Muhammad, and we can rely on a similar level of incomprehension along with, on current conditions, a great level of violent reaction to these findings. One of the pioneers of research of this kind is **Ibn Warraq**.

Further reading: Irshad Manji, *The Trouble with Islam.*

FOUNDATIONALISM. The claim that some beliefs rest upon indisputable foundations of truth and as such are self-evident (are their own proof), and can support a comprehensive ideology of life. Foundationalist arguments have been the traditional favorite of religious apologists, in particular Alvin Plantinga (1932–), who has argued that belief in God is a basic belief that is warranted even if it lacks **evidence**.

But foundationalism has come under severe attack over the past century, mainly on the grounds that there are no infallible foundations upon which a philosophical system can rest. There is also the problem of arguing that *my* beliefs rest upon self-evident foundations of truth, but the other fellow who makes the same claim, is actually incorrect. As a result of criticisms such as these, it has become difficult to hold foundationalist views without resorting to **dogmatism**.

FOUNDATIONS. A large work edited by seven theologians and published in 1912, which sought to reconcile Christian thinking with modern thought. *Foundations* was conscious of its intellectual predecessors, particularly *Essays and Reviews* (1860), which had attempted something similar, and had gotten its editors in a great deal of trouble. As B. H. Streeter (1874–1937) observed, a "Christ whom apologists first have to 'save' is little likely to save mankind."

Foundations received a hostile reception from the more conservative elements within the Church of England leadership. In fact, the Anglicans went into a period of doctrinal controversy that lasted for ten years, and was never fully resolved. The coeditors of *Foundations* stressed the need for freedom of academic inquiry and recognizing the damaging effect of modern scholarship on comparative religion and higher criticism. The conservatives insisted that the liberal theology favored by men like Streeter undermined the authority of the church as the fountainhead of bringing the unchanging word of God to men.

In an attempt to resolve the growing factionalism, the archbishop of Canterbury convened a commission in 1923 to investigate these issues. It didn't report until 1938 (after Streeter had died) and attempted a series of unconvincing compromises. While some of the issues have changed, the dividing lines between religious liberals and conservatives in the Church of England remain today where they were in 1923.

FOUR BEGINNINGS. A series of axioms devised by Mengzi, known to Westerners by his Latinized name, Mencius (371–289 BCE). Mencius stressed the primary importance of the people to a well-run polity, and of the justification for revolt against a badly run polity. The Four Beginnings accepted by virtually all Confucians as the innate moral qualities is the view that:

- commiseration is the beginning of **human-heartedness**;
- shame and dislike is the beginning of righteousness;
- deference and compliance is the beginning of propriety; and
- right and wrong is the beginning of wisdom.

Mengzi believed that people are innately good and that we all have these four beginnings in us as a matter of course. They are, he taught, what distinguish humans from the beasts. With proper attention to the Four Beginnings, we may achieve the four Constant Virtues: human-heartedness, righteousness, propriety, and wisdom.

Further reading: Fung Yu-lan, *A Short History of Chinese Philosophy*.

FOUR CAUSES. A method of inquiry championed by **Aristotle**. The four causes are the material, the formal, the final, and the efficient. They can then be characterized like this:

- *the material cause*: what is the object in question made of?
- *the formal cause*: how is the object structured?
- *the final cause*: what purpose does the object serve?
- *the efficient cause*: why did this object come into being?

Aristotle criticized the **Pre-Socratic** philosophers for being unduly concerned with the material cause (the first question) and the followers of **Pythagoras** with concentrating too much on the formal cause (the second question). **Plato** was also thought to have been confused about the formal causes.

Further reading: Anthony Gottlieb, *The Dream of Reason*.

FOUR FREEDOMS, THE. The ideals as outlined by President Franklin Delano Roosevelt (1882–1945), which inspired the war against Nazism. In a speech to Congress on January 6, 1941, Roosevelt ended by calling for rearmament and support for the Allies with his vision of the four freedoms. They were, in Roosevelt's actual words:

- *freedom of speech and expression—* everywhere in the world;
- *freedom of every person to worship God in his own way*—everywhere in the world;
- *freedom from want*, which, translated into worldly terms, means economic understandings that will secure to every nation a healthy peacetime life for its inhabitants—everywhere in the world; and
- *freedom from fear*, which, translated into worldly terms, means a worldwide reduction of armaments to such a point and in such a thorough fashion that no nation will be in a position to commit an act of physical aggression against any neighbor—anywhere in the world.

Roosevelt added that these need not be the

vision of a distant millennium, but "the definite basis for a kind of world attainable in our own time and generation." Roosevelt's four freedoms are an admirable basis for **planetary humanism**, with the proviso that freedom to worship God in one's own way includes the freedom not to indulge in worship of any god.

FOUR NOBLE TRUTHS. Subsequent to the notion of **dependent arising**, the Four Noble Truths constitute the core of the **Asian tradition** known as Buddhism. The Buddha (**Siddhartha Gautama**) believed that ignorance is the root cause of suffering and that both are endemic in life as normally lived. In the Four Noble Truths, the Buddha offered a down-to-earth program to rise above a life of ignorance and suffering, while avoiding the related mistake of succumbing to the **transcendental temptation**. By "noble," the Buddha meant "relevant" or "fruitful," rather than "excellent." The Four Noble Truths are:

- life in this world is full of suffering;
- all things, including suffering, have a cause;
- it is possible to stop suffering; and
- there is a path that leads to the cessation of suffering.

Built into the fourth Noble Truth is the Eightfold Path that leads to no desire:

- *right belief*, i.e., belief in and understanding of the Four Noble Truths;
- *right resolve*, i.e., overcoming sensuality, suppressing misery-inducing desires;
- *right speech*, i.e., avoiding gossip, lies, slander, etc.;
- *right conduct*, i.e., practicing chastity, sobriety, restraint;
- *right livelihood*, i.e., choosing an occupation consistent with Buddhism;
- *right effort*, i.e., maintaining constant intellectual alertness to distinguish wisdom from foolishness;

- *right mindfulness*, i.e., understanding the four awakenings: one's body, feelings, thoughts, and objects of thoughts; and
- *right meditation*, the climax of the first seven steps, i.e., achievement of trance states, which are the advanced stages of *arahat*ship, or sainthood.

The Eightfold Path is not to be seen as some brand of **command morality**, but as a way of life. By integrating these precepts into one's life, ignorance and suffering can be risen above. Scholars generally agree that, despite its focus on ignorance and suffering, Buddhism should not be seen as a pessimistic philosophy. See the entry on **Faustian Bargain**.

Further reading: David Kalupahana, *A History of Buddhist Philosophy*.

FOUR-PART CURE. A piece of advice offered by the **Epicurean** thinker Philodemus of Gadara (first century BCE), which encapsulates the Epicurean outlook. It's uncertain which work of Philodemus this came from, but it is preserved in a papyrus found at Herculaneum. The Four-Part Cure advises:

- Don't fear God,
- Don't worry about death;
- What is good is easy to get; and
- What is terrible is easy to endure.

The Four-Part Cure urges us to concentrate on what really matters, namely contentment within a modest range of our **human needs**. Know the limits of what you need, and place tight limits on what you don't need, because things you don't need will not bring you **peace of mind**. Pain and suffering can be endured, if only because they are an inevitable part of life. It is a mistake to waste away one's health fretting about the hopefully short periods when we will be unwell.

The Four-Part Cure begins with a sound attitude toward the gods. Philodemus is reminding us that the Greek gods were far too happy and preoccupied up in Olympus to concern themselves with our fate, so we are better off proceeding with our lives without reference to them. This is a characteristically cheerful piece of Epicurean advice. It is free of **anthropocentric conceit** and philosophically wise without being unduly academic.

Further reading: Brad Inwood, L. P. Gerson, and D. S. Hutchinson, eds., *The Epicurus Reader*.

FRANCE, ANATOLE (1844–1924). Pseudonym for Anatole Francois Thibault, a brilliant and prolific novelist. Son of a bookseller, Thibault was first employed as a publisher's reader, later becoming a blurb writer and critic. His first major work was a biography of Alfred de Vigny (1868), but he was chiefly known for his novels, the first of which was *The Crime of Sylvester Bonnard* (1881).

France was a fearless defender of Alfred Dreyfus, a Jew subjected to years of persecution, culminating in a famous trial at the turn of the twentieth century. The Dreyfus case was brought up in his novel *Monsieur Bergeret in Paris* (1900). He also wrote *Penguin Island* (1908), a biting satire of Roman Catholicism and contemporary France. Other novels critical of religion included *The Gods Will Have Blood* (1912) (which features one of literature's rare atheist heroes) and *The Revolt of the Angels* (1914). But France was not only a novelist. As well as his early biography, he wrote a groundbreaking study of Joan of Arc, puncturing many of the more sentimental myths that had developed around her name. He was awarded the Nobel Prize for Literature in 1921 and, no less an honor, his entire corpus of writing was placed on the Roman Catholic **Index of Forbidden Books** in 1922.

FRANCIS, SAMUEL (18th century). English medical doctor who wrote a book called *Watson Refuted* (1796), which was a defense of **Thomas Paine**'s *Age of Reason* from the criticisms made by a certain Watson, but with the extra point of interest in going further, by condemning the constant vilification of atheists. *Watson Refuted* was later reprinted by **Richard Carlile** during his campaign for freedom of the press.

FRANKLIN, BENJAMIN (1706–1790). American Enlightenment icon. Benjamin Franklin was born in Boston and was originally intended for the church, but was apprenticed into the printing trade, where he educated himself.

After a short sojourn in England, Franklin set up a printing business in Philadelphia, and in 1729 bought the *Pennsylvania Gazette*. Two years later he established the Philadelphia library and in 1744 he founded the American Philosophical Society. Franklin then devoted much of his time to scientific pursuits, including the famous experiment with a key tied to a kite string on June 15, 1752, which demonstrated that lightning is indeed electrical. In 1762, Franklin became a fellow of the Royal Society. From 1764 until 1775, he represented the American colonies in London. He was ambivalent about independence to begin with but signed the Declaration of Independence in 1775.

Franklin's single most valuable contribution lay not in any of his achievements, but in his suggestion in 1774 to **Thomas Paine** that he should go to America. This had momentous consequences for America, and for the world.

Franklin's views are hard to describe with certainty, as they changed considerably through the course of his life. While still a youth he had abandoned belief in most items of Christian dogma, although he remained sympathetic to religious practice. He is best described as a deist. Franklin also gave support to the hierarchical view of the universe now known as the **great chain of being**. Only a month before his death, Franklin told a friend that he thought the Christian moral system had been corrupted over the centuries, and that he doubted the divinity of **Jesus Christ**.

FRANKLIN, ROSALIND (1920–1958). Pioneer molecular biologist whose work was essential for the discovery of the structure of DNA. From a well-to-do Jewish family, Franklin went to university, despite the opposition of her father. From early childhood, Franklin was an atheist and rationalist. By the age of twenty-six, Franklin had published five outstanding scientific papers on the nature of coal and charcoal, which are still referred to today, and had been awarded her PhD. After the war, Franklin worked in Paris, using x-rays to create images of crystalized solids, and again made pioneering advances in this area.

In 1950, Franklin returned to England, where she was invited to work at King's College, London, studying living cells. Franklin came up against something of an old-boys network, being barred from eating in the common room, for instance, because she was female. Not one to suffer fools gladly, Franklin came into conflict with some of her male colleagues, and working conditions became difficult.

These difficulties aside, Franklin was making excellent progress taking x-ray photographs of DNA in an attempt to discover DNA's structure. Unknown to her, and without her permission, some of her photographs were shown to James Watson and Francis Crick, who used them to arrive at the structure of DNA in March 1953.

She soon left King's College and spent the rest of her career at Birkbeck College in London, where she worked once again on coal, and also with viruses, publishing seventeen influential papers on the subject. During this time, Franklin developed ovarian cancer, in all probability acquired from long exposure to x-rays. She died at thirty-seven.

Further reading: Brenda Maddox, *Rosalind Franklin: The Dark Lady of DNA*.

FREE INQUIRY. The great **Greek playwright** Euripides (484/480–406 BCE) caught the spirit of free inquiry when he wrote, "Blessed is he who learns how to engage in inquiry, with no impulse to harm his countrymen or to pursue wrongful actions, but perceives the order of immortal and ageless nature, how it is structured." It would be difficult to encapsulate more effectively why it is we owe such a massive cultural debt to the ancient Greeks. See the entry on **ancient Greece and Rome, legacy of**. In the **Enlightenment**, free inquiry was given the rallying cry of *sapere aude*, or "dare to think." The ideal of free inquiry was also given a splendid voice by **Joseph McCabe** in 1920 when, during the famous debate with Sir Arthur Conan Doyle (1859–1930), he said "I will respect any man or any woman, no matter what their conclusions may be, if they have used their own personality, their own mind, and their own judgment, rigorously and conscientiously. I do not care what conclusions they come to." See the entries on **freethought** and **rationalism**.

The point of free inquiry is that the inquiry is free, which means the inquirer will be allowed to pursue the line of inquiry without regard to where it leads. In other words, there are no areas that are out of bounds to genuine free inquiry. This was the motive behind the original freethinkers. They wanted to be able to think freely even in socially prescribed areas like **religion**. And it is only a partial exaggeration when **Percy Shelley** wrote, "The crime of inquiry is one which **religion** has never forgiven." The society that allows, even encourages, free inquiry can properly be called an **open society**.

What makes **humanism** unique as a **life stance**, is its commitment to free inquiry. It is significant that the first feature of **Paul Kurtz**'s four-part definition of humanism is that it is a method of inquiry. Humanism is not, first and foremost, this or that set of beliefs, it is a way of inquiring about the world. It is with the goal of pursuing that tradition that Kurtz called the official magazine of the **Council for Secular Humanism**, *Free Inquiry*.

FREE SPIRIT. A term used by **Friedrich Nietzsche**, which he used to mean a human who has become free, who has "seized possession of itself." Most of us are bound by cultural protocols and notions of good and **evil**. The free spirit is not bound by any of these notions but is beyond good and evil.

While Nietzsche's conception of the free spirit is too romantically self-absorbed, it can nevertheless serve as a guide for us to avoid the pitfalls of peer pressure and mindless conformism.

FREE WILL. An idea vital to traditional religious defenses of the goodness of **God** in the face of the presence of **evil** in the world. Free will is a **dualistic** view of the world, because, in most cases, it presupposes the existence of a **soul**. More recent, nonreligious conceptions of free will have been proposed by **existentialists** such as **Jean-Paul Sartre**. Their arguments are intended not so much to rescue the idea of a loving God in the face of human evil, as to give an account of the scope of human freedom in the *absence* of God.

Neither the traditional religious conception of free will, nor the more recent existentialist understanding overcome the problems inherent in the idea. Free will works as an idea only insofar as it ignores scientific reality. The truth of the matter is that human beings are circumscribed in their choices to a very significant degree. Defenders of free will are bound to say that *every* significant moral choice that *every* person makes is entirely free, that is, uncaused. But this becomes unsustainable in the light of all recent physiology and psychology, which has shown complex webs of interaction and genetically derived templates that favor certain behaviors in some people. The way these behavior templates operate depend on the vicissitudes of life.

Free will also leaves some unpalatable options for people with mental illnesses or handicaps. By this standard, the offensive behavior of the retarded adolescent is an absolute black mark against him in the annals of heaven. And yet such an attitude lacks basic compassion as well as scientific coherence.

Free will has traditionally been juxtaposed as the opposite of **determinism**. As usual the truth is more complex than that. While there is no validity in traditional conceptions of free will, the current consensus is that human beings have a certain measure of free will within a general environment of determinism. As one popularizer put it, we are dealt our hand, but how we play it is our business.

FREETHINKER, THE. The oldest extant **freethought** journal in the world. Founded in 1881 by **G. W. Foote**. This was a time when a bewildering array of freethought and related papers were coming and going, so it is remarkable that this journal has survived. It began as a monthly, but by September 1881, it became a weekly, which it remained for ninety years. Since 1971 *The Freethinker* has been monthly once more.

In 1893, after the demise of the *National Reformer*, a journal made famous during the life of **Charles Bradlaugh**, *the Freethinker* became the principal freethought journal in the world. It lost that primacy within ten years once the *Literary Guide*, the journal of the **Rationalist Press Association**, got into its stride.

After Foote's death, the *Freethinker* was edited for many years by **Chapman Cohen**. Cohen kept Foote's memory alive by keeping his mentor's style of writing and attitude toward organized religion. *The Freethinker* has had a succession of prominent humanists edit it since then, including **Jim Herrick, Peter Brearey**, and the Australians **David Tribe** and Nigel Sinnott. *The Freethinker* is currently edited by Barry Duke and remains a valuable and readable journal.

FREETHOUGHT. A term that summarizes as well as any what **humanism** is about. While the *idea* of thinking freely has been around ever since human beings have thought about thinking, the word itself is of recent origin. The word "freethinker" was first used in a letter written by William Molyneux to the philosopher **John Locke** in April 1697. It reached a broader audience in 1713 when **Anthony Collins**'s book *Discourse on Freethinking* was published. Nowadays freethought is best thought of as the general umbrella word that covers all the various types of nonreligious **life stances**. **Atheism, rationalism,** humanism, **skepticism, secularism, agnosticism**—they are all subsets of freethought. The novelist George Meredith (1828–1909) described freethought as "**the best of causes.**"

As these terms suggest, freethinkers believe a variety of things, but what brings them together is a refusal to be bound by any static formulas of thought. The Russian philosopher Valerii Kuvakin describes freethought as "thinking that, from the very beginning, does not place any limitations on itself, in terms of either the content or the forms of thinking." **George Jacob Holyoake** maintained that freethought is founded upon the exercise of our rational faculties, arguing that those who are afraid to know both sides of a question cannot really think about the question. Freethought implies three conditions:

- *free inquiry*, which he called the pathway to truth;
- *free publicity of ideas*, in order to learn whether they are useful; and
- *free discussion of convictions*, without which it is not possible to find out whether they are true or false.

As an organized movement, freethought went into decline in the 1880s. Among the issues which divided it include:

- the relationship between secularism and atheism;
- the different emphases of the **abolitionists and substitutionists**; and
- personality disputes and issues of organization and control.

But the three conditions of freethought that Holyoake outlined are as relevant today as they were in his day. This has helped freethought retain its appeal as an umbrella term. Recent attempts to coin a new umbrella term, like **brights**, have enjoyed only limited success.

Further reading: Valerii Kuvakin, *In Search of our Humanity*; Edward Royle, *Radicals, Secularists and Republicans*; and Susan Jacoby, *Freethinkers, A History of American Secularism*.

FREETHOUGHT HISTORY RESEARCH GROUP. As the title suggests, a group dedicated to **freethought** history, established in London in 2003. The FHRG produces an annual journal and a newsletter.

Freethought history is scandalously under-researched. It tends to fall into the gaps between intellectual history, religious history, sociology, and philosophy. As a result there is no university department that sees freethought history as part of its legitimate area of interest. The result has been that few people are even aware of this fascinating field of history. And when researchers wander into the area, they frequently make elementary mistakes for lack of examining primary materials, and because there are too few historical works there to guide them. It is to be hoped that the FHRG will help address this problem.

FREUD, SIGMUND (1856–1939). Flawed genius. Born to a Jewish family in a region of Austria which is now part of the Czeck Republic. Freud made significant contributions to twentieth-century thinking with his invention of **psychoanalysis**. From 1882, when he joined the staff of Vienna General Hospital, until 1900, when he published *The Interpretation of Dreams*, Freud built up the body of theory that became psychoanalysis. It was Freud's view that human beings are driven fundamentally by **sex**, and that our **human nature** is constructed around that essential fact. Freud constructed a hierarchy of **consciousness**, starting from the primeval id, through to the ego and on to the superego. Central to Freud's thinking was the notion of the unconscious, access to which we tend to guard ferociously.

While almost every aspect of psychoanalysis has been thoroughly discredited, Freud's importance as a thinker cannot be denied. He can justifiably be claimed as one of the most influential thinkers of the first decades of the twentieth century. Today, Freud's criticism of religion in works like *The Future of an Illusion* (1927) is still valuable.

FRIEDAN, BETTY (1921–). American feminist pioneer. She was born Elizabeth Goldstein in Peoria, Illinois, and educated at Smith College, where she graduated in 1942 with a degree in psychology. Her father was a great admirer of **Robert Ingersoll**, whose works he read frequently to her. In 1947 she married Carl Friedan and took on the life expected of her—that of wife and mother. For ten years Friedan fulfilled this role while trying to pursue a freelance-writing interest.

Friedan is best known for what has become a classic of feminist writing: *The Feminine Mystique* (1963), which looked at the plight of millions of American housewives. *The Feminine Mystique* was rich with her own experience and that of other women who felt deeply frustrated and dissatisfied with their lives. Heavily influenced by **humanistic psychology**, Friedan argued that women should look to forging careers for themselves as a way to assert their own status as human beings. She criticized the expectation that women should look to fulfilling their lives vicariously through the lives of their husbands and children. It articulated what so many women felt that it quickly became a national bestseller.

Friedan was the cofounder and first president of the National Organization for Women in 1966, and the National Women's Political Caucus in 1971, both of which are still an influential voice for women in the United States. She headed the National Women's Strike for Equality in 1970. In 1969 Carl and Betty Friedan divorced.

Her later books included *It Changed My Life: Writings on the Women's Movement* (1976) and *The Second Stage* (1981). In 1993, Friedan wrote *The Fountain of Age*, which looked at issues of aging, and challenged the general view that aging involves a decline of capabilities. She was elected to the **International Academy of Humanism** in 1988.

Further reading: Betty Friedan, *Life So Far: A Memoir*.

FRUITS OF PHILOSOPHY, THE. A pamphlet on birth control originally published in 1832 by an American physician, Dr. Charles Knowlton (1800–1850). The work achieved notoriety in England in 1877 when **Charles Bradlaugh** and **Annie Besant** reprinted it. *The Fruits of Philosophy* sold 100,000 copies in its first three months, and it greatly stimulated the sale of other birth-control literature. **Charles Watts**, the pamphlet's printer, was arrested for printing it. Watts pleaded guilty to publishing obscene literature, which occasioned a split between him and Bradlaugh and Besant, who went on to found the Freethought Publishing Company and publish *The Fruits of Philosophy* as its first title. Bradlaugh and Besant were convinced of the value of working people having access to reliable birth-control information. This is now widely recognized as wise, but in the nineteenth century was a novel innovation, and thought by many to be profoundly immoral.

Bradlaugh and Besant were themselves prosecuted for publishing obscene literature and were sentenced to six months imprisonment, but were released on a technicality. Bradlaugh continued to advance the cause of birth control until his death in 1891. Besant wrote *The Law of Population* in 1878, which espoused the case for birth control with particular eloquence.

Further reading: Walter Arnstein, *The Bradlaugh Case*.

FUN. One of the more important implications of **atheism** is the importance of having fun. We only live once, and our life is not a grim preparatory test for some sort of graduation in the sky. Having fun comes in lots of different ways, but it usually involves the harmless frittering of some time in a leisurely pursuit that has no point to it besides that it is fun. Things like sports, films, barbecues, reading, gardening, listening to music, shopping, walking through beautiful parks, **sex**, fairgrounds, circuses, drinking with friends, and so on. Most of these activities make little or no sense apart from their ability to provide fun.

Fun has come in for a surprisingly large amount of criticism. The mandarins of higher culture worry about the vulgarity of many popular entertainments. Pessimistic academics warn that many styles of fun are ways to anaesthetize people into an unreal world, far from the corridors of power. See the entry on **manufacturing consent**. And religious **virtuecrats** want to corral the sort of fun people can enjoy, when they can enjoy it, and who they can enjoy it with.

Each of these criticisms has some validity. Many popular entertainments *are* vulgar and even destructive; off-road driving is doing significant damage to the environment and many video games are violent and encourage a sedentary lifestyle among young people who should be more active. And if more people cared as passionately about the behavior of their politicians as that of sports or rock stars, we may well have more responsible democracies. And some fun is downright exploitative—pornography, in particular.

But humorless regulations and controls achieve little. See the entry on **comstockery**. One of the cornerstones of the **open society** is that people are going to do things you really don't like. See the entry on **toleration**. The main justifications for the prohibition of fun are when it involves the exploitation of children or the defenseless, the willful destruction of the environment, or when it comes at a significant cost to other people's right to peace and quiet. Where fun ends and exploitation begins is a legitimate topic for debate as part of the **social intelligence**. Fun is not to be confused with **hedonism**, **narcis-**sism, or self-indulgence. For the humanist, fun is most special when it means time spent with friends and family. What people call fun is up to them, and long may they enjoy it.

FUNDAMENTAL FORCES, THE. Contemporary physics has identified four fundamental forces in the universe:

- strong force;
- electromagnetism;
- weak force; and
- gravity.

The *strong force* is the strongest of the four, and is responsible for holding the nucleus together. *Electromagnetism* holds together electric charges and magnets. The *weak force* is responsible for emitting radiation and gravity. Electromagnetism and the weak force become unified at very high energies. *Gravity*, the weakest of the four, is the force that attracts objects toward each other. What is being worked on at the moment is a **theory of everything**, which can accommodate all four forces.

It is also worth adding that these are fundamental forces whether humans like it or not. The existence of the four fundamental forces is a foundational element of **reality** as we understand it today. They are, in the language of John Searle, intrinsic facts, as opposed to observer-related facts, which we as humans from our fallible perspectives, can hope to unravel. See the entries on **facts** and **external realism**.

FUNDAMENTALISM. A form of religious reaction to the increasingly divergent and pluralistic world we live in. Fundamentalism is in the paradoxical position of owing its existence to the very modernity it loathes so much. But because it consists largely of this hostility to everything around it, fundamentalism can offer no positive guidance to its adherents. While secular movements can and do breed intolerant fanatics, confusion can arise when the term fundamentalism is applied to secular movements. Fundamentalism is best used in a specifically religious context. Fundamentalism presumes to be the authentic voice of whatever religious tradition it is part of, but this is not the case. Fundamentalism rests upon these presuppositions:

- that the core of **religion** is doctrine, usually in the form of **scripture**;
- that this doctrine can be fixed with precision and finality; and
- that fundamentalists are the only ones able to undertake this task.

The emphasis on doctrine is why (with the partial exception of Hindu extremists) fundamentalism is largely confined to the **monotheistic** faiths of Judaism, Christianity and Islam. The **Asian traditions** do not emphasize doctrine to anything like the same extent. Very often there is also an element, sometimes said openly, though usually simply implied, that those who disagree cannot do so in good faith. In this way, their opponents are more than simply *wrong*; they are *wicked* as well. This provides a powerful sense of moral superiority and righteousness to fundamentalists, who may in many other senses, be on the margins of society. See the entries on **monopoly on truth** and **demonizing the opposition**. This **certainty** also gives them powerful advantages over religious liberals. See the entry on the **fatal flaw at the heart of religious liberalism**.

Many commentators have noted that fundamentalism is deeply political. Most varieties of fundamentalism are opposed to **pluralism**, multiculturalism, many of the principal findings of modern **science**, religious diversity and **toleration**, **secularism**, **free inquiry** and artistic expression, and equal **rights** for women. Together these forces opposed by fundamentalism are the building blocks of the modernity they despise so much. Among American fundamentalists, all these features of modernity are frequently bundled up together and labeled **secular humanism**. Among Muslim fundamentalists the principal enemy is usually "the West," and in particular the United States. Among supporters of the **Hindutva** variety of Hindu extremism, Muslims are the main target, as they are for ultra-Orthodox Jews, although **secularists** and liberals are a favorite target for each of these groups. See the entries on **Intolerance, Principle of**, and **theopathic condition**.

FUTURISM. An art movement best known before World War I. Its most vociferous champion was the Italian writer Filippo Marinetti (1876–1944) who published the *Futurist Manifesto* in 1909. Futurism, as conceived by Marinetti, was an idealistic celebration of technology, in particular the ability of technology to challenge and overturn the past. The Futurists celebrated what they saw as the liberating power of the machine and of movement. They welcomed the onset of war in 1914. After the war Marinetti became an early and ardent Fascist, and remained so until his death. It is a sobering fact, writes the art historian Robert Hughes, that Futurism was the most influential art movement of the twentieth century.

Further reading: Robert Hughes, *The Shock of the New*.

G

GAGE, MATILDA JOSLYN (1826–1898). American pioneer for women's suffrage. Matilda Joslyn was the only daughter of a prominent New York abolitionist Dr. Hezekiah Joslyn and his wife Helen Leslie Joslyn. When she was only eighteen she married Henry H. Gage. They had five children, four of whom survived.

Gage joined the feminist movement in 1852, speaking at the National Convention, held in Syracuse, New York. She joined the National Woman Suffrage Association (NWSA) when it formed in 1869 and remained active in the suffrage movement for the rest of her life. Among her many roles, she coauthored with **Elizabeth Cady Stanton** the *Declaration of Rights for Women* (1876) and edited the suffrage paper, the *National Citizen and Ballot Box* between 1878 and 1881 and served as president of the NWSA in 1872. After **Susan B. Anthony** effected the union of the NWSA and the more conservative American Woman Suffrage Association, Gage went on to found the Women's National Liberal Union (WNLU) in 1890.

From the 1880s onward, Gage became increasingly interested in the causes of the resistance to women's rights. Along with Stanton, Gage came to see the role of the church as central in the suppression of women. At the opening convention of the WNLU, Gage said that in "order to secure victory for women we must unfetter the minds of men from religious bondage." Gage cooperated with Stanton in producing the first three volumes of *The History of Woman Suffrage* (1881–1889). Under her own pen, she wrote *Woman, Church and State* (1893), which criticized the church's record on feminist issues since the Middle Ages.

Gage was a **freethinker** for most of her adult life. In her later years, she was supportive of **Theosophy**. Gage is best known for her catchphrase: "There is a word sweeter than Mother, Home, or Heaven. That word is Liberty."

GAIA. A name given to what began as a scientific hypothesis but quickly degenerated into a **New Age** hodgepodge. The Gaia hypothesis began with the scientist James Lovelock. Lovelock's original term for Gaia was Biocybernetic Universal System Tendency (BUST). The name for the hypothesis was apparently suggested by Lovelock's friend, the novelist William Golding (1911–1993). Gaia was originally a Greek mythical symbol of the Earth, personified as the daughter of Chaos. The term was first used by Lovelock in the journal *Atmospheric Environment* in 1972.

The Gaia hypothesis can be defined thus: "Life, or the biosphere, regulates or maintains the climate and the atmospheric composition at an optimum for itself." What has so excited the New-Agers is the consequences of the last two words: *for itself.* Lovelock himself has denied that Gaia implies any untenable **mysticism** or teleology, but he has been criticized for doing little to counter those who have interpreted Gaia in this way. In fact, Lovelock has himself been instrumental in the new-aging of the Gaia hypothesis. It was Lovelock who discovered the ozone-depleting effect of chlorofluorocarbons (CFCs) in the atmosphere, but for fifteen years denied it would damage the environment because Gaia would "sort things out."

In its more extravagant forms, Gaia falls foul of the **Stratonician Presumption**, but its more modest variation, which stresses the interdependence of all things, is a worthwhile contribution to ecological thought.

GALEN (129–199 CE). Greek physician, born in Pergamos. Galen was a prolific writer on a wide variety of subjects, but was known in his own day, and to posterity, mainly for his works on anatomy and medicine. He acquired his knowledge of anatomy as a physician to gladiators. He went on to become the court physician to the great **Stoic** emperor **Marcus Aurelius**. Aspects of Galen's thought were in tune with contemporary thinking, for example, he emphasized preventing illnesses rather than curing them. Galen was a pagan who criticized Christians for not thinking rationally.

Galen's medical writings had an extraordinary career. They survived the **Dark Ages** and remained almost unquestioned until the sixteenth century. One of the very few people to revolt against Galen's authority was Theophrastus Paracelsus (1493–1541), who was shunned by the medical community as a result. Galen's physiology was not replaced satisfactorily until William Harvey (1578–1657) discovered the circulation of blood. In parts of the Muslim world, Galen's works, translated by Avicenna, retained unquestioned authority until early in the twentieth century.

GALILEI, GALILEO (1564–1642). Italian scientist who developed the proofs of the **heliocentric universe**. Galileo was strongly influenced by the Greek **atomists**, the **Epicureans**, and **Giordano Bruno**, who was burned at the stake for his free thinking. It was inevitable that Galileo should also excite the suspicion of the Catholic authorities, who feared that Galileo's atomism left no room for Catholic dogma like transubstantiation.

What Bruno had come to through abstract speculation, Galileo came to using experimentation and **mathematics**. He made the first astronomical observations from the newly invented telescope. While looking at the moons of Jupiter in 1609, he confirmed the heliocentric universe as put forward by the Polish astronomer Nicholas Copernicus (1473–1543). And looking at spots on the sun, Galileo observed that heavenly bodies are not the perfect spheres classical cosmology inherited from **Aristotle** assumed them to be. He presented his findings in 1632 in a book which now goes under the title *Dialogue on the Two World Systems*. Here the Ptolemaic and Copernican cosmologies were debated, much to the disfavor of the former. The following year the **Inquisition** forced Galileo to retract his findings. It is possible that the Inquisition was reacting to Galileo's atomism as much as to his Copernicanism. Responding to the threat posed by Galileo, the Inquisition included astronomy in its orbit, and passed two propositions:

- "that the sun is the centre and does not revolve about the earth, is foolish, absurd, false in theology, and heretical, because expressly contrary to Holy Scripture . . ."; and
- "that the earth is not the centre, but revolves about the sun, is absurd, false in philosophy, and, from a theological point of view at least, opposed to the true faith."

The church forbade the teaching of the heliocentric universe, and works espousing that idea remained on the **Index of Forbidden Books** until 1835. It was not until 1992 that the Vatican finally decided that Galileo had been wrongly condemned.

Galileo's truly brilliant contribution was as the first physicist of the modern age by virtue of his initiating the study of the mechanics of moving bodies. What has become known as the Principle of Galilean Relativity is about the basic similarity between the state of rest and the state of uniform motion. A person, situated as he is in one place at one time, can make no observations or experiments of an absolute velocity, because any measurement of velocity is between one body and another body. Galileo's discovery of relative motion was an essential break from the fixed universe of Aristotle to the Einsteinian understanding we have today.

Further reading: Pietro Redondi, *Galileo: Heretic.*

GALLIO. Roman proconsul of Achaea, probably between 51 and 52 CE and brother of the famous **Stoic** thinker **Seneca**. Gallio was an educated and cultured man, whose main ambition was to write a distinguished work on natural history. According to the New Testament Book of Acts (18:11–17), Gallio was pressed to adjudicate in a dispute between **Paul**, then proselytizing in Corinth, and the local Jewish authorities who were incensed by Paul's claims. Gallio refused to be drawn into the conflict and allowed Paul to go free. By this historical chance was Paul allowed to continue on his way and become responsible for much of the material used by contemporary fundamentalists to vent their hatred of humanists and other non-Christians. Would that Paul could have learned a lesson from Gallio in **toleration** and **humanism**.

GAMBETTA, LEON (1838–1882). An architect of contemporary French democracy. Born in modest circumstances, Gambetta was the child of a French woman and an Italian immigrant to France. Against his father's wishes, the precocious boy was able to leave his remote Gascon town and study law in Paris.

Gambetta's talents moved him toward politics and in 1869 he was elected as a deputy to the French parliament. After France's defeat by the Prussians in 1871, he became an important spokesman for the opposition to the hapless Emperor Napoleon III. His courage during the war, and his dramatic escape from Paris in a balloon, inspired his countrymen at a dark time. So important did Gambetta become that, although he only briefly held the position of premier, he is seen as one of the most important figures in the creation of the Third Republic. He was a very significant presence behind the 1875 republican constitution.

Gambetta was also a leader in the struggle against clerical reaction between 1871 and 1879. He spoke of clericalism as the enemy. He was a leading influence behind what are known as the Ferry Laws of 1881–1882, which established free, secular education and the right to a civil marriage and limited access to divorce. Each of these reforms was gained in the face of bitter clerical opposition. Gambetta died at only forty-four from complications after he accidentally shot himself in the arm. To this day there is hardly a town in France that does not have a "Rue Gambetta."

GARRISON, WILLIAM LLOYD (1805–1879).

American abolitionist and social reformer. Garrison was the son of a drunken father and fiercely Evangelical mother, even by the standards of the time. At only seven, Garrison was left in his home town of Newburyport, Massachusetts, while his mother sought employment elsewhere. He was apprenticed as a young boy to the local paper and rose to become a journalist, much to his mother's dismay.

In 1829 he took up the cause of abolitionism. After a short term of imprisonment he founded *The Liberator* in Boston in 1831 and the New England Antislavery Society in 1833. But Garrison's campaigning zeal got into gear after he became aware of the works of **Thomas Paine**. Paine's name had been so thoroughly demonized by the Baptists he grew up with, it took until middle age before Garrison was even familiar with Paine's writings (see the entry on **demonizing the opposition**). Garrison's earlier Evangelical beliefs were replaced by a thoroughly heterodox and anticlerical theism, very much in Paine's stamp. Later in his life, Garrison turned increasingly to **spiritualism**.

Garrison also campaigned for women's rights, which earned him the hostility of religious conservatives no less than his support for abolitionism. Women like the fearless abolitionist campaigners Sarah (1792–1873) and Angelina (1805–1879) Grimké got a fair hearing in *The Liberator* that they got in few other journals, and women were welcome as decision makers in the Antislavery Society, in sharp contrast to other antislavery organizations. Only after the Civil War did the alliance break between abolitionists and the women's rights movement, when Garrison stopped short at advocating the extension of the franchise to include black women. Garrison did this mainly on pragmatic issues of what he thought Congress would tolerate.

GAUTAMA, SIDDHARTHA (563–483 BCE, approx.).

Indian reformer and moralist in whose name the **Asian tradition** known as Buddhism was created. The facts of Gautama's life are disputed and shrouded in layers of myth. These are the most commonly used dates for his birth and death, although others have been used, with birth dates ranging between about 600 and 450 BCE. Siddhartha was the son of Suddhodana, the ruler of a little kingdom on the foothills of the Himalayas. He was of the Sakya clan, and the main settlement of the kingdom was Kapilavastu. Siddhartha's mother is said to have died while giving birth, leaving him to be raised by his sister Pajapati Gotami. Siddhartha may have married; tradition has him marrying Yasodhara and fathering

Rahula. This is not known for sure.

Most of the tales told of Siddhartha's quest for wisdom and eventual enlightenment are apocryphal and as such, tell us about what his followers said about him, rather than what actually happened. And as with Christianity, the multiplicity of beliefs which came to be known as Buddhism diverge in very significant ways from the teachings of the "founder." Like the word "Christ," "Buddha" is not a name, but a title. The Buddha means "the enlightened one."

The Buddha was dissatisfied with the formalism and aridity of the rituals and asceticism that dominated Indian practice in his day. He rejected the saving efficacy of the *Veda*, and some crucial Hindu notions, such as *atman*, but he retained most other important Hindu ideas, in particular *dharma* and rebirth. He saw himself as a *yana*, or a vehicle others may use on their road to wisdom. He was adamant in rejecting the **transcendental temptation** and extravagant metaphysical theorizing. His two main innovations were the notions of **dependent arising** and the **Four Noble Truths**.

The Buddha forbade his followers to perform **miracles** for display. He insisted that acquiring **supernatural** powers does not mean one is spiritually superior. In fact, the Buddha rejected claims of supernatural knowledge and was broadly atheistic. However, he had to be persuaded to change his opinion of the role of women. For much of his career, he urged men to keep their distance from women. Neither can he be credited with abolishing caste. Indeed, his philosophy remained quite aristocratic.

That said, Gautama's knowledge and eventual enlightenment was the result of his own efforts, and his genius lay in his ability to convince others that they too could achieve enlightenment if they were open and honest enough. Instead, people have preferred to believe that they can achieve enlightenment if they are sufficiently slavish to the Buddha. Among the few points Buddhists have in common is a faith in the full enlightenment of the Buddha. But in actual fact, the Buddha insisted that people should not blindly follow his dicta but should work things out for themselves. **Therevada Buddhism** emphasizes this aspect of the Buddha's teachings most closely.

GAUVIN, MARSHALL JEROME (1881–1978). Rationalist lecturer and writer called "the Canadian antichrist" by his opponents. Marshall Gauvin was born in Dover, New Brunswick, on May 3, 1881, the eighth of ten (some say eleven) children. His mother, Madeleine Dorion, was a devout Roman Catholic but his father, Israel Gauvin, had converted to the Baptist faith. Gauvin's youth was spent in a climate of bitter religious acrimony. During a visit to Boston in 1899, Gauvin heard firsthand about **Robert Ingersoll**, whose name he had heard denounced from the pulpit. For the next ten years Gauvin read all the important **freethought** works, as well as becoming intimately familiar with the Bible. He would hold single pages of **scripture** in one hand while continuing to work as a carpenter with the other.

In 1912, Gauvin left his work as a carpenter and began his career as a full-time rationalist lecturer. After several years in Pittsburgh in 1914 and a two-year tour of North America on behalf of the *Truthseeker*, Gauvin took up in 1921 a position in Minneapolis for the Twin City Rationalist Society. In the same year he married Martha L. Becker, herself the product of a German freethinking family. They had one daughter. In 1926, Gauvin moved to Winnipeg, where for fourteen years he was the full-time lecturer for the Winnipeg Rationalist Society, which in 1934 he renamed the Winnipeg Humanist Society. Gauvin finally retired from active lecturing in 1940, noting that the day of the lecturer was over as radio and the cinema were becoming more popular ways to spend leisure time. Between 1921 and 1940, Gauvin gave more than eight hundred lectures.

After spending the war working as a carpenter, Gauvin's freethought career seemed once again to come back to life when he was elected president of the newly reformed National Liberal League in 1946. For much of the next eight years, Gauvin lived in New York trying to build the league. His efforts, though considerable, came to nothing, falling victim to infighting and dissension. In 1954 he returned to Winnipeg. From then until shortly before his death he continued to write for *Truthseeker*, although he was increasingly alarmed by the racism and **anti-Semitism** that was characteristic of the paper at that time. Marshall Gauvin died on September 23, 1978, at 97. The best collection of his work is in *The Fundamentals of Freethought* (1923), a selection of his more important lectures.

GEE, MAURICE (1931–). New Zealand author described as one of the world's finest writers working in English. Maurice Gee, the son of a carpenter, was born in the small town of Whakatane and raised in Henderson, then a small town (now a suburb) west of Auckland. Henderson appears frequently in his novels in various guises. Gee attended Avondale College, then Auckland University, where he took a MA in English in 1954. He worked as a teacher for two years in the rural town of Paeroa before spending three years doing casual work. He spent 1961 in England on a grant from the New Zealand Literary Fund. Gee had had several short stories published through the 1950s, but his name became better known with the publication of *The Big Season* (1962), his first novel. He captured the pressures of small town living in New Zealand brilliantly.

Since then Gee has produced a string of powerful novels, all of which explore family relationships, and themes of loneliness, social constraints, and the strength of **character** needed to challenge societal norms. A couple of Gee's novels explore the dynamics of **rationalism** in New Zealand. *In My Father's Den* (1972) and *Plumb* (1978) are especially important in this respect. *Plumb* is the fictionalized account of the life of Rev. James Henry George Chapple (1865–1947), a Pres-

byterian minister who was thrown out of the church for chairing a meeting of **Joseph McCabe** (who is also mentioned in the book). Chapple ended his life an active rationalist. More recent novels include *Going West* (1992), *Crime Story* (1994), and *Living Bodies* (1998). He has also achieved the rare double of also writing excellent children's novels, in particular *The Halfmen of O* (1982), *The Priests of Ferris* (1984), and *Motherstone* (1985). See the entry on **humanist-themed novels**.

Gee has received almost every award and honor available. He was named one of New Zealand's ten greatest living artists in 2003, and received an honorary doctorate in literature from the University of Auckland in 2004. He describes himself as an evolutionary humanist and is an honorary associate of the **New Zealand Association of Rationalists and Humanists**.

GELLNER, ERNEST (1925–1995). Humanist philosopher, defender of the **open society**, and **smiter of humbug**. Ernest Gellner was born in Paris and educated at Prague Grammar School, before moving to England, where he studied at Balliol College, Oxford. He was on the staff of the London School of Economics from 1949 until 1984, being professor of philosophy there from 1962. From 1984 he was William Wyse professor of social anthropology at Cambridge University and a professorial fellow at King's College, Cambridge.

Gellner made his reputation with a stinging attack on linguistic philosophy. The polemical fire in *Words and Things* (1959) was a shock to the sheltered world of British academic philosophy, and many never forgave Gellner for the ferocity of his attack. **Bertrand Russell** wrote a foreword for the book. Many years later Gellner wrote *The Psychoanalytic Movement* (1985), a devastating criticism of **psychoanalysis**. He was also a strong defender of the concept of **reason** from its many detractors, particularly in books like *Reason and Culture* (1992). Not surprisingly, Gellner was an outspoken critic of **postmodernism**. This was expressed most strongly in *Postmodernism, Reason and Religion* (1992). Gellner's last book, *Language and Solitude* (1998) was published after his death. It was a criticism of **Wittgenstein**. "We are," Gellner wrote, "a race of failed Prometheuses. Rationalism is our destiny. It is not our option, and still less our disease."

Gellner was a humanist is the fullest sense of the word. He was a defender of **Enlightenment values** of rationality, **secularism**, **pluralism**, and an authentic compassion not mired in sentimentality. He developed the concept of the **civil society** in *Conditions of Liberty* (1995) in the last book published during his lifetime. This was the most positive of all his books. Gellner was an honorary associate of the **Rationalist Press Association** from 1979 until his death. He was one of the most broadly intelligent social critics of his generation.

GEMEINSCHAFT AND GESELL-SCHAFT. German terms referring to different theories of society. They were brought together by the German historian Ferdinand Tönnies (1855–1936) in an influential work of theoretical sociology, published in 1887. Gesellschaft refers to the **open society** of anonymous individuals who engage in contractual arrangements with one another, whereas Gemeinschaft refers to the more **romantic** blood and soil links of tradition and hierarchy. Influenced by **Arthur Schopenhauer** and **Friedrich Nietzsche**, Tönnies saw the influence of gesellschaft as enervating on an otherwise vital and authentic racial tradition.

GENDER. The differences between males and females that are determined by culture. By contrast, **sex** differences are biological. However, it is important not to harden the gap between natural and cultural so that a new form of **dualism** is the result. This was a problem in some of the earlier feminist thinkers like **Betty Friedan** and **Simone de Beauvoir**. Gender theory, which downplays biological differences or denies biological constants such as human nature, is never going to be able to provide satisfactory explanations of, let alone solutions for, the differences between men and women.

Notions like femininity have traditionally been defined in the context of what is *not* male. Softness, passivity, sensuousness, irrationality have all been seen by philosophers as essential characteristics of the feminine, not infrequently to act as complements to the different set of male virtues. This is a gender issue, whereas the lower toleration of women to alcohol, for example, is a biological difference with gender implications.

Until 1955, gender applied only to grammar, but that year John Money, a sexologist at Johns Hopkins University, spoke of gender in the sense now understood, although in the context of a study of hermaphrodites. The term became popular with feminists in the 1960s, becoming mainstream in the 1980s. Gender studies are increasingly coming to terms with **evolutionary psychology**, leading to some grounds for optimism that a comprehensive understanding of the various roles of nature and nurture can be achieved.

Further reading: Jean Grimshaw, *Philosophy and Feminist Thinking*; Helena Cronin, *The Ant and the Peacock*; and Janet Radcliffe Richards, *Human Nature after Darwin*.

GENERAL WILL. An idea made popular by the philosopher **Jean-Jacques Rousseau** in his book *The Social Contract* (1762). The general will is not the same as the sum of all individual wills. Rather, it is a semimystical pulling together of the commonality in the same direction. Individual wills were to be voluntarily subordinated to the general will. And the state would be the instrument of the general will.

The idea has some romantic appeal, but it assumes that when people think rationally, they will eventually all come to the same conclusion. This is simply not true. As other thinkers from the **Enlightenment** like

Voltaire and **Diderot** recognized, there are many different ways of being rational. The idea of the general will is inimical to **pluralism** and runs a strong risk of descending into **totalitarianism**.

Rousseau never made clear whether the general will was an ideal, or whether he seriously thought a country the size of France could seek to acquire legitimacy from the general will of the people. He wrote in *The Social Contract*: "My argument, then, is that sovereignty, being nothing other than the exercise of the general will, can never be alienated; and that the sovereign, which is simply a collective being, cannot be represented by anyone but itself—power may be delegated, but the will cannot be." It is a small step from this for one man, **Adolf Hitler** for example, to see himself as the embodiment of the general will.

Many postmodernist critics have drawn attention to the totalitarian tendencies of Enlightenment thought, without stopping to ask who among the thinkers of the time was responsible for such ideas. It is one thing to recognize the totalitarian implications in Rousseau's ideas, but it is altogether another thing to then assume the entire period known as the Enlightenment can be written off. Rousseau's ideas ran counter to the general direction of most of his contemporaries.

GENERALIZED COPERNICAN PRINCIPLE. The principle that says there is no center of the universe—in other words that any point in space is equivalent to any other point. See the entry on **heliocentric universe**.

GENETIC MODIFICATION. One of the most contentious and ill-informed debates currently running. This is often seen as a new issue, arising out of an emerging science. This is not true; people have been genetically modifying plants and animals for centuries, with the effect of producing significantly larger, better quality products, and feeding an ever-growing population. Norman Ernest Borlaug (1914–) received a Nobel prize in 1970 for his work developing new strains of rice and wheat, which have fed millions of people. Ironically, opponents argue that genetically modified food is unnecessary because we already have enough food to feed the world. One of the reasons we have enough food is the genetic-modification work of scientists like Borlaug.

Genetic research also has the chance to effect some significant breakthroughs in medical research. Among the wider public, there is general agreement that genetic research is acceptable with respect to medicine but not with respect to food. In the laboratory, however, it is not always easy to make this distinction, as research in one area may yield an unintended benefit in another area.

Much of the opposition to genetic research is based on a prescientific notion of the fixity of species, namely that everything was created as it is now and is best left that way. Images of pigs crossed with tomatoes make for graphic posters, but are hardly a constructive contribution to the debate. More sensible opposition to genetic modification revolves around the **precautionary principle**, which states that change should be predicated upon caution, and that we should wait for more test results to emerge before we rush into changes that could be unsafe or have some other unintended consequence.

The real objection should not be against genetic research as such, but the way large multinational companies are coercing farmers to use genetically modified seeds, which are produced by themselves. The objection is more against the arrogance and shortsightedness of multinational companies, not against genetic research itself.

The other core issue in today's debate on genetic modification is the growing realization that the time is approaching when we will be able to modify and improve *Homo sapiens*. See the entry on the **human genome project**. There are very good reasons to be concerned about this, but banning things will not work. It will only drive the research underground. Some are excited by the prospect; see the entry on **transhumanism**. Others are absolutely terrified by it. There is an element of **anthropocentric conceit** to see that *Homo Sapiens* can't be improved upon. This will be one of the major issues of **bioethics** of the coming century. As the situation with nuclear power has shown us, clear codes of practice, transparency, and global regulations and control will be essential to harness the best in genetic research and limit the risks.

GENOCIDE. The systematic attempt to destroy an entire people. For a campaign of slaughter to be sufficiently systematic to be called genocide, it needs to be planned, focused, and informed by some sort of ideology which casts the victim people as posing a mortal danger to one's own people. The two most common reasons given to justify genocide are religious or racial differences, although the racial differences are frequently informed by religion, most notably **anti-Semitism**.

The word was only coined in 1944, by the Polish Jewish jurist Raphael Lemkin (1900–1959), but the practice has been around since humans began living in groups.

Many ancient struggles had genocidal goals, with some gruesome examples recorded in the **Hebrew scriptures**. Between 1492 and 1990 there have been at least thirty-six genocides, twenty of them since 1950, two of them (Bangladesh and Cambodia) costing more than a million lives. Most successful recent genocide was the destruction of the Tasmanians. In the century after Europeans landed on Tasmania in 1772, they systematically destroyed the aboriginals on the island. The most recent genocide was the slaughter in 1994 in Rwanda in which at least 800,000 people lost their lives.

In December 1948, the **United Nations** sponsored a genocide convention, which helped provide a standard definition of genocide and focused international attention on the subject. The provisions of the 1948 conference were ratified by the United Nations in 1951. Since the end of the **cold war** the United Nations has been able to play a more effective role in helping prevent genocides and bringing those responsible to justice. The trails at the International Court of Justice of Serbian and Rwandan perpetrators of genocide are hopeful signs of the growing willingness of the world community to confront this ancient evil. Bringing the perpetrators of genocide to justice and alleviating the suffering of the victims is yet another example of the pressing need for transnational solutions to our problems. See the entry on **global governance**.

GENUINE PROGRESS INDICATOR. A model designed to measure more effectively than the gross domestic product (GDP) the level of national prosperity. The GDP is a crude measure of overall economic activity that makes no attempt to evaluate this activity. An environmental disaster can actually be good for the GDP as new employment is stimulated, lawsuits are flying back and forth, and an expensive cleanup has to be undertaken. Similarly, a divorce, or a crime will help the GDP go upward because of the economic transactions they stimulate. But few people would argue that environmental disasters, divorce, or crime should therefore be encouraged.

What is needed is an index that *evaluates* the economic transactions and includes activity which is good for the economy without economic transactions taking place. In the GPI, economic growth resulting from undesirable activity would not be counted, whereas, things like volunteer work, housework, or helping sick family members (and thus saving the health system that expense) would be included. Measuring economic activity in this way would give a far truer indicator of the economy in terms of making a better society where people are happier, rather than simply richer. See the entries on **affluenza** and **positive and negative sustainability quotient**.

Further reading: www.redefiningprogress .org.

GEOCENTRIC UNIVERSE. The idea of the universe that was dominant before the breakthroughs of the scientific revolution of the seventeenth century, particularly by **Galileo** and **Isaac Newton**. The geocentric universe put planet Earth at its center and infused it with meaning for human beings, who were its central focus. Because human beings were the focus of the universe, special human beings—shamans, witch doctors, priests—were able to propitiate the heavens with their spells and **magic**. The idea of the **great chain of being** was also integral to the geocentric universe.

The most comprehensive account of the geocentric universe was given by Ptolemy of Alexandria (90–168 CE, approx.) in 150 CE, although the idea had been around for a long time even then. See the entry on **Anaximander**. Ptolemy's account of the geocentric universe remained the standard for more than fifteen hundred years until the scientific revolution of the seventeenth century rendered it redundant. Christopher Columbus had a copy of Ptolemy's works with him when he set out in 1492 to discover a westward route to the Indies.

The geocentric universe is centrally relevant to the **monotheist** religions, with their claim that the creator of the universe is interested in the welfare of each and every one of us. A clear example of the geocentric world-view is the Creation Psalm (Psalm 8), which arrogates to "man" a position "little less than heavenly beings" and in dominion over all other things of the earth. The Qur'an makes similar observations (36:38, 40, and so on). See the entry on **dominionism**. The geocentric universe is now seen as a special brand of **anthropocentric conceit**. It has been replaced by the **heliocentric universe**.

GEROETHICS. A term coined by American scholar Gerald Larue that refers to the consideration of ethical principles with regard to the needs and interests of the elderly. It is Larue's contention that society's changes have an ongoing impact on the elderly, and the elderly, in turn, have a sufficiently coordi-nated series of responses to these changes. See the entry on **agequake**.

Further reading: Gerald Larue, *Geroethics*.

GLOBAL CORPORATE CITIZENSHIP INITIATIVE. A concept created in 2001 by the **World Economic Forum**. The initiative consists of forty World Economic Forum member corporations which have demonstrated a commitment to corporate citizenship. The forum's Web site defines global corporate citizenship as "the contribution a company makes to society through its core business activities, its social investment and philanthropy programs, and its engagement in public policy." It goes on to note that a company's impact is determined by the manner in which it handles economic, social, and environmental relationships.

Following the lead of **United Nations** secretary-general Kofi Annan, many multinational corporations are realizing that business cannot prosper in a climate of massive poverty and malnutrition. Some of the more philanthropic corporations like Microsoft have lead the way with a series of programs to combat **AIDS** and to close the digital divide. It is worth taking facts such as this into consideration when judgments on **globalization** are being made. The picture of avaricious corporations is part of the truth, but only part.

GLOBAL GAG RULE. Informal title given to the decree by President George W. Bush on January 22, 2001, which denied American funding to foreign nongovernmental organizations that are associated with any sort of planned parenthood program or pro**abortion** position. The rule was first imposed by President Reagan. It was then repealed by President Clinton and reapplied, along with its current informal title, by President Bush.

Bush's Global Gag Rule has had calamitous effects on many organizations involved with the reproductive rights and healthcare of women in some of the poorest countries of the world. Access to contraceptives has become more difficult in many parts of the world. The Global Gag Rule was accompanied by a total withdrawal of American funding for the **United Nations** Population Fund (UNFPA). Ironically, this has resulted in a massive increase in the number of women having abortions in the poor countries of the world. In the absence of sensible reproductive information for women to make an informed choice, the incidence of abortions always rises. And yet religious conservatives want to limit the provision of reproductive information *and* access to abortions. Such mutually defeating policies have only one thing in common—a hostility to women having power over their own bodies.

President Bush covered his tracks on the Global Gag Rule with a heavily advertised announcement of a $15 billion HIV/**AIDS** prevention program. What escaped media attention was the subsequent reduction of that amount to $2 billion in the first year, and the requirement that the money should be spent only on ideologically motivated "Abstinence only" programs. While there is no doubt that **abstinence** works as a measure against HIV/AIDS, it is hardly a practical solution, particularly in societies where girls often have little direct say in when their sexual activities begin.

The Global Gag Rule and the preference for abstinence programs are significant victories for the American Religious Right who imposes its misogynist policies not just on its own citizens, but on the world. It constitutes an impediment to the **sexual and reproductive rights** of women around the world.

GLOBAL GOVERNANCE. A term given to the style of transnational political management that is developing in the post–cold war world. It is increasingly obvious that the global problems of environmental deterioration, whether in the form of overfishing, deforestation, climate change, global warming, desertification, or population pressure, as well as the **war on terror**, all need to be managed at a global level. Global governance is the political manifestation of **planetary humanism**.

The catchphrase used to be "world government," but what really is needed is global governance. World government suggests a single global authority with coercive power, but the experience of the Soviet Politburo suggest that this is not a model conducive to democracy. Global governance is the messier reality of nation-states, the **United Nations**, international treaties like the **Kyoto Treaty**, and the major multinational corporations, international governmental organizations (IGOs) and nongovernmental organizations (NGOs) all having some input in preserving the planet for the future. Global governance doesn't presuppose the end of the nation-state, nor does it seek to usurp all power into the hands of a tiny elite that decides what is good for the rest of us. World government would be more likely to give rise to some form of hegemonic **globalism** than the looser process of global governance. Global governance is the product not of globalism but of **globalization**.

Global governance may well be less tidy, less heroic, and more prone to fits and starts than world government, but at the current stage in the development of our planetary consciousness, is the best we can hope to achieve. As we begin the twenty-first century there are more than two hundred forty IGOs and more than two thousand multilateral treaties and intergovernmental agreements in operation. These are at the heart of the notion of global governance. The success of the **Montreal Protocols**, and the partial success of the **Kyoto Treaty**, are illustrations of how global governance works. The main problem with global governance as described here is its chaotic nature. The very variety of organizations, groups, treaties, and protocols, makes some form of coordination between them essential in the long run. The challenge is whether this can be done without global governance becoming precisely the over-bureaucratized central authority that people fear world government would become.

Further reading: Carl Coon, *One Planet, One People—Beyond "Us vs. Them"*; and Mike Moore, *A World Without Walls*.

GLOBALISM. Not to be confused with **globalization** or **global governance**, globalism is the doctrine that all regional and particular interests around the planet should be subsumed to the global interests as defined by one regional and particular interest. Many see the United States, the world's only genuine superpower following the end of the **cold war**, as the world's main proponent of globalism. Others have seen **Islamism**, with its specific aim to Islamize the whole world, as an example of globalism. Sometimes specific institutions are accused of globalist tendencies, for example, activists on the left sometimes speak of multinational corporations, the **World Trade Organization**, the **International Monetary Fund**, or the **World Bank** in these terms. Activists on the right are more inclined to target the **United Nations**. Religious fanatics and **anti-Semites** have accused the Jewish people of tendencies toward globalism.

The point of all this is that globalism is an easy charge to make, not least because it is next to impossible to verify. The clearest evidence so far of globalism, is the worldwide growth in American-style consumerism. The important task is to move toward global governance without slipping into the temptations of globalism. This is the long-term objective of **planetary humanism**.

GLOBALIZATION. A term used to refer to the process whereby national economies, identities, and outlooks are replaced by transnational economies, identities, and outlooks. The American theorist Samuel P. Huntington characterized post–**cold war** politics as becoming multipolar and multicivilizational. The trend was first noticed in the 1960s and 1970s and accelerated in the 1990s, after the end of the cold war. Since then the pace of globalization has increased. Globalization is generated by the move to free trade, the growth in air travel, the Internet, and the rising need for global solutions to global problems. Having said this, globalization is not a new phenomenon. **Joseph McCabe** noted in 1923 that there "is

only one world-wide civilization today, and it will never again die. It is essentially the same in Tokyo and New York, London and Sydney, Paris and Buenos Aires, Warsaw and Mexico."

Huntington also has noted that state governments "have in considerable measure lost the ability to control the flow of money in and out of their country and are having increasing difficulty controlling the flow of ideas, technology, goods, and people. State borders, in short, have become increasingly permeable." It is not that the nation-state is going to wither away, but it is going to change very markedly indeed. These changes have had significant impact on the **welfare state** model of governance, which dominated the scene after World War II.

A good example of globalization is the little label in your trousers that says which country it is made in. That label is becoming increasingly meaningless as raw materials, white- and blue-collar staff, marketing, distribution, and retailing of the item depend on a transnational effort.

The economist A. T. Kearney claims that Singapore is the most globalized country in the world. This is measured by:

- levels of cross-border contact;
- per capita outgoing telephone traffic;
- tourist numbers exceeding native population by a factor of three; and
- commitment to free trade.

Other highly globalized nations are Sweden, Finland, and the Netherlands, and it is not coincidental that each of these countries is a highly developed, civilized, secular democracy. At the opposite end of the spectrum, North Korea and Turkmenistan would be candidates for the world's least globalized country. There would be little dispute as to where most people would prefer to live.

Klaus Schwab, the convener of the **World Economic Forum**, has outlined seven principal challenges to globalization:

- the need to create conditions for faster growth;
- the need for environmental and social sustainability;
- developing an effective international peacekeeping;
- narrowing the technological and social gap between the rich and poor;
- the need for higher standards of health and nutrition;
- the need for a common understanding of human rights and values; and
- safeguarding cultural identity in an increasingly homogenized world.

At its best, globalization allows for a range of new freedoms to explore the world and immerse oneself in the fabulous **diversity** of life on this planet. Globalization is helping the move toward **global governance**. At its worst, it is the means by which that very diversity will be inexorably expunged by a soulless, largely American-driven **affluenza**. Which of those becomes predominant will depend on us.

Further reading: Samuel P. Huntington, *The Clash of Civilizations and the Remaking of the World Order*; Naomi Klein, *No Logo*; and Mike Moore, *A World Without Walls*.

GLOSSOGONOUS WORD-SALAD. A wonderful phrase taken from the philosopher Susan Haack to refer to the **jargon**-filled verbiage that passes for profound scholarship among certain types of **postmodernists** and others. Glossogonous (like **glossolalia**) derives from the Greek *glossa*, or tongue. See the entries on **différance** and the **Incontinence Principle of Continental Philosophy**.

GLOSSOLALIA. The practice of speaking in tongues that is popular among several religions and even outside of a religious context altogether, but is best known among fundamentalist Christians. The claim usually made is that the person speaking in tongues has become a mouthpiece of **God** and is speaking an unfamiliar language, most commonly with the purpose of making some sort of prophecy. The practice is mentioned several times in the New Testament but even Paul, although he admits to speaking in tongues, condemns the practice as evidence of immaturity and exhibitionism (1 Cor. 13:11 and 14:20).

No independent study has ever demonstrated that glossolalia is anything more than a psychological condition brought on by the emotional intensity of an occasion or the need to secure the attention of one's associates.

GNOSTICS. A strain of mystical religious belief that sought a greater spiritual commitment by passing beyond the worldly instruction of bishops and **scriptures** and seeking instead a higher awareness, or *gnosis*. This often came in the form of mystical knowledge and secret codes and phrases. The Gnostics were radical **dualists**, in that they saw the world as intrinsically evil and the human body was our connection to the evil world. So everything we could do to negate the body would be for the good of the soul. Gnosticism predated Christianity; what it gained from that religion was the idea of redemption, which helped accentuate even further the huge gap between the divine realm and the worldly realm, a division central to Gnostic thought.

From about 80 to 150 CE, Gnostic groups came into conflict with other styles of messianic belief, including Christians. The Gnostics took Jesus as a teacher who could help them overcome the body in the interests of the soul. But the Gnostic approach to Jesus soon brought them into conflict with other types of Christians. The conflict with **Marcion**, in particular, helped stimulate the need many Christians felt for some authoritative texts by which true from false Christians could be distinguished. Indeed, a great deal of early Christian doctrine was formulated in response to the challenges of Gnosticism.

Little was known about Gnosticism until the discovery of the Nag Hammadi papyri in 1945. Until then, most of what we knew about Gnostics came from the works of their enemies. This remains the case for many naturalists and freethinkers of the ancient world.

Further reading: Elaine Pagels, *The Gnostic Gospels*.

GOD. A concept devised by human beings in an attempt to explain to themselves what they don't understand and to accord to themselves a status in the cosmos they do not deserve. Theologians have argued for centuries as to the nature of God, and wars and persecutions have been conducted on behalf of one interpretation or another. Generally, the idea of God is described as being:

- incomparably good and glorious;
- uncreated and unchanging;
- interested in human welfare above all others in the universe; and
- **beyond human understanding**.

The problems inherent in these contradictory understandings are so immense that **monotheist** religions have resorted to recommending **faith** as the surest means by which this sort of God can be known. This is sensible, because once reason is applied to this notion its instability quickly becomes apparent. See the entry on **omniscience**.

Many people have found purpose and meaning through faith in God, and freethinkers have often said that good people are usually going to be good anyway and that the idea of God is actually a barrier to goodness, or at least unnecessary to it. See the entry on **godless morality**.

The principal reason for the power of the God idea is the ability it has to stimulate our **anthropocentric conceit**. Instead of seeing ourselves as one species among many on one planet among countless billions, the God idea allows us to see ourselves as being of central interest to the creator of the entire universe. On top of this, it also allows believers to see themselves as humble.

GOD, DENIAL OF. One of the more popular **prejudices against atheists** is that they are simply denying **God** for some disrep-

utable motive known only to themselves. But this is to base an argument on what can only be speculation about the motives of other people, a procedure both philosophically suspect and impertinent. It is another form of **demonizing the opposition**. On top of this, there are several important weaknesses to the denying God argument, as the Canadian philosopher Kai Nielsen has noted:

- not all defenders of Christianity regard themselves as defenders of theism— Paul Tillich (1886–1965), for example, regarded a theistic God as idolatry;
- not all theists seek to rationally justify God, e.g., Kierkegaard (1813–1855); and
- not all those who deny God are atheists, e.g., Karamazov.

It is not that God is being denied, but the *existence* of God; a very different point. See the entry on **religion, criticism of**.

Further reading: Kai Nielsen, *Philosophy and Atheism*.

GOD IS LOVE. A worthy but incoherent idea, because it requires **God** to be a corporeal agent, in other words a physical entity, in order to experience and give expression to this love. In which case, God could also be prone to other bodily processes like lust, jealousy, and so on. For most **monotheist** systems the notion that God is love is also made very problematic by the behavior of this God in other circumstances. If God is love, what does one do with all the passages of scripture that tell of a jealous, vindictive God who sanctions brutality and oppression?

GOD OF THE GAPS. A phrase referring to the tendency among theologians and religious apologists to insert **God** into areas still without a coherent or widely accepted scientific explanation. It is possible that this type of argument (though not the term itself) originated with **Isaac Newton**, who, when faced with calculations of planetary orbits that did not quite fit, attributed the discrepancy to

God's working in the universe. The term was first used by the Scottish Evangelist Henry Drummond (1851–1897) who criticized the practice of scanning "the fields of Nature and the book of Science in search of gaps—gaps which they fill up with God."

The main problem with this approach, as Drummond recognized, is that it concedes to **science** the primary role as a provider of authoritative explanations of phenomena. It also allows that God's role as an explanation will decline as the gaps in our **knowledge** are filled. And it is entirely arbitrary that the gap in our knowledge should be filled in by God.

GOD, VARIATIONS OF. It is an elementary mistake to think there is only one type of **god**. Because God is a human creation, there is a bewildering variety of forms that God is said to take. Among the more common are, at least in the tradition of Western religions:

- the anthropomorphic God of most forms of **monotheist** fundamentalism;
- the nonanthropomorphic god of more sophisticated believers and many Western theologians;
- the nonanthropomorphic deistic God of the universe;
- the mystical idea of God as the cosmic source of the universe and ourselves;
- the modern view of God as a symbolic term or allegory; or
- the set of equations that physicists usually mean when they speak of "the mind of God."

So, when George Bernard Shaw (1856–1950) was asked if he denied God, his answer "Which one?" was not without point. This multiplicity of god-ideas underscores the wisdom of **Charles Bradlaugh**'s negative **atheism**, where he says he is not denying god, but is simply without a coherent idea of god, because no theist can provide a clear definition.

Once again, the problem of the wide range of ideas about God is not as significant in

Asian traditions, which are either agnostic, like Buddhism and philosophical **Taoism**; unconcerned about the question, like Confucianism; or comfortable with leaving it up to individuals to construct the most suitable god-idea their **dharma** requires, like Hinduism.

GÖDEL'S THEOREM. A proof developed in 1931 by Kurt Gödel (1906–1978) from the University of Vienna, which established a clear limit on mathematical proof. Following on from the work of **Bertrand Russell** and A. N. Whitehead (1861–1947) in *Principia Mathematica* (1910–1913), Gödel demonstrated that in any system of formal mathematics there are sentences of arithmetic that, while being true, cannot be shown to be true within that system of **mathematics**. The further implication of this is that trying to settle on some foundational set of mathematical axioms in order to determine the truth of all mathematics is bound to fail.

Many theorists have employed Gödel's Theorem in various metaphysical or anti-science projects, but usually at the cost of misinterpreting or overestimating the consequences of the theorem. While Gödel's Theorem is undoubtedly important, its importance is limited principally to mathematics.

GODLESS MORALITY. Even many prominent churchmen are beginning to recognize that it is a mistake to mix **God** up with questions of morality. This was persuasively argued in 1999 by Richard Holloway, at the time a prominent British churchman. Holloway conceded the important point that talk of God in a moral debate is so fraught with difficulties as to be pretty well worthless. This is because we have no reliable way of determining who is actually speaking on God's behalf and who is not, or of what bits in the various **scriptures** to ignore and what bits to take as valid.

Once we have abandoned some things mentioned in the Bible, like child sacrifice, then we have moved irrevocably toward an ongoing understanding of biblical ethics.

While Holloway was speaking of Christianity, this observation is just as true for Judaism and Islam, the two other religions based on scriptures.

What we are left with is a range of moralities, but this moral pluralism does not necessarily mean moral **relativism**, at least not in its more dire forms. What it means is that there are many ways of looking at any issue, and we are going to need to understand these various approaches, and continue with our own search for values that can work in harmony with the fact of this pluralism. The difficulty, even impossibility, of this venture means that our search for values has a tragic element to it. But this in no way means that we should cease the search. Quite the contrary, we must continue, undaunted. One thing which must remain certain, however, is that our search must leave God out of the picture entirely.

Further reading: Richard Holloway, *Godless Morality: Keeping Religion Out of Ethics.*

GOETHE, JOHANN WOLFGANG (1749–1832). One of the most influential German humanists. Born in Frankfurt, he was educated privately and prepared without enthusiasm for a legal career similar to his father. He deserted his legal career for a life of letters, and in 1771 published *Götz von Berlichingen*, which was inspired by an unsuccessful love affair. This work was a landmark in the ***sturm und drang*** movement then beginning in Germany. But even more important for *sturm und drang* was Goethe's next work, *The Sorrows of Young Werther* (1774). Following from the phenomenal success of this book, Goethe was invited to the court of the grand duke of Weimar. While there Goethe helped transform the city into the Athens of Germany. It was during this time (1773) that Goethe wrote his justly famous words on **Prometheus**. They were originally intended as the opening piece to act 3 of a major work on Prometheus, but alas the work was never written; the fragment stands as an isolated poem.

While in Weimar, Goethe was a lusty, indulgent youth and then a frugal, unsocial ascetic. But after his trip to Italy in 1786 to 1788, he had discovered the balance between the two. There are few better illustrations of Aristotle's **Doctrine of the Mean**. As his biographer **Joseph McCabe** put it, "Nature was divine, the human body glorious: the senses were the appointed gates to admit happiness to the heart. . . ." All of Goethe's career was, in fact, devoted to exploring the many moods of love. He had little time for the traditional Christian dogmas of **sin** or **immortality**.

After his return to Germany, his scientific and literary work continued without a break until his death. He became friends with Johan Friedrich Schiller (1759–1805) and the two cooperated on projects and acted as friends and rivals throughout their lives. Goethe's most brilliant creation during these years was *Faust*, of which part 1 appeared in 1808 and part 2 in 1832, the year of his death. Part 1 is usually considered one of the classics of German literature.

Goethe was also a capable scientist, and while his own scientific quest proved to be a dead end, his authority inspired many people to go on to distinguished careers in the sciences.

GOLDEN CURTAIN. While the iron curtain was said to separate the communist bloc from Western Europe and the bamboo curtain shielded China, at least before its recent liberalization, the talk in Europe now is of a golden curtain. This refers to the no less daunting divide between the prosperous West and an impoverished Eastern Europe. For those from the former communist bloc, the enticements of Western prosperity are as elusive as ever.

GOLDEN RULE. A fundamental ethical maxim for civilized societies. The golden rule has a positive version: Do to others what you would wish others to do to you. It also has a negative version: Never do to others what you wouldn't want done to you. Probably the oldest expression of the golden rule can be found in the Indian classic, the Mahabharata, which says that the sum total of duties is contained in the maxim, "Thou shalt not do to others what is disagreeable to thyself." **Bertrand Russell** worked on a variation of the golden rule in what he called the **Supreme Moral Rule**.

Some variation of the golden rule is found in virtually every system of belief. This is not surprising, as the golden rule is the ethical expression of a biological imperative known as **reciprocal altruism**. As part of our evolutionary development, *Homo sapiens* have learned that some level of reciprocity is a basic requirement to any sort of cooperation. For this reason it is unreasonable to insist that the golden rule expresses some essentially religious imperative. The golden rule is entirely explicable in naturalistic terms.

The value of the golden rule has also been questioned by some philosophers, who cite various difficulties it can lead one into. For instance, the masochist may want pain done to him, but that is no reason to inflict pain on others. **Immanuel Kant** dismissed the golden rule as trivial and unable to serve as a standard or principle. Kant preferred his alternative, the **categorical imperative**. It is with these criticisms in mind that Mario Bunge, an Argentinian philosopher working in Canada, has developed the concept of **agathonism** as a refinement of the golden rule.

Agathonism solves the problems philosophers have raised about the golden rule, but even then we need to exercise **judgment** in every moral question we come across. The practical application of the golden rule was put best by **Paul Kurtz** when he wrote, " The general rule of moral decency is to cooperate as best we can, to tolerate the differing views of others, and to negotiate."

GOOD LIFE, THE. The good life is not the same as the moral life. One may lead a moral life and be desperately unhappy. The good life involves being moral, but is not subsumed or defined by it. One of the best conceptions of what constitutes the good life is from the Buddha. In the *Anguttara-nikaya*, the fourth in a collection of dialogues (this one with the banker Anathapindika), the Buddha outlined four characteristics of the good life:

- well-being relating to resources, or sufficient means, honestly acquired;
- economic well-being, **happiness** resulting from enjoyment of lawfully acquired wealth;
- happiness consequent upon being free from debt; and
- happiness of being free from blame.

For the Stoic thinker **Epictetus**, the good life had three main features:

- the ability to master one's desires;
- performing one's duty to the best of one's ability; and
- being able to think clearly about oneself, one's loved ones, and the wider community.

Epictetus's idea of performing one's duty to the best of one's ability has much in common with the notion of **dharma** and the third feature has lots in common with the idea of taking a **cosmic perspective**. See the entry on **value meaning**.

Further reading: David Kalupahana, *A History of Buddhist Philosophy*; and Epictetus, *The Art of Living* (interpreted by Sharon Lebell).

GORA. Familiar name of Goparaju Ramachandra Rao (1902–1975). Gora was born in Chatrapur, in Orissa, to a high-caste family. Conventionally religious until his middle twenties, Gora took an MA at Presidency College, Madras. His marriage was arranged by his parents. Gora was twenty-two, Saraswati, his bride, was ten. Gora's first job was as a lecturer in natural science at the American Mission College in Madurai, Tamil Nadu. The principal offered him the chance for further study at Yale if he embraced Christianity, but

Gora turned the offer down. Gora left the Mission College soon after this and took a position at the Agricultural Research Institute in Coimbatore. Here he was joined by his wife, now 14, who since her marriage had been involved in the religious ceremonies appropriate for married girls.

Gora taught at Coimbatore for a year, then at Ananda College in Ceylon, an institution run by the Buddhist Theosophical Society, where he taught botany for a year. In 1928 he and his family returned to Kakinada in Andhra Pradesh to teach at PR College, his alma mater. By this time Gora and Saraswati were both atheists. Gora taught well but his views were unacceptable to the school authority, who fired him despite protests from the students. This discrimination came to the attention of Sarvepalli Radhakrishnan (1888–1975), a prominent philosopher who later became president of India. Radhakrishnan recommended Gora be appointed to teach botany at the Hindu College, Masulipatanam, Andhra Pradesh. Gora taught there for five years before resigning in 1940, after pressure from the college which blamed Gora for the rising influence of Marxism among the students.

Tired with constant pressure from narrow-minded believers, Gora and his family went to the remote village of Mudunur in Andhra Pradesh to begin a new kind of life. Living in two thatched huts built just for them, Gora engaged in adult education in the village. He taught people of all castes, who sat together and drank from the same well.

Gora was imprisoned in 1942 for involvement with the Quit India Movement. And it was at Mudunur that Gora founded the **Atheist Centre**, now one of the most respected centers of practical atheism in the world.

Gora built up an acquaintance with Mahatma Gandhi (1869–1948) and can be credited with breaking down some of Gandhi's misconceptions about atheism. Gora spoke with Gandhi during his visit to the Sevagram Ashram in November 1944. During that visit, Gandhi found Gora too intellectual and did not like his atheism. In January 1945

Gora returned to the Sevagram Ashram and stayed there for three months. Gandhi still could not bring himself to endorse Gora's atheism, but he was considerably more positive about Gora's outlook on life after the longer conversation. Gandhi agreed to officiate at the marriage of Gora's eldest daughter to an untouchable but was assassinated before the ceremony, which took place at the Sevagram Ashram on March 13, 1948.

Gora went on to build the Atheist Centre and advocate what he called **positive atheism**. He articulated his outlook best in *Positive Atheism*, published in 1972. Since Gora's death, Saraswati Gora has taken on the leadership of the Atheist Centre.

GORHAM, CHARLES TURNER (1856–1933). English rationalist, journalist, and author. Educated privately and brought up with conventional religious beliefs. After a brief adolescent spell as a fervent Evangelical, Gorham turned to **rationalism**. While working as a solicitor's clerk in London, he chanced upon the **Rationalist Press Association**, which he was then closely linked to for the rest of his life. Gorham was a frequent contributor to the RPA's journal, the *Literary Guide*, and from 1912 until 1928, he served as the association's secretary. From 1916 until 1919 Gorham was the editor of the *Humanist*, a journal of the Ethical Union.

Gorham's first book began life as his own researches on the authority of the scriptures. It was published as *Is the Bible a Revelation from God?* in 1894. Gorham was a capable popularizer of rationalist thinking for the nonspecialist. Among his books are *Ethics of the Great French Rationalists* (1900), *The First Easter Dawn* (1908), *The Spanish Inquisition* (1918), *Why We Do Right* (1924), *Religion as a Bar to Progress* (1930), and *The Gospel of Rationalism* (1942).

GORHAM, GEORGE CORNELIUS (1787–1857). The victim of the last trial for heresy in England. Gorham, an Anglican minister but with Calvinist leanings, denied the standard view that at baptism a person is cleansed of **original sin** and born again into Christ. Gorham's views became relevant during an application in 1847 to the bishop of Exeter for a curacy in his diocese. Anywhere else in England, Gorham's application would probably have gone ahead with little more than raised eyebrows. But the bishop of Exeter was Henry Phillpotts (1778–1869), a litigious man with grand theories on the role of the church and the dignity of bishops. Having been warned of his views, the bishop subjected Gorham to an intensive grilling, effectively a trial, in December 1847 and again in March 1848. The bishop found Gorham's views unacceptably unorthodox and refused him the position. Gorham appealed to the Judicial Committee of the Privy Council which, on August 6, 1851, overruled the bishop's decision. Enflamed with pious indignation, the bishop gathered his clergy together in synod and affirmed his position as the true one.

The Gorham case weakened the Church of England, because it emerged from the affair looking oppressive and pedantic. What it illustrates is just how much things have changed since the middle of the nineteenth century. Such a dispute would hardly make waves in the parishioner's newsletter now, let alone become a serious and divisive national issue. For those who scoff at the thesis of **secularization**, the Gorham case stands as a reminder of its essential validity.

GOTT, JOHN WILLIAM (1866–1922). English atheist campaigner and the person with the distinction of having been tried for **blasphemy** more often than anyone else in British history. In 1894, along with two colleagues, Gott launched a journal called the *Truthseeker*, which was designed to act as a focus for freethought activity and opinion in the Bradford area. The *Truthseeker* lasted until about 1905. **Chapman Cohen** was involved with it in its early years.

Gott was charged with blasphemy in 1903 for publishing a cartoon that had appeared

without comment in the ***Freethinker*** fifteen years previously. For technical reasons, this charge was dropped. In 1911 Gott again came under official scrutiny, this time for publishing the supposedly blasphemous pamphlet called *Rib Ticklers, or Questions for Parsons*, a collection of jokes and satirical observations about the Christian religion. *Rib Ticklers* had been on sale without incident for about eight years and Gott always made a point of announcing that he would refund the penny pamphlet for sixpence for anyone distressed by its contents. Even the prosecuting policeman acknowledged this offer had been made public. Despite all this Gott was found guilty of blasphemy and sentenced to four months in prison.

Gott was again prosecuted and imprisoned for distributing *Rib Ticklers*, this time in Birmingham in 1917. And incredibly, in 1921 Gott once again faced a blasphemy charge for distributing *Rib Ticklers*, and on this occasion a birth-control pamphlet as well. This time he was sentenced to nine months' hard labor. The sentence was appealed the following year and upheld. Despite being unwell when the sentence was given, Gott served his full term. He was released in August and died on November 8, his health having been ruined by his last term of imprisonment.

GOVERNMENT, PRIMARY FUNCTIONS OF. Freethinkers of all types have agreed in maintaining strict limits on the pretensions of government. In particular, they agree that the role of government is the betterment of the human condition. How this is to be done, of course, has been a matter of debate. **Baruch Spinoza** perhaps summarized this view best when said the "ultimate aim of government is not to rule or restrain, by fear, nor to exact obedience, but contrariwise, to free every man from fear, that he may live in all possible security; in other words, to strengthen his natural right to exist and work without injury to himself or others."

Three centuries later, in the 1949 Reith Lectures, **Bertrand Russell** said much the same things as Spinoza when he itemized the three primary functions of government as security, justice, and the conservation of resources. Half a century later, this list still looks good.

How these three primary functions of government are best achieved remain a source of disagreement among freethinkers as among all other communities. **Freethought** encompasses political views from libertarianism on the right to socialism on the left. However, freethinkers of all persuasions agree that **democracy** is the best form of government to enact these primary functions.

Further reading: Baruch Spinoza, *Tractatus Logico-Philosophicus* and Bertrand Russell, *Authority and the Individual*.

GRAHAM, PHYLLIS (1905–1978). Former Carmelite nun who lost her faith and left the church. Phyllis Graham was born in Woodford, Essex, and grew up with an intense drive for religious experience. After twenty years as a Carmelite nun, Graham left the church and wrote *The Jesus Hoax* (1974), one of the most moving renunciations and denunciations of religious faith ever written. The book ended with a sixteen-page appendix of cruel passages from the New Testament, concentrating on the doctrine of **hell**, which Graham was most repelled by. Graham was in the process of having her autobiography published when the publishing firm the book was contracted to collapsed. A fragment of it appeared as a pamphlet *The Nun Who Lived Again*, published by the **National Secular Society**. Oppressed with age and infirmity, Graham took her own life in May 1978.

GREATEST HAPPINESS PRINCIPLE. See **UTILITY, PRINCIPLE OF**.

GREAT CHAIN OF BEING. Preevolutionary notion of order in the cosmos, providing for a special place for humanity. This idea was not called the great chain of being until the twentieth century. The idea of a hierarchy of order in nature is a very old one. **Aristotle** is usually blamed for this idea, although he articulated a sense of order that long preceded him. The great chain of being idea is also fundamental to Christianity, **Neoplatonism**, and Islam.

The hierarchy can be roughly traced as flowing downward from **God** or gods, through to man, to woman, to higher animals, lower animals, plants, and then rocks. This is a top-down chain, as it is inconceivable that lower stages can have any sort of influence on higher stages. There is a clear and essential qualitative difference between each stage. Men are most like God, and so are essentially superior to women. But even women have souls (though this concession came late in Christian history), and so are superior to the animals, and so on. The Muslim philosopher Ibn Sina (980–1037 CE) developed the idea of **holy reason**, which has strong resemblances to the great chain of being.

Despite its preevolutionary, and indeed antievolutionary, implications, ideas reminiscent of the great chain of being can be found among several of the earlier defenders of evolution. For example, **Ernst Haeckel** spoke in these terms in his populist classic *The Riddle of the Universe*. However, the great chain of being is a prescientific idea that no longer has any intellectual standing.

Further reading: Arthur Lovejoy, *The Great Chain of Being*.

GREAT COMMISSION, THE. A term given to the passage in the gospel attributed to Matthew (28:19–20), which has **Rabbi Yeshua**, now known as Jesus Christ, commanding his followers to make disciples of all the nations, baptizing them in the name of the Father, the Son, and the Holy Ghost. This passage is often used by Evangelicals as their scriptural authority for missionary activity.

The problem with this is that the passage is not from Jesus at all but is a very late addition to the text of the Matthew gospel. The passage presupposes practices such as baptism, which weren't recognized Christian activities during the life of Rabbi Yeshua. It also supposes that Gentiles were part of Yeshua's outlook, which was not the case.

GREAT DECEPTION, THE. The practice among theologians to put their own beliefs into the mouth of **Jesus Christ** is described by the German biblical scholar **Gerd Lüdemann** as the great deception. One of the foundational pillars of Jesus scholarship over the past century and a half is the recognition that writing a life of Jesus runs the greater risk of outlining the beliefs of the person writing the book than of Jesus Christ. We know so little about this person, we don't even give him his proper title and name, and to insert our own beliefs into his mouth, without regard for the piety of the motives underlying such an action, is to deceive one's reader. See the entries, **Rabbi Yeshua** and **Jesus Christ, creation of**.

Further reading: Gerd Lüdemann, *The Great Deception*.

GREAT DIVIDE, THE. A term used by **Hector Hawton** that referred to the real division, which was not between theism and atheism but between **reason** and unreason. Hawton argued that the first tenet of **irrationalism** is that truth is unattainable. From this the irrationalist was then able to conclude that our beliefs are nothing more than an arbitrary choice, and that no form of accumulation of **knowledge** is meaningful or even possible. The full-blooded irrationalist, Hawton argued, would feel terribly estranged from the world unless there existed full freedom to accept utter nonsense without any need to justify oneself.

Hawton argued this in the context of the then-fashionable **existentialism**, which was sweeping the Western world. Existentialism made clear that **atheism** and **rationalism** don't necessarily go together. His thoughts are just as relevant today, in the context of **postmodernism**, which takes **narcissism** and **nihilism** even further than existentialism. See also the entry on the **passes-for fallacy**.

Further reading: Hector Hawton, *The Feast of Unreason*.

GREAT FEAR, THE. The period of growing national hysteria in the United States dating approximately from Winston Churchill's "iron curtain" speech in Fulton, Missouri, in 1946 and lasting for about a decade. Features of the great fear included the perceived threat of world communism, including internal communist subversives within the United States. America went through a similar, though less hysterical, red scare after World War I as well. The great fear also built on the precedent of the hysterical anticommunism of prominent Catholics like Fulton Sheen (1895–1979) and Father Charles Coughlin (1891–1979) from the 1930s. Coughlin, dubbed "the father of hate radio," was a firm and consistent apologist for Hitler and Mussolini.

The most visible manifestation of the great fear was Senator Joe McCarthy (1909–1957), whose campaign of hunting down communists had all the hallmarks of a witch hunt, with the communists being only slightly less mythical than the witches. President Harry Truman (1884–1972) felt moved to describe McCarthy as a "pathological character assassin." The more substantial figures behind McCarthy were Richard Nixon and FBI boss J. Edgar Hoover.

The longest-lasting effect of the great fear was the link made between godliness and patriotism and **atheism** with "godless communism." Even though communism has now gone, this link remains, to the lasting disadvantage of atheism.

GREAT MORALE, THE. A concept developed by the great Chinese humanist Mengzi (371–289? BCE), known in the West as Mencius. The great morale [*Han Jan Chih Ch'i*] involved the morale of the man who identifies himself with the universe. There are two ways of cultivating the great morale:

• understanding the **Tao**, or the way of

principle that leads to the elevation of mind; or

- the accumulation of **human-heartedness**, or the constant doing what one ought to do because one is a citizen of the universe.

Through the constant accumulation of understanding of the Tao and cultivation of human-heartedness, the great morale will gradually develop within oneself. Mengzi also believed the it was achievable by everyone, because we all have the same nature. By "everyone," Mengzi meant all men, but there is no reason now why everyone cannot now be extended to actually include *everyone*.

Further reading: Fung Yu-lan, *A Short History of Chinese Philosophy*.

GREAT PERSECUTION, THE. The so-called persecution of Christians by the Roman emperor Diocletian (245–313 CE). The persecutions, of which that by Diocletian was the last, were part of Christian mythology for many centuries, most notably in *The Book of Martyrs*, published originally in 1554. The evocative image of Christians being thrown to the lions for their faith has been an enduring image for two thousand years.

As always, the facts tell a different story. The story of Nero persecuting Christians in the Colosseum is problematic because the Colosseum was not built until the reign of Vespasian (69–79 CE), after Nero's death. In fact recent evidence suggests the Christians were involved, if not actually starting the fire, but fanning its growth, in the expectation of it hastening on the second coming.

From the second century, the Roman empire granted religious liberty to a large range of eastern cults and philosophies, the principal exception being the orgiastic cult of Bacchus. On occasions, there were periods of persecution, when it was felt the state religion was in need of protection in troubling times. Many Christians (not the only minority cult caught up in these times) were, like Muslim fanatics today, ecstatic at the thought of martyrdom, and refused the simple test of giving public praise to the emperor at Roman shrines, and so brought on their own deaths.

There were only two persecutions that were general throughout the empire; that of Decius, from 249 to 251, and that of Diocletian from 303 to 305. The so-called great persecution of Diocletian was directed largely against Christian property and not against Christian people. Not one Christian was executed under Diocletian's reign, according to the historian Henry Chadwick. Only with his more fanatical successor Galerius (d. 311 CE) did the persecution extend to people, and even then it was haphazard, depending on the vigor of the local authorities. Reputable sources put the *entire* toll over all the persecutions at about 2,000. Christian theologians as early as Origen (185–254 CE) admitted that the number of actual victims of the persecutions was very low. While any persecution is unacceptable, this falls far short of the persecutions perpetrated by Christians against those of other beliefs, and even of other Christians. Another point about the so-called persecutions that often escapes notice is that the persecutors, like **Hierocles** of Bithynia, were themselves theists. The immediate consequence of the persecution was that Galerius' successor, **Constantine**, decided on a different way of dealing with the Christian minority.

GREAT ULTIMATE, THE. A term given its fullest shape by the Confucian philosopher Zhu Xi, or Chu Hsi in the old spelling (1130–1200). Zhu Xi is credited with reworking Confucian thought to such a degree that it has been called Neo-Confucianism by scholars since his day. The great ultimate, the central idea of Zhu Xi's philosophy, brings together several strands of Confucian thinking, notably principle (*li*) and material force (*qi*). The great ultimate, or *tai ji* (*t'ai chi* in old spelling) is the highest principle in the universe. It has no physical form and yet exists in all things, animate and inanimate. Principle explains the universality and interdependence of things, whereas material force explains the physicality of things. This is not a **dualist** picture, but one that stresses the entire interdependence of things. The great ultimate is Zhu Xi's variation on the concept of **Dao**.

GREATEST HAPPINESS PRINCIPLE. See **UTILITY, PRINCIPLE OF**.

GREEK PLAYWRIGHTS. The three great Greek playwrights were Aeschylus (525–456 BCE), Sophocles (496–405 BCE), and Euripides (484/0–406 BCE). **Tragedy** is one of the noblest forms of expression, and it was invented in ancient Greece, and some of its finest examples came from these three men. Not until **William Shakespeare** would any playwrights reach those heights of literary brilliance and profound human understanding. This is not, of course, to undervalue the comedies that these playwrights also wrote.

Aeschylus was the first of them, and is often called the father of Greek tragedy. He was born in Eleusis, the town where the Mysteries were performed. He saw active service as a young man, being wounded at the battle of Marathon in 490 BCE and may well have seen action at the battle of Salamis ten years later, which destroyed the Persian invasion. Aeschylus is thought to have written sixty plays, but only seven have survived. Of these, *Prometheus Bound* stands out as his most sublime effort, although some recent scholarship has detected sufficient textual and grammatical differences in this play from his others to raise a doubt over authorship. It was Aeschylus who explored the themes of responsibility and power in the Prometheus story. A general theme of his plays is that fate is not necessarily the relentless teleological force it is sometimes made out to be.

Sophocles was in the middle of the three great Greek playwrights. He was more conventionally respectful of the gods than Aeschylus or Euripides, and his plays were about the consequences and fulfillment of prophecy. Sophocles' plays reworked the notion of *sophrosyne* in the self of the Oracle of Delphi's dictum that we should know ourselves. His tragic heroes are people who, in some crucial way, do not know themselves, and suffer because of their self-delusions. And yet, the tragic irony is heightened because the heroes could not be heroes if they *did* know themselves. Sophocles' masterpieces are often thought to be *Oedipus the King* and *Antigone*. Once again, only seven of Sophocles' output (123 plays) has survived.

Euripides, the latest of the three great Greek dramatists, began life as a painter, but moved to literature. His first success in the theater didn't come until he was forty-four. He never achieved the fame during his life that Aeschylus and Sophocles enjoyed, but his plays have enjoyed a long career since his death. We know of about ninety-two dramas by Euripides, and of them eighteen are complete. Among his best-known plays are *Medea*, *Hippolytus*, *Bacchae*, *Electra*, and *Iphigenia in Aulis*.

Euripides was naturally clearheaded and skeptical. His divine and mythical characters are presented in down-to-earth guises, much to the chagrin of the conservatives of the day. The *Bacchae* was a very late play and widely thought to be his finest masterpiece, and *Hippolytus* (428 BCE) one of the best-organized tragedies of them all. The *Trojan Women* (425 BCE) was written at the height of Athens's wartime hubris and, under the guise of retelling an aspect of the tale of Troy, makes some important points about life.

Euripides underplayed the importance that the chorus had in Aeschylus's plays.

Sophocles had used the notion of *sophrosyne* as a tragic device which the hero must reject in order to be a hero, and then to suffer the consequences of such a rejection. Euripides was slightly more nuanced in his questioning the adherence to one virtue or set of virtues at the expense of other sets of equally noble virtues.

The deaths of Sophocles and Euripides at about the same time as the defeat of Athens in the Peloponnesian war marked the end of the great era of Greek tragedy and signaled the enduring value of comedy. Chief among them was Aristophanes (448–388 BCE, approx.) who brought a caustic dislike of charlatanism and public pretentiousness into his comedies. Aristophanes subjected the gods and famous people to biting, though good-humored satire; in one play Prometheus is represented cowering under an umbrella, hiding from the other gods. In *The Clouds*, **Socrates** is caricatured as the ultimate **Sophist**. Ancient Greece understood the value of being able to laugh at itself.

GRESHAM'S LAW. A truism attributed to the British politician Sir Thomas Gresham (1519–1579) who observed that bad money drives out good. He had in mind the practice of coins made of inferior metals driving out of circulation those made of purer metals. This is because people would tend to spend the base coinage first and to hoard the purer coinage. But, of course, this has the effect of driving the pure coinage out of circulation.

Now, Gresham's Law has been employed in the wider sense of saying that **corrupt** practices will always prevail over honest practices: dishonest politicians will prevail over honest ones; degrees from inferior colleges will put pressure on high quality degrees from ivy league institutions; and so on. See the entry on **Sturgeon's Law**.

GROUP OF SEVEN. An informal coalition of the seven major industrial and financial nations in the world, which meet periodically to discuss world trends and issues of common interest. The Group of Seven, or G7, as it is usually known, was originally composed of five nations: the United States, Great Britain, Japan, Germany, and France. In 1986 Canada and Italy were invited to join. Russia has been lurking around the periphery, and for some meetings the group has been the G8.

The G7 is only one of several coalitions of nations (see the entry on the **Group of 77**), but it is the most powerful. The G7 nations have the greatest influence over the **World Bank** and the **International Monetary Fund**, but the increasing economic muscle of China is having a negative impact on the G7's ability to have things all their own way. As a result, there is talk of replacing the G7 with the G4, which would consist of the United States, the Euro zone, China, and Japan. This would reflect more closely the actual balance of world capital at the present stage.

GROUP OF 77. A coalition of developing countries whose goal is to articulate their special economic needs to relevant world bodies such as the **United Nations**, the **World Bank**, and the **International Monetary Fund**. The Group of 77, usually known as G77, was established on June 15, 1964, with the Joint Declaration of the Seventy-Seven Countries. The G77 came together at the conclusion of the United Nations Conference on Trade and Development (UNCTAD) when it became apparent that less-developed countries had essential interests in common. The coalition first met in Algeria in 1967. It is now comprised of 132 countries, but the name is retained for its historical significance. Ministers from member countries meet regularly prior to important international congresses in order to coordinate their priorities and policies.

The basic priority of the G77 was stated in the Joint Declaration of the G77, when it first convened in 1964: The "efforts of developing countries to raise living standards of their peoples, which are now being made under adverse external conditions, should be supplemented and strengthened by constructive international action." More recently, the G77 has expanded its activities. As well as redressing North-South inequalities, the G77 has also worked to increase cooperation between member states, what it calls "South-South Cooperation." The Group of 77 was the logical next step in the growing awareness of less-developed nations of their many shared interests. See the entries on the **Group of Seven** and the **Five Principles of Coexistence**.

GROUP POLARIZATION. A term employed by sociologists that refers to the growing tendency of people to congregate among others like themselves, and for a process of self-reinforcement to then take place. In many parts of the United States, communities are becoming more homogeneously liberal or conservative, secular or religious. A consequence of like-minded people associating primarily with each other is that the original tendencies of that group, whether liberal or conservative, tend to become more so, with liberal communities becoming more liberal and conservative communities becoming more conservative. With communities polarized in this way, it becomes more difficult for them to relate to one another, which only intensifies the polarization process.

These divisions are not solely along racial lines, although they remain very strong in the United States. These are divisions of attitude, not infrequently determined by one's level of education and the range of jobs one has access to. The racial element to group polarization remains a factor by virtue of the, on average, lower educational attainments of African Americans and Latinos.

In the way the old segregation posed a threat to the **open society**, so does the newer phenomenon of group polarization. If people don't have neighbors whose views are different than their own, the stimulus toward **toleration** is not aroused. "Celebrating diversity" has always been little more than an empty slogan, but the process of group polarization will only drain the slogan of whatever force it once had.

GROUPISHNESS. A term coined by the science writer Matt Ridley to denote the human propensity to join or identify with a collective. Whether a sewing circle, football club, race, or religion, human beings are drawn toward clustering in groups. Less helpfully, we also have a tendency to identify positive virtues with our group and negative virtues with other groups.

The tendency to groupishness has an evo-

lutionary origin, as group membership enhanced survival chances, in terms of larger pools of information and physical resources being shared. Our group loyalties can inspire us to deep levels of sacrifice for others and willingness to subordinate our interests for the wider group interests. By the same token, groupishness has a long record of inspiring savage persecution and butchery of people for no other reason than that they belong to another group.

GULLIBILITY. Described by **Paul Kurtz** as the **original sin** of **human nature**. All human beings are to some extent gullible, but for too many people there is a tendency to accept the testimony of those in authority or to believe claims made without sufficient, or even any, supporting evidence. The only known antidote to gullibility is **critical thinking**. See the entry on **critical receptiveness**.

GURDJIEFF, GEORGE IVANOVITCH (1877?–1949). To his disciples a brilliant and original mystic; to his detractors, a charlatan. Gurdjieff was a compulsive liar and few facts are known with any real certainty about his life. Even his date of birth is not known for sure. Any date between 1870 and 1886 is credible, with most people seeming to go for 1877 as the least unlikely.

Gurdjieff was strongly influenced by Madame Blavatsky, the creator of **Theosophy**. Like Blavatsky, Gurdjieff's writings were monumentally long, covering every conceivable subject but exhibiting no particular order. His philosophy revolved around the common preoccupation of mystics: harmony, cosmic unity, and learning to Be. Gurdjieff's writings are gathered in a thousand-page tome appropriately called *All and Everything*.

After a suitably mysterious youth in the mystic East, Gurdjieff established the Institute for the Harmonious Development of Man near Paris and collected a large, though constantly changing, group of disciples. He died in a car accident in 1949.

H

HABERMAS, JÜRGEN (1929–). The most influential German philosopher of his generation. Habermas is best known for his comprehensive work *The Philosophical Discourse of Modernity* (1985, English translation 1987).

Habermas trained under Theodor Adorno (1903–1969), one of the most extreme opponents of the **Enlightenment** tradition. Habermas has sought to avoid the unhelpful extremes of Adorno and others. He shares some of their concerns about the universalist notions of **reason**, but is unprepared to then jump to the conclusion that all is lost and we can do little but wallow in **nihilism**. Habermas's career has been an extended campaign to rescue what he calls practical reason. He has advocated what he calls communicative action, which rejects **foundationalism**, and has some similarities to **John Dewey**'s notion of **social intelligence**. Unlike the postmodernists, Habermas retains some confidence that a communicative action and practical reason can bring forth something akin to **progress**. However, some critics have accused Habermas of simply legislating that all emancipated reasoners be the sort of European-style social democrat that Habermas seems to hold up as the ideal. Habermas was elected to the **International Academy of Humanism** in 1994.

HADITH. The source of religious authority for Muslims second in importance only to the Qur'an. In principle, the Hadith are collections of sayings from **Muhammad** and anecdotes from his life that can be used by Muslims for moral instruction. Sunni Muslims recognize six authoritative Hadith traditions. Muslim theologians see the Hadith as the practical application of the Qur'an in everyday life.

In fact none of the Hadith traditions are thought to reach earlier than the time of the Abbasids, 120 years after Muhammad's death. Even the six authoritative traditions exist in various forms and are riddled with later interpolations. Hadith were concocted to serve contending Ummayad, Shi'ite, and Abassid political interests, and they even became a source of income for itinerant storytellers.

As with the Qur'an, the Hadith can be used in whichever way the reader wants to use them. Those who want to kill unbelievers, ascribe fanciful **conspiracy theories** to Jews, and impose barbarous restrictions on the lives of women will find a plenitude of Hadith sources to back them up. Similarly, those who want to speak of peace, **truth**, **love**, and **toleration** will also be able to cite some Hadith sources in their support.

Further reading: Ram Swarap, *Understanding the Hadith*.

HAECKEL, ERNST HEINRICH (1834–1919). German evolutionist and champion of **Charles Darwin** in Germany. Ernst Haeckel was born in Potsdam, the son of a lawyer. After studying in Wurzburg as a doctor, he spent a year working in a hospital in Vienna. His experiences with suffering, and his contact with freethinkers, eroded his belief in a benevolent Providence. But it was his reading of *The Origin of Species* by **Charles Darwin** that changed his life. Darwin's book crystallized Haeckel's own thinking. He is reputed to have said, "I might have written much of this book myself."

Haeckel devoted his life to spreading knowledge of **evolution**. If **T. H. Huxley** was "Darwin's bulldog," Haeckel was Darwin's rottweiler. While he was Germany's most prominent advocate of Charles Darwin, Haeckel was by no means a **Darwinian**. It was Haeckel's intention to synthesize the evolutionism of Darwin, **Lamarck**, and **Goethe**.

In 1900 Haeckel became known to a much larger audience thanks to a popular work he wrote which, in its English translation, was called *The Riddle of the Universe*. The translator was **Joseph McCabe**, who went on to become Haeckel's most important English-speaking popularizer. *The Riddle of the Universe* was tremendously influential and sold very well indeed. Its huge sales helped propel Watts and Co., its English publisher, to levels of financial stability it could only dream of. Watts and Co. was the publishing house connected to the **Rationalist Press Association**. Haeckel was an honorary associate of the RPA from 1899 until 1915, when he resigned over differences over World War I.

Further reading: Ernst Haeckel, *The Riddle of the Universe*, with introduction by H. James Birx.

HALDANE, RICHARD BURDON (1856–1928). British philosopher, jurist, and politician. Richard Burdon Haldane was born into a very prominent family. His parents were strict Baptists, but Haldane lost his religious beliefs during adolescence, after reading **David Friedrich Strauss**, **Ernest Renan**, and **Lucretius**. After undergoing adult baptism to please his parents, Haldane made a public declaration of his abandonment of Christianity. Anticipating later trends in theology, Haldane declared that "God is not outside us, but within our breasts." Religious creeds were of symbolic significance only.

Haldane went to pursue distinguished careers in law and politics, serving several liberal governments and the first labor government, led by Ramsey Macdonald in 1924. His more important contributions include his role in establishing tertiary institutions alongside Oxford and Cambridge, which until then had existed solely to educate the ruling classes. Haldane also oversaw many of the changes in British military organization that had become necessary after the indifferent performance of British arms against the Boers between 1899 and 1902.

Haldane never dropped his interest in philosophy. He was offered the chair in moral philosophy at St. Andrews after presenting the Gifford Lectures of 1903–1904. The lectures were later published as *The Pathway to Reality* (1903). Haldane turned the invitation down and continued his career in law and politics. Another important work of his is *The Philosophy of Humanism* (1922).

HALDEMAN-JULIUS, EMANUEL (1889–1951). American publishing entrepreneur and pioneer. Emanuel Julius was born in Philadelphia on July 20, 1889 (although several sources say July 30), the son of Russian Jewish migrants. He left school very young and worked a variety of jobs before entering the newspaper world. His experiences with class discrimination and **anti-Semitism** also steered him into radical politics. He was inspired to a life in **freethought** when he read **Thomas Paine**'s classic *The Age of Reason* and, later on, Oscar Wilde's poem *The Ballad of Reading Gaol*. His drift to radicalism and freethought estranged him from his parents, a rift which never healed.

Julius left Philadelphia in 1906 and never looked back. He had a successful, busy career in socialist journalism and politics in New York, Wisconsin, California, and then back in New York. There he met Anna Marcet Haldeman, the daughter of a wealthy Kansas banker and farmer. The two relocated to her home town of Girard, Kansas, and were married in 1916, taking on the double-barreled name. They had two children and adopted a foster daughter.

With access to considerable funds, he began publishing. The works which had inspired him as a youth were purchased at a cheap secondhand bookshop, and he wanted to provide this opportunity for others. In 1919 he began the People's Pocket Series, publishing the *Rubaiyat of Omar Khayyam* and Wilde's *Ballad of Reading Jail* (complete with American spelling). Over his career, he sold more than three hundred million books and pamphlets. Known as the "Prince of Pamphleteers," he published 2,241 titles. The key to his success was simple: the price. Originally they sold for 25 cents, but large demand meant he could drop the price to ten cents.

By 1924 he was looking for a new direction for the People's Pocket Series. Along came **Joseph McCabe**, at the time estranged from the **Rationalist Press Association** and in need of a new publisher. The relationship was highly beneficial for both parties. Haldeman-Julius replaced the People's Pocket Series with the Little Blue Books and, a short while later, the Big Blue Books. McCabe was commissioned to write the first fifty Little Blue Books, which were later published as *The Story of Religious Controversy* (1929). Overall McCabe's titles sold very well; 1,892,000 of the larger Big Blue Books, not counting his 126 Little Blue Book titles. Later in his career, Haldeman-Julius said that his involvement with McCabe "had been enough to build a career for anyone." Many other important freethinkers were published by Haldeman-Julius, including **Bertrand Russell** and **Rupert Hughes**.

Haldeman-Julius continued publishing until his death. He came under increasing surveillance from the FBI, not least because of the "Black International Series," written by McCabe, which was strongly critical of the Catholic Church. While fighting a conviction for income tax evasion, Haldeman-Julius drowned in his swimming pool on July 31, 1951.

HAMAS. A radical Muslim organization based in Palestine that broke away from the **Muslim Brotherhood** in 1987 to pursue its more specifically conceived goals of total eradication of the state of Israel and its replacement by a Palestinian Muslim theocracy. The literal meaning of "Hamas" is "zeal," but it is also an acronym in Arabic for "Islamic Resistance Movement."

Hamas is particularly strong in the impoverished Gaza Strip, where it runs a popular social-welfare wing, which distributes aid to the poor and to families of martyrs. It also has a political wing and another that pursues terrorist activity. Hamas is funded by many Muslim countries across the Middle East, particularly Syria.

Hamas has a difficult relationship with the Palestinian authority, which in 1996 launched a crackdown against them, but without daring to extinguish the organization altogether—which it knew it could not do. The military wing of Hamas is known as the Izzedine al-Qassam brigades and is responsible for the planned assaults on Israeli targets and training suicide volunteers for their missions.

The religious leader of Hamas was Sheikh Ahmad Yassin (1939–2004), a quadriplegic cleric living in Gaza, who was responsible for fiery rhetoric against Israel. Such is the degree of hatred in the area that Yassin was seen locally as something of a moderate. He devoted a lot of energy to the social-welfare arm of the movement. He was assassinated on March 22, 2004, by the Israelis in retaliation for a terrorist attack in Ashdod that killed about twenty people. Within weeks, his successor was also assassinated.

HANLON, JAMES OGDEN (1899–1986). New Zealand rationalist and journalist. Hanlon spent most of his life in Auckland, New Zealand's largest city. His father had been a Catholic but at some point became a rationalist and brought his son up that way. Hanlon worked as a journalist before enlisting for service in World War I. After his demobilization, he returned to journalism, working most of his life at the *Auckland Star*. As a young reporter for the *Star* in 1923, he covered the lectures given by **Joseph McCabe** in Auckland.

After ten years in the United Kingdom, he returned to the *Star* and began an association with the rationalist movement in New Zealand which lasted the rest of his life. He was vice president three times between 1945 and 1961, and was president from 1955 until 1958 and again, briefly, between August 1958 and May 1959. But his main contribution was his role as editor of the *NZ Rationalist*, which in October 1964 became the *NZ Rationalist and Humanist*. He served as editor from September 1939 to March 1942, late 1943 to May 1953, May 1955 to August 1958, October to December 1959, August 1961 to

November 1973, and February 1974 until September 1975. During these 29 years he wrote 218 editorials and a great many other articles and shorter contributions. He was one of the longest-serving editors of any publication in freethought history, ranking alongside **Charles Watts** and **Chapman Cohen**. In some ways, he stayed on too long, and became something of a liability in his later years. Very appropriately, however, Hanlon was made a life member of the Rationalist Association in 1955.

He was also active in the WEA, Chess Club, Howard League for Penal Reform, the Auckland Debating Association, and the Voluntary Euthanasia Society of England. He married Alice Horspool in 1928. They had no children. See the entry on the **New Zealand Association of Rationalists and Humanists**.

Further reading: Bill Cooke, *Heathen in Godzone: Seventy Years of Rationalism in New Zealand*.

HAPPINESS. That fine balance between living well and doing well. It is easier to say what happiness does not consist of. Happiness is not the same as a constant succession of pleasures. Neither can it be bought, except perhaps temporarily, with the possession of new objects. Happiness is elusive, as people who actively seek it can attest. Happiness can also be seen as a property of the wider notion of welfare. The Finnish philosopher **Henrik von Wright** spoke of welfare as an umbrella term that covers all aspects of what is good for people, and happiness is surely an important part of that.

Robert Owen was correct when he said that happiness cannot be achieved alone. Happiness is only real when others can experience it as well. **John Dewey** spoke in a similar vein when he said that happiness is found "only in enduring ties to others, which reach to such depths that they go below the surface of conscious experience to form its undisturbed foundation." **Bertrand Russell** was also correct when he said that for many people, happiness is an achievement rather than a gift of

the gods. One of his most successful works of popular philosophy was called *The Conquest of Happiness* (1930). His use of the military word "conquest" was deliberate, because in order to be happy, we must "find ways of coping with the multitudinous causes of unhappiness which with each individual is assailed." Russell also warned against seeking happiness by believing things that, while they may be consoling, are not necessarily true. In this respect, happiness also requires **veracity**. Russell wrote that the secret of happiness consists in letting one's interests be as wide as possible and letting one's reactions to the world to be friendly rather than hostile. See the entry on the **good life**.

HARD AND SOFT NEWS. The distinction, particularly with regard to television, between serious, intelligently delivered international and national news, and lightweight stories about pets, celebrities, and sports games. Soft news is appealing to program directors because it is cheaper to produce and less likely to offend advertisers. It may also have local interest, which will fulfill a requirement for the channel. And soft news items with a local flavor also ensure a local audience, which is good for advertising.

Hard news, by contrast, is expensive; it may require a journalist to be on the ground at some dangerous and distant part of the globe. Or, at least, it may require payment to another station that has a journalist on the ground. Hard news is also more demanding intellectually, which may tax the resources of the viewers who will then reach for the remote. See the entry on **dumbing down**.

As a general rule, privately operated broadcasting stations find the provision of hard news more difficult because of the economic arguments against it. Some broadcasting stations, like FOX News in the United States, have specific preferences for soft news. These stations are vulnerable to accusations of **manufacturing consent**.

Government-funded broadcasting stations—in democracies—are often better equipped to provide viewers with hard news. They will have a charter to uphold high standards of journalism and provide intelligent and accurate analysis of the news. And, more importantly, they are not under the same obligation to pander to the interests of advertisers. The BBC remains the standard for others to emulate in this respect.

Further reading: Benjamin Radford, *Media Myth Makers.*

HARDY, THOMAS (1840–1928). Brilliant and prolific English novelist and poet. Over his long life, Hardy wrote fourteen novels, fifty short stories, a three-volume epic, and more than a thousand poems. He was born at Higher Bockhampton, Dorset, six months into the marriage of Thomas Hardy Sr., a stonemason and church musician, and Jemima (Hand), an embroiderer.

At an impressionable age, Hardy witnessed the public hanging in 1856 of Martha Browne, who had killed her husband. She was possibly the model for Tess in *Tess of the d'Urbervilles* (1891). This, and a later visit to London during his twenties, helped Hardy jettison his Christian belief. Hardy was, to all intents and purposes, an atheist, although he was always distrustful of labels.

Hardy married Emma Gifford in 1874, but their marriage was unhappy; they were fully estranged by 1898, partly exacerbated by the reaction to another of Hardy's masterpieces, the gloomy *Jude the Obscure* (1895–96). In fact, the reaction to *Jude* was so splenetic that Hardy wrote no more novels after that, turning to poetry instead. The bishop of Wakefield led the protest when he publicly burned his copy. Hardy's poetry is dark and deeply aware of the tragic sense of existence without the sentimentality or nostalgia that lessens the impact of many other thinkers concerned with our tragic condition.

Hardy's worldview is best expressed in his poem *God's Funeral.*

Hardy's other main novels were *Under the Greenwood Tree* (1872), which was the first to win widespread acclaim, *The Return*

of the Native (1878), *The Trumpet Major* (1880), and *The Mayor of Casterbridge* (1886). A retiring man, Hardy declined a knighthood but did accept the Order of Merit in 1910. He also refused an invitation in 1899 to become an honorary associate of the **Rationalist Press Association** because he didn't want to be pinned down, rather than because of any disagreement with the RPA's principles.

HARPER'S ILLUMINATED AND NEW PICTORIAL BIBLE. A lavishly produced and vastly profitable marketing publication of the Bible from 1844, which stands as a milestone in the commodification of religion, which has since reached epic proportions in the United States. In discovering a large market for this sort of religious material, encouragement was given to commercial printing which inevitably looked to filling the demand for brightly produced material by printing attractive books that were not of a religious character. In this way, the mix of piety and profit has helped turn American religion into simply another consumable, in competition for the American public's discretionary dollar. See the entry on **Jesus junk**.

Further reading: R. Laurence Moore, *Selling God: American Religion and the Marketplace of Culture.*

HARRISON, HUBERT HENRY (1883–1927). Influential African American educator, described as not only the "foremost African-American intellect of his time, but one of America's greatest minds." Hubert Harrison was born in St. Croix in what was then the Danish Virgin Islands. He was born on the same day (April 27) as **Herbert Spencer**, who was a major influence on his thought. At only seventeen, he migrated to the United States where took a series of menial jobs while putting himself through night school. Even after graduating with excellent marks, he could still only get a job as a post-office clerk.

Fired up by his experiences of discrimination, he broke from organized Christianity, joined the Socialist Party, and became a very capable soapbox orator. He didn't stay there long, as he came across much of the same racist attitudes among his socialist colleagues. In June 1917 Harrison left the Socialist Party and founded the Liberty League for Afro-Americans. In that capacity he worked hard to bring equal opportunity for black Americans in the booming theater industry as well as in trade unions. As editor of the Liberty League's journal, *The Voice*, Harrison became an important leader of black opinion in New York. The league split up over internal quarrels and Harrison moved to a paper called *Negro World*, which he transformed into another important source of black opinion. Harrison's two major works, *The Negro and the Nation* (1917) and *When Africa Awakes* (1920) emerged out of his journalism. He also wrote for the ***Truthseeker***.

In 1926 Harrison began giving lectures for the New York City Board of Education, and even appeared at New York University and the Institute for Social Study, a considerable achievement for someone entirely self-taught. He claimed to have acquired qualifications that in all probability he had not earned, but nobody doubted his intellectual ability to have acquired those qualifications had his upbringing been less impoverished. He died penniless while still relatively young.

Harrison was enormously influential on people as diverse as Marcus Garvey (1887–1940) and A. Philip Randolph (1889–1979). He worked with Garvey for a few years but broke with him in 1920. Unlike Garvey, Harrison believed that the discrimination against black people would end only when all poor people, regardless of color, were freed from bondage. An obituarist wrote: "The soul of Hubert Harrison knew neither black nor white, race nor religion. If a more universal man has been created in our day we have not met him."

Further reading: Norm R. Allen Jr., ed., *African American Humanism: An Anthology*; and Jeffrey B. Perry, ed., *The Hubert Harrison Reader*.

HARRISON, JANE (1850–1928). Pioneering Classicist scholar, suffragist, and said-to-be "the cleverest woman in England." Harrison was born in Cottingham, Yorkshire, and was educated privately. Between 1874 and 1879 she studied classics at Newnham College, Cambridge, showing herself to be a gifted scholar. Her original training in the 1870s was in classical philology, but in her middle years she branched to broader ranges of subjects. She was responsible for some seminal studies on Greek **mythology** and **religion**.

In 1879 she moved to London to study archaeology at the British Museum. It was there she began her career of reinterpreting Greek myths in terms of archeology, putting special emphasis on ritual. She was vice president of the Hellenic Society from 1889 to 1896, and in 1896 she became a corresponding member of the Berlin Classical Archaeological Institute. As well as Latin and Greek, Harrison was fluent in Spanish, Swedish, Persian, and Hebrew. In 1915 she learned Russian, which she added to her teaching portfolio at Newnham. She retired in 1922.

In all probability, Jane Harrison was a lesbian. Her first serious relationship was with the gifted Roman scholar Eugénie Sellers (1860–1943). Her next significant relationship after she broke with Sellars in 1893 was with Hope Mirrlees (1887–1978), which lasted until Harrison's death. Harrison was an agnostic, albeit of an unusual type. In 1927 she became an honorary associate of the **Rationalist Press Association**. Her main works include *Prolegomena to the Study of Greek Religion* (1903), *Themis* (1912), *Ancient Art and Ritual* (1913), and *Epilegomena to the Study of Greek Religion* (1921).

HAUGHTINESS-ISM. See **ARROGANTISM.**

HAWTON, HECTOR (1901–1975). Humanist, editor, and author. Born into an ardently Protestant family and raised on *Foxe's Book of Martyrs* and *Pilgrim's*

Progress, Hawton converted to Catholicism at fifteen. Further study of science and philosophy led him out of Catholicism and briefly to Marxism before becoming a humanist. He worked as a journalist and developed a prodigious capacity to write. During World War II he worked for Bomber Command's Group 4 at Heslington Hall in York. After the war, he was secretary of the **South Place Ethical Society** from 1948 until 1954.

One of his many writing assignments was to serve as editor of the *Humanist*, which he edited from 1953 until 1971 and again from 1974 until his death in 1975. During his editorship the *Humanist* was a very good magazine indeed, with a wide range of high-quality articles from capable authorities. Most of the main thinkers of postwar Britain had an article in the *Humanist* at some time or other. Under a series of pseudonyms, Hawton contributed mightily himself. His most important pseudonym was "R. J. Mostyn," though "Humphrey Skelton," "James Plender," "George Robinson," "Jonathan Yeo," and "W. B. Pengelly" also had frequent assignments.

His major nonfiction works include *Men Without Gods* (1948); *Philosophy for Pleasure* (1949), which had a long career on the American paperback market; *The Thinker's Handbook* (1950); *The Feast of Unreason* (1952), a brilliant demolition of **existentialism**; and *The Humanist Revolution* (1963).

And in the best traditions of **Renaissance man**, Hawton also wrote detective novels, women's romances (under the pseudonym "April Brooks"), and children's adventure (under the pseudonym of "John Sylvester"), as well as a series of novels under the pseudonym of Jack Lethaby. One feature of his novels was his ability to create female characters who were real. Oddly, it was his male characters who often seemed two-dimensional.

As if this wasn't enough, he also ghostwrote most of the books attributed to the popular psychologist Eustace Chesser (1902–1973). Hawton knew Chesser through their membership in the Hampstead Humanist Group, of which Chesser was president for two decades. Chesser's titles written by Hawton include *Love Without Fear*, *Unmarried Love*, and *Grammar of Marriage*. And between all this, Hawton always enjoyed socializing with his friends. As a Fleet Street journalist, Hawton had developed a formidable capacity for drink, and enjoyed an evening at the pub with friends. See the entries on the **great divide** and **Rationalism, Principles of**.

HAYWARD, HENRY J. (1866–1945). Entrepreneur, rationalist, and showman. Henry Hayward was born in Wolverhampton in 1866 in modest circumstances. After a career with the highly successful musical troupe "The Brescians," he emigrated to New Zealand in 1905 and quickly became interested in the cinema. Before long he was a very wealthy man. His brother, Rudall, became a pioneer New Zealand filmmaker. Despite his ability as a capitalist, Hayward had distinctly left-leaning sympathies, ensuring his cinemas were available for left-wing speakers when no other hall was open to them.

His financial prospects collapsed during the Depression, and in his early sixties he was forced to rebuild his financial fortunes. Extraordinarily, he also became president of the Rationalist Association during this demanding time. When the rationalists began their Sunday evening cinema and talks, he made his cinemas available to them. For the next fourteen years, he was the highest-profile president the New Zealand Rationalist Association ever had. In 1942 he was made an honorary associate of the **Rationalist Press Association**. During his time as president he made public stands in favor of academic freedom, and against censorship in the cinema and the persecution of Jehovah's Witnesses.

He had a florid writing style, but his work was full of life and **humor**. Among his works are *Christian Principles*; *A Torchbearer of Science* (on Marie Curie); *Christians and Freethinkers*; *Krishna and Christ* (all 1941); *The Churches are Emptying; Creeds are Dying: Why?* (both 1942); and an autobiography entitled *Here's to Life! The Impressions, Confessions and Garnered Thoughts of a Free-Minded Showman* (1944).

Further reading: Bill Cooke, *Heathen in Godzone: Seventy Years of Rationalism in New Zealand.*

HEBREW SCRIPTURES. What Christians call the "Old Testament" are in fact the Hebrew scriptures, or the Hebrew Bible. The Hebrew scriptures were written by a wide variety of different people for different political, social, and religious ends. Most of the scriptures were written between the ninth and fourth centuries BCE. The contradictory texts were brought together, probably by Ezra, in the fifth century BCE, after the Jews had been allowed to return to their homeland by the Persian leader Cyrus (d. 529 BCE). To mark their appreciation, Cyrus was spoken of in the scriptures as a messiah.

The Hebrew scriptures entered a new phase after the third century BCE when they were translated into Greek, an event known as the Septuagint because seventy scholars were supposedly employed in the translation. The Hebrew scriptures became known as the "Old Testament" by Christians in the second century CE, when the Christian communities, no longer part of the Jewish religion, felt the need to create their own **scripture** (the "New Testament") and to relegate the Hebrew scriptures to the secondary role as the vehicle which foretold the coming of Christ, and is now superseded. The Christian habit of using the Hebrew scriptures as little more than a textual quarry for passages which supposedly herald the coming of **Jesus Christ** is insupportable and disrespectful of an older religious tradition. See the entries on **anti-Semitism**, **Marcion**, and **supersessionism**.

HEDENIUS, INGEMAR (1908–1982). One of Sweden's greatest secularists and humanist philosophers. Hedenius was born into an upper class family who were conventionally religious. He went to Uppsala University originally to study **theology**, but lost his

belief during the course of that study. His career was spent as a philosopher at Uppsala. Only twenty years later did his mother learn he was an atheist; his father was never told.

Hedenius developed a lifelong interest in ancient Greece, and had a very high opinion of Greek culture, which he thought superior in many ways to Christianity. Over his career he wrote more than thirty books which had a significant impact on Swedish public life.

Among his most important books are *Faith and Knowledge* (1949), which outlined Hedenius's atheism; *Life and Usefulness* (1961), which discussed his thoughts on humanism; and *About the Dignity of Man* (1982), which dwelt on a number of issues.

Hedenius was by nature melancholic and developed a theory of absurdism to give expression to that side of him. See the entry on **absurdity**. Hedenius's contribution to Swedish life was immense and civilized. His works deserve to be better appreciated among English-speaking readers.

Further reading: Finngeir Hiorth, *Secularism in Sweden.*

HEDONISM. Traditionally seen as the idea that pleasure is the principal good. However, **Paul Kurtz** argues that there is more to hedonism than that. Hedonism can be divided into three categories, two of which are harmful to the individual, while the third, with important conditions, is healthy. The two unhealthy varieties of hedonism are:

- *hedonicphobia*, or the condition in which the individual has forgotten how to relax, and fears pleasure, whether sexual, gastronomic, aesthetic, or in any other form, often seeing it as some form of weakness or compromise. The hedonicphobe is often opposed to other people's pursuit of pleasure as well; and
- *hyperhedonism*, or the ever more frenetic search for more and more pleasure. Hyperhedonism is almost always counterproductive, as the pleasures gradually cease to thrill and so have to

be taken in larger and larger doses, usually resulting in physical harm. See the entry on **affluenza**.

The middle ground between these two unhealthy and counterproductive extremes is what Kurtz calls *robust hedonism*. This involves a healthy love of life and what life has to offer, and an open, unafraid attitude to sampling life's joys. Robust hedonism, unlike its two opposites, recognizes that the pleasures of life are most enjoyable when taken in moderation, when they are justly earned, and when they do not involve harm to oneself or others. See the entries on **fun**, the **Doctrine of the Mean (Aristotle)**, and the **activist frame**.

Further reading: Paul Kurtz, *Exuberance: An Affirmative Philosophy of Life*.

HEIDEGGER, MARTIN (1889–1976). One of the most important and controversial philosophers of the twentieth century. Martin Heidegger was born in southwest Germany and raised in a sternly traditionalist Catholic environment. While he lost his faith in the specifics of Catholic Christianity, he retained an abiding interest in preserving a mystical or transcendental element in life.

Heidegger was a lifelong opponent of **democracy**, and indeed of most elements of Western society. His philosophy was about finding an **authentic** way of living in the face of the technological frenzy he saw as underlying both Soviet communism and Western capitalism. He called for a throwing off of Western metaphysics and returning to a primordial state of Being. Much of his work is devoted to articulating what he meant by Being. Many people have observed that his Being is a transformed notion of **God**.

The core of his philosophy was the notion of *Volk*. German *volkish* thought feared and distrusted modernity and sought various forms of spiritual renewal, either through racial purity, clean country living, or **romanticism**. Many *volkish* thinkers were **anti-Semitic**. He probably wasn't anti-Semitic on principle, but simply on grounds of expedience. He has been

called a cultural anti-Semite.

For a relatively short time, all of 1933 and on to about 1935, he was an enthusiastic Nazi, serving as rector of Freiburg University. His enthusiasm waned only when it became apparent that the Nazis weren't going to grant him the role of intellectual sage of national socialism. Even after he stopped being a card-carrying member of the party, he remained inclined toward fascism. He never retracted his support for fascism. Indeed, he never could, because the cultural chauvinism and **mysticism** of fascism is built into his philosophy.

Heidegger's main work was *Being and Time* (1927), although he wrote a great deal. His turgid writing style has attracted a lot of attention. Supporters see it as deliberately blocking in an attempt to drive us into deep thought. Opponents say that his cloudy writing is a sure sign of cloudy thinking. Both Heidegger's philosophy and writing style were deeply influential on **postmodernism**. His contemporary Karl Jaspers (1883–1969) wrote of Heidegger, "Among contemporaries the most exciting thinker, masterful, compelling, mysterious—but then leaving you empty-handed."

Further reading: Hugo Ott, *Martin Heidegger: A Political Life*; Julian Young, *Heidegger, Philosophy, Nazism*; and Paul Edwards, *Heidegger's Confusions*.

HELIOCENTRIC UNIVERSE. The understanding of the universe that does not involve the Earth being at its center. The earlier view, the **geocentric universe** favored by most Greeks and taken over by the Christians, had the Earth at the center of the universe. But for this view to work, all planetary movements had to be regular and predictable. The geocentric view was unable to account for the irregular appearances of stars and planets. What seemed to them erratic trajectories can only make sense in a universe where the Earth is part of a very much larger context.

Astronomers like **Heraclides of Pontus** and **Aristarchus of Samos** made brave attempts to deal with these problems, but their ideas faced too much opposition and died stillborn. The followers of **Pythagoras** posited a heliocentric universe, and while their theories had little explanatory power, they helped persuade Nicholas Copernicus (1473–1543) and **Kepler**, many centuries later, to develop the idea more effectively. Copernicus worked in secret for thirty years, mindful that his research would get him in trouble with the church. His book, *On the Revolutions of the Heavenly Spheres* (1543) demonstrated that, contrary to **scripture** and church teaching, the earth went around the sun and was not at the center of the universe. But he retained the belief that the sun was at or near the center, and that earth's orbit took the form of a perfect circle, the geometric shape most likened to perfection. It was Kepler who determined that the planetary orbits are elliptical.

The heliocentric universe was recognized as true by most scientists by the 1630s, despite at-times virulent church opposition. In the name of strict biblical literalism, Martin Luther (1483–1546) lambasted Copernicus, calling him an upstart astrologer. The Catholic Church condemned Copernicus, mainly because it didn't like its authority attacked by Protestants. In 1610, Catholics were forbidden to read the works of Copernicus. This ban lasted until 1822. See the entry on the **Index of Forbidden Books**.

The heliocentric universe represents the first major assault on our **anthropocentric conceit**. From being at the very center of the universe, a universe created by **God** for us, human beings found themselves on one planet in what quickly turned out to be a limitless universe. The old style anthropomorphic god ceased to be credible from that day on. See the entry on **spiritual schizophrenia**. The first people to attempt new understandings of God and the universe in light of the new knowledge were **Giordano Bruno** and **Baruch Spinoza**. The next major assault on our anthropocentric conceit would come in the nineteenth century: **evolution** by **natural** **selection** as discovered by **Charles Darwin**. See the entry on **evolution, consequences of** and **Hubble's Law**.

HELL. In Western understanding, a fiery underworld where those who are wicked or who are not of the preferred religion (the two are often seen as the same thing) spend an eternity in torment as a punishment. Hell is an important element of the **Divine Command Theory**, which emphasizes the virtue of obeying **God**'s commands and the dire consequences of not doing so.

The authority for the Christian version of hell derives principally from the influential passage in Matthew 25:31–46, although since at least the nineteenth century, hell has fallen from favor among religious thinkers. A particularly ferocious book called *The Sight of Hell* contributed toward creating that backlash. Some liberal theologians have tried to refashion hell as a place not of physical torment but a place where one is separated from God. Fundamentalists will have none of this, and remain committed to the old notion as a place of torment. As is frequently the case, the fundamentalists are more consistent with **scripture**, but at the cost of appearing more judgmental and harsh. The religious liberals have the advantage of coming across as more compassionate, but at the cost of reinterpreting scripture to suit their own needs. See the entry on the **fatal flaw in religious liberalism**.

The naturalistic understanding of hell is simple: there isn't one. Human beings are quite capable of making their lives a misery without needing supernatural assistance in the matter. The doctrine of hell has been responsible for impoverishing the lives of millions of people; people who have denied their true nature or their real beliefs, or spurned their true love in the name of some religious prejudice.

HEPBURN, KATHARINE (1907–2003). American actress, widely thought the best and most beautiful actress of her age. Born in Hartford, Connecticut, and educated at the liberal Bryn Mawr College. Hepburn's acting career began with a role in the film *The Czarina* (1928). Her New England patrician grace and diction won her a glorious career. She won a series of Academy Awards, among them for her roles in *Morning Glory* (1933), *Guess Who's Coming to Dinner?* (1967), *The Lion in Winter* (1968), and *On Golden Pond* (1981). Some of her most notable films were with Spencer Tracy (1900–1967), such as *African Queen* (1951). Hepburn remains the only woman to win three Best Actress Oscars.

Toward the end of her life, Hepburn suffered from Parkinson's Disease, but she was not deterred from continuing her career. Among her later work included television shows such as *Mrs. Delafield Wants to Marry* (1986).

She had little time for established religion. She declared in the October 1991 issue of the *Ladies' Home Journal*, "I'm an atheist, and that's it. I believe there's nothing we can know except that we should be kind to each other and do what we can for other people."

HERACLIDES OF PONTUS (388–310 BCE). Greek astronomer and early advocate of a form of **heliocentric universe**. Heraclides of Pontus introduced two disturbing ideas into ancient astronomy. Noting that Venus and Mercury are never seen at any great distance from the sun, Heraclides suggested that this could mean they revolve not around the Earth, but around the sun. Heraclides also suggested that the daily rotation of the heavens was just as well explained by the Earth rotating on its axis as that the heavens rotate the Earth. These ideas disturbed familiar ideas favored by the religions that the Earth was the center of the universe.

HERACLITUS (d. 480 BCE, approx.). Prominent philosopher of ancient Greece. As with most **Pre-Socratic** thinkers, very little is known about his life except that he was part of the ruling echelons of the Ionian city of Ephesus. And very little of his work remains apart from a few fragments and quotations

from later thinkers. He had a grim reputation; he was disdainful of the masses and indeed of human nature generally. And he was known as "the riddler" because of the cryptic style of his utterances.

It is thought that Heraclitus flourished not long after the Ionian thinkers **Thales** and **Anaximander**, and **Pythagoras**. Heraclitus differed from both in that he tended to look more within himself than the outward-looking Ionians, and had little interest in the metaphysical speculations of the Pythagoreans. Unlike the Pythagoreans, Heraclitus believed that the universe had not been created, but had always existed. One of the lengthier quotations of his that has survived says, "This world, which is the same for all things, was made by no god or man. It has always been, it is, and will be an ever-living fire, kindling with measure being quenched with measure."

He believed that it was important to appreciate the governing principle of the universe; something that he thought no other thinkers, and certainly not the common people, came near to understanding. If he expressed the governing principle, it has not come down to us. The closest we can get to it is the notion that everything is in a constant state of flux. This is illustrated by his famous declaration that one can never step into the same river twice, because the water and the river bed will have moved on. But in this constant flux we can discern the underlying oneness of all things—the governing principle.

HERD INSTINCT. A term coined by **Friedrich Nietzsche**, which epitomized his attitude toward the general citizen. He described the herd instinct as that "of the *sum of zeroes*—where every zero has 'equal rights,' where it is virtuous to be zero" (*Will to Power*, 53). Nietzsche saw Christianity, **freethought**, and liberalism as decadence—forms of man which ultimately reduce to their lowest common denominator—the herd instinct. The herd instinct was held to value whatever sustained inertia. Nietzsche mentioned trustfulness, veneration, the sense of truth, sympathy, impartiality, integrity, and toleration as herd instincts that permitted people to avoid thinking and engagement with life.

Nietzsche didn't want to overthrow herd instincts so much as confine them to the herd. With that in mind, Nietzsche advocated a philosophy of rank, singling out the Indian caste system as codified in the *Laws of Manu* for special praise. Nietzsche recommended **Dionysianism** as the antidote to succumbing to the herd instinct. It is Nietzsche's concept of the herd instinct that separates him most severely from the humanist tradition.

HERESY. Defined by Leonard George as a crime of perception, "an act of seeing something that, according to some custodian of **reality**, is not truly there." This means that heresy is always relative to whatever orthodoxy is being defended. It also means that heresy is very largely a problem confined to cultures dominated by a **monotheistic** brand of religion. In the **Asian traditions** of Hinduism, Buddhism, Confucianism, and **Taoism**, it is pretty well impossible to find space for the concept of heresy, because these traditions do not revolve around notions of one **god**, whose message is inscribed in **scripture**. The philosopher **Baruch Spinoza** observed "no heretic without a text."

The word derives from the Greek word *hairesis*, which means "choice." Even in the New Testament, Christians were described as heretics. Acts 24:5, for example, which refers to the "sect of the Nazarenes" should, if translated honestly, read "the hairesis of the Nazarenes," which places the emphasis not on the sect but on the beliefs (*hairesis*) which characterize that sect. In the tolerant world of Roman polytheism, no opprobrium was attached to the term, but once Christianity became the official religion of the Roman Empire in the fourth century, heresy became a serious crime. Part of the reason for this was that church property had been exempted from taxes, so it became important to have a clear idea as to who was part of the church and who was not.

Heresy was beginning to take on its recognized form in 2 Peter 2:1, one of the latest works included in the New Testament, which warns against false prophets and damnable heresies. This approach became the dominant one. St. Jerome (342–420), one of the more influential early saints, outlined this policy when he declared that anyone against the church was by default with **Satan**, and as such had relinquished the right to life. This fanaticism took on a new menace when Christianity became the official religion of the Roman Empire. The first known execution of a heretic Christian by other ecclesiastics happened in 385. The man was Priscillian, a bishop, scholar, and ascetic based in Spain. In the **Theodosian Code** of 438 it was decreed simply that all "heresies are forbidden by both divine and imperial laws and shall forever cease." For more than one and a half thousand years people were executed, often with great cruelty, for this crime.

Only with the development of **humanism** after the Renaissance did heresy become problematic as a crime. From the nineteenth century, in the West, heresy was no longer taken seriously. It was left to Christian apologists to retain some meaning for the term. Early in the twentieth century G. K. Chesterton wrote a book about a variety of prominent people of his time who he considered to be heretics. Such people, wrote Chesterton, have philosophies which are "quite solid, quite coherent, and quite wrong."

One of the most recent examples of a heresy trial in the western world was in New Zealand in 1967 when Lloyd Geering, a prominent Presbyterian theologian was charged with heresy by some of his coreligionists, scandalized by Geering's concessions to modern biblical criticism. He was acquitted.

Further reading: Leonard George, *Crimes of Perception: An Encyclopedia of Heresies and Heretics*.

HERMENEUTICS. The discipline of textual interpretation. The word invokes the Greek god Hermes, the messenger of the gods. Hermeneutics means "the art of interpretation," or, more literally, "to track down." The French nihilist Michel Foucault (1926–1984) defined hermeneutics as "the totality of learning and skills that enable one to make the signs speak and to discover their meaning." This definition serves to obscure as much as it clarifies, and this has been an ongoing problem with hermeneutics as a discipline.

Hermeneutics works on the assumption that "text" contains **symbols** that stand in need of interpretation. In this way scholars of hermeneutics can take on the mantle of a secular priesthood. The emphasis on text means that hermeneutics has little ability to shed light on nontext-based methods of research, such as statistics-based research. It also finds itself indifferent to actual human suffering, as this is resistant to textual interpretation. The logical conclusion of hermeneutics is **deconstruction**. When used in concert with other disciplines, hermeneutics is a valuable discipline. But when it presumes to supersede them, it ceases to be academically useful.

HERMENEUTICS OF SUSPICION. A term coined by Paul Ricoeur (1913–2005) which refers to the tendency to attack one's opponents not by criticizing their arguments but by impugning their motives. In popular language, this practice is close to what is meant by the term **demonizing the opposition**. The closest parallel in philosophy is the *ad hominem* **argument**.

HEROSTRATUS. The world's first **nihilist**. The story goes that Herostratus was desperate to be remembered forever but realized that he could not achieve this by doing something noble, so he would do something ignoble. Hence, in 356 BCE, he burned down the two-hundred-year-old temple of Artemis in Ephesus, thought of as one of the seven wonders of the world.

The Ephesians, in their anger at Hero-stratus's action, forbade his name to be mentioned, on pain of death. This novel idea failed. Contemporaries in the manner of Herostratus are legion. The teenage murderers at Columbine High School in Denver spring to mind.

HERRICK, JIM (1944–). English humanist thinker. Educated at Trinity College, Cambridge, before working as a schoolteacher for about seven years. He then changed careers to devote his time to the British **freethought** movement, and he has worked at some time for most freethought associations in the country. For a while he worked for the **British Humanist Association**, and then was general secretary of the **National Secular Society**. From 1977 until 1981 he edited the **Freethinker**, and in 1982 wrote that magazine's centenary history. After a year as acting editor, Herrick served as editor of the **Rationalist Press Association**'s journal, the *New Humanist*, from 1985 until 2003. Since then he has been *New Humanist*'s literary editor. And from 1992 until 1998 Herrick was editor of the *International News*, the journal of the **International Humanist and Ethical Union**.

Jim Herrick is the author of *Vision and Realism: A Hundred Years of the Freethinker* (1982); *Against the Faith: Essays on Deists, Skeptics and Atheists* (1985); and *Humanism: An Introduction* (2003).

HIDDEN ENCYCLICAL. The name given to a draft encyclical condemning racism which was suppressed by **Pius XII**. The draft, to be called *Humani Generis Unitas*, specifically condemned Nazi persecution of Jews. The draft encyclical even went on to mention the context of past **anti-Semitism** in Europe, much of which was carried out under the auspices of Catholic teaching, although it claimed credit for "censuring" such conduct.

All this was too controversial for Pius XII, however. One of his first actions after becoming pope in April 1939 was to suppress this document and prevent it from becoming an official encyclical. So effective was this suppression and the subsequent covering up of the document's existence, that it became known as the hidden encyclical.

Further reading: Georges Passelecq and Bernard Suchecky, *The Hidden Encyclical of Pius XI.*

HIDEOUS SCHIZOPHRENIA. The description of the **separation of church and state** by **Sayyid Qutb**, the Muslim philosopher and inspiration to **Islamism**. Qutb argues that the very idea of separating church and state is not merely wrong, but illustrative of the moral decadence of the West. The only possible condition for moral and spiritual health is where religion (by which he means Islam) and the state mesh in total harmony. Qutb saw **secularism** (incorrectly) as a Christian legacy to the world, ignoring the ancient Greek precedents for secularism.

HIEROCLES (third–forth centuries CE). Proconsul of the province of Bithynia during the reign of Diocletian (284–305 CE) and author of a now-lost work called *Logoi Philaletheis*, which outlined the many contradictions in the Christian Bible and compared **Jesus Christ** unfavorably to **Apollonius of Tyana**, who nevertheless was credited only with being a God-beloved man. The only knowledge we have of this book is limited to minor references to it in later Christian scholars who criticized it. Hierocles was a pagan thinker and a theist. He was thought to have been involved in the so-called **great persecution** of Christians under Diocletian.

HIGHER DISMISSIVENESS. A phrase coined by Anthony Gottlieb to refer to the sneering condescension of **postmodernist** academics and commentators, especially when faced with issues of scientific truth or ethical judgment. It is the habit of proponents of the higher dismissiveness to put words like truth, objectivity, or rationality in **scare quotes** (not truth but "truth"), partly as a display of their being **beyond** such follies. The

mistake they make is to observe, correctly, that many judgments are **fallible**, open to error or rival interpretation, only then to leap to the conclusion that all knowledge is no more than posturing. See the entries on **hissing suffix** and **glossogonous word-salad**.

HIGHER REPULSION. A term coined by the Indian atheist thinker Parasram Vehromal Kanal (1883–1954) to refer to things which have so offended people that they have devoted years to their eradication. **Slavery**, suttee (widow-burning), child labor, untouchability, and abuse of animals are all examples of activities that have motivated a higher repulsion. But to be driven to eliminate such evils does not mean one is driven by negativity. One is motivated by repulsion, but it is a higher repulsion. See the entry on **dalits**.

HINAYANA BUDDHISM. See **THERAVADA BUDDHISM**.

HINDUTVA. A word derived from *Hindu Tattva*, or Hindu Principles. It is a claim of proponents of Hindutva that Hindu culture is the oldest civilization in the world and, as such, constitutes a prototype for all later cultures. Proponents of Hindutva describe it as a rationalist and humanist outlook, while opponents of Hindutva call it a brand of fascism.

The word was coined by Vinayak Damodar Savarkar (1883–1966) in a 1923 pamphlet called *Hindutva: Who is a Hindu?* Publishing under the pseudonym "A Maratha," Savarkar advocated a two-nation theory of India, as being divided between Hindus and Muslims. As Muslims recognize a holy land outside of India, their commitment to India must be suspect as a result, Savarkar argued. He later became an enthusiastic supporter of Nazism, and was implicated in the assassination of Gandhi in 1948. Hindutva ideologues reject the notion of an **open society** where, under a secular banner, all worldviews can live in peace.

A bust of Savarkar was unveiled in the Central Hall of Parliament Buildings by the president of India in February 2003. India was at the time ruled by the Hindu nationalist party, the BJP, the party most closely affiliated with Hindutva theories. In the last two decades of the twentieth century, Hindutva rose from being a slogan for marginal fanatics, to a favored ideology of the government. The parallel with the rise to power of Evangelical Protestantism in the United States, with its similar ideology of division and confrontation, is chilling. Most Hindutva-sponsored violence has taken place in the western state of Gujarat and in the holy city of **Ayodhya** in Uttar Pradesh.

HIORTH, FINNGEIR (1928–). Norwegian philosopher and atheist. Born in the Dutch East Indies to a family of Norwegian Salvation Army missionaries. By the age of nineteen, he was a confirmed atheist and materialist. In 1946 he returned to Norway, where he began an academic career, studying in Norway, the Netherlands, France, and Germany. He obtained his doctorate in Germany in 1962, and from 1963 to 1993 taught **philosophy** at the University of Oslo. During his academic career, he produced a string of books on Leibniz (1966), **Hume** (1973), Chomsky (1974), the notion of power (1975), and *Philosophers in Indonesia* (1983). He has also written a history of Timor.

Since his retirement Hiorth has been equally prolific, producing a series of introductory works for the nonspecialist reader of aspects of **rationalism, humanism**, and **atheism**. These titles include *Introduction to Atheism* (1995), *Introduction to Humanism* (1996), *Atheism in India* (1998), and *Ethics for Atheists* (1998). These titles were published by the Indian Secular Society, whereas the next string of works were produced by the **Human-Etisk Forbund**; they include *Secularism in Sweden* (1995), *Values* (1999), *Studying Religion* (2000), *Atheism in the World* (2003), and *Positivism* (2004).

HIRD, DENNIS. See **FORMER PREACHERS**.

HIROHITO, EMPEROR (1901–1989). Japanese emperor from 1926 until his death, who oversaw dramatic changes in the way his country was governed and in his own status. Following Japan's defeat in World War II, on January 1, 1946, Hirohito formally announced to his people that he was not divine. Until this time the emperor was revered as a direct descendant of the sun goddess Amaterasu. Hirohito was counted as the one hundred twenty-fourth emperor in succession from Amaterasu, and the Japanese nation was counted as having a special destiny among all the nations. It was this attitude that culminated in the militarism and aggression which had led them to war and defeat.

The emperor's announcement was an epochal moment in Japanese history. Against the worst fears of mystics and conservatives, the emperor retained a useful role in Japanese society and politics as a symbolic focus of unity but without the damaging and chauvinistic assumptions of divinity.

HISSING SUFFIX. The suffix "-ism" can spell doom to any word it is appended to. **Science** becomes **scientism**, history become **historicism**, and so on. One victim of this form of academic controversy was the scientist **E. O. Wilson**, creator of the concept of **sociobiology**, which has since developed into **evolutionary psychology**. Wilson was accused, quite incorrectly, of genetic **determinism**. In his excellent book *Consilience*, Wilson writes amusingly of "sins made official by the hissing suffix."

HISTORICISM. A term with two contradictory meanings, depending on where one lives. For readers of **Karl Popper**, historicism is the tendency, most notoriously obvious with **Marxism**, to see history as following inexorable laws which, in turn, make the course of the future a **certainty**. Thus Marxists see the future apotheosis of communism as objectively certain, as it is nothing more than the inevitable outcome of the laws of history. Popper described historicism in this sense as requiring sociology to be theoretical history. This understanding of historicism is a version of **teleology**.

But for most people operating within the North American intellectual climate, historicism is quite different than Popper's **determinism**. In North America, historicism usually means the belief that different peoples and places live by and value different sets of norms and values than we do today. This understanding of historicism is a version of **relativism**.

HITLER, ADOLF (1889–1945). German dictator. The only thing about Hitler that is relevant to this dictionary is to put to rest the old canard that Hitler was an atheist. No serious scholar makes this mistake, but unfortunately it comes up periodically in the fundamentalist media in the United States, which is now too powerful to simply ignore.

Adolf Hitler was born into the Roman Catholic Church and died without ever having been disowned by the church. He paid his church dues till the end of his life. While Hitler cannot be described as a practicing Catholic, many of his views, in particular his **anti-Semitism**, have deep Catholic roots. Hitler was a theist for all his life, while also being an opponent of Christianity. In *Mein Kampf*, Hitler wrote: "I am convinced that I am acting as the agent of our Creator. By fighting off the Jews, I am doing the Lord's work." Hitler repeatedly invoked Providence, in whose name he felt he was working for the German people. As late as 1944, Hitler reiterated his position. "I am a pious man," he said in a speech, "and believe that whoever fights bravely in defense of the natural laws framed by God and never capitulates will never be deserted by the lawgiver, but will, in the end, receive the blessings of Providence."

Hitler, and most of the Nazi leadership, opposed the churches because they saw them as rival sources of political power. But most of them remained theists, and as the example of the **Cult of the Supreme Being** illustrates, opposing the church does not make one an atheist. Some German **freethought** organiza-

tions were banned in 1932, with enthusiastic support from the Nazi party, and the rest were banned after the Nazis came to power the following year. They remained banned until 1945 and freethinkers were persecuted throughout the Third Reich, although little acknowledgement of this suffering is made.

Further reading: Richard Steigmann-Gall, *The Holy Reich: Nazi Conceptions of Christianity, 1919–1945*.

HIZBULLAH. Lebanese Shi'ite terrorist organization that seeks to create a Muslim theocracy modeled on Iran. Hizbullah means "party of God." It is funded by Syria and Iran and operates in Lebanon at the behest of Syria, who controls much of what goes on in that country. Hizbullah has the dubious honor of having pioneered the use in modern times of the **suicide bomber**. Its leader is Hassan Nasrallah.

HOAX. Defined by Alex Boese as an outrageous and public act of deception. An act of deception that is not public is simply an act of deception between one person and another, and lacks the quality of being a hoax. A hoax is a deception that has engaged public attention, and it does this by virtue of being in some way outrageous or sensational.

Not all hoaxes are conceived in a malicious spirit. Some are simply done for fun, like most April Fools jokes. Others even have a noble intention, like the famous **Sokal Hoax** of 1996, which punctured the academic pretensions of **postmodernism**.

Further reading: Alex Boese, *The Museum of Hoaxes*.

HOBBES, THOMAS (1588–1679). Radical English philosopher. Thomas Hobbes was born in Malmesbury, Wiltshire, the son of an independent-minded country vicar. It was one of Hobbes's favorite stories that his premature birth was due to his anxious mother hearing the news of the approaching Spanish Armada. He was raised by his uncle, who had him educated at Magdalen Hall, Oxford, between 1603 and 1608. Hobbes spent most of his adult life in the service of wealthy patrons, in particular the Cavendish family, who were the earls of Devonshire.

Hobbes's philosophical career did not begin in earnest until he was forty, when he came across the works of the ancient mathematician and astronomer Euclid (300 BCE, approx.). Hobbes was inspired by the elegance and **certainty** of Euclid's proofs to attempt a similar project for the fields of politics and society. But the England of Hobbes's adulthood was not a suitable place to look for certainties in. The English Revolution, the beheading of Charles I, and the puritan commonwealth of Oliver Cromwell (1599–1658) combined to turn the world upside down for Englishmen. This instability and uncertainty only strengthened Hobbes's desire to write something that would stabilize his country.

Hobbes is best known for his classic work of political philosophy, known as *Leviathan* (1651). His account of the world was thoroughly naturalistic. He gave an account of how we are supposed to behave in a **state of nature**, that is without any rules to guide and admonish us. Against the chaos and brutality of the state of nature, Hobbes postulated giving the sovereign very broad powers as the undisputed ruler. He did this, though, for secular and pragmatic reasons and with none of the usual appeals to the divine right of kings, or any other of the popular religious-based arguments of the day.

Hobbes argued that fear and ignorance are the driving forces behind religion, but he was happy they remain as consolations for the people. Like many thinkers of the time, fear of punishment imposed an equivocal style in Hobbes's writing on religion. See the entry on **parallel theology**. But few of his contemporaries were fooled. So widespread were the suspicions of his being an atheist that the English parliament investigated his beliefs to see whether, as an atheist, he could be blamed for an outbreak of plague in London. As the philosopher J. C. A. Gaskin has noted, it is

difficult to imagine that someone of Hobbes's intellect could have been unaware of, or not to have intended, the serious criticisms of religion that everyone else read into his work.

HOBHOUSE, LEONARD TRELAWNEY

(1864–1929). Influential English sociologist and liberal humanist. From 1897 to 1903, Hobhouse was a leading figure at the *Manchester Guardian*, and a significant force behind the tolerant liberalism of that newspaper. From 1907 until his retirement, he was professor of sociology at London University, the first professional sociologist at that institution.

Hobhouse was a leading spokesperson for a newer, more intellectually rigorous liberalism at the end of the nineteenth century. Where liberals of the nineteenth century extolled the virtues of *laissez-faire* capitalism, Hobhouse was, along with Graham Wallas (1858–1932) an articulate proponent of the newer, more interventionist brand of liberalism.

Hobhouse's main books include *Mind in Evolution* (1901), *Morals in Evolution* (1906), *Liberalism* (1912), and *Development and Purpose* (1913). In his underappreciated work *The Rational Good* (1921), Hobhouse gave an account of rationality that belies most of the caricatures of the rationalist faith in reason so beloved by opponents. Instead, he spoke of **impulse-feeling** as the primary motivating force in people.

HOGBEN, LANCELOT (1895–1975).

English scientist and writer. Born in Southsea and educated at Cambridge. He held academic positions in Britain, Canada, and South Africa before becoming Mason professor of zoology from 1941 to 1947 and then professor of medical statistics at Birmingham until his retirement in 1961. He was best known for his successful works of popular science, *Mathematics for the Million* (1936) and *Science for the Citizen* (1938), both of which went through many editions.

Hogben was an uncompromising rationalist and opponent of all grandiose ideologies. He quickly came to see communism as a greater threat to intellectual freedom even than Christianity. He had a strong distrust of any sort of "true believer." He was also an outspoken critic of **eugenics**.

HOLBACH, BARON PAUL HEINRICH DIETRICH (1723–1789). Wealthy pioneer of **atheism** and **rationalism**. Born in Germany, Holbach spent his life in France, where he set his house up as one of the leading social and intellectual centers in Europe.

Holbach was an important supporter of the *Dictionnaire Encyclopédie*, writing over four hundred entries to it over many years. His most important work, *Le Système de la Nature* (two volumes in 1770), though long and poorly organized, was a thorough defense of atheism and materialism. The first half laid down the scientific foundations of materialism and the second half was an attack on religion. He was a rigid determinist with regard to questions of **free will**, but it would be wrong to characterize him, as has often been done, of arrogance. In fact, his attitude is quite humble with regard to claiming to understand the entire workings of nature. See the entry on **cosmic modesty**. Holbach's advocacy of negative atheism was one of the more thorough of its types until **Michael Martin** more than two centuries later.

To protect himself from Christian persecution, he wrote *Le Système de la Nature* under the name Mirabaud, who had been dead ten years when the book was published. His friends also shielded him from persecution until his death. Holbach attracted this sort of loyalty because of his own record as a generous benefactor of writers down on their luck. He supported many writers, without regard to their religious views. See the entry on the *Looking-Glass of Atheism and Ignorance*.

HOLISM. See **SYSTEMISM**.

HOLLAND, HENRY EDMUND (1868–1933). Socialist politician, rationalist, and atheist. Harry Holland was born in Ginninderra, New South Wales, the son of a farmer. He left school at ten and worked as a farm hand until he was fourteen, when he was apprenticed as a compositor to a newspaper. He joined the Salvation Army at this time and met his future wife, Anne McLachlan. They married in 1888. Holland left the Salvation Army in 1890, dissatisfied with its irrelevance to the real-life difficulties of the workers. Holland was a rationalist and an atheist for the rest of his life.

For the next twenty-two years, he was deeply immersed in socialist politics in Australia, going to prison on two occasions as a result of his activities. In May 1912 he and his family migrated to New Zealand and he found himself immersed at once in the wave of industrial action gripping the country, culminating in the General Strike of 1913. In April of that year Holland took over the editorship of the *Maoriland Worker*, a radical journal of the militant left-wing in New Zealand. Once again, he was sent to prison for his activities, this time being found guilty of sedition.

In May 1918 Holland was elected to parliament as MP for Grey, a constituency on the West Coast of the South Island. The following year Holland became leader of the parliamentary Labor Party, retaining a militant socialist position while retaining the support of all party factions Holland led the Labor Party until his death in 1933, although widespread suspicion of him by moderates probably helped prevent his party from becoming government during his lifetime. He was succeeded as Labor Party leader by **Michael Joseph Savage**.

Holland died of a heart attack after climbing a steep hill to attend the funeral of the prominent Maori chief Te Rata Mahuta. A wave of enthusiasm and sympathy for Holland after his death, something he had never achieved in his life, helped propel the Labor Party to power in 1935.

Further reading, P. J. O'Farrell, *Harry Holland: Militant Socialist*.

HOLLOWS, FREDERICK (1929–1993).
Australian physician who became a leader in
the campaign to fight eye diseases among
Australian aborigines. Hollows was born in
Dunedin, New Zealand, to a family of modest
circumstances. The son of a railway worker,
the young Hollows thought at one point of
entering the church but discovered that "sex,
alcohol, and secular goodness are pretty keen
instruments and they surgically removed my
Christianity, leaving no scars."

From experience in Eritrea, Vietnam, and
Nepal, he developed a program for performing eye surgery in severe conditions. In
Australia, he cofounded the Aboriginal Medical Service and was instrumental in setting
up a chain of community clinics devoted to
the health of aborigines. In 1990 Hollows
was given the Australian of the Year award by
the Australian government, and in 1991 he
was honored as the Humanist of the Year by
the Council of Australian Humanist Societies.
He was an outspoken atheist.

HOLOCAUST DENIERS. A symptom of
postwar **anti-Semitism**. Since World War II,
anti-Semites have had to confront the difficulty posed in projecting their ideas to a
world with fresh memories of the suffering of
Jews during World War II. Their recourse has
been to deny the Holocaust took place at all,
or at least to revise radically the level of persecution the Jews suffered.

The denial of the Holocaust has become
common among Muslims. Educators in
Western countries have experienced a significant minority of Muslim students who deny
the Holocaust took place. But the problem is
by no means limited to Muslims. In the West,
one of the more prominent people accused
recently of denying the Holocaust was Hutton
Gibson, father of the American actor, Mel
Gibson, who in 2003 was quoted in a *New
York Times* article as describing the Holocaust
as a charade. Gibson, a traditionalist Roman
Catholic, also condemned the developments
in the Catholic Church since Vatican II as a
Masonic plot backed by the Jews.

There is no historical doubt whatsoever
that the Holocaust took place, and revisionist
attempts to write it out of history are done not
according to sound historical scholarship, but
in the service of a preset hatred.

HOLY LIE, THE. An idea brought up by
Friedrich Nietzsche in 1888 but not used
until *The Will to Power* (1901), a posthumous
work put together by other people. The holy
lie referred to the ages-old attempt by priests
and philosophers—**Plato** above all—to
ensure their control by dulling the people
with false notions of the world and of
morality. The holy lie seeks to replace natural
purpose with fulfillment of the law, to create
the conditions where service to **God** appears
as a purpose and where natural consequence
can be interpreted in supernatural terms. With
this in mind, the holy lie was invented, and
consists of:

- a God who punishes and rewards, and
  who obeys law books and is serious
  about priests;
- an afterlife and promise of **immortality**;
- conscience in man in order to believe
  good and evil are permanent and set by
  God;
- morality, as a denial of natural
  processes; and
- truth, as given by priests.

Nietzsche wrote that the idea of God is
nothing more than a turning away from life
and where truth becomes the lies priests tell.
Needless to say, Nietzsche warned us against
falling victim to the holy lie. A more recent,
and more secular version of the holy lie is
Noam Chomsky's notion of **manufacturing
consent**.

Further reading: Friedrich Nietzsche, *The
Will to Power*; and Plato, *The Republic*.

HOLYOAKE, GEORGE JACOB (1817–
1906). Pioneer of secularism and cooperation, Holyoake was born into a poor family in

Birmingham, and as a young man became a teacher and organizer for the movement led by **Robert Owen**. He also became a leading spokesman for the radical anti-Christian wing within Owenism. While lecturing in Cheltenham, Holyoake responded to hostile clerical interrogation, saying that, while poverty existed in the land, God could be put on half-pay. For this he was charged with **blasphemy** and was jailed as an atheist.

After his spell in prison, he changed his emphasis. Holyoake decided the increasingly antireligious trend in Owenism was harmful while also wanting to retain the interest in ethical renewal that the Owenite movement was then moving away from. He went on to bring this new program together under the label of **secularism**. He sought out, and was remarkably successful at maintaining, the friendship of men of higher standing than he.

Holyoake's legacy is important but uneven. He was the only person whose career spanned both of the legacies of Owenism: the cooperative movement and the secular movement. He also believed that he spanned the divide between the radical and moderate critics of religion, although the radicals, led by **Charles Bradlaugh** and his followers were less convinced of this.

Holyoake's written work is uneven in quality. Being largely self-taught, he did not always follow a line of argument with required diligence. This notwithstanding, he was a popular author, and unusually for freethinkers, had a significant middle-class audience. His *Logic of Death* (1850) sold sixteen thousand copies within a year and is thought by many to be his most powerful **freethought** work.

HOLY REASON. An idea with a long pedigree but with poor credentials. **Plato**'s version of **reason** was more akin to mystic insight than to evidence-based reasoning. But his **Neoplatonist** successors developed this trend to its (il)logical conclusion. It can be seen to best effect in the work of the Muslim Neoplatonist philosopher Ibn Sina (often known by his latinized name Avicenna

(980–1037 CE). Ibn Sina conceived of a hierarchy of reason, and a concomitant hierarchy of reasoners. There is practical reason, which is our day-to-day reasoning, and then there is theoretical reason, a superior form of reasoning which is directed to the great truths of the universe. But the apex of the hierarchy is holy reason—a special quality of reason accessible to a select few. Only by virtue of this special quality of reason can the select few hope to grasp the universal truths. Ibn Sina saw prophecy as the highest stage of human reason, and solely the prerogative of this select few. See the entry on **Taqlid**.

The problems in this approach are apparent. First of all, this hierarchy of reason owes whatever credibility it has to a prescientific view of the cosmos, and implies the existence of some variety of a **great chain of being**. It is also profoundly **totalitarian**. It offers no ground upon which to challenge someone's claim to possess the fruits of holy reason. Everyone is able to reason; reason is inherently democratic. It is part of our evolutionary heritage. Some people can reason more effectively than others, but this difference is not imprinted in the cosmos and is always open to challenge.

Further reading: Majid Fakhry, *A History of Islamic Philosophy*.

HOMER (ninth–eighth centuries BCE). One of the most important people in history and about whom we know next to nothing. His dates are uncertain, as is his birthplace. Most scholars are fairly happy with the idea that Homer came from Ionia or Smyrna, the home of the **Pre-Socratic** philosophers. Tradition says Homer was the son of Maeon, and that he lived until old age, dying blind and penniless. He is credited with writing the *Iliad* and the *Odyssey*, two of the greatest literary masterpieces of all time. The *Odyssey* came together in the form we have it around 725 BCE and described a world that was disappearing even then.

There remain credible doubts that the same person wrote both works. Either way, everybody should read the *Iliad* and the *Odyssey*, not simply because they are foundational documents of Western civilization, but because they remain, after almost three thousand years, genuinely enjoyable reading experiences.

Homer's books were the backbone of Greek learning and culture during its finest age. The achievement of the **Greek playwrights** would be vastly different had Homer not lived. The *Iliad* and *Odyssey* bequeathed many of the noblest thoughts of Greece to the later Roman and Christian ages, and arose to prominence once again during the Renaissance and contributed mightily to the climate of **Renaissance humanism**. To this day, the *Iliad* and the *Odyssey* are regularly translated, or adapted for poetry or films. The recent translations of both books by the American scholar Robert Fagles help bring them alive once again to a new generation of readers.

Further reading: Charles Freeman, *The Greek Achievement*; and Homer, *The Iliad* and *The Odyssey* (translated by Robert Fagles).

HOMO RELIGIOSUS. Literally "religious man," or more loosely, "man is a religious animal." This phrase, usually left in Latin to provide gravitas, is frequently employed by liberal religious scholars and some **Unitarians** to insist that humans have some essential impulse for **religion**. By claiming that we are *Homo religiosus*, they can include **unbelievers** as part—albeit an errant part—of the world religious community. The Canadian theologian Wilfred Cantwell Smith (1916–2001) was especially prone to this form of condescension.

Others use the claim of *Homo religiosus* to accuse humanists of dishonesty to their "real" selves. This use of the *Homo religiosus* argument is just as exclusivist as the fundamentalists who love to quote Psalm 14:1, which declares "the fool has said in his heart 'there is no God.'" In fact there is no evidence for any essential religious sensibility among *Homo sapiens*, particularly not in the sense meant here.

HOMO SAPIENS. The term coined by **Carolus Linnaeus** to identify human beings within the vast scheme of nature. Rather optimistically, *Homo sapiens* means "man the wise." *Homo sapiens* is only the most recent version of the human animal to have evolved. Our human ancestors are thought to have been first distinguishable around seven million years ago. Our more direct, big-brained ancestors date from about two and a half million years ago. *Homo sapiens* is no more than about 150,000 years old.

We used to tell ourselves that *Homo sapiens* represented the pinnacle of evolution, and some have gone so far as to claim that evolution was primed for the specific purpose of creating us. We now know these theories to be the presumptions of **anthropocentric conceit**. *Homo sapiens* has survived as much by luck as by judgment, let alone by design, particularly through the five major **extinctions** that have wiped out many other species. *Homo sapiens* is no more foreordained than any other species, which is to say not at all. And only when we take that lesson to heart will *Homo sapiens* truly deserve the title of man the wise.

Further reading: Richard Leakey and Roger Lewin, *The Sixth Extinction*.

HOMO SYMBOLICUS. The label given to humanity by the German philosopher Ernst Cassirer (1874–1945), which referred to what he saw as humanity's innate tendency to reduce all social communication to **symbols**. This claim is more credible than that surrounding ***Homo religiosus***, but is still something of an overstatement.

HONDERICH, TED (1933–). Canadian-born British philosopher and **smiter of humbug**. Ted Honderich was born in Baden, Ontario, and educated at the University of Toronto. After a short spell as literary editor of the *Toronto Star*, he left Canada for Britain to study philosophy. He studied philosophy at University College, London, under his mentor **A. J. Ayer**. Honderich has remained loyal to Ayer's memory ever since.

Honderich has written widely, but his philosophical specialism is on the study of **determinism**. His major work in this area is *A Theory of Determinism* (1989) and with an excellent popular version of his argument called *How Free Are You?* (1993). He has also written controversial works on the death penalty, conservatism, **terrorism**, and a remarkably candid autobiography, *Philosopher: A Kind of Life* (2001). He also edited the *Oxford Companion to Philosophy* (1995). Honderich is a convinced atheist, and has been an honorary associate of the **National Secular Society** and the **Rationalist Press Association** since 1988. See the entries on **Equality, Principle of**, and **Desert, Principle of**.

HONEST TO GOD. A small book published in 1963 by J. A. T. Robinson (1919–1983), at the time the Bishop of Woolwich, which was enormously influential. Robinson's thesis was not new or that radical. It was a rehash of Dietrich Bonhoeffer (1906–1945) and Paul Tillich (1886–1965) in particular, so most clergymen who had gone through seminary education were familiar with Robinson's argument. Robinson argued that out of the wreckage of the traditional arguments for **God** and religion, it was still possible to create a Christianity without religion—in effect, a deified **humanism** not dissimilar to what humanists had been scorned for advocating for over seven decades. What made the argument new was that it was a bishop saying it.

Honest to God provoked a storm of controversy and debate in Britain about religion and its role for people and society. However, it was not popular with most religious believers, and certainly not with the church leadership. Archbishop Michael Ramsey expressed his disapproval of *Honest to God* to Robinson on several occasions, although he later regretted his obscurantism. Since Robinson's day, the Church of England has become significantly more conservative and hostile to views such as those he advanced in *Honest to God*. And Robinson's book did

little in the long run to help gather support for religious liberalism. *Honest to God* is a classic example of the **fatal flaw at the heart of religious liberalism**.

HONOR KILLINGS. An example of traditional cultures not being as benign as is often made out by gullible Westerners. Honor killings are an ancient practice, found particularly in the Middle East and parts of South East Asia, which usually affect women whose sexual conduct is thought to bring dishonor to their families. As punishment for this dishonor, the women are often subjected to brutal beatings, having acid thrown in their faces, or even being killed to protect the honor of the family name. It is estimated there are a thousand honor killings in Pakistan every year. Pakistani president Pervez Musharraf called honor killings a "curse which blights the nation." Westerners became more aware of the problem of honor killings in 2001 and 2002 after Muslim migrants in Britain, Sweden, and the Netherlands went on trial for murdering their daughters. The problem is not limited to Islam, however. Informal Hindu caste courts known as *panchayats* in the northern states of Uttar Pradesh and Haryana have also decreed honor killings against women thought to have brought dishonor to their families.

Two crucial points need to be understood: in the vast majority of cases it is only women's sexual misconduct that can bring shame and dishonor to the family, and only women are held responsible for sexual activity, despite it also involving a man's participation.

Several Muslim and Hindu sources recognize honor killings to be a problem. Some of the Muslim activists have lamented the "distortion" of traditional Islam by this practice. Other sources, while not actually endorsing honor killings, contribute to the general culture which holds women as inferior to men and in need of male supervision. See the entry on *Women in Islam*. Nothing less than a comprehensive reformation of male attitudes toward women in these societies will deal with this problem, but this in turn will involve a very fundamental reformation of Islam itself. Freed from the shackles of a **scripture**, Hindu activists have been able to campaign against honor killings without having to justify their actions.

HOOK, SIDNEY (1902–1989). American philosopher of **naturalism** and **pragmatism**. Born and raised in New York, Hook's entire career was also spent there. He worked as professor of philosophy at New York University from 1932 to 1972, during which time he was politically active. In his youth Hook was a fervent Marxist, which can be seen in his early work *Towards an Understanding of Karl Marx* (1933). He quickly changed his mind on this and for the rest of his life was a staunch opponent of communism. This was manifested in some trenchant anticommunism during the **Great Fear** (which earned him the lasting dislike of many leftist thinkers, including **Corliss Lamont**) and support for the Vietnam War. Hook's later thoughts are well covered in *Marx and the Marxists: An Ambiguous Legacy* (1955). Hook was also influenced by Morris Cohen (1880–1947) and **John Dewey**, although he differed with Dewey on the degree to which **humanism** is religious in nature. Hook was of the opinion that humanism is inevitably secular.

Later on, Hook tended more toward supporting social democracy and philosophical naturalism. Important books in this regard were *The Quest for Being* (1961), a collection of some of his best essays. Other important books include *The Hero in History: A Study in Limitation and Possibility* (1943), and his autobiography, *Out of Step* (1987). He was a great influence on his students, including **Paul Kurtz**. Hook was elected a foundation member of the **International Academy of Humanism** in 1983. In 1986 the Reagan administration awarded Hook the Medal of Freedom, the highest civilian award in the United States.

HOOPS, WALTER (1902–1997). German-American freethinker. Walter Hoops was born in Hanover, Germany, and raised in the *freidenker* (freethinker) movement in that country. As a member of the political left in turbulent Weimar, Germany, Hoops often found himself in physical confrontations with the Brown Shirts.

In 1932 he saw the writing on the wall and emigrated to the United States, where he lived for the rest of his life. He lived in St. Louis and worked as an export manager and was a prominent rationalist for more than half a century. For many years he was editor, or on the editorial team of the ***American Rationalist*** magazine and his work formed the intellectual backbone of that magazine. He also edited a small work called *Our Rationalist Heritage* (1968), an anthology of the thoughts of great thinkers with special emphasis on freedom of thought. In 1991 Hoops received the Lifetime Achievement Award at the **Council for Secular Humanism** conference in Kansas City.

HOUSMAN, ALFRED EDWARD (1859–1936). English poet and classical scholar. Born in Worcestershire, Housman was educated at Bromsgrove School, where he won a scholarship to St. John's College, Oxford. Despite failing his study of Greats, Housman went on to become a respected classical scholar, publishing critical editions of Juvenal in 1905 and Lucan in 1926. Housman was professor of Latin at University College, London, from 1892 and at Cambridge from 1911. He is best known as a poet, in particular for his poem *A Shropshire Lad* (1896).

He abandoned any connection with Christianity. For a while he described himself as a **deist**, but soon moved on to **atheism**. He specifically rejected the term **agnostic**. He noted drily that the Church of England was the best religion ever invented, because it was less disturbing than any of the others, and got rid of "so much Christian nonsense." Housman's atheism is expressed best in a variety of his poems, most notably *Laws, The*

Carpenter's Son, and *The West*.

HOYLE, FRED (1915–2001). English theoretical astrophysicist, popularizer of **science**, science fiction writer, and **smiter of humbug**. Hoyle was born in Bingley, Yorkshire, and educated at Cambridge University. In 1956 he became the Plumian professor of astronomy at Cambridge, and in 1967 became the founder-director of the Institute of Theoretical Astronomy, also at Cambridge. He resigned from his professorial positions in 1973 to devote himself to public issues and the popular understanding of science.

Hoyle is best known for his seminal contributions to the theory of the structure of stars and on the stellar origin of the chemical elements. Along with Sir Hermann Bondi and Thomas Gold, he was a joint proponent of the steady-state model of the universe, which was replaced by the **big bang** theory. And in collaboration with Chandra Wickramasinghe he pioneered the modern theory of **panspermia**. He was also a strong advocate for nuclear energy.

He was elected a fellow of the Royal Society in 1957, was awarded the **Kalinga Prize** in 1968, and was knighted in 1972. He has published over forty books, including works on technical science, popular science, and science fiction. Notable among the fiction is *The Black Cloud* (1957) and *October the First Is Too Late* (1966, cowritten with his son, Geoffrey).

HUBBLE'S LAW. An axiom of modern physics, discovered by Edwin Hubble (1899–1953), the chief consequence of which is the understanding that the universe is expanding. What Hubble noticed in 1923 was that the redshift is proportional to distance. Redshift is the move of light toward red, which is caused by a body's motion away from Earth. Hubble's law is expressed mathematically as $V=HD$, with V being the velocity of a galaxy, D as the distance, and H as the Hubble constant, which is derived from the speed at which a galaxy is moving from the **big bang**.

Not only has Hubble's Law helped us determine that the universe is expanding, it also helped us determine the age of the universe, which we now estimate to be 15 billion years old. See the entry on **heliocentric universe**.

HUGHES, LANGSTON (1902–1967). Regarded by many as the African American poet laureate. Langston Hughes was born in Joplin, Missouri, to a white father and a black mother. His parents divorced when he was very young, and he was brought up by his grandmother until he was thirteen. In the 1920s, as he was emerging as a major poetic talent, he became a significant figure in the Harlem Renaissance, a period of great intellectual and cultural vitality in African American thought, which lasted from about 1917 until 1935. Two of the strongest influences on Hughes were **Walt Whitman** and **Claude McKay**.

As a youth he lost his faith, and some of his most powerful poems relate his views on religion. His early poem *Goodbye Christ*, written after a trip to the Soviet Union, attacked the church and praised communism. Not surprisingly, *Goodbye Christ* got Hughes into a lot of trouble, particularly during the **Great Fear**. Hughes later apologized for writing it. There were other poems that made his views on **religion** quite clear, including *Christ in Alabama*. Hughes's work *I Too, Sing America* influenced Martin Luther King Jr. (1929–1968), the principal figure of the civil rights movement in America.

His first published work of poetry was *The Weary Blues* (1926). He went on to publish twelve more volumes of poetry. A collection of his works, the *Collected Works of Langston Hughes*, appeared in 1994. Hughes also wrote novels and drama. His first novel, *Not Without Laughter* (1930) won the Harmon gold medal for literature.

Hughes's life was not easy. Though he earned a living from his writing, he was never far from the poverty line. He also struggled with being homosexual. He did not use the word "humanist" to describe himself, but was explicitly atheist. Hughes's biographer describes him as "secular to the bone."

Further reading: Norm R. Allen Jr., ed., *African-American Humanism: An Anthology.*

HUGHES, RUPERT (1872–1956). Prolific American author and uncle of the reclusive millionaire Howard Hughes (1905–1976). Rupert Hughes was born in Lancaster, Missouri, and raised in Keokuk, Iowa. With a great deal of encouragement from a loving family, he rose to become one of America's most successful writers of his generation, producing highly thought-of poetry, novels, reference works, biographies, and film and radio scripts. Among the biographies was the three-volume biography of George Washington: *The Human Being and the Hero, 1732–1762* (vol. 1, 1926); *The Rebel and the Patriot, 1762–1777* (vol. 2, 1927); and *The Savior of the States, 1777–1781* (vol. 3, 1930). Despite high praise for these volumes, the fourth and last volume was never completed. Hughes was also a capable musician, and many of his works had a musical theme or were about aspects of music. In 1903 he produced a biographical dictionary of American musicians, which remained the standard reference work on the subject and went through many editions.

Hughes also had an interesting transition from believer to agnostic, which he detailed in *Cosmopolitan* magazine in 1924 and which the following year became the book *Why I Quit Going to Church*, published by the Freethought Press Association, run by **Joseph Lewis**. Hughes then wrote for the **Haldeman-Julius** press, including two Little Blue Books, *The Ghastly Purpose of the Parables* (1927) and *The Lord and Mr. Ford.* Despite his reputation as a freethinker, Hughes was honored later in his life with public dinners and other celebrations of his work. It would be difficult to imagine that happening now.

Further reading: James O. Kemm, *Rupert Hughes: A Hollywood Legend.*

HUMAN DIGNITY. The notion that, alone among the animals, ***Homo sapiens*** deserve special consideration. Traditionally, the idea of human dignity rested on the assumption that we alone possessed a **soul**, marking us off as favored by **God**. The idea got its first specific attention during the Renaissance. To the twenty-first-century observer, Renaissance humanists were altogether too extravagant in their praise of human dignity. It was necessary at the time because it served as a corrective to the miserable pessimism and fatalism of the Middle Ages. But today it smacks of **anthropocentric conceit**. So as to deal effectively with the planetary scope of the problems facing us, human beings need to reconsider our understanding of human dignity. The concept is still important, but it must be tempered with our appreciation of the planet and the other animal species we share it with.

Today it is the quiet dignity of those who suffer that we should extol. But we should extol it not with words and sentimental twaddle about the virtue of suffering, but with practical assistance to end that suffering. The dignity of human beings lies not in their souls, for we have no such accoutrement. Our dignity lies precisely in our ability to carry on in the knowledge of not flattering ourselves with anthropocentric conceit.

HUMAN-ETISK FORBUND. Or in English, the Humanist-Ethical Society of Norway. The Human-Etisk Forbund is one of the most successful humanist organizations in the world, not least because it enjoys significant government funding.

The Human-Etisk Forbund was founded in 1956 by Kristian Horn (1903–1981), a biologist at the University of Oslo. It had a great deal of support from the academic community, but did not really prosper until Levi Fragell (1939–) became its secretary-general in 1976. It was Fragell's belief that, to be successful, a humanist organization must combine the three traditional strands of organized **humanism**, namely:

- *the view-of-life strand*, which focuses on the propagation of positive humanist ethics;
- *the tradition strand*, which provides secular ceremonies for important occasions; and
- *the freethinker strand*, which is involved in the criticism of **religion**.

Under Fragell's leadership, the society broadened the range of services it offered to members, in particular, naming and funeral ceremonies and secular counseling. Fragell also modernized some of the organization's attitudes which, until his tenure, held fairly conservative views on women's rights, homosexuality, and **abortion**. The Human-Etisk Forbund also plays a leading role in humanist activism outside India. It has a long track record of working with the various projects run by the **Atheist Centre** in India. Fragell went on to play a leading role in the **International Humanist and Ethical Union** for many years.

The Human-Etisk Forbund also has a vigorous publishing program, including the broad range of material in English written by the philosopher **Finngeir Hiorth**.

HUMAN GENOME PROJECT. A loosely coordinated project, with almost forty countries taking part, to build up a complete picture of the sequences of bases in human DNA. The human genome is composed of twenty-three pairs of chromosomes, each of which is a DNA molecule. DNA consists of varying patterns of the four bases: guanine, cytosine, adenine, and thymine, commonly known by their initials: A, T, G, and C. A always teams up with T and G always teams up with C. The primary role of **DNA** is to encode the information needed to build proteins, which are commonly called the building blocks of life. In compiling a complete picture of the base sequence, scientists will have a complete map of the genetic structure of *Homo sapiens*.

The project began in 1990 and it was completed early in 2003, two years ahead of schedule. Its goals were to provide a map of all the genes in human DNA and determine the chemical sequences by which A, T, G, and C interact. Even by 2003 there were still gaps in the picture, but the basic outline had been mapped by then. The next tasks are to discern more clearly the variations of DNA which contribute to diseases. The consequences of this new knowledge are enormous. See the entries on **bioethics** and **neuroethics**.

HUMAN-HEARTEDNESS. One of the better translations of the word *jen*, used by **Kongfuzi** (Confucius), and a notion that was central to his philosophy. Kongfuzi spoke of the superior man who acts according to his duties, according to what ought to be done, as opposed to lesser people, who operate only for gain. But the superior man acts according to what ought to be done, not merely out of a grim sense of duty, but because of his human-heartedness. Confucius said in the *Analects* that human-heartedness consists in extending oneself so as to include others.

HUMAN KNOWLEDGE: ITS SCOPE AND LIMITS. A book written by **Bertrand Russell**, which was published in 1948. *Human Knowledge* was intended as the summing up of his life's work. The purpose of it was to show the strict limits to what we can really know about the world around us, the impossibility of **foundationalism** (though he didn't use that term), and then providing a guide to what we could count as very probably true.

Russell demonstrated and then tried to solve the disconnection between the private nature of human experience and the public nature of scientific knowledge. He noted that knowledge is a significantly less precise concept than is generally assumed, and that the roots of knowledge are in our "embedded and unverbalized animal behavior." This has since been shown to be very much the case, although Russell has not received the praise he deserves for noting this in 1948. At the end of the book Russell proposed five postulates, the job of which was to justify **external**

realism and in so doing, provide a means by which we can acquire reliable **knowledge** about the world.

Human Knowledge received an almost universally negative reception. Much of this was due to the change in intellectual fashion. Linguistic philosophy was king and **Ludwig Wittgenstein** was very much the philosopher of choice. Since then, linguistic philosophy has fallen into disfavor, having been charged with not having any real philosophical problems to ask. *Human Knowledge*, by contrast, had some pressing questions to ask, took the subject seriously, and made a valiant attempt to provide an answer. The current strength of external realism owes a debt to *Human Knowledge*.

Further reading: Bertrand Russell, *Human Knowledge: Its Scope and Limits*; and Ronald Jager, *The Development of Bertrand Russell's Philosophy*.

HUMAN NATURE. One of the most difficult notions to understand comprehensively. One thing we can be confident about is that most traditional theories of human nature are wrong, because they posit some sort of **soul**, **mind**, **psyche**, or vital spark, which are essentially different from, and usually superior to, the body. Each of these theories, deriving from religion or **idealist** philosophy, has collapsed over the past century. No less fallacious are the theories that no such thing as human nature exists. Thinkers as diverse as **Jean-Paul Sartre**, **Ayn Rand**, and Michel Foucault have all advocated this. We also need to take care with theories of human nature which seek to draw conclusions about the proper sphere of activity of men and women, or different races.

All these caveats aside, it is absurd to claim that human beings are not constrained in very significant ways by biological constants like birth, **death**, aging, and sickness. It is clear that there is such a thing as human nature, and that it can be understood through sciences such as **evolutionary psychology**. E. O. Wilson, one of the most important nat-

uralists of the early twenty-first century, has spoken of human nature as "the epigenetic rules, the hereditary regularities of mental development that bias cultural evolution in one direction as opposed to another, and thus connect genes to culture."

Further reading: E. O. Wilson, *Consilience: The Unity of Knowledge*.

HUMAN NEEDS. **Paul Kurtz** has argued that there are two categories of human needs. First there are *biogenic needs*, which involve the physicochemical needs for basic sustenance: salt, oxygen, water, calcium, and so on. The other main biogenic need is the need to be able to grow, mature, and develop. Then there are *sociogenic needs*, which include the:

- need for a sense of psychological security;
- need for a reciprocal love, or commitment;
- need for a sense of belonging;
- need for self-respect;
- need for avenues for self-expression; and
- need for avenues for cognitive development.

It is the task of the civil society to address these needs, for without any one of them, humans are unlikely to develop to anything like their full potential.

Further reading: Paul Kurtz, "Need Reduction and Normal Value" in *Philosophical Essays in Pragmatic Naturalism*.

HUMAN RIGHTS COMMISSION. An agency of the **United Nations** charged with promoting human rights around the world. Its job is to oversee the gradual acceptance and implementation of the **Universal Declaration of Human Rights**. As of 2004, there are fifty-three member nations of the Human Rights Commission.

The HRC is composed on the one hand of delegations representing countries and on the other hand of representatives of nongovernmental organizations (NGOs). It has frequently been observed that the countries with the poorest human-rights records are well represented on the HRC, which they use to defend their human rights record, or deflect attention from it. The NGO representatives, on the other hand, are there to attract as much attention as possible to countries with poor human rights records. This can result in some tense sessions. Such is the grim reality of extending the reach of human rights around the world. But while this is a grossly unsatisfactory system, it is better than nothing.

HUMANAE VITAE. The papal encyclical described by Garry Wills (1934–), in other respects an outspoken Catholic apologist, as "the most disastrous papal document of the twentieth century" on a par with its nineteenth-century equivalent, the *Syllabus of Errors* (1864). Issued on July 25, 1968, *Humanae Vitae* was the authoritative papal condemnation of all forms of birth control except the largely fictional rhythm method. *Humanae Vitae* has been strongly supported by Paul's successors, John Paul II in particular.

Pope Paul VI, who issued the encyclical, was stunned by the negative reaction to it, and never issued another one. Many prominent Catholic thinkers and spokespeople publicly opposed *Humanae Vitae*, while many others lost their faith over it and left the church for good. Catholics in the developed world have largely ignored *Humanae Vitae*, posing a standing challenge to papal authority as a consequence. Birth rates have declined in nominally Catholic countries like France, Spain, and Italy at rates commensurate, even greater than, the European average. But among poorer believers in less-developed nations, where enforcement has been stricter, the consequences have been catastrophic. Not only has *Humanae Vitae* contributed significantly to an unsustainable population growth, it has also accelerated the spread of sexually transmitted diseases, **AIDS** in particular.

HUMANE-ISM. A term suggested by the American scholar Floyd Matson. While admitting the word is awkward, Matson saw it as concentrating on "the prospective act of human becoming, of the unfolding of 'the best qualities of mankind,'" rather than on the simple rejection of **dogmatism**. Intellect, wrote Matson, is not sufficient to make a humanist. "The authentic humanist is not to be identified as one who has a great deal of mind: the humanist is one who minds a great deal."

Further reading: Floyd Matson, "Humaneism," *Free Inquiry* 4, no. 2 (Spring 1984): 48.

HUMANIC. A word coined by the Serbian political philosopher Svetozar Stojanovic, to suggest that, like the Titanic, the ship of humanity may well be sailing to disaster. Stojanovic sees a half-understood capacity within human beings for what he calls self-apocalypse. Symptomatic of that incapacity is our inability to transcend our limited conceptions of power from their current nation-state conceptions to a genuinely global understanding. Stojanovic lists the main problems that threaten a global apocalypse:

- the growing gap between the rich and the poor;
- ecological stress caused by overpopulation in many parts of the world; and
- growing divide between those with access to technological development and those without.

Stojanovic argues that the slogan should now read "Think and Act Globally." He sees little hope unless we can move on from nation-state–based orientations and interests. He doubts both the ability of world religions to adapt themselves to the new requirements, and the possibility of their successful replacement by a **planetary humanism**.

Further reading: Svetozar Stojanovic, *Serbia: The Democratic Revolution*.

HUMANISM. One of the oldest and certainly the most transcultural worldview in humanity's history. The American philosopher **Paul Kurtz** has provided the best understanding of humanism when he defined it in terms of its four constituent features:

- humanism is a method of inquiry;
- humanism presents a cosmic world-view;
- humanism offers a set of ethical recommendations for the individual's life stance; and
- humanism expresses a number of social and political ideals.

It is important to note the order in which these characteristics have been listed. Number four is the least important of them, not because social and political ideals are unimportant, but because the nature of those ideals has changed most over time and between continents. Numbers two and three are more important because the details of the worldview and the ethical recommendations have greater commonality between the various humanist civilizations of the world.

But the most important feature of humanism, because it is the most constant, is feature number one: humanism as a method of inquiry. From the **Carvakas** and **Ajivikas** in India, from **Kongfuzi** and **Wang Chong** in China, from **Thales** and the Greek thinkers, through the Renaissance to the **Enlightenment** to the twenty-first century, humanism is best understood as a method of inquiry. The *conclusions* of that inquiry—numbers two, three, and four in Kurtz's definition—change between cultures and between centuries, but the *method* of inquiry has remained essentially the same. The method of inquiry is based solidly in **naturalism**. See the entry on **humanist philosophy, three strands of**.

Symptomatic of the uniqueness of humanism is that for most of its life it has functioned very well without the word. The word derives from the Latin root *humilis*, or humble. Humility is a core feature of humanism, something not appreciated fully, even by many humanists. Grounded as it is in the notion of humility, humanism is a rejection of notions that serve to inflate our sense of self-importance. In this way, humanism is a rejection of the **transcendental temptation** and other forms of **anthropocentric conceit**.

Humanism as a *concept* has its origins in ancient India, China, and Greece—each one arising independently—but the actual *word* was not coined until 1808, by the German educationist **Friedrich Immanuel Niethammer**. To make things more complicated, *humanist* existed as a word long before *humanism*, originating in the Renaissance. See the entry on **Renaissance humanism**. But as humanism is defined principally by its method rather than by its conclusions, the lack of a word to act as a catchall for those conclusions is a trivial issue.

HUMANISM, AFFIRMATIONS OF. Devised by **Paul Kurtz**, the affirmations are one of the best comprehensive summaries of what **humanism** is about. They first appeared in *Free Inquiry* magazine in the Spring 1987 issue, and since then have been a regular feature on the inside cover of each issue. They are as follows:

We are committed to the application of reason and science to the understanding of the universe and to the solving of human problems.

We deplore efforts to denigrate human intelligence, to seek to explain the world in supernatural terms, and to look outside nature for salvation.

We believe that scientific discovery and technology can contribute to the betterment of human life.

We believe in an open and pluralistic society and that democracy is the best guarantee of protecting human rights from authoritarian elites and repressive majorities.

We are committed to the principle of separation of church and state.

We cultivate the arts of negotiation and compromise as a means of resolving differences and achieving mutual understanding.

We are concerned with securing justice and fairness in society and with eliminating discrimination and intolerance.

We believe in supporting the disadvantaged and the handicapped so that they will be able to help themselves.

We attempt to transcend divisive parochial loyalties based on race, religion, gender, nationality, creed, class, sexual orientation, or ethnicity, and strive to work together for the common good of humanity.

We want to protect and enhance the earth, to preserve it for future generations, and to avoid inflicting needless suffering on others.

We believe in enjoying life here and now and in developing our creative talents to their fullest.

We believe in the cultivation of moral excellence.

We respect the right to privacy. Mature adults should be allowed to fulfill their aspirations, to express their sexual preferences, to exercise reproductive freedom, to have access to comprehensive and informed healthcare, and to die with dignity.

We believe in the common moral decencies: altruism, integrity, honesty, truthfulness, responsibility. Humanist ethics is amenable to critical, rational guidance. There are normative standards that we discover together. Moral principles are tested by their consequences.

We are deeply concerned with the moral education of our children. We want to nourish reason and compassion.

We are engaged by the arts no less than the sciences.

We are citizens of the universe and are excited by the discoveries still to be made in the cosmos.

We are skeptical of untested claims to knowledge, and we are open to novel ideas and seek new departures in our thinking.

We affirm humanism as a realistic alternative to theologies of despair and ideologies of violence and as a source of rich personal significance and genuine satisfaction in the service of others.

We believe in optimism rather than pessimism, hope rather then despair, learning in the place of dogma, truth instead of ignorance, joy rather than guilt or sin, tolerance in the place of fear, love instead of hatred, compassion over selfishness, beauty instead of ugliness, and reason rather than blind faith or irrationality.

We believe in the fullest realization of the best and noblest that we are capable of as human beings.

HUMANISM AS A RELIGION. There is a great deal of confusion about the status of humanism as a **religion**. Some religious-studies scholars, quite rightly, want to include humanism in their field of study by virtue of humanism being a comprehensive worldview. And from the other end of the spectrum, some of the more extreme fundamentalists in the United States want to call humanism a religion for the political reason of then being able to banish all modern learning, which they see as the tainted fruits of humanism, from the classroom. And then, just to confuse the issue still further, there is a section of humanists who are known as **religious humanists**.

The truth is that humanism is a comprehensive worldview that is not a religion. It is apparent with the **Asian traditions** that the concept of "religion" is problematic as an explanation. Much the same objection applies to humanism as well. Humanism has no founder, no **scripture**, no supposedly timeless creed, no acknowledgement of a sacred dimension with which we need to commune in some way. And yet, humanism has a comprehensive way of looking at the world. Humanism is not a religion but a **life stance**.

Unmoved by this, American fundamentalists often insist that humanism is a religion, not because they believe the claim, but because it would be politically useful to them were this to become a widely held view. They often cite a reference in *Torcaso v. Watkins* (1961) where **secular humanism** is listed along with Buddhism and some other beliefs as a religion without belief in **God**. What the fundamentalists don't say is that this reference is in a footnote, not in the actual legal decision, and what is said in footnotes has no legal standing whatsoever.

Far more important, however, is the Ninth Circuit's decision on *Peloza v. Capistrano Unified School District* (1994). There the court said quite clearly that "neither the Supreme Court, nor this circuit has ever held that evolutionism or secular humanism are "religious" for Establishment Clause purposes." It went on to define religious belief as involving a belief in a divine creator. This understanding was reiterated by the DC Circuit in 2000 in *Kalka v. Hawk*.

But just because humanism is not a religion doesn't mean that an unbridgeable gulf exists between the two worldviews. With goodwill on both sides, meaningful dialogue could take place. Contrary to common supposition, humanists have a lot in common with religious people. See the entries **talking past one another**, **moral truisms shared by us all**, and **what atheists and religious believers have in common**.

HUMANISM, BOOKS ABOUT. There is a large literature on humanism from a variety of standpoints. The best single volume introductions to humanism are *Embracing the Power of Humanism* (2000), *The Courage to Become* (1997), and *Affirmations* (2004), all by **Paul Kurtz**. Then there is *On Humanism* (2004) by Richard Norman; *Humanism: An Introduction* (2003) by **Jim Herrick**; and *Introduction to Humanism* (1996) by **Finngeir Hiorth**. *Humanism* (1997) by Tony Davies, is less reliable, dragging with it a lot of postmodernist baggage. Longer works on humanism include *What is Good? The Search for the Best Way to Live* (2003) by A. C. Grayling. This is excellent and accessible to nonspe-

cialist readers. Then there is *Forbidden Fruit: The Ethics of Humanism* (1988) by Paul Kurtz; *Humanism: Beliefs and Practices* (1999) by Jeaneane Fowler; and *In Search of Our Humanity* (2003) by Valerii Kuvakin.

The two best anthologies of humanism are *The Humanist Anthology* (1995, revised edition of 1961) edited by **Margaret Knight** and revised by Jim Herrick; and *Skepticism and Humanism: The New Paradigm* (2001) by Paul Kurtz.

The most accessible single-volume history of humanism is *The Humanist Tradition in the West* (1985) by Alan Bullock. While *What is Good?* is not strictly a history of humanism, it also serves very well in that capacity. Of more scholarly interest is *The Question of Humanism: Challenges and Possibilities* (1991) edited by David Goicoechea, John Luik, and Tim Madigan; and *Philosophy in Crisis: The Need for Reconstruction* (2001) by Mario Bunge.

HUMANISM, FOUNDATIONS OF. The true sign of the greatness of any **life stance** is whether it can be stated simply. Humanism is backed by great philosophical wealth, but it is also able to be expressed in simple truisms. The foundations of humanism are:

- Know yourself;
- Remember your humanity and forget the rest; and
- Live well and help others to live well.

The rest, as they say, is details. The foundational principles of a **good life** include these three outlooks, each of which is very ancient, predating all **monotheist** religions. See the entries on **Agathonism** and **only connect**.

HUMANISM IN THE ANCIENT WORLD. Humanism is one the oldest and most transcultural worldviews on Earth, beginning quite independently in India, China, and Greece. The **Carvakas** were the materialist school of thought (*darshana*) in India, being traceable to the sixth century BCE. Carvaka philosophy regarded the universe as interdependent and subject to perpetual **evolution**, with no deity, **immortality**, **soul**, or karma. The aim in life is to get the maximum amount of pleasure from it. This had various interpretations, from unalloyed hedonism on the one hand to an altruistic service to others on the principle that this will maximize both their **happiness** and one's own.

In contrast to India, the humanist strand in China became the principal strand of thought. This is largely, though by no means exclusively, due to the influence of **Kongfuzi**, who is known in the West by his latinized name, Confucius. Kongfuzi's genius involved transforming the **naturalism** and **humanism** latent in Chinese thinking into the strongest forces in Chinese thought to this day. He said that maintaining a distance from spiritual beings was a sign of wisdom; he expressed no opinion on the fate of **souls**, and never encouraged **prayer**.

In Greece, humanism can be traced back to the philosophers known as the **Pre-Socratics**, that is, philosophers active before **Socrates**. The first of them was **Thales**, the man credited as being the father of philosophy. Thales' claim to fame rests on being the first person who tried to explain the world not in terms of myths but by observation of the world as he actually saw it. Where **Homer** attributed the origin of all things to the **God** Oceanus, Thales taught that water was the prime element in all things.

The other thinkers who succeeded Thales took his thoughts in different directions, but their emphasis on studying the natural world and humanity's place in it remained the same. The humanist spirit was given its best voice by Socrates who, during the trial for his life, declared that the unexamined life is not worth living.

The humanist tradition of Greek thought received a check in the philosophy of **Plato**, and never fully recovered. Several Hellenistic movements, in particular **Epicureanism** and **Stoicism**, reflected important elements of humanist thought, but all in the end were incorporated or crushed by Platonism and then by Christianity. But the humanism of the ancient world was not extinct, only dormant, and its rediscovery in the Renaissance was the single most important cause of the cultural and intellectual reawakening of that age after centuries of darkness. See the entry on **Renaissance humanism**.

Further reading: J. M. Robertson, *A History of Freethought: Ancient and Modern*; James Thrower, *The Alternative Tradition*; Dale Riepe, *The Naturalistic Tradition in Indian Thought*; and Charles Freeman, *The Closing of the Western Mind*.

HUMANISM, PLANETARY. The broadest manifestation of **humanism**. And it makes sense, because humanism cannot work effectively on a scale lower than planetary. To speak of English humanism or Indian humanism is to limit humanism to one group of humans. To speak about Renaissance humanism is to speak about humanism at one point in time. To speak of **secular humanism** or **religious humanism** is to limit humanism along ideological lines. Even to speak about humanism runs the risk of making **speciesist** presumptions about *Homo sapiens* being of special interest or importance. And the monotheistic religions are careful to limit themselves in this way, creating a severe abyss between believers and **unbelievers**. But only with planetary humanism do the points that divide us take second place to the fact of our essential interdependence as a species, as well as our collective charge to protect and nourish the earth.

Paul Kurtz was the first person to speak of planetary humanism. Kurtz said, "Our actions should be judged by their effects on those we encounter in our communities of interaction. This must be extended to the larger planetary focus: the blue-green dot as viewed from outer space." Planetary humanism is the current expression of the **cosmic perspective**, which is so vital for us to adopt.

Planetary humanism is more than just

pious intention, it is the way the world is headed, however haphazardly. As **globalization** reshapes our world, and we find that the problems that afflict us are global problems which require global solutions, planetary humanism is the standard that can provide the framework in which *Homo sapiens* work out their problems in a sustainable, interdependent way. The **United Nations** is the organizational manifestation of planetary humanism and the **Millennium Development Goals**, the **Montreal Protocols**, and the **Kyoto Treaty** are some of the means by which it is given expression. See the entries on **Declaration of Interdependence: A New Global Ethics**, **cosmopolis**, and **global governance**.

Further reading: Paul Kurtz, *Humanist Manifesto 2000: A Call for a New Planetary Humanism*, and *Affirmations*.

HUMANISM, SEVEN THESES OF. A statement, in a specific order, of the intellectual foundations of **humanism** as conceived by Mario Bunge. As an proponent of **systemism**, which argues for a complex, interdependent understanding of things, Bunge begins with the cosmological, and works "up" from there. The seven theses of humanism are as follows:

(1) *Cosmological*: whatever exists is either natural or man-made.

(2) *Anthropological*: common features of humanity and more significant than the differences.

(3) *Axiological*: there are some basic human values, such as well-being, honesty, loyalty, solidarity, fairness, security, peace, and knowledge, and these are worth working, even fighting, for.

(4) *Epistemological*: it is possible to find out the truth about the world and ourselves with the help of experience, reason, imagination, and criticism.

(5) *Moral*: we should seek salvation in this world through work and thought.

(6) *Social*: liberty, equality, solidarity,

and expertise should be used in the management of the commonwealth.

(7) *Political*: while allowing freedom of and from religious worship we should work toward the attainment or maintenance of a secular state.

It is important to note the order in which these theses are given. Based solidly in the hard sciences, and on through the **social sciences**, Bunge's systemist account of humanism grounds it solidly in reliable information.

Further reading: Mario Bunge: *Philosophy in Crisis: The Need for Reconstruction*.

HUMANISM, SOCIAL PRINCIPLES OF. As noted in the entry on **humanism**, the political and social ideals of humanism have changed over the centuries more than the other three core components of humanism. **Paul Kurtz** has outlined what he called the basic principles of humanist **eupraxsophy**. These principles have been more or less constant throughout the history of humanism:

• the value attached to **social intelligence**;
• preference for democratic methods of persuasion;
• recognition of the value of education;
• giving reign to the peaceful negotiation of differences and compromise;
• the need to satisfy basic economic and cultural needs of the citizens;
• the need to end discrimination; and
• the ethical commitment to the world community as the object of our highest moral devotion.

Different branches of humanist civilization have supported these social principles with varying degrees of commitment, but no branch of humanist civilization has entirely ignored or disowned any of these principles. As with the other entries on aspects of humanism, there is no intention here to insist that humanists alone espouse these principles. Humanists do not have a **monopoly on** the truth. The point is that humanism is consistent with these principles. See the entry on the **Humanist's Decalogue**.

Further reading: Paul Kurtz, *Eupraxsophy: Living Without Religion*.

"HUMANISM," SOME ABERRANT USES OF. One of the problems with the term "humanism," is the variety of uses it can be put to. Two instances from recent literature are worth alerting the reader to.

Among some postmodernist writing and among artists influenced by such work, "humanist" is often employed to mean someone who retains a **dualist** view of life, with an immortal **soul** or some essential essence. These scholars then compete with one another to rid themselves of any last vestiges of what they call "residual humanism." This understanding is derived from the outlook of the thinkers we now call **Renaissance humanists**, and takes no account of more recent trends.

And with no little irony, the other aberrant use of the word "humanist" is from thinkers of the left or in the hard sciences. For many of these thinkers, "humanist" means someone in the social sciences—the humanities—who has little scientific understanding and has a preference for **glossogonous word-salad**. In other words, the very postmodernist thinkers who themselves are desperately ridding themselves of residual humanism!

Neither of these accounts of humanism is accurate because neither of them takes any account of what humanists themselves have been saying over the past three hundred years.

HUMANISM, WEAKNESSES OF. Humanism is unique among the major systems of belief in that it is candid about its weaknesses. When summing up humanist philosophy **Corliss Lamont** finished with this principle: "Humanism, in accordance with **scientific method**, believes in the unending questioning of basic assumptions and convictions, including its own." See the entry on **humanist philosophy, ten propositions of**. In that spirit, it is worth examining

the weaknesses of humanism, which would seem to include:

- its inability to offer traditional consolations in the face of suffering;
- the confusion arising from the many competing and incompatible understandings of the word (see the entry on **"humanism," some aberrant uses of**);
- its apparent inability to express itself simply;
- related to the above point is the overly cerebral image of humanism;
- its vulnerability to charges of **speciesism**; and
- the fact that much of its energy is devoted to the negative tasks of combating religious error rather than promoting the positive humanist outlook.

These are serious weaknesses. But no system is incapable of improvement, and the more fully one recognizes that fact, the better. See the entry on **atheism, insufficiency of**.

HUMANIST BELIEFS, THE TEN CORE. The Humanist Association of Canada has compiled this list of ten core beliefs. It defines **humanism** as "the betterment of humanity through the application of **reason** and **democracy**." The ten core beliefs of humanism are:

- the human species has evolved as, and remains as, part of nature;
- human **consciousness** is a function of the activity of the human brain;
- human beings require, to some extent, a system of belief in order to function;
- all forms of the **supernatural** are a myth;
- we are capable of great achievement, both for the good and for the worse;
- our range of behaviors has not been preordained;
- those of us who are aware of how our beliefs impact on others are more likely to act ethically;

- we all deserve equality of opportunity;
- human life on earth is fragile and requires our care and attention; and
- our destiny is not preordained but is in our hands.

The compilers insist that these ten core beliefs are not just another **command morality**. They are simply a set of beliefs that bring humanists together and as such "shows how Humanist beliefs are different from those of organized religions—and also from those of political parties." See the entries on **humanist family values**; **humanist principles**; **humanist values**; **humanist virtues**; **Humanist's Decalogue**; and **Affirmation of Humanism for Kids**.

Further reading: Humanist Association of Canada, *The Ten Core Beliefs of Humanists*.

HUMANIST FAMILY VALUES. In response to the avalanche of invective from the American Religious Right, in the beginning of 1999, the **Council for Secular Humanism** outlined a set of humanist family values. They go as follows:

(1) People should be free to choose their own family structure without fear of discrimination, whether they be nuclear family, single parent, extended family, married, or unmarried.

(2) People should be able to marry across any racial, religious, or creedal divide. People of the same sex should also be able to marry.

(3) All marriages, regardless of their structure, should be based on the equality of each partner.

(4) Family members should be free from all forms of mental, physical, and sexual abuse, including marital rape.

(5) Children have a right to the full love, care, and attention of their caregivers.

(6) Adoption or custody decisions should be made in the interests of the children's welfare, not on some religious or social test.

(7) Children have the right to proper medical care and caregivers do not have the right to withhold treatment or impose bizarre treatments in accordance with their religious beliefs.

(8) Children have the right to an education free from indoctrination and with as little regard to the financial circumstances of the caregivers as possible.

(9) People must be free to choose the birth control measures best suited to their needs and sexual health, without being subjected to outside interference.

(10) In a world of rapid change, we must not become bogged down in stale formulas from the past as to how families should be constituted.

See the entries on **family values**; **humanist principles**; **humanist beliefs, the ten core**; **humanist values**; **humanist virtues**; **Humanist's Decalogue**; and **Affirmation of Humanism for Kids**.

Further reading: Matt Cherry and Molleen Matsumura, "A Vision of Families for the Twenty-First Century," *Free Inquiry* 19, no. 1 (Winter 1998/99): 25–26.

HUMANIST MANIFESTO I. A document signed in 1933 by thirty-three American Unitarian ministers and **John Dewey**, the pragmatist philosopher. The manifesto was drafted principally by the philosopher Roy Wood Sellars (1880–1973) and the Unitarian minister Raymond Bragg (1902–1979). The *Humanist Manifesto*, as it was originally called (the "I" was added later) brought together developments in liberal religious thinking that had taken place since the turn of the twentieth century.

It is an important document in **religious humanism** but was never able to galvanize the wider humanist community. For example, **Corliss Lamont** didn't sign the manifesto, being unhappy with the references to religious humanism and thinking it altogether too vague. And representatives of the **ethical**

culture movement refused to sign it because they deemed it too secular. And apart from Dewey and Sellars, the manifesto was ignored by all major philosophers who were otherwise sympathetic to **humanism**. An attempt by the Unitarian minister Charles Francis Potter (1885–1962) to release a revised version came to nothing.

Further reading: William F. Schulz, *Making the Manifesto: The Birth of Religious Humanism*.

HUMANIST MANIFESTO II. A document signed in 1973 by 261 prominent thinkers and leaders from around the world. *Humanist Manifesto II* was drafted as the successor manifesto to the *Humanist Manifesto I*, which was then forty years old. It was drafted by **Paul Kurtz** and Edwin H. Wilson (1899–1993), an important signatory of the *Humanist Manifesto I*. The *Humanist Manifesto II* was a great improvement on the original for three main reasons:

- it was much more specific about what humanism actually is;
- it dropped the confusing attempt to characterize humanism as a religion; and
- it attracted a great deal more support from prominent thinkers.

While the *Humanist Manifesto II* was a more consistently secular document, it was not antireligious in an unhelpful way. It acknowledged that religion can inspire dedication to commendable ethical ideals. However, it also noted that dogmatism does a great disservice to human welfare.

It made eighteen main points, grouped into the fields of religion, ethics, the individual, democratic society, and humanity as a whole. The main points were:

- moral values derive from human experience;
- reason and intelligence are humanity's most effective instruments;
- economic systems should be judged by

how they help humanity, rather than along ideological lines; as well as
- affirming the moral equality of all;
- calling to transcend the limits of national sovereignty; and
- adopting planetary solutions to planetary problems.

Without using the phrase, the *Humanist Manifesto II* was a call for **planetary humanism**. "What more daring a goal for humankind," the *Manifesto* concluded, "than for each person to become, in ideal as well as in practice, a citizen of a world community. It is a classical vision; we can now give it new vitality." See the entry on **cosmopolis**.

HUMANIST MANIFESTO III. A one-page affirmation of humanist principles devised in 2003 by the **American Humanist Association**. The main points of the Humanist Manifesto III are:

- knowledge of the world is derived by observation, experimentation, and rational analysis;
- humans are an integral part of nature, the result of unguided evolutionary change;
- ethical values are derived from human need and interest as tested by experience;
- life's fulfillment emerges from individual participation in the service of human ideals;
- humans are social by nature and find meaning in relationships; and
- working to benefit society maximizes human happiness.

Further reading: www.americanhumanist.org.

HUMANIST MANIFESTO 2000. Issued by the **International Academy of Humanism**, the *Humanist Manifesto 2000* is by far the most authoritative restatement of the humanist position. It introduced the concept of **planetary humanism**, which was a logical step from the principles outlined in the academy's earlier **Declaration of Interdependence**, issued in 1988. As no one country is able fully to master its own economic destiny in a globalized world, the manifesto called for an awareness of needs at the planetary level, rather than at the national level. It outlined **fundamentalism** and **postmodernism** as the principal adversaries to a program of planetary humanism. It made a point of distinguishing **religion** in general from fundamentalism in particular. As part of outlining a new global agenda, the manifesto called for:

- backing the **United Nations** as the principal coercive agency of the world;
- recognizing overpopulation as one of the most fundamental causes of world distress;
- supporting the existing international conventions regarding human rights;
- fighting **tax avoidance** among the largest multinational corporations;
- developing a suitably transnational system of international law; and
- promoting a greater effort to raise awareness of and to combat environmental deterioration.

In order to put this agenda into effect, the *Humanist Manifesto 2000* advocated:

- an effective world government based on popular elections;
- a workable international security system;
- increasing the powers of the World Court;
- the creation of an effective planetary environmental monitoring body;
- planning an international system of taxation for the sole purpose of assisting the underdeveloped nations;
- development of global institutions to monitor and regulate the behavior of multinational corporations; and
- a system to keep alive the free market of ideas.

Humanist Manifesto 2000 was a visionary plea for rationality and **global governance**. It was signed by a wide variety of some of the most reputable academic and other leaders in the world at the time.

Further reading: Paul Kurtz, *Humanist Manifesto 2000*.

HUMANIST PHILOSOPHY, TEN PROPOSITIONS OF. The humanist thinker **Corliss Lamont** wrote an influential work of humanist thought which went through several editions. In that book he outlined what he called the ten central propositions of humanist philosophy.

(1) Humanism believes in a naturalistic metaphysics or attitude toward the universe that considers all forms of the supernatural as myth.

(2) Man is an evolutionary product of the nature of which he is a part and has no survival after death.

(3) Having its ultimate faith in man, humanists believe that human beings possess the power of solving their own problems, through reliance primarily upon reason and scientific method applied with courage and vision.

(4) Humans possess genuine freedom of creative choice and action, and are, within certain objective limits, the masters of their own destiny.

(5) Humanism grounds all human values in this-earthly experiences and relationships, and holds as its highest goal the this-worldly happiness, freedom, and progress—economic, cultural, and ethical—of all mankind.

(6) Humanism believes that the individual attains the good life by harmoniously combining personal satisfactions and continuous self-development with significant work and other activities that contribute to the welfare of the community.

(7) The widest possible development of art and awareness of beauty, including the appreciation of nature's loveliness

and splendor is encouraged, so that the aesthetic experience may become a pervasive reality in the life of man.

(8) Worldwide democracy, peace, and a high standard of living on the foundations of a flourishing world order are essential.

(9) The complete social implementation of reason and scientific method, and thereby in the use of democratic procedures, including full freedom of expression and civil liberties, throughout all areas of economic, political, and cultural life is essential.

(10) Humanism, in accordance with scientific method, believes in the unending questioning of basic assumptions and convictions, including its own.

Most of Lamont's formulations of the philosophy of humanism still make excellent reading, although the wording of one or two of them would now be considered unfortunate. Proposition three, for instance, has a flavor of **anthropocentric conceit** to it. However, the danger of getting carried away with ourselves is countered in the tenth proposition. Humanism is the only major system of belief that includes as an item of central importance the questioning of its own assumptions. See the entry on **humanism, weaknesses of**. Also, see the entries on **humanist family values**; **humanist beliefs, the ten core**; **humanist principles**; **humanist values**; **humanist virtues**; **Humanist's Decalogue**; and **Affirmation of Humanism for Kids**.

Further reading: Corliss Lamont, *The Philosophy of Humanism*.

HUMANIST PHILOSOPHY, THREE STRANDS OF. The Dutch humanist philosopher **Jaap van Praag**, outlined what he saw as three main strands of humanist philosophy over its long history:

• *moral and reflective humanism*, such as the **Epicureans**, **Epictetus**, philosophical

Taoism, and German humanist thought down to Karl Jaspers (1883–1969);

• *social humanism*, with **Kongfuzi**, **Jeremy Bentham**, and **M. N. Roy** as prime exemplars; and

• *empirical humanism*, stretching from the **Atomists** and **Wang Chong** down to logical positivism, **Bertrand Russell**, and **humanistic psychology**.

This is a very worthwhile observation. It helps reveal the complexity and range of **humanism**. I have given a broader range of examples of these traditions than van Praag, who limited himself mainly to European examples. Van Praag dated humanism from the European Renaissance, and took little notice of the tremendous contributions of ancient Greece or the **Asian traditions**.

Further reading: Jaap van Praag, *The Foundations of Humanism*.

HUMANIST PRINCIPLES. The principles of **humanism**, as outlined by **Paul Kurtz**, are as follows:

• commitment to **free inquiry** and the open mind;

• belief in the courage to live without fear or trembling;

• confidence in the power of human creativeness, inventiveness, and achievement;

• constant efforts to improve the human condition, mitigate suffering, and combat disease, war, and cruelty;

• respect for the **rights** of others;

• dedication to the preciousness and dignity of the individual;

• cultivation of happiness and the full life;

• emphasis on **love**, shared experience, and human joy;

• **tolerance** of other points of view and styles of life;

• belief in social justice and humanitarian aid;

• encouragement of a world community

which transcends national, ethnic, sexual, and racial barriers;
- emphasis on compromise and negotiation of differences; and
- belief in a free, open, pluralistic, and democratic society.

Kurtz drew up this list in 1983 and deliberately abstained from lengthy commentary upon it. He added that humanist morality is not cast in stone; we can always look to improving our principles and, in the light of new evidence, are morally required to do so. See the entries on **humanist beliefs, the ten core**; **Humanist Decalogue**; and **humanist family values**.

Further reading, Paul Kurtz, *In Defense of Secular Humanism*.

HUMANIST-THEMED FILMS. A complete list of humanist-themed films would be unwieldy, impossibly broad, and quickly outdated. However, here is a sample of films in English which contain important and interesting humanistic elements. Films such as *Black Robe* and *At Play in the Fields of the Lord* (both 1991) explore the arrogance inherent in **monotheism**; missionaries sent to convert godless Indians find that the tribes are neither barbaric nor in need of Christian salvation. On the topic of plurality of belief, the infamously libertine Marquis de Sade (1740–1814) is the subject of *Quills* (2000), a film that embraces freedom of inquiry and expression. *The Magdalene Sisters* (2003) tells the true story of tens of thousands of Irish women sent to Catholic asylums after being outcast by their strongly moralistic society. Instead of being sheltered, the women were exploited and abused, forced to toil for decades in slavelike conditions in penance for their real and imagined sins.

Humor, an important (and often overlooked) element in **humanism**, is seen in films such as the classic **Monty Python**'s *The Life of Brian* (1979), which follows a hapless and reluctant Jesus-type character through an irreverent and hilarious persecution and cru-

cifixion. More recently, the comedy *Saved!* (2004), though ultimately a proreligion film, challenges blind **dogmatism** and shows how the religious mind can misdivine and rationalize an unknowable deity's desires.

Turning to science, *Contact* (1997), based on the book by **Carl Sagan**, features a cinematic rarity—a strong, intelligent, independent atheist women as a hero. Literate and imaginative, the film shows how the universe's natural beauty can inspire a **cosmic perspective** entirely without any religious or supernatural significance, and reminds us of our literal and figurative place in the universe.

Not surprisingly, many horror films have touched on the evils of religion. *Frailty* (2002) is a taut, original horror film about what happens when people believe that **God** directs them to do evil. The title refers to the fallibility of human belief and perception, and how easily we can be deceived. Ironically, *The Passion of the Christ* (2004) might be considered a humanist film insofar as it exposes a visceral sadism rarely acknowledged in Catholic doctrine. It highlights varied passionate (yet incongruous) interpretations that religious texts can produce among fervent believers. Finally, and perhaps most improbably, there is George Romero's overlooked gem *Martin* (1978), about a young man who may (or may not) be a vampire yet is persecuted as one. The title character utters a simple yet profoundly skeptical and humanist message: "There is no magic."

Further reading: www.radfordreviews .com/rr.html.

HUMANIST-THEMED NOVELS. As with the entry on **humanist-themed films**, this entry can only be a partial and subjective survey. But for what it's worth, here is an assortment of excellent novels, each of which explores some theme significant to humanists.

There are a lot of fine books that explore the theme of people's lives having been impoverished by particularly misanthropic versions of **religion**. Among the best would be *Shame* (English translation, 1994) by

Taslima Nasrin, *The Lonely Passion of Judith Hearne* (1955) by Brian Moore (1921–1999), and the *Dark Materials* trilogy (1995–2001) by **Philip Pullman**. In *Babbitt* (1922) and *Elmer Gantry* (1927), Sinclair Lewis (1885–1951) takes a slightly more satirical tone, although these novels remain serious criticisms of the banality of modern religion, among other things. In the same vein is **H. G. Wells**'s undervalued classic *Christina Alberta's Father* (1925). Also well worth reading is *Messiah* (1959) by Gore Vidal. The specific genre of criticism of the Catholic Church has also been attempted on many occasions, but in few cases better than **Emile Zola**'s *Lourdes* (1894) and *Rome* (1896), or **Anatole France**'s satire, *Penguin Island* (1908). In France's *The Gods Are Athirst* (1912) we are treated to a truly rare event; the hero of the book is an atheist, and he is heroic *because* he is an atheist. Much more grim is **Margaret Atwood**'s *The Handmaid's Tale* (1982), a story set in a fundamentalist state of the future. Other books about religion, but less clearly opposed to its more destructive features is *The Bell* (1958) by **Iris Murdoch**, *Plumb* (1978) by **Maurice Gee**, *Knowledge of Angels* (1994) by Jill Paton Walsh, and *The Book Against God* (2003) by James Wood.

There is a huge literature of dystopias about the future, but among the best would be *The War of the Worlds* (1898) and *Mr. Blettsworthy on Rampole Island* (1929) both by H. G. Wells, *Brave New World* (1932) by Aldous Huxley, *Nineteen Eighty-Four* (1948) by George Orwell, *Oryx and Crake* (2003) by Margaret Atwood, and *Jennifer Government* (2003) by Max Barry. The focus of the warnings range from science, government, or corporations, but in each case the guilty party is beyond reasonable social control. These books also give lie to the frequently repeated charge of the optimism of **humanism**. Each of these authors is a humanist, and each is pretty pessimistic about human nature generally.

Truly excellent books about the mystery of being human would include *Nausea* (1938) by

Jean-Paul Sartre, *The Grapes of Wrath* (1939) by John Steinbeck (1902– 1968), and *A Fine Balance* (1995) by Rohinton Mistry. A surprisingly successful attempt to articulate what could be called **Enlightenment** values in novel form is *The Curious Enlightenment of Professor Caritat* (1995) by Steven Lukes. Another attempt at a similar idea, though a very different sort of book, is *Message to the Planet* (1989) by Iris Murdoch.

Obviously this by no means exhausts the range of excellent novels there are to read. But each of them remains well worth reading.

HUMANIST-THEMED WEB SITES. Most of the organizations mentioned in this dictionary maintain a Web site of some sort. And a growing number of intellectuals have their own site. Most of them are worth exploring. Among those with a broadly freethinking theme, a few are particularly worth mentioning. Without doubt, the *Secular Web* is the most comprehensive Web-based resource on the Net. It is maintained by a nonprofit organization called Internet Infidels. It is well organized and has a range of different approaches, services, and styles of discussion and interaction. The *Secular Web* also maintains the *Atheist Web*. It is the stated goal of Internet Infidels to promote and defend **atheism** on the Net, and they certainly do that very effectively.

Another good site is *About Atheism and Agnosticism*, maintained by Austin Cline. This is a section of the *About* site, which maintains a "Religion and Spirituality" section and, very evenhandedly, includes this one on **agnosticism** and atheism. Cline studied German literature at Princeton, and while there, founded the Princeton Freethought Association. The best site devoted to **humanism** is *Secularhumanism.org*. A site with a scientific bent is *Naturalism.org*, an excellent site for reviews, discussion, and other material related to **naturalism**. It is run by Tom Clark.

One of the best of the many skeptic sites is the *Skeptiseum*, overseen by **Joe Nickell**.

The *Skeptiseum* features images from a variety of subjects close to contemporary skepticism, including the Shroud of Turin, weeping icons, UFOs, and many other bizarre and wacky things.

Among the sites with selections of articles from a wide range of sources, none is better than *Arts and Letters Daily*. This site alone makes the Web worthwhile. Also excellent is *Butterflies and Wheels*, a site devoted to the **smiting of humbug**, particularly in its **postmodernist** forms. Other good sites are *Philosophynews.com* and *Criticalrealism .demon.co.uk*. An excellent news site from a **freethought** perspective is the *Rationalist International*, run by Sanal Edamaruku from New Delhi, India (http://www.rationalist international.net).

One of the cleverest satires on the Net is the *Landover Baptist Church* site (http://www.landoverbaptist.org). To begin with, you can be forgiven for thinking you've strayed onto another splenetic Evangelical site. But then it starts to dawn on you that all is not right. The site's subtitle is "The Largest, Most Powerful Assembly of People to Ever Exist! Unsaved are NOT Welcome." By this time you are ready for other clues, for instance the advertisement for "This month's banned book: Jesus says 'Burn it now!'" This site is a very clever satire on the follies of **fundamentalism**.

HUMANIST VALUES. According to the Norwegian philosopher **Finngeir Hiorth**, the classical humanistic values are freedom, **reason**, and **tolerance**. Contemporary secular humanists are committed to an open and pluralistic society and emphasize the value of tolerance. Social and political problems should as far as possible be solved by democratic methods.

Hiorth then goes on to itemize the highest values of **secular humanism** as compassion, democratic pluralism, equality, fairness, a **good life**, honesty, **human dignity** (or personal worth), justice, human **rights** (including the right to privacy), peaceful means in solving conflicts, **reason**, responsibility, **scientific methods** and results, self-determination, sincerity, and **toleration**. From this it follows that discrimination, whether because of class, creed, ethnicity, **gender**, nationality, race, **religion**, sexual orientation, intolerance, irrationality, or **supernaturalism** are to be condemned.

The British philosopher A. C. Grayling outlined a similar list of humanist values. After making a historical survey of humanist values through the ancient world, the Renaissance, the **Enlightenment**, and the modern world, Grayling summed them up:

- individual liberty;
- the pursuit of **knowledge**;
- the cultivation of pleasures that do not harm others;
- the satisfaction of art;
- personal relationships; and
- a sense of belonging to the human community.

This series of values is also shared by Confucian thinkers. See the entry on the **Three Ways and the Eight Steps**.

Neither Hiorth nor Grayling are saying that these values are exclusive to humanists. No system of belief has a **monopoly on truth**. What they are saying is that these values are entirely consistent with humanism. See also the entries on the **Principle of Countermisery**, **Humanist Decalogue**, and **humanist family values**.

Further reading: Finngeir Hiorth, *Values*; and A. C. Grayling, *What is Good? The Search for the Best Way to Live*. See also Valerii Kuvakin, *In Search of Our Humanity*.

HUMANIST VIRTUES. Virtues are slightly different from **values** in that **virtues** are qualities we possess, or should seek to possess, as human beings. The core humanist virtues as outlined by **Paul Kurtz** include:

- *courage*, the affirmation of life and self-reliance;
- *cognition*, the rational powers we pos-

sess to enrich our lives; and

- *caring*, the benevolence toward others that enrich us all.

These, Kurtz argues, are the core virtues we need to take control of our lives and live them fully. It is interesting to see that the American moral philosopher James Gouinlock has determined a similar list of what he calls core virtues. Gouinlock does not call them humanist virtues, although clearly they are humanist in outlook. Gouinlock's list of core virtues is:

- *rationality*, the sincere attempt to seek the truth;
- *courage*, the willingness to question our own beliefs; and
- *respect for persons*, the quality of being impartially respectful of everyone.

Gouinlock sees these core virtues because they are irreducible and interdependent. Apart from the slight differences of order and emphasis, these virtues are the same and can provide a simple framework by which people can live a morally sound, intellectually vigorous and laughter-filled life. See the entries on **veracity**, **Humanist's Decalogue**, and **humanist family values**.

Further reading: Paul Kurtz, *The Courage to Become*; and James Gouinlock, *Rediscovering the Moral Life*.

HUMANISTIC JUDAISM, SOCIETY OF.

American-based organization representing the humanistic wing of Judaism, created by Sherman Wine in 1969. It is the purpose of Humanistic Judaism to extol Judaism as a culture, rather than as a **religion**. Composed originally of eight families outside of Detroit, Humanistic Judaism now claims about forty thousand members in forty different locations around the United States.

Wine grew up in the shadow of the holocaust, and his principal conclusion from those years was that there isn't any supernatural or **magic** dimension and that one must make the best of one's life for oneself. He studied phi-

losophy at the University of Michigan before enrolling at the progressive Hebrew Union College in Cincinnati, Ohio. After his ordination in 1956, Wine worked at a synagogue in his hometown of Detroit, before a spell as army chaplain in Korea in 1957 and 1958.

After three years running a Reform congregation in Windsor, Ontario, Rabbi Wine's long trajectory to **humanism** came to a head. In 1963 he founded the Birmingham Temple on the outskirts of Detroit, and was immediately plunged into a great deal of acrimonious opposition. In 1969 he founded the Society for Humanistic Judaism to act as an advocacy organization for his brand of humanism. It took many years before humanistic Judaism was acknowledged by other Jewish organizations as a legitimate expression of Jewish identity.

HUMANISTIC PSYCHOLOGY.

An influential branch of psychology associated with Abraham Maslow (1908–1970), Erich Fromm (1900–1980), and Carl Rogers (1902–1987). Humanistic psychology owed a large intellectual debt to **existentialism**. And as articulated by Maslow, it understood things in terms of a hierarchy. Only when basic **human needs** are satisfied can the higher needs be addressed. This conforms closely to the distinction of human needs into biogenic and sociogenic needs as articulated by **Paul Kurtz**.

According to humanistic psychology, any success in the higher needs of love, fulfillment, and self-actualization can happen only on the solid foundation of our lower needs having been seen to. Self-actualization or, in Rogers's language, becoming a person, is a process of understanding oneself and achieving a sense of autonomy. This is not the same as aloofness. Self-actualization is where our love for, and interaction with, others is not determined by external considerations of seeking approval or avoiding censure, but for internal reasons of recognizing the intrinsic value of the other person.

Humanistic psychology has been very

influential, not least in the **feminism** of writers such as **Betty Friedan**. It has been criticized as being overly individualistic, and undervaluing the role of **community** in our lives. Perhaps more importantly, and particularly in the case of Maslow, humanistic psychology had the fault of being aggressive in its attitude toward egalitarianism. Failure to achieve self-actualization was often couched in contemptuous terms reminiscent of earlier puritanism. Somehow, failure to achieve self-actualization implied some moral fault on the individual. Maslow was an admirer of **Friedrich Nietzsche**, and concepts like self-actualization start looking rather like the **Overman**. Maslow coined the word "Eupsychia," which was his future utopia and was run by (and, it would seem, for) the self-actualized few.

HUMANISTICS. A word used mainly by Dutch humanists, which refers to the theory of **humanism**. Humanistics is often spoken about in the language of **phenomenology**. **Jaap van Praag** spoke of humanistics as "the systematic, phenomenological reproduction of a model of the humanist conviction." Rather unhelpfully, van Praag recommended humanistics as taking "humanist thinking out of the area of a certain vagueness, while its content maintains the openness that is characteristic of this thinking."

More recently, the **University of Humanist Studies** (UVH) speaks of humanistics as a multidisciplinary science drawing from the "humanities, the social, behavioral and cultural sciences, epistemology and methodology." Much of the UVH is dedicated to training counselors, so humanistics in this context is the actively engaged empathizing with others.

Further reading: Jaap van Praag, *Foundations of Humanism*; and Annemie Halsema and Douwe van Houten, eds., *Empowering Humanity: State of the Art in Humanistics*.

HUMANIST'S DECALOGUE. A restatement of humanist morals, composed by the English sociologist Ronald Fletcher (1921–1992). The Humanist's Decalogue originally appeared in the English magazine *New Society*, and was reprinted in 1964 by Pioneer Press, which was aligned with the **National Secular Society**. The Humanist's Decalogue says:

(1) Never accept authority unless, in your own seriously considered view, there are good grounds to do so.
(2) Base your conduct upon simple human principles.
(3) Strive to eliminate war.
(4) Strive to eliminate **poverty** and work for greater prosperity for everyone.
(5) Don't be a snob, don't worry about labels, and work for a broader fellowship in society.
(6) In sexual behavior, use your brains as well as your genitals, and always in that order.
(7) Take the necessary steps to enjoy family life and **marriage**.
(8) Keep the law.
(9) Commit yourself to active citizenship.
(10) Have confidence in the modern world and in your powers to improve it.

As this decalogue suggests, Fletcher was a civilized and humane man, and not without a sense of **humor**. It is also a code of behavior which is admirably suited to inculcating the responsibility, civic virtues, and **altruism** that is central to humanist morals. And it shouldn't need to be said, but the Humanist's Decalogue was not being offered as an alternative **command morality**. As Fletcher said, "I cannot lay claim to having had conversations with the Almighty, and, perhaps in consequence, I possess neither the certitude of Moses nor his extreme simplicity of mind and utterance." See the entries, **humanism, social principles of**; **humanist principles**; **humanist values**; and **humanist virtues**.

Further reading: Ronald Fletcher, *Ten Non-Commandments: A Humanist's Decalogue*.

HUMBUG, SMITER OF. "Humbug" is a wonderful word, and usually refers to pompous or windy nonsense spouted by hypocrites. There is an awful lot of it about. Every hypocritical televangelist or **virtuecrat** is liable to spout humbug. The word can quickly become a noun, referring to the person himself as a humbug.

With this in mind, a smiter of humbug is a person who calls nonsense by its proper name and exposes the double standard which lurks behind it. **Ted Honderich** had the same thing in mind when he described **A. J. Ayer** as a "hussar against nonsense." Some of the greatest atheists, skeptics, and humanists have been smiters of humbug: **Voltaire**, **T. H. Huxley**, **Joseph McCabe**, **Emanuel Haldeman-Julius**, **L. Susan Stebbing**, **Ernest Gellner**, and **Richard Dawkins**. Smiting humbug, like **debunking**, is a noble profession, although usually a thankless one. And neither should smiting humbug be seen exclusively as a negative activity. Eradicating falsehood, if done with due humility and awareness of one's own fallibility, is a profoundly noble and positive activity. A classic work of humbug smiting is *An Outline of Bunk* (1929) by Haldeman-Julius, while *Leaps of Faith* (1996) by Nicholas Humphrey is an outstanding recent example.

HUME, DAVID (1711–1776). One of the most significant philosophers of all time as well as being of the more pleasant personalities from the ranks of philosophers. Hume lived most of his life in Edinburgh, Scotland, where he was loved by his friends and respected for his generosity as much as for his intellect. One of his close friends was **Adam Smith**. But even some of his friends couldn't believe that Hume could be these things and not be a Christian. And neither was Hume's genius apparent to his contemporaries: he was never thought sufficiently highly of to be given a university chair.

Bertrand Russell wrote that Hume's *Treatise of Human Nature* (1739–40) blew the temple of reason sky high. This is because Hume took **René Descartes** to task for his belief that **reason** is, and always will be, the most powerful force within us. Far from being able to dominate the passions, Hume wrote that reason can only ever be the slave of the passions. This did not mean that Hume believed we should obey our passions. His point was that we should be skeptical about grand theorizing about either reason or passion. Hume also concluded that nothing external to human beings can be morally normative. Hume's philosophy has cast a shadow over **command moralities** and **foundationalism** ever since. He carried these thoughts into the area of **ethics** in *Enquiry Concerning the Principles of Morals* (1748), which he thought his best book.

In *Dialogues Concerning Natural Religion* (1777), he contrived a dialogue between three people, each taking clearly recognized philosophical positions regarding **religion**. The character Hume clearly identified with was Philo, who was generally skeptical. It is possible that the *Dialogues* are an example of **parallel theology**. *Dialogues* has some of the most incisive arguments against the cosmological and teleological arguments for the existence of **God**. Predictably, all of Hume's works were placed on the **Index of Forbidden Books**.

One area of Hume's thought, which has not carried the day to the same extent, is his theory that we do not have a coherent, overall view of ourselves, but only a bundle of different perceptions. **Ernest Gellner** called this view "bundleman." If Hume means by this that human personality is complex and multifaceted, then the point is sound, but if he means we can have no coherent view of ourselves, that would be implausible.

Further reading: A. J. Ayer, *Hume*.

HUMMER. Presumably the last word in selfish, self-defeating consumerism. As if the large and gas-guzzling SUV's (Suburban Assault Vehicles in popular parlance) aren't bad enough, along come the Hummers. The Hummer is the civilian version of the military

Humvee, which stands for "High Mobility Multipurpose Wheeled Vehicle." Hummers are built on the same production line as Humvee's. The only differences are the creature comforts. And because they weigh more than 8,600 pounds, the US government does not require Hummers to meet federal fuel-efficiency regulations. No information on fuel economy is provided on Hummer's Web sites, but they are believed to get about ten miles to a gallon. Most Hummer fuel tanks hold thirty-two gallons.

They cost between $50,000 and $117,000, weigh 3,900 kg (8,600 pounds), and are 2.05 meters (six feet, nine inches) wide and 1.98 meters (almost six feet, five inches) high. Hummer Web sites exploit the military connection, talking about a "patented military paratrooper folding frame" and pedals of "military spec." However, the FAQ (frequently asked questions) page warns us the Hummer is not bullet proof.

Sir Harry Kroto, the Nobel Prize winner in chemistry and laureate of the **International Academy of Humanism**, has devised a scale, running from ten down to minus ten, which can provide consumers a clear assessment of the environmental impact of the item they are purchasing. This is called the **Positive and Negative Sustainability Quotient**. By any standard, the Hummer would attract the lowest possible negative sustainability quotient. The next question is, does anyone care?

HUMOR. One of the most important senses a human being can possess. The **absurdity** of life and the foolishness of so much of what human beings do puts a high value on humor. A sense of humor is often the key to a successful marriage; married couples often say that the thing they value most in their partner is their sense of humor. The Greek **atomist** philosopher **Democritus** was known as the laughing philosopher, for his unwavering sense of humor. The great English novelist **E. M. Forster** noted that the New Testament lacks the merest trace of humor, which accounts for much of Christianity's subsequent history.

And of course, **laughter** is good for you. While hatred and anger damage our bodies, laughter helps them. Humor is one of the most effective antidotes to **anthropocentric conceit**. See the entry on **fun**.

HUNGER. Along with thirst, the most primal lack that humans can suffer from. No human can develop when such a basic condition as hunger exists. Sustenance is a biogenic need (see the entry on **human needs**).

A **United Nations** report in 2003 found that hunger was once again on the rise around the world in the 1990s. After three decades of decline in world hunger, the UN report estimated that 840 million people (one in seven of the world's population) went hungry between 1999 and 2001 and that 4.5 million people join that number each year. Even in the United States, it is thought that ten million people go hungry, and a further twenty-one million stave hunger off thanks to charity food relief.

In virtually all cases, hunger is an avoidable condition which requires political will to solve. Hunger and its endpoint of famine do not occur because there is insufficient food to go around, but because the poor and defenceless cannot afford the food that is available. This is why many people go hungry, or even starve, in conditions of sufficiency of food. See the entry on **democracy**.

Further reading: Amartya Sen, *Development as Freedom*.

HUXLEY, JULIAN (1887–1975). Biologist, humanist, and prolific popularizer of science. Julian's pedigree was excellent, being the grandson of the famous biologist **T. H. Huxley**, and brother of the writer Aldous Huxley (1894–1963). Educated at Eton and Balliol College, Oxford, Huxley graduated with a zoology degree in 1909. He then roamed for many years, in and out of various academic institutions in Britain and abroad, but he was not suited to teaching. He was research associate at the Rice Institute in Houston, Texas, for six years until 1916, and in 1921 he organized an expedition to Spitzbergen. In 1932 he wrote *Problems of Relative Growth*, a study of the different rates of growth of different body parts, but his real strength was as a public intellectual with a broader range of interests. In the 1920s Huxley became involved with the **Rationalist Press Association**, which published many of his works of popular **science**.

Huxley's career as a popularizer of science took off after the publication of *The Science of Life* (1932), an influential popularization project undertaken with **H. G. Wells** and his son. Huxley is widely credited with recognizing the importance of the **neo-Darwinian synthesis**, about which he wrote in *Evolution: The Modern Synthesis* (1942). He was a pioneer in nature documentaries, being a coproducer of *Private Life of the Gannet* in 1934. Huxley received many honors and awards: he served as secretary of the Zoological Society of London from 1935 till 1942, he was elected a fellow of the Royal Society in 1938, and was knighted in 1958. He received the prestigious **Kalinga prize** for popularization of science in 1953.

He became a household name in Britain after World War II because of his regular appearances on the popular and influential BBC program, *Brains Trust*. In 1946 he was appointed as the first director-general of the newly founded United Nations Economic and Scientific Organization (UNESCO). He used this position to alert people to the growing problems associated with population expansion and environmental destruction. In 1952 Huxley was the elected the first president of the **International Humanist and Ethical Union**, and in 1963 he was the first president of the British Humanist Association.

His brand of **humanism** has not been his most successful legacy, largely because it persisted in recycling religious idioms and notions in a secularized context. His most important work in this field was *Religion Without Revelation*, published originally in 1927, and rewritten, not by Huxley, but by the prominent English humanist **H. J.**

Blackham, in 1957. Huxley also championed what he called evolutionary humanism, most notably in a series of essays he edited called *The Humanist Frame* (1961), which went off on an eccentric trajectory by endorsing the teleological notions of Pierre Teilhard de Chardin (1880–1955). He also advocated some blatant forms of **anthropocentric conceit** and **eugenics** long after both notions had dropped from favor.

HUXLEY, THOMAS HENRY (1825–1895). Scientist, **smiter of humbug**, public intellectual, and promoter of **Darwinism** in its earliest years. Huxley was the son of an impoverished schoolmaster and had only two years' formal schooling, but his prodigious talent ensured he received more chances than his humble origins would normally have allowed him. After a period in London as a medical apprentice, during which time he saw firsthand the poverty of many Londoners, Huxley joined the navy. From 1846 until 1850 he served as naval surgeon on the HMS *Rattlesnake*, which toured the Great Barrier Reef and New Guinea. This allowed Huxley to collect material for his research on various species of invertebrates. He was admitted into the Royal Society in 1851 for his work in this field. In 1854 he was appointed lecturer on natural history at the Royal School of Mines, from where he became an influential public intellectual.

When **Charles Darwin**'s *Origin of Species* appeared in 1859, Huxley quickly appreciated its revolutionary significance. He reportedly berated himself for not having thought of **natural selection**, the method Darwin showed was the driving force of **evolution**. Huxley's contribution came later, when he became Darwin's principal apologist in the English-speaking world. He reportedly wiped the floor with Samuel Wilberforce (1805–1873) at a famous debate on evolution in 1860 when he replied to a supercilious question about which side of his family descended from the apes. Huxley followed this up with his important book, *Evidence of Man's Place in Nature* (1863), which was the first serious application of Darwin's principle to human beings.

Huxley is also famous for coining the word "agnostic," in 1869. He felt that both **atheism** and theism inferred degrees of certainty about metaphysical questions that was inappropriate. **Agnosticism** was tremendously influential for the better part of a hundred years, although it is now a redundant concept.

But Huxley was by no means a thoroughgoing secularist. He secured election to the newly created school board in London in 1870 by opposing secularists and advocating the continued use of the Bible in schools. He saw the Bible as being well suited to cultivating a historic sense in young people. Later in his life he accepted that strict secularity of education was the better course, but by this time he had served his time on the school board.

Huxley received just about every major public prize and award the English-speaking world could bestow, and he was widely admired. He was also deeply admired by the founders of the **Rationalist Press Association**, which published many of his writings. Huxley was grandfather to the famous biologist **Julian Huxley** and Aldous Huxley, (1894–1963) the novelist.

Further reading: Adrian Desmond, *Huxley*.

HYLOZOISM. A name given by later Greeks to the **Pre-Socratic** philosophers from Ionia, where **philosophy** and **science** were born. The hylozoists were said to be those who think matter is alive. They didn't bring in supernaturalist notions to explain the world. It is an important fact that science and philosophy began by people whose philosophy was naturalist and whose method of inquiry was scientific. Critics of hylozoism argue that the idea is so general as to be meaningless.

HYPATIA (355?–415 CE). Pagan philosopher, mathematician, and astronomer who worked in Alexandria. Hypatia was the first woman to make a substantial contribution to mathematics. The daughter of Theon, an important philosopher and mathematician, Hypatia rose to become head of the Platonist school in Alexandria in about 400 CE, where she earned a reputation for teaching with greater scientific precision and liveliness than was customary. Her main work revolved around improving notions of the cone, an important concept in Ptolemaic astronomy. She cowrote with her father learned commentaries on Ptolemy's works, and in her own right on Apollonius's work *Conics*, and Diophantus's work *Arithmetica*.

Hypatia was murdered by a Christian mob incited to violence by Cyril (later St. Cyril), bishop of Alexandria. It is said that her skin was scraped off her still living body with conch shells. Cyril whipped up hysteria among the mob about the impropriety of a woman philosopher, accusing her of witchcraft. Hypatia was known for her support of Orestes, the principal civil leader in the city. Orestes, a Christian, was a powerful counterbalance to the aspirations of Cyril.

I

IAROSLAVSKII, EMELIAN (1878–1943). One of the early leaders of militant **atheism** in the Soviet Union. Minei Izrailovich Gubelman was born in the remote Siberian town of Chita, where his father was in exile. Under his assumed name of Emelian Iaroslavskii, he began his career as a revolutionary while still a young man. In 1917 he participated in the Bolshevik takeover of Moscow and became the first commissar of the Moscow region. Through the 1920s he was secretary of the Central Control Commission of the Communist party and was on the editorial board of a number of important papers and journals, including the main antireligious paper *Bezbozhik* (until 1941). He led the Society of Old Bolsheviks and in 1924 was put in charge of the newly created League of the Godless, a position he held until his death. Apart from an antireligious tract written in 1907, Iaroslavskii had no particular qualifications to run the league. He oversaw the publication of *The Bible for Believers and Non-Believers* (1923–24), which went through ten editions through the 1920s and 1930s. Among his other works were *Party Ethics* (1924) and *Morals and the Way of Life* (1926). The League of the Militant Godless began cooperating with the **World Union of Freethinkers** in 1936.

Despite being an Old Bolshevik and having been specifically criticized by Stalin in 1931, Iaroslavskii survived the purges of the 1930s. In fact, a saccharined account of the purges (in their early stages) entitled *Bolshevik Verification and Purging of the Party Ranks*, appeared under his name in 1933. He died of natural causes in 1943, although the activities of the league had been drastically curtailed after the Nazi invasion in June 1941.

Iaroslavskii was, by Bolshevik standards, a voice of moderation. He was opposed to direct legislation to penalize the churches or the practice of religion. He supported the importance of instruction on the iniquity of **religion**, particularly for the peasantry. He wanted cadres involved in this process to be educated with respect to the history of the orthodox church and, mythology, as well as Marxism-Leninism. Iaroslavskii also encouraged the creation of a series of secular ceremonies which could replace the religious rites of passage. His death coincided with the Russian rapprochement with the orthodox church, in the interests of the war effort. See the entry on **Bonch-Bruevich, Vladimir**.

Further reading: Daniel Peris, *Storming the Heavens: The Soviet League of the Militant Godless*.

IBSEN, HENRIK (1828–1906). Norwegian dramatist who changed the face of modern theater. When Ibsen was still young his father went bankrupt, leaving him to fend for himself. From the age of sixteen he worked as a chemist's assistant, then as a journalist in Bergen. He became involved in a theater in Bergen, quickly becoming its director and resident playwright. In 1857 he moved to Christiania (Oslo), where he was appointed director of the national Norwegian Theater. When that enterprise went bankrupt in 1863, Ibsen went to Europe, mainly Germany, for several years.

His best known plays are *Peer Gynt* (1867), *A Doll's House* (1879), and *Hedda Gabler* (1890). In *The Emperor and the Galilean* (1876) Ibsen depicted Roman **paganism** favorably against Christianity. He stripped the theater of its many fripperies and fantasies and made it a vehicle for serious discussion of contemporary social issues. He had no patience for the many hypocrisies that attended conventional manners and morals. Neither was he prepared to take on the role of prophet. And while he was more than usually aware of the role irrational forces play in determining our behavior, he was not prepared to go as far as his contemporary **August Strindberg** did.

Ibsen was very influential across Europe and attracted some powerful advocates, among them the Danish critic Georg Brandes (1842–1927) and George Bernard Shaw (1856–1950) in Britain. Brandes was influential in crystallizing Ibsen's genial **agnosticism** into a more militant rejection of **religion** as illusion. Ibsen was an honorary member of the International Freethought Federation, which later became the **World Union of Freethinkers**.

IDEAL OBSERVER THEORY. A theory of justification in **ethics** derived originally from British thinkers in the eighteenth century but developed in the twentieth century by the American philosopher Roderick Firth (1917–1987). Firth developed the ideal observer theory as a way for us to imagine a moral problem not from our own, flawed, and incompletely informed perspective, but someone who is fully informed and completely impartial. It is in this sense an act of imagination. In this way the question would become not how do I respond to this moral question, but how would a completely impartial and fully informed person—an ideal observer—respond? Would an ideal observer consider such and such with a feeling of disapproval?

The ideal observer theory is not perfect; critics have suspicions that it relies on circular arguments within it. Others have worried that it has the flavor of being a "God-like" sort of argument. **Michael Martin**, a recent defender of the theory, has argued that a way to avoid the circularity of an ideal observer with moral beliefs is to posit an ideal observer in terms of feelings and experiences. The atheist would frame the issue as "act *a* would be morally wrong if and only if there were an ideal observer under ideal conditions, and act *a* would be disapproved of by this ideal observer." Martin has rejected the Godlike argument by reiterating that the ideal observer is an entirely hypothetical construct for human use when dealing with moral questions.

Further reading: Michael Martin, *Atheism, Morality, and Meaning.*

IDEALISM. An ancient strand of **philosophy** and **theology**, the core insight of which is the conviction that an understanding of the ultimate nature of reality can be had, but only through those parts of us which can be deemed spiritual. Knowledge of this absolute is gained not by experience or experiment, but by inner workings—pure reason among some idealists, **meditation** or **prayer** among others. By whichever of these routes being recommended, the individual is promised that all perceived contradictions, inconsistencies, and contingencies will eventually disappear or be shown to be fallacious in the face of the full certainty and purity of the absolute.

Among many problems that idealism has been unable to surmount include its inability to establish the existence of whichever variation of the absolute that is being urged from our belief. G. E. Moore (1873–1958) pointed

out in his important work *Principia Ethica* (1903) that the supreme good becomes problematic when conceived as an absolute by virtue of being impervious to any sort of human interaction with it. Idealism is also essentially **dualistic**, which involves a fundamental divergence from contemporary understanding of the cosmos.

IDEOLOGICAL TOTALISM. A concept developed by Robert Jay Lifton, originally from a study of victims of Chinese "thought reform" methods on prisoners during the Korean War. Looking at the concept now, it is clearly applicable to the cultist and/or terrorist mindset. The eight basic characteristics of ideological totalism include:

- *milieu control*: strict control on comings and goings, who one can associate with, and what one can read;
- *mystical manipulation*: disciplines and practices adopted apparently spontaneously, or without explanation, but in fact coming from the sources of authority;
- *demand for purity*: only the believer can fail; no failure can be ascribed to the system or to the leader;
- *call of confession*: confession, often in public, of one's sins or weaknesses;
- *sacred science*: the believers, and only the believers, have a **monopoly on the truth**;
- *loading the language*: words are loaded to convey hidden doctrines and to delimit behavioral constraints;
- *doctrine over person*: if feelings and doctrine conflict, then the doctrine is at all times to be preferred; and
- *dispensing of existence*: if the doctrine demands the supreme sacrifice, whether of believer or unbeliever, then so be it.

All varieties of **freethought** have opposed the methods and goals of ideological totalism. See the entry on **cults**.

Further reading: Robert Jay Lifton, *Thought Reform and the Psychology of Totalism.*

IGNORANCE, VEIL OF. A term coined by the American philosopher **John Rawls** and meant as a positive condition. Rawls insisted that the fact we hold certain social, religious, or philosophical views is no reason for us to propose, or for others to accept, a notion of justice that favors our own views and those who hold them. It is beholden upon policy makers, then, to conceive of justice for their citizens behind a veil of ignorance as to their views.

Critics have argued that the requirement for total and complete impartiality of those operating behind the veil of ignorance is impossible to achieve. Nobody can operate entirely divorced from their own beliefs and prejudices. This is not to say, however, that the effort should not be held as an ideal. It has been achieved with a measure of success by the civil-service tradition in Great Britain and some English-speaking countries of the **Commonwealth of Nations**, and in Scandinavia. It is worthwhile to note that these countries are consistently shown to be the least **corrupt**. They are also the most secular.

IGTHEISM. A word coined by **Paul Kurtz** to denote what he thinks underlies the theism of many theologians. The prefix "ig" is derived from ignorant. Kurtz argues that when theologians speak in abstractions about the "ground of being," or even "God the Father," or "maker and ruler of the universe," they are really employing murky language as a dodge to cover up our ignorance about how the universe actually operates. Phrases such as these, Kurtz argues, are unfalsifiable, unhelpfully vague, and unintelligible.

Further reading: Paul Kurtz, *The New Skepticism: Inquiry and Reliable Knowledge*.

IJTIHAD. A tradition within Islam which literally translates as "strenuous endeavor" and which refers to a conscientious examination of the sacred texts in order to discover for oneself the truths of Allah. It can also refer to the more problematic scenario of finding one's way in circumstances where believers find themselves uncertain of the proper Muslim response to a situation, where the sacred sources are unclear. In Sunni Islam it is permitted to make a decision oneself as to the correct course of action (albeit within strict bounds), whereas in Shi'ite Islam this is forbidden. Shi'ites believe there is no situation not foreseen in some capacity in either the Qur'an, the **Hadith**, or in **Sharia Law**. The practice of *ijtihad* in Sunni Islam became more problematic after the triumph of Qur'anic literalism and the doctrine of *taqlid*.

There has recently been an attempt to reinterpret *ijtihad* as a tradition of independent reasoning which encourages believers to reexamine their faith in the light of new knowledge or circumstances. This is too generous a reading of *ijtihad*, for three reasons:

- there is no room for inquiry that leads to a rejection of Islam;
- the practice of *ijtihad* is restricted to scholars; for the general public, *taqlid* is the preferred option; and
- individual study is generally frowned on in favor of group study.

These problems notwithstanding, the notion of *ijtihad* stands as a dormant possibility for a reformation and liberalization of Islam, unlikely though such an eventuality may look today.

IMAGOLOGY. A word coined by the Serbian political philosopher Svetozar Stojanovic as part of his argument that we are now in the post-Gutenberg age where images rather than words are the crucial tool. An ideology is a comprehensive program for understanding the world and acting in it based on words, but an imagology is a comprehensive program for understanding the world and acting in it based on images.

Imagology is that set of images that social groups use to justify their actions, usually while casting aspersion on their opponents as well. A case in point is the care those opposed to abortion use to call themselves "pro-life" while those who support abortion insist they are "pro-choice." It is the image these words portray which carry the message for most people, not the lengthy written arguments on either side.

Stojanovic has conjured up a series of terms that illustrate his notion of imagology. For instance, the *image accomplie* is a *fait accomplie* done in images. An *image accomplie* is the image of a person or section of society that gets embedded in the popular imagination first, and nothing will change it. An actor might be forever typecast by his best-known role. Think of Leonard Nimoy as Mr. Spock. Stojanovic also talks of imagolatry, the buzz image, image bite, and image tank.

Stojanovic is critical of the reluctance of many scholars to take images seriously, noting that scholars (people who produce words) are notoriously prone to overstate the power of words to affect actions.

Further reading: Svetozar Stojanovic, *Serbia: The Democratic Revolution*.

IMMACULATE CONCEPTION, DOG-MA OF.

Announced on December 8, 1854, as a required article of **faith** for all Roman Catholics. This decree declared it Catholic dogma that Jesus, through Mary, was conceived immaculately. It was inconceivable to Pius IX that Mary could have engaged in **sex** in order to give birth to Jesus. It was also necessary, within the confines of Catholic theology, that Mary be free from the curse of **original sin**, which would have been impossible had she had conceived Jesus the normal way. It was an important milestone in the sanctification of Mary.

The dogma of immaculate conception was symptomatic of the increasing intellectual isolation of the Catholic Church from the world as it was progressing in the nineteenth century. It was the first time a pope had inaugurated a new item of dogma without the authority of a general council. Exactly ten years later Pius enacted the **syllabus of errors**, which condemned eighty propositions that amounted to a comprehensive rejection of the values of modernity. The infallibility of these papal pronouncements was left implied though unsaid until papal infallibility was announced on July 18, 1870.

IMMORTALITY. The ultimate wish fulfillment, or **transcendental temptation**.

As a response to the fact of **death**, the desire for immortality has three main features:

- an attempt to overcome death by explaining it away;
- an attempt to contrive a direction for oneself in a purposeless universe; and
- the provision of consolation to the bereaved and fearful.

At its worst, belief in immortality has two negative consequences:

- it robs life of its focus, making it little more than a preparation for death; and
- it enables people to avoid responsibility for ethical decisions because of the transference of moral authority to a source outside of humanity.

It is an important part of humanist thinking that the fact of death—its permanence—has to be taken seriously. This requires us to avoid the temptation to assign a corner of the cosmos for one's **soul** to spend eternity. Avoiding the transcendental temptation is the first step to a full, mature acceptance of life on *its* terms, and not according to *our* preferences.

The ancient Chinese thinkers understood this when, instead of yearning for immortality in heaven, they focused more on being remembered on earth. This was done by what were called the "three establishments":

- *establish virtue*, or to be known as an upright and honest person;
- *establish achievement*, or be known by what one achieved in life; and
- *establish words*, be known by one's written legacy.

In other words, it is how one lives one's life that counts, and that is what will be remembered. See the entry on **Xu Fuguan**.

Further reading: Corliss Lamont, *The Illusion of Immortality*; Paul Kurtz, *Exuberance: An Affirmative Philosophy of Life*.

IMPLAUSIBILITY, ARGUMENT FROM. An argument devised by **Michael Martin** which follows on from the **argument from conflicting theories**. The argument from implausibility goes like this: In order for one to reasonably believe that life has meaning in a Christian worldview there must be a plausible account of salvation, but there is no plausible account of salvation. Therefore, one cannot reasonably believe that life has meaning in a Christian worldview. Because to base a worldview on an implausible foundation is to render the entire worldview vulnerable.

Further reading: Michael Martin, *Atheism, Morality, and Meaning*.

IMPOSSIBILITY THEOREM. A theorem in **social sciences** devised by Kenneth Arrow (1921–), an American Nobel Laureate (1972) in economics. The theorem was devised originally as part of Arrow's doctoral thesis and presented to the public in *Social Choice and Individual Values* (1951, second edition 1962). The theorem has several applications. Its specific application is to methods of voting, but in its broader application, the theorem says that a society has as many preferences for social policy as there are individuals within it, so that it is impossible to satisfy every preference, or insist that the winning preference was the more rational of the choices available. Given this basic inability to satisfy every preference, there arises a need for some sort of social-choice function which can categorize and rate all the preferences according to some agreed-upon properties. Arrow listed these properties as including:

- a meaningful voting mechanism;
- a limiting of preferences to those that

are, even in principle, achievable;
- the presence of a working democracy, or at least the absence of dictatorship;
- a climate conducive toward changing one's mind in the face of new evidence; and
- the ability to channel irrelevant preferences to one side, without dismissing them altogether.

More recently, the impossibility theorem has been put to other uses, for instance demonstrating that the notion of "sustainable growth" is an oxymoron, because unlimited growth in a finite, nonrenewable resource like planet Earth doesn't work. Others have been critical of some uses of the impossibility theorem, saying it is wielded as an excuse for nonaction. Others have noted that "impossibility" is not the right word, as everything depends on the breadth of information available to any social-policy decision.

Further reading: www.informationgenius .com; and Amartya Sen, *Development as Freedom*.

IMPULSE-FEELING. What really moves people, according to the English thinker **L. T. Hobhouse**. In his book, *The Rational Good* (1921), Hobhouse was one of the first thinkers to ditch the presumptions about rationality as an independent and exalted principle, without going as far as many others who concluded that rationality has no place in our lives.

Impulses, Hobhouse noted, need to be converted into some sort of purpose, and it is this purpose that is the beginning of rationality in action. By placing rationality firmly within our biological makeup, Hobhouse anticipated contemporary studies on rationality and the brain. And like the contemporary theorists, Hobhouse was sure that, rather than rendering rationality irrelevant, the vulnerability and weaknesses of it are precisely what makes it so important.

Some important elements of Hobhouse's thoughts on impulse-feeling had been anticipated by the **Stoic** thinker Panaetius (185–

110 BCE, approx.), who thought that virtue has its origins in impulses.

Further reading: L. T. Hobhouse, *The Rational Good*.

INCONTINENCE PRINCIPLE OF CONTINENTAL PHILOSOPHY, THE. An unbreakable law of the universe noted by the philosopher Matthew Stewart. The Incontinence Principle states that if you think you understand continental philosophy, you don't understand it. And anyway, what can be understood with Western concepts is trivial and **logocentric**. See the entries on **différance**, **glossogonous word-salad**, and **jargon**.

Further reading: Matthew Stewart, *The Truth About Everything*.

INCREMENTALISM. An idea made fashionable after the success of the second Bush administration to bring about a ban on partial birth abortion. This success was seen by progressive and liberal media as an incremental step toward achieving a complete ban. With each restriction of choice, itself not worthy of full protest, a reaction by stealth can be achieved against the **open society**. See the entry on **dominionism**.

INDEX OF FORBIDDEN BOOKS. The list of books that Roman Catholics were forbidden to read or even to possess. The index was officially begun in 1557 by Pope Paul IV (1555–59) and lasted until 1966. Unofficial indices had been circulating for some time prior to this. For instance, the University of Louvain circulated a printed index of forbidden works in 1546, and the first official index in Spain was published in 1551. The papal index was administered by the **Inquisition** and contained some of the most significant works of **philosophy**, **science**, and literature ever written. Indeed, once the physical dangers of being proscribed in this way had been removed, having one's books placed on the index was a badge of pride.

Most indices had conditions by which a book would be placed on them. They in-

cluded books written by heretics, anything that could be construed as anti-Catholic, and vernacular translations of the Bible. It was the practice of the Roman index to prohibit books entirely if were held to include errors, whereas the various Spanish indices generally permitted a book to circulate if the offending passage was excised from it.

The Spanish index of 1583, one of the most comprehensive issued in that country, included literary names such as Boccaccio (1313–1375), Dante (1265–1321), Petrarch (1304–1374), Rabelais (1494–1553), and Thomas More (1477–1535). The first half century of the index in Spain usually discriminated between Latin works and those in the vulgate. Later on, the classification was changed to include three categories:

- authors whose entire corpus was prohibited;
- books that were prohibited regardless of the author; and
- anonymous works.

This system worked oddly, as Tycho Brahe's (1546–1601) and Johannes Kepler's (1571–1630) works were both in the first category and yet their works all appeared in Spain, having only received minor excisions. As well as this, importing foreign books into Spain carried the death penalty. See the entry on **Intolerance, Principle of**.

INDIAN HUMANIST UNION. Originally the Society for the Promotion of Freedom of Thought, and founded in Allahabad in 1954, the society became the Indian Humanist Union in 1960. The leader of the IHU was Narsingh Narain (1897–1972) who was a respected member of the international humanist community until his death. Narain wrote widely and edited the *Humanist Outlook*, a quarterly journal of humanist thought. Since his death the IHU has organized the Narsingh Narain Memorial Lecture as an annual event. In recent years this event has been held in cooperation with the India International Centre in New Delhi.

INDIAN RADICAL HUMANIST ASSO-CIATION. Founded on November 2, 1969, from the Radical Humanist Movement, which was the reconstituted Radical Democratic Party, founded in 1940 by **M. N. Roy.** The IRHA is still largely built on the intellectual foundations laid by Roy, in particular his concept of radical humanism. The IRHA was led from 1969 until 1980 by **V. M. Tarkunde,** a scholar and honorary associate of the **Rationalist Press Association**. Tarkunde's book *Radical Humanism* (1983) is the best single summary of the IRHA's position. Since 1986 the IRHA has been led by **Indumati Parikh**, a doctor based in Mumbai. Parikh has a long record of fighting for women's rights and health issues in that city.

The IRHA published an English-language monthly magazine, the *Radical Humanist*, to a subscription-only readership. Some of the regional branches publish journals in local languages. The IRHA owns no property and operates from no single place, fearful of the perversion of priorities that can occur when voluntary organizations become guardians of property and money. Its membership is small but includes a number of influential academics and people involved in public life.

INDIAN RATIONALIST ASSOCIA-TION. An Indian **freethought** association with a long, if broken, history. It is difficult to trace the history of the IRA with certainty. The organization began as the Anti-Priest-craft Association in Bombay in January 1930. This group was composed of influential men in that city, some of them with connections to the **Rationalist Press Association** in Britain. It was led by Dr. G. V. Deshmukh. In 1931 the organization changed its name to the Rationalist Association of India and in July that year it began its quarterly journal, called *Reason* under the editorship of Dr. Charles Lionel d'Avoine (1875–1945). *Reason* earned notoriety in September 1933 when d'Avoine wrote an article called "Religion and Morality" that gave offense to English ecclesiastical authorities in Bombay.

D'Avoine simply drew attention to the gap between words and deeds by prominent churchmen. He faced charges relating to the article but was acquitted. The case attracted national attention and stimulated interest in rationalism. Soon after d'Avoine's acquittal, the Rationalist Youth League was formed, which nurtured some future leaders of Indian unbelief, such as Abraham Solomon. *Reason* suspended publication in 1936 and started again in February 1937 under the editorship of Prof. R. D. Karve (1881–1953). D'Avoine became president. *Reason* continued until the end of 1942 and the RAI became dormant after that.

Meanwhile in Madras, the Indian Rationalist Association was formed in December 1949. This was founded at an all-India conference of rationalists hosted by the Madras Group of the Rationalist Press Association. It was the intention of the conference to form a rationalist organization that would represent all India. Many members of the moribund Rationalist Association of India joined the IRA. The IRA continued a fitful existence through the next three decades, troubled by financial and organizational difficulties. Under the editorship of S. Ramanathan it published the *Indian Rationalist* intermittently through the 1950s and 1960s, finally ceasing publication in December 1966. The IRA discontinued its activities at the end of 1970. Since then it has been revived on several occasions in different parts of the country. Today there are at least two groups claiming the mantle of the Indian Rationalist Association.

INDIFFERENTISM. The condition of being entirely unmoved by beliefs or enthusiasms that motivate others. With regard to questions of religion, indifferentism is not the same as **atheism** or **agnosticism**, and certainly not the same as **humanism**. Atheists and religious believers have in common a conviction that time spent thinking seriously about religious and philosophical questions is time well spent. The indifferentist would dispute that claim. See the entry on **what atheists and religious believers have in common**.

INDIVIDUALISM. A word coined in the nineteenth century, which was used almost exclusively in a negative sense to begin with, mainly by conservatives. Individualism was criticized as a manifestation of what happens when you take notions like the **rights** of man seriously.

Among the surprisingly large number of beliefs Marxist revolutionaries and Christian conservatives have in common is the belief that the self is determined largely in a social context and that individualism is an egoistic fancy designed to break up **community** or betray vital class interests.

However, it is equally true that individualism only works in the context of being with others. Robinson Crusoe, alone on his island, has no need for individualism. True individuals have a developed awareness of themselves without being self-centered or narcissistic. An individual is an authentic person *in the presence of others*. **Narcissism** is not the final terminus of the individual—it is the admission of the inability to be a full person in the presence of others. See the entry on the **minimal self**.

Further reading: Steven Lukes, *Individualism*.

INDUCTION. See **DEDUCTION AND INDUCTION**.

INEQUALITY. The condition whereby people are treated according to different values. There are two main types of inequality:

- that which arises from physical or natural causes, such as a disease; and
- that which arises from social conventions.

This distinction between the physical and the social is very basic; it is paralleled in our understanding of **human needs** and **facts**. Nothing humans can do will ever eliminate inequality of the first type. People who are struck down at birth with a lingering illness or handicap are not going to enjoy the same sort of opportunities as those born healthy and strong. This is part of the unfairness of life. The best that can be done is that the extent of the inequality suffered can be mitigated. And thanks to the advances in technology and secular principles of equality before the law, great advances have been made in mitigating this sort of ineradicable inequality.

Inequalities suffered from social conventions, however, are another matter altogether. Illegitimate children used to suffer severe social inequalities for a "crime" committed before they were born. Civilized societies have abolished this most unnecessary inequality. Both types of inequality can, and frequently do, result in **poverty**. Women also suffer some very basic inequalities, the most widespread and debilitating of which is the inequality in the division of food. Many other **gender**-related inequalities persist, many of them tied up with traditional religious injunctions.

Another commonly recognized inequality is that between the rich, mostly northern hemisphere nations, and the developing world to their south. Not only is inequality between the wealthy West and developing rest widening, the gap is also widening within the West. The top 20 percent of American society earns almost as much as the bottom 80 percent. This balances out as 49 percent of the national income going to the top 20 percent, while the remaining 51 percent is distributed among everyone else. Moreover, the very wealthy can maximize their earnings by the many ingenious forms of **tax avoidance** that expensive accountants can appraise them of. See the entry on **ecological footprint**.

INFIDEL DEATHBEDS. One of the oldest and most popular **prejudices against atheists**. The story goes that atheists spend their last moments screaming in terror for a priest, or else groaning in regret of their lives devoted to the propagation of untruth. This prejudice is old enough that **G. W. Foote** wrote a book called *Infidel Deathbeds* in 1886 to counter it. *Infidel Deathbeds* was revised, enlarged, and reissued through the 1930s.

The first point about this slander is how primitive it is. Like the **atheists in foxholes** prejudice, it is based on a simple unwillingness to believe that atheists can die in accordance with their convictions. It also implies that atheists are cowards. More unsettling for religious believers is the unsaid implication that they believe in the afterlife for less than noble reasons themselves.

This prejudice is widespread enough that prominent atheists often feel the need to have witnesses to their death, so that they may testify that the atheist died without screaming for a priest. Were such aspersions cast against religious believers by atheists there would be no end to the righteous anger, but when atheists are the targets, no slander is too vile. The infidel-deathbeds prejudice has been applied most notoriously to **Thomas Paine**, **Voltaire**, **Herbert Spencer**, **Charles Darwin**, and **Bertrand Russell**, although **Jean-Paul Sartre** is being mentioned more frequently. And less than a year after Foote's own death came tales in the religious media that Foote himself had undergone a deathbed conversion.

Further reading: G. W. Foote, *Infidel Deathbeds*.

INGERSOLL, ROBERT GREEN (1833–1899).

The son of a Presbyterian minister, Robert Ingersoll was born in the village of Dresden, on the shores of Lake Seneca in central New York state. Though his father was from the more progressive end of the Protestant spectrum, Ingersoll's upbringing was pious and joyless. He had very little formal education, but was inspired to a life of learning when he came across the works of **William Shakespeare** as an adolescent. Shakespeare, along with **Thomas Paine**, remained a source of inspiration for the rest of Ingersoll's life. After training as a lawyer, he set up business in 1857 with his brother in Peoria, Illinois. His marriage in 1862 to Eva

Parker (1841–1923) was genuinely happy and produced no scandal that religious opponents thought inevitable in the private life of infidels. Parker came from a prominent family of progressive thinkers, who counted **Abraham Lincoln** as one of their friends. Unable to slander his home life, his opponents resorted to calling him "Robert Injuresoul."

Once the civil war began, he helped form the 11th Illinois Cavalry Regiment, and became its commanding officer with the rank of colonel. He served until the end of 1862, when he returned to civilian life as a result of a parole with Confederate forces that had captured him.

For the next thirty years, Ingersoll built a career as a lawyer, public speaker on **freethought**, and Republican politician. His political career foundered because of his public expression of religious unbelief. Had he been of a compromising character, Ingersoll could well have had a significant political career, as even his opponents acknowledged. Ironically, his political legacy lived on not in the Republican Party, but among left-leaning politicians like Eugene Debs (1855– 1926) and Robert LaFollette (1855–1925). At no point did Ingersoll tailor his views to suit his audience. His outspoken support for racial and **gender** equality put him at odds with many other freethinkers, let alone the religious conservatives.

Ingersoll outlined his creed in this way: "The time to be happy is now. The place to be happy is here. The way to be happy is to make others so." Ingersoll apologized that his creed was short, but noted that it is nevertheless long enough. In his massive history of nineteenth-century freethought, **J. M. Robertson** declared Ingersoll the most widely influential platform propagandist of the century. The deepest source of his influence was the eloquence of his indictment of orthodox religion. And yet he was able to retain the friendship of many people who disagreed with his views, whether religious or political.

In 1987, the house where Ingersoll was

born was bought by the **Council for Secular Humanism**, and in 1993 it opened as a museum. It is the only freethought museum in the United States.

INQUIRY, TOOLS OF. Honest inquiry needs a range of interdependent skills and aptitudes. The most important of them are:

- *the ability to make informed conjectures* about things and check how their conjectures fit the evidence;
- *imagination* to think up plausible explanations for their questions, and ways to gather the needed evidence;
- *care, skill, and persistence* to seek out all possible relevant evidence;
- *intellectual honesty* to seek out evidence that may falsify one's ideas and to confront openly what negative evidence one does come up with;
- *rigorous reasoning* to figure out the consequences of these conjectures; and
- *good judgment* in assessing the weight of one's evidence.

These used to be seen as the foundation of the **scientific method**. While it is true that scientists need these qualities, they are not exclusive to them. All inquirers, whether they be professional academics at universities, or the intellectually curious general reader need to exercise these aptitudes.

Further reading: Susan Haack, *Defending Science—Within Reason*.

INQUISITION. The Roman Catholic Church's answer to heterodoxy. The first reference to the title of inquisitor was at the Council of Tours in 1163. This council was deeply concerned with the Cathar **heresy** then very powerful in southern France and elsewhere. There was talk of a stern, official response to it. This came in the form of Pope Lucius III's *Ad abolendum* decretal of November 4, 1184, to "make inquisition" for heresy. The work of the Inquisition was carried out by encouraging neighbor to spy on

neighbor. All reports to inquisitors were anonymous and once charged, the accused had no defense and no right of appeal. The guilty were handed over to the civil authorities for punishment, not wanting to be directly responsible for the deaths.

In 1252, Innocent IV in *Ad Extirpanda*, permitted the torture of heretics. Amended versions of this bull allowed the inquisitors themselves to be present at the torture. Composed primarily of Dominicans and Franciscans, the Inquisition soon acquired a special immunity from conventional lines of ecclesiastical authority. It got a new lease on life in Rome by Pope Paul III in 1542 as part of the Counter Reformation against Protestantism and heresy. Only in 1816 did Pope Pius VII officially condemn the practice of torture.

The propensity to embark on inquisitions is a feature of **monotheist** religions, which find it difficult to acknowledge the good faith of those who reject their beliefs. Islam never had an organized Inquisition in the way Christianity had, a fact about which Muslims are justly proud. Nevertheless, Islam has maintained an informal series of controls which have probably been more effective at eliminating or discouraging dissent than the more vulgar Christian variety. There have been no inquisitions in any of the **Asian traditions**. See the entries on the **Spanish Inquisition** and **Intolerance, Principle of**.

INSTITUTE OF HUMANIST STUDIES. A nonprofit humanist foundation based in Albany, New York, founded by a local businessman, Larry Jones, in 1999. The IHS has set as its main goals assistance in Web hosting, providing online training courses for young humanists, and granting financial support for worthwhile humanist projects around the world.

INSTITUTE OF SCIENTIFIC ATHEISM. An institute, founded in 1964, attached to the Central Committee of the Communist Party of the Soviet Union, and dedicated to the propagation of **atheism**. The institute trained graduate social scientists in the theory of scientific atheism and the history of **religion**. It published a journal called *Questions of Scientific Atheism*.

The institute was profoundly disliked by the Russians, not because they nurtured any special love of religion, but because they resented its position as the sole source of legitimate and allowable thoughts. Indeed, it is a prime example of the dangers of any official endorsement of a religion or an ideology. The arguments of the **separation of church and state** function just as well against the Soviet experiment in official atheism. The institute was an early casualty of the collapse of the Soviet Union.

All this said, it is to be hoped that some of the works produced by it will eventually be published in English. Russian scholarship is excellent, and there must be some classics of the history of and theory of atheism, **freethought**, and religion, which would repay translation.

INTELLIGENT DESIGN THEORY. A variant of **creationism** that arose in the United States in the 1990s. In fact, intelligent design has been described as "Creationism Lite." In the wake of creationism's failure, proponents of intelligent design are prepared to jettison strict biblical literalism, a young earth, and most notions of the fixity of species. Their central claim is that human **evolution** is impossible to understand without some idea of a guiding intelligence. The main advocates of this approach include Philip Johnson (a lawyer), William Demski (a mathematician), and Michael Behe (a biologist). The principal divisions within intelligent design revolve around their conflicting attitudes toward **naturalism**.

Some of the more pointed criticisms of intelligent design theory have come from the Catholic theologian John F. Haught, who notes the theory's unwillingness to come to terms with the disorderly, undirected streams of evolution that are nonetheless part of the life process. Not only that, intelligent design

can say nothing about the breakdown of fixed order, which is no less vital for life to continue. And because **God** is linked so closely with design and order, there is little choice left for them but to attribute disorder in nature to **Satan**, or some sort of demonic principle. To ignore the contingency and randomness of evolution, or to attribute them to other supernatural agents which themselves require explanation does not make any worthwhile contribution to the debate. Furthermore, sidelining God as an intelligent designer, makes the **problem of evil** even more difficult to solve from a religious point of view.

Neither can intelligent design explain why God should have seen fit to create such a complicated universe for something as straightforward (for God) as having one planet with human beings on it. There is an awful lot of superfluous design out there for such a limited result.

Intelligent design is no more a science than was creationism. Beyond the assertion that an intelligent designer must be responsible for the universe, no evidence is given of *how* this might happen. It is best seen as a thinly disguised form of Christian apologetics. William Dembski acknowledged as much when he said intelligent design is simply a crossover between the **logos** theory of the Gospel of John and information theory.

Further reading: John F. Haught, *God After Darwin*; and Paul Kurtz, ed., *Science and Religion: Are They Compatible?*

INTERNATIONAL ACADEMY OF HUMANISM. A body of distinguished humanist academics and thinkers. The members, called humanist laureates, are nontheists who have distinguished themselves by their use of the principle of **free inquiry** in their specialty, by their commitment to the use of **reason** and **scientific methods** in acquiring **knowledge** about the universe, or by their upholding of **humanist values** and principles. The academy operates mainly through publications, conferences, and press releases on important issues. Composed originally of thirty, the academy is now limited to eighty laureates at any time. Among its number are some of the most prominent men and women in the world today. A lot of them have separate entries in this dictionary.

The academy was established in 1983 and has met on six occasions: 1985 at the University of Michigan; 1986 at the University of Oslo; 1988 at the State University of New York at Buffalo; 1992 at the Universiteit voor Humanistiek (the **University of Humanist Studies**) at Utrecht in the Netherlands; 1995 at the Delphi Academy in Delphi, Greece; and 1996 in Mexico City.

Its publications include: "Education and Free Inquiry," *Free Inquiry* 5, no. 3 (Summer 1985): 4; *Neo-Fundamentalism and the Humanist Response* (1988); "A Declaration of Interdependence: A New Global Ethics," *Free Inquiry* 8, no. 4 (Fall 1988): 4–7; "Science, Technology, and Ethics in the 21st Century," in *Building a World Community* (1989); *Challenges to the Enlightenment: Defending Science and Reason* (1994); "Declaration in Defense of Cloning and the Integrity of Scientific Research," *Free Inquiry* 17, no. 3 (Summer 1997): 11–12; and *Humanist Manifesto: A Call for a New Planetary Humanism* (1999).

INTERNATIONAL ASSOCIATION FOR CRITICAL REALISM. See **CRITICAL REALISM**.

INTERNATIONAL ATOMIC ENERGY AGENCY. The world's foremost transnational agency to ensure nuclear material is used responsibly and in a way open to inspection. The agency was established as a response to **cold war** concerns about nuclear proliferation. In December 1953 US president Dwight Eisenhower addressed the **United Nations** on "Atoms for Peace," which stimulated the IAEA statute three years later and the formal establishment of the agency in 1957. The IAEA is headquartered in Vienna, Austria. There are three main strands to its activities:

- *verification and security*, ensuring nuclear material is not used for military purposes;
- *safety*, monitoring safety levels at nuclear facilities; and
- *promoting technology*, including nuclear technology to solving development problems and encouraging sustainable development.

As well as its high-profile work in monitoring nuclear proliferation, the IAEA has also conducted scientific research into various aspects of nuclear energy and genetic engineering. Since the end of the cold war, the IAEA has been active in finding and overseeing the safe decommissioning of nuclear weapons from the former Soviet bloc. The IAEA is an important example of **global governance**.

INTERNATIONAL FEDERATION OF FREETHINKERS. See **WORLD UNION OF FREETHINKERS**.

INTERNATIONAL HUMANIST AND ETHICAL UNION. A federation of humanist and ethical societies founded in Amsterdam in 1952. The IHEU was an amalgamation of many member organizations of the **World Union of Freethinkers** (WUF), which had been founded in 1880 but by then was all but defunct, and the International Ethical Union, which had been founded in 1896. A rump WUF continued after 1952 and still exists today. The two leading founders of the IHEU were **Harold Blackham**, representing the Ethical Union and **Jaap van Praag**, representing the Dutch Humanist League. Other organizations from the Netherlands, Great Britain, United States, Germany, and India were involved. After van Praag's long term as president, it was decided the IHEU should be run by a troika of three copresidents. This system worked pretty well for more than twenty years. Having served on the IHEU board since 1969, **Paul Kurtz** served in this capacity from 1986 until 1994.

The inaugural congress of the IHEU issued the **Amsterdam Declaration**, which was a five-part statement of the fundamentals of **humanism**. Since then the declaration has grown to the seven-part statement released at the IHEU's fiftieth anniversary conference in 2002. The IHEU has three main functions:

- to stimulate and coordinate the activities and policies of member organizations;
- to help create new organizations where they do not exist; and
- to participate in international organizations to advance humanist interests.

Because of the interest Jaap van Praag had in the IHEU, it remained based in the Netherlands for more than forty years. In 1997 the IHEU moved its headquarters to London and appointed Babu Gogineni as its executive director.

The IHEU now has about a hundred member organizations. It enjoys official non-governmental-organization (NGO) status at the **United Nations** and general-consultative status at UNICEF and the Council of Europe. And in 2004 the IHEU received a grant from the Appignani Foundation to establish a Humanist Center for Bioethics in New York.

The problem of inadequate resources has been a problem for the IHEU ever since its inception, but it has nonetheless been a stalwart voice for humanism over the past half century.

INTERNATIONAL MONETARY FUND. An international agency with the stated purpose of facilitating monetary stability and promoting economic growth around the world. The IMF grew out of a meeting at Bretton Woods, New Hampshire, in July 1944 between forty-five countries looking to rebuild a postwar prosperity. The **World Bank** (or, more properly, the World Bank Group) was created at the same meeting. It was widely thought that World War II had been brought on in part by the protectionism which brought on the Great Depression of the

1930s, and it was the intention of the Bretton Woods gathering to create a new system of monetary relations that would ensure such a calamity never happened again. The IMF was formally created in December 1945.

The cornerstone of the IMF was the agreement to peg the value of all member currencies on the United States dollar, which in turn would be valued in terms of gold. This became known as the Bretton Woods system and lasted until 1971. It ended when the United States ended the practice of pegging the US dollar with gold. Since 1971 member governments have been able to peg their currencies against any currency (but not against gold) or to float freely. It was also in 1971 that the **World Economic Forum** first met.

The IMF is careful to mention it is owned by 184 countries. Each member country is represented by a board of governors which technically has the final say in deciding policy. However, the board of governors meets only once a year and while it is absent, the day-to-day running of the IMF is undertaken by a twenty-four-person executive board. Eight countries have guaranteed places on the board: the United States, Great Britain, Germany, Japan, France, Russia, China, and Saudi Arabia. Votes are not apportioned equally, but are determined on the size of the contributions. The United States makes the largest contributions. The IMF's headquarters are in Washington DC.

The focus of the IMF is on the big picture, in particular with economic policies and financial-sector policies pursued by member countries. The IMF is neither an aid agency nor a development agency. Aid and development are more the stated goals of the World Bank. The IMF provides financing to countries whose balance of payments is in difficulties or whose international reserves have been weakened. Whether the recipient of a loan or not, member countries agree to have their exchange-rate policies overseen by the IMF. In practice this means member countries agree to implement policies toward the goals of "orderly economic growth with reasonable price stability, together with orderly underlying economic and financial conditions, and to avoid manipulating exchange rates for unfair competitive advantage."

IMF loans are always conditional on the recipient country undertaking to revise their policies in favor of redressing its balance of payment problems, freeing up spending and private investment, and repaying debt. Opponents of the IMF have accused it of insisting on long-term changes that are more to the benefit of the rich lenders than the impoverished borrowers. And even supporters of the IMF have noted its role in providing the conditions for the theft of billions of dollars in Russia in the 1990s. However, supporters note that the IMF conditions also have the effect of making financial dealing more transparent, and thus exposing **corruption**, which is surely a major problem for the world's poor. What is needed now is greater transparency in the IMF's own dealings. So, it is too simplistic to see the IMF simply and exclusively as an uncaring oppressor of the poor, but it is also fair to question its economic preferences.

Further reading: www.imf.org; Amartya Sen, *Development as Freedom*; and Mike Moore, *A World Without Walls*.

INTOLERANCE, PRINCIPLE OF. A principle, identified by the philosopher J. C. A. Gaskin, which reads: "We know what is right and true, and for your sake it is our duty to see to it that you know nothing else." Gaskin notes that the Principle of Intolerance is "appropriate to the exclusive claims of **monotheism**" and was effectively used by the Roman Catholic Church for many centuries. Many types of Protestants, particularly those of **fundamentalist** persuasion, are also well disposed to the Principle of Intolerance.

It was this principle that motivated the **Inquisition**, the **Index of Forbidden Books**, and **Comstockery**, not to mention the destruction of the **Alexandria Library**, the closing of the **Academy** by the emperor Justinian, the murder of thousands of heretics through the centuries, and many other crimes against **freethought**.

Further reading: J. C. A. Gaskin, ed., *Varieties of Unbelief from Epicurus to Sartre*.

INTUITION. A quality often seen as some sort of direct, primal relation between the mind and the **soul**. Intuition as used in this sense often appears in **New Age** or mystical literature, but virtually no philosophers speak of it in this way. Part of the reason intuition has fallen into disfavor is that it has been misused for irrational ends. People have spoken of their "women's intuition," "psychic intuition," even "racial intuition." And the assumption has always been that intuition works at a "deeper" level than mere **reason**. See the entry on **mereymustification**. Some exponents of **phenomenology** also tried to speak of intuition, when the problems with speaking about essences became apparent.

However, it is wrong to see intuition as necessarily working against the interests of **reason**, or even that they are two separate qualities. Intuition and reason are both biological tools we have developed as mechanisms by which we make sense of the world. We can be deceived by our reason no less than by our intuition. The **flow** of the creative artist or thinker, the inspiration of the scientist and inventor, the hunch of the psychologist: all of these are the creative fusion of intuition and reason. **Aristotle** described wisdom as the combination of intuition and rational **knowledge**.

INVESTIGATION OF THE ESSENCE OF THE DEITY, AN. One of the first specific defenses of **atheism** written in the modern age. Because even Britain at the time was not an entirely **open society**, it was necessary for the author to shelter under the pseudonym of "Scepticus Britannicus." The book was published in 1797 and went through the contradictions inherent in the idea of **God**. Most of them are now familiar to us, but in 1797, it took courage, even in England, to say these things. Scepticus Britannicus also attacked **deism**.

IRENAEUS OF LYONS (140–202 CE). The first Christian theoretician of **original sin**. As bishop of Lyon, Irenaeus was a prominent critic of **Gnosticism** in his work *Against the Heretics*. Part of Irenaeus's objection to the Gnostics was that their attributing all that was wrong in the world to the **evil** force had the effect of absolving humanity of responsibility for its **sins**. In the wake of God's gift of free will, Irenaeus argued, **Satan** was able to exploit our weaknesses. Humanity's proclivities to evil was endemic as a consequence of the crimes of Adam and Eve. Irenaeus was also responsible for inventing the first list of popes. See the entry on **Linus**.

IRRATIONALISM. The condition of being in active opposition to rationality and emphasizing instead some other faculty or value within the individual as deserving priority. What this fundamental faculty or value is held to be varies widely, depending on the situation of the propounder. It has been intuition, **faith**, race, nationality, *der Führer*, the Inner Light, **gender**—anything, just so long as it is not **reason**.

Irrationalism is not the same as simple irrationality, which everyone displays at various times. Being irrational is part of being human, but elevating irrationality into a body of thought or code of practice is altogether another thing. **Humanism** is opposed to all attempts to systematize irrationalism (what should be an oxymoron), whether from a theistic or atheistic standpoint. It is not that intuitive or nonrational judgments are without value—quite the contrary. It is merely to say that such **judgments** or values should be open to scrutiny, testing, and criticism.

The first step in the struggle against irrationalism is to defend the existence of brute facts, and therefore of a real world these **facts** alert us to. Irrationalism prefers to posit fantasy worlds or, at the very least, to put the real world in **scare quotes**.

It is also important to recognize that irrationalism is not value neutral. The claim that we are fundamentally irrational leaves some other element to provide the understanding of our essence. This has usually been the tool of the demagogue. See the entry on **the great divide**.

IRRATIONALISM, FOUR DANGERS OF. A formula devised by the Norwegian humanist and former president of the **International Humanist and Ethical Union**, Levi Fragell. When he speaks of **irrationalism**, Fragell specifically excludes irrationality in the sense of emotions, art, drama, music, and so on. It is when irrationality is promoted into a serious body of thought and used to combat rational programs for change that Fragell sees the problem. With this in mind, Fragell sees the four dangers of irrationalism as:

- it is *dysfunctional*, in that it hinders the fulfillment of goals and aims set by society or the individual—for instance faith healers inhibit the path to health, rather than aid it;
- it is *harmful*, in that it breeds sectarianism and ethnic hatreds;
- it is *evil*, in that it can positively encourage atrocities and other hateful acts; and
- it is *ridiculous*, in that the pretensions of some its practitioners defy the most basic common sense.

In the sense of giving strength to these forms of irrationalism, Fragell says that religions "have misled all cultures, cheated and betrayed all new generations and hindered the development of a global society based on truth and honesty."

ISLAMIC JIHAD. A fundamentalist terrorist organization committed to the destruction of Israel. Islamic Jihad is smaller than **Hamas**, and without its other social programs. It is a looser-knit organization, particularly after the Israelis assassinated Fathi Shikaki, the group's founder, in Malta in 1995.

ISLAMIC RESURGENCE. A term given to the comprehensive revitalization of all branches of Islamic thought since the 1970s. This resurgence was fueled by a sharp rise in population throughout the Muslim world between the 1970s and the first decade of the twenty-first century. This population bulge will have a greater significance than the earlier **baby boom**, which transformed Western societies after World War II. While the population in Muslim countries grows rapidly, those countries have not enjoyed any remotely comparable levels of economic growth, leading to widespread **poverty** and frustrated expectations. Neither have these societies made significant moves to **democracy**.

The Islamic resurgence has been manifested by a truly massive return to traditional religious observances and ritual and a more pervasive observance of dietary, clothing, and other social codes perceived to be characteristically Muslim. The rise of **Islamism** is only one aspect of the Islamic resurgence.

ISLAMISM. One of the consequences of the **Islamic resurgence** is a political form of Islam, sometimes called political Islam. The three principal strands of Islamism, according to Paul Berman, are:

- recognition of the need to counter infidel barbarism;
- preference given to **jihad**, in its most aggressive sense; and
- commitment to the creation of an Islamic state.

Islamism can manifest itself in terrorist acts, but also in the form of political conservatism, and less overtly political ways which concentrate on internal purity or social reform. The ultimate expressions of Islamism were Ayatollah Khomeini, who led the revolution against the Shah in Iran and founded an Islamic state, and the Taliban in Afghanistan. The philosophical inspiration of Islamism is **Sayyid Qutb**. See the entry on the **war on terror**.

Further reading: Paul Berman, *Terror and Liberalism*.

IS/OUGHT GAP. See **NATURALISTIC FALLACY**.

J

JAINS. An unorthodox variation of Hinduism and a prime example of the difficulty of speaking of **Asian traditions** as religions. The Jains credit Mahavira as their founder. Mahavira's dates are uncertain, but the traditional dates for him are 540–468 BCE. *Mahavira*, which means "Great Hero," was the last of a succession of twenty-four sages who had handed down knowledge from the deep recesses of history. Mahavira is said to have left his home near the Ganges when he was thirty to wander from place to place in search of enlightenment, which he eventually achieved.

The Jains specifically reject notions of **God** or gods. The Jain text, the *Mahapurana* (*The Great Legend*) is explicitly atheist. Jains believe that the universe is uncreated and eternal, which leads them to argue against **arguments to design** and generally to consider that the qualities attributed to God are contradictory and unreasonable. The Jains are opposed to any theory that does not emphasize ethical responsibility, and they maintain, correctly, that ideas of God or gods do just that.

Jains subscribe to the doctrine of *syadvada*, which holds that all judgments are held to be **falsifiable** because of the imperfect viewpoint of each observer. Everyone must work out their own salvation and liberated souls can only serve as guides, since it is a mistake to consider them infallible or supernatural.

Jains argue that everything except souls and space are created from matter. In physics, the Jains are broadly **atomistic**. Souls from the dead can, if having reached perfection, become a Parmatman, or supreme soul. Jains opposed the passive readings the **Ajivikas** gave to the doctrine of *niyati*. Against their pacifism, the Jains taught *kiriya* (action, dynamism, or vitalism), which became a central component of Jain thought. While remaining broadly naturalistic, Mahavira defended notions of **free will**.

Jains are a small minority in India, but are respected for their industriousness and integrity.

Further reading: Dale Riepe, *The Naturalistic Tradition in Indian Thought*.

JAMES, WILLIAM (1842–1910). Very influential American psychologist and thinker. James was raised in a freethinking family environment. His brother was the eminent novelist Henry James (1843–1916). James qualified as a doctor and from 1872 to 1882 taught comparative anatomy at Harvard. In 1882 he transferred to philosophy, and three years later to psychology. His writings from this period were later published as *The Principles of Psychology* (1890), a landmark work in the history of that discipline. In philosophy, James was an important proponent of **pragmatism**. Like most thinkers of his day, he was anxious to eschew Cartesian **dualism**. Inspired largely by his understanding of **Charles Darwin**, he sought to place **human nature** in the context of the individual responding to, and being formed by, the environment.

James did not want to rescue **God**, or even the idea of God, from the clutches of **science**. He was not, even unwittingly, a proponent of the **God of the Gaps**. God could not be used as an explanation of the world, but went some way toward providing an explanation of human behavior. However, James was just as adamant that **consciousness** could not be explained entirely in scientific terms. Rather, the mind is an instrument for coming to terms with, and explaining, the world.

James's other major works are *The Will to Believe* (1897); *Varieties of Religious Experi-ence* (1902), his Gifford Lectures in Edinburgh; and *Pragmatism* (1907). James's later works show the influence of Henri Bergson (1859–1941), the French thinker best known for his notion of elan vital, or vital spark.

JARGON. An enemy of learning and knowledge. Jargon is the collective name for words used as a vehicle to parade the user's profundity, rather than because it helps develop understanding. The philosopher **John Locke** spoke of jargon as the "pedantic terminology to make things dark." Complicated words or phrases are often used in technical writing and sometimes the need is felt to coin a new word in order to make a point which cannot be made with the existing range of words. All this is perfectly legitimate because they help move knowledge along.

Jargon, however, is the *unnecessary* addition of technical language or coined words. They may be unnecessary because there are words already in use which in fact perform the function of the jargon. Worse, the jargon may actually serve to obscure sound understanding of the argument being offered. And worse still, the use of jargon may be a deliberate ploy to affect the impression of brilliance which is not in fact warranted. Without doubt the worst offenders in each of these categories have been some of the more extravagant European **postmodernists** and **psychoanalytical** thinkers.

Contrary to widespread perception, dense and obscure writing need not necessarily be profound. In the case of **Immanuel Kant** it was, but Kant set an unfortunate precedent, encouraging lesser minds to write as he did but with less excuse. True brilliance is best shown by the ability to write lucidly and clearly and not to muddy things with jargon and verbiage. Few people illustrate this better than **Bertrand Russell**.

JEFFERSON, THOMAS (1743–1826). Third president of the United States, **Enlightenment** man, and architect of the **separation of church and state** in that country. A native of Virginia, Jefferson trained as a lawyer and was admitted to the bar in 1767. He quickly became embroiled in federal politics and was instrumental in drafting the Declaration of Independence, which was signed on July 4, 1776. After independence Jefferson held a variety of official posts in France until 1789 when George Washington appointed him as secretary of state. After a temporary withdrawal from public life, Jefferson became vice president to his friend John Adams in 1797, and from 1801 until 1809 he was president. He won the presidency despite a concerted attempt by religious conservatives to blacken his name and caricature his deist beliefs. During his first term, Jefferson oversaw the Louisiana Purchase, the largest purchase of land in history. As a result of the purchase, the United States doubled its size and it became only a matter of time before it extended still further to reach the Pacific Ocean and become a continental power.

But Jefferson's finest achievement was his contribution to the separation of church and state in America. In 1779 he proposed a bill to establish in the state of Virginia the complete equality of all (white) people regardless of religious belief or their lack thereof. This idea scandalized religious conservatives, who wanted to extend to non-Christians the same discriminations currently in place against blacks. Jefferson's bill was eventually passed in Virginia in 1786 and became the template for the federal constitution. Jefferson also showed great courage in 1802 when he invited his old friend **Thomas Paine** to return to live out his days in the United States, a move which brought down an avalanche of spleen from outraged religious conservatives. Jefferson also resisted a campaign in 1808 to institutionalize a day of **prayer**, noting that a refusal was required by the constitution. He was opposed to too great a concentration of power at the center. After his terms as president, Jefferson retired to his estate at Monticello in Virginia. Much of his time in his last years was devoted to establishing the University of Virginia, becoming its rector in 1819.

As a young man, Jefferson shed his early conventional religious beliefs in favor of a **deism** bordering on **skepticism**. He had been especially unable to accept the doctrine of the **Trinity**. Later in his life, Jefferson moved to a highly unorthodox and demythologized version of Christian humanism. His thoughts were expressed in two short works *The Philosophy of Jesus* (1804) and *The Life and Morals of Jesus* (1819–20) which anticipated **Ernest Renan** in placing Jesus in a human context, without the trappings of **supernaturalism**. Jefferson saw Jesus as uniquely good without being divine.

Jefferson would be pretty much the ideal Enlightenment hero, but for his double standard with respect to his ownership of slaves and his sexual dalliance with one of them, Sally Hemings. Ever since his death, people have not known what to make of a champion of liberty who kept slaves. He had no doubts of the iniquity of **slavery**: in 1782 he called for its abolition. But it seems that Jefferson could not persuade himself of the equality of black people. In the end we can say that Jefferson is the personification of the legacy of the Enlightenment: an inspiring and noble program, but far from perfectly implemented. See the entry on **Enlightenment, legacy of**.

JEMAAH ISLAMIYAH. A fundamentalist Muslim terrorist organization active in several countries across Southeast Asia, but primarily based in Indonesia. Jemaah Islamiyah, which simply means "Islamic group," seeks to create a Muslim theocracy covering all of Southeast Asia. It emerged in the 1970s, although little is known about its structure. Its intellectual roots come from Darul Islam, an Islamist group formed while Indonesia was still a Dutch colony.

It is thought that Jemaah Islamiyah is led by Abu Bakar Bashir (1938–), a longstanding extremist and **anti-Semite** of Yemeni extraction who has lived in Indonesia for most of his life. Perhaps even more significant is Nurjaman Riduan Ismuddin, known as Hambali, who is thought to be in charge of operations in the region.

Indonesia was reluctant to inflame its large and increasingly restive Muslim population by pursuing Jemaah Islamiyah too forcefully until the bombing of a nightclub in the popular tourist resort island of Bali in October 2002, which killed 180 people. Bashir served a nominal prison sentence after the Bali bombing. The new government in 2004 under Susilo Bambang Yudhoyono seems set to pursue a tougher line against the terrorists. See the entry on **war on terror**.

JEPTHAH. One of the judges of Israel and a God-fearing man who, in return for the Lord's favor in slaughtering thousands of Ammonites, honored a pledge to sacrifice his daughter (and only child). Jepthah went on to slaughter forty-two thousand Ephraimites, who were resentful at not being invited to help slaughter the Ammonites. The Lord rewarded Jepthah's behavior with a generous posterity.

JERUSALEM CONFERENCE. The first major betrayal of the teachings of **Rabbi Yeshua**. The Jerusalem Conference is the name given to a gathering in about 49 CE of Jewish conservatives and radicals. The radicals, led by **Paul**, were determined to preach what they interpreted as the Gospel of Jesus Christ to Gentiles, against the wishes of the conservatives, who had known Yeshua.

The specific issues involved the ongoing validity of Jewish practices such as male circumcision and dietary laws, and the degree to which these were required of non-Jewish converts. The larger issue was the authority of Jewish law and the validity of non-Jewish converts in the first place. Rabbi Yeshua had made it quite plain (Matthew 5:17–19 in particular) that he had come to uphold every jot and tittle of the law as recorded in the **Hebrew scriptures**, and his followers and disciples were determined that this should continue to be the case.

But Paul wanted to extend his preaching to non-Jews, for whom the circumcision and dietary laws would be a barrier to conversion.

The two parties argued it out. The conservatives made the reasonable point that they had been with Rabbi Yeshua and knew what his views were. Paul, who had never met Yeshua, insisted his authority came from visitations from the risen Christ. Technically the two parties reached a compromise, in which Gentile converts need not be circumcised but that they should observe some of the dietary restrictions and abjure adultery. But in reality, it was a victory for Paul, because the combined authority of the very people who had known Rabbi Yeshua had been overruled.

The Jerusalem Conference was a significant milestone in the overshadowing of Rabbi Yeshua and the **creation of Jesus Christ**. There is an interesting account of the debate in Acts 15:4–29, and, in all probability, Galatians 2:1–10. Naturally, these accounts favor Paul's reading of events.

JESUS CHRIST. See **YESHUA, RABBI**.

JESUS CHRIST, BOOKS ABOUT. There is a huge literature on Jesus Christ, but relatively few titles are entirely forthright about the consequences for Christianity of recognizing the essential Jewishness of **Rabbi Yeshua**. Among the most responsible of recent literature on Jesus for the nonspecialist is *Jesus* (1992) by A. N. Wilson. Slightly more demanding, but still accessible to nonspecialist readers are *The Changing Faces of Jesus* (2000) by Geza Vermes; *The Jesus Legend* (1996) by G. A. Wells; *The Historical Figure of Jesus* (1993) by E. P. Sanders; *The Incredible Shrinking Son of Man* (2003) by Robert Price; and *A Credible Jesus* (2002) by Robert Funk, founder of the **Jesus Seminar**.

Much longer but still readable by nonspecialists is *The Historical Jesus* (1991) by John Dominic Crossan. Equally long though less easy to read is *Jesus After 2000 Years* (2001) by **Gerd Lüdemann**. And, while by no means bedtime reading, *The Life of Jesus Critically Examined* (1835) by **David Friedrich Strauss** and *The Quest of the Historical Jesus* (1910) by Albert Schweitzer (1875–

1965) are still worth reading. These books don't all say the same thing by any means, but they are all honest attempts to get beyond the clearly untrue caricature of Jesus Christ as presented by conventional Christianity.

JESUS CHRIST, CREATION OF. The idea of "Jesus Christ" arose out of a slow transformation of the Jewish prophet **Rabbi Yeshua**, into a cosmic principle, rich with Greek and Eastern religious notions quite foreign to the intellectual world Rabbi Yeshua inhabited. The process was already underway when it was debated at the **Jerusalem Conference** in about 49 CE. The historian Jaroslav Pelikan has written that to "the Christian disciples of the first century the conception of Jesus as a rabbi was self-evident, to the Christian disciples of the second century it was embarrassing, to the Christian disciples of the third century it was obscure."

The New Zealand liberal theologian Lloyd Geering (1918–) has itemized six stages in the gradual replacement of Rabbi Yeshua, the Jewish prophet, with Jesus Christ, the Christian prototype. The stages went like this:

- Rabbi Yeshua, the Jewish messiah;
- Jesus as *a* son of **God**;
- the Lord, the Savior, the *only* Son of God;
- the **logos** or Word of God and Creator of the World;
- the incarnation of God; and
- the second unit of the Holy **Trinity** as defined by the Council of Chalcedon (451 CE).

This process took about four hundred years, and by its end the Jewish origins of Christianity and of its founder has been almost entirely expunged, and a new system which had developed incrementally, had risen in its stead. And in the saddest of ironies, an offshoot of the creation of Jesus Christ from Rabbi Yeshua was a vicious **anti-Semitism**.

Further reading: Jaroslav Pelikan, *Jesus Through the Centuries*; Lloyd Geering, *God in the New World*; and John Rowland, *Christian Origins*.

JESUS CHRIST, MYTH THEORY OF. The theory that **Jesus Christ** never existed. There had been since the Middle Ages the story of the three imposters: Moses, Jesus, and **Muhammad**, which **freethinkers** of various stripes developed over the centuries. The first clear assertion that Jesus Christ never existed can be traced to a popular work by Count Volney (1757–1820) called *Ruins of Empires* (1791). It was given fuller expression by **J. M. Robertson**, especially in *Christianity and Mythology* (1900) and *Pagan Christs* (1903). Robertson was deeply impressed by the amount of pre-Christian material in the Jesus story, and his works are an impressive collection of that material. But it is one thing to give an account of the mythical origins of many of the stories attached to Jesus, and it is quite another to then conclude that Jesus Christ never lived. Robertson also had an awkward tendency to write off inconvenient New Testament passages as interpolations.

A more sophisticated proponent of the myth theory was the English rationalist G. A. Wells, a lecturer in German at Birkbeck College, London. Thanks to his excellent command of the language, Wells was intimately familiar with German theology. His main books stressed pre-Christian origins less than Robertson, and talked more of **Paul**'s complete ignorance of, and lack of interest in, the details of Jesus' life.

But if there have been prominent supporters of the myth theory in the ranks of organized **freethought**, they have not been the sole voice of the movement. Some very prominent rationalist thinkers like F. C. Conybeare (1856–1924), **Joseph McCabe**, and **Archibald Robertson** have written more standard historical accounts of the life of Jesus. These writers all understood the vast gulf between the historical Jesus and the Christ of faith, but without then feeling the need to conclude that the historical Jesus did not exist.

The myth theory is built on a kernel of truth, but then concludes too much. The mythicists were building on the realization of nineteenth-century biblical scholarship that the Gospels were not a historical narrative but were ahistorical accounts loaded with later Christian interpretation. There is still a great reluctance among theologians to admit this, and the myth scholars were decades ahead of their orthodox rivals in this respect. But they then jumped one conclusion too far, and this undermined the valid points they were making. See the entries on the **quest for the historical Jesus**; **Jesus Christ, creation of**; **Jesus Seminar**; and **Rabbi Yeshua**.

JESUS JUNK. A derogatory term used in the Christian trinket trade for the plethora of Jesus-related junk that can be bought in the United States; everything from Jesus night-lights, to WWJD ("What Would Jesus Do?") T-shirts and armbands. What Jesus would have made of this trivializing of his message in his own name can only be imagined. One suspects he would have felt moved to undertake another rampage through the Temple of Mammon.

Jesus Junk is just one example of the decline of **religion**, even in an as apparently religious country as the United States. Jesus Junk is part of the commodification of religion, where billboards advertise a church or the visit of an Evangelist in just the same manner they would advertise a new brand of toilet paper or car insurance.

The ubiquity of this heavily marketed and commodified Christianity is evidence of its weakness in the more important field of ideas, where it has lost all the important philosophical battles of the past four hundred years, and is now left with a tarnished, shop-soiled product past its use-by date.

Further reading: R. Laurence Moore, *Selling God: American Religion and the Marketplace of Culture.*

JESUS SEMINAR. A regular gathering of a wide range of scholars whose main goal has been to revise understanding of Jesus Christ more in keeping with the authentic historical setting in which he lived and thought. The Jesus Seminar is an important force in the **third quest for the historical Jesus**. When the seminar first met in 1985, thirty scholars took part. By 2004, more than two hundred scholars were involved. While most members of the seminar were left-leaning Protestants, there was a smattering of Jews, Roman Catholics, and **Unitarians**.

The seminar comes together twice a year and hears academic papers that have been prepared and circulated in advance. The seminar fellows then vote, using colored beads, to indicate the degree of authenticity they attach to the words or deeds of Jesus under scrutiny. The black beads indicated the word or deed was thought to have little or no chance of being authentic. The colors went through grey to pink to red, which indicated a high degree of confidence. By this form of majority voting, the seminar has come up with a small set of phrases that it believes are the genuine words or deeds of **Rabbi Yeshua**. This form of arriving at scholarly consensus has come in to a great deal of criticism, not all of it from religious conservatives who are hostile to the seminar's program. The seminar recognizes that voting does not automatically determine the truth, but it maintains that it is the best way to achieve a scholarly consensus.

The first phase of the seminar lasted from 1985 until 1991 and focused on the words of Jesus. It concluded that 18 percent of the words of Jesus were likely to be authentic. These findings were published in *The Five Gospels: The Search for the Authentic Words of Jesus* (1993). The second phase, which lasted from 1991 until 1996, focused on the deeds of Jesus. This time 16 percent of the 176 deeds attributed to Jesus were deemed to be genuine. These findings were published in *The Acts of Jesus* (1998). As well as these works, individual members have produced important books, notably the founder, Robert Funk, who wrote *Honest to Jesus* (1996) and *A Credible Jesus* (2002). See the entries on **Yeshua, Rabbi** and **Jesus Christ, creation of**.

JEWISH WAR. A bloody struggle between the Jews in Palestine and their Roman overlords between 66 and 70 CE, and one of the most significant events in the history of Christianity, because it spelled the end of it as a strand of Jewish religious thinking. The Jews revolted at what they saw as tyrannical government by the Roman procurators, although the war was a protest against the principle of foreign domination, whether benign or cruel.

The Romans sent in Vespasian with three legions to suppress the revolt, which he succeeded in doing in 70 by taking Jerusalem. The Jewish remnants are then thought to have taken refuge on the mountain of Masada (although some credible recent scholarship has questioned the historicity of these events). A lengthy siege ensued and, at the moment of defeat in 73, the Jewish defenders killed themselves rather than surrender to the Romans.

After the war, the Jerusalem temple, the centerpiece of Judaism, was destroyed and the priesthood which worked there was dispersed. The Wailing Wall is said to be part of the foundations of the temple. Along with the temple, the Jewish national council, the Sanhedrin, a collaborationist governing body established by Pompey in 66 BCE, was also dismantled. And Jews left Jerusalem and settled around the Mediterranean and Near Eastern world, adding to the already broad Jewish diaspora.

This scattering of the Jews from Palestine fatally weakened the Jewish element in Christianity, already weakened after the **Jerusalem Conference** of 49 CE. Relations between them and the Jews who saw **Rabbi Yeshua** more in terms of **Jesus Christ** continued to worsen, leading to the expulsion of Jewish Christians from synagogues. From then on, Christians were on their own, and needed to justify their existence as against the Jews. This gave rise to the doctrine of **supersessionism** and goes a long way to explaining the **anti-Semitism** in the New Testament.

JIHAD. An Islamic notion involving the defense of their religion. Islam divides humans into the *Dar el-Islam* (House of Submission) and the *Dar el-Harb* (House of War). The **Qur'an** features some passages that demand war between the two houses, and other passages can be read in a more pacific way. In historical fact, however, jihad became associated with struggle against *Dar el-Harb*. In most cases, jihad is waged as a response to provocation from the *Dar el-Harb*. Jihad is a continuation of the Jewish and Christian thoughts on the **just war**.

After the attacks of September 11, 2001, many Western scholars and Islamic apologists tried to argue that jihad is a peaceful concept involving an internal struggle against one's own weaknesses, or a social struggle, such as a campaign against drugs, or some such social malady. This understanding of jihad may have been well intentioned, but it failed to do justice to the basic meaning of the term, which is military. The politically correct reading of jihad has its origins in some writings of Sufi mystics, but the more commonly understood use of the term is to denote the war against unbelievers. Ibn Taymiyah (1268–1328), an important precursor of **Wahhabi** Sunni Islam, extended the notion of jihad to include war against other Muslims who are insufficiently orthodox. This understanding of jihad is what is employed by Muslim terrorists when they target Muslim governments, not some sanitized notion of inner struggle. The logical goal for jihad is the conversion, surrender, or death of all infidels.

JOAD, CYRIL EDWIN MITHCINSON (1891–1953). English popularizer and journalist. Through much of the 1920s and 1930s, Joad was the most widely known popularizer of **freethought** in Britain. Joads's brand of freethought was an unstable mix of Platonism, vitalism, and **empiricism**, which collapsed under the strain of World War II. From about the end of 1942, Joad drifted into an equally eclectic version of Protestant Christianity. The height of Joad's influence was at the end of World War II, when he was part of the popular radio program *The Brains Trust*, along with **Julian Huxley**.

Joad's conversion to Christianity is still cited frequently in works by Christian apologists. What they neglect to mention is that Joad's propaganda value diminished significantly in 1948 after he was prosecuted for travelling on the train without a ticket. Following that debacle, Joad was dropped from the BBC's *Brains Trust*, and his public standing declined.

JOUISSANCE. A term much loved by postmodernists of a psychoanalytical bent. The word tends to remain untranslated because of its ambiguous meaning in French. It can mean a bewildering variety of things, depending on the author, ranging from sexual pleasure to religious bliss. The main value of the word for people who use it is its very ambiguity, allowing it to be slipped in whenever one wants a suitably foreign word to add tone to one's writing.

JOURNET, NOËL (d. 1582). French **freethinker** burnt at the stake in Metz in 1582. Journet's two manuscripts were burned with him; one that outlined the inconsistencies of the Bible, another that dismissed the Bible as a fable. The inconsistencies Journet exposed are now acknowledged by all but the most literal fundamentalists. Journet did not deny that a **God** existed; he argued that the Christian God was wicked. He also denied the˘ divinity of Christ.

Further reading: Michael Hunter and David Wootton, eds., *Atheism from the Reformation to the Enlightenment*.

JOYCE, JAMES (1882–1941). Hugely talented and original novelist. Born in Dublin and educated by Jesuits, Joyce reacted against the stifling bigotry of his Catholic education and went to Europe in 1902. He returned to Ireland little more than a year later to be with his mother at her death. While in Ireland, Joyce met Nora Barnacle, who remained his companion for the rest of his life.

Most of the remainder of Joyce's life was spent in Paris in a state of genteel poverty. He became known for his series of short stories called *Dubliners* (1914) and the autobiographical work, *Portrait of an Artist as a Young Man* (1916). Joyce's masterpiece is *Ulysses* (1922), which is often seen as one of the literary highlights of the twentieth century. In an attempt to recover the past in existential detail, *Ulysses* is a snapshot of several people's lives in Dublin in the summer of 1904. Joyce's work has remained deeply controversial ever since its publication. *Dubliners* was ready for publication in 1906, but it took eight years to overcome the objections of timid publishers and **virtuecrats**. *Ulysses* was banned in many countries and was not published in the United States until 1933 and Britain until 1936. Joyce's last major publication was *Finnegan's Wake* (1939).

"JUDEO-CHRISTIAN," MYTH OF. From the 1980s it became more common to speak of "Judeo-Christian" values or "Judeo-Christian" heritage. This trend began as a tactic by the Religious Right in the United States to allay growing alarm about their rhetoric among Jewish communities. Since then, the term has entered popular usage. "Judeo-Christian" is usually employed in the defense of a range of conservative issues, such as opposition to **abortion**, contraception, or homosexuality, and support for a restricted vision of **family values**. More recently, religious liberals have tried to appropriate the "Judeo-Christian" term in the interests of their causes, though with less success.

However, the "Judeo-Christian" tag is very unsound historically. It assumes a close alliance between Judaism and Christianity, and ignores the long centuries of Christian **anti-Semitism**. It also ignores the many differences in approach and emphasis between the **Hebrew scriptures** and the New Testament.

Perhaps the most blatantly incorrect usage of the "Judeo-Christian" tag is when it is applied to supposedly "Judeo-Christian" values. The least that can be said of this is that it ignores the invaluable contribution of Greece and Rome to the values most people hold dear. And a more serious charge is that it is an attempt, made against the grain of history, to claim for conservative Christianity a **monopoly on the truth**. This is a dangerous claim to make because it suggests that **toleration** of other points of view is tantamount to doing a deal with **Satan**, a claim frequently made in the more fundamentalist denominations. The fact is that the values many assume to be "Judeo-Christian" had been articulated and propagated centuries before Christianity was invented. See the entries on **ancient Greece and Rome, legacies of** and **humanism in the ancient world**.

JUDGMENT. A very valuable and underappreciated skill. Judgment entails the ability to cope with a new situation effectively. A new situation is where our principles and beliefs cease to operate. In this case we will need to evaluate that situation, assess the relevant **evidence**, and arrive at a reasonable decision without following rules. When we follow rules, we don't need to exercise any judgment beyond the simple decision to continue following the rules. But in a situation where we find the rules don't apply, or for some reason we are not going to follow the rules, then we need to exercise judgment.

All judgments are **fallible**, and are best made when the individual has command of an appropriate body of information. In this way, judgment is a learned ability, a skill acquired by the individual. And as such, judgment is entirely within the naturalistic realm. Another important fact about judgment is that different people will of course judge things differently, as the information they have access to will vary as will their ability to decipher and manage information. This makes toleration and empathy a necessary corollary to judgment.

Command moralities do not allow independent judgment to grow and develop, because they subscribe to the **principle of universalism**, which says that in all times and circumstances, there is only one acceptable response to any situation. See the entries on **reason** and **inquiry, tools of**.

Further reading: Harold Brown, *Rationality*.

JULIAN THE APOSTATE (331?–363 CE). The last pagan emperor of Rome. Julianus Flavius Claudius was the son of a half-brother of **Constantine** who, along with seven members of his family, had been murdered in the bloodletting that followed the death of the first Christian emperor. Orphaned at six, Julian was brought up by his half-brother Gallus, who was executed in 354. Julian was revolted by the violence and hypocrisy of his Christian upbringing and secretly returned to **paganism**. He enjoyed a successful military career against the Germanic barbarians before being appointed Caesar in 355, and in 361 he became emperor at the urging of his troops.

As soon as he took office, Julian determined to reverse the decrees which discriminated against paganism. He allowed all people, including Christians, to worship as they saw fit. No less significant, Julian ordered the reconstruction of the Jewish temple at Jerusalem, and the return of Jews there. Julian did this knowing that a rebuilt temple would seriously weaken Christian claims to have replaced Judaism as the New Covenant. Like his mentor **Marcus Aurelius Antoninus**, Julian was a philosopher-king, and left some important writings, in particular his study of Christianity, *Against the Galileans*.

These potentially explosive actions came to an abrupt end in 363 when Julian was killed while fighting in Mesopotamia. His death is one of the great "what-ifs" of history. We can only speculate whether he could have succeeded in restoring paganism to its former glories. Either way, the experiment was a shock to the Christians. After Julian's death, all the previous privileges for Christians were restored and persecution of Jews and pagans intensified and became more violent, most notably under **Theodosius**. Julian proved to be paganism's last gasp. His career as emperor lasted less than two years, but had an impact on history out of all proportion to the length of his tenure. His life is the subject of an excellent historical novel simply called *Julian*, by Gore Vidal. And in his poem, *Hymn to Prosperine*, **Algernon Swinburne** puts into Julian's mouth the words, "Thou has conquered, O pale Galilean; the world has grown gray from thy breath."

Further reading: Charles Freeman, *The Closing of the Western Mind*; and R. Joseph Hoffmann, ed., *Julian's "Against the Galileans."*

JUNG, CARL GUSTAV (1875–1961). Influential mystic. Jung was an early follower of Sigmund Freud, the founder of psycho-analysis. But Jung broke with Freud in 1913, largely over differences of opinion over the role of sexuality as a motivating force for people. Jung's early opinions were a standard blend of German racism and pseudoscience. He considered himself the living reincarna-tion of **Goethe**. He saw his mission in life to rescue German civilization from the cultural depredations of superficial urban living, par-ticularly as manifested in Judaism.

Under the influence of the gifted but unstable thinker Otto Gross (1877–1920), Jung was introduced to sexual anarchy, which he blended in with his commitment to extolling the virtues of what he saw as the unrestrained sexuality of the pre-Christian pagans. He then became a proponent of a spiritualized sexuality, which he came to see as vital for his psychic health. His wife, the mother of his five children, was not encour-aged to experiment in a similar way.

Jung brought his theories together in the book *The Psychology of the Unconscious* (1912, English translation 1916). Here he developed some of his central ideas, notably that of the collective unconscious, which posited a common racial memory, which was the task of psychically healthy people to rediscover.

As he developed his own following, he became less amenable to criticism. Some of his lectures in the 1920s were kept secret until almost thirty years after his death. He gradually came to believe he was the deified incarnation of the pagan Germanic deity Abraxas. He also felt himself to have a very close relationship with the Norse god Wotan, although he claimed to be surprised when the Nazis used his writings on the subject.

After World War II Jung reinvented him-self as the grandfatherly and spiritual leader for the age. Some skillful popularizations of his work made him accessible to a new gener-ation of readers who were unaware of Jung's racist past. See the entry on **mythology**.

Further reading: Richard Noll, *The Aryan Christ*; and Jeffrey Moussaieff Masson, *Against Therapy*.

JUPITER COMPLEX, THE. A term coined by the British atomic scientist P. S. M. Blackett that refers to the godlike and de-tached feeling of righteousness of bombing the enemy. Language reminiscent of the Jupiter Complex was used during World War II by both axis and allied forces. Both justi-fied their bombing in terms of righteous smiting of the evildoers. See the entry on **coventrate**.

More recently the Jupiter Complex has taken on an even more sinister form. It has been widely observed that the televised pic-tures of guided bombs going down air-condi-tioning shutes of buildings in Belgrade or Baghdad bear disconcerting likeness to video games. In the technological age, the Jupiter Complex sounds less like the righteous anger of the gods and the whoops of teenagers living out a fantasy.

JUST SO STORIES. A pejorative title given to the tendency, particularly within **evolu-tionary psychology**, to give explanations of how something in nature has come about. The term comes from Rudyard Kipling's (1865–1936) *Just So Stories* (1902), which told of how the elephant got its trunk and so on. Critics argue that evolutionary psychologists are prone to answering why human traits are as they are with "just so" stories.

JUST WAR. A controversial idea with a long history. In the ancient world any provocation against one's nation or tribe was considered sufficient for a war to be thought just. Things became more problematic after the advent of Christianity, which saw an increase in the ferocity of warfare, much of which pitted Christian against Christian. The idea was first canvassed specifically by Augustine of Hippo (354–430 CE) who proposed three principles to determine whether a war was just. They were:

- the cause for which the war is fought is just;
- the war is fought with the right intention; and
- the war is fought under duly constituted authority.

Augustine was able to reconcile his conditional support for a just war with the commandment to kill by observing that, outside the City of God, we are all locked in **original sin**, and so these measures are necessary. The Muslim notion of **jihad** was a continuation of Jewish and Christian notions of a just war.

More recent theories have emphasized that war is a measure of last resort, which takes place only when all possible nonviolent means have been exhausted. And the notion of "right intention" has been expanded to include the desire to reestablish peace. In an age of seriously destructive weapons, it has also been added that the war should be in some proportion to the injury received. So initiating a nuclear holocaust over some trivial diplomatic slight would be unjust by this reckoning. Other theorists have wanted to delineate as clearly as possible between combatants and noncombatants.

Another criterion of a just war is that the peace established must be a clear improvement on the situation that existed before the conflict. This criterion rules out a very large number of wars, the protagonists of which have insisted was justly fought. Still others, such as the Argentinian-born philosopher Mario Bunge, insist that the notion of a just war is an oxymoron, because all wars are unjust to their victims. The best that can be hoped for, Bunge argues, is that there may be one side of a war which is just, for example the victims of an unprovoked aggression. The American scholar Joyce Salisbury makes the most pertinent point when she says that we can only know whether a war has been just or not in the light of the quality of peace established. Millions of people believed World War I was a just war, but the peace betrayed that vision. After World War II, by contrast, while the peace was far from perfect, even the populace of the defeated nations generally conceded that their defeat served the cause of a just world more than their victory would have done. Salisbury's warning is all the more valid in the light of the fact that the so-called **war on terror** is rewriting most of the traditional rules of warfare.

The first attempt at an international agreement on the rules of war was the Geneva Convention, which is the name given to any agreement on the rules of war signed in Geneva. The first such meeting was 1864, which, among other things, established medical facilities as out of bounds as a war target. Other conventions followed in 1906, 1929, and 1949. An attempt in 1977 to widen the scope of the Geneva Conventions to include the casualties of guerilla war has been only partially successful. The United States, for instance, has not ratified it. With the war on terror now changing the rules once more, there is need for another look at the Geneva Conventions.

Further reading: John Keegan, *A History of Warfare*; Jimmy Carter, "Just War—or Just a War?" *New York Times*, March 9, 2003; www.wagingpeace.org; and Micheline Ishay, *The History of Human Rights*.

JUSTICE AS FAIRNESS. An idea conceived by the American political philosopher **John Rawls**. Justice as fairness is Rawls's most important idea and was the central theme in his books *A Theory of Justice* (1971, revised edition 1999) and *Political Liberalism* (1993). The idea was refined in *Justice as Fairness: A Restatement* (2001).

Justice as fairness envisages **society** as a fair system of cooperation that has been developed over generations and works in conjunction with the idea of the citizen as a free and equal person, and a **well-ordered society** being one which is effectively regulated by a public political conception of justice.

Justice as fairness is a recasting of the notion of the **social contract** and says that free and equal citizens can agree to the terms of social cooperation they wish to be bound by. Justice as fairness appeals to the reasonableness of people, rather than to their rationality: a rational person need not involve any notion of moral sensitivity in the way a reasonable person must. See the entry on **rationality and reasonableness**.

Neither is justice as fairness morally neutral. It has a built-in preference for the virtues of fair social cooperation such as civility, **toleration**, reasonableness, and a sense of fairness. The aim of justice as fairness is the practical one of becoming a notion of justice that citizens can share by virtue of exercising their shared **public reason**.

One of the contrary arguments to justice as fairness is that of justice as harmony. This has been favored by more authoritarian thinkers like **Plato** and **Thomas Hobbes**. This sees justice as a stable society where everybody knows his place, and social cohesion is the prime goal of justice. More recently, the British philosopher Stuart Hampshire (1914–2004) argued that justice is conflict. Hampshire said that, since there are no ideals of justice written across the sky, the ideals of justice have to arise out of society, and these ideals are generated by conflict, as people argue over what those ideals should be. Hampshire was following in the long tradition going back to **Heraclitus**, who said "justice is strife."

K

KAABA. A cubelike building in the center of the Sacred Mosque in Mecca that houses the black stone. The Kaaba is said to have been built by Adam and later destroyed in the flood. At the time of its reconstruction, when Ishmael was looking for a foundation stone, the angel Gabriel donated the black stone. In fact the worship of sacred stones was an old pagan practice that Islam took over. The black stone is most probably a piece of meteorite.

The Kaaba represents an unlikely intrusion of paganism into the otherwise stern **monotheism** of Islam. It was common practice among the pre-Islamic Arabian tribes to worship a deity in a sanctuary on top of a hill. The Muslim adoption of this practice eased the transition of pagan tribes into the faith. The seven circuits of the Kaaba required of pilgrims probably has an astrological origin.

The Kaaba took on its sacred status only once it had become apparent that Jews and Christians weren't going to convert en masse to Islam. Otherwise Jerusalem would have been the holy city and center of Islam.

KAHL, JOACHIM (1941–). German philosopher and **atheologian**. Kahl was born in 1941 and graduated from the University of Marburg as a Christian theologian. But his studies brought him to the realization that the whole structure of Christianity and all its truth claims were untrue, so he left the church in 1967 and began a new course of study at the University of Frankfurt, specializing in philosophy, sociology, and political science.

Kahl became well known after his short and fiery critique of Christianity, *Das Elend des Christentums,* was published in 1968. The work was translated and published in English as *The Misery of Christianity* in 1971, and included a preface by **Gerhard Szczesny**. *The Misery of Christianity* is widely recognized as a landmark in postwar criticism of Christianity. Part one, "What is Christian?," was a passionate and wide-ranging general critique of the crimes and falsity of historical Christianity. Part two, "Irrationality in Theology," was a more scholarly critique of German theology since the war. Kahl has had a distinguished career since *The Misery of Christianity*, but his works have not been translated into English.

KALINGA PRIZE. An award created by UNESCO in 1952 to recognize outstanding popularizers of science. The funds for the award came from its initial promoter, Indian philanthropist and progressive politician Bijayananda Patnaik (1916–1997). Kalinga is the ancient name for Orissa, Mr. Patnaik's home state, where his memory is widely respected.

Each member state can, through their respective national science organization, nominate a candidate, and the decision is made by the director general of UNESCO on the advice of a four-member panel. The laureate is awarded on World Science Day, receives the UNESCO World Science Medal, a modest honorarium, and usually undertakes a speaking tour. Past prizewinners include Louis De Broglie (1952, the first laureate), **Julian Huxley** (1953), **Bertrand Russell** (1957), **Arthur C. Clarke** (1961), **Fred Hoyle** (1967), Sergei Kapitza (1979), David Attenborough (1981), Peter Medawar (1985), and Marisela Salvatierra (2002).

KANAL, SATYAVAN P. (1911–). Son of P. V. Kanal (1883–1954), an educator and member of the **Dev Samaj**. S. P. Kanal was born in Ferozepur, Punjab, and studied philosophy in England where he was exposed to the works of **Bertrand Russell**, G. E. Moore (1873–1958), and **L. Susan Stebbing**. In 1948 he became head of the philosophy department at the Panjab University Camp College in Delhi. In 1957 he moved to Delhi University as head of postgraduate evening studies. In 1970–71, he was guest professor at Newport News, Virginia.

Kanal was an important atheist philoso-

pher in twentieth-century India. His main books are *The Philosophy of Religion* (1984) and *The Ethics of Devatma* (1991). Devatma is the honorific title given to Satya Nand Agnihotri (1850–1929), the founder of Dev Samaj. Sections from these books have been released separately as pamphlets, notably *Atheism in North India* and *Secular State and Religion* (both 1990). Kanal's atheism is unusual by Western standards, combining a Platonist confidence in intrinsic values such as beauty, goodness, and **altruism** with an insistence on our obligations to each other and to life itself. It is because of the **tragedy** of life, he writes, that **religion** was invented and justified. Kanal stresses the differences between religion and **humanism**, the former being based on **supernaturalism**, the latter on **naturalism**. But he also sees humanism as both a philosophy and a religion, and by grounding one's world in **science** and **reason** and immersing one's life in the teachings and example of Devatma, one can be imbued with the goodness to live the ideal life.

Further reading: Finngeir Hiorth, *Atheism in India.*

KANSEI EDICT. An official edict pronounced by the shogunate of Japan in 1790 that declared neo-Confucianism as the official philosophy of Japan and forbade the propagation of any rival system. The edict established two government positions whose responsibility was to oversee and censor any heterodox material. The edict was part of a general conservative crackdown aimed at creating a closed society and bolstering the power of the Tokugawa Shogunate. The edict, and the conservatism which attended it, brought to an end a productive period of Japanese neo-Confucian thinking.

KANT, IMMANUEL (1724–1804). Probably the most brilliant philosopher of all time, although it is one of the paradoxes—and triumphs—of **philosophy** that one can be utterly brilliant and make a seminal contribution, without necessarily being right in all things.

Kant's period of philosophical activity was relatively short. His three most important works are the *Critique of Pure Reason* (1781), the *Critique of Practical Reason* (1788), and the *Critique of Judgment* (1790), although the *Groundwork of the Metaphysic of Morals* (1785, known usually as *The Moral Law*) is also important.

What Kant tried to do was to effect a compromise between the two great and conflicting strands of philosophy that had arisen, in the West at least, with the **rationalism** of Plato and the **empiricism** of **Aristotle**. Kant was inspired by the Scottish genius **David Hume** to address this long-standing philosophical impasse. Kant dismissed both the rationalist and empiricist accounts of how we come to know things. Concepts are not derived, as empiricists said, by sense experience, nor, as claimed by rationalists, through logical abstraction. These categories of thoughts are, he argued, the common language of humanity and form a foundational program with which we can make sense of the world. Kant is best known for his contribution to moral philosophy, where he postulated the **categorical imperative**. See also the entry on *sapere aude*.

Kant also made tremendous contributions to the comprehensive demolition of traditional arguments for the existence of **God**, such as the **ontological argument**, the **cosmological argument,** and the **argument to design**. Kant was happy to retain the notion of God to act as a symbolic ideal. Though he believed that religion had little or nothing to offer morality, Kant was convinced that notions of God and **immortality** were essential in justifying morality. God, freedom, and immortality were postulates of pure practical reason in Kant's mind. The *Critique of Pure Reason* ended up on the **Index of Forbidden Books**.

Kant's scientific work is less well known, but hardly any less extraordinary. In the *General History of Nature and Theory of the Heavens* (1755) he made some significant predictions which were later confirmed by others: the nebula hypothesis (later confirmed by **Laplace**); the description of the Milky Way as one of many lens-shaped collections of stars (later confirmed by Herschel); and the proposal that friction from tides slowed the rotation of the earth (confirmed a century later).

KARMA. An important concept among the great **Asian traditions** of Hinduism and Buddhism. Central to karma is the idea that all our thoughts and actions produce a result, no matter how distant, and that result must play itself out. In this way, one's strengths and weaknesses now are the product of past thoughts and actions, and our current thoughts and actions will help shape our future existences. What is required is developing the ability to accrue Karma that no longer craves for things and for life, for such craving is symptomatic of our fundamental ignorance. Karma is what keeps our life processes going through many rebirths, but we must seek enlightenment by which we can stop this endless cycle of rebirths and enter nirvana.

Karma has many troubling consequences. It requires the belief that the world is just, so that all actions will reap their appropriate reward or punishment at some time or other. In this way, karma functions as a unique answer to the **problem of evil**. Evil exists in the world, but the apparent flourishing of evildoers in this life is illusory, for their misdeeds will be accounted for in the manner in which they live their next life. A wicked person now may be reincarnated as a **dalit** or a cockroach in the next. Not only that, but those suffering in this world are in fact paying the price for misdeeds in a previous life. This means that all human suffering one sees is deserved suffering. This also means that karma can only ever be seen as being wise after the event.

Further reading: Paul Edwards, *Reincarnation: A Critical Study*.

KAZANTZAKIS, NIKOS (1883–1957). Brilliant and eclectic Greek thinker and novelist. Nikos Kazantzakis was born in Iraklion on the island of Crete. After studying law in

Athens he went to Paris where he studied under the French philosopher Henri Bergson (1859–1941). Along with **Friedrich Nietzsche**, Bergson exerted a profound influence on Kazantzakis's thinking.

After a career writing travel books, Kazantzakis turned to novels. His two best known works are *Zorba the Greek* (1946, translated 1952) and *The Last Temptation of Christ* (1951, translated 1960), for which he was excommunicated by the Greek Orthodox Church. Not to be outdone, the Roman Catholic Church placed the book on the **Index of Forbidden Books** in 1954. Kazantzakis also wrote the epic poem *Odyssey: A Modern Sequel* (1938).

Kazantzakis is sometimes described as intensely religious, but this confuses intensity of feeling with religious feeling. He lived his life with passion and was deeply interested in religious questions, but his actual religious beliefs were heterodox, to say the least. A less well-known work of his was *The Saviors of God: Spiritual Exercises* (1927) where Kazantzakis acknowledges **God**'s nonexistence and urges, in Nietzschean style, a heroic refusal to succumb to the **transcendental temptation**. Kazantzakis was also strongly influenced by Buddhism, and spoke of saving God by our own efforts at a fulfilled life.

KELLER, HELEN (1880–1968). Humanist writer and activist for the blind. Keller was born in Tuscumbia, Alabama, and lost her eyesight at nineteen months. With the assistance of a devoted tutor, she slowly learned to speak. In 1904 she graduated with honors from Radcliffe College.

Keller became an outspoken advocate for disabled women and minorities. She was a founder of the **American Civil Liberties Union** and an early activist in the Humanist Society of New York and the National Association for the Advancement of Colored People. She was a supporter of women's suffrage and reproductive rights, and after the atomic bombs were dropped on Hiroshima and Nagasaki, of the peace movement. Predictably, Keller came to the attention of the FBI and the Committee for Un-American Activities during the **great fear**. Keller was a longstanding friend of **Joseph Lewis**, a fellow Alabaman. Among her best-known works include *The Story of My Life* (1903), *Let Us Have Faith* (1940), and *The Open Door* (1957).

KEMAL, MUSTAPHA (1881–1938). The founder of modern Turkey. Mustapha Kemal was born in Salonika, at the time part of the Ottoman Empire, now part of Greece. His father was a career soldier and made sure Mustapha received a secular education. Even after his father's death when he was only seven, his mother persisted with a secular education. While at school, he was given the name Kemal, or "perfect one," because of his proficiency in mathematics.

He followed his father into the armed services, and while stationed in Salonika, became involved in the reform movement known as the Young Turks, although he was on the losing side of internal quarrels within the reformist ranks. After this, Kemal devoted his energies to the military, where his reformist ideas won him widespread admiration. When the Ottoman Empire entered World War I on the side of Germany, Kemal was given the responsibility of defending the strategically important Gallipoli peninsula. When British, Australian, and New Zealand forces (the ANZACs) landed there on April 25, 1915, Kemal led a brilliant defense, which ultimately forced the invaders to relinquish their precarious foothold on the peninsula.

In the chaos after the empire's defeat in 1918 it looked as if Turkey would be reduced to a rump state in northern Anatolia, or even disappear altogether, as European countries tried to parcel bits of the country off for themselves. Over the next five years, Kemal led the fight against each of these invaders and saved Turkey from dismemberment. It was an incredible achievement, against all odds, and Kemal became known as Attatürk, or "father of the Turks."

He did not just rescue Turkey from the consequences of military defeat. He can properly be called the father of modern Turkey. He achieved this by importing ideas from outside Turkey that he thought were essential to the country's future. In 1923 he abolished the **Khalifat** and established Turkey as a secular republic. But it was his changes in education that were probably the decisive factors in the success of the social revolution he achieved. He enacted the Law for the Unification of Education in Turkey in 1924. This law brought all the small, parochial schools in the country under the control of the Ministry of Education. Boys and girls received the same education and all convents run by religious sects were banned and primary education was made secular and compulsory. And in 1928, the Arabic script was replaced by the Latin script. Attatürk said as early as 1922 that "nations which want to preserve logically unjustifiable traditions and beliefs can scarcely develop, if they develop at all." With this in mind, Turkish women got the right to vote in 1934, the first country in the Middle East to do so.

Attatürk's secularist legacy has been under attack for the past thirty years. After a military government took power in 1980, religious education was made compulsory and the number of Muslim clerics being trained increased by 300 percent. More recently, terrorist organizations have sought to destroy his memorial in Ankara as a protest against **secularism**. However, the second article of the Turkish constitution states that Turkey is a "democratic, secular, and social state governed by the Rule of Law." Today, Turkey stands on the brink of joining the European Union. It is inconceivable that this could be possible were it not for the reforms overseen by Attatürk. And the secular reforms in Turkey stand as an example of what can be achieved in the Middle East.

KEPLER, JOHANNES (1571–1630). Brilliant German astronomer who established beyond doubt the **heliocentric universe**, although his brilliance is not without paradox. For instance, he worked out successfully the correct orbits for the six planets known at the time, although his figures depended on there being only six planets, and yet we now know there are nine, so Kepler's success here is accidental.

Another paradox was his twenty year attempt to confute the findings of Copernicus (1473–1543), which succeeded in verifying them instead. Working from a **faith** derived from **Pythagoras** that the universe is a harmonious series of relations, Kepler worked out that the planetary orbits of the sun do not happen in a perfect circle, as Copernicus (following **Aristotle**) maintained. Instead, Kepler found that planetary orbits are elliptical. These are known as Kepler's Laws of Planetary Motion. And all this was written in *Harmonices mundi* (1619), which was written primarily to describe the harmonies in music!

KEYNES, JOHN MAYNARD (1883–1946). The most influential economist since **Adam Smith**. Born into a privileged family, John Maynard was the son of John Neville Keynes, a Cambridge philosopher and economist. From Eton, Keynes studied at King's College, Cambridge, where he lectured between bouts in senior administrative positions in London, including the India office between 1906 and 1908.

Until the end of World War I, Keynes was content with his secluded and privileged life. It was only after a posting at the treasury during the war that Keynes became active in public life. Keynes resigned from the treasury in protest at the terms of the draft treaty about to be imposed on defeated Germany. He outlined his opposition in his angry work *The Economic Consequences of the Peace* (1919), which criticized strongly the manner in which the peace negotiations after World War I had been conducted.

Keynes took an active part in public life after this, combining his intellectual and political work. Keynes's two masterpieces of economics were *A Treatise on Money* (1930) and *General Theory of Employment, Interest, and Money* (1936). These two books combine the economic theory now described simply as Keynesianism. In particular, Keynes argued that unemployment need not be a permanent state of affairs, and set out a new account of planning the management of money to support his views. Keynes's views were strongly influential on Franklin Roosevelt's New Deal, which helped reform the American economy battered by the depression. The newly elected Labor Government in New Zealand was similarly influenced, and in 1935 began a fourteen-year term of office founded largely on Keynesianism.

Keynes's interests were not limited to economics. In *Treatise on Probability* (1921), he advanced a dauntingly complicated argument that distinguished logical relationships between something being "highly probable" and "justifiable induction." Keynes was also an important member of the literary Bloomsbury Group and was instrumental in setting up the Arts Theatre at Cambridge. He also made a fortune on the stock market, both for himself and for King's College.

After World War II, Keynes played a leading role in establishing the postwar international monetary system at Bretton Woods. See the entries on **World Bank**, **International Monetary Fund**, and **global governance**. Keynes also negotiated the postwar loan for the British economy, bankrupted by its effort in defeating **Adolf Hitler**.

KHALIFAT. Or in Western spelling "Caliphate" is the office of the Khalif, or Caliph, the successor to Muhammad. The Khalifat-i-Rashida is the model government of the four caliphs after Muhammad: Abu Bakr (632–634 CE), Omar (634–644), Othman (644–656), and 'Ali (656–661).

The word "khalif" means "successor." The problem was that **Muhammad** left no direct male heir to succeed him, nor, according to Sunnis, had he made any provision for a successor, and so on Muhammad's death in 632, Abu Bakr was chosen as the Caliph. However, according to Shi'ites, Muhammad had appointed his cousin 'Ali as the successor. 'Ali did not become Caliph until 656 and his rule was contested throughout, culminating in his murder in 661, and an irrevocable split between Sunni and Shi'ite Muslims.

After the four orthodox or "rightly guided" successors of the Khalifat-i-Rashida, the Khalifat continued through what are called the Umayyad (661–750) and Abbasid (750–1517) dynasties. But at this point the Ottoman Turks took the Khalifat to Constantinople and the Shi'ite Fatimids of Egypt set up their own Khalifat in Cairo. The split was exacerbated by different attitudes to the Khalifat. Most Sunnis believe that the institution is simply a stopgap given that Muhammad chose no successor. But because Shi'ites believe that Muhammad did in fact appoint a successor, the office of Khalif is of divine provenance. See the entry on the **Mahdi**. The Sunni Caliphate carried on with few breaks until it was abolished on March 3, 1924, by **Mustapha Kemal**, Turkey's leader after World War I.

It is the ambition of militant Islamist groups like **al Qaeda** to restore the Khalifat. A **fatwa** signed on February 23, 1998, by Osama bin Laden, Ayman Zawahiri (his lieutenant), and Fayher Rehman Khalil, head of the militant organization Jamiat ul Ansar (group of helpers) based in Pakistan announced the restoration of the Khalifat as their goal. They believe that all Middle Eastern governments have fallen short of their divine responsibility to propagate Islam.

KIMBERLEY PROCESS. A system of certification of diamond transactions established in 2000 on the initiative of a group of diamond traders in southern Africa. The process now involves seventy countries, and hopes to end the illicit trade in diamonds out of Africa, which is funding the chronic ethnic and warlord violence on that continent. The first meetings of the traders were held in Kimberley, South Africa. The Kimberley Process was finally worked out at a meeting in Interlaken, Switzerland, in November 2002.

The Kimberley Process has been criticized as inadequate because it applies only to rough diamonds. Supporters of the process defend this on the grounds that, if buyers are offered processed diamonds without proper certification, then they can be justifiably suspicious as to its provenance.

KNIGHT, MARGARET (1903–1983). Academic based at the University of Aberdeen who made history in January 1955 when she gave a series of broadcasts on BBC radio called *Morals Without Religion*. This was one of the first instances in the United Kingdom when religious beliefs were openly challenged on air. The reaction was volcanic, with Knight being subjected to a storm of abuse by religious listeners unused to having their views criticized, however mildly.

Knight denied that Christianity and communism were the great alternatives of the day, suggesting instead that both are dogmatic systems and, as such, stood together against scientific humanism. Children, Knight said, should be taught Bible stories in the same way they are taught any other ancient myth. The essence of humanism was held to be disinterestedness, or not letting our own claims blind us to those of other people. The furor over the *Morals Without Religion* broadcasts made Margaret Knight a popular speaker for a long time and contributed materially to spreading humanist views. Ten years later, far more militant humanists, like David Tribe and **A. J. Ayer** were on radio and television with hardly a murmur of protest. Christians, however, continued to enjoy the overwhelming majority of air time.

Outside of the *Morals Without Religion* affair, Margaret Knight was known for a study of *William James* (1950) and a defense of telepathy. She edited the very successful *Humanist Anthology* in 1961 and wrote a concise restatement of rationalism called *Honest to Man* (1974).

Further reading: Bill Cooke, *The Gathering of Infidels: A Hundred Years of the Rationalist Press Association*.

KNOWLEDGE. A general term covering a huge range of data produced throughout the body and processed by the brain. There are three main types of knowledge:

- *propositional knowledge*: the knowledge that something is so;
- *procedural knowledge*: the knowledge of how to do something; and
- *knowledge by acquaintance*: the knowledge based on our direct personal experience.

Knowledge, wrote **Bertrand Russell**, is a matter of degree. All human knowledge, he went on, is "uncertain, inexact, and partial"; a declaration he could see no limitations to whatever. This intellectual modesty is an essential part of **freethought**. **Socrates** was an early exemplar of this attitude. The Oracle at Delphi was supposed to have declared Socrates the wisest of men. Socrates was under no illusions, however, as to what this meant. The basis of the wisdom of Socrates lay in his awareness of just how little knowledge he really had.

The less knowledge there is, the harder to add to it, which is why the intellectual development of humanity was so slow for so long. See the entry on **meliorism**.

Further reading: Bertrand Russell, *Human Knowledge: Its Scope and Limits*.

KONGFUZI (551–479 BCE). Known to the West by his Latinized name Confucius, Kongfuzi is the most significant Chinese thinker in Chinese history. He also deserves to be thought of as one of the most outstanding humanists of all time. Kongfuzi was born into an aristocratic family in the state of Lu, now part of Shantung province in China. Kong's family, though aristocratic, had fallen on hard times and was impoverished, especially after his father's early death, when Kong was only three. Kong became a government official in Lu and was very successful, too successful for his own good. In 497 he left Lu after falling foul of government intrigue and was a wandering sage, going from court to court, in search of a sympathetic patron. He attracted a group of followers through these dark years.

In about 485 he returned to Lu where he taught his disciples. After his death his disciples compiled a series of sayings and aphorisms of the master. This work, the *Analects*, is the most authentic of all the works attributed to Kongfuzi. Most of the other works attributed to him, while Confucian in flavor, were compiled by his followers. See the entry on **Qu Yuan** for an interesting parallel.

Kongfuzi's genius involved transforming the **naturalism** and **humanism** latent in Chinese thinking into the strongest forces in Chinese thought down to this day.

Master Kong said that having a distance from spiritual beings was a sign of wisdom. He expressed no opinion on the fate of **souls** and never encouraged **prayer**. For him, education was the key.

He is usually portrayed as a conservative. In many respects this is true; he was concerned with good government and harmonious social relations. But this view overlooks how radical his new interpretations of traditional concepts were. In particular, Kong realigned the concept of *chun-tzu*, which had traditionally meant "son of the ruler" into "superior man," with the effect that nobility was no longer a matter of blood or birth, but of **character**. This was a very radical departure from customary Chinese thinking that preceded him. Along with this, Kong radically transformed the notion of *jen* from meaning "kindliness" to the more general "man of the **golden rule**," or perfect *chun-tzu*. *Jen* was expressed in terms of chung and **shu**, or conscientiousness and altruism.

Kongfuzi's ideas of harmonious relations are articulated most thoroughly in a work which reflects his ideas, though was not actually written by him called *The Great Learning*. They are also an important feature of his notion now called the **Doctrine of the Mean**.

KOVOOR, ABRAHAM (1898–1978). Longtime rationalist campaigner. Born in Tiruvalla, Kerala, to a prominent priest in the Syrian Christian Church at Malabar. Kovoor studied botany and zoology at Bengabasi College in Calcutta. His **skepticism** developed when he was young. When asked to return home with some water from the Ganges, reputed to have miraculous healing power, Kovoor would fill his bottle at the railway station nearest home. But sure enough, the water would be ascribed healing powers.

Kovoor had a long teaching career in India and Sri Lanka. Early in his career, he was asked to teach **scripture** study. He did so with great success, with all his students passing, many with distinction. But they also become atheists. He was not asked to teach the class again.

After his retirement he devoted his time to the eradication of superstition. Along with his wife, Professor Jacqueline Kovoor, he founded in 1960 the Sri Lanka Rationalist Association, serving as president until his death. He toured India and Sri Lanka extensively, giving examples of the simple tricks wandering godmen use to allegedly demonstrate their spiritual powers. He slept in haunted houses and undertook important actions at times the astrologers deemed inauspicious. He challenged Sai Baba to submit to a test of his special powers, but Sai Baba refused to consent. In 1963 he issued a challenge, promising to pay 100,000 Sri Lankan rupees to anyone who could demonstrate supernatural powers under fraud-proof conditions. To this day nobody has been able to claim the prize. Not surprisingly, Kovoor attracted substantial media interest in his work.

In 1976 he put many of his experiences together into his book *Begone Godmen! Encounters with Spiritual Frauds*, which has gone through many editions. His work has been continued since his death by B. Premanand (1930–). As well as running a hospital and an institution for intellectually disabled children, Premanand is busy travelling and appearing on television exposing magic and fraud.

KRISHNAMURTI, JIDDU (1895–1986). Son of an Indian civil servant who was "discovered" by the prominent Theosophist **Charles Leadbetter**, who hailed the boy as a reincarnation of the Buddhist Lord Maitreya and of identical cosmic spirit to **Jesus Christ**. From this moment on, Krishnamurti was sequestered away and indoctrinated in the ways of **Theosophy**. Leadbetter and **Annie Besant** established the Order of the Star of the East as a vehicle for Krishnamurti.

Once able to decide for himself, he split from the Theosophical movement in August 1929 and began his own highly successful career as a **New-Age** prophet. Krishnamurti advocated that people find their own way to peace. Truth, he said, was a pathless land, and he urged those who had followed him to shun churches, sects and cults, and materialism. In the process, he went on to become a very rich man.

KRISHNAMURTHY, AVULA GOPALA (1917–1966). Indian humanist campaigner. Krishnamurthy, commonly known as "AGK," was born and raised in Andhra Pradesh and lived most of his life there. He was educated at Lucknow University, graduating in law and literature. He was part of the rebirth of the **Indian Rationalist Association** in 1949, serving for many years as its vice president. He was also active for many years in the radical-humanist movement.

Krishnamurthy was influenced by **M. N. Roy**, although he never shared Roy's commitment to Marxism. He translated Roy's *New Humanism* into Telugu, the language spoken in Andhra Pradesh. During his career in Andhra Pradesh he championed intercaste marriages and defended the rights of **dalits**. He also opposed, successfully, a textbook designed for elementary school children, which described the Buddha as Satan. He became widely respected for his work and was widely influential throughout Andhra Pradesh.

KUNDALINI. An idea beloved by several generations of **New-Age** enthusiasts. Kundalini is said to be a hidden psychic force, often referred to as the coiled serpent. It is unclear exactly what or where the kundalini is; it is held to lie at the base of the spine by some, it is semen according to others. Either way, the coiled serpent is roused by stimulating activities during **yoga** and then rises to activate the psychic powers of whichever psychic center is being called upon.

KÜNG, HANS (1928–). Swiss theologian whose teaching license was revoked by Pope John Paul II in 1979, the first year of his papacy. Küng had questioned papal infallibility in his book *Infallible? An Inquiry* (English translation, 1971). John Paul II responded by using the formidable powers to enforce doctrinal orthodoxy that the papacy had acquired over the twentieth century. The process was overseen by the Congregation for the Doctrine of the Faith (the renamed Holy Office or **Inquisition**) under the control of Cardinal Joseph Ratzinger. The cardinal had originally been a liberal, but was shocked into reactionary conservatism by the events of the 1960s.

Küng has developed a reputation as a skilled and sensitive theologian, particularly with such books as *On Being a Christian* (1974) and *Does God Exist?* (1978). He at least recognizes some intellectual and even moral force in **atheism**, but his critique is deficient by not then going on to make a thorough analysis of positive **humanism**. Despite recognizing that the atheist does not have to be a nihilist, his argument proceeds pretty much on that assumption. Predictably, **God** ends up looking very good indeed.

KURTZ, PAUL (1925–). Secular humanist philosopher, organizer, and entrepreneur. Paul Kurtz was born in Newark, New Jersey. Soon after enrolling at New York University, he volunteered for military service. Not quite eighteen, his unit was rushed to the front during the height of the Battle of the Bulge. Later on he was among the forces that liberated Dachau concentration camp. He stayed with the American forces in Germany for eighteen months after the war before being demobilized.

Upon his return to civilian life, Kurtz resumed his studies at New York University before moving on to Columbia University, where he took his PhD in 1952. He was a student of **Sidney Hook** and retained a lifelong relationship with the older philosopher. And through Hook, Kurtz stands in direct line from **John Dewey**. His doctoral dissertation was called *The Problem of Value Theory*. His whole academic career was devoted to justifying the methods of objective inquiry. He was never happy restricting his activities to the academic ghetto, and when he was offered the editorship of the *Humanist*, the magazine of the **American Humanist Association**, in 1967, he took it. In 1976 he was instrumental in establishing the **Committee for the Scientific Investigation of Claims of the Paranormal**, and in 1980 he set up the **Council for Secular Humanism**.

The core of Kurtz's philosophy of life can be found in *The Transcendental Temptation* (1986), *Forbidden Fruit: The Ethics of Humanism* (1988), *Eupraxophy: Living without Religion* (1989), and *Skepticism: Inquiry and Reliable Knowledge* (1992). In the tradition of Dewey and Hook, Kurtz outlines a **naturalist**, joyful, and invigorating philosophy of life. Perhaps the most significant difference between Dewey and Kurtz is in their respective attitudes toward **religion** and religious language. Kurtz warned against the **transcendental temptation** and rather than insisting humanism is a "me too" religion, coined the word **eupraxsophy** to explain the humanist love of life, profound respect for nature, and willingness to live an active life. See the entries on **activist frame**, **common moral decencies**, and **transcendental temptation**.

Shorter works which have explored these themes include *Exuberance: An Affirmative Philosophy of Life* (1978), *The Courage to Become: The Virtues of Humanism* (1997), and *Affirmations* (2004). Edited collections of his works include *Toward a New Enlightenment: The Philosophy of Paul Kurtz* (1994), *Embracing the Power of Humanism* (2000), and *Skepticism and Humanism: The New Paradigm* (2001). And Kurtz has edited some other important books like *Challenges to the Enlightenment: In Defense of Reason and Science* (with Timothy J. Madigan, 1994) and *Science and Religion: Are They Compatible?* (with Barry Karr and Ranjit Sandhu, 2003).

Among the organizations Kurtz founded or cofounded include: **Prometheus Books** (1969); CSICOP, the Committee for the Scientific Investigation of Claims of the Paranormal (1976); the Council for Secular Humanism (1980); the **International Academy of Humanism** (1983); the **Committee for the Scientific Examination of Religion** (1983); the **Secular Organizations for Sobriety** (with James Christopher, 1988); **African Americans for Humanism** (with Norm Allen, 1989); the **Center for Inquiry** (1991); the Council for Media Integrity (1996); the Society of Humanist Philosophers (1997); the Council for Scientific Medicine (1997); and the **Commission for Scientific Medicine and Mental Health** (2003).

Further reading: Paul Kurtz, *Embracing the Power of Humanism*.

KYOTO TREATY. An important step toward an effective transnational environmental policy. The Kyoto Treaty was the first agreement to set binding restrictions on emissions of gases that are known to help contribute to global warming.

The Kyoto Treaty was signed in 1997 by 170 nations, including the United States. It rose out of the **United Nations** Framework Convention on Climate Change in 1992. It was becoming clear by the mid-1990s that the targets set in 1992 were not going to be met, hence the need for the Kyoto meeting. The treaty could not take effect until it had been ratified by enough industrialized nations to account for 55 percent of the combined level of emissions as of 1990. As a result, ratification was delayed for seven years, mainly because of the refusal of the United States, which is responsible for 36 percent of all emissions, to sign. President George H. W. Bush signed the original 1992 convention but President George W. Bush refused to ratify the Kyoto Treaty. It was only when Russia became a signatory in October 2004, that the 55 percent threshold was overtaken.

Nobody argues that the system established at Kyoto is perfect. Signatory nations can reach their targets without reducing their own emissions by purchasing credits from other nations. Each signatory nation is allotted a set of credits, which represents its permissible levels of emissions. So Russia, which is producing emissions below its set level, is sitting on a bonanza of credits it can sell to other countries. And China, though a signatory of the Kyoto Treaty and a major polluter, is not bound by its restrictions because it is a developing economy. Many American economists have complained of this as giving China an unfair economic advantage over the United States.

But, more serious than any of these problems is that even if the Kyoto levels were reached, they would still be inadequate to stem the levels of greenhouse emissions into the atmosphere. Calculations differ, but some scholars estimate it would take upwards of 40 times the level of current percent restrictions to even begin to make any meaningful difference.

But despite all these significant drawbacks and failings, the Kyoto Treaty represents an important milestone in **global governance** on environmental issues. Effective solutions can no longer be worked at a national level. Our problems are global and interdependent, so our solutions must be global and interdependent. It has also transpired that conforming to the Kyoto protocols has not been as costly as critics feared. BP, the world's second largest oil company, decided in 1997 to voluntarily reduce its emissions to 10 percent below 1990 levels. It met its targets eight years ahead of schedule and at no net economic cost, because the savings from lower energy costs balanced the

costs of implementation. None of this would have happened without the leadership of the United Nations. See the entry on the **Montreal Protocols**.

L

LADDER OF RELIGIOUS CRUELTY, a conception of the history of religions devised by **Friedrich Nietzsche**, who wrote of a ladder with many rungs—but the three most important were:

- at one time we sacrificed other human beings to **God**, not infrequently the human beings we loved the most: our firstborn children;
- then, as we became more moral (so called), we learned to sacrifice our own natures to God and take on a joyless demeanor; and
- finally, when nothing else is left to sacrifice, we sacrifice God himself out of a masochistic cruelty toward oneself, and worship instead stone, stupidity, fate, and nothingness.

This final act of sacrificial cruelty was what Nietzsche meant by the **death of God**.

Further reading: Friedrich Nietzsche, *Beyond Good and Evil*.

LAICITY. A concept being developed by European humanist thinkers as the proactive union of **secularism** and human **rights**. Ideas of laicity (laïcité in French, laicità in Italian) began among nineteenth-century campaigners for the **separation of church and state**. In the twenty-first century, laicity has a broader meaning. It begins with the recognition of each citizen's freedom of conscience and proceeds from that to a neutral and impartial state as a necessary condition for this to take place. Most nations in Europe are multicultural and post-Christian, and the concept of laicity is designed to give voice to making a genuinely multicultural society a success for all its citizens.

LAMARCK, JEAN-BAPTISTE DE
(1744–1829). Influential evolutionist before **Charles Darwin**. Lamarck coined the term "biology" and was the first to recognize the significance of fossils as a means to understanding **evolution**. He worked on a formula of simple-to-complex, but the mechanism he suggested to explain evolution was incorrect. Lamarck's mechanism was known as the inheritance of acquired characteristics, which postulated that evolving life-forms have an instinct for improvement and that, over many generations, this instinct for improvement can be passed on to succeeding generations.

Lamarck's theory of the inheritance of acquired characteristics remained very influential even after Darwin conceived natural selection. Lamarck's theory remained valid for those who wanted to retain a sense of purpose in history, whether libertarians such as **Herbert Spencer** or Marxists, through to Christians anxious to save a place for a creator. Even Darwin subscribed to the inheritance of acquired characteristics, despite also adhering to natural selection. Lamarckism remained influential until the **neo-Darwinian synthesis** of the 1930s, although it remained powerful in the Soviet Union until well into the 1950s.

LAMONT, CORLISS (1902–1995). A significant figure in the development of American humanism. Lamont was born in Englewood, New Jersey, to a very wealthy family. His father was a business partner of the industrialist J. P. Morgan (1867–1943). Lamont was born on Good Friday, which his mother took as a good omen for his future piety. She was to be disappointed.

While studying at Harvard, Lamont became familiar with socialist thinking. He took his PhD in 1932 at Columbia, studying under **John Dewey**. His PhD was later pub-

lished as *The Illusion of Immortality* (1935), which remains a classic study of the subject.

As his socialist views developed, so did his admiration of the Soviet Union. It took Lamont much longer than most people of his generation to review his attitude toward it. This attitude dogged him for the rest of his life, involving him in some testy spats with the staunch anticommunist **Sidney Hook**.

Lamont was a major target of Senator Joseph McCarthy (1909–1957) during the **great fear**. Lamont also had to fight some important legal battles to obtain his due civil rights. He had to go to the Supreme Court to regain his right to have a passport, without regard to his political beliefs. He also fought suits against the CIA and FBI with respect to the surveillance these agencies had put him under.

Lamont's major work was *Humanism as a Philosophy* (1949), which developed out of his course at Columbia called "Philosophy of Naturalist Humanism." Later editions, retitled *The Philosophy of Humanism*, were very influential statements on humanism. See the entry on **humanist philosophy, ten propositions of**. He also wrote an autobiography, *A Lifetime of Dissent* (1988). Lamont was an honorary associate of the **Rationalist Press Association** from 1982 until his death.

LAND ETHIC. An idea posed by the American conservationist and pioneer of wildlife ecology, Aldo Leopold (1887–1948), which says that things can be judged right or wrong according to the degree by which they preserve, or fail to preserve, the integrity, stability, and beauty of the land. Clearly, the development of a coherent land ethic would contribute significantly to the **principles of sustainable development**. See the entry on the **positive and negative sustainability quotient**.

LANGUAGE GAMES. An idea invented by **Ludwig Wittgenstein** and put to many uses since his death. Sociologists of knowledge, advocates of the **strong program**, and **postmodernists**, have all used the notion of lan-

guage games as support for their various schema. Wittgenstein's understanding of language changed dramatically over his career. In his first book, The *Tractatus Logico-Philosophicus*, he argued for a single calculus underlying the whole of language, but in his the last work written before his death, *Philosophical Investigations*, he spoke of many different language games, each with its own set of use-rules. These rules are determined simply by the uses made of language within the boundaries of each "game," there being no general rules to cover all games. According to Wittgenstein, we can never explain them. This was an important part of his attempt to dissociate **philosophy** from **science**.

But, as was noted in Ray Monk's biography, Wittgenstein was shown a roulette table on one occasion. Roulette tables involve the world of gambling, and so have a language game associated with them. But Wittgenstein commented to his host, "I don't see how you *can* win!" As Monk observed, maybe there is a point to scrutinizing the rules.

Many religious apologists have employed the idea of language games to protect religious language from criticism, claiming that such criticism comes from those who are from another language game, say that of **humanism**. See the entry on **social worlds**. But this is a double-edged sword, because if religious truth claims are exempt from criticism on the grounds of being a specific language game, then it also means that proselytizing is no less inappropriate. See the entry on **external realism**.

LAPLACE, (MARQUIS) PIERRE SIMON DE (1749–1827). Greatest of the eighteenth-century French astronomers. The son of a farmer, Laplace studied in Caen before going to Paris, where his genius was quickly recognized. He became professor of mathematics at the École Militaire. While there, Laplace broke new ground with his researches on the inequalities in the orbits of Saturn and Jupiter. His main work was *Exposition du Système de Monde* (1796). In this work,

Laplace developed the nebular hypothesis, although the idea was anticipated by **Giordano Bruno** and **Immanuel Kant**.

Laplace is credited with replying to Napoleon's question about where God fits into his system: "Sire, I have no need for that hypothesis." As with most stunning one-liners, this is probably apocryphal, although it also probably represents his views accurately. This didn't prevent Laplace spending his declining years as a faithful scion of the restored Bourbon monarchy and the church. In 1817 Laplace was made a marquis by Louis XVIII.

LASKI, MARGHANITA (1915–1988). Novelist and critic. Born in Manchester to a prominent Orthodox Jewish family, the niece of the prolific socialist author Harold Laski (1893–1950), and educated at Oxford University. Laski married the publisher John Howard in Paris in 1937.

She wrote widely. In *Ecstasy* (1961) she explored the nature of religious belief and in *Everyday Ecstasy* (1980) the social effects of religious belief, both from a secular perspective. See the entry on **adamics**. Other important works included the novels *Little Boy Lost* (1949) and *The Victorian Chaise Longue* (1953) as well as studies of Jane Austen and **George Eliot**. She achieved notoriety in 1962 when she declared herself an atheist on television, during a dialogue with the Rev. Leslie Timmins on the BBC program *Meeting Point*.

LATERAN TREATY. The concordat between fascist Italy and the Vatican, signed on February 11 and ratified on June 7, 1929. This was a particularly important deal for both sides. For the papacy, it regularized their political and constitutional status, which had been in doubt since the Italian state had incorporated the larger papal territories in 1870, leaving the Vatican isolated and brooding. And for Benito Mussolini's (1883–1945) dictatorship, the treaty brought legitimacy and secured the quiescence of a potentially powerful rival.

The fascist government made a payment to the Vatican of about $100 million and placed Catholic clergy on the state payroll. Roman Catholicism was declared the sole religion of the state and, most important of all, Mussolini recognized Vatican City as an independent state.

The two sides then conferred awards upon each other. Pius XI conferred the Order of the Golden Spur upon Mussolini, and Cardinal Gasparri, who signed the concordat, was in turn awarded the fascist medal, the Order of the Annunziata. The first political payoff for the Lateran Treaty came a month after it was signed when most of the Catholic clergy instructed their flock to vote for fascist candidates.

The terms of the concordat were altered in 1984 when Roman Catholicism was no longer declared to be the official state religion.

LAUDAN, LARRY (1945–). Professor of philosophy at the University of Hawaii and defender of **science** and **reason** against the encroachments of **relativism** and **postmodernism**. Laudan is known particularly for his stout opposition to the **strong program** in the sociology of science.

Laudan's main books include *Progress and Its Problems* (1977), *Science and Values: The Aims of Science and Their Roles in Scientific Debate* (1984), *Science and Relativism: Some Key Controversies in the Philosophy of Science* (1990), *Beyond Positivism and Relativism: Theory, Method and Evidence* (1996), and *Danger Ahead: The Risks You Really Face on Life's Highway* (1997).

LAUGHTER. Quoting French philosopher Henri Bergson (1859–1941), the English comic genius John Cleese described laughter as a socially sanctioned protest against unduly conformist behaviors and attitudes. This notion captures well the subversive nature of laughter. It pricks the bubbles of pretentious **virtuecrats**, and, even more valuable, enables us not to take ourselves too seriously. **Plato** thought that laughter was undignified. Essential to the freethinker's worldview is the ability to take the **cosmic perspective** without being crushed. To recognize our irrelevance in the grand scheme of things is made so much easier by laughter. **Anthropocentric conceit** is not merely wrong, it is humorless, no less a crime. So despite all the conceit, all the pomposity, all the stupidity, life is still infinitely worth living. And it is made worth living in no small measure by our ability to have **fun** and to laugh.

LAWAL, AMINA. A Muslim woman from northern Nigeria who got caught up in a moral and religious controversy that reverberated around the world. Lawal was found guilty in March 2002 of adultery by a local **Sharia** court, which, since 1999 has had legal authority in several northern Nigerian states. Lawal was not provided any defense counsel. The punishment for women found guilty of adultery is death by stoning. The man escaped any charge when he declared on the Qur'an that he was not responsible.

News of the case became internationally spread when, on August 19, 2002, a Sharia court of appeal upheld the decision, and by implication, the method of punishment. At this point other agencies stepped in and provided Lawal with legal support. Over the next year Brazil and Italy offered Lawal asylum, and the case went before the Sharia Court of Appeals. The appeal was called for in August 27, 2003, and was then delayed until September 25. Then, in a 4–1 decision, Lawal was acquitted, on a series of technicalities of Muslim law, most notably, the absence of witnesses to the original act of fornication, and the refusal of the lower Sharia court to permit Lawal to retract her confession.

It is hard to believe that the Muslim authorities had not also considered the serious political implications of upholding the decision. Nigeria's president Obasanjo, a born-again Christian, had already declared that, if it had come to that, he would have overruled the Sharia court's decision, on the grounds that the Nigerian constitution does not permit death by stoning. At the time of Lawal's acquittal, however, there were other people under sentence of death by stoning for various crimes, and once the media glare has passed from the Lawal case, who knows what will go on?

LEADBETTER, CHARLES (1854–1934). Scandalous progenitor of the **New-Age** movement. Leadbetter contrived a romantic account of his childhood, which involved courage and adventure in South America and being born in 1847. In fact he was the son of a railway clerk who entered the Church of England in 1878, but whose interest in the occult led him to join the Theosophical movement in 1884.

Leadbetter moved to Sri Lanka and India, where he helped found the Theosophical headquarters and commune at Adyar. Whether there or in London, Leadbetter made sure he was in charge of the education of adolescents, so as to indulge his pederastic preferences. In 1910 Leadbetter "discovered" the new guru in the fifteen-year-old boy **Jiddu Krishnamurti**. He refused to shake hands with women, or to stay in a house alone with one, lest he be polluted. With boys, however, his attitude was very different indeed. His whole career was dogged with accusations of pederasty, but he enjoyed the solid support of **Annie Besant**, and so he survived. Leadbetter's books, in particular *The Astral Plane*; *Man, Visible and Invisible*; and *The Chakras* are still recommended New-Age reading. Leadbetter also had an inordinate love of pomp and ceremony and was severely criticized by other Theosophists for transforming the movement into just another church.

This accusation had some validity as Leadbetter went on to help found the Liberal Catholic Church, which was founded in 1918 and still exists today. He became the Church's second bishop. The first was James Wedgwood, a fellow traveler in Theosophy and pederasty. Wedgwood was eventually driven mad by his sexual promiscuity and drug use. Leadbetter's book *The Science of the Sacraments* combined the Mass and magic, and is still used by the Liberal Catholic Church.

Further reading: Peter Washington, *Madame Blavatsky's Baboon.*

LEAGUE OF THE GODLESS. See **IAROSLAVSKII, EMELIAN**

LEE THESIS. The informal name given to the theory that economic development is promoted best in conditions where democratic freedoms are curtailed. The theory is named after Lee Kuan Yew (1923–), longtime prime minister of Singapore. Under Lee's leadership, Singapore experienced rapid and sustained growth at a time when many civil liberties were withheld and genuine democracy was kept at bay.

The Lee Thesis may apply in certain countries at early stages in their social development, providing the levels of political control are not unduly onerous and are gradually released. A version of it has operated with some success in Uganda since 1986. Uganda had suffered under corrupt multiparty systems and military dictatorship when Yoweri Museveni led what is called a no-party democracy under an all-embracing structure known as the Movement. Under this system, Uganda has experienced its longest period of peace and development since becoming independent in 1962.

But the Lee Thesis presupposes that development must entail "blood, sweat, and tears." And it cannot explain the high and consistent levels of growth in genuinely democratic though poor countries such as Botswana. It also presupposes that poor people care little for democratic freedoms. However, there is a great deal of evidence against this, not least the opposition in India to Indira Gandhi's (1917–1984) suppression of civil liberties during the emergency of 1975–77. There is little doubt that economic growth is hindered in countries which are overly authoritarian. The general rule still applies that the **open society** is the surest guarantee of economic prosperity.

Further reading: Amartya Sen, *Develop-*

ment as Freedom; and Justus Mugaju and J. Oloka-Onyango, eds., *No-Party Democracy in Uganda*.

LEGISLATOR MODEL OF MORALITY. An account of morality employed by many religions, authoritarian ideologies, and **command moralities**. The legislator model, and its related paragon model, posit a supreme legislator, and moral paragon, to act as an example to his followers. The Ten Commandments is a classic example of the legislator model of morality. These commandments are thought to provide a complete framework for a moral life, with simple rules and clear penalties for transgressing them.

The problem with the legislator model of morality is that the legislation laid down in some holy **scripture** is always going to be circumscribed by the time in which it was written, and is going to have difficulties adapting to new situations. Because of this, religions have developed extensive literatures of commentary to act as supplements and updates to the original legislation. But a tension always exists between the original legislation, particularly if it is thought to be divinely inspired, and the recognition that it needs to be updated. Because of the failings of the legislator and paragon models of morality, in real life, religious people often use the interested party model, which works on the assumption that gods and spirits have access to all relevant information about our actions, and *therefore* have the moral opinions that we get as intuitions. The ex post facto religious justification of our own intuitions gives our own intuitions more authority than they would normally carry.

The humanist understanding of morality does not work according to the legislator model of morality. **Humanism** recognizes that legislation is never absolute, always open to criticism and change, as conditions and levels of knowledge grow. Humanism also prefers each individual to be his or her own paragon, to live up to moral ideals not prescribed from primitive times and obeyed by fear and habit, but freely developed and logically understood injunctions to living in a humane and compassionate way.

LEGITIMACY OF THE DEMOCRATIC SYSTEM. According to the Canadian sociologist John O'Neill the legitimacy of the democratic system lies in the following things being able to happen:

- people have access to information whereby social goals are articulated;
- people are aware of and feel entitled to exercise their rights in effecting resource reallocations; and
- peoples' problems with institutions constitute *prima facie* cases for their reform.

O'Neill argued that the complementary interactions of these three processes constitute the democratic legitimation of society, because the general citizen is communicating effectively with the expert elites in power.

Further reading: John O'Neill, *The Poverty of Postmodernism*.

LENNON, JOHN (1940–1980). Phenomenal musical and songwriting talent. Born in Liverpool, England, in 1940, Lennon's parents split up when he was five. Lennon grew up rebellious and with little will to concentrate at school. While at the Liverpool College of Art in 1956, he was introduced to Elvis Presley's song "Heartbreak Hotel," which reignited an interest in music instilled in him by his mother. He was introduced to Paul McCartney in 1957 and the Beatles was formed in 1960. The group developed its distinctive sound in nightclubs in Liverpool and Hamburg, Germany. When the group returned to England in 1962, Beatlemania was an established phenomenon. The Beatles went on to produce a series of records that transformed the music scene around the world.

From the simple pop of *Hard Day's Night*, to the soulful ballads of *Rubber Soul*, and on to the raw, experimental sounds of the *White Album*, Lennon was the creative leader of the

Beatles, notwithstanding the talent of McCartney, George Harrison, and Ringo Starr. The Beatles cemented their fame with a punishing schedule of touring. In 1966 Lennon enraged American fundamentalists with an off-the-cuff comment about the Beatles being more popular than Jesus. Fundamentalists indulged their indignation with a riot of album burning, but their antics did nothing to diminish the Beatles' popularity.

In March and April of 1968 the Beatles went to India, ostensibly to sit at the feet of Maharishi Yogi and learn some timeless subcontinental truths. In fact, Lennon used the trip as another opportunity to practice his playing and learn new ways to express himself musically. The title song from Lennon's album *Imagine* (1971) has become something of a humanist anthem, being used in anthologies of systems of belief which include **humanism**. The song was heartfelt and reflected genuinely Lennon's thoughts and fears, as well as the ideals that motivated him. "God," Lennon wrote, "is a concept by which we measure our pain."

Lennon moved to New York in 1972 with his second wife Yoko Ono (1933–), although the American authorities made trouble with his visa application, disapproving of Lennon's active opposition to the Vietnam War. The last album of Lennon's life was *Double Fantasy*, released only three weeks before his assassination by Mark Chapman on December 8, 1980.

LENNSTRAND, VIKTOR (1861–1895). Pioneering Swedish freethinker. Born into a devout family, Lennstrand was expected to follow the family tradition of working actively for religion. An active Evangelical, Lennstrand entered Uppsala University in 1881. There he came across the leading thinkers of Europe at the time. The seeds of doubt were sown by reading **Feuerbach**, **Haeckel**, **Darwin**, **Spencer**, and **Mill**. After several years of intellectual turmoil, Lennstrand in desperation prayed to **God** for assistance and received none. He finally declared himself an atheist in 1887.

Lennstrand began his career as an active **freethought** lecturer. One of his first lectures, "Is Christianity a Religion for Our Time?" was disrupted by the police. He then moved to Stockholm where he lectured on freethought topics. Late in 1888 he founded the Utilitiska Stamfund (Utilitarian Association) and the following year he established the *Fritänkaren* (*Freethinker*). Lennstrand continued to attract the attention of the authorities as well. In November 1888 he was imprisoned for three months for freethought lecturing. In October the following year he served another three months' imprisonment for **blasphemy**. In December he went back to prison for the same offense, with the prospect of a lengthy term ahead of him. He was so badly treated in prison that his health was broken. Eventually a public meeting attended by over five thousand people, followed by a petition signed by eight thousand persuaded the king to have him released. In December 1894 illness forced him to retire from all his activities. He died on November 1, 1895.

Further reading: Finngeir Hiorth, *Secularism in Sweden*.

L'ESPIRIT DE SPINOSA. One of the earliest compendiums of **freethought** ever to be compiled, and as such a book that deserves a special place in the history of freethought. The book itself has had a varied and interesting history. Its authorship was uncertain for centuries and very few copies of it exist. *L'Espirit* was probably written in the first years of the eighteenth century and was published in 1719 alongside an early biography of the life of **Baruch Spinoza**. Two years later *L'Espirit* was published separately under the title *Traité des trois imposteurs*, which reflected some new material that had been added to the original text. *L'Espirit* is an important work for three main reasons:

- it's the first freethought compendium;
- it disseminated the thought of Spinoza; and

• it influenced radical Enlightenment thought in the century that followed.

After centuries of scholarly debate, a credible theory by the Italian historian Silvia Berti, has solved many of the mysteries surrounding this book. It now transpires that the author of *L'Espirit* was the freethinker Jan Vroesen (1672–1725), a senior official in the court of Brabant. *L'Espirit* was a bold, though not always accurate, reinterpretation of Spinoza's thought in the service of a materialist view of the universe. The work also used sections from works by **Thomas Hobbes**, **Guilio Vanini**, and others. It brought these thinkers together in its attack on the divine character of prophecy and the dangers of ignorance. It also criticized clergy and theologians who are paid to preserve that ignorance, and was critical of **anthropocentric conceit** in Spinozistic terms. The prose was improved and some extra chapters were added by a friend of Vroesen's, Jean Rousset de Missy (1686–1762), the person thought for a long time to have been the author of the entire work.

L'Espirit is also important as an example of a series on anonymous heterodox tracts that were published in the seventeenth and eighteenth centuries. As the risks of imprisonment and death were very great for questioning the veracity of religion, it was obviously tempting to publish anonymously. See the entry on *Looking-Glass of Atheism and Ignorance*.

Further reading: Silvio Berti, "The First Edition of the *Traité des trois imposteurs* and its Debt to Spinoza's Ethics," in Michael Hunter and David Wootton, eds., *Atheism from the Reformation to the Enlightenment*.

LEVY, HYMAN (1889–1975). Mathematician, Marxist, and rationalist. Born to a poor Jewish family in Edinburgh, Levy was inspired to a life of science by **Joseph McCabe**, whose lectures he attended as a youth. Against the odds, Levy secured a university education and his brilliance was soon

recognized. He succeeded A. N. Whitehead (1861–1947) as professor of mathematics at Imperial College in London in 1924 and remained there until his retirement in 1957.

Levy was also concerned to share his knowledge with nonspecialist audiences. He was a very popular, witty, and eloquent lecturer. He made a name for himself in a BBC radio series called *Science in a Changing World*; the transcripts were later published in 1934 by Watts and Co. as *The Web of Thought and Action*. Levy also wrote *The Universe of Science* (1932), which attempted to popularize physics and mathematics to nonspecialist readers. *The Universe of Science* was published in the **Rationalist Press Association**'s influential **Thinker's Library** series and remained in print until the 1950s. In 1949, Levy's magnum opus, *Modern Science*, attempted to bring contemporary science together in a synthesis.

He was active in the Left Book Club until its demise and in the Rationalist Press Association until his death. He was a member of the Communist Party for more than thirty years, resigning in 1957. He remained a Marxist for the rest of his life.

LEWIS, JOSEPH (1889–1968). American atheist campaigner. Joseph Lewis was born to a family of nonpracticing Jews in Montgomery, Alabama. The family moved to Selma when he was still young, and Lewis's short school career was there. While working in the family store, a family friend gave the boy some books to read, including those by **Robert Ingersoll**. Through Ingersoll, Lewis learned about **Thomas Paine**, for whom Lewis became a lifelong champion. In 1912 the family moved to New York, where Lewis attended night school for a while. His ambition to be a lawyer was frustrated by poverty and the ever-changing and costly requirements to qualify. For a short while he worked for **Margaret Sanger**, selling her books on birth control.

Eventually, Lewis started out on his own, founding the Eugenics Publishing Company (later the Freethought Press Association) and the Freethinkers of America movement. And in 1937 he founded the *Age of Reason* magazine, which survived until his death. He did well for himself by distributing **freethought** material through mail order. In 1926 he published his first book, *The Bible Unmasked*, a work in the Paine tradition. Lewis was a fearless promoter of Paine's memory for the rest of his life. He took leading roles in building and preserving several statues to Paine, both in the United States and in Europe, and was an important figure in establishing the Thomas Paine memorial in his birthplace of Thetford, Norfolk. The Paine statue in Paris was designed by the American sculptor Gutzon Borglum (1867–1941), who achieved fame as the creator of the carving of the four American presidents into Mt. Rushmore in South Dakota.

Lewis was also a tireless campaigner against preachers he considered dishonest. He was one of the few people to conduct effective campaigns in opposition to Billy Graham and Oral Roberts. Among Lewis's friends he counted **Helen Keller**. Late in life, while convalescing after his second heart attack, Lewis wrote *An Atheist Manifesto*. He died on November 4, 1968.

LIBERAL DECALOGUE. Set of ten liberal tenets outlined by **Bertrand Russell** in an article for the *New York Times*, December 16, 1951 called "The Best Answer to Fanaticism —Liberalism." They subsequently appeared in the third volume of Russell's autobiography. Russell's Liberal Decalogue went thus:

(1) Do not feel absolutely certain of anything.
(2) Do not think it worthwhile to proceed by concealing evidence, for the evidence is sure to come to light.
(3) Never try to discourage thinking for you are sure to succeed.
(4) When you meet with opposition, even if it should be from your husband or your children, endeavor to overcome it by argument and not by authority, for a victory dependent upon authority is unreal and illusory.
(5) Have no respect for the authority of others, for there are always contrary authorities to be found.
(6) Do not use power to suppress opinions you think pernicious, for if you do the opinions will suppress you.
(7) Do not fear to be eccentric in opinion, for every opinion now accepted was once eccentric.
(8) Find more pleasure in intelligent dissent than in passive agreement, for, if you value intelligence as you should, the former implies a deeper agreement than the latter.
(9) Be scrupulously truthful, even if truth is inconvenient, for it is more inconvenient when you try to conceal it.
(10) Do not feel envious of the happiness of those who live in a fool's paradise, for only a fool will think it is happiness.

Further reading: Bertrand Russell, *The Autobiography of Bertrand Russell*.

LIBERTARIANISM. The idea that personal liberty is meaningful only when restrictions on that liberty are reduced to the absolute minimum. In political and economic thinking, libertarianism tends to stress the absolute priority of certain types of **rights** over the pursuit of social goals, in particular the rights involving personal liberties and property rights. With this in mind, libertarians tend to speak of the "priority of liberty," although this term is also used by nonlibertarian liberals, most notably **John Rawls**. Libertarians are closely related to objectivists, the name assumed by followers of **Ayn Rand**.

Consistent with the priority of liberty, libertarians are usually open-minded about the sexual peccadilloes of their neighbors, unlike their religious-conservative allies. But critics of libertarianism have noted its restricted understanding of **poverty**, which is reduced simply to having limited financial means. Poverty is far more complex than simply having less money than other people. Economists like Amartya Sen have demonstrated that poverty is better understood as the deprivation of capabilities. Opponents of libertarianism argue that freedom is better served when all people are given some degree of opportunity, by way of the state assistance if necessary.

LIFE, SANCTITY OF. A **dualistic** outlook that imbues human life with special status by virtue of having a **soul**, which is the everlasting essence of us given by **God**. The sanctity-of-life argument is fundamental to the opposition to **abortion** and **voluntary euthanasia**, although many sanctity-of-life proponents rather inconsistently support capital punishment for criminals. A few of the more fanatical sanctity-of-life extremists have favored killing abortion doctors because of their apparent lack of respect for life.

The sanctity-of-life argument runs up against the **naturalist** understanding of the world, which has shown that souls do not exist and that beliefs about an afterlife or a God or supernatural agency can be maintained only by **faith**. The sanctity-of-life worldview also has elements of outdated **great chain of being** views about being human. Some **Asian traditions** like the **Jains** are more consistent when they care for the lives of animals in the same measure as they do for human beings.

The naturalist view of the world stresses the interdependence of all things. *Homo sapiens* cannot afford the **anthropocentric conceit** of seeing theselves as the only species favored by God with a soul. Humans need to think of their needs in the broader context of the species and the planet. It is also worth reminding ourselves that there is no such thing as the abstraction "life." There is my life, your life, her life, his life. Life does not exist outside the creatures whose hearts are beating.

LIFE-STANCE. A term coined in 1996 by the English philosopher Harry Stopes-Roe to refer to the beliefs and practices an individual or a community feel define who they are and are therefore significant to them in the way they live their lives. Stopes-Roe was unhappy to see **humanism**, which is a life-stance, also be seen as a religion. He argued that there are two meanings usually implied when people speak of "religion." On the one hand they are referring to the focus of what is most important in life. But on the other hand, religion very often involves speaking of God. While Stopes-Roe was content that religion should retain its supernaturalist implications, on the grounds of this being how most people understand the term, he was *not* content that religions should be permitted to retain their self-declared monopoly on the focus of what is most important in life.

Stopes-Roe was also happy for religious people to see their worldview in terms of a life-stance as well, indeed one of the advantages of "life-stance" was its sensitivity to their position *and* to that of nonbelievers. As for humanism, he was quite clear that the naturalistic view of the universe is fundamentally at odds with the religious worldview, which posits some sort of superpurposive agency. "The definition of humanism excludes superpurposive realities and therefore the idea of a god; this must be a root element." As many societies grope their way toward becoming genuinely pluralistic, the idea of life-stance has become quite popular and has found its way into legal and educational documents in several countries.

LIMITLESS COMMUNICATION. A notion explored by the German philosopher Karl Jaspers (1883–1969), which he made a central feature of his philosophy. Limitless communication (*Grenzenlose Kommunication*) refers to the ongoing dialogue between people as the reliable way to arrive at **truth**. Truth is communicative, in that it cannot be arrived at without people talking about what truth is. So with limitless communication, and its necessary corollary of limitless listening, we can arrive at truth. The alternative is to insist we are in exclusive possession of the truth and that it is the duty of everyone to listen to us. This is the method of **command moralities** and **absolutism**, which limitless communication rejects. See the entry on **social intelligence**.

LIMITS REACHED BY TWENTIETH-CENTURY SCIENCE. Newton Garver and Seung-Chong Lee have observed that the twentieth century was an age of limits. And these limits will have an important series of effects on our thinking. The limits we reached in the twentieth century include:

- the speed of light, beyond which it is impossible to go faster, as revealed in the **theories of relativity**;
- a limit on the application of continuous functions in mechanics, as revealed in **quantum mechanics**;
- a limit reached on our ability to determine both the position and the momentum of particles, as outlined in the **Uncertainty Principle**; and
- difficulty in proving a logical system to be both complete and consistent, as outlined in **Gödel's Theorem**.

Garver and Lee note that these limits act as opportunities rather than restrictions, because what lie beyond these limits are impossible anyway. **Bertrand Russell** had already outlined the limits of knowledge in *Human Knowledge: Its Scope and Limits* (1948). See the entry on **external realism**.

Further reading: Newton Garver and Seung-Chong Lee, *Derrida and Wittgenstein*.

LINCOLN, ABRAHAM (1809–1865). The sixteenth American president, architect of the abolition of slavery, and freethinker. Lincoln was born in modest circumstances near Hodgenville, Kentucky. His family moved several times, and settled in Indiana in 1816 and Illinois in 1830. Though his formal schooling was brief, he developed a deep respect for learning, thanks largely to his stepmother. He worked for a while as a clerk in New Salem, Illinois, where he rose to become village postmaster and deputy county surveyor. He also studied law and began to practice in 1836. And from New Salem, he began a political career. A long and difficult political career culminated with nomination, after three ballots, as Republican candidate for the presidency. Lincoln served as president from 1861 to 1865.

Throughout his political career Lincoln was underestimated and scorned by those who felt themselves more qualified, either by birth or education, to hold responsible office. They all failed to appreciate Lincoln's political genius, manifested mostly by his common touch and facility with words. The issue that defined Lincoln's life was the emancipation of the slaves. For many years his position on this divisive issue was timid. Even after becoming president, Lincoln was not wholeheartedly in favor of emancipation. But he was wholeheartedly in favor of maintaining the Union and came to see that the Union could not be saved without the question of slavery being addressed head on. Against the advice of many people, Lincoln issued the Emancipation Proclamation, which came to effect on January 1, 1863. The wording of the proclamation and Lincoln's speeches, in particular the Gettysburg Address, were so eloquent that doubters were won over and a new conception of the promise of America was born.

Despite this, Lincoln was fortunate to win a second term. He was saved by the military victory of Union forces under General Sherman, who captured Atlanta only weeks before the election. On Good Friday, April 14, 1865, only weeks after beginning his second term, he was assassinated by J. Wilkes Booth (1838–1865), a Confederate sympathizer. Lincoln died the next day.

He would qualify as the most saintly man ever to have occupied the White House. He was also one of the most heterodox on religious matters. It worried him greatly that

Confederate troops invoked the support of **God** with every bit as much sincerity of belief as many Union soldiers. Lincoln was steeped in the Bible, but was unwilling to identify himself with any religious denomination. As a young man in New Salem, Lincoln read *The Age of Reason* by **Thomas Paine**, and Count Volney's (1757–1820) *Ruins of Empires*, an important work of Enlightenment skepticism. It was probably with these reading habits in mind that a party of Protestant clergy opposed Lincoln in his early political career. Lincoln's law partner in Illinois, William Herndon, was a known agnostic. Like **Thomas Jefferson**, Lincoln's brand of belief was entirely his own. It was broadly theistic and specifically non-Christian.

LINNAEUS, CAROLUS (1707–1778). Swedish naturalist and the first person to establish rational general principles for the classification of plants and animals. Until his time, the authority of **Aristotle**'s increasingly nonsensical categories had been dominant. Linnaeus based his categories on two concepts: the idea of a distinct species and the concept of a hierarchy of living forms. The living world was divided into five kingdoms, which were in turn split into classes. The five kingdoms were the Monera, single-celled organisms without nuclei including bacteria and some algae; Protista, single-celled organisms with nuclei; Plantae, the higher plants; Fungi, lower plants not using the sun as a source of energy; and Animalia, the animals.

It was Linnaeus who gave us the term *Homo sapiens*. The principal difficulty with Linnaeus's work was that it was pre-Darwinian, and assumed the fixity of species.

LINUS. The first bishop of Rome. It is part of Catholic mythology that the popes extend in an unbroken line from St. Peter, who was authorized by Jesus Christ to succeed him. This is not true, and even some Catholic historians now recognize this fact. The first list of popes was compiled by **Irenaeus of Lyons** around 180 CE, and the list began with Linus.

This was endorsed by the Christian historian Eusebius (263–339 CE). What is more, the list is highly suspect; the sixth in the list is called Sixtus.

Stories about Peter's activities after the death of Jesus were progressively embellished in the decades after his death and were generally accepted by the second century of the common era—it is now generally acknowledged that those were pious frauds, and that no reliable accounts of Peter's life exist. See the entry on the **Petrine Text**.

Further reading, Eamon Duffy, *Saints and Sinners: A History of the Popes*.

LISBON EARTHQUAKE. A devastating earthquake that destroyed the Portuguese capital on November 1, 1755, and was accompanied by widespread fires and the flooding of the Tagus river. Thirty thousand people are thought to have lost their lives, many of whom were in church at the time the earthquake struck.

The disaster provoked a fiery response from **Voltaire**. *The Poem on the Lisbon Disaster* was subtitled "An Examination of the Axiom 'All Is Well.'" Voltaire was sickened by the complacent reply of orthodox religionists and of Deists. His poem is a brooding polemic against the callous defenses for the existence of **evil** in the world. For example, he asked:

> But how to conceive a **God** supremely
>   good,
> Who heaps his favors on the sons he
>   loves,
> Yet scatters evil with as large a hand?

Attempts to answer this sort of problem are called theodicies. There have been no successful theodicies. See the entry on **theodicy**.

LOCAL HOLISM. A term used by Thomas Kuhn (1922–1996) to refer to the notion that ideas in **science**, or any other discipline, cannot be learned in isolation, but must be learned in the context of the cluster of related terms and ideas. Ideas are associated with generalizations and theories, and knowledge of the ideas is incomplete without the knowledge of the generalizations and theories they give rise to. This was one of the notions Kuhn used in succession to the much-abused notion of **paradigms** and paradigm shifts, from which Kuhn distanced himself in later years.

LOCKE, JOHN (1632–1704). Hugely influential English philosopher, whose works lay the foundation for the **Enlightenment** and the American Revolution. Locke influenced the Enlightenment in the same fundamental way that Petrarch (1304–1374) influenced the **Renaissance**. Both men served as patrons, even founder figures, for the movements that followed them. Locke was also one of the most important proponents of **empiricism**. His main argument was that all our **knowledge** came through the senses. The mind at birth was a blank slate upon which sense-impressions are etched.

Locke's most important book, in terms of influence, was the *Second Treatise on Civil Government*, which provided the intellectual justification for the so-called Glorious Revolution in England in 1688 that overthrew the Catholic king James II (1633–1701) and set limits to the monarchy. It also established the principle of the separation of powers, which was adopted in the United States. Locke set out a contractual view of government which allowed for the contract to be unilaterally ended by the people if it has been violated by rapacious government, as James II was widely felt to have done. It was Locke's view that the source of authority in society was not the divine right of kings, or tradition, or **religion**, as had previously been argued, but the people. Following on from this, Locke's *Letter Concerning Toleration* (three parts: 1689, 1690, 1692) argued that a person's religious allegiance was of no concern to the sovereign, but was a matter of personal conscience, although even Locke could not bring himself to extend toleration to include

Catholics, Jews, or atheists. See the entry on **toleration**.

Locke's own religious views leaned toward heterodoxy. Recent scholarship has raised the likelihood that Locke was a Socinian, one who believed the Gospel stories, including the resurrection, but who denied the virgin birth and **Trinity**. Locke was adamant that revelation was subordinate to **reason** and had little time for the **argument from universal consent**.

In his *Essay Concerning Human Understanding* (1690), Locke disputed the claims of **Descartes** that human ideas were innate, arguing instead that they come from sense-impressions. It followed from this that our codes of morals are the creations of our sensations. This led the way to the radical rethinking of **human nature** and how society can be managed that characterized the **Enlightenment**. Locke's views were brought to the attention of a wider reading public by **Voltaire**. And, as a final badge of honor, Locke's works were placed on the **Index of Forbidden Books**.

LOGOCENTRISM. A term coined by Jacques Derrida (1930–2004) that refers to the purportedly rationalistic spirit of Western thought. Deriving from the word **logos**, which itself is a notoriously slippery notion, logocentrism refers to the dominating tendency of Western thought to find some "singular logic of presence" beyond signs and representation. As revealed in the "centrism" part of the word, there is a built-in condemnation of the practice; a stern rebuke of the tendency to trample on the other ways of seeing things. It is the self-appointed task of **postmodernists** to rediscover the victims of logocentric domination and release them in a flurry of densely written texts. See the entry on the **hissing suffix**.

One of Derrida's many critics is the humanist philosopher Peter Levine, who notes that it would be practically impossible to disprove Derrida's claim that "the West"—itself a vague term—is logocentric, because "logocentric" is so vague a term it is not open to empirical contradiction. What is more, it may well be true that thoughts are expressed in the form that thought takes (Derrida calls this "writing"), but such a statement is empty of meaning.

Further reading, Peter Levine, *Nietzsche and the Modern Crisis of the Humanities.*

LOGOS. Greek concept with several contrasting meanings. On the one hand, *logos* means the underlying principle of order in the universe, but, on the other hand, it means the spoken word. **Heraclitus** and the **Stoics** used *logos* in the former sense. But giving a principle a name runs the risk of anthropomorphizing it, which in turn becomes a pretext for others to succumb to the **transcendental temptation**. This was especially true of a word which had a double meaning to begin with. **Anaxagoras** turned Heraclitus's inanimate *logos* into a more mystical entity called Nous which **Socrates** took further by transforming Nous into Spirit. Platonists used logos in the sense of the divine power of reason. As logos became progressively grander, the original idea that logos was always open to critical scrutiny was slowly lost.

By the time the word was applied by Greek translators to the Gospel of John, the mystical understanding of the *logos* concept was in the ascendant. And John took the next step by claiming the *logos* becomes flesh in Jesus, an idea which would have been incomprehensible to the classical Greeks. The word is now lost forever in the mists of **theology**.

Further reading: Charles Freeman, *The Closing of the Western Mind.*

LOKAYATA. A term given to an Indian materialist thinker. Derived from the Sanskrit *loka* (world) and *ayata* (unrestricted), it originally meant anyone devoted to study of the universe without being bound by prescriptive brahmanical formulas. A lokayata was not necessarily opposed to Vedic or brahmanical thinking, although they developed in that direction. Eventually, a lokayata was invari-

ably linked to the materialist **Carvaka** school of thought (or *darshana*). "Lokayata" became a term of abuse in the way that "atheist" was for many centuries in the West. "Lokayata" and "Carvaka" are now used interchangeably in many texts.

LOMONOSOV, MIKHAIL (1711–1765). The outstanding Russian Enlightenment thinker and humanist, called by Alexander Pushkin (1799–1837) "the first Russian university." Lomonosov was born in the remote Archangel region bordering on the White Sea, the son of a fisherman. He quickly showed an unusual intellect, working his way through the few books that could be found in his locality. In 1730 Lomonosov walked to Moscow in search of an education. Many obstacles were put in the way, by the church and the aristocrats, who scorned his lowly origins. Slowly Lomonosov overcame them, and in 1736 he went to Germany to study. After his return to Russia in 1741, he began an intense program of building a public program based on his own learning. Once again, he faced ongoing opposition from entrenched, conservative interests. The ongoing struggle with reactionary interests undermined his vigorous health and brought on his premature death.

He persevered, and in the long run he effected a comprehensive reorganization of the St. Petersburg Academy, where he worked. His work culminated in the central role he played in the foundation of Moscow State University, where he was also instrumental in initiating the teaching in the Russian language. A fine statue of him stands in front of the central building of the university.

Lomonosov was a great supporter of the program begun by Peter the Great (1672–1725) to bring the Enlightenment to Russia. For Lomonosov, Peter was a model of the ideal leader. However, he was no propagandist for monarchy or serfdom. His many writings on social and political philosophy were suppressed by the czars and were not published in full until the 1950s.

So only two hundred years after his death can we appreciate the scope of his wide-ranging thought. He excelled in a wide variety of disciplines: mathematics, astronomy, history, poetry, linguistics, politics, sociology, and philosophy, among others. Lomonosov was a naturalist and materialist. Nature exists independently of humanity and has no properties or substances outside nature.

Further reading: Valerii Kuvakin, *A History of Russian Philosophy.*

LOOKING-GLASS OF ATHEISM AND IGNORANCE. A work of Russian atheist literature dating from the late eighteenth century. *Looking-Glass of Atheism and Ignorance* was published anonymously and to this day its author remains unknown. It has seven chapters, each of which refutes one particular religious dogma. Most of the traditional Christian dogmas are included: the perfection of **God**, God's omniscience, and God as creator of the world. The book concludes that no such entity as God exists and that the world is not dependent on such an entity. The dating of the book is set by the evidence that **Baron d'Holbach**'s work *Le Système de la Nature* (1770) was influential.

Looking-Glass of Atheism and Ignorance is also interesting as an example of the surprisingly large number of anonymous atheist and heterodox tracts circulating in the seventeenth and eighteenth century. See the entry on *L'Espirit de Spinosa*.

LORD'S RESISTANCE ARMY. A brutal Christian private militia operating in northern Uganda, particularly among the Acholi people. The Lord's Resistance Army (LRA) was founded by Joseph Kony in about 1986, having emerged out of an earlier group called the Holy Spirit Movement. Kony is thought to have been born in the 1960s and is a fundamentalist Christian with a mystical bent who wants to rule Uganda along the lines of the **Ten Commandments**. He claims to be in touch with spirits.

The LRA is notorious for its deployment of child soldiers who are so brutalized that they become inured to the pain they cause in others. The LRA is responsible for a long line of child abductions, village massacres, rapes, and other violence. It has been supported by the Sudanese government, which led Uganda to sever diplomatic relations with that country in 1995. Under pressure from the United States in 2002, Sudan permitted the Ugandan army to attack the LRA's bases in the southern reaches of its territory. The operation was not successful and a partly revitalized LRA has resumed a round of savage violence, abductions, and rapes in northern Uganda. Late in 2003 the LRA became the official subject of investigation by the International Criminal Court at the Hague.

LOVE. The most important of the human emotions and among the most abused. Love is the sense of commitment to someone or something else. It is the feeling a person has that the **happiness** and fulfillment of their partner is an essential factor in one's own happiness and fulfillment. Much of the value love has comes from it being a gift from one person to another, not born out of contractual obligation, but out of a desire to give of oneself.

Love is not the same as **sex**, although sex is one way love may legitimately be expressed. Love and sex are intricately bound together, particularly among younger people, but as we grow older, love can be manifested in more varied ways, often in simple, unspoken companionship.

The American philosopher Marvin Kohl has distinguished *benevolent* love from *caring* love. The essential difference between the two is that benevolent love is abstract and inert concern whereas caring love involves active participation. It is one thing to be benevolently disposed, but the next step is to act on that benevolence. Benevolent love can be extended to the entire universe while caring love can only have a limited application. Kohl's distinction is reflected in the emphasis **eupraxsophy** has for active involvement in making the world a better place, rather than simply expounding on it.

LUCIAN OF SAMOSATA (117–180s CE). Often seen as the **Voltaire** of the ancient world, Lucian was a classical satirist, imaginative writer, and **smiter of humbug**. Lucian was raised in the backwater of Samosata on the periphery of the Roman Empire, now in Turkey. He was by nature a **rebel**. He rebelled against his provincial upbringing, not least by learning Greek and preferring it to the Aramaic he spoke as a child. He practiced law in Antioch before becoming a professor of rhetoric in Athens and finally a senior law official in Egypt. He wrote prolifically. Between seventy and eighty works of his survive; doubts inevitably arise as to the authenticity of some of them.

Lucian should be credited with inventing the whole genre of humorous dialogue. His satirical style is surprisingly modern. He poked fun at public piety regarding deities nobody seriously believed in anymore and questioned the hypocrisy of wise men who lived foolish lives. One work, *The Passing of Peregrinus*, was a critique of a Cynic thinker who had a career as leader of a band of Christians midway through the second century. He criticized Peregrinus as being a charlatan. Another important satire has been translated as *Fishing for Phonies*. He also deserves credit for being the first person to write fictional accounts of interplanetary travel. In about 160 CE, Lucian wrote *Vera Historia* (*True History*), where the hero is sailing past the Pillars of Hercules (Gibraltar), long regarded as the edge of the known world. The hero's ship is caught in a waterspout and deposited on the moon. In another work, *Icaromenippus*, the hero reaches the moon using a vulture's wing on one arm and an eagle's on the other. By this method of flight, the hero reaches the sun as well.

Beneath the satire was a genuine concern for the standards of philosophy and indignation at its perversion in the interests of junk science or rampant **irrationalism**. The imagination of Lucian's writing inspired playwrights and thinkers from **Shakespeare**; the English satirist Jonathan Swift (1667–1745);

Erasmus, whose sensational *Praise of Folly* (1511) owed a direct debt to Lucian; and the French writer François Rabelais (1494–1553). Lucian was a friend of the great pagan philosopher **Celsus**. Conventional Christian histories have pilloried Lucian, and tell of him being torn apart by mad dogs as divine punishment for his criticism of Christianity. For centuries the word "Lucianism" was a term of abuse in the same way "atheist" has become.

Further reading: Christopher Robinson, *Lucian*.

LUCRETIUS (100–55 BCE). One of the greatest poets of the ancient world. His full name was Titus Lucretius Carus, and his poetic masterpiece, *De rerum natura* (*On the Nature of Things*), which was completed in 60 BCE, is the greatest surviving example of **Epicureanism**. As a follower of **Epicurus**, Lucretius shared his mentor's wish to rid nature and history of the arbitrary interference of supernatural forces. Mankind had created the idea of gods, so that meant they existed, but they had no interest in humankind at all. Lucretius was strongly opposed to the view commonly held among thinkers of his day that superstitions were useful means of keeping the common herd docile. See the entries on **bread and circuses** and the **holy lie**. Brian Silver describes Lucretius well when he says he was "a thinker standing out against the irrational, but not the mysterious; against **superstition**, but not against **awe**."

The writings of Lucretius are among the finest examples of the capacity of Roman writers to assimilate a mass of Greek learning and create a new organic whole out of it. As well as Epicurus, Lucretius was familiar with **Heraclitus**, **Anaxagoras**, the **Atomists**, and Thucydides. But the core of Lucretius's **naturalism** was the **atomism** of Leucippus and **Democritus**, partially revised in the light of the criticisms of **Plato** and **Aristotle**. Most interesting was Lucretius's talk of the sideways swerve atoms are prone to, and which are responsible for atomic collisions. Platonist and religious scholars scoffed at this idea for centuries, but the onset of **quantum mechanics** reveals that he was onto something after all.

He was very influential among the thinkers of the Renaissance who wanted to overthrew the religious dogma of the Middle Ages. His work was rediscovered in 1417 by Poggio Bracciolini and quickly entered Renaissance thought. The atomism of Lucretius was a strong influence on the thinking of **Galileo**. The Catholic Church tried to suppress reprintings of *The Nature of Things*, but to no avail. Lucretius and Epicureanism went on to become vastly influential on the development of **Enlightenment** thought.

LÜDEMANN, GERD. German New Testament scholar who has been subjected to a campaign of harassment from his religious colleagues. Lüdemann taught at McMaster University in Canada between 1977 and 1979 and Vanderbilt University between 1979 and 1982. In 1983 he was appointed to a chair in New Testament Studies at the theological faculty of the University of Göttingen, in Germany. Göttingen has a long history of important New Testament scholarship and is associated in particular with the History of Religions School, which works from the idea that religions change over time and that their job is to chart and account for those changes. Lüdemann, who is a fellow of the **Jesus Seminar**, sees himself as continuing that tradition of New Testament exegesis. He is also a fellow of the **Committee for the Scientific Examination of Religion**.

Lüdemann's earlier faith was lost during the course of his study, as he came to recognize that the biblical message "has become impossible, because its points of reference, above all the resurrection of Jesus, have proved invalid and because the person of Jesus is insufficient as a foundation of faith once most of the New Testament statements about him have proved to be later interpretations by the community." His willingness to follow his convictions has got him in a lot of trouble with his more timorous colleagues. After making his opinions public, his colleagues pushed for his dismissal from his position. They were unable to achieve his dismissal, but his opponents managed to have his position recategorized as a chair in the History and Literature of Early Christianity.

The dispute has resulted in a series of costly legal struggles. The campaign against Lüdemann is the first of its kind in a Protestant theological faculty in Germany. It has called into sharp relief the pretension of these faculties to support scientific research while also requiring an oath of fealty to the principles of the Lutheran Church. His recent books include *The Great Deception: And What Jesus Really Said and Did* (1999), *Jesus After 2000 Years* (2001), *Paul: The Founder of Christianity* (2002), and *The Resurrection of Christ: A Historical Inquiry* (2004). These books constitute a formidable indictment of the traditional truth claims of Christianity. See the entry on **authenticity, criteria of**.

LYCZYNSKI, KAZIMIERZ (1634–1689). Polish atheist who wrote a book called *About the Non-existence of God*. Lyczinski was executed and for many years it was assumed that his **atheism** was the direct reason for his death. However, recent work suggests that his atheism was a convenient excuse for his destruction as part of a wider dispute over property and inheritances.

M

MACDONALD, GEORGE E[VERETT] (1857–1937). American freethinker and veteran journalist. Born in modest circumstances, MacDonald began his working life as a farm hand. While still a teenager he moved to New York where he worked for the **freethought** paper the *Truthseeker*, the creation of **D. M. Bennett**. In 1888, he went to San Francisco and along with **Samuel Putnam** founded the journal *Freethought*. That paper folded in 1891, and MacDonald went on to work in provincial journalism for a couple of years before returning to New York. In 1909 he took over the editorship of the *Truthseeker* from his brother, Eugene Montague MacDonald (1855–1909) who had run the paper since 1883. MacDonald remained the editor of the *Truthseeker* until his death in 1937.

The best years of the *Truthseeker* were under the two MacDonald brothers. During those years it was a respectable and intelligent voice of reason. Tragically, that heritage was betrayed after his death. He shares with **Chapman Cohen** of Great Britain and **James Hanlon** of New Zealand the distinction of being one of the longest-standing editors of a freethought magazine.

MacKAY, JEAN (1920–1986). English humanist author, artist, and activist. MacKay was born into a tolerant family; her father was agnostic and her mother was religious. Her mother died of cancer when she was only sixteen. Her war years were spent enjoying the sort of freedom that men take for granted. Her first book was a popular introduction to **humanism**, *What Humanism Is About* (1963). She also wrote a pamphlet, *An Introduction to Secular Humanism*, as well as several volumes of poetry. She was an editor of the *Freethinker* for a short while, between 1966 and 1967.

MacKay was also involved in practical humanism. She was the first secretary of the Agnostics Adoption Bureau (later the Independent Adoption Society) and founder of the Humanist Letter Network and Cancer Contact, a support group for people with cancer. She wrote under the pseudonym "Kit Mouat," mainly to shield her husband, a senior diplomat. She died of cancer in 1986.

MADISON, JAMES (1751–1836). Fourth president of the United States and an important contributor to the principle of the **separa-**tion of church and state**. Madison was born in Port Conway, Virginia, and educated at the College of New Jersey, now Princeton University. He trained as a lawyer and became active in state and later federal politics. As a delegate in 1776 to the drafting of the state constitution for Virginia, Madison had a pivotal role in securing complete freedom of conscience in that state. Later, in 1784, he was instrumental in opposing state contributions to churches. As part of his campaign he penned the *Memorial and Remonstrance against Religious Assessments*, which was signed by two thousand Virginians. Once again, Madison had enshrined an important foundation of the separation of church and state.

Like **Thomas Jefferson**, Madison was concerned to limit the deleterious effects **sectarianism** can have on a transparent civil government. He also led the Congress that ratified the Bill of Rights, which begins with the declaration that "Congress shall make no law respecting an establishment of religion, or prohibiting free exercise thereof. . . ." He was also careful to add that the First Amendment was binding on the states in equal measure as it was on the federal government, an important addition, and one with important implications for the future of civil rights in America.

Madison went on to serve his friend Jefferson as secretary of state and then two terms as president of the United States, from 1809 to 1817. He was not religious in any conventional sense. "Religious bondage," Madison wrote in 1774, "shackles and debilitates the mind and unfits it for every noble enterprise."

MAGIC. A prescientific idea that the universe can be made to bend to our will. The German philosopher Ernst Cassirer (1874–1945) observed that magic operates on the general principle that one can gain possession of objects in the real world by a symbolic representation of them accompanied by a ritualized performance. Magic made some sense in the **geocentric universe**, where shamans and magicians could speak to the gods, who controlled the universe and guided the destiny of human beings. And magic was very important among **Renaissance** thinkers. But in a universe defined by mathematic equations and principles understood through **science**, there is no serious place for magic.

Magic has now found its true vocation as an amusement which we know is sleight of hand, but we can suspend skeptical faculties for a while in the interests of **fun**.

MAHDI. A figure of special importance in Shi'ia Islam. The closest translation of "mahdi" is "divinely guided one." The idea of Mahdi has several uses in Sunni Islam, none of them being anything like as important as it is to Shi'ites. In Shi'ia Islam, the Mahdi is the single most important figure in the future of the religion and of the world generally. It is entirely guided by Allah and will return at a time when Muslims are oppressed around the world and will bring peace and justice to all and usher in a new golden age.

There is no mention of the Mahdi in the Qur'an, and the veracity of the references to the Mahdi in the Hadith are disputed between Sunni and Shi'ite Muslims. The idea of the Mahdi developed two to three hundred years after the beginning of Islam. The first time the idea was mentioned was in 686 CE by Mukhtar Thaqafi bin I-Hanafiya. Several people in the history of Islam have laid claim to the title. In light of the subsequent failure of all of them, they are usually written off as heretics. Despite this, belief is strong that the prophecy of the Mahdi will definitely come to pass.

Various sources prophesy that the Mahdi will be tall, fair, have a slight stutter, which will cause him to occasionally slap his thigh in frustration, and will be forty years of age at the time of his emergence. These variations notwithstanding, it is hard not to see the many parallels with Christian thinking about the second coming of Christ. Neither is this surprising, as the theme of a returning savior is an old one. King Arthur was said to be waiting to return to save his people in their darkest hour.

MAHMOUD, ZAKI NAGUIB (1905–1995). Influential Egyptian philosopher and critic. Born in Damietta on the Nile Delta and educated in Cairo, Mahmoud taught philosophy in secondary schools for much of his career. He argued that we live in a scientific age, and that abstract speculation in the manner of medieval philosophy or divine inspiration is no longer a credible form of thinking upon which to depend.

In the manner of **Bertrand Russell** and **A. J. Ayer**, he argued that universal statements that range beyond the realm of verifiable particular facts are likely to be meaningless. In *The Renewal of Arabic Thought* (1971) Mahmoud picked out authoritarianism, traditionalism, and verbalism as the three principal impediments to Arabic thought and advocated their replacement with modes of thinking that are not, as he put it, "fake," but which rest on reliable **knowledge**. Mahmoud was particularly concerned about the tendency to verbalism, by which he meant the veneration of the Arabic language in its own right, as an obstacle to progress. He was opposed to the power of **religion** to act as brakes to progressive thought and open debate in Arabic societies.

Mahmoud wrote widely, but his main books include *The Myth of Metaphysics* (1953), *Towards a Scientific Philosophy* (1959), and *The Renewal of Arabic Thought* (1971). He will be an important figure for any future Muslim Renaissance.

MALLEUS MALEFICORUM, THE. A book best translated as *The Hammer of Witches*, published in 1486. The *Malleus Maleficorum* was written as a sober manual for those intent on the elimination of **witchcraft**. It quickly became indispensable in that role and as a textbook for the **Inquisition**. The book's authors, Heinrich Kramer, Dean of Cologne University, and Jacob Sprenger, Dominican Inquisitor-General in Germany, were quite clear that misfortune, of whatever variety, could be explained by the intervention of **Satan**. The *Malleus Maleficorum* and the thinking behind it was reinforced by successive papal decrees throughout the sixteenth century. While the *Malleus* was a Catholic document, the belief in witches was also actively supported by all leading Protestant thinkers of the time as well. Over the next two centuries the *Malleus* went through nineteen editions.

Every **superstition** then believed about witches was confirmed to be true: witches did kidnap and eat children, they did lust after sex with the devil, and they were responsible for climatic and economic calamities. While purporting to be hostile to witches, the *Malleus* did more than any other book to propagate belief that witches existed. It won important endorsements from theologians of the day, including from the faculty at Cologne University. The most conservative estimate is that half a million people, the vast majority of them women, perished during the witch craze encouraged by the publication of the *Malleus Maleficorum*.

Belief in witches died out due, in part at least, to the advance of **science**. For instance, William Harvey (1578–1657), the Englishman who discovered the circulation of blood, dissected a toad that was reported to be possessed of a demon. Harvey found no such demon, and ceased to believe in witches.

MALTHUS, THOMAS ROBERT (1766–1834). English churchman and theorist on population growth. Born in Dorking, Surrey, Malthus studied at Cambridge, where he was elected a fellow of the Jesus College in 1793. In 1797 he became curate at Albury in Surrey. While at Albury he published anonymously the book he is best known for, *Essay on the Principle of Population* (1798, with a heavily revised edition in 1807). In 1805, Malthus was appointed professor of political economy at Haileybury, at the time the college for the East India Company. While there he wrote a book on rent and *Principles of Political Economy*, another enormously influential work.

Malthus was not the first theorist of **overpopulation**. The great **Enlightenment** thinker **Marie Jean Antoine Condorcet** aired most of the ideas later ascribed to Malthus. But where Condorcet spoke of solving the problem through the education of women, Malthus took a more gloomy view, inspired by his Christian ideas on the prevalence of evil. Malthus criticized what he saw as complacent prognostications of unlimited growth, because the natural rates of population growth would inevitably increase faster than any growth in food production to sustain such a growth in numbers. Malthus argued that this Law of Population as he called it, could be contained by rates of death from war, pestilence, famine, and so on, and by causes that prevent birth, which he listed as sexual **abstinence** and "vice," by which he meant birth control. While his hostility to birth control was counterproductive and his fear that food production will lag behind population growth has been shown to be wrong (so far, at any rate), his general fears of the debilitating effects of population growth were prescient.

He was reviled for his views in the *Essay*, and was subjected to vicious criticism, both from progressives, who believed growth could cater to any population increase, and from conservatives, whose objections were of a moral nature. His most important reader was **Charles Darwin**. Reading the *Essay* put the last piece in the jigsaw of evolution together. Realizing Malthus was right, Darwin then understood that only **natural selection** could deal with the otherwise inexorable growth in population.

Half a century after Malthus's death his influence gave rise to what became known as Malthusianism. From the right this was expressed as **social darwinism**, but on the left it was expressed as promoting knowledge of birth control. An early champion of this approach was the great atheist campaigner **Charles Bradlaugh**. See the entry on **overpopulation**.

MANN, THOMAS (1875–1955). Important German novelist and thinker whose work focused on the decline of the very tradition he became a master of. Mann was born and raised in Lübeck, but much of his life in Germany was spent in Munich. Through his life, he struggled with his conservative and puritanical character on the one side and his artistic tendencies on the other. While still only twenty-five, he wrote *Buddenbrooks* (1901), which told the tale of a German family, not unlike his own, which declined over a few generations as the family's robust business abilities give way to artistic leanings. This book is cited as the principal reason Mann was awarded the Nobel Prize for Literature in 1929.

For much of his early life, he was politically and socially conservative. His views found expression in *Confessions of an Unpolitical Man* (1918), where Mann distinguished between the debilitating notion of civilization, with its implications of internationalism, and *Kultur*, with its more nationalistic focus. He advanced the old German idea of **Bildung**, which feared that association with politics only coarsened the individual. But as German politics went from bad to worse, he slowly revised this view, seeing it as an evasion of responsibility. When the Nazis took power in Germany, Mann was advocating a more active and humanistic notion of Bildung, which encouraged involvement in political life. All this came too late for Germany.

In *The Magic Mountain* (1924), he told the story of Hans Castorp's confinement at a sanatorium in Switzerland in the years leading up to World War I. The people Castorp comes into contact with typify attitudes in Europe at the time and go some way to describing the intellectual poverty of European thinking. In *Dr. Faustus* (1947), Mann returns to the Faust theme, very influential in German cultural history, to explore the ghastly reality of what Germany had recently been through. Shortly before his death, Mann wrote an uncharacteristically humorous novel called *The Confessions of Felix Krull, Confidence Man* (1954).

Critics argue that Mann's writing is cloudy and unclear. His supporters see him as a profound thinker and humanist.

MANSON, MARILYN (1969–). Controversial American entertainer. Brian Warner was born in Canton, Ohio, and at eighteen moved to Tampa Bay, Florida, where he worked as a music journalist. There, in 1990, he set up his band called Marilyn Manson, which has been described as "industrial rock" and "androgynous rock." Each of the band members takes the name of a female pop culture icon and a serial killer. Marilyn Manson combines the names of Marilyn Monroe and Charles Manson.

Marilyn Manson's brand of rock is calculated to attract attention, and it has been successful in doing that. As well as the sexual ambiguity, there are the nihilistic and violent lyrics and the parodying of religious themes and images. Manson calls himself the "Antichrist Superstar" and is reported to have links to the Church of Satan. Religious conservatives and **virtuecrats** have had plenty of opportunities to be offended by Manson's songs and videos. The band was even blamed for society's ills after the Columbine High School massacre in 1999, when two alienated youths went on a shooting rampage, killing twelve fellow students and a teacher. That neither of the killers was a fan of the band counted for little.

What the outraged virtuecrats fail to realize is that bands like Marilyn Manson are products of the society they emerge from. The growing power of Evangelical **command moralities**, with all the opportunities for hypocrisy such a climate encourages, are bound to produce an equal and opposite reaction. And tut-tutting is not going to help.

Marilyn Manson is a test case for our commitment to **toleration**. It is easy to tolerate those things we approve of, but what of those we don't? Nobody is being exploited in this case (at least not beyond the bounds of normal commercialism) and there are no genuine victims. People can choose to partake of this form of entertainment or not, as they see fit. We should have learned from the lessons of **comstockery** and prohibition that banning things is part of the problem, not part of the solution. Warner made the case well in a talk to philosophy students at Temple University in Philadelphia in 2004 when he said, "I'm not someone who doesn't respect **religion**, but I don't care for the way religion is used to manipulate people." He went on to say "We create our own gods. We create our own devils."

MANUFACTURING CONSENT. A phrase used by Noam Chomsky (1928–) and his coauthor Edward Herman as the title of their influential 1988 book. Chomsky's vision of contemporary society is chilling. He argues that the United States is not a **democracy** in any meaningful sense, but is run by a cabal of corporate leaders, government mandarins, and the top men in the military. See the entry on **Oligarchy, Iron Law of**. In order to retain its power, it diverts the people with a never ending parade of conforming and trivial events. See the entry on **bread and circuses**. Elections are won by the rich and consent is manufactured by the highest bidder. With the mass media being owned and operated by a small coterie of super-rich men, the business of manufacturing consent is all the easier.

Sport is a prime example of a massively costly diversion to amuse the masses while the power elite get on with the business of governing without interference. The notion of manufactured consent is a more recent, and more secular version of **Friedrich Nietzsche**'s idea of the **Holy Lie**. See also the entry on **imagology**.

Further reading: Noam Chomsky and Edward Herman, *Manufacturing Consent: The Political Economy of the Mass Media*.

MARCION (85–160 CE). one of the most significant people in the development of Christianity. Marcion was to have a seminal influence on the development of the New Testament and Christian theology. He was also to be a significant influence in the **anti-Semitism** that is rife in the New Testament.

The great New Testament scholar F. C. Conybeare (1856–1924) called Marcion the greatest anti-Semite in antiquity. He could also be said to be the principal **supersessionist**.

Born to Syrian parents in Sinope on the Black Sea coast of what is now Turkey, Marcion became a wealthy man as a shipowner. Sometime late in the 130s he went to Rome and joined the Christian community there, only to be expelled as a heretic in 144.

He was a **Gnostic** who found it difficult, and distasteful, to relate the Jewish **Yahweh** to the God spoken about by **Paul**. Marcion believed the Jewish Yahweh to be a malevolent spirit. And, in this vein, he was determined to strain as much Jewishness away from his image of Jesus Christ as possible. Marcion was the first person to gather together the Epistles of Paul, and felt free to excise passages that violated his image of Jesus. The significant hostility toward the Jews in the New Testament can be explained largely by the agenda of Marcion who, more than anyone, was responsible for putting it together. However, he failed to excise the **Hebrew scriptures** entirely. They came to be included in the slowly evolving Christian scriptures, although in the debased form as being the "Old Testament," which had been superseded by the New.

To this day, it is a common device by religious apologists to explain away the follies and cruelties of the Old Testament and declare that the revelation of Jesus and the New Testament can be treated apart from the Old Testament. This ploy both ignores Jesus' own words on the issue and commits what is known as the Marcionite Heresy.

MARLOWE, CHRISTOPHER (1564–1593?). Brilliant and rebellious dramatist, thought by many to be the most brilliant before **Shakespeare**. Son of a shoemaker, Marlowe received a first-class education, graduating MA from Benet (now Corpus Christi) College, Cambridge, in 1587. Marlowe achieved greatness for his stage plays *Tamburlaine the Great* (1587), *The Tragical*

History of Dr. Faustus (1588), *Edward II* (1592), and the epic poem *Hero and Leander* (1598), which was completed by George Chapman. His works were characterized by towering passions and violence, and beautiful language.

There has long been speculation that Marlowe had a part to play in the production of some of Shakespeare's plays. This is quite possible, as some parts of *Dr. Faustus* betray another hand than Marlowe's. It is possible that Marlowe was involved in parts of *Henry VI* and *Titus Andronicus*, although it is unreasonable to argue that he, or anyone else, wrote entire plays now attributed to Shakespeare.

Marlowe was an outspoken freethinker and opponent of Christianity. He was on the verge of being arrested when, some say, he was killed in a pub brawl. Others say a strong case can be made that Marlowe, knowing of his imminent arrest, staged the fight to cover his flight to Italy, where he lived for the rest of his life, dying sometime in the 1630s.

MARRIAGE. An ancient institution that serves as a legal statement of two people being bound together as one unit. For many centuries this usually meant that the woman had simply given up her status as an individual and had been subsumed into the person of her husband. As society has become more secular and old religious taboos have declined, this exploitative notion of marriage has declined too, although it is far from dead historically.

Conservative Christians favor the idea of marriage as an insoluble sacrament, but this is actually a relatively recent development. In ancient Rome marriage was a civil contract and divorce a domestic act, which was validated by a written document drawn up with a witness. It wasn't until about the eleventh century that the church had secured general control over the institution of marriage. It was only when the Italian theologian Peter Lombard (1100–1164 CE, approx.) brought together various church documents into a coherent package and developed the seven sacraments, of which marriage was one, that the church position on marriage was set in stone. And it was at this time that divorce technically became impossible for Christians, although churchmen were able to find loopholes when it suited their interests to do so. Martin Luther argued that marriage was a holy thing, but not a sacrament. This allowed marriage once again to be seen as a secular commitment.

For many people nowadays, marriage has a looser meaning. It means a public declaration of love for and commitment to another person. The religious sanctions surrounding the ceremony are either irrelevant or simply provide a pleasing backdrop. It is every bit as possible now, in the West particularly, to enjoy a loving and long-lasting relationship outside of marriage. The important point is whether the relationship is a loving one, not whether it conforms to some preset commandment as to what constitutes a marriage. See the entries on **family values** and **humanist family values**.

MARTIN, EMMA (1812–1851). English **freethought** pioneer. Brought up in a Baptist family from Bristol, Emma Martin began as a critic of infidelity, denouncing it as an effusion of weak minds and the resource of guilty ones. Her faith was shaken by the trials of **George Jacob Holyoake** and **Charles Southwell** for **blasphemy**, and after a lengthy period of study and thought, she became a freethinker. She also had to struggle with a desperately unhappy marriage, eventually having to maintain her children on her own, something nineteenth-century England made formidably difficult for women.

Martin became a prominent proponent of women's rights and of freethought. Fluent in Italian, she translated the *Maxims* of Guicciardini into English. She also penned several short tracts, including *Baptism: A Pagan Rite*, *Religion Superseded*, *Prayer*, *A Conversation on the Being of God*, and a protest against capital punishment. She also wrote a novel called *The Exiles of Piedmont*. George Jacob

Holyoake, who spoke at her funeral, described her as "a handsome woman, of brilliant talent and courage."

MARTIN, MICHAEL (1932–). American philosopher, and one of the twentieth century's most brilliant defenders and articulators of the philosophy of **atheism**. After a short spell at the University of Colorado, Martin moved to the University of Boston, where he remained for the rest of his professional career.

In *Atheism: A Philosophical Justification* (1990) Martin demolishes the traditional arguments for religious belief, and the more recent attempts to resurrect them. He then proceeds to argue the case for negative atheism, before arguing the case for the stronger version, known as positive atheism. There has been no serious attempt to refute this book, which remains a milestone of contemporary atheism. His next work was *The Case Against Christianity* (1991), in many ways a companion volume to *Atheism*. In the same methodical way, Martin proceeds through all the arguments for Christianity and refutes them point by point. In *Atheism, Morality, and Meaning* (2002), given as one of the **Prometheus Lecture Series**, Martin examines some other defenses of religion and shows them to be wanting. And most recently, Martin has coedited an authoritative collection of essays on atheism called *The Impossibility of God* (2003). He is a fellow of the **Committee for the Scientific Examination of Religion**.

Martin's work requires concentration and effort, and in an attempt to present his findings to a nonspecialist audience, he wrote, at the suggestion of his wife, *The Big Domino in the Sky* (1996). This collection of short stories illustrates Martin's philosophical conclusions in a more accessible way. This dictionary is another such attempt.

MARTINEAU, HARRIET (1802–1876). English scholar and popularizer of immense range. Harriet Martineau suffered throughout her life from a variety of serious ailments, in particular deafness and heart disease, but still went on to make a serious contribution to intellectual life in England.

Martineau's principal work was her translation of Auguste Comte's (1798–1857) *Positive Philosophy*, a translation thought so good that Comte had it retranslated from English into French, considering it an improvement on his own work. James Mill (1773–1836) had earlier said to her it was impossible to make Comte's work, dubbed the "dismal science," readable, and yet this was Harriet Martineau's achievement. See the entry on **positivism**. She also wrote a two-volume study of Comte's philosophy, as well as popularizations of the works of **Thomas Malthus** and the economist David Ricardo (1772–1823), as and a series of novels.

After a trip to the Middle East Martineau shed her liberal **Unitarian** views. She now described herself as an atheist in the vulgar sense of rejecting popular theology but not in the philosophic sense of rejecting a first cause. Every conception of **God**, Martineau wrote, was degrading and offensive to her, and she preferred to roam "the unfenced universe." She was also an enthusiastic supporter of the movement to abolish **slavery**. The powerful Whig politician Lord Brougham (1778–1868) said of her, "There is at Norwich a deaf girl who is doing more good than any man in the country."

MARTYRDOM. In its current context, the religious delusion that dying violently in the service of **God** is an act of particular righteousness that will be rewarded in heaven. The well-educated young men who flew planes into the World Trade Center in 2001 and the desperadoes who killed three hundred people, half of them children, in Beslan in Russia three years later, performed these deeds with a clear conscience. They knew, because the Qur'an told them so, that dying while killing the infidels is a specially honorable form of death (see 9:73, 9:123, 4:74–78, or 4:95–101, among others). Many **hadiths** give a similar account.

Martyrdom in the Muslim context has particular appeal for young men because of the popular belief that the paradise that awaits them consists of seventy black-eyed virgins and a state of permanent intoxication without the hangover. However, recent scholarship suggests the "black-eyed virgins" is actually a mistranslation, and could really refer to raisins. The incidence of martyrdom might well decline if this becomes better known.

Martyrdom is not peculiar to Islam. The early saints venerated by the Roman Catholic Church acquired their status by virtue of having died as a martyr, whether they did or not. And for centuries Protestant Christians were reared on *Foxe's Book of Martyrs* (1563), a grisly account of those who were burned at the stake for their Protestant beliefs. Martyrdom is a phenomenon most common in **monotheist** religions, which have an **absolutist** sense of God's authority and a corresponding inability to see any good in those who would choose to live differently. It is the most virulent form of **anthropocentric conceit**.

MARXISM. Body of thought named after Karl Marx (1818–1883), although others, notably Friedrich Engels (1820–1895) developed the theory as well. Essentially, Marxism is a metaphysical analysis of history. On the basis of the Marxian analysis of history, the prediction was made that capitalism would lead to widespread misery and oppression. Eventually, through these and other internal and inherent contradictions, capitalism would collapse to be replaced by socialism. The agent for this change would be the proletariat, a politically aware vanguard of the working class. This transition to socialism would happen in the most industrially advanced countries, as this is where the largest proletariat would be found. In due course, the rest of the world would catch up and experience its own decay of capitalism. At this stage socialism would develop to an even more advanced stage, called communism. National barriers would have broken down and all contradictions of production would have been solved. Under communism, each would work and consume to the level of their needs. **Religion** would have withered away because nobody would be experiencing the frustrations that were held to be religion's greatest reason for existence. See the entry on **opium of the people**.

Needless to say, the Marxist predictions about the future, despite being held to be objective, have not transpired. No proletariat ever developed, the first revolution took place not in the advanced industrialized countries of the West, but in Russia, which was still overwhelmingly agrarian and precapitalist in economic development. Capitalism has not decayed on the Marxist model at all, and in fact it was the Marxist bloc that collapsed under the weight of its own internal contradictions toward the end of the twentieth century. **Karl Popper** described Marxism as a metaphysical dream married to a cruel reality.

Marx had many penetrating insights into the nature of capitalism and religion in the nineteenth century, but as a prophet of the future his work was wrong, and indirectly responsible for the terrible crimes committed in his name. Since the collapse of Marxism as a political model, many Marxist intellectuals in the West drifted into a variety of brands of **postmodernism**.

MATARISVAN. Hindu deity to whom fire was first disclosed, or who first created fire from fire-sticks and then gave it to the a caste of celestial fire-priests who in turn gave it to humanity. This is an interesting parallel to the Greek myth of **Prometheus**.

MATERIALISM. A word with two quite different uses. In popular discourse, materialism is the tendency to value possessions and to measure one's self-worth by how many possessions one owns. Materialism in this sense is almost always used as a term of condemnation. In this sense, a materialist is portrayed as shallow and unmoved by the finer things of life.

The other understanding of materialism is as an ancient strand of philosophy, with prominent traditions in India, China, and Greece, down to the modern world. The core assumption of philosophical materialism is that there is no reality other than the material order in which we live. This core assumption has stood the test of time; what has changed is the question of what the material order actually consists of. Materialism is closely aligned, although not absolutely the same as, **naturalism**.

It has been a long-standing tactic of religious apologists to contrive some sort of link between the two understandings of materialism in an attempt to discredit philosophical materialism. There is in fact no necessary link between the two at all. In fact, virtually all philosophical materialists would condemn the materialism just spoken of just as roundly as religious critics. Good examples would be **Epicurus** and **Lucretius**.

The earliest form of materialism was **atomism**, the view that matter consists of indivisible atoms. This view dominated materialist thought until the end of the nineteenth century. But the twentieth century saw a revolution in materialist philosophy. In the nineteenth century, materialism defended the notion that there are no entities that exist independent of material entities. This thesis is no longer credible, although the many gleeful prophecies of the death of materialism have all proved false. In fact, materialism has become the dominant intellectual paradigm of the twentieth and twenty-first centuries, albeit in a new version.

Highlights of twentieth-century materialism include J. J. C. Smart's *Philosophy and Scientific Realism* (1963) and Patricia Churchland's *Neurophilosophy* (1986). Contemporary materialism views matter not as indivisible atoms, or even of solid objects at all, but of a quantizable force field. Neither is materialism deterministic in the traditional sense. See the entry on **determinism**. **Quantum mechanics** have shown that nature, at the quantum level at least, is probabilistic. But the basic materialist claim that all things in the universe are connected in a web of interdependence has been vindicated by contemporary science.

Further reading: Richard Vitzhum, *Materialism: An Affirmative History and Definition*.

MATHEMATICS. Described by **Bertrand Russell** as the alphabet of the book of nature without being the book itself. Galileo said much the same thing when he said that without mathematics we have no chance of comprehending a single word of the book of nature. This is because mathematics can express patterns of the universe in the simplest and most concise way, and by virtue of that conciseness, reveal the underlying simplicity and unity. Mathematics also has the distinction of being the only discipline where **proofs** can in principle be found for any controversy.

The paradox of this provability, simplicity, and unity is that it makes science less accessible for the nonspecialist, for whom mathematics is daunting in the extreme. There are some brave attempts to make mathematics accessible to the nonspecialist, but it may well be in the nature of the subject that this exercise is always going to be problematic.

See the entry on **Gödel's Theorem**.

Further reading: Simon Gowers, *Mathematics: A Very Short Introduction*; and Lancelot Hogben, *Mathematics for the Million*.

MATUBBAR, AROJ ALI (1900–1985). Rationalist philosopher from Bangladesh. Born into a poor family in rural Bengal, Aroj Ali Matubbar had to take on the role of chief provider for his family at the age of eleven when his father died. His formal schooling lasted only one year, but he borrowed books from wealthier families in his locality, and later from public libraries. He became a rationalist after the death of his mother. When he went to a nearby town to develop a photograph of his dead mother, the local mullahs issued a **fatwa**, declaring that photographs could not be taken of dead people, especially of women. They insisted that prayers be sent to Allah for her soul instead. This led

Matubbar to question Qur'anic teaching and then the existence of Allah himself.

He dedicated his life to the alleviation of poverty and ignorance, and the righting of civil-rights abuses. Over his long life he worked quietly in his region to educate and empower some of the world's poorest people. His **rationalism** was not so much a doctrine but a system of learning the truth by the use of reason. **Skepticism** was the driving force of his rationalism. He put these thoughts together in *The Quest for Truth* in 1952, although it was not published until 1973. He had been under legal and social pressure from Muslim leaders not to publish, and it was only in the first years of newly independent Bangladesh, which declared itself a secular republic, that Matubbar was able to do so. He also published *Smaranika* (*Remembrance*) in 1982 and *Anumn* (*Conjectures*) in 1983 and left two unpublished works.

McCABE, JOSEPH MARTIN (1867–1955). The twentieth-century's most neglected polymath. Joseph McCabe was born in Macclesfield, the son of William McCabe, an Irish migrant silk worker, and Harriet Kirk, an English convert to Catholicism. As the second-born, the young McCabe was destined for the priesthood. While still a pious altar boy at eleven and twelve, McCabe was subjected to sexual abuse he only felt able to speak of when he was seventy-three years old. He was a talented youth and he rose quickly through the ranks. His novitiate year was spent at Killarney in Kerry, at a monastery he later learned was a dumping ground for priests who had committed moral indiscretions or had ruined themselves with drink.

Partially arising from this experience, McCabe became an outspoken campaigner for improving the educational standards of the priesthood. He was appointed professor of philosophy at only twenty-three. He went on to study Oriental languages at Louvain University in 1893–94 and was offered a PhD for his work, but was required by the rules of the Franciscan Order to refuse. McCabe's

long-held doubts assumed crisis proportions, culminating on Christmas Day, 1895, when he admitted to himself he had lost his **faith**. He left the church on Ash Wednesday, 1896, and began a career of writing and speaking that was to span fifty-eight years.

Over his long life he wrote a staggering amount, most of it popularizations of the academic consensus of the day as he perceived it. The first half of his career was divided between being an independent author, publishing works with a range of companies, and working with the **Rationalist Press Association**. His two most enduring areas of interest were the Roman Catholic Church and **evolution**. McCabe was one of the twentieth century's most consistent critics of the Roman Catholic Church, without descending into hatred or vulgarity that tarnished so much Protestant criticism. His works of popular evolution were of outstanding quality, and avoided all of the most frequent errors of the day: **Social Darwinism**, **eugenics**, and Lamarckism. McCabe was an outspoken feminist from early in the twentieth century, specifically applying that label to himself. These opinions, and his difficult personality, slowly lost him most of his publishing contacts.

He was his own worst enemy. He was thin-skinned and resentful of what he saw as unearned success of some of his contemporaries—people like **Charles Gorham** and **Adam Gowans Whyte**, whose paths to rationalism had been easier than his own. By 1928 he had worn out his welcome at the Rationalist Press Association. For much of the second half of his career, he published with **Emanuel Haldeman-Julius**, although after 1934, a partial reconciliation with the RPA was reached. All this said, McCabe's strengths were as extraordinary as his weaknesses. He was courageous in expressing opinions that were unpopular. He never told his readers what they wanted to hear. He told them what he thought was the **truth**. And in nearly all cases it was, because McCabe had an uncanny ability to distinguish a genuine shift in intellectual direction from a mere fad—an ability many of the academics of time, who looked down on McCabe as a mere popularizer, did not have. He wrote clearly and felt no need to parade his vast learning. And despite the volatility of his own personality, his opinions were surprisingly moderate and expressed in a civil way. He had this in common with **Bertrand Russell**.

It is difficult to single out the most important works from such a huge corpus, but a minimum list would include *Twelve Years in a Monastery* (1897), *The Story of Evolution* (1912), *The Sources of the Morality of the Gospels* (1914), *A Biographical Dictionary of Modern Rationalists* (1920), *The Story of Religious Controversy* (1929), *The Rise and Fall of the Gods* (1931), *The Riddle of the Universe Today* (1934), *A History of the Popes* (1939), and *A Rationalist Encyclopedia* (1948). Whether they realize it or not, every popularizer of the second half of the twentieth century walks in McCabe's shadow.

Further reading: Bill Cooke, *A Rebel to His Last Breath: Joseph McCabe and Rationalism.*

McCALL, COLIN (1919–2003). English rationalist activist and writer. Born into a family of rationalists, McCall grew up entirely without any form of religion. He was a polymath, with a wide range of interests. The young McCall wrote his first contribution to the *Freethinker* in 1939 and his last shortly before his death. In 1957 he joined the editorial board of the *Freethinker* and was editor until 1965. Until 1963 he was also general secretary of the **National Secular Society**.

Through the 1960s and 1970s McCall was a freelance writer, wrote for an architectural journal, and was deputy editor of *Yours*, an advocacy magazine for Help the Aged. In 1990 McCall returned to the *Freethinker*, contributing a regular column called "Down to Earth," as well as a stream of articles and reviews.

McKAY, CLAUDE (1889–1948). Jamaican-American poet and an early source of inspiration for the Harlem Renaissance, a period of great intellectual and cultural vitality in African American thought, which lasted from about 1917 until 1935. Claude McKay was born in Jamaica and his only education was provided by his older brother, Theo. The rest of his family was strongly religious, but Theo, and through him, Claude, grew up as staunch agnostics and rationalists. McKay was also fortunate to have attracted the attention of Walter Jekyll, an Englishman living in Jamaica. Jekyll introduced McKay's works to the **Rationalist Press Association**, which published *Constab Ballads* in 1912. In the same year, *Songs of Jamaica* was published. McKay was a strong influence on later poets such as **Langston Hughes** and black politicians like **Leopold Senghor**.

In 1912 he left Jamaica for the United States. After a brief spell at the Tuskegee Institute, he studied agriculture at Kansas State University. In the 1920s he traveled to the Soviet Union, although his enthusiasm for communism did not last long. In 1934 he returned to the United States and lived in Harlem, New York. He wrote no new poetry after the 1920s. After his return to New York he wrote *A Long Way from Home* (1937), *Harlem: Negro Metropolis* (1940), and *The Negroes in America*, which wasn't published until 1979. Toward the end of his life, after many experiments with various forms of belief, McKay converted to Catholicism.

Further reading: Winston James, *A Fierce Hatred of Injustice: Claude McKay's Jamaica and His Poetry of Rebellion*; and Norm R. Allen Jr., ed., *African-American Humanism: An Anthology.*

McLAUGHLIN, EMMETT. See **FORMER PREACHERS**.

McTAGGART, JOHN McTAGGART ELLIS (1866–1925). British Hegelian philosopher who achieved the rare double of combining a commitment to **atheism** with an equally serious commitment to **immortality**. McTaggart, who spent his entire academic career, between 1897 and 1923, at Cambridge University in England developed an idiosyncratic blend of Hegelian idealism and atheism. He argued for immortality in the form of a disembodied mind, in the manner of **Plato**. This was argued principally in his work *Some Dogmas of Religion*, published in 1906, with a second edition in 1930, and *The Nature of Existence* (1921). A weakness in McTaggart's thinking was his almost complete ignorance of **science**, and his inability to see its value.

MECCA. A city in Saudi Arabia and, according to traditional Muslim accounts, the birthplace of the prophet **Muhammad**. However, the role Mecca played in the formation of **Islam** is far from clear. Scholars of Islam have shown that there are no references to Mecca in any early non-Muslim sources and early mosques point not to Mecca but to a point in northwest Arabia. Jerusalem played a very significant role in early Islam until relations with the Jews broke down seriously, after which Muslims felt the need to relocate their origins within Arabia as part of fashioning an independent religious identity. It was only then that Mecca became a place of central importance in Muslim thinking.

MEDITATION. A popular practice, usually involving sitting still and freeing one's mind from day-to-day cares and ultimately from entrapment in one's sense of self. Meditation seeks to find peace by stilling our seemingly neverending process of thinking. One can do this by a variety of ways, such as focusing on a single point, or on one's breathing, or simply on nothing at all.

Meditation is a worthwhile exercise insofar as it is designed to eliminate **stress** and encourage the individual to relax. It is less valuable when it is presumed to be a way to gather priceless insights about the nature of the universe.

MELIORISM. The doctrine that the world may be made better by human effort. Freethinkers have frequently been accused of having a superficial confidence in the unlimited **progress** of humanity. This accusation was never more than a caricature. What has distinguished freethinkers from indifferentists is that freethinkers have consistently recognized that, if we are to survive, much less prosper, it will depend on our own efforts. Indifferentists are more inclined to shrug their shoulders and claim they can make no effective contribution. Freethinkers have usually been prepared to do their bit, however humble, to help improve the human condition.

MEME. A termed coined by **Richard Dawkins** to refer to replicators or units of cultural transmission. An abbreviation of mimeme, "meme" was chosen specifically to sound like "gene," and thus give the correct impression. Just as genes propagate themselves in the gene pool, Dawkins writes, by transference from body to body, so do memes propagate themselves by transference from brain to brain in a process that can be called imitation. For example, the newly acquired skill of English blue tits to peck through milk bottles to get at the milk is a meme which spread rapidly through that population. The value of this chance discovery soon made itself felt to the blue-tit population and the skill to distinguish the bottles and peck through the foil lids was quickly imitated.

However, memes can also catch on simply because they are easily learned, rather than for any intrinsic advantage to be had from them. Thus, notions that are easily imitated or remembered have a high rate of infection. Among humans, for example, items of trivia have a higher rate of infection than sophisticated philosophical concepts. The word has caught on, having been used by psychologists such as Nick Humphrey and Susan Blackmore and philosophers like **Daniel Dennett**.

Further reading: Richard Dawkins, *The Selfish Gene* and *Unweaving the Rainbow*; and Susan Blackmore, *The Meme Machine*.

MEMEPLEX. A collection of memes that have gathered together for mutual benefit.

For instance a **religion** is a collection of memes of a similar order and with a structure designed to preserve and propagate those memes. New memes conducive to the survival and prosperity of the memeplex will be accepted; those not conducive will not be.

MENCKEN, H[ENRY] L[OUIS] (1880–1956). American journalist and **smiter of humbug**. Mencken was born in Baltimore, Maryland, to a family of German origin. His parents were agnostics. Precociously intelligent, Mencken read voraciously, and was particularly well read in the sciences. In 1898 he began work as a journalist, and in 1906 moved to the *Baltimore Sun*, which he remained associated with for the rest of his working life.

Mencken was a prolific writer and editor. He was editor of the *Smart Set* between 1914 and 1923 and the *American Mercury* until 1933. He is remembered for his fiery prose and damning indictments of fundamentalism and small-mindedness. His biting ridicule and sense of the absurd was a formidable weapon against obscurantism. His wit was particularly influential during the Scopes trial in 1925 when John Scopes (1900–1970), a biology teacher in Tennessee was charged with teaching evolution. Mencken is credited with inventing the term "Bible belt," among many others, in his long career.

His written output was prodigious, including twenty-eight books and innumerable introductions, editorials, and reviews. His best-known books were Treatise *on the Gods* (1930) and *Treatise on Right and Wrong* (1934). In the first of these titles, Mencken articulated his **agnosticism** and his admiration of **T. H. Huxley**. Another important influence on Mencken was **Friedrich Nietzsche**, about whom he wrote a book in 1908. However, Mencken was also an **anti-Semite**, and this drastically reduces his value to contemporary freethinkers.

Further reading: S. T. Joshi, *H. L. Mencken on Religion*.

MEREYMUSTIFICATION. A term used to denote the tendency of supernaturalist apologists to favor words like "mere" and "must" in their arguments against **naturalism**. Many apologists are prone to insist that there *must* be some extra dimension and that *mere* matter cannot explain the beauties and complexities of the universe. See the entry on **sothingist**. Many readers don't appreciate the emptiness of claims that resort to asserting that something *must* exist or that something that does exist is *merely* this or that. The American philosopher Morris Cohen (1880–1947) understood the problem, however, when he wrote that "mere" is the "most dangerous word in our language because it is the only one that has a superlative but no comparative."

MESLIER, ABBÉ JEAN (1664–1729). To all outward appearances Abbé Meslier was an undistinguished Catholic country priest from the Etrépigny region of the Champagne district of France. But Meslier was in fact a fervent atheist, materialist, and political radical with a visceral dislike of the hypocrisy and oppressiveness of his church, and of **religion** generally. He was a great admirer of **Pierre Bayle** and **Montaigne**. In the last decade of his life Abbé Meslier decided to write his thoughts down, to be published after his death. In *Testament*, he described religion as a means by which the masses are duped. It was he who wrote the much-quoted passage of wanting to hand "with the bowels of the priests all the nobles and rulers of the world." Meslier was unusually candid. One part of the *Testament*, addressed to his parishioners, read:

> I would have enlightened you sooner if I could have done so with safety. You are my witnesses that I have never exacted the fees which attach to my office as curate. I discouraged you from bigotry and I spoke to you as seldom as possible of our wretched dogmas. I had to carry out the duties of my office but how I suffered when I had to preach to you those pious lies

that I detest in my heart! A thousand times I was on the point of breaking out publicly and opening your eyes but a fear stronger than myself held me back and forced me to keep silence until my death.

Upon his death, he left all his property to his parishioners. **Voltaire** came across Meslier's work and was influenced by it, as was **Diderot**. Voltaire ensured a partial publication of Meslier's work came out in 1762, although it was not until 1864 when the whole work was published. It has still not been translated into English. Voltaire proposed for Meslier the following epitaph: "Here lies a very honest priest, who at death asked God's pardon for having been a Christian."

METACOGNITION. The ability to realize when you don't know something. This ability is more useful than the ability to realize you do know something, because the recognition of ignorance is a spur to further activity. It used to be thought that metacognition was one of those unique skills the *Homo sapiens* has, and which marks us off from other animals. This is no longer the case, as chimpanzees have been shown to possess some level of metacognitive ability. This is yet another example of the redundancy of old **great chain of being** presumptions of the uniqueness of humanity. See the entry on **fallibilism**.

METAETHICS. Questions *about* ethics rather than questions *within* ethics. Where ethics is the discipline of what is right and wrong, metaethics focuses on the broader questions of what it means to make **judgments** about right and wrong. Questions about the meaning of **morality**, or whether moral judgments are true across cultures are metaethical questions.

META-MORAL CONVICTIONS SHARED BY US ALL. An important element of **planetary humanism** is the sense that, underlying all the things that divide us

(religion, politics, race, money, and so on), there are important meta-moral convictions that virtually all of us would accept. The American humanist philosopher Kurt Baier has outlined these:

- we should have moralities;
- all members of a society should be taught what is condemned or valued;
- following those moralities should become second nature; and
- the beneficial effects of the morality depends in large measure on its being true.

So, rather than **demonizing the opposition** or claiming a **monopoly on the truth**, planetary humanism begins with the assumption of a common humanity and works from there. Whatever may divide us, these at least we can all agree upon. And it follows from this that there may also be items of moral belief that many of us share as well. See the entries on **moral truisms shared by us all** and **common moral decencies**.

Further reading: Kurt Baier, *Problems of Life and Death*.

METANARRATIVES. Grand accounts of history that usually posit history moving inevitably toward some goal or other. **Marxism** is a metanarrative, for instance, because its sense of history is predetermined. Capitalism will definitely be succeeded by socialism, which in turn will be succeeded at some future date by communism. Christianity is also a metanarrative. Some of the more perceptive feminists have also observed that **feminism** has a metanarrative, which is endangered by the **postmodernist** critique. The feminist view of history involves a series of struggles culminating in a hard-won freedom being implemented. From this new vantage point, new attitudes can develop and attention can move on to righting other wrongs which previously were beyond reach. See the entries on **teleology** and **historicism**.

METAPHYSICIANS AND IRONISTS. A distinction made by the American philosopher, **Richard Rorty**. In *Contingency, Irony, and Solidarity* (1989), Rorty talks about what he calls our final vocabulary. This is the collection of words we carry around with us—and the ideas they are connected to—which we use when we describe ourselves to ourselves or to others. We will use our final vocabulary when we express admiration or condemnation, and generally when we try to make sense of the world.

But Rorty goes on to say that there are two main personality types, which are understood in terms of how they relate to their own final vocabulary. He calls these two groups the metaphysicians and the ironists:

- *Metaphysicians* are those who search for the one true final vocabulary.
- *Ironists* have deep doubts about their own final vocabulary, and are impressed by the strength with which others express theirs, but rather than adopt someone else's final vocabulary, remain ambivalent about the whole process.

Rorty has a distinct preference for the ironist, for a number of reasons. His main point is that the metaphysicians are deluding themselves when they seek out the ultimate final vocabulary. Doing this assumes there is one final **truth** above all others, and this, Rorty argues, is not a valid assumption. For Rorty, the ironist is wise to abandon this futile quest, and to enjoy the spirit of **free inquiry** as a sufficient end in itself. However, see the entries on **external realism**, **critical commonsensism**, and **critical realism**.

Further reading: Richard Rorty, *Contingency, Irony, and Solidarity*.

METROSEXUAL. The latest word to capture the mood of louche **narcissism** observed among the young. The word was first used by Mark Simpson in the British newspaper the *Independent* in 1994. The metrosexual is young, male, urban, and narcissistic. He is familiar with the latest fashion looks, the places to eat, to drink, and the right company to keep. He may well be straight, he may well be gay; the important thing is that he is into pleasure—his own pleasure. The person most often associated with the term is the English soccer star and celebrity David Beckham.

But before we get too self-righteous, it is well to notice that this is hardly a new phenomenon, even though it now has a new name. In London during the 1770s, many older people noticed the prevalence of young men with money to burn and an appetite for excess and display. These men were said to have macaroni manners, a reference to the lascivious Continentals thought to be the source of the decay. Since then we've had fops, dandies, nancy boys, and Sloane Rangers. The metrosexual fits neatly into this tradition.

MILL, JOHN STUART (1806–1873). English philosopher and social reformer. As a boy, Mill was brought up in what even by nineteenth-century standards was an unloving and exceptionally demanding home environment. Throughout his life Mill suffered from **depression**, from which the poetry of Wordsworth and contemplation of the beauties of ancient Greece were important cures. He wrote of his upbringing very movingly in his revealing and honest *Autobiography* (1873). It is easy to mock Mill and many have taken the opportunity to do so. His melancholy and his championing of **positivism** have brought him critics. But his wisdom, humanity, and desire to overcome his deficits are all admirable traits.

Mill's essay *On Liberty* (1859) remains one of the foundational documents of the humanist tradition. Mill declared liberty was essential to the health of the individual and the wider society. "The worth of the State," he wrote, "is the worth of the individuals composing it. . . ." Mill said the dangers lay in intolerance and the tyranny of the majority, messages just as valid in the twenty-first century as in his own. Mill defended **Richard Carlile**'s right to publish books the majority disapproved of, and was a staunch supporter of the North during the American Civil War. Other causes Mill supported included proportional representation, votes for women, national education, and the abolition of discrimination based on **religion**. He also gave public support to the courageous atheist campaigner **Charles Bradlaugh**, which probably cost him his seat in parliament in 1868.

Other important works include *Utilitarianism* (1863) where Mill developed **Jeremy Bentham**'s idea in a creative way. Critics of the **Principle of Utility** have noted that it leads logically to the problematic conclusion that the end justifies the means. Mill extended the idea of utilitarianism by arguing that we should seek to maximize the **happiness** not of ourselves, but of others. He also spoke more of the *quality* of happiness than its *quantity*. This is why we should value liberty, Mill wrote. Who knows what sort of happiness is right for us? The good society, therefore, is the one that allows us maximum scope to find our happiness.

Mill was an instinctive **feminist**, outlining his thoughts in *The Subjection of Women* (1869). This book, and several others (notably *On Liberty*), were written with the help of Harriet Taylor (1807–1858), Mill's longtime companion and eventual wife. He developed his liberal and heterodox views on religion in separate works which were published as *Three Essays on Religion* (1874).

His integrity won him respect from fellow parliamentarians and from radical activists alike, something very few people in England could manage at the time. The Catholic Church placed Mill's works on the **Index of Forbidden Books**.

MILLENNIUM DEVELOPMENT

GOALS. A series of goals set by Kofi Annan, secretary-general of the **United Nations**, on September 8, 2000. All the 191 member nations of the UN have agreed to ratify these goals by 2015:

(1) Eradicate extreme poverty and hunger.

(2) Achieve universal primary education.

(3) Promote gender equality and empower women.

(4) Reduce child mortality.

(5) Improve maternal health.

(6) Combat HIV/**AIDS**, malaria, and other diseases.

(7) Ensure environmental sustainability.

(8) Develop a global partnership for development.

These goals are not simply a set of fine words. The United Nations has been devoting as many resources as it has available to bringing them about. The UN is working with nongovernmental organizations around the world to bringing these goals to fruition. Needless to say, many of the governments that have signed their assent to these goals are less than conspicuous in realizing them. Each of these goals could be achieved at about the same cost of the subsidies the European Community provides each year to insulate their farmers from cheap imports. The Millennium Development Goals are the clearest practical instance of **planetary humanism**.

Further reading: www.un.org/millennium goals/.

MILLENNIUM ECOSYSTEM ASSESSMENT.

An international program launched in June 2001 by the **United Nations** secretary-general Kofi Annan. The MA, as the program is known, was completed in March 2005. Its purpose was to provide accurate data on ecosystem changes around the planet to help policymakers address the issues appropriately. Of particular interest are questions of biological **diversity**, the conservation of fundamental resources like **water** and arable land. The MA involved more than thirteen hundred authorities from ninety-five countries.

The main findings of the MA are:

- Change to ecosystems over the past fifty years has been at an unprecedented level and has resulted in "a substantial and largely irreversible loss in the diversity of life on Earth";

- These changes have helped human prosperity in the short term, but at the cost of long-term problems which threaten to overwhelm all the progress made; and
- The degradation of the Earth's ecology is likely to worsen significantly in the first half of the twenty-first century. At risk are the **Millennium Development Goals**, which are concerned with addressing the growing issues of **inequality** in the world.

The enormity of the problems the MA has drawn our attention to highlights the fact that global problems require nothing less than global solutions. See the entries on **global governance**, **sustainable development**, and **planetary humanism**.

Further reading: www.millennium assessment.org.

MIND. A linguistic term for the brain. There is no such thing as the mind separate from the brain. Mind, as many thinkers in this field have observed, is what the brain does. Giving any grander role to the mind runs the risk of advocating some form of **dualism** between mind and body. See the entries on **consciousness** and **astonishing hypothesis**.

MINIMAL SELF. A concept developed by the American historian Christopher Lasch (1932–1994). Lasch wrote several insightful critiques about the shallowness of American consumer culture, in which he analyzed the destruction of coherent notions of selfhood. Lasch was pessimistic, arguing that the increasing pressures of modern society encouraged not an inflated sense of self, but a minimal self, a beleaguered, lightweight self honed down to the minimum level necessary for survival. See the entry on **affluenza**.

Further reading: Christopher Lasch, *The Minimal Self*.

MIRACLES. Events supposed to have happened which, by virtue of their extraordinariness, are attributed to some supernatural agency, usually **God**. A miracle is so extraordinary that those who believe it took place, cannot believe it could have happened without divine fiat.

Miracles have a plethora of conceptual and practical problems attached to them. What is a manifestation of God for one **faith** tradition is usually dismissed by those of other traditions as either the product of superstitious credulity or **Satan**. Miracles seemingly never take place in conditions where their effects may be verified. Skeptics have traditionally argued that the more extraordinary the claim being made, the more extraordinary the **evidence** needs to be. But it usually works the other way round: in most cases, the more extraordinary the claim, the weaker the evidence is. See the entry on **burden of proof**. And the miracles of history are very often in the service of some ignoble end, usually the destruction of one's enemies.

David Hume's essay on miracles remains unanswerable when he says that "no testimony is sufficient to establish a miracle, unless the testimony be of such a kind, that its falsehood would be more miraculous than the fact which it endeavors to establish." And **Richard Dawkins** illustrates this by using the example of the alleged miracle at Fatima; a miracle officially endorsed by the Vatican. Here it is alleged that the sun apparently tore itself from its moorings and hurtled toward the seventy thousand onlookers, only to return to its place in the sky. Now, according to Hume, it would be less fantastic to believe the incident at Fatima never happened than to believe the sun behaved in that way with nobody else on earth noticing anything odd.

Milton A. Rothman summarizes this conceptual incoherence when he writes:

The concept of supernatural forces presents a paradox to **science**. If supernatural forces were real in the sense that they could be identified, measured, and their laws determined, then they would become part of nature. They would no longer be supernatural. On the other hand, if supernatural forces work completely outside the domain of the natural, then how can they have physical effects on things within nature?

But perhaps the most devastating weakness of miracles was pointed out by **Baruch Spinoza** when he denounced the **anthropocentric conceit** that beliefs in miracles imply. Believers in miracles, Spinoza wrote "conceive nature as so limited that they believe man to be its chief part!"

Further reading: Milton A. Rothman, *The Science Gap*; Richard Dawkins, *Unweaving the Rainbow*; and David Hume "Of Miracles."

MISANTHROPE. Someone motivated by a dislike, envy, or even hatred of human beings. This may take the form of a mental illness, or be an advanced form of antisocial behavior. Certain religions, particularly those inclined to stress the inherent wickedness of human beings, increase the chance of the belief descending into misanthropy. While there are more than enough reasons to be disgusted with *Homo sapiens*, there is little to be gained by adopting a hatred for one's own species as an article of **faith**. And neither does avoiding misanthropy mean that we should fall inevitably into shallow optimism or **anthropocentric conceit**.

Aristotle wrote about the **Doctrine of the Mean**, where he encourages us to find the mean position between two extremes. The challenge for contemporary humanity is to find a mean between the extremes of misanthropy on the one hand and anthropocentric conceit on the other.

MIURA BAIEN (1723–1789). Japanese Confucian scholar, scientific-naturalist philosopher, and the founder of economics in his country. This is on the strength of his book *Kagen* (*Source of Value*), in which he asked

the same questions as his contemporary **Adam Smith**. Miura concluded, as Smith did, that value is the sum of labor and materials, which makes those practices very important indeed.

Miura formed a school called *Jorigaku*, or rationalist studies. His main works were *Gengo* (variously translated as *Deep Words* or *Abstruse Language*), which studied the principles that underlie the universe; *Zeigo* (*Superfluous Language*); and *Kango* (*High-flown Language*); which came together to criticize the deadening effects of tradition while appealing to **science** and nature. He came slowly to appreciate that the **geocentric universe** he originally favored was no longer credible, and with commendable honesty he incorporated the new **heliocentric** system into his thinking.

Miura believed in a supreme being in the manner of **deism** and was a critic of Christianity. He opposed the Buddhist view of emptiness and spoke instead of a dynamic and eternal universe in which our **death** is simply a small part of ongoing change. See the entries on **Giordano Bruno** and **dynamic integrity** for similar ideas. Miura dismissed the idea of some people being accorded special status as sages or buddhas, insisting instead that "Heaven and earth is the teacher." He applied this to his own works, attributing only what was erroneous to himself. Miura was also ahead of his time in believing in the essential equality of the races and sexes. For an interesting parallel in Chinese Confucianism, see the entry on **Dai Zhen**.

Further reading: Rosemary Mercer, *Deep Words: Miura Baien's System of Natural Philosophy*.

MODERN ART. A term which is taking on an increasingly pejorative flavor. When used by some religious and social conservatives, "modern art" has come to mean all contemporary nonrepresentational art, which, they claim, lacks significant levels of skill and therefore constitutes some sort of perversion of "real art." This debate over modern art is one of the frontlines in the **culture wars**.

Arguments not dissimilar to this have been given against artistic innovation since time immemorial. Much of the confusion revolves around archaic understandings of what constitutes a **piece of art**. It is true that a lot of contemporary art focuses less on skill than on the underlying idea or ideas. This means that much of the assessment of the work's quality now involves the viewer's response to the underlying idea. This leads to another confusion that underlies a lot of suspicion of contemporary art. Many people want to have a clear idea of what the piece is about, but frequently the underlying idea or ideas are unclear (often deliberately so), leaving the viewer feeling uncomfortable.

At this point all that is required is for the viewer to have some confidence in their own preferences. The first question to ask is a simple one: "Do I like it?" If not, simply move on and don't give the work another thought. If so, the viewer might want to ask why the piece appeals. The important point is that there is often no definitive answer. And this is precisely why many critics of modern art are so worried by it. See the entry on **telic art**.

MODES OF RELIGIOUS TRANSMIS-SION. There are, according to anthropologist Harvey Whitehouse, two principal modes of religious transmission, which activate different cognitive processes in the brain, and probably appeal to different personality types:

- *imagistic* mode, where people perform emotional rituals or dramatic rites, and slip into ecstatic states; and
- *doctrinal* mode, which presents coherent, systematic sets of messages.

These two modes follow one another in a ceaseless cycle. People tire of lifeless doctrine and formalist ritual and this need fuels a charismatic renewal. The renewal eventually exhausts itself or is brought under control by the religious authorities, who have modified their doctrine to try and accommodate the new situation. The new doctrines work for a while until they in turn become stale and lifeless and provoke fresh outbursts of imagistic thinking. Whitehouse's idea has strong parallels to **Friedrich Nietzsche**'s distinction between Apollonianism and **Dionysianism**.

MOLHED. Muslim term for an atheist. Thus, the Molhedeen are the atheists. Islam has no way of acknowledging that an atheist can be in good faith. The existence of **God** is not regarded as a proposition to be assented to or dissented from. It is a foundational and obvious fact from which dissent can only be taken in the form of incomprehensible stupidity or malevolence. **Atheism** constitutes a willful rejection of an obvious **truth**, and as such, any sort of **toleration** is not only unnecessary, it would be morally wrong.

MONOPOLY ON TRUTH. It is widely recognized that no worldview has a monopoly on truth. This means that however satisfied we may be with our own worldview, it is important that we do not close our minds to the possibility that it is in error in places or even in its entirety. Hindus may well have things to learn from Jews, and Christians may well have things to learn from atheists; at the very least we need to be alive to the possibility. See the entry on **fallibilism**.

For most worldviews this is not particularly problematic. For the great **Asian traditions** of Hinduism, Buddhism, Confucianism, and **Taoism**, this insight is either acknowledged or specifically reinforced. In the humanist tradition, the insight that nobody has a monopoly on truth is central. It is only in the **monotheist** religions that this idea becomes difficult. Christianity and Islam both have inflexible **scriptures** that claim to have a monopoly on truth. The best-known example is the Christian insistence, repeated throughout the New Testament, that nobody is saved except those who believe in the crucified and resurrected Jesus. The Qur'an makes similar claims about the exclusive truth of Islam. See the entries on **"Judeo-Christian,"** myth of, and **demonizing the opposition**.

Liberals in the monotheist faiths have tried to soften this harsh exclusivism, but often at the cost of jettisoning those bits of scripture that do not suit their purpose. Unfortunately for them, however, this illustrates the **fatal flaw at the heart of religious liberalism**.

MONOTHEISM. The belief that there is only one **God**. There are three major monotheist **religions**—Judaism, Christianity, and Islam—all of which worship the same god, although under different names. The Christian notion of the **Trinity** has tended to obscure and even put into question that religion's commitment to monotheism. Certainly Islam is the most unambiguously monotheist religion in existence. None of the great **Asian traditions** are monotheist.

Monotheism as a style of belief is highly useful as an imperial ideology because of its simple division of people into believers and unbelievers. And this division can be given a moral as well as an intellectual dimension. Unbelievers can be portrayed as not simply wrong, but *wicked*, and as such, worthy of fearsome persecution. Monotheism provides people as well as states a clear view of the world, a **certainty** untainted by ambiguity or doubt. It also is the purest form of **anthropocentric conceit**, because this one God, supposedly the creator of the entire universe, is thought to be interested in our welfare.

Recent scholarship on monotheism has noted that its technique is to create scarce resources. They are best summed up as:

- *inscripturation*: the reduction to writing to what is believed to be authoritative information about supernatural forces. This creates divisions between rival **scriptures**, both of which make claims to possessing a **monopoly on the truth**;
- *sacred spaces*: where a section of land is seen as more valuable from surrounding land for religious reasons, e.g., Jerusalem or **Ayodhya**;

- *group privilege*: where privileges, whether sacred or profane, are distributed on the basis of religion. The sharpest example is **genocide**; and
- *salvation*: a commodity with long-term benefits, and, once again, distributed solely on terms of religious exclusivism.

The scientific advances of the past five hundred years have helped demonstrate the error of a monotheist view of the cosmos. The scarce resources being competed for are socially constructed figments of the imagination, rather than actually existing entities. And even if they did exist, the division of people into "us" and "them" simply by virtue of what we believe, is a primitive and violent mode of operation. Indeed, many scholars of religion now recognize that monotheism is inherently violent.

These insights have helped reveal the grave moral failings of monotheism. Sadly, these advances have done little to dent the hubris of the monotheist outlook, and the battle for hearts and minds will go on into the distant future, so long as our planet can cope with the consequences of our anthropocentric conceit that monotheism has done so much to encourage. See the entries on **Intolerance, Principle of** and **spiritual schizophrenia**.

Further reading: Regina Schwartz, *The Curse of Cain: The Violent Legacy of Monotheism*; and Hector Avalos, *Fighting Words*.

MONTAIGNE, MICHEL EYQUEM DE (1533–1592). Significant humanist thinker of the late Renaissance. Born into a very wealthy family in Perigord, France, Montaigne had a privileged, if eccentric, education, speaking nothing but Latin until he was six years old. He studied law and for thirteen years was on the governing council of Bordeaux. He also served at the royal court in Paris for a while. But, in 1571, during the French **wars of religion**, Montaigne withdrew to his family estates. There he devoted the next twenty years to writing a series of essays, for which he became famous.

His essays were an extended self-examination without being in any way self-absorbed, let alone self-satisfied. Instead, he observed his behavior and subjected it to scrutiny and criticism. Montaigne was greatly influenced by the **Stoic** thinker **Epictetus**, who was translated into French in 1566. Most unusually, Montaigne was able to rid himself of self-delusion and self-praise, but without simply falling into morbid self-hatred. He openly expressed his skepticism regarding revealed religion. He believed that the accident of our birth determines our beliefs. "We are Christians," he wrote, "for the same reason we are Perigordians or Germans." Montaigne's essays are among the finest examples of **Renaissance humanism**, and without the grandiloquence that often accompanied the writings of his contemporaries. Montaigne, whose works were placed on the **Index of Forbidden Books** in 1676, was a strong influence on **William Shakespeare**.

MONTERREY CONSENSUS. The name given to a statement made by the 2002 Summit of Financing for Development, an initiative of Kofi Annan, secretary general of the **United Nations**. The Monterrey Consensus states that a "universal, rules-based, open, nondiscriminatory and equitable multilateral trading system, as well as meaningful trade liberalization, can substantially stimulate development worldwide, benefiting countries at all stages of development." The summit at which this declaration was announced was attended by more than fifty heads of state and significant senior staff, allowing for serious decisions about **global governance** to be put into effect. It also had representatives of important nongovernmental organizations (NGOs) sitting around the table, and not having to make themselves heard from the other sides of barricades.

The Monterrey Consensus helped produce agreement as to how to stimulate growth and development in all parts of the world, and began the process of streamlining the many

transnational organizations whose role it is to work in this area. It is agreements such as this that help coordinate development programs and tackle planetwide problems at a planetary level. Nothing less than that will do.

MONTESQUIEU, CHARLES DE SECONDAT, BARON (1689–1755). Important voice of the **Enlightenment**. Montesquieu performed his civic duties as governor of Bordeaux until poor eyesight forced him to retire. He then devoted himself to writing, the importance of which remains with us today. In *Persian Letters* (1721) he engaged in satirical criticisms of social and religious hypocrisy. He used visiting Persian dignitaries as the narrative focus for his criticisms. His writing was among the first to criticize European customs and imply that those of other cultures may have little to learn from them. This marked an important milestone in what we now value as cultural **toleration**.

Montesquieu's masterpiece is *The Spirit of the Laws* (1748), thought by the English historian Alan Bullock (1914–2004) to have as good a claim as the starting point for modern sociology as **Adam Smith** has for economics. Montesquieu sought to outline and **analyze** what he saw as the general laws, which underlie change, whether political, moral or social. Where earlier commentators had resorted to supernatural notions like fate or fortune to explain change, Montesquieu explained change in terms of climate, and geography, which he would then call the spirit of the laws. But Montesquieu was not saying that we have no ability to determine our own future. On the contrary, he argued passionately for the overriding importance of freedom over despotism.

Like most intellectual Frenchmen of the day, he admired the English constitution, and described at length what he saw as its separation of powers as an important explanation for the freedoms the English enjoyed. Montesquieu's argument was to be taken up by the Americans, when they came to write their own constitution after gaining independence from Britain. He was a passionate opponent of **slavery** and his ideas on the separation of powers were influential on the **Declaration of the Rights of Man and of the Citizen**, which became the symbol of the French Revolution. The Catholic Church placed *The Spirit of the Laws* on the **Index of Forbidden Books**.

MONTREAL PROTOCOLS. An international agreement signed in 1987 and amended on several occasions since then, in which the signatories agreed to a plan to reduce the amount of chlorofluorocarbons (CFCs) into the atmosphere. The agreement required most CFCs to be phased out of use by 2000 and 2005 for the rest.

The Montreal Protocols built upon the Vienna Convention for the Protection of the Ozone Layer, which met in 1985. By this time the scientific evidence of the harmful effects of CFCs had become indisputable and it was clear that worldwide action was needed. Twenty-four countries were signatories to the original agreement, which came into effect in 1989, and now more than 162 countries have signed up. The Montreal Protocols have been largely successful; in the first eight years after the signing, use of ozone-depleting CFCs declined by 73 percent. But much more needs to be done to protect the escalating damage to the ozone layer. Despite the pressing need, consideration was given to developing countries with low levels of CFC emission.

The Montreal Protocols are a cause for optimism in that it was one of the first international agreements to include trade sanctions, fines, and other coercive measures in order to ensure compliance with them. There has also been an encouraging level of cooperation between businesses and governments on the issue. India and China are among the worst offenders at present.

MONTY PYTHON'S FLYING CIRCUS. One of the highlights of twentieth-century **humor**. Monty Python's Flying Circus was a television program that was broadcasted on the BBC between 1969 and 1974 and was the brainchild of Graham Chapman (1941– 1989), John Cleese, Terry Gilliam, Eric Idle, Terry Jones, and Michael Palin. Each show consisted of a series of comic skits punctuated by animations. The skits and the animations came together to create an innovative new style of **absurdist** humor, in the tradition of The Goons, Beyond the Fringe, and Spike Milligan.

Chapman and Cleese had been friends at Cambridge University, while Palin and Jones had known each other at Oxford. Idle was at Cambridge, though a year behind Chapman and Cleese. Each show was the result of cooperative effort; any sketch the majority found funny would be included and stitched together by Gilliam's animations. Chapman and Cleese tended to write as a team, as did Palin and Jones while Idle, perhaps the most talented writer among them, wrote alone. Some of the sketches from the television show have become part of the collective memory of the English-speaking world.

After Monty Python had run its course as a television series (much, much later than anyone had predicted), the Pythons took to films: *And Now for Something Completely Different* (1972), *Monty Python and the Holy Grail* (1977), *The Life of Brian* (1979), and *The Meaning of Life* (1983). *The Life of Brian*, which received important financial assistance from the former Beatle George Harrison (1943–2001), was criticized by church leaders and became a cult classic for most other people.

From there the Pythons went on to pursue successful solo careers, with the exception of Graham Chapman who died of spinal cancer in 1989. More films were produced, among the best of which were the comic dystopia *Brazil* (1985, directed by Gilliam and written by Gilliam and Palin) and *A Fish Called Wanda* (1988) starring Cleese and Palin. See the entry on **humanist-themed films**.

The absurdist humor of the Pythons is part of a British tradition while also being a unique innovation of their own, and a gift to the world. Absurdist humor is best employed in pricking the more humorless pretensions people are liable to adopt. The Pythons are responsible for some of the most successful, and certainly some of the most influential, critiques of **anthropocentric conceit** ever made.

MOORE, CHARLES CHILTON (1837–1906).

The last person to have gone to prison for **blasphemy** in the United States. Moore originally trained as a Baptist minister, but was increasingly estranged from his denomination because of the widespread support for **slavery** among his colleagues. Moore left the church, now calling himself a "durned old infidel." In 1884, after a few years as a coffee salesman, Moore began a paper, the *Blue Grass Blade*, which advocated **freethought** and prohibition. Based in Lexington, Kentucky, the *Blade* was influential out of proportion to its print-run and pretty soon it attracted the attention of the **virtuecrats** of the day, in particular Anthony Comstock (1844–1915), longtime secretary of the New York Society for the Suppression of Vice. In 1899, Moore was sentenced to two years in jail for "obscenity," which was later reduced to six months.

During his incarceration Moore wrote an autobiography called *Behind the Bars: 31498*. The freethought historian Susan Jacoby notes that this would be one of the few pieces of jailhouse literature to include letters of support from the author's fellow inmates *and* warders. On returning to Lexington, Moore was met by a crowd of five hundred people who welcomed him home. The *Blue Grass Blade* continued until 1905.

Soon after his release from prison, in the case of *United States v. Moore*, the District Court D., Kentucky, ruled that it is not enough that material be offensive to religious opinion for it to be barred from the postal system. It had to be lewd and lascivious as well as obscene in such a way as to lead on toward sexual immorality. See the entry on **comstockery**.

Further reading: Susan Jacoby, *Freethinkers: A History of American Secularism*.

MORAL TRUISMS SHARED BY US ALL.

It is an important, but rarely appreciated, point that the vast majority of human beings share a core range of moral beliefs. Because they are so universal they are often called moral truisms. The Canadian philosopher Kai Nielsen has identified these moral truisms, which are shared by atheists and religious believers:

- truthfulness is a virtue;
- promises should be kept;
- integrity is something to be cultivated;
- human well-being is desirable;
- understanding one's situation in life is a good thing;
- human suffering and pain are bad;
- caring for others is good;
- cooperation on fair terms is essential to a decent life;
- mutual respect and recognition are essential for human flourishing; and
- the care of children is morally obligatory.

Nielsen adds that while these moral truisms are indeed universal, they are not enough in themselves. What each of us then needs to do is to rework these universal moral truisms into a coherent view of the world. This is **what atheists and religious believers have in common**. Both groups see the process of doing this as valuable. This in itself constitutes a valuable point of commonality.

However, we also have a duty not to then claim that the worldview we have built up from these moral truisms that are common to us all is better than all the other worldviews which have drunk from the same well. That, sadly, is a feature of religious **fundamentalism**.

Further reading: Kai Nielsen, *Naturalism and Religion*.

MORALITY.

The name given to the need human beings have to live in social groups successfully. Morality is not simply memorizing some set of commandments; that is memory. Morality involves an active process of living together in peace and at some more pleasing level than the **state of nature**. Recent developments in **evolutionary psychology** have shown that the principle of reciprocity is fundamental to morality. This is called **reciprocal altruism**. The philosophical version of reciprocal altruism is the **golden rule**, "do unto others as you would have others do unto you."

While the basic principles of reciprocity have a biological foundation, it is still important to train the young in moral principles. But simply parroting a series of do's and don't's is not the same as learning how to **reason** morally or to put oneself in another person's shoes. It has been frequently observed that morality is not taught, it is caught. Crucial to effective moral growth and understanding is a balanced self-esteem. For a discussion on objective morality, see the entry on **objectivity**.

MORALNETS. A term coined by the American anthropologist Raoul Naroll (1920–1985) to refer to the community of friendships and obligations that help provide focus and support in people's lives. Any individual may live as part of several different and even competing moralnets. Family, work, community, football clubs, church, political parties; each of these provides sets of rules and norms that help regulate a person's behavior. Preserving these moralnets, without undue self-righteousness about the standards of other moralnets about which we may disapprove, is an important aspect of preserving the **civil society**.

MORRIS D. FORKOSH BOOK AWARD. An award offered by the **Council for Secular Humanism** for the most outstanding work of **science** or **philosophy** that has promoted **free inquiry** and the **open society** during the previous year. To date, the recipients of the award have been:

1988, Arthur N. Strahler, *Science and Earth History: The Evolution/Creation Controversy*
1989, **Sidney Hook**, *Convictions*

1990, Stephen Jay Gould, *Wonderful Life*
1991, **Steve Allen**, *Steve Allen on the Bible, Religion, and Morality*
1994, **Antony Flew**, *Atheistic Humanism*
1996, **Ibn Warraq**, *Why I am Not a Muslim*
1997, Kurt Baier, *Problems of Life and Death: A Humanist Perspective*
2000, **E. O. Wilson**, *Consilience: The Unity of Knowledge*
2003, Taner Edis, *The Ghost in the Universe: God in the Light of Modern Science*

MORTALISM. The view that the **soul** is material and not immortal. **Thomas Hobbes** held a variation of this view in his major work, *Leviathan* (1651). More recently, Peter Heinegg has written on mortalism, characterizing it as the understanding that **death** means extinction, with no possibility of any sort of **immortality**. Heinegg writes that metaphysicians and priests "preach and prate about immortality, but the body knows better." Heinegg calls mortalism the open secret of our culture; open in that no argument for personal immortality is credible any longer. Heinegg has edited a book, giving examples of what he sees as mortalist thinking. Mortalism is a type of **cosmic modesty**.

Further reading: Peter Heinegg, *Mortalism*.

MOTT, LUCRETIA COFFIN (1793–1880). American antislavery campaigner, woman's rights advocate. Born into a Quaker family in Nantucket, Lucretia Coffin received a better education than was normally available to women at the time. She married James Mott, a successful merchant.

For many years Mott was a respected abolitionist, serving as secretary of the Philadelphia Female Anti-Slavery Society, but was still denied a seat by the abolitionist movement at an important conference in London in 1840. And her interest in feminism was sparked when she discovered that male teachers were paid twice that of female teachers.

Her religion was a highly refined **deism**,

bordering on **atheism**, informed by Enlightenment ideas of **progress**, **reason**, and natural **rights**. For her views, Mott was ostracized by the Quaker community and was the target of a rioting mob, which came close to burning her house down. **Elizabeth Cady Stanton** wrote that no topic was out of bounds to Mott and no opinion unworthy of consideration.

MOUAT, KIT. See MacKAY, JEAN

MOZI (470–391 BCE, approx.). Chinese humanist philosopher. Little is known of his life. Mozi (Mo Tzu or Mo Ti in old spelling) was born at the beginning of the period of unrest in China known as the "Warring States." In the face of the **violence** and upheaval of his times, he traveled around China and worked to prevent conflicts and bloodshed. He attracted followers and a body of writings grew in his name, most of which fairly closely resembles his views. It is interesting that Mozi's life was roughly contemporary with **Socrates** in Greece. His writings are gathered in a large body of works known as the *Mozi*, or *The Works of Mozi*. His thought was influential in China for about two hundred years after his death, but lost out in the end to Confucianism.

Mozi saw self-centeredness, or what he called partiality as the root cause of the distress of his times. He advocated what he called benevolence as the counter to partiality. If we are capable of loving our family, why can this love not be extended to all others? In fact, the inability to extend this love *to* all is tantamount to a failure to be loving *at* all. In an anticipation of the **Principle of Utility**, Mozi said that benevolence brings good to others while partiality brings only ill. He used the Chinese idea of the Will of Heaven in a more expressly religious way than **Kongfuzi** or Mengzi, although it would still be a mistake to conflate the Will of Heaven into a **God** in the Western sense.

Mozi also held to a **state of nature** theory that all was **chaos** until people came together to cooperate toward peace and harmony.

Mozi favored a hierarchical society, but departed from the norm when he advocated that positions of authority be held by the most capable candidate, not simply the most privileged. In some respects Mozi was unhelpfully puritan. For instance, he saw little value in music, seeing it as a distraction. Neither did he favor any sorts of foods other than the strictly nutritious. His puritanism came from his view that partiality is fueled by greed, which comes from desire for these fripperies. Kongfuzi, by contrast, saw music as a noble pursuit in its own right. Mozi also opposed the Confucian indifference to **religion** and fussiness on matters of ritual.

MUHAMMAD. The prophet of Islam. As with Jesus, it is very difficult to separate fact from fiction when dealing with the life of Muhammad. Interest in Muhammad as a historical person began relatively late, so little reliable information is known about him. The traditional story has him born around 571 CE in Mecca to a family once prosperous but since fallen on hard times. Muhammad was born into the Arab tribe of Quraysh, who are much discussed in the Qur'an. An orphan, Muhammad grew up with his uncle, Abu Talib, a trader. He probably accompanied his uncle on trips to Syria. He later worked as a commercial agent for a rich widow, Khadija, whom he eventually married. He claimed that in 610, while sitting on Mount Hira, he had a revelation from **God**. Soon he found himself offending the sensibilities of the pagan Meccans, and he fled the city.

His flight to Yathrib (now known as Medina) was later elevated into the starting point for Muslim chronology. He made friends in Medina, not least by enriching them by raids on Meccan caravans and the plundering and slaughtering of the people of the three significant Jewish clans in the city. He also demanded the murder of a prominent Jewish opponent, the poet Kab ibn al-Ashraf. While being a small minority in Mecca, Muhammad was content to preach **toleration**, but once he achieved dominance in

Medina, his message was less conciliatory toward those who disagreed with him. Muhammad's power grew, culminating in his return to Mecca in triumph in 630. At the time of his death he had united most of the Arabian peninsula behind him.

This traditional picture of Muhammad in the Qur'an is the result of a steady accretion of accounts, each developed in response to felt needs at the time. The slow accumulation of stories about him arose in response to sectarian and theological needs of the time, and, when based on any sources at all, rest on unreliable sources. The earliest material on him was written by Ibn Ishaq in 750, but that has only survived in the form of a subsequent edited work by Ibn Hashim, who died in 834. As with the Gospels of the New Testament, the various historical works on Muhammad were not written as objective works of history but as idealized accounts of the past and of the prophet.

Further reading: Ibn Warraq, ed., *The Quest for the Historical Muhammad.*

MUNZ, PETER (1921–). Wide-ranging scholar. Born in Chemnitz, Germany. After the early death of his father, and the growing **anti-Semitism** in Germany, his mother took his family to Italy, where they lived from 1933 to 1940. Having heard of the progressive policies of New Zealand, they moved there, via Palestine, in 1940.

Munz studied at Canterbury University in New Zealand and St. John's College, Cambridge. He was at the infamous poker incident at the Cambridge Moral Science Club between **Karl Popper** and **Ludwig Wittgenstein** in 1946. Munz's first published work was a defense of **Plato** from Popper's attack in his classic, *The Open Society and Its Enemies*, which was written in New Zealand. While he was no acolyte of Popper, it is fair to say he was one of Popper's most articulate defenders in the postwar intellectual scene. He returned to New Zealand in 1948 and was in the history department at Victoria University of Wellington until 1987, serving as the head of the department from 1965.

Munz wrote widely, making serious contributions in history and philosophy. His most valuable works are *The Problem of Religious Knowledge* (1959), a title in the important Library of Philosophy and Theology series published by SCM; *Relationship and Solitude* (1964); *Frederick Barbarossa: A Study in Medieval Politics* (1969); *When the Golden Bough Breaks: Structuralism or Typology?* (1973); *Our Knowledge of the Growth of Knowledge: Popper or Wittgenstein?* (1985); and *Philosophical Darwinism* (1993).

Further reading: Miles Fairburn and Bill Oliver, eds., *The Certainty of Doubt: Tributes to Peter Munz.*

MURDOCH, IRIS (1919–1999). Brilliant novelist and public intellectual. Born in Dublin to an Irish mother and an English father, Iris moved as a child to London. After a youthful dalliance with communism, she spent the rest of her life pondering the nature of freedom. After studying at Cambridge under **Ludwig Wittgenstein**, she was elected in 1948 as a fellow of St. Anne's College in Oxford, working there until 1963.

Her first book, published in 1953, was a short study of French **existentialist** thinker **Jean-Paul Sartre**, and is still one of the best introductions to this thinker. The influence of Wittgenstein and Sartre were evident in her first novel, *Under the Net*, published in 1954. There followed a succession of novels, almost one a year, for the next three decades. Highlights among them are *The Bell* (1958); *The Sea, The Sea*, which won the Booker Prize in 1978; *The Good Apprentice* (1985); and *Message to the Planet* (1989). Central themes are the integrity of personality, the contingency of life, and the dark strength of fanaticism and obsession.

She also wrote some works of formal philosophy: *The Sovereignty of Good* (1970), *The Fire and the Sun* (1977), and her largest nonfiction work, *Metaphysics as a Guide to Morals* (1992). A good collection of her works was put together by Peter Conradi in

1997, titled *Existentialists and Mystics*. Conradi has also written an excellent biography and literary study of Murdoch's books. See the entry on **humanist-themed novels**.

Ironically, Murdoch became best known after she had contracted Alzheimer's Disease. Her last few years were described poignantly, but without sentiment, by her husband, John Bayley in *Elegy for Iris*, which was also made into a film starring Judi Dench, Kate Winslet, and Jim Broadbent. She was made a dame of the British Empire in 1987.

She had no time for traditional religious conceits of **immortality** or **God**, but wanted religion, when understood as a sense of commitment, to survive. She was enamored of Buddhism for this reason. See the entry on **Brigid Brophy**.

MUSLIM BROTHERHOOD, THE.

founded by Hassan al-Banna (1906–1949) in Egypt in 1928 originally as a religious organization with the sole intention of fostering the Muslim religious life and certain charitable works. But the brotherhood soon took on a more specifically political flavor when it adopted the policy of seeking the restoration of the **khalifat**, an ancient religious and political position analogous to the papacy, which had been abolished by **Kemal Attatürk**, the founder of modern Turkey. The Muslim Brotherhood not only wanted the khalifat to be restored, but for it to be restored to full political sovereignty over the Muslim world, and for the full imposition of **Sharia Law**.

When **Sayyid Qutb** returned from the United States in 1951, he joined the Muslim Brotherhood and quickly became its leading intellectual. For a while it looked as if the brotherhood would exert an influence on the new nationalist regime of Gamal Abdel Nasser (1918–1970), which took power in a coup in 1952, but the brotherhood's religious **fundamentalism** ran counter to Nasser's secular pan-Arabism. In 1954 Nasser banned the Muslim Brotherhood, sending its leaders into exile, and thus helping expand its influence much further than would normally have been the case.

After the death of Nasser, his successor Anwar Sadat (1918–1981) lifted restrictions against the Muslim Brotherhood in the hope they would combat the left wing in Egyptian politics. Since the middle 1980s the brotherhood has established control over most of the professional life and much of the financial life of the nation. In January 2004 Muhammad Mahdi Akef, a long-standing member of the brotherhood's militant old guard took over leadership from Mamoun el-Hodeibi (1921–2004).

The growing power and establishment look of the brotherhood has spawned a new era of radical terrorist organizations in Egypt, some of which have been responsible for the murder of secular intellectuals, Jews, and foreign tourists.

MU'TAZILISM.

A school of Islamic **rationalism** that flourished from the eighth to eleventh centuries CE. Mu'tazilism was profoundly influenced by Greek philosophy, especially Aristotle and the Neoplatonists. The first principle of Mu'tazili thinkers was that it is incumbent on all human beings to exercise speculative **reason** in order to know **God**. Speculative reason is to be based on rational argument, the **scriptures**, the paradigmatic practice of the prophet, and the consensus of the community.

On the basis of this first principle, Mu'tazili thinkers grouped around the Five Usul, or Fundamentals. These were divine unity, divine justice or theodicy, the promise of reward or threat of punishment in the hereafter, the intermediate position on who is and who is not a good Muslim, and the commanding of the good and prohibiting the evil. For a while Mu'tazilism held sway among the leaders of political Islam, and some of them permitted authoritarian measures to ensure Mu'tazili doctrines be adhered to. Ironically, given they advocated open debate, the Mu'tazili theologians acquiesced in this contradictory enforcement of their views.

By the eleventh century Mu'talizism was in decline and for many centuries the word "mu'tazili" became a term of abuse to mean little more than an unbeliever. In the twentieth century, Mu'tazilism has undergone a limited revival as Muslim scholars have sought ways that contemporary Islam can resist the encroachments of the West while adopting Western practices felt to be necessary in order to preserve Muslim independence. Mu'tazilism has also been seen by some Muslim intellectuals as a necessary bulwark against **Islamism**, with its threats against democracy and free speech.

Further reading: Richard Martin and Mark Woodward with Dwi Atmaja, *Defenders of Reason: Mu'tazilism from Medieval School to Modern Symbol.*

MYSTICISM. A style of experience that assumes the unity of all things and focuses on giving the individual an **intuition** about it. Mystical knowledge is supposed to be direct **knowledge**, and therefore **beyond** rationality, ideology, or **religion**.

Psychologists have distinguished two contrasting styles of mystical experience. There is the outward-directed visionary experience where the mystic encounters Vishnu, Jesus, the Buddha, or whoever. It often comes after winding oneself up by dance, drugs, or ecstatic experience. This is the type of mystic experience most common in the realm of popular religion. Then there is what is called depth mysticism, a more inward-directed experience. This variety of experience is the result of lengthy **meditation** or solitude and involves plumbing the depths of a quieted **soul**. See the entry on **modes of religious transmission**.

Mysticism often runs afoul of both religious orthodoxy and **skepticism**. The **monotheist** religions have traditionally been suspicious of freelance paths to **God** or ultimate meaning, because they fear, justifiably, that these intuitions will lead to **heresy**. Mystics frequently claim that their intuition of the unity of all things transcends the exclusive claims to truth of organized religion. Mystics have often been enthusiasts for the **perennial philosophy**. Paradoxically, however, mys-

tical claims are often bitterly criticized by supporters of rival faiths. What is a celestial mystical experience for one person is a dangerous flirtation with demons for another.

Atheists and skeptics, by contrast, suspect the extravagant language of much mystical writing is little more than a smokescreen to cover their ignorance. It is not that ignorance is the preserve of mystics; far from it. The important point is the attitude one takes to one's ignorance. Skeptics have also noted that, despite their universalistic rhetoric, mystics experience things that are invariably grounded in their own culture, and even in their own personalities. Medieval mystics saw visions of Christ and the **Trinity**, whereas Hindu mystics confer with one of the many gods from the Hindu pantheon. The day a Buddhist mystic sees the Virgin Mary and a Sufi mystic jives with Elvis Presley is a day skeptics still wait for. **Friedrich Nietzsche** probably got it right when he said: "Mystical explanations are considered deep. The truth is that they are not even superficial." See the entry on **No Free Communion, Principle of**.

MYTHOLOGY. A catch-all word for a wide spectrum of stories, tales, beliefs, cultural norms, and practices. Because it is a catch-all term, we should not expect a single, easy definition of mythology. Most attempts at presenting a theory of it have suffered from this universalism. Even less should we believe that we can somehow be saved or redeemed by myths. See the entry on **Carl Gustav Jung**. Most egregious of all is Joseph Campbell (1904–1987) whose work was very popular but of little academic value. The philosopher Paul Edwards described Campbell as a "purveyor of mush," and the more sympathetic Robert Elwood lamented that "something very narrow" lurks in Campbell's supposedly broad understanding of mythology.

But if we need to resist the more extravagant uses mythology is sometimes put to, we can recognize that we have much to learn from these beautiful stories. There is a widely held prejudice that rationalists cannot appreciate myths. This is simply not true. Freethinkers have long been inspired by the story of **Prometheus**. There is no necessary conflict between enjoying a tale which falls under the label "myth" and having a naturalist view of the world. See the entry on **Jane Harrison**. No one can or should live by **reason** alone. All myth traditions are edifying or beautiful to some extent, although we should resist the temptation to read great spiritual depths into them. See the entry on **Homer**.

Further reading: Robert Ellwood, *The Politics of Myth* and G. S. Kirk, *The Nature of Greek Myths*.

N

NAGASENA. Rationalist Buddhist sage. Described by Radhakrishnan as an "acute dialectician" and "thoroughgoing rationalist." Nagasena appears as the Buddhist teacher and sage who answered the questions of King Menander about Buddhism. Nothing else is known about Nagasena, even his historicity is uncertain. Menander was one of the Bactrian kings, who ruled over the Indus and upper Ganges valleys between 125 and 95 BCE, and the dialogue between the king and his teacher was composed about a century later. The dialogue became known as the *Milinda Panha* or *Questions of King Milinda* and is considered one of the more authoritative texts among **Therevada Buddhists**.

The Buddha, as portrayed by Nagasena, was opposed to concocting a make-believe world of **religion** simply as an escape for the sufferings of mankind. Nagasena emphasizes the atheistic and materialist aspects of the Buddha's thought, dismissing the concept of an immortal **soul** as an illegitimate abstraction. In a similar vein, he sees nirvana as extinction, the closure of all becoming, contrary to other Buddhist thinkers who have

preferred to portray nirvana as eternal peace and stillness above the neverending whirligig of desire. This can also be seen with notions of **God**. He interprets the Buddha's **agnosticism** on the matter into a firmer **atheism**. Therevada Buddhism retains this essentially atheistic cosmology to this day. See the entry on **Asian traditions**.

NAGEL, ERNEST (1901–1985). American philosophical naturalist. Nagel was born in the Austro-Hungarian empire and his family emigrated to the United States in 1911. Nagel became an American citizen in 1919. He took a PhD at Columbia University and spent his entire academic career there. **Sidney Hook** was a longtime friend and ally.

His philosophical interests included symbolic logic, probability, mathematics, biology, law, and history. He was a staunch defender of rational methods of inquiry and of academic freedom. He was also a convinced atheist. But neither was Nagel a reductive materialist. He saw change in terms of the transformations that material things undergo in their interactions with each other. Nagel was also a strong defender of human rights, but without believing that rights are written into the fabric of the cosmos.

His most important book was *The Structure of Science* (1961), which gave a model of scientific change. His work continued to be influential, despite the publication of Thomas Kuhn's work, *The Structure of Scientific Revolutions* the year after. After Kuhn's work was appropriated for antiscientific purposes, he subsequently retreated to a position nearer where Nagel had been all along. See the entry on **paradigm**. Nagel was a laureate of the **International Academy of Humanism** from its inception in 1983 until his death.

NANNY STATE. Term often used by objectivists and **libertarians** to refer pejoratively to the **welfare state**, or indeed of any attempt by the state to coordinate or regulate the lives of its citizens. The assumption being that a life free of the domineering clutches of the nanny state will be a freer and more vital life.

The problem with this idea is that it reduces the options to a simplistic *either* total freedom unfettered by regulation *or* total subjection under a tyrannical state. See the entry on **either black or white, fallacy of**. There are many credible options for expanding individual opportunity through proactive government programs, regulation, and taxation that do not impinge unduly on individual freedom. And in the case of environmental controls, it may well be necessary to monitor and regulate those at the planetary level. See the entry on **global governance**. The question boils down to the extent one feels part of a wider society of individuals. As the British prime minister Margaret Thatcher famously observed, "There is no such thing as society." By this she meant that there is only a collection of individuals and that **social capital** and **social intelligence** are illusory ideas.

When considered in a **romantic**, man-alone context, the hostility to the state can be rhetorically pleasing, but if one recognizes the needs of others around one, many of whom have not had the same range of educational and other opportunities, it becomes clear that larger institutions—the state among them—has a positive role to play in the promotion of individual freedom. One interpretation of this is the **Difference Principle** of **John Rawls**.

NANSEN, FRIDTJOF (1861–1930). Norwegian explorer, scientist, and humanitarian—one of the greatest Norwegians of all time. He was born near Christiana (now Oslo), the son of a prosperous lawyer and educated at Christiana University where he studied zoology. He made his first voyage to the Greenland Sea in 1882, making useful observations of seals and bears during his trip. On his return he was appointed curator of the natural history museum in Bergen. Nansen was awarded a doctorate in zoology in 1888, the year he made his next trip to Greenland. This trip was actually a trip across Greenland, something that had never been attempted before. The two-month long trip

took the six-man party through temperatures reaching minus 45 Celsius and upward of 9,000 feet above sea level.

More trips followed in 1893, and 1895–96, when he got closer on foot to the North Pole than any other person. On his return he was professor of zoology at Christiana University. He later moved to oceanography and in that capacity made three expeditions around various parts of the north Atlantic in 1900 and again between 1910 and 1914. He wrote about his explorations in *The Norwegian North Polar Expedition* (1893–96) and *Northern Mists* (1911).

After Norway became independent from Sweden in 1905, Nansen took some interest in politics, serving as Norwegian minister to Great Britain until 1908. He returned to public life during World War I, serving as head of the Norwegian delegation to the United States between 1917 and 1918, helping to negotiate ways in which food could get through the Allied blockade to his country. He represented Norway at the Treaty of Versailles which ended World War I and was active in the League of Nations until his death. On behalf of the league, Nansen worked in the early 1920s to help rehabilitate tens of thousands of refugees and displaced ex-prisoners of war. He invented what became known as Nansen Passports, which served as documentation for people who had nothing left. He then devoted his energies to channeling food to victims of the brutal famine in Russia during 1921 and 1922. He can be credited with saving the lives of millions of people. Later on he worked in Greece, helping the repatriation of refugees who had fled Turkey. His last major relief effort was with Armenians still suffering from the attempted **genocide** at the hands of the Turks in 1915. He was awarded the Nobel Prize for Peace in 1922 for his work.

He was an outspoken agnostic. In an essay on **religion** published by the **Rationalist Press Association** in 1909, Nansen said that the religion of one age is the literary entertainment of the next.

NARCISSISM. The tendency, becoming more widespread with each succeeding generation, toward obsession with oneself—one's own needs and wants—without reference to, or in open defiance of, larger wants and needs. The word comes from the Greek myth of Narcissus, who failed even to notice the love of Echo because he was so infatuated with his own self-image. Narcissus couldn't leave the pond for a moment for fear of missing his image staring back at him.

One of the most insightful scholars of narcissism was the American historian Christopher Lasch (1932–1994), who agreed with earlier scholars that narcissism is a denial of bourgeois values of thrift, individual choice and responsibility and, above all, freedom. But, Lasch added, these very values are the ones that created the conditions in which narcissism has flourished. And where conservative critics attack narcissism as contrary to the spirit of free enterprise, Lasch has demonstrated that the opposite is the case. Narcissism is one of capitalism's most characteristic features. Consume now, because you're worth it.

A narcissistic culture is characterized not so much by selfish egoism as the weakened belief that the world survives us who live in it at the moment. This brand of narcissism has the effect, among other things, of rendering unreal the environmentalist call for us to see ourselves as stewards of the planet for future generations. See the entry on **affluenza**.

Further reading: Christopher Lasch, *The Culture of Narcissism*; and Frank Hearn, *Reason and Freedom in Sociological Thought*.

NASRIN, TASLIMA (1962–). Bangladeshi author and activist. Her father was a progressive secularist, though rather strict and distant, and her mother was an unsophisticated Muslim wife and mother. Nasrin recalled the frightening descriptions of hell and the penalties for uppity women being spoken about by the local Muslim cleric her mother took her to. On her father's urging, she had a thorough education, graduating from Mymensing University and working in a hospital while slowly building a reputation as a poet and author. She won national awards in 1992 and 1993, but it was only when her first novel, *Lajja* (*Shame*) was banned by the Bangladesh government that Nasrin developed an international reputation. *Shame* records the smouldering Muslim reaction to the destruction to the Babri Masjid mosque in **Ayodhya**, which ignited religious violence in the subcontinent that has still not abated. *Shame* was translated into English in 1994.

"Religion," Nasrin writes, "is the cause of fanaticism, bloodshed, hatred, racism and conflict. Only **humanism** can make people humane and the world livable." While in exile in Sweden she also wrote *My Girlhood* (2001), an autobiography, and *French Lover*, another novel, published in 2002. See the entry on **humanist-themed novels**.

In 2004 Nasrin was awarded the UNESCO-Madanjeet Singh Prize for the Promotion of Tolerance and Nonviolence.

NATIONAL SECULAR SOCIETY. The oldest extant association in the world devoted to **freethought** in all its forms. The National Secular Society was founded in 1866 by **Charles Bradlaugh**, who remained its president almost without a break until 1891. Many prominent members of the society were also active in campaigning for reform of stifling Sunday laws, press freedom, republicanism, and abolition of the House of Lords.

Bradlaugh was succeeded as president by **G. W. Foote**, who achieved national celebrity during a prominent trial for **blasphemy** in 1883. Foote was also responsible for creating the National Secular Society Ltd. Until then, bequests to secularist bodies had frequently been challenged in the courts, on the ground that one could not be sane and donate to a non-Christian organization, despite the law recognizing that one could criticize Christianity legally. Foote's registration of the National Secular Society under the Company Laws meant that bequests could now be given to the organization without fear of it being retracted. This was tested in the Bowman Case in 1915 to 1917, which eventually reached the House of Lords. Charles Bowman had left a substantial sum to the NSS, the legitimacy of which was challenged by his family. Eventually the legitimacy of the bequest was upheld, thus establishing an important civil right.

Foote was succeeded as president by **Chapman Cohen**, who held the office from 1915 until 1949 and carried on very much in Foote's style. The society had a rocky time adjusting to postwar conditions, but it still enjoyed a succession of capable presidents, including **David Tribe** from 1968 to 1971 and **Barbara Smoker** from 1971 until 1996. The society has mounted many successful campaigns to end unjust religious privilege and hypocrisy. Its magazine is the *Freethinker*, which has been published without a break since 1881.

NATIONALISM. An ideology of identity that can take a benign form of a simple love of one's country and a more malignant form of preference for one's kind at the expense of people from other nationalities.

In Europe there was very little sense of nationalism as currently understood before the French Revolution. The great civilizations of Asia, in particular China and Japan, had strong understandings of their status as a people, which approximated European nationalism, but was less tied up with state-territorial notions of national identity.

Nationalism ceases to be a positive virtue when identification with one's country overrides any consideration of justice. It is to be hoped that *Homo sapiens* can learn to find its chief source of identity on a planetary level, as one species among others living interdependently on our pale blue dot. See the entry on **planetary humanism**.

Further reading: Ernest Gellner, *Nationalism*; and Carl Coon, *One Planet, One People*.

NATURAL SELECTION. The method by which **evolution** works. After the Copernican revolution established the principle of the **heliocentric universe**, natural selection is the second major blow to the pretensions of humanity of having a special status in the cosmos. The Copernican revolution destroyed our pretensions of being the center of the universe, and the Darwinian revolution ended our claim to being the apogee, only below **God**, on the **great chain of being**.

Natural selection was discovered by **Charles Darwin**. In the words of **E. O. Wilson**, natural selection is the "differential survival and reproduction of different genetic forms [which] prepares organisms only for necessities." This means that organisms achieve a structure that works effectively enough for it to maximize its fitness. This is not done by that organism deciding to improve. It usually means that the changes it does make, usually through mutation, will soon enough be tested for their effectiveness. Organisms that make a certain change may die out whereas organisms that make some other change, or don't change at all, survive. Nature, in effect, has "selected" the organisms best suited to the conditions. Now, of course, conditions may change, in which case all bets are off. See the entry on **extinction**.

Further reading: Charles Darwin, *On the Origin of Species*.

NATURALISM. One of the oldest and most transnational understandings of the world ever devised. The simplest definition of naturalism is from **Michael Martin**, who describes it as "the system of thought holding that all phenomena can be explained in terms of natural causes and laws without attributing spiritual or **supernatural** significance to them." A fuller account of naturalism is supplied by the philosopher Dale Riepe, who described the naturalist as one who:

- places a high value upon **reason** and sense experience as the most reliable avenues of **knowledge**;
- believes that knowledge is not mystical, innate, or intuitive;
- believes that the external world, of which humans are an integral part, is

objective and therefore has existence apart from anyone's **consciousness**;

- believes that the world manifests order and regularity and that, contrary to some opinion, this does not exclude human responsibility;
- believes that this order cannot be changed merely by thought, **magic**, sacrifice, or **prayer** but requires the actual manipulation of the external world in some physical way;
- rejects supernatural **teleology**, believing instead that the direction of the world is caused by the world itself; and
- is humanistic by virtue of believing that humans are not a mirror of some supernatural deity or absolute principle but a biological existent whose goal is to do what is proper for humans' continued existence and fulfillment.

Naturalistic thinking can be traced back to the Indian **Carvaka** school and thinkers like **Uddalaka**, as well as the **Pre-Socratic** thinkers of Greece, and followers of **Kong-fuzi** and **Wang Chong** in China. In the twenty-first century, naturalism has become the predominant outlook among educated people. All attempts to sustain some supernatural view of the world have failed.

There are two approaches to naturalism:

- *methodological naturalism*, which is committed to the **scientific method** of inquiry; and
- *cosmological naturalism*, which is a series of ideas that revolves around the central notion of the interconnectedness of things.

Some thinkers like **Richard Rorty**, Kai Nielsen, and others, have limited themselves to methodological naturalism. This is not because they want to preserve some supernatural belief, but because they are worried about endorsing some brand of **foundationalism**. Other thinkers see no reason to divorce the methodological approach of naturalism from its cosmological outcomes. These people include **Richard Dawkins**, **Daniel Dennett**, **Bertrand Russell**, **Paul Kurtz**, and others.

The victory of naturalism comes in the wake of the collapse of supernaturalist notions like the **geocentric universe**, the **great chain of being**, and the **soul**. As each foundation of our **anthropocentric conceit** has been removed, *Homo sapiens* has adjusted to seeing itself as part of an interdependent fabric of nature. Naturalism is an essential component of developing part of this new **cosmic perspective**.

Further reading: Dale Riepe, *The Naturalistic Tradition in Indian Thought*; Paul Kurtz, *Philosophical Essays in Pragmatic Naturalism*; and Kai Nielsen, *Naturalism and Religion*.

NATURALISTIC FALLACY. An important and highly controversial idea, first developed by **David Hume**, but made known by G. E. Moore (1873–1958) in his 1903 book *Principia Ethica*. Moore believed that any attempt to define "good" was bound to fail, because "good" is a simple, nonnatural (though not **supernatural**) quality that could not be analyzed. With this is mind, Moore was critical of some of the **Social Darwinist** theories fashionable at the time, which claimed to be able to derive notions of good from their readings of **science**. Moore drew on the insight of Hume, who criticized the tendency to draw conclusions about what *ought* to be the case from information that only speaks about what the case actually *is*. A graphic example is the tendency of deformed animals to die or be killed by their mother (the "is" in the equation) as evidence that humans suffering from some disability *ought* be similarly dealt with.

An important, though neglected, point about the naturalistic fallacy is that it applies not only to naturalistic theories but to *all* ethical theories. For instance, the claim made by many Evangelical Christians that the Bible says *a*, therefore we ought to *a*, is one of the clearer examples of this fallacy in operation. So while the naturalistic fallacy has some worthwhile things to say about the more simple forms of inappropriate is-to-ought rationalizing, it is far from established that any attempt to treat the concept of "good" as something open to analysis is, by definition, mistaken. To take a simple example, polluted water causes illness in people, therefore we ought not to pollute water. Is this really such a bad argument?

At best, the naturalistic fallacy serves as a useful corrective to making unduly confident is-to-ought conclusions. But we should not shy away from using science as a tool to help us improve life and happiness on the grounds of a supposed fallacy in philosophy from a century ago. As with most other difficult questions, it requires us to use our **reason**, **judgment**, and **critical thinking** skills.

NECESSITY. See *AMOR FATI*

NEGRI, VITALI (1887–1972). Scholar and freethinker. Born to a Jewish family in Constantinople, then the capital of the Ottoman empire, where he studied medicine and psychology. Negri emigrated to the United States in 1912, eventually settling in Los Angeles. He studied at USC and UCLA, receiving a doctorate and establishing the Philosophical Institute in 1923. His career was spent working as a psychiatrist, counting many famous businessmen and film stars among his clients. He served as president of the Western Institute of **Psychoanalysis** in 1942. He also taught psychology and **philosophy** for twelve years and was the author of over thirty books, the most important of which were *The Creator and the Created* (1933), *Psychoanalysis and the Care of the Inferiority Complex* (1947), *Psychoanalysis and the Sexual Life* (1949), and *Your Complexes and You* (1959).

Negri was an opponent of **superstition** all his life. He was honorary president of the Freethinkers of Southern California and president of the Los Angeles Humanist Society of Friends, and was active in the Masons. After the death of his wife, Negri carried on his work in organized humanism.

NEHRU, JAWAHARLAL (1889–1964). Indian freedom fighter, prime minister, thinker, and one of the most significant humanists of the twentieth century. Jawaharlal Nehru was born into a very privileged family of Brahmins, originally from Kashmir. His father, Motilal Nehru (1861–1931) was a close friend and ally of Mohandas Gandhi (1869–1948), the figurehead of the Indian resistance movement. Nehru was educated privately until 1905, when he was sent to Harrow, one of England's most prestigious private schools. He went on to Trinity College, Cambridge, and practiced law in London before returning to India in 1912. In 1916 he married Kamala Kaul (1899–1936). The couple had one daughter, Indira, who, using her married name Gandhi, went on to have a long and significant career in Indian politics.

At the same time, a growing interest in Indian independence led Nehru to become politically active. He met Gandhi at a meeting of the Indian National Congress in 1916 and one of the firmest, most important political partnerships of the twentieth century was underway. Gandhi and Nehru were very different personalities, and yet their contrasting strengths complemented each other's. Nehru went to prison for the first time in 1921, the first of nine periods of incarceration under the British. Overall, he spent nine years in prison in the cause of freedom. It was during his terms of imprisonment that he did most of his writing.

After the death of Motilal Nehru in 1931, he became even more closely allied with Gandhi, and it was soon apparent that Nehru was Gandhi's preferred successor, although Gandhi did not make that specific until 1942. As another war became more likely, Nehru, despite struggling against the British for independence, made it quite clear that he, and India, were on the side of the Allies against fascism. Ironically, Nehru spent much of the war years in prison. After the war, it was clear that British rule could not last and he took a central role in guiding the process to independence. Nehru made a mistake, we can now see with the advantage of hindsight, in not involving the rival Muslim League more closely in the lead-up to independence. There is more than enough blame for the horrors of the partition, during which hundreds of thousands of Hindus and Muslims were killed in bitter religious fighting. However, on August 15, 1947, India became independent, and Nehru was its first prime minister.

Until his death in 1964 he was prime minister of India, and was loved by the people—one of the few twentieth-century leaders about whom that can genuinely be said. His four guiding principles were democracy, socialism, national unity, and secularism. Each of these contributed substantially to making India the vibrant nation it has become. He was also a leader of what became known as the nonaligned countries. Nehru also helped steer India through the crisis of the assassination of Gandhi by a Hindu fanatic. Nehru's two biggest failures during his long term as leader of India was his inability to resolve the ongoing dispute over Kashmir and the disastrous war with China in 1962, in which Indian troops performed poorly and Indian territory was lost.

And finally, he helped set the tone intellectually in India by virtue of his writing. Books like *The Discovery of India* (1946) and his autobiography (1936) influenced millions of people for more than two generations. Both these books outlined Nehru's commitment to humanism.

Further reading: M. J. Akbar, *Nehru: The Making of India*; and John Keay, *India: A History*.

NEO-DARWINIAN SYNTHESIS. The coming together of Darwinian theory and genetics is known as the neo-Darwinian synthesis. Until the synthesis Darwinism and genetics, then known as Mendelism, were often thought to be at loggerheads, and many people supposed that Darwinism was dead. Even today **creationists** do not scruple to cite

Mendelians criticizing Darwinians and claim that this is evidence that **evolution** itself is being contested.

The synthesis between Darwinism and genetics happened via the development of microevolution, which showed that genetics was responsible for geographic differences in species rather than the **Lamarckian** inheritance of acquired characteristics, which was the most widely accepted explanation until then. This meant that natural selection and genetics were not merely compatible, but were indissolubly linked, contrary to what had hitherto been thought.

The science behind the synthesis was first aired by R. A. Fisher (1890–1962) in *Genetics and the Origin of Species* (1930), and the fact that a synthesis of Darwinism and genetics had been effected was covered by **Julian Huxley** in *Evolution: The Modern Synthesis* (1942). The neo-Darwinian synthesis has had many consequences in the history of evolutionary thinking. The most important consequence was the collapse of any vestige of scientific credibility for non-Darwinian theories like **Social Darwinism** and **eugenics**.

Further reading: Peter Bowler, *Evolution: The History of an Idea*.

NEOPLATONISM. A miscellany of ideas gathered from **Plato**, **Pythagoras**, **Aristotle**, and the **Stoics**, which had an extraordinary influence through the **Dark Ages** and Middle Ages. Platonism denotes the developments in Platonist thought until 200 CE or so, but after then the changes became great enough to justify the term Neoplatonism. Neoplatonism is more **mystical** and **dualistic** than its predecessors.

The two people most responsible for these changes to what we now call Neoplatonism were Plotinus (204–270 CE) and Iamblichus (250–325 CE). Plotinus was a deeply religious pagan whose thoughts on supernaturalism, immortal souls, bodily shame, and the folly of enjoying life was adapted by St. Augustine to Christian needs. Iamblichus carried even further the trend toward magic and supernaturalism.

The pagan strand of Neoplatonism was extinguished by Justinian when he closed down the **Academy** in 529 CE. The other branch of Neoplatonism, as practiced in Alexandria, became indistinguishable from Christianity, and went on to have an influence lasting almost a millennium. Neoplatonism was also profoundly influential in Muslim philosophy during its golden age. See the entry on **holy reason**.

NEUROETHICS. A subset of **bioethics** that examines the ethical issues raised by the growing ability of **science** and **technology** to influence brain states. We are at the dawn of an era where brain-enhancing drugs will be available to all who can afford them. This is one of the countless consequences of the new level of data about the human body we now have access to thanks to the successful completion of the **Human Genome Project**. In some ways the rise of neuroethics is not surprising. We have had neurophilosophy and neuroscience for a couple of decades; it was only a matter of time before neuroethics entered the fray.

To take a couple of examples, is it ethical for a company to use brain scans to probe people's memories, sexual history, drug habits, and proneness to disease? How will we test for children who have taken these— legal—drugs before exams? How will we ensure equality at an exam when some children will not be able to afford them? These are the sorts of questions that will be the stuff of neuroethics in the years to come.

However, some examples may not be as controversial. As research into finding cures or long-term palliatives for conditions like **depression** or Alzheimer's Disease continues, we may well come across drugs that stimulate brain performance. Medicines are often discovered in this way: they begin as a proposed cure for one ailment, but it transpires that it is excellent in curing another ailment, or in stimulating some other part of the body altogether. Either way, neuroethics is a

field with a huge future. See also the entry on **transhumanism**.

NEUTRAL MONISM. A term referring to a philosophy of the mind which rendered obsolete the lengthy disputes that had dominated philosophy for four centuries on the relative priority of "**mind**" or "matter." The theory is anticipated somewhat in the speculations of the Greek philosopher **Anaxagoras**, but was articulated most clearly by **Bertrand Russell**.

Everything in the universe, Russell wrote, is composed of events that have some duration in time and extension in space. "Mind" and "matter" are merely convenient shorthand terms for the various events that fall under the rubric of psychology and physics respectively. Until neutral monism, the debate had see-sawed back and forth as to whether mind or matter was the fundamental constituent, or substance, of the universe. In the wake of the theory of **relativity**, it transpired that there is no "substance," fundamental or otherwise, in the universe. Neutral monism understood this development when it argued that neither mind nor matter is the basic explanation. What there is, is stuff, some of which is called mental, some physical, depending on the circumstances of the investigation.

What neutral monism could not deal with satisfactorily was how to explain this more elemental stuff from which both mind and matter derived. Neutral monism is not a serious contender in the philosophy of mind anymore. There is no longer any need felt to reconcile mind and matter because there is no such thing as "mind."

NEW AGE MOVEMENT, THE. An eclectic coalition of ideas that, since the 1970s, has become influential in the Western world. Central to the New Age movement is a suspicion that traditional Western values and practices are fundamentally flawed. Western scientific and rational values are held to be, at best, incomplete truths and, at worst, betrayals of the essential truth. But the New Age movement also rejects traditional

Western religion and metaphysics, rejecting its dogma and its perceived inability to provide a sufficiently radical critique of Western scientific and rational values.

In the place of rejected Western values, the New Age movement embraces a wide range of practices held to be more in keeping with the rhythm of the universe. Most of these practices are **pseudosciences**. They include chakra balancing, faith healing, acupuncture, homeopathy, palmistry, alchemy, **kundalini**, martial arts, and many others.

Many New Age ideas revolve around notions of healing. Many strands of New Age thinking view the universe as essentially a spiritual phenomenon and our maladies as essentially spiritual maladies, hence the emphasis is on what are deemed holistic cures. At its best, New Age ideas are an acceptable way of comprehending the obvious truth that the mind has a significant role to play in healing physical maladies. At its worst, the New Age movement is an excuse for a cloying **narcissism**.

NEW CYNICISM, THE. A term given by the philosopher Susan Haack to a spectrum of critics of **science**. Prominent among the New Cynics are **postmodernists** and proponents of the **strong program** in sociology and supporters of "feminist science" or some such form of advocacy.

Partisans of the New Cynicism assert that any claims of honest inquiry, respect for **evidence**, and disinterested search for truth are illusions behind which the real players of power, politics, and special interests arrange things. Haack notes that the New Cynics recognize correctly that the uncritical cheerleaders of science (Haack calls them the Old Deferentialists) went too far in their claims on behalf of science. But the New Cynics then threw the baby out with the bathwater and concluded that all science is therefore discredited. This is called the **passes-for fallacy**.

Against the follies of the New Cynicism, Haack proposes what she calls **Critical Common-Sensism**, which has a great deal in common with **Critical Realism**.

Further reading: Susan Haack, *Defending Science—Within Reason.*

NEW ZEALAND ASSOCIATION OF RATIONALISTS AND HUMANISTS. One of the longest-running humanist associations in the world. Many short-lived rationalist and freethought organizations were set up around the country in the 1880s, largely as a result of the interest generated by the discrimination against **Charles Bradlaugh** in Britain. The most substantial of them was the New Zealand Rationalist Association, which formed in 1910 from the Canterbury Freethought Association, which was centered in Christchurch, on the South Island. And in the North Island, the Auckland Rationalist Association (ARA) reformed in 1927 from earlier groups in that city. After a couple more changes of name, the association took over in 1954 the title of New Zealand Rationalist Association from the defunct Christchurch-based group. And in 1997 the association renamed itself once again, this time in an attempt to unite the rationalist and humanist branches of the movement, which had broken apart in 1967. And by speaking of rational*ists* and huma*nists*, rather than rational*ism* and huma*nism*, the emphasis was put on the people rather on the beliefs.

When the ARA reformed in 1927 it established a journal, called the *Truthseeker*. In 1938 this became the *New Zealand Rationalist* and in 1964 the *NZ Rationalist and Humanist*, and 1997 it broadened its appeal when it renamed itself *The Open Society*. At various times, this journal has featured writing from prominent New Zealand thinkers, novelists, poets, and philosophers. It was edited for many years by **J. O. Hanlon**. See the entry on **Henry J. Hayward**. The current editor is **Bill Cooke**.

In 1960 the association purchased a property in the center of Auckland, close to the university. This building, called Rationalist House ("Rat house" for short) has been a vital center for heterodox thought in New Zealand.

Each year the NZARH gives the **Charles**

Southwell Award for the New Zealander who most conspicuously promoted the cause of humanism and the open society in the previous year. The award is named after **Charles Southwell**, the first declared freethinker in New Zealand's history.

Further reading: Bill Cooke, *Heathen in Godzone: Seventy Years of Rationalism in New Zealand*.

NEWMAN, CHARLES ROBERT (1802–1884). Brilliant but unstable brother of better-known John Henry Newman (1801–1890) who converted to Roman Catholicism, eventually becoming a cardinal, and Francis William Newman (1805–1897), who became a liberal theist and rationalist. Charles was educated at Ealing and went on to study literature at Bonn, but left without getting his degree. He was a schoolmaster in Sussex for a while but was unable to hold the job down. From 1853 until his death he lived in an attic on a subsistence stipend in Tenby provided by his brothers.

During this time he wrote some brilliant expositions of **atheism** which appeared in **George Jacob Holyoake**'s periodical the *Reasoner*. In 1891 Newman's atheist writings were collected together under the title *Essays in Rationalism*, complete with an introduction by Holyoake and biographical sketch by J. M. Wheeler (1850–1898).

NEWTON, SIR ISAAC (1642–1727). Alongside **Immanuel Kant**, probably the most brilliant mind in all history. Isaac Newton was born into a farming family in Woolsthorpe, Lincolnshire. Isaac's father, also Isaac, died when he was only three months old and the boy had a lonely childhood being raised by his grandmother. His indifferent health meant he was unsuited to most practical pursuits, so he was sent to Cambridge to be a clergyman. But it was soon apparent that Newton's genius lay in other areas.

He read widely at university but it was in 1665 and 1666, during a period of exile back in Lincolnshire while Cambridge was closed due to an outbreak of plague, that the young genius worked out the core of his new ideas. Working on the observations of **Galileo**, Newton developed the three laws of motion, which remain foundational to modern physics. While elements of them have been replaced by the **theory of relativity**, the basic soundness of Newton's laws remains. Alongside these three laws, Newton developed a four-part **scientific method**:

- no more causes of natural things should be sought beyond what is true and sufficient to explain their appearances;
- the same natural effects must be attributed to the same causes;
- qualities of bodies are to be thought of as being universal; nd
- theories derived from observation of phenomena should be thought accurate until such time as other phenomena contradict them.

Newton's most famous book was the *Mechanical Principles of Natural Philosophy* (1687), usually known as the *Principia*. It was here he articulated the three laws and the four-part scientific method, although he had been thinking about them for many years prior to publication. He had been elected a fellow of the Royal Society in 1672. Newton's other important book is *Opticks* (1704), where he used mathematics to explain some vital aspects of the universe. Newton is also credited with the invention of calculus, although the German philosopher G. W. Leibniz (1646–1716) is credited with independently arriving at some similar points of calculus, and of improving Newton's method of representing mathematical terms.

Newton's first law is now seen as being less significant than the second law. He envisaged a universe operating like a gigantic mechanism operating according to natural laws. His law of universal gravitation states that "the gravitational force varies directly as the mass and inversely as the square of the distance." This is because one object is held to exert a force on another. His theory of gravity showed that what makes things fall on earth is exactly the same force that works on planets and stars. Up until then these had been explained by different theories. This is the context behind the apocryphal story of the apple falling on Newton's head, which led him to ponder these things.

Later in his life, Newton devoted most of his time to alchemy and biblical exegesis. These writings are of great interest to the historian of ideas, but have no contemporary value. Newton's **religion** was highly heterodox, being a form of Arianism, a **heresy** dating back to the fourth century CE, for which he would have been killed in most earlier ages. His vision of how the universe works was a major step away from the **anthropocentric conceit** of medieval metaphysics, which saw the universe in terms of a cosmic drama between **God**, **Satan**, and humanity. The Newtonian God was the original clockmaker, who saw only an occasional need to tinker with his original design. But Newton was first and foremost a freethinker. He wrote: "**Plato** is my friend, **Aristotle** is my friend, but my best friend is **truth**."

Further reading: James Gleick, *Isaac Newton*.

NICKELL, JOE (1944–). The world's only professional **paranormal** investigator. Nickell has had a colorful life, being at various periods a stage magician, private detective, and journalist before returning to the University of Kentucky where he took a master's (1982) and a PhD in English (1987), with special reference to folklore and literary investigation. He was an instructor at the University of Kentucky until 1995 when he became senior research fellow of the **Committee for the Scientific Investigation of Claims of the Paranormal** (CSICOP). He writes the "Investigative Files" column for the *Skeptical Inquirer*.

Skeptics are often accused of being mere **debunkers**, and Nickell is alive to that objec-

tion. His approach is to decry both unduly credulous and dismissive stances prior to an investigation, and to enter the investigation with an open mind. Nickell has three main investigative approaches:

- *on-site investigations*, sometimes working undercover or in disguise;
- *experimentation*, such as when he recreated one of the giant Peruvian Nazca lines; and
- *forensic analysis and scholarly research.*

He is a very popular speaker at conferences, is a regular guest on television and radio programs, and has had articles in journals as diverse as the *Journal of Police Science and Administration* and *Indiana Folklore*. He has written more than twenty books. His most important skeptical works are *Inquest on the Shroud of Turin* (1983, 1998), *Secrets of the Supernatural* (1988), *Mysterious Realms* (1992), *Looking for a Miracle* (1993), *Real-Life X-Files* (2001), and *The Mystery Chronicles* (2004). He has also written children's books, *The Magic Detectives* (1989) and *Wonder-workers!* (1991), and several works on forensic science, including *Camera Clues* (1994), *Detective Forgery* (1996), and, with John F. Fischer, *Crime Science* (1999). See the entry on **humanist-themed Web sites**.

NIEMOJEWSKI, ANDRZEJ (1864–1921). Rationalist author and poet. Andrzej Niemojewski was born to Polish parents in Dorpat, Russia, now part of Estonia. He originally studied law and worked as a businessman, but after 1897 he devoted himself to his main loves, writing and the study of **religion**. He was a freethinker whose works, which were critical of religion, repeatedly got him in trouble with the law. He was imprisoned for three months in 1899, narrowly missed the same fate on several later occasions, and was imprisoned once more in 1911 for "**blasphemy**."

Between 1906 and 1921 he edited the

journal *Independent Thought*. He wrote socially engaged poetry and novels, in particular *People of the Revolution* (1906). He also translated **Ernest Renan** into Polish and was a skilled orientalist.

Niemojewski was a devotee of the then-fashionable theory that Jesus could be explained in the context of ancient solar myths. One of his pamphlets was entitled *God Jesus: The Sun, Moon and Stars as Background to the Gospel Stories*. If this theory is of little value today, it is not notably more fanciful than the orthodox story it sought to replace. Of more lasting value is Niemojewski's socially engaged writing.

NIETHAMMER, FRIEDRICH IMMAN-UEL (1766–1848). German educationist credited with coining the word **humanism**. In a book called *The Quarrel of Philanthropinism and Humanism in the Theory of Educational Instruction of Our Time* (1808) Niethammer advocated a broad-ranging moral education and gave this education the name humanism. The important point about all this is that humanism was the conservative strand of Niethammer's education theory. Philanthropinism, about which Niethammer wrote, was an eccentric, antireligious education theory which had a brief vogue at the time. In humanism, Niethammer was trying to find a middle way between unthinking hostility to the new ideas while preserving what he thought best of the traditional values.

While the use of the word humanism has developed out of sight from Niethammer's understanding, there remains a characteristic feature of it. Humanism is not a radical departure from traditional values, as some reactionaries like to suppose. But neither is it quite as radical as its more militant supporters like to imagine. Niethammer's conception of humanism has much in common with the idea of **Bildung**, which was spoken of in Germany at the time, and of **eupraxsophy**, which **Paul Kurtz** coined almost two centuries later.

Further reading: Nicolas Walter, *Human-ism: What's In the Word?*

NIETZSCHE, FRIEDRICH (1844–1900). Dangerous genius. With little risk of exaggeration, Nietzsche can be described as one of the most influential philosophers of all time. He was a philosopher of **atheism**, being one of the first to understand that traditional notions of **God** were no longer credible. Nietzsche's description of the situation was compelling, more so than his proposed solutions.

Nietzsche's main ideas were *amor fati*, or love of necessity, the **death of God**, the **eternal recurrence** of the same, the **overman**, and the **will to power**. Nietzsche's most important works are *Thus Spake Zarathustra* (1883–85) and its immediate successor *Beyond Good and Evil* (1886), along with *The Gay Science* (1882), *Toward a Genealogy of Morals* (1887), and *Twilight of the Gods* and *The Anti-Christ* (both from 1888). One of his more influential books was put together after his death and given the title *The Will to Power*. This consisted of a series of aphorisms and observations from Nietzsche's notebooks that were given headings by his sister, whose politics and racial opinions were sharply different than Nietzsche's. *The Will to Power* is worth reading, but it needs to be treated with caution.

Beyond Good and Evil is probably Nietzsche's most impressive work of philosophy, formally understood, but *Zarathustra* is a poetic or operatic masterpiece that is in a class of its own. There is a lot in *Zarathustra* against which one should shudder, but it is difficult to resist the incredible power of his writing and imagery. There are lots of wonderful books on Nietzsche, but it would be hard to improve on *Nietzsche in Turin*, by Lesley Chamberlain as a place to begin. See the entry on **Zarathustra**.

Further reading: Lesley Chamberlain, *Nietzsche in Turin*.

NIGERIAN HUMANIST MOVEMENT. One of the most important humanist movements in Africa. For many years there was no organized humanist movement in Nigeria, but the presence of **Tai Solarin** helped keep humanist issues before a wide audience. Nigerian **humanism** emerged in the 1990s in response to the advance of Islam in the north and Evangelical Christianity, funded in large part from the United States, in the south. The increasingly sectarian nature of Nigerian politics and society has made it crucial that a secular voice for toleration and pluralism be heard.

Nigerian humanism first made itself known outside its own country when Leo Igwe attended the **International Humanist and Ethical Union** congress in Mumbai in January 1999. Igwe's speech outlined the urgent need for humanism in Nigeria and across Africa. Igwe condemned the intrusion of foreign religions with the sectarian ways which shattered the "cohesion that once marked the traditional life of African people."

The NHM has led a series of campaigns, including one against the imposition of **Sharia law** in the northern provinces of the country. It has also campaigned against child-killing, a practice common among practitioners of traditional beliefs. The NHM also produces a journal called the *Humanist Inquirer*.

In December 2000 the NHM hosted a major conference on development issues in Nigeria, and in October the following year it hosted an even more ambitious international conference. This conference was funded by the **Center for Inquiry**, which entered into an agreement with the NHM to create a Center for Inquiry—Nigeria. See the entry on **African Americans for Humanism**.

NIHILISM. Described by **Friedrich Nietzsche** as the state where "why" gets no answer, or, less poetically, a state of complete **relativism**, an assertion that nothing can be known with any confidence. Nietzsche scholars see his idea of the spirit of revenge as the essence of nihilism. The spirit of revenge is a vague, generally directed sense of resentment against the world.

More recent understandings of nihilism speak of the state where all values are held to be equal, simply because there are no values at all. Following on from this, no distinctions can be made and there are no differences in the quality of anything. Some fundamentalists have claimed that **humanism** is nihilistic, but this is clearly not the case. While humanism doesn't offer pat formulas or certitudes, the answers it does suggest to the problems of living clearly indicate the gulf that separates it from nihilism. See the entry on **believe in nothing**.

Further reading: Peter Levine, *Nietzsche and the Modern Crisis in the Humanities*.

NINE DEMANDS OF LIBERALISM. A political program that was published in the American journal the *Index*, operating out of Toledo, Ohio, on April 6, 1872, which led to the creation of the National Liberal Association (NLA). The list was compiled by Francis Ellingwood Abbot (1836–1904), who became the NLA's first president. The NLA was the predecessor to the American Secular Union. The nine demands were:

(1) We demand that churches and other ecclesiastical property shall be no longer exempt from taxation.

(2) We demand that the employment of chaplains in Congress, and in the legislatures, in the navy and militia, and in prisons, asylums, and all other institutions supported by public money, shall be discontinued.

(3) We demand that all public appropriations for educational and charitable institutions of a sectarian character shall cease.

(4) We demand that all religious services now sustained by the government shall be abolished; and especially that the use of the Bible in the public schools, whether ostensibly as a textbook or avowedly as a book of religious worship, shall be prohibited.

(5) We demand that the appointment, by the president of the United States or by the governors of the various states,

of all the religious festivals and fasts shall wholly cease.

(6) We demand that the judicial oath in the courts and in all other departments of the government shall be abolished, and that a simple affirmation under the pains and penalties of perjury shall be established in its stead.

(7) We demand that all laws directly or indirectly enforcing the observance of Sunday as the Sabbath shall be repealed.

(8) We demand that all laws looking to the enforcement of "Christian" morality shall be abrogated and that all laws shall be conformed to the requirements of natural morality, equal rights, and impartial liberty.

(9) We demand that not only in the Constitution of the United States and of the several states, but also in the practical administration of the same, no privileges or advantage shall be conceded to Christianity or any other special religion; that our entire political system shall be founded and administered on a purely secular basis; and whatever changes shall prove necessary to this end shall be consistently, unflinchingly, and promptly made.

The Nine Demands of Liberalism served as the clarion call for the NLA for many years, and constituted its appeal to preserve the **separation of church and state** and combat the authoritarian tendencies of **Comstockery**.

Further reading: Stephen Kevin Green, "The National Reform Association and the Religious Amendments to the Constitution, 1864–1876." An unpublished Master's Thesis, University North Carolina, Chapel Hill, 1987, p. 37, Appendix A–149–150.

NIRVANA. The goal among Buddhists of the final extinction of the self and its permanent and total identification with the Buddha-nature or, among Chinese Buddhists, the Universal Mind. Among some Chinese Buddhists, Nirvana involves total identification with the principle of *Wu*, or nonbeing. Other Chinese Buddhists speak poetically of reaching the other shore; this shore being the cycle of birth and **death**, the other shore being nirvana.

The rival thoughts on the afterlife constitute one of the more significant differences between the **monotheist religions** of the West and the **Asian traditions**. The monotheist notion of the **soul**, which is grand enough to warrant a place somewhere in the cosmos for all eternity is at sharp odds with the more humble idea of nirvana, which involves the extinction of all notions of the self. See the entries on **Eastern philosophy** and **anthropocentric conceit**.

NITSCHKE, PHILLIP (1947–). Australian campaigner for **voluntary euthanasia**. Phillip Nitschke was born and raised in Adelaide, South Australia. He studied at Adelaide before moving to Flinders University to take a PhD in physics. Nitschke then moved to the Northern Territory where he worked with Aboriginal communities. His experiences persuaded him to retrain in medicine, so he moved to Sydney where he took a medical degree.

Back in the Northern Territory, he created controversy when he was critical of hospital facilities in Darwin being able to cope in the event of a nuclear alert. This was during the visit of an American nuclear-powered ship to the city. The hospital refused to renew his contract, but after a legal battle, it changed its policy and renewed his appointment.

Nitschke's life changed forever in 1996, when, running against the political tide, Marshall Perron, the chief minister of the Northern Territory, oversaw legislation that decriminalized voluntary euthanasia. Perron's legislation ran into concerted opposition from the Australian Medical Association (AMA) which declared that no doctor in the state would cooperate with the Perron bill. Nitschke then gathered the signatures of twenty doctors who said they would. In the short time the voluntary euthanasia legislation was in place (it was later overturned by the Australian federal government), Nitschke helped several people who came to him for help to die with dignity. The Northern Territory legislation was used by four people before it was overturned. The wishes of two more were denied by parliament.

Since then Nitschke has become a tireless campaigner for the right of people to choose the time and place of their own death when faced with terminal illness. He runs workshops that detail ways people can manage their own death. These workshops are very popular and are usually booked months in advance. In 1998, Nitschke was awarded the Australian Humanist of the Year award by the **Council of Australian Humanist Societies**.

NO FREE COMMUNION, PRINCIPLE OF. A tongue-in-cheek, though very perceptive, maxim devised by the irreverent philosopher Matthew Stewart. The Principle of No Free Communion states that any **philosophy** which has as its aim the union of humanity and the universe and which conceives this union as something grander than simply someone doing philosophy cannot be said to have achieved this by philosophical means.

This means that if we want to construct some grand metaphysical system that claims to unite humanity and the universe, we have ceased to work philosophically and have entered the realm of **mysticism**, the **paranormal**, or **religion**.

Further reading: Matthew Stewart, *The Truth About Everything*.

NO TRUE SCOTSMAN MOVE. An **ad hominem** line of argumentation, identified by **Antony Flew**. Rather than consider the validity of the argument being put forward, the No True Scotsman move changes the subject by saying "No true Scotsman (or Christian, communist, American, Muslim, or whoever) would say that."

This argument is used quite often by Christians and Muslims, who, when asked about atrocities or injustices committed by coreligionists, often answer, "Ah, but they're not proper Christians/Muslims." This assumes there is such a thing as a "proper" Christian or Muslim, and more specifically, that a proper Christian or Muslim would agree with me. And, in the Christian context at least, it ignores the passage of **scripture** that says "By their fruits you shall know them" (Matthew 7:16–18). See the entry on **perfumed smokescreen**.

Further reading: Antony Flew, *Thinking About Thinking*.

NONBELIEF, ARGUMENT FROM. An argument, articulated by **Michael Martin**, against the existence of **God**. This argument is most effective against all three **monotheist** religions, particularly their more fundamentalist manifestations. This argument proceeds from the fact that there are more than a billion freethinkers in the world, not to mention the other three billion or so followers of the **Asian traditions**. How, then, can a supposedly loving God who is anxious for humans to be saved, not provide clear **evidence** of his existence and proof of the need for salvation? How loving is it that billions of people are condemned to eternal **hell** when so many of them never even knew about the existence of this God? Could God not have made his message universal, so everyone could hear it, or comprehensible, so everyone could understand it?

Apologists usually provide three types of answers to this dilemma. There is the *free will defense*, which says God gave us **free will** to choose as we see fit. But by making his message clear, God could at least reduce the room for confusion. And what sort of God would want his creation to believe in him on such flimsy and irrational evidence? Then there is the *testing defense*, which says God is testing our **faith**. Why a loving God should want to do this, presumably knowing that millions will fail the test and go to hell for all time, when God could have done otherwise, is left unexplained. And some apologists fall back on the *unknown purpose defense*, which says God has a reason, but we don't know what it is. This is a very weak argument, and supposes a worryingly irrational God.

It follows from this that it is reasonable to doubt the existence of God as conceived by the fundamentalist wings of monotheist religions.

Further reading: Michael Martin, "Three Arguments for Nonbelief," *Free Inquiry* 21, no. 4 (Fall 2001): 50–53.

NONOVERLAPPING MAGISTERIA. A term coined by Stephen Jay Gould (1941–2002) to refer to the completely separate areas of interest of **science** and **religion**. Gould endorsed a notion long preferred by religious apologists that science asks the "how" questions while religion asks the "why" questions, and that neither magisteria has any reason to encroach on the territory of the other. In this way, Gould insisted, there is no necessary **conflict between science and religion**.

Gould's concept is wrong, for many reasons. First, it ignores the many specific historical and factual truth claims that religions make: Jesus rose from the dead, the Qur'an is the inspired word of God as dictated by the Angel Gabriel to the Prophet Muhammad, and so on. It would be irresponsible to leave the answers to these questions solely to those who already believe them to be true. Furthermore, Gould's **dualism** relinquishes to religion all the crucial moral and ethical questions. This is indefensible, both because secular moralists have many valuable things to say, and because religious moralists cannot agree on what they are saying, despite claiming to be speaking on God's behalf. It is also flawed in principle to set up intellectual no-go areas. In an open society, nothing should be beyond the reach of critical scrutiny. Gould notwithstanding, there is a conflict between science and religion.

Further reading: Stephen Jay Gould, *Rock of Ages*; and Paul Kurtz, ed., *Science and Religion: Are They Compatible?*

NORMATIVE ETHICS. The style of **ethics** best known to nonphilosophers because normative ethics is the ethics that seeks to provide us with general guidelines about how we should act. There are three main strands of normative ethics:

- *virtue ethics* of **Aristotle** and his followers;
- *deontological ethics* of **Kant** and his followers; and
- *utilitarian ethics* of **Bentham**, **Mill**, and their followers.

Both Kant and the utilitarians were interested in what sorts of actions we should perform and why they are good while others are bad. But while they asked similar questions, they came up with very different answers. Kant and deontological ethics talk in terms of duty, which leads to what Kant called the **categorical imperative**, which operates as a sort of universal law. Also, see the entry on **supreme moral rule**.

Contemporary utilitarians, by contrast, speak of maximizing human **happiness**. They concentrate on the consequences of an action, arguing that the moral value of an action can only be known by the consequences the action has, rather than in examining the action itself. See the entries on **Utility, Principle of**.

The most recent variety of ethics, although it has ancient roots, is virtue ethics Virtue ethics can be said to begin with Aristotle and tackles the problem from a different angle. Virtue ethics is more about **character**, or what makes a virtuous person. It works on the theory that the virtuous person will know what actions to do because he or she is virtuous. Aristotle's ethical ideas are captured in his ideas of **eudaimonia** and the **doctrine of the mean**. See the entry on **values**.

NOT ENOUGH FAITH TO BE AN ATHEIST. One of the more popular throwaway lines against atheists. This line is related to the many **prejudices against atheists** although it is as much a misrepresentation of atheism as it is a prejudice against it. The thinking behind this claim is that it stretches credulity too much to believe the universe was created by **chance**, or out of nothing, and the unsaid insult implied is that to think in such credulous ways amounts to faith.

As with most other one-liners against atheists, the not-enough-faith argument fails on several grounds. First, it misrepresents how atheists see the universe as beginning. To the extent that atheists theorize on this matter, they do not postulate the fortuitous concourse of atoms, so beloved by Christian apologists. **Quantum mechanics** consists of random events, but events at an atomic level and above conform to some chain of causes that humans call the laws of nature. With this in mind it requires no bizarre degree of faith to accept the big-bang account of the beginning of the universe.

The second problem with the not-enough-faith argument is that it is subversive of any positive notion of **faith**, which is surprising as the argument comes from religious apologists. The not-enough-faith argument casts faith as an irrational grasping at straws in order to support some outlandish view of life. When atheists have portrayed religious faith in this way they have been castigated as being irreverent, insensitive, and vulgar in their understanding of the relationship people have with God. But when the argument is used by religious believers against atheists, none of these objections apparently apply.

The third problem with the not-enough-faith argument is that it is usually given in complete ignorance of the wealth of atheist philosophy that has been produced over the last seventy years. Few of them have read any of the **books on atheism** mentioned in this dictionary. In the light of this ignorance, the not-enough-faith argument does nothing more than attack a straw man. The only real damage it inflicts is on the conventional religious conception of faith.

NOTHING BUTTERY. A derogatory phrase applied to those who are thought to explain subjects like **consciousness** in materialist terms: i.e., consciousness is *nothing but* neurons interacting with other neurons. Proponents of **dualistic** theories of mind, usually people with a religious or New Age bent, condemn this approach as a "nothing buttery" sort of **reductionism**.

This sort of criticism is deceitful because the preferred conclusion is smuggled in under false pretenses. The argument goes:

- nobody fully knows the working of the human mind;
- therefore, it is impossible to understand the working of the human mind on a naturalist basis;
- therefore, it is necessary to bring in a supernatural or other dualistic explanation before we can understand how the mind works.

Not fully knowing how the mind works is one thing; to then presume a supernatural explanation as the only valid one is quite another. In philosophical terms, this is a variant of the **argument from ignorance**. It is also related to **mereymustification**.

Further reading: Milton Rothman, *The Science Gap*.

NUN, THE. A satire written by **Denis Diderot** on the elements of injustice and suppression against nuns. In 1752 a French nun, Marguerite Delamarre tried through the courts to be released from her religious vows on the grounds that she had made them under duress. She was unsuccessful and was forced to return to her convent, where she remained for the rest of her life. The publicity surrounding this case attracted Diderot's attention, whose own sister, Catherine, had died insane in a convent at only twenty-seven years old. Most of the book was written in 1760, although it was not published until 1796, twelve years after Diderot's death.

Unlike many other of Diderot's works, *The Nun* was not put on the **Index of For-**

bidden Books, but it was actively resisted by the Roman Catholic Church even into the twentieth century. In 1962, Jacques Rivette, a French filmmaker, found that his attempts to produce a film version of *The Nun* ran up against official censorship, effectively postponing its production for three years. The Roman Catholic Church launched a major campaign to stop production of the film in 1965. The film passed the censors in 1966 and had a short season at Cannes, but was then banned in France.

O

OBJECTIVE MORALITY. A notoriously difficult subject that is easily susceptible to collapsing into a simple **command morality**. The requirement for objectivity is demanding; for something to be objective, there can be no exceptions, it must hold for all people at all times. This rules out the prohibition on killing, for instance, because we can all imagine a scenario when one person's death in order to save millions is justifiable.

The New Zealand philosopher Raymond Bradley speaks of objective morality in the sense of moral truths being true without regard to what an individual or social group thinks or desires. Objective morality has these three features:

- our moral beliefs are either true or false and not merely expressions of emotion;
- the truth or falsity of our moral judgments is a function of whether the objects of moral appraisal have the moral properties we ascribe to them; and
- we must recognize the possibility of other moral truths that await our discovery.

The last of these is important because it prevents us from succumbing to the conceit of seeing the beliefs of our own time and informed by our current levels of scientific knowledge as somehow "objective." There are big differences between objective morality and command morality. The other danger with items of objective morality is that, in order for them to be genuinely exceptionless, they have to be expressed in general terms and risk becoming truisms. See the entry on **moral truisms shared by us all**. So, even with a list of moral truisms shared by us all, we still need to apply them to our lives through the processes of **judgment** and **rationality**. Not even objective morality absolves us of these responsibilities. Here is where **wide reflective equilibrium** is so helpful. And, as Bradley shows to devastating effect, the notion of objective morality lends decisive weight to **atheism**. See the entry on **atheism, moral argument for**.

OBJECTIVITY. A word many people suppose to be the same as their opinions. Genuine objectivity, however, is a far more difficult condition to reach. The American philosopher **John Rawls** outlined five conditions for objectivity:

- the ability to establish a public framework of thought sufficient for conclusions to be reached on the basis of reasons and evidence after full discussion and reflection;
- having the aim of being reasonable or true;
- the ability to specify an order of reasons;
- the ability to distinguish an objective point of view from a partisan one; and
- having an account of agreement in **judgment** among other reasonable people.

Rawls concluded that a moral or political conception can be deemed objective if and only if it answers to each of these five points. Other scholars have noted that objectivity is ultimately not a matter of conforming to methodologies, but of **character**. Respecting all evidence, even when it is inconvenient, remaining aware at all times of our fallibility, and studying in good **faith** are, in the end, tests of character.

Another philosopher, John Ryder, has observed that it is a mistake to confuse objectivity with **absolutism**. It is possible for the humanist to value objectivity while also denying the value of absolutism. This is because an absolute is that which is unrelated and unconditional to anything at all. This is an altogether different state than objectivity.

Further reading: John Rawls, *Political Liberalism*; and Susan Haack, *Defending Science—Within Reason*.

OCCIDENTOSIS. A word coined only half in jest to refer to the widely held attitude that "the West" is responsible for all the evils of the world. Even Edward Said (1935–2003), the person more responsible than most for giving Occidentosis its vogue, has described it as "extremely tiresome and boring." Occidentosis is the major presupposition behind some of the more hysterical forms of the subdiscipline known as postcolonial studies and much of **postmodernism**. Significant elements of the anti**globalization** campaign are also motivated by Occidentosis, although that movement remains intellectually credible if those elements are expunged from it, unlike most of postmodernism or postcolonial studies.

Occidentosis, of course, makes the same mistake that **orientalists** were accused of doing, namely lumping a complex civilization with many competing and contradictory elements into one uniform idea, and then accusing it of a variety of sins. There is nothing wrong in being proud of one's cultural heritage, even if it is European. Pride in one's heritage does not mean one is not alive to the many errors, crimes, and follies committed by people presuming to act in its name. But it is no less an error to then assume a greater degree of virtue to the oppressed, as **Bertrand Russell** noted in 1950. Pride in one's own heritage is best accompanied by joy that others are proud of theirs, followed

by dialogue and debate so as to appreciate the basis of their cultural pride and how to learn from it. That is the basis of **planetary humanism**.

OCCULT ARTS. A general term to include astrology, alchemy, divination, feng shui and many others. Occult arts share with **science** a desire to interpret nature and to then use those interpretations in the service of humankind. Many occult arts developed into genuine sciences when they ceased attributing real powers of intervention to the **supernatural**. The best-known example is alchemy which gave rise, however accidentally, to the science of chemistry. It is worth noting that the word "occult" comes from the Latin *occulere*, which means literally "to cover up." This illustrates well the difference between occult arts and the sciences. See the entry on **New Age**.

OCKHAM'S RAZOR. Also known as the **Principle of Parsimony**, this is an extraordinarily influential rule of philosophy. Attributed to William of Ockham (1285–1349) who said, "Entities are not to be multiplied beyond necessity." This means that when two theories that explain the same facts collide, the simpler of the two should be preferred as the most likely to be accurate. This is because the more convoluted theory has more in it which can go wrong and thus compromise the theory. It has frequently been observed that some of the most stunning breakthroughs in thought are really quite simple ideas.

Ockham was also responsible for systematically dismantling the five proofs for the existence of **God** that Thomas Aquinas (1225–1274) had devised the previous century. For Ockham, God could only be grasped through **faith**. See the entry on the **burden of proof**.

O'HAIR, MADALYN MURRAY (1919–1995). The loose cannon of twentieth-century **atheism**. Madalyn Evalyn Mays was born on April 13, 1919, in Pittsburgh, Pennsylvania.

She was awarded a BA from Ashland College in Ohio in 1948 and a law degree from South Texas College of Law in 1953. Too intelligent and restless for the cramped choices available to women of her generation, Mays moved around, physically, emotionally, and intellectually. She may or may not have been married to William Murray, a wealthy Roman Catholic then serving in World War II. Either way, they had a son, William. Later she married Richard O'Hair, a shady character with an excessive love of drink.

She shot to national prominence in 1963 after her successful fight, which went to the Supreme Court of the United States, to defend the rights of her son from the practice of compulsory prayer in school. The case, known as *Murray vs. Curlett*, in fact was in tandem with an identical case, *Abington Township vs. Schempp*. But unlike the Schempp's, O'Hair was prepared, even keen, for the publicity the case engendered, although the level of hostility and harassment she faced took a severe toll on the family.

Out of this case, O'Hair formed **American Atheists**, an organization still going today. Over the next thirty years she led the American Atheists through some worthwhile campaigns on behalf of the rights of atheists as citizens. Most of her legal challenges ended in failure, but she did win a case that overturned a Texas regulation requiring employees on the state payroll to believe in **God**. But she also held atheism up to ridicule by her increasingly bizarre antics, the frequent schisms within her organization, and the estrangement of her son, William, who became a born-again preacher in 1980.

In August 1995 O'Hair, her son Jon, and Robyn, her adopted daughter—who had been abandoned by William while a baby—were abducted by three criminals and were forced to sign over significant sums of money before they were murdered.

Further reading: Bryan F. Le Beau, *The Atheist: Madalyn Murray O'Hair*.

OH REALLY? FACTOR. A satirical response to the program on the FOX channel in the United States called *The O'Reilly Factor* with Bill O'Reilly as the host. This term suggests a healthy level of **skepticism** regarding some of the more sensational and politically motivated "news" programs in the United States.

OIL SHOCKS. A series of pricc increases by the Organization of Petroleum Exporting Countries (OPEC) in 1974 and again in 1979 that shook the Western economies and altered the balance of world power. The initial stimulus for the price rises was the Yom Kippur War, which was the fourth major conflict between Arab countries and Israel, this time resulting from a surprise attack by Egypt and Syria against Israeli forces on October 6, 1973, the day of Yom Kippur, a Jewish holy day. Despite the element of surprise, the Arab attack was a failure with Israeli forces quickly recovering and going on the offensive.

The significance of Yom Kippur lay in the growing unwillingness of the Arab world to continue selling oil to the Western world while the West continues to support Israel. Before the war began, oil was sold for $3 a barrel, but on October 16, OPEC raised the price per barrel to $4.50 while also reducing their output. This brought on the "oil shocks," which had destabilizing effects on the developed world's economy for at least the rest of the decade, and has radically reshaped world politics. Both oil shocks were followed by recessions in the Western economies.

OLIGARCHY, IRON LAW OF. A pessimistic theory of political power. The idea was first expounded by the German political scientist Robert Michels (1876–1936) from a study of German socialist parties and unions. Michels concluded that the open, democratic ideals of small organizations inevitably give way to the need for organizational efficiency and rational decision making. This trend inevitably favors the officeholders at the time, who are more aware of how the organization works. In time, the original ideals of transparency and openness are lost and the organization hardens into a self-supporting structure. Because Michels saw no exception to this process he spoke of the iron law of oligarchy.

There are many who would argue that Michels's gloomy conclusions, if not an iron law, at least shed a lot of light on the almost inevitable way organizations can be relied upon to betray their original purpose and atrophy into a self-serving bureaucracy.

OMAR KHAYYAM (1048–1122 CE, approx.), Persian poet, mathematician, and astronomer. Born in Nishapur, the son of a tentmaker, Omar Khayyam nevertheless received a good education. He went to Samarkand as a young man, where he wrote an important work on algebra. On the strength of that work, he was invited by the Seljuk sultan Malik Shah to serve as an astronomer and to help reform the calendar. After the sultan's death, Omar Khayyam made his pilgrimage to Mecca (the *hajj*). The *Rubaiyat* achieved lasting fame as a scathing indictment of joyless orthodoxy and a celebration of life and sensuality. One quatrain reads:

> Lord of the fatwa, what a rogue you
>   are!
> Drinker I may be, I prefer by far
> From the juice of grapes to secure a
>   thrill
> Than to cheat orphans of their father's
>   will!

Omar Khayyam's quatrains were rediscovered in the nineteenth century when they came to the attention of the English poet Edward Fitzgerald (1809–1883), who translated the quatrains and rearranged their order. Fitzgerald's work was published in 1859 as the *Rubaiyat of Omar Khayyam*. Rubaiyat means quatrain. The *Rubaiyat* achieved immediate fame and has been translated into most of the major languages of the world. Fitzgerald's valuable work also stands as a rebuke to the pretensions of **Orientalism**, which insist that Westerners have made no positive contribution to non-Western cultures.

OMNISCIENCE. The quality of infinite **knowledge** traditionally attributed to **God**, although even some religious philosophers have acknowledged that attributing omniscience to God is incoherent. The British theistic philosopher Richard Swinburne (1934–) has admitted that God cannot be omniscient because he can't know what all his future actions will be. This is because God's moral perfection is incompatible with being omniscient. If God knew about the Holocaust, to take an obvious example, before it happened and yet did nothing to prevent it, what does that say for the perfect goodness of God? Swinburne tried to patch up a theory of limited omniscience to deal with this problem.

Furthermore, omniscience means knowledge of *everything*, including all the dark, mean, and ugly things of life. But having full knowledge of hate, greed, envy, and sexual deviancy and exploitation raises another set of serious problems for God's moral perfection. And for God to know fear, frustration, and failure, as he would have to in order to be omniscient, would mean that he can't at the same time be omnipotent, which is to be all powerful, quite the opposite of these emotions.

OMPHALOS. A book published in 1857, written by Philip Gosse (1810–1888) which argued that **God** created the Earth very recently, in accordance with biblical teaching, and had then inserted the complete fossil record into his creation to give the impression of greater age. "Omphalos" is a Greek word that refers to a stone at Delphi in Greece, which was regarded by them as the central point of the earth.

Reaction to *Omphalos* was uniformly critical, even among churchmen otherwise hostile to **evolution**. There are still some fundamentalists who take this line, though without attributing it to Gosse. The story of Philip Gosse's desperate attempts to retain his biblical literalism are movingly told in *Father* *and Son* (1907), the autobiography written by his son, Edmund (1849–1928), an important literary critic and agnostic. See the entry on **degenerationism**.

ONAGROCRACY. A term coined by the Italian philosopher Benedetto Croce (1866–1952). With Italian fascism in mind Croce described onagrocracy as government "by braying asses." Croce intended onagrocracy as an addition to the three traditional types of government posited by **Aristotle**: tyranny, oligarchy, and **democracy**. Unfortunately there are still plenty of examples of government by onagrocracy.

ONLY CONNECT. A passage from a novel by the humanist author **E. M. Forster** and one of the most poignant formulations of **humanism**:

> Only connect! That was the whole of her sermon. Only connect the prose and the passion, and both will be exalted, and human love will be seen at its highest. Live in fragments no longer. Only connect, and the beast and the monk, robbed of the isolation that is life to either, will die.

The passage comes from Forster's novel *Howards End* (1910). It encapsulates the essential simplicity of humanism, which is about people recognizing their common humanity and seeing past all the things that divide us. See the entry on **humanism, foundations of**.

Further reading: E. M. Forster, *Howards End*.

ONTOLOGICAL ARGUMENT. One of the hardy perennials in the existence of **God** arguments. The argument was first used by the Catholic theologian St. Anselm (1033–1109). It was refuted comprehensively by **Immanuel Kant**. It resurfaces from time to time, but is the least salvageable of the classical arguments for the existence of God.

This argument can be summarized in this way: God, by definition, is incomparable and unsurpassable, the greatest thing we could imagine. Such a perfect, all-powerful being has to be greater than our imagination, therefore it exists. But, as Taner Edis has shown, this argument also works for proving the existence of Mildred the unicorn. The ontological argument is merely an attempt to define God into existence. It also assumes— incorrectly—that everything must have a cause. **Quantum mechanics** has shown this not to be true.

Further reading: Taner Edis, *The Ghost in the Universe*.

ONUOHA, ENYERIBE. Nigerian educator and humanist leader. Onuoha was a traditional ruler of the Umuchieze people of southeastern Nigeria. He was a Catholic priest for twelve years, before leaving the church in 1972. Since then he has described himself as a secular humanist. Onuoha was active in the **Nigerian Humanist Movement** once that organization was founded. Onuoha taught at the Institute of Management and Technology in Enugu for twenty-five years.

In his capacity as a critic of the church, he was subjected to criticism for his troubles. His book *The Land and People of Umuchieze* (2003) outlines the beliefs of his people and is strongly critical of many church practices and beliefs. In line with other critics, he is critical of the attitudes of dependence and passivity many of the Western Evangelical churches encourage.

OPEN CONSPIRACY, THE. A term given by **H. G. Wells** to his attempt at creating a groundswell of popular opinion in favor of world government and planetary cooperation and planning. The idea was articulated principally in his two works, *The Open Conspiracy: Blueprints for a World Revolution* (1928) and *What Are We To Do with Our Lives?* (1931). Unknown to Wells, the term had already been used by **Arnold Ruge**, the German thinker and popularizer of the concept of **humanism**.

OPEN SOCIETY. A phrase made known by **Karl Popper** in his book, *The Open Society and Its Enemies* (1945), one of the most influential philosophical works of the twentieth century. Popper defined an open society as one where the individual is presented with personal decisions. Developing this theme, an open society is based on the recognition that nobody has a monopoly on **truth**. If nobody has a monopoly on the truth, it follows that different people have different views and interests, and that there is a need for institutions to protect the rights of all people to allow them to live together in peace.

An open society must by definition be a **democracy** where the rule of law is transparent and reliable. Dominant political or religious dogmas, before which minorities are expected to submit, are antithetical to an open society. See the entries on **civil society** and the **Kansei Edict**.

Further reading: Karl Popper, *The Open Society and Its Enemies*.

OPEN SOCIETY INSTITUTE. Living proof that ideas have consequences. Founded by **George Soros**, the Open Society Institute is inspired by **Karl Popper**'s notion of an **open society**. Soros, a Hungarian-born capitalist and humanist, founded this philanthropic foundation in 1993. The institute is one of several such foundations founded by Soros, which are active in more than fifty countries. Based primarily in the former communist countries, but also in Africa, Latin America, and Asia, it helps fund a range of programs focusing on civil society, education, media, public health, and human **rights** as well as social, legal, and economic reform. In 2003 the institute and other Soros foundations had spent a total of about $400 million annually to support projects in these and other focus areas. It has its main offices in New York and Budapest. It would be difficult to find a clearer example of **planetary humanism** in action.

OPIUM OF THE PEOPLE. One of the most famous lines in the history of the criticism of religion. It was written by Karl Marx (1818–1883) in *Contribution to Hegel's Philosophy of Right* (1844). The passage reads: "Religion is the sigh of the oppressed creature, the sentiment of a heartless world, and the soul of soulless conditions. It is the opium of the people." In making this criticism, Marx noted that the "abolition of religion as the illusory happiness of men is a demand for their real happiness." Marx's article appeared in a journal that came out only once, during his brief period of cooperation with **Arnold Ruge**.

However, the narcotic analogy was not new to Marx. It went back to **Baron d'Holbach** in 1767. And **Ludwig Feuerbach** spoke of the opiate of religion in his book on **Pierre Bayle** in 1838. Only a year later the German writer Heinrich Heine (1797–1856) expanded on the opium idea when he wrote: "Heaven was invented for people who no longer expect anything from earth . . . Hail this invention! Hail to the religion that poured into mankind's bitter chalice a few, sweet, narcotic drops, spiritual opium, drops of love, hope, and faith." And in 1841 the German theologian Bruno Bauer (1809–1882) spoke of the "opium-like haze" of religion.

The religion-as-opium argument works on the recognition of religion deriving its power by providing illusory consolations to otherwise powerless and disenfranchised people. By succumbing to the **transcendental temptation**, people have abrogated responsibility for their own lives and deferred real power to others.

OPUS DEI. A secret Roman Catholic fraternity. Founded in 1928 by a Vincentian priest, Fr. Josemaria Escriva de Balaguer (1902–1975), Opus Dei (Work of God) was established as a countermeasure to the perceived threat of Freemasonry. Opus Dei is strongly Marian in flavor and is reactionary and secretive. In the atmosphere of post–civil war Spain, Opus Dei thrived. In 1943 the organization inaugurated an inner order called the Sacerdotal Society of the Holy Cross, which was, and remains, an invitation-only gathering of influential politicians and clergymen. General Franco (1892–1975), the fascist dictator of Spain from 1939 until his death, relied heavily on Opus Dei members, and the organization held its most significant positions in Franco's administration. Opus Dei also became influential in South America, where it owned television and radio stations and had members in successive Argentinian governments. Opus Dei was involved in the military junta of 1971.

Opus Dei enjoyed the patronage of John Paul II, who was responsible for Escriva's rapid beatification in 1992, despite strong opposition. John Paul also gave Opus Dei the canonical status of a "personal prelature," thus making it clear that the organization had his support. These moves have strengthened the conservative forces within the Catholic Church.

ORIENTALISM. An academic bone of contention that achieved prominence after Edward Said's book *Orientalism* (1978) that accused Western scholars of looking at all non-Western societies through the filter of their imperialist worldview. Since then "Orientalism" has become a standard term of abuse (ranking alongside "essentialism") among postmodernists and others anxious to despise everything Western. The Orientalist fad has given a tremendous boost to the pseudodiscipline of postcolonial studies, which shares with **theology** or **psychoanalysis** the weakness of having an original premise no one is encouraged to question. In postcolonial studies, the original, unquestionable thesis is that all colonialism is wrong and all colonials wicked. In contrast to this **dogmatism**, genuinely academic disciplines include the responsibility to question original premises.

There have, moreover, always been problems with the sweeping generalizations made by Said (1935–2003) and his followers. Contrary to the standard orientalist line, many of the scholars now deemed orientalist acquired their interest in Asian cultures not from imperialist arrogance but because of their disillusionment or even disgust at the materialism and philistinism they perceived as the dominant values of Europe. And as Charles Allen has shown in *The Search for the Buddha*, the contributions made by European scholars in the nineteenth century have been absolutely indispensable in recovering some very important strands of Buddhist history and thought. For example, Dr. T. W. Rhys Davids (1843–1922) and his wife Caroline Rhys Davids (1858–1942) made invaluable contributions to the growing understanding of Buddhism in the West in the twentieth centuries. For another example, see the entry on **Omar Khayyam**.

Another standard prejudice among supporters of the Orientalism thesis is that rationalists and humanists are particularly vulnerable to the crime of Orientalism. In actual fact, rationalists have frequently warned against Orientalism. To take one example among many, in 1916 **Joseph McCabe** wrote, "We set up a fictitious 'Oriental imagination,' and try to make the Orientals live down to it." His career it peppered with warm appreciations of Chinese and Japanese cultures, not infrequently at the expense of estranging his popular audiences. See the entry on **Occidentosis**. Few scholars now take the Orientalism thesis as presented by Said seriously.

Further reading: Ibn Warraq, "Debunking Edward Said," http://www.secularism.org/articles/debunking.htm.

ORIGIN OF SPECIES, THE. One of the most influential books of the modern era. The book (full title: *On the Origin of Species by Means of Natural Selection, or The Preservation of Favored Races in the Struggle for Life*) was published on November 24, 1859, after more than twenty years of close scientific research and thinking. Every one of the 1,250 copies of the first edition sold out on the first day. **Charles Darwin** had been gathering research for this book for twenty years, but when he heard from Alfred Russel Wallace (1823–1913), then working in Borneo, who had arrived at similar solutions, Darwin was motivated to speed up work on his proposed book. Darwin and Wallace avoided an unseemly conflict over priority by presenting their findings jointly to the Linnaean Society in 1858.

Origin of Species had two main functions. On the one hand, Darwin set himself the task of giving evidence for the historical fact of **evolution** as the cause of the origin of species. In this he was overwhelmingly successful. On the other hand, he made the case for **natural selection** as the vehicle by which evolution takes place. Here his case was solid but not overwhelming. The main weakness in Darwin's argument was his complete ignorance of genetics.

These weaknesses notwithstanding, *The Origin of Species* is a masterpiece of scientific reasoning. It confronted the human race with the second of its great demotions from **anthropocentric conceit**. Where the Copernican revolution had removed *Homo sapiens* from being the center of the universe, the Darwinian revolution dethroned humans from their privileged position in the **great chain of being**. See the entry on **heliocentric universe**.

ORIGINAL SIN. One of the most deeply rooted and influential Christian concepts, even though the scriptural support for it is weak. Hinted at in the writings of Paul, the idea was first mooted by **Ireneaus**, Bishop of Lyon, in his struggle against the **heretics** of his day. Original sin was given its most systematic treatment by St. Augustine (354–430 CE). The dogma of original sin has never been as influential in the Orthodox Christian countries as it is in the West.

The dogma of original sin says that all people are inherently sinful, by virtue of the choice made by Eve and condoned by Adam to eat from the tree of knowledge of good and evil in the garden of Eden. By disobeying an order from **God** not to eat from that tree, Adam and Eve were expelled from Eden and

brought death, misery, and an ineradicable evil upon all mankind. Original sin is said to weigh so heavily upon us that it compromises our ability to reason clearly and honestly.

The bleakness and misanthropy of the idea of original sin has become something of an embarrassment to many Christian theologians, and attempts have been made to allegorize the story away. But Christianity needs original sin, or else there would be no need for the death of the son of God on the cross to redeem the sinful by believing in him. Once the death of Jesus becomes pointless, the whole Christian story collapses. See the entry on **anthropodicy**.

Original sin is one of many ideas that cannot survive intact after contact with scientific thinking—in this case **evolution**. In evolutionary thinking, there is no place for a **soul**, or a time when *Homo sapiens* were all fitted with one. Through **natural selection** humans have acquired a range of behaviors, some of which are unattractive, but many of which are noble. There is little room for accommodation between the theological view and the scientific view on this question, and to that extent it is reasonable to speak of a **conflict between science and religion**.

OUSPENSKY, PETER DAMIAN (1878–1947). Russian-born mathematician, mystic, and eccentric. He was originally a disciple of **Gurdjieff**, but broke with him in 1924.

Widely read in **Theosophy**, Ouspensky wrote a series of works that blended **Kant**, notions of sacred geometry, Theosophy, Sufism, and elements of Buddhism. He adapted **Nietzsche**'s theory of the **eternal recurrence** with notions of **reincarnation** to claim we have lived our lives before and will live them again, forever, unless we can break out of this ceaseless pattern. His most popular work was *Tertium Organum*, which, in theosophical style, tried to blend Eastern and Western thought, as he conceived them.

OUTSIDER, THE. A term coined by the English writer Colin Wilson and used as the title of a very successful book in 1956. The outsider, as Wilson conceived him, was the person excluded from normal society, not by virtue of some defect or social stigma, although he may have those as well. The outsider had this status by virtue of seeing through the vacuity, conformism, and emptiness of societal norms. The outsider was something of an existential hero, a **rebel**. Where the bourgeois conformist saw only order, rationality, and hierarchy, the outsider saw the truth of chaos and dark ambitions.

The idea of the outsider had a certain vogue for the better part of two decades. But as its inherent **romanticism** became more apparent it died an unlamented death. Wilson's notion of the outsider was a new take on **Rousseau**'s noble savage idea, with the savage brought into the city. Wilson's idea lacked the intellectual or emotional depth of the rebel as conceived by **Albert Camus**.

Further reading: Colin Wilson, *The Outsider*.

OVERBELIEF. The capacity we all have to hold positive illusions about ourselves, in particular about our abilities. To take a trivial example, most of us believe our driving abilities are above the average, and these beliefs are held consistently, even among people with long records of driving accidents. People also tend to hold overbeliefs about their self-worth and their ability to change things for the better.

The evolutionary advantages of these overbeliefs are obvious. People who have overbeliefs about their ability to handle **stress** are often better able to cope when faced with stressful situations. Overbelievers are more likely to take manageable risks, or to engage in constructive problem solving. Overbelief can of course spill over into megalomania and self-defeating arrogance, which is why rationality is so important as a counterbalance to our built-in ability to deceive ourselves. The opposite of overbelief is, not surprisingly, underbelief, the capacity of

holding unreasonably negative opinions about our abilities.

OVERLAPPING CONSENSUS. An idea conceived by the American political philosopher **John Rawls**. Overlapping consensus refers to the existence in most societies of several competing comprehensive religious, political, moral, and social views of the world, each with their own notions of right and wrong and the limits of **toleration**. What Rawls wanted was to establish a **well-ordered society** in which competing groups could live in harmony together.

Overlapping consensus is a goal to be reached: it is not a mere *modus vivendi* in lieu of an apparently genuine national consensus. Overlapping consensus rejects the idea of society being dominated by a single, overarching consensus. Neither does an overlapping consensus imply indifference to the various comprehensive doctrines competing in society.

What the overlapping consensus seeks is that partisans of the many competing religious and philosophical worldviews accept the same basis of public justification in matters of justice, on the basis of their otherwise different and competing worldviews.

OVERMAN, THE. A conception of the German philosopher **Friedrich Nietzsche**, and one of the more controversial ideas of modern philosophy. And not by any means a humanist concept. The word in German is *Übermensch*, which used to be translated as "superman," but the notion of heroes in capes and underpants cannot help but creep in to a word like this. The better translation is "overman."

Contrary to common portrayal, the overman is not an outstanding individual, military leader, or philosophical or artistic genius. Rather, the overman is a metaphor, even a proposal, for the future of humanity—a humanity that can transcend the shackles of dualistic and conformist moralities. The overman is the sort of person who is reconciled to the truth of the **eternal recurrence** without descending into complete madness at the prospect.

The overman concept can be found mainly in Nietzsche's poetic classic, *Thus Spake Zarathustra* (1886), but he neglected the idea after that because his interest moved on to the notion of the **will to power** being exercised by the superior man, usually in the form of dominating the weak and powerless. This new emphasis left little room for a generalized type of humanity that has transcended existing limitations.

Nietzsche's notion of the overman spawned a great number of imitations, most of them unhelpful. While most of them, like the Nazi ideal of the blond beast, involved some form of misreading of Nietzsche's work, they also captured elements of his ideas quite accurately. The overman was an important influence in Abraham Maslow's conception of self-actualization in **humanistic psychology**.

Further reading: Ofelia Schutte, *Beyond Nihilism: Nietzsche without Masks.*

OVERPOPULATION. Still the most pressing problem of the twenty-first century. First discussed systematically by **Thomas Malthus**, the question of population remains one that many people prefer to ignore or deny. It took two million years for the world's population to reach a billion in 1825; it then took a century to reach the second billion, thirty-five years for the next billion, fifteen for the next billion, twelve or so years for the next, and a decade for the next. In the decade 1980–1990, world population increased by about 923 million. Forecasts are now talking of a world population of eleven billion by the middle of the twenty-first century.

Overpopulation is caused not only by more babies being born, but by more babies surviving, and more elderly living much longer than was ever the case traditionally. The main reason more people survive is that many infectious diseases have been conquered, or at least kept at bay.

It is true that there is still enough food to feed the world's population, but this ignores the fact that the world's population goes hungry because of unequal food distribution. The problem is not simply that there are too many people, but that the ecological cost of feeding, housing, and finding employment for so many people is beyond the capacity of the earth to provide. In many countries the water table has dropped significantly, raising fears of drastic water shortages and even water wars. See the entries on **ecological footprint** and **water**.

The nature of overpopulation has changed over the past few decades. A feature of the overpopulation threat is its regional concentration. Some parts of the world, notably Japan and Europe are likely to experience not merely a slackening in population growth by the middle of the twenty-first century, but a positive decline. Japan, in particular, is looking at a potentially disastrous population decline over the next half-century. And once the **baby boomers** have shuffled off the mortal coil by the 2030s or so, Europe may also experience an actual decline in population.

But it is far too early to become complacent. At the start of the twenty-first century, half the world's population growth was in six countries: India, China, Indonesia, Pakistan, Nigeria, and Bangladesh. The ecological and political consequences of further growth in these already overcrowded countries are dire. Increasing strain will be put on fragile ecosystems to feed, house, and clothe these people. A significant population bulge has also been detected in Muslim countries in North Africa and the Middle East. The emerging baby boomers of these societies are helping feed the mood of militant **Islamism** and even **terrorism**.

And the irony is that the solution to overpopulation is relatively simple, in principle at least. It is a simple fact that the two best ways to reduce birth rates is to improve women's education and employment. This will inevitably mean that many traditional and religious attitudes toward women and birth control must change. Prosperity and freedom for women are not merely good in themselves; they can also save the planet. This is not, of course, the same as advocating unrestricted economic growth across the planet. We are all going to need to adjust our understanding of prosperity in the century ahead. **Affluenza** is not the same as prosperity. See the entry on **sexual and reproductive rights**.

OWEN, ROBERT (1771–1858). Along with **Thomas Paine**, the most extensive influence for **freethought** in the first half of the nineteenth century. Owen's style of freethought involved not so much a criticism of dogma but, in the words of **J. M. Robertson**, "a calm impeachment of **religion** in a spirit of philanthropy." Criticism of religion was not Owen's main theme, though. His main theme was a generalized critique of laissez-faire capitalism on economic and moral grounds.

Owen rejected any variety of supernatural religion as a teenager after reading the **Stoic** philosopher **Seneca**. But the turning point in Owen's life was a public meeting in 1817 when he spoke of the "gross errors that have been combined with the fundamental notions of every religion that has hitherto been taught to men." From then on Owen was branded a freethinker and earned the undying hostility of much of the clergy and the upper classes. Through most of his most creative years Owen was agnostic.

He passionately advocated a system of communal living that would protect people from the brutality of the world, and in particular of capitalist exploitation. Working to improve the environment in which people live, especially children, was the focus of his work. In the face of strong opposition from businessmen and churchmen, Owen transformed a factory setting at New Lanark in Scotland to a model of planning and welfare. He stopped employing children under ten years of age, providing them with nursery care instead. And older children took part of the day off to attend school. Within years the drunken workforce was won over by the obvious improvements in the quality of their lives. Productivity went up too. **Jeremy Bentham** cooperated with Owen in the New Lanark project.

This was the only major practical experiment established by Owen that succeeded. His main gifts were providing the moral vision to inspire others rather than serving as practical organizer himself. After his death Owenism broke up into two movements: the cooperative movement and the **secularist** movement. Owen's book *A New View of Society* (1816) was also very influential. Among its suggestions included universal education and trained teachers, a ban on child labor, poor law and prison law reform, discouraging gambling, and reform of the church. It was under Owen's influence that Sir Robert Peel (1788–1850) drafted legislation to abolish child labor in Britain.

One of Owen's less-celebrated legacies can be traced in the garden-city idea. In the late 1870s, George Cadbury, a prominent Quaker and heir to the business empire of that name, transferred his plant out of Birmingham to a planned, suburban setting he called Bournville. This community was reminiscent of New Lanark. Every worker owned his own home, the children went to school rather than work, and standards of sanitation were high. Led by Ebenezer Howard, the garden-city movement was known throughout England before World War I. After World War II, the newly elected Labour government launched enthusiastically into the creation of planned garden cities as a means of easing congestion in London and introducing people to a cleaner, brighter life.

P

PAGANISM. A collective name given to every possible pre-Christian belief and practice, ranging from simple **superstitions**, folk beliefs, tribal deities, and on to sophisticated non-Christian religions. In this way, primitive beliefs about fertility are lumped in with obtuse **Neoplatonist** philosophy as being pagan. This is to serve as a warning that paganism is a notoriously vague term, which has traditionally been used as a catchall term of abuse and, more recently, has taken on a similarly catchall chic. It has become fashionable to associate paganism with more ecologically friendly attitudes, although this ignores the long history of animal and even human sacrifice among many pagan religions.

The decisive downfall of classical paganism can be dated to 384 CE, in the wake of a series of discriminatory legislation by the Christian Roman emperors Gratian and, even more so, **Theodosius**.

PAIDEIA. One of the foundational concepts of **humanism**. The term comes from classical Greek philosophy and is derived from the Greek word *pais* or *paides*, which translated literally, means "boy," but in its broader meaning can be defined as "education for responsible citizenship." It was understood by the Greeks that this sort of education was an effective democracy. *Paideia* had four characteristics:

- it offered a unified and systematic account of human knowledge;
- it provided a technique of reading and disputation based upon mastery of language and intellectual precision;
- it worked on the assumption that the human personality can be improved by education; and
- it valued the qualities of persuasion and leadership as important qualities for the vital task to taking part in public affairs.

The ideals of *paideia* were imitated by the Romans, from which the Latin word *humanitas* is derived. See the entry on **eupraxsophy**.

Further reading: Alan Bullock, *The Humanist Tradition in the West*.

PAINE, THOMAS (1737–1809). Journalist, campaigner, and prophet of the modern world, and, in the tradition of prophets, one without honor in his own land. Paine was born in Thetford, Norfolk, the son of a Quaker father and Anglican mother. Coming from a poor family, Paine's formal education was negligible. At thirteen he began work in his father's corset-making workshop and at sixteen he ran away to sea. As a young man he worked as a tax collector, which gave him ample insight into the injustices of the system, in particular, the plight of the Jews, who were obliged to pay taxes and yet were denied the right to vote. Paine became active in radical circles and soon lost his job as a tax collector. On the recommendation of **Benjamin Franklin**, Paine moved to America in 1774, where he immediately felt at home amidst the political ferment then dominating the colonies.

Paine's seminal contribution to the American revolution came in the form of his writings, in particular *Common Sense* and *The American Crisis*, both of which appeared in 1776. *Common Sense* caught the mood of the American people at the crucial time in the Revolution, selling more than 500,000 copies in the 1770s alone. Paine earned nothing from his bestseller, preferring instead that people read his words rather than fill his coffers. *Common Sense* argued that government is the delegation of power for the benefit of society at large. *The American Crisis* came out at a low period of the Revolutionary War and had an important galvanizing effect on flagging spirits, especially among the soldiers. George Washington (1732–1799) had *The American Crisis* read to his shivering soldiers on Christmas Eve of 1776, on the eve of a crucial engagement with the enemy. The only issue Paine misread was the question of **slavery**. Unlike most of his contemporaries, Paine did not exempt the African slaves from the promise of freedom. He was instrumental in the state of Pennsylvania's abolition of slavery in 1780, the first place in the world to do so.

With freedom won in America, Paine returned to England in 1787, in time to be embroiled in the French Revolution. Once again, Paine's extraordinary contribution came in the form of his writing. His next major book, *Rights of Man*, part 1 of which was endorsed by **Thomas Jefferson**, appeared in 1791 and part 2 the following year, after Paine had fled England to France. *Rights of Man* was written in a matter-of-fact way to highlight the histrionics that Edmund Burke had employed in *Reflections on the Revolution in France* (1790). *Rights of Man* broke every existing publishing record and remained relevant until the twentieth century. It was read aloud to the illiterate, expanding its influence. It remains a landmark on the development of the idea of **rights**.

In France, Paine also worked tirelessly for the cause of popular emancipation. But his innate sense of justice got him in trouble because he opposed the execution of the king. Paine was thrown in prison, being accused of being a traitor to France. His reputation in the United States had already declined after *Rights of Man* appeared there, but his next major work, *Age of Reason* (1794–95) substantially damaged his reputation in America. No longer welcome in France or England, Paine returned to America in 1802 at the invitation of Thomas Jefferson, by then president of the United States. There he lived out the rest of life in poverty and isolation.

Paine's legacy has been extraordinary. He was a spokesperson for emancipation from tyranny, in whatever form it takes. His condemnation of tyranny and oppression was bolder than Karl Marx's and his practical proposals to alleviate poverty were more cognizant of the complexities of life and society than Marx was able to muster. Paine was one of the first to detect the dishonest motives behind the calls made by those in power to speak on behalf of "the people." And contrary to the slanders of priests and apologists, Paine was not an atheist but a Deist. *Age of Reason* was written to defend his notion of God from the vulgarity and superstition of the anthropomorphic God of the Bible.

Further reading: John Keane, *Tom Paine: A Political Life*.

PALMER, ELIHU (1764–1806). A tempestuous American religious radical. Less well known than **Thomas Paine**, Palmer deserves comparison with the equally flamboyant **Charles Southwell**. Palmer was born in Canterbury, Connecticut, and trained for the church, a profession for which he was distinctly unsuited, for Palmer was not given to circumlocution or timidity of expression.

His public career began as a Presbyterian minister in Queens, where he lasted less than a year. He then moved to a Baptist church in Philadelphia, where he lasted no longer than in his earlier appointment. Palmer then declared himself a Universalist, although it quickly transpired he was too radical even for this generally tolerant sect. By 1791 he was a convinced **Deist**. His options as a Christian minister exhausted, Palmer studied law, but unwisely chose to set up practice in Philadelphia, where he had so recently scandalized so many people with his radical views. An epidemic of yellow fever that swept through the city killed his wife and left him blind for the rest of his life. His legal career now at an end, he became an itinerant lecturer of Deism before taking up with the Deistical Society of New York in 1797.

While in New York, he published two Deist newspapers, *Temple of Reason* and *Prospect, or View of the Moral World*. He also dictated a book, *Principles of Nature; or, A Development of the Moral Causes of Happiness and Misery Among the Human Species* (1801), which sold very widely. Unlike many Deists (**Anthony Collins** or **Benjamin Franklin** come to mind), Palmer wrote for readers of modest station. This fact alone was enough to worry the guardians of conventional morality. *Principles of Nature* was reprinted and sold in England thanks to the courageous **Richard Carlile**. After Palmer's death, his widowed second wife was saved from destitution by **Thomas Paine**, then in grave financial straits himself.

PANENTHEISM. A term devised to distinguish itself from **pantheism**. Whereas pantheism is the state where everything is **God**, panentheism is the more theological notion that everything is *in* God. The word was coined by the German philosopher Karl Krause (1781–1832) to act as a middle ground between pantheism and theism.

Panentheism was an attempt to escape the naturalistic implications of pantheism without falling back into conventional theism, which maintained a strict distance between God and humanity. If everything is in God, this allows room for God to still be more than the sum of all its parts. And into this state have entered many theologians, anxious to fill in all the blanks.

PANSPERMIA. The thesis that life reached planet Earth from deep space. The idea behind the panspermia hypothesis is ancient, being traceable back to **Anaxagoras**. But the modern, more scientifically sophisticated version was broached by the physicist **Fred Hoyle** and the Sri Lankan astronomer Chandra Wickramasinghe. Comets, meteorites, and space dust seem capable of carrying amino acids which, after impact on earth, find the warm, moist atmosphere highly congenial. Critics of panspermia say that it doesn't help with the fundamental question of the origin of life; all it does it push the problem out into space.

PANSY. The flower used to symbolize **freethought**. This is because "pansy" derives from the French word "pensée," or "thought." Pansies are also notable for their facelike flower. It is thought the tradition began in Europe and was picked up in the United States in the 1880s or 1890s. It is possible that the tradition of associating the pansy with thought is quite old. **William Shakespeare** has his character Ophelia say "And there is pansies, that's for thoughts" (*Hamlet*, 4.5).

Further reading: Annie Laurie Gaylor, "A Pansy for Your Thoughts," *Freethought Today* (June/July 1997).

PANTHEISM. The doctrine that humanity and nature are not independent from **God**, but

are parts of God's all-inclusive being. The word was invented in 1705 by the religious radical John Toland (1670–1722) and literally means "the All is God." Toland's most concentrated use of the word was in his book *Pantheisticon* (1720).

Though the word is relatively recent, the concept has been around for centuries, being observable in elements of Hinduism and in **Pre-Socratic** philosophy. The most sophisticated articulation of pantheism can be found in the works of **Giordano Bruno** and **Baruch Spinoza**. Christian theologians have always been suspicious of pantheism, because they recognize it as a stepping-stone to **atheism**. More mystically inclined thinkers have preferred the concept of **panentheism**. The faults with pantheism were expressed most succinctly by **Arthur Schopenhauer**, who said that saying the world is God explains nothing, but serves only "to enrich language with a superfluous synonym of the word 'world.'"

PARADIGM. Once a word confined to linguists, since the publication of Thomas Kuhn's (1922–1996) influential work, *The Structure of Scientific Revolutions* (1962), the notion of "paradigm" has become part of everyday language. Kuhn spoke of paradigms in terms of governing sets of principles that tend to settle into orthodoxy until such time as they become manifestly unable to explain events. At which time they are swept away by the next revolution in ideas. The classic example is the fundamental shift in physics brought about by Einstein's discovery of the theory of **relativity**.

The notion of a paradigm has filtered into popular language, with people speaking of a "paradigm shift," by which they mean a very significant movement of opinion. Kuhn has also been used by **postmodernists** and proponents of a bogus discipline known as the sociology of science, especially its most extreme form, called the **strong program**. Kuhn has been taken by these groups to have shown that there is no **progress** in **science**.

These criticisms do a serious injustice to Kuhn, particularly in view of his later corrections and clarifications, when he spoke less about paradigms. Other critics have noted that the paradigm notion of science overstates the unity of science, and understates its prolific and untidy dynamism.

If the paradigm notion overstates the case, it is valid to observe that science has built up a massive body of **knowledge** and is understandably reluctant to shed large sections of it each time the trumpets herald some supposed new breakthrough. Slightly tongue-in-cheek, the American psychologist Arthur S. Reber called this the Principle of Psychological Inertia. This inertia is not peculiar to science, all bodies of thought develop it. And occasionally it results in conflict between the conservative guardians of the current knowledge and the young turks. But the point the critics of science miss is that, sooner or later, the side that is right wins the day. And that is not something that can be said for all bodies of thought.

PARADISE SPELL. A term used by the American columnist David Brooks to describe what he means by the "American dream." It is, Brooks says, the "controlling ideology of American life." Many societies have creation myths but in the Paradise Spell, Americans have a fruition myth. The Paradise Spell is the tendency to see the present from the vantage point of the future. **Peace of mind**, so the Paradise Spell goes, is just around the corner. Once I get that raise, buy that **Hummer**, have that born-again experience, attend that motivational lecture series, get on that reality TV program, relocate to the South, or whatever it is—*then* I will have reached my paradise and will have achieved **happiness**.

The Paradise Spell has a wider application too. Once the moral regeneration program I am participating in, once the enemy (apply to taste) are out of government; once the Rapture takes place—*then* we will all have reached paradise. But until then I must continue to consume, preach, berate, and gener-

ally live a restless, discontented life. The Paradise Spell is a by-product of the emptiness of **affluenza**. For an interesting parallel, see the entry on **adamics**.

PARALLEL THEOLOGY. Name given to the large body of literature that set out to criticize one system of belief by criticizing a parallel system. This practice was widespread in seventeenth- and eighteenth-century Europe, although it can be detected in many authoritarian systems even today. When freethinkers wanted to criticize Christianity, they would often disguise their work as a criticism of "heathenism" or Islam. This was done to protect the author from the harsh laws that punished any sort of criticism of Christianity.

More recently this practice has been called theological lying, by the British historian of atheism, David Berman. Theological lying is Berman's term for the sort of dissimulation forced upon freethinkers who risked their lives by writing their real thoughts. It is an unfortunate term, as it casts a shadow over freethinkers who face stern legal dangers to expressing themselves openly, as **Thomas Aitkenhead** found to his cost. Theological lying is detectable by three main techniques:

- *protecting* oneself by conventional declarations of piety;
- *communicating* one's true position to discerning readers; and
- *insinuating* one's position to the undiscerning readers.

Berman notes that each technique was directed toward different readers. The protecting passages were directed toward the authorities; the communicating passages to fellow freethinkers; and the insinuating passages to open-minded believers and the unwary. Prime examples of parallel theology/theological lying would be the works of Charles Blount (1654–1693) and John Toland (1670–1722), two English freethinkers widely thought to be Deists, but who Berman argues were in fact atheists. Other examples would be Conyers Middleton (1683–1750) who was almost certainly a Deist, and not the Christian he claimed to be.

Theological lying is not peculiar to Christian Europe. Undemocratic societies from time immemorial have forced freethinking people to resort to some form of dissimulation. "Theological lying" is an unfortunate term for this practice, because it implies a want of honesty on the part of the heterodox writers, and not on the society which requires such practices if one is to escape persecution.

Further reading: David Berman, "Disclaimers as offence Mechanisms in Charles Blount and John Toland," in Michael Hunter and David Wootton, eds., *Atheism from the Reformation to the Enlightenment.*

PARANATURAL. A term coined by **Paul Kurtz** in 2000 to illustrate the fact that **naturalism** is normative. In the way that **paranormal** refers to what is beside or **beyond** what is normal, so paranatural is beside and beyond what is natural. It is an axiom of philosophy that the **burden of proof** lies with those making the larger claim. Thus, those claiming some sort of paranatural condition, such as life after death or **miracles**, have the burden of proof to provide evidence why the natural explanation should, in this instance, be rejected. In point of fact, Kurtz argues that any "para" arguments, whether paranormal or paranatural, are little more than substitutes for our ignorance. See the entry on **skepticism, core principles of**.

Further reading: Paul Kurtz, ed., *Science and Religion: Are They Compatible?*

PARANORMAL. The term given to that which is held to exist beside or **beyond** what is normal. Supporters of the paranormal believe that there exist conditions, properties, and agents which cannot be explained by the standards of conventional science, but can be explained by some other means. Unlike breakthroughs in conventional science, paranormal "discoveries" usually come about by flashes of inspiration by people without any

special training in the relevant branches of **science**. Similarly, the reports of paranormal phenomena are almost always by way of anecdote and are thus not open to repetition or refutation. In this way, claims of the paranormal are not scientific claims.

Many aspects of paranormal phenomena such as ESP, precognition, or telepathy require a transmission of energy to the brain from elsewhere, but no such medium has ever been shown to exist. Transmission of information can only take place when elementary particles interact with each other. With ESP and other forms of "extrasensory" communication, no credible explanation has been given for how such interaction could possibly take place. The paranormal is a **pseudoscience**. See the entry on **skepticism, core principles of**.

PARAPSYCHOLOGY. A **pseudoscience** that purports to study mental phenomena not explainable by conventional **science**. Phenomena include telepathy, clairvoyance, prophecy, ESP, and so on. Parapsychology is a pseudoscience because it has not succeeded in producing any honestly arrived at and repeatable results that have stood scrutiny of scientists. See the entry on **occult arts**.

In the United States, the National Research Council undertook a two-year study of the claims of parapsychology and concluded in 1988 that there is no worthwhile evidence for any claims of parapsychology. In Britain some dramatic evidence for parapsychology was given by **George Soal**, but his figures were discovered after his death to have been tampered with. See the entry on **skepticism, core principles of**.

Further reading: Paul Kurtz, ed., *The Skeptic's Handbook on Parapsychology.*

PARIKH, DR. INDUMATI (1918–2004). Outstanding Indian leader. It is one of the ironies of contemporary life that Mother Teresa (1910–1997), whose charitable activities in India were minimal at best, is lionized around the world as the embodiment of virtue, while Indumati Parikh, whose record of achievement was incomparably greater, is unknown outside India.

In 1964, alarmed by the burgeoning population in their city of Bombay (now Mumbai), Dr. Parikh and her husband sold their home in the affluent part of the city and moved to the slums, where she established Streehitakarini, a self-help organization dedicated to providing the women of the slums with contraceptives and advice on contraception. Streehitakarini soon expanded into a range of activities related to women's health and education. Acknowledging the influence of the great Indian humanist **M. N. Roy**, Dr. Parikh always sought to work *with* the women of Mumbai, rather than *for* them.

Dr. Parikh was an active humanist, serving as president of the **Indian Radical Humanist Association** since 1986. She was also a laureate of the **International Academy of Humanism**. In 1992 she took an active part in calming religious tensions in Mumbai, after the destruction of the mosque in **Ayodhya**. Speaking about her beliefs, Dr. Parikh described humanism as "the only ideology that would cut across boundaries and help men and women to understand their basic humanness."

PARMENIDES (510s–460s BCE, approx.). An important though eccentric Greek philosopher. As with most **Pre-Socratic** philosophers, we know very little about Parmenides except that he lived in Elea, a Greek city on the southern shores of Italy. Parmenides was unusual in that he wrote his philosophy in verse—the *Way of Truth*, of which quite a lot has survived, and *Way of Seeming*, of which little has survived.

Like **Heraclitus**, Parmenides explored the interconnection of things, but from a radically different perspective. Parmenides thought everything was eternal and uncreated because it doesn't make any sense to conceive of that which is not. This means we can only speak sensibly of that which is. It also means nothing ever changes.

The problem with all this is that it is clearly untrue, because we can think about things that do not exist: aliens, leprechauns, and so on. Nevertheless, Parmenides is important because he supplied **Plato** with the idea that truly valuable things must be truly unchanging things. And Parmenides' other great service was to inspire his pupil, Zeno (not to be confused with Zeno of Citium, the founder of **Stoicism**), who devised some fiendishly clever paradoxes that were designed to defend his mentor's ideas. They didn't succeed in that, but they have retained their value as philosophical puzzles to the present day.

PARSIMONY, PRINCIPLE OF. See **OCKHAM'S RAZOR**.

PASCAL'S WAGER. An argument for the existence of **God** still popular with many religious apologists. The best-known variation of this argument comes from Blaise Pascal (1623–1662), although it was around before him, possibly coming originally from Muslim theologians. The argument concedes that nothing can be known about God using human reason, but Pascal went on to say that it is nonetheless sensible to believe in God, because if God and Christianity are true, then the believer enjoys eternity in heaven as a reward, but if it is false, nothing has been lost, because we all end up dead anyway.

Pascal's Wager is surprisingly popular among religious apologists, despite the unflattering light it shines on the motivations for religious belief. It is one of the most blatant forms of **anthropocentric conceit**, because not only does it presume the cosmos is here for our eternal delectation, but it trivializes religious commitment to being merely a safe bet. Neither does Pascal's Wager help with respect to which God is paramount. A Christian might resort to Pascal's Wager to argue for the rationality for his faith, but he can't use it for proof that the God he has faith in is the Christian God.

Humanism operates along quite different lines. In contradistinction to Pascal's Wager, humanism acknowledges our irrelevance in the grand scheme of things, and on the basis of this **cosmic modesty**, builds up an outlook on life that rejects the **transcendental temptation**, and fashions a life replete with meaning and joy in full knowledge that our life will end.

PASSES-FOR FALLACY. A term introduced by the British-born American philosopher-scientist Susan Haack. The passes-for fallacy works like this. Many scientific theories have been thought to be **true** but have turned out to be false. In other words the so-called facts underlying these false theories have passed for truth rather than actually being true. From this valid premise many people have leapt to the entirely invalid conclusion that, because these facts proved not to be true, therefore, *all* notions of facts, sound evidence, and honest inquiry are specious.

Haack points out that not only does the conclusion not follow from the premise, if the conclusion were true, the premise could not be true either, thus becoming self-defeating. And yet despite the glaring weakness of this fallacy, it has been very influential among **postmodernists**, supporters of the **strong program**, and other opponents of **science**.

Further reading: Susan Haack, *Defending Science—Within Reason.*

PASSMORE, JOHN (1914–2004). Brilliant Australian philosopher. John Passmore was raised a Catholic but quickly rebelled against the moral consequences of the Christian story. He studied **philosophy** at the University of Sydney and was one of the several important Australian philosophers influenced by **John Anderson**. From 1950 until 1955 he taught philosophy at the University of Otago in New Zealand, before moving to the Australian National University in Canberra. He became professor of philosophy there in 1958 and remained there the rest of his academic career.

Passmore was more than a brilliant man, he also shaped his discipline. Much of what is now called applied philosophy developed under his influence. Reflecting Anderson's influence, Passmore was interested in the larger context in which philosophical ideas play themselves out. His work in applied philosophy surveyed political theory, art, **science**, and, most importantly, the environment. With respect to the environment, Passmore argued strongly that *Homo sapiens* needs to change its attitudes toward the environment, which can lead to the necessary drastic curtailing of our current levels of consumption. But, having said this, Passmore insisted with equal force that we need to do this without adopting flaky **New Age** nostrums about Western **science** and **reason**. Science and reason are essential tools by which we may survive.

Passmore is also responsible for *A Hundred Years of Philosophy* (1957), quite in any way the most learned account of the philosophical developments in the century roughly 1850 to 1950. Other important books are *The Perfectibility of Man* (1970) and *Serious Art* (1991). See the entry on **telic art**.

He received most of his honors due to his contribution and genius. He was corresponding fellow of the British Academy, and honorary foreign member of the Danish and American Academies of Science and Letters, and a founding member of the Australian Academy of the Humanities. In 1987 he was elected a laureate of the **International Academy of Humanism**. Passmore described himself as a "pessimistic humanist" in light of humanity's ongoing capacity for wickedness and stupidity.

PATHETIC FALLACY. A term coined by the English critic John Ruskin (1819–1900) which drew attention to the literary habit of attributing human emotions to nonhuman objects in nature, as in happy sunshine or grim clouds. The crocus, he wrote, is not spendthrift, and only willful fancy can make that true. These literary turns tell us more about the author than of the subject at hand. But Ruskin was not opposed per se to these flourishes. What he wanted to draw our attention to was that we learn about the *author* through them, not about nature, and insofar as it does that, then the pathetic fallacy tells the truth. What the pathetic fallacy does is to allow the writer to dramatize emotions against a larger backdrop than simply oneself. In Ruskin's mind, this was the purpose of art.

In the twentieth century, the pathetic fallacy was given slightly different uses. For instance the writer Llewelyn Powys (1884–1939) wrote *The Pathetic Fallacy* (1930), in which he said:

> The human race has suffered three grave humiliations: when Copernicus showed that the earth was not the center of the universe; when Darwin proved that man's origin was not the result of a direct creation; when Freud explained that man was not the master of his own thoughts and actions. It must endure an increment of ignominy before it will be prepared to temper its demands.

Powys had reinterpreted the pathetic fallacy to now become a protest at humans presuming greater significance for themselves in the universe than the facts would warrant. The pathetic fallacy had been transformed into a call for **cosmic modesty** by resisting the **transcendental temptation** and rejecting **anthropocentric conceit**. Powys's book was quickly taken up the following year by the **Rationalist Press Association** as a title in its influential **Thinker's Library**.

PATRIARCHY. A term important to feminist discourse, but which has never been defined effectively. Patriarchy is usually taken to mean the management of society by, and in the interests of, men. Occasionally this has been taken one step further by seeing patriarchy as the systematic oppression of women. Patriarchy has functioned as a historical, even a **teleological**, vehicle of oppression. It has also been used in the sociological sense as a form of discriminatory social organization.

Some of the more extreme variations of patriarchy, for instance Mary Daly in *Gyn/Ecology* (1979) draws a vivid picture of patriarchy as a planetary conspiracy of men to tyrannize and destroy women physically, psychologically, and spiritually. Women, by contrast, are pure of heart and perennial victims of men's violence. Since then, patriarchy has been subjected to more sober scholarship. In particular, Gerda Lerner has outlined the historical roots of patriarchy and has avoided most of the more extravagant theses of Daly and others. However, it remains a moot point whether there was any specific time in history when predominantly matriarchal societies were replaced by patriarchal systems. What is useful is the warning against patriarchal *attitudes*, and a historical awareness of this form of presumption is valuable.

Further reading: Gerda Lerner, *The Creation of Patriarchy*.

PAUL (1/5–65 CE, approx.). The founder of Christianity. The central pillar of Christian **theology**—the death and resurrection of Jesus—was Paul's work. The traditional story is that Saul, a Hellenized Jew from Tarsus, had a conversion experience on the road to Damascus, changed his name to Paul, and became Jesus Christ's most important disciple. In fact, Paul never met **Rabbi Yeshua**, and expressed little interest in him as a person. Paul's "Jesus Christ" is a construction of his own, which owed little to the actual message of Rabbi Yeshua and contradicted it in important ways. Paul won a victory against the disciples of Yeshua at the **Jerusalem conference** in about 49 CE, a significant milestone in the process of the **creation of Jesus Christ**.

The crucial fact about Paul is that his writings predate the Gospels, and as such, are the earliest writings about Jesus. Most authorities attribute Romans, 1 and 2 Corinthians, Galatians, 1 Thessalonians, and Philemon as genuine products of Paul. There is argument about the status of 2 Thessalonians and Colossians, while few people link Paul to Ephesians and virtually nobody links Paul to any of the other books traditionally attributed to him. The fact that Rabbi Yeshua's message was hijacked so comprehensively by Paul is one of the tragedies of Christianity, and of the world. See the entry on **Jesus Christ, myth theory of**.

The heart of Paul's message was the need to prepare for the imminent return of Jesus Christ and to refocus fractious Christian communities in the face of the delay in Christ's return. But the Jesus Christ Paul spoke of was a concept laden with esoteric (possibly **Gnostic**) ideas about salvation and redemption that had little to do with the straightforward and specifically Jewish message of Rabbi Yeshua.

Paul's fiery exclusivism was dictated by his conviction of the imminent coming of Christ. For instance, he encouraged celibacy not only because he loathed the flesh, but because fleshly matters were held to be of little account in the short time left before the coming of the kingdom. Once it was apparent that the kingdom of God had, for some reason or other, been delayed, Paul's injunctions became a more generalized warning against enjoying life and preparing for afterlife. Either way, it is hard to see what relevance Paul's teachings have two thousand years after the imminent arrival of the kingdom of God has failed to arrive. See the entry on monotheism.

Further reading: Hyam Maccoby, *Mythmaker: Paul and the Invention of Christianity*; and Gerd Lüdemann, *Paul: the Founder of Christianity*.

PEACE OF MIND. A very elusive property. There are so many formulas for the achievement of peace of mind, despite the ancient realization that peace of mind is rarely, if ever, achieved by the slavish devotion to formulas.

For the ancient **skeptics**, the suspension of **judgment** was the key to *ataraxia*, or tranquility. By contrast, the great **Cynic** thinker Diogenes of Sinope (400–325 BCE, approx.) thought that peace of mind comes from stepping out of the conventional rat race, with all its acquisitive goals of more possessions, more money, and promotion. For Diogenes, peace of mind comes through self-reliance, indifference to the world, and freedom from other people. He was also a stern critic of **religion**, seeing its fixation on **death**, enslavement to **superstition**, and support for moral conventions and priestcraft as impediments to peace of mind. While these criticisms are valid, Diogenes' plan to achieve peace of mind is too limited. For most of us, our ties with other people—no matter that they limit our freedom—are the most important feature of our lives, and of our peace of mind. Diogenes said wise things about scorning material possessions and not bowing down to dreary conventions and expectations, but he goes too far when he also prefers us not to bond with others.

For the **Epicureans**, peace of mind involved the absence of pain. This happy state is reached by understanding the demons that lurk to make us miserable in notions like God, death, pleasure, and suffering. By relinquishing all the vain hopes, fancies, and fears that linger in these ideas, we can attain peace of mind. And contrary to the popular misconception, **Epicurus** did not advocate indulgence in animal pleasures as a means to peace of mind. And unlike the Cynics, Epicureans held very great store on the value of friendship as a boon to peace of mind.

For the **Stoics**, peace of mind came when one lived in accordance with nature, which involved wisdom, balance, and temperance (*sophrosyne*). Like the Cynics and Epicureans, the Stoics taught indifference to material possessions and honors, but unlike those groups, Stoics advocated that nonetheless, we should take part in public affairs. We can avoid the hypocrisy and disillusionment that so often attends a public life only if we do so with little regard to the normal inducements of wealth, fame, and honor.

Perhaps the Chinese classic, the *Laozi* (later known as the *Tao te Ching*) puts things best when it says: "There is no crime greater than having too many desires; there is no disaster greater than not being content; there is no misfortune greater than being covetous. Hence in being content, one will always have enough." If only we could manage that! The trick with peace of mind is to attain stability within oneself without turning one's back on the suffering of others. It also means finding a sure cure for **affluenza** and the **Paradise Spell**. See the entry on the **activist frame**.

Further reading: A. C. Grayling, *What is Good? The Search for the Best Way to Live*.

PECKSNIFF, MR. A character in Charles Dickens's early novel *Martin Chuzzlewit* (1843). In public Mr Pecksniff is a pillar of society and prone to high-sounding declarations about universal love, but is in actual fact a self-serving hypocrite. Sadly, the type was common enough for "Pecksniffian" to enter common usage denoting any public person who says one thing and does another. American public life is littered with tub-thumping **virtuecrats** whose private life is as debauched or driven by greed as the system they so eloquently condemn on the public platform. Televangelists are a case in point.

What makes Pecksniffian hypocrisy so repulsive is its creation of a gap between our words and our deeds. One solution is to judge people by their speech and not by their deeds. In this way, pious declarations would excite no admiration unless and until people were satisfied they were matched by actions and deeds consonant with those words. This is the approach of **humanism** and the **Asian traditions**, but the **monotheist** religions (Judaism, Christianity, and Islam) tend to judge people by what they believe, or what they say they believe. This makes Pecksniffian hypocrisy a problem especially prevalent among those systems of belief.

PERCEPTUAL AMPLIFICATION. A term used by the Indian entrepreneur Vivek Paul in the context of American perceptions toward outsourcing of jobs to India. At a time when millions of jobs were being lost in the United States, a small percentage of which were being taken up in India, if each newly unemployed American happened to think that his or her job went to India, then a perceptual amplification has taken place.

Perceptual amplification is a useful term in many other contexts. Seeing a report on television about violence can often lead to the perceptual amplification that we live in more violent times, often contradicting the figures, which show a decrease in violent crime. Or, reports of violent Muslims can lead to the perceptual amplification that Muslims are generally prone to violence. Perceptual amplification is one of those tricks of fallacious reasoning we can play on ourselves, and we need to guard against its temptations. See the entry on **inquiry, tools of**.

PERENNIAL PHILOSOPHY. An idea beloved by romantics and mystics that stresses an underlying unity, usually dressed in religious garb, to all human thought. The phrase was originally used by neoscholastic thinkers as a familiar honorific to the work of Thomas Aquinas (1225–1274). This had dogmatic consequences because it assumed Aquinas's blending of Christian theology and Aristotelian philosophy constituted a final synthesis of philosophy and theology in favor of Roman Catholicism. The Renaissance scholar Agostino Steuco (1496–1549) wrote a ten-volume work, *De Perenni Philosophia* (1540), which articulated strongly this understanding of the perennial philosophy.

The term was popularized in the twentieth century by Aldous Huxley, but in the service of quite different purposes than the neoscholastics would have countenanced. In *The Perennial Philosophy* (1946), Huxley defined the perennial philosophy as "the metaphysic that recognizes a divine **reality** substantial to the world of things and lives and minds."

Enthusiasts of the perennial philosophy consider it to be the highest common denominator of all existing theologies. It requires the advocate to downplay religious specifics and overemphasize the areas of common ground. And this is often done at the expense of the specifics of any single belief system that its adherents are most attached to, specifically the exclusive, normative claims and excoriation of their enemies.

PERFUMED SMOKESCREEN. A term given by A. C. Grayling to the religious defense that all the crimes of religion (think of the **Inquisition, slavery,** the Crusades, misogyny, etc. in the case of Christianity) are the crimes of people, and imply no blame to the religion itself. To that plea, Grayling cites one of Christianity's own teachings: "Ye shall know them by their fruits. . . . A Good tree cannot bring forth evil fruit, neither can a corrupt tree bring forth good fruit" (Matthew 7:16, 18).

Grayling says that the real perfume in the religious defense is the unsaid claim that contemporary religion is free from these sorts of failings. Behind every charity and aid program lies an attitude toward women, or toward contraception, or toward **abortion,** which contributes significantly to the very ills the charities seek to provide help for. See the entry on the **no true Scotsman move.**

Further reading: A. C. Grayling, *What is Good? The Search for the Best Way to Live.*

PERICLES (490?–429 BCE). Athenian statesman and exemplar of the civic humanism of ancient Greece. As befitting someone wellborn, Pericles was well educated and destined for an important role in Athenian civic life. As a young man, he had a successful career as a soldier, increasing the naval strength of Athens. But he was not satisfied to live by the sword alone. He also attempted to end the internecine warfare among the Greeks by forming a grand federation of the Greek states. Sparta, however, was not interested in cooperation and the scheme came to nothing.

Pericles was a friend of all the greatest **Greek playwrights** and philosophers of his day: **Aeschylus, Sophocles, Euripides, Anaxagoras, Socrates, Protagoras,** and Phidias (the architect of the Parthenon)

among others. The years of Pericles' power in Athens represent one of the most noble periods of human history. During this time most of the buildings we associate with the glories of Athens were begun, and many of the most brilliant Greek plays were written and performed. Pericles is remembered for his beautiful oration on behalf of victims of the Peloponnesian war which had just begun. His funeral oration extolled the civic virtues of Athens at its best. So powerful was Pericles that his enemies often had to attack him through his allies, and through **Aspasia,** his influential mistress. Phidias and Anaxagoras suffered in this way. Pericles died of fever in 429, two years after the Peloponnesian war had begun, and which would bring the golden days of Athens to an end.

PERIYAR. Honorific title given to E. V. Ramasami Naicker (1879–1973), one of India's greatest atheist campaigners. Periyar in Tamil means great, great one. He was born in Erode, Tamil Nadu, on September 17, 1879, to a family of fair means and conventional Hindu belief. After a brief elementary education, he started work in his father's business, at which he did well. At nineteen he married Nagammai who was at the time thirteen. They had a girl who died after five months and had no children after that. Nagammai died in 1933, at fifty-eight.

Periyar's leadership skills were seen early, and he held a variety of offices in his home town. It is not known for certain when he became an atheist, but his visit to Varanasi in 1904 shocked him when he saw that this supposedly holy city was no holier than anywhere else. In 1919 he joined the Indian National Congress and worked actively in the party for several years. His leadership skills became apparent in 1924 when he led a Congress agitation in Vaikam in neighboring Kerala against a custom whereby low-caste people were prohibited from walking down a street near a Hindu temple. Periyar led a satyagraha (a nonviolent protest involving fasts and civil disobedience, made popular by

Gandhi) against the practice, and was imprisoned for a month and told to leave Vaikam. He refused to do so and was imprisoned for a further six months.

Growing support for Periyar and his wife, as well as the supporting work of the other activists, brought the discrimination to an end. Not long after that all the temples of Kerala rescinded this practice.

Soon after this victory Periyar left the Congress, dissatisfied with its attitude against freeing low-caste people from restrictions. While giving some support to the Justice Party, he devoted most of his efforts to the Self-Respect Movement, founded in 1926 by S. Ramanathan. Like many southern Indians, Periyar resented the born-to-rule assumptions of brahmins. Not only did this involve caste and class discrimination but, as many southerners feel, it also involves the south being dominated by the north. He campaigned fiercely against Hindi becoming the national language of independent India, since Hindi is the language of the north alone. His **atheism** was intimately bound up with his Dravidian nationalism.

Periyar remarried in 1949, when he was seventy, to his twenty-eight-year-old secretary Annaiyar Maniyammai. This led to widespread discontent among his followers. One of his main campaigns over the years had been for equality in **marriage**. His opponents felt that the age difference between them undermined the chance of any equality in the marriage.

In 1953 he led a campaign against images, and encouraged his followers to destroy their Ganesha images. Periyar saw **religion** as consisting of little more than superstition, repression, ignorance, and exploitation. These ills could be countered only by the consistent application of reason. "Rationalism," Periyar wrote, "must improve morality." His three core virtues were good behavior, honesty, and **truth**.

On a statue of Periyar in Chennai, the plaque reads, "There is no God. There is no God. There is no God at all. He who invented God is a fool. He who propagates God is a scoundrel. He who worships God is a barbarian."

PERSONAL INCREDULITY, ARGUMENT FROM. A title given by **Richard Dawkins** to the standard objection to the **argument to design**. Dawkins characterizes the argument as "I can't believe that this complex thing evolved by chance." The argument from personal incredulity sets up the creationists' own inability to think in terms of the periods of time required by **evolution** as the standard by which evolution is judged. Dawkins notes dryly that this is a weak argument. Chance, he adds, is a minor ingredient in **natural selection**, but the central ingredient of cumulative selection is, by definition, nonrandom.

Further reading: Richard Dawkins, *The Blind Watchmaker*.

PERSUASIVE DEFINITION. The practice, first noted by the American philosopher C. L. Stevenson, of disguising an argument in a definition. The habit of dictatorships to describe themselves as true democracies or people's democracies is a case in point. Another good example can be found in the titles of some organizations. For instance the militant antiabortion group Operation Rescue, turns the title of a dogmatic and violent group into a rosy and affirmative persuasive definition of its purpose. This trick is endemic in advertising. It requires people to have their wits about them at all times so as not to be fooled.

PETRINE TEXT. The passage in Matthew (16:18) used by Roman Catholic apologists to provide biblical authority for their church. The passage says "Thou art Peter, and on this rock I will build my church, and the gates of hades shall not prevail against her."

Many contemporary non-Catholic scholars argue that this passage is inauthentic, as **Rabbi Yeshua** had no intention of founding a church, because, being a Jew, there was already the Jewish religion, which he had come to purify and prepare for an imminent apocalypse. The Catholic understanding of this passage forces upon Jesus something quite foreign to his actual intentions. Others see it as a text originally used by Matthew to buttress Peter's status within the Christian community against Paul, but with no thought to the use it was later put to.

Authorities disagree when the Petrine Text was first used to buttress the church's authority. Some credit Irenaeus in 180 CE, although he used the authority of Paul as well as Peter. Others say the text was not used before the middle of the third century CE, when during a ferocious controversy against Cyprian of Carthage, Stephen of Rome invoked the passage to support his authority.

PETWHAC. An acronym coined by **Richard Dawkins** that stands for "Population of Events That Would Have Appeared Coincidental." Dawkins gives several illustrations of the actual numerical probability of a coincidence occurring, such as, two people on the same football team sharing the same birthday. What are frequently touted by psychics as proofs of their **paranormal** power are in fact reasonably probable odds. All that is required is a little time spent with a calculator.

The petwhac of a coincidence can easily grow, depending on our vigilance. In this way the coincidence of receiving a letter from someone we dreamt about for the first time in years last night becomes even more remarkable if it is not that person who turns up, but her brother, or someone else with the same name, or birthday, and so on. As Dawkins notes, most people's lives involve a large number of opportunities for coincidence, so it would be remarkable if one did not happen every now and then.

Further reading: Richard Dawkins, *Unweaving the Rainbow*.

PHENOMENOLOGY. The notoriously slippery range of philosophic methods that have come to mean different things to different people. It was founded by the German philosopher Edmund Husserl (1859–1938). The original idea involved a methodology of thinking. It claimed to begin with a thorough examination and bracketing of one's own intellectual habits and assumptions. But rather than see this as a primarily psychological process of self-examination, Husserl insisted that phenomenology could get to transcendentally prior essences. These essences were held to be able to be known directly, as opposed to a mere object, which we have to perceive first.

Faced with the difficulties inherent in this process, phenomenology slowly moved from a theory of how we think to a form of **idealism**, where it spoke of the essence of **consciousness**. This project has come almost entirely unstuck as neither "consciousness" nor "essences" have survived as coherent notions. The same fate befell later attempts of speaking of **intuition**. Some of the more naturalistic phenomenologists like Nicolai Hartmann (1882–1950) tried to steer the discipline away from the more idealist interpretations. Another important early proponent was **Marvin Farber**, but he ended up changing his mind on the validity of the discipline and became one of its most important critics, most notably in *Naturalism and Subjectivism* (1959). Another critic, **John Passmore**, summed up phenomenology's failure as not realizing that the isolated essence, even assuming the coherence of such a notion, cannot be the starting point of reflection. See the entry on **external realism**.

PHILOSOPHY. A word replete with scholarship and, because of that, likely to frighten off many people. This is unfortunate, because philosophy is best seen as systematic inquiry into life and a love of wisdom for its own sake. These are qualities many people have, not all of them philosophers by any means. In all likelihood the word *philosophia* was first used by the followers of **Pythagoras**. Fung Yu-lan (1895–1990), who wrote the definitive history of Chinese philosophy, described philosophy as "systematic, reflective thinking on life." One of the most succinct and poetic encapsulations of philosophy came from Chrysippus, one of the founders of **Stoicism**.

Philosophy, Chrysippus said, is an orchard with logic as its walls, the **sciences** as its trees, and **ethics** as its fruit. This said, philosophy has generally asked questions about:

- **knowledge** and **reason**;
- **human nature**;
- the nature of government and **society**; and
- the meaning of life.

Philosophy's specific contribution is in helping us to think *clearly* on these topics. At its best, philosophy helps us clear away nonsense and spot foolish or extravagant claims. It is less helpful in determining what we should put in its place, but perhaps that's not a bad thing.

The recognized field of philosophy has changed over its two-and-a-half-thousand-year life span. In the Middle Ages philosophy meant anything that wasn't **theology**. But as knowledge has advanced, philosophy has slowly relinquished whole areas of its earlier purview to new disciplines; in particular the life sciences and social sciences. Philosophy has now become confined to a relatively narrow academic ghetto.

However, there are still many talented philosophers who are able to write for a larger, nonspecialist audience. Among the best of them active today are **John Searle**, Susan Haack, **Daniel C. Dennett**, A. C. Grayling, Peter Singer, and Mary Midgley.

PHILOSOPHY, BOOKS ON. There is an enormous literature on philosophy, with a growing amount written in ways accessible to the nonspecialist. For instance, there are four good magazines which cover philosophy in ways suitable for the nonspecialist: the *Philosophers' Magazine*, *Free Inquiry*, *Philosophy Now*, and *Zeitschrift fur Philosophie*. Another journal, called *Think*, is also well worth looking at.

There are lots of handbooks on philosophical terms. The best are *Thinking from A to Z* (Routledge, 2003) by Nigel Warburton and

How to Think Straight (latest edition) by **Antony Flew**. The best single volume dictionaries of philosophy are both called *Dictionary of Philosophy*; one by Antony Flew, the other by Mario Bunge. Still the best multi-volume resource is the *Encyclopedia of Philosophy*, edited by Paul Edwards.

The best general survey of philosophy across its major areas is *An Introduction to Western Philosophy* (1995) by Antony Flew. The best single-volume overview of Asian thought is *Understanding Eastern Philosophy* (1997) by Ray Billington.

The simplest history of philosophy is *A Passion for Wisdom* (1997) by Robert Solomon and Kathleen Higgins. Then there is *The Dream of Reason* (2000) by Anthony Gottlieb. This book is excellent. It has become fashionable to sneer at **Bertrand Russell**'s *History of Western Philosophy*, but this book is still well worth reading, although the chapters on **Nietzsche**, Hegel, and **Kant** are best read with a large pinch of salt.

For Muslim philosophy, see Majid Fakhry, *A History of Muslim Philosophy* (1970). For Buddhist philosophy see *A History of Buddhist Philosophy* (1992) by David Kalupahana. Neither of these is really suitable for the nonspecialist but both are worth the effort. For Chinese philosophy see *A Short History of Chinese Philosophy* (1948) by Fung Yu-lan, or his shorter version called *The Spirit of Chinese Philosophy* (1947). I am not familiar with any single-volume history of Indian philosophy suitable for the nonspecialist that doesn't descend into windy nonsense. Still the best is *A History of Indian Philosophy* (1922–1952) by Surendranath Dasgupta. However, this runs to five volumes and was incomplete at Dasgupta's death.

PHILOSOPHY, CRISIS OF. Many critics have noted the failure of the discipline of philosophy to provide much in the way of intellectual leadership over the past thirty or more years. There are more philosophers in universities now than at any time in the history of *Homo sapiens*, and yet we hear so little from the vast majority of them. And those we do hear from are given the condescending title of "public intellectual," or, even worse, "popularizer." At a time when **fundamentalism** and ethnic hatreds are rampant and organized **religion** is so clearly unable to provide a coherent intellectual or moral lead, why has philosophy been so passive? Mario Bunge, a very senior and respected Argentinian-born philosopher, now working in Canada, has outlined these main reasons:

- *Excessive professionalization*: philosophers have larger teaching loads and more need to publish or perish in order to secure promotion, which leaves them with little time to worry about much else;
- *Mistaking obscurity for profundity*: it has become fashionable to write densely, in the hope of being thought "deep." See the entry on **glossogonous word-salad**;
- *Obsession with language*: while clarity is important, philosophy needs to be concerned with more than language. Bryan Magee has made a similar point;
- *Idealism*: philosophy in general is an exhausted school of thought with nothing new to add;
- *Undue importance to micro-problems and fashionable puzzles*: this comes at the expense of serious thinking on important questions;
- *Tough-minded dealing with insubstantial issues and tender-minded dealing with serious issues*: this reveals that philosophy has lost its direction;
- *Fragmentation*: this is the price paid for the collapse in philosophical system building;
- *Detachment from science and technology*: these are the engine-rooms of modern civilization; and
- *The ivory tower mentality*: philosophers write for each other in academic journals nobody else reads.

"Most contemporary philosophers," Bunge writes, "have neither their feet on the ground nor their eyes fixed on the stars." The result is an intellectual vacuum being filled with easy certitudes of **command moralities**, tribalism, or widespread withdrawal from the democratic process. See the entry on the **minimal self**.

The outstanding exceptions to this general lament, apart from Bunge himself, would be **John Searle**, **Daniel C. Dennett**, A. C. Grayling, Mary Midgley, **Richard Dawkins**, Peter Singer, and **Paul Kurtz**.

Further reading: Mario Bunge, *Philosophy in Crisis: The Need for Reconstruction*; and A. C. Grayling, *What is Good? The Search for the Best Way to Live*.

PHRONESIS. A Greek word that means "practical common sense" and which **Aristotle** praised. The phronimos was the man of practical wisdom and was a person capable of deliberating on those practical matters, as distinct from (though not opposed to) the more theoretical wisdom in the phrase sophia. The closest modern-day equivalent of this ideal can be found in **Paul Kurtz**'s notion of **eupraxsophy**.

PHYSICAL SCIENCES. The group of disciplines such as physics, chemistry, biochemistry, biology, physiology, and, in some people's opinion, physical geography, psychology, and anthropology. The physical sciences are united in their use of the **scientific method**. And the physical sciences are contrasted with the **social sciences**.

PHYSICS ENVY. Satirical title given to the predilection among some **social scientists** to employ needless formulas and other supposed paraphernalia of the **physical sciences** in their writing, so as to be thought properly "scientific." The phrase is usually attributed to the American physicist Richard Feynman (1918–1988) and is a play on the notion of penis envy that **Sigmund Freud** supposed girls to suffer from.

PIECE OF ART. One of the debates within contemporary art is where the boundaries of art lie. What is a work of art? When does a piece of elephant dung or the fender from a car become a work of art? Uncertainty about questions like this has left many people feeling anxious about, and often hostile toward, forms of art they don't understand.

The problem began in 1913 when Marcel Duchamp (1887–1968) started using **ready made** objects as elements in his art. Since then the debate has raged as to where the boundaries of art lie.

The simplest way to solve this problem is to change the way one defines what a work of art is. The American visual-arts scholar Timothy Binkley said that a piece of art is simply any object an artist says is art. Binkley prefers to speak of a *piece* of art rather than a *work* of art, because an artist might have used a **ready made** object and not worked on it at all, and yet it has, in this new context, become art. So, anything in a gallery (or some other art space) is a piece of art. At a single stroke, much of the tortured debate over whether the work is "art" or not becomes irrelevant, and leads on to the more worthwhile question of whether the work is *good* art. See the entry on **modern art**.

Further reading: Timothy Binkley, "Piece: Contra Aesthetics," in Philip Alperson, ed., *The Philosophy of the Visual Arts*.

PIGEON HOLE FALLACY. The widely observed phenomenon of experts recognized in one field who make pronouncements outside their field of expertise and expect to be taken seriously as "an expert." In this way, it is difficult to take seriously the fiery criticisms of **evolution** by the "**intelligent design**" apologist Phillip Johnson, who is a lawyer. This problem is closely related to **Clarke's Law**.

PILLARIZATION. A term used to refer to the once-strict division of people in the Netherlands into groups divided by religion, but which, with the **secularization** of Dutch society, took on a quite different aspect. Between 1917 and the mid-1960s, pillarization came to mean the way public funds were apportioned between these sectarian groupings or pillars. The leaders of each pillar had the task of reaching agreement with the leaders of other pillars on issues of common concern or national interest. This pillarized system was connected to a specific interpretation of the constitutional **separation of church and state**. In the Netherlands, this separation did not prevent the government from spending tax money on the facilities and activities of churches and similar institutions. What it did mean was that the government may only provide money to worldview organizations if it treats all of them in a just and proportionally equal way.

This arrangement has had important effects for the humanist movement. When in 1946 the Dutch humanists, led by **Jaap van Praag**, started a campaign for the equal treatment of atheist and agnostic Dutch citizens, it was able to use the constitution as a lever to acquire government funds for all kinds of humanist activities. Because, for example, when the government gave money to a Protestant and Roman Catholic development organization, it could almost (it is always a question of interpretation) be required by law to also give money to a humanist development organization. And so on.

The pillarization system began to be dismantled after 1965 as part of the recognition of the reality of secularization, particularly when it came to be recognized that the system locked people into whichever pillar they began with. The depillarization (*ontzuiling*) process since 1965 is generally seen as having increased the freedom of the individual. It has not been a painless process, however, not least because of the financial costs involved.

PINK FLOYD. English supergroup thought by many to be the best rock group ever. Known for haunting music and existentially challenging lyrics, Pink Floyd has been hugely influential for more than thirty years. The group played for the first time in October 1965, having slowly come together from the original friendship between Roger Waters (1943–) and Syd Barrett (1946–) in London. The band's name was devised as a tribute to two blues players, Pink Anderson (1900–1974) and Floyd Council (1911–1976). The group signed with EMI records in 1967, the year they released their first album, *Piper at the Gates of Dawn*.

A succession of extraordinary albums followed. Pink Floyd is thought to have sold 140 million albums over its career, making it one of the most successful groups in the history of contemporary music. *Atom Heart Mother* topped the UK LP charts when it was released in 1970, but was eclipsed by the phenomenal success of *The Dark Side of the Moon*, which was released in 1973 and went on to sell 15 million copies and spend 741 weeks on the Billboard Top 100 Album Chart. Their 1979 double album *The Wall* beat that, selling 23 million records and coming in as the third highest-selling album ever (after the Eagles' *Greatest Hits 1971–75* and Michael Jackson's *Thriller*). Many Pink Floyd fans rate *Wish You Were Here* (1975) as their greatest album.

Their success was due to the quality of the music and lyrics, as opposed to many later bands, whose success owed more to marketing. After the departure of Syd Barrett, the intellectual powerhouse of the group was Roger Waters while many of the melodies came from Dave Gilmour (1946–). Between the two a special magic was created, at least for the years they could work together. From the early 1980s disputes in the band became too great and Waters finally left the band in December 1985. Official Web sites give grudging acknowledgment of Roger Waters's lyrical brilliance, but claim his misanthropy became tiresome and he outstayed his welcome. Waters and his former colleagues came to a guarded understanding in 1988 and have since gone their own way. Waters and Pink Floyd have continued to release albums since

then. The Floyd albums were *A Momentary Lapse of Reason* in 1987 and *The Division Bell* in 1994. Neither Waters nor Floyd has been as brilliant since their split.

Further reading: Nicholas Shaffner, *A Saucerful of Secrets: The Pink Floyd Odyssey*.

PIOUS FRAUD. An act of deception undertaken not for reasons of pecuniary gain, but for the advancement or vindication of one's church. Good examples include the **donation of Constantine**, and the works falsely attributed to **Dionysus the Areopagite**. See the entry on **pseudepigraphy**.

PITT PRINCIPLE. A political principle identified by the American economist Paul Krugman. It is named after the Securities and Exchange Commission chairman Harvey Pitt, an appointee of George W. Bush. The Pitt Principle is a continuation of the long-standing Peter Principle, which states that managers fail because they rise to their level of incompetence. The Pitt Principle goes one step further and states that sometimes people are promoted precisely because of their incompetence.

Facing unprecedented levels of corporate fraud, insider trading, and dishonest accounting, Pitt made sure to appoint people who were unqualified to examine thoroughly the abuses they were, in principle, supposed to uncover. In this way the seriously wealthy friends of the Bush administration, and in all likelihood Pitt himself, were able to prosper.

Further reading: Paul Krugman, *The Great Unraveling*.

PIUS XII (1876–1958). Reactionary pope. Born Eugenio Pacelli in Rome to a family of papal loyalists at a time the papacy felt besieged by the foreign influences of nationalism and **democracy**, as manifested in the new state of Italy, which had subsumed the Papal States. Pacelli was deeply pious from a very young age and surprised no one when he declared his intention to enter the priesthood.

From the start of Pacelli's church career, he was an uncompromising centralist. Under Pope Pius X, Pacelli was deeply involved in drafting the Code of Canon Law, which was completed in 1917. The Code of Canon Law gave unprecedented powers to the papacy over the church, particularly regarding the appointment of bishops and the enforcement of orthodoxy.

Pacelli was also entrusted with drafting and seeing through to a successful conclusion a concordat with Serbia. This concordat, signed on June 24, 1914, undermined the influence Austria-Hungary traditionally exercised over Catholic interests in Serbia and the Balkans and was widely regarded in Austria as a national insult. When Franz Ferdinand was assassinated by Gavrillo Princip (1894–1918), a Serbian nationalist, four days after the concordat was signed, Austria-Hungary was in a very belligerent mood and presented Serbia with the drastic ultimatum that began the tragic slide into World War I.

Nevertheless Pacelli remained committed to the policy of securing concordats with secular governments as a means of protecting and enhancing Catholic interests and papal power. The most notorious concordat that Pacelli was central in securing was with the fledgling Nazi regime in Germany. His efforts were inspired by the Lateran Treaty, which was drafted by Pacelli's elder brother, Francesco, and signed by the papacy and Fascist Italy in 1929. As with the Lateran treaty, both sides got what they wanted from the concordat. The Vatican secured command over the powerful German Catholic Church and the freedom of religion in Germany. Hitler, in turn, was promised a complete withdrawal of Catholic interests from German politics. This involved the betrayal and isolation of the Centre Party, the last party still with a voice in German politics. The Centre Party had been a powerful Catholic party which could well have been the focus for opposition to the Nazis. But the papacy of the time saw no place for Catholic political parties. The concordat was signed on July 20, 1933.

Despite habitually breaking the terms and spirit of the concordat, and ever-growing harassment of Catholics in Germany, the papacy remained committed to it. Pacelli became pope on March 2, 1939, as the shadow of war darkened Europe. Despite his personal opposition to Nazism, Pacelli consistently saw communism as the greater menace and was prepared to do business with fascism in order to preserve a narrowly conceived idea of church interests in those countries. Pacelli was continually pressured by Allied representatives to issue some condemnation of Nazi atrocities, and continually refused to do so, even once he became familiar with the details of the Holocaust. Pacelli did not issue an unequivocal condemnation of Nazism until June 1945. By contrast, his condemnations of communism were regular and unambiguous. In contrast to the deafening silence of the war years, he issued three encyclicals over the period of ten days that condemned the Soviet invasion of Hungary in 1956.

Pacelli was also responsible for returning the church to a period of deep conservatism and hostility to theological inquiry or debate. In *Humani Generis* of 1950, Pius XII banned historical contextualization of dogma on the grounds it would lead to relativism. Pius insisted that future papal encyclicals were to be accepted without argument of discussion from bishops or theologians. One of the better-known victims of this policy was the liberal theologian Pierre Teilhard de Chardin (1881–1955). See the entries on **assumption of Mary**, **concordat**, **Lateran Treaty**, and **Opus Dei**.

Further reading: John Cornwell, *Hitler's Pope: The Secret History of Pius XII*.

PLACEBO. A word first seen in 1785, derived from Latin, meaning "I shall please" and which has come to mean make-believe medicine. The placebo effect recognizes the critical role the mind plays in recovery from many ailments. On some occasions it has been difficult to distinguish healing rates among patients using conventional medicine and those using placebos. The danger comes when quacks and charlatans ascribe what is actually a natural recovery, possibly based on the placebo effect, on their alleged cures.

Placebo-effect-driven improvements are quite common in **alternative medicine** because of the level of care and attention the patient receives, and the heightened expectations of recovery that are often associated with high-stakes belief in the efficacy of the alternative medicine practice in question. However, it is the placebo effect which should get the credit, not the alternative medicine.

All this notwithstanding, the placebo question is far from straightforward. Recent research by two Danish scientists has questioned whether placebos are as effective as assumed here, and other studies differ on what actually takes place when somebody's condition improves under a placebo. So, while the apologists for alternative medicine are wrong to claim that the placebo effect cures as the result of their procedure, the jury is still out on how and to what extent the placebo effect actually works.

PLATO (428–347 BCE). One of the most influential philosophers of all time. Born into a privileged and influential Athenian family, Plato grew up at a time of political and social strife. He saw firsthand the failings of tyranny and **democracy** as forms of government. After the government-inspired trial of his mentor **Socrates**, Plato resolved to have nothing to do with flawed politics of this sort. Of vastly more historical importance was his establishment of the **Academy**, a school of higher learning, in about 387 BCE.

His main goals in philosophy were to oppose the **Pre-Socratic** philosophers who had gone before him, and whose theories he thought dangerous. In contrast to the **naturalism** of most of the Pre-Socratics, Plato taught the immortality of the **soul** and the central significance of the battle between good and evil, and the need for a class of philosopher-kings who understood this and who would rule accordingly. From **Parmenides** Plato developed the idea that only

things which are eternal have any real value. Plato taught that all things were but facsimiles of the pure forms of them, which reside in heaven. The highest form was the form of the good. Later Platonists equated the form of the good with **God**, but Plato insisted that this was not the case. The form of the good was more important than God in Plato's scheme of things.

His politics inclined to **totalitarianism**, a legacy of the civil unrest he experienced as a youth. In the *Republic*, Plato postulated an ideal society that has disturbing parallels with dictatorships like North Korea. **Bertrand Russell** noted during a visit to the Soviet Union in 1920 that the society being built there was the closest parallel to Plato's republic. **Karl Popper** explored the same point in greater detail in his masterpiece *The Open Society and Its Enemies*. Plato traveled twice to Syracuse in Sicily, where he spent some time hoping to put his ideas in the *Republic* into practical fruition. The attempt was a dismal failure. The story of this has been brilliantly written about by **Mary Renault** in her novel *The Mask of Apollo*.

Plato wrote extensively, and about twenty dialogues and some letters survive, although there has been controversy among scholars about which of these are actually his. He originally set himself the task of outlining the thoughts of his hero Socrates. Plato's earlier works, like the *Apology*, are fairly faithful renderings of what Socrates thought. But as he got older, Plato's works, though continuing to speak in Socrates' name, bear less and less resemblance to his thoughts.

A particularly influential work is *Timaeus*, which has Plato's cosmogony and was translated by Cicero (106–43 BCE), and was the only dialogue known to the West during the Middle Ages, and is thus very important for its influence as much as its actual ideas. The *Timaeus* was strongly influenced by the ideas of Pythagoras. A full translation of Plato's works was completed by the Renaissance thinker Marsilio Ficino (1433–1499).

PLATO'S PHILOSOPHY, CONTRIBU-TIONS OF. Alfred North Whitehead (1861–1947) famously said that all Western philosophy is but a series of footnotes to Plato. While that overstates the case, there is no denying Plato's extraordinary influence on thought. This is as much a product of accident as well, in that Plato's writings survived to be passed on to later generations, whereas those of his **Pre-Socratic** predecessors did not.

The historian of ideas C. D. Hardie listed four main contributions made by Plato's philosophy, three of them positive with one negative:

- valuing highly the role of **reason** in human life;
- describing the basic virtues of wisdom, courage, temperance, and justice;
- valuing the role of education in society; and
- setting the conditions for a hostile attitude toward **science** to prevail.

Another way of looking at it is to see the tremendous influence of Plato's work *Timaeus*, which stood as the principal work of cosmology until the end of the Middle Ages. It provided intellectual support for myth and fantasy over hard science for all those centuries, but it also inspired many scientists who did in fact make significant discoveries in various branches of science.

Further reading, C. D. Hardie, *Background to Modern Thought*.

PLAYING GOD. One of the more commonly used arguments against a variety of ethical issues, such as **abortion**, cloning, **voluntary euthanasia**, or genetic engineering. The argument goes that interfering in the natural order is somehow unnatural and an arrogant usurpation of a role only **God** can play. Sometimes this argument is used even though no serious reference to God is being made.

The playing-God argument makes several untenable assumptions. First of all, of course, it assumes there is a God that exercises minute control over all elements of nature, including human beings. Even if this assumption is rejected and the "God" part of the argument is rhetorical, an assumption about the orderly and planned forces of nature is still being made. This overlooks the fact that **evolution** is a random process with no sign of outward control or purpose.

The playing-God argument would also, if taken to its logical conclusion, rule out *any* intrusion into the workings of nature. Prevention of disease, ensuring the supply of clean water, breeding livestock, keeping domestic pets; all these are instances of playing God. It would also rule out capital punishment, which many people who use the playing-God argument are happy to resort to in other circumstances.

PLEDGE OF ALLEGIANCE. A formula recited in American public schools, the original intention of which was to help assimilate the many thousands of new immigrants to the United States. The pledge was written in 1892 by Francis Bellamy (1855–1931), a former Baptist minister who had been thrown out of his Boston church for his anticapitalist views. He then joined the Christian Socialist movement. Eventually Bellamy stopped attending church altogether because of the racial bigotry of the church members.

Bellamy was a strong supporter of the separation of church and state, making it reasonable to assume he would have opposed the addition in 1954 of "under God" to the pledge. He was a cousin of the radical utopian writer Edward Bellamy (1850–1898), author of the wildly popular utopian romance *Looking Backward* (1888). Despite their suspicion of the secular nature of the pledge, Roman Catholic schools began using the pledge during World War I, in an attempt to display their patriotic credentials. By the beginning of World War II, the pledge was compulsory in many states. This resulted in a spate of persecution against Jehovah's Witnesses, who refused on religious grounds to cite it. Their case was taken up by the **American Civil Liberties Union** among other groups. And in 1954, the words "under God" were added during the period of anticommunist fervor now known as the **Great Fear**.

Bellamy's original pledge was simple. It read: "I pledge allegiance to my Flag and to ("to" was a later addition) the Republic for which it stands, one nation, indivisible, with liberty and justice for all." In most cases the pledge now reads "I pledge allegiance to the Flag of the United States of America and to the Republic for which it stands, one nation, under God, indivisible, with liberty and justice for all." In 2004 Michael Newdow, an atheist from California, challenged the pledge on the grounds that it violated in First Amendment of the Constitution. Newdow's challenge reached the Supreme Court and attracted widespread respect, even from many who opposed his views. Despite being widely acknowledged to be a sound case, Newdow was turned down on a technicality.

PLINY THE ELDER (22–79 CE). Born Gaius Plinius Secundus but known to history as Pliny the Elder, to distinguish him from his nephew, Pliny the Younger. Pliny had a long and successful career as a Roman soldier, diplomat, and scholar. He died during the eruption of Vesuvius which destroyed the town of Pompeii.

Of the great deal that Pliny wrote, the only piece to survive was the *Natural History* (77 CE), a thirty-seven-volume **encyclopedia** of most branches of **knowledge** known to the Roman world. Pliny's *Natural History* was not the first encyclopedia, but it was one of the best organized of Roman encyclopedias. It was one of the first to include a table of contents and references to cited works at the end of each chapter. He claimed to have researched from two thousand books and to have discussed twenty-thousand topics. It was a mixture of intelligent **skepticism** and pseudoscientific credulity. But together it is an invaluable record of the ancient world.

PLURALISM. One of the most important legacies of the **Enlightenment**. Pluralism involves a reasoned support for the existence in harmony of different cultures and ways of life within the same political system, with no, or at least a minimum of, discrimination between them. Pluralism does not require that all the various cultures slowly assimilate into the dominant culture, although that can be an unintended consequence. This is why pluralism is the *reasoned* support for diversity. See the entry on the **general will**.

For the individual, pluralism is an opportunity to shed unsuitable **command moralities** and develop a moral outlook involving a small set of **core virtues**, or dispositions to act. Contrary to the claims of **fundamentalists** and some **postmodernists**, pluralism is not the same as **nihilism**. While pluralism does not issue forth one-size-fits-all commandments, it can provide individuals with legitimate confidence in their own convictions alongside a genuine respect for the different views of others. This process of slowly understanding one's own position and those of others is what **John Dewey** called the **social intelligence**.

The only point on which a successful pluralist society must insist is that it be a **secular** society. Religious habits of absolutist truth claims, **command moralities**, and **demonizing one's opponents** simply cannot persist long without **toleration** of **diversity** becoming an early casualty. As if to illustrate this, in 1999 the Catholic Church issued a decree condemning pluralism, which it equated with **Marxism**. It is true that this requires some element of adjustment from religious minorities least inclined to toleration of diversity, but that price does not seem unreasonable. However, pluralism need not require these religions to abandon their beliefs. It only requires a willingness to put aside absolute claims to truth and exclusive access to God and to learn to understand their God in less authoritarian ways. Using academic **jargon**, this is called the privatization of religion.

Further reading: James Gouinlock, *Rediscovering the Moral Life*.

POLITICAL ISLAM. See **ISLAMISM**.

POLITICAL VALUES. The Russian philosopher Valerii Kuvakin has identified these as the most important political values:

- political freedom and responsibility;
- national security;
- patriotism;
- cosmopolitanism;
- international security;
- civil peace; and
- political concord.

Political values, Kuvakin argues, are directly related to social values and are concentrated around the idea of justice, a wise social order, and the ways of maintaining this order. Political values are also historical, and reflect the political experience of the people in question. In some societies, for instance, patriotism is a more important value than in others. These values do not necessarily all sit comfortably with one another, and each political culture is largely determined by the relative weight given to one of these values over another. What is clear, however, is that each of them requires an **open society** in order to show themselves off to best advantage.

Further reading: Valerii Kuvakin, *In Search of Our Humanity*.

POLITICAL VIOLENCE, CAUSES OF. There are many theories of political violence, but most theorists agree on the fundamental causes of political violence throughout history. The political scientist Paul Wilkinson has itemized these:

- ethnic conflicts, hatreds, discrimination, and oppression;
- religious and ideological conflicts, hatreds, discrimination, and oppression;
- socioeconomic relative deprivation;
- stresses and strains of rapid modernization which tend to exacerbate socioeconomic relative deprivation;
- perceived political weaknesses, in-

fringements of **rights**, injustice, and oppression;
- lack of adequate channels of peaceful communication of protests;
- existence of a tradition of violence, disaffection, and popular turbulence;
- the availability of a revolutionary leadership equipped with a potentially attractive ideology;
- weakness and ineptitude of government, police, and judiciary;
- erosion of confidence in the regime and its values and institutions; and
- deep divisions within the governing elites.

The best antidote to the danger of political violence is the **open society**, where people get as much opportunity as is practicable to make their voices heard.

Further reading: Paul Wilkinson, *Terrorism and the Liberal State*.

POP ART. An influential art phenomenon of the 1960s. Pop Art was a complex mix of a celebration of mass culture and a form of aggression against the established order. The term was first used by the English critic Lawrence Alloway, and it made its debut in an exhibition at the London Institute of Contemporary Art in 1956. One of Pop Art's first proponents was Richard Hamilton (1932–) then teaching at Newcastle University and a practicing artist. Hamilton's prophetic collage *Just What Is It That Makes Today's Homes So Different, So Appealing* (1956) has a muscleman holding a phallic sucker with the word "pop" on it. Hamilton described Pop Art as:

- *popular*, designed for a mass audience;
- *transient*, short-term solution;
- *expendable*, easily forgotten; and
- *low cost*.

Critics have seen Pop Art as a reaction against the grandiosity of Abstract Expressionism. This is true, but far from a complete explanation. Pop Art owed as much to Dada as to its dislike for Abstract Expressionism. Pop Art was an optimistic celebration of the material plenty of the 1950s and 1960s, and when that plenty and the euphoria that accompanied it evaporated at the end of the decade, so did Pop Art.

Further reading: Robert Hewison, *Too Much: Art and Society in the 1960s, 1960–1975*.

POPPER, KARL RAIMUND (1902–1994). Thought by many to be the greatest philosopher of the twentieth century. Karl Popper was born in Vienna to parents Jewish in origin and Protestant by adoption. Popper's life was radically altered by World War I, which destroyed the culture he was brought up in. After working on the land and as a cabinet maker, he went to Vienna University, where he took a doctorate in psychology.

In 1935 the British philosopher **L. Susan Stebbing** invited Popper to Britain. There he met **Bertrand Russell** and **A. J. Ayer** and other leading British thinkers. In 1937 he took a position lecturing in philosophy at Canterbury College, at the University of New Zealand (later the University of Canterbury). While in New Zealand, Popper wrote one of his best-known books, *The Open Society and Its Enemies* (1945), which he described as his "war book." This two-volume work took up the notion of the **open society** and gave it its classic rendering, and spoke of **critical rationalism**. *The Open Society and Its Enemies* was a powerful criticism of the totalitarian implications in the philosophy of **Plato**, G. W. F. Hegel (1770–1831), and Karl Marx (1818–1883). It remains one of the classics of contemporary humanist philosophy. Another work to come out of his spell in New Zealand was *The Poverty of Historicism*, although it was not published until 1957. Here he criticized the directional view of history employed by **teleological** worldviews like **Marxism**. See the entry on **Peter Munz**.

If Popper's political philosophy was controversial, his philosophy of science was even more so. His main work in this field was *Logik der Forschung* (1934), which appeared in English as the *Logic of Scientific Discovery* (1959). His rejection of the inductive method of reasoning, and his **falsification** theory have attracted serious opposition, not least from scientists. See the entry on **deduction and induction**. And Popper won few friends for his work with the Australian neurophysiologist John Eccles (1903–1997), *The Self and Its Brain* (1977), which defended a type of **dualism** and opposed **determinism**. Popper's greatest contributions remain his political and social philosophy, and his exposition of critical rationalism. These alone are enough to justify his inclusion among the top few philosophers of the twentieth century.

Popper was a lifelong atheist and rationalist. He was an honorary associate of the **Rationalist Press Association** from 1976 and a laureate of the **International Academy of Humanism** from its inception in 1983.

Further reading: Bryan Magee, *Popper*.

PORPHYRY (232/4–305 CE). Pagan philosopher and early critic of Christianity. Porphyry is thought to have written seventy-seven treatises on various topics, from commentaries on **Aristotle** to arguments for vegetarianism. Only fragments of his fifteen-volume work *Against the Christians* have survived, which was publicly burned in 448 CE by the order of the Christian emperor Theodosius II (reigned 408–450 CE).

R. Joseph Hoffmann, a scholar of early Christianity, contends that Porphyry's philosophy can be unearthed in a work called *Apocriticus*, by the fourth-century theologian Macarius Magnus. Using this method, Hoffmann shows that Porphyry observed the many contradictions in the Gospel accounts of Jesus and exposed most of the Christian theological claims to searching critique.

Further reading: R. Joseph Hoffmann, ed., *Porphyry's Against the Christians: The Literary Remains*.

PORTEOUS, SKIPP. See **FORMER PREACHERS**.

POSITIVE AND NEGATIVE SUSTAIN-ABILITY QUOTIENT. The Nobel prize-winner in chemistry and laureate of the **International Academy of Humanism**, Sir Harry Kroto has devised a scale, running from ten down to minus ten, which can provide consumers a clear assessment of the environmental impact of the item they are purchasing. For instance, a gas-guzzling **Hummer** would attract a very negative sustainability quotient, because they are wasteful of gas, take up more road space, and are responsible for considerable damage to open country and beaches.

The PSQ and NSQ scales could also apply to industries. New industries powered not by fossil fuels but by hydrogen and oxygen, and developing energy from the sunlight we get free every day would be high PSQ industries, and could attract tax breaks and subsidies as a result. More controversially, developing genetically modified strains of wheat and rice that have no need for inorganic fertilizers could, on its own, save up to 20 percent of the world's fossil fuel supply. See the entry on **affluenza**.

POSITIVE ATHEISM. Variety of atheism articulated in India by **Gora**, founder of the **Atheist Centre**. Gora's version of positive atheism is not to be confused with the positive atheism as articulated by **Antony Flew** or **Michael Martin**. See the entry on **atheism**. Gora's version of positive atheism combines an active profession of atheism with a life of moral seriousness. It has a lot in common with **Paul Kurtz**'s notion of **eupraxsophy**.

Positive atheism grew out of an earlier piece of writing, simply called *Atheism* (1938), but Gora's employers refused him permission to have the piece published. After a great deal more thought and reading, Gora had developed his larger view of atheism, which was first published as *Positive Atheism* in 1972. Gora emphasized the twin phenomena of freedom and responsibility as central tenets of his view. Empowered by free-

dom and motivated by responsibility, Gora pictured the atheist as a socially active person, working politically to eradicate suffering in all its forms. The many social programs of the Atheist Centre are a faithful reflection of Gora's vision of positive atheism.

This has been influential in the West. In 1991 Harry Stopes-Roe argued that positive atheism and humanism are the same thing, because they are "animated by the same principles."

Further reading: Gora, *Positive Atheism*.

POSITIVE ATHEISM, JUSTIFICATION FOR. The American philosopher **Michael Martin** has provided five conditions for justifying positive atheism as a coherent philosophical position. Martin speaks of positive atheism in the sense outlined in the **atheism** entry, not the **positive atheism** championed by **Gora**. Positive atheism is justified if:

- all the available evidence used to support the view that **God** exists can be shown to be inadequate;
- God is the sort of entity that, if it existed, would reasonably lead to the presumption that it would leave sufficient evidence of its existence;
- the above presumption is not undermined despite many attempts to do so;
- all the areas where evidence may be expected to appear has been comprehensively examined; and
- there are also no acceptable beneficial reasons to believe that God exists.

All the developments in philosophy, science, and history have satisfied these criteria, and therefore positive atheism is justifiable.

Further reading: Michael Martin, *Atheism: A Philosophical Justification*.

POSITIVISM. A term inaccurately used by some writers to describe **rationalism** and **humanism**. Properly used, positivism refers to the body of thought created by Auguste Comte (1798–1857). The term was used in his main work, which was translated into English as *Positive Philosophy* (1830–42). Comte's system of positive philosophy identified three stages of history. The first phase of history, the theological, was dominated by the immediate action of supernatural beings. The second, or metaphysical, stage was said to be characterized by the use of abstract forces. The third and final stage of history is the positive state, which is reached when people abandon **supernaturalism** and metaphysics in favor of an empirical approach to things. See the entry on **historicism**. Comte's philosophy of history was accompanied by some sensible, if dreamy, observations about the brotherhood of man.

The second half of Comte's career was devoted mainly to developing an extravagant and rigid "Religion of Humanity" that would become the social glue for a new utopia. This change of direction was brought about by the early death of a woman Comte had fallen madly in love with. The months of the year (there were to be thirteen) were to be renamed after famous role models, Moses, **Homer**, **Aristotle**, and so on, and each day would honor some lesser figure in the same general mold as the figure after whom the month is named. Sundays would be reserved for some figure held to deserve special respect. Women, though held to be morally superior to men and worthy of receiving an education, were nonetheless denied access to the significant rites of passages in the Religion of Humanity. For example, one of the significant sacraments was to achieve "Maturity" at age forty-two. Women were not eligible for Maturity, nor were they able to take the next sacrament of "Retirement" at age sixty-three.

There was to be a priestly class, complete with high priests and a supreme pontiff, whose job was to look over the affairs of society and in particular ensure that the next caste down, that of capitalists, would not get ideas above their station. Thus established, the Religion of Humanity would then go on to solve the three great world problems: sub-ordinating **progress** to order, analysis to synthesis, and egoism to **altruism**.

Positivism had little influence in France, but lingered for a while in England. The Religion of Humanity even developed its own version of the **Trinity**, prompting **Thomas Henry Huxley** to observe acidly, though not inaccurately, that Positivism resembled "Catholicism minus Christianity." Comte's successor in France, Pierre Lafitte (1823–1903), went on to emphasize the social and ethical aspects of Positivism, while Richard Congreve (1818–1899), a leading follower in England, emphasized the Religion of Humanity. Organized Positivism in Europe failed to take deep root or to attract a new generation of leaders. In one of those strange historical quirks, it was exported to South America, where it found, particularly in Brazil, a receptive environment. In South America, Positivism meant a bit more than simply Comtism; there was a general commitment to evolution and progress.

Unlike **rationalism** and **humanism**, Positivism relied on an extravagant historicism and had leanings to **totalitarianism**. Its Religion of Humanity was too close to the Christianity it sought to displace to offer any real alternative. By the end of the nineteenth century, it was pretty much bankrupt, only to reappear quite out of context as a means by which rationalism and humanism could be attacked.

POSTMODERN   CHURCHES. See **EMERGING CHURCHES**

POSTMODERNISM. An academic trend that arose in universities in the late 1960s and exercised considerable influence until the middle 1990s. It is very difficult to give a single, coherent account of postmodernism. Postmodernists themselves acknowledge their movement is incapable of definition, but when a definition is attempted, it is usually put in terms of decline and disintegration. Possibly the most extravagant description comes from the Polish sociologist and ardent postmodernist, Zygmunt Bauman, who described postmodernism as a "state of mind marked above all by its all-deriding, all-eroding, all-dissolving *destructiveness*." Slightly less polemically, the American political theorist Gregory Bruce Smith saw postmodernism as "fundamentally a sign of disintegration, of transition, of waning faith in the modern ideas of Reason and Progress, and the Enlightenment project in general." The philosopher Mario Bunge has discerned five traits shared by most postmodernists:

- *mistrust of reason*, particularly logic and **science**;
- *subjectivism*, the idea that the world is but our representation;
- *relativism*, or the idea that all truth is relative to one's culture, **gender**, class, etc.;
- *obsession with myth*, symbol, metaphor, and rhetoric; and
- *pessimism* and the denial of the possibility of **knowledge**.

Postmodernists have been anxious to undermine any claim to reliable knowledge, although this has been applied selectively. It has been seen most commonly in a hostility to science and **humanism**, but has been more indulgent toward **religion** and **supernaturalism**, the claims of the latter to knowing their beliefs are founded on certainties notwithstanding.

The first major counterattack against postmodernism came in the form of the book *Higher Superstition* (1994), edited by Paul Gross and Norman Levitt. Influenced by this book, the New York physicist Alan Sokal perpetrated the most comprehensive hoax against postmodernist intellectual pretensions, and the postmodernist movement has been in decline ever since. See the entries on **postmodernity**, the **Sokal Hoax**, and **passes-for fallacy**.

Further reading: Zygmunt Bauman, *Intimations of Postmodernity*; Gregory Bruce Smith, *Nietzsche, Heidegger and the Transi-*tion to Postmodernity;* and Kurtz and Madigan, eds., *Challenges to the Enlightenment*.

POSTMODERNITY. Not to be confused with **postmodernism**. Postmodernity is a title given to the stretch of time since between 1968 and 1973 (accounts vary). To label these years postmodernity suggests a different style of experience than was the norm before. Opinions differ as to whether postmodernity is a new stage and therefore a *departure* from modernity, or is an altered set of emphases *within* modernity. Postmodernism is a series of ideas and theories advanced to give some explanation to postmodernity.

POSTULATORY ATHEISM. A term used originally by Max Scheler (1874–1928), which refers to a particular variety of atheism, of which existentialist atheism and Objectivism are examples. Postulatory atheism requires the rejection of **God** in order to then postulate some other principle more central to its form of thinking. In both existentialist atheism and Objectivism, the more central principle is the affirmation of humankind's freedom. The atheism is generally taken for granted in forms of postulatory atheism as being so obvious as not worth arguing for, and less important than the central principle that follows on from the original atheism.

Further reading: William A. Luijpen, *Phenomenology and Atheism*.

POVERTY. A debilitating condition with many causes. Extreme poverty is defined by the **World Bank** as living on less than one US dollar (set at 1985 rates) per day. It is estimated that 1.2 billion people are, by this standard, extremely poor. In Africa, 40 percent of the population lives on under a dollar a day. And around the world a further 2.8 billion people live on only two dollars a day. But poverty is more than simply having less money than other people. Poverty is a broader lack of access to a variety of **rights** and opportunities, and education and **human**

needs—what the Nobel Prize–winning economist Amartya Sen summarizes as capability deprivation. Seeing poverty as capability deprivation is the better approach because:

- capability deprivation is intrinsically important whereas low income is only instrumentally important;
- there are more influences on capability deprivation than on low income; and
- instrumental relation between low income and low capability varies with cultures.

What could be considered poverty in one society may well be inappropriate for another. Understanding poverty in these terms also has implications for education and health policies, in that educating people with the sole or primary aim of reducing low incomes will not necessarily help reduce poverty. Poverty is also linked, though in various ways, to **inequality**.

Another feature of poverty that has been properly understood only recently is its prevalence among women. The United Nation's Convention on the Elimination of All Forms of Discrimination against Women estimates that in developing countries, women receive between a third and a half of the—already modest—pay that men receive. As with respect to reproductive rights, it is also true that the key to economic progress is to ensure the rights of women.

Further reading: Amartya Sen, *Development as Freedom* and Micheline Ishay, *A History of Human Rights*.

POWER. Defined by Karl Deutsch (1912–1992) as "the ability to afford not to learn." This, as Deutsch well knew, is a privilege given to only a very few, and even then is an illusory condition. In philosophical terms, power is what is exercised against others or through the filter of coercion. Authority, by contrast, is the condition of exercising responsible leadership over a people who have granted the sovereign that right to lead. Working on this definition, it

can be said that power is a dangerous thing, and is against the interests of **democracy** and **global governance**. See the entry on **reciprocity, criterion of**.

PRAGMATISM. A philosophical movement that began in the United States in the later part of the nineteenth century and centered around the works of Charles Peirce (1839–1914), **William James**, and **John Dewey**. Pragmatism fell into disuse from the 1930s and was revived in the 1970s, principally by **Richard Rorty**, to the extent that his name is often now seen as synonymous with pragmatism.

The main insight of pragmatism is that intellectual activity is not so much a process of coming to grips with transcendental questions for which answers exist, independently of the observer, as of practical problem solving in day-to-day activity. The two main targets of early pragmatist criticisms were the notions of **certainty** and independence. Pragmatists argued against the related notions of independent agents finding certainty through the dispassionate application of reason. Pragmatists have had an ambivalent relationship with **external realism**, which argues for the independence of the natural world in relation to human **knowledge** and beliefs about the world. Generally, pragmatists have sought to distance themselves from external realism without seeing themselves as irreconcilable with it. The relationship with truth was put most succinctly by William James with respect to **religion**. In what has become known as the pragmatic criterion, James said "religion doesn't work because it's true, it's true because it works."

Pragmatism has been described as a subspecies of **postmodernism**, an observation related to the importance of Rorty in contemporary pragmatism. However, other variations of pragmatism are considerably closer to notions of **naturalism** than postmodernists. See the entries on **reality** and **critical common-sensism**.

Further reading: John R. Shook, ed., *Pragmatic Naturalism and Realism*.

PRAYER. The ability to talk to oneself without feeling silly. Frederick Denison Maurice (1805–1872), an English liberal churchman, proposed an argument against prayer that has remained relevant. Maurice asked if God's will is good then why try to change it by petitions and intercessions? And if God's will is not good, then praying to change God's will is completely futile, given his omnipotence. The Indian philosopher Sarvepalli Radhakrishnan (1888–1975) spoke of prayer as "bargaining with **God**. It seeks for objects of earthly ambitions and inflames the sense of self."

For a short while in 2001, there were rumors that a major scientific study, led by three Columbia University medical scholars, had proved the efficacy of prayer. The study purported to show that infertile women who had been prayed for had a spectacularly higher rate of becoming pregnant than the women who had not been prayed for. Pretty soon, the flawed and even fraudulent nature of the study became known, and it has been dropped. Rogerio Lobo, once touted as the leader of the study, has now distanced himself from it. Another of the study's authors, Daniel Wirth, is now in prison for a long list of frauds, many of them committed in **paranormal** circles. And Kwang Yul Cha, the third author of the study, is no longer with Columbia University and is trying to keep low and ride the storm out. The "Miracle Study," as the media touted it, turns out to have more in common with the frauds perpetrated on behalf of parapsychology by **George Soal**.

The most positive value of an activity like prayer is the opportunity for a period of calm and quiet for the person. Prayer can be worthwhile, not because God or some other supernatural entity will hear and respond, but because the person doing the praying has a chance for a little bit of quality time to him- or herself. But equally, of course, this can be achieved by **meditation**, listening to a favorite piece of music, or just sitting quietly watching the world go by. And these methods have the advantage of not succumbing to the **transcendental temptation**.

Further reading: Bruce Flamm, "The Columbia University 'Miracle' Study: Flawed and Fraud," *Skeptical Inquirer* 28, no. 5 (Sept.–Oct. 2004): 25–31.

PRECAUTIONARY PRINCIPLE. A principle of science management which states that if the consequences of an action are uncertain or a matter of serious dispute between knowledgeable people, then that action should not be proceeded with. The precautionary principle emerged from European environmental thinking in the 1970s, but did not acquire this title until later in the 1980s. The principle is usually cited in the context of technological, climatic, or genetic research that does not have the support of the overwhelming majority of the scientific community. See the entry on **genetic engineering**.

The precautionary principle has the important consequence of shifting the **burden of proof** onto the advocates of the change, rather than those who oppose it. Supporters of the principle say this is entirely appropriate when considering some potentially dangerous new idea. Critics of the principle say that this amounts to a "guilty until proven innocent" approach to **science**, which, if taken seriously, would bring to an end any major scientific research.

PRE-SOCRATIC PHILOSOPHERS. A general term to describe the Greek philosophers who were active before **Socrates**. Many historians and philosophers have had reason to admire the general attitude of the Pre-Socratics, even if their actual opinions are of less value than the attitudes which underlie them. **Bertrand Russell** praised them for not only having an open, **scientific attitude** of inquiry but for their creativity and imagination. In fact, most of the basic categories of philosophy began with them. And the first Pre-Socratic philosopher, **Thales**, is credited with the invention of **science**. The Pre-Socratic philosophers can be divided into five major strands:

412   Presumption of Atheism

- *Ionians*, including **Thales**, **Anaximander**, **Anaxagoras**, and **Anaximenes**;
- *Pythagoreans*, including **Pythagoras** and his followers;
- *Eleatics*, including **Xenophanes**, **Parmenides**, and Zeno;
- *Sophists*, including **Protagoras**, Gorgias, Hippias, and **Socrates**; and
- *Atomists*, including **Democritus** and Leucippus.

The Pre-Socratic philosophers had little in common apart from the historical accident of being born before Socrates. They represented a variety of viewpoints, although it's fair to say that most of them were naturalistic in approach. Tragically, very few works of any Pre-Socratic philosopher has survived in full. Their work was destroyed by religious zealots at the **Alexandria Library**. Often we only know the thoughts of the Pre-Socratic philosophers from their enemies.

PRESUMPTION OF ATHEISM. An idea introduced by **Antony Flew** that claims the **burden of proof** in the argument about the existence of **God** lies with the theist. It is up to the theist to introduce and defend his idea of God and to demonstrate that his idea has some application. Flew gives the example of a work associate suspected of having behaved discreditably. The proper course of action for his colleagues is to refrain from asserting they know the action did happen until there is sufficient evidence to warrant such a claim. Flew goes on to say that if this is the right action in everyday matters such as this, it is also the right action with regard to claims about God and eternal life. We don't vilify our work associates without sufficient evidence, so why make claims about the entire universe on similarly weak grounds?

Many people then evade this challenge by declaring their belief in God to be a matter of **faith**. But Flew points out that, if one's faith is not going to be frivolous and arbitrary, the theist must at some point present some sound reasons to justify the particular construct one's faith allegedly demonstrates.

Contrary to the claims of the more populist style apologists, the presumption of atheism is not the same as the presumptuousness of atheism. As Flew points out, the notion has been employed by theist philosophers for centuries. It is also geared toward inculcating a modesty in the claims one is prepared to make and defend, which is the opposite to presumptuousness. See also the entry on the **Stratonician Presumption**.

Further reading: Antony Flew, *God, Freedom, and Immortality*.

PRICE, ROBERT M. See **FORMER PREACHERS**

PRIMITIVE CHRISTIANITY. One of the more enduring myths people have believed about Christianity is that it began with a period of primitive simplicity, which was later lost by growing sophistication and worldliness. This myth has been particularly important for people seeking to effect some sort of reform within Christianity. Many strands of Protestantism, for instance, hold great store by this myth, for it is their claim to legitimacy against the Roman Catholic Church, which has its own, different, myth of its legitimacy having been bestowed upon by the **Petrine text**.

What twentieth-century scholarship has revealed is very different. Far from a period of primitive simplicity, the earliest decades of Christianity were characterized by a great variety of contradictory and antagonistic viewpoints, with each side anathematizing each other as heretics. Only slowly did certain views achieve dominance and, as history is written by the victors, they then cast themselves as the true believers from the earliest times.

PRINCIPLE. Described by **Paul Kurtz** as "a rule of conduct, a standard, or norm governing action." So, a person of principle is a person who can be relied upon to act in a predictable way, and more than that, predictable in a way favorable (or at least not harmful) to others. See the entry on **character**.

It does not follow, of course, that a person's principles can't change. It would be surprising if a person could go through a full life without experiencing some need to alter one's principles in the light of new **evidence**. This suggests maturity and a willingness to recognize error in one's own view of the world. In fact, principles invite their application in various contexts. **Command moralities** have a problem with this adaptability, and prefer a more inflexible code that is more attuned to ascribing blame than facilitating the ability to take personal responsibility, which is implied in the notion of principle. See the entry on **Doctrine of the Mean (Kongfuzi)**.

PRISCA THEOLOGIA. A brand of Renaissance **mysticism**. *Prisca theologia* means "first theology," and is related to, though not the same as, the **perennial philosophy**. *Prisca theologia* arose as an idea in the **Renaissance** and was concerned with the so-called original pagan theology which gave birth to Christianity. Thinkers like Marsilio Ficino (1433–1499) and Giovanni Pico della Mirandola (1463–1494) sought to harmonize Platonism, **Neoplatonism**, and **Pythagoreanism** with Christian theology in the belief that at the core of all these philosophies lay an essential harmony. The idea of *prisca theologia* was later taken up by mystical sects such as the Rosicrucians and **Theosophy**.

While the details of *prisca theologia* hold little water academically, it is interesting to note that even among the Renaissance thinkers who remained enraptured by supernaturalism, the orthodox Christian account was no longer adequate.

PROGRESS. A view of history that is essentially secular in its orientation, although it does not follow that **secularism** must therefore involve a belief in progress. The first serious discussions of progress developed in Britain and France in the seventeenth and eighteenth centuries, but it was not until the nineteenth century that the idea of progress became very influential across a wide body of people.

In the nineteenth century the essentially liberal notion of progress was taken over by Marxists, who strapped on to progress the idea of historical inevitability. This view became known as **historicism** and was brilliantly demolished by **Karl Popper** in *The Poverty of Historicism* (1957) and *The Open Society and Its Enemies* (1945).

The nonhistoricist idea of progress was expounded in the most systematic way by the English scholar J. B. Bury (1861–1927). In his work *The Idea of Progress* (1920), Bury saw progress as a synthesis of the past and a **prophecy** of the future. Progress is an entirely secular notion, he maintained, because otherwise it would merely become a theory of providence. It was, he added, the achievements of physical science that did more than anything else to instill the idea of progress.

The basic argument against a guarantee of progress, according to **Antony Flew**, is that humans can make choices, which implies that we can make choices of an unprogressive nature. But many authors have defended a modest notion of progress. After all, they argue, it is difficult to deny that we know more facts about the world as each year goes by. This steady accumulation of **knowledge** is most evident in the sciences, as Bury observed in his theorizing about progress at the beginning of the twentieth century. So, if progress is not written into the fabric of the cosmos, it is true that we have more knowledge than was ever the case previously. And with that greater knowledge, at least in principle, we have more options. See the entry on **meliorlism**.

PROLIFERATION SECURITY INITIATIVE. An initiative sparked by the recognition of the Bush administration late in 2002 that it had no international authority to seize a shipment of missiles heading to Yemen from North Korea. By June 2003 the initiative was fully operational.

At the time of its writing the initiative comprises eleven countries: Australia, France, Germany, Italy, Japan, the Netherlands, Poland, Portugal, Spain, the United Kingdom, and the United States. The idea is for this grouping to share intelligence on the passage of weapons of mass destruction to and from countries of "proliferation concern," in particular, North Korea and Iran, the two countries against which the initiative is primarily directed. It also allows for the search and detention of vessels thought to be carrying weapons of mass destruction (WMD) material as they pass through a member's territory.

The initiative remains highly controversial, as it is still unclear whether members have any more right to detain vessels than the United States on its own. The initiative's relationship to international law and the United Nations is, at the time of writing, far from clear.

PROMETHEAN ETHICS. A concept advanced by the American philosopher Marvin Kohl. Promethean ethics, Kohl argues, combines the audacity traditionally associated with **Prometheus** with the virtues of disinterested sympathy, benevolence, and beneficence. Promethean ethics require more than **love** and **knowledge**, which are not enough on their own. In order to be effective, love and knowledge need to be fired with energy and praxis. This is a very similar idea to that championed by **Paul Kurtz** in his notion of **eupraxsophy**.

Promethean ethics require of us an active engagement in the welfare of humanity through acts of "sympathetic imagination and beneficence." Promethean ethics, Kohl says, "reminds us that fear, whether it be of the gods or physical nature, ultimately gives rise to a self-defeating conservatism." We cannot be compelled to admire something because it is "natural." Cancer is natural, as is disease, infirmity, and **death**. To combat these and other natural evils is not wrong. And Promethean ethics is specifically atheistic. It rejects the idea of a beneficent providence on the grounds of there being little evidence for

such a notion and a huge amount of evidence against it. Because "Prometheus" means "forethought," Promethean ethics are committed to human beings taking **responsibility** for building a better world in the future. But that better world will not be rushed into without forethought. Scientific or technological innovations will be thought about carefully before they are implemented.

And Promethean ethics, once again because of the emphasis on forethought, understands that making the world a better place for human beings, means ensuring it is a better place for all nonhuman beings as well. As opposed to the simplistic **dominionism** of the **monotheist** religions and the even more widespread **speciesism**, Prometheanism sees a place for all living and nonliving things on the planet. It recognizes the complex interdependence of living and nonliving things and is not given to the **anthropocentric conceit** of according human beings an exalted place on a **great chain of being**. See the entries on **humanist virtues** and **humanist values**.

Further reading: Marvin Kohl, "The Nature of Promethean Ethics," *The Humanist*, Jan-Feb 1996.

PROMETHEUS. The mythological symbol of **freethinkers**. **Bertrand Russell** wrote that the essential character of civilization is forethought, and it is significant that "Prometheus" means "forethought."

Prometheus was one of the titans, the earliest of the divinities. Unlike the other titans, Prometheus could see that their days were over and the rule of the gods, led by Zeus was about to begin, so he sided with the gods. All sorts of evocative stories are attached to Prometheus, which has made him a rich mine of imagery. Chief among them is the story of Prometheus stealing fire from Zeus and giving it to humanity. Armed with fire, humans were able to grow and learn. This enraged the overbearing Zeus, who had Prometheus chained forever to Mount Caucasus where an eagle (or a vulture in other versions) would return at nightfall and slowly pick his liver out. By morning the wound would heal, in time for the torment to begin again the following nightfall. After thirty generations of suffering, Prometheus was freed from his chains by Heracles. But his release was not through the magnanimity of Zeus, but rather Zeus's continuing need for Prometheus's power of forethought. The story goes that Greeks would wear a ring on their finger in memory of the suffering Prometheus endured on their behalf. Prometheus is in this sense an early prototype of **dying and resurrected gods**.

Freethinkers have always responded to the warmth, tragedy, even the elements of comedy in the Prometheus story. Prometheus is a model of fiery anger against unreasoning authority and the caprice of the gods. Prometheus is the primal **rebel**. Conservatives have maligned Prometheus as an exemplar of hubris, or arrogance, or merely as a trickster. But freethinkers don't see it as arrogant to redress injustices. The **Greek playwrights**, **Goethe**, **Shelley**, Robert Graves (1895–1985), and **Carl Spitteler** have all expressed the humanist value of the Prometheus story in different ways. Lord Byron (1788–1824) put it best:

> Thy godlike crime was to be kind,
> To render with thy precepts less
> The sum of human wretchedness.

The two central themes in the Prometheus story for freethinkers are the themes of forethought and rebellion against oppression. See the entries on **Promethean ethics** and **mythology**.

PROMETHEUS BOOKS. The publishing house founded in August 1969 by **Paul Kurtz** with the aim of providing an outlet for works of a naturalist, humanist, and skeptical perspective. Originally little more than a part-time activity, Prometheus Books slowly became recognized as one of the premier publishing houses of its kind in the world. Its first publication was called *Tolerance and Revolution* (1970), an account of a series of Marxist/humanist dialogues. Since then it has published more than 3,000 titles, at a rate of about 110 new titles a year.

Prometheus Books can be seen as the successor to Pemberton Books, the publishing wing of the **Rationalist Press Association** (RPA). Some of Prometheus's earliest titles were from the Pemberton list. And like Watts and Co., the RPA's original publishing house, Prometheus Books does not restrict itself to publishing **freethought** material only. This is one of the reasons for its success. For example, it has published series of works for children, for gays and lesbians, and for senior citizens. Prometheus has also taken on publishing works of contemporary politics and social issues. With respect to **religion**, perhaps most notable has been its willingness to publish scholarly works critical of Islam. This was not common practice before the intensification of the **war on terror** after 2001. See the entry on **Ibn Warraq**.

Prometheus also runs some comprehensive series, the more important being *Contemporary Issues*, the *Great Minds Series*, and *Great Books in Philosophy*. Prometheus raised its standing with respect to philosophy in 1998 when it bought Humanity Books, which has become its scholarly imprint. And in 2004 it inaugurated its science fiction imprint called **Pyr**. Science fiction is very popular among freethinkers, from **H. G. Wells** through to **Isaac Asimov**. Interest in science fiction began in 2000 with the publication of *Galactic Rapture* by *Free Inquiry* editor **Tom Flynn**. Pyr's foundation editorial director is Lou Anders, a prolific science fiction writer. Anders has edited four anthologies, including *Live Without a Net* (2003) and has published over five hundred magazine articles. Previously, Anders was executive editor of an online publishing site, an agent for Titan Publishing Group, and senior editor of *Argosy Magazine*.

PROMETHEUS LECTURE SERIES. A series of lectures, which are then published, by eminent philosophers on various aspects of **naturalism**, **atheism**, and **humanism**. The publications in this series constitute a very significant contribution to the ongoing intellectual credibility of these outlooks. The books in the series include:

- **Antony Flew**, *Atheistic Humanism* (1993);
- Kai Nielsen, *Naturalism without Foundations* (1996);
- Kurt Baier, *Problems of Life and Death: A Humanistic Perspective* (1997);
- Mario Bunge, *Philosophy in Crisis: The Need for Reconstruction* (2001);
- Richard H. Schlagel, *Vanquished Gods: Science, Religion, and the Nature of Belief* (2001); and
- **Michael Martin**, *Atheism, Morality, and Meaning* (2002)

At the time of this writing, plans are afoot for the expansion of the Prometheus Lecture Series.

PROOF. A sequence of sentences, each of which follows without contradiction from its predecessor, ending in a theorem in which a degree of confidence can be attested. Proofs require different levels of confidence, depending on the discipline. For example, in law, proof is when something has been established beyond *reasonable* doubt, but in **mathematics**, proof is when something has been established beyond any *possible* doubt. So, outside of mathematics, we need to exercise our **judgment** as to what constitutes being beyond reasonable doubt. See the entries on **evidence**, **reason**, and **certainty**.

PROPHECY. Usually thought of as polemical or threatening warnings of doom to all who disagree with the prophet in question. The **Hebrew scriptures** are full of this sort of prophet: Elijah and Ezekiel being perhaps the classic examples. American **fundamentalism** would be out of business without prophets of this sort, whose warnings of

imminent apocalypse are the bread and butter of the fundamentalist fear factor.

But prophets come in different shapes and sizes. Two of the most interesting and visionary prophets were **H. G. Wells** and **Friedrich Nietzsche**, whose different works foresaw significant aspects of the modern world.

Arthur C. Clarke has distinguished two common forms of the failure of prophecy: failures of nerve and failures of imagination. Failure of nerve is the more common of the two. This involves the inability to see the obvious facts in the face of all the relevant evidence. The frequent declarations by many prominent scientists early last century that a heavier-than-air flying machine was impossible is a prime example. The other failure lies in the imagination, which is the situation when all available facts are known and understood, with one critical exception. An example of this is Lord Rutherford (1871–1937), who frequently made fun of those who thought his discovery of splitting the atom could lead to harnessing energy locked up in matter. The truly great prophet is able to then infer the existence of that extra, as yet unknown fact, and move learning along as a result.

PROTAGORAS (485–411 BCE, approx.). Greek thinker associated with the **Sophists** and one of the world's first known agnostics. Protagoras was born in Abdera (the city of **Democritus**) but spent most of his life in Athens where he taught for forty years, becoming a wealthy man in the process.

The most oft-quoted saying of Protagoras is his statement that man is the measure of all things. He has been criticized for arrogantly writing humanity across the cosmos, but this is not what Protagoras was saying. What he meant was that, like it or not, we are the standard by which we understand things. Centuries later, **Ludwig Wittgenstein** wrote that if a lion could talk, we would not understand him because we don't understand the lion's world. This is all Protagoras was saying: we can only understand the universe on the terms of the equipment we have to understand it with.

In his book *Of the Gods*, Protagoras gave expression to one of the earliest declarations of agnosticism when he said: "About the gods I have no means of knowing either that they exist or that they do not exist or what they are like to look at; many things prevent my knowing—among others, the fact that they are never seen and the shortness of human life." *Of the Gods* was publicly burned in Athens and Protagoras was brought to trial in 411 BCE for impiety. It is likely that he drowned while on his way to exile in Sicily.

PSEUDEPIGRAPHY. The false attribution of an author to a particular body of writing; a kind of **pious fraud**. The word derives from the Greek *pseudos* (liar, deceiver) and *epigraphy* (write on something). Many books of the **Hebrew Bible** and New Testament, for example, are attributed falsely to someone who did not, and often could not, have actually written the work. The easiest example is the book of Deuteronomy, which is traditionally said to have been written by Moses, and yet, toward the end of the book, "Moses" writes about his own death (34:5). In the same vein, none of the Gospels of the New Testament were actually written by the people later said to be the authors: Matthew, Mark, Luke, and John. These names were not given to the Gospels until late in the second century CE.

Closely related to pseudepigraphy is the pseudepigrapha, which refers to a body of writings, none of which were included in the Hebrew Bible or the New Testament, and which were written between 250 BCE and 200 CE. Many of these works were ascribed to some prominent person from the Hebrew or Christian Bible, usually in order to increase the authority the work might enjoy among the readers.

PSEUDOMORPHOSIS. A word used to describe a metamorphosis that is not as complete as is generally thought. André Chastel spoke of the cultural pseudomorphosis of Renaissance art from the models derived from the ancient world. More recently the Serbian political philosopher Svetozar Stojanovic used this term to describe the transition from state socialism under Josip Broz Tito to the supposedly democratic state under Slobodan Milosevic.

A characteristic feature of pseudomorphosis is that the elites from the previous system are fundamentally unchanged and have merely reinvented themselves for the new system. Behind that showy reinvention, however, the essentials of state power and of who wields it remain the same. The pseudomorphosis model applies well to Serbia, but also to Romania and several of the former Soviet republics, in particular Belarus, Uzbekistan, and Turkmenistan.

Further reading: Svetozar Stojanovic, *Serbia: The Democratic Revolution*.

PSEUDO-RATIONALISM. Described by **Karl Popper** as an immodest belief in one's own superior intellectual gifts, or a claim to be among a select few of initiated people, those with special knowledge. It is an overweening intellectual arrogance. Popper mentioned **Plato** as an exemplar of pseudo-rationalism. Popper distinguished pseudo-rationalism from true or **critical rationalism**.

PSEUDOSCIENCE. Notions believed to have some form of scientific validity but which have been comprehensively **debunked** or shown to be erroneous by the scientific community. Examples of pseudoscience include astrology, crop circles, faith healing, claims of psychic powers or clairvoyance, **UFOs**, Nostradamus, pyramid power, **creationism**, and its recent sibling, **"intelligent" design**.

The Australian geologist Ian Plimer has itemized fifteen characteristic features of pseudoscience, and contrasted them with their opposite scientific characteristic. The characteristics of pseudoscience are:

- **dogmatism**, as opposed to openness to criticism;

- fixed ideas, as opposed to having a willingness to change;
- selected favorable discoveries, as opposed to absorbing all new discoveries, whether or not they are conducive to one's theory;
- absence of any peer review process;
- cultic, depending on personalities rather than on the substance of the idea;
- claims of widespread usefulness, often in moral areas, outside the field's actual area;
- narrow, constrained and bigoted as opposed to transnational in outlook;
- criticism viewed as conspiracy rather than as an important and welcome part of the process;
- many benefits to the proponent of the theory, as opposed to abstract benefits to humanity;
- arranged to be unfalsifiable, in direct contradiction to scientific practice;
- cherished ideas valued without regard to their veracity;
- appeals to authority, again, in direct contradiction to scientific practice;
- measurements at the limit of detection, as opposed to accurate measurements;
- nonrepeatable, as opposed to being repeatable by peers; and
- inability to predict, unlike scientific theories, which usually do have the ability to predict.

Plimer noted that **creationism** fulfils all fifteen criteria of pseudoscience. Where scientific ideas are developed on the basis of observation, measurement, calculation, and experiment, pseudoscience is characterized by **dogmatism**, avoiding peer review, appeals to authority, viewing criticism as evidence of conspiracy or dishonesty, and a cultic dependence on charismatic individuals. Evidence for pseudoscience is usually secondhand or anecdotal, and the photographs are grainy. Frequently, as was the case with crop circles, the phenomenon turns out to be simple fraud. See the entries on **science** and **skepticism, core principles of**.

Further reading, Ian Plimer: *Telling Lies for God: Reason vs. Creationism.*

PSEUDOVALUES. Identified by the Russian philosopher Valerii Kuvakin as a catchall word for the values emanating from errors, delusions, prejudices, and myths (popularly understood) which, as well as being doubtful in principle, serve to undermine more positive human values because of their pretension to truth. Kuvakin acknowledges that pseudovalues may even produce some good, but says that, because of their having originated in error, delusions, prejudices, and myth, such effects are necessarily accidental, short lived, and unreliable. See the entries on **rationalism, principles of** and **veracity**.

Further reading: Valerii Kuvakin, *In Search of Our Humanity.*

PSYCHE. Greek word often mistranslated as **soul**. This understanding of the word would be misleading, however. The Greeks had no hard and fast opposition between **mind** and body that is a characteristic of supernaturalist worldviews. For the Greeks, psyche meant more the animating principle of life, rather than a discrete part of our body which can be separated at **death**. Anaximenes, for instance, thought the psyche was air.

PSYCHOANALYSIS.   Long-discredited pseudoscientific fad invented by the Austrian thinker **Sigmund Freud** and developed by the Swiss physician **Carl Gustav Jung**. The central idea of psychoanalysis is the belief that there is something called the unconscious, which is home to all the essential human traits, and that only by a technique known as free association can the secrets of the unconscious be unlocked. Freud took almost no notice of the critical role the conscious mind has in determining the unconscious. According to psychoanalysis, any method of understanding the unconscious apart from free association is bound to fail, because all other methods will fail to overcome the resistance of the unconscious to being unraveled.

And of course the only people who are able to conduct free association properly are authenticated psychoanalysts.

Psychoanalysis has three very significant weaknesses. One is that it is inclined to see psychological reasons for the client's complaint, but if the problem is actually physical, it is often too late for the illness to be treated by the time it has been properly diagnosed. Another weakness is Freud's attitude toward women, which is the hallmark more of his own failings rather than the sober conclusions of an advanced science. And finally, because the person being psychoanalyzed is also a paying customer, there is a strong incentive to prolong the treatment.

Part of the appeal of psychoanalysis is its ability to provide answers to everything, but as many critics of it have observed, it is precisely this that is its chief failing. Psychoanalysis further protects itself from any criticism by simply pigeonholing any disagreement with psychoanalysis as evidence of "resistance." In this way it renders itself impervious to criticism. This circularity of psychoanalysis is one of the reasons it should be seen as a **pseudoscience**. The intellectual antecedents of psychoanalysis are pseudosciences like clairvoyance, phrenology, and mesmerism. See the entry on **rational-emotive behavior therapy**.

Further reading: Karl Popper, "The Problem of Demarcation" in *A Pocket Popper*; and Jeffrey Moussaieff Masson, *Against Therapy*.

PSYCHOLOGICAL INERTIA, PRINCIPLE OF. See **PARADIGM**.

PUBLIC REASON. A concept with its origins in the thought of **Immanuel Kant** but which became known in its current form through the work of the political philosopher **John Rawls**. Public reason is one of Rawls's most important concepts. It is, he says, the characteristic of a democratic people. Public reason is the reason of free and equal citizens: it takes place in public and is about the good of the public and about matters of fundamental justice.

Public reason is not about creating an overarching conformity of thought or zeal of commitment. On the contrary, public reason allows for more than one reasonable perspective on any issue. The point is that public reason is about not bringing our political and religious viewpoints into public debate on constitutional matters or the limits on rights and responsibilities. Public reason is the mechanism whereby citizens in a democratic society exercise coercive powers over one another.

Rawls saw the American Supreme Court as an exemplar of how public reason operates. The job of the Supreme Court is to reconcile the ideals and provisions of the Constitution with the various precedents regarding the case at hand, and in doing so, furthering the application of the Constitution in a way broadly consonant with its original aims. The political and religious views of each Supreme Court justice is, in principle, irrelevant to their professional work. Using Rawlsian language, there should be a **veil of ignorance** regarding the personal views of the justices themselves. Americans will know how far from that ideal we are.

Further reading: John Rawls, *Political Liberalism*.

PUBLIC WORSHIP REGULATION ACT. An act of the British parliament, passed in 1874, which was designed to combat the perceived menace of too great an emphasis upon ritualism in Protestant churches. England was sensitive to what it perceived as undue Roman Catholic influence on the English church. The act was a failure because it attempted to coerce a minority of ritualist-inclined churchmen into order. The few who were determined to continue were able to assume the moral high ground by posing as martyrs to the true **faith**. The ritualists, relatively unpopular before the act, became much more widely respected, even by those who continued to oppose them.

And the Church of England came out of the whole exercise looking small-minded and foolish.

The Public Worship Regulation Act is also a noteworthy milestone in the making of post-Christian Britain. Not only was it a textbook case in the failure of legislating **morality** and belief, it was also the last time a session of the British parliament was preoccupied with ecclesiastical matters.

PULLMAN, PHILIP (1946–). English novelist and **smiter of humbug**. Philip Pullman was born in Norwich on October 19, 1946, the son of a Royal Air Force serviceman. When he was eleven his family moved to North Wales. He studied English at Exeter College, Oxford, before embarking on a teaching career. He then moved into adult education at Westminster College, Oxford, before becoming a full-time writer.

Pullman has managed the difficult task of writing books accessible both for children and adults. His *Dark Materials* trilogy, *Northern Lights* (1995), *The Subtle Knife* (1997), and *The Amber Spyglass* (2001) have been especially successful. *Northern Lights* won the 1996 Carnegie Medal and *The Amber Spyglass* won the 2001 Whitbread Prize. The *Dark Materials* trilogy is a classic tale of a struggle against the dark forces of the Inquisition, witch burning, and fanatical religious zeal. Rather than seeing the Fall as a catastrophe for humanity, Pullman sees the onset of human freedom and knowledge as something to celebrate. Pullman is an unabashed agnostic. Referring to Blake's observation that Milton was of the Devil's Party without knowing it, Pullman said "I am of the Devil's party, and I know it." Pullman is a fellow of the **Committee for the Scientific Examination of Religion**.

Other works by Pullman include *The Ruby in the Smoke* (1985), *The Shadow in the North* (1987), *The Tin Princess* (1994), and *I Was a Rat!* (1999). He is an authority on Victorian Britain, and his novels are often set at that time. See the entry on **humanist-themed novels**.

PUNISHMENTS AND REWARDS, ARGUMENT FROM. One of the older and more popular variations of a broader argument from motivation, used by theists to claim an exclusive access to morality. The argument from punishments and rewards, which declares that people who do not believe in **God** will not follow an **objective morality**, is widely used by religious fundamentalists. The argument founders on two simple observations:

- there are in fact, and have always been, people who do not believe in God but who do espouse an objective morality; and
- there are many people who do believe in conventional religious punishments and rewards who nevertheless behave immorally.

It is highly problematic, then, to claim that nonreligious people are less likely to behave morally because they are not constrained by fears of punishment or hope of reward. The argument also cheapens the value of moral behavior by linking it up with a simplistic system of punishments and rewards. This eliminates the possibility of doing good without thought of personal reward.

Further reading: Michael Martin, *Atheism, Morality, and Meaning*.

PUTNAM, SAMUEL PORTER (1838–1896). Leading nineteenth-century American freethinker. Samuel Putnam was born in Chichester, New Hampshire, on July 23, 1838, the son of a Congregational minister. In 1864, after three years active duty in the Union army, Putnam had a religious conversion and resigned from the army to pursue a career as a minister. After studying at the Chicago Theological Seminary, he worked as a Congregationalist preacher. But his stay with religious orthodoxy was brief. In 1871, Putnam joined the **Unitarians**, but even this move could not keep pace with his evermore radical religious views. Within a few years he left the Unitarians and turned to organized **freethought**. Putnam's radicalization also helped destroy his marriage of eighteen years to Louise Howell, which ended in 1885 on the ground of "religious and temperamental differences."

From 1879 until the end of his life Putnam was involved in the freethought movement, traveling extensively around the United States. He estimated that he traveled one hundred thousand miles during his lecturing career. In the summer of 1895, he made a successful lecture tour of Great Britain. Between 1888 and 1891, he was based in San Francisco where, with his friend **George E. Macdonald**, founded and ran the journal *Freethought*, which was funded largely by Putnam's tireless traveling and lecturing. The Depression forced Putnam and Macdonald back to New York in 1892, where he turned to the question of freethought organization. At a meeting he called in Chicago on September 4, 1892, he formed the Freethought Federation of America, with himself as president. It was Putnam's goal to create an effective political voice for freethought. He remained president of this organization until his death.

Putnam also found time to write poetry and articles, but his most sustained effort was *Four Hundred Years of Freethought*, a massive work, put out to coincide with the four-hundredth anniversary of the discovery of America. The title notwithstanding, the book was really a celebration of freethought as it stood at that time.

Putnam died on December 11, 1896, in mysterious circumstances. He, along with an attractive, twenty year old protégé, Miss May Collins, were both found dead in her hotel room in Boston. Putnam had been waiting for Collins to accompany her out to the theater when they were "poisoned by illuminating gas." Putnam's friend George Macdonald hastened to add that the "bodies of both, dressed for the street, were found on the floor."

PYRRHONISM. A strand of Greek thought that began with Pyrrho the Skeptic (365–270 BCE). Pyrrhonists were the original philosophers of **skepticism**. The Greek word *skeptikoi* means inquirer or searcher. As with so many Greek thinkers, we know little about Pyrrho, and he left no writings of his own. It was said that he was a soldier in the army of Alexander the Great (356–323 BCE) and that he learned his skeptical attitude in India from the naked philosophers there, who may well have been **Jains**. However, there was no shortage of skeptical thinking in the Greek tradition. Like the **Epicureans** and the **Stoics**, the Skeptics were keen to find ways to tranquility. The method of the Skeptics was to do so by avoiding the tensions raised by taking dogmatic positions on things.

For a while the finest Skeptics were teachers at **Plato's Academy**, in particular Arcesilaus (315–240 BCE, approx.) and **Carneades**. But the next great Skeptic thinker was Sextus Empiricus (third century CE), who continued the work of Carneades by tidying up the thoughts of Pyrrho. Sextus argued that Skeptics should live without opinions. This was not so much, as had earlier been argued, that because for every good argument for something there is an equally good argument against it. Sextus's argument was more that we should not rush to conclude that our argument is right and cannot be improved upon. Sextus was strongly critical of those he called **dogmatists**, that is, those who are confident they have found the **truth**. We also owe our knowledge of ancient skepticism to Sextus Empiricus, whose two books, *Outlines of Pyrrhonism* and *Against the Dogmatists* summed up the movement so far. Ancient Pyrrhonism was summarized brilliantly by the little-known thinker Aenesidemus (first century CE) who compiled what are known as the **Ten Tropes of Judgment**.

Pyrrhonism died out after Sextus Empiricus, but, along with other important strands of Greek thought, was rediscovered in the Renaissance and contributed mightily to the scientific revolution of the seventeenth century and beyond. Influenced by Sextus Empiricus, thinkers like Pierre Gassendi

(1592–1655) reintroduced aspects of classical skepticism into European thought.

Further reading: Myles Burnyeat, ed., *The Skeptical Tradition*.

PYTHAGORAS. Vastly influential **Pre-Socratic** philosopher, although very little is known about him. To the degree he was a historical character at all, he was probably born between 580 and 550 BCE on the island of Samos. He is thought to have left Samos when in his forties and moved to Croton, a Greek colony in southern Italy, where he became active in town politics. Late in his life, the people of Croton rebelled against him and his followers, and he was sent into exile. The revolt was probably against the rather joyless and puritanical conditions the Pythagoreans wanted to impose on their fellow citizens. For a couple of centuries Pythagorean communities lingered; these were religious communes brought together for the practice of asceticism and the study of **mathematics**, which was seen as a religious vocation.

Nothing that Pythagoras wrote himself has survived, so most of what is attributed to him is found in the works of others. He was essentially a **mystical** thinker who believed in a rational cosmos, and by rational he meant divine. His was an early **dualist** philosopher of good and evil, which taught the transmigration of souls. The purpose of life, he thought, is to purify the **soul** by an understanding of the arithmetical purity of the universe and a life of sober piety.

Quite in any way the most important admirer of Pythagoras was **Plato**, who reproduced his thought in the *Timmaeus*. Pythagoras as rendered by Plato was read by Boethius (480–525 CE), who in turn bequeathed it to the Middle Ages. The ascetic and dualist strand of Pythagoreanism found its way into Platonism, **Neoplatonism**, and Christianity. The first crack in the Pythagorean worldview came when they discovered the existence of irrational numbers—something they had not expected.

More helpful was the Pythagorean cosmology, which dissented from the usual picture of Earth as the center of the universe. The Pythagoreans spoke of the mutually balancing forces of the central hearth and the counter hearth, around which everything revolved. These observations were an inspiration for Nicholas Copernicus (1473–1543) and **Kepler** to pursue their studies that established the **heliocentric universe**.

Q

QU YUAN (343–278 BCE, approx.). The father of Chinese poetry and crusader against —and victim of—misgovernment and **corruption**. Qu Yuan (Ch'u Yuan in old spelling) was born into the ruling elite of the state of Qu. While still a young man, he was appointed to a senior advisory position to his relative Huai Wang, the ambitious ruler of Qu. Qu Yuan quickly learned some hard lessons about politics when he fell foul to court intrigue. Qu Yuan had opposed Huai's aggressive foreign policy, particularly with respect to Ch'in, the largest country during the troublesome Warring States period. Qu's advice was ignored and in 303 BCE he was sent into exile. Huai Wang went to Ch'in to negotiate, only to be imprisoned by them, never to return. Huai Wang's son signed a humiliating peace, but this did not prevent Ch'in from invading Qu and destroying the capital.

Qu watched these events from his exile. Saddened by the fate of his country, he wandered and wrote the poetry that became so influential in subsequent Chinese culture. When he heard of the occupation of his country, his despair knew no bounds, and he drowned himself in the Mo-li, a tributary of the Yangtze.

Qu Yuan's poems were collected in a work later called the *Elegies of Qu*. Some of the works are probably not his, but his masterpiece is "On Encountering Sorrow." One of the elegies, "Crossing the River," (translated by Yang Hsien-yi and Gladys Yang) is a fine example of the **cosmic perspective** that Qu Yuan had been able to achieve.

> One sage of old had head shaved like a slave,
>> Good ministers were killed,
> In nakedness one saint was forced to roam,
>> Another's blood was spilled.
> This has been so from ancient times till now,
>> Then why should I complain?
> Unflinchingly I still shall follow truth,
>> Nor care if I am slain.

To this day Qu Yuan is remembered in the annual Dragonboat race, which had its origins in the attempt to find his body.

QUANTUM MECHANICS. Along with the theory of **relativity**, quantum mechanics is the science that shaped the twentieth century. The revolutions in telecommunications, the Internet, and personal computers all rest on the insights of quantum mechanics. The term "quantum" was coined by Max Planck (1858–1947), the German theoretical physicist who formulated the first quantum theory in 1900. The core of quantum theory is that energy changes take place by unpredictable and unmeasurable leaps called quanta. One of the major tenets of quantum mechanics is the **Uncertainty Principle**, which states that one cannot know with infinite precision both the position and the momentum of a particle.

It is said that there are two interpretations of quantum mechanics. The most widely accepted is what is known as the *Copenhagen interpretation*. It stresses the nebulousness of any quantum system and the altering effects of any attempt to observe the system from the outside. This understanding works well for all practical demands quantum mechanics is put to, such as designing a laser. Some physicists are concerned that, when dealing theo-retically with the whole universe, the Copenhagen interpretation falls down. In practical matters (so far as that word isn't absurd when discussing quantum mechanics) there is no difference between the Copenhagen interpretation and its rival, the *many-worlds theory*. When looking at the universe through the Copenhagen interpretation, the universe has no shape or order unless measured from elsewhere. In the many-worlds theory, all possible universes exist.

Much has been made by **postmodernists** and followers of various **pseudosciences** of the unpredictability of quantum mechanics in general and the Uncertainty Principle in particular. The claim has been made that this inability to predict precisely spells the end of **determinism** and even the rule of **science**. This is, of course, nonsense. The whole universe is causal. The causation at the quantum level appears at this stage to be indeterministic, whereas the causation at all other levels is, to some extent or other, deterministic. The causation, however, remains universal. Nobody yet knows where the barrier between deterministic and indeterministic causation lies.

The current attempts to arrive at a **theory of everything** are basically an attempt to reconcile relativity, which operates on the universal scale, with quantum mechanics, which operates at the subatomic scale. Both systems work in their own spheres but seem incapable of working together in the same universe. Some physicists think **string theory** will be the means by which this breakthrough is made.

Further reading: Brian Greene, *The Elegant Universe*.

QUASARS. A controversial idea in astronomy. Quasar is short for quasistellar radio source, which were thought originally to be stars but turned out on closer inspection to be intense sources of light emanating from a very great distance. One quasar can produce more energy than an entire galaxy and yet be no bigger than our solar system. The measurement of the energy from quasars can help us determine the age of the universe. Because quasars burn energy so ferociously, they tend to have, by astronomical standards, fairly short lives. It is thought there are more dead quasars than there are live ones, and that dead quasars could well be black holes, but dormant black holes, because they are starved of fuel.

QUEST FOR THE HISTORICAL JESUS. The attempt by scholars over the past two centuries to place **Rabbi Yeshua** in some reliable historical context. Each of the quests for the historical Jesus have acknowledged that the entity called **Jesus Christ** is not a credible figure outside of a faith context.

It is generally understood there have been three quests for the historical Jesus. The first was led mainly in the nineteenth century by German theologians and historians. This quest was determined to detach the historical Jesus from the Christ of theology and myth. Leading scholars in this quest were **David Friedrich Strauss** and Ferdinand Christian Baur (1792–1860). The first quest was summarized brilliantly by Albert Schweitzer (1875–1965) in *The Quest of the Historical Jesus* (1901, translated 1910). Schweitzer brought the first quest to a close with his recognition that most attempts to write a life of Jesus shorn of theological and mythical additions ended up as little more than the author's own projections superimposed onto "Jesus."

The second quest for the historical Jesus took place after World War II. This quest was influenced by the failure of the first quest and the vogue of **existentialism**, which was then strong. Prominent thinkers of the second quest were the German theologian Rudolf Bultmann (1884–1976) and James M. Robinson. The second quest was prepared to abandon the historical Jesus in favor of making a deliberate existential decision to have **faith** in Christ in full knowledge of the mythical character of most of the facts connected to his name.

The third quest for the historical Jesus has been going since the 1980s, and is concerned primarily with understanding the Jewish cultural conditions that determined Rabbi Yeshua's real message. The third quest recognizes that "Jesus Christ" is a theological invention with little or no bearing on the thoughts, values, and priorities of the Jewish rabbi known as Yeshua. The **Jesus Seminar** has been an important force in the third quest. Other important scholars of the third quest are Geza Vermes (1924–), particularly in books like *Jesus the Jew* (1973) and *The Changing Faces of Jesus* (2000), and Robert Funk with *Honest to Jesus* (1996) and *A Credible Jesus* (2002). See the entries on **Jesus Christ, creation of**, and **Jesus Christ, myth theory of**.

QUIETISM. Philosophical/religious stance best articulated by **Ludwig Wittgenstein**, when he said in the *Tractatus Logico-Philosophicus*, "What we cannot speak about we must pass over in silence." Quietism assumes when a topic is so complex or **beyond human understanding** that, rather than deciding on flimsy or uncertain evidence, the best response is to say nothing.

The American philosopher Owen Flanagan has recommended quietism as a response to the question of the existence of **God**. He maintains nothing sensible can be said, either in favor of or in denial of, God's existence. Flanagan denies this position is tantamount to either **atheism** or **agnosticism**. This position would be more credible if good reasons were given for showing why the arguments for atheism put forward by people like **Antony Flew**, J. L. Mackie (1917–1981), J. J. C. Smart, **Michael Martin**, and others are not sensible, but this has not been done. As a result, quietism is not an adequate response to the collapse of arguments for the existence of God.

QUINE, WILLARD VAN ORMAN (1908–2000). One of the most important American philosophers of the twentieth century. Quine was born in Akron, Ohio. After taking a BA at Oberlin College, he moved on to Harvard University to work under A. N. Whitehead, coauthor with **Bertrand Russell** of *Principia Mathematica*. Quine received his PhD from

Harvard in 1932 after only two years. After traveling in Europe, he returned to Harvard in 1936, and, apart from war service in Washington DC, spent the rest of his professional life there. He retired in 1978.

His main works are *Two Dogmas of Empiricism* (1951), *From a Logical Point of View* (1953), *Word and Object* (1960) where Quine outlined his understanding of **naturalism**, and *The Roots of Reference* (1973). Much of Quine's importance is in relatively technical areas of mathematical logic. However, the general trend of his work was to reject the tidy contrast many different groups were trying to make between science and philosophy. With this in mind, he was a critic of the linguistic philosophy of **Ludwig Wittgenstein** and J. L. Austin (1911–1960), as well as **phenomenology**. He also opposed the **falsification** theory of **Karl Popper**, when he noted that scientific generalizations are no more prone to decisive falsification than they are to decisive **verification**. Despite Quine's clear intentions, some of his writings have been cited by opponents of science as supporting their attack on notions like scientific evidence. Quine summarized his philosophy in *Pursuit of Truth* (1990) which, while not easy for the beginner, is nonetheless clear and concise. Quine was one of the original fellows of the **Committee for the Scientific Investigation of Claims of the Paranormal**.

QUOTE WHORES. The term applied to film reviewers who will sacrifice their integrity by spinning a succession of superlatives about a film they know to be rubbish in the hope the quote will be picked up and used in the advertisements.

QUR'AN. A body of writing treated by Muslims as the holy **scripture** of Islam. Traditional accounts of the Qur'an's origins vary. One sura (book of the Qur'an) claims it was revealed in its entirely on one night, a night "better than a thousand months." (Qadr. 97:1) Elsewhere, it is said to have been brought down by an unnamed "trusted spirit" (The Poets 26:193).

The Qur'an has been subjected to significantly less higher criticism than the Bible. Study of it so far has revealed that it was brought together from a wide variety of unconnected sources and for an equally wide variety of theological, political, and literary reasons. The consequences of this have hardly begun to be felt inside orthodox Islam.

The orthodox accounts of the origins of the Qur'an are inconsistent, but revolve around the immediate successors being anxious not to lose knowledge of the sayings of **Muhammad**, many of which were memorized by heart by men serving as soldiers. Most orthodox accounts have the Qur'an complete within a few decades after Muhammad's death. Few scholars accept this view. Most accept a later date for the compilation, usually up to the ninth century.

Even the word "qur'an" has a less clear meaning than is commonly supposed. Muslim tradition says the word means "to read" or "to bind together," but recent scholarship has shown that the word is an Arabized form of a Syriac word, which is best translated as "recitation" or "reading." Among the many important consequences of this is that it puts the Qur'an later than the orthodox account, and places it in Syria and/or Iraq, not in Arabia. It also makes it unlikely any of it was written by Muhammad.

Further reading: Ibn Warraq, ed., *The Origins of the Koran*.

QUTB, SAYYID (1906–1966). Egyptian philosopher widely seen as the father of Islamic fundamentalism and **Islamism**. Qutb was born in the village of Mush in Upper Egypt, and had a conventional, secular education. As a young man he wrote a novel, which attracted little attention, and a work entitled *Literary Criticism: Its Principles and Methodology* which was well received. In 1948, Qutb was sent to the United States to study American education. There is some doubt about whether Qutb was already on the path toward **fundamentalism** before his trip to America, but there is no doubt he was repelled and shocked by the racism and sexual freedoms in the United States. He was especially disturbed by the freedoms allowed to women. Upon his return to Egypt in 1951, Qutb joined the **Muslim Brotherhood**.

In 1954 he was arrested and spent much of the rest of his life in prison, during which he wrote his best-known work, the thirty-volume *In the Shade of the Koran*, a series of commentaries on the Qur'an. Sayyid's brother, Muhammad, fled to Saudi Arabia, where he became a professor of Islamic Studies. Osama bin Laden was one of his students. Sayyid Qutb railed not only against the Jews and Christians, but also against the corrupt rulers in the Arab world.

His **anti-Semitism** was relentless, portraying the Jews as irrevocably hateful, perfidious, and malevolent. Qutb was also alarmed at the growing freedoms accorded to women, which distanced them from their natural role as child rearers. Christianity and Judaism were locked in mortal combat with Islam, Qutb argued, because they recognized the superiority of Islam, and knew they had to destroy it in order to survive.

Not surprisingly, Qutb was a bitter opponent of the **separation of church and state**, which he denounced as a **hideous schizophrenia**. Against this, Qutb advocated a totalitarian Muslim **khalifat** under **sharia law**, where religion encompassed every aspect of society. He saw this renaissance being brought on by a vanguard of true believers who would destroy the secular and collaborationist Arab leaderships and effect, through *jihad*, a transformation of the Muslim world which would in turn inspire the rest of the world to follow its shining example. If this meant **martyrdom**, so much the better. Qutb spurned offers of exile in Libya or Iraq and went to his death in Egypt as a martyr. He was hanged on August 29, 1966, as part of the Egyptian government's retaliation for the Muslim Brotherhood's attempted assassination of Nasser (1918–1970).

R

RADEST, HOWARD (1928–). Leading American religious humanist thinker and educator. Educated in New York, Radest has been a major figure in the **Ethical Culture** movement in the United States and the **International Humanist and Ethical Union**. He has had a long career in moral education. For a decade he was director of the Ethical Culture Fieldston School, which enjoyed a high reputation under his management. Radest was the founding dean of the Humanist Institute and founded Columbia University's Seminar on Moral Education.

He wrote a history of the Ethical Culture movement, *Toward Common Ground* (1969) and *The Devil and Secular Humanism: The Children of the Enlightenment* (1990), a lament of **humanism** taking seriously its secular and naturalistic origins. He recycled a series of postmodernist critiques of **rationalism** and **atheism** and suggested humanism started down the wrong path around 1973, the year the ***Humanist Manifesto II*** was released (which Radest signed). It is not that Radest is wrong about the importance of the moral dimension of humanism. He is right about that. Where he is wrong is to believe that somehow this dimension cannot be given full justice from an atheist and rationalist perspective. Other books include *To Seek a Humane World* (1971), *Can We Teach Ethics?* (1989), and *Humanism with a Human Face: Intimacy and the Enlightenment* (1996).

RAND, AYN (1905–1982). Eccentric radical for a society entirely free from the constraints of government. Alice Rosenbaum was born in St. Petersburg to a prosperous Jewish family. In 1925 she secured permission to leave Russia and arrived in the United States in February 1926. Soon after arriving in America Rosenbaum reinvented herself, soon taking on her new name: Ayn Rand.

Almost as soon as she landed in the United States, she became a vocal anticommunist. She participated enthusiastically in the McCarthyite show trials against suspected communists, later known as the **Great Fear**. Rand went on to build a worldview that articulated her anticommunism in the form of a **Romantic** individualism. Her ideas were propagated most successfully in some long and didactic novels, principally *The Fountainhead* (1943) and *Atlas Shrugged* (1957).

In *The Virtue of Selfishness* (1961) Rand tried to rescue selfishness from its universally held position as a term of abuse and transform it into a noble concern for one's own interests. Her attitudes to this were inconsistent in that, on the one hand Rand wanted selfishness to be seen in a value-neutral way, but on the other hand she imbued selfishness with a Romantic power to redeem (her word) man and morality. Rand contrasted selfishness with **altruism**, which became the most evil quality, one which condemns people to cynicism and guilt. See the entry on **either black or white, fallacy of**.

From this, Rand proceeded to advocate untrammeled capitalism as the system most suited to **human needs** and for personal growth and development. She was also an atheist, but saw little point in stressing this aspect of her thought, as the arguments for religion she felt to be too incoherent to bother with.

Since her death in 1982 the Objectivist movement has been riven by splits, with one group posing as guardians of the sacred flame, and others wanting to push Rand's ideas on in ways she had not addressed. Objectivism is the more cultic extreme of **Libertarianism**.

Further reading: Barbara Branden, *The Passion of Ayn Rand*.

RATIONAL BELIEFS. Those beliefs that can withstand the scrutiny of people who themselves are critical of their beliefs. This has the effect of making these beliefs open to refutation and/or modification. It ensures they are **fallible**. The Canadian philosopher Kai Nielsen drew up a list of six standards for the rationality of a belief:

- the most efficient and effective means are to be taken to achieve one's ends;
- in the event of several compatible ends, we should, as far as we can ascertain, take the option which is most able to realize the largest number of these ends;
- if facing two ends that are equally desired and equal in other respects, we should choose the end most likely to be achieved;
- in the event of the same probabilities for two plans of action which secure entirely different ends, we should choose the one we most prefer;
- in the event we are unclear what our preferred ends are, we should postpone our decision until such time as more information becomes available; and
- we should seek to fulfill ends that we value the most before fulfilling other ends.

These are guides; a rational belief can't be judged simply by following some litmus test, and this was not Nielsen's intention. See the entries on **inquiry, tools of**; **testing our beliefs**; and **belief**.

Further reading: Kai Nielsen, *Philosophy and Atheism*.

RATIONAL-EMOTIVE BEHAVIOR THERAPY. A form of action-oriented therapy which focuses on substituting positive thoughts, feelings, and actions for the negative ones that have been hampering the client's life thus far. Rational-Emotive Behavior Therapy (REBT) is predicated on a few basic principles:

- you are responsible for your own emotions and actions;
- your harmful emotions and behaviors are the product of your irrational thinking;
- you can learn more realistic views and incorporate them into your life; and

- by incorporating a reality-based perspective into your life, you will experience a greater acceptance of yourself and of your life.

REBT draws heavily on the wisdom of the **Stoics, Spinoza,** and **Bertrand Russell**. Their Web site features a quotation from **Epictetus**: "What disturbs people's minds is not events but their judgments on events." REBT works differently than the passive procedures used by psychoanalysts. REBT's methods are more direct; clients are challenged and questioned, even confronted about the beliefs that are holding them back. Ellis believes that this procedure works more quickly. Its advantages are clear; not only is the client happier sooner than with other therapies, it also saves the client money that longer therapies would require. In this way, the **narcissism** of endless self-analysis, and the dishonesty of unnecessarily drawn-out sessions are avoided. REBT also encourages clients to develop a **cosmic perspective**.

REBT was developed in 1955 by the American psychologist Dr. Albert Ellis (1913–). Ellis developed REBT after becoming disillusioned with the fallacies of **psychoanalysis**. He was written extensively, though his most important books are *The Art and Science of Love* (1960), and *A Guide to Rational Living* (1975). The **humor** of the REBT method is apparent in some of Ellis's popular titles, like *How to Stubbornly Refuse to Make Yourself Miserable about Anything— Yes, Anything*. REBT centers have now developed around the world. In 2003, the **Center for Inquiry** entered into a partnership with the Albert Ellis Institute in Tampa, Florida.

RATIONAL WORLD INITIATIVES. A program of social improvement by an Indian forum of the same name. The objectives of the Rational World Initiatives are:

- to understand the world in terms of concept, functions, and development;
- to promote scientific and rational thinking;

- to promote human rights and values;
- to strengthen and safeguard measures for vulnerable sections of society;
- to promote and protect the health of people to the highest achievable level;
- to promote the sustainable development of mankind; and
- to adopt and promote all measures that can save humanity and the environment of the planet.

Rational World Initiatives plans to advance this program with a series of conferences, debates, and school programs. The president is Dr. J. Kishore.

RATIONALISM. A term with two major, and opposed, uses. On the one hand, rationalism refers to a tradition of philosophy whose principal representatives include **Plato** and G. W. Leibniz (1646–1716). The rationalism of these men was geared toward creating a single, **absolutist** worldview based upon the findings of what was often called pure **reason**, which was held to represent closely the way the universe actually is. This rationalism was framed by, or at least tended toward, ethically and politically **totalitarian** outlooks.

But on the other hand, and the sense in which it will be employed here, is to refer to a tradition of **freethought** that places an emphasis on the process of reason in solving problems and giving meaning to one's life. See the entry on **Rationalism, Principles of**. The exemplars of rationalism in the context meant here are the **Pre-Socratic** thinkers in Greece, the **Enlightenment** philosophers, and more recently, people like **Bertrand Russell** and **Paul Kurtz**. The first point to note is that the rationalism of Plato and Leibniz are quite different in approach and their conclusions than the rationalism of the Pre-Socratics or Bertrand Russell.

The word "rationalist" was first employed by a London newsletter on October 14, 1646. **Rational beliefs** are beliefs that have stood up against scrutiny from others who are no less critical of their own beliefs. The scrutiny of people unable to subject their own beliefs to the same level of scrutiny is significantly less valuable. Rational beliefs, in contrast to the dogmas held by extremists, are **fallible** and open to modification and development. The core of the rationalist program is its unwillingness to accept the reality of the world, or truth claims about it, simply on **faith**.

One of the most courageous declarations of what rationalism is about came from **Joseph McCabe**, who said during a debate in 1920: "I represent Rationalism. That is to say, I want the whole world to use its reason, every man and woman in the world. I will respect any man or any woman, no matter what their conclusions may be, if they have used their own personality, their own mind, and their own judgment, rigorously and conscientiously. I do not care what conclusions they come to."

RATIONALISM, PRINCIPLES OF. The British polymath **Hector Hawton** outlined the main principles of **rationalism** as:

- *disinterested* pursuit of truth;
- *compassion* for suffering, combined with a determination to use all available knowledge to end, or at least alleviate, it; and
- *freedom of thought* and the freedom to express those thoughts, without which cultural and intellectual life would be impoverished.

The sort of judgment a rationalist passes on a creed, Hawton wrote, is not on its **utility** or aesthetic beauty, but on its truth, for the other **values** depend on its being true. For the rationalist, nothing can have truly good effects and consequences if its foundations are built on untruths. This is what **Bertrand Russell** meant when he said "It is not by delusion, however exalted, that mankind can prosper, but only by unswerving courage in the pursuit of truth." See the entry on **veracity**.

Further reading: Hector Hawton, *The Thinker's Handbook*.

RATIONALIST INTERNATIONAL. An organization, based in India, dedicated to the propagation of rationalism there and around the world. It is run by Sanal Edamaruku (1955–), who is also secretary of the **Indian Rationalist Association**. The Rationalist International hosts excellent Web-based news bulletins and holds conferences at regular intervals.

It presents the International Rationalist Award to a person who has made an outstanding contribution to **rationalism**, **humanism**, and the **open society** around the world. In 2000 the award went to **Paul Kurtz**, founder of the **Center for Inquiry**, **Committee for the Scientific Investigation of Claims of the Paranormal**, the **Council for Secular Humanism**, and their respective magazines, as well as **Prometheus Books**, and other achievements. In 2002 the award went to **Jim Herrick**, editor of the *New Humanist* from 1985 to 2003 and author of three books on aspects of the history of **freethought**.

RATIONALIST PRESS ASSOCIATION. One of the most significant **freethought** organizations through the course of the twentieth century. Most freethought organizations in the nineteenth century had brief lives and revolved around one or two towering individuals. It was the genius of **Charles Albert Watts** to see the need for a new type of organization and to succeed in creating it. Watts himself was an unassuming man who worked best outside the public glare, but he was brilliant at attracting lifelong loyalty from people wealthier and more outgoing than himself. He also inherited a tiny publishing firm from his father **Charles Watts**. Young Charles Albert developed Watts and Co. into a profitable business, unlike most previous freethought publishing operations, which had brief, cash-strapped lives before becoming insolvent. His ability lay in the confidence he inspired among people wealthier than himself to supply him with capital. Watts's transparent honesty and willingness to take only a minimal wage from his publishing ventures helped boost that confidence.

The RPA's golden age was the years from its inception in 1899 until the onset of World War I. During that time it made some significant contributions to the secularization of Great Britain. It did this by showing its competitors that there was a large market for low-cost reprints of serious nonfiction. The series was called the **Cheap Reprints**. Light fiction had been published in this form before, but nobody believed that the poor, who could not afford the price of a hardcover book, would want to buy this material in cheap form. With its small stocks of borrowed money, the RPA proved that such a market existed.

Watts and Co. suffered from its own success. Its Cheap Reprints series attracted a host of competitors, among them Penguin, who began issuing cheap paperbacks in 1935. In 1929 Watts and Co. responded with the **Thinker's Library**, which ran to 140 volumes over its twenty-two-year career. But after World War II, it was all downhill for Watts and Co. Charles Albert Watts died in 1946 and his son Fred worked himself into an early grave in 1953. The RPA sold the company in 1961 and persisted with a smaller publishing wing, Pemberton Books, until the mid–1980s. But as Pemberton faded away, **Prometheus Books**, under the management of **Paul Kurtz**, was rising to take its place.

Another important publication of the RPA was its annual. It began in 1884 as the *Agnostic Annual*, becoming the *RPA Annual* in 1907, the *Rationalist Annual* in 1927 and *Question* in 1968. The series finally came to an end in 1980. During those years some of the best minds of the century were published in the annual: **Bertrand Russell, Karl Popper, A. J. Ayer, Antony Flew, Subrahmanyan Chandrasekhar**, J. B. S. Haldane (1892–1964), **H. G. Wells**, and many others. The annual was one of the most important vehicles for rationalist scholarship and criticism in the world until the rest of the academic literature caught up.

But the only wing of the original RPA to survive is its magazine. Originally *Watts's Literary Guide*, then between 1894 and 1956 the *Literary Guide*, then the *Humanist*, and since 1972 the *New Humanist*, the RPA's magazine is a remarkable record of intellectual and social thought since the 1880s. As with the *Rationalist Annual/Question*, some of the finest minds of the past century have contributed to the *New Humanist* and its predecessors. From the days of Gladstone to those of Tony Blair, the *New Humanist* has been giving a humanist perspective on the issues of the day.

Further reading: Bill Cooke, *The Gathering of Infidels: A Hundred Years of the Rationalist Press Association*.

RATIONALITY AND REASONABLENESS. Rationality is the condition of habitually subjecting one's **judgments** to evaluation by one's peers, and that this evaluation be listened to seriously and reacted to in a mature way. This notion of rationality does not require everyone to agree with everyone else, and does not mean that the majority view is therefore the rational view. Neither does this view of rationality presume that rational is the same as "truthful" or "**objective**."

This understanding of rationality is derived from **Karl Popper**. However, several other important philosophers have sought to distinguish rationality from reasonableness. By this version, rationality is given a less favorable reading of seeking to fit the universe into a preconceived schema. By this thinking rationality differs from reasonableness in that a rational plan need not include an element of moral sensitivity that a reasonable plan would. This problem is paralleled in the divergent understandings of **rationalism**.

The important point about this is that the division between rationality and reasonableness should not be over-emphasized. Rationality and reasonableness are complementary processes. If rational agents may not include a moral or compassionate element, reasonable agents will find it impossible to determine their ends and decide the best ways to achieve them.

Further reading: Stephen Toulmin, *Return to Reason*.

RAWANDI, IBN AL- (d. 910). Freethinking philosopher of the early Islamic period. The rationalist **Mu'tazilite** theologians had generally been able to balance their debt to Greek **rationalism** with their Islamic faith, but Ibn al-Rawandi took this line of questioning a great deal further. Showing extraordinary courage, al-Rawandi was prepared to question what to virtually all of his contemporaries was beyond question. And as is so often the case with early **freethinkers**, all of his works have been lost or destroyed, and we can only rebuild his thoughts through the passages attributed to him by his enemies.

His enemies said that he repudiated the entire supernaturalist system of revelation and miracles and was frankly **agnostic** on the question of the existence of **God**. Other sources interpreted his views more in terms of denouncing revelation as unnecessary and irrelevant, in that unaided human reason was sufficient to determine knowledge of God and good and evil. Al-Rawandi was said to have rejected monotheism in favor of dualism, and to have disparaged the vanity of divine wisdom. He even parodied the **Qur'an** and **Muhammad**. He was accused of being an atheist (which he almost certainly was) and executed.

RAWLS, JOHN (1921–2002). The most prominent political philosopher of the second half of the twentieth century. Rawls was born in Maryland to a prosperous, socially active, and liberal family. Rawls originally planned to enter the ministry, but his experiences during World War II led him to change his mind. He enrolled at Princeton in 1946 and was awarded a PhD in 1950. He married in 1948. Rawls taught at Princeton, Oxford, Cornell, MIT, and finally at Harvard, where he stayed from 1962 until his retirement.

Rawls's career was devoted to establishing how to arrange fair terms of cooperation between rational citizens who hold different political, philosophical, and religious worldviews. In doing this, he restated and revitalized liberal philosophy in a way not achieved since **John Stuart Mill**. Rawls's classic was *A Theory of Justice* (1971) which has been translated into twenty-seven languages and has become a bestseller, despite not being an easy or elegant read. Not since *Das Kapital* has a work of political theory been so influential among politicians and activists; *A Theory of Justice* was a significant influence among prodemocracy protesters at Tiananmen Square in China in 1989. Rawls went on to develop his ideas in *Political Liberalism* (1993) and *The Laws of Peoples* (1999); a revised edition of *A Theory of Justice* appeared in 1999.

Rawls was offered literally hundreds of honorary doctorates and other awards. He accepted only three honorary doctorates (Oxford, Harvard, and Princeton) and among the few awards he accepted included the National Humanities Medal, given by the National Endowment for the Humanities, in 1999. Rawls was no less reticent about involving himself in political issues: one of the few exceptions was his cooperation with three others defending the right to **voluntary euthanasia** in 1997.

RAZI, ABU BAKR MUHAMMAD B. ZAKARIYYA AL- (854–925/35). Along with **Ibn al-Rawandi,** one of the most freethinking Muslim philosophers. Al Razi was one of the first freethinkers to find the concept of **God** incompatible with a **scientific outlook**. Known to the West for many centuries as Rhazes, Abu Bakr Muhammad al-Razi was born in Rayy where his youth was spent as a lute player or money-changer, according to different traditions. He soon gained recognition for his breadth of knowledge and was put in charge of the hospital. His fame spread and he was later appointed in charge of the hospital in Baghdad.

Al-Razi wrote widely, reputedly being responsible for more than two hundred works. His medical treatises remained influential until well into the sixteenth century. Few of al-Razi's works survive, and he is mostly known through his detractors, who bitterly attacked his tendency to think independently. Symptomatic of this was al-Razi's criticisms of the pervasive **Aristotelianism** then dominating Muslim philosophy. Al-Razi's own views, those on the transmigration of the soul for instance, reflected more closely those of **Plato** and **Pythagoras**.

Like his near-contemporary Ibn al-Rawandi, al-Razi declared revelation to be superfluous, since **reason** was sufficient for knowledge of the **truth**, and morally questionable, because of the rivers of blood that have been spilled in the name of revelation. Along with this he rejected the validity of prophecy. These views earned him long-lasting hatred from the orthodox as an infidel. The story of the end of his life has him refusing to have a cataract removed because he had seen enough of the world and didn't want to see any more.

READE, WILLIAM WINWOOD (1838–1875). Writer and visionary. Born into a comfortable middle-class family, and nephew of Charles Reade, the successful dramatist and novelist. Best remembered for his visionary work *The Martyrdom of Man* (1872) which looked to an age when **science**, having freed humanity from its material needs, would permit us to attend to our psychological and emotional needs and build a perfect society on Earth. Reade was only thirty-three when he wrote *The Martyrdom of Man*, which went through twenty-two editions and sold more than two hundred thousand copies over the next fifty years. It influenced many people, perhaps the most notable being Winston Churchill (1874–1965) and **H. G. Wells**. Ironically, it was as a novelist that Reade wished to be remembered, but his novels, the best of which was *The Outcast* (1875) failed to capture the Victorian imagination.

Contrary to popular prejudice, Winwood Reade's vision of progress was not a brash and vulgar optimism. It was in fact, wistful and melancholic. He understood the sacrifices that must be made in building a humane society of the future. With admirable **cosmic modesty**, Reade wrote, "The **soul** must be sacrificed; the hope in **immortality** must die. A sweet and charming illusion must be taken from the human race, as youth and beauty vanish, never to return." See the entry on **doubt**. Reade was an agnostic and humanist. He died at thirty-seven of tuberculosis. A maniacal salvationist woman broke into the house where Reade was dying and prayed noisily for his soul before being removed.

READY-MADE. A term coined by the French artist Marcel Duchamp (1887–1968) in 1913 to denote an everyday object, which, when put in a gallery setting, becomes a work of art. Duchamp set the scene for this new development in art when he fixed a bicycle wheel on top of a wooden stool and declared it a work of art. He did the same four years later with a ceramic urinal, which he turned upside down, signed it "R. Mutt," and displayed it as a work of art.

Duchamp's innovation has had a revolutionary effect on art making and appreciation. Many people outside the art world are skeptical about the artistic value of lengths of piping, items out of rubbish bins, and so on, but what the artists want us to do is to look at things in a new way, and to appreciate the beauty or interest in things we might otherwise ignore. See the entries on **piece of art** and **culture wars**.

REALITY. The universal term for the natural world and all things within it. Whether we like it or not, there is a real world out there, and it proceeds along by its own rules with total indifference to our philosophizing about its existence. **Science** has proved itself by far the best means we possess to understand reality and to frame laws about it.

The American philosopher Murray Murphey described reality as whatever our best theory says it is. This clever definition recognizes that the problem lies with us, but runs the risk of presuming that humans somehow determine what reality actually is. **John Searle** has solved this problem with his distinction between intrinsic and observer-related **facts**. Intrinsic facts are facts about the world about which a sufficient quantity of **evidence** exists to render **doubt** about little more than a nominal duty. Observer-related facts are more subject to the chance variations of perspective. The process of **reliabilism** is also of central importance in this process of determining the level of confidence we should ascribe to the elements of reality we experience.

Following on from this, it is also a mistake to cast "real" as the opposite of "socially constructed." As Susan Haack points out, socially constructed institutions and customs are just as real in the effect they have on people's lives as are items from the physical world, like rocks or birds. See the entries on **social worlds** and **relativism**. The two best current philosophical accounts of reality are John Searle's **external realism** and Susan Haack's **critical common-sensism**.

Further reading: John Searle, *The Construction of Social Reality*; and Susan Haack, *Defending Science—Within Reason*.

REASON. An activity rooted firmly in our physical constitution. Reason is a product of **natural selection**, and has helped humans understand their surroundings and relate to other people. It is a method of data **analysis** which allows us to comprehend our situation most effectively. It is not some timeless ideal writ across the cosmos that we need to look up to. Neither is it a watertight compartment of the mind which is immune to other influences. And neither is it a cold activity divorced from spontaneous warm humanity, as irrationalists and apologists like to portray it. Because it is firmly rooted in our physical constitution, reason is as human an activity as any other, and to suggest otherwise is to force

a **dualism** onto humanity which itself is a cold and foreign abstraction. See the entry on **intuition**. The English philosopher **Richard Robinson** distinguished three main senses of reason:

- giving reasons;
- the ability to think; and
- the ability to think well.

In the third sense, to think well becomes an ethical act. It follows that the first principle of reason is to believe or disbelieve or suspend **judgment** in accordance with the balance of reasons for and against any particular proposition. He simplifies this by saying that reason demands respect for reasons. See the entry on **evidence**.

It is important to say that it is the very fragility of reason that makes it so important. We know we can deceive our rational faculties in the interests of self-deception. We know that the conclusions we reach can be faulty if the premise we begin our chain of reasoning with is inadequate. But, for all the weaknesses of reasoning, it is all we've got and we'd better make the best of it.

Further reading: Richard Robinson, *An Atheist's Values*; and Donald B. Calne, *Within Reason: Rationality and Human Behavior*.

REBEL, THE. In many ways the rebel is the default archetype for freethinkers. Following the lead of **Prometheus**, freethinkers rebel against tyranny, even when the tyrant is Zeus himself. It takes a rebellious spirit to rebel against the conformism and **anthropocentric conceit** implicit in the **god** idea. The great twentieth century rationalist **Joseph McCabe** asked that his tombstone should read: "He was a rebel to his last breath." And **Bertrand Russell** said: "Without rebellion, mankind would stagnate, and injustice would be irremediable."

The rebel as a model for living was conjured up by the French playwright and thinker **Albert Camus** and was the subject of a book by that name, published in 1951. The rebel is the person who says no, but who, in saying no, is not simply mouthing a renunciation. That primary act of rebellion is the essential preliminary to thinking for oneself.

Camus' rebellion is different from Christian forms of rebellion, which are quickly rendered futile by its promises of eternal life. It is of first importance to Camus that the rebellion takes place in the face of the certainty and utter finality of our death. The rebel is an atheist and the rebellion is against anthropocentric conceit. Camus' insight has provided the hitherto underappreciated tragic dimension to atheist thought. See the entry on **Promethean ethics**. See also the entry on **the outsider**.

Further reading: Albert Camus, *The Rebel*.

RECIPROCAL ALTRUISM. A principle in human evolution of being most generous to those who are most generous to you. The idea developed from the work of Robert Trivers in 1971 and has attracted an impressive range of supporting studies since then. Contrary to many popular notions of **evolution** as a constant and bloody struggle for supremacy, there is a great deal of cooperation in nature as well. Reciprocal altruism plays an important role in **evolutionary psychology**.

While unending generosity is costly on time and resources and brings no advantage to oneself at all, constant suspicion and miserliness only has, at best, short-term advantages. Consequently, humans learned the habit of reciprocal altruism, of initiating kindness and gifts, and measuring the degree to which they were reciprocated, or responding to kindness or gifts in suitable proportion. This sort of behavior had obvious advantages when hunting large animals, and ensuring full advantage of it is had before the animal runs off or is stolen. As our ethical thinking developed, reciprocal altruism developed into the **golden rule**.

Further reading: Susan Blackmore, *The Meme Machine*; and Robert Wright, *The Moral Animal*.

RECIPROCITY, CRITERION OF. A notion outlined by the American philosopher **John Rawls** as a guide to the way we can share power. The criterion of reciprocity says that "our exercise of political **power** is proper only when we sincerely believe that the reasons we offer for our political action may be reasonably accepted by other citizens as a justification of those actions." By this criterion, many, probably most, of the instances of the exercise of political power would be illegitimate. It would certainly invalidate most actions from the more ideologically rigid administrations.

Reciprocity lies between impartiality, with its implications of altruism, and the idea of mutual advantage. Reciprocity is the aim of reasonable people.

Further reading: John Rawls, *Political Liberalism*.

REDUCTIONISM. A fashionable term of abuse that obscures many positive features of this style of inquiry. In its role as a term of academic abuse, reductionism has come to mean the process of simplifying a complicated issue to a few inappropriate and arbitrary fundamentals. Milton A. Rothman identifies three main kinds of so-called reductionism:

- *methodological reductionism* is the application of research techniques from one discipline to another;
- *theoretical reductionism* is the related notion of believing that the subject matter from one discipline can be presented in terms of another; and
- *ontological reductionism* is the most commonly understood sense in which the term reductionism is used, and refers to the scientific understanding of the universe as composed of elementary particles and the forces by which they interact.

The flip side of reductionism is the wholly praiseworthy process of working in an interdisciplinary way. **Richard Dawkins**, **E. O.**

Wilson, and **Daniel C. Dennett** have all defended reductionism as the most successful research method ever devised. Understanding that human beings are collections of molecules subject to the laws of chemistry is only reductionistic in the bad sense if the **analysis** stops there. But to incorporate this basic **truth** into a larger synthesis of understanding what it is to be human can only be a good thing. It is the lifeblood of science. In Dennett's terms, reductionism is what grounds our research in the cranes and not in the skyhooks. See the entry on **cranes and skyhooks**.

Further reading: Milton A. Rothman, *The Science Gap*; and Daniel C. Dennett, *Darwin's Dangerous Idea*.

REEVES, AMBER (1887–1981). Oldest surviving daughter of prominent New Zealand politician and historian William Pember Reeves and his wife Maud, a Fabian and suffrage campaigner. After a political career in New Zealand, the Reeves family moved to England when Amber was nine years old. She went to Newnham College, Cambridge in 1905 and blossomed in student life, joining, among other groups, the Cambridge University Fabian Society, which boasted **H. G. Wells** as one of their speakers. Their mutual admiration became a physical affair, news of which caused a huge scandal that almost wrecked Wells's career and Amber's life. In 1909 Amber was pregnant with his baby. A marriage with Rivers Blanco White took place on May 7, 1909, and Anna Jane was born on December 21, 1909. Wells wrote a novel, *Ann Veronica*, based on the affair, which was very controversial. There was also a lot of Amber in Amanda, a figure in Wells's 1915 novel, *The Research Magnificent*.

Amber never regretted her affair with Wells. She went on to work actively for women's suffrage and in the early 1930s she provided important assistance to Wells, who was working on *The Work, Wealth and Happiness of Mankind*, which appeared in 1932. Reeves stood as Labor candidate for Hendon in 1933 and 1935, but made her name as a lecturer through thirty-seven years at Morley College, becoming an inspiration for successive generations of younger women. Her novels include *The Reward of Virtue* (1911), *A Lady and Her Husband* (1914), and *Helen in Love* (1916). Nonfiction titles included *The New Propaganda* (1938) and *Worry in Women* (1941). But it was in *Ethics for Unbelievers* (1948) that she felt most closely expressed her own views.

REINCARNATION. The belief, widespread among **Asian traditions**, that an essential core of each human being survives **death** and is planted in a new body, often as part of an ongoing spiritual development which lasts over the course of many lifetimes.

Reincarnation requires a bewildering array of beliefs and assumptions, some of which are implausible in the extreme, while others are frankly immoral. To begin with, reincarnation requires confidence that the world is completely just, so that all misfortune that befalls a person is deserved. Reincarnation also requires the belief that the **soul** is completely independent of the body. In this way, all Holocaust victims must have merited their death because, whether occupying the Jewish body being gassed by fate or choice, that grisly death had be to be their destiny so as to atone for some ghastly crime in the past.

The reincarnationist needs to believe that when a person dies, that person's pure essence survives for a protracted time in some place apart from the physical world, then, without any sort of physical organs or sense or cognition, goes to the appointed (or chosen, depending on the variation) woman to begin the next round, without showing any signs of the old age of physical malady which resulted in the death of the earlier incarnation. But then, oddly in the light of having all this ability, the pure essence most commonly enters a woman in miserably poor circumstances, for a nasty, brutish, and short life. As with the Holocaust example, this only makes sense if the starving child in some way deserves to die that way.

Not surprisingly, most people who claim to remember past lives, usually occupied the bodies of the rich and famous, some of whom must have been positively rattling with the unborn incarnations of future generations. Few people claim to be reincarnations of a child prostitute from some twelfth-century slum. Although as the world's population has grown over the centuries, everyone from earlier ages would have had to carry around dozens, even hundreds, of putative essences in preparation for their future appearance.

But if reincarnation is absurd when considered scientifically, it has some important moral points which are worth considering as well. It is, for instance, a more nuanced view of death than the simple promise of **monotheist** religions of everlasting life. The final aim of reincarnation is extinction and total identification with the cosmos. There is less **anthropocentric conceit** in reincarnationist views of death than the monotheist views.

Further reading: Paul Edwards, *Reincarnation: A Critical Examination.*

RELATIVISM. The notion that the truth of any idea is confined only to the person believing it. Relativism is about more than a simple variety of beliefs. It is about the idea that all beliefs have a similar value without regard to whether they are correct or not. The main failing of relativism is that it falls apart in the face of some pretty firmly established scientific principles. Gravity, the speed of light, **death**, and invariant properties are not matters of cultural taste. Step off a tenth floor roof and you will fall to the ground, whether you are wearing a Muslim veil or jeans and sneakers.

Relativism appears on the surface to be an important condition of **toleration**. It is wrong, goes the argument, to judge the practices of other cultures because their standards are different from ours, and who are we to say their customs are wrong? But, of course, this attitude is contradictory of itself. The very act of saying judging across cultures is wrong is to make a universal judgment. The surface appearance of toleration and humility in fact hides a deeper arrogance than the attitudes it seeks to replace.

Most relativists also run into trouble when faced with pressing moral issues. In the case of child sexual exploitation, for instance, most people are inclined to condemn this practice in whatever society it appears, but the relativist has no coherent way to express disapproval, even in cases such as this. Relativism makes the mistake of thinking each culture is infallible, an idea not only mistaken but dangerous.

Neither can relativism explain how attitudes in society come to change over time. If everyone's opinion is as good as anyone else's, why bother to change? Neither can relativism explain how conflict over ideas arises. If everybody is right in their own way, then how could conflicts involving the notion that the other people are wrong arise?

It is apparent, then, that relativism is incoherent. All this said, relativism points to an important truth, which is that people's opinions are radically different, and are usually impervious to change, in particular change by rational persuasion. The trick of twenty-first century people is that we need to hold our beliefs with a passion, but also be able to avoid fanaticism and **dogmatism**. And we also need to understand the difference between truths being absolute and being objective. See the entries on **facts** and **objective morality**. The ability to do this is a notable achievement.

RELATIVITY, THEORIES OF. Breakthroughs in science by **Albert Einstein**. There is the special theory of relativity, which was developed in 1905 and the general theory of relativity which was developed in 1915. What made the theories of relativity so important was that they showed all previous notions of absolute space and time to be erroneous.

The term "relativity" was not one Einstein cared for. He wanted the theory to be known as the theory of invariants, which better described what relativity is about. To this day, some people still confuse relativity with **rel-**

ativism, making the mistake that the theory of relativity means we can declare that "everything is relative." This is nonsense, and misunderstands fundamentally what relativity is about. Another misconception is that relativity renders Isaac Newton's conception of the universe redundant. This is also not as clearly true as is commonly supposed. Newtonian mechanics still works for everything but the subatomic scale, where we defer to quantum physics, and on the universal scale, where we defer to general relativity.

As the title suggests, the special theory is the narrower of the two. It is concerned with velocities, or steady motions in straight lines. It says that the laws of nature are the same for all observers whose frames of reference are moving with constant velocity with respect to one another. Einstein proposed that light travels through space in quantum form, which revived the old debate about whether light consisted of waves or particles. Einstein said that light consists of particles, but they were new types of particles, which sometimes had the properties of a wave, sometimes of a particle. The special theory is summed up in the famous equation $E=mc^2$.

Many writers have observed that the special theory was waiting to be discovered and if Einstein had not come up with it, someone else would have. However, the general theory remains a tribute to Einstein's unique genius. So ethereal was the general theory that it remained largely unused for forty years after its discovery. But all current theories of black holes, the big bang, and quasars and pulsars could not have been developed without the general theory of relativity.

The general theory extended relativity to involve a new theory of gravitation based on the geometry of space-time. It holds that the laws of nature are the same for all observers with respect to each other. Unlike Newton's law, which saw one object exerting force on another object, general relativity sees one object distorting space-time and thereby causing changes in the motion of other objects. In other words, general relativity is about the curving of space-time.

General relativity only becomes important when objects are very massive, or when measurements have to be very precise. Newton's law suffices all other times. The general theory was shown to be true in 1919 when Sir Arthur Eddington (1882–1944) showed that Mercury, which has a peculiarity in its orbit, moved exactly as Einstein predicted it would.

Further reading: David Bodanis, *E=mc²: A Biography of the World's Most Famous Equation*; and Brian L. Silver, *The Ascent of Science*.

RELIABILISM. A theory of knowledge that avoids most of the pitfalls of other theories. Many theories of knowledge are internalist, in that they rely on some sort of inner light to provide justification for true beliefs. The problem with these theories is that no version of inner light, whether a soul, mind, psyche, or unconscious has ever been shown to exist. Reliabilism is the direct opposite of foundationalism and is antithetical to command moralities.

Reliabilism is different; it is externalist, and allows for a much wider range of sources by which knowledge can be acquired and judged reliable. These sources, called belief-forming processes, can be many and varied: visual, auditory, perceptual, and so on. With this array of different sources, taken from all parts of our life, we can build up an interdependent web of knowledge. A belief-forming process is reliable when it produces more true beliefs than false beliefs. By this method, we can learn which sources have a poor record of reliability for us in the past, and learn to take it less seriously than other sources with a better track record. In this way, astrology will give way to astronomy or creationism to evolution. Reliabilism depends on exposing our minds to as broad a range of belief-forming processes as possible. We can continue to believe in astrology if our belief-forming processes consist solely of women's magazines and Shirley Maclaine books, but once we broaden our range, the unreliability of astrology will become apparent. See the entry on **social worlds**.

We are all going to carry around some false beliefs, and the solution to this is to keep our eyes open, and keep our reading, watching, and listening as broadly based as possible, so as to increase the opportunity of new knowledge, which will lead in turn to new beliefs.

Further reading: Robert Nola, *Rescuing Reason: A Critique of Anti-Rationalist Views of Science and Knowledge.*

RELIGION. Defined by the distinguished anthropologist **Raymond Firth** as a "**life stance** that includes at minimum a belief in the existence and fundamental importance of a realm transcending that of ordinary experience." **Paul Kurtz** expanded on this when he itemized six criteria for a religion:

(1) " The belief that there is some realm of being that transcends experience or **reason**, that this realm is sacred, numinous, or holy, and that it is related to the world as its ultimate cause or final purpose."

(2) " The belief that human beings have some obligation to the sacred."

(3) The ability of that other realm and the religion that honors it to offer solace.

(4) The existence of institutions, hierarchy, and priesthoods to act as an intermediary between the two realms.

(5) Prophets who receive the word of **God**, Jesus, Muhammad, etc., who are venerated.

(6) Existence of Holy **scriptures** which also are venerated.

Other scholars, such as Stewart Guthrie, have seen religion in terms of systematic **anthropomorphism**. Human beings are inevitably anthropocentric, Guthrie argues, and it is this part of us that provides the foundation for our commitment to religion. Anthropomorphism in religion comes in two guises: on the one hand is the claim that gods exist, which is to attribute human characteristics to nature, and on the other hand is the attribution of human characteristics to those gods. Both these activities are incurably anthropocentric. **Science**, by contrast, is humanity's principal weapon against anthropomorphism, because science tries to understand nature as much as is possible on its own terms. This constitutes the fundamental point of the **conflict between science and religion**.

Whether looking at religion from the viewpoint of Firth and Kurtz, or from the viewpoint of Guthrie, it is clear that the essential division is between the naturalistic sciences, which study nature with at least an understanding of the problem of **anthropocentric conceit**, or religion, which, at least in its monotheist variety, sees the entire universe as a mirror of human beings.

It is important to note that the **Asian traditions** of Hinduism, Buddhism, Confucianism, and Taoism do not conform to these understandings of religion and, indeed, a good case can be made that when we speak of "religion," we usually mean only the three **monotheistic** religions of Judaism, Christianity, and Islam.

Further reading: Raymond Firth, *Religion: A Humanist Interpretation*; Stewart Guthrie, *Faces in the Clouds: A New Theory of Religion*; and Paul Kurtz, *Eupraxophy: Living without Religion* (1989)

RELIGION, CRITICISM OF. It has become unfashionable to criticize religion. Criticism of religion is very often seen as demonstrating some sort of intolerance, whereas a profession of religious **faith**, even if it is quite discriminatory, is tolerated as a legitimate expression of personal views. This is an unsatisfactory, and potentially dangerous, situation. Religion, like any other human construct, is capable of error and can benefit from criticism. Indeed, because the conservative wings of the **monotheistic religions** frequently claim possession of absolute truth, the close scrutiny of such claims is a public duty.

The criticism of religion, as of any other

institution, is an important part of the ongoing **social intelligence**. No institution should be above criticism. And neither is the criticism of religion necessarily the same as hostility to religion. Some of the most biting criticism of religion has come from religious believers. Among the more extreme religious apologists, the claim is often heard that freethinkers are motivated primarily by **anti-Semitism**, a hatred of Christianity, or "Islam-ophobia." This is untrue. Making a claim like this is an attempt to **demonize the opposition** and to deny that any rejection of, or opposition to, religion can be done honestly.

Bertrand Russell got to the heart of the matter when he wrote, "Find more pleasure in intelligent dissent than in passive agreement, for, if you value intelligence as you should, the former implies a deeper agreement than the latter." See the entry on the **Liberal Decalogue**. Ironically, the practice of criticizing religion is one of the things that freethinkers have in common with religious believers. As against the mass of **indifferentism**, freethinkers take religious claims seriously enough to subject them to serious investigation. Religious believers do the same. While the conclusions reached are obviously different, the sense that this is a worthwhile activity unites us both.

Open, informed and civil dialogue between freethinkers and religious believers is a priority. Religious organizations need to abandon the policy of demonizing the opposition and take nonbelievers as seriously as nonbelievers have been taking them.

RELIGION, DIMENSIONS OF. The British scholar of religion Ninian Smart (1927–2001) itemized seven dimensions of **religion**:

- practical and ritual dimension;
- experiential and emotional dimension;
- narrative or mythic dimension;
- doctrinal and philosophical dimension;
- ethical and legal dimension;
- social and institutional dimension; and
- material dimension.

Smart had originally discerned six dimensions, but they became seven and altered their focus as he studied further. Looking at religion in this way allows one to appreciate the complexity of religion and its ability to be a force for good and a force for violence, often in the same person.

Further reading: Ninian Smart, *The Religious Experience of Mankind.*

RELIGION, DYNAMICS OF. In a historical survey of **religion**, written at the end of the nineteenth century, **J. M. Robertson** outlined what he thought was the principle by which organized religion survives over time. Religion, Robertson wrote, depends on accumulated financial power to enable it to maintain its educational, propaganda, and other forms of outreach with little or no regard to the changing intellectual conditions that swirl around it.

While Robertson may have underestimated the degree to which institutionalized religion has had to change with the times, his basic point about the crucial importance of the financial power as a buttress to religion's continuation remains valid.

Further reading: J. M. Robertson, *The Dynamics of Religion.*

RELIGION OF THE OPEN MIND. A phrase employed by **Adam Gowans Whyte** and used as the title of a book published in 1913. The essence of **rationalism**, Whyte wrote, is the duty to apply to areas of religion the same standards of investigation and honest criticism we value in every other area of life. Saints and apostles, Whyte wrote, have long dreamt of the day when we would all believe the same thing. Happily, he added, that day will never arrive. The religion of the open mind atones for the loss of a delusional "other world" by leading us to realize fully the possibilities of this world. "Moreover, by an apparent paradox, this yea-saying of life is the best preparation for the acceptance of death."

Further reading: Adam Gowans Whyte, *The Religion of the Open Mind.*

RELIGIOUS ATTITUDE, THE. While acknowledging the difficulty of generalizing in this area, several scholars have laid down some useful guidelines. Among the best attempts to present a basic taxonomy of religious attitudes comes from the American philosopher Tad S. Clements. Characteristics of the religious attitude include:

- feeling that the supernatural, and one's relationship with it, are of primary importance;
- having sure **faith** in the immutable verities of one's religion;
- a passive receptivity toward supernatural influences;
- a willingness to accept a *feeling* of assurance over evidence-based knowledge;
- a readiness to add new supernatural ideas to explain supernatural ideas that already exist;
- the feeling that what has happened ought to have happened, and a hostility to examination of the way things work;
- the willingness to feel awe, reverence, etc., for supernatural verities; and
- the tendency to anthropomorphize their relationship with the supernatural.

A clear conclusion from this list is the differences between the religious and the scientific attitudes. Unfashionable though such a theory is, there are nonetheless some fundamental differences in the premises of the ideal religious believer and those of the ideal secular humanist. See the entry on **conflict between science and religion**.

Further reading: Tad S. Clements, *Science versus Religion.*

RELIGIOUS EXPERIENCE. There has been a popular strand of thinking which has dismissed as irrelevant any discussion of religious *ideas*, and insisting that the real debate is over the religious *experience*. The most prominent advocate of this approach was the American psychologist **William James**.

Among the many fallacies of this approach is to see religious experience as something special, over and above other forms of experience, and requiring a different form of propagation. But work in **evolutionary psychology** has shown this to be incorrect. As with other forms, religious forms only work because they can fit into notions, needs, and desires that are already active in the brain. This is not to say that there is a "religion gene." There is not. It is to say that we have established templates for understanding the world and our place in it, and the many religious explanations have had a long career of providing those explanations.

And on a popular level, there has been a tendency to try to shield religious beliefs by describing them as experiences, which it would be impolite and irrelevant to subject to empirical scrutiny. In this way, a superficially held prejudice can escape examination and be passed off as an expression of a deeply held sense of natural right. This is not good for the **social intelligence** or the **open society**. See the entry on **six suggestions for religious believers**.

Further reading: Pascal Boyer, *Religion Explained.*

RELIGIOUS HUMANISM. A branch of **humanism** that sees value in retaining some elements of religious language while rejecting the supernaturalist meanings inherent in them. The core contention of religious humanism is that *Homo sapiens* is *Homo religiosus*, in other words, naturally inclined toward thinking in religious terms. Unlike more secularly oriented humanists, religious humanists see value in bringing words like "**God**," "**faith**," "transcendence," and "**spirituality**" out of their religious habitat and employing them for secular purposes. Secular humanists, by contrast, contend that only confusion can result from doing that, as well as providing ammunition for extremist American fundamentalists who are trying to have humanism branded a **religion** so as to banish **evolution** and other fruits of humanism (as they see it) from the classroom. See the entry on **secular humanism**.

The *Humanist Manifesto I* (1933) remains the most influential document of religious humanism. It no longer represents the opinion of mainstream humanism, having been replaced by the *Secular Humanist Declaration* and the *Humanist Manifesto 2000*.

Outside the United States, where these political considerations are not as important, religious humanism has been more overtly religious, with specific theistic commitments being retained among thinkers like Pierre Teilhard de Chardin (1881–1955) and Albert Schweitzer (1875–1965). See the entries on **Sea of Faith**, **ethical culture**, and **Radest, Howard**.

RELIGIOUS IDEAS, CAUSES OF. As conceived by **Sigmund Freud** in his most brilliant book, *The Future of an Illusion* (1927), include:

- the necessity to defend oneself against the crushing supremacy of nature; and
- the felt need to correct the many injustices and imperfections of nature.

Freud went on to ask on what bases we have to believe religious ideas. He said there are three answers, which do not sit well alongside each other. They are:

- because our ancestors believed them;
- because we have proofs which have come down to us from a long time ago; and
- because it's not right to question their truth anyway.

Freud saw religious ideas as illusions derived from what we wish to be true rather than from what actually is true. Without these illusions we will have to abandon our **anthropocentric conceit** and adopt some **cosmic modesty**.

Further reading: Sigmund Freud, *The Future of an Illusion*.

RENAISSANCE HUMANISM. The years between 1400 and 1600 in the broadest understanding, or more narrowly between about 1450 and 1527, are now known as the Renaissance. Most scholars agree that its intellectual precursor was the Italian scholar Petrarch (1304–1374) and that it ended with the death at the stake of **Giordano Bruno** in 1600. This period only began to be known as the Renaissance in the nineteenth century. The **humanism** of the Renaissance was characterized mostly by a revolt against stifling orthodoxy, mainly represented by orthodox Catholic theology and its distorted **Aristotelianism**. It is important to note that the humanism of the Renaissance was not a single program, but a collection of individuals who were united more by the value they placed on independent scholarship than on developing a coherent understanding of the world, let alone one that could be called humanist. But behind the varying ideas of people as different as **Erasmus**, Machiavelli (1469–1527), and Thomas More (1478–1535) was the interest they shared in seeking human solutions to human problems.

Against the orthodoxy of the theologians, Renaissance humanists were inspired by the works of the pagan ancient Greeks, whose works were slowly being unearthed, or imported from the Muslim world. A central element of Renaissance humanism was the belief that the values of the pagan Greeks and Romans were superior, or at least had much to teach a Europe emerging out the gloom of the Middle Ages, where Christianity had been dominant. Among theologians like Erasmus, there was a strong desire to extend at least the possibility that the pagan Greeks, whose lives had been exemplary despite not being Christians, could be saved. For the conservatives, if they weren't Christians, they weren't saved, no matter how good their lives were.

Medieval thinking had been dominated by cultural pessimism: weariness with this world and a suspicion, derived mainly from St. Augustine (354–430 CE), that human affairs are inevitably tainted with corruption and selfishness. Renaissance thinking, by contrast, was positive and optimistic. While renaissance humanism differed on many points, it was pretty unanimous in its condemnation of the monastic life, with all its implications of defeatism and withdrawing from one's civic duties.

Renaissance humanism was distinctive in several ways. The very idea of the Renaissance came from the idea that this age was the first to rediscover and appreciate fully the cultural grandeur of the ancient world. While **Aristotle** had long been known, his influence had not always been a force for good. In the hands of Catholic theologians, scholasticism had deteriorated into an arid and dogmatic impediment to **freethought**. The thinkers of the Renaissance saw themselves as the scourge of medieval dogma and pioneers of a new cultural and intellectual orientation centering on the majesty of the ancient world. The new style of thinking was stimulated by the rediscovery of ancient thinkers, in particular **Lucretius**, Cicero (106–43 BCE), and **Plato**. While Plato was often embraced simply as a rejoinder to the overarching influence of Aristotle, **Lucretius** and Cicero were deeply influential for their own messages.

Renaissance humanists scorned the doomladen fears of the medieval thinkers who saw any social change as driven by base, even satanic, motives, and therefore inevitably bound to fail. The renaissance humanists were optimistic about the power of culture to effect positive social change. They were also optimistic about the power of ideas to effect real changes. Where the Middle Ages tended to see things in theological terms, renaissance humanists saw things from a more naturalistic perspective. St. Augustine had taught that the city of **God** could only be built in heaven where humans were no longer in control. But the renaissance humanists were more of a feeling that humanity could create, if not the city of God, at least a city of godly humans, right here on earth. Only after the sack of Rome in 1527 did this optimism decline and a return to contemplation and an escape from the world once more became a discernable trend in Renaissance thought.

Another feature of this optimism in the ability of humans to create their own destiny was the significant changes in the understanding of **religion**. Very few Renaissance thinkers were atheists: almost all were theists, the majority of them remained Christians, though of heterodox sympathies. There was also a strong leaning toward mysticism. See the entry on *Priscia theologia*. But the understanding of God changed. God was something that could be understood by our learning and study. Indeed, learning and study was a deeply pious activity, in that learning about nature meant, ipso facto, learning about God. The Renaissance was a period of significant historical and scriptural research. For instance, **Lorenzo Valla** was responsible for exposing the fraud known as the **Donation of Constantine**, upon which the papal claims to own its large territories in Italy was based. Far from being a document dating to the Emperor **Constantine**, Valla proved that the document was composed five hundred years later, in the eighth century. Valla was influential in teaching people the need to read scriptures with a skeptical frame of mind. This religious scholarship of Renaissance scholars was usually undertaken with a mind to reform religion and purging it of its recent and harmful additions. This drive led directly to developing some of the first ideas since the ancient world of religious toleration. This trend only came to an end when the religious reformer Savonarola (1452–1498) was burned at the stake.

By the end of the sixteenth century, much of the optimism that underlay the spirit of the Renaissance had evaporated. This pessimism can be seen in the works of **Montaigne**. In the way the pagan humanism of the ancient world was slowly stifled by religion and reaction, so Renaissance humanism was closed down by the combined effects of the Counter-Reformation and Protestantism.

Further reading: Eugenio Garin, *Italian Humanism: Philosophy and Civic Life in the Renaissance*; and Lisa Jardine, *Worldly Goods: A New History of the Renaissance*.

RENAISSANCE, LEGACY OF. We don't remember the Renaissance for its achievements in philosophy as much as for its cultural brilliance. However, the overall effect was extraordinary. **Bertrand Russell** noted that the Renaissance helped prepare the way for the scientific breakthroughs of the seventeenth century. The legacy of the Renaissance includes:

- breakdown of the straitjacket of scholastic philosophy;
- revival of the study of **Plato**, thereby requiring a choice between him and **Aristotle**; and
- encouragement of the habit of regarding intellectual activity as a "delightful social adventure, not a cloistered meditation aiming at the preservation of a predetermined orthodoxy."

A parallel development was the invention of printing, which very quickly helped produce a larger reading public than had been the case before, and a greater demand for books. In this way, the ideas current at the time had a far larger circulation than could ever have been the case before the advent of printing.

Another legacy of the Renaissance is that orthodox Christian theology was no longer thought to be adequate, even among those who thought in supernatural terms. The popularity of ideas like *prisca theologia* is evidence of that dissatisfaction.

Further reading: Bertrand Russell, *History of Western Philosophy*.

RENAISSANCE MAN. This refers to the ability of a person to combine a well-rounded education in the arts and sciences with being active in public life. In this way the person's education is being put to good use, in helping along the **social intelligence**. This general education and public spiritedness amounted to possessing a full **character**. The ideal of Renaissance man was reached most completely in **Leonardo da Vinci**.

What we call Renaissance man was in fact one of the many ideals the Renaissance human-ists borrowed from the ancient world. A. C. Grayling has noted that the ideal of Renaissance man was inspired largely by the life of Cicero (106–43 BCE). Once again, a social ideal owes its origin not to Christianity, but to their pagan forbears. See the entry on *paideia*.

Further reading: A. C. Grayling, *What is Good? The Search for the Best Way to Live*.

RENAN, ERNEST (1823–1892). Vastly influential French writer and thinker. Ernest Renan was raised by his sister after his father drowned when he was five years old. He was destined for the church, and in 1838 went to a seminary in Paris, but soon became disillusioned with the insincerities of the Catholicism he was immersed in. In 1845 he left the church, earning a living teaching at a night school. Under the influence of Pierre Berthelot (1827–1907), an eminent chemist teaching at the same school, Renan abandoned formal Christianity and adopted a Hegelian **pantheism**. He studied in Lebanon between 1860 and 1861 and upon his return was appointed professor of Hebrew, Syriac, and Chaldaic at the College de France.

Renan's name was made when he wrote the *Life of Jesus* (1863), which became enormously popular as a whimsical, though naturalistic account of Jesus' life, shorn of the usual miraculous trappings. The work sold 300,000 copies in France alone, and was translated into most European languages. His influence was widespread, not least because of his beautiful writing style. In a revealing example of **anti-Semitism**, the Catholic Church accused Renan of being subsidized by Rothschild to oppose the faith. There followed a series of studies of the people and conditions of early Christianity: *The Apostles* (1866), *Saint Paul* (1869), *The Antichrist* (1873), and *History of the People of Israel* (1888–94). He also wrote a series of ethical dramas which were published in 1888.

Renan disbelieved in a personal **god** and **immortality**, but taught that we must behave *as if* God and the soul exist. He died enormously popular and influential.

RENAULT, MARY (1905–1983). Pseudonym of Mary Challens, who was born in London, the daughter of a doctor. Despite an early desire to become a writer, Challens took a degree in nursing in 1936, so as to expand her knowledge of the human condition. Her mother had wanted her to take an interest in her appearance and marriage prospects, but this was not Challens's style. Her first published novels were written off-duty, while serving in World War II. Her first novel was *Promise of Love* (1939), and then *Return to Night* (1947), which received the MGM award.

After the war Renault migrated to South Africa, where her most famous novels were written. She wrote a succession of historical novels on various themes of classical Greece, the best of which were *The Last of the Wine* (1956), *The King Must Die* (1958), *The Mask of Apollo* (1966), her trilogy on Alexander the Great: *Fire from Heaven* (1970), *The Persian Boy* (1973), and *Funeral Games* (1982). These remain unsurpassed novels of historical imagination.

A notable feature of Renault's is her ability to convey the thoughts of men, in particular homosexual men. Her earlier work, *The Charioteer* (1955), is notable in this regard. Renault was a lesbian; her lifelong companion was Julie Mullard. She also wrote a biography of Alexander, *The Nature of Alexander* (1975).

Further reading: David Sweetman, *Mary Renault: A Biography*.

RESPONSIBILITIES. It is true that, alongside the **rights** we claim for ourselves, we also have a set of responsibilities which accompany them. Talk of rights runs the risk of being empty unless this important corollary is understood.

Humanists have always embraced the importance of our responsibilities, although it has been expressed in different ways. For example, the American philosopher James Gouinlock speaks of two kinds of responsibilities: *obligations* and *duties*. Obligations are moral calls upon our time and energy that are enshrined in custom rather than strict legality. Anyone who has made a promise has an obligation to keep it. This is not an absolute obligation because there may well be good reasons to break the promise. But generally speaking, we have that obligation. Teachers have obligations to their students, friends have obligations to each other.

But we also have duties, which are more specific than obligations. We have a duty to observe road rules and return library books and live up to our contractual obligations. These may well be backed up by the weight of the law. See the entry on **Declaration of the Rights of Man and of the Citizen**.

An essentially similar point has been made by two Dutch humanists, Johanna van Noordwijk and Jacobus van Noordwijk, who discerned four different responsibilities:

- for our own health and **life stance**;
- for our loved ones, relatives, and friends;
- for all other humans; and
- for all life on earth.

The first two, they note, are part of our evolutionary heritage. See the entry on **reciprocal altruism**. The second two are typical only for *Homo sapiens* and are cultural achievements. Each of these responsibilities can only be nurtured through education and recognition of the urgent need for **planetary humanism**.

Further reading: James Gouinlock, *Rediscovering the Moral Life*; and Johanna van Noordwijk and Jacobus van Noordwijk, "Humanist Thoughts on a Sustainable Human Existence," *New Humanist* 108, no. 4 (November 1993): 11–12.

RETREAT FROM PYTHAGORAS. The title of an essay by **Bertrand Russell** in which he summarized his life's work as such. What he meant by this is that he had progressed (or retreated, as he put it) from the **transcendental temptation** posed by thinkers like Pythagoras to a more tentative worldview, one without resplendent absolutes and consolations, but one which is also free from **anthropocentric conceit**. Specifically, the retreat was from, not so much Pythagoras, as from **Plato**'s idealist views (derived from Pythagoras) of the universal authority of logic and mathematics.

But even at this stage in his life, Russell still insisted that while no philosophy can mirror perfectly the world we live in, we still have a duty to make the mirrors we do use as undistorted as possible. This sums up the task of humanist philosophy.

Further reading: Bertrand Russell, *My Philosophical Development*.

REVERENT AGNOSTICS. A term applied to a type of **agnostic** thinker in the late-nineteenth and early-twentieth centuries. The typical reverent agnostic had undergone a long and painful loss of faith and retained a genuine respect for the religious life and religion as a social institution. The main focus of criticism of religion by reverent agnostics was directed against superstition and the cruder forms of **anthropomorphism**. They were often strongly critical of **atheism**, which they saw as just as obscurantist as the anthropomorphic religion they had rejected. These criticisms are no longer valid, as the philosophy of atheism has expanded and deepened immeasurably since the nineteenth century. Reverent agnostics are the natural predecessors of today's **religious humanists**.

REVISIONIST HISTORY. A term used most often in a negative sense. A revisionist history contrives to affect a significant shift in conventional wisdom on the subject at hand by advocating a radically new thesis. The most extreme variety of revisionist history is that of the **Holocaust deniers**. It is often the case that the revisionist history is unsuccessful at overturning the conventional account of the subject at hand, either because the revisionist's account is short on evidence, or places too much emphasis on particular pieces of evidence, or for some other reason. Not infrequently, it is because revisionists are

party to some ideology which underlies their objection to the conventional account.

This is not to say that historical accounts cannot be changed—far from it. Bold new historical insights and meticulous new research can, and sometimes do, lead to new accounts of how history has proceeded. But the brash new accounts that are too clever often justify the label "revisionist history."

RICHTER, GERHARD (1932–). German painter. Born in Dresden, Germany, in 1932, Richter was raised in Nazi Germany and then the Soviet zone, which later became the communist satellite state of East Germany. He enrolled in the Dresden Art Academy in 1952 and learned the foundations of traditional painting. His early work consisted of public murals proclaiming the glories of socialism. He escaped to West Germany in 1961, not long before the Berlin Wall was built.

Richter enrolled in the art academy in Düsseldorf, and was exposed there to some very influential artists and art ideas. The formidable technical skills he acquired in Dresden were put to use, and Richter blossomed into one of the postwar world's preeminent artists.

Richter's art works across many boundaries, incorporating photo-based paintings, paintings about painting, abstraction, and photo realism. In the 1970s he ignored the increasingly shrill insistence that painting was now dead. He also tacked from abstraction to photo realism whenever he felt he was being bracketed as one sort of artist.

A lifelong atheist and humanist, he ignored the demands of all totalizing ideologies, having experienced them as a youth. To the extent that any one theme pervades his work, it would be giving visual evidence of the discrepancies between what we see and what we think we see.

RIGHTS. A set of entitlements that people can expect to claim from the societies in which they live. Rights are not absolute entitlements. It is not written in the cosmos that

Homo sapiens should have inalienable rights. This was the claim that **Jeremy Bentham** mocked as "nonsense upon stilts." Rights are relations, and the extent of entitlements and the inevitable conflicts between them are the sorts of issues which ongoing democratic discussion needs to work out. We may, for example, be getting to the end of the period of history when we can breezily claim the right to drive a car. This ongoing debate about what society will and will not tolerate is what **John Dewey** called **social intelligence**.

There are three main categories of rights:

- *classical* rights: the rights to life, liberty, pursuit of happiness;
- *welfare* rights: the rights to a job, education, housing, medical care; and
- *contractual* rights: the rights emanating from any sort of contract or agreement.

The classical rights are those most essential to a stable society composed of fulfilled individuals. These rights speak to our **human needs**; our biogenic needs are fundamental, followed by our sociogenic needs. The main limitation on the rights we can legitimately claim is that they not be used to violate the rights of others. This is the legal application of **reciprocal altruism** and the **golden rule**. The welfare rights are the most contentious types of rights, and a great deal of political debate is involved in where to set the boundary to these rights, and how many of them can be afforded.

We also need to distinguish between having a *right* to something and *deserving* something. The person who deserves something has earned a particular distinction and it is legitimate that that person enjoys his just desert. Rights, however, are everybody's entitlements, without regard to merit. It is here where welfare rights can be most problematic. A child-abusing drunk may have a right to subsidized accommodation, but he can hardly be said to deserve it. There is no straightforward answer. Each society needs to work out its own priorities based on its own social intelligence.

All varieties of rights are evenly balanced with **responsibilities**. If we choose to exercise the right to listen to loud music in earphones, then we have the responsibility to pay for the cost of hearing aids in later years. Understanding this balance between rights and responsibilities is integral to humanism. It is also important to balance speaking of rights with speaking of **character** and **virtue**. See the entry on **duty of the well-informed citizen**.

Discussion of rights is no longer an abstract recreation of philosophers. All member states of the **United Nations** that have ratified the 1966 Covenant on Civil and Political Rights and the Covenant on Economic, Social, and Cultural Rights can no longer evade responsibility by saying that their rights are their business. Rights are now a global concern and can now be spoken of as human rights. Other major statements of human rights include the Declaration of the Rights of the Child (1959), the Convention on the Elimination of All Forms of Racial Discrimination (1966), and the Convention on the Elimination of Discrimination against Women (1967).

Further reading: James Gouinlock, *Rediscovering the Moral Life*; and Micheline Ishay, *The History of Human Rights*.

RITCHIE-WILMOT SYNDROME. A syndrome named by Paul Edwards to refer to the gulf which often appears between a claim being made, usually by advocates of some **pseudoscience**, and the evidence being offered in its support. The syndrome is named in honor of Dr. George Ritchie and Mr. Wilmot, two supporters of **astral travel**.

We often hear of some remarkable new phenomenon, about which "scientists are baffled," but once the breathless testimony has finished and the media spotlight moved on, it often transpires that the claim was based on little more than the testimony of a secondary source. When push comes to shove, and evidence is demanded, it is often found to be extremely flimsy or simply nonexistent. This was found to be the case with both Ritchie and Wilmot in their claims on behalf of astral travel. Hence the Ritchie-Wilmot Syndrome.

Further reading: Paul Edwards, *Reincarnation: A Critical Examination.*

ROALFE, MATILDA (1813–1880). English **freethought** pioneer and activist. During the **blasphemy** persecutions in 1843, Roalfe left London and went to Edinburgh to take part in the struggle to win the right to a free press. She issued a manifesto declaring that she would sell works according to whether she thought them useful, "whether they did or did not bring into contempt the Holy Scriptures and the Christian Religion." Inevitably she was prosecuted for selling freethought material and was sentenced to two months' imprisonment on January 23, 1844. She was advised that a plea of ignorance of the content of the material might earn her an acquittal. She refused. She also refused to exploit a legal technicality which might have enabled her to escape confinement. In fact she vowed to continue selling freethought material upon her release: a vow she honored. She later married Walter Sanderson, a close associate of **George Jacob Holyoake**. She ended her life in Galashiels, Scotland.

ROBERTSON, ARCHIBALD (1886–1961). English socialist and rationalist. Archibald Robertson was the son of a senior Church of England figure, who ended his career as bishop of Exeter between 1903 and 1916. While still at school, the young Robertson was alerted to **atheism** by a schoolmate's disparaging reference to **Percy Bysshe Shelley**'s poem "Queen Mab." By the time he was at Oxford, Robertson was an atheist and socialist. While his father was still alive, Robertson wrote under the half-hearted pseudonym of "Robert Arch." In 1938 he joined the Communist Party. He remained a Marxist for the rest of his life.

Robertson's friend Belfort Bax (1854–1926) introduced him in 1920 to the **Ration-**alist Press Association**, and from 1925 he served on the RPA's board of directors. But he became increasingly impatient with the evolutionary rationalism of the RPA and in 1931 took part in an attempted palace coup with the goal of modernizing the association. Robertson's group, including **C. E. M. Joad**, wanted the RPA to adopt a scientific humanist stance. The coup, which became known as "the Great Conway Hall Plot," was a complete failure and the old guard survived. Robertson resigned from the board in 1932 but soon returned to the RPA, and remained a loyal member for the rest of his life. He even returned to the board in 1954. Most of his works were published by Watts and Co., the publishing house linked to the RPA. It was Robertson who gave the famous **Thinker's Library** series their name. He contributed several volumes to the series: *The Bible and Its Background* (two volumes, 1942); *Jesus: Myth or History?* (1946), a very sensible refutation of the **myth theory of Jesus**; *Man His Own Master* (1948); and *The French Revolution* (1949).

Some of his late works include *How to Read History* (1952), an introduction to the Marxist account of history; *Rationalism in Theory and Practice* (1954); and *The Reformation* (1960). Robertson was a capable scholar and a clear writer, but had a somewhat formidable personality, which tended to turn people away.

Further reading: Bill Cooke, *The Gathering of Infidels: A Hundred Years of the Rationalist Press Association.*

ROBERTSON, JOHN MACKINNON (1856–1933). Scholar, liberal, and politician. One of the ablest thinkers of the **freethought** movement in the first decades of the twentieth century. Born in modest circumstances on the Isle of Arran, he only received schooling until he turned thirteen, but became one of the most widely read men of his generation. In 1878 he joined the staff of the *Edinburgh Evening News* as a feature writer. His own path to freethought was completed after hearing a lecture by **Charles Brad-laugh** in Edinburgh on **Giordano Bruno**. Robertson joined the **National Secular Society** and in 1884 went to London and worked for Bradlaugh's paper, the *National Reformer*.

After Bradlaugh's death, Robertson soldiered on with the *National Reformer*, but the paper folded in 1893, unable to continue without Bradlaugh's personality to back it. Robertson continued to work as a journalist until he was elected to parliament as Liberal MP for Tyneside in 1906. He rose to become Parliamentary Secretary to the Board of Trade from 1911 to 1915 and served on the Privy Council from 1915 until his election defeat in 1918.

As well as his journalistic work, he produced an extraordinary range of books, covering history, politics, economics, literature, and comparative religion. In a series of works, Robertson argued passionately for the mythical theory of Jesus. *Christianity and Mythology* (1900) and *Pagan Christs* (1903) were the main works, with three more, *The Historical Jesus* (1916), *The Jesus Problem* (1917), and *Jesus and Judas* (1927), which dealt with objections and pursued lesser points. Robertson's myth theory works are clumsily written and pursue an eccentric thesis, which tended to obscure rather than highlight the layers of myth the Jesus story is buried in. However, Robertson deserves credit for questioning the historicity of Judas, and seeing the creation of Judas as a gambit to discredit the Jews. This has since become a serious argument in religious-studies circles. As so often happens, a rationalist first made the point, but suffers from being ahead of his time.

Of greater scholarly and literary value are Robertson's histories. Over a period of thirty years he added to a general history of freethought which went through several editions, ending up as two double-volume works: *A History of Freethought: Ancient and Modern* (1936) and *A History of Freethought in the Nineteenth Century* (1929). These are brilliant, scholarly, and invaluable. And oddly, they are also better written than the myth books. Also worth reading is his intellectual history *A Short History of Morals* (1920).

Following his mentor, Charles Bradlaugh, Robertson was a lifelong republican, arguing in 1887 that the monarchy was simply a vehicle for the production of snobs and sycophants.

ROBERTSON,   PRISCILLA   SMITH (1910–1989). American historian, humanist, and activist. Priscilla Smith was born in Paris but raised in upstate New York. Her father was Preserved Smith (1880–1941), also a historian. In 1934 Priscilla married Cary Robertson, who went on to become a longtime Sunday editor of the *Courier-Journal*, based in Louisville, Kentucky. They had three children.

For a while, Smith Robertson chaired the Kentucky Civil Liberties Union and was a member of the American Friends Service Committee. In 1956 she took on the editorship of the *Humanist*, the journal of the **American Humanist Association**. Three years later she resigned, citing censorship of her views and interference with her editorial decisions. Her entire staff resigned in support of her.

She lectured at Indiana University in Bloomington and, during her time at Radcliffe as a fellow between 1966 and 1968, at Harvard. Her books were *Revolutions of 1848: A Social History* (1952) and *An Experience of Women: Patterns of Change in Nineteenth-Century Europe* (1982).

ROBINSON,   RICHARD (1902–1996). English scholar and atheist. Born in Watton, Norfolk, to a deeply religious family. When Robinson wrote to his mother that he no longer believed, his mother replied that the family had suffered a great disaster.

Robinson became a member of Oriel College, Oxford, in 1921, where he studied for a B. Litt and MA. He was at Marburg University in Germany in 1927–28 and Cornell University in the United States from 1928 to 1946, where he obtained his doctorate. He tutored philosophy at Oriel from 1946 until his retirement in 1969. Chiefly known for his works of philosophy, in particular *Plato's Earlier Dialectic* (1941), and *Definition* (1954), Robinson surprised many when he came out with *An Atheist's Values* in 1964, one of the most successful articulations of liberal **atheism** in the twentieth century. See the entries on **reason** and the **Principle of Countermisery**.

ROCK MUSIC. One of the most significant cultural by-products of the 1960s social revolution. Rock's musical roots were in rock 'n' roll, blues, and pop music, but until the 1960s this sort of music was a peripheral entertainment that would only alarm humorless pastors. Some historians have dated the birth of rock music to July 5, 1954, the day when Elvis Presley recorded "That's All Right."

Rock music, notes the social historian Robert Hewison, was expressive of feelings; it enacted **violence** and attempted the transcendental. Its subversive and hedonistic messages were then broadcast by a powerful communications industry. This blend of music and technology meant rock music could be enjoyed in private and en masse, at large concerts and festivals. But the coalition between rock music and capitalism has always compromised rock music's capacity to articulate political grievances. One of the few major bands to combine successfully a critique of capitalism with commercial success was **Pink Floyd**, especially during the years Roger Waters was its lead lyricist.

Since the 1960s, rock has become a multi-billion-dollar industry, spawning a vast array of subcultures and musical genres, the most important of which are:

- *psychedelic rock*, such as early **Pink Floyd**;
- *progressive rock*, such as the later Beatles, later **Pink Floyd**, Jethro Tull, and the Alan Parsons Project;

- *hard rock*, such as Led Zeppelin, Deep Purple, Uriah Heep, and Guns N' Roses
- *heavy metal*, a louder, more manic spin-off of hard rock, like AC/DC and Def Leppard;
- *industrial rock*, like Devo and **Marilyn Manson**;
- *glam rock*, the greatest examples of which were Queen and Meat Loaf;
- *folk rock*, such as Lynyrd Skynyrd; and
- *punk rock*, the ultimate protest music.

Few entries will date the author of this work as closely as this entry does.

Further reading: Robert Hewison, *Too Much: Art and Society in the Sixties, 1960–1975*.

RODDENBERRY, GENE (1921–1991). American television producer and creator and executive producer of the cult television series *Star Trek* and its sequel *Star Trek: The Next Generation*. Eugene Wesley Roddenberry was born in El Paso, Texas, and brought up in Los Angeles. He became an atheist when he was a teenager, and began writing when he was a pilot in World War II. He flew B–17 bombers against the Japanese during World War II, taking part in eighty-nine missions, for which he received the Distinguished Flying Cross and the Air Medal. After the war he worked as a crash investigator for Pan Am, surviving a crash in the Syrian desert himself on one occasion.

Roddenberry gave up his flying career when he saw television. He immediately grasped its importance for the future and moved to Los Angeles in the hope of selling scripts for television shows. After successfully preparing scripts for several different shows, he came up with the idea for *Star Trek*. Television executives originally turned *Star Trek* down, fearing it was too cerebral. But once it hit the screen it quickly attracted a loyal following and went on to become one of the most influential television series of all time. It ran for three seasons from 1966 to 1969 and *The Next Generation* ran from 1987 until 1994. The original series was cancelled not so much because of any fall in audience, but because the audience was too young for advertisers to market to.

Roddenberry did not think of *Star Trek* as science fiction, but as being about people. He encountered a series of problems with cautious television networks. He wasn't allowed to have a woman as the ship's second-in-command, and against his wishes, early programs had sexist costumes for women. Roddenberry had to struggle to keep black officers in the cast and there was pressure from Christians to have a chaplain on board the ship. Roddenberry survived all this and ensured *Star Trek* had a positive, even optimistic humanist message. His basic message was that to enrich our lives fully, we need to develop the warmth of human emotions because reason and logic are not enough. He received a total of eleven Emmy Awards throughout his career.

ROGERS, WILL (1879–1935). American cowboy actor, humorist, and irreverent wit. William Penn Adair Rogers was born in Indian Territory (which later became Oklahoma) in 1879, the son of a successful rancher. After trying to work as a cowboy in Argentina, Rogers joined a wild-west show in Texas, where he could combine his love of the cowboy lifestyle with his theatrical talents. Between 1905 and 1915 he worked for the Ziegfeld Follies, the most famous vaudeville stage show in the country.

By now quite famous, Rogers moved in 1918 to Hollywood where he began a spectacularly successful film career, starring in seventy-one films. He survived the transition to the "talkies," even prospered, as he managed this new change. In 1922 he began an additional career as a syndicated columnist, and yet again he was very successful. "I don't make jokes," Rogers wrote, "I just watch the government and report the facts." Over his journalistic career, he wrote twenty-eight hundred articles. In 1930 he also began giving radio addresses. His addresses were extremely popular, being listened to by forty million people. **H. L. Mencken** called Rogers "the most dangerous man alive" because of the influence he wielded.

Rogers had a ready wit, in the manner of **Mark Twain** or **Ambrose Bierce**. He noted that "everybody is ignorant, only on different subjects." Rogers's irreverence was illustrated well in 1920 when he participated in a debate with a local preacher at the Los Angeles Advertising Club. The moot was that "cowboys have contributed more to civilization than preachers." Tongue-in-cheek, Rogers asked that the debate be confined only to facts, because if lies were allowed, his opponent as a preacher, would have an unfair advantage over him. The advertising club declared the debate irrelevant as neither cowboys nor preachers had done anything for civilization.

Anticipating the Monster Raving Loony Party in Britain many decades later, Rogers stood for president in 1928 on an absurdist ticket. He promised to resign if elected, and his platform was to do whatever the other fellow won't do. There was a serious side to his **humor**. Commenting on the growing **inequality** during the Great Depression, he noted drily that America "will be the first nation in the world to go to the poor house in an automobile." He worked for the election of Franklin Delano Roosevelt in 1932. Rogers was killed in a plane crash in Alaska in August 1935.

ROGUE STATE. A term used for a state that supports terrorist activities or supplies weapons of mass destruction to irresponsible nations or networks. As rogues are people whose activities help undermine civic society, so rogue states help undermine transnational cooperation and **global governance**. The classic example is Libya, which was involved in the destruction of a Pan Am flight over Lockerbie, Scotland, in 1988. This was part of a large-scale, state-supported effort to destabilize other countries by resorting to **terrorism**. It was also developing weapons of mass destruction, a fact not acknowledged until 2003, after the United States and Britain destroyed another rogue state: Iraq under Saddam Hussein. Ironically, the destruction of Saddam's rogue state has converted Iraq into a **failed state**, an even more frightening prospect for world peace.

ROMANTICISM. An antirational reaction to the **Enlightenment**. Romanticism was not a school of thought. It was more a mood or style, whose principal spokespeople were to be artists and poets. While the **Enlightenment** had extolled **reason** and technology, the Romantics extolled the emotions, **intuition**, spontaneity, and a sense of history. Romanticism was popular from about the 1810s until the 1840s.

The groundwork of Romantic thought was laid down by the **Sturm und Drang** movement in Germany and by **Jean-Jacques Rousseau** who epitomized what **Bertrand Russell** called the revolt of solitary instincts against social bonds. Many of the leaders of Romantic thought were poets and artists, and so it is not surprising to find them seeing poets and artists as uniquely qualified to carry the world's soul on their shoulders.

Lord Byron (1788–1824), John Keats (1795–1821), **Percy Bysshe Shelley**, and Friedrich Hölderlin (1770–1843) were some of the more important Romantic poets. They all qualify not merely because of their talent but also by virtue of dying Romantically young or, in Hölderlin's case, mad. The notion of **art for art's sake** is a deeply Romantic one, imbued as it is with notions of escaping the vulgarity of the multitude into an appropriately **sublime** cocoon. It also elevated the moral authority of poets and artists—such as themselves.

Romanticism also reacted against the internationalism of the Enlightenment and was moved by appeals to **nationalism**, even racism, as nonrational calls to ourselves. Anticipating **postmodernism** in the next century, the Romantics affected a loss of confidence in the future, which they replaced with nostalgia for idealized images of the past. Only in Shelley or **Beethoven** is the genius enough to forgive some of the more extravagant excesses of Romanticism.

If overdoing the rationality of the Enlightenment is a mistake, it is more of a mistake to take too far the self-absorbed **irrationalism** of the Romantics. **Goethe**, one of the most significant influences on Romanticism said, "Classicism is health, romanticism disease."

RORTY, RICHARD (1931–). American **pragmatist** philosopher. After beginning as a conventional analytical philosopher, Rorty established his reputation with his book *Philosophy and the Mirror of Nature* (1979). Here Rorty broke out against much of the Western intellectual tradition. His rebellion against traditional metaphysics and epistemology lies in what he sees as the long-standing mistake of philosophers to assume that their task was to reflect accurately a reality which is capable of accurate reflection. Rorty continued this exploration in *Contingency, Irony, and Solidarity* (1989) when he distinguished between **metaphysicians and ironists**.

Critics of Rorty accuse him of throwing the baby out with the bathwater. It is one thing, they say, to see problems in getting an accurate picture of the world—an insight hardly original to Rorty. It is quite another to then declare that attempts at a comprehensive understanding of the world should be abandoned. For a while Rorty spoke of himself as a **postmodernist**, although he came to regret that usage. He was elected as a member of the **International Academy of Humanism** in 1988.

ROSE, ERNESTINE LOUISE (1810–1882). Campaigner for abolitionism, women's rights, and atheism. Rose was radical even among the radicals of her day, a position made even more uncomfortable because of her Jewish birth. Born E. L. Süsmond Potowsky, the daughter of a Jewish rabbi in Poland. While still in her teens, Potowsky had to fight a legal battle against her father's wish to impose a husband on her. She won that battle and left Poland for good and traveled through Europe.

In 1829 she traveled to Britain, surviving a shipwreck on the voyage. Once ashore, and penniless, she immersed herself in the radical movement, then being led by **Robert Owen**. In 1832 (or 1836, the accounts vary) she married William Rose, an English radical, and in 1836 migrated to the United States. From then until 1855, she was a regular speaker and campaigner around the country, becoming known as the "Queen of the Platform." Unlike most of her abolitionist and women's-rights colleagues, Rose saw **religion** as part of the problem that held blacks and women in subjection. While most women's-rights campaigners were accused at some time in their career of being atheists, in the case of Ernestine Rose, it was true. Being feminist, Jewish-born, *and* atheist, she received more vicious abuse than most of her colleagues—no mean feat. One newspaper editor warned that listening to Rose would be "a thousand times below a prostitute." And she was not just incidentally an atheist; she publicly defended **atheism** throughout her career. In 1861 she produced a pamphlet, *A Defence of Atheism*, based on a talk on that subject in Boston. Her radicalism notwithstanding, she won the staunch support of **Susan B. Anthony** and **Lucretia Mott** in particular.

In 1873 William and Ernestine Rose returned to Britain for good, where they largely dropped out of public life, though they maintained their association with the English radicals **George Jacob Holyoake** and **Charles Bradlaugh**. Rose's public defense of atheism is the main reason she has been all but forgotten, even by historians.

ROUSSEAU, JEAN-JACQUES (1712–1778). Hugely influential French thinker and representative of the less helpful ideas of the **Enlightenment**. Rousseau was born in Geneva, with his mother dying during his birth. Rousseau had little formal education. In 1728 he ran away and lived with Barone Louise de Warens (1700–1762). Eventually the two became lovers. During this time he was baptized a Catholic. In 1741 he moved to Paris where he took up with an illiterate maid, Thérèse le Vasseur.

Rousseau was very argumentative. He eventually fell out with all the prominent Enlightenment thinkers, including **Voltaire**, **Diderot**, and **David Hume**. The estrangement was both personal and ideological, as Rousseau became increasingly convinced that, while human beings were essentially good, they were being corrupted by civilization. He argued that civil society was inherently corrupt and degrading, particularly in contrast with the noble simplicity of primitive societies, which are unencumbered with the trappings of modernity. He was the creator of the noble-savage stereotype. He wanted people to recognize our corrupt state and advocated fundamental reform. We all have, Rousseau argued, an "inner voice" which provides for us a reliable source of justice and virtue. This natural tendency to goodness is then ground down by society and revealed **religion**.

Rousseau's most influential idea was also his least helpful: the **general will**. Some see Rousseau as a philosopher of freedom, but others see him as a precursor of **totalitarianism**. The latter view has more to recommend it. No less influential were his works on education. *Emile* (1762) was a runaway bestseller which, in the form of a simple romance, outlined Rousseau's views on education. He argued that **reason** is the faculty we develop last, so the education system that focuses on reason and words is doomed to fail. He wanted Emile's mind to be stimulated imaginatively, by combining mental and physical activity. However, education for the girl, Sophie, was geared exclusively toward pleasing Emile. *Emile* outraged the Catholic Church and forced Rousseau to flee France. He also angered **Mary Wollstonecraft**, who wrote *A Vindication of the Rights of Women* (1792), as a vehicle to criticize Rousseau.

Rousseau was not troubled by a poor opinion of himself. "I dare to believe," he wrote in his *Confessions*, "that I am different from any man who exists." On one level, of course, this is true, but not on the level he had in mind.

ROUT, ETTIE (1877–1936). Rationalist, feminist, and campaigner for safe sex, described by **H. G. Wells** as an "unforgettable heroine." Sadly, this hasn't stopped Ettie Rout from being forgotten. She was born in Tasmania but the family moved to New Zealand when she was seven. Despite being an intelligent girl, her education was brief because the family was too poor for her to stay in school. She became active in socialist and rationalist circles, becoming the first editor of the radical journal the *Maoriland Worker* in 1910.

Once World War I started, she founded the New Zealand Volunteer Sisterhood, to arrange for young women to attend the troops. Rout was quickly shocked by the prevalence of venereal disease among the soldiers. She worked up a prophylactic kit for distribution among them, which in 1917 was officially adopted by the New Zealand Expeditionary Force as part of a soldier's kit. At about this time, and the time the French awarded Rout the Reconnaissance Française for her efforts, the puritanical news media in New Zealand banned any mention of her on the grounds of her work being "obscene." A bishop in the House of Lords called her "the most wicked woman in Britain." But the soldiers called her a saint.

Rout followed up her war work with *Safe Marriage* (1922), a guide to safe sex, but the work was banned in New Zealand. Only the rationalist movement was brave enough to recommend the book publicly. After the war, she settled in London and in 1920 she married the physical-culture publicist Fred Hornibrook (1877–1965). There she worked in the birth-control movement.

Rout's life ended tragically. Her marriage to Hornibrook had come to an end by 1936 and in May that year she returned to New Zealand. But few people were prepared to welcome her even then. She took a ship to Rarotonga, where on September 17 she died by her own hand. Rout's memory was preserved appropriately when the New Zealand AIDS Foundation called its Christchurch office the Ettie Rout Center. See the entries on **Margaret Sanger** and **Marie Stopes**.

Further reading: Jane Tolerton, *Ettie: A Life of Ettie Rout*.

ROUX, EDWARD RUDOLPH (1903–1966). Botanist and political activist. Born in the north of South Africa to an Afrikaner father and English mother, Roux grew up in Johannesburg. His father owned a pharmacy and was a freethinker. Eddie Roux grew up on the far left, helping found the Young Communists League in 1921 and joining the Communist Party of South Africa (CPSA) two years later. After graduating at the University of the Witwatersrand, he completed a PhD at Cambridge University in 1929, doing research on plant physiology. Between finishing his studies at the university and 1936, Roux was deeply committed to communism, attending in 1928 the sixth Congress of the Communist International in the Soviet Union. Back in South Africa, he was active in Communist Party politics until falling foul of a purge in 1935 and leaving the party altogether the following year. In 1945 he joined the faculty at the University of the Witwatersrand, where he became professor of botany in 1962.

In 1957 he returned to active politics by joining the Liberal Party of South Africa, which was committed to a multiracial future for South Africa. One of Roux's more important books was called *Longer Than Rope* (1948), the first history of African nationalism in South Africa. At about this time he also founded a rationalist association. Early in the 1960s he was listed officially as dangerous to the regime, and as such came under a raft of restrictions. In 1963 he was forced to leave the Liberal Party and the following year was forcibly retired from his position at the university. Under that legislation, Roux was barred from any teaching, political activity, or from even being quoted. His health suffered under this persecution and he died, it was said, of a broken heart, in 1966, at sixty-three. The rationalist association he founded did not long survive him, although a small amount of money from that organization was bequeathed to a humanist society, which formed in 1979.

ROY, M. N. (1887–1954). Born Narendranath Bhattacharya in Arbelia, near Calcutta, the son of a village priest and teacher of Sanskrit. He changed his name to Manavendra Nath Roy when he visited the United States in 1916. Roy was deeply religious as a youth, but became a revolutionary in his teens, participating in eight robberies with the purpose of collecting funds for the cause. He was sent to prison in 1910. During World War I, and under the name of Charles A. Martin, Roy traveled Asia in search of arms for their planned insurrection. In 1916 he arrived in the United States, posing as a theology student. He was arrested in 1917 and fled to Mexico while on parole. He stayed in Mexico for about two and a half years and, under the influence of Michael Borodin, an official in the Communist International, became a Marxist. In 1919 he traveled to the Soviet Union and for the next ten years, rising to a senior position in the Comintern. But from 1927 onward, he fell into disfavor from Stalin and in 1929 was expelled from the Comintern. The following year he returned to India, where he remained for the rest of his life.

After a brief spell as a member of the Indian National Congress, Roy founded his own party, the Radical Democratic Party in December 1940. He dissolved the party in December 1948 and increasingly turned his attention away from politics and toward educational and cultural activities. Alongside this process Roy slowly shed his Marxism in favor of what he came to call radical humanism. He founded a magazine in 1945 called the *Marxian Way* but it was later renamed the *Humanist Way*.

In 1946 he unveiled to the Radical Democratic Party the **Twenty-two Theses of Radical Humanism**. These theses have become the foundation of radical humanism as it has operated in India. His work as philosopher of humanism was carried on by **V. M. Tarkunde**. Chief among Roy's books are *New Orientation* (1946), *22 Theses of Radical Humanism* (1947), reissued as *New Humanism* (1981), *Materialism* (revised edition, 1951), and *Reason, Romanticism and Revolution* (two volumes, 1952 and 1955).

RUGE, ARNOLD (1802–1880). Philosopher and humanist pioneer, described by **J. M. Robertson** as one who "gave his life to a disinterested propaganda of democracy and light." Ruge did more than anyone else to bring the word "**humanism**" to an English audience. He had a stellar career ahead of him, but for his radical views. He was educated at Halle, Jena, and Heidelberg universities. In 1825 he went to prison for five years for his activities in the cause of a united Germany. During his incarceration he translated Thucydides and a play of Aeschylus into German and wrote a **tragedy** of his own. After his release, he went to Halle, where he became professor of pedagogy and aesthetics at Halle University. But in 1838 he once again jeopardized his future when he cofounded a Hegelian journal, the *Hallische Jahrbücher* in 1838, which came under critical scrutiny from the clergy, who hounded it with constant censorship and in 1843 managed to have it closed down. For a short while after that he cooperated with Karl Marx, but didn't follow him into socialism. See the entry on **opium of the people**. In 1847 he opened a bookshop in Leipzig, but continued harassment forced him to leave Germany, first for France, then for Britain, where he lived the rest of his life, earning his money as a schoolmaster.

In his various publications, Ruge was a leading proponent of using the word "humanism" in the sense of a comprehensive worldview, rather than simply a philosophy of education. See the entry on **Friedrich Immanuel**

Niethammer. Ruge spoke of humanism as "realized Christianity," although this passage was excised by his censors. He wanted humanism to transcend both Christianity and philosophy. He wrote, "Only the free man is a real human being—the realization of the theoretical freedom is free humanity. Such humanizing of the world we call Humanism."

RUNYON, G. VINCENT. See **FORMER PREACHERS**.

RUSHD, IBN (1126–1198). Thought by many scholars to be the most significant Muslim philosopher of all time. Rushd, known in the West by his Latinized name Averroës, was also vastly influential in Christian circles. He was born into a privileged family of civil and religious professionals in Cordoba, the intellectual heart of Muslim Spain. He spent his life traveling between Cordoba and Seville in Spain, and Marrakesh in Morocco. In 1195 or so he retired from public duties, or was forced into exile, having come under a political cloud or in the face of rising opposition to him from conservative clerics. His death, which has long been suspected of not being natural, spelled the beginning of the end for the golden age of Muslim philosophy.

A prime concern of his was the reconciliation of **philosophy** and **religion**. He approached this question through commentaries on the works of **Aristotle**. His main work was called *The Incoherence of the Incoherence* (1180, approx.) and was a criticism of earlier philosophers who questioned the power and relevance of **reason** in all areas of human investigation.

Rushd's harmonizing of religion and philosophy was sophisticated. On the one hand, he tried to avoid simply allegorizing the anthropomorphisms in the Qur'an as he felt the **Mu'tazilites** had done. But he was no less careful to avoid the crude literalism of Hanbal (d. 855 CE) and others. He did this by acknowledging that the Qur'an has passages that are ambiguous and passages that are unambiguous. Following from this, he argued that it addresses itself to different orders of people in different ways. What is appropriate to one group is not appropriate to others. While he accorded religion higher status than philosophy, he also said that reason has a vital part to play in religious life. His thoughts were later translated, not entirely correctly, as advocating a double-truth idea which purportedly allowed religious truth to sit alongside conflicting philosophical truth.

Ibn Rushd worked in the puritanical and anti-intellectual climate of the Almohads, in the context of which his voice came across as a champion of reason. And while it would be overstating it to call Ibn Rushd a champion of **gender** equality, he was at least open in principle to the idea that women may well have greater ability than they were generally credited with.

In the face of growing **fundamentalism** in the Middle East, two courageous scholars, Mourad Wahba and Mona Abousenna, created in 1994 the Ibn Rushd and Enlightenment International Association, which in 2004 became a branch of the **Center for Inquiry** movement. They put out a journal called *Averroes Today*.

RUSSELL, BERTRAND (1872–1970). Philosophical genius and social gadfly. Born into the very highest reaches of English society, Russell studied at Cambridge University. Along with his colleague G. E. Moore (1873–1958), Russell was instrumental in overturning the prevailing orthodoxy of Hegelianism in English philosophy at the time. His early works of philosophy, in particular *The Principles of Mathematics* (1903) had a profound effect on trends in logic and understanding the importance of language. The most productive years of Russell's life were devoted to producing, with Alfred North Whitehead (1861–1947), the monumental three-volume (it was meant to be four) *Principia Mathematica* (1910–13) which was designed to show that pure mathematics follows from logical premises and only uses concepts that are definable in logical terms. This project was later shown to be flawed, not least from the work of **Kurt Gödel**. Nevertheless, the *Principia* remains one of the most daunting monuments to raw intellectual power ever produced.

It was during World War I that Russell felt the need to write a new sort of book, one that could extend beyond the cloistered world of academic philosophy, and be accessible to the general citizen. The first of these was *Principles of Social Reconstruction* (1916), a series of lectures on issues surrounding postwar reconstruction. This book was enormously successful and established a wider audience for Russell than philosophers had hitherto thought possible, or desirable. He went to prison for several months in 1918 for his opposition to the war.

Much of his later career was spent as a public intellectual, with occasional forays back into technical philosophy. Reversing the usual trend, he became increasingly radical as he got older. In 1955 he wrote what became known as the Russell-Einstein Manifesto. It was cosigned by **Albert Einstein**, one of the last things he did before his death. The Russell-Einstein Manifesto laid the foundations for the peace movement. In 1958 Russell was instrumental in setting up the Campaign for Nuclear Disarmament, serving as its first president. Two years later he founded the even more radical Committee of 100 to participate in civil disobedience against Britain's nuclear policies. Russell led from the front, going to prison in 1961, for the second time in his life. In 1963 he established the Bertrand Russell Peace Foundation as a vehicle to further world peace.

He was married four times. The first, to the American Quaker Alys Pearsall Smith (1865–1951) ended in 1911, although they were not divorced until 1921. The second, to Dora Black (1894–1986) ended disastrously in 1932. See the entry on **Dora Russell**. The third, to Patricia Spence, ended in 1952. Russell's fourth marriage, in 1952 to Edith Finch, was the happiest of the four and continued until his death in 1970. His son by his third wife, Conrad Russell (1937–2004), went on to become a respected historian, peer in the House of Lords, and honorary associate of the **Rationalist Press Association**.

The most important of the later technical works were *Analysis of Mind* (1921) and *Analysis of Matter* (1927), *An Inquiry Into Meaning and Truth* (1940), and *Human Knowledge: Its Scope and Limits* (1948). The themes that were constant in Russell's work were the analytical method, **empiricism**, realism, and the relations between things. The best of his popular writings are *The Scientific Outlook* (1931), *Religion and Science* (1936), *History of Western Philosophy* (1946), and *Why I am Not a Christian and Other Essays* (1957). It has become fashionable to dismiss much of this writing, as if writing for nonspecialist audiences is somehow disreputable. Happily, this attitude has little effect on the ongoing popularity of him and his work.

Further reading: Caroline Moorhead, *Bertrand Russell: A Life*.

RUSSELL, DORA (1894–1986). Atheist activist and author. Dora Black was born on April 3, 1894, in Thornton Heath, Surrey, the daughter of a senior civil servant who was later knighted for his work. She attended Sutton High School and won a scholarship to attend Girton College, Cambridge, taking her first degree in 1915. During her time at Cambridge she was a member (and later the secretary) of the Heretics, the notorious **freethought** society on campus. She was also an active Suffragist. Black was awarded an MBE in 1917 for her work at the British War Mission in the United States during World War I.

Black met **Bertrand Russell** in 1916 and again in 1919, when they became lovers. She followed Russell to Russia in 1920 after he refused to take her with him. On his return, they collaborated on *The Practice and Theory of Bolshevism* (1920), by far the most prescient book on the Soviet Union at such an early date. The two married in 1921, and had two children, John (1921–1987) and Katherine (1923–). Their ten-year marriage was hectic, with political campaigns, speeches, and books. And in 1927 they established Beacon Hill School, designed to educate the whole child along the lines of what is now known as the Montessori system. The marriage broke up amid great bitterness. Financial difficulties with the school, and Bertrand's inability to cope with Dora's enthusiastic interpretation of their "open marriage" were probably the main reasons. Bertrand was never again able to see Dora in a positive light. Dora was, eventually, more forgiving. She is widely thought to have been an important influence on her husband's move to a more militant **atheism** in the 1920s.

She remained active in progressive issues for the rest of her life. She was a founding member of the Progressive League in 1932, the National Council of Civil Liberties in 1934, and the Abortion Law Reform Association in 1936. And she struggled to keep Beacon Hill School open until 1943. After World War II, she was involved more in feminist and pacifist issues. Dora Russell was an honorary associate of the **Rationalist Press Association** from 1974 until her death in 1986.

She wrote a great deal during her long life. Her best-known work is the three-volume autobiography, *The Tamarisk Tree* (1975–1985). Other books included *Hypatia, or Woman and Knowledge* (1925), *The Right to be Happy* (1927), *In Defense of Children* (1932), and *The Religion of the Machine Age* (1983). There is also a good collection of her journalism under the title *The Dora Russell Reader* (1983).

RUSSIAN HUMANIST SOCIETY. Formed in 1995. Following the collapse of the Soviet Union, the idea of **atheism** was widely unpopular, as it was associated with the former regime, and with the KGB in particular. And yet there was a pressing need to develop a sense of civil society and secular values. It was with this in mind that the Russian Humanist Society was founded. The word "Russia" is

licensed in that country, so any organization seeking to have that name in their title must apply for official permission. The RHS applied and permission was finally granted in 2001. At this point, the official name of the society became Inter-regional Social Organization for Promoting the Development of Humanism (Russian Humanist Society).

The RHS has ten branches stretching from St. Petersburg to Irkutsk and from Komi to Dagestan. In cooperation with the Russian Academy of Sciences, the RHS publishes the journal *Common Sense*, which is the premier scourge of **pseudoscience** in Russia. The RHS has also published *Humanism in Civil Society* (2003), which is intended as a textbook for students and an introductory work for nonspecialist inquirers.

The RHS also supports the United Democratic Opposition, a group of human-rights exiles from Turkmenistan. The RHS works in close cooperation with two **Centers for Inquiry** in the country—one in Moscow and one in Kolomna.

S

SACRA VIRGINITAS, an encyclical issued by **Pius XII** on March 25, 1954, which insisted upon the retention of clerical celibacy. The encyclical began with this declaration: "Holy virginity and that perfect chastity which is consecrated to the service of **God** is without doubt among the most precious treasures which the Founder of the Church has left in heritage to the society which He established."

The encyclical criticized modern trends of questioning clerical celibacy and forcefully restated the superiority of virginity, or at least chastity, for those disenfranchised from the former condition. Only then, so the argument goes, can the individual devote his entire time to the glory and worship of God. It also restated the more general preference for virginity over **marriage**. The urge to promote marriage as the only method by which the harmonious development of the human personality can be achieved was censured as a "dangerous error." *Sacra Virginitas* endorsed flight and constant vigilance as the preferred methods to avoid the temptations of the flesh. See the entries on **family values** and **humanist family values**.

SAGAN, CARL (1934–1996). Brilliant scientist and popularizer of science. Born and raised in New York City, he studied at Chicago and Berkeley before working for a while at Harvard. He then moved to Cornell where he spent the rest of his academic life. During his scientific career, Sagan was David Duncan Professor of Astronomy and Space Sciences at Cornell and Distinguished Visiting Scientist at the Jet Propulsion Laboratory, California Institute of Technology. His scientific work involved the nature of planetary atmospheres and surfaces, and the origin of life.

It is as a popularizer of science that Sagan, often working with his third wife, **Ann Druyan**, is best known. He was author, coauthor, or editor of thirty books, of which the later popularizations are the best known. The most important was *Cosmos* (1980), which also became a fifteen-part television series and was hugely influential, being seen in sixty countries by up to 400 million people. Other important works of popular science included *Intelligent Life in the Universe* (1966, with I. S. Shklovskii), *The Dragons of Eden* (1977), *Contact* (1985, later turned into a film), *The Demon-Haunted World* (1996), and ***Billions and Billions*** (1997).

Sagan was the recipient of a large number of awards. Among the most prestigious include the NASA Medal for Exceptional Scientific Achievement, the NASA Apollo Achievement Award, and (twice) the NASA Distinguished Public Service Award and the Joseph Priestley Prize for distinguished contributions to the welfare of mankind. Sagan, after whom Asteroid 2709 is named, was cofounder of the Planetary Society. He was a laureate of the **International Academy of Humanism** from its inception in 1983. Incredibly though, Sagan's nomination for membership to the National Academy of Sciences was rebuffed because of a condescending attitude among members for his works of popularization.

He was a difficult personality, being imperious and insufferably self-assured. But his contributions to the public understanding of science far outweigh his faults.

Further reading: William Poundstone, *Carl Sagan: A Life in the Cosmos*; and Keay Davidson, *Carl Sagan: A Life*.

SAKHAROV, ANDREI (1921–1989). Russian theoretical physicist, dissident, and humanist described by **Paul Kurtz** as the **Galileo** of his day. Born in Moscow, the son of a distinguished scientist, Sakharov graduated in physics from Moscow State University in 1942. He quickly became a senior figure in the Soviet nuclear program, helping to develop the Soviet hydrogen bomb in the 1950s. He was the youngest person ever elected to the Soviet Academy of Sciences.

However, Sakharov also had a conscience of extraordinary depth as well. During the 1960s, he became opposed to the Soviet nuclear effort and took a leading role in campaigning for disarmament and peace. In December 1966 he led a group of dissidents to protest in Pushkin Square in Moscow in favor of constitutional guarantees of freedom for Russian citizens. He was also part of the creation of the Human Rights Committee, which was founded in November 1970.

Despite considerable difficulties in communication, Sakharov signed the ***Humanist Manifesto II*** in 1973 and was elected unanimously to the **International Academy of Humanism** in 1983. In 1975 Sakharov was awarded the Nobel Peace Prize but was refused permission by the Soviet authorities to travel to Oslo to accept the award. His wife, Elena Bonner, made the trip on his behalf.

In 1979 Sakharov spoke publicly against the Soviet invasion of Afghanistan and called for a boycott of the upcoming Moscow Olympics. This was too much for the Soviet authorities, who had Sakharov dragged bodily from his car and arrested. All his state honors were stripped from him and he was confined to his home city of Gorky (now Nizhny Novgorod). Through these years the international humanist community was loud in its support for Sakharov and protested against his confinement, especially once it was apparent his health was declining. Thanks to continuous pressure from humanist organizations, he was finally allowed to travel outside the Soviet Union in 1988. He went to New York, where he received the International Humanist Award, which he had been granted two years previously. Shortly before his death, Sakharov was elected to the Congress of People's Deputies, the Soviet parliament.

SAMKHYA. One of the oldest and most influential of the schools (*darshanas*) of Indian philosophy, being mentioned first in the fourth century BCE, although probably flourishing a century earlier than that. The earliest known Samkhya work is the *Samkhya Karika*, written by Iswara Krishna about 200 CE.

Samkhya has developed an elaborate metaphysics which, broadly speaking, is atheistic, recognizing only two ultimate realities: *purusa* (sentience) and *praktri* (matter). *Praktri* is uncaused and eternal and in a state of constant **evolution**. It is composed of three essential substances: essence, energy, and inertia. Cosmic history began with these elements being in total equilibrium. Evolution began with the arrival of *purusa*, and is the principle for which evolution continues. *Purusa* is itself entirely uncreated and is neither **God** nor some sort of prime mover, although some strands of Samkhya thinking tend to promote *purusa* as a variation of universal spirit. It would be a mistake, however, to equate this notion of a universal spirit with **God** in the Western sense. What divides Samkhya thinkers is whether the notion of

God is capable of any proof, or whether it is a mistaken belief.

For humans, the Samkhya system advocated liberation from the bondage of *praktri* by knowledge. But this liberation isn't like a Western notion of salvation. It is more like philosophical wisdom. In most Samkhya thinking, this philosophical wisdom involves the rejection of **anthropocentric conceit**.

Samkhya thinking has been dogged by a series of inconsistencies, mainly involving the nature of and relationship between *praktri* and *purusa*. The school went into something of a decline around the first century CE and when it was revived more than a thousand years later, it was less naturalistic than it had originally been.

Further reading: Dale Riepe, *The Naturalistic Tradition in Indian Thought*.

SANGER, MARGARET (1879–1966). American social reformer for the rights of women. Born in Corning, New York, to a poor family, Margaret Higgins was deeply influenced by her mother's eighteen pregnancies, and eleven live births, which brought on her early death. While working as a nurse in New York before World War I, she had further opportunities to see the unnecessary toll taken on women's health by unwanted pregnancies. The young Higgins came under the influence of the charismatic atheist Emma Goldman (1869–1940). Sanger's credo, "No Gods—No Masters," reflects the influence of Goldman's anarchism. Higgins was married to William Sanger in 1900, and after a divorce from him, to J. Noah H. Slee in 1922.

In 1912 Sanger gave up nursing to devote herself to the cause of birth control, a term she is credited with coining. To begin with even the suffrage campaigners kept aloof from Sanger, fearing the negative effect of associating their work with the highly controversial idea of birth control. The older, more conservative suffragists feared a repetition of the controversy over **Elizabeth Cady Stanton**'s controversial work, *The Women's Bible*.

Sanger edited a magazine called the *Woman Rebel* and distributed a pamphlet entitled *Family Limitation*. She soon got into legal trouble for her activities, being indicted for using the postal services for the purposes of promoting birth control. These were the same Comstock Laws that caused the suicide of **Ida Craddock**. The charges were dropped in 1916, the same year Sanger opened the first birth-control clinic in the United States, in Brooklyn, New York. For this, Sanger went to prison for a month in 1917. The publicity her imprisonment provoked helped sway public opinion her way and also helped in the move against the fiercely discriminatory Comstock Laws. See the entry on **comstockery**.

Like her contemporaries, **Marie Stopes** and **Ettie Rout**, Sanger argued that the ongoing success of a **marriage** could be enhanced by safe **sex**. What today would seem like common sense, in Sanger's day was portrayed as an outrageous assault on God's order. In 1921 she formed the American Birth Control League, and served as its president until 1928. This organization had several changes of name and amalgamations until it became the Planned Parenthood Federation of America in 1942, which still serves Americans wanting to make rational family-planning decisions. In a sad reply of the suffragists' spurning of Stanton, Sanger went on to downplay and even deny the contribution Goldman made to Sanger's own efforts and to the wider campaign for birth control. She also pursued an interest in **eugenics** that does her little credit. At one point she appointed a notorious racist, eugenicist, and **anti-Semite**, **Lothrop Stoddard**, to the board of Planned Parenthood.

Late in her life, Sanger helped fund the scientific research that led to the development of the pill, which women could take to avoid pregnancy while being sexually active. A significant contributor to the scientific development of the pill was the scientist John Rock (1890–1984), a devout Catholic who nonetheless was convinced that the pill was morally right. In the wake of **Humanae Vitae**, Rock was slowly estranged from the church.

Among Sanger's numerous books are *What Every Mother Should Know* (1917), *My Fight for Birth Control* (1931), and *Margaret Sanger: An Autobiography* (1938). She died in Tucson, Arizona, on September 6, 1966.

SANTAYANA, GEORGE (1863–1952). Philosopher, poet, novelist, and critic. Jorge Augustín Nicolás Ruiz de Santayana was born in Madrid to Spanish parents, and was brought to Boston at the age of nine and educated at the Boston Latin School. He studied at Harvard under **William James** and the idealist philosopher Josiah Royce (1855–1916). Santayana spent his academic career at Harvard where he was professor of philosophy. Then, quite abruptly in 1912, he left Harvard and emigrated to Europe. In 1924 he settled in Rome and remained there for the rest of his life.

Santayana wrote a great deal, but is best remembered for *The Life of Reason* (five volumes, 1905–1906), which is deeply imbued with the ideals of the **naturalism** and **humanism** of ancient Greece. He eschewed **dualism** and advocated what he called the Aristotelian principle; all ideals have a natural basis but all natural processes are capable of ideal fulfillment. By **reason**, Santayana simply meant a higher-order impulse. After World War I, Santayana turned to **critical realism**, contributing to an important collective work called *Essays in Critical Realism* (1920).

Though an atheist and materialist, he could see good in religion, when understood properly. Santayana saw little value in literal belief and **supernaturalism**. But as a way of memorializing and celebrating what matters in life, it is of inestimable value. Santayana remains quite influential in American philosophical circles particularly with respect to American philosophical naturalism, but elsewhere his influence is not great, where he is often seen as long-winded and discursive.

SAPERE AUDE. What should be the rallying cry for the **freethinker**. *Sapere aude* in Latin means "dare to know." The phrase can be traced back to the Roman writer Horace (65–8 BCE), although it was also used by **Denis Diderot** when in 1771 he wrote, "Have the courage to free yourself from the yoke of religion." Perhaps the best-known use of the term *sapere aude* comes from **Immanuel Kant**'s famous essay, *What is Enlightenment?*

> Enlightenment is Man's emergence from self-imposed tutelage, that is to say, from the inability to use the intellect without guidance by another. It is self-imposed if its cause does not lie in a deficiency of the intellect but of the courage and determination to use it autonomously. *Sapere aude*! Have the courage to think! is therefore the motto of the Enlightenment.

Sapere aude sums up the humanist project. Daring to know means being ready to abandon cherished beliefs in the light of new evidence, eschewing static formulas of thought, and never being satisfied with what one knows now. When we reject the **transcendental temptation**, when we think seriously about Nietzsche's idea of the **eternal recurrence**, or when we try to build a **cosmic perspective** into our way of living and thinking, we are daring to know.

SARPI, PAOLO (1552–1623). Historian, scientist, senior church official, and critic of Christianity. Pietro Sarpi was born in Venice, and joined the Servite Order when he was only thirteen at which point his first name was changed to Paolo. At twenty years old, Sarpi became a professor of canon law and **theology**. His propensity for freethinking got him into trouble early on in his career. On more than one occasion complaints were lodged against him to the **Inquisition**. And on October 5, 1607, there was an attempt on his life by his clerical enemies. He had good reason to fear; only seven years earlier, **Giordano Bruno** was burned at the stake for his **freethought**.

In science, he made some useful speculations about the circulation of the blood, but his most important work was as a historian. His major work was *History of the Council of Trent* (1619), which is seen to this day as a landmark work. He wrote about church history in entirely secular terms and was a source of encouragement to those who opposed clerical interference in society and religious **dogmatism**. Sarpi's work has been seen as a precursor to Edward Gibbon's *Decline and Fall of the Roman Empire*. Not surprisingly, he wrote under the pseudonym of Pietro Soave Polano to protect himself from persecution. See the entry on **parallel theology**.

But more important even than that, in 1606 Sarpi became the legal advisor to the Venetian rulers. In that position, he played an important role in shielding Venice from the brutality of the Roman Catholic Counter-Reformation. He was one of the earliest defenders of the rights of secular sovereigns. See the entry on **Thomas Hobbes**. As well as the clear evidence that Sarpi was a secularist and freethinker, recent scholarship also suggests he was an atheist.

Further reading: David Wootton, *Paolo Sarpi: Between Renaissance and Enlightenment*.

SARTRE, JEAN-PAUL (1905–1980). Influential French journalist, novelist, and campaigner. Sartre's father, Jean-Baptiste, died when he was very young, and his mother, who was related to Albert Schweitzer (1875–1965), moved in with her parents. Sartre grew up a precocious youth, reading widely. The presence of religious discord between his Catholic mother and grandmother and Protestant grandfather gave young Jean-Paul his first tastes of religion. By his teens he was an atheist.

In 1928 he met **Simone de Beauvoir**, and the two remained friends and lovers for the rest of his life. As well as working in the field of literature, he also studied **phenomenology** in Germany, which was to exercise a large influence over his later work.

His legacy is very mixed indeed. On the one hand, he is responsible for *Nausea* (1938), one of the most powerful novels of the twentieth century. And he had a distinguished record in the French resistance to Nazism, and popularized the philosophy of **existentialism** for millions of people. Later in his life he was a tireless campaigner for civil **rights** and for the righting of injustices. But on the other hand, he wrote some well-nigh unreadable philosophy, much of which was secondhand from **Martin Heidegger**, and some of his philosophy was downright dangerous.

Sartre's best-known work of philosophy was *Being and Nothingness* (1943) in which his debt to Heidegger is particularly strong. It is here that Sartre articulated most of the concepts associated with his name, such as **bad faith** and **authenticity**. He was wrong to argue, as he did, that we can determine our personality as if writing on a blank slate. See the entry on **free will**. But his emphasis on freedom and responsibility was important and influential.

One of his last major works, *Critique of Dialectical Reason* (1960), was an unsuccessful attempt to affect a synthesis between **Marxism** and existentialism. The *Critique* also provided one of the most **misanthropic** and **nihilist** interpretations of **human nature** and democracy of the twentieth century. He proposed a brutal state of nature in which the motive force in history is scarcity, with each person being in mortal and eternal combat with the Other, a merciless enemy and the next pathetic victim for yet another merciless enemy. Against this he proposed the Marxist salvation myth of a revolutionary struggle in the future, which would bring the world's workers together in a new dispensation, whereby scarcity would be forever banished. But, for all his faults, nobody can accuse Sartre of being uninvolved in the politics and causes of his day.

SATAN. Mythical idea with a roller-coaster career. The core idea of Satan as an ally of **God** being cast out for disobedience is an old one. Greek myths tell of Hephaestus who was ejected from Mt. Olympus by Zeus and who lived in the underworld making armor for gods and heroes. Satan's earliest appearances in the **Hebrew scriptures** portray him as a loyal lieutenant to God. He is often an adversary of humanity, but not of God. Only in later Jewish writings is Satan given a more thoroughgoingly evil nature. Predecessors of the Satan idea can be found in Egyptian, Mesopotamian, Persian, Canaanite, and Greek sources. The Satan figure that came to play an important role in the Christian imagination is an amalgamation of all these influences, brought together in a Christian melting pot.

By the time the New Testament came to be put together, Satan had developed into a full-scale adversary of both God and humanity. Indeed the New Testament is the story of the battle between Satan and Jesus. Christianity makes no sense without Satan, because without the Fall and the consequent **original sin** of humanity, Jesus' message of redemption has little point. Satan also has a role to play in the origin of **anti-Semitism**. Contemporary embarrassment about Satan among churchmen has some unsettling theological consequences which haven't been resolved at all successfully. Modern fundamentalists have sought to evade the question by continuing to insist on the historical reality of Satan.

There are some very good books about Satan. The best nonspecialist one is *The Devil: A Biography* (1995) by Peter Stanford. More specialized, but well worth reading, are *Satan: The Early Christian Tradition* (1981) by Jeffrey Burton Russell, and *The Origin of Satan* (1995) by Elaine Pagels. Between these three scholars, the growth of the idea of the devil is chronicled, as is the important role it has played in Christian thinking, not least in its anti-Semitism.

SATANIC VERSES, THE. A book written by the prominent novelist Salman Rusdie and published in 1988. In this novel, Rushdie referred to a section of the Qur'an (chapter 53: "The Star") which purports to have the Prophet **Muhammad** being advised by Allah that three pre-Islamic jinn (spirits) might help him in his quest to have the people hear his message. These jinn, al-Lat, al-Uzza, and Manat, appeared in the Qur'an as the "daughters of Allah." This passage is known as the satanic verses, although the Qur'an itself does not use the term. Muhammad soon came to the view that these three jinn, important deities to the pagan Meccans, were not in fact, messengers from Allah, but interpolations from Satan.

The incident remains a source of embarrassment to orthodox Muslims, and helps explain the splenetic reaction to Rushdie's book. There is no suggestion in the Qur'an that Muhammad received his advice from Satan or any satanic agent, but a significant section of Muslim opinion soon inferred that Rushdie was making such an implication. And it was this that led to Ayatollah Khomeini's judgment against Rushdie. See the entries on **blasphemy** and **fatwa**.

SATISFICERS AND MAXIMIZERS. Terms coined by American psychologist Barry Schwartz in a book that looked at the paradox of choice. Western consumer society has extolled the importance of choice to such an extent that consumers are increasingly paralyzed by the choices. Even for such trivial purchases as a coffee or shampoo, the consumer is required to exercise a bewildering number of choices. The range of choice has got to the point where it has become largely meaningless. And underlying this seemingly endless range of choices is the reality that very few of these choices are meaningful or even honest. In the face of this dishonesty, people's freedom is actually restricted and impoverished rather than enhanced. The result is anxiety, **stress**, **depression**, and **affluenza**.

Schwartz posits two types of responses to the avalanche of choice. He calls them satis-

ficers and maximizers. *Satificers* are those who purchase something that is good enough for their needs. They've not invested too much time fretting about product research. They bought what approximated their needs and moved on. *Maximizers*, by contrast, are out to get the very best product; they research the product carefully, shop around, and after buying the product are often anxious that they haven't secured the best possible deal. Schwartz recommends the satificers' attitude as being more conducive to one's health and happiness.

Schwartz has tapped into something very important, and about which philosophers have written for centuries. The ability the satisficer has shown, that the maximizer has not, is the ability to set a limit on his or her desires. When the **cynic** philosopher Diogenes was asked by Alexander the Great what he wanted, Diogenes was reported to have wanted nothing more than for Alexander to step aside, so as not to block his light. We need not go as far as Diogenes for his point to be valid.

Further reading: Barry Schwartz, *The Paradox of Choice: Why More is Less.*

SAVAGE, MICHAEL JOSEPH (1872–1940). Pioneering New Zealand prime minister. Savage was born in Tatong, Victoria. His mother died when he was five years old and he was then raised by his older sister, Rose, until her premature death in 1891. Raised as a Catholic, Savage became a militant rationalist. Only at the very end of his life did he return to an idiosyncratic form of messianic Catholicism.

Savage migrated to New Zealand in 1907, settling eventually in Auckland. He never married, and he lived his entire adult life as a boarder, in the home of Alf and Elizabeth French. He quickly became deeply involved in union and party politics. He represented the Socialist Party at the 1911 election, and the Social Democratic Party in 1914, polling respectably both times. Savage was intimately involved in the formation of the Labor

Party in 1916, and in 1920 he entered parliament as Labor MP for Auckland West.

After his election as deputy leader in 1922, Savage guided the Labor Party toward a more moderate stance than the more militant **Henry Edmund (Harry) Holland** was comfortable with. On Holland's death in October 1933 Savage became leader of the party. The combined effects of the Depression and Savage's personality resulted in a landslide victory for the party in 1935, winning fifty-five of the eighty seats in parliament. Once in government, the Labor Party set new standards of social-security legislation, race relations, and financial and political independence. See the entry on the **welfare state**. Savage's last year of life was marred by a losing struggle against cancer and a vicious dispute with a Labor Party renegade (and, incidentally, also a rationalist) John A. Lee (1892–1980). This dispute did little to affect Savage's popularity. A moving memorial to him was built on the foreshore in Auckland, the only New Zealand prime minister to be so honored.

SCAM. An organized scheme to defraud people of their property which involves some level of participation from the victim. Unlike a **hoax**, a scam is never anything but dishonestly motivated, but, unlike a fraud, a scam isn't necessarily illegal. Some major companies, for instance, operate as thinly disguised pyramid schemes, and are quite legal. Pyramid schemes are scams, so are most of the e-mails from Nigeria offering us huge returns on some dubious investment, if only we would. . . . These sorts of scams appeal to the greed of people who should know better. Scams that most resemble frauds are the most likely to be illegal, and will be most likely to involve a victim who is blameless, as when someone earns the trust of a vulnerable person, has them sign their assets over on some plausible account, and then disappears.

SCARE QUOTES. The practice of putting quotation marks around a word to alert the reader to some grave problem with it. Accordingly, we frequently see writers speak of "truth" when they mean **truth**, "knowledge" when they mean **knowledge**.

It is not always invalid to use scare quotes, although it is certainly overused at the moment. It might be appropriate, for instance, if one is talking about the *idea* of truth, rather than truth itself.

SCHILLER, FERDINAND CANNING SCOTT (1864–1937). An important philosopher in his day, though now forgotten, who popularized his eccentric idea of **humanism** in Great Britain and the United States. Schiller was born in Denmark to a German family which had made its money in India. He was educated at Rugby and Balliol colleges, Oxford. In 1897, after a short but significant spell at Cornell University in the United States, he returned to Corpus Christi College, Oxford, where he taught until 1926. While in the United States, Schiller had been exposed to the emerging philosophy of **pragmatism**, especially as articulated by **William James**. He spent his career arguing for pragmatism, but which he chose to call humanism. From 1926 onward, Schiller spent part of each year lecturing at the University of Southern California. In 1935 he moved there permanently. He died on August 9, 1937.

While acknowledging James's importance, Schiller took pragmatism in more of a **relativist** direction than James had advocated. Schiller resolutely opposed any form of **foundationalism** or claims of **objectivity**. All truths are human creations, he argued. In the face of stern criticism, chiefly at the hands of **Bertrand Russell**, Schiller slightly modified his views later in life. Schiller was famous for his sense of humor. One of his later essays was titled, "Must Philosophy Be Dull?"

In speaking of humanism, Schiller wanted to anthropomorphize pragmatism. He often returned to the saying attributed to the **Pre-Socratic** philosopher **Protagoras** that man is the measure of all things. Where **naturalism** spoke of humanity's accommodation with nature, humanism spoke of its control of nature. It is now apparent that Schiller's understanding of humanism suffers from an element of **anthropocentric conceit**, although, in his defense, he did criticize this aspect of human nature, which he called **yahoo-manity**. Schiller's understanding of humanism did not survive him. He wrote a great deal, though his main works were *The Riddle of the Sphinx* (1891), *Humanism: Philosophical Essays* (1903), and *Studies in Humanism* (1907).

SCHOPENHAUER, ARTHUR (1788–1860). Very influential German philosopher. Born in Danzig (now Gdansk in Poland), the Schopenhauer family moved to Hamburg when Arthur was still a boy. His father was a banker and his mother a novelist. Under his father's pressure, Schopenhauer trained originally for business, but he had more of his mother's preferences. After the death of his father in 1805, he was able to embark on an academic education, graduating from the University of Jena in 1813.

Schopenhauer's most important work was *The World as Will and Idea* (1819). While Schopenhauer had no doubt of the book's brilliance, it took a generation before many other people shared his opinion. He was ignored and unread until after the failure of the 1848 revolutions and the return of a fashionable **Romantic** pessimism. Germany was in the grip of G. W. F. Hegel (1770–1831) and **Immanuel Kant**, against whom Schopenhauer raged.

Schopenhauer was deeply influenced by Indian philosophy, the first major philosopher to be so influenced. He emphasized the active role of the will, and stressed that the only **authentic** path of liberation which was free from illusion was art, particularly music. Art and music alone can provide us with a release from the material world of illusion. Schopenhauer was also a confirmed atheist, although he did not develop this part of his philosophy in any great degree. He refrained from criticizing religion because, though he thought

them wrong, he appreciated their central role of compassion.

Schopenhauer has had a mixed reputation among professional philosophers: among those from the Anglo-American schools, which value critical analysis, his reputation is not high. But among Continental philosophers, and among many literary thinkers and nonspecialists, he has been very important indeed. His reputation was not helped by his unpleasant personality; he was self-centered and misanthropic beyond the pale of what could be deemed eccentricity.

SCHWERNER, MICHAEL (1939–1964). Atheist martyr for the civil-rights movement. Schwerner was a New York–raised secular Jew; he even forwent his bar mitzvah. Educated at the Columbia University School of Social Work, he was set on a life of social activism for the underprivileged. In January 1964 he and his young wife moved to Mississippi to work for the government-sponsored organization Congress of Racial Equality (CORE). He had been recruited into CORE by its founder **James Farmer**, one of the "Big Four" civil-rights leaders and a secular humanist. Schwerner was posted to the city of Meridian, were he managed a community center and took part in voting-registration campaigns and other civil-rights work.

Schwerner came to the attention of the local Ku Klux Klan leader, who determined that he should die. While returning home after visiting some black Americans recovering from a beating and whose church had been burned, Schwerner, along with Andrew Goodman and James Chaney were ambushed and murdered. They died on June 21, 1964, one day after the US Senate passed the Civil Rights Act which outlawed racial discrimination in the public sector. The killers originally only planned to murder Schwerner, but when faced with all three activists in the car, two atheist Jews and a black man, the logic of their hate sealed the fate of them all.

The story of their deaths (though not the atheism of Schwerner and Goodman) are the inspiration for the film *Mississippi Burning* (1988). The progressive campus organization COOL (Campus Outreach Opportunity League) sponsors an annual Michael Schwerner activist award in his memory.

SCIENCE. The defining feature of our age. The American scientist **E. O. Wilson** defined science as "the organised, systematic enterprise that gathers **knowledge** about the world and condenses the knowledge about the world into testable laws and principles." What makes scientific ideas especially useful is that they are produced without reference to our social context. Science is neither a philosophy nor a belief system, but is a combination of operations. The word science derives from the Latin noun *scientia*, which in turn derives from the verb *scire*, or "to know." Unlike **religion**, there are no forbidden zones in science; all things and all people are open to question, and it is this built-in error-detection machinery that makes science so valuable. **Philosophy**, at its best, works in the same way.

The British embryologist Lewis Wolpert has outlined these five criteria for a subject to qualify as a science:

- the phenomena it deals with should be capable of confirmation by independent observers;
- ideas should be self-consistent;
- explanations should be able to be linked to other branches of science;
- a small number of laws should be able to explain a wide variety of phenomena; and
- ideally, it should be quantitative and able to express its theories mathematically.

Victor Stenger, an American physicist, picked May 28, 585 BCE, as the day science was born because that was the day an eclipse occurred in Ionia, precisely when the **Pre-Socratic** philosopher **Thales** had predicted. In this incident, observation of the universe had resulted in a prediction about how things operate, which was subsequently vindicated, leading to a clearer general understanding of the universe. This is the stuff of science.

Science does involve **progress** for the simple reason that more is known now about the workings of the world than was known at any time previously. See the entry on **pseudoscience**.

Further reading: E. O. Wilson, *Consilience: The Unity of Knowledge*; and Lewis Wolpert, *The Unnatural Nature of Science*.

SCIENCE, BASIC PRESUPPOSITIONS OF. Science is founded on some basic presuppositions. These consist of foundational principles which underpin whole areas of science and the idea of scientific inquiry. The basic presuppositions of science include:

- space-time is real;
- matter is real, and it exists spatially and temporally;
- the things that constitute the natural world form organized and interdependent systems;
- on the macroscopic level, all events have causes;
- nature can be explained nonteleologically; and
- nature is intelligible in naturalistic, scientific terms.

Some opponents of science have argued that these basic presuppositions are no different from religious articles of **faith**, or are simply culturally derived arbitrary assertions. Both of these claims are false. These are basic presuppositions of science because they are both the fruit of centuries of scientific work, and are so fundamental to human understanding that they have an evolutionary basis. Some of these basic presuppositions are not simply true, they are essential to our survival, as individuals and as a species.

Further reading: Tad S. Clements, *Science versus Religion*.

SCIENCE, BOOKS ABOUT. There are many excellent books on various branches of science, but relatively few on science as such. These are among the best introductions to science written for the nonspecialist.

The simplest reference work I know is, *1001 Things Everyone Should Know About Science* (1993) by James Trefil. Still designed for the nonspecialist is *A Brief History of Science* (1998) edited by John Gribbin, with seven chapters on the various sciences, complete with excellent illustrations. General introductions to science include *The Unnatural Nature of Science* (1992) by Lewis Wolpert; *The Trouble with Science* (1995) by Robin Dunbar; and (the most complicated of the three) *The Ascent of Science* (1998) by Brian Silver. An excellent introduction to technology, which is frequently confused with science, is *The Power of the Machine* (1994) by R. A. Buchanan.

Two good books (though less suitable for nonspecialists) on the general methods of science are *Consilience: The Unity of Knowledge* (1998) by **E. O. Wilson** and *Defending Science—Within Reason* (2003) by Susan Haack.

SCIENCE, ELIMINATIVE CRITERIA OF. Science has built-in procedures by which legitimate scientific claims or theories may be distinguished from **pseudoscientific** ones. They are called eliminative criteria, and they are the mirror image of the **plausibility criteria**, which help determine which claims or theories justify further study. Eliminative criteria by which claims may be deemed unscientific:

- the claim must be **falsifiable**, at least in principle;
- there must be logical connections between the system proposed and with publicly accessible facts;
- the language used in formulating the claim must not be hopelessly ambiguous; and
- the principle of parsimony (**Ockham's Razor**) should be observed.

A claim or theory that fails all four of these eliminative criteria can safely be dismissed as **pseudoscience**.

Further reading: Tad S. Clements, *Science versus Religion*.

SCIENCE, METHODS OF. There are three major types of scientific work:

- *sorting*, classifying and measuring accurately—incongruities that arise here can lead on to
- *experimental research*, where little-understood relationships are explored, and which will provoke
- *theoretical work*, where law-making can be speculated from the experimental data.

Further reading: Hyman Levy, *The Universe of Science*.

SCIENCE, PLAUSIBILITY CRITERIA OF. Just as science has **eliminative criteria** by which **pseudoscientific** claims can be identified and dismissed, so too does it have criteria by which claims or theories may be seen as warranting further consideration. Plausibility criteria by which claims may be deemed scientific include:

- *relevance*, it must be logically possible to infer the fact to be explained from the explanation being offered;
- *testability*, it must be possible to predict observational data that tend to confirm or disconfirm the explanation;
- *compatibility*, it must be compatible in some areas with previous, well-established and relevant hypotheses;
- *predictive or explanatory power*, it must have some predictive or explanatory ability; and
- *simplicity*, the claim or theory must conform to the principle of parsimony, otherwise known as **Ockham's Razor**.

Further reading: Tad S. Clements, *Science versus Religion*.

SCIENCE, PRESUMPTION OF. An idea, though not outlined under this title, by several current philosophers of science. It argues that science deserves a privileged place in the theory of knowledge for the simple reason that science has a record of providing accurate and reliable **knowledge** that no other discipline can hope to match. If, therefore, any other system of belief or method of thought arrives at a conclusion at variance with science, the **burden of proof** lies with the other discipline to show why, in this case, it is right and science is wrong.

Other philosophers of science like Susan Haack, have not wanted to go quite this far, claiming that science is not so much *privileged* as *distinguished*, by virtue of its unparalleled record of success. See the entry on the **Stratonician Presumption**.

Further reading: Norman Levitt, *Prometheus Bedeviled: Science and the Contradictions of Contemporary Culture;* and Susan Haack, *Defending Science—Within Reason.*

SCIENCE, SUSPICION OF. The English historian Eric Hobsbawm has noted that suspicion of science is fueled by four feelings:

- that science is incomprehensible;
- that its practical and moral consequences are uncertain and/or disastrous;
- that it underlines the helplessness of the individual; and
- that it is inherently dangerous in its interference with the natural order.

These fears are not all without some foundation; the first two fears are shared by scientists and laypeople. The second two fears, however, are mainly held by laypeople. It is interesting that the third of them refers to the challenge science makes to our **anthropocentric conceit**. See the entry on **aristoscience**.

Further reading: Eric Hobsbawm, *Age of Extremes: The Short Twentieth Century 1914–1991.*

SCIENCE, THE GOAL OF. The ultimate goal of science, according to Susan Haack is

"substantial, significant, explanatory truth." Haack elaborated by saying that scientists seek true answers to questions that concern them and that the questions which concern them are substantial and significant. **Paul Kurtz** also has a twofold goal for science:

- *to develop* theories that serve us as powerful instruments that we can use in understanding nature and applying this knowledge to technological uses, but also
- *to approximate* as far as we can what nature is really like, in some way independent of the stuff of human experience and conceptualization.

Further reading: Susan Haack, *Defending Science—Within Reason*; and Paul Kurtz, *The New Skepticism: Inquiry and Reliable Knowledge*

SCIENTIFIC ATTITUDE. There is no single scientific attitude, in the same way that there is no single **religious attitude**. However, a general taxonomy can be attempted. General characteristics of the scientific attitude include:

- curiosity;
- the desire for defensible, reliable knowledge;
- the tendency to think of the subject of study as related to other elements of nature in lawful ways;
- the recognition that anyone may be mistaken;
- tendency to **skepticism**;
- a predilection to creating conditions whereby experiments can be undertaken;
- a preference for logical simplicity;
- an aversion for vague or confused concepts;
- preference for the ideal of moral neutrality when seeking knowledge; and
- the tendency to avoid **anthropomorphism**.

This list comes from Tad Clements, but others, who would agree with this list, would also say that this attitude is not limited to scientists. Susan Haack has argued that this attitude is critical to all **free inquiry**.

Further reading: Tad S. Clements, *Science versus Religion*; and Susan Haack, *Defending Science—Within Reason*.

SCIENTIFIC METHOD. A phrase that has become unfashionable but which remains important nevertheless. The phrase can be traced back to 1581, in the writings of Francisco Sanchez (1552–1623), a scholar at Toulouse University and a distant relative of **Montaigne**. Sanchez invoked the ancient **Pyrrhonists** to argue against claiming **certainty** in our **knowledge**. Certainty, Sanchez said, belonged only to **God**. For humans, we can hope for nothing more than a provisional account of knowledge, but one that can slowly gather greater authority.

The modern methods of achieving scientific understanding were ushered in by **Galileo** and systematized by **Isaac Newton**, who can truly be said to be the father of modern science. Today, the understanding of the scientific method is entirely naturalistic. The scientific method is not an intrinsically superior method floating above all other methods. It was put best by **Bertrand Russell** when he described it as the techniques and rules we use to make degrees of belief correspond to their degrees of credibility.

Neither is the scientific method a property exclusive to the sciences. Any serious scholar will exercise the intellectual qualities known as the scientific method. See the entry on the **tools of inquiry**.

Further reading: Bertrand Russell, *Human Knowledge: Its Scope and Limits*; and Anthony Gottlieb, *The Dream of Reason*.

SCIENTISM. The process of showing too much confidence in the powers of science, even of placing **faith** in science as an agency of salvation. This is an oft-repeated accusation against rationalists and humanists, who are held to be replacing **God** with science. While this accusation is frequently repeated, very rarely are any concrete examples given.

SCIENTIST. A word coined only in 1834. If we need any more graphic indication of how the world has changed since the **Enlightenment**, this is it. The word is generally credited to the English polymath William Whewell (1794–1866).

For many centuries there was no need for a separate word like "scientist." Science began as a branch of **philosophy**, being called natural philosophy. There was no distinction between science and philosophy, but the increasing specialization in the sciences, which can be traced back to the Hellenistic Age (300 BCE–100 CE, approx.), began to test those links. The developments in **mathematics** and science in the seventeenth and eighteenth centuries intensified those divisions, so that by the nineteenth century there was a need for a word to describe the people engaging in science, because "philosopher" would no longer do.

SCRIPTURE. A distinctly religious form of writing. For a body of writing to be called a scripture the claim needs to be made that it is directly inspired by **God** or gods, often from a divine revelation. Clear examples of this would be the Qur'an, the Bible, or the Book of Mormon.

Because they can be as vague or elusive as any other body of writing, scriptures tend to develop extensive commentaries to help explain them. Prime examples of this are the Hadith among Muslims and the Talmud among Jews. Elsewhere, specialized groups of theologians or priests emerge who claim authority to interpret scripture for everyone else.

Scriptures are most clearly in evidence among the **monotheist** religions. Among the **Asian traditions**, it is more problematic to speak of scriptures. Among Hindus, the **Veda** have great authority, as do Confucian writings among the Chinese, but it is not correct to describe them as having the authority of scripture. Hindus and followers of Confucius can reject or question aspects of their writings without aspersions being cast on their beliefs or **character**, as can happen in the Judeo-Christian religions.

Freethinkers, whether atheists, humanists, or skeptics, have no scripture. They have a large body of writing from which to draw, but none of it is accepted without question. Furthermore, freethinkers can see value in writings from all traditions, not simply from their own.

SCYLLA AND CHARYBDIS. A story from ancient Greece which has been referred to ever since by writers wanting to draw attention to two competing and contrasting dangers. The story of Scylla and Charybdis is told by **Homer** in the *Odyssey*, the undisputed classic of Western civilization. Scylla is "a fiend not born for death"—a creature with a dreadful bark, twelve legs, and six heads, each with triple rows of teeth, that pick up sailors from passing boats to eat them. Against Scylla there was no defense. Facing Scylla was Charybdis, who lived under a rock and would suck whole boats into the water and vomit them up against the jagged rocks. The combined terrors of Scylla and Charybdis were the talk of the seafaring community in the time of Odysseus. Both Herakles and Odysseus came up against Scylla and Charybdis during their careers.

The most recent reworking of the Scylla and Charybdis tale comes from the German humanist **Jürgen Habermas**. For contemporary freethinkers, Habermas wrote, the challenge is to chart the dangerous waters between, on the one hand, the Scylla of absolutism and **fundamentalism** and the Charybdis of **relativism** and **nihilism**, on the other. Fundamentalism has the dangers of closed and exclusionary thinking—what could be called thinking by numbers. Nihilism, by contrast, is intellectually sloppy and self-serving. So, contemporary humanists need to have sufficient confidence in their method of learning and the conclusions of that learning to resist relativism and nihilism

but without succumbing to the temptations of absolutist thinking. This is a difficult goal to achieve. The Canadian philosopher Kai Nielsen has written that it is "a cultural achievement to be able to abandon the quest for **certainty**, to live comfortably with **fallibilism** and, all the same, not to be at all caught up by skepticism, nihilism, or **cynicism**." See the entry on **Doctrine of the Mean (Aristotle)**.

Further reading: Jürgen Habermas, *The Philosophical Discourse on Modernity*; and Kai Nielsen, *Naturalism and Religion*.

SEA OF FAITH. A movement created by Don Cupitt (1934–), a radical English theologian. Cupitt had already become a controversial figure in the Anglican Church with his book *Taking Leave of God* (1980), which earned him a personal reprimand from the Archbishop of Canterbury. The Sea of Faith movement began in 1984 after a six-part television series and a book, both of that name, written by Cupitt, created a great deal of interest. The phrase "Sea of Faith" was taken from Matthew Arnold's poem *Dover Beach*, which lamented the decline of orthodox Christianity. Cupitt is frankly atheistic and humanistic, but the Sea of Faith movement has charted a slightly more eclectic course. Cupitt's goal is to help create a "post-dogmatic and nonsupernatural religion of the future." He is a fellow of the **Jesus Seminar** and the **Committee for the Scientific Examination of Religion**. The Sea of Faith's Web site includes elements of **postmodernism**, **religion**, nonrealist philosophy, and **humanism**. The English organization puts out a journal called *A Reasonable Faith*, edited by David Boulton.

The Sea of Faith has spread to a few other countries, in particular New Zealand, where it is under the influence of a similarly radical theologian, Lloyd Geering (1918–), another Jesus Seminar fellow. The Sea of Faith has been a voice for **religious humanism** in that country. Most Sea of Faith groups agree that, while the actual truth-claims of religions are invalid, there nonetheless remains a valuable experiential core to religion that is useful.

SEARCH FOR EXTRATERRESTRIAL INTELLIGENCE (SETI). A program originally undertaken by a wing of NASA, but cuts in funding encouraged the establishment of the privately financed SETI Institute in 1984. Since then the SETI Institute, which employs 120 people, has established a reputation for conducting impeccable science and has eroded the distrust of the program which had built up in NASA. The search for extraterrestrial intelligence is only one part of the SETI Institute's activities, much of which is concerned with astrobiology.

SETI's main technique has traditionally been to look for alien radio signals. Early efforts in this field ran into problems of not being able to distinguish the source of the signals. An announcement in the Soviet Union in the early 1960s of intense radio signals turned out to be emissions from a quasar.

SEARLE, JOHN (1932–). One of the foremost contemporary philosophers. John Searle was born in Denver, Colorado, and studied at the University of Wisconsin from 1949 to 1952 before going to Oxford University as a Rhodes Scholar. He took his D.Phil there and taught at Christ College, Oxford, until 1959, when he moved to the University of California at Berkeley, where he spent the rest of his academic career. His first work, *Speech Acts* (1969), reflected the influence of the linguistic philosopher J. L. Austin (1911–1960).

More recent works have been on questions of **artificial intelligence**, **consciousness**, rationality, and what used to be called our knowledge of the external world. In *The Construction of Social Reality* (1995), Searle talks about our ability to create an objective reality. He does this by distinguishing between different levels of **facts**. Other important books by Searle include *The Rediscovery of the Mind* (1992) and *Rationality in Action* (2001).

Searle is an atheist and humanist. As a young man, he was at dinner when **Bertrand Russell**, then eighty-five, made his famous comment regarding what he would say to **God** in the event of coming before him after his earthly demise: "You didn't give us enough **evidence**."

Searle has also been one of the most intelligent critics of the more pretentious forms of **postmodernism**, in particular during his several dogfights with the French deconstructionist Jacques Derrida (1930–2004). See the entries on **external realism** and **facts**.

SECTARIANISM. An attitude of mind most apparent among adherents of a sect. The British sociologist Bryan Wilson (1926–2004) has discerned eight tendencies that characterize a sect:

- exclusivity, not permitting dual membership with other groups;
- claims to hold a monopoly on the truth, again to the exclusion of others;
- a preference for being lay organizations, without complex hierarchies, which leads in turn to;
- a rejection of religious labor and
- a strong preference for voluntarism;
- an expectation of sustained standards among members and a willingness to punish or exclude those who contravene those standards;
- demanding the total allegiance of members; and
- being essentially a protest organization, usually against moral conditions of the day.

Wilson insists that this is an ideal type. Many groups do not include all eight of these tendencies, or do so in variable quantities, and yet can still be described as sects.

Further reading: Bryan Wilson, *Religion in Sociological Perspective*.

SECULAR HUMANISM. Defined by **Tom Flynn** as "a comprehensive nonreligious **lifestance** that incorporates a naturalistic philosophy, a cosmic outlook rooted in **science**, and a consequentialist ethical system." This is a sound enough definition but has the problem of itself needing clarification. See the entry on **normative ethics** for consequentialism. Secular humanism sits in-between the value neutrality of **atheism**, which is nothing more than the belief that the evidence for **God** or gods is unconvincing, and **religious humanism**, which seeks to preserve a religious attitude while rejecting religious beliefs. As a generalization, secular humanists are more positive toward science as a discipline. The division between secular and religious humanism also parallels in some ways the divide between **abolitionists and substitutionists**.

The need to add "secular" to humanism reflects the conditions in the United States, where the threat of **fundamentalism** has been greatest. In the United States, there has been a concerted effort to label **humanism as a religion**, in an effort to expunge all traces of humanism from the public education curriculum. This has resulted in a greater need to stress the secular nature of humanism than has been the case elsewhere. The addition of "secular" probably dates back to the important case *Torcaso v. Watkins* (1961), which included a marginal note referring to the relationship between humanism and **religion**.

Humanists have also been at greater pains to distance themselves from communism which has meant they dropped earlier labels like "scientific humanism" or "**socialist humanism**," both of which had a certain vogue. But the main point of contention has been the relationship of humanism with religion. Paul Beattie (1937–1989), a religious humanist, discerned three major differences between religious and secular humanists:

- the meaning of the word "religion";
- the value of the church as an institution; and
- the attitudes toward religious traditions.

Despite the differences in approach, Beattie concluded, correctly, that secular and religious humanists have a great deal more in common than the attitudes which divide them. See the entry on **secular humanism, ten myths about**.

Further reading: Tom Flynn, *Secular Humanism Defined*; and Paul Beattie, "Humanism: Secular or Religious," *Free Inquiry* 1, no. 1 (Winter 1980–81): 11–13.

SECULAR HUMANISM, TEN MYTHS ABOUT. Few **life stances** are caricatured and slandered as regularly as **secular humanism**. This has been a particularly severe problem in the United States. With this in mind, the **Council for Secular Humanism** thought it worthwhile to pen this response. The ten myths about secular humanism are:

(1) Secular humanists have no morals.
(2) Secular humanists derive their morals from Christianity.
(3) The Supreme Court has ruled that secular **humanism is a religion**.
(4) Secular humanism worships mankind.
(5) Secular humanists believe all nature should be subjugated to human desires.
(6) Secular humanism is the same as communism.
(7) Secular humanists are unpatriotic.
(8) Secular humanists want to outlaw religion.
(9) Secular humanism is the official religion of the public education system.
(10) Secular humanists don't exist, but are simply a bogeyman invented by the Religious Right.

Each of these myths has been dealt with in entries in this dictionary. It is remarkable how frequently these quite incompatible myths are repeated by the same person. See the entry on **six suggestions for religious believers**.

Further reading: Matt Cherry and Molleen Matsumura, "Ten Myths about Secular Humanism," *Free Inquiry* 18, no. 1 (Winter 1997–98): 25–28.

SECULAR HUMANIST DECLARATION. Conceived and drafted by **Paul Kurtz**, the *Secular Humanist Declaration* originally appeared in the inaugural issue of *Free Inquiry* magazine in Winter 1980 and later that year as a pamphlet. The declaration appeared at a time when **secular humanism** was becoming the target of hysterical attack by fundamentalist Christians in the United States. Secular humanism was blamed for all the nation's ills and, in the face of this torrent of abuse, Kurtz and fifty-eight leading academics and writers put their name to the declaration both to redress the balance and to make clear to the public what secular humanism was actually about. The declaration reached the front page of the October 15, 1980, issue of *New York Times*.

The declaration affirmed that secular humanism was concerned with the following ideals:

- *free inquiry*, the first principle of a democratic society;
- *separation of church and state*, as the best guarantee of an open society;
- *the ideal of freedom*, as a cornerstone of an open society;
- *ethics based on critical intelligence*, rather than **command moralities**;
- *moral education*, as opposed to dogmatic indoctrination;
- *religious skepticism*, of supernatural claims and the supposed essential link to morality;
- *reason*, as opposed to **irrationalism** as the dominant form of public discourse; and
- *science and technology*, as agents of positive change.

Among the signatories included Francis Crick (1916–2004), **Dora Russell**, Albert Ellis (1913–), B. F. Skinner (1904–1984), **Isaac Asimov**, **A. J. Ayer**, and Zhores Medvedev (1925–). Thirty-six of the signatories came from the United States, with others coming from Britain, Canada, France, India,

Norway, Israel, and Yugoslavia. "In a world engulfed by obscurantism and irrationalism," the declaration concluded, "it is vital that the ideals of the secular city not be lost."

Further reading: Paul Kurtz, *The Secular Humanist Declaration*.

SECULAR ORGANIZATIONS FOR SOBRIETY. An organization devoted to helping people overcome substance abuse without resorting to the religious dicta preferred by competing groups. Conventional groups build their programs for recovery on recognizing a higher power, but for those who have no such belief, the program is useless, and can be detrimental to their recovery. SOS contends that its program emphasizes the need to take control of one's life, rather than substituting one addiction (alcohol) for another (religion). It advances a method of alcohol and drug abstention which focuses on being honest with oneself and taking back control of one's life.

SOS began from an article in the Summer 1985 issue of *Free Inquiry*, written by James Christopher, a recovered alcoholic and son of an alcoholic. Interest in the article was so high that Christopher went on to found SOS. Since then, SOS has been a major social program affiliated with the **Center for Inquiry**. In November 1987 the California state courts recognized SOS as an alternative to Alcoholics Anonymous as a place people being required to undertake rehabilitation could be sent. Several states have now followed this example. SOS is now an internationally respected organization with a distinguished advisory board.

Christopher has written a series of books which outline his views; *How to Stay Sober* (1988), *Unhooked: Staying Sober and Drug-Free* (1989), and *SOS Sobriety: The Proven Alternative to 12-Step Programs* (1992).

Further reading: www.sossobriety.org.

SECULARISM. One of the most essential preconditions for democracy. People understood the value of secularism long before there was a word for it. The term was coined by the English reformer and journalist **George Jacob Holyoake** in 1841 and has taken on a worldwide significance. Holyoake brought together two traditions of **freethought** into secularism: the radical, republican, activist, and anticlerical tradition of **Thomas Paine**, and the ethical, utopian, and rationalistic tradition of **Robert Owen**. In *The Origin and Nature of Secularism* (1896) Holyoake defined secularism as a "code of duty pertaining to this life for those who find **theology** indefinite or inadequate, unreliable or unbelievable." The three essential principles of secularism were held to be:

- the improvement of life and human effort;
- that **science** can have a material part to play in that improvement; and
- that it is good to do good.

Holyoake was adamant that secularism was not antireligious. Holyoake wanted secularism to avoid the excesses of both Christianity and atheism. See the entry on **secularist rules for human conduct**. Secularism in the sense of a moral **life stance** without religion is now better understood as **humanism**.

The core understanding of secularism today involves the idea of the neutrality and noninvolvement of the government with regard to religion. Thus, the secular state is neither a religious nor an atheistic state, but a state where government, especially in areas of education and health and public policy, is independent of religion. In this understanding, Albania during its years of state-sponsored atheism was not a secular state.

Few people have expressed the value of secularism better than Sheikh Mujibur Rahman (1920–1975), the founder of the state of Bangladesh. In a speech to the Bangladeshi parliament in 1972, Sheikh Mujib said:

Secularism does not mean absence of religion. The seventy five million people of Bengal will have the right to religion. We do not want to ban religion by law. We have no intention of that kind. Secularism does not mean absence of religion. Muslims will observe their religion and no body in this state has the power to prevent that. Hindus will observe their religion and nobody has power to prevent that. Buddhists and Christians will observe their respective religions and nobody will be allowed to use religion as a political weapon.

In August 1975 Sheikh Mujib and his entire family were assassinated and Bangladesh has since become an Islamic Republic.

A state run on secular principles is best suited to ensuring the peace among all its citizens, who may practice one of a number of faiths, or none. The secular state is not a perfect idyll where all find contentment, but then neither is any other sort of state. Secularists have a responsibility to resist those irresponsible claims for a promised perfection of society. See the entry on **Adamics**. But the secular society is the best type of society to ensure the basic standards of **pluralism** and **toleration** are met.

SECULARIST RULES FOR HUMAN CONDUCT. As defined by **George Jacob Holyoake**, the first spokesperson for **secularism**. Holyoake thought of secularism as a moral movement, unconcerned with abstruse theological battles about **God**. In Holyoake's mind the secularist rules for human conduct are:

- truth in speech;
- honesty in transactions;
- industry in business; and
- equity in reward.

His secularist rules were given in the same vein as the various outlines of **humanist values** which more recent thinkers have outlined. It was not claimed that these virtues were the sole preserve of secularists, but that they are entirely consistent with secularism. See the entry on **monopoly on the truth**.

Further reading: George Jacob Holyoake, *The Origin and Nature of Secularism*.

SECULARIZATION. The process relating to the separation of religious and worldly concerns. This usually, though not inevitably, involves the diminution of the role of religion in society. Neither does secularization necessarily imply a decline in interest in religion.

Bryan Wilson (1926–2004), a leading theorist of secularization, notes that it is not only a change occurring *in* society, but it is also a change *of* society at the level of its basic organization. Among the educated classes, a significant degree of religious unbelief had been apparent since the late seventeenth century, but it took a long time before this gradual erosion in religious belief occurring in society grew into a change of society as a whole. This was due largely to a reticence among the wealthy to express their views in public, for fear of reprisals from the church and of setting a poor example to the downtrodden. Other features of secularization include:

- the decline of organized religion to enforce moral sanctions;
- the ability of people not to attend church without suffering physical or social persecution as a result;
- the decline of religious controversy as a significant example of children's intellectual development; and
- the commodification of religion as a measurement of its decline.

Further reading: Bryan Wilson, *Religion in Sociological Perspective*; and R. Laurence Moore, *Selling God: American Religion and the Marketplace of Culture*.

SEEDS OF MORAL SKEPTICISM IN CHRISTIAN ETHICS. The American philosopher **Michael Martin** has shown that Christian ethics, thought by many to be a sure foundation for ethical **certainty**, in fact has the potential to collapse into any of the following four different kinds of moral skepticism:

- *moral nihilism*, stemming from the moral anarchy which would follow from the **divine-command theory** if **God** doesn't exist;
- *moral epistemological skepticism*, from the difficulty in choosing a source of God's commands and interpreting them accurately;
- *amoral skepticism*, arising from doubts about the morality of religious actions, such as the many atrocities and immoralities in the Old Testament; and
- *pragmatic moral skepticism*, arising from a perceived inability to behave at the morally perfect standards prescribed by one's religion.

In order to avoid any of these pitfalls built into Christian ethics, Christians have to employ just the same doses of rationality, moral **relativism**, and ethical choice they condemn in humanists. They have to explain away the atrocities and immoralities of the Bible, and justify their inability to live up to the better injunctions of the Bible, not to mention their unwillingness to live according to the worst ethical codes (owning slaves, exploiting children, and so on). See also the entry on **atheism, moral argument for**.

Further reading: Michael Martin, *Atheism, Meaning, and Morality*.

SELFISH GENE, THE. An idea introduced by **Richard Dawkins** in a very influential book by that name which was published in 1976. The book was a bestseller and has been translated into thirteen languages. The idea of the selfish gene, and Dawkins as the creator of the idea, has come under sustained, and often misinformed, criticism ever since. What made *The Selfish Gene* an important book is that it took a gene's eye view of things. Genes have only one object, and that is to replicate themselves. This process favors genes which help work toward the reproductive success of its host entity.

The catchy title of this book captured attention no less than the superb prose in which it was written. Many critics reacted mistakenly to what they thought was a celebration of selfishness as a psychological state, Dawkins's denial of this notwithstanding. DNA has no feelings, so "selfish" means operating in such a way as to make one's own replication as likely as possible. In this way being healthy, having a full stomach, and access to sex is more fun than illness, starvation, or celibacy. *The Selfish Gene* went into a revised and expanded edition in 1989.

SELFPLEX. Like a **memeplex**, a large collection of **memes** brought together for common benefit. Some memes may gain an advantage by becoming closely associated with a person's concept of themselves. Once a meme is entrenched in this way, the person is more likely to propagate this meme in such a way as to induce more people to copy it. In contemporary society, with more and more memes bombarding us, it is to the advantage of memes to secure a high rate of acceptance and retention by people who will take the meme on and treat it like a cherished belief.

Further reading: Susan Blackmore, *The Meme Machine*.

SEMANTIC HOLISM. A doctrine in the philosophy of language championed by Hilary Putnam (1926–), although the term was coined by Michael Dummett (1925–), an opponent of semantic holism. The principal insight of semantic holism is that interpreting a word is a holistic manner. This means that the broader your search for the meaning of a word, the better your understanding of the word is likely to be.

The philosophy of language has had every kind of ideologue, from those who insist that the essential meaning of a word is locked in for all time, to those who deny any word has any meaning outside of what we choose to give it. Semantic holism appreciates that the meaning of a word is partly the result of our use of it and partly the result of the context in which the word is used outside ourselves. The wider and more open our search for the contexts of a word is, the surer our own use of the word will be.

Semantic holism is an outlook which emphasizes **judgment**, or **critical receptiveness**. It is closely associated with **reliabilism**. We can't rely on a stable body of facts which we simply look up. Each context for a word's meaning will be slightly different, and so will require of us a different exercise of judgment.

By looking closely at how the word is used externally from us, the chief objection to semantic holism can be avoided. Critics have said that with semantic holism, coming to an agreement about the meaning of a word is next to impossible, as each person exercises their own judgment. This is a valid objection, and it is avoided by watching closely what happens to the meaning of the word around us. The sound application of critical receptiveness and reliabilism will avoid that danger.

Further reading: Hilary Putnam, *The Threefold Cord: Mind, Body and World*.

SENECA (4 BCE/1 CE–65 CE). Roman thinker and jurist. Lucius Annaeus Seneca was born in Cordoba into a family of comfortable, but by no means plush, circumstances. One of Seneca's brothers was **Gallio**, who played a cameo role in the New Testament. Seneca never enjoyed robust health, but became an accomplished scholar, specializing in the natural sciences. For a while he dallied with Pythagorean mysticism and eastern cults, but settled on a mature acceptance of the **Stoic** philosophy.

He had a tumultuous political career. He trained in law and became a leading speaker in the Senate, attracting the hostility of the new emperor Caligula in the process. Early in the reign of Claudius, Seneca was exiled to Corsica, where he spent eight miserable years. He was recalled to Rome by Claudius's second wife, Agrippina, where he was given high office and became tutor to her son, Nero. It is not widely appreciated that the first five years of Nero's reign were among the best years of Roman administration, and for this Seneca can take much of the credit. But serving a dictator can be a tricky business and in 65 CE, Seneca was forced to commit suicide by Nero.

Not surprisingly for a man whose career was so unstable, his philosophy focused mainly on moral edification. He didn't presume to be a sage, simply a man trying to grow morally. Seneca was an outspoken critic of **slavery**, gladiatorial combat, and all other forms of cruelty and inhumanity. His philosophy found expression in nine tragedies and ten moral essays. His writings were very influential in setting the tone for **Renaissance humanism**, and served as models for many noble thinkers, such as **Montaigne**.

SENGHOR, LEOPOLD (1906–2001). Outstanding African political and intellectual leader. With the encouragement of his mother, Senghor originally trained for the Catholic priesthood, but at the age of twenty, he realized that was not the right calling for him. In 1928 he was sent to Paris for further study. It was in Paris that Senghor was made fully aware of the influence African art had on contemporary European painting and sculpture. He excelled in his studies, and qualified as an *agrégé*, the highest standard of teacher at the time, one who could teach at secondary and tertiary levels. Senghor saw military service from 1939 until his capture in 1940. During his imprisonment he wrote some of his finest poems.

After the war, he became politically active, representing Senegal in the French Constituent Assembly. In the years leading toward independence, he tried to create a federation of several French-speaking colonies, fearing, correctly as it turned out, that if each colony became an independent state, each one would be too small to stand up for itself internationally. Senghor's federation was not a success, and he became the first president of independent Senegal. He was president from 1960 to 1980. He was one of very few independence-era leaders who stepped down

from office voluntarily (another being Julius Nyerere of Tanzania).

He was an inspirational independence-era leader. He was a leading proponent of the notion of negritude, which sought to give expression to black experience through the arts. He also articulated a form of African socialism and was an opponent of **corruption**. He retired to France, where he wrote *That Which I Believe: Negritude, Frenchness, and Universal Civilization* (1988). Senghor was a laureate of the **International Academy of Humanism** from 1991 until his death in 2001.

SEPARATION OF CHURCH AND STATE. Described by Susan Jacoby, the American historian of **freethought**, as a river that divides and nourishes the banks on either side.

The first country to attempt a radical separation of church and state was the United States. Influenced by **Thomas Paine**, **John Locke**, and the **Enlightenment**, **Thomas Jefferson** wrote in 1802 of the "wall of separation between Church and State." Following Locke, Jefferson said that religion "is a matter which lies solely between man and his **God**." During the presidency of George Washington (1732–1799), in a government treaty with the Muslims of North Africa, it was declared that "the Government of the United States of America is not in any sense founded on the Christian religion." It is simply not true to assert that the United States of America was founded as a Christian nation.

Freedom of religion must mean freedom to hold *or not to hold* a religious belief. If freedom *from* religion is not an integral part of freedom *of* religion, the phrase is meaningless.

Across the world the separation of church and state has been an essential prerequisite to building a genuine democracy. In some countries the struggle for separation of church and state was long and bitter. In France, moderate opinion moved progressively toward the idea of separation with each new example of Catholic intransigence and abuse of privilege. Separation was finally achieved in 1905 in the face of ongoing opposition from the church and from reactionary political groups. The extremist antimodernism of the pontificate of Pius X played into the hands of the government. In fact, so bitter and violent was the opposition that the government was able to rally moderate religious opinion to its side in the interests of preserving the peace.

Similarly in Portugal following a 1910 revolution, church influence in schools and universities was ended, religious orders were expelled, and the church was formally disestablished. Sadly, much of this good work was undone in 1926 when the Portuguese republic foundered and was replaced by a clerico-fascist military junta. Since the collapse of that regime in 1974, Portugal has moved, hesitantly at first, toward an **open society**.

Elsewhere, newer nations were able to learn the lessons of history. Australia, known as "the lucky country," is an example. Article 116 of the Australian constitution, which was drawn up for the creation of the Australian Commonwealth in 1901, says, "The Commonwealth shall not make any law for establishing any religion, or for imposing any religious observance, or for prohibiting the free exercise of any religion, and no religious test shall be required as a qualification for any office or public trust under the Commonwealth."

The separation of church and state is an essential precondition for any genuine democracy. See the entries on **secularism** and **hideous schizophrenia**.

SERAPIS. An interesting example of a manufactured **religion**. The cult of Serapis is the Scientology of the ancient world. In an attempt to strengthen their position in Egypt the Greek Ptolemaic dynasty created this cult. In response to a dream, Ptolemy I Soter (reigned 305–284 BCE) ordered a statue of Jupiter to be brought from Sinope to Egypt. It formed the basis of a specially built temple which was designed to become the center of the cult. The Egyptian priest Manetho and the Greek priest Timotheus reworked old Egyptian deities, devised the attributes of the new god, and decided upon its name. Serapis was portrayed as a regal figure whose right hand rested on Cerberus, the three-headed dog who guarded the underworld in Greek mythology, and whose left hand held a scepter raised to the sky.

Within a century there were forty-two Serapeums around Egypt and the cult spread through the Roman Empire. Notwithstanding the obvious and recent evidence of human creation of Serapis, the Roman historian Tacitus (56–120 CE, approx.) thought that the **miracles** attributed to Serapis was reliable history. The Serapeum at Alexandria was destroyed in 391 CE by the Christian followers of the patriarch Theophilus.

SEX. The means by which most species procreate and ensure the continuation of their kind. Many species have developed elaborate ways of overcoming the tremendous wastefulness of **evolution**. Methods range from producing so many offspring that some should survive from sheer chance, to carefully nurturing few offspring until they are strong enough to look out for themselves.

Homo sapiens has favored both these approaches at various times and places. But its other achievement has been to make sex fun. Making sex fun means it will happen as often as possible and, before the advent of contraception, ensure a constant supply of offspring.

One of the few core features shared by **monotheist** religions and **Asian traditions** is an ambivalent attitude toward sex, in particular toward the part played by women. Christianity and Islam probably have the most perverse and restrictive philosophies of sex. Islam, the youngest of the monotheist religions, has taken the old desire to control women for the sake of men to the greatest extent. The fear and hostility toward women is still there to be seen in Christian scriptures, but much of the venom of those passages has been pulled by biblical criticism, the **secularization** of society, and the evolution of religious values. Many feminists now use the word **gender** when they mean sex.

One of the oldest **prejudices against atheists** is that they seek to free themselves of the moral rules they were brought up in so as to indulge some horrible sexual passion. In fact, most types of **freethinkers** have been positively prudish with regard to sex, even when they have supported a freer climate in principle. Sex has become commercialized and trivialized in consumer society, and this is a trend atheists, skeptics, and humanists can dislike no less than their religious neighbors. All varieties of freethinkers reject the prurient and antifemale proscriptions of the religious past, without then jumping to the conclusion that complete sexual license is justified. The sexual ethics of freethinkers is based on a greater respect for one's sexual partner than has been customary among traditional faiths. Most atheists and humanists refuse to condemn homosexual or bisexual practice among consenting adults. Any form of sexual exploitation is unacceptable to all varieties of freethinker for the simple reason that it is not based on free and informed consent and violates the **golden rule**.

SEXUAL AND REPRODUCTIVE RIGHTS. Fundamental to any serious consideration of women as people of equal worth to men is a full charter of sexual and reproductive rights. Diana Brown, cofounder of the **World Population Foundation**, composed this charter of rights early in 2004:

(1) The right to own one's own body, which includes the right to decide whether, when, and with whom one has sexual experiences.
(2) The right to adequate education and information about sex and reproduction.
(3) The right to distinguish sexual experiences from reproduction, which entails access to reliable contraception.
(4) The right to choose whether or not to marry.
(5) The right to choose one's marital partner.
(6) The right to decide whether and when to have children and to cease childbearing.

(7) The right to end a marriage that is unhappy or violent, so long as adequate provision is made for any children.
(8) The right to a reasonable standard of sexual and reproductive healthcare, which assumes, among other things, the right to safe abortion.
(9) The right to joint responsibility for children born during a marriage or committed relationship.

Alongside this charter of rights, Brown adds three basic protections that females of all ages can reasonably expect:

• protection against all forms of sexual abuse, including sexual activity while still a minor;
• protection from genital mutilation; and
• protection from all other forms of violence.

The list of rights Brown has outlined for women covers the field of rights entitlements. Her charter invokes classical, welfare, and contractual rights (see the entry on **rights**). It is also apparent that for this charter to come anywhere near realization, there will need to be a comprehensive change of mood among each of the world's religions and traditions.

Further reading: Diana Brown, "Women's Sexual and Reproductive Rights," *International Humanist News*, February 2004.

SHAH, AMRITAL BHIKKUBAI (1920–1981). Indian scholar and humanist born into a **Jain** family in Gujarat. In 1937 Shah went to Pune to study science, graduating BSc in 1941. For several years he taught science and was active in the teachers' union. In 1946 he met the Indian Marxist **M. N. Roy**, and the two men had a long friendship, despite disagreeing politically. While admiring much of Roy's thought, Shah criticized Roy's **twenty-two theses of radical humanism**. Shah was critical of Marxism and advocated an **open society**. Shah also campaigned against the prohibition of cow slaughter and the veiling of Muslim women. He was particularly supportive of equal rights for **dalits**, or untouchables, forming the Renuka Devi Association for the education of children of prostitutes.

In April 1969 Shah was central in establishing the Indian Secular Society and served as its founder president, which he remained for the rest of his life. He was a prolific and successful journalist and author. He coedited a multivolume series called *Social Structure and Change*, which traced changes in Indian society. Among the other works Shah edited or coedited include: *Jawaharlal Nehru: A Critical Tribute* (1965), *Tradition and Modernity in India* (1965), and *Cow Slaughter: Horns of a Dilemma* (1967).

SHAKESPEARE, WILLIAM (1564–1616). The greatest playwright since the **Greek playwrights** and one of the most incisive commentators on human emotions who ever lived. He was the son of John Shakespeare and Mary Arden and was probably born on April 23, 1564, in Stratford-on-Avon, in Warwickshire, England. The Shakespeare family was relatively well off. William was educated locally and in 1582, at eighteen, married Anne Hathaway. They had three children.

Around 1588 Shakespeare went to London and began working as an actor. Anne remained in Stratford her whole life. He showed considerable talent and before long began writing plays of his own. For the next twenty years he worked in London and wrote most of the plays he has become famous for. The first half of his career was devoted mainly to comedies and historical dramas, the tragedies were written mainly in the second half. He retired to Stratford in 1610 a fairly wealthy man and continued writing until his death, at only fifty-two on April 23, 1616.

The best of Shakespeare's plays have exercised an influence unmatched by any other playwright in history. He admired the writing of the great skeptic **Montaigne** and is thought to have been strongly influenced by **Giordano Bruno**. Kenneth Clark has written of Shakespeare that he "must be the first and

may be the last supremely great poet to have been without a religious belief, even without humanity's belief in man." Critics have long observed that Shakespeare's characters who evince religious faith are rarely pillars of rectitude. Their piety is safe, formulaic, and self-serving, and not above petitioning **God** for the comeuppance of others. Recent suggestions that Shakespeare may have been Catholic are no more likely than any other claim. Certainly, the Catholic characters in the plays are no more outstanding than the Protestants. It is not unlikely that Shakespeare's own views are apparent when he says in *All's Well That Ends Well*:

Our remedies oft in ourselves do lie
Which we ascribe to heaven.

Shakespeare was a critic of formal, organized religion and of the **anthropocentric conceit** it so often gives rise to. He articulated his **cosmic perspective** in the *Tempest*, when he has Prospero say, "We are such stuff as dreams are made of, and our little life is rounded with a sleep." This passage seems important as it is also thought to be Shakespeare's farewell speech to the stage. Clark concluded that "the human spirit has gained a new greatness by outstaring this emptiness."

SHARIA LAW. The body of Muslim law that emanates from the Qur'an and its complementary source, the **Hadith**. Other sources of Sharia law are *ijma* (consensus of the community), *qiyas* (analogy, usually only undertaken by scholars) and *ijtihad* (reasoning by analogy). Sharia law governs all aspects of day-to-day life, including sexual behavior, eating, praying, and business practices. Sharia law contains the rules to which Muslims should conform.

Shi'ite Sharia is slightly less harsh against women. A man has to go before a cleric to get a divorce whereas the Sunni can simply say "I divorce you" three times. In Shi'ite Sharia, a woman's inheritance is divided only between her brothers, whereas in Sunni a woman's inheritance is divided between all male relatives, no matter how distant.

There is a wide variety of responses to the observance of Sharia Law around the Muslim world, ranging from Turkey's predominantly secular constitution to the attempt by the Taliban in Afghanistan to fully implement Sharia Law as the law of the land. Most Middle Eastern nations run a combination of secular and Sharia law, with Sharia being reserved in most cases for marriage and inheritance issues.

Sharia Law came to the attention of Westerners with the case of **Amina Lawal**, a woman from northern Nigeria who was under threat of being stoned to death for adultery according to the Sharia Law in her region.

SHEIKH, YOUNAS (1952–). Pakistani doctor imprisoned for **blasphemy**. After living and working in the United Kingdom for some years, Sheikh returned to his native Pakistan to practice and teach medicine. In 1992 he established the Enlightenment, a humanist group committed to democracy and secularism in Pakistan.

In October 2000, he was arrested following a complaint from a student. Sheikh was alleged to have observed that, since Muhammad only became a Muslim after receiving his first revelation at forty, it follows that Muhammad's parents weren't Muslims. This observation was held to be objectionable to Muslims and mobs were incited to howl for his arrest. It later transpired that the complainant was not present at the time the statement was supposed to have been made, but the pressure to continue with the prosecution was kept up by the mobs led by fanatical Mullahs.

In August 2001 Dr. Sheikh was found guilty of blasphemy, which in Pakistan carries the death penalty. He then remained in prison for two years while waiting for an appeal. Meanwhile an international campaign around the world, led by the humanist movement, protested his arrest and petitioned his release. He was also declared a prisoner of conscience by Amnesty International. In November 2003

he was quietly released from prison and soon afterward sent to Europe for his own safety.

SHELLEY, JAMES (1884–1961). Teacher and broadcasting pioneer. James Shelley was born in modest circumstances in Coventry in England, only migrating to New Zealand in 1920. He saw active service in World War I, and contrary to the prejudice of there being no **atheists in foxholes**, he lost his religious faith at Passchendaele in 1917. Shelley rose to the rank of major and also played a role in the education corps. After arriving in New Zealand, he quickly became an important figure in education circles, pioneering, among other things, a program of rural adult education.

In 1938 **Michael Joseph Savage** appointed Shelley as director of broadcasting, a position he held until 1949. During that time he expanded and strengthened the national broadcasting system. He was responsible for establishing the *Listener*, which went on to have a significant role in New Zealand cultural and intellectual life for the next half century. He was also instrumental in the formation of the New Zealand Symphony Orchestra.

Shelley was also a vice president of the Rationalist Association and the Sunday Freedom League between 1936 and 1943, relinquishing the position only when the association decided to restrict the number of its vice presidents to two. In 1949 he returned to the United Kingdom, where he died in 1961.

Further reading: Ian Carter, *Gadfly: The Life and Times of James Shelley*.

SHELLEY, MARY WOLLSTONE-CRAFT (1797–1851). The daughter of William Godwin (1756–1836) and **Mary Wollstonecraft Godwin**, who died soon after giving birth to her. In 1814, at only seventeen, Mary Godwin eloped with the brilliant poet **Percy Bysshe Shelley** and married him two years later. Two years later again she wrote her first novel *Frankenstein*, which became one of the most evocative and long-lasting images of a human creation rising against its creator. *Frankenstein* was conceived in Switzerland, in the company of Percy Shelley and Lord Byron (1788–1824), another brilliant romantic poet. Frankenstein was a major source of inspiration for *The Rock Drill* (1913–14), a sculpture by Jacob Epstein (1880–1959), which has become emblematic of the estrangement of humans in the twentieth century. Shelley wrote a series of novels: *Valperga* (1823); *The Last Man* (1826), a dystopia about human society after a catastrophic pestilence; *Lodore* (1835); and her last novel, *Falkner* (1837).

SHELLEY, PERCY BYSSHE (1792–1822). Poetic genius and freethinker. While still a youth at Eton, Shelley was known as "Shelley the atheist." His radical views got him expelled from Oxford University when, in 1811, he wrote the tract *The Necessity of Atheism*. This work (which was refused copyright on the grounds of its pernicious views) and his early poem *Queen Mab* (1813) served as an inspiration to several generations of radicals and revolutionaries in Europe. The following year, he was involved in a protest in London against the continued persecution of booksellers for selling **Thomas Paine**'s *Age of Reason*. His most brilliant defense of **atheism** was in his 1814 work *Refutation of Deism*.

In the short interval between 1818 and 1821 Shelley produced some of the other poems his fame still rests upon. *Revolt of Islam* was written in 1818, *Prometheus Unbound* was written the following year in Rome and published in 1820. These poems alone mean we can forgive many of the follies and excesses of **romanticism**, of which these are prime examples. Shelley also wrote some powerful prose and was more interested in alleviating real misery suffered by real people than many of his fellow romantics were.

Later in life Shelley repudiated his youthful atheism and materialism and embraced a refined form of **pantheism**, derived principally from **Plato**. At the time of his death, he had agreed to cooperate in a translation of

Spinoza's *Tractatus Theologico-Politicus*, but this project never went ahead. He remained disdainful of Christianity throughout his life. Shelley drowned, at only twenty-nine, off the Italian coast on July 8, 1822.

SHU. When asked whether his philosophy could be put into just one word, **Kongfuzi** (Confucius in Latin spelling) answered that it could, and the one word was *shu*, which can be translated as "Do not impose on others what you yourself do not desire." Shu is a variation of the **golden rule**.

SHUMAYYIL, SHIBLI (1860–1917). Prominent Lebanese Egyptian popularizer of **evolution**. Shumayyil was the first Arab thinker to defend evolution to Muslim readers. He translated **Ludwig Büchner**'s work *Force and Matter* into Arabic, and introduced his readers to the thoughts of **Charles Darwin**, **Ernst Haeckel**, **Herbert Spencer**, and other prominent evolutionists. A thoroughgoing naturalist, Shumayyil argued that only a **naturalism** informed by the sciences, evolution in particular, could serve as an antidote to **superstition** and reaction.

SIGHT OF HELL, THE. A booklet, first published in 1861, designed to educate children into what they may look forward to if they end up in **hell**. *The Sight of Hell* was one of a series of fourteen inexpensive booklets penned by the appropriately named Father Furniss, a Catholic priest from Sheffield. Its companion publication was *The Terrible Judgment and the Bad Child*. The series was influential and sold widely, but by the second half of the nineteenth century was instrumental in fueling a backlash against the whole idea of hell.

Further reading: Hypatia Bradlaugh Bonner, *The Christian Hell*.

SILVER, QUEEN (1910–1998). American child prodigy, described by the famous scientist Luther Burbank (1849–1926) as the "Girl Wonder." The daughter of a socialist activist,

Queen Silver spent her childhood traveling the country as her mother campaigned for women's rights and rights of labor. In this atmosphere, the girl grew up quickly. She also had a precocious intelligence and had read the works of **Charles Darwin**, **Ernst Haeckel**, and others at a very young age.

More extraordinary than this was her ability to stand in front of large crowds and synthesize the thoughts of these people at such a tender age. Queen Silver was an experienced speaker at the age of eight. Her learning was not easy. Librarians in Los Angeles tried to deny her the right to read books on science on the grounds that they were "male" books. Her protest was loud enough to have that discrimination ended, although it continued elsewhere. Her reputation had grown to such an extent that in 1919, the eight-and-a-half-year-old girl was commissioned by the London Society of Social Science to give six lectures in Los Angeles. The lectures, given without notes, were a sensation. In 1921, she created another sensation when she gave a series of lectures which explained in popular language Einstein's **theory of relativity**.

In 1923 she began *Queen Silver's Magazine*, a **freethought** journal which attracted more than five thousand subscribers around the world. It ceased publication in 1931, because of the Depression. She also helped the progressive cause during the Scopes Trial in 1925. An article she wrote for the *Truthseeker* called "Evolution from Monkey to Bryan" was widely reprinted and turned into a pamphlet. When Bryan challenged evolutionists to come out of the trees and debate the subject, Queen Silver accepted the challenge, but Bryan declined.

As the 1920s wore on, the socialist side of her mother's campaigning began to attract violent attention from right-wing groups. Their socialist bookshop was burned down while the police looked on, and hirelings of businessmen's groups disrupted their meetings. The ongoing strain of this harassment took a toll on her mother's health and with the onset of the Great Depression, Queen left public life to help care for her mother. She fell out of the public eye for four decades. And despite her obvious intelligence, she never secured any position commensurate to her abilities. Late in life, she returned to active life, working for a variety of civil rights and feminist causes. Queen Silver was so well known that in 1929 Cecil B. de Mille (1881–1959) made a film called *The Godless Girl*, which was modeled on her life.

Further reading: Wendy McElroy, *Queen Silver: The Godless Girl*.

SIMPLICITY. An important concept of the Chinese philosopher Laozi (Lao Tzu is the former spelling). According to Laozi, the overarching universal principle is the **Tao**; that which cannot be named. Nothing is simpler than the Tao, which also means that nothing is simpler for any individual thing, including humans, than the Te, which is the little part of the Tao in each thing. If nothing is simpler than the Tao, and the Te, then it follows that a life free from arbitrary and unnecessary complications is a life well spent, and in harmony with the Tao.

This is a noble idea, although Laozi insists that **knowledge** too is a dangerous diversion from simplicity. He also scorned the Confucian notion of **human-heartedness** as a further degeneration of the original Te, and counsels inactivity from the sage ruler.

SIN. Described by **Bertrand Russell** as one of the most important of the underlying causes of unhappiness. Sin is held to have this peculiar power by virtue of its being an offense against **God**. Given that God is all-powerful and all-good, sin can only come either from our essential wickedness or from the machinations of **Satan**. Sin is, in this sense, a defilement of our **soul**, which traditional **monotheist** theology insists is the repository within us of the essence of God.

The concept of sin was given its fullest expression in the writings of St. Augustine (354–430 CE), who did more than anyone else to integrate the notion of sin into the Western understanding of human nature. It is with this in mind that **Nietzsche** spoke of sin as having been invented alongside its sister concept of **free will** as an instrument of torture to confuse and make people distrust their own instincts. Certainly the concept of sin has little meaning once the related concepts of God or soul are found to be illusory.

More recently, liberal theologians, embarrassed by traditional notions of sin, have defanged the concept by trying to portray it in an existential way by speaking of being separated or estranged from God. Few people have been impressed with this. Whether religious liberals like it or not, sin is inevitably bound up with **command moralities**. Sin has no place in naturalistic ethics. The Greeks, in their wisdom, had no conception of sin as discussed here.

This is not to say, of course, that people are not inclined to act or think badly. Of course we are. The point is that these behaviors are part of being human and are best addressed in that context, and without reference to supernatural notions of God, the soul, or **evil**.

SINGAPORE ISSUES. The name given to a series of pressing problems of **globalization** and free trade. They are also referred to as "new issues." Most of the issues were identified and took on their current status as recurringly difficult issues at a **World Trade Organization** meeting of ministers held at Singapore in 1996. After some tense negotiations they found their way into the WTO agenda at the next major round of world-trade talks, which began at Doha in Qatar in 2001. Developed countries are in favor of securing agreements on these issues, while less-developed nations are worried about the implications of these issues on their own economies. The issues are:

- investment;
- competition policy;
- transparency in government procurement; and

- trade facilitation.

Developing countries are worried about these issues because they fear that giving ground here will only increase the power of the multinational corporations, at the expense of their own economic development. Critics say that these countries are fearful of exposing their corrupt government processes to international scrutiny. See the entry on **corruption**. Attempts have been made to unbundle these issues, or in other words, to try to deal with each one separately, but without much success. The issues, in the end, are too interrelated to be broken up.

The issues, as well as the equally pressing question of agricultural subsidies, came to a head at the WTO meeting held at Cancún in Mexico in September 2003. The failure to reach any sort of agreement resulted in these talks collapsing. Solving the Singapore issues is a major priority if **global governance** is going to proceed satisfactorily.

SIX SUGGESTIONS FOR RELIGIOUS BELIEVERS. In the spirit of honest criticism, the following six suggestions could help pave the way toward genuine **dialogue** between religious believers and freethinkers. It is not suggested, of course, that all religious apologists are privy to all of these failings.

(1) Don't assume that someone who disagrees with you must also be dishonest or in some other way morally deficient.

(2) People who don't share your beliefs are not **unbelievers**, they are people who have other beliefs than yours.

(3) Remember that atheists have just as much capacity for humility as religious people, because they believe as they do with no thought to their own personal reward.

(4) Claiming that criticisms of religion are "offensive" or that they "insult one's faith" is to evade responsibility for answering the criticisms.

(5) Try examining what humanists actually believe, not what you think they believe.
(6) Take responsibility for your condemnations; you're not "just following scripture."

Were religious apologists to take seriously these six suggestions and implement them in their apologetic work, the debate between them and freethinkers would at least have the chance of rising above the level of *ad hominem* abuse, and some genuine issues could be broached.

SKEPTICAL ENVIRONMENTALIST, THE.

A controversial book written by Bjørn Lomborg (1965–), a Danish political scientist, and published by Cambridge University Press in 2001. The book called into question many of the projections of growing ecological distress and population pressure, and upheld the ability of the world economy to sustain its production without undue environmental damage. The controversy surrounding his book rapidly projected Lomborg to celebrity status. He became a regular guest on television and radio shows and was invited to comment for the *New York Times*, the *Daily Telegraph*, and the *Economist*. In November 2001 he was nominated as a global leader for tomorrow by the **World Economic Forum**, and early in 2002 he was appointed director of Denmark's Environmental Assessment Institute.

However things did not all go Lomborg's way. Responding to a series of complaints from eminent scientists, the Danish Committees on Scientific Dishonesty (DCSD), an officially recognized government-funded body, issued a report which concluded that *The Skeptical Environmentalist* does constitute dishonest science. Among the evidence given was Lomborg's tendency to use secondary sources and to resort to peer-reviewed literature only when the arguments supported his point of view.

The DCSD concluded that the book's systematically biased representation of data constituted a perversion of the scientific message and, as such, constituted scientific dishonesty. The DCSD went on to exonerate Lomborg of gross negligence, noting that many of his errors and omissions may simply have been the result of the lack of specialist knowledge of the areas he was writing about. It is clear from these criticisms that Lomborg's work has to be treated with extreme caution—at best —and that the fears of the environmentalists remain valid ones.

SKEPTICISM. It is not so much a body of thought as a method of thinking. Skepticism is the intellectual offspring of **Pyrrhonism** in the ancient world. The original meaning of the word was "to look about," but it came to mean "considered examination." As the standards for a *considered* examination are high, it follows that many ideas and beliefs fail to provide sufficient reasons to be upheld. This led to the current understanding of skepticism as refraining from accepting an idea or belief without sufficient **evidence**.

When being confronted by an assertion or a piece of information the skeptic may do any of several things: (1) examine how the claim or datum was put together, and attempt to replicate the conditions in which it was generated; (2) search for counterexamples and check the effectiveness of the claim or datum against its various consequences; or (3) determine whether the claim can be shown to be false, even in principle. What the skeptic does *not* do is accept uncritically the claim or datum immediately.

Skeptics, in the words of Mario Bunge, can be grounders and grinders. They can ground their beliefs around rational and verifiable evidence, and they can also grind away at the unsupported flights of fancy beloved of paranormalists, **creationists**, **postmodernists**, and others. Skepticism is an essential ingredient in science and technology. In either case, skepticism is more than simply **debunking**.

Skepticism can also be total or tactical. Total skepticism is radical and systematic whereas tactical skepticism is moderate and methodological. Early Pyrrhonism was a type of total skepticism, whereas Sextus Empiricus (third century CE) and most contemporary skeptics are tactical skeptics. Their skepticism is moderate and methodological. Tactical skepticism is the better approach.

Skepticism is by no means always a good thing. Claiming to be skeptical that the world is spherical, say, in the face of all the evidence to the contrary, is little more than burying one's head in the sand. It amounts to listening to reasons against something but rejecting out of hand reasons for the same thing. The surer and more grounded the **knowledge**, the less reason there is for total skepticism. However, we need to remember that any knowledge is **fallible**, and a degree of tactical skepticism is always a useful corrective against **dogmatism**. See also the entry on the **Ten Tropes of Judgment**.

Further reading, Paul Kurtz, *The New Skepticism*; and Mario Bunge, *Philosophy in Crisis*.

SKEPTICISM, BOOKS ABOUT. The best source on skepticism is the *Skeptical Inquirer* magazine, published by the **Committee for the Scientific Examination of Claims of the Paranormal**. There are many excellent skeptical magazines around the world, in many different languages, but the *Skeptical Inquirer* remains the standard by which all the others are judged.

Among the books, *Skeptical Philosophy for Everyone* (2001) by Richard Popkin and Avrum Stroll is the best introduction. Good introductions to skepticism from a specifically philosophical standpoint are *Scepticism* (1973) by Kai Nielsen and the more recent *Scepticism* (2003) by Neil Gascoigne. *The New Skepticism: Inquiry and Reliable Knowledge* (1992) by **Paul Kurtz** is an important single-volume study of contemporary skepticism, and *Skepticism and Humanism: The New Paradigm* (2001) is a useful collection of Kurtz's essays on skepticism and **humanism**. *Skeptical Odysseys*

(2001) is an interesting collection of personal accounts from leading skeptics.

The Skeptic Encyclopedia of Pseudoscience (2 vols., 2002) edited by Michael Shermer is a useful compendium of various **pseudosciences**, but sheds little light on pseudoscience as a phenomenon or on skepticism as a tool.

Some of the better historical accounts of skepticism include *The Skeptical Tradition* (1983) edited by Myles Burnyeat, and *Skepticism in Renaissance and Post-Renaissance Thought* (2003) edited by José R. Maia Neto and Richard Popkin. However, this book is not suitable for nonspecialists. And then there are a plethora of books on all aspects of pseudoscience, looked at from a skeptical point of view.

SKEPTICISM, CORE PRINCIPLES OF. The American psychologist Arthur S. Reber has itemized three core principles of **skepticism**. Reber argues that it is the recognition of these three principles which makes someone a skeptic:

- nature is reliable;
- **science** is coherent; and
- explanation is mechanistic.

The skeptic believes that nature operates along the same principles in Beijing as it does in Brooklyn. Each discipline has demonstrated its credentials by improving our understanding of how nature is reliable within its field. No **pseudoscience** has ever made a contribution in this area, which is why they remain a pseudoscience. And across all the disciplines of science there are some basic principles which apply—principles of energy and mass, cause and effect, time and so on. See the entry on **science, basic presuppositions of**. So if one of these principles is being challenged, we are either on the threshold of a fundamentally new understanding of science, or, more likely, we have a **paranormal** claim on our hands. And science also rests on the explanation of the processes under examination being plausible. It is not enough to wave one's hands and talk of **miracles**, the invisible hand, or the mystery of the unknown. For something to be called science, its processes need to be reliable and repeatable. In pseudoscience, these conditions are never met.

Devotees of the pseudosciences often think they have made a telling point when a skeptic has declined to investigate their claims. They then accuse the skeptic of being close-minded. But this accusation fails when the paranormal claim has violated one of the three core principles of skepticism. And as the **burden of proof** lies with those making the larger claim, the skeptic is not required to investigate each and every shrill assertion. It is up to the paranormalist to provide **evidence** that his claim is worthy of investigation. After all, it is the paranormalist who is claiming scientific status, not the other way round.

Further reading: Arthur S. Reber, "On the Paranormal: In Defense of Skepticism," *Skeptical Inquirer* 7, no. 2 (Winter 1982–83): 55–63.

SLAVERY. An ancient institution whereby one person can own, or at least have a controlling say over, the activities of another person. The first person to denounce slavery as being wrong in principle was the **Stoic** orator Dio Chrysostom (d. 112 CE, approx.). The early Christians were indifferent to slavery as an institution because of the respect for the law laid down in the New Testament book of Romans. The law, as recorded in the **Hebrew scriptures**, takes slavery for granted. Once Christianity became the established religion of the Roman Empire, its conservatism hardened. At the Council of Gangra (340 CE), for instance, Christians who encouraged slaves to disobey their masters were anathematized. St. Augustine (354–430 CE) accepted slavery as all part of a world dominated by **original sin**. Many Christians were slave owners and took slavery for granted in just the same way their pagan neighbors did. The record of Islam with regard to slavery is, if anything, even worse.

The Qur'an has several passages which enjoin Muslims to treat their slaves well, but there is no condemnation of slavery. Indeed, slavery existed in some Muslim societies until the second half of the twentieth century. While the **Asian traditions** all have strongly hierarchical elements in their teaching, there is very little mention of slavery. Neither Buddhism nor Confucianism advocated it.

Widespread popular opposition developed during the Enlightenment, on secular grounds of the natural equality of human beings and of the sheer injustice of the institution. A prominent secular opponent to slavery in England at the time was Thomas Day (1748–1789). Christian apologists often try to avoid their religion's dismal record with regard to slavery by emphasizing the role of the Christian abolitionist William Wilberforce (1759–1833). However, this is to forget the countries, like Denmark and Haiti, which had abolished slavery before Britain. The first country to formally abolish slavery was the dreaded French revolutionary government, in 1794, although Napoleon restored it in the French colonies in 1802. And neither were Wilberforce's own views on slavery free from ambiguity. Speaking to the House of Commons in 1813, Wilberforce insisted that securing missionary access to the heathen of India was more important than abolition of slavery. This was because Indian religion was, in his words "mean, licentious and cruel." This prejudice also overlooks the crucial role played by non-Christian abolitionists, like **William Lloyd Garrison** and **Lucretia Coffin Mott**.

While formal slavery has been abolished throughout the world, particularly since the Slavery Convention (1926) and the Supplementary Convention on the Abolition of Slavery (1957), widespread poverty has thrown up new types of indentured work that differs only nominally from the slavery of old. It is estimated that there are people, in the area of twenty-seven million people, who are, for all intents and purposes, slaves. Upward of twenty million of them are on the Indian subcontinent.

SLIPPERY SLOPE. A popular but poor, and often dishonest, argument that can be used against a variety of scientific or social innovations. The slippery slope argument contends that A should be banned or halted because it would lead to B. An example: stem cell research (or euthanasia, or many other things) should be banned because it will lead to . . . (add some ghastly scenario). The problem with the slippery slope argument is that it doesn't allow for the possibility of A happening *without* leading to B. Neither does it encourage the debate about having A and not having B.

SMITH, ADAM (1723–1790). Scottish economist and architect of the capitalist economy. Adam Smith was born in Kirkcaldy, Fifeshire, the son of a customs official. His father died before he was born, but Smith was able to proceed with an education. He spent most of his working life as professor of moral philosophy at the University of Glasgow. He was a close friend of the philosopher **David Hume**.

The book that made Smith historically important is *The Wealth of Nations* (1776), which made the case for enlightened self-interest as the surest guiding principle for the management of society. He surveyed the historical patterns of the hunter-gatherer, nomadic agriculture, feudalism, and international commerce, and argued for the superiority of the fourth—and, in Smith's view, final—stage.

Smith didn't address the issue of which form of government would best suit the economy he favored, although it was clear he preferred laissez-faire capitalism. He recognized that a government established with the purpose of defending property rights would be, in part, a defense of privilege and **inequality**, but argued that market forces would keep prices sufficiently low to offset these inequalities. This feat would be achieved by what he called the "invisible hand" of providence. Smith's other important book was the *Theory of Moral Sentiments* (1759) where, in contrast to the rational self-interest of *The Wealth of Nations*, Smith spoke

of sympathy as a guiding human emotion.

He is usually credited with founding the discipline of economics, but quite independently of Smith, the Japanese thinker **Miura Baien** arrived at similar conclusions.

SMITH, WILLIAM ROBERTSON (1846–1894). Scottish theologian and victim of religious bigotry. Born in Keig, Aberdeenshire, Smith was raised as an Evangelical Presbyterian. He studied at Aberdeen and Edinburgh before further study at Bonn and Göttingen in Germany. In 1870 he became professor of Hebrew and the Old Testament at the Free Church College, Aberdeen.

He attracted a storm of hostile attention for his article on the Bible for the *Encyclopedia Britannica* in 1875. So angry were his coreligionists that, in 1880, he was charged with **heresy** by the General Assembly of the Free Church of Scotland. He was acquitted of that charge, but the following year, in response to an article, "Hebrew Language and Literature," Smith was relieved of his position at Aberdeen University by a vote of 491 to 113. His enemies were not content with that, and Smith faced a series of private legal assaults over the next few years. This persecution notwithstanding, he remained a theist, though he rejected the supernatural claims of Christianity.

In 1883 Smith moved to Cambridge, where he switched his academic focus to the study of Arabic. And in 1887 he joined the editorial board of the *Encyclopedia Britannica*. As well as his encyclopedia articles, Smith wrote *The Old Testament and the Jewish Church* (1881) and *The Religion of the Semites* (1889). His work was influential on J. G. Frazer (1854–1941), author of the monumental study, *The Golden Bough*.

SMOKER, BARBARA (1923–). Born into a devout Roman Catholic family in London, Smoker was originally convinced she wanted to become a nun. Wartime service in Ceylon (now Sri Lanka) exposed Smoker to different ways of living and believing. A great deal of reading and thinking about her religious views led her to renounce Christianity altogether in 1949. She was then active in radical and **freethought** organizations for her entire life: Campaign for Nuclear Disarmament, the Committee of 100, and Vietnam-protest organizations in particular. But her main attention was devoted to the freethought movement. Smoker was president of the **National Secular Society** from 1971 to 1996, and chairperson of the Voluntary Euthanasia Society from 1981 to 1985.

An active debater, journalist, and controversialist, Smoker also wrote a monograph called *Humanism*, published in 1973 and reissued in 1998. Unlike the weightier tomes designed for adults with much leisure, *Humanism* was written for secondary-school-age readers. Smoker also produced a book of satirical verse called *Good God!* (1977), and a pamphlet on embryo research called *Eggs Are Not People* (1985). A longtime contributor to the *Freethinker*, a selection of her articles were anthologized as *Freethoughts: Atheism, Humanism, Secularism* in 2002. She has represented the atheist viewpoint on radio and television in the United Kingdom and on speaking tours in the United States and India.

SNOW, CHARLES PERCY (1905–1980). English novelist, public intellectual, and humanist. Born and raised in Leicester, Snow went on to Christ's College, Cambridge, where he became a fellow from 1930 until 1950. During World War II he worked in an advisory capacity for the ministry of labor and from 1945 until 1960 was a civil service commissioner. This experience of the inner reaches of government provided the material for a series of novels which went under the collective label of *Strangers and Brothers*. This series ran from 1940 until 1968. Since his death, Snow's fiction has become militantly unfashionable, but books like *The New Men* (1954) and *Corridors of Power* (1964) raised important issues of power and responsibility. He was an admirer of **H. G. Wells**, and his civic **humanism** and interest in the boundaries of **science** reflect that influence.

Snow's early career had been in science, and though he left that world for the world of government and writing, he retained his interest in the sciences for the rest of his life. His last book was a popularization of developments in twentieth-century physics called *The Physicists* (1981).

In his role as public intellectual, he gave the 1959 Rede Lectures entitled *The Two Cultures*, where he suggested a growing rift between the world informed by the sciences and the world informed by literature. The **two cultures** debate proved to be very bitter and protracted. Snow was knighted in 1964. In 1950 he married the novelist Pamela Hansford Johnson.

SOAL, SAMUEL GEORGE (1889–1975). In his day a widely respected scientist but who proved to be a charlatan. In research between 1936 and 1939, Soal provided a series of impressive data which gave striking evidence for psychical phenomena, such as mindreading, telepathy, and clairvoyance. His work had seemingly given **parapsychology** a genuine scientific status. In later work, published as *The Mind Readers* in 1955, Soal produced examples from a study of two Welsh boys which further confirmed these findings. He served as president of the Society for Psychical Research from 1950.

Widespread **skepticism** about his findings prompted a supporter of Soal to vindicate his findings. What he found instead was evidence of Soal having cheated and manipulated results on a large scale. Problems had already arisen over the shoddy control protocols in the study of the Welsh boys. It transpired that the boys had been able to communicate to one another and had misled Soal over the entire experiment. When the protocols were tightened, the boys' mindreading abilities vanished. All of Soal's work is now completely discredited, and much of parapsychology along with it.

SOCIAL CAPITAL. A concept that is difficult to define and yet essential to any healthy society. Among some theorists social capital refers mainly to attitudes: our neighborliness, our willingness to pick up litter dropped by others, or to donate our time to the local school, library, or community center. Each of these intangible acts of **altruism** help keep the fabric of society strong and healthy. Others have spoken of institutions like schools, libraries, universities, and public parks as social capital. They cost money to run and don't turn a profit, but does that mean they are liabilities, as some on the political right argue?

Even the **World Bank** has belatedly recognized the value of social capital. In fact the World Bank's definition of social capital, from a 1999 report, is one of the best currently available. Social capital "refers to the institutions, relationships, and norms that shape the quality and quantity of society's social interactions . . . Social capital is not just the sum of the institutions which underpin a society—it is the glue that holds them together."

People who are actively engaged in society should help maintain the social capital, so long as they are not preaching some sort of intolerance. All constructive **moral-nets** are important threads in the social capital. It will be apparent that social capital is a fragile flower. It presupposes **pluralism**, and that society needs to be held together to prevent it from splitting up into so many mutually uncomprehending groups. **Command moralities** find it difficult to accommodate the pluralism and **toleration** required in the delicate balancing act of maintaining social capital. The busybody and **virtuecrat** is as much of a liability to social capital as is the selfish egotist who never joins any social network and takes no interest in the wider society.

SOCIAL DARWINISM. A misreading of **Darwinism** that was popular and influential from the 1850s to about the 1930s. Social Darwinism made the mistake of extrapolating a whole theory of society, not from a close

reading of Darwin's works, but from a few phrases, the most notorious being "the survival of the fittest," which was said originally not by **Charles Darwin** but by **Herbert Spencer**.

Social Darwinism claimed to extend Darwinism into the **social sciences**. They argued that, as **evolution** was thought to favor the fit and strong, so we see the same in society. People rise to positions of wealth and power because they are better adapted to struggle and survive. Conversely, those who fail in life do so because they are less well adapted in the struggle to survive. Many Social Darwinists took this one step further by concluding that any sort of assistance to the disadvantaged was going to run counter to nature by helping the unfit survive. It would be wrong, they argued, to try to undo what nature is doing. It would be better in the long run for the unfit to be allowed to perish, in this way the biological fitness of the race would slowly improve.

This more extreme version of Social Darwinism became known as **eugenics**, and was influential between the 1910s to about the 1940s. The supposed scientific credentials of Social Darwinism was finally demolished by the **neo-Darwinian synthesis** of the 1930s, and its social observations were rendered obsolete by the advent of the **welfare state**. However, with the widespread restructuring of welfare states around the world in the 1990s and early twenty-first century, some Social Darwinist ideas underwent a revival at the hands of the political right.

Further reading: Peter Bowler, *The Non-Darwinian Revolution*.

SOCIAL INTELLIGENCE. A term coined by the American philosopher **John Dewey** which referred to the ongoing dialogue society has with itself to determine how its priorities change over time. The concept of social intelligence has been described by the American moral philosopher James Gouinlock as Dewey's greatest contribution to moral thought.

Social intelligence assumes that there are no permanent moral injunctions somehow intrinsic to the universe. It also emphasizes the social nature of moral thinking over other theories that stress moral thinking as something we do alone. Rather, morality is what people determine together to be right or wrong at one particular time. To take one example among many, public hanging, once considered acceptable, even edifying, is no longer considered in a positive light. That change took place by the ongoing social intelligence.

Social intelligence, like **social capital**, is a fragile flower, and requires people to be actively involved in their community, ideally with a spirit of **toleration** for different opinions and recognition of the value of **pluralism**. Social intelligence can easily be skewed by unbalanced ownership of media outlets, strident language, and harsh **command moralities** which see no value in other viewpoints. See the entry on **limitless communication**.

Further reading: James Gouinlock, *Rediscovering the Moral Life*.

SOCIAL SCIENCES. A group of academic disciplines, usually identified as history, sociology, political science, pedagogy, and human geography. There seems to be less unanimity as to where disciplines like physical geography and anthropology fit; some see them as social sciences and others see them as physical sciences. All these disciplines can and do use the **scientific method**, in the sense that they involve disinterested research using repeatable methodologies. But these disciplines, unlike the hard sciences, can also employ more interpretive procedures like **hermeneutics**, about which there is a great deal of controversy.

SOCIAL WORLDS. An idea conceived by sociologists Peter Berger and Thomas Luckmann in *The Social Construction of Reality* (1971). Berger and Luckmann saw social worlds as coherent sets of institutions, social identities, and behaviors that come together to produce a worldview that those within the social world believe to be true. A classic example of a social world is fundamentalist Christianity which opposes **evolution**. People adhering to this social world are able to maintain their outlook, despite its obvious falsity, because they rarely go outside their social world and therefore are rarely exposed to any challenges to their outlook. Berger and Luckmann argued that all social worlds involved some element of delusion. The task of the sociologist was to sort out the various illusions into some manageable order.

This interesting and worthwhile theory of Berger and Luckmann was later taken up and turned on its head by **relativists** and **postmodernists**, who claimed that it was problematic at best and imperialist at worst to even attempt any sort of cross-cultural analysis or judgment. Into this morass stepped the American philosopher **John Searle**, whose provocatively titled book *The Construction of Social Reality* (1995) overthrew the pessimistic notion of being unable to make distinctions between various social worlds. Searle did this by his masterly exposition of what **facts** actually are. See the entry on **moralnets** and **external realism**.

SOCIALIST HUMANISM. A movement of intellectuals that tried to give Marxism a humanist face. The need for a realignment in **Marxism** was felt by many left-wing intellectuals, particularly after 1956, when the Soviet Union invaded Hungary and squashed an uprising against Stalinism and Russian occupation. In the same year Nikita Krushchev had denounced Stalinism and its brutal ways. Socialist humanism wanted to expunge the dogmatism that Marxism had degenerated into and reinvigorate it with a more humanistic orientation.

A center of socialist humanist thought was Yugoslavia, which had been expelled in 1948 by Stalin from the international communist community. Since its expulsion, socialist intellectuals had been trying to articulate a new vision of popular Marxism. Socialist-humanist thought slowly centered on a small but influential group of philosophers who became known as the Praxis Group. These thinkers emphasized the earlier Marx, particularly as seen in what became known as the *Paris Manuscripts* (1844). Here, Marx was taken to be more open and free in his thinking, and less inclined to the **historicism** of his major works. The Praxis Group was a source of great annoyance to Marshall Tito (1892–1980), Yugoslavia's dictator, but Tito was anxious not to lose his reputation in the West as a maverick leader of a freer brand of Marxism. In January 1975, however, Tito's patience snapped, and the Praxis Group was shut down. Most of the philosophers lost their academic positions, but Tito shrank from imprisoning them. Most of the group went on to have important roles in building Serbia's postcommunist future in the 1990s. One of them, Svetozar Stojanovic, was a leading opponent to the dictatorial regime of Slobodan Milosevic, which was ousted in a popular revolution in 2002. Stojanovic is a member of the **International Academy of Humanism**. A leading ally of the Praxis Group in the United States was the philosopher **Paul Kurtz**. A Marxist-Humanist dialogue became the first book published by **Prometheus Books**.

In Britain, the movement became organized around a new journal called the *New Reasoner*, which was founded in 1957. Subtitled "A Quarterly Journal of Socialist Humanism," the *New Reasoner* was coedited by the historian E. P. Thompson (1924–1993). Thompson led the counterattack against the strident antihumanism of the French Marxist Louis Althusser (1918–1987) in brilliant polemical critiques such as *The Poverty of Theory* (1978).

In the end, socialist humanism failed to sort out its own contradictions. It failed to reconcile orthodox Marxism with liberal humanism. It failed to provide a stable ground for **pluralism** and freedom of thought within a Marxist dialectic of history which discounts such things as bourgeois irrelevances. Ironically, socialist humanism had the same sort of contradictions and difficulties liberal Christianity has between reconciling the authority of **scripture** and the shifting moral imperatives of a diverse and ever-changing world.

The most comprehensive anthology of socialist humanist thought can be found in *Socialist Humanism* (1965), a collection edited by Erich Fromm (1900–1980). But the most impressive intellectual achievements of socialist humanism were the histories by E. P. Thompson, in particular *The Making of the English Working Class* (1963) and *Whigs and Hunters* (1975).

SOCIOBIOLOGY. See **EVOLUTIONARY PSYCHOLOGY**.

SOCRATES (469–399 BCE). Hugely influential philosopher of Athens. Reputedly the son of a midwife and a stonemason who had worked in the Parthenon; Socrates styled himself the midwife of the mind. Apart from a stint in the army, Socrates had no conventional achievements to his credit. His adult life was spent arguing with his fellow Athenians in the agora, the outdoor marketplace of the city.

Socrates is remembered as much for his method of thinking as for the conclusions he arrived at. The Socratic method involved asking searching questions and drawing attention to problems underlying the answer. In this way, people could see that the views they hold with great confidence in fact are problematic or even contradictory. Socrates' thoughts are known only through the writings of his pupil **Plato** whose earlier dialogues are generally thought to give an accurate indication of Socrates' thought, although Plato's later works are more his own thoughts wrapped up in Socrates' words.

In 399 BCE, Socrates was put on trial on charges of refusing to recognize the official gods of Athens, indeed of introducing new ones, and of corrupting the young. He had long angered the conservative powers-that-be with his wit and questions, particularly at a time when Athens was at war. Free thinking at such a time was thought by many to be tantamount to treason. Socrates' speech in his own defense can be found in Plato's *Apology*. Though not Socrates' exact words, Plato probably captures them pretty accurately. It is here that Socrates makes his famous declaration that the unexamined life is not worth living.

The values Socrates sought to impart were admirable: know thyself; never be afraid to ask questions; value your friends and grow with them; nurture your psyche. His criticism of the **Pre-Socratic** philosophers on behalf of a **dualism** of mind and body was less helpful. **Bertrand Russell** praised Socrates for his indifference to worldly success, courage in the face of death, and concern for truth, but also criticized him for some no less significant defects. They included his tendency to be bullying and dishonest in his arguments, the unwarrantable consolation of an afterlife to ease his fear of **death**, and his determination to prove his philosophical views, even at the expense of critical thinking.

To this could be added Socrates' indifference to the **naturalist** spirit of the Pre-Socratic philosophers who preceded him.

SOCRATES FOUNDATION. A foundation established in 1950 by the Dutch Humanist League with the purpose of promoting **humanism** in the broadest sense of the word. This has mostly been done by a steady production of publications, as well as seminars, summer schools, and conferences. The three main vehicles used by the foundation are the annual Socrates lecture (beginning in 1984), the publication since 1954 of the quarterly journal *Rekenschap* ("to account"), and the establishment of Socrates chairs at various universities. As of 2004, there are eight Socrates chairs in various Dutch universities, with diverse specialisms, including education, cultural studies, philosophy, technology, and anthropology. The Socrates Foundation is an important voice for humanism in the Netherlands.

SÖDERBERG, HJALMAR (1869–1941). Swedish novelist and **smiter of humbug** who gravitated from **skepticism** to open criticism of Christianity during his writing career. Söderberg lost his faith as a teenager and spent the rest of his life in an attempt to find some meaning to life without religion. Söderberg was influenced by the dark style of **August Strindberg**, Sweden's greatest literary genius. Another favorite of his was **Anatole France**.

Söderberg attracted attention with his first novel, *Martin Birck's Youth* (1901, translated 1930), the story of a dreamer living a humdrum, conventional life. Other novels on this sort of theme include *Doctor Glas* (1905, translated 1963) and *The Serious Game* (1912). *Doctor Glas*, which considers issues of **abortion** and conventional hypocrisy, is surprisingly relevant to contemporary society. Söderberg also wrote an important play, *Gertrud* (1906), which later was turned into a film by Carl Dreyer. Söderberg was a relentless critic of conventional pieties and acquired the reputation as an immoralist as a result of his early writing. However, his writing was not bitter, rather it was melancholic and wistful. His loss of faith and criticisms of religion made him unpopular in Sweden, and after 1917 he lived in Denmark.

A selection of his short stories was translated into English by the rationalist scholar Carl Lofmark (1936–1987) and published shortly before his death from cancer.

Further reading: Carl Lofmark, "Hjalmar Söderberg (1869–1941): Swedish Freethinker," *Question* 11 (1978): 3–14.

SOKAL HOAX. The scandal that brought about the collapse of the claims of **postmodernism** to any sort of academic credibility. In 1996 Alan Sokal, a professor of physics at New York University, submitted a paper to the postmodernist journal *Social Text*. The paper had the impeccably postmodernist title of "Transgressing the Boundaries: Toward a Transformative Hermeneutics of Quantum Gravity" and demonstrated that even the laws

of **science** are nothing more than social con-
structs—one of the central points of postmodernist orthodoxy. Sokal proposed a new
model of quantum gravity, which would be
more in keeping with the **feminism**, post-
colonialism, and **relativism** favored by the
Social Text editors. So enamored were the
Social Text editors that they made no attempt
to have other academics read over Sokal's
article and check it for errors, and it duly
appeared in the spring issue of the journal.

But on the same day that issue of *Social
Text* hit the newsstands, *Lingua Franca* published a letter from Sokal exposing the whole
article as **hoax**. Everything he had written
about the social relativity of science was nonsense. Indeed, he had even included basic
errors of scientific fact in the article, which
had gone unnoticed.

The editors of *Social Text* were caught in
a double bind. Not only were they made to
look foolish for having published such
obvious nonsense, but the very credibility of
the postmodernism they espoused was fatally
undermined as well. This is for two reasons.
First, postmodernists have often scorned the
academic process of academic verification
and the search for **truth** as little more than
culturally constructed narratives of Late Capitalist (suitably capitalized) elites, but here
were shown how badly things can go wrong
when these processes are abandoned.

And then, to make things worse, when it
transpired they had been fooled into publishing something because they agreed with
it and had been seduced by the **jargon** rather
than because it was true, the *Social Text* editors resorted to personal attacks and smears.
If they had scorned the standard processes of
academic verification and the search for truth
as they claimed, why should they have
reacted so venomously? This dilemma was
never resolved and postmodernist pretensions to academic credibility have not fully
recovered.

Further reading: The Editors of Lingua
Franca, *The Sokal Hoax*.

SOLARIN, TAI (1922–1994). Nigerian educator and humanist, described by **Wole
Soyinka** as a "passionate warrior in the cause
of democracy." Solarin was a very prominent
educator and social critic in Nigeria, reaching
wide audiences there through the Nigerian
newspaper the *Guardian*. After an education
in missionary schools, Solarin received
higher education in the United Kingdom,
where he discovered the writings of **H. G.
Wells**, **Robert Ingersoll**, and others. From
his readings, Solarin became convinced that
religion served only to instill submissive attitudes to white domination, and later, to a general underdevelopment and passivity which
worked in the interest of ruling elites.

Solarin returned to Nigeria in 1952, becoming the headmaster of a local school. When he
determined to remove religious instruction
from the school, he was sacked. In 1956 he
established his own school, calling it the
Mayflower, which went on to become one of
the leading educational institutions in his
country. Mayflower graduates developed a reputation for working harder, and for possessing
greater technological competence and independence of mind. The first woman engineer in
Nigeria was a graduate of the Mayflower.

Solarin was a fearless and public advocate
of **atheism**, **humanism**, and **democracy** in a
country used to uncritical acceptance of religious dogmas and superstitions. He suffered
detention on several occasions, the longest in
1984–85 when he was imprisoned for seventeen months for criticizing the military
regime then in power. He was survived by his
wife, Sheila, who has carried on his work.

SOLON (638–559 BCE, approx.). Athenian
lawmaker who anticipated many of the fundamental values of Western **democracy**. As
Archon, or chief magistrate, of Athens in 594
BCE, Solon was given the job of reforming
the Athenian constitution. In particular, Solon
saw that the wealthy enjoyed too strong a
hold over their dependants and debtors.
Without attacking the principle of **inequality**,
Solon reduced the permissible privileges of

the wealthy. He also introduced the notion of wealth being a determinant for participation in the political process, rather than the privilege of birth. These and his other actions established the principle that no individual is above the law. Solon entrenched this principle by formulating the principle of trial by jury and the right of appeal. Solon could easily have made himself the unquestioned tyrant of Athens, as others had done before him, but he had refused the title.

Solon was also a poet and an enthusiastic moralist. Some of his poems were political, while others praised love and the **good life**. Hundreds of years after Solon, Diogenes Laertius, an influential historian, wrote a book variously titled *Lives of the Greek Philosophers*, or *Lives of Eminent Philosophers*, in which he credits Solon with these ten moral maxims:

(1) Trust good **character** more than promises.
(2) Do not speak falsely.
(3) Do good things.
(4) Do not be hasty in making friends, but do not abandon them once made.
(5) Learn to obey before you command.
(6) When giving advice, do not recommend what is most pleasing, but what is most useful.
(7) Make reason your supreme commander.
(8) Do not associate with people who do bad things.
(9) Honor the gods.
(10) Have regard for your parents.

Solon's influence on later Greek thought was immense, and via the Greeks, his influence on the development of Western institutions should also be recognized as profound.

SOPHISTS. Traveling philosophers of ancient Greece who, for a fee, could speak on most subjects. The Sophists were, along with the other **Pre-Socratic** thinkers, pioneers of **philosophy**, social theory, and critical think-

ing. The principal Sophists were active in the fifth and fourth centuries BCE, although others who fit the title were active in later centuries. The Sophists were not so much a school of philosophy as they were a philosophical trade. They were valued because Greeks emphasized civic-mindedness and an ability to articulate one's views clearly and eloquently. These were the sorts of skills the Sophists imparted. As a rule, the Sophists were skeptics and agnostics.

They were hated by social conservatives who feared their teaching of **critical thinking** and questioning of **theology**, especially among the young. Three of the best known Sophists were **Protagoras**, Gorgias, and Hippias, all of whom are known only through the works of their opponents. This is a fate that has befallen nearly every single humanist and skeptical philosopher of the ancient world. **Plato** scoffed at the Sophist's habit of accepting fees for philosophizing, but such an attitude was easy for him, as he had an independent means of income. Plato was also suspicious of the idea that civic responsibility could be taught to anyone. For him, these skills belonged to a privileged few. Plato's hostility generally won the day, however, as the words "sophistry" or "sophistical" came to mean a subtle and dishonest playing with words. But the Sophists do not deserve the bad press they have had. The American historian Marvin Perry wrote: "The Western humanist tradition owes much to the Sophists, who examined political and ethical problems, cultivated the minds of their students, and invented formal secular education."

SOPHOCLES. See **GREEK PLAYWRIGHTS**.

SOPHROSYNE. A word used by Greek thinkers, from **Homer** to **Aristotle** and beyond, and for which there is no direct equivalent in English. The word derives from *sophron*, which means "of sound mind." It is best understood as a mix of self-knowledge, self-restraint, and moderation. **Greek play-wrights** like Aeschylus used sophrosyne in the sense of the mean between vices, much as **Aristotle** did later on in his **Doctrine of the Mean**.

Plato elevated sophrosyne to sit with justice, courage, and wisdom as the one of four cardinal virtues. He spoke of it as the condition where our emotions, our passions as he called them, acknowledge that Reason should have pride of place. The capital "R" for reason is not accidental. Plato did not just mean our human reasoning faculty, but our ability to grasp the cold, clear Reason which is the underlying principle of the world. Having made this step, Plato thought we could be called wise.

Plato's notion of Reason is illustrative of the weaknesses of the rationalist tradition in philosophy (see the entry on **rationalism**). The **Pre-Socratic** philosophers were closer to the truth when they argued that our passions are just as important as our reason (which the Pre-Socratics tended not to treat as worthy of a capital letter). Aristotle tended to speak of sophrosyne as the balanced point between the opposite vices in his ethical theory known as the Doctrine of the Mean. See the entries on **eupraxsophy** and **phronesis**.

SOROS, GEORGE (1930–). Capitalist, philosopher and philanthropist. George Soros was born in Hungary, living through the pro-fascist Horthy regime and subsequent Nazi and Soviet occupations. He fled Hungary in 1947 and moved to London, where he studied at the London School of Economics, graduating in 1952. While there, he came under the influence of the seminal Austrian-born philosopher **Karl Popper**. In 1956, Soros moved to the United States, where he built up a huge fortune through an international investment fund he created. He then created and ran the Soros Fund Management LLC.

He started a second career as one of the world's most active philanthropists in 1979. His first initiative was to provide funding for black students to attend the University of Cape Town in apartheid South Africa. In 1993 he founded the **Open Society Institute** (OSI) and a series of philanthropic organizations that are active in more than fifty countries.

Soros is the author of seven books, most on themes reminiscent of Karl Popper. They include: *The Alchemy of Finance* (1987), *Opening the Soviet System* (1990), *Underwriting Democracy* (1991), *Soros on Soros: Staying Ahead of the Curve* (1995), *The Crisis of Global Capitalism: Open Society Endangered* (1998), *Open Society: Reforming Global Capitalism* (2000), and *George Soros on Globalization* (2002). He is also a respected journalist and commentator. He has received honorary degrees from the New School for Social Research, the University of Oxford, the Budapest University of Economics, and Yale University. In 1995, the University of Bologna awarded Soros its highest honor, the Laurea Honoris Causa, in recognition of his efforts to promote open societies throughout the world. In 2004 he was elected to the **International Academy of Humanism**.

SOTHINGIST. Tongue-in-cheek term for the person who, when asked whether he believes in **God**, replies, "Well, there must be so'thing." Polls on religious belief often come up with sothingists: people who reject the idea of a personal god, but assume there must be "some sort" of higher power. See the entry on **mereymustification**.

SOUL. A religious concept involving the essence of the individual having no physical constitution of any kind and yet having the ability to control and regulate the physical body it is temporarily housed in. Ideas of the soul first took root in the West among Pythagoreans and slowly became a religious idea aiming at ultimate salvation consisting of liberation from the bondage of the body. For **Aristotle**, the soul simply meant being alive, or animate, so when we die, our soul dies too. All that lives on is **reason**. For **Descartes** it meant a substantial self, housed in an alien body. Following on from Descartes, some religious thinkers have even attempted to locate the soul in the human body. Needless to say, none of these attempts have been successful.

Scientific explanations require some verifiable causation for events, but the soul, according to most **monotheist** accounts, is accountable to **God** alone. But as concepts of God vary greatly, we find people's accounts of what a soul is, and what a soul is for, vary no less greatly. For centuries Christian theologians believed that the male embryo acquired a soul at the fortieth day, while the female embryo took eighty days. Most notions of the soul which are linked to monotheist religions have it vacating the body on **death** and carrying that individual's essence into some **supernatural** realm. By contrast, the **Asian traditions** place less emphasis on the soul as something worthy of an eternal existence. The Asian traditions talk more about the soul ultimately being fused into the universal reality. See the entry on **Eastern philosophy**.

There is no **evidence** that anything like a soul exists, and there is a great deal of evidence to show that the idea is impossible. It is an advanced form of **anthropocentric conceit** to consider our essential selves sufficiently grand to warrant cluttering up some corner of the universe for all time. See the entries on **astonishing hypothesis** and **cosmic modesty**.

Further reading: Jerome Elbert, *Are Souls Real?*; and Francis Crick, *The Astonishing Hypothesis*.

SOUL-MAKING DEFENSE. An attempt by the respected religious philosopher John Hick (1922–), to account for the **problem of evil**, one of the most intractable problems in the philosophy of religion. Hick's point is that evil in the world is necessary for the creation of conditions which can lead to acts of compassion between people—acts which build character and enrich the soul, thus enhancing people's chances for salvation.

Hick notes that the very randomness of natural evil (which is evil arising from natural disasters, as opposed to evil arising from the actions of people) is necessary to stimulate the sort of **character** that shows compassion and then fills a **soul** with goodness.

Critics of this defense include **Michael Martin**, who has countered that **God** could just as easily have created ways for us to develop these traits without all the suffering. Another criticism is that we could have had enough opportunities for character-building compassion simply from the acts of human evil without adding in acts of natural evil as well.

Further reading: Michael Martin, *Atheism, Morality, and Meaning*.

SOUTH PLACE ETHICAL SOCIETY. The world's longest-running **freethought** society. The society began in London as a nonconformist sect known as the Philadelphians in 1793 under the guidance of an American, Elhanan Winchester (1751–1797). More than anything, the Philadelphians were rebels against the calvinism inherent in much of the established church's doctrines and ways. Under the leadership of William Vidler (1758–1816), the congregation became **Unitarian** in 1802, and in 1816, the drift away from Christianity gathered pace under the leadership of William Johnstone Fox (1786–1864), who preached a vaguely deified **humanism**, stressing that the congregational bond should not be **faith**, but virtue. In 1824 the congregation moved into a new building on South Place in Finsbury.

Fox left the congregation under a cloud in 1852 and things looked bad for South Place for several years. During his brief tenure, Henry Barnett (1830–1872) tried to take the society back to traditional Christianity, but met with opposition from the congregation. All this changed in 1864 when **Moncure Conway**, recently arrived from the United States, took over the ailing organization. Over the next twenty years, Conway led South Place away from Unitarianism to an ethical **agnosticism**. He returned to the

United States in 1885, and was replaced by **Stanton Coit**, who transformed South Place into an ethical society with an open platform for rationalist and nonreligious ethical thinkers. See the entry on **ethical culture**. Conway returned in 1892, having completed his magisterial biography of **Thomas Paine**. Conway was the last of SPES's formal ministers. After him, South Place appointed a number of lecturers to take his place. They included some of the most famous freethinkers of the day like **Joseph McCabe** and **J. M. Robertson**.

In 1929 the society moved to new, custom-built premises at Red Lion Square in London called Conway Hall. The society is still there, and Conway Hall provides rooms for groups to meet and a large hall for chamber concerts. Since 1910, the society has hosted the Conway Memorial Lecture, which has attracted some very prominent thinkers, most notably **Bertrand Russell**, **A. J. Ayer**, **Margaret Knight**, **Marghanita Laski**, **Ted Honderich**, **Ernest Gellner**, and Sir Hermann Bondi (1919–2005). The society also publishes a regular journal, now called the *Ethical Record*, which has been published without a break since 1895, making it one of the oldest extant freethought periodicals in the world.

Further reading: I. D. MacKillop, *The British Ethical Societies*.

SOUTHWELL, CHARLES (1814–1860). Described as one of the romances of rationalism. The youngest of thirty-three children, Southwell had a tumultuous career as a **freethought** lecturer and journalist in Britain, Australia, and New Zealand. He came to freethought as a reaction to the smugness of a prominent Calvinist lecturer he had heard. He worked for the movement lead by **Robert Owen** before volunteering to fight for the British Legion in Spain against the reactionary Carlists. Upon his return Southwell worked for eighteen years as a freethought lecturer and writer, during which time he founded the explicitly atheist paper, the *Oracle of Reason*. In February 1842 he and his friend **George Jacob Holyoake** went to prison for **blasphemy** as a result of remarks made in that paper.

An argument with Holyoake after their release made it difficult for Southwell to earn money as a freethought lecturer, so he left for Australia. He quickly got into trouble there and moved on to New Zealand, becoming the first acknowledged freethinker to appear on New Zealand shores, arriving in Auckland from Sydney on January 29, 1856. Less than three months after arriving in Auckland, Southwell was in public life, giving lectures in support of the allies against Russia in the Crimean War, and on items of local politics. On December 11, 1856, the first issue of the *Auckland Examiner*, Southwell's last and most enduring newspaper, rolled off the press. The *Examiner* was a project close to Southwell's heart, and he persevered with it despite financial hardship and the decline in his own health.

He had mellowed since his early days of aggressive **atheism** in England, where he had been imprisoned for a fierce denunciation of the Bible. In the *Examiner*, he directed his attention more toward local politics. When he commented on **religion**, it was usually in the context of religion being used as a cloak for public righteousness. Southwell died, apparently of tuberculosis, in 1860. The **Charles Southwell Awards** are named after him.

Further reading: Bill Cooke, "Charles Southwell: New Zealand's First Freethinker," www.nzarh.org.nz/document/southwell.htm.

SOYINKA, WOLE (1934–). One of the most prominent living Nigerians. Wole Soyinka was born in Abeokuta, in southwestern Nigeria. He studied at Ibadan and at Leeds University in England. He abandoned his budding career in theater and returned to Nigeria after his homeland became independent in 1960. There he became politically active in opposition to the military regime led by General Gowon, serving a term of imprisonment between 1967 and 1969. This became the subject of his book *The Man Died* (1972). Upon his release, he was involved in academia in Nigeria and abroad and was particularly active as a writer. He won the Nobel Prize for Literature in 1986—the first black African to win this distinction.

Growing respectability did not prevent Soyinka from continuing to oppose military regimes in Nigeria. Things got so bad during the dictatorship of Sani Abacha that he fled the country to escape a death sentence. While in exile, he wrote *The Open Sore of a Continent* (1996) which was a strong criticism of misrule in Africa, particularly in Nigeria. He dedicated that book to **Tai Solarin**. In this and other writings Soyinka made no secret of his opinion that religious extremism played an important role in the problems besetting Africa. As if to vindicate this view, a Muslim cleric issued a *fatwa* calling for Soyinka's death.

Soyinka has written: "Humanism for me represents taking the human entity as the center of world perception, of social organization and indeed of ethics, deciding in other words what is primarily of the greatest value for humans as opposed to some remote extraterrestrial or ideological authority."

SPANISH INQUISITION, THE. A long-standing attempt by the Roman Catholic Church to coerce uniformity of belief among Catholics and those outside the church. It was in Spain where the Inquisition took on its most systematic form. The main task of the Inquisition in Spain, originally at least, was to test the orthodoxy of the forcibly converted Jews. A succession of **anti-Semitic** legislation in the fourteenth and fifteenth centuries led to the creation of a large community of newly converted Jews, or *conversos*. It was widely believed that most *conversos* still practiced their Jewish faith in private and the Inquisition was established to test this thesis out.

A papal **Inquisition**, run by the Dominicans but directly responsible to Rome, had operated in Aragon for about a century. It was in November 1478 that Sixtus IV empowered

an Inquisition for all of Spain, once more under Dominican supervision. The Inquisition began its activities in Seville in 1480, burning six *conversos* at the stake and forcing thousands to flee their homes. This encouraged the establishment of other Inquisitions around the country. Tomas de Torquemada (1420–1498) was appointed along with six others on February 11, 1482, and a year later became the first inquisitor-general over all of Spain. Torquemada set the standard for inquisitorial zeal by organizing a large book burning at his monastery in Salamanca, a precedent followed by his successors. In its first eight years of service the Inquisition in Seville alone burned seven hundred people and punished in other ways seven thousand. Ironically, Torquemada had a strong component of Jewish ancestry, something which may have fueled his hatred for Jews.

After the conquest of Granada in 1492 the Moors were granted the free exercise of their religion and were to be regarded as free subjects of the crown. But it seems unlikely that Ferdinand and Isabella took these guarantees seriously. Nor was the Inquisition happy with this example of **pluralism**. From 1499 attitudes toward the Moors hardened and persecutions became more frequent. In 1567 all Moorish customs and language were outlawed and Moorish religious literature was destroyed. This precipitated a desperate Moorish rebellion in 1568, which was put down with great brutality. The Inquisition supported the eventual expulsion of the Moriscos from Spain in 1609.

The rise of Lutheranism in Germany gave the Inquisition its next danger. Reading any Lutheran works was formally banned in April 1525 and persecution of Erasmian Catholics proceeded apace after that. The Dutch scholar **Erasmus** enjoyed a brief popularity in Spain in the early decades of the sixteenth century, but got caught up in the general persecution of Protestantism. The Spanish Inquisition issued its first **Index of Forbidden Books** in 1559, and by 1612 it included all the works of Erasmus.

The chief point of difference between the Inquisition and secular justice of the time was the practice of protecting the identity of informers and conducting the trials in secret. Neither of these practices existed at the beginning of the Inquisition, but they developed quickly after its first few years. The Inquisition was responsible for creating a climate of fear, when the most trivial comment or action made one liable to being denounced to the Inquisition.

The normal procedure was that the charge against the accused was put before a theologian who would determine if in fact **heresy** was involved. In practice, this often involved lengthy delays and many people were in prison for two or more years before facing a trial, or being told they were free to go. The cost of maintaining the prisoner was, in most cases, met by the family, which often resulted in complete destitution. It is thought about a third of prisoners were subjected to torture.

The accused usually waited for days, weeks, sometime even years before even being told what they were accused of. Instead the inquisitors would visit the accused on three occasions asking him to search his conscience, confess the **truth**, and trust the mercy of the Inquisition. Eventually the accused would be told of the charges and would be required to respond to them immediately. Occasionally the accused would have some sort of legal counsel, usually an Inquisition appointee. Even when told the charges the accused would not be told the identity of his accusers or what evidence existed to support the charge.

The Inquisition slowly lost its popular support in the eighteenth century as it turned its face against the works of **Enlightenment** thinkers who were advocating reforms, justice, and **toleration**. These matters had less to do with the Inquisition's core role of eliminating heresy and more to do with politics, and so lost popularity among the intellectuals and, most crucially, the political machinery. The last victims of the Spanish Inquisition were in 1826: a Jew burned at the stake and a Quaker who was hanged for introducing a Protestant hymn into his school assembly.

Further reading: Henry Kamen, *The Spanish Inquisition.*

SPECIESISM. The assertion that one's own species is of prime concern, and that all other species can be treated or mistreated in the interest of that one species. Peter Singer, DeCamp Professor of Bioethics at the University Center for Human Values at Princeton University, has been credited with coining the term. Speciesism is the highest form of **anthropocentric conceit.** *Homo sapiens* is the only species capable of operating along speciesist lines. **Humanism** is not the same as speciesism because humanism understands humanity's place as one species among many that share our planet. There are examples of speciesist thinking among evolutionists, but it is the old **supernaturalist** worldviews that succumb most openly to the temptations of speciesism. Speciesism is built into the **scriptures** of **monotheist** religions and in the notion of the **great chain of being**. Even setting aside the intrinsic right of other species to their place on the planet, it is in humanity's interest to think and act interdependently with all the other species we share the planet with. See the entry on **diversity**.

A more charged question is whether or not the scientific testing of animals amounts to speciesism. Animal liberationists would argue that it does whereas most scientists would reject the charge. The charge is not valid in the end because the use of animals for scientific purposes does not imply an attitude that this is all the animals are good for, or that humans have an inalienable right to this sort of usage. Using animals for scientific experiments actually reinforces the sense of interdependence *Homo sapiens* has with other animal species. Few people argue, however, with the need to reduce suffering and exploitation of animals when it is unnecessary.

Some of the worst instances of speciesism are rarely, if ever, criticized. For example, many traditional cultures have notoriously speciesist attitudes toward certain animals, the parts of which are thought, quite incorrectly, to be an aphrodisiac or some such thing.

SPENCER, HERBERT (1820–1903). The man with the dubious honor of having risen to and fallen from prominence more quickly and more totally than any other serious thinker. It is almost required to sneer at Herbert Spencer now; his prose is always turgid, his nonacademic background as an engineer is held against him, as are his vanity and sexual hangups. But in his own day, Spencer was hailed as the most profound new philosopher since **Aristotle** and his books influenced two generations of thinkers in the second half of the nineteenth century.

Spencer was a philosopher of evolution who, in 1857, conceived of a vastly ambitious program of reimagining the world in terms of evolutionary thinking. This project he called synthetic philosophy and included some works already written, in particular *Principles of Psychology* (1855), to which was added *First Principles* (1862) and followed with *Principles of Biology* (1864, 1867). Other works, not all of which were part of the synthetic philosophy, include *Education* (1861), *The Man versus the State* (1870), *Data of Ethics* (1879), and *Autobiography* (1904).

It was Spencer's goal to understand **evolution** in terms of **progress** as conceived in nineteenth-century terms. His work can be seen as a libertarian mirror image of the project Karl Marx (1818–1883) undertook with regard to **Marxism**. Spencer understood evolution in the progressionist terms inspired largely by **Jean Baptiste de Lamarck**. Also, Spencer is often saddled with the blame for **Social Darwinism**, although he was far from alone in expounding those sorts of thoughts. Spencer's single biggest contribution here was to coin the phrase "survival of the fittest," which **Charles Darwin** later adopted and later still was taken up by social Darwinists. With the advantage of hindsight we can now see that Spencer's progressionism and social Darwinism were mistaken—as Marxism has also been proven to be wrong.

Several points about Spencer should be borne in mind before we rush to condemn. For one thing, Spencer was admired as much for his method as for his conclusions. Spencer was hailed as the epitome of the **scientific attitude** by people across the religious divide. He was also very influential among the growing class of wealthy businessmen in the United States because he gave them a *modus operandi*. He also deserves recognition for his tremendously important role in providing much of the terminology and conceptual apparatus for the discipline of sociology. And finally, he deserves credit for attempting, no matter how clumsily as we would now see it, a **consilience** of the universe. Spencer can hardly be accused of **reductionism**.

SPINOZA, BARUCH (1632–1677). Thought by Bertrand Russell to be the most lovable of all the great philosophers. Spinoza was the first great philosopher to attempt a comprehensive philosophy in the light of the new thinking about the heliocentric **universe**, particularly as articulated by **Giordano Bruno**. Spinoza spoke in terms of *sub specie aeternitatis*, or "from the viewpoint of eternity." His was truly a **cosmic perspective**.

Spinoza was born in Amsterdam to Jewish parents who had fled Catholic persecution in their native Portugal. His brilliance was soon apparent, and was to cost him dearly. He was given a rabbinical education, but his interest in the new sciences of optics and astronomy as well as his unorthodox religious views led to his expulsion from the Jewish community in 1656. After his excommunication he changed his name to Benedict and took employment in various cities around Holland, before settling in the Hague in 1670, the year his most famous book was published. Even in relatively tolerant Holland it would have been dangerous to acknowledge publication of the *Tractatus Theologico-Politicus*, but despite being published anonymously, the book was banned in 1674.

The *Tractatus Theologico-Politicus* looked at biblical authority and sources in secular and scholarly terms, and without the distracting lens of **faith**. Rather optimistically, Spinoza claimed that the Bible, when properly understood, supports freedom of scientific and philosophical research. But "properly understood" meant relinquishing most of the facts and doctrine of the Bible, and focusing instead on its spirit. Spinoza also championed the secular state.

His other great work, *Ethics* (1677), was published after his death. *Ethics* was no less radical than the *Tractatus*. It rejected notions of a personal creator, **free will**, and personal **immortality**, and spoke instead of **God** as an all-encompassing substance which pervades mind and matter. Spinoza's God was pantheistic. Spinoza also rejected the strict dualism between **mind** and matter that **Descartes** had advanced. Instead, he argued that the universe was composed of one fundamental substance, which he called at various times nature or God.

Spinoza died young, from the combined effects of consumption and the accumulation of glass dust in his lungs from the lens grinding and polishing business he lived by.

SPIRITUAL EXCELLENCES. A term used by English philosopher **L. Susan Stebbing** in the context of her account of humanist **ethics**. Stebbing listed the spiritual excellences as:

- **love** for other human beings;
- delight in creative activities of all kinds;
- respect for **truth** and the satisfaction in learning to know what is true about the world and about ourselves;
- loyalty to other human beings;
- generosity of thought and sympathy with those who suffer, and hatred of cruelty and other evils;
- delight in the beauty of nature and in art; and
- to have experience of pain and of for-

going what would be good for oneself in order that the needs of others may be met.

Stebbing had no problem with using the word "spiritual," although she recognized many humanists object to the term. She made it quite clear, however, that these "excellences are to be found in *this* world; no heaven is needed to experience them." See the entry on **spirituality**.

Further reading: L. Susan Stebbing, *Ideals and Illusions*.

SPIRITUAL SCHIZOPHRENIA. The condition among Christians of inhabiting an intellectual world which takes cognizance of the Copernican revolution, while still inhabiting the emotional world of the pre-Copernican Bible, which features a prominent personal **God** who is interested in our welfare and who created earth at the center of the universe. See the entry on **heliocentric universe**. This is the world inhabited by a growing number of **fundamentalists**.

This condition was identified and named by the New Zealand religious humanist theologian Lloyd Geering (1918–) in his book *God in the New World* (1968). This book, and the crisis in modern religion he identified, came after an unsuccessful charge of **heresy** was brought against him by conservatives in the Presbyterian Church of which Geering was an ordained minister. Geering's solution, pursued over the next thirty-five years, was a form of **religious humanism** strongly influenced by Wilfred Cantwell Smith (1916–2001) and Paul Tillich (1886–1965).

SPIRITUALISM. An unorthodox religious movement that flourished between the 1850s and 1930s. The basic principle of spiritualism was the belief that human beings survive bodily death and that those still living can, on occasions, communicate with them. At a time when confidence in traditional religious dogmas was in decline, spiritualism provided a new vehicle for people anxious to reconcile science and **religion**.

Spiritualism began in western New York and was dogged from the beginning by charlatans and fraudsters. Many people genuinely believed they had discovered a new fact of science, one that could reconcile it to a broader reality of theism. But others saw an opportunity to extract money from gullible people. So pervasive was the tendency to fraud that the movement never established fully its reputation as either a new science or a new religion.

Spiritualism also gave room for various other movements to grow, such as vegetarianism, **Theosophy**, dress reform, and **alternative medicine**. Spiritualism became very popular toward the end of World War I, fueled by the grief of people who had lost loved ones in the war and were willing to grab onto anything that would help them deal with the tragedy. But after some photographs of fairies which Sir Arthur Conan Doyle (1859–1930) made the mistake of believing genuine were exposed as a fraud, the craze fell away.

Further reading: Ruth Brandon, *The Spiritualists*.

SPIRITUALITY. Oddly enough, a divisive issue among freethinkers. Is it appropriate for people who don't believe in **God** or a **supernatural** dimension to speak of "spirituality" or "having a spiritual dimension"? Some believe that the word is inevitably bound up with its supernatural associations and shouldn't be used. Others see no harm in using this word to express our strongest convictions or, in the language of the theologian Paul Tillich (1886–1965), our ultimate concern. **Bertrand Russell** expressed the problem well when he said with respect to his use of "atheist" or "agnostic," it depends who the audience is. Among philosophers he would speak of himself as an agnostic, but to general audiences he would describe himself as an atheist, in both cases, so as not to be misunderstood.

As with many disputes, it depends what is

meant by "spirituality." So long as no supernatural element is understood by it, it probably does no harm. But, as opponents of the term say, one cannot use "spirituality" meaningfully without presupposing some dimension above and beyond what is natural. See the entry on **cranes and skyhooks**. **Tom Flynn**, the editor of *Free Inquiry* magazine, opposes the use of the word, and in 2002 gathered ninety-five words that could be used as alternatives. But many of those who use the word argue that it is a mistake to get too tied up over semantics. Spirituality has an important meaning, and it is wrong to concede to the religious people a monopoly over this term.

Some freethinkers who use the word *spirituality* include the American philosopher Robert C. Solomon, who speaks of spirituality as "the thoughtful love of life." And **Carl Sagan** used the word more in the sense of **awe** and wonder when he wrote that "Science is not only compatible with spirituality; it is a profound source of spirituality." And see the entry on **spiritual excellences**.

Further reading: Robert C. Solomon, *Spirituality for the Skeptic*; and Tom Flynn, "When Words Won't Die," *Free Inquiry* 22, no. 3 (Summer 2002): 50–51.

SPITTELER, CARL FRIEDRICH GEORG (1845–1924). Influential Swiss poet and Nobel Prize winner (1919, literature). Spitteler originally trained for the church at Heidelberg, but lost his faith during his study. He remained non-, even antitheist for the rest of his life.

After spending his early years as a private tutor in Russia and Finland, Spitteler returned to Switzerland where he wrote his epic poem, *Prometheus and Epimetheus* (1881), which is thought to have exercised a strong influence on **Friedrich Nietzsche**. Spitteler's other great poem, *The Olympic Spring*, was originally composed between 1900 and 1905, and then revised in 1910. This was the work that earned Spitteler his Nobel Prize. It was later published under the title *Prometheus the*

Long-Suffering. He also wrote short stories, a novel called *Imago* (1906), memoirs, and a criticism of one-sided pro-Germanism.

STALINISM. A perversion of **Marxism** which helped drag the whole Marxist enterprise into the very dustbin of history it had so enthusiastically consigned to other ideas. Stalinism was built up in the Soviet Union by Joseph Stalin (1878–1953) into one of the most centralized forms of **totalitarianism** ever devised. Other countries whose political systems could fairly be described as Stalinist include Albania under Enver Hoxha, Iraq under Saddam Hussein, North Korea under Kim Jong Il, and Turkmenistan under "Turkmenbashi," Suparmurat Niyazov. Stalinism usually involves a massive, state-run program of terror, a personality cult around the leader, and a bunker mentality regarding the outside world.

Several people have noted the religious parallels in Stalinism. Like a cult, Stalinism had an infallible leader and an imposing set of dogmas, scriptures, and rituals. And, just as important, Stalinism offered a clear vision of the enemy. Being branded a "kulak," "capitalist," "reactionary," "insurrectionist," or "bandit," was important in terms of the religious nomenclature (think of the differences between "heretic," "heathen," "apostate," and so on) but usually brought about the same deadly conclusion.

STANTON, ELIZABETH CADY (1815–1902). Pioneering American freethinker and feminist. Stanton began her career as a campaigner against **slavery** but moved on to concentrate on the plight of women's **inequality**. Stanton, with her mentor **Lucretia Coffin Mott**, was instrumental in convening the first convention devoted to the issues of women's inequality, in particular, the right to vote. The convention took place on July 19–20, 1848, in Seneca Falls, New York, and produced what was called the *Declaration of Rights and Sentiments*. The declaration attacked infringements on women's rights in the language of the American constitution, with its talk of universal **rights**. It also recognized the role religion has played in restricting women's lives. Today, a fine museum stands on the site of the conference.

Over the next half century, Stanton fought tirelessly for the rights of women. With her lifelong friend **Susan B. Anthony**, Stanton founded the National Woman Suffrage Association (NWSA) in 1869 and remained its president until 1893. The title of the organization notwithstanding, Stanton and Anthony saw women's emancipation as a wider program than simply getting the vote. The vote was simply the first step. Along with Susan B. Anthony, Stanton edited the four-volume *History of Women Suffrage* (1881–1886).

As she got older, Stanton became more impatient with the stultifying effects organized religion had on women, and she devoted more of her attention to liberating women from religious superstition. Stanton was a friend and admirer of **Robert Ingersoll**. Her last major work was a controversial project called *The Woman's Bible* (1895), a commentary on the passages in the Bible that discuss women and women's roles, with criticisms of the misogyny inherent in most of them. *The Woman's Bible* was a very bold project, and has not received the respect it deserves as a landmark of biblical criticism. It sold very well, going through seven impressions in its first six months and being translated into several languages. This project lost Stanton a lot of friends and helped marginalize her from the women's movement. In the same way that **Thomas Paine**'s posthumous reputation was ruined after he wrote *The Age of Reason*, so did Stanton's reputation suffer after her publication of *The Woman's Bible*. Stanton's more conservative successors as leaders of the suffrage movement strove to diminish her contribution to the cause.

Further reading: Kathi Kern, *Mrs. Stanton's Bible*; and Susan Jacoby, *Freethinkers: A History of American Secularism*.

STATE OF NATURE. An idea made famous

by the English philosopher **Thomas Hobbes**, who wanted to make a case for the existence of **morality** without the traditional recourse to **supernatural** power or innate moral senses. Hobbes wrote about the state of nature in his masterpiece, *Leviathan* (1651). He is widely believed to have been an atheist. What he did was to postulate that humanity's natural condition is the moral free-for-all, which he called the state of nature. In the state of nature there are no rules and no political authority to enforce rules. Even the strong person can be brought down by a coalition of the weak. This is the context for his famous passage that life in the state of nature is "solitary, poor, nasty, brutish and short." So, it is in everyone's interest to negotiate the end of this condition and to devise rules which all will agree to abide by.

The pivotal idea in Hobbes's conception of the state of nature is negotiation. Only when people recognize the basic evils and dangers of the state of nature will they be prepared to negotiate away the total freedom the state of nature provides them for a measure of stability and order. Hobbes went on to advocate a strong, centralized state under a powerful sovereign as the only effective force to counter our native disposition toward the conditions of the state of nature.

John Locke also used the idea of the state of nature, but not in the service of a powerful sovereign. Rather, Locke used the state-of-nature motif in the service of a free people who make contracts with their rulers—contracts that can be rescinded if the rulers overstep the mark. And **Jean-Jacques Rousseau** spoke of the state of nature, but this time in the context of the idyllic space where the noble savage was free from the trammels of urban corruption. See the entry on **Romanticism**.

STEBBING, L. SUSAN (1885–1943). The first female professor of philosophy in Britain and an unjustly forgotten thinker. The youngest of six children of Charles Stebbing, a London barrister, and Elizabeth Elstob, a granddaughter of George Elstob, the earl of Durham. Both her parents died while she was still very young and Lizzie (her first name) was brought up by a guardian.

Stebbing always suffered from indifferent health. Her preferred course of study while at Girton College, Cambridge, was classics, but this was considered too demanding, so she studied history. A chance discovery of F. H. Bradley's *Appearance and Reality*, then an influential work of metaphysics, led her on to philosophy.

Before 1920 she had a variety of appointments before being appointed a full-time lecturer at Bedford College, London, in 1920. In 1933 she became full professor of philosophy, the first woman in Britain to attain this honor. Her areas of interest were mathematical logic, philosophy of science, and the theory of language. Under the influence of **Ludwig Wittgenstein**, she helped found the academic journal *Analysis*, which looked to publishing philosophical articles which were short, to the point, and free from any of the aimless theorizing that Wittgenstein so abhorred.

A formidable **smiter of humbug**, Stebbing came down strongly against pretentious or woolly thought. Chief among her targets were the theistic astronomers Sir James Jeans and Sir Arthur Eddington, both of whom had strayed from their area of specialty to pronounce on the role of God in the universe. In *Philosophy and the Physicists* (1937) the two men were subjected to some stern criticism. Stebbing also wrote a well-regarded popular work *Thinking to Some Purpose* and *Ideal and Illusions* (1941).

This said, she was deeply admired by her students, for whom her door was always open. She produced her account of the **spiritual excellences**, one of the most moving summaries of humanist ethics ever written. She died at her home in Tintagel, Cornwall, at only fifty-seven. Stebbing was an agnostic and was active in the Ethical Union. She served as honorary associate of the **Rationalist Press Association**.

STEIN, GORDON (1941–1996). American scholar of **freethought**. Stein obtained a PhD in physiology from Ohio State University in 1974, and taught for a while at the University of Rhode Island. At the time of his death he was director of libraries at the **Center for Inquiry**. He was instrumental in bringing together the most comprehensive freethought library in the world. His own large collection went to the Center for Inquiry upon his death.

Stein had a long career in the freethought movement. He was editor of the *American Rationalist* from 1978 until 1996, and became a senior editor of *Free Inquiry* in 1993. He compiled an annotated guide to the works of **Robert Ingersoll** in 1969 and a descriptive bibliography of freethought in the United States in 1978, and Britain and the Commonwealth in 1981. In 1990 he compiled *God Pro and Con: A Bibliography of Atheism*. He also edited *An Anthology of Atheism and Rationalism* (1980) and *A Second Anthology of Atheism and Rationalism* (1987) and three substantial reference works: *The Encyclopedia of Unbelief* (1985), *The Encyclopedia of Hoaxes* (1993), and the *Encyclopedia of the Paranormal* (1996).

STEPHEN, LESLIE (1832–1904). English scholar and agnostic. Born into a privileged family, Stephen was educated at Eton, King's College, London, and Trinity Hall, Cambridge. Less usual for someone of his background, Stephen was raised a fervent Evangelical, being part of the Clapham Sect. He was ordained as a minister but lost his **faith**. This was not that unusual, but Stephen's next step was. He left the church in 1870 and became known as an outspoken agnostic. While the word was coined by **T. H. Huxley**, it was Stephen's writings on the subject that gave **agnosticism** its vogue, in particular *An Agnostic's Apology* (1893). This essay had a long life, as it was reprinted by an organization he helped to found: the **Rationalist Press Association**. He argued that there are limits to the **knowledge** humans can acquire, and beyond those limits it is foolish to dog-matize, whether for or against **religion**. But within what we can know, it is apparent that evidence for God's existence is absent, and that religious systems are but metaphysical creations.

Stephen's two great contributions to English scholarship were writing *The History of English Thought in the Eighteenth Century* (1876) and serving as the first editor of the *Dictionary of National Biography* (1882–1891). He also helped found the influential *Pall Mall Gazette*. Another important work was *Science of Ethics* (1882), where he explored the conditions for objective ethics in the absence of an afterlife to act as an inducement and threat.

Stephen was a generous benefactor to young talent he saw coming along. In particular, he did much to encourage the career of the young **Joseph McCabe**, who maintained a lifelong admiration of Stephen in return. Stephen was the father of the artist Vanessa Bell (1879–1961) and the novelist Virginia Woolf (1882–1941).

Further reading: Noel Annan, *Leslie Stephen: The Godless Victorian*.

STODDARD, LOTHROP (1883–1950). Proof, if any is needed, that no system of belief has a **monopoly on truth** or virtue. Lothrop Stoddard was an American writer and **Unitarian**, and author of a book called *Scientific Humanism* (1926). He was the only child of a privileged Massachusetts family, and he took a PhD at Harvard University in 1914, having already studied law there.

Scientific Humanism was a popular study of the humanist idea as he understood it. Stoddard pleaded for open-mindedness, a scientific spirit of inquiry, and a reconciliation between **religion** and **science**. Little hint was given of his principal area of interest, the tone of which had been set with his PhD. Entitled *The French Revolution in Santo Domingo*, Stoddard told of the horrific slaughter of whites by black slaves. His fifteen other books all pursued this theme; they followed his grand theory of a **clash of civilizations**. Excerpts of his books can be found on extremist and white supremacist Web sites to this day.

His best known book was *The Rising Tide of Color Against White-World Supremacy* (1920) in which he warned of the dire consequences of the white races relinquishing their hold on the inferior colored peoples of the earth. *The New World of Islam* (1921); *The Revolt Against Civilization: The Menace of the Underman* (1922), a study of Bolshevism; and *Racial Realities in Europe* (1924) all continued the theme.

Not surprisingly, Stoddard was also an enthusiastic eugenicist and **anti-Semite**; his works were used in Nazi textbooks. Stoddard actually met **Adolf Hitler** and Joseph Goebbels in 1940. The outcome of the war and the erosion of any scientific credibility for **eugenics** meant that Stoddard was largely ignored in his last years.

STOICISM. A noble worldview from ancient Greece, founded by Zeno of Citium (333–262 BCE), a student at Plato's **Academy**. Much of the thought that is characteristically Stoic was developed by Cleanthes and, especially, Chrysippus (280–207 BCE). Later prominent Stoics included **Seneca**, **Marcus Aurelius**, and **Epictetus**. As is sadly common with these ancient philosophies, most of their writings of the earlier Stoics has been lost or destroyed by enemies.

The main focus of Stoicism was to live virtuously, which meant following nature, or living according to natural law, another idea developed by Stoics. To live according to natural law required us to understand nature, and stoic ethics derived from that study. The Stoics counseled a brand of wisdom that involved the submission of our desires while giving free rein to our thoughts. They spoke of **cosmopolis**, as the universal city, where, united by our human reason, we could live together. These themes of cosmic determination and human freedom remained constant throughout the career of Stoicism.

Stoic thought shared with **Epicureanism** a firm **naturalism**. Stoics opposed **Plato's** theory of forms, arguing that these forms were just constructions of the mind, itself a physical phenomenon. Similarly, the Stoics did not believe in an immortal **soul** or in any sort of afterlife. However, Stoics did believe in an orderly universe and usually posited a fiery breath, or *pneuma*, which exercises control, a very distant control, over it. So thoroughly planned was the universe, that it unfolds again and again in exactly the same way, for all time. More than two thousand years later the German philosopher **Friedrich Nietzsche** would say the same thing, although he called it the **eternal recurrence**.

In the face of this onward cosmic march, Stoics advocated acceptance of what we cannot change. Once again, this principle has a later parallel in Nietzsche's notion of *amor fati*, or love of necessity. But unlike Nietzsche, the Stoics set a high value on a life of public service and the commonwealth of man.

Stoicism has been subjected to several lines of criticism. On the one hand Christians and others have disparaged Stoicism's inability to provide consolation for the poor and dispossessed, but this undervalues the role played by Epictetus, a former slave and advocate of clear-minded acceptance of the inevitable and detachment from what is not in our power to alter. This criticism also confuses providing consolation and offering illusions as a consolation. The Stoics were opposed to peddling illusions as a means of consolation. See the entry on the **good life**.

Other critics have accused the Stoics of accepting injustices in the world too placidly. Neither is this fair, as Stoics did not—like the **Cynics**—preach withdrawal from public affairs, but developed a mature acceptance of what one can realistically hope to achieve. The Stoic ideal was the active citizen, involved in the affairs of his city, but not getting too carried away with it all. Marcus Aurelius did not write his *Meditations* while idling in Rome, but while campaigning against barbarian invasions. Perhaps the most just criticism of Stoicism is that it is without **humor** or lightness of touch, but much of what happens in the world is not conducive to either of these.

Stoic thought was very influential, being the outlook most followed by educated Romans for five hundred years. Stoicism bequeathed significant ideas in ethics and philosophy to **Neoplatonism** and Christianity which followed it. Many of the elements of Christianity that its apologists think are unique to it were in fact part of Stoic thought centuries earlier. By the third century CE Stoicism had very largely disappeared, its most important teachings having been taken over by Christianity.

STOPES, MARIE CARMICHAEL (1880–1958). English scientist and pioneer for birth control. Born in Edinburgh, Marie Stopes was educated privately until she was twelve. She went on to University College, London, and the University of Munich, where she took a PhD in 1904. That year she became a lecturer in botany, and in the process became the first female science lecturer in Britain. In her capacity as a scientist, Stopes wrote *Ancient Plants* (1910) and the two-volume *Cretaceous Flora* (1913–15).

Her first marriage, to a Canadian botanist, R. R. Gates, was unhappy and ended in 1916. Her experiences from this marriage provided the stimulus for her work in talking about women's health and **sex** issues. Her own experiences also provided the background for her sensitive book *Married Love* (1916), which argued that sex could become a positive force for the ongoing satisfaction of a marriage. Her book caused a sensation and was banned in the United States. Of her vast output, her most important books were *Wise Parenthood* (1918); *Contraception: Its Theory, History and Practice* (1923), and *Sex and Religion* (1929). These books sold very well, which did nothing to allay the opposition from conservative church groups to her work.

In 1921 Stopes and her second husband Humphrey Roe founded their first birth-control clinic, in the London district of Islington. Until Stopes's work, it was pretty much

impossible to speak about contraception. Stopes faced bitter opposition to her work from the churches and the medical profession, both of which feared a diminution of their respective areas of authority. Her legal struggles went all the way to the House of Lords.

Toward the end of her life, she became enamored of **mysticism**, and wrote some poetry to give expression to her thoughts on the subject. She died of cancer in 1958. Her son, Harry Stopes-Roe (1924–) went on to become a prominent British philosopher and humanist. See the entries on **Olympe de Gouge**, **Margaret Sanger**, and **Ettie Rout**.

STOPPARD, TOM (1937–). Born Tom Straussler in what is now the Czech Republic, his family fled the Nazis in 1939 by moving to Singapore. In 1941, Straussler along with his mother and brother left for India to escape the Japanese. His father stayed behind and was killed. After the war his mother married Captain Kenneth Stoppard and they went to Britain to live.

Stoppard left school at seventeen and became a journalist, soon showing great talent as a theater critic. His first television play was *A Walk on the Water* (1963), but his major breakthrough was with *Rosencrantz and Guildenstern are Dead* (1966), which took a new look at Hamlet through the eyes of the two minor Jewish characters.

Stoppard has also been responsible for some very influential screenplays, most notably *Brazil* (1985) coauthored with Terry Gilliam and Charles McKeown. He has won many awards, including sharing an Oscar with Marc Norman for Best Screenplay Award for *Shakespeare in Love* (1998).

A longtime supporter of progressive issues, he has worked actively with Amnesty International for many years. Among other work done for Amnesty was the television play *Professional Foul* (1977), which was Stoppard's contribution to the Prisoner of Conscience Year (a UN initiative to raise awareness of political prisoners). He is also an atheist, and is an honorary associate of the

National Secular Society. In 2000 he was made a member of the Order of Merit, an order limited to no more than twenty-four people at any one time.

STRATEGIC INFORMATION. A term employed by anthropologist Pascal Boyer to refer to information that activates the part of our brain that regulates social interaction. Different information can be strategic to different people, but gossip and personal confidences constitute some of the most widespread strategic information in the world. Any information that affects our **knowledge** of ourselves and others in social contexts, thus affecting our relative statuses, is strategic information. The widespread human anxiety about being the subject of gossip boils down to the anxiety that others have access to strategic information about ourselves. This anxiety has an evolutionary origin.

Part of the explanation of the popularity of supernatural agents like gods and spirits, is that they are usually deemed to have access to a lot more strategic information than mortals. See the entry on **memes**.

Further reading: Pascal Boyer, *Religion Explained*.

STRATO THE PHYSICIST (340s/30s–269 BCE). An important person in history, science, and philosophy, but about whom we know very little. Strato was born in Lampsacus and had clearly become a very well-known scholar by the time Ptolemy I Soter called him to Egypt to supervise the education of his son Ptolemy II Philadelpus, who himself went on to found the **Alexandria library** and museum. Strato was summoned from Alexandria to succeed **Theophrastus** as head of the Lyceum, **Aristotle**'s school. Strato is known to have written about forty treatises, but none of them have survived except as excerpts in the works of others. Strato was known after his death as "the physicist"—physics in the Greek sense of natural philosopher. He is also known as Strato of Lampsacus.

His chief contribution was to take further than any other thinker in antiquity the **scientific method** of observation, even to the point of constructing apparatus for the solution of a specific problem. He developed ideas concerning vacuums to a point not surpassed for fifteen hundred years. His contributions to psychology were also significant. And he dismissed all notions of anthropomorphic gods and **teleology**. See the entry on the **Stratonician Presumption**.

Strato also disagreed with Aristotle's idea of the mortality of the **soul** (*psyche*) and **immortality** of the intellect (*nous*). This had the effect of recognizing the kinship of man with the animals. Unlike many earlier thinkers, Strato taught that humans were superior animals, rather than animals being degenerate humans. Diogenes Laertius said of him that he "excelled in every branch of learning but most of all in that which is styled the philosophy of nature, a branch of philosophy more ancient and serious than the others."

STRATONICIAN PRESUMPTION, THE. A formula developed by **Antony Flew** to demonstrate the presumption of atheism. Named after **Strato the physicist**, the next but one successor to **Aristotle** as head of his school, the Lyceum. Flew developed Strato's **naturalism** into an ingenious argument for the priority of **atheism**.

It is one of the most fundamental premises of **philosophy** that the least complicated argument is to be favored over the more tortuous or convoluted argument. This is because an economical argument has fewer possibilities for error. This is known as **Ockham's Razor**. Now, the Stratonician Presumption begins with the universe explaining itself entirely in its own, natural, terms. So, if a theist then wants to add **God** or gods into the equation as the explanation, the **burden of proof** lies with the theist to justify this violation of Ockham's Razor. Thus, any discussion of the universe must begin with a presumption of atheism. See the entry on **science, presumption of**.

STRAUSS, DAVID FRIEDRICH (1808–1874). German theologian who changed forever the ability to see the Gospels as an authentic historical source, and who suffered persecution as a result. Strauss came to fame through his massive work *Leben Jesu* (1835), which reached English speakers via a translation from **George Eliot** in 1846. It was Strauss's intention to rid the religious core of the Gospel story of its supernaturalist and mythological excrescences. Strauss tried to soften the blow by claiming that Christianity retains a philosophic truth even if it doesn't have the historical truth it has traditionally claimed.

Upon publication of *Leben Jesu*, Strauss was subjected to an unparalleled level of abuse and calumny. He was promptly removed from his university post at Tübingen and transferred to an unimportant post in his home town of Ludwigsburg. Faced with severe disapproval from his father, Strauss moved to Stuttgart in 1836 and in 1839 was offered a professorship of theology at Zürich. After a storm of clerical indignation, this offer was withdrawn, and Strauss withdrew into a world of private scholarship. For years to come, even a suspicion of sympathy with the views of Strauss was enough to end the academic career of theologians.

Strauss devoted 1840 and 1841 to a second major work, a review of Christian dogma, but this attracted significantly less critical attention than *Leben Jesu*. In 1864 he wrote a second version of his *Life of Jesus*, this one written specifically for the German people. Once again, Strauss tried to explain events of the Jesus story in naturalistic terms.

By the time Strauss had finished *The Old Faith and the New* (1872) it was clear he had abandoned even the fig-leaf of Christian belief he had hitherto retained. He argued that traditional Christianity was doomed and that a new system of belief embedded in art and science needed to arise in its place. See the entry on **Gerd Lüdemann**, for a contemporary rerun of the Strauss persecution.

STRAUSS, RICHARD (1864–1949). Brilliant German composer. The son of a successful musician, Richard Strauss started learning the piano at age four and composing music at seven. At Munich University, he studied philosophy and aesthetics as well as music.

Strauss had a stellar career, composing his first works in 1883. In 1885 he became conductor at Meiningen and the following year the third conductor in Munich. In 1889 he went on to conduct at the chapel of the grand duke of Weimar and in 1894 at Bayreuth. In 1908 he was appointed general musical director for Prussia. Other major works included *Till Eulenspiegel* (1894–95) and *Don Quixote* (1898). His best known work is *Also Sprach Zarathustra* (1896) which was inspired by his reading of **Friedrich Nietzsche** and won him considerable criticism from the churches. This music was introduced to later generations of people in the film *2001: A Space Odyssey* (1968), a cooperative venture by **Arthur C. Clarke** and Stanley Kubrick (1928–1999).

Strauss also wrote operas such as *Salome* (1905) and *Elektra* (1909), and various songs. He retained important positions after World War I, and for a while was used as a cultural symbol by the Nazis, but came under suspicion because his son was married to a Jew and because Strauss refused to drop his Jewish friends such as the writer Stefan Zweig (1881–1942). In January 1944 Martin Bormann forbade all further contacts with Strauss. Strauss, his son, and daughter-in-law all survived the war.

STRESS. An amount of pressure beyond one's ability to deal with well. Many people operate better under pressure. Stress is the dividing line between pressure, under which we work well, and stress, which gets the better of us.

Stress levels are increasing, and is exacerbated by conditions like sleeplessness or being overweight or inactive, all of which are much more common than has ever been the case. In the developed world, stress levels are increasing because of growing uncertainty and workloads at work. In the United States, it pays—at least in the short run—to have less staff working longer hours. A smaller staff means fewer people to provide expensive health benefits for. But this smaller staff has to work longer hours, and is more likely to take work home, resulting in greater levels of stress. Companies undergoing downsizing, outsourcing, or even when experiencing periods of growth, all help produce higher stress levels among employees.

Another type of stress that is hard to deal with is the sort that emphasizes our powerlessness. Depressing world events, illnesses in the family, and so on, are very stressful, not least because we are relatively powerless to effect any change. Medication can help to some extent, but better approaches include not becoming too absorbed by the stress-creating events, enjoying the support of one's friends, and keeping fit. And while the **transcendental temptation** is powerful in this context, it is not going to provide any real solution.

STRINDBERG, AUGUST (1849–1912). Tempestuous Swedish novelist and dramatist. Born in humble circumstances, Strindberg was lucky to receive any education, let alone study at Uppsala University. He studied Chinese and worked in Stockholm's Royal Library, while developing a reputation as a man of letters. His reputation began in 1879 with a satirical novel called *The Red Room*, which was a controversial study of Swedish life and manners. When his second novel, on the same theme, was published in 1882, the furor drove Strindberg abroad. In 1884 he was charged with **blasphemy**, arising from comments made in one of his short stories. He returned from exile to answer the charge and was acquitted. His next major work, a lighter piece called *The People of Hemsö* (1887), has become a popular classic in Sweden. Toward the end of his life, during a period of acute distress, verging on madness, he turned to an eccentric form of Swedenborgian mysticism.

Altogether his works comprise fifty-five volumes. Strinberg's plays set new standards for expressing inner realities and turmoil and had a long-term influence on contemporary theater. His influence was most pronounced in the tumultuous days after World War I, when people were ready for Strindberg's unstable genius. He is frequently thought to have been Sweden's greatest literary genius.

STRING THEORY. One of the most complicated attempts being undertaken to arrive at a **theory of everything**. String theory emerged early in the 1980s as an attempt to see the fundamental items of the universe not as waves or particles, but as stringlike membranes. String theory may have provided a mechanism whereby the four **fundamental forces** of the universe (gravity, electromagnetism, the strong force, and the weak force) can all work together at the quantum level.

Dr. John Schwarz, now at Cambridge University, was the first person to speculate that a string structure may eliminate some of the problems that beset particle theory.

Among the problems string theory has yet to solve is that it needs ten dimensions in which to operate, and yet we know at the moment of only four. There are also problems related to the relationship between string theory and the **cosmological constant**.

It remains impossible at a practical level to conduct experiments to corroborate string theory, so much of the thinking is at the theoretical level of mathematical modeling. It is still an open question whether it will succeed in bringing about the theory of everything.

Further reading: Brian Greene, *The Elegant Universe*.

STRONG PROGRAM. Name given to a strand of thought, found chiefly within the sociology discipline, which seeks to portray **science** as a discourse of power in which the accepted scientific account owes its authority not so much to being the best argument, but because it has the most powerful backers. The Strong Program is the end point of a long movement, much of which is perfectly legitimate, to understand science better by also appreciating the social context in which science is developed. But it is one thing to recognize that science *develops within* a social context, and quite another thing to then conclude that this social setting *determines the results* of science. This arises principally from a confusion between knowledge and belief.

Advocates of the strong program differ in their explanation of the mechanics by which scientific beliefs are constructed. Some offer quite deterministic theories of causality, while others prefer **postmodernist, Wittgensteinian**, or **phenomenological** accounts. Ironically, proponents of the strong program almost unanimously invoked the authority of Thomas Kuhn (1922–1996), although the second half of Kuhn's career was spent in evermore direct opposition to the Strong Program. Kuhn's work, *The Structure of Scientific Revolutions* (1962) was widely interpreted as the founding work for the program, but this was never unambiguously the case, and it was even less so with Kuhn's later work.

Advocates of the program claim that politics, personalities, and social conditions play a significant role in the life of science. Virtually nobody denies this trivial point. The more important claim, and the one which is so much more controversial, is that these interests also help determine scientific outcomes. Advocates of the Strong Program regularly fall foul of the **passes-for fallacy**. There is also the problem that if we are not justified in believing the theories of science by virtue of their being socially derived, then surely the same is true for the Strong Program.

Further reading: Robert Nola, *Rescuing Reason: A Critique of Anti-Rationalist Views of Science and Knowledge*; and Susan Haack, *Defending Science—Within Reason*.

STRUCTURES OF DECEIT. A term employed by the otherwise faithful Catholic apologist Garry Wills (1934–) to describe the well-nigh inescapable labyrinth of precedents and past mistakes and evasions that make any contemporary recognition of error inside the church a virtual impossibility. To take one example, even if the church was willing to admit the extent of its culpability in regard to the sexual exploitation of children by priests, it would need to call into question long-standing edicts about clerical celibacy, among other things.

To admit that any of these things were a mistake would mean admitting that the pope who took the decision had not been acting with clear authority as God's vicar on earth. And having admitted that, the whole structure would come tumbling down. The equivocal and dishonest attitude taken by the church in dealing with its long history of **anti-Semitism** runs up against the same structures of deceit. Wills acknowledges that the very legitimacy of the papacy, long shown to rest on spurious historical claims and forgeries like the **Donation of Constantine**, is upheld only by the mutually reinforcing structures of deceit.

Further reading: Garry Wills, *Papal Sin: Structures of Deceit*.

STURGEON'S LAW. An unbreakable rule of the universe that observes that 90 percent of everything is crap. The law was discovered by the American science fiction writer Theodore Sturgeon (1918–1985), who admitted that 90 percent of science fiction is crud, but only because 90 percent of everything is crud. Since then "crud" has given way to "crap" and the law has taken on a universal application.

STURM UND DRANG. A German phrase meaning storm and stress which infected the middle classes and intellectuals, partly as a reaction to **Enlightenment** rationalism. *Sturm und Drang* was a precursor to **Romanticism**. The young intellectuals of the Sturm und Drang movement extolled spontaneity of feeling and the unpredictability of artistic genius. The book that epitomized Sturm und

Drang was the novel by **Johann Wolfgang Goethe**, *The Sorrows of Young Werther* (1774). The movement in Germany also had an element of nationalist resentment against the cultural hegemony of France.

Another influential thinker was the historian Johann Gottfied Herder (1744–1803) whose histories decried universal trends, moral laws, and **human nature**, stressing instead the essential differences of nations and peoples, who could only be judged by their own standards.

SUBLIME. A word that arose in the nineteenth century in the context of the individual's reaction to nature. A sublime experience of nature was a mixture of joyful wonderment at the beauty of what one is seeing, but also some fear at its power, and recognition of the brevity of one's own existence in the face of this beauty. Americans who saw the Grand Canyon often feel this sense of the sublime. German painters like Caspar David Friedrich (1774–1840) were particular exemplars of this style of painting.

The sublime experience is often described as religious, spiritual, or **mystical**, and yet none of these things fully express it. The sublime experience is a human experience: life is short, nature is old and incomparably beautiful, and I am lucky to have seen this sight. See the entry on **cosmic perspective**.

SUICIDE BOMBERS. People so filled with **faith**, usually in **God**, that they are willing to kill other people solely because their version of faith in God differs in particulars. Faith is essential to the logic of the suicide bomber, and **martyrdom** is the reward. While most **monotheistic** religions have some sort of proscription against suicide, they are either ambiguous, or can be ignored in favor of calls to martyrdom and dying for the faith.

Suicide bombers are only the latest manifestation of a long history of suicide terrorism. Fanatical Jews in the first century CE, known as Sicarii, or "dagger man," were people who attacked political and religious opponents with little thought of escape. Then there were the Assassins, a Muslim cult active from the eleventh to the thirteenth centuries in Iran and Syria. The Assassins targeted people they supposed to be insufficiently zealous in their faith. The assassin was usually high on hashish at the time of the attack, normally done in broad daylight, in public, and with no means of escape. Suicide tactics came to formal warfare in the form of the kamikaze pilots who flew their explosive-filled planes into American warships toward the end of World War II.

Contemporary suicide bombers made their debut in 1983 in an attack organized by the Islamic group **Hizbullah** against the American troops based in Beirut in which 241 people were killed. In the first four years of the Palestinian *intifada* more than four hundred Israelis were killed by suicide bombers. However, the largest user of suicide bombers as a weapon of terror has been the Tamil Tigers, who have been fighting a war of autonomy in northern Sri Lanka since the 1980s.

It was originally thought that the stereotypical suicide bomber was a young male with relatively little education and no hope for the future. This is not the case, as many suicide bombers have been educated people from stable families. Some of them have not been overtly religious until shortly before their decision to volunteer themselves. One of the more articulate suicide bombers was Reem al-Reyashi, a twenty-two-year-old mother of a three-year-old boy and one-year-old girl. In her televised address before the attack, Reyashi said that "God gave me the ability to be a mother of two children who I love so . . . but my wish to meet God in paradise is greater, so I decided to be a martyr for the sake of my people. I am convinced that God will help and take care of my children." On January 14, 2004, she, operating on behalf of the terrorist organization **Hamas**, blew herself up at an Israeli checkpoint, killing four security personnel and wounding seven others. See the entry on the **Principle of Intolerance**.

SUMANIYA, THE. A little-known Indian school that expounded an agnostic and skeptical philosophy and regarded supernatural knowledge as impossible.

SUPERNATURALISM. The tendency to posit some sort of power, principle, **God**, or force that operates and has its being at a level **beyond** the natural world and not bound by its rules. Because supernatural claims purport to go beyond the limits of what is natural, the **burden of proof** lies with the person making any sort of claim involving a supernatural dimension. What is more, extraordinary claims require extraordinary amounts of **evidence**.

All forms of inquiry are part of nature, including those which claim to transcend it. But, unlike naturalist claims, the claims of supernaturalism cannot be repeated, tested, or verified, and rely in the end solely upon assertion and can be believed only by **faith**. It is for these reasons that supernaturalism is not opposed to **naturalism**, but is a subset of naturalism. This does not involve, however, a complete rejection of supernaturalism as a factor worthy of consideration. Supernaturalism is a valid subject of study as a cultural phenomenon within naturalism—a way some people choose to interpret the universe. But it is not an alternative to naturalism. See the entries on **cranes and skyhooks**, **transcendental temptation**, and **anthropocentric conceit**.

SUPERSESSIONISM. Deriving from *supersedere*, which means "to sit upon," supersessionism is an old Christian doctrine whereby it accorded to itself the honor of having superseded the earlier revelation of Judaism. The outstanding example of Christian supersessionism is the New Testament, which claims to have superseded the **Hebrew scriptures**, which was then tagged with the dismissive title "Old Testament." This was largely the work of **Marcion**.

An important feature of supersessionist thinking is the mining of the superseded faith's scriptures for prophecies that are claimed to be fulfilled by the new revelation. In this way, Christianity uses Old Testament passages as prophecies that "prove" its role as the fulfillment of the superseded faith. The assumption underlying supersessionism is that the old revelation had no reason, or even right, to exist. In this way, supersessionism led directly to **anti-Semitism**. If the new revelation has superseded the old one, so the reasoning goes, then it is perverse of the followers of the old revelation to hold stubbornly to their outmoded beliefs.

While the official doctrine of supersessionism was rescinded at Vatican II, the scriptural underpinnings and foundational theology remain. After all, the New Testament is supersessionism's greatest vehicle.

Further reading: James Carroll, *Constantine's Sword: The Church and the Jews*.

SUPERSTITION. A simplistic manifestation of **anthropocentric conceit**. Superstition is the frame of mind that sees significance for oneself in everyday acts of nature, and believes that the performance of some sort of ritual act or sacrifice will mollify whatever spirit or agency is aggrieved in this instance. Superstition is completely incompatible with a naturalistic view of the world. And **Baruch Spinoza** noted wisely that superstition "seems to account as good all that brings pain, and as bad all that brings pleasure."

It has become unfashionable, among Westerners who like to think themselves sophisticated, to speak of superstition. They imagine this to involve some sort of cultural arrogance toward those cultures where such practices are common. But among the cultures where superstitious practices are common, people know better. Among those who live with the consequences of superstition, there is a greater understanding of its harmful effects, particularly for women. In the West, superstition remains strong, although it has been effectively neutralized, and is little more than an idle diversion.

SUPREME BEING, CULT OF. A state cult

implemented by the radical wing of the French revolutionary government, known as the Hebertists, in the autumn of 1792. The radicals, who were led by Jacques-Rene Hébert (1757–1794) were heavily influenced by **Jean-Jacques Rousseau**'s idea of the **general will**. The French leader, Maximilien Robespierre (1758–1794) was a devotee of Rousseau and considered Rousseau's views the surest foundation for society. Robespierre was strongly antagonistic to **atheism**. As part of the cult, a goddess of reason sat on a throne installed in the Cathedral of Notre Dame, now the principal Temple of Reason. Hébert and his closest followers went to the guillotine in March 1794. The Cult of the Supreme Being was abolished after the fall of the Jacobins in July 1794.

Religious apologists have long used the Cult of the Supreme Being to highlight the dangers of a society without **religion** or of the weaknesses of enthroning reason. These attacks ignore several important points:

- Hébert and his followers were anticlerical, even anti-Christian, but were not atheists;
- The intellectual inspiration of the cult was Rousseau, hardly an apologist for rationalism; and
- Few rationalists in the naturalist tradition would support an idea as absurd as reason being enthroned, since that is just another form of **anthropocentric conceit**.

The Cult of the Supreme Being is testimony to the follies of taking **deism** to its logical conclusion. The Cult of the Supreme Being is not to be confused with **Theophilanthropy**.

SUPREME MORAL RULE. An ethical maxim among people who reject **command moralities**. There are many examples of atheists and humanists who have proposed some version of a supreme moral rule. The phrase was actually used by **Bertrand Russell** in *An Outline of Philosophy* (1927). We tend to call good that which we desire and bad that which we seek to avoid, Russell observed. The problem here, of course, is that by these definitions, it becomes impossible for everyone to be good, since many of our desires will impinge on the welfare of others.

Russell's solution? The supreme moral rule, which is: *Act so as to produce harmonious rather than discordant desires.* In this way, **love** is a desire more conducive to the good than hate, knowledge more conducive to the good than ignorance, and so on. In other words, love, mutual respect, knowledge, and **toleration** are harmonious desires rather than their opposites. This is another version of the **Golden Rule**. The philosopher Mario Bunge has also developed a supreme moral rule, though without using the term. See the entry on **Agathonism**.

Other great thinkers have spoken of what are, in effect, supreme moral rules without naming then as such. For instance, the **Stoic** thinker and Roman Emperor **Marcus Aurelius** wrote: "Since it is possible that we may depart from life this very moment, regulate every act and thought accordingly." **Friedrich Nietzsche** implied a similar thing with this notion of the **eternal recurrence**.

More recently, **Joseph McCabe** wrote: "*Our* supreme law for men and women is: Thou shalt be happy. Our fundamental counsel is: Do unto others as you would they should do unto you. Make no man or woman weep, as old Egypt said. Enjoy the sun, and cloud not the lives of others. Cultivate those qualities which, if generally cultivated, will make life a joy for all: virility, wisdom, tenderness, delicacy, justice, kindliness, truthfulness, straightness. Then yours is the kingdom of earth, and it has no other laws."

None of these thinkers claim that their supreme moral rule is writ into the cosmos. They are not lapsing into **absolutism**; they all appreciate that others will think differently. Consequently, their supreme moral rules should not be thought of as commands, but as guidelines, which are meaningless without the open decision of the individual to live his or her life in accordance with the supreme moral rule that resonates best with them. See also the entry on **Equality, Principle of**.

SUSTAINABLE DEVELOPMENT. One of the most important concepts to be developed in the past half century, and one which most people agree on the value of, even when they have different understandings of what it means. The original attempt at an authoritative definition of sustainable development came from the World Commission on Environment and Development (WCED) which, in 1987, defined it as a kind of development that "meets the needs of the present without compromising the ability of future generations to meet their own needs." In 1989 the Food and Agriculture Organization gave an expanded definition, with particular attention on its area of interest:

> Sustainable development is the management and conservation of the natural resource-base, and the orientation of technological and institutional changes, in such a manner as to ensure the attainment and continued satisfaction of human needs for present and future generations. Such sustainable development (in the agriculture, forestry, and fishery sectors) conserves land, water, plant, and animal genetic resources, is environmentally nondegrading, technically appropriate, economically viable and socially acceptable.

It is plain that sustainable development cannot be undertaken seriously without some form of transnational regulation. The interdependence of humanity means that transnational planning and regulation is essential. A dam built in one country can have serious consequences for the climate and prosperity for the citizens of a neighboring country. The **Montreal Protocols** are a successful example of transnational regulation. A laissez-faire economic climate is unable to allow for the degree of regulation and education a full commitment to sustainable development would entail.

The other essential requirement for any serious attempt to apply the principles of sustainable development is a change of attitude from all people, but especially from the developed nations, toward thinking at a planetary level. See the entries on **affluenza** and **voluntary simplicity**.

SUSTAINABLE DEVELOPMENT, PRINCIPLES OF. The Nepalese conservationist Dr. Gopi Upreti has outlined the principles of sustainable development in the following terms:

(1) Maintaining ecological integrity in a way that sustains ecosystems, diversity, and life-support services.
(2) Achieving a harmony between population growth and the ability of the planet to sustain such a population level.
(3) Integration of people and the needs of the **ecoregions** they inhabit.
(4) Equity and social justice, without which the second and third principles are illusory.
(5) Adopting consumption patterns that are ecologically sustainable.

These principles can best be given effect by great commitment, transnational regulation, oversight, and by Westerners living more frugally.

Further reading: Gopi Upreti, "Environmental Conservation and Sustainable Development Require a New Developmental Approach," *Environmental Conservation* 21, no. 1 (Spring 1994): 18–29.

SWINBURNE, ALGERNON CHARLES (1837–1909). English poet and playwright. Born in London, the son of an admiral, and educated at Eton and Balliol College, Oxford, though he left before taking his degree. Swinburne traveled around Europe where he met and came under the influence of Victor Hugo. He returned to London and a life of serious dissipation until his health broke down. He then moved into the home of his friend Theodore Watts-Dunton and lived there as a semirecluse for the rest of his life.

Swinburne first came to public attention in 1865 for his play *Atalanta in Calydon*, which was infused with rebellion against religious correctness. This was quickly followed by *Poems and Ballads* (1866), a collection of uninhibited, antireligious though deeply romantic poems, which established his reputation. There was a second series of *Poems and Ballads* in 1878 and a third in 1889. Swinburne lent his support for Italian liberation (and for republicanism and **anticlericalism**) in *Songs Before Sunrise* (1871). This work also featured a segment known as the *Hymn to Man*, which is often found in anthologies. His *Tristram of Lyonese* (1882) was an Arthurian romance that is generally thought the finest example of its kind. He also wrote some highly regarded criticism, in particular *Essays and Studies* (1875) and *Studies in Prose and Poetry* (1894).

He was raised a pious Christian and was a fervent believer until late in his teens. The vicious bullying he suffered from at Eton and his widespread experience of religious hypocrisy opened his eyes to the other side of religion. In 1878, he represented English poetry at the centennial celebration of the death of **Voltaire**. Among the best poems that express his worldview include *Before a Crucifix*, *The Garden of Prosperine*, *Cor Cordium*, *The Storms of Time*, *Hertha*, and his late work *The Altar of Righteousness*.

SYMBOLS. An artificial sign invented by humans to stand for something. The word derives from the Greek word *sumbolon*, which meant a token or means of identification by which people could recognize each other. Only later did it come to mean a signifier for some deep and esoteric reality.

Mario Bunge observes that a symbol can

designate a concept, like a number, or it can *denote* something, like the name of a city. Symbols give us the ability to refer to what the symbol designates or denotes. So the three squiggles d, o, and g, when put together, denote (stand for), in a way other people can understand, a dog.

Many people have been carried away by symbols, forgetting along the way that symbols do not *create* the objects they are stand-ins for. With this is mind, we need to be skeptical when symbol slips into symbol*ism*.

Further reading: Mario Bunge, *Philosophical Dictionary*.

SYMBOLISTS. A school of painting that flourished in the last twenty years of the nineteenth century and was inspired in large part by the poets Stéphane Mallarmé (1842–1898) and **A. C. Swinburne**, and the philosophers G. W. F. Hegel (1770–1831) and **Arthur Schopenhauer**.

The Symbolists followed on from the **Romantics** in their interest in symbols, although theirs was a different focus. Although both movements were reacting against the materialism of nineteenth-century Europe, the Romantics were more political than the Symbolists. The Romantics valued notions like the noble savage and revolt, but the Symbolists were more quiescent. Their interest was beauty, which they sought to idealize in their art. In their quest for an ideal beauty, the Symbolists looked outside Christianity. They looked instead toward the **Asian traditions** or toward more eclectic and individual **mysticisms**.

Some of the main painters of the period were Odilon Redon (1840–1916) and Gustave Moreau (1826–1898) in France, Gustav Klimt (1862–1918) in Austria, and Fernand Khnopff (1858–1921) in Belgium. The Symbolist movement lost steam with the death of Mallarmé in 1898 and was pretty much dead by 1910.

SYSTEMISM. A method of learning that stresses the interdependence of things. More specifically, it states that every thing and every idea is a system in itself and is part of a wider system. And every research field is a component of the system of human knowledge. It follows from this that trying to study any one thing in isolation is almost bound to fail, by definition. To take one example, a human society is a system composed of four major subsystems:

- *biological system*, whose members are bound together by sexual selection, kinship relations, and child rearing;
- *economic system*, whose bonds are those of production and exchange;
- *political system*, whose functions are to manage the **social capital** and activities; and
- *cultural system*, propagated by teaching and learning, designing and recording, planning, engaging in controversies, and so on.

Systemism argues that the study of human society without acknowledging this essential interdependence will lead to **reductionism** of the unhelpful variety and an impoverished understanding. Systemism is more than holism, which is prone to admitting wooly notions into the debate. See the entry of **humanism, seven theses of**, for an example of Systemism in action, because the theses are in a set order.

Further reading: Mario Bunge, *Philosophy in Crisis: The Need for Reconstruction.*

SZCZESNY, GERHARD (1908–2002). German author, broadcaster, and controversialist. Gerhard Szczesny was born in East Prussia. He studied philosophy, literature, and journalism at Königsberg, Berlin, and Munich. After World War II he acquired a reputation as an intellectual leader, largely through a series of essays under the title *Europe and the Anarchy of the Soul*. In 1947 he became vice director of the culture and education section of Radio Bavaria and the following year created the night radio section of the station. In October 1957 he became the director of special programs.

Szczesny published *The Future of Unbelief: Contemporary Observations of a Non-Christian* in 1958. It won the Heinrich Droste Literature Foundation award for the most outstanding treatment of a historicocultural theme. The book created a tremendous controversy, much of which was later collected in *Belief and Unbelief.*

Szczesny worked as a broadcaster in Bavaria until 1961 when, in a highly controversial broadcast, he compared West German chancellor Willi Brandt (1913–1992), East German leader Walter Ulbricht (1893–1973), and Nazi propaganda chief Joseph Goebbels (1897–1945). Szczesny then went on to found the Humanist Union in Munich after the Roman Catholic Church engineered the banning of Mozart's *Figaro* on the grounds of immorality. The Humanist Union has defended the **open society** against several other encroachments since then.

Szczesny's later titles include *The Answer of the Religions* (1982), *A Buddha for the Evening Country* (1976), and *The Mischief of Total Democracy: Experiences with Progress* (1983).

T

TAGORE, RABINDRANATH (1861–1941). India's most outstanding poet of the twentieth century. Rabindranath Tagore began and ended his life in Calcutta (now Kolkata). His was a privileged upbringing as the son of the Maharishi Debendranath Tagore, an important Hindu reformer, and Shrimati Sharada Devi, who died in his infancy. Tagore's prodigious output was inspired by the Bengali culture into which he was born. As well as being a poet he was an accomplished playwright, artist, composer, philosopher, and storyteller. He is venerated by Bengalis, and is seen as the most brilliant proponent of Bengali culture. Some of his more elitist contemporaries found it disquieting that Tagore wrote in the vernacular so that ordinary Bengalis could read his work.

In 1901 Tagore founded Shantiniketan with the intent of recapturing the rural simplicity of India while also incorporating what was valuable from the West. In 1921 this institute became a university. Among his important books are *Nashtanir* (*The Broken Nest*, 1901) and *Chocher Bali* (*Eyesore*, 1903), and the short story *Punishment*, which spoke of the oppression of women in low-caste society. One of his poems, *Our Golden Bengal*, became the national anthem of Bangladesh. He won the Nobel Prize for Literature in 1913 for his collection of poems known as *Gitanjali*, or *Song Offerings* (1912). The Nobel Prize alerted European readers to Tagore's work, and he has retained a wide European readership from then on.

Tagore was knighted in 1915, but in 1919 he renounced his knighthood in protest of the British policy in the Punjab, which had resulted in the massacre at Amritsar. While Tagore was an opponent of colonialism, he was reluctant to embrace the strong **nationalism** of the freedom struggle. His work was very influential on Mohandas Gandhi (1869–1948) who went on to lead India to independence. Tagore's **humanism** was deeply rooted in Indian philosophy and history. He looked forward to the day when nationalism will be replaced by transnational values, what he called "unity consciousness." Tagore was an early proponent of **planetary humanism**, albeit in a mystical vein.

TAI CHEN. See **DAI ZHEN**.

T'AI CHI. See **GREAT ULTIMATE**.

TALKING PAST ONE ANOTHER. It is often claimed that humanists and religious believers are talking past one another. Each side, so the argument goes, is set in its own mindset; neither is going to change its position. Each side begins from completely different propositions, or occupies different **social worlds**, so that no common ground is possible and arguing between them is a waste of time.

There is some truth in this claim, but it would be dangerous to accept it unconditionally. First of all, humanists and religious believers both have a commitment to their beliefs and are keen to defend them. It is one of the things these groups have in common. It is something that distinguishes both groups from the **indifferentists**. See the entry on **what atheists and religious believers have in common**.

Second, the notion of talking past one another assumes there is no possible area of agreement. It assumes a radically **relativist** view of the universe. By contrast, humanists and religious believers usually believe that certain things about the universe can be established within a degree of confidence. Religious believers are more inclined to express **certainty** than humanists, and of course the content of the beliefs are different, but the willingness to make that effort and the confidence that it can be done, to varying degrees of perfection, are things both groups have in common.

And third, the ongoing humanist-religious debate is actually a positive contribution to the **social intelligence**. The most insidious assumption lurking behind the "talking past one another" claim is that the principles being disputed are unimportant, or that arriving at a sound conclusion about them is not a good use of time. The "talking past one another" argument is intellectually lazy. It says that questions about the meaning of life or the proper alignment of morals, or the existence of **God** are irrelevant, unanswerable, or in some other way marginal. Neither humanists nor religious believers consider this to be the case.

Having said all this, there is a great deal to be desired about the nature and quality of humanist-religious debate. It is becoming increasingly dominated by the practice of **demonizing the opposition**. This is extremely unhelpful. One side assumes it has a **monopoly on the truth**, and so makes no effort to engage in meaningful debate. Or, just as frequently, there is no debate because of some skewed notion of "respecting faith," as if allowing outrageous claims to go unchallenged shows respect to anything. There is a crying need for serious, informed debate on religious and moral issues across the humanist-religious divide. And one of the definitions of informed debate is that it doesn't talk past the opponent.

TAO. A concept of central importance to Chinese thought. The first point to make is that the Tao (also spelt Dao) is not to be confused with the different notion of **God**. When Taoists say that all things come from the Tao they do not mean God, particularly not in the Western sense of the word. The Tao is essentially impenetrable and ungraspable and yet we must direct our lives toward comprehending it. The Tao can be understood in an **existential** sense as the Way, which means the way we live our lives that is most in harmony with how we should live our lives. But the Tao can also be taken in the more cosmological sense of being the name to refer to the essential principle of things.

Taoists often say that those who say they know what the Tao is are the ones who definitely know the least about the Tao. The Tao embodies being and nonbeing. A life spent trying to understand the Tao through study or asceticism is not usually recommended. Indeed, comprehending the Tao is most likely to come to those not trying to comprehend it.

Confucianists, by contrast, are more confident in their own ability to at least grasp the question. At one stage, Confucianists argued that not only is the Tao namable, it is the only truly namable thing. Later Confucianists also distinguished *Tao*, about which we have been speaking, with *tao*, the primordial essence of each and everything, which are all part of the Tao. This idea is not dissimilar to **Plato**'s theory of forms.

Further reading: Fung yu-Lan, *A Short History of Chinese Philosophy*.

TAOISM. An ancient strand of Chinese thought. The notional founder of Taoism is Laozi (or Lao Tzu), but his name means "Old Master" and there is serious doubt whether Laozi was an actual historical person. The odds are that there was no such man. Taoism is the more metaphysical and paradoxical understanding of the Tao than is common elsewhere in Chinese thought.

The two classical works of Taoism are the *Tao Te Ching* (otherwise known as the *Lao Tzu*) and the *Chuang Tzu*. The *Tao Te Ching* is ascribed to Laozi but is in fact an anthology of works by several hands, possibly being put together between 300 to 230 BCE. The *Tao Te Ching* is obscure and difficult. Its main focus is the eternal, unchanging **Tao** which produces all things without actually creating them. However, it also condemns tyranny, overtaxation, and warfare. It urges an ideal of responsible government based on rulers genuinely loving the people.

The *Chuang Tzu* is named after Chuang Tzu (369–286 BCE, approx.), after Lao Tzu the most important Taoist thinker. However little of the book was written by him. It was probably put together by Quo Xiang (third century BCE, Kuo Hsiang in old spelling). The *Chuang Tzu* is no less mystical, but approaches the questions in a slightly more existential way. It argues that personal freedom, and understanding the Tao, lies in liberation from knowledge and words.

Taoism is usually broken into philosophical and religious branches. Philosophical and religious Taoism don't differ on beliefs so much as on emphasis. Neither strand has any time for notions of personal immortality or reincarnation. Religious Taoism is more inclined to see the Tao as a supreme reality and more inclined to occult and **superstition**. It was an important influence in the development of **Zen Buddhism**. Philosophical Taoism is a refined form of **humanism**.

TAOIST VIRTUES. The prime Taoist virtue is the ability to achieve a truly **cosmic perspective**. Each of us is a microcosm of the universe, and we can look to our own mental, physical, and spiritual health best when we keep that basic fact in mind. In this way, Taoism rejects the **anthropocentric conceit** of **monotheist** religions. Laozi praised three virtues in particular:

- compassion;
- frugality; and
- inaction (*wuwei*).

These virtues are highlighted because they are the most conducive to understanding the essence of the Tao, and therefore more useful to ourselves. Taoists usually portray the Tao as the producer and sustainer of all things while also being inactive. Things are not produced by great bouts of activity, and it is wise for us to behave in a similar way. Too much activity can actually undo the original action.

The doctrine of inaction led Taoists to oppose the Confucian ideas of active involvement in society. In particular, the notion of **human-heartedness** was subjected to criticism.

TAQLID. An Islamic doctrine that has had devastating effects on the quality of Islamic science, philosophy, and **critical thinking**. *Taqlid* means "to imitate" and refers to the requirement to follow Muslim clerics on all matters without asking for any sort of justification of their decisions. The *Taqlid* doctrine states that there are no truths revealed beyond those revealed in the Qur'an. This sort of literalism has the effect of shutting down **free inquiry** and banishing scholars. The Qur'an is inconsistent on this (as on many other) issue, with passages that extol and condemn blind, uncritical **faith**. See also the entry on *ijtihad*.

TARKUNDE, VITHAL MAHADEV (1909–2004). Human rights activist, scholar, educator, judge, and humanist. Vithal Mahadev Tarkunde was born on July 3, 1909, and rose to become a prominent judge at Bombay (now Mumbai) High Court and eventually the Supreme Court of India. He was a close associate of **M. N. Roy**, a communist in his earlier life who turned to **radical humanism**. Tarkunde worked closely with Roy and devoted considerable time and energy to the radical-humanist movement. He eventually resigned his position as judge so he could devote more to time the movement. In 1969 he founded the **Indian Radical Humanist Association** and went on to serve as its chairman until 1986. He edited the IRHA's journal, the *Radical Humanist* and published articles and books, the best known of which was *Radical Humanism* (1983, second revised edition 1992). He was also the founder-president of the Peoples Union of Civil Liberties of India.

Tarkunde fought bravely for democratic rights during the Emergency of 1975–77, during which time Indira Gandhi (1917–1984) limited many political freedoms. Tarkunde was an important figure in a group called Citizens for Democracy.

Tarkunde was widely honored for his work. He was made an honorary associate of the **Rationalist Press Association** in 1976, and the **International Humanist and Ethical Union** acknowledged his work for freedom of speech and civil liberties during the Emergency with the Humanist Award. He has been a member of the **International Academy of Humanism** since 1983 and the Indian government decorated him with the prestigious Padmabhushan Award in 1998.

TAX AVOIDANCE. A form of **corruption** which, if unchecked, will contribute very significantly to the erosion of democracy in the world. In 1950 about 17 percent of government revenue in the United States came from corporate taxes. In 2000 that figure had dropped to just 7 percent. This decline is due in large part to the growing willingness of large corporations to evade their legitimate tax obligations and thus impoverish their fellow countrymen.

In 2004 it was estimated that in the United States alone, $250 to $300 billion of legitimate tax revenue will be lost to tax avoidance. Most of this is done through the use of tax shelters and a series of sham transactions whereby corporations can move their money in ways that can to evade taxation. Between 1996 and 2000 no less than 60 percent of US corporations paid no tax at all.

Tax avoidance on this scale widens the gap between the rich and the poor and undermines the effectiveness of the **welfare state**'s ability to provide minimum assistance to the needy. Mike Moore, head of the **World Trade Organization** between 1999 and 2002, made the important point that "tax is the price you pay for civilization." That is true, and every taxable dollar that avoids the taxman also avoids schools, museums, art galleries, national parks, and the public-health system. See the entry on **social capital**.

TAYLOR, ROBERT (1784–1844). English eccentric and **freethinker**. Taylor was persuaded to leave a promising career in medicine to enter the church. In January 1813 he graduated with a BA and took holy orders. While serving as a curate in Midhurst, Sussex, Taylor had a series of discussions with a tradesman, which introduced doubt in his mind, soon turning into a full rejection of religious belief. After preaching a sermon on Jonah which traumatized his congregation, Taylor resigned and took up a career as a freethinking lecturer. He then scandalized the clergy by lecturing on freethought platforms in full clerical regalia. Taylor went to prison two times for **blasphemy**, for a year from February 1828 and for eighteen months over 1831–32. During his first imprisonment he wrote *The Diegesis* (1829) which explored the origins, evidences, and early history of Christianity. He was an early advocate of the **myth theory of Jesus**.

Taylor also wrote a weekly letter to the *Lion*, a periodical **Richard Carlile** began on his behalf. These letters were later published as *The Devil's Pulpit* (1830). Taylor suffered from mistreatment in his second term of imprisonment. Soon after his release he married a wealthy lady and retired from public life. See the entry on **former preachers**.

TECHNOLOGY. The study of human techniques for making and doing things. The core study of technology is the study of the sources of power. Technology assumes a degree of confidence in human rationality and creativity. It is considerably older than **science**, which is more concerned with the systematic understanding of our universe. It was not until the nineteenth century that science had a significant impact on technology. By contrast, technology has, until very recently, had a profound influence on science.

The state of modernity has made plain the technological dilemma. On the one hand, the world has become dependent on technology as a means of generating wealth in order to maintain living standards. But at the same time, it threatens to destroy society. What is certain is that technology and science will both play a vital role in resolving this dilemma.

Further reading: R. A. Buchanan, *The Power of the Machine*.

TELEOLOGY. The belief that everything has some higher purpose, be it **God**, the dialectic, **progress**, or some other abstraction. **Historicism** as understood in Europe is a variation of teleology.

One of the most ubiquitous problems with teleology is that the higher purpose is never obvious; it always seems to need a human being to explain this purpose to us. And invariably it is the bearer of the teleological truth who presumes the pivotal role as ambassador between the higher agency and mere mortals. The postmodernist criticism of **metanarratives** is useful insofar as it is critical of teleology. Unfortunately, much of the postmodernist critique overstates its case by criticizing against *any* coherent historical understanding. It also fails to acknowledge the criticisms of teleology made by earlier, nonpostmodernist philosophers like **Bertrand Russell** and **Karl Popper**.

TELIC ART. A term used by **John Passmore** to denote art that exhorts us to care for some cause or other. Examples include religious art, feminist art, and environmental art. Perhaps the finest piece of telic art in the twentieth century was Picasso's *Guernica*, painted in 1937 as a protest against the German bombing of the Spanish town in Guernica as part of their contribution toward the fascist cause in the Spanish Civil War. Unlike *Guernica*, most telic art doesn't outlive the cause it is championing and at its weakest, it collapses into simple propaganda. See the entry on **modern art**.

Further reading: John Passmore, *Serious Art*.

TEMPLETON,   CHARLES.   See **FORMER PREACHERS**

TEN TROPES OF JUDGMENT. The name given to a set of ten observations made by the **Pyrrhonist** philosopher Aenesidemus (first century CE). Aenesidemus was a scholar at **Plato**'s **Academy** before leaving for Alexandria. None of Aenesidemus's works survive, and they are only known from later commentators. In order to serve his core conviction that nothing can be known for certain, Aenesidemus arranged these ten tropes as a reminder of the difficulties in making any sort of dogmatic utterance. The ten tropes were probably first articulated in his work, the *Pyrrhoneia*. The ten tropes are:

- everyone has different perceptions and feelings;
- equally, everyone has different mental and physical attributes, which also color their outlook;
- each of our different senses gives us different types of information;
- our perceptions of things depend on the state of our mental and physical senses at the time;
- the world looks different from different positions and viewpoints;
- we never see anything directly—everything comes to our senses from some sort of medium, such as air or water;
- impressions will also depend on varia-

tions in factors like color, motion, temperature, or the number of objects being observed;
- we are differently impressed by things which are familiar than with those which are unfamiliar;
- all knowledge is predication, and predicates are more about the relation between the object and our senses than about the object itself; and
- opinions and values differ between people of different countries.

While each of these is a relevant point to bear in mind and is a valuable corrective against facile dogmatism, it doesn't follow that we must suspend any sort of judgment, as Aenesidemus probably would have preferred us to do. It is these contingencies that **reliabilism** is so effective in countering. See the entries on **skepticism**, **fallibilism**, **critical receptiveness**, and the **scientific method**.

TERRORISM. One of the most ancient forms of psychological warfare, which has returned with a vengeance to the forefront of political activity at the beginning of the twenty-first century. Terrorism need not be politically motivated; criminals and psychopaths have long used terrorism. But we are mostly used to thinking of it in its political and religious contexts. Paul Wilkinson, an authority on terrorism, defined it as "coercive intimidation": the "systematic use of murder and destruction, and the threat of murder and destruction in order to terrorize individuals, groups, communities or governments into conceding to the terrorists' political demands." There are three main forms of political terrorism:

- *Repressive terrorism*, which is used by **totalitarian** states to subdue its own population, for example, Saddam Hussein's Iraq;
- *Subrevolutionary terrorism*, which is employed for a variety of reasons excluding political revolution, for

example, the IRA; and

- *Revolutionary terrorism*, which is employed to effect a major political revolution, for example, **al Qaeda** or **Jemaah Islamiyah**.

Wilkinson noted that terrorism is based on three assumptions about human nature, which are either false or at least unproven:

- when faced with threats to life and limb, people will always surrender their beliefs and principles to save themselves;
- terrorism invariably leads to the intended victims being terrorized; and
- that terrorist victims will inevitably suffer a collapse of will to resist.

Terrorist violence is generally indiscriminate in its effects, which is an important component in creating the terror. Because of this it is also arbitrary and unpredictable, and very often involves denial of the normal rules of war. Terrorists almost always have the political initiative. They can launch a new attack any time they please, and any destruction caused is a success for them. Law enforcement authorities, by contrast, have the much more difficult problem of anticipating their moves and employing their necessarily limited resources in what seems to them at the time the most effective way. As there will always be more opportunities for targets than there are people to protect them, the terrorist has a built-in advantage.

It doesn't always go the way of the terrorists though. Terrorism can often end up being counterproductive in that it often results in:

- widespread revulsion against them by the mass of the population, including those intended to sympathize with them; and
- the acquisition of harsher methods of reprisal from the government.

Also, the protracted exhaustion of all the people involved can, in the long run, lead to a decline in appreciation of the values which motivated the terrorists to take up arms in the first place. See the entry on **war on terror**.

Further reading: Paul Wilkinson, *Terrorism and the Liberal State*.

TESTING OUR BELIEFS. One of the problems with **humanism** is the perceived difficulty in establishing any reliable foundation for one's beliefs. Religious fundamentalists accuse humanists of being moral relativists, by which they mean immoral and self-serving. This, of course, is a caricature—at best. Humanism rejects **foundationalism** and **absolutism** in the interests of a reasonable **fallibilism**.

Paul Kurtz has outlined eight ways we can test the quality of our beliefs. Even so, he warned, these methods won't provide rock-solid foundations for one's beliefs. Humanism doesn't work like that. If they can't be absolutely objective, they can, however, be objectively relative.

(1) Our beliefs should be held as hypotheses, ideas which may prove on further research to be mistaken.

(2) We should feel the need for adequate **evidence** before accepting any hypothesis.

(3) The evidence we do accept should not simply be secondhand or passively received; we should have made some effort to provide evidence for ourselves.

(4) We shouldn't rely on subjective evidence, evidence that is unavailable to public scrutiny, or the testimony of others.

(5) No hypothesis should be treated in isolation; everything has some sort of context which is relevant and which should be considered.

(6) We can judge beliefs by their consequences.

(7) We should be skeptical of any ideas which are offered as infallible, ironclad assertions.

(8) We need to remain open to new ideas that may weaken ones we already hold.

The trick, according to the British philosopher Bernard Williams (1929–2003) is to develop confidence in our **values** rather than **certainty** in them.

Further reading: Paul Kurtz, *The New Skepticism: Inquiry and Reliable Knowledge*.

THALES (624–548 BCE, approx.). The man credited as being the world's first philosopher, although credit might have to go to **Uddalaka** for that. Thales is the first of the **Pre-Socratic** philosophers. Little is known about his life, except that he was a native of the Ionian city of Miletus, and that he traveled widely in the Eastern Mediterranean. Thales's claim to fame rests on being the first person who tried to explain the world not in terms of myths but by observation of it as he actually saw it. Where **Homer** attributed the origin of all things to the god Oceanus, Thales taught that **water** was the prime element in all things.

These two approaches are fundamentally opposed. Homer's assertion is just that, and is not open to verification or refutation. Thales's contention, by contrast, was made in the scientific spirit—that is as something to be discussed and either verified or refuted. Victor Stenger has even dated the birth of **science** to a day in Thales's life. On May 28, 585 BCE, an eclipse of the sun took place in accordance with estimates of Thales. The eclipse happened on that date, because his **mathematics** and his science were right, not because he divined the gods or conferred with oracles. Others have expressed some skepticism that Thales made anything more than an inspired guess.

THEOCRACY. Literally, a polity ruled by **God**, but which in effect means a polity ruled by people who claim to be ruling in God's name. Few surer recipes for **totalitarianism** have ever been provided. The opposite of a theocracy is an **open society**, which, by definition, needs to be secular.

THEODICY. A philosophical stratagem used to provide some sort of explanation for why **God** permits **evil** in the world while, it is claimed, being utterly perfect and compassionate at the same time. The **problem of evil** is one of the abiding issues religious apologists need to come to terms with, but even serious apologists recognize that few of them are at all compelling. Most theodicies have the effect of looking like special pleading for God in a way that trivializes or wants to explain away the real suffering people have endured. See the entry on **anthropodicy**.

THEODOSIAN CODE. Or *Codex Theodosianus*, was promulgated in 438 CE by the Roman emperor Theodosius II (reigned 408–450 CE). It was a very large-scale collection and codification of about twenty-five hundred Roman laws, going back to the reign of **Constantine**. The Theodosian Code gave significant political power and privileges to the Christian ecclesiastical hierarchy, especially in the sphere of municipal government where local officials now had to share rights and duties with churchmen. The code was the first time in the history of the Roman Empire that the benefits of citizenship now depended on correct religious belief. Among the decrees of the Theodosian Code:

- examination of entrails of sacrificed animals is linked with treason, and thus a capital offense;
- most other forms of pagan worship is condemned on penalty of loss of property or exile, or fine;
- all idol worship is banned on pain of death;
- all pagan temples are closed and entry of them is prohibited; and
- wills and testaments made by pagans are declared void.

The code marked a new departure in the growth of Christian **anti-Semitism**. It condemned "the madness of Jewish impiety or the error and insanity of foolish **paganism**" and legitimized an attitude of persecution of non-Christians that lasted for many centuries.

Chapter 16 began with the declaration, "It is necessary that the privileges which are bestowed for the cultivation of religion should be given only to followers of the Catholic faith. We desire that **heretics** and schismatics be not only kept from these privileges, but be subjected to various fines." After all this, the code rather half-heartedly spoke against the direct assault against Jews and pagans. It greatly increased the strength of the church across the Mediterranean world, to the lasting detriment of free expression. It was an important landmark on the way to the **Dark Ages**.

THEODOSIUS I (347–395 CE). The first Roman emperor to persecute his pagan subjects on the grounds of their religious beliefs. Having demonstrated his military ability, Theodosius was made coemperor by Gratian in August 379. Theodosius was more genuinely Christian in his beliefs than his predecessors; he was the first emperor not to take the pagan title *pontifex maximus*, although he was not formally baptized until 380.

In February 380 he decreed that the Nicene Creed was now formally binding on all Roman citizens and that belief in the creed was what constituted a Catholic Christian. The following year, he declared the **Trinity** to be formal orthodoxy, dismissing those who disagreed as **heretics**. These decrees were ratified by the Council of Constantinople later in 381. This inaugurated a new climate of religious intolerance. From the reign of Theodosius I on, pagans were faced with increasing persecution and harassment by Christian authorities. Theodosius enacted further edicts against the pagans in 383, 385, 386, 391, and 392. For instance, in 386 Theodosius confirmed Constantius's death penalty for pagans and ordered all pagan temples to be closed or destroyed. And in 392 Theodosius made his decrees of the previous year even stronger by imposing a complete ban on the worship of pagan gods. Other actions included the prohibition of bequests for the maintenance of pagan cults. In this climate of increasing persecution, the Olympic Games were held for the last time in 395, after 1,200 years. They were not to be reinstated until 1896.

Given this political climate, it is not surprising that the first person sentenced to death in Christendom for **heresy** was in 385. And when the temple of Serapis and the **Alexandria Library** were destroyed by a Christian mob in 389, and upward of half a million manuscripts were destroyed, Theodosius I congratulated the city on the destruction. He also ordered the works of the pagan philosopher **Porphyry** to be destroyed. It was left to Honorius (reigned 395–423) and Theodosius II (reigned 408–450) to exclude pagans from governmental posts. These measures were confirmed by the **Theodosian Code** of 438 and continued by Leo (reigned 457–474) who excluded pagans from the legal profession, and to Justinian (reigned 527–565) who excluded pagans from academic chairs. In 529 Justinian ordered all pagans to receive compulsory Christian instruction and baptism, with penalties of confiscation of property and exile. And in the same year Justinian closed down the **Academy**, founded by **Plato** more than nine hundred years previously. The **Dark Ages** had begun.

THEOGRAPHY. A word to denote works thought to have been written, or dictated, directly by **God**. Biography, historiography, and so on, are written by people, but theography is said to be written by God. There are, of course, significant problems attached to this claim. What for some people is obviously the work of God, is for others the work of humans, and sinful humans at that: the *Book of Mormon*, for example. It also requires the believer to either accept as literally true all the writings said to be theographic.

THEOLOGY. The discipline of making palatable to others what theologians already know to be true. This puts theology at odds with academic disciplines, which look to questioning everything, including the foundations of one's own discipline. The truth criteria of theology, by contrast, are the doctrinal assertions of their particular **religion**, which makes any critical study of those assertions very problematic indeed. In particular, theology is different from the secular discipline of religious studies, which is the open-minded study of the phenomenon of religion. Theology also stands apart from the **scientific attitude**. Indeed, the logical (though not necessary) conclusion of theology is the Muslim doctrine of *Taqlid*.

In an article called "On the Inner Call to Scholarship," Max Weber (1864–1920), the great German sociologist, pointed out that any theology that wishes to remain true to itself will call for the sacrifice of the intellect. This is because theology must presuppose revelation, whereas any secular academic discipline cannot presuppose anything, let alone revelation. From a slightly different vein, the English philosopher Frank Ramsey (1903–1930) noted that theology along with absolutist ethics is one of the two famous subjects which we have realized to have no real objects. More light-heartedly, **Denis Diderot** made a similar point in this little tale: "I was lost in a great forest at night, with only a tiny light to guide me. A stranger approached and said 'My friend, put out your candle, so that you will find your way better.' That person was a theologian."

Pascal Boyer has spoken of the tragedy of the theologian, referring to the neverending custom of people to avoid **theological correctness**. In order to render one's theology immune from popular distortion and manipulation, the theologian's message must become so uninteresting as to make it unworthy of adulteration. See the entry on **demotheology**.

THEOLOGICAL CORRECTNESS. A term coined by anthropologist Justin Barrett to refer to the widespread tendency among people of being able to give a coherent account of their religious beliefs, while in actual fact endorsing, and living in accordance with, divergent sets of beliefs. Often people will present the theologically correct account of their beliefs, but in actual fact, they believe slightly different things, or extra things, and it is often those different and extra things that actually inform their actions.

This phenomenon is not restricted to areas of religion; it can also be observed in politics and elsewhere. Neither is theological correctness to be dismissed simply as hypocrisy. The aberrant behavior is not so much reshaping doctrines to suit our needs, but people insisting that doctrines must be accepted whole and unchanged. See the entry on **Cafeteria Catholics**.

Further reading: Pascal Boyer, *Religion Explained*.

THEOLOGICAL LYING. See **PARALLEL THEOLOGY**.

THEOPATHIC CONDITION, THE. A condition of religious fanaticism identified by **William James**. Fanaticism, James argued, is found only in aggressive and dominating personalities. And when such a personality is religious, then "all human loves and human uses" are expelled. We have found more than ample evidence for this condition in the rise of religious fundamentalism, which insists there is only one way to know **God**, one way to honor God, and one way to live in accordance with his principles. And, wouldn't you know it, that one way is identical to the preferences of the fanatic.

Such single-mindedness is not the exclusive preserve of religious fanatics, but the presence of the **absolutist** notions of God and the **transcendental temptation** make the theopathic condition particularly virulent in its religious guise. See the entries on **certainty** and **command moralities**.

Further reading: William James, *The Varieties of Religious Experience*.

THEOPHILANTHROPY. A **pantheist** movement that had a brief vogue during the French Revolution. The Theophilanthropical Society was formed in September 1796 and came to an end in 1801, after Napoleon concluded a concordat with Pope Pius VII. Theophilanthropy brought together three words: "God," "love," and "man." **Thomas Paine** was briefly involved with the society, lecturing to it in January 1797 on the existence of **God**. Theophilanthropy advocated a pantheist vision of God and the immortality of the **soul**. "The universe," wrote Paine, "is the bible of a true Theophilanthropist." Meetings of the society would hear readings from the Bible and from **Asian traditions**, as well as Greek and Chinese sources. It was critical of fanaticism and **atheism**. Paine revived the idea of Theophilanthropy in New York and a paper called the *Theophilanthropist* appeared for a short while between 1810 and 1811. Contributors included **Elihu Palmer**.

In his biography of Paine, **A. J. Ayer** claimed that the Theophilanthropical Society was the precursor of the **South Place Ethical Society**. This is unlikely since the South Place Ethical Society was originally formed in 1793, before the Theophilanthropical Society, and the latter was well and truly dead by the time the South Place Ethical Society held similar beliefs. This said, the two societies shared a similar outlook. Theophilanthropy also has much in common with contemporary **Unitarianism**. Theophilanthropy is not to be confused with the **Cult of the Supreme Being**.

THEOPHRASTUS (373–287 BCE). **Aristotle**'s successor as leader of the Lyceum. Unlike Plato's **Academy**, which did little to develop the founder's philosophy after his death, Aristotle's Lyceum, especially under Theophrastus and his successor, **Strato the Physicist**, made significant contributions to thought. Theophrastus left a large body of writing, of which little has survived.

Theophrastus continued Aristotle's line of scientific **naturalism**, criticizing extravagant teleological thinking. He also demolished the fashionable thinking about the four elements, being among the first thinkers to observe that fire is not an element at all, but a compound, and that hot and cold are not first principles,

but attributes of something else. This spelled the end of Aristotle's conception of physics, although that was not fully appreciated at the time.

THEORIES OF EVERYTHING. Name given to attempts by mathematicians and theoretical physicists to arrive at a theory regarding particles and forces that would explain and contextualize every item of the universe. An element of matter would not be independent of the space which surrounds it, but simply another element of that space. There would, in short, be no independent entities.

The core problem that theories of everything will have to overcome is to reconcile **quantum mechanics**, which explains much of the subatomic world, and general **relativity** (specifically gravity), which explains the universe in its immensity. These two principles of physics work well in their respective areas but seem incompatible when set beside each other. Some physicists think that **string theory** will provide the breakthrough toward a theory of everything.

Some physicists, notably Stephen Hawking (1942–) and Paul Davies (1946–) have tried to portray the monism of the theory of everything as the "mind of **God**," but just what this god would be is far from clear. Several critics have observed that it would amount to little more than a set of equations. As often happens, the title of the theory gives rise to as many misconceptions as clarifications. Even if a theory of everything is successfully worked out, this will not at all mean the end of physics. It would, at best, open for us, the rule book of the universe, without having been explained all the rules.

Further reading: Brian Greene, *The Elegant Universe*.

THEOSOPHY. Extravagant but harmless cult. The word probably came from the writings of the mystic writer Johann Valentin Andreae (1586–1654), in particular his book *Christianopolis* (1619). Andreae is usually credited as the founder and inspiration for the Rosicrucians. Modern Theosophy was inspired by the writings of Helena Petrovna Blavatsky (1831–1891), a wildly eccentric Russian émigré.

Theosophy as a movement grew from the waves of **spiritualism** that had gripped Europe and North America in the 1850s and 1860s. It combined diverse strands of **pseudoscience**, occult thinking, and Eastern philosophy. Blavatsky claimed to have visited Tibet, then safely remote and unknown, and to have learned important mystical insights. The Theosophical Society was founded in the United States in 1875 and was soon accompanied by a compendious work, *Isis Unveiled* (1875–77) which Blavatsky claimed had been dictated to her by divine presences. Her writings were panned by scholars but had a wide appeal to sections of the general public who were looking for this sort of esotericism and were not unduly worried by its incoherence.

Outwardly, Theosophy involved an open-minded search for the laws of nature and psychic powers in people, as well as propagating notions of the brotherhood of man and the study of comparative religion. Theosophy as a movement went through a series of scandals involving stolen correspondence, pederastic leaders (see the entry on **Charles Leadbetter**), forged documents, and high-profile defectors (see the entry on **Jiddu Krishnamurti**), but the movement remained influential until the 1920s. One of Blavatsky's more influential admirers was Heinrich Himmler (1900–1945), who adapted her racial theories into the ostentatious mythology he built for the SS. An altogether more positive legacy of Theosophy was that it commanded the allegiance of three of the twentieth century's greatest artists: Piet Mondrian (1872–1944), Constantin Brancusi (1876–1957), and, at least until 1914, Wassily Kandinsky (1866–1944). Another convinced Theosophist was L. Frank Baum (1856–1919), author of *The Wonderful Wizard of Oz*. And Baum's mother-in-law, the great American feminist pioneer **Matilda Joslyn Gage**, was also supportive of Theosophy.

Apart from the artists, the most important convert for Theosophy was **Annie Besant**. While still an atheist Besant was given a copy of *The Secret Doctrine* to review by George Bernard Shaw (1856–1950), although other accounts say it was the journalist W. T. Stead (1849–1912) who gave her the work. Besant surprised everyone by being converted. By 1896 Besant was the leader of the movement and remained staunchly attracted to Theosophy for the rest of her life. She led the move to deemphasize its supernatural elements.

THERAVADA BUDDHISM. The brand of Buddhism which most accurately reflects the teachings of **Siddhartha Gautama**, the Buddha. Theravada Buddhism is practiced in Sri Lanka and Southeast Asia, as opposed to Mahayana Buddhism, which is widespread in China and Japan. The smallest variation is Vajrayana Buddhism in Tibet. This is the branch of Buddhism linked with the Dalai Lama. Theravada Buddhism is sometimes known as Hinayana, or "Lesser Vehicle" Buddhism, a derogatory title given by its Mahayana opponents. Contrary to Buddhism's popular image as a pacific religion, the division between Theravada and Mahayana Buddhism has been bitter. Theravada Buddhism became organized around 250 BCE, around the time of **Ashoka**, the Maurya emperor, although the split began at what is called the Second Council, which took place around 377 BCE between Theravada and the Mahasangikas, who predated the Mahayana.

Theravada teaching took on its modern form between the fifth and tenth centuries CE. Some of its most important thinkers were Buddhaghosa ("the voice of the Buddha") in the fifth century CE, and two later thinkers, both called Dhammapala. Theravada is the most atheistic of the great **Asian Traditions** and is a good reason why calling them religions is problematic at best. Eschewing any notion of a **god**, or any other form of **transcendental temptation**, Theravada Buddhism follows the Buddha's teaching to "be a light unto oneself." Different branches of Theravada extol different versions of the ideal known as the *arahat*, or "worthy one." *Arahats* are those who have fully understood the Buddha's teachings and incorporated them fully into their lives. See the entries on **dependent arising** and the **Four Noble Truths**.

THINKER'S LIBRARY. A very successful series of books published by the **Rationalist Press Association** between 1929 and 1951. The idea behind the library was much the same as for the RPA's highly successful **Cheap Reprints** program almost thirty years earlier. The Thinker's Library was designed to make the works of leading thinkers available to people of modest means. The inexpensive hardbound volumes were originally sold at one shilling each, though prices soon rose in the wake of the Great Depression. More than five million Thinker's Library titles were sold during the series' career, the best single title being **H. G. Wells**'s *A Short History of the World*.

Altogether there were 140 titles in the Thinker's Library series, covering a wide range of topics from a wide range of perspectives. Many different shades of opinion were published in the series, from **reverent agnostics** and **religious humanists** to atheist liberals and post–Spanish Civil War Marxists. The series ranged from sober histories to essays and light relief, from complicated works of science to undemanding novels, from **Charles Darwin** to **Charles Gorham**, from Samuel Butler (1835–1902) to the gothic novelist Marjorie Bowen (1885–1952). For several decades people spoke of coming across a Thinker's Library title as being the turning point on their road to **freethought**.

Further reading: Bill Cooke, *The Gathering of the Infidels: A Hundred Years of the Rationalist Press Association*.

THIRD CULTURE, THE. An idea that can

be traced back to a lecture in 1959 by **Sir C. P. Snow** called "The Two Cultures," where Snow commented on the growing communication gulf between the humanities and the sciences. He was bombarded with an avalanche of criticism for making this observation, notably from the literary critic F. R. Leavis (1895–1978), whose criticisms were especially vindictive. When he revisited the issue in a 1963 essay, Snow speculated on a third culture arising, whereby literary scholars were resuming dialogue with scientists.

Thirty years later the notion of a third culture was taken up by John Brockman, an American writer, thinker, and entrepreneur. But Brockman saw the third culture not being peopled by literary thinkers conversant with the sciences, but with scientists themselves. He edited a work titled *The Third Culture* (1995) featuring essays by the sort of people he had in mind; scientists taking on the role of public intellectual. They included **Richard Dawkins**, **Daniel C. Dennett**, Steven Pinker, Nicholas Humphrey, Stephen Jay Gould (1941–2002), and Roger Penrose. *The Third Culture* was an influential work. See the entry on **two cultures**.

Further reading: John Brockman, ed., *The Third Culture*.

THIRD WAY, THE. An attempt to create a new brand of progressive politics that has been very influential. The idea was first given expression by the British sociologist Anthony Giddens. Third Way thinking became most popular among European and Australasian Labor parties in the 1980s and after. These parties recognized the problems the **welfare state** was getting into: overregulation, increasing costs, and a declining stream of revenue to pay for it all. See the entry on **Eurosclerosis**. Of particular concern was the skyrocketing costs pension schemes face once the **baby-boomer** generation starts to retire. See the entry on **agequake**. The most prominent example of third-way politics has been the Labor Government under Tony Blair in Britain. Even the party's new name, New

Labor, is emblematic of the change. Another important example was the Labor Government in New Zealand between 1984 and 1990, and again since 1999, which has reworked the management of the welfare state in that country.

Third-way thinking wants to work more creatively with business and government than earlier left-of-center politics saw as appropriate. Third-way thinkers want to avoid the older talk of class conflict and big bureaucracy as much as they avoid the rhetoric of the right about the virtues of laissez faire. Critics have argued that the third way is nothing more than warmed-over conservatism.

Further reading: Anthony Giddens, *The Third Way*.

THIRD-WORLD DEBT. A serious problem before the 1980s, which has become a lot more severe since then. What stimulated third-world debt was the huge amounts of cash floating around the world's banks coming from oil-producing countries newly enriched by price rises which led to the **oil shocks** in the West. This money had been deposited in Western banks, which then lent large sums out to third-world countries, usually for expensive infrastructure projects, such as dams. But recession soon took hold and interest rates on the loans began to increase unexpectedly, and at the same time the value of the goods third-world countries produced declined. In some cases the loans had been ill-considered in the first place.

Third-world debt stood at $130 billion in 1973, but after the first wave of loans went out after the price rises, the debt in 1982 had ballooned up to $612 billion. By 1997 the total was 2.17 *trillion* dollars. This amounts to the third world paying $717 million in debt repayment every day. To take one example among many, the national debt of Uganda in 2003 was 4.3 billion dollars, the equivalent of 70 percent of the country's GDP or 186 percent of the country's export earnings.

For many of the poorest nations, more money was being spent on servicing the debt than in developing education and health services. Africa spends four times more on servicing the interest on their loans than on healthcare. In fact, many loans are made on the express condition that cuts to these services be made, so as to ensure the debt is repaid. What is more, the debts have to be repaid in hard currencies (the currencies of wealthy developed nations) which third-world currencies have to buy at an enormous disadvantage. As countries began to default on their loans, pressure on the Western banks rose, with some of them not surviving.

Third-world debt is one of the most pressing economic and ethical issues that need to be addressed in the twenty-first century. See the entries on **World Bank Group** and **International Monetary Fund**.

THOMSON, JAMES (1834–1882). Brilliant, self-destructive Scottish poet. While working as a schoolmaster in the army, Thomson met **Charles Bradlaugh**, and the two became fast friends. Thomson's life was a continual catalog of tragedies, and he resorted to alcohol more and more frequently.

Thomson wrote a lot for the **freethought** press, but is best remembered for his unutterably bleak poem, *The City of Dreadful Night* (1874), one of the most concentrated examples of sublime melancholy ever written. The American author Herman Melville described *The City of Dreadful Night* as "the modern Book of Job, duskily looming with the same aboriginal verities." Thomson wrote his poems under the pseudonym of "BV," which stood for Bysshe Vanolis, which in turn stood for the poets **Shelley** and Novalis, who Thomson admired above all others.

He never succeeded in establishing a stable way to live, and he died at only forty-eight, penniless and ruined by drink.

Further reading: Tom Leonard, *Places of the Mind*.

THREE DENIALS, THE. Christian apologists are prone to three denials when faced with unpleasant or otherwise inconvenient passages in the New Testament:

- *ignoring the passage altogether*, such as Jesus' injunction to hate the family;
- *explain it away as symbolic or allegorical*, such as eternal torment for unbelievers; or
- *insist that it is out of character and must be a later interpolation*, such as Jesus speaking in parables so as not to enlighten the unbeliever.

But, as **Margaret Knight**, who made these observations (without giving them this title) noted, if some passages can be explained away, it makes it very difficult to then provide any convincing reason why we should take seriously the passages that remain.

Further reading: Margaret Knight, *Honest to Man*.

THREE WAYS AND THE EIGHT STEPS, THE. The formulation of **humanist values** as articulated in *The Great Learning*, the classical work of Confucian ethics. Originally part of a large Confucian work called the *Book of Rites*, *The Great Learning* was later extracted from it and made a stand-alone Confucian work. Probably not written by **Kongfuzi** (Confucius) himself, but by Zengzi (a disciple) or Zi Si (his grandson). The reference to great learning is to distinguish it from small learning, which children are in need of. The great learning is what adults need to comprehend.

The power of *The Great Learning* is that it encapsulates the Confucian educational, moral, and political program in a simple format. First are the Three Ways, or Three Aims:

- clear character;
- loving the people; and
- abiding in the highest good.

These Ways are achieved by the Eight Steps:

- investigation of things;

- extension of knowledge;
- sincerity of the will;
- rectification of the mind;
- cultivation of the personal life;
- regulation of the family;
- national order; and
- world peace.

The Three Ways and the Eight Steps encapsulate the Confucian emphasis upon reforming one's **character** and building social cohesion and the intimate links between the two notions. It is important to see how both processes begin with oneself, working on the basic premise that one can play no useful role in society if one's own personality and family are in disorder. At no point is there any reference to any **supernatural** order or **command morality**.

THYMOS. Greek word meaning spiritedness, which refers to our desire for recognition being the most fundamental drive within us. Thymos was first discussed in **Plato**'s *Republic*, and has been a theme in Western philosophy ever since. Thymos is not simply desire, nor is it **reason**—it is the basic drive for understanding our value in the world, as opposed to the value of those things and people around us.

In its most vulgar manifestation thymos is the dog-eat-dog combativeness of competitive people. **Nietzsche**'s **will to power** is a brand of thymos. Thymos is capable of generating all the most destructive fanaticisms and hatreds. More helpfully, it is an innate sense of justice, so that when we feel we have been dealt with unjustly, we feel anger, and when we feel we have been dealt with justly, we feel pride. Each of these scenarios involves a public understanding of our sense of value. Much human activity can be understood as the means by which we go about ensuring that other people share the sense of value of ourselves as we do. It also helps explain why each generation will feel the need to **rebel** against its elders. It doesn't matter whether the older generation has done things well or poorly. What matters is that it was them, and not us, who did these things.

Further reading: Plato, *The Republic* (bk. 2); and Francis Fukuyama, *The End of History and the Last Man*.

TIELMAN, ROBERT (1946–). One of the most important humanist thinkers and activists since World War II. Rob Tielman was born in Hilversum, the Netherlands, on August 19, 1946. His father, a socialist, had been imprisoned during the war, and his mother had spent much of the later part of the war in hiding.

Tielman spent much of his career as professor of sociology at the University of Utrecht. He has written widely; his best known work is *Homoseksualiteit in Nederland* (1982); he coauthored several works: *Bisexuality and HIV/AIDS: A Global Perspective* (1991) with Manuel Carballo and Aart Henriks; *The Third Pink Book: A Global View of Gay Liberation and Oppression* (1993) with Aart Henriks and Evert van der Veen; and he coedited *Building a World Community: Humanism in the Twenty-First Century* (1994) with **Paul Kurtz** and Levi Fragell. From 1987 through 1994 Tielman was active on the National Commission of the Fight against AIDS, a government agency. He is at present serving as president of the Netherlands Pluralist Public Schools Foundation.

He has held a large number of important posts within the humanist movement. He has been president of the **International Humanist and Ethical Union** and of the Dutch Humanist League and vice-president of the European Humanist Federation.

Tielman was knighted by the Queen of the Netherlands for his social work in 1987 and in 1998 he was awarded the Rob Angelo Medal, the premier award of the Culture and Recreation Centre, a gay and lesbian organization which he has given long service to. He is also a laureate of the **International Academy of Humanism**.

TIT FOR TAT. A remarkable ethical model that began life in 1981 as a computer simulation of the prisoner's dilemma, an ethical conundrum to which there is no solution. Based on the problem of the prisoner's dilemma, the American social theorist Robert Axelrod developed a computer test for methods of cooperation. To his surprise a simple model, called tit for tat, devised by Anatol Rappaport, was the winner. It also won a more difficult second test Axelrod devised.

The tit-for-tat model quickly showed itself to be among the most flexible and has subsequently become a model for ethics. This was because of its simplicity. Tit for tat has only two rules:

(1) Start by being ready to cooperate.
(2) Then repeat exactly your opponent's move.

The core strategy of tit for tat is to reciprocate the behavior of the opponent. Although there are varieties of it, they mostly begin with a gesture of cooperation. If that gesture is reciprocated in an equally friendly manner, acts of cooperation continue. But if the gesture of cooperation is responded to with betrayal, then that sets the tone of the relationship until the other party changes its tune.

Things got more complicated after that, but the basic pattern of tit for tat was set, and the lessons it can teach humans with regard to ethical behavior remain valid. Tit for tat provides support for Robert Trivers's theory of **reciprocal altruism**.

TOLERATION. In many ways, the most important tool *Homo sapiens* can use to ensure its future survival. The great **Enlightenment** thinker **Voltaire** called toleration "the appurtenance of humanity," by which he meant the essential corollary to the fact that we are prone to weakness and error. "We are all products of frailty," Voltaire wrote, "and prone to error. So let us mutually pardon each other's stupidities. This is the first principle of the law of nature." See the entry on **doubt**.

Toleration is an essential component of any **democracy**. A democracy is, at best, an **open society**, and in open societies we need to develop tolerance for things we may not personally approve of. Toleration rests on the assumption of **diversity** in the world and the need to respect those whose views we may not share. Toleration is the expression of **reciprocal altruism** in practice. The limits of toleration are reached when moral responsibility has been abandoned or jeopardized. In this way, toleration of **terrorism** or child pornography is not appropriate.

The pressing need for toleration grew in Europe in the wake of the **wars of religion**, during which millions of people died in the name of **God**. The primary goal of the early proponents of toleration was that people's religious allegiances were their own concern, and not those of their rulers, as had previously been the case. This case was put most clearly in **John Locke**'s *Letter Concerning Toleration* (three parts—1689, 1690, 1692), although even Locke could not bring himself to extend toleration to include Catholics, Jews, or atheists. It was partially from the inspiration of Locke that the Enlightenment placed such an emphasis on toleration.

Some scholars have shown how tolerance is often given lip service to rather than honored in any serious way. Others have said we need more than mere toleration, we must have an active celebration of diversity. These arguments have some validity, but we still stick to toleration for the time being. Toleration can only take root where a genuine feeling for people's **rights** exists, and where a transnational ethos prevails. **Humanism** is a system of belief which meshes with these feelings intimately. **Monotheistic** religions have a problem with toleration because they believe themselves to be in possession of absolute truth, which has to come to them from **God** himself, in the form of **scripture**. Islamic toleration extends only as far as Jews and Christians. No toleration can be extended to those who do not subscribe to the monotheistic **command morality**. See the entry on **Intol-**

erance, Principle of. Within this framework, disagreeing with God's truth can't simply be a difference of opinion, it has to bring with it some moral taint, hence the need for words like "heretic" and "apostate." The **Asian traditions**, while being far from models of toleration, have a better record than the Western religions, mainly because of their lesser concern for the content of people's beliefs than for the manner in which they live.

TOMINAGA, NAKAMOTO (1715–1746). An important influence on the Japanese Enlightenment. Quite independently from the European **Enlightenment**, Tominaga employed the methods of scholarly criticism, **empiricism**, and rationality in his studies. In *Shutsujo kogo* (1745) he made some pioneering criticisms of the historicity of Buddhism. He is thought to be the first scholar to question whether the Mahayana sutras came directly from the Buddha. By close reading of the sutras, he concluded that they were written upward of five hundred years after the Buddha's death. Some later Buddhist scholars like Murakami Sensho (1851–1929) admitted the validity of Tominaga's scholarship.

It was Tominaga's belief that ideas and religious practices are not revealed at one time and place, but are the product of slow cultural evolution, and when misused in the service of **dogmatism**, betray their value. In *Jottings of an Old Man* Tominaga criticized each of the main belief systems prevalent in Japan. Confucianism was criticized for obscuring its original clarity with rhetoric. Buddhism was attacked for lapsing into **magic** and **supernaturalism**, and Shintoism was criticized for obscurantism. Tominaga wrote "I am not a follower of Confucianism, nor of Taoism, nor Buddhism. I watch their words and deeds from the side and then privately debate them."

TOTALITARIANISM. A term coined by Italian philosopher Giovanni Gentile (1875–1944) to symbolize the complete unity of human consciousness into an ideal, the embodiment of which was the state. Not surprisingly, Gentile became an enthusiastic supporter of Italian Fascism, eventually being murdered by communist partisans for his troubles.

The idea of totalitarianism only became widely known with the publication of **The Origins of Totalitarianism** (1951) by the German scholar Hannah Arendt (1906–1975), who made some telling observations about the many features shared by fascism and **Stalinism**.

Without using the word, totalitarianism has been warmly recommended by thinkers over a long period, but it became more prominent in the second half of the nineteenth century, as some thinkers worried about the effects of mass **democracy** on their beloved hierarchies and predemocratic values. The most brilliant European thinker whose work had clear totalitarian overtones was **Martin Heidegger**, and in the Muslim world it was perhaps **Sayyid Qutb**. Totalitarianism was taken up by the Baathi thinkers in the Middle East, and it found its fullest expression in Saddam Hussein's Baath Party regime in Iraq, prior to its destruction in 2003. Also, see the entry on the **general will**.

Almost without exception, the humanist community throughout history has been vocal in its opposition to totalitarianism. The **humanist values** of freedom, **reason**, and **toleration** are all vulnerable in a totalitarian society. Humanism operates most successfully in an **open society**.

TRAGEDY. Described by Karl Deutsch (1912–1992) as the condition, inevitable in human life, when awareness exceeds power. Tragedy as an art form found its true home in ancient Greece, where it worked and reworked the themes of the hero brought low by a crucial failure to recognize the limits of self-assertion. The German philosopher Karl Jaspers (1883–1969) said that what we learn from tragic knowledge is what makes us suffer, what makes us fail, and what we will attempt to do in the face of this knowledge. In its tra-

ditional sense, tragedy, which is not to be confused with mere misfortune, is the preserve not of the common run of a person, but of an aristocracy—an aristocracy of feeling or intellect. Thus Hamlet, King Lear, or any other tragic hero is both graced with more talent than the rest of us, but also with greater flaws.

Christianity cannot accommodate tragedy, because of its myth of redemption, open to all, as long as there is faith in the redeemer. In contrast to this, the English sociologist Ronald Fletcher (1912–1992) noted that **humanism** recognizes an "inescapable undertone of tragedy in the world" because, in the knowledge of the shortness of our life and the transitoriness of our achievements, humanism can offer no consolation. It can only counsel us to persevere, because life will be over all too soon. In this sense, humanism has democratized tragedy. See the entries on **Greek playwrights** and **William Shakespeare**.

TRAGEDY OF THE COMMONS. The notion devised by Garret Hardin (1915–2003) in an address to the American Association for the Advancement of Science in 1968 which has since become very influential. Hardin wanted to illustrate the principle of the finiteness of the planet's resources. He posited a village with a block of common land near it. The villagers use the commons to graze their cattle, and when one villager decides to graze more of his cattle on the commons to raise his level of prosperity, other villagers feel bound to follow suit. Pretty soon the overgrazing has destroyed the commons and now nobody can use it and the village suffers accordingly. It doesn't take much to apply this notion to the planet as a whole.

The crisis of world overfishing is a good illustration of the tragedy of the commons. It only takes one country to extend its fishing fleet to encourage others to do the same. And as stocks deplete, the logic of the tragedy of the commons is to fish even more aggressively, to get what is left. This ruinous situation is fueled in no small part by subsidies of $20 billion annually, and protection. Any credible notion of **sustainable development** will have to take the tragedy of the commons seriously. See the entries on **ecology** and **ecological footprint**.

TRANSCENDENTAL PRETENSE, THE. A term coined by American philosopher Robert C. Solomon to refer to the habit of some religious leaders of invoking some scriptural authority to impose their commandments on the world. This is a common practice of **fundamentalists**, who wrap their prejudice up in the language of "only doing God's work." The transcendental pretense is a variation of the **argument from authority**.

Further reading: Robert C. Solomon, *Spirituality for the Skeptic*.

TRANSCENDENTAL TEMPTATION, THE. A term coined by **Paul Kurtz** to refer to the temptation to look to the consolations of **magic** and **religion** rather than take responsibility for one's life and face reality. The transcendental temptation is the clearest form of **anthropocentric conceit** we are prone to succumbing to. The ability to resist the transcendental temptation is an essential step in forging an autonomous, responsible **eupraxsophy**. Submitting to the transcendental temptation traps one in the **command moralities** of the past and prevents any serious exploration of life and nature in its own terms. Valerii Kuvakin has isolated the principal transcendental temptations as:

- the temptation of **immortality**;
- the temptation of forgiveness and perfection;
- the temptation of a guarantee of safety and protection; and
- the temptation of absolute happiness.

Some people have tried to argue that these are inherent **human needs**, but this claim founders on the fact that millions of people around the world live productive lives without having succumbed to any of these temptations.

Further reading: Paul Kurtz, *The Transcendental Temptation*; and Valerii Kuvakin, *In Search of Our Humanity*.

TRANSFERRED AUTHORITY, FALLACY OF. A common practice, where an authority in one discipline makes pronouncements in another discipline, expecting his authority to be transferred to the new context. Scientists speaking about **God** or theologians speaking about some area of science are among the groups most likely to commit this error.

TRANSHUMANISM. Described in 2004 by the right-wing commentator Francis Fukuyama as "the world's most dangerous idea." The word was originally coined by **Julian Huxley**, largely under the influence of the **mysticism** of Pierre Teilhard de Chardin (1881–1955). Transhumanism is the term under which a loose coalition of individuals support the transformation of human ability through the technology and science that is now available to us.

A group of transhumanists got together in 1998 and created the World Transhumanist Association (WTA). The WTA then issued a seven-point Transhumanist Declaration in the same year, of which the following is a summary:

(1) Humanity will be radically changed by technology in the future with possibilities for redesigning human beings in fundamental ways.
(2) Research into these developments should be undertaken.
(3) We should be open to this new technology rather than try to ban it.
(4) The individual has a right to explore these technologies if she so chooses.
(5) It would be tragic if we let these opportunities slip through our fingers, or if we allowed *Homo sapiens* to become extinct.
(6) There is a need for appropriate forums for these issues to be discussed.

(7) Transhumanism supports the well-being of all forms of sentience, without regard to the form that sentience takes.

Transhumanism is one strand of thought that emerges once one has taken seriously the findings of modern science with regard to the nonexistence of a **soul**, or any sort of supernatural essence. Given that we are biological entities, it follows that, if these entities can be improved upon, what reason is there not to do so? It is clearly incorrect to insist that our current biological and anatomical and neurological structure is the best that could possibly be devised.

However, one doesn't have to be religious to be troubled by this idea. There is a sense in which it violates the **precautionary principle**, which is a cause for concern. There are enormous bioethical implications in transhumanism that we have barely begun to explore. The issues raised by the transhumanists will be the cutting edge of moral philosophy, **bioethics**, and the **conflict between science and religion** for much of the twenty-first century. Nevertheless, the challenge of building better *Homo sapiens* is clearly upon us, and we would be shortsighted to hope the issue goes away simply by banning research or pious condemnation of those who are in favor of pushing the changes.

Further reading: www.transhumanism.org.

TRIBE, DAVID (1931–). Australian thinker, activist, and poet. David Tribe was born in Sydney and educated in Brisbane. As a young man he moved to Britain where he immersed himself in the **freethought** movement as a speaker, journalist, broadcaster, and public-relations advisor. He served as chairman of the Humanist Group Action (1961–64) and was on the executive committee of the National Council for Civil Liberties from 1961 until 1972. He was president of the **National Secular Society** from 1963 until 1971 and in 1966 was editor of its magazine the *Freethinker*. In 1972 Tribe returned to Australia, where he took a less active role in freethought.

He has written extensively. His major books include *Freethought and Humanism in Shakespeare* (1964); *100 Years of Freethought* (1966), a particularly valuable centenary history of the freethought movement; *President Charles Bradlaugh MP* (1971), still the major twentieth-century study of **Bradlaugh**; *Nucleoethics* (1972), a quirky attempt to set a new agenda for new humanist ethics; and *The Rise of the Mediocracy* (1976). He is an honorary associate of the **Rationalist Press Association**, the **Rationalist International**, and the **New Zealand Association of Rationalists and Humanists**.

TRINITY. A Christian doctrine which states that, though **God** is one substance, he reveals himself in the three divine persons of God, **Jesus Christ**, and the Holy Ghost. The Trinity developed as a response to the widely differing views among early Christians over how best to reconcile the divinity of Jesus with the fatherhood of God. The word came from the early Christian thinker Tertullian (160–240 CE, approx.), but the formula was devised at the Council of Nicaea, convened by the emperor **Constantine** in 325 CE. The result was a barely comprehensible formula over which theologians have struggled for the best part of two thousand years, and over which many people have lost their lives. The difficulty was exacerbated by the lack of support in Christian **scripture** for the Trinitarian position. After decades of dispute, the Trinity was declared orthodox by **Theodosius** in 381 CE, leaving those who disputed the formula to be branded as **heretics**. Even St. Thomas Aquinas conceded that the Trinity could not be defended using **reason**, but only through **faith**.

Disputes over the status of a word in the Nicene Creed led to the permanent estrangement between the Catholic and Orthodox churches in 1054. The word at issue was *filioque* (proceeds), which Catholics considered a part of the creed and Orthodox did not. In fact, the word was not part of the original creed, it was added as a move against the Arian heresy in the fourth century. The filioque controversy involved the relative standing of the Father, Son, and Holy Ghost. The Orthodox felt that the added word *filioque* overemphasized the Son over the Father and the Holy Ghost. Orthodox worship the Trinity as an indivisible whole. The Catholic church, by contrast, focused attention on Jesus Christ, and hence needed the word "proceeds" in the formula so as to give Jesus the required level of spiritual authority as proceeding from the Father. Upon this rather technical controversy, the two largest Christian churches have been bitterly at odds for over a thousand years. Even in the United Kingdom, it was an offense to deny the Trinity until 1813. Since then the Trinity has become an increasingly arcane theological relic.

TRUELOVE, EDWARD (1809–1899). Secularist bookseller in London who suffered persecution for his beliefs. Truelove was a veteran of all the major **freethought** struggles in nineteenth-century Britain. After working with **Richard Carlile**, **George Jacob Holyoake**, and for the Owenite movement, Truelove opened a bookshop on the Strand in 1852. In 1858 an unsuccessful prosecution was brought against him for publishing W. E. Adams' *Tyrannicide*, and in 1878, at the instigation of the Society for the Suppression of Vice in 1878, he was arrested, fined £50, and sentenced to four months imprisonment for selling two birth-control pamphlets: *Moral Physiology* by Robert Dale Owen (1801– 1877) and *Individual, Family and National Poverty* by J. H. Palmer. Truelove was supported morally and financially by the secularist movement.

TRUTH. The clearest possible understanding people can achieve of the world in which we live. A statement can be deemed true when the object described coheres with what is said about it. Our perceptual and intellectual faculties are limited and **fallible**, so there is always a chance that error has crept into our understanding of what is true. This requires that we should always be ready to abandon what we may today consider to be true if it turns out not to be. The **geocentric universe** was held to be true for many centuries until it turned out not to be. However, just because notions once thought to be true are now known to be false does not mean that all notions of facts, sound **evidence**, and honest inquiry are specious. This is what Susan Haack calls the **passes-for fallacy**.

It is also important to note that while humans have difficulties explaining notions of truth to themselves, there is a real world out there, one that existed long before we evolved sufficiently to undertake a study of it. Much of what we know about the real world is true, but there is always room for improvement in our understanding.

There is also a difference between a *true* argument and a *valid* one. A valid argument is one that is internally consistent and meaningful, but without necessarily being true. Consider this example from the **deduction and induction** entry:

- Only gods can arrange a virgin birth.
- Jesus had a virgin birth.
- Therefore, the gods arranged Jesus' birth.

This deduction is perfectly valid; it just happens not to be true. The deduction is valid because it makes sense to argue this; it's not gibberish. But the problem is that the premises are untrue, which automatically means that the conclusion is untrue.

TRUTH, COHERENCE THEORY OF. The theory of truth which says that something is true when it is coherent with a series of related facts. This is not simply a pedantic difference with the **correspondence theory**. The coherence theory rose in response to the various difficulties of the correspondence theory with respect to notions of "correspondence" and of "**facts**." Opponents of the coherence theory worry that it is tantamount to **rela-**

tivism. In the face of this challenge, some coherentists have conceded that some beliefs are more equal than others. Beliefs deriving from **science**, for instance, can justifiably lay claim to this distinguished status. See the entries on **reliabilism** and **foundationalism**.

TRUTH, CORRESPONENCE THEORY OF. The theory of truth which says that something is true if and only if it corresponds with the **facts**. The correspondence theory relies on defending the coherence of concepts such as "truth," "correspondence," and "facts." Once the dust from the often highly technical nature of the debate over the validity of the correspondence theory has settled, there remains a need for the concept of truth.

Further reading: John Searle, *The Social Construction of Reality*.

TRUTHSEEKER, THE. A long-running American **freethought** paper. The *Truthseeker* was founded by **De Robigne Mortimer Bennett** in 1873. Bennett came to this decision after a journal refused to print his letters disputing a local clergyman. It began publication in September 1873 in Paris, Illinois, then it was moved to New York early the next year, and became a weekly in January 1876. As soon as the *Truthseeker* arrived in New York, it began to attract the hostile attention of Anthony Comstock (1844–1915), after whom the notorious Comstock Laws were named. See the entry on **comstockery**. Having been imprisoned because of these laws, Bennett handed over the editorship to Eugene Macdonald (1855– 1909) who edited the *Truthseeker* until his death. Eugene's position was taken over by his younger brother **George E. Macdonald**, who retained the position until his death in 1937.

These were the glory years of the paper, which outlived, and in most cases took over, all its fellow freethought periodicals. Under the influence of the Macdonald brothers, the *Truthseeker* was an intelligent voice of liberal, evolutionist freethought, inspired mainly by **Herbert Spencer** and **Ernest Haeckel**. It was a tribute to the paper's popular support that it survived the Great Depression and the death of George Macdonald in 1937. Charles Lee Smith (1887–1964), a founder of the **American Association for the Advancement of Atheism**, bought the *Truthseeker* from Macdonald in 1930 and turned it into a monthly. Smith remained editor until his death, although during his editorship it began to lose circulation. The main reason for this was Smith's racism and **anti-Semitism** which, particularly after 1950, became significant features of the paper. Smith's assistant editor Woolsey Teller (1890–1954) shared Smith's views and was a bad influence.

Faced with sharply declining circulation, Smith was persuaded to sell the paper to James Hervey Johnson (1901–1988) who moved the paper to his home town of San Diego. Under Johnson's control, the *Truthseeker* retained all the hatreds of his predecessor, plus a few more. By the time of the paper's centenary issue in 1973 it had only a few subscribers.

The *Truthseeker* died a squalid death during a prolonged legal struggle. **American Atheists** engineered a takeover of the paper in 1987 and Johnson was engaged in the legal struggle to retrieve his paper at the time of his death.

TURING, ALAN (1912–1954). Brilliant and sensitive English mathematician and scientist. Alan Turing is credited with pioneering the development of the computer and the discipline of **artificial intelligence**. Born into a comfortable upper-middle-class family, he received an excellent education, studying at Kings College, Cambridge, and taking a PhD at Princeton University, graduating in 1938.

During World War II, Turing worked for the Department of Communications at Bletchley Park in Britain, where he played a major role in cracking the German code used for military communication, known as Enigma. The Germans were confident that the code, which changed constantly, was impossible to break. But Turing and his colleagues built a machine known as Colossus, which was, in effect, a computer, and broke the code in a relatively short time. The military advantage to the Allies of cracking the Enigma code is pretty well impossible to exaggerate. Turing was awarded an OBE in 1946 for his work breaking the code.

After the war, he worked for the National Physical Laboratory, where he worked on what was known as the Automatic Computing Engine. His research from this time is generally regarded as some of the earliest investigation into what is now called artificial intelligence. Turing believed that a well-designed computer could match or surpass all brain activities, a view that got him into heated arguments with some of his colleagues.

In what has become a landmark paper, written in 1950, Turing postulated a test involving a person asking questions via keyboard to both a person and an intelligent machine. Turing believed that if the questioner could not tell the machine apart from the person after a reasonable amount of time, the machine could usefully be described as intelligent. This is now known as the Turing Test and remains a central topic of contention within the artificial-intelligence community.

In 1948 Turing left the National Physical Laboratory and moved on to the University of Manchester, where he worked on the development of the Manchester Automatic Digital Machine (MADAM). He created algorithms and programs for MADAM, while also developing his mathematical knowledge to develop brilliant new insights in biology. He also had time and energy to take up running as an exercise, and at which he reached close to Olympic status.

Turing died in mysterious circumstances in 1954. The general consensus is that he committed suicide in a state of depression over being homosexual. He became a fellow of the Royal Society in 1951.

Further reading: Andrew Hodges, *The Alan Turing Home Page*, www.turing.org.uk.

TURNER, JOSEPH MALLORD WILLIAM (1775–1851). Brilliant and eccentric English painter. Despite a poor and unhappy upbringing, Turner received an education in art from the age of fourteen, and his first picture was exhibited in the Royal Academy when he was fifteen. At only twenty-eight, Turner was appointed academician, and in 1808 became professor of perspective at the Academy.

Turner's painting, particularly after he switched to oils in 1793, became stronger and stronger. Between *Ulysses Deriding Polyphemus* (1829) and *Fighting Temeraire* (1839), he produced paintings of such quality that they revolutionized artmaking. He was also fortunate in having an influential admirer in the person of John Ruskin, who did a great deal to publicize his works.

Ruskin called his friend an infidel, and subsequent biographers have noted with varying degrees of embarrassment, Turner's complete indifference to religious questions. Turner left his pictures to the nation and donated his considerable fortune to founding a home for destitute British artists.

TWAIN, MARK (1835–1910). Thought by many to be the most important American writer. Samuel Langhorne Clemens was born in and educated in Florida, Missouri. He went to work as a compositor in 1851, and from 1857 until 1861 as a riverboat pilot on the Mississippi. It was there he took the name that the world came to know him by. "Mark Twain" refers to the river being two fathoms deep at that point. Clemens was not the first person to use that *nom de plume*.

One of Twain's strongest gifts was his natural sense of **humor**. Until his later years, Twain was a genuinely funny man. His satire is used to good effect in *The Celebrated Jumping Frog of Calaveras County* (1865) and *The Innocents Abroad* (1869). But he is justly remembered for his classics *Tom Sawyer* (1876) and *Huckleberry Finn* (1884), the latter title sold more than fifty thousand copies in its first two months. To this day, these two books are often miscategorized as children's books. This is not true. They are well written enough to still be accessible to young readers, but these two masterpieces are worth reading at any age.

Twain was also a prolific journalist. He took a leading role in denouncing the widespread looting of Chinese property undertaken by missionary organizations in China during the Boxer Rebellion of 1901. He was always ready with a witty rebuke to the **virtuecrats** who every now and then would try to have his works banned from local libraries. He was a great admirer of **Robert Ingersoll**, who he regarded as the voice of the new age. Twain's **freethought** was best illustrated in his private correspondence, although works like *Christian Science* (1903), *Eve's Diary,* and *What is Man?* (both 1906) reveal Twain's total rejection of all forms of theism. A late work *The Mysterious Stranger* was unfinished at the time of his death and explored still further his attitude toward religion. It was not published fully and accurately until 1969.

TWENTIETH-CENTURY PHILOSO-PHY, MAIN FEATURES OF

In his book *Philosophy in the Twentieth Century*, **A. J. Ayer** began with a summary of the main features of twentieth-century philosophy:

- the growth of philosophy's own self-consciousness;
- the total eclipse of system building;
- retreat from pretentious moral philosophy that tells people what to do; and
- progress made, through greater attention to language, in the study of **evidence**.

The first point alludes to the attention philosophers have given to the actual purpose of philosophy, and its relation to the natural and social sciences. The second refers to system building in the sense of philosophers like G. W. F. Hegel (1770–1831), who attempted grandiose philosophies which attempted to answer all questions and in this way were a system. The third point pretty well explains itself, and the fourth refers to the greater awareness of language as a highly relevant factor in a philosophical argument. Ayer's outline is a very useful summary of a hundred years of—dare one say it—**progress** in philosophy.

Further reading: A. J. Ayer, *Philosophy in the Twentieth Century*.

TWENTY-TWO THESES OF RADICAL HUMANISM

A program outlined by **M. N. Roy** in December 1946 before the Radical Democratic Party in Bombay. The twenty-two theses are the intellectual foundation of radical humanism as understood in India. The theses are:

(1) Man is the archetype of society.
(2) The quest for freedom and search for **truth** constitute the basic urge of human progress.
(3) The purpose of all rational human endeavor, individual as well as collective, is attainment of freedom, in ever-increasing measure.
(4) Rising out of the background of the law-governed physical nature, the human being is essentially rational. **Reason**, being a biological property, is not the antithesis of will.
(5) The economic interpretation of history is deduced from a wrong interpretation of **materialism**. It implies **dualism**, whereas materialism is a monistic philosophy.
(6) Ideation is a physiological process resulting from the awareness of environments. But once they are formed, ideas exist by themselves, governed by their own laws.
(7) For creating a new world of freedom, revolution must go beyond an economic reorganization of society.
(8) Communism or socialism may conceivably be the means for the attainment of the goal of freedom. How

far it can serve that purpose must be judged by experience.

(9) The state is the political organization of society, and its withering away under communism is a utopia which has been exploded by experience.

(10) State ownership and planned economy do not by themselves end exploitation of labor, nor do they necessarily lead to an equal distribution of wealth.

(11) Dictatorship tends to perpetuate itself. Planned economy under political dictatorship disregards individual freedom on the pleas of efficiency, collective effort, and social progress.

(12) The defects of parliamentary democracy have also been exposed in experience.

(13) Liberalism is falsified or parodied under formal parliamentary democracy. The doctrine of laissez faire only provides the legal sanction to the exploitation of man by man.

(14) The alternative to parliamentary democracy is not dictatorship; it is organized democracy, in the place of the formal democracy of powerless atomized individual citizens.

(15) The function of a revolutionary and liberating social philosophy is to lay emphasis on the basic fact of history that man is the maker of his world—man is a thinking being, and he can be so only as an individual.

(16) The method and program of social revolution must be based on a reassertion of the basic principle of social progress. A social renaissance can only come about through determined and widespread endeavor to educate the people in regard to the principles of freedom and rational cooperative living.

(17) Radical Democracy presupposes economic reorganization of society so as to eliminate the possibility of exploitation of man by man.

(18) The economy of the new social order will be based on production for use and distribution with reference to human needs.

(19) The ideal of Radical Democracy will be attained through the collective efforts of spiritually free men united in the determination of creating a world of freedom.

(20) In the last analysis, education of the citizen is the condition for such a reorganization of society as will be conducive to common **progress** and prosperity without encroaching upon the freedom of the individual.

(21) Radicalism integrates **science** into social organization and reconciles individuality with collective life; it gives to freedom a moral and intellectual as well as a social content.

(22) Radicalism starts from the dictum that "man is the measure of everything" (**Protagoras**) or "man is the root of mankind" (Marx), and advocates reconstruction of the world as a commonwealth and fraternity of free men by the collective endeavor of spiritually emancipated moral men.

The nineteenth and twentieth theses were originally more specifically directed to political action, but after the Radical Democratic Party was abolished in December 1948, the theses were altered to allow for a more general method of realization. Most of the theses consist of several sentences, but only the first one or two have been included here.

TWO CULTURES. A term introduced by **C. P. Snow** to denote the different mental worlds occupied by the sciences and the humanities, particularly as represented by literature and **religion**. Snow spoke of the two cultures in the 1959 Rede Lecture at Cambridge called "The Two Cultures and the Scientific Revolution." Snow was subjected to a venomous attack by a scholar of English literature, F. R. Leavis (1895–1978), three years later. As if to underscore Snow's original claim, the two-cultures term has been consistently criticized, even ridiculed, by scholars in the humanities, but has met with favor by scholars trained in the sciences. Lewis Wolpert, for instance, has noted that scientific work is essentially creative whereas creativity within the humanities is of a more private nature.

Amid the avalanche of spleen, few people noticed that Snow looked forward to the day when a **third culture** would emerge which could bridge the gap between the sciences and humanities. This idea was taken up in an innovative way in John Brockman's book, *The Third Culture* (1995).

TYRANNOPHOBIA. A term coined by the English philosopher **Thomas Hobbes** which referred to an unreasoning phobia to being governed. Hobbes, whose political aim was to provide the conditions for a stable, autocratic state, saw any resistance or dislike of even oppressive government as evidence of being an enemy of the state.

The twenty-first century versions of tyrannophobia include the suspicion that the government is always, as a matter of definition, a source of oppression or, even more fanciful, that government is involved in some long-running conspiracy against "the people." Both these perceptions are widely held, and both do the principle of government and the practice of governing a disservice.

If we are to survive the twenty-first century, we are going to need to be governed. Worldwide agreements to limit pollution, some of which, like the **Montreal Protocol**, are already successful. Others, like the **Kyoto Treaty**, are less so, and the various population policies are even less so. Hysterical opposition to world government, motivated by some form of tyrannophobia, is a very unconstructive response to the urgent problems the planet faces.

U

UDDALAKA. The earliest representative of naturalistic thought in India, and if the dates ascribed to him are correct, the world. His historicity is uncertain, but his dates have been put at 640–610 BCE. This would put him before **Carvaka** and **Thales** as the first recorded naturalistic thinker. Uddalaka was a teacher-philosopher who enjoyed disputation and developed a sizable following, which helped preserve some of his teachings from oblivion. Like his father Aruna, Uddalaka was one of the most prominent teachers of the **Veda**.

Uddalaka held that breath was the essential element in a human being. Many **idealist** thinkers of the time held that thought is the essential element, but Uddalaka argued that thought is itself made up matter, in the same way breath is. Uddalaka was also skeptical of **reincarnation**. The story goes that Svetaketu, Uddalaka's son was upbraided by a prince for knowing nothing about reincarnation. When Svetaketu spoke to his father about this, Uddalaka said he knew nothing about the doctrine. Reincarnation doesn't appear in the Rgveda, the earliest and most important of the Veda, at all.

One passage attributed to Uddalaka expresses **skepticism** about the power of the Veda. "If when a man knew a thousand Veda and yet could not be free from misery, so long as he did not know the right path, my opinion is that the Veda are useless, the path of self-restraint is the truth." Uddalaka was also an optimist, against the run of Indian thought at the time and since. He was very important to the development of Indian **naturalism**. He gave the first Indian versions of a monistic universe, **atomistic** physics, and deliberation based on appeal to what is physically observable rather than to mystical slogans.

Further reading: Dale Riepe, *The Naturalistic Tradition in Indian Thought*.

UGANDA HUMANIST ASSOCIATION. An organization begun in 1993 by a group of students at Makerere University in Kampala, along with some of the staff at the university and members of the police force. Out of this group Deogratiasi Ssekitooleko has emerged as the leader. The Uganda Humanist Association (UHASSO) was formally started in 1994, with help from the **British Humanist Association** and **African Americans for Humanism**. For ten years UHASSO worked quietly, with several autonomous groups around the country doing their bit to combat superstition and ignorance. UHASSO achieved international recognition in 2004 when the **International Humanist and Ethical Union** hosted a conference in Kampala, during which UHASSO was formally brought together. The **Center for Inquiry** has supplied UHASSO with several hundred books and provides regular financial assistance for an office located near the university. UHASSO doubles as the Center for Inquiry–Uganda.

UHASSO has taken an innovative approach to **humanism**. Far from importing European notions to combat local superstitions, UHASSO has sought to work with Uganda customs and forms of social organization to promote its values. With this approach, interpreted differently in the various regions of the country, UHASSO has done work far out of proportion to its size.

ULRICHS, KARL HEINRICH (1825–1895). The first known gay activist. The son of a surveyor who died when he was ten years old, Ulrichs studied theology and law at Göttingen and Berlin universities, writing a doctoral dissertation on the Treaty of Westphalia of 1648. He was a civil servant between 1857 and 1859 but was hounded out of the service for his homosexuality. He then supported himself as a freelance journalist. He wrote a series of books, many of which were banned by state library services. The ban was lifted on May 26, 1864, which some gays take as the symbolic date for the start of the gay movement.

Ulrichs coined the world "Uranians," which was for many years the preferred slang word for homosexuals. Before he came out, Ulrichs used the pseudonym *Numa Numantius*. He devoted his life to the cause of the public acceptance of homosexuality, and arguing for it as entirely natural rather than a **sin** worthy of supernatural penalties. He even argued for homosexuality as being an ethical lifestyle.

Ulrichs was the first person to "come out" in public, declaring himself to be homosexual before five hundred members of the Congress of German Jurists in August 27–29, 1867. In 1879 Ulrichs left Germany forever, and spent the rest of his life in Italy, dying there penniless in 1895.

ULTRAMONTANE CATHOLICISM. A staunchly conservative form of Catholicism that grew after the shock of the French Revolution. "Ultramontane'" means "beyond the mountains," a reference to Rome. Ultramontanism was bitterly antirationalist, even antimodern. It preferred a sentimental, unthinking piety centered around home and hearth, with women quietly at home producing lots of Catholic babies.

UNBELIEF. A term defined best by the American historian James Turner as the "continuing absence of a conviction that any such superhuman power exists." The British philosopher J. C. A. Gaskin defined unbelief as:

- lack of belief in supernatural agents or abstractions;
- lack of belief in **miracles** or supernatural interventions; and
- lack of belief in any form of a future state.

Gaskin prefers "unbelief" over a word like "**atheism**" because "unbelief" means no more and no less than not believing in certain things, whereas "atheism" involves a harder position of denying these things. However, this is not a strictly accurate portrayal of contemporary atheism. Another problem with the word "unbelief" is that it defines itself as a negative other to religious belief, and seems to concede to religious belief the status of being the norm. This becomes particularly problematic when "unbelief" becomes "**unbeliever**." However, "unbelief" and "unbeliever" are useful terms when used historically, when it is difficult to determine with precision what a person's beliefs actually were, beyond a general awareness of them not being orthodox.

Further reading: J. C. A. Gaskin, ed., *Varieties of Unbelief* ; and Michael Hunter and David Wootton, eds., *Atheism from the Reformation to the Enlightenment.*

UNBELIEVER. Derogatory term applied to anyone who rejects a religious belief. **Freethinkers** of all persuasions believe many things, and it is a great mistake, as well as an insult, for them to be defined simply by what they don't believe. This dictionary exists as a standing reminder to the many noble things freethinkers believe. To describe oneself as an unbeliever assumes—quite incorrectly— that *religious* belief sets the standard for what constitutes belief. This is not, and has never been, true. It also gives strength to the prejudice that people without religious belief **believe in nothing**.

UNCERTAINTY PRINCIPLE. Discovered in 1925 by Werner Heisenberg (1901–1976) and one of the most important tenets of **quantum mechanics**. The Uncertainty Principle states that one cannot know with infinite precision both the position and the momentum of a particle. The Uncertainty Principle rests on the bedrock assumption of continuous motion, and therefore precludes the existence of a stationary particle. Among the many consequences of the principle is that there are limits on the predictability of future events. There exists at the subatomic level a fundamental randomness, known as quantum fluctuation.

As with other elements of quantum mechanics, the Uncertainty Principle has been taken up by **postmodernists** to announce the end of **science** and of **reason**. This is nonsense. The inability to know the movement of subatomic particles with infinite precision does not mean that we cannot make reliable and intellectually sound predictions about the world and act in accordance with them.

UNIDENTIFIED FLYING OBJECTS (UFOs). Strictly speaking a UFO is an object seen to be flying which cannot be identified. Few people doubt the existence of objects in the sky that remain unidentified by observers. But many people then leap to the wild conclusion that an object they cannot identify must be a spacecraft from another planet.

An interesting feature of the UFO craze is that people only claimed to have seen UFOs after science fiction and the mass media had made these ideas available. The first UFO sightings were in the 1940s. Interest in the craze grew until the 1970s but then slowly declined. By the beginning of the twenty-first century very few people were taking UFOs as alien spaceships, let alone "flying saucers," seriously.

The UFO craze does two foolish things. First, it presumes to identify what is unidentified, and second, it ignores the laws of physics. There are some absolutes in the laws of physics as presently understood. One of them is that no object can travel faster than the speed of light, which would be necessary to make practicable the sort of space travel assumed here. The other is the law of gravity. Both of these laws of physics are habitually ignored by those who claim to have seen space travel vessels from other planets. Most space travel vessels have no visible means of propulsion or means by which they remain aloft and no explanation is usually given for how they managed to get here.

UNITARIANISM. Once a radical Christian movement, now a religiously inclined assemblage of liberals, progressives, and religious humanists. Unitarianism emerged first in the

Reformation as a radical protest against the orthodox dogma of the **Trinity**, although it traces its theological roots to the Arian controversy in fourth-century Christianity. The leaders in the new Unitarianism were Faustus Socinus (1539–1604), who, with his uncle Laelius Socinus (1525–1562) helped develop anti-Trinitarian thought, which soon became known as Socinianism. Unitarians, rightly, saw no warrant for the Trinity in **scripture**, and as they wanted to model their lives entirely on the scriptures, the Trinity had to go. Faustus Socinus went further, denying the divinity of Christ, **original sin**, the value of propitiating the gods through sacrifice, and justification by **faith**. Inevitably, Socinus was denounced by the **Inquisition**, his possessions seized, and he was forced into exile, where he died destitute. Socinus's example gave the Unitarians a powerful reason to advocate **toleration** of **heretics**. Another important critic of the Trinity was Michael Servetus (1511–1553) who wrote *On the Errors of the Trinity* (1531) and for which he was burned at the stake in Geneva.

An important eighteenth-century Unitarian was the scientist Joseph Priestley (1733–1804), who was branded an atheist and whose home was ransacked in 1791. Denying the Trinity was illegal in Britain until 1813. Priestley ended his days in the United States where Unitarianism took root. The American Unitarian Association was founded in 1825 and can boast six American presidents among its number. In 1961 they merged with the Universalist Church to form the Unitarian-Universalist Association. Unitarians were strongly represented among the signatories of the *Humanist Manifesto I*. Contemporary Unitarianism is a complex coalition of liberal religious believers, supporters of various styles of **New Age** thinking, **religious humanists**, and freethinkers. Unitarians are natural allies with the **Sea of Faith** movement in Commonwealth nations. The principal difference between Unitarians and **secular humanism** is their contrasting notions about the idea of *Homo religiosus*, or the idea that humans are naturally religious. The points in common, however, are far more significant than the points of difference.

UNITED NATIONS. Flawed institution though it may be, the United Nations represents one of the few vehicles to preserve some hope for the future. When the United Nations began in 1945 it had fifty-one member states. As of 2002 it had 190, most of which did not exist in 1945. The United Nations is made up of five main organs:

- the *General Assembly*;
- the *Security Council*;
- the *Economic and Social Council*;
- the *International Court of Justice*; and
- the *Trusteeship Council*.

The General Assembly is the discussion and policy-making forum at which each of the 190 member nations has a seat. Resolutions passed at the General Assembly do not have binding effect on member nations, but can and do exert a strong moral influence, or can be used by other nations against errant members. The General Assembly makes important decisions on the operation of the UN. For instance it appoints the nonpermanent countries to the Security Council as well as judges to the International Court of Justice. Most of its work is done by six committees: Disarmament and International Security; Economic and Financial; Social, Humanitarian, and Cultural; Special Political and Decolonization; Administrative and Budgetary; and Legal.

The Security Council, by contrast, can pass resolutions that are binding on member countries. When the United Nations began in 1945, five Security Council members (Great Britain, the United States, France, the Soviet Union, and China) were given the power to veto resolutions they thought conflicted seriously with their national interest. As well as the five permanent members, there are ten nonpermanent members, who sit at the council for two years. More recently, there have been moves by Germany, Japan, India, and Brazil to be given permanent seats. This would help make the permanent members more representative of the post–**cold-war** world balance. See the entry on the **Yalta Conference**.

The power of the veto helped create the cold-war stalemate which made the United Nations appear ineffectual to some people. There is some truth in this, but the veto also preserved the UN from suffering the fate of the League of Nations, its hapless predecessor. There have been fewer vetoes since the end of the cold war, and the Security Council has become a more effective institution as a result. It has sent peacekeeping forces to conflicts around the world more frequently than throughout the entire cold war.

The Economic and Social Council (ECOSOC) operates under the authority of the General Assembly and incorporates the welfare arm of the UN, in particular UNESCO and UNICEF. ECOSOC also oversees aspects of transnational postal services and civil aviation. These organizations are the clearest illustration of **planetary humanism** in action. **Julian Huxley** was the first director-general of UNESCO, from 1946 until 1948, and Sir Alfred Zimmern (1879–1957) was its first secretary-general (see the entry on the **welfare state**). The **Human Rights Commission** operates under the auspices of the ECOSOC.

The International Court of Justice (ICJ) was formally inaugurated on April 18, 1946, at the Hague with a view to deciding international disputes that UN member states submit to it. The court's decisions are binding. The court also serves as an advisory body for any international agency that should wish to seek advice from it. The ICJ was simply the latest in a series of major attempts at international arbitration. The League of Nations had its own international court, which in turn had been modeled on the Hague Peace Conference in 1899—a landmark event in international law.

The Trusteeship Council is the least important of the bodies. It was responsible for overseeing some colonial territories that had changed hands after war. All of these territories are now independent and in 1994 the Trusteeship Council ceased operation. There is talk of reviving it with a new role, for instance, with respect to the environment.

The problems the United Nations face are many. Many nations do not pay their dues, which leaves the organization unable to conduct all its operations to full effect. The sheer size of the organization makes it unwieldy. And most countries are willing to use the language of **global governance** when it has no effect on their national interests, but will balk and obstruct when it does. And in the United States a powerful lobby led by the Religious Right nurtures a bitter hatred of the UN. The UN often turns up in fundamentalist literature as behind some satanic cabal to undermine the "**Judeo-Christian** values" of the United States. See the entry on **conspiracy theories**. And the UN has failed often enough to give ground for pessimism—its failure to intervene in Rwanda being a prime example. But despite all these problems, the UN remains one of the few bright lights on the international scene today, and is overwhelmingly a force for good.

Carl Coon, an American former diplomat, has argued that humanists need to "adopt" the United Nations as the organization which most articulates its principles. Religious believers have traditionally had church institutions they could direct their devotion to. But the United Nations, as the best example of planetary humanism in action, is an obvious candidate for practical, applied **humanism**. The practical application of planetary humanism can be seen in the **Universal Declaration of Human Rights** and in the **Millennium Development Goals**.

Further reading: Carl Coon, *One Planet, One People: Beyond "Us vs. Them."*

UNIVERSAL CONSENT, ARGUMENT FROM. An interesting example of an argument for the existence of **God** which was once very effective and widely used but is now almost completely forgotten. It was once popular to argue that since all nations believe in God, no sane person could dispute what everyone else knows to be true. But then along came the explorers who found that other cultures believed in other gods altogether, and, even worse, civilizations like China had no belief in God. There followed a delay while Christian theologians debated whether the followers of **Kongfuzi** were genuinely atheistic. Once it was conceded that they were, the writing was on the wall for the argument from universal consent. As if these discoveries weren't bad enough, then came the rediscovery by Western scholars of the **freethought** heritage of the ancient Greeks and Romans. This spelled the end of the argument. So for those who think no **progress** can ever be made in the seemingly interminable existence-of-God debate, they should recall the decline and fall of the argument from universal consent.

UNIVERSAL DECLARATION OF HUMAN RIGHTS (H. G. Wells). A statement drawn up by Wells that went on to become an important influence on the **United Nations**. Wells wrote and revised the declaration between 1939 and 1944, and devoted a considerable amount of his last years to publicizing it to as wide an audience as possible. Wells devised the declaration to serve as a guiding set of principles for the pursuit of the war against fascism and building a peaceful world order after the war. In their baldest form the rights are as follows:

(1) Right to live.
(2) Protection of minors.
(3) Duty to the community.
(4) Right to knowledge.
(5) Freedom of thought and worship.
(6) Right to work.
(7) Rights of personal property.
(8) Freedom of movement.
(9) Personal liberty.

(10) Freedom from violence.
(11) Right of lawmaking.

Wells first outlined the need for such a declaration in a Penguin Special, *The Rights of Man* (1940). The declaration then appeared, in slightly amended forms, in *Guide to the New World* (1941), *The Outlook for Homo Sapiens* (1942), and *'42 to '44: A Contemporary Memoir* (1944). David Smith, an important biographer of Wells, has also noted the influence of the declaration on the Atlantic Charter, signed by Franklin Roosevelt and Winston Churchill in 1941, and on Roosevelt's **Four Freedoms**. Wells's declaration was also a guide for Eleanor Roosevelt (1884–1962), who played a pivotal role in seeing the **United Nations' Universal Declaration of Human Rights** through.

Further reading: David Smith, *H. G. Wells: Desperately Mortal.*

UNIVERSAL DECLARATION OF HUMAN RIGHTS (United Nations). Called "the Magna Carta for all humanity," the declaration is the most significant humanist vision ever created. After two years of deliberation, it was adopted by the **United Nations** on December 10, 1948, since designated as Human Rights Day. The declaration was intended to serve as a "common standard of achievement for all peoples and all nations. . . ." It was drawn up from people from all corners of the earth.

The declaration is not a binding document, but is designed to act as an inspiration to member countries as the ideal to work toward. It has thirty articles and is overseen by the United Nations **Human Rights Commission**, the first chairperson of which was Eleanor Roosevelt (1884–1962). The declaration was endorsed by all United Nations member states with the exception of the Soviet Union, Byelorussia, Ukraine, Poland, Czechoslovakia, Yugoslavia, Saudi Arabia, and South Africa, which abstained. Byelorussia (now Belarus) and Ukraine were parts of the Soviet Union at the time, but were given UN votes as part of the horse-trading to entice the Soviets into the UN. The official explanation most of the abstainers gave was their concern at the individualist orientation of the declaration. Its successful passage by the UN owed a great deal to the skill and dedication of Eleanor Roosevelt.

Nobel Peace Prize winner and human-rights campaigner René Cassin (1887–1976) had an important role in drafting the 1948 Declaration of Human Rights. He drew on the battle cry of the French Revolution, and identified the four main pillars of the declaration as "dignity, liberty, equality and brotherhood." See the entry on the **Declaration of the Rights of Man and of the Citizen**. Each of those pillars is dealt with successively through the articles of the declaration. Articles 1–19 deal with individual liberties; articles 20–26 deal with issues of social and economic equality, and articles 27–28 deal with rights associated with community.

This is the text of the first three articles of the declaration:

Article 1: All human beings are born free and equal in dignity and rights. They are endowed with reason and conscience and should act towards one another in a spirit of brotherhood.

Article 2: Everyone is entitled to all the rights and freedoms set forth in this Declaration, without distinction of any kind, such as race, color, sex, language, religion, political or other opinion, national or social origin, property, birth or other status.

Furthermore, no distinction shall be made on the basis of the political, jurisdictional or international status of the country or territory to which a person belongs, whether it be independent, trust, nonself-governing or under any other limitation of sovereignty.

Article 3: Everyone has the right to life, liberty and the security of person.

The provisions of the Universal Declaration of Human Rights was taken several steps further in 1966 with ratification of the Covenant on Civil and Political Rights and the Covenant on Economic, Social, and Cultural Rights.

Further reading: Micheline Ishay, *A History of Human Rights.*

UNIVERSAL ISLAMIC DECLARATION OF HUMAN RIGHTS. A declaration prepared in 1981 by the Islamic Council, a private London-based organization affiliated with the Muslim World League. The declaration says that it is divine revelation that has given us the "legal and moral framework within which to establish and regulate human institutions and relationships." Furthermore, that divine revelation is best manifested in the teachings of Islam.

Unfortunately, the rights of humanists, or any other sort of nonreligious person, would be tenuous in the extreme under this dispensation. Section XII (a) accords to every person "the right to express his thoughts and beliefs so long as he remains within the limits prescribed by the Law. No one, however, is entitled to disseminate falsehood or to circulate reports which may outrage public decency, or to indulge in slander, innuendo or to cast defamatory aspersions on other persons." Now the law, as prescribed in the Qur'an accords very few rights to nonbelievers, and frequent exhortations to their destruction can also be found.

The rights of women are no less circumscribed. There is a section on the rights of married women, but not one for women in general. Chapter 19, revealingly titled "The Right to Found a Family and Related Matters," begins with some vague assurances of equality, however section g reads: "Motherhood is entitled to special respect, care and assistance on the part of the family and the public organs of the community." The next section apportions duties in this way: (h) "Within the family, men and women are to share in their obligations and responsibilities according to their sex, their natural endowments, talents and inclinations, bearing in mind their common responsibilities toward their progeny and their relatives."

The flaws and evasiveness of the Universal Islamic Declaration of Human Rights reveal clearly that **monotheist** religions are constitutionally incapable of providing the framework for **rights** and responsibilities on a strictly equal basis. By dividing people into the "us and them" of believer versus unbeliever, monotheist religions can only parody the values of **planetary humanism**.

UNIVERSALISM, PRINCIPLE OF. The principle that, in all instances of X, we should do Y. This principle is favored by proponents of **command moralities** and religious fundamentalists with simplistic ideas that, if we just follow the Ten Commandments, then everything will be all right. In fact, things are more complicated than that, and we need to be confident enough to exercise our individual **judgment** in each situation.

There are times when even killing someone may be justified. If we are able to kill a terrorist who is just about to detonate a bomb in a crowded room, a very good case can be made that killing the terrorist is the right thing to do. The principle of universalism, however, is too inflexible to permit that sort of judgment call in unique situations, and in cases where the standard rules don't apply. The vital skill to learn is not unthinking obedience to an allegedly universal principle but fearless **critical thinking**.

UNIVERSITY OF HUMANIST STUDIES. A fully accredited university, founded in the Netherlands in 1989, with the principal purpose of training counselors wishing to work in schools, hospitals, the armed forces, or prisons. It has since expanded to provide education for prospective teachers and those wishing to work as policy makers for government departments or NGOs, and for academics. The university, which is also known as the University of **Humanistics**, offers a three-year bachelor program, a series of vocationally specific master's programs, and a doctoral degree. The university usually has about three hundred twenty students and a staff of forty-five, of whom six are full professors and six are holders of endowed chairs.

The university is based in two attractive buildings in the old part of Utrecht, one of the Netherlands' most beautiful towns. The University of Humanist Studies is an important center of humanist thought.

Further reading: Annemie Halsema and Douwe van Houten, eds., *Empowering Humanity: State of the Art in Humanistics*.

UNKNOWABLE, THE. An interesting example of a word that had a brief career doing what its creator intended of it before being put to altogether different uses. The term has been traced to the English high churchman Henry Mansel (1820-1871), who argued in *Limits of Religious Thought* (1858) that the human mind could never hope to comprehend the glory of **God**, which means that we cannot hope to question his inspired word. But if Mansel spoke of the Unknowable as the bastion of church authority, the idea was quickly taken up for altogether different purposes when **Herbert Spencer** transformed the Unknowable into something so remote from our **knowledge** that it is futile to speculate as to any aspect of its activities. And this in turn prepared the way for **T. H. Huxley**'s coining of the word **agnostic** in 1869.

UNMOVED MOVER. A notion conceived by **Aristotle** to explain how the heavenly motions began. Whatever began the heavenly motions, Aristotle argued, had itself not to move; it had to be an unmoved mover. Aristotle conceived of the cosmos as a sphere, and the unmoved mover as the unchanging and nonphysical quality toward which the universe gravitated in graceful concentric circles. The cosmos was complicated enough to require many unmoved movers, but with a senior one at the edge of the cosmos, keeping the clockwork motions regular.

Aristotle's unmoved mover has little in common with the **monotheist** God of Judaism, Christianity, and Islam. Aristotle had no conception of **God** as a being who was interested in human affairs. There was no **anthropocentric conceit** in Aristotle's unmoved mover. This notwithstanding, Aristotle's unmoved mover was slowly transformed by Christian apologists into the first-cause argument: nothing is created without a cause and God is the first cause. The Swedish novelist **Hjalmar Söderberg** noted that "[t]o posit a First Cause is to assume a law of causality and in the same breath require an exception to it." See the entry on **Aristotelianism**.

UNTOUCHABLES. See **DALITS**.

UPANISHADS. A series of texts which are a continuation of the **Veda** with a bent toward philosophical speculation. "Upanishads" translates literally as "sittings near the teacher." As with the **Veda**, the Upanishads are not to be thought of as **scripture**.

The Upanishads are generally thought to have been composed between about 750 and 500 BCE. Much of that time was marked by cultural turmoil and uncertainty. It is unwise to attempt a summary of the message of the Upanishads, mainly because they say many different and contradictory things. Nevertheless, they can be categorized broadly as monistic or **pantheistic** in cosmology. The ethics of the Upanishads range from sophisticated **idealism** to crude **superstition**.

However, some ideas seen as central to what is now known as Hinduism arose from the Upanishads, notably the notions of **karma**, the wheel of rebirth, and of the essential unity of the individual soul with ultimate reality, or Atman and Brahman.

USTINOV, PETER (1921–2004). Author, comedian, actor, and champion for the children of the poor. Peter Ustinov was born in London but was always happy to boast his polyglot ancestry, with Russians and Ethiopians among others. He was educated at Westminster School and served in the Royal Sussex Regiment and RAOC during World War II. While still serving, Ustinov's first play, *House of Regrets*, was produced in 1942. He went on to produce a series of successful plays and films including *The Man in the Raincoat* (Edinburgh Festival, 1949), *The Love of Four Colonels* (1951), *Romanoff and Juliet* (1956, later made into a film and a musical), *Photo-Finish* (1962), and *The Unknown Soldier and His Wife* (1967).

Ustinov wrote and directed the films *School for Secrets* (1946) and *Vice-Versa* (1947), directed, produced, and acted in *Billy Budd* (1961), and directed and acted in *Hammersmith is Out* (1971). He also wrote an autobiography, *Dear Me* (1977). He said his novel *Krumnagel* (1971) was "certainly one of my better works." Later works, all published by **Prometheus Books**, include *Still at Large* (1995), *A Dash of Pity, and Other Short Stories* (1996), and *Monsieur René: A Novel* (1999). He received the Benjamin Franklin Medal from the Royal Society of Arts in 1957.

As if to complement his lighter side, Ustinov also worked as a cultural ambassador for UNICEF and later for UNESCO. He lent his name and time to a variety of projects and fundraising activities for the relief of **poverty**. Shortly before his death, the University of Vienna created the Ustinov Institute, dedicated to the study of the effects prejudice has on individuals and on societies. Ustinov was a humanist and atheist. In 1993 he was elected a laureate of the **International Academy of Humanism**. Peter Ustinov was survived by his third wife Hélène.

UTILITY, PRINCIPLE OF. An ethical principle devised by the radical English liberal **Jeremy Bentham**. Also known as the Greatest Happiness Principle. Bentham rejected the universalist moral principles of Christianity and philosophers like **Immanuel Kant**. Instead, Bentham insisted that people have a right to **happiness** and that a society's value is determined by the amount of happiness it can facilitate in its citizens. With this in mind, Bentham devised his Principle of Utility, which stated that an object or an action's value is determined by its ability to produce benefit or avoid harm for the people concerned.

The Principle of Utility has been criticized on many grounds, the most common one being that it makes no distinction between pleasure and happiness. Others have accused utilitarians of reducing pleasure/happiness to what is measurable. Still others have accused utilitarians of being unrealistic in their demand that we overcome our **groupishness** and think evenhandedly in the interests of those we love and of complete strangers.

John Stuart Mill developed and broadened the range of the Principle of Utility in ways Bentham was unable to do. For Mill, the emphasis was not simply on how *much* happiness could be mustered, but what *quality* of happiness can be achieved. Mill's view of the quality of happiness often gets him into trouble with people who accuse him of the new crime of elitism. Mill was elitist in the sense that intellectual and cultural pleasures were held by him to be superior to physical pleasures.

More recent understandings of utility ignore the problematic issue of comparative happiness (how does one judge who is more happy?) and focus instead on utility as a means by which a single person's choices can be represented. And philosophers such as Peter Singer have become champions of what is known as preference utilitarianism, a modified version of the Principle of Utility. All the problems with the Principle of Utility notwithstanding, it remains an invaluable contribution to social philosophy and ethics. See the entry on **normative ethics**.

VALLA, LORENZO (1405–1457). Italian humanist scholar, best known for exposing the document known as the **Donation of Constantine** as a fraud. Valla also wrote *Dialogue on Freewill*, a frankly skeptical work, and a very sympathetic account of **Epicurus**. Another work was *De Voluptate* (*About Pleasure*), which criticized monasticism and the pleasures of this world, only to portray the pleasures of heaven in very worldly terms. *De Voluptate* is probably an example of **parallel theology**, whereby the surface orthodoxy of the account masks the actual heterodoxy of the author's opinions.

Valla was influential in teaching people the need to read **scriptures** with a skeptical frame of mind. This was recognized at the time, and for which he was praised by leading scholars such as **Erasmus**. Indeed, Valla's work was a direct inspiration for Erasmus to commence his own work on the New Testament. The Vatican, however, was less enamored by his work, and Valla had to flee Rome in 1443 to the safety of Naples, where he was protected from the **Inquisition**. Only when the more tolerant Pope Nicholas V was elected in 1447 could Valla return to Rome.

VALUE MEANING. A term coined by **Michael Martin** to express how we can live a **good life**, and how we can understand that it is a good life. Martin notes that there is a difference between having meaning in life and having purpose in life. This is because some purposes have no meaning. So, Martin proposes what he calls purpose meaning. A human life has purpose meaning if it has a purpose (or purposes) that are significant and can provide psychological satisfaction. It is also important that it is possible to fulfill one's chosen purpose meaning (or meanings) and that they aren't simply arbitrary and implausible.

This means that the meaning of life is different for different people. The meaning of life will vary according to people's circumstances and background. Some may regret this, others will simply see that the theory is taking account of the real world.

Martin then concludes that a human life has value meaning "if and only if it is, on the whole, good for the person who leads it." After all, **Adolf Hitler**'s life had meaning, but it can't be said to have purpose meaning, and certainly not value meaning. Again, this recognizes the fact that different people will have different value meanings for their lives. We can come to understand whether our purpose meaning is good for us, i.e., has value, by employing techniques like the **wide reflective equilibrium**.

Further reading: Michael Martin, *Atheism, Morality, and Meaning.*

VALUES. A concept related to, although broader than, **ethics**. Ethics is a theoretical investigation into the fundamental principles which do, or which ought to, inform a given field of activity. Thus, the study of ethics is the study of a branch of **philosophy**. A theory of value, by contrast, answers the more practical question of what quality or qualities are good. Value often stands for a quality or a property rather than for a physical object. Values are not independently existing entities; they exist only when, where, and among whom they have meaning.

It is common to think of values as nice things like honesty, trustworthiness, and so on. But these are best thought of as **virtues**. Values is a broader concept, because as well as the virtues, there are also basic values, which are needs, such as drink, food, shelter, sex, and so on. There are also negative values like pain, hunger, thirst, and humiliation. These are related to our **human needs**.

There are subjectivist and objectivist theories of value. The emphasis in a subjectivist theory is the value a community places on a quality or property. Values, therefore, are held to be subjective because they will vary

according the community being considered. Against this approach is the objectivist theory. Plato epitomizes this philosophy. Contrary to the **relativism** of subjectivist values, objectivists would claim that values exist in the cosmos independent of human beings, in other words, that they are objective. As a result of this, reasoned public debate in an **open society** about our respective values is of paramount importance.

Values can also be thought of as either intrinsic or instrumental. Instrumental value is when something has value as an instrument to something else, the easiest example being money. Intrinsic value is if something has value in itself. It is more difficult to find examples of intrinsic value, but the best example might be **happiness**. This has problems, however, because happiness for some might well entail misery for another. This means that happiness is not an intrinsic value. One way out of the problem is not to speak of intrinsic value at all, but "highest value." This, of course, is a matter of opinion, and therefore a subjectivist value.

Further reading: Finngeir Hiorth, *Values;* and Valerii Kuvakin, *In Search of Our Humanity.*

VANINI, GUILIO CESARE (1585–1619). Italian atheist and martyr. Educated in philosophy, theology, science, and law, Vanini entered the church but soon found the atmosphere oppressive. He was notable for the courage he demonstrated in portraying his **atheism** honestly and openly, without resorting to the dissimulation so many of his contemporaries did in order to avoid the persecution of the church. Vanini traveled widely in Europe, gathering powerful enemies to his naturalistic message. He became a formidable opponent of Scholasticism, arguing that the only true worship was the worship of nature. He was skeptical about the existence of supernatural entities, and he thought that religions were fictions created and supported by rulers for their own advantage. The second of his books, *De admirandis*

(1616), was a thoroughgoing demolition of the pretensions of Christian theology and the hypocrisy of Christian practice.

In 1614 Vanini sought refuge from persecution in England only to spend forty-nine days in the Tower of London. He returned to France in 1615 but quickly ran into more serious trouble. His books were ordered to be burned by the Sorbonne and he was charged with atheism. In Toulouse, Vanini's tongue was cut out and he was burned at the stake. His courage led to an early death and served as a warning to other unbelievers to keep their thoughts to themselves or at least to express them cryptically. See the entries on **parallel theology**, **Giordano Bruno**, and **Paolo Sarpi**.

Further reading: Nicholas Davidson, "Unbelief and Atheism in Italy, 1500–1700," in Michael Hunter and David Wootton, eds., *Atheism from the Reformation to the Enlightenment*.

VAN PRAAG, JAAP (1911–1981). Important leader of Dutch and international **humanism**. Van Praag exercised leadership intellectually and organizationally. He was for many years a professor of philosophy at the University of Leiden, eventually holding the chair there. However, his influence among English speakers is not as great as it deserves to be, as much of his work remains untranslated. One of his main works which has appeared in English is *Foundations of Humanism* (1982). See the entry on **humanist philosophy, three strands of**.

Van Praag was also a central figure in postwar Dutch humanism, and he was a central force behind bringing the **International Humanist and Ethical Union** (IHEU) together in 1952. It was a tribute to van Praag's influence that the foundation congress of the IHEU was held in Amsterdam. The Dutch Humanist Ethical Society offers the J. P. van Praag Award for the promotion of human **rights**.

VAN RYSWYCK, HERMANN (d. 1512). Dutch priest turned atheist burned at the stake

for heresy at the Hague in 1512. Not only was van Ryswyck a priest—he was from the order of Inquisitors—but this did not prevent a dramatic loss of faith, for which he was tried. Van Ryswyck denied an afterlife, **hell**, the divinity of Christ and every other principal tenet of Christianity. He was sentenced in 1502 to life imprisonment, but ten years later was dragged once again before the court, found not to have changed his mind, and executed.

VEDA. Ancient Indian texts. It is not claimed that the Veda were written by the gods—the claim is that they were always there. In this sense it is not accurate to describe the Veda as **scripture**. "Veda" means "knowledge" in Sanskrit. The Veda are frequently referred to as "the Vedas," but this is not strictly accurate, as there are four collections of the Veda. However, the Veda are not in fact four seamless collections, all moving in the same direction and in the same spirit. The collections are known as:

- *Rgveda*, or Veda of poetry, the oldest, and philosophically most important;
- *Samaveda*, or Veda of songs, most of which is from the *Rgveda*;
- *Yajurveda*, or Veda of sacrificial texts, verses for chanting and ritual application; and
- *Atharveda*, or priestly Veda, mainly magic and spells, and added later to the original Veda.

The most significant of them is the oldest of them, the *Rgveda*. It may well have been composed around 1100 BCE, and was transmitted orally for more than five hundred years before being written down sometime after 500 BCE. The *Rgveda* consists of ten cycles of hymns and liturgies. The *Samaveda* and *Yajurveda* add to and reiterate the *Rgveda* while the *Atharveda* is of altogether later provenance. It is only then that the notion of the cow as sacred appears.

It is a mistake to equate the Veda with scriptures in the tradition of the **monotheist** religions. Certainly, the Veda are held in high esteem, but a body of writing does not need to be a scripture to achieve that status. In Hinduism, one can question in good faith the divine origin of the Veda without this necessarily subjecting you to any disfavor. Neither does questioning the divine origin of the Veda imply a lack of interest or even reverence for them. The tradition of doubt is known as *nastikya*. The **Carvaka** school of Indian philosophy was *nastikya*. This openness to **reason** and unwillingness to cast those one disagrees with as heretics, as the monotheist religions tend to do, is an admirable feature of the **Asian traditions**.

The Indian philosopher Sarvepalli Radhakrishnan (1888–1975) identified three competing strata of thought in the Veda: naturalistic polytheism, monotheism, and monism. As he says, "[t]he process of godmaking in the factory of man's mind cannot be seen so clearly anywhere else as in the Rgveda."

VERACITY. One of the key **humanist virtues**. The English philosopher **John Locke** defined veracity as not holding any proposition with greater assurance than the **proofs** it is built upon will allow. This means that the sketchier our **evidence** for an idea, the greater caution we should employ in believing it.

In his timeless pamphlet *The Faith of a Rationalist* **Bertrand Russell** declared that he finds two original sources for his opinions: kindly feeling and veracity. In the absence of veracity, Russell wrote, kindly feeling can simply slip into self-deception. Russell acknowledged that religious belief may well make some people better and it certainly provides a powerful consolation, but is that good enough? "No sound morality," Russell wrote, "can need to be based upon evasion, and a **happiness** derived from beliefs not justified on any ground except their pleasantness is not a kind of happiness that can be unreservedly admired." See the entry on **Rationalism, Principles of**.

Further reading: Bertrand Russell, *The Faith of a Rationalist*.

VERDI, GUISEPPE (1813–1901). The greatest Italian composer of the nineteenth century. Born the son of an innkeeper, Verdi's musical genius was appreciated by locals, who helped fund his early musical training. After failing to succeed the organist at the local cathedral, he was given a grant by the Philharmonic Society. His first opera was *Oberto*, but it was with *Nabucco* (1842) that Verdi achieved lasting fame. He went on to produce a succession of brilliant operas: *Rigoletto* (1851), *La Traviata* (1853), *Aida* (1871), *Otello* (1887), and *Falstaff* (1893) all of which are staples to this day.

Verdi's first wife and their two children died in 1839 and 1840. In 1859 he married Guiseppina Strepponi, an operatic soprano. They remained happily married for the rest of their lives. He was also active in politics for a while. He was an enthusiastic Italian nationalist and **anticlerical**, and was happy that his choruses were popular with nationalist demonstrators. He was politically active on two occasions, but only for short periods, as political life did not suit him. Verdi's success made him a rich man, but he continued to live a relatively simple life. In 1898 he founded a refuge in Milan for elderly musicians. Verdi was an atheist. He insisted that his funeral have no religious element to it.

VERIFICATION, PRINCIPLE OF. A principle outlined by **A. J. Ayer** in his classic work of philosophy, *Language, Truth and Logic* (1936). Ayer contended that there are two types of meaningful statements:

- *analytic statements*, which determine their truth or falsity by virtue of their own terms, such as "all bachelors are unmarried men"; and
- *synthetic statements*, which determine their truth or falsity by looking out at the world, such as "the sun rises in the east."

Statements in **mathematics** and logic would be analytical statements and scientific, historical, and everyday life statements would be synthetic, based on Ayer's terms. Because synthetic statements need some sort of outside measure of justification, Ayer posited the Verification Principle as the measure to achieve that. Any statement that can't be verified, in Ayer's view, is neither right nor wrong, but *meaningless*.

The Verification Principle has huge implications on most religious and ethical beliefs, for instance, none of which can be independently verified.

The Verification Principle is still very valuable as a tool, but it ran into some serious problems, not least its failure to verify itself. **Karl Popper** outlined some problems with it, and postulated the idea of **falsification** as a solution.

VIOLENCE. Defined by the British political scientist Paul Wilkinson as the "illegitimate use or threatened use of coercion resulting, or intended to result in, the **death**, injury, restraint or intimidation of persons or the destruction or seizure of property."

Wilkinson saw the advantage of this definition as that it doesn't confuse the capacity to inflict violence with its actual infliction, while also implying a clear distinction between physical violence and aggressive rhetoric.

More recently, and in a different context, the religious-studies scholar Hector Avalos has distinguished two types of violence: *somatocentric* violence, which is physical violence against the body, and *pneumatocentric* violence, which is psychological violence, or, more poetically, violence against the soul.

Avalos maintains that **monotheist** religions are inherently violent by virtue of the competition they set up for scarce resources. These resources are the rewards that monotheist religions offer their followers: **immortality**, feelings of **certainty**, and a clear understanding that those who disagree are not just wrong but wicked. In this way, religious violence is of a different nature than secular violence.

Further reading: Paul Wilkinson, *Terrorism and the Liberal State*; and Hector Avalos, *Fighting Words*.

VIRGIN-WHORE DICHOTOMY. The long-standing no-win situation allocated to women in traditional Christianity. In traditional Christian thinking, Eve is the first woman and the person saddled with the responsibility of introducing **sin** into the world because she had the temerity to pick an apple from the tree of **knowledge** of good and evil. As a result of being cast out from Eden, women were doomed to the pains of childbirth as well as the inevitability of death and suffering we were all now subject to.

The only woman to have escaped this fate was Mary, the mother of Jesus, who was able successfully to have been both a mother and a virgin. In the grim world of traditional Christianity, women either walked in the steps of Eve, or of Mary. There was no escape from this virgin-whore dichotomy. All women bore the curse of Eve in the form of a heightened sexuality, which required severe restraint. The only women able to escape this were those who joined nunneries or committed themselves to perpetual virginity, in emulation of Mary. It was not until societies became predominantly secular that a wider choice was offered women as to how they choose to live their lives. Even now, these victories are under threat. See the entry on *The Nun*.

VIRTUE ETHICS. See **NORMATIVE ETHICS**.

VIRTUECRAT. The term given to professional moralizers, particularly in the United States. The term achieved widespread recognition in 2003 after the discovery that prominent morals campaigner William Bennett was also a high-stakes gambler who, during his gambling forays, smoked three packs of cigarettes a day.

VIRTUES. Dispositions to behave in certain beneficial ways. Different societies will extol different virtues. Dictatorships and **command moralities** will value obedience over intellectual inquiry. **Aristotle**, in an idea known as the **Doctrine of the Mean**, spoke of virtue as the middle ground between opposite vices. Unlike Plato, Aristotle believed that virtue is learned. Virtue is a capacity that needs to be instilled and developed. **Jeremy Bentham** had a simpler idea, equating virtue with whatever maximizes pleasure and minimizes pain. **Paul Kurtz** has outlined what he calls the **humanist virtues**.

VIRUSES OF THE MIND. In a famous essay, **Richard Dawkins** likened some elements of religious thought to viruses. By their nature, viruses are hard for their victims to detect, and the victims may even deny strongly that they suffer from any virus at all. Dawkins offered some symptoms to look out for:

- believing very strongly that something is true or right without feeling any need for **evidence** to justify that belief;
- making a virtue of having strong beliefs, in spite of their not being based on any sort of evidence, even thinking them superior to beliefs which do rely on evidence;
- believing that "mystery" is a good thing and that solving mysteries is a bad thing;
- behaving intolerantly or aggressively toward those who do feel a need for evidence to justify their beliefs, and toward those who have deeply held, though different beliefs;
- a dim awareness that one's belief is the result (usually) of an accident of birth rather than deliberate choice on one's part;
- even when the belief has been especially chosen, it is usually the result of exposure to "a particularly potent infective agent," i.e., an Evangelist of some sort; and

- the recognition that one's beliefs often simulate a repressed sexuality.

Dawkins expressed these seven points in a more tongue-in-cheek manner than shown here, using medical language to bring out the link he saw between religious belief and a virus. Citing the case of the English philosopher Anthony Kenny, who took thirty years to overcome his commitment to Roman Catholicism, Dawkins noted that the religious virus can be beaten, but recognized gloomily how hard it is to shake free of.

Further reading: Richard Dawkins, "Viruses of the Mind," in **Paul Kurtz** and Tim Madigan, eds., *Challenges to the Enlightenment*.

VISUAL ARTS. A term being preferred to the more traditional idea of fine arts, because the latter term is too bound up with aesthetic notions of beauty and gentility. Fine arts has traditionally been limited to painting, sculpture, and printmaking, but there are so many newer forms of artmaking, such as installation art, video art, performance art, and so on, that a new term is a good idea. Visual arts attempts to be more value-neutral than fine arts, and more accommodating toward the new genre. See the entries on **aesthetics**, **piece of art**, and **ready made**.

VIVEKANANDA, SWAMI (1863–1902). Indian reformer and humanist. Born into a privileged family in Calcutta, Narendranath Datta had a full education, including the Indian classics, Western philosophy, riding, and swimming. In 1881 he came under the influence of Swami Ramakrishna (1836–1886), who became his mentor and guide for the rest of his life. After Ramakrishna's death, Vivekananda (as he had now become) wandered India as an ascetic monk. During his travels he concluded that, though India had a brilliant intellectual tradition, it needed more for its people to be lifted from the grinding **poverty** that blighted so many lives.

In 1893 he accepted an invitation to represent Hinduism at the World Parliament of Religions in Chicago. His wide reading and brilliant speaking won him a wide celebrity in the United States and Europe and was a significant factor in the rise in interest in Hinduism in the West at the time. He traveled through the West once again in 1899. Upon his first return to India, he founded the Ramakrishna Ashram at Belur near Calcutta and undertook a program of social reform. The Ramakrishna Mission has gone on to become the largest charity in India.

Vivekananda's thought was grounded in a sophisticated understanding of Vedanta philosophy, although he was convinced that all ideas need to be reinterpreted for the conditions of the day. He was also influenced by Buddhism, Christianity, and Western philosophy and was happy to take wisdom from whatever source. He had little patience with superstition and mindless orthodoxy, and he favored the strict **separation of church and state**. For him, service to one's fellow human being constituted the essence of the godhead. This was an adaptation of the Vedantist teaching that one is not free until everyone is free. Vivekananda had a great impact on Mohandas Gandhi (1869–1948), who described Vivekananda's words as "great music."

His four main written works are the *Jnana-Yoga*, the *Bhakti-Yoga*, the *Karma-Yoga*, and the *Raja-Yoga*. He also gave a large number of lectures, many of which have been published since his death. Vivekananda had been offered the chair of Oriental philosophy at Harvard University, but he turned it down to return to the poor of India.

Vivekananda died in 1902 at only thirty-nine and after a public career of ten years. A beautiful shrine to his memory was built at Kanniyakumari, a tiny islet at the southernmost tip of the Indian subcontinent. It is said that, before his first trip abroad, he swam to the islet so he could contemplate whether to do so.

Further reading: Mohit Chakrabarti, *Swami Vivekananda: Vibrant Humanist*.

VOLTAIRE (1694–1778). One of the most influential campaigners and **smiters of humbug** of all time. Born François Marie Arouet, son of a notary who wished him to study law. Arouet's heart was not in law, however, preferring literature. In 1716 he was forced into exile after writing a scorching lampoon of the corrupt Prince d'Orléans. The following year he was imprisoned in the Bastille, where he adopted his pen name of Voltaire. He was exiled again in 1719 and went to the Bastille a second time in 1726. During his exile in England between 1726 and 1729, he became an enthusiast for English liberties and humanitarianism, in particular those expressed by **John Locke**. For a while he lived in Prussia at the court of Frederick the Great, but their relationship soured, and in 1758 Voltaire settled in Ferney, just inside the French border, but far enough away from his beloved Paris to qualify as exile.

Voltaire's writing career, spanning fifty-four years, was spent attacking clerical and other abuses of power, often in works of brilliant wit and caustic power. His *Poem on the Lisbon Disaster* (1755) questions how a loving god can permit so many innocent people, many of them in church at the time, to die a horrible death during the earthquake which devastated Lisbon that year. His *Treatise of Toleration* (1763) told the well-known story of the Calas family, whose tragedy had been brought about by religious prejudices. The Hugenot Jean Calas was broken on the wheel and strangled to death on the charge of killing his son to prevent him from becoming a Catholic. The charge was patently false, and Voltaire campaigned for justice over many years. He pleaded for Christians to learn to tolerate people of other beliefs.

His best-known story is *Candide* (1759), which ridiculed complacent theism and rationalist optimism, among other things. His most sustained work was his *Philosophical Dictionary* (1764), which took about twelve years to compile, and which was publicly burnt in Protestant Geneva and the Netherlands as well as in Catholic France and the

Holy See. His entire works were placed on the **Index of Forbidden Books** in Spain in 1762. But Voltaire was not cowed. "Every honorable man," Voltaire wrote, "must hold the Christian sect in horror." Such was Voltaire's fame that he attracted a series of legends about him screaming for a priest on his deathbed. See the entry on **infidel deathbeds**.

Further reading: **A. J. Ayer**, *Voltaire*.

VOLUNTARY EUTHANASIA. One of the last basic **rights** not yet accorded to people. Euthanasia comes from the Greek, and means "good death." Voluntary euthanasia refers to the right people should have to end their lives in dignity when faced with terminal illness and when all possible medical avenues have been exhausted. Once it is apparent an illness is terminal and the patient is certain to decline into a lengthy, painful, or undignified final phase, the patient should have the right to decide not to subject himself or his families to the prolongation of the agony. Voluntary euthanasia, in this context, does not refer to cases of whether to prolong a person in a coma on life support. It only refers to cases when a terminally ill but otherwise rational person has a right to decide the time and circumstances of his or her **death**.

Opponents of voluntary euthanasia have two major complaints:

- voluntary euthanasia violates the **sanctity of life**; and
- voluntary euthanasia is open to abuses.

The main argument is that voluntary euthanasia violates the sanctity of life. This is the gist of what people mean when they say it is tantamount to "**playing God**." In this argument, life is given to us by **God**, which means only God can take it away from us. This, of course, is a very flimsy argument because it rests on the highly contentious and, in the opinion of this dictionary, fallacious, assumption that God does indeed exist. Even were we to ignore this weakness, we can also legit-

imately ask what purpose God would see in prolonging unnecessary suffering.

There is also an odd hypocrisy in religious conservatives being apostles of choice in some areas but not in others. Religious conservatives are often keen to espouse choice and the responsibility that goes with it when it comes to material objects, but to oppose the same principle being applied to more serious questions of life and death.

The argument of the possibility of the system being abused is a stronger one. But there are some relatively sure safeguards to prevent abuse. A person who, in full soundness of mind, gives specific instructions in his or her will about the conditions under which life support services should be withdrawn, should have those wishes honored. In other cases, the opinion of medical professionals about the chance of remission would obviously carry weight. No decision to end one's life should be taken without lengthy consultation with medical professionals and with family members. Family members likely to benefit substantially from the dying person's will would need either to be exempted from the consultation process or at least declare their interest.

The other important point to make is that voluntary euthanasia is not being advocated *instead* of palliative hospice care or other methods of prolonging life. It should be one choice among many that a range of parties have a hand in making. But if the hospice care involves little more than pumping the dying patient full of morphine to hide the pain until death, then it is quite reasonable for a terminally ill person to wish not to go down that road. When offered as a choice alongside hospice care, it is likely that relatively few people would avail themselves of their right to voluntary euthanasia. The numbers would be no larger than the people who take this path now, often in more difficult circumstances, particularly for family members. Joseph Fletcher (1905–1991), dubbed the "father of biomedical ethics," said that "[w]hen continued life is not wanted by such patients, and their deaths would not injure others in any substantial way, there is no ethical excuse for forcing them to stay alive."

VOLUNTARY SIMPLICITY. The idea that one can live simply *and* happily. The scourge of **affluenza** tells us we need this one extra thing to be happy. One commentator called it the **paradise spell**. But most of us know this is not true. There is no correlation between the more we buy and our level of happiness. In fact, there is good evidence to the contrary. Now voluntary simplicity doesn't mean we all have to live in the forest and eat acorns. It means we buy only what we need, not want we may want, or what advertisers tell us we want.

Voluntary simplicity understands that time is infinitely more valuable than money, so a promotion at work which will entail even more time away from one's home and family might not be worth it. Voluntary simplicity also entails sacrifices we may not want to make: fewer overseas flights to exotic locations, fewer new toys, even using public transport! See also the entries on **buyer's remorse** and **positive and negative sustainability quotient**.

Further reading: Duane Elgin, *Voluntary Simplicity*.

VON WRIGHT, GEORG HENRIK (1916–2003). One of the most important philosophers of the second half of the twentieth century. Georg Henrik von Wright was born in Helsinki, then still part of Russia, to a family of Swedish Finnish aristocrats. From 1934 to 1937 he studied philosophy, history, and politics at Helsinki University. He was influenced by the logical positivists of the Vienna Circle. The Nazi takeover of Austria in 1938 prevented von Wright from studying there, so he went to Britain, where he studied at Cambridge. He divided his career between spells in Finland and Great Britain. From 1968 until 1977 he was chancellor of Abo Academy in Finland.

While in Britain, he met **Wittgenstein** and remained deeply influenced by him throughout his life. Von Wright was a central figure in the posthumous publication of Wittgenstein's works. In fact, von Wright was one of relatively few disciples of Wittgenstein who went on to forge a successful career of his own. Unlike Wittgenstein, von Wright was a rationalist and a humanist.

Von Wright wrote widely, covering several areas of formal **philosophy**, most notably the problem of induction and questions of logic and the philosophy of **science**. Outside of formal philosophy, he wrote as an essayist and cultural critic. Most of this writing is still in Swedish and awaits translation into English. His major books included *The Logical Problem of Induction* (1941, with several reprints), *The Varieties of Goodness* (1963), *Freedom and Determination* (1980), *In the Shadow of Descartes* (1998), and an autobiography in 2001.

WAHHABI ISLAM. The puritanical brand of Sunni Islam that is the official creed of the Saudi dynasty and of the Saudi kingdom over which they exercise direct rule. The Wahhabi brand of Islam is named after Muhammad b. 'Abdul-Wahhab (1703–1792) although it has roots in Islam going back to Hanbal. The Wahhabis were enamoured of the works of Ibn Taymiyah (1262–1327), whose ferocious style denounced the pernicious influence of foreign ideas and processes into the pure truth of Islam as revealed in the Qur'an and the commentary of the ancients. Ibn Taymiyah's works opposed all attempts of Muslim theologians and philosophers before him to comment and expand on the Qur'an and the commentary of the ancients.

Wahhabi Islam has also learned from Ibn Taymiyah an emphasis on ritual observance and a degree of intolerance to Shi'ite Islam, which is dismissed as a Jewish conspiracy, or Sufi mysticism. To this day in Saudi Arabia, criticism of Ibn Taymiyah can lead to trouble. See the entry on **foundamentalism**.

By 1814 the Wahhabis had conquered Arabia and, following in the footsteps of **Muhammad** himself, were poised to extend their conquests north into Syria. But a combined force under Muhammad Ali of Egypt and Western forces drove them back. Wahhabi ideas nevertheless spread around the Muslim world and were very influential. The Islam of **al Qaeda** is heavily influenced by Wahhabi.

WAL-MART. The world's largest corporation which specializes in discount retailing in a way that undercuts most smaller businesses. Wal-Mart is a $220-billion-a-year business, and the United States' largest single employer—more than a million people. Wal-Mart is the property of the Walton family, one of the richest on the planet. Five of the ten richest people in the world (according to some lists) are Waltons. S. Robson Walton is thought to be worth $65 billion, which is more than Bill Gates.

Wal-Mart came out of Bentonville, Arkansas, and parades itself as an honest-to-goodness, real American firm, which espouses real American values. These values are difficult to discern with respect to employees, however. Despite being required to take part in a morning chant through each of the letters that make up "Wal-Mart," employees are paid less-than-subsistence wages, full-time work is defined as twenty-eight hours, and unionized labor is strictly forbidden. Wal-Mart has faced more suits for workplace discrimination than any other American corporation. Wal-Mart's reputation as an employer, particularly of women and African Americans, was so bad in 2003 that the firm decided to address the issue—by hiring a public relations firm to conduct an expensive advertising campaign.

Wal-Mart is also a major importer of cheap produce from China, where work conditions are little different from slave labor. The sweat shops producing Wal-Mart goods

offer wages of thirteen cents an hour, below China's minimum wage of thirty cents an hour, and then charge usurious rents and charges for food. Wal-Mart tried to hide its dependence on Chinese goods with a hugely expensive advertising campaign, telling consumers it "buys American." It abandoned the campaign in 1998 when it became all too obviously untrue. In 2001 it moved its worldwide purchasing headquarters to China.

The growing financial might of Wal-Mart has meant that it has been able to undercut small businesses around the United States, as well as being instrumental in the closure of thousands of small retail businesses. But Wal-Mart is unrelenting in promoting its brand of folksy conservatism, religious **fundamentalism**, and right-wing politics.

WANG CHONG (Wang Ch'ung) (27–97 CE). Chinese naturalist and skeptic philosopher. He was a minor official in Zhejiang and Anhui who never reached high office. His main work, *Lunheng* (*Discursive Equilibrium*) covered eighty-five chapters and was written over 82 and 83 CE. At a time when the intellectual quality of Confucian thought was in decline and **Confucius** himself was slowly being deified, Wang Chong relentlessly criticized **mysticism** and **irrationalism**.

Wang Chong was a stern critic of the airy mysticism of the **Yin and Yang** school, arguing that Heaven takes no action in the lives of human beings, that natural events are simply that—natural events without any supernatural implications. He opposed the widespread superstitions about attracting fortune to oneself and preventing misfortune. Moral virtue has no essential connection with personal destiny. He insisted that any theory must be tested by concrete **evidence**, and he tried at all times to argue in a rational manner, supporting his claims with appropriate levels of evidence.

Wang founded no school and attracted no lengthy commentary on his works, which are the usual paths to a lasting influence in China. Nevertheless, he is credited with doing much to eradicate **superstition** in China. Perhaps his lasting legacy is as a role model for subsequent Chinese thinkers working within the rationalist tradition. Wang deserves closer study as one of the foremost premodern rationalists from anywhere in the world.

Further reading: Ian P. Greal, ed., *Great Thinkers of the Eastern World* (1995); Wing tsit-Chan, *A Source Book in Chinese Philosophy* (1963).

WAR CRIMES TRIBUNALS. A series of specialist international courts established under the aegis of the **United Nations** to deal with specific cases of suspected war crimes. The first War Crimes Tribunals were established in the 1990s in response to widespread outrage at the slaughter in former Yugoslavia and Rwanda. The International Criminal Tribunal for the former Yugoslavia (ICTY) was formed in May 1993 and by 2004 had indicted seventy-eight people for war crimes. The International Criminal Tribunal for Rwanda was formed in November 1994 and has so far indicted about twenty-five people for war crimes. The sight of former Yugoslav president Slobodan Milosevic facing charges before ICTY has greatly helped the cause of universal human **rights** and transnational cooperation. In a perverse betrayal of its founding principles, the **World Union of Freethinkers** actually supported Milosevic.

Most countries support the war crimes tribunals, although support is far from universal. The United States, for instance, is not a member country. It is easy to find fault with any transnational organization such as this, but global cooperation is essential to our survival as a species. The tribunals are the most practical illustration of **planetary humanism** in action. See the entry on **global governance**.

WAR ON TERROR. The catchphrase of the post–September 11 world. It has become a truism to observe that the war on **terrorism** is a war like no other ever fought. The war is fought not against rival nations but against shadowy groups like **al Qaeda**, **Hamas**, and others. This has become known as "asymmetrical war." For the war on terrorism to be successful, it must be fought simultaneously on three fronts:

- *the intelligence war*, to preempt terrorist strikes, seize sources of finance and weapons, and so on;
- *conventional war*, when necessary, against **rogue states** or **failed states** which harbor terrorist cells; and
- *the battle of ideas*, to win the hearts and minds of all people to the ideals of **democracy** and **pluralism**.

The intelligence war is going to be vital in winning the war on terror. It is a messy, murky sort of conflict, one which necessarily operates undercover and away from public scrutiny. The intelligence war will require new thinking from human-**rights** supporters, as some powers to search and detain are an inevitable part of this conflict. But clear limits will need to be set, or else the opponents of the terrorists risk losing the moral high ground.

The war on terror cannot be won solely by conventional military means. Indeed, it is likely to be the least effective method, and the one most likely to produce counterproductive results. The debacle in Iraq has demonstrated this. It is not that conventional war is inappropriate at all times, but it needs to be, and be seen to be, the last resort. And it needs to be understood without ambiguity as a **just war**.

Another danger is that authoritarian regimes around the world use the "war on terror" as the excuse to crack down on legitimate dissent in its own country. There have been enough troubling instances of this in Uzbekistan, Turkmenistan, and elsewhere, while in Russia, the democratic process has suffered some important reverses in the name of fighting terrorism. It will be important that the West and the international community don't avert their eyes from these abuses in the way they tolerated authoritarian regimes during the **cold war**, so long as they were on "our side."

What is becoming increasingly clear is that the war on terrorism is going to be, more than anything else, a battle of ideas. This battle of ideas will be fought on three fronts:

- showing that democracy, pluralism, **secularism**, and **planetary humanism** are the best means by which we can all live on the planet together in peace;
- discrediting the religious **fundamentalism** which gives rise to terrorism; and
- redoubling efforts to address issues of **poverty** and **inequality** in the world.

It is folly to assume the war on terror means that the struggle for human rights is just a luxury that can come later, once the war is won. The struggle for human rights will be a significant front in the war on terror. In the end, one of the surest ways of winning the war on terror is the full implementation of the **millennium development goals**.

Further reading: Paul Berman, *Terror and Liberalism*; and Sam Harris, *The End of Faith*.

WARRAQ, IBN. Pioneering scholar of Islamic and Qur'anic criticism. "Ibn Warraq" is a pseudonym to protect this scholar from violence at the hands of Muslims who are unused to any form of criticism. The name refers to Abu Isa Muhammad b. Harun Warraq (d. 909) a freethinking scholar and teacher to **Ibn Rawandi**.

Ibn Warraq's first book was *Why I am Not a Muslim* (1995), which has become a bestseller. Since then he has edited three important collections of scholarly essays on various aspects of Islamic Studies and Qura'anic criticism: *The Origins of the Koran* (1998), *The Quest for the Historical Muhammad* (2000), and *What the Koran Really Says* (2002). *Leaving Islam* (2003) features a series of accounts, some of them very moving, of people's paths away from Muslim belief toward **freethought**. All these books are published by **Prometheus Books**, and are

thought by many to lay the foundations for an era of Qur'anic criticism which is long overdue. In 2003, Ibn Warraq received the Distinguished Secular Humanist Award from the **Council for Secular Humanism** for his contribution toward a new look at Islam.

Further reading: http://www.secularislam .org.

WARS OF RELIGION. A name given to a series of religious-political-dynastic conflicts in France, eight in all, between 1559 and 1598, provoked by persecution of Protestant Hugenots by the Roman Catholic political leadership. They were described by the prominent humanist **Montaigne** as "a true school of treachery, inhumanity and brigandage." The Hugenots had become significant among the nobility and among the rising class of artisans and small businessmen. The peasants remained staunchly Catholic in all areas except the southwest of France.

The first three conflicts lasted without interruption through the 1560s and secured for the Hugenots some freedom of worship at the cost of surrendering some strategic fortresses. This fragile compromise was shattered by the murder of some Hugenot leaders and general massacre of thousands of their followers at the Massacre of St. Bartholomew (August 23–24, 1572).

Five more conflicts flared up and wore down over the next twenty-five years. Eventually an exhausted country arranged a compromise known as the Edict of Nantes (April 15, 1598), which secured for Hugenots a measure of political equality with Catholics. This religious toleration lasted until 1685, when the edict was revoked (October 18), and any form of non-Catholic religious practice was forbidden. Despite a ban on emigration, about fifty thousand Hugenots fled the country, resulting in a serious financial and intellectual impoverishment of the country.

The French wars of religion were only part of a broader series of religious-political-dynastic conflicts of the time. The Dutch revolted against Spanish rule between 1567 and 1579, the Spanish Armada fought England in 1588, there were struggles between Catholics and Protestants in England, and, most bloody of all, the Thirty Years' War (1618–1648) broke out, which devastated much of central Europe for several generations. Not until World War I did Europe see such bloodshed again.

The widespread disgust with the seemingly endless rounds of killing, rapine, and plunder in the name of **God**, along with the extraordinary advances in science which saw the collapse of the **Geocentric universe**, gave rise to the concept of **toleration** of different opinions. And toleration was only one of the main threads of the **Enlightenment**, which wanted a different sort of world than one torn apart by wars of religion.

WATER. The most undervalued resource on the planet. Many people have predicted that the twenty-first century will see a series of water wars. It is estimated that water consumption has increased sixfold since 1990. And only 2.5 percent of the world's water is fresh, and three quarters of that is in the polar icecaps. This makes conflict over this valuable resource quite likely, as 40 percent of the world's population lives in regions with some degree of water shortage and 23 million people die each year as a consequence of unsafe water.

Some wealthy countries, like Saudi Arabia, Kuwait, and Japan rely heavily on the expensive process of the desalination of sea water, but this option is not open to poorer countries. Those countries that possess plentiful quantities of fresh water are going to find themselves as prosperous as oil-rich nations are today. Few issues underscore the need for transnational planning and cooperation more clearly than the management of water resources. See the entry on **global governance**.

WATTS, CHARLES (1836–1906). English **freethought** lecturer described by **George E. Macdonald** as "one of the ablest men who ever stepped upon a platform." Born in

Bristol, the son of a Wesleyan minister, Watts was inspired into freethought after hearing lectures by **George Jacob Holyoake** and **Charles Southwell**. Watts gave his first lecture when he was only fourteen. It was called "The Curse of the Nation and Its Remedy." The curse was the demon rum, the remedy teetotalism. Shortly afterward, Watts went to London where, in 1864, he joined his brother John in the printing business. As part of his trade, he became subeditor of the *National Reformer*, the journal edited by **Charles Bradlaugh**. The two men remained firm friends until 1877 when they disagreed strongly on the right course of action with regard to a birth-control pamphlet called *The Fruits of Philosophy*. Bradlaugh thought it an important enough issue to risk arrest and imprisonment. Watts thought differently, so when arrested for publishing an obscene tract, Watts pleaded guilty, much to Bradlaugh's disgust.

Soon after his estrangement from Bradlaugh, Watts took over another freethought periodical, the *Secular Review*, from Holyoake. He worked on this journal with **G. W. Foote** and W. Stewart Ross (1844–1906) until 1886, when he left for Canada. In Toronto, he founded another journal, *Secular Thought*, and was a vigorous campaigner around Canada and the United States. Increasingly precarious income from this activity forced him back to Britain in 1891, although he visited North America three more times in 1896, 1899, and 1902. Shortly before he left for Canada, he bequeathed his publishing operation to his son, **Charles Albert Watts**, who built it up into Watts and Co., the **Rationalist Press Association**, and the *Literary Guide*, which is still published as the *New Humanist*.

Watts gave between 150 and 200 lectures a year over much of his adult life. Most of his written output was taken from his lectures. A selection of them was brought together under the title *The Meaning of Rationalism* (1905).

Watts's obituary summed up his life, and a great deal about the core of **humanism** in the process: "He firmly maintained the necessary limitations of **human knowledge**, but never claimed to determine fully the scope of human capacity. Avoiding alike **mysticism** and shallow denial, he was a true agnostic, anxious not merely to beat down error, but to build up truth."

WATTS, CHARLES ALBERT (1858–1946). English publishing pioneer. Born in modest circumstances, his father was **Charles Watts**, one of the most important **freethought** leaders of the nineteenth century. Young Charles Albert Watts learned the printing and publishing trades from the bottom up, serving lengthy and impoverished apprenticeships. Not given to leadership from the front in the style of **Charles Bradlaugh**, Watts built up Watts and Co., a publishing firm which was to enjoy extraordinary success, and the **Rationalist Press Association**, which is still with us today. Watts and Co. and the RPA were Watts's life.

In 1883 Watts established *The Agnostic Annual*, which continued publication under several different names until 1980. And in 1885 he founded the *Literary Guide*, which served as a vehicle for promoting his books and went on to become one of the premier humanist journals in the world. Today it is published as the *New Humanist*.

Watts's genius was in understanding how the publishing trade actually worked, and in being able to inspire confidence in men richer than himself to finance his innovative publishing ventures. The most daring of these was his plan to reprint substantial works of freethought, history, **science**, and biblical criticism in paperback form for only sixpence or hardback for a shilling. These prices would make these works accessible to working-class readers. Conventional wisdom was that poorer people lacked the inclination or ability to read works of this sort. Watts proved them wrong. Between 1902 and 1912 Watts and Co. produced the **Cheap Reprints** series which made works by **T. H. Huxley**, **Ernst Haeckel**, and others available to readers of modest means.

Many titles in this series sold in the tens of thousands, often to the alarm of church leaders, who were unused to poor people thinking for themselves. Eventually changes to copyright laws and pressure against railway vendors forced the Cheap Reprints series to come to an end. But in the mean time, publishing history had been made. Watts repeated this success with the **Thinker's Library**, which ran from 1929 until 1951.

Things became more difficult for Watts after World War I, and even his skills weren't sufficient to prevent Watts and Co. from suffering at the hands of aggressive new competition that imitated his earlier successes in the form of the cheap Penguin paperbacks and rival popular science series. A surge of book buying during World War II delayed the problem until after Watts's death in 1946. The problem was left to his son F[rederick] C. C. Watts (1896–1953) to try to solve. That Fred Watts failed was through no lack of effort on his behalf. In 1954 the RPA took over direct ownership of Watts and Co., and in 1960 they sold the firm to Sir Isaac Pitman and Sons.

Further reading: Bill Cooke, *The Gathering of Infidels: A Hundred Years of the Rationalist Press Association*.

WAVE FUNCTION OF THE UNIVERSE. A theory devised in the 1980s and 1990s by Stephen Hawking, Andre Vilenkin, Alex Linde, and others that postulates a law of nature they call the Wave Function of the Universe, which implies that it is highly probable that a universe with the features we observe in ours could emerge without a cause. The theory works mathematically by assigning a number to all possible universes and finding out that they cancel each other out except in cases of a universe such as the one we inhabit, giving a 95 percent probability that our universe could come into existence uncaused. In other words, our universe came into existence because of its inherent mathematical properties, not because a **god** on one planet in that universe decided to create it. See the entry on **mathematics**.

WEASEL WORDS. Words that have a benign surface meaning, but are used as a smokescreen for the less benign reality. Advertising abounds with them. Something may be strawberry *style*, but this of course does not mean the product has been anywhere near a strawberry.

More serious is the use of weasel words in politics. An "enemy combatant" is a prisoner of war by any other name, but an enemy combatant is not protected by the Geneva Convention the way prisoners of war are. The Israeli government of Ariel Sharon was anxious that the wall it built around the Palestinian Authority should not be called a wall because of unpleasant ties with the Berlin Wall. Instead it is called a barrier or a fence. Other examples of weasel words could include "protective custody" when we mean arrest and detention; "intelligence activity" when we mean spying; "liberation" when we mean occupation; and "negative profit" when we mean financial loss.

Bureaucrats often speak of "constructive ambiguity," whereby a document is phrased sufficiently vague that its real intent is missed and the politicians who have to sell it to the public can divert attention from its primary intent. Weasel words work against the free and open communication of ideas, and a skeptical attitude to what we are told is always sensible. See the entry on **manufactured consent**.

WELFARE STATE, THE. A term coined in the 1930s by Professor Alfred Zimmern (1879–1957) that did not come into widespread use until World War II, when it was used to contrast the Allies with Hitler's "warfare state." The term has come to mean the political system where the state assumes significant responsibility for a "cradle to grave" provision of healthcare, education, pensions, unemployment, and other allowances. These provisions are given out in the form of government benefits for a range of conditions, the most common being unemployment, sickness, or old age. Revenue is raised by taxation.

The sentiment behind the idea of the welfare state is ancient. There are incidental references to the duty of kings to their subjects throughout ancient literature, but perhaps the most comprehensive notion of a welfare state can be found in the works of the Buddhist sage, Nagarjuna (150–250 CE, approx.). Nagarjuna advocated limiting the incomes of some of the better-off members of society so that the poor could afford their services. He also saw a positive role for the state in the construction of canals, wells and irrigation systems, the provision of shelters for the needy, and the prevention of bankruptcy.

However, the welfare state could not emerge as a serious idea until the state had the resources to effect the sort of changes asked of it. This did not happen until the nineteenth century. Ironically, the first comprehensive program of welfare measures was enacted by Bismarck's Germany in the 1880s, more with the intent of buying the workers off, rather than from solicitude for their welfare. The first welfare program enacted with welfare motives was in New Zealand in the 1890s. Interestingly, New Zealand was also among the first countries to scale back its welfare provisions, this beginning after 1985.

The problem for the welfare state since World War II has been to determine the right balance between the distributive goals of leveling the playing field for the disadvantaged while retaining as open a society as possible so that others may strive for goals they have set for themselves. The bureaucratic muddle in Europe has led to what has been dubbed **Eurosclerosis**. But many countries where the welfare state has been pared back significantly are beginning to look once again like the nineteenth-century societies the original proponents of the welfare state were reacting against. In the United States, the gap between the rich and poor is unhealthily wide and getting wider. Such levels of **inequality** are inconsistent with a stable society in the long run. The right balance has not yet been reached. See the entry on **baby boomers**.

WELL-ORDERED SOCIETY. The American philosopher **John Rawls** conceived that the ideal well-ordered society would involve these features:

- everyone accepts, and this acceptance is on the public record, the same principles of justice;
- the political institutions are streamlined and work together in a way the public knows about and approves of; and
- citizens have a coherent sense of justice and confidence in society's institutions, and are thus willing to comply with them.

Rawls made a point of contrasting a well-ordered society with potentially more authoritarian notions of a **community**, which involves all citizens sharing the same religious and political views.

A basic feature of a well-ordered society is that there exists a widespread public awareness of what sort of claims are appropriate for citizens to make regarding political justice, and how those claims should be supported. See the entry on **civil society**.

Further reading: John Rawls, *Political Liberalism*.

WELLS, GEORGE ALBERT (1926–). English scholar of great depth and range. Wells is best known for a series of thoroughly researched works on the historical Jesus. His Jesus books need to be read in the order in which they were written to appreciate the development of his thought. His first was *The Jesus of the Early Christians* (1971), which outlined just how sparse the contemporary knowledge of Jesus really was. Then in *Did Jesus Exist?* (1975, revised second edition 1986), *The Historical Evidence for Jesus* (1988), *Who Was Jesus?* (1989), and *The Jesus Legend* (1996), Wells went over the New Testament and other accounts and called into question the conventional theological account of **Jesus Christ**. Following the example of **J. M. Robertson**, Wells argued for a mythical reading of Jesus, although his

version of the myth theory was always more nuanced than Robertson's. Wells's scholarship is to be taken seriously, not least because of his perfect command of German, and his wide familiarity with German biblical criticism. For most of his career, Wells was professor of German at Birkbeck College in London.

Wells also edited a long-overdue study of Robertson's huge corpus. This study, *J. M. Robertson (1856–1933): Liberal, Rationalist, and Scholar* (1987), brought together some of the best thinking on Robertson. Wells's other main book was *Religious Postures* (1988), a collection of essays on some prominent Christian apologists and their arguments.

Wells was active in the **Rationalist Press Association**, serving as chairman of its board of directors from 1981 until 1989, and editor of its annual research journal *Question* from 1976 until it was closed due to financial restraint in 1980. He was an honorary associate from 1989 until 2003.

WELLS, H[ERBERT] G[EORGE]. (1866–1946). Novelist, prophet, and thinker — one of the twentieth century's most multitalented geniuses. Born in modest circumstances in Kent, Wells narrowly avoided a life of penury and obscurity in the drapery trade his mother planned for him. He studied at the Normal School of Science at South Kensington (now the Royal College of Science and part of the University of London) under **T. H. Huxley**, and taught for a while, before being able to earn a living as a writer. His first published writings were a series of scientific romances. This genre, now known as science fiction, was then in its infancy. The best of these works, *The Time Machine* (1895), *The Island of Dr. Moreau* (1896), *The Invisible Man* (1897), and *The War of the Worlds* (1898), remain classics in their field to this day.

Common wisdom says that these works represent Wells at his best, but his writing career lasted another forty-five years and included some very significant books. After the scientific romances, Wells moved on to novels about life, the best of which were *Kipps* (1905), *Ann Veronica* (1909), *Tono-Bungay* (1909), *The History of Mr. Polly* (1910), and *The New Machiavelli* (1911). These were followed by what Wells later called his prig novels: *Marriage* (1912), *The Passionate Friends* (1913), and *The Wife of Sir Isaac Harman* (1913). These were the first of a series of novels centering around ideas of social reform and personal commitment to living one's life fully and in the public interest.

The onset of World War I produced a series of conflicts within Wells, as it did for many people. While being suspicious of patriotism, Wells deeply loved England, and his wartime books, both fiction and non-fiction reflected this tension. The best of his wartime works were *Mr. Britling Sees It Through* (1916) and *The Undying Fire* (1919). After the war, Wells embarked on a series of what have been called textbooks for the world. They were the hugely popular *Outline of History* (1920), *The Science of Life* (1931), and *The Work, Wealth, and Happiness of Mankind* (1932). Each of these was very influential, despite receiving sniffy reviews from academics.

Wells's novels continued through these years, the most outstanding being *Christina Alberta's Daughter* (1925), *Mr. Blettsworthy on Rampole Island* (1928), and *The Bulpington of Blup* (1932). *Mr Blettsworthy*, in particular, deserves much more recognition than it has had. It is a study of the breakdown of the easy Edwardian consensus about progress. Wells is unfairly said to have been an apostle of **progress**, only to have been disillusioned in his last days. This is untrue. There was a stream of pessimism about humanity's **anthropocentric conceit** from the very early days of his writing career. This underlies the lasting appeal of his science fiction, and reappears periodically, as in *Mr. Blettsworthy*. See the entry on **humanist-themed novels**.

Wells continued to produce outstanding work until the last year of his life, highlights

being *The Brothers* (1938), *The Outlook for Homo Sapiens* (1939), and *You Can't Be Too Careful* (1941), his last novel. During World War II, he was instrumental in composing a **Universal Declaration of Human Rights**, which went on to have enormous influence.

Further reading: David Smith, *H. G. Wells: Desperately Mortal*.

WHAT ATHEISTS AND RELIGIOUS BELIEVERS HAVE IN COMMON. Too often it is assumed that atheists and religious believers have nothing in common. But in fact, the two groups have a large number of things in common. Whether they are more significant than what separates them may well become an issue about whether the **open society** can survive the twenty-first century. This issue is not really relevant to the **Asian traditions**, where the opposition of believer/atheist is hardly possible. Sadly, the history of intolerance toward atheists has primarily been a feature of **monotheist** religions.

The first and most common point atheists and religious believers have in common is a shared humanity. This may sound trite and obvious, but it is worth saying, because the demonization of atheists which is now so ubiquitous, tends to obscure this basic fact. See the entry on **demonization of the opposition**. Atheists and religious believers share the same biogenic needs and virtually all of the sociogenic needs (see the entry on **human needs**). We also have a series of **moral truisms shared by us all**. So, as well as the common human needs and moral truisms, atheists and religious believers also have these important things in common:

- recognition that time spent working out a coherent plan for living constitutes a valid, even an important, use of our time;
- belief that the answers we arrive at when working out this worldview matter; and
- opposition to a life given over to **narcissism** and **nihilism**.

Atheists and religious believers also share a large number of ethical beliefs. This is not surprising as many ethical precepts of Christianity were borrowed from Greek philosophies like **Stoicism** and **Neoplatonism**.

These common points center not so much around what we believe, but our shared conviction that a comprehensive view of the world is a valuable thing to work toward. See the entry on **indifferentism**. Ironically, atheists and religious believers also have in common a sense of being besieged in an unfriendly environment. Both groups have some reason to feel this, although in the case of religious believers, the hostility is often directed toward modernity as a whole. And see the entry on **talking past one another**.

WHITE, ANDREW DICKSON (1832–1918). American scholar. Born in Homer, New York, White received a BA from Yale in 1853 before spending time in Europe, including serving as attaché in the US delegation to St. Petersburg between 1854 and 1855. The following year he returned to Yale where he completed his MA, before taking up a teaching position at the University of Michigan, where he stayed until 1863. White then returned to his native New York where he served in the state's senate. With his friend Ezra Cornell (1807–1874), White helped established Cornell University in 1867, and was its first president, serving until 1885. White ensured that Cornell was not dominated by religious interests, and also looked to establishing a sound science training at the university.

He faced a barrage of criticism and hostility for his efforts to free Cornell from sectarian interference. It was partly to respond to this criticism that he began research for his masterpiece: *A History of the Warfare of Science with Theology in Christendom*, which was first published in 1896. This work quickly established itself as a classic of scholarship and is still well worth reading. This book represents the most scholarly rendition of the **conflict between religion and science** thesis.

After his retirement, White again served in Russia and elsewhere as a diplomat, and was the chairman of the International Peace Conference, held at the Hague in the Netherlands in 1899. White's other main works were *Autobiography* (1905) and *Seven Great Statesmen in the Warfare of Humanity with Unreason* (1910). Cornell University has honored White with the Andrew D. White professorship-at-large. One of its most prominent recipients was **Georg Henrik von Wright**.

WHITE-COLLAR CRIME. A term coined only in the 1930s, by an American sociologist, Edwin Sutherland (1883–1950). Until then, people tended to think of crime as something done by poor people, usually against rich people. But Sutherland was the first to make a systematic study of the now obvious fact that socially privileged people can be criminals too. He studied the legal counts against seventy of America's largest corporations, and found that not a single one had not at some stage been indicted of serious white-collar crimes.

Sutherland had little patience for the bad-apple myth, arguing that white-collar crime is a learned behavior. Later on, another important American sociologist, C. Wright Mills (1916–1962), wrote of the structured immorality of corporate culture. Few people, in the wake of the corporate scandals at the end of the twentieth century (Worldcom, Enron, and others) would dispute this idea. Executives began each Worldcom board meeting with a Christian prayer. They then engaged in large-scale crime.

White-collar crime has some different features than blue-collar crime. With white-collar crime the criminal and victim seldom come face to face. Indeed, there are often many victims, separated both geographically and temporally. White-collar criminals are still treated differently than their blue-collar colleagues. To this day, an embezzler of millions, assuming he is caught, is likely to receive easier sentences than someone who robbed a store of a few thousand.

WHITMAN, WALT (1819–1892). Brilliant American poet. Walt Whitman was born in West Hills, on Long Island, near New York, the son of a freethinking carpenter. He was brought up in Brooklyn and began work doing a variety of menial positions in offices. He then tried teaching in rural areas before he returned home and took up journalism. For about ten years he worked as a journalist in Brooklyn and New Orleans. Through these years he also experimented with poetry, to give some expression to feelings he found no avenue for in journalism.

The publication of *Leaves of Grass* in 1855 unleashed a series of **culture wars** which lasted for more than thirty years, as Whitman was pilloried by religious conservatives and thrown out of a government job by his Evangelical boss, and his publishers were subjected to threats and harassment. The treatment of Whitman is one of the clearest examples of **comstockery** in action. Despite this ongoing persecution, *Leaves of Grass* went through eight editions and grew from ninety-five to four hundred forty pages. Unlike his religious persecutors, Whitman's poetry was more in the spirit of **Jesus Christ**, when he said, "Not till the sun excludes you do I exclude you."

Whitman was greatly admired by many prominent freethinkers and suffrage campaigners, in particular **Robert Ingersoll** and **Elizabeth Cady Stanton**. However, Whitman was closer to **pantheism** than the **agnosticism** of either Stanton or Ingersoll. Unlike the religious conservatives, the freethinkers were either unperturbed or chose to overlook Whitman's homosexuality. His funeral was attended by many thousands of people whose lives had been enriched by his poetry.

WHYTE, ADAM GOWANS (1875–1950). Scottish journalist, novelist, and activist. He was the seventh of nine children. Whyte's father was a dentist of gentle, epicurean habits, who hoped his son would become an artist. Adam's skills lay elsewhere, however, and his father died when he was only twelve

years old. In 1898 Whyte moved south to London where he remained for the rest of his life, and earned his living as a journalist. He joined the board of the **Rationalist Press Association** on its foundation in 1899, and remained a board member for fifty-one years, a record nobody has come near to matching.

Whyte's formal job after 1901 was editor of the journal *Electrical Industries*, but his real love was rationalist writing. His best book was *The Religion of the Open Mind*, originally published in 1913; it went through four editions, remaining in print until the late 1940s. This book is still worth reading. Earlier in his career he had to write under a pseudonym, so as not to endanger his employment. As "J. A. Hedderwick," Whyte wrote *Do We Believe? A Brief Exposition of the Rationalist Faith* in 1904. Whyte was also a successful children's author, most notably *The World's Wonder Stories* in 1916. His best known novel was *Christabel's Fairyland* (1926). He was also a successful popularizer of the biological sciences for children, publishing *Our World and Us* (1930), *How Life Goes On* (1932), and *The Ladder of Life: From Molecule to Mind* (1951), which went through publication just after his death. He was also a prolific journalist. For twenty-one years until his death, he wrote a regular column called "The Open Window" for the *Literary Guide*, under the pseudonym Protonius.

WIDE REFLECTIVE EQUILIBRIUM. A theory that argues that moral judgments can be justified without having to resort to a discredited **foundationalism**, but by a broader approach which looks for the coherence of a belief with other beliefs, whether they be moral or other spheres of thought. What the wide reflective equilibrium brings is an ability to juggle many balls at once, assessing the merits of one belief against another in terms of their overall coherence in the larger scheme of beliefs that one holds, and not by some litmus test against a preordained set of commandments. This method fits well with the reliabilist method of assessing **knowl-**

edge, and is a valuable tool whereby the free-thinker can assess moral issues in a balanced way. Wide reflective equilibrium complements **reliabilism** as a method of understanding the world.

It was originally developed by Nelson Goodman and **John Rawls** in **ethics**, and later employed by Kai Nielsen in *Naturalism Without Foundations* and **Michael Martin**'s book *Atheism, Morality, and Meaning*, both of which are titles in the **Prometheus Lectures Series**.

WILL TO POWER. One of the less helpful of the ideas generated by **Friedrich Nietzsche**, the will to power is also one of his least developed. It is often thought of as the idea Nietzsche moved on to after neglecting the notion of the **overman** he had developed in *Thus Spake Zarathustra* (1886). But in moving from the overman to the will to power, Nietzsche was not moving from one idea to another, but to a sharper version of the same idea. Both were an attempt to assert the primacy of **thymos** over desire and reason.

Like the overman, the will to power is an attempt to transcend human limitations, particularly those imposed by reason and nature. The will to power can be seen as the will to dominate. **Immanuel Kant** had the opposite in mind when he said that no one has a moral entitlement to use others as a means to their own ends.

WILSON, E[DWARD]. O[SBORN]. (1929–). The foremost American biologist of his generation. E. O. Wilson was an only child, brought up in a fundamentalist Baptist family in Alabama. At fifteen he "accepted **Jesus Christ**" at a revival meeting. But when he began at the University of Alabama two years later, he found that none of the **creationism** he had been brought up with could possibly be true. He was studying genetics and evolutionary biology, and none of it confirmed the tenets of his biblical indoctrination. "I saw that all I had learned and hoped to accomplish in natural history studies," he

wrote much later, "made sense only from the vantage of scientific materialism."

Liberated from the fundamentalist baggage, Wilson went on to have a stellar career. He was invited to join the doctoral program at Harvard in 1951. In 1956 he joined the faculty at Harvard, and remained there for the rest of his career. Just as J. B. S. Haldane (1892–1964) made his reputation with the study of beetles, so Wilson specialized in the study of ants, writing a seminal work on them in 1971. Wilson became a public figure with his controversial book *Sociobiology: The New Synthesis* (1975). This book caused a storm of controversy, much of it thoroughly ill informed. What *Sociobiology* sought to do was to integrate the findings of biological evolution with the social sciences. It is a truism that our biological constitution, in the form of our genes, plays a determinative role in our lives. *Sociobiology* sought to explain this linkage. Opponents were worried about the future of their prescientific notions of the **soul**, or of **free will**, and mounted an acrimonious campaign against sociobiology. Sociobiology is now generally known as **evolutionary psychology**.

Wilson's next major public work was the Pulitzer Prize–winning work, *On Human Nature* (1978). **Human nature** has also been a very unfashionable concept, but Wilson's arguments helped redress the balance. More recently, he wrote *Consilience: The Unity of Knowledge* (1998), which tried to look at the bigger picture. See the entry on **consilience**. He was elected to the **International Academy of Humanism** in 1983, part of the academy's inaugural intake. Wilson writes, "Today, I would call myself a scientific humanist, someone who believes in humility toward other people but not toward the gods." See the entry on **biophilia**.

WINGED ANCHOR, THE. A motif for **humanism**. In the face of the widespread sense of uncertainty abroad and dreary **affluenza** at home, many people have turned to religious **absolutism** in the hope of finding an anchor of purpose for their atomized lives. But, as many commentators have noted, the anchor of religious **certainty** has also provided inspiration for the frenetic struggle against modernity by religious fanatics and terrorists, and some of the more imperious and heavy-handed responses from the West.

So we cannot rely on anchors alone. What we need is an anchor with wings; an anchor that provides confidence *and* the willingness to explore. In the context of dissolving certainties and diminishing national sovereignty rising alongside renewed national and religious fanaticisms, there is a desperate need for a coherent alternative—for an anchor with wings. **Planetary humanism** has the authority of an ancient tradition, spanning the great civilizations of India, China, and Greece. But it can also look ahead. Planetary humanism can combine the invigorating cross-fertilization of ideas and people that constitute the great promise of **globalization** with the quiet reassurance that comes from being part of a noble intellectual, cultural, and artistic heritage. The winged anchor is also a way to take full responsibility for adopting a **cosmic perspective**. See the entries on **Scylla and Charybdis** and **the best of causes**.

WITCHCRAFT. A form of misogyny and supernaturalist **superstition**. In the West, the attitude toward witches can be traced back to the **Hebrew scriptures**, where Exodus 22:18 has the fateful injunction, "Suffer not a witch to live." This passage was the inspiration for the frenzy of witch-hunting in the sixteenth and seventeenth centuries. While the passage comes from the Hebrew scriptures, it has been applied in this cruel way by Christians rather than by Jews.

The witchcraft frenzy took on truly dangerous proportions after the publication in 1486 of *Malleus Maleficarum* (*Hammer of Witches*), a book written by two Dominican friars and designed as a handbook for inquisitors. The inherent sinfulness of women was a central theme of the book because women were held to be more prone to the allures of witchcraft than men. Particularly misogynistic passages from the Bible and quotes from St. John Chrysostom (347–407 CE) and others were used as evidence. The basic drive behind witchcraft was held to be sexual lust, women's appetite for which, thanks to the curse of Eve, was insatiable. See the entries on **original sin**, the **virgin-whore dichotomy**, and the **Inquisition**.

The witchcraft craze was brought to an end by an increase in scientific knowledge. Nowadays, in the West at least, witchcraft has been sufficiently defanged that it is little more than a harmless amusement for people wanting to appear different. In many parts of the developing world, however, witchcraft is still practiced and continues to impact mainly upon women.

WITTGENSTEIN, LUDWIG (1889–1951). Austrian-born genius who became one of the twentieth century's most important philosophers, although his legacy was far from positive. Wittgenstein was born into one of the richest families in Europe. He could have done anything he wanted.

His early influences were a mixed bag of Germanic pessimists, ranging from the philosopher **Arthur Schopenhauer**, to the historian Oswald Spengler (1880–1936), author of *The Decline of the West* (1918) and, strangest of all, Otto Weininger (1880–1903), who in a bizarre work *Sex and Character* (1903) gave vent to **anti-Semitism** and a pathological fear and hostility of women. Each of these thinkers retained an influence on Wittgenstein throughout his philosophical career.

Wittgenstein began his career studying aeronautics, which brought him to the University of Manchester. A growing interest in mathematics led him to seek out the greatest mathematician and philosopher of the day, **Bertrand Russell**, who quickly appreciated Wittgenstein's genius, and worked hard to support him.

Of all the books that now appear under

Wittgenstein's name, only one was written by him during his lifetime. This was the *Tractatus Logico-Philosophicus* (1921). The other major work written by Wittgenstein was still being revised when he died. This was *Philosophical Investigations* (1953). All the other works which appear under his name were either compilations of Wittgenstein's lecture notes, or notes taken during his lectures by students. See the entry on **Georg Henrik von Wright**.

Wittgenstein's career reflected his personality: tumultuous and intense. Throughout his philosophical career, he believed that philosophers were prone to talking nonsense and adding to the problems of the discipline by their attempts to formulate grand answers. The real task of philosophy, as he saw it, was not so much to end our ignorance with words but to recognize that words all too often lead to further and greater ignorance.

The *Tractatus* was Wittgenstein's attempt to illustrate this problem and outline his solution. It is a unique work of **philosophy**, with whole traditions of thought encapsulated into formidably dense assertions. It is both dazzlingly clear and infuriatingly opaque. Wittgenstein argued that language has an underlying logical structure, but that the more we understand that structure, the more we realize how little can meaningfully be said. The very last sentence of the *Tractatus* says, "What we cannot speak about we must pass over in silence."

Philosophical Investigations is a fuller account and partial repudiation of his earlier thoughts. Here he placed greater stress on our tendency to end up in conceptual and linguistic muddles. Indeed, he went a step further by saying that even relying on traditional philosophical tools like explanation is to misunderstand how language works, and to fail to understand that analysis will not help us understand anything truly important. Bertrand Russell expressed impatience with this approach, saying that Wittgenstein had given up even trying to think the issues through and had invented a doctrine to invalidate the whole process. This is only slightly unfair. The English philosopher A. C. Grayling put it better when he said that Wittgenstein's hostility to clarity, rigor, and accuracy provided a rationale for charlatans to avoid the scrutiny these qualities could bring against them. Grayling is correct to see Wittgenstein's importance not strictly as a philosopher but as a philosophical poet and personality.

Further reading: A. C. Grayling, *Wittgenstein*; Ray Monk, *Wittgenstein: The Duty of Genius*; and **A. J. Ayer**, *Wittgenstein*.

WOLLSTONECRAFT, MARY (1759–1797). Feminist pioneer who, in the words of **Samuel Putnam**, "stands like a radiant prophetess at the opening of woman's new career." An unloved child; Mary's parents were disappointed she was not the second son they hoped for. Her childhood and youth were spent caring for her ailing mother and keeping out of her violent father's way. In 1787 she went to London and became immersed in radical activities. There she wrote a short tract on the education of girls and a novel, *Mary*. The activities of the English revolutionaries, no less than the revolution in France, provoked the Tory Edmund Burke to write *Reflections on the Revolution in France* (1790), which attacked radicalism and progressive politics. Burke's book in turn stimulated two famous rejoinders: **Thomas Paine**'s *Rights of Man* (1791) and Mary Wollstonecraft's *A Vindication of the Rights of Women* (1792).

Wollstonecraft's first published response to Burke had been a short, unsigned tract called *A Vindication of the Rights of Men*, which appeared at the end of 1790. But she soon discovered that many people did not make the assumption she did that by speaking of men she meant humanity. With that in mind Wollstonecraft rewrote her tract, and gave it a new title, *A Vindication of the Rights of Women*. Here she argued that neither **reason** nor **virtue** have gender. Girls should study history, classics, and literature alongside the boys. She criticized the tendency for girls to be taught what she called fascinating graces rather than a faculty for reasoning. Women, Wollstonecraft argued, are no less capable of reasoning than men. Another of Wollstonecraft's targets was **Jean-Jacques Rousseau**, who supported a blatantly sexist philosophy of education.

After four years in France, Wollstonecraft returned to England in 1796 and began a romantic relationship with a longtime radical ally William Godwin (1756–1836). They married later that year, but Wollstonecraft died from complications from the birth of their child, who went on to become **Mary Wollstonecraft Shelley**.

Wollstonecraft was ridiculed for her views for the better part of a century, by women no less than men. Horace Walpole (1717–1797), a respected man of letters, called her a hyena in a petticoat. But today Mary Wollstonecraft is recognized as a pioneer of women's rights and organized **feminism**. See the entry on **Olympe de Gouge**.

WOMEN IN ISLAM. A book published in 2000 by the Egyptian-born imam Mohamed Kamal Mustafa. *Women in Islam* elaborates on Qur'anic advice to husbands about the management of their wives. When dealing with rebellious women, Mustafa recommends the husband deliver a "serene dialogue" as the first form of control. Should that fail, the next step is to refuse to sleep in her bed. Should the wife remain obdurate in the face of this withdrawal, then the husband should administer corporal punishment, though "without excess," Mustafa warns.

He then gives advice on the method of beating: "If one needs to use blows, they should be administered to specific parts of the body like the feet and hands, using a light and thin stick so it will not leave scars or bruising on the body."

Mustafa was living in Spain acting as a prayer leader in a mosque in Malaga at the time his book was published. Early in 2004 Spanish authorities charged the imam with violating civil **rights** of women. Mustafa's defense was that his advice was based on the Qur'an, which is quite true (see Women 4:34; The Cow 2:228; and Sad 38:44; among others). This, however, was not a sufficient defense for the court and Mustafa was fined 2,160 Euros. This incident is an interesting example of the problems of incorporating presecular ideas into a secular, **civil society**.

WOOLNOUGH, JAMES (1915–1992). Pioneering abortion doctor in Australia and New Zealand. Jim Woolnough was born in Sydney and studied medicine there. During that course of study he worked in the abortion ward of Crown Street Women's Hospital and was impressed by the unnecessary suffering and death of women who hadn't been able to have the choice of a safe abortion. He joined the newly created Humanist Society of New South Wales in 1960 and was instrumental in steering the society to publish in 1962 a report entitled *Termination of Pregnancy*. He worked at a private abortion clinic in Sydney until 1973, when he moved to New Zealand to manage New Zealand's first abortion clinic. The following year the clinic he managed became the focus of antiabortion protests.

Soon after taking over control of the center it was raided by the police leading to an arrest in February 27, 1975, for illegally procuring miscarriage. This quickly became a test case for the legality of abortion in New Zealand. On December 27, 1975, Woolnough was acquitted of the charges. The verdict was appealed the following year, but was upheld on July 22, 1976. In December 1977 the Sterilisation and Abortion Act was passed, which determined the manner in which legal abortion could be undertaken in New Zealand.

Woolnough was an active member of the **NZ Association of Rationalists and Humanists** until his death.

WORLD ATHEIST CONFERENCES. A series of conferences devoted to the practical implementation of **positive atheism** in society. The theme of the 2005 conference, for instance, was "Atheism and Social Progress." The World Atheist Conferences are sponsored by the **Atheist Centre**, based in Vijayawada, Andhra Pradesh, India. There have been five World Atheist Conferences (1972, 1980, 1983, 1996, and 2005). All conferences were held at the Atheist Centre except the one in 1983, which was held in Helsinki, Finland.

WORLD BANK. A consortium of five international corporations whose stated purpose is the reduction of world **poverty**. The five corporations are the International Bank for Reconstruction and Development (IBRD), the International Development Association (IDA), the International Finance Corporation (IFC), the Multilateral Investment Guarantee Agency (MIGA), and the International Center for the Settlement of Investment Disputes (ICSID). Technically speaking, the World Bank refers only to the IBRD and IDA, while the World Bank Group refers to all five corporations. The group is headquartered in Washington, DC, but claims more than a hundred offices around the world.

The two World Bank corporations are in the business of making loans and providing advice. The IBRD provides loans and policy advice to poor and middle-income countries whose credit rating is thought to be sound. The IDA focuses on the poorest countries, and provides grants and interest-free loans for measures it thinks will reduce poverty and conform to standards of "accountable governance," and an improved private investment climate.

The other three corporations which make up the World Bank Group have more limited roles. The IFC works to support private enterprises with capital. The MIGA provides guarantees against war and unrest and other factors that could harm foreign investment in developing countries. And the ICSID is concerned with arbitrating in international investment disputes.

The World Bank is careful to mention it is owned by 184 countries. Any country wanting to join the World Bank must already be a member of the **International Monetary Fund** (IMF). Each member country is represented on a board of governors which technically has the final say in deciding policy. However, while the board is absent, the day-to-day running of the World Bank is done by a twenty-four-person board of executive directors. It is this board that is responsible for the approval of all the loans and other policy decisions the bank makes. Five countries have guaranteed places on the board of executive directors: the United States, Great Britain, Germany, Japan, and France. This board selects the president who, by custom, is nominated by the United States and is a United States national.

The World Bank grew out of a meeting at Bretton Woods, New Hampshire, in July 1944 between forty-five countries looking to rebuild a postwar prosperity. The World Bank's first loan was $250 million to France for reconstruction. The IMF was created at the same meeting. The Bretton Woods system was largely the brainchild of **John Maynard Keynes**.

There are many valid objections that can be laid against the World Bank, and not simply from the political left. The most common complaint is that it promotes styles of growth more in the interests of the rich nations and in ways harmful to local ecosystems and agricultural practice. For instance, it is alleged the World Bank promotes increasing yield by massive quantities of fertilizer and pesticides, without regard to the soil contamination and dependency on Western markets this approach creates in the long run.

In response, the bank claims it has shifted its focus nowadays to the reduction of poverty. During the 1990s, the World Bank recommended an increase of foreign aid by $10 billion annually to help eradicate the worst instances of poverty around the world. James Wolfensohn, World Bank president, talks in terms of a "comprehensive development framework," by which he means rejecting unduly narrow, one-size-fits-all economic programs which looked solely at privatizing, open markets, and so on. Contemporary development, Wolfensohn argues, must be flexible and multifaceted. As with the IMF, the World Bank's main problem has been its lack of accountability and transparency. See the entry on **global governance**.

Further reading: www.worldbank.org; www.whirledbank.org; and Mike Moore, *A World Without Walls*.

WORLD BRAIN. An idea conceived by **H. G. Wells**, who worried that, while human knowledge was expanding at an unprecedented rate, our coordination of that knowledge was lamentably amateurish. Rather than single universities, research centers, and separately published **encyclopedias**, all pursuing their various agendas, Wells urged the bringing together of all these bodies into a world brain.

While Wells did not have the Internet in mind, he would certainly be very excited by it. The Internet has an enormous amount of junk, but it also has a great deal of valuable information. Just as people have to use their **judgment** to discriminate between worthwhile and worthless books, so must they do the same for Web sites. But the ease of access and universality of the Internet means it is the closest we are likely to get to having the world brain that Wells called for in the 1930s.

Further reading: H. G. Wells, *World Brain*.

WORLD ECONOMIC FORUM. A powerful body of the world's largest corporations that seeks to give **globalization** a human face. Founded in 1971 in Switzerland by the Swiss academic and entrepreneur Klaus Schwab, following an informal gathering of business and academic leaders at the Swiss mountain retreat of Davos the year previously. Since then the forum has met annually at Davos (with the exception of 2002, when they met in New York as an act of solidarity with that city) to discuss world affairs and how to influence them in ways they see as beneficial. The forum now consists of the foremost one thousand corporations in the world. Since 1998 it has operated out of its new headquarters in Geneva.

Among its many initiatives includes the Global Leaders for Tomorrow, which was established in 1992 to identify and support promising young leaders in business and global policy, and the **Global Corporation Citizenship Initiative**. Other projects include the Global Digital Divide Initiative and the Global Health Initiative.

Critics note that the one thousand corporations that participate in the World Economic Forum are overwhelmingly from the developed world, and so have an interest in giving the status quo the best face possible in order that their giant profits continue to roll in.

WORLD GOVERNMENT. See **GLOBAL GOVERNANCE**.

WORLD POPULATION FOUNDATION. A highly respected nonprofit organization based in the Netherlands dedicated to raising awareness of issues related to **overpopulation**, poverty, and the oppression of women. The foundation was established by the English entrepreneur and humanist Roy Brown. It is premised on the principle of every person having the right to determine their reproductive lives as they think fit. The foundation has had field offices in Vietnam and Pakistan since 1999, and it works with kindred organizations in ten other countries, including Indonesia, Nepal, Thailand, Kenya, South Africa, Tanzania, Uganda, and Zambia.

The foundation concentrates on young people. Whereas many programs focus rather unhelpfully on promoting sexual abstinence (see the entry on the **global gag rule**), the foundation alerts young people to sexual health risks, and provides information with no sense of condemnation or moral smugness. In 1997, the foundation created the Dutch Council on Youth and Population, which has since grown into a strong voice advocating international **sexual and reproductive rights**.

WORLD TRADE ORGANIZATION. For all its faults, a positive force for the good, if only because of its focus on solving problems at a transnational level. The WTO was formed on January 1, 1995, with the stated purpose of liberalizing world trade. The WTO headquarters is in Geneva, Switzerland, and was the by-product of the so-called Uruguay Round of trade talks, which lasted between 1986 and 1994. The Uruguay Round ended with the Marrakesh Agreement, signed in Marrakesh, Morocco, which decided, among other things, to create the WTO.

It was originally thought to establish a body such as the WTO in 1944 and 1945, when the **World Bank** and **International Monetary Fund** were established. That didn't happen, and for many years trade issues were handled principally through the General Agreement on Tariffs and Trade (GATT). The WTO replaced the GATT as the principal agency overseeing world-trade issues.

As of 2003, the WTO was composed of 146 member countries, and publicly acknowledged a staff of 560 and a fund of the rather modest sum of 154 million Swiss francs. Any country can apply to join the WTO, and membership is growing. The WTO lists its activities as administering world-trade agreements, providing a forum for trade talks, dealing with trade disputes, monitoring trade policies, and helping developing nations boost their trade. Of particular value is its role in mediating trade disputes, a process which places each disputant, regardless of size and power, on an equal footing.

The WTO administers what is called the Trade Policy Review Mechanism (TPRM), which is a noncoercive mechanism for scrutinizing free-trade policies among member nations. Critics are skeptical, and have accused the WTO of opposing environmental legislation and overriding elected governments in the interests of free trade as defined and policed by major corporations. Even the WTO Web site acknowledges that the level of benefit from world trade by developing countries is a matter of debate. But the accusations

of authoritarianism are unsound. The WTO policy of free trade is set by the member nations; the executive and secretariat have relatively little authority to act on their own initiative. However, the poorest countries inevitably have less clout, particularly those that cannot afford to maintain WTO liaison offices. The problem is not an authoritarian WTO dictating policies to the world. The two main problems are administrative inefficiency and careerism within the WTO, and the North-South split within the WTO itself. This latter problem was made clear at the 2003 meeting in Cancún in Mexico.

Opponents of **globalism** gathered in the thousands in Seattle in November 1999 and effectively shut down the WTO meeting taking place in the city at the time. The WTO was to have launched what it called the "Millennium Round" of trade talks. Since the Seattle debacle, WTO meetings have been in considerably more out-of-the-way places or made inaccessible to protestors. In 2003, things took a new step when the WTO meeting at Cancún was scuttled, not by protestors, but by the delegates themselves. Representatives of developing countries walked out of the talks because they felt they were getting a raw deal at the hands of the developed world. Of particular concern was the raft of trade barriers and subsidies which protect farmers in the United States and Europe from competition from cheaper agricultural produce from the developing world.

Further reading: Mike Moore, *A World Without Walls*.

WORLD UNION OF FREETHINKERS. an international union of **freethought** organizations from around the world organized in Brussels in 1880 by a group of European freethinkers, including **Charles Bradlaugh**. The organization Bradlaugh helped establish was known as the International Federation of Freethinkers. It became the World Union of Freethinkers in 1936. It existed as a conduit for communication for freethought organizations around the world and a mobilizing agent for organizations suffering persecution.

After 1887, the single most important activity of the federation was its congresses, which were usually held biannually. The congresses from 1890 until 1910 represented the high point of the federation. They attracted some of the most prominent thinkers of the day and represented the thought of the age. The 1893 congress, which met in Madrid, so alarmed the government that it was forcibly broken up. Perhaps the Rome congress of 1904 and the Paris congress the year later were the zenith of international freethought. The Rome congress was held with high-level government support and in the teeth of opposition from the papacy, and the Paris congress took place the year France passed its legislation on the **separation of church and state**. Those who attended these congresses returned to their various organizations around the world and reported excitedly about the important people they had met and the powerful arguments they had heard.

Things started going wrong for the federation after World War I when it drifted to the hard left. Its change of name in 1936 was part of an amalgamation with the Soviet-backed Proletarian League. The WUF congress of that year featured representatives of the Soviet League of the Militant Godless, led by **Emelian Iaroslavskii**. After World War II, the WUF's hardline political stance started costing it support. For instance, the 1949 WUF congress moved that accommodating **humanism** would amount to weakening its antireligious message, which was thought to be the heart of the WUF program. See the entry on **abolitionists and substitutionists**. It was largely through dissatisfaction with this policy that the **International Humanist and Ethical Union** (IHEU) was formed in 1952. By the 1960s the WUF had been reduced to a tiny rump organization as freethought organizations joined the IHEU. The WUF is now based in Switzerland with about twelve member organizations that keep in touch through e-mail. It follows an eccentric line of politics. In 2004, for instance,

Klaus Hartmann, the WUF vice president, was a speaker at a gathering in Belgrade to protest the arrest of Slobodan Milosevic for crimes against humanity.

Further reading: David Tribe, *100 Years of Freethought*.

WRIGHT, FRANCES (1795–1852). Abolitionist, author, and atheist. Born to a freethinking family of independent means in Dundee, Scotland. Wright survived despite being orphaned as a young girl and grew up precocious and enthusiastic about life. At eighteen she wrote a short sketch called *A Few Days in Athens*, which was a polemical defense of **Epicureanism**. **Samuel Putnam** called this book "one of the wisest and best books ever written, sparkling with genius and learning." *A Few Days in Athens* was dedicated to **Jeremy Bentham**. She also wrote a volume of letters about life in the United States, and a tragedy called *Altorf* (1819).

An early fascination with America encouraged Wright to visit that country when only twenty-three years old. After a three-year stay in Paris, Wright returned to the Unites States where she undertook an ambitious plan to place emancipated black slaves on a large estate in Tennessee, but ongoing hostility from neighboring farmers drained her health and the project failed. She assisted the emancipated slaves in resettling to Haiti. This experience, as well as ongoing opprobrium from the proslavery Presbyterian Henry Ward Beecher (1813–1887) deepened her hostility to the Christian religion. She cooperated with **Robert Owen**'s utopian experiment at New Harmony, Indiana, for as long as it lasted. In 1829 she published a series of lectures called *A Course of Popular Lectures*, which outlined her heretical views on religion. The clergy responded by calling her "The Red Harlot of Infidelity." While at new Harmony, Wright became involved with William S. P. D'Arusmont, although this relationship quickly soured. They married in about 1838 and were divorced ten years later. She died in 1852 from injuries received after slipping on ice.

X

XENOPHANES (560–470 BCE, approx.). One of a succession of Greek rationalists reacting to the mysticism of **Pythagoras**. A citizen of Colophon, in Ionia, Xenophanes cast doubt on the pretension of claiming to speak what is completely true. None of us can do that, he argued. The best we can do is to express opinions resembling things that are true.

Not surprisingly, Xenophanes was a critic of **anthropocentric conceit** as well. He observed that "each group of men paint the shape of the gods in a fashion similar to themselves; the Ethiopians draw them dark and snub-nosed, the Thracians red-haired and blue-eyed." Xenophanes proposed a **deistic** vision of god, an unusual idea for Greeks of his day.

XU FUGUAN (1903–1982). Chinese philosopher who contributed a great deal to articulating a reformed, practical Confucian **humanism**. Xu Fuguan was born in Hubei province to a farming family. Xu's first career was in the army, where he rose to the rank of major-general, before retiring midcareer, disillusioned with politics and politicians. The second half of his career was spent as a writer, journal editor, and university professor, during which time he sought to revitalize the Chinese cultural tradition.

Xu's family name was Binching, but he changed it to Fuguan, which served as a summary of a passage from the *Daodejing*, which says "All things come into being, and I see [*guan*] thereby their return [*fu*]." This passage epitomized Xu's outlook. See the entry on **Taoist virtues**.

Xu postulated a variation of anxiety as the basic characteristic of Chinese tradition. This was not anxiety in the **existentialist** sense of dread, fallenness, or despair, but a more positive understanding of anxiety as the motivating agent for a life of virtue. He went on to restate classical Chinese humanism as a life of practical virtue in which the **transcendental temptation** is rejected. See the entries on **immortality** and **eupraxsophy**.

Further reading: Chung-ying Cheng and Nicholas Bunnin, eds., *Contemporary Chinese Philosophy*.

XUNZI (300–215 BCE, approx.). After **Kongfuzi** (Confucius) and Mengzi (Mencius), the next greatest Confucian scholar. Xunzi (Hsün Tzu in the old spelling) is counted among the famous "hundred philosophers," who are credited with establishing the intellectual heritage of Chinese civilization. The main work through which we know his thoughts is the *Xunzi*, which in all likelihood was written by him, although it was edited later by followers.

Xunzi differed from Mengzi, in that he thought **human nature** was intrinsically evil, although, as a true Confucianist, he was convinced that proper training in the norms of society, chiefly by means of paying due respect to rituals and ceremonies so valued in the Confucian tradition, could bring out the best in people.

Unlike Christian theories of **original sin**, Xunzi valued what human effort could produce. Value comes from culture and culture is a human creation. Xunzi was a forthright naturalist, who advised his readers to marvel at supernatural phenomena but not to fear them. He scorned undue concentration on religious notions. One attends to the ceremonies and rituals, not because we believe all the supernatural claims being intoned, but because it provides social cohesion. Despite having a lower opinion of the essentials of human nature, Xunzi was just as convinced that anyone could become a sage. Whereas Mengzi thought we could all become sages because we are intrinsically good, Xunzi thought we could because we are intrinsically intelligent and able to overcome our evil propensities.

Y

YAHOO-MANITY. A term used by the humanist philosopher **F. C. S. Schiller**. He used the term in a short work called *Tantalus, or the Future of Man* (1924), part of an influential series of pamphlet-length tracts linked by a title taken from mythology, and designed for nonspecialist audiences. Schiller, though normally known for according humanity a unique position as thinker as maker of reality, conceded in this work that humanity's behavior was often uncivilized. That tendency he dubbed yahoo-manity. Schiller would have little reason to revise his opinions in light of recent history.

YAHWEH. Warrior or mountain god, originally of the land of Midian who was taken over and amalgamated into earlier Hebrew tribal deities. The Hebrews originally spoke of "the gods of our fathers," probably tribal chiefs turned into gods; but in the extreme crisis of the exile in Egypt, the Hebrews discovered in the Midianite deity the characteristics of aggression they felt they needed. Considerable effort was later made in the Pentateuch to equate Yahweh with the earlier "gods of our fathers." Eventually, Yahweh also came to supersede and overwhelm El Shaddai, the god of the northern Hebrews.

This process of gods coming and going and being amalgamated into newer and more powerful coalitions was established practice in the ancient world. For a long time the Hebrews acknowledged the existence of the gods of other peoples. Their claim was simply that their god, Yahweh, was the best of them. But in the next major crisis of their society, the exile to Babylon in 587 BCE, Yahweh came to be viewed as the only possible god. What is more, knowledge of this god could only be arrived at by **faith** and revelation.

Among the Greeks, by contrast, god—for those who believed in such an idea—was accessible to human **reason**. This tension has never been resolved. It is an aspect of the divide known by the shorthand of Athens and Jerusalem, with Athens standing in for the tradition of rationality and **humanism**, and Jerusalem standing in for the tradition of faith and revelation. It was this absolute Yahweh that the Christians inherited and wrote about in the New Testament.

Further reading: Werner Schmidt, *The Faith of the Old Testament*; and Jack Miles, *God: A Biography*.

YALTA CONFERENCE. A summit meeting held at a Crimean resort town of the political leadership of Great Britain, the United States, and the Soviet Union on February 7–11, 1945, to outline plans for the postwar world. The participants at Yalta revisited some problems with respect to the functioning of the **United Nations**, left unresolved from the meeting the year before at Dumbarton Oaks, Scotland. But Yalta also set the scene for the **cold war**, which was to dominate politics for the next half century.

The participants at Yalta determined the new boundaries for postwar Poland and Germany, and issued the Declaration on Liberated Europe, which, in a restatement of the principles of the Atlantic Charter (1941), called for self-determination, internal security, and free elections among the liberated nations of Europe. Tension between the United States and the Soviet Union escalated rapidly as the Russians were determined to ensure their national security above all other considerations, and the Americans received a lesson in *realpolitik*.

The Russians went to Yalta feeling that they had burdened the lion's share of suffering in defeating Hitler, and deserved consideration of their security needs. The Americans, by contrast, were anxious to convert the noble intentions of the Declaration on Liberated Europe into a blueprint for a peaceful future, and didn't really appreciate the Russians' sense of grievance. These two outlooks very quickly turned to indignant anger and a sense of betrayal on both sides. The cold war had begun.

YAROSLAVSKY, YEMELYAN. See **IAROSLAVSKII, EMELIAN**.

YEN YÜAN (1635–1704). One of a long line of practical-minded Chinese intellectual leaders. Yen Yüan (or Yen Hsi-chai) was born in Chilhi and for many years was a conventional philosopher, with strong interest in classical Chinese ethics and a work on the ideal form of government to his name. But he became increasingly dissatisfied with what he came to see as irrelevant bookish learning with no practical outcome.

While still retaining his deep respect for the Chinese classics, Yen Yüan now emphasized the practical qualities, which he characterized as the six duties and the six arts. The six duties were filial piety, brotherliness, kindliness toward relatives by blood, kindliness to relatives by law, responsibility to one's friends, and compassion. These duties could best be expressed through the six arts: etiquette, music, archery, charioteering, writing, and **mathematics**.

In 1696 Yen had the opportunity to put his thoughts into practice when he was appointed director of the prestigious Chang-nan Academy. As well as the conventional subjects, Yen's students learned the practical arts of fencing, weightlifting, dancing, and singing. He took a dim view of **meditation** or reading unless balanced by healthy activity. It was not through abstract study that one understood things, but the combination of learning from experience and solving problems as they arise in one's actual life. His academy ran a four-part program of learning, centering around classics and history, literature, military science, and the practical arts.

Yen Yüan was an influential figure in his day, and helped reorient neo-Confucian thinking away from the more abstract emphasis it had been dominated by until then. He is relevant today as an exemplar of **eupraxsophy**.

YESHUA, RABBI (4 BCE–30 CE, approx.). Jewish reformer from the outlying province of Galilee. There are very few reliable facts about his life. Indeed, it is a credible question whether he existed at all. The evidence would suggest that he probably did, though certainly not in the form popularly envisaged by most Christian believers. See the entry on **Jesus Christ, myth theory of**. So distorted has Christian understanding become that Yeshua's name has been rendered into the Greek (*Jesus*), and his actual title of rabbi dropped, and a more controversial title of messiah, again rendered into Greek (*Christ*), has then turned into a surname. The Christian rebranding of Jesus Christ disguises and confuses the true identity and purpose of Rabbi Yeshua. See the entry on **Jesus Christ, creation of**.

The main sources of information about Rabbi Yeshua are the Gospels of the New Testament, which are problematic from a historical point of view because they were not written primarily as histories, but as pericopes, or short passages designed to be read aloud during acts of public worship. What is more, many of the incidents said to have formed Yeshua's life have clear legendary and mythological features to them. See the entry on **dying and resurrected gods**.

Once all the myth and propaganda has been set aside, the true account probably runs something like this. Rabbi Yeshua lived entirely within the Jewish culture he was raised in; all his thoughts, values, and goals were Jewish, and he had no intention of speaking to anyone outside the Jewish community. The few passages in the New Testament that can reliably be credited to Rabbi Yeshua reveal him as a magician, a prophet, and an exorcist. He saw his role as a prophet sent to warn his fellow Jews that the kingdom of God was imminent and that all those with eyes to see and ears to hear should prepare for this event. Some theologians have argued that Rabbi Yeshua was familiar with some Greek thinking, in particular with **Cynicism**. This is possible, but it would be a mistake to see this influence as running counter to Yeshua's essentially Jewish outlook.

Either way, Yeshua's preaching got him into trouble when he entered Jerusalem and challenged political and religious authorities in the city. It is possible that Yeshua entered Jerusalem with a view to hasten the imminent coming of the kingdom of God, about which he had preached. Like so many other radicals of the time, he was executed by the Romans because he was seen as a threat to stability and order in the city. The collaborating Jewish council, the Sanhedrin, in all likelihood, colluded with the Romans in engineering his death. But this is very far from the standard Christian account that "Jesus" was executed by "the Jews," who persuaded a diffident Pontius Pilate to do the deed for their own warped reasons. This misperception marks the beginning of **anti-Semitism**. The latest and most egregious version of the standard story came in Mel Gibson's film *The Passion of the Christ* (2004). See the entries on **quest for the historical Jesus** and **Jesus Christ, books about**.

Further reading: Geza Vermes, *The Changing Faces of Jesus*; and E. P. Sanders, *The Historical Figure of Jesus*.

YIN AND YANG. An ancient and occultic element of Chinese thinking, yin-yang is a **dualistic** conception of constant transformation. Yin and yang are complementary opposite elements of the **Tao**. Yin and yang has played an important part in the Chinese emphasis on establishing harmony in oneself and in the universe. The classic text of yin and yang is the *I Ching*, or *Book of Changes*. The constituent parts of humanity are the earth (yin) and heaven (yang) which come together in combination during life and return to their respective abodes in death. Yin is female, negative, dark, cold, and passive while yang is male, positive, light, hot, and active.

The yin-yang concept has been cheapened and opened to ridicule by some particularly sentimental uses of it by **New Age** pundits. While the yin-yang notion has no scientific value, at its best it is a useful reminder against according humanity too much cosmic status. See the entry on **anthropocentric conceit**. Properly understood, yin-yang is about humans finding a cosmic harmony without recourse to gods or the supernatural.

Further reading: Michael Shermer, ed., *The Skeptic Encyclopedia of Pseudoscience.*

YOGA. An ancient brand of exercise which is very valuable, so long as all the **New Age** nonsense that often accompanies the practice is ignored. The great sage of yoga was Patanjali, about whom next to nothing is known. The book Patanjali is credited with writing, the *Yoga-Sutra,* was probably written between 100 and 300 CE. The *Yoga-Sutra* is composed of four books (*padas*) with 195 sayings and aphorisms, which, being short and cryptic, have encouraged a veritable industry of commentaries. Through the commentaries, the *Yoga-Sutra* is purported to show how yoga can be a form of physical and spiritual exercise that can help the practitioner overcome the delusions of desire, egoism, and worldly ambitions.

Today, yoga is being exploited by entrepreneurs like Bikram Choudhury, who is creating a McDonald's-style New Age brand empire based around his style of yoga for the masses.

Z

ZARATHUSTRA. The first thinker to take **dualism** seriously. Very little is known for sure about Zarathustra, who is also known by his Greek name Zoroaster. Zarathustra is the Persian rendering of his name. Zoroastrian tradition talks about him living around 6000 BCE, but this seems very unlikely. However, scholars date him anywhere from around 1700 BCE to 600 BCE. His teachings are preserved in a collection of seventeen hymns,

known as *Gathas* and which form a significant part of the *Avesta*, the **scripture** of the
Zoroastrian religion.

Zarathustra's dualism involved the universe divided into black and white, with no
one omnipotent power in control. Ahura
Mazda was the supreme god on the side of
good and light, while Ahriman was in charge
of **evil** and darkness. We could choose
whether to follow good or evil; the righteous
would choose wisely, the wicked would not.
The Zoroastrian deity Mithra (or Mithras in
Roman rendering) had many features of a
dying and resurrected god.

The influence of Zoroastrian thought on
Jewish and Christian religious thinking has
been extensive and, in most cases, unhelpful.
The harsh and clear division between good
and evil that is characteristic of Zoroastrianism can be seen in **Gnosticism** and apocalyptic brands of Judaism, which found its
way into Christianity via **Paul**. Centuries
later **Friedrich Nietzsche** took Zarathustra's
name for one of his most important works,
Thus Spake Zarathustra (1883–85). Zarathustra created morality, Nietzsche wrote, so
he could preside over the self-overcoming of
morality as well.

**ZAYED CENTRE FOR COORDINA-
TION AND FOLLOW-UP**. A think tank
based in Abu Dhabi, funded largely by Abu
Dhabi's Sheikh Zayed (1918? 2004), and
linked with the Arab League. The Zayed
Centre was established in 1999 with the pur-
pose of operating as a research center for
Arab opinion on all matters relating to the
Middle East.

Early in its career the center made the
mistake of giving platform space to a ragtag
crew of political, religious, and social
extremists from the West. This opened it up
to criticism from Western intellectuals, who
accused the center of trading in **anti-Semitism**, unreasoning hatred of Israel, and **conspiracy theories**. But this criticism ignored
the wide range of high-level internationalists
and moderates, such as former US president

Jimmy Carter and former US vice president
Al Gore, who also spoke there. As a result of
the criticism the Zayed Centre closed down.
It is strongly to be desired that it reopens,
because it has an important role as an intellectual leader for moderate Arab opinion.

ZEITGEIST. German word meaning "spirit
of the times" which has recently become
fashionable to drop into conversation. *Zeitgeist* is usually used in the context of the prevailing attitudes and beliefs of a particular
society at a given time. However, it is wise to
be skeptical of the term, which is often used
simply to discredit views one disagrees with
or to accord majority status to views one does
agree with. Even more peculiar is that people
are often willing to speak approvingly of
Zeitgeist while speaking disapprovingly of
metanarratives.

ZEN BUDDHISM. An esoteric branch of
Buddhism. Zen is the Japanese name for
Ch'an Buddhism, which developed as an
independent form of Buddhism at the hands
of Huineng (638–713 CE), who rose from
very humble origins to become one of
China's most influential thinkers. He is credited with a work called *The Platform Scripture of the Sixth Patriarch*, which is generally
regarded as the classic work of Ch'an/Zen
Buddhism. Huineng, in turn, owed a debt to
the *Vajracchedika*, an early Buddhist attempt
to deconstruct absolutist metaphysics. It
would be contrary to the spirit of Zen, however, to describe this work as a **scripture**, or
even as a work to be imitated or emulated.

As with most **Asian traditions**, it is misleading to describe Zen Buddhism as a **religion**. Zen acknowledges no **god**, no rites, no
afterlife, no scripture, and no **soul**. But neither is Zen a philosophy in the formal sense
of the term, because it is no less averse to
logic and **reason**. Its preference is for inner
spiritual experience. The **Tao** is not to be
sought in **philosophy**, worship, or speculation. The Tao is one's everyday life.

Zen Buddhism is about clearing the mind

of the temptation to think in religious or philosophical terms. It wants people to look at the essence of things with a mind unclouded by these concepts. It looks to achieving this by **meditation** on its many *koans*, which are paradoxical aphorisms designed to subvert conventional religious or philosophical chains of thinking. It was these *koans* that attracted popular attention in the West in the 1960s and which were parodied as "What is the sound of one hand clapping?" Zen Buddhism, particularly as popularized in the West, is open to parody, but it remains an authentic path to peace without recourse to the usual range of **transcendental temptations**.

Further reading: D. T. Suzuki, *An Introduction to Zen Buddhism*.

ZINDIQ. A term which has come to be used by Muslims as a catchall word loosely understood as "heretic." The word may have derived from the Zoroastrian scripture *Zend Avesta*, which was of course a heretical work in Muslim eyes. See the entry on **Zarathustra**. It can also refer to those who hold an interpretation of Islam that is not mainstream, or it can mean a philosophical materialist. It can also refer to a female pagan religion. See the entry on **heresy**.

ZOLA, ÉMILE (1840–1902). Brilliant French novelist and crusading journalist. Émile Edouard Charles Antoine Zola was the son of an Italian engineer working in France at the time. Despite the death of his father when he was only seven, Zola received a good education. From early on, Zola had wanted to earn his living as a writer. He first worked in a publishing firm before his own works began to gain a following.

Zola established his reputation with his brilliant naturalistic novel, *Therese Raquin* (1867), which is available in paperback. He is best remembered for his monumental twenty-volume cycle of novels, known as Les Rougon-Macquart series, which followed the fortunes the Rougon-Macquart family during the reign of Napoleon III (1852–1870). Zola

later attracted the fierce hostility of the Roman Catholic Church thanks to his three novels, *Lourdes, Rome*, and *Paris* (1894–98), which subjected Catholic superstition and **corruption** to scathing satire and criticism.

Just as this series was ending, Zola intervened in the Dreyfus Affair, which had been tearing France apart since 1894. His intervention was something of a turning point in the affair. Alfred Dreyfus (1859–1935) was a Jewish officer who had been sent to Devil's Island on trumped-up charges of treason. It was Zola's opinion that the treatment of Dreyfus was the worst miscarriage of justice since the Calas case, which **Voltaire** spent so much time fighting a century earlier. He wrote a scathing indictment of the religious prejudice and **anti-Semitism** underlying the affair and accused several of the leading people in the scandal, knowing full well he was inviting prosecution himself. The articles were originally in *Le Figaro* but were withdrawn by a timid editor. Zola then sent them to a smaller paper *L'Aurore*, edited by Georges Clemenceau (1841–1929), a veteran politician and secularist. It was Clemenceau who suggested the article's title: *J'Accuse*. The article appeared on January 13, 1898, and circulation of *L'Aurore* increased tenfold.

Zola was then put on trial himself, accused of libeling government ministers. The trial attracted worldwide press coverage and the case against Dreyfus was shown to be without foundation. Zola lost the case but won the argument. After a second trial, brought by a technicality arising from the first one, Zola fled to England to escape imprisonment. His intervention also set a precedent for the active participation of intellectuals in politics. Even the word "intellectuals" developed at this time.

Zola's death was engineered by people who were outraged by his participation in the Dreyfus Affair. Masons working on the building next door to his blocked his fireplace, and Zola died of carbon monoxide poisoning on September 29, 1902. After his death the obstruction was removed.

A Calendar of Atheism, Skepticism, and Humanism

JANUARY

January 1, 1801: First asteroid, named Ceres, is discovered.

January 1, 1802: Thomas Jefferson first uses the phrase "wall of separation between church and state."

January 1, 1863: Abraham Lincoln issues Emancipation Proclamation.

January 1, 1946: Emperor Hirohito of Japan disclaims his divine status in his New Year's message.

January 1, 2000: Sweden formally disestablishes the Lutheran Church.

January 2, 1492: Granada falls to Spanish Christian troops, ending seven hundred years of Muslim rule in Spain.

January 2, 1920: Birth of Isaac Asimov.

January 3, 1889: Friedrich Nietzsche collapses into insanity after seeing a cab driver beating a horse in Turin.

January 3, 1915: Church of England organizes mass prayer to ask God to end the war.

January 4, 1960: Death of Albert Camus.

January 4, 1961: Death of Erwin Schrödinger, German theoretical physicist.

January 5, 1933: Death of J. M. Robertson.

January 5, 1948: Warner Brothers shows the first color newsreel.

January 6, 1884: Death of Gregor Mendel, discoverer of genetics.

January 6, 1941: Franklin Delano Roosevelt delivers his famous "Four Freedoms" speech.

January 7, 1697: Thomas Aitkenhead becomes the last person to be executed for blasphemy in Britain.

January 7, 1972: Date of the end of the world as predicted by Herbert W. Armstrong, founder of the *Plain Truth* magazine.

January 7, 1979: Fall of the Khmer Rouge regime in Cambodia.

January 8, 1642: Death of Galileo Galilei.

January 8, 1877: Charles Watts arrested for printing *The Fruits of Philosophy*.

January 9, 1929: Alexander Fleming discovers penicillin.

January 9, 1951: The United Nations headquarters in New York is opened.

January 10, 1776: Thomas Paine's *Common Sense* is published.

January 10, 1946: First meeting of UN General Assembly.

January 10, 1955: Death of Joseph McCabe.

January 11, 1850: Birth of G. W. Foote, editor of the *Freethinker* from 1881 to 1915.

January 11, 1928: Death of Thomas Hardy.

January 11, 1970: Gora opens the first World Atheists Meet, in Vijayawada, India.

January 12, 1863: Birth of Vivekananda, Indian religious humanist reformer.

January 12, 1896: Dr. Henry Louis Smith takes the first x-ray photograph.

January 13, 1886: Charles Bradlaugh finally takes his seat in parliament after five by-elections.

January 13, 1898: Émile Zola's article "J'Accuse" is published, electrifying the Dreyfus case.

January 14, 1321: Death of Dante Alighieri.

January 14, 1898: Death of Lewis Carroll, author *of Alice's Adventures in Wonderland.*

January 15, 1535: Henry VIII declares himself head of the Church of England.

January 15, 1925: Bishop Montgomery Brown found guilty of heresy by an Episcopalian church court in the United States.

January 16, 1932: Birth of zoologist Diane Fossey.

January 16, 1980: Scientists in Boston invent interferon, a natural virus-fighting substance through genetic engineering.

January 17, 1706: Birth of Benjamin Franklin.

January 17, 1946: UN Security Council meets for the first time.

January 18, 1689: Birth of French philosopher Montesquieu.

January 18, 1908: Birth of Jacob Bronowski.

January 19, 570 CE: Traditional date for the birth of Muhammad.

January 19, 1724: Birth of Confucian philosopher Dai Zhen.

January 19, 1943: Birth of Janis Joplin.

January 20, 1790: Death of John Howard, after whom the Howard League for Prison Reform is named.

January 20, 1920: Roger Nash Baldwin creates the American Civil Liberties Union.

January 20, 1942: Top Nazi officials meet at Wannsee to outline plans for the Final Solution.

January 21, 1738: Birth of Ethan Allen, pioneer American freethinker and freedom fighter.

January 21, 1793: Louis XVI executed by the revolutionary French government.

January 22, 1906: Death of George Jacob Holyoake.

January 22, 1973: *Roe v. Wade* decision legalizes abortion in the United States.

January 23, 1911: The all-male French Academy of Sciences rejects Nobel Prize winner Marie Curie's application for membership.

January 23, 1918: Soviet government enacts separation of education from the churches.

January 23, 1944: Death of Norwegian artist Edvard Munch.

January 24, 1839: Charles Darwin elected to the Royal Society.

January 24, 1891: John Ballance, a freethinker, is sworn in as premier of New Zealand.

January 24, 1965: Death of Winston Churchill.

January 25, 1874: Birth of Somerset Maugham, English author and atheist.

January 25, 1955: Columbia University develops an atomic clock, which will be accurate to one second every three hundred years.

January 26, 1945: Russian troops liberate Auschwitz.

January 27, 1832: Birth of Lewis Carroll, author *of Alice's Adventures in Wonderland.*

January 27, 1967: The Treaty of Principles Governing the Activities of States in the Exploration and Use of Outer Space, which forbade territorial claims and weapons making or dumping in space, is signed by sixty-two nations.

January 28, 1935: Iceland becomes the first country to legalize abortion.

January 29, 1737: Birth of Thomas Paine.

January 29, 1989: The University of

Humanist Studies is founded in Utrecht.

January 30, 1649: Charles I is beheaded in London.

January 30, 1891: Death of Charles Bradlaugh.

January 30, 1933: Adolf Hitler becomes chancellor of Germany.

January 30, 1948: Mahatma Gandhi assassinated by Hindu fanatic.

January 30, 1969: The Beatles perform live for the last time.

January 31, 1944: In *Prince v. Massachusetts*, the US Supreme Court upholds decision to impose limits on using children for distributing religious literature.

FEBRUARY

February 1, 1851: Death of Mary Wollstonecraft Shelley.

February 1, 1865: Thirteenth amendment prohibits slavery in the United States.

February 1, 1924: Pope Pius XI forbids priests from belonging to political parties, which spelled the demise of large Catholic parties that might have acted as opponents to the rising threat of Fascism.

February 1, 1979: Ayatollah Khomeini returns to rapturous reception in Iran.

February 2, 1943: German VI Army surrenders in Stalingrad.

February 2, 1970: Death of Bertrand Russell.

February 3, 1919: League of Nations first meets.

February 3, 1983: President Reagan declares 1983 the "Year of the Bible."

February 4, 1794: French National Convention abolishes slavery.

February 4, 1954: Death of Chapman Cohen.

February 4, 1921: Birth of Betty Friedan.

February 5, 1971: Third manned landing on the moon takes place.

February 6, 1918: Women over thirty granted the vote in the United Kingdom.

February 6, 1843: Charles Southwell released

from prison, serving for blasphemy.

February 6, 1913: Birth of Mary Leakey, paleoanthropologist.

February 7, 1828: Robert Taylor imprisoned for "blasphemy."

February 7, 1945: Victorious Allied leaders meet at Yalta to outline plans for postwar Europe.

February 7, 1947: Dead Sea Scrolls discovered at Qumran.

February 8, 1564: Birth of Christopher Marlowe, English dramatist.

February 8, 1999: Death of Iris Murdoch.

February 9, 1619: Guilio Vanini burned at the stake for atheism.

February 10, 1931: Birth of Austrian novelist Thomas Bernhard.

February 10, 1993: Death of Fred Hollows, atheist, physician, and philanthropist.

February 11, 1482: Tomas Torquemada appointed chief inquisitor of all Spain.

February 11, 1929: Mussolini receives the Papal Order of the Golden Spur on the occasion of the Lateran Treaty between Italy and the papacy.

February 11, 1990: Nelson Mandela released after twenty-seven years in South African jails.

February 12, 1789: Death of Ethan Allen, pioneer American freethinker and freedom fighter.

February 12, 1804: Death of Immanuel Kant.

February 12, 1809: Birth of Abraham Lincoln.

February 12, 1809: Birth of Charles Darwin.

February 13, 1633: Galileo detained by the Inquisition in Rome.

February 13, 1945: Allied forces begin a twenty-four-hour bombing of Dresden.

February 14, 1975: Death of Julian Huxley.

February 14, 1989: Ayatollah Khomeini issues a fatwa against Salman Rushdie.

February 15, 1820: Birth of American suffrage pioneer and agnostic, Susan B. Anthony.

February 15, 1564: Birth of Galileo Galilei.

February 16, 1906: Death of Charles Watts.

February 16, 1890: Charles Bradlaugh

resigns as president of the NSS for health reasons.

February 17, 1958: CND formed in London; Bertrand Russell becomes its president.

February 18, 1546: Death of Martin Luther.

February 18, 1984: Italy and the Vatican agree to end Roman Catholicism's status as official religion of Italy.

February 19, 1473: Birth of Nicholas Copernicus.

February 19, 1600: Giordano Bruno burned at the stake.

February 19, 1861: Czar Alexander II abolishes serfdom in Russia.

February 19, 1896: Joseph McCabe leaves the priesthood.

February 20, 1835: Charles Darwin experiences an earthquake in Chile, which confirms some important claims made by geologist Charles Lyell.

February 20, 1901: Birth (and death in 1982) of French microbiologist Réne Dubos.

February 21, 1677: Death of Baruch Spinoza.

February 21, 1953: James Watson and Francis Crick discover the structure of DNA.

February 22, 1788: Birth of Arthur Schopenhauer, German philosopher.

February 22, 2002: Death of Raymond Firth, New Zealand–born anthropologist.

February 23, 1886: Charles Hall isolated aluminium from its ore.

February 23, 1997: Scottish scientists announce the cloning of Dolly the sheep.

February 24, 1848: *The Communist Manifesto* is published.

February 24, 1871: *Descent of Man* is published.

February 24, 1943: Birth of George Harrison, one of the Beatles.

February 25, 1616: Galileo forced by the Roman Catholic church to renounce his belief that the earth orbits the sun.

February 25, 1988: Jimmy Swaggart, prominent American televangelist, banned from preaching after being discovered consorting with a prostitute.

February 26, 1869: Fifteenth amendment prohibits the denial of African Americans the right to vote.

February 26, 1899: Charles C. Moore goes to prison for blasphemy for distributing a freethought newspaper in Kentucky.

February 27, 380 CE: Emperor Theodosius I declares Christianity the state religion of the Roman Empire.

February 27, 1836: Birth of Charles Watts.

February 27, 1902: Birth of American author John Steinbeck.

February 27, 1975: Jim Woolnough arrested on the charge of illegally procuring miscarriages, which becomes a test case, leading to the legalization of abortion in New Zealand.

February 27, 2003: United States House of Representatives votes to ban embryonic stem-cell research.

February 28, 1901: Birth of theoretical chemist Linus Pauling.

February 28, 1953: James Watson and Francis Crick announce their discovery of the structure of DNA.

February 29, 1692: Sarah Osborne, Sarah Good, and a slave called Tituba are arrested on charges of witchcraft, beginning the Salem Witch Trials.

MARCH

March 1, 1896: Antoine Henri Becquerel discovers radioactivity.

March 1, 1922: Birth of peace-oriented Israeli prime minister Yitzhak Rabin.

March 2, 661 CE: The murder of 'Ali, cousin of Muhammad, now the holiest day in the Shi'ite calendar.

March 2, 1939: Eugenio Pacelli, "Hitler's Pope," elected as Pius XII.

March 3, 1875: Bizet's opera *Carmen* opens in Paris.

March 3, 1879: Death of W. K. Clifford.

March 4, 1966: John Lennon announces that the Beatles are more popular than Jesus.

March 4, 1989: Pope John Paul denounces Salman Rushdie's *The Satanic Verses* as "blasphemous."

March 5, 1616: Galileo receives an "absolute injunction" from the papacy and his works are placed on the Index of Forbidden Books.

March 5, 1946: Winston Churchill gives his "iron curtain" speech in Fulton, Missouri.

March 6, 1927: Bertrand Russell delivers his address "Why I am Not a Christian" to the South London Branch of the National Secular Society.

March 6, 1937: Birth of Valentina Tereshkova, the first woman in space.

March 7, 1965: "Bloody Sunday" civil-rights march in Selma, Alabama is broken up by the police.

March 7, 1996: First photos of the surface of Pluto are taken.

March 8, 1857: March against exploitation of women in America, which later is used as the commemoration of Women's Day.

March 8, 1918: Birth of Dr. Indumati Parikh, Indian crusader for women's health.

March 8, 1983: Ronald Reagan gives his "evil empire" speech to the National Association of Evangelicals.

March 9, 1822: American inventor Charles Graham gets patent for false teeth.

March 9, 1934: Birth of Yuri Gagarin, the first man in space.

March 10: Commonwealth Day.

March 10, 1876: Alexander Graham Bell makes the first telephone call.

March 11, 1818: Mary Shelley's *Frankenstein* is published.

March 11, 1920: Joseph McCabe debates Sir Arthur Conan Doyle on the truth of spiritualism at Queen's Hall, London.

March 11, 1985: Mikhail Gorbachev becomes the leader of the Soviet Union.

March 12, 1938: The Anschluss, the German occupation of Austria, begins.

March 12, 2001: Taliban soldiers destroy ancient Buddhist sculptures at Bamian, Afghanistan.

March 13, 1733: Joseph Priestley, discoverer of oxygen, is born.

March 13, 1791: *Rights of Man* (part 1) by Thomas Paine is published.

March 13, 1906: Death of American suffrage pioneer and agnostic, Susan B. Anthony.

March 13, 1930: Pluto discovered by Clyde Tombaugh at Lowell Observatory.

March 14, 1492: Ferdinand and Isabella of Spain decree the expulsion of all Jews in the kingdom.

March 14, 1879: Birth of Albert Einstein.

March 15, 44 BCE: The Ides of March, the assassination of Julius Caesar.

March 16, 1190: Jews in York commit mass suicide rather than take forced baptism.

March 16, 1751: Birth of James Madison.

March 16, 1819: Dr. John Bostock gives the first clinical description of allergies.

March 17, 180 CE: Death of Marcus Aurelius, and the decline of Rome begins.

March 17, 1861: The kingdom of Italy is formally announced.

March 18, 1965: Aleksey Leonov becomes the first person to leave a space capsule and walk in space.

March 18, 1898: Death of American suffrage pioneer and freethinker Matilda Joslyn Gage.

March 19, 1987: Televangelist Jim Bakker resigns as head of PTL ministries after it is disclosed he had an affair with Jessica Hahn.

March 20, 1838: Birth of Norwegian playwright Henrik Ibsen.

March 20, 1934: Dr. Rudolph Kuenhold gives first practical demonstration of radar.

March 21, 1834: Date given for the end of the world by William Miller, founder of Seventh Day Adventists.

March 21, 1844: Another date given for the end of the world by William Miller, founder of Seventh Day Adventists.

March 22, 1832: Death of Goethe.

March 22, 1963: The Beatles' first album, *Please Please Me*, is released.

March 23, 1832: House of Commons passes

the Third Reform Bill, which broadens male suffrage and made the election process more democratic.

March 24, 1826: Birth of American suffrage pioneer and freethinker Matilda Joslyn Gage.

March 24, 1882: Robert Koch tells the Berlin Physiological Society he has found the bacillus responsible for tuberculosis.

March 25, 1901: Birth of Raymond Firth, famous New Zealand anthropologist.

March 25, 1954: Papal encyclical *Sacra Virginitas* endorses clerical celibacy.

March 25, 1957: Treaty of Rome establishes the European Economic Community, now the European Union.

March 26, 1827: Death of Ludwig van Beethoven.

March 26, 1953: Jonas Salk announces a new vaccine to immunize against polio.

March 26, 1999: Jack Kevorkian is found guilty of second-degree murder for helping the terminally ill Thomas Youk (with the support of his family) end his life.

March 27, 1968: Yuri Gagarin, first man in space, dies in a plane accident.

March 27, 1997: Heaven's Gate members commit mass suicide as comet Hale-Bopp passes Earth.

March 28, 1902: Birth of American humanist Corliss Lamont.

March 28, 1939: Last Republican forces in Spain surrender, giving victory to Franco's Fascists.

March 28, 1979: Accident at the Three Mile Island nuclear facility in America.

March 29, 1824: Birth of Ludwig Büchner.

March 29, 1974: *Mariner 10* takes the first close-up photographs of Mercury.

March 30, 239 BCE: Chinese astronomers first record the orbit of Halley's comet.

March 30, 1853: Birth of Vincent van Gogh.

March 31, 1727: Death of Isaac Newton.

March 31, 1903: New Zealander Richard Pearse becomes the first person to make a powered flight.

March 31, 1903: Birth of H. J. Blackham.

APRIL

April 1, 1908: Birth of Abraham Maslow, founder of humanist psychology.

April 1, 1960: *Tiros I*, the first weather satellite, goes into orbit.

April 2, 1838: Birth of French reformer Leon Gambetta.

April 2, 1840: Birth of French novelist and crusading journalist Emile Zola.

April 3, 1507: Martin Luther ordained as a Catholic priest.

April 3, 1973: First portable phone call made.

April 4, 1968: Assassination of Martin Luther King Jr.

April 5, 1588: Birth of English philosopher Thomas Hobbes.

April 5, 1753: British Museum founded by an act of Parliament.

April 6, 1697: First use of the word "freethinker," in a letter to John Locke.

April 6, 1896: Revival of Olympic Games at Athens.

April 6, 1903: Birth of Erwin Schrödinger, German theoretical physicist.

April 6, 1992: Death of Isaac Asimov.

April 7, 1948: World Health Organization founded.

April 7, 1994: Civil war, leading to genocide, starts in Rwanda.

April 8, 563 BCE: Traditional date for the birth of the Buddha.

April 8, 1938: Birth of Kofi Annan, United Nations secretary-general.

April 9, 1865: General Robert E. Lee surrenders at Appomattox court house, effectively ending the American Civil War.

April 9, 1929: Birth of Fred Hollows.

April 10, 1861: Ernestine L. Rose publicly advocates atheism in Boston.

April 10, 1972: Seventy nations sign treaty banning biological warfare.

April 11, 1876: W. K. Clifford delivers his famous lecture "The Ethics of Belief."

April 11, 1955: Albert Einstein signs the Russell-Einstein Declaration condemning nuclear weapons.

April 11, 1968: Civil Rights Act extends rights to African Americans in the United States.

April 12, 599 BCE: Traditional date for the birth of Mahavira, the founder of Jainism.

April 12, 65 CE: Death of the Stoic thinker Seneca.

April 12, 1633: The Inquisition begins its formal interrogation of Galileo.

April 12, 1961: Yuri Gagarin becomes the first man to go into space.

April 13, 1743: Birth of Thomas Jefferson.

April 13, 1817: Birth of George Jacob Holyoake, who introduced the term "secularism."

April 13, 1919: Birth of Madalyn Evalyn Mays (Madalyn Murray O'Hair).

April 13, 1999: Judge Jessica Cooper imprisons Jack Kevorkian for 10 to 25 years for helping a terminally ill man to die, with the full support of his family.

April 14, 1891: Birth of Dr. Ambedkar, tireless campaigner for the rights of untouchables in India.

April 14, 1986: Death of Simone de Beauvoir.

April 15, 1865: Abraham Lincoln dies of wounds from an assassination attempt.

April 15, 1912: *Titanic* sinks, having been struck by an iceberg.

April 15, 1921: Albert Einstein introduces time as the fourth dimension.

April 15, 1938: First *Superman* comic makes its appearance.

April 15, 1980: Death of Jean-Paul Sartre.

April 16, 1844: Birth of French novelist Anatole France.

April 16, 1921: Birth of the author, actor, and agnostic Sir Peter Ustinov.

April 16, 1958: Death of Rosalind Franklin, pioneer molecular biologist.

April 17, 1790: Death of Benjamin Franklin.

April 18, 1775: Paul Revere's ride begins the American revolution.

April 18, 1946: International Court of Justice inaugurated in the Hague.

April 18, 1955: Death of Albert Einstein.

April 19, 1995: US federal building in Oklahoma City is bombed by American right-wing extremists, killing 168 people.

April 20, 1889: Birth of Adolf Hitler.

April 20, 1902: Pierre and Marie Curie isolate the radioactive element in radium.

April 20, 1986: Madalyn Murray O'Hair steps down as president of the American Atheists in favor of her son Jon Garth Murray.

April 21, 753 BCE: Traditional date for the foundation of Rome.

April 21, 1869: T. H. Huxley coins the word "agnostic."

April 21, 1910: Death of Samuel Clemens, "Mark Twain."

April 22, 1970: The first Earth Day is celebrated.

April 22, 1724: Birth of Immanuel Kant.

April 22, 1915: Poison gas used in warfare for the first time.

April 23, 1564: Likely birth date (and death in 1616) of William Shakespeare.

April 23, 1858: Birth of Max Planck.

April 23, 1984: Existence of AIDS virus announced to the world.

April 24, 1184 BCE: Traditional date when Greeks are said to have entered Troy with the wooden horse.

April 24, 1981: IBM unveils its first personal computer.

April 25, 1933: German Catholic Church supplies Nazis with information on the racial stock of all German Catholics.

April 25, 1953: DNA discovery announced.

April 25, 1990: Hubble Telescope sent into orbit.

April 26, 121 CE: Birth of Marcus Aurelius, Stoic emperor of Rome.

April 26, 1995: Death of American humanist Corliss Lamont.

April 26, 1937: German planes bomb the Spanish town of Guernica.

April 26, 1986: Chernobyl disaster.

April 27, 1994: South Africa holds its first elections open to all citizens.

April 27, 1759: Birth of Mary Wollstonecraft, pioneer feminist.

April 28, 1937: Birth of Saddam Hussein.

April 28, 1945: Benito Mussolini shot by partisans and hung upside down in Milan.

April 29, 1925: Dr. Florence Sabin becomes the first woman to be elected to the US National Academy of Sciences.

April 29, 1980: Death of Alfred Hitchcock.

April 30, 1803: The Louisiana Purchase is the largest block of territory ever to be sold from one nation to another.

April 30, 1899: Death of Ludwig Büchner.

April 30, 1905: Albert Einstein submits his PhD dissertation, *On a New Determination of Molecular Dimensions*, to the University of Zurich.

April 30, 1945: Adolf Hitler commits suicide in his Berlin bunker.

April 30, 1975: Final surrender of South Vietnam, ending the Vietnam war.

April 30, 1976: Conference opens in Buffalo, New York, at which the Committee for the Scientific Investigation of Claims of the Paranormal (CSICOP) is founded.

MAY

May 1, 1918: Bertrand Russell's appeal against imprisonment for pacifism rejected.

May 1, 1933: The first *Humanist Manifesto* is issued.

May 1, 1976: The Committee for the Scientific Investigation of Claims of the Paranormal (CSICOP) is created.

May 2, 1519: Death of Leonardo da Vinci.

May 2, 1880: Reception in New York for D. M. Bennett, editor of the *Truthseeker*, following his release from prison under the Comstock laws.

May 2, 1994: Nelson Mandela wins South Africa's first multiracial election.

May 3: Designated by the United Nations as world press freedom day.

May 3, 1675: Massachusetts decrees church doors to be locked during services, to prevent people leaving during long sermons.

May 4, 1825: Birth of T. H. Huxley.

May 4, 1845: Birth of W. K. Clifford.

May 4, 1970: Four American students killed by the national guard during student unrest at Kent State University.

May 5, 2349 BCE: Date, according to Archbishop Ussher, that Noah's Ark landed on Mt. Ararat.

May 5, 1818: Birth of Karl Marx.

May 5, 1925: John Scopes arrested for teaching evolution in Dayton, Tennessee.

May 6, 1527: German and Spanish mercenaries sack Rome, effectively ending Rome's preeminence in the Renaissance.

May 6, 1856: Birth of Sigmund Freud.

May 7, 1711: Birth of David Hume.

May 7, 1748: Birth of Olympe de Gouge, author of the *Declaration of the Rights of Woman*.

May 8, 1737: Birth of Edward Gibbon, author of *The Decline and Fall of the Roman Empire*.

May 8, 1945: VE day, or Victory in Europe declared.

May 9, 1983: Vatican rescinds its condemnation of Galileo.

May 9, 1985: Designated by the enlarged European Union as Europe Day.

May 10, 1267: Church officials order Vienna's Jews to wear distinctive clothing.

May 10, 1941: German bombing destroys large stocks of RPA books.

May 11, 330 CE: Constantine inaugurates Constantinople as the capital of his empire.

May 11, 1998: India conducts its first nuclear tests.

May 11, 2001: Death of Douglas Adams.

May 12, 1521: Henry VIII publicly burns the heretical works of Martin Luther.

May 12, 1907: Birth of Katherine Hepburn.

May 12, 1949: The Soviets abandon the blockade of Berlin.

May 13, 609 CE: Pope Boniface IV converts the Pantheon at Rome into a Catholic church.

May 13, 1940: Winston Churchill rallies Britain with his "blood, toil, tears, and sweat" speech.

May 14, 1771: Birth of Robert Owen.

May 14, 1948: The state of Israel is proclaimed.

May 15, 1876: First meeting of the ethical-culture movement.

May 15, 1946: Death of Charles Albert Watts, founder of the RPA.

May 15, 1980: Pope John Paul II confirms his support of the papal infallibility doctrine.

May 16, 1943: German troops destroy the Warsaw synagogue.

May, 17, 1954: In *Brown v. Board of Education*, the US Supreme Court rules that segregated schools are unconstitutional.

May 17, 1963: British Humanist Association founded.

May 17, 1967: Tennessee repeals the legislation under which John Scopes had been prosecuted for teaching evolution in 1925.

May 18, 1048: Birth of Omar Khayyam.

May 18, 1804: Napoleon becomes emperor of France.

May 18, 1872: Birth of Bertrand Russell.

May 18, 1941: Pope Pius XII receives Ante Pavelich, the Nazi puppet of Croatia, and publicly defends Pavelich's record.

May 19 1487: The theology faculty at Cologne University endorses the *Malleus Maleforicum*, which unleashed the witch craze.

May 20, 1806: Birth of John Stuart Mill.

May 20, 1947: Bertrand Russell reads "The Faith of a Rationalist" as part of a BBC radio series titled *What I Believe*.

May 21, 1921: Birth of Soviet scientist and dissident Andrei Sakharov.

May 21, 1924: American Presbyterian Church declares evolution "untenable."

May 22, 427 BCE: Traditional date for the birth of Plato.

May 22, 1592: Giordano Bruno arrested for heresy.

May 23, 1928: Suffrage in the United Kingdom extended to women twenty-one and over.

May 24, 1543: Death of Nicholas Copernicus.

May 24, 1689: Act of Toleration passed by English parliament.

May 24, 1842: George Jacob Holyoake gives a talk in Cheltenham which results in him being imprisoned for blasphemy.

May 25, 1521: Martin Luther declared a heretic at the Diet of Worms.

May 25, 1925: John Scopes indicted by a Tennessee court for teaching evolution.

May 26, 1592: The formal Inquisition of Giordano Bruno begins.

May 26, 1864: Ban on gay books in Germany lifted, seen by gay activists as the symbolic date for the start of the gay-rights movement.

May 26, 1899: Rationalist Press Association formally registered as a company.

May 27, 1858: Birth of Charles Albert Watts, founder of the Rationalist Press Association.

May 27, 1964: Death of Jawaharlal Nehru.

May 28, 585 BCE: Eclipse predicted by Thales, the first known philosopher, on scientific principles, rather than astrological premonition. This date has been described as the day science was born.

May 28, 1588: Spanish Armada sets out to conquer England for the true faith.

May 29, 1453: Constantinople falls to the Ottoman Turks.

May 29, 1953: Edmund Hillary and Tenzing Norgay climb Mt. Everest.

May 30, 1431: Joan of Arc burned at the stake at the authority of the bishop of Beauvais and the English.

May 30, 1778: Death of Voltaire.

May 31, 1819: Birth of American poet Walt Whitman.

May 31, 1962: Adolf Eichmann executed for war crimes in Israel.

JUNE

June 1, 1593: Christopher Marlowe dies (or stages his death) in a pub brawl.

June 1, 1946: Fawn Brodie excommunicated from the Mormon Church for writing the truth about Joseph Smith, the cult's founder.

June 2, 1840: Birth of Thomas Hardy.

June 2, 1899: Robert Ingersoll gives his last public address, "What is Religion," to the Free Religious Association in Boston.

June 2, 1923: Birth of Barbara Smoker.

June 2, 1924: American Indians become citizens of the United States.

June 3, 1098: Crusaders sack Antioch and put thousands to the sword.

June 3, 1657: Death of William Harvey, the discoverer of the circulation of blood.

June 4, 1913: Emily Wilding Davison runs under the king's horse as a protest for votes for women, dying four days later from her injuries.

June 4, 1968: UN general assembly approves the Nuclear Non-Proliferation Treaty.

June 5, 1883: Birth of John Maynard Keynes.

June 5, 1947: The Marshall Plan for the reconstruction of Europe is unveiled.

June 5, 1996: The Council for Democratic and Secular Humanism (CODESH) changes its name to the Council for Secular Humanism.

June 6, 1683: Elias Ashmole opens the Ashmolean Museum of Art and Archaeology in Oxford, the first public museum in the world.

June 6, 1832: Death of Jeremy Bentham.

June 6, 1944: D-Day, when British, American, and Canadian troops land in Normandy.

June 7, 1832: British parliament passes the first Reform Bill, which expands the franchise and reforms the electoral system.

June 7, 1954: Alan Turing, pioneer of the computer, commits suicide.

June 8, 632 CE: Traditional date given for the death of Muhammad.

June 8, 1809: Death of Thomas Paine.

June 8, 1970: Death of Abraham Maslow, founder of humanistic psychology.

June 8, 2000: Texas Governor George W. Bush declares this day the "Day of Jesus."

June 9, 1889: Statue of Giordano Bruno unveiled in Rome.

June 9, 1978: Following federal pressure, Spencer Kimball, the Mormon president, has a "divine revelation" that blacks aren't, in fact, inferior, as previous Mormon doctrine taught.

June 9, 1993: In *Peloza v. Capistrano*, a US court ruled that a teacher does not have a right to teach creationism in a biology class and that evolutionism is not a religion.

June 9, 1995: Center for Inquiry in Amherst, New York, is opened.

June 10, 1692: Bridget Bishop becomes the first of the people executed during the Salem witch trials.

June 10, 1929: Birth of E. O. Wilson, father of evolutionary psychology.

June 11, 1889: Birth of Joseph Lewis, American freethought campaigner.

June 11, 1910: Birth of Jacques Cousteau, French environmentalist.

June 11, 1963: Vietnamese Buddhist monk Quang Duc sets fire to himself to protest American involvement in Vietnam.

June 12, 1929: Birth of Anne Frank.

June 12, 1964: Nelson Mandela sentenced to life imprisonment.

June 13, 323 BCE: Death of Alexander the Great.

June 13, 1949: Birth of Ann Druyan.

June 14, 1648: Margaret Jones becomes the first person to be hanged for witchcraft in Massachusetts.

June 14, 1928: Death of Emmeline Pankhurst.

June 14, 1954: "Under God" added to US Pledge of Allegiance.

June 14, 1966: The Vatican announces it has

abolished the Index of Forbidden Books.

June 15, 1215: King John of England signs the Magna Carta at Runnymede, apportioning rights and responsibilities more equitably.

June 15, 1752: Benjamin Franklin and his son confirm that lightning is electrical with their experiment with a kite and key.

June 16, 1871: Gladstone repeals the Test Acts, which forbade non-Anglicans to enter the elite universities.

June 16, 1902: Birth of prominent evolutionist George Gaylord Simpson.

June 16, 1904: Bloomsday, the day James Joyce's *Ulysses* is set.

June 16, 1918: American socialist Eugene Debs makes antiwar speech which leads to his imprisonment for ten years and revocation of his citizenship.

June 16, 1963: Valentina Tereshkova becomes the first woman to go into space.

June 16, 2000: Pope John Paul II ratifies encyclical *Dominus Iesus*, which confirms the superiority of Catholicism to all other forms of belief.

June 17, 1834: Henry Hetherington's paper *The Poor Man's Guardian* declared legal, despite not including stamp tax in its price, thus ending the British "taxes on knowledge."

June 17, 1963: US Supreme Court rules compulsory Bible reading in schools as unconstitutional.

June 17, 1972: Offices of the Democratic Party broken into in the Watergate building, Washington, DC.

June 17, 2004: Death of Indian pioneer activist and humanist Dr. Indumati Parikh.

June 18, 1815: Napoleon finally defeated at the battle of Waterloo.

June 18, 1981: First genetically engineered vaccine (to prevent hoof and mouth disease) was announced.

June 19, 1945: Birth of Aung San Suu Kyi, leader of the Burmese struggle for democracy.

June 19, 1947: Birth of Salman Rushdie.

June 20, 1789: French deputies sign the Tennis Court Oath.

June 20, 2002: China announces it will build desalination plants using used fuel from nuclear reactors.

June 21: World Humanist Day (northern summer solstice).

June 21, 1905: Birth of Jean-Paul Sartre.

June 21, 1964: Atheist civil-rights workers Michael Schwerner and Andrew Goodman are murdered with James Chaney by the Ku Klux Klan in Mississippi.

June 21, 1994: Bradlaugh House inaugurated in London.

June 22, 1633: Galileo forced to recant his views on the heliocentric universe by the Inquisition.

June 22, 1887: Birth of Julian Huxley.

June 23, 1902: Albert Einstein starts work at the Swiss Patents Office in Berne.

June 23, 1912: Birth of Alan Turing, pioneer of the computer.

June 24, 1842: Birth of satirist Ambrose Bierce.

June 24, 1915: Birth of Fred Hoyle.

June 25, 1894: Statue of Charles Bradlaugh unveiled in Northampton, with thousands in attendance.

June 25, 1908: Birth of W. V. O. Quine.

June 25, 1973: In front of a Senate committee, John Dean implicates Richard Nixon in the Watergate scandal.

June 25, 1997: Death of Jacques Cousteau.

June 26, 1945: United Nations Charter signed.

June 26, 2002: Ninth Circuit Appeals Court votes that the Pledge of Allegiance, which had the words "under God" inserted in 1954, is unconstitutional because it transgresses the separation of church and state.

June 27, 1844: Joseph Smith, founder of Mormonism, is killed by a mob in Illinois.

June 27, 1954: The world's first nuclear power station starts producing electricity in Obninsk, USSR.

June 28, 1836: Death of James Madison.

June 28, 1914: Assassination of Archduke Franz Ferdinand.

June 29, 1895: Death of T. H. Huxley.

June 29, 2003: Death of Katharine Hepburn.

June 30, 1860: T. H. Huxley confronted "Soapy Sam" Wilberforce at the British Association debate on evolution.

June 30, 1908: Meteorite destroys 2,200 square kilometers of forest at Tunguska, Siberia.

JULY

July 1, 1777: Death of Confucian philosopher Dai Zhen.

July 1, 1913: A radio signal emitted from the Eiffel Tower allows clocks around the world to be synchronized for the first time.

July 1, 1963: Maryland Committee for Church-State Separation, the precursor to American Atheists, is founded.

July 2, 1877: Birth of Hermann Hesse, Swiss German novelist and poet.

July 2, 1890: Propagandist Press Committee, predecessor to the Rationalist Press Association, first meets.

July 2, 1964: US Civil Rights Act passed.

July 3, 1904: Death of Theodor Herzl, founder of the Zionist movement.

July 3, 1927: First issue of the New Zealand freethought paper the *Truthseeker* is published.

July 4, 1776: United States declaration of independence is signed.

July 4, 1780: Thomas Paine awarded an Honorary Masters of Arts degree by the University of Pennsylvania.

July 4, 1826: Death of Thomas Jefferson.

July 4, 1826: Robert Owen gives his "Declaration of Mental Independence" address.

July 4, 1902: Death of Vivekananda, Indian religious-humanist reformer.

July 5, 1948: National Health Service Act creates publicly funded health service in Britain.

July 5, 1996: Dolly the cloned sheep is born at the Roslin Institute, Edinburgh.

July 6, 1415: Jan Hus burned as a heretic in Constance, Switzerland.

July 7, 1668: Isaac Newton receives his MA from Trinity College, Cambridge.

July 7, 1907: Birth of Robert Heinlein, science fiction author.

July 7, 1981: Sandra Day O'Connor becomes the first woman to serve on the American Supreme Court.

July 8, 1822: Percy Bysshe Shelley drowns in Italy.

July 8, 1853: Commodore Perry anchors in Tokyo Bay, opening up Japan to Western influence.

July 9 1595: Johannes Kepler publishes *Mysterium Cosmographicum*.

July 10, 1953: KGB boss Lavrenti Beria is arrested.

July 10, 1955: "In God We Trust" added to US currency.

July 11: World Population Day.

July 11, 1533: Pope Clement VII excommunicates Henry VIII.

July 12, 1555: Paul IV issues *Cum Nimis Absurdum*, which restricts Jews to a ghetto and institutes a large number of discriminatory measures against them.

July 12, 1906: All convictions against Alfred Dreyfus are annulled, ending France's most shameful episode of official anti-Semitism.

July 13, 1934: Birth of Nigerian humanist author Wole Soyinka.

July 13, 1995: The Galileo spacecraft releases the first probe to Jupiter.

July 14, 1789: Parisian mob storms the Bastille, launching the French Revolution.

July 14, 1858: Birth of Emmeline Pankhurst, suffragette pioneer.

July 15, 1099: Christians on the First Crusade liberate Jerusalem by massacring many thousands of its inhabitants.

July 15, 1919: Birth of Iris Murdoch.

July 16, 622: Day one of the first year of the Muslim era.

July 16, 1918: The Romanov royal family is murdered in Ekaterinburg, Russia.

July 17, 1945: Churchill, Truman, and Stalin meet at Potsdam to arrange the shape of the postwar world.

July 17, 1959: Mary Leakey discovers *Zinjanthropus boisei* in Olduvai Gorge, Tanzania.

July, 18 1870: Dogma of Papal Infallibility declared at First Vatican Council.

July 18, 1918: Birth of Nelson Mandela.

July 19, 64 CE: In the grip of apocalyptic fervor, Christians fan the flames of Rome, which burns to the ground.

July 19, 1848: Elizabeth Cady Stanton opens the first Women's Rights Convention in the United States, in Seneca Falls, New York.

July 19, 1856: Birth of George Bernard Shaw.

July 20, 1304: Birth of Petrarch, patron of Renaissance humanism.

July 20, 1889: Birth of Emanuel Haldeman-Julius.

July 20, 1933: Vatican signs concordat with Nazi Germany.

July 20, 1944: The bomb plot against Adolf Hitler fails.

July 20, 1969: Neil Armstrong sets foot on the moon.

July 21, 356 BCE: Herostratus destroys the temple of Artemis in Ephesus in an attempt to be remembered forever.

July 21, 1542: Universal Inquisition established in Rome.

July 21, 1899: Death of Robert Ingersoll.

July 21, 1925: John Scopes found guilty of teaching evolution in Dayton, Tennessee.

July 21, 1990: Roger Waters plays *The Wall* in Potsdamer Platz, Berlin.

July 22, 1822: Birth of Gregor Mendel, discoverer of genetics.

July 22, 1988: Five hundred American scientists agree to boycott Pentagon germ-warfare research.

July 23, 1858: British parliament ends legal discrimination against Jews.

July 24, 1911: Hiram Bingham rediscovers the lost Inca city of Machu Picchu, in Peru.

July 24, 1974: During the Watergate scandal, President Nixon is told he must hand over the tapes of Oval Office conversations.

July 25, 1909: Louis Bleriot crosses the English Channel in a plane, the first international flight ever made.

July 25, 1920: Birth of Rosalind Franklin, pioneer molecular biologist.

July 25, 1943: Mussolini is arrested; fascist regime collapses.

July 25, 1968: In *Humanae Vitae*, Pope Paul VI bans all forms of birth control for Roman Catholics.

July 25, 1978: Birth of Louise Brown, the world's first test-tube baby.

July 26, 1894: Birth of Aldous Huxley.

July 26, 1956: Nasser nationalizes the Suez Canal.

July 27, 1586: Sir Walter Raleigh brings the first consignment of tobacco to Europe.

July 27, 1656: Baruch Spinoza expelled from the synagogue in Amsterdam for his beliefs.

July 28, 1804: Birth of Ludwig Feuerbach.

July 28, 1902: Karl Popper born in Vienna.

July 28, 2004: Death of Francis Crick, codiscoverer of the structure of DNA.

July 29, 1099: Death of Pope Urban II, who preached the crusades.

July 29, 1890: Death of Vincent van Gogh.

July 31, 1941: Hermann Goering orders Reinhard Heydrich to prepare the "final solution" to the Jewish problem.

July 31, 1951: Emanuel Haldeman-Julius drowns in his swimming pool.

July 31, 2001: Judge Roy Moore unveils his 5,000 Ten Commandments slab in Alabama, which was later declared unconstitutional.

AUGUST

August 1, 1744: Birth of Jean-Baptiste de Lamarck, pre-Darwinian evolutionist.

August 1, 1774: Joseph Priestley identifies oxygen.

August 2, 1492: Ferdinand and Isabella expel Jews from Spain.

August 2, 1990: Saddam Hussein invades Kuwait.

August 3, 1492: Christopher Columbus sets off to discover the Indies.

August 3, 1546: Etienne Dolet, printer to Erasmus and Rabelais, burned at the stake.

August 4, 1792: Birth of Percy Bysshe Shelley.

August 4, 1892: Death of Ernestine Rose, freethought and feminist pioneer.

August 4, 1944: Anne Frank is arrested by the Nazis.

August 4, 1965: Bodies of murdered atheist civil-rights martyr Michael Schwerner and his two colleagues are found.

August 5, 1858: First transatlantic telegraph sent.

August 5, 1963: Test Ban Treaty signed between USA, USSR, and Britain in Moscow.

August 6, 1945, atomic bomb dropped on Hiroshima.

August 6, 1862: Alfred Domett becomes New Zealand's first freethinking premier.

August 6, 1962: Birth of Taslima Nasrin.

August 6, 1991: Tim Berners-Lee announces the existence of the World Wide Web.

August 7, 1860: Death of Charles Southwell, New Zealand's first freethinker.

August 7, 1941: Death of Indian poet Rabindranath Tagore.

August 8, 1588: Spanish Armada defeated by the English fleet.

August 8, 1902: Birth of theoretical physicist Paul Dirac.

August 9, 1936: Jesse Owens outruns Nazi athletes at Berlin Olympics.

August 9, 1945: Plutonium bomb dropped on Nagasaki.

August 9, 1962: Death of Hermann Hesse, Swiss German novelist and poet.

August 9, 1974: Richard Nixon resigns as president of the United States.

August 9, 1977: First meeting of the Committee for the Scientific Investigation of Claims of the Paranormal (CSICOP) executive council.

August 10, 1675: King Charles II lays the foundation stone of the Royal Observatory, Greenwich.

August 10, 1846: Legislation is passed in Washington to create the Smithsonian Institution.

August 11, 3114 BCE: Beginning of the world according to Mayan Indians.

August 11, 1833: Birth of Robert Ingersoll.

August 12, 1887: Birth of German physicist Erwin Schrödinger.

August 12, 1961: Barrier constructed around West Berlin, later strengthened to become the Berlin Wall.

August 13, 1876: Richard Wagner's epic *Der Ring des Nibelungen* opens in Bayreuth.

August 13, 1899: Birth of Alfred Hitchcock.

August 14, 1941: Churchill and Roosevelt sign the Atlantic Charter.

August 14, 1945: President Truman announces the unconditional surrender of Japan.

August 15, 1947: India becomes independent and the largest democracy on earth.

August 15, 1969: The Woodstock concert opens in the United States.

August 16, 1819: The Peterloo Massacre, in which eleven people protesting for reform in England are killed by government troops.

August 16, 1842: George Jacob Holyoake is sentenced to six months prison for blasphemy.

August 16, 1884: Robert Stout, freethinker and rationalist, becomes premier of New Zealand.

August 16, 1977: Elvis Presley found dead.

August 17, 1896: Bridget Driscoll of Croydon, Surrey, is killed by a car traveling at four miles per hour, becoming the first pedestrian fatality from a car.

August 17, 1932: Birth of novelist and essayist V. S. Naipaul.

August 18, 1227: Death of Genghiz Khan.

August 18, 2001: Dr. Sheikh sentenced to death for blasphemy in Pakistan on trumped-up charges.

August, 19 14 CE: Death of the first Roman Emperor, Augustus.

August 19, 1921: Birth of Gene Roddenberry, creator of *Star Trek*.

August 20, 1880: First meeting of the International Federation of Freethinkers, in Brussels.

August 20, 1884: Birth of German demythologizing theologian Rudolf Bultmann.

August 20, 2001: Death of Fred Hoyle.

August 21, 1817: In a major public address in London, Robert Owen announces his rejection of religious belief.

August 21, 1952: First congress of IHEU begins in Amsterdam.

August 22, 1862: Birth of composer Claude Debussy.

August 22, 1864: Twelve countries sign the Geneva Convention, which protects the rights of prisoners of war.

August 22, 1974: Death of Jacob Bronowski.

August 23, 1609: Galileo demonstrates his telescope.

August 23, 1939: Hitler and Stalin shock the world by signing a pact, which includes the dismemberment of Poland.

August 24, 79 CE: Mt. Vesuvius erupts, destroying Pompeii and Herculaneum.

August 24, 410 CE: Alaric the Goth sacks Rome.

August 24, 1661: Act of Uniformity is passed, which required all clergymen, academics, and teachers in England to be members of the Church of England.

August 25, 325 CE: Council of Nicaea, which established Christian orthodoxy, ends.

August 25, 1776: Death of David Hume.

August 25, 1900: Death of Friedrich Nietzsche.

August 25, 1973: The first CAT scan is made.

August 26, 1789: French Assembly approves the Declaration of the Rights of Man and Citizen.

August 26, 1952: The International Humanist and Ethical Union (IHEU) inaugural congress issues the Amsterdam Declaration.

August 26, 1970: Betty Friedan leads the Women's Strike for Equality on the fiftieth anniversary of women getting the vote in the United States.

August 26, 1973: *Humanist Manifesto II* is released.

August 27, 1660: The works of John Milton are burned on the orders of the newly restored English monarch, Charles II.

August 27, 1867: Karl Heinrich Ulrichs becomse the first person to publicly state his homosexuality, at a conference of German Jurists in Munich, Germany.

August 27, 1996: Death of Gordon Stein.

August 28, 1749: Birth of Johann Wolfgang Goethe.

August 28, 1963: Martin Luther King Jr. gives his "I have a dream" speech, igniting the civil-rights movement in America.

August 29, 1632: Birth of John Locke.

August 29, 1949, USSR tests its first atomic device.

August 29, 1966: Sayyid Qutb, godfather of Islamic terrorism, is executed in Egypt.

August 30, 1797: Birth of Mary Wollstonecraft Shelley.

August 30, 1831: Charles Darwin invited to travel aboard the HMS *Beagle*.

August 30, 1871: Birth of Ernest Rutherford, New Zealand–born physicist.

August 30, 1891: Annie Besant gives her farewell address to the secularist movement.

August 30, 1963: The hotline between Washington and Moscow goes into operation.

August 31, 1989: Norm Allen and Paul Kurtz found African Americans for Humanism.

August 31, 1997: Death of Princess Diana.

SEPTEMBER

September 1, 5509 BCE: Creation of the world, according to the Byzantine calendar.

September 1, 1868: Birth of Chapman Cohen.

September 2, 1945: VJ Day, as Japan signs unconditional surrender aboard US battleship *Missouri*.

September 2, 1969: NBC cancels *Star Trek*.

September 3, 1260: The Mongol advance is halted by the Mamelukes at the battle of Ain Jalut, north of Jerusalem.

September 3, 1759: Pope Clement XIII instructs all Catholics to hand in copies of Denis Diderot's *Encyclopedia* for destruction.

September 3, 1939: World War II begins.

September 4, 476 CE: Romulus Augustulus is deposed, bringing the Western Roman Empire to an end.

September 4, 1905: Birth of Mary Renault, English author.

September 4, 1965: Death of Albert Schweitzer.

September 5, 1793: French National Convention votes to begin the "Reign of Terror" in defence of the revolution.

September 5, 1972: Palestinian terrorists attack Israeli athletes at Munich Olympics.

September 6, 1795: Birth of Frances Wright.

September 6, 1966: Death of Margaret Sanger.

September 7, 1978: The first genetically engineered insulin is produced.

September 8, 1966: First screening of *Star Trek*.

September 8, 2000: UN devises the Millennium Development Goals.

September 9–10, 1889: Charles Bradlaugh debates Rev. Marsden Gibson on the question of "Has Humanity Gained from Unbelief?"

September 9, 1971: John Lennon's album *Imagine* is released in the United States.

September 10, 1797: Death of Mary Wollstonecraft, pioneer feminist.

September 10, 1941: Birth of palaeontologist Stephen Jay Gould.

September 11, 1857: Mormons instigate massacre of 120 settlers heading for California, including seventeen children, at Mountain Meadows.

September 11, 1973: Salvador Allende is murdered during a CIA-inspired coup in Chile.

September 11, 2001: Twin Towers and Pentagon bombing.

September 12, 490 BCE: Athens defeats the Persian Empire at the battle of Marathon.

September 12, 1961: Bertrand Russell imprisoned for his part in antinuclear demonstrations.

September 12, 1977: Murder of Steve Biko, antiapartheid activist, by South African police.

September 13, 1872: Death of Ludwig Feuerbach.

September 14, 1879: Birth of Margaret Sanger.

September 14, 1919: Adolf Hitler joins the Nazi Party.

September 15, 1835: HMS *Beagle*, with Charles Darwin aboard, reaches the Galapagos Islands.

September 15, 1940: Battle of Britain Day, the turning point in the air war.

September 16, 1327: Cecco d'Ascoli is burned at the stake as a heretic by the Inquisition.

September 16, 1987: Montreal Protocols are signed, which agrees to reduce production of CFCs in an attempt to protect the ozone layer.

September 17, 1743: Birth of French *philosophe* Marquis de Condorcet.

September 17, 1787: United States Constitution is signed.

September 17, 1994: Death of Karl Popper.

September, 18 1899: First meeting of the Rationalist Press Association.

September 18, 1970: Death of guitarist Jimi Hendrix.

September 19, 1991: The iceman corpse is discovered on the Austrian Italian border.

September 20, 1792: France passes law legalizing civil marriage and permitting divorce in cases of adultery, ill-treatment, and mutual consent.

September 20, 1870: Collapse of the Papal States, which become part of Italy.

September 21, 1860: Death of Arthur Schopenhauer.

September 21, 1866: Birth of H. G. Wells.

September 22, 1792: French revolutionary government declares this day as the first day of year one.

September 22, 1927: Bertrand and Dora Russell open Beacon Hill School.

September 23, 480 BCE: Greeks defeat the Persian invasion at the battle of Salamis.

September 23, 1846: German astronomer Johann Galle discovers Neptune.

September 24, 2001: Taliban calls for a jihad against the United States.

September 25, 1789: James Madison steers the Bill of Rights through Congress.

September 25, 1890: God tells the Mormons to give up polygamy.

September 26, 1833: Birth of Charles Bradlaugh.

September 27, 1791: French revolutionary government becomes the first country to extend full civil rights to Jews.

September 27, 1919: Sir Arthur Eddington confirms the truth of the general theory of relativity by observing the perihelion of Mercury.

September 28, 551 BCE: Birth of Confucius.

September 28, 1978: Pope John Paul I dies in mysterious circumstances in the Vatican.

September 28, 1995: The last day Madalyn Murray O'Hair is seen alive.

September 29, 1902: French novelist and crusading journalist Emile Zola dies in suspicious circumstances.

September 29, 1938: The Munich Agreement dismembers Czechoslovakia.

September 29, 1995: Most likely date of the death of Madalyn Murray O'Hair.

September 30, 1784: Immanuel Kant finishes his famous essay "What is Enlightenment?"

September 30, 1997: Roman Catholic Church in France apologizes for its inaction in regard to Jews during World War II.

OCTOBER

October 1, 1847: Birth of Annie Besant.

October 1, 1893: Final issue of Charles Bradlaugh's paper, the *National Reformer*.

October 2, 1836: Charles Darwin returns to England after his voyage on the *Beagle*.

October 2, 1869: Birth of Mohandas Gandhi.

October 2, 1958: Death of Marie Stopes, British birth-control pioneer.

October 3, 1793: Thomas Paine denounced as a traitor by the French revolutionary government for opposing the death of the king.

October 3, 1925: Birth of American novelist and critic Gore Vidal.

October 4, 1947: Death of Max Planck.

October 4, 1957: The Soviet Union launches *Sputnik*, the first trip into space.

October 4, 2000: Dr. Younas Sheikh is arrested in Pakistan on blasphemy charges.

October 5, 1713: Birth of Denis Diderot.

October 5, 1969: *Monty Python's Flying Circus* airs for the first time.

October 5, 1989: Televangelist Jim Bakker is convicted of multiple fraud.

October 6, 1981: Egyptian president Anwar Sadat is assassinated by fundamentalists.

October 6, 1984: Death of prominent evolutionist George Gaylord Simpson.

October 6, 1998: Fatal beating in Wyoming of Matthew Shepard by two fundamentalist homophobes.

October 8, 1906: Birth of Sayyid Qutb, Muslim philosopher of terrorism.

October 8, 1958: Dr. Åke Senning implants the first internal heart pacemaker.

October 9, 1940: Birth of John Lennon.

October 10, 1813: Birth of composer Giuseppi Verdi.

October 10, 1963: The Nuclear Test Ban Treaty comes into operation.

October 11, 1957: Britain's radiotelescope at Jodrell Bank comes into operation.

October 12, 1998: Death of Matthew Shepard, after fatal beating by two fundamentalist homophobes.

October 13, 1909: Freethinking radical Francisco Ferrer is executed in Spain.

October 13, 1988: Shroud of Turin is proven to be a Medieval forgery.

October 13, 2002: Islamic terrorists blast a nightclub in Bali, killing two hundred young people.

October 14, 1646: The word "rationalist" is used for the first time, in an English newspaper.

October 14, 1893: Congress of the International Federation of Freethinkers is forcibly broken up by the Spanish government.

October 14, 1964: China joins the nuclear club, exploding its first nuclear device.

October 14, 1999: World population reaches six billion according to the UN Population Fund.

October 15, 70 BCE: Reputed birth date of the Roman poet Virgil.

October 15, 1844: Birth of Friedrich Nietzsche.

October 15, 1880: Birth of Marie Stopes, British birth-control pioneer.

October 15, 1980: Council of Secular Humanism founded.

October 15, 1980: *Secular Humanist Declaration* appears on the front page of the *New York Times*.

October 16, 1854: Birth of Oscar Wilde.

October 16, 1902: In the face of religious persecution, feminist pioneer Ida Craddock commits suicide in New York.

October 17, 1915: Death of G. W. Foote.

October 17, 1952: New Zealand Rationalist Association is prosecuted under Indecent Publications Act for promoting the *Journal of Sex Education*, which advocated contraception and safe sex.

October 18, 1685: Revocation of the Edict of Nantes, which forbids all religious belief and activity that is not Catholic.

October 18, 1931: Death of Thomas Edison.

October 19, 1781: General Cornwallis surrenders at Yorktown, ending the American War of Independence.

October 19, 1812: Napoleon begins his retreat from Moscow.

October 19, 1900: Max Planck outlines the basics of quantum physics to the Berlin Physical Society.

October 20, 1859: Birth of John Dewey.

October 21, 1833: Birth of Alfred Nobel.

October 21, 1945: Women can vote for the first time in France.

October 22, 1962: Cuban Missile Crisis begins, and the world hovers on the brink of nuclear war.

October 22, 1965: *Time* magazine asks the question on its front cover, "Is God Dead?"

October 22, 1996: Pope John Paul II acknowledges that evolution is "more than a hypothesis."

October 23, 4004 BCE: The day of creation, according to Archbishop Ussher.

October 23, 1997: The day the world should have ended in rapture according to Archbishop Ussher.

October 24, 1648: Treaty of Westphalia is signed, which ends the Thirty Years' War and establishes a new order in Europe.

October 24, 1827: Robert Taylor faces his first conviction for "blasphemy."

October 24, 1945: Creation of the United Nations, now celebrated as United Nations Day.

October 24, 1991: Death of Gene Roddenberry, creator of *Star Trek*.

October 25, 1838: Birth of Georges Bizet, French composer.

October 25, 1946: Karl Popper is menaced with a poker wielded by Ludwig Wittgenstein at the Cambridge Moral Science Club.

October 26, 1902: Death of Elizabeth Cady Stanton.

October 26, 1947: Birth of Hillary Rodham Clinton.

October 27, 1553: Michael Servetus is burned at the stake in Geneva for being a heretic.

October 27, 1939: Birth of John Cleese.

October 28, 312: Constantine wins the battle of Milvian Bridge, and converts to Christianity.

October 28, 1965: Pope Paul VI issues *Nostra Aetete*, which absolves the Jews of the collective responsibility of having killed Jesus.

October 29, 1783: Death of French encyclopedist Jean le Rond d'Alembert.

October 29, 1910: Birth of A. J. Ayer.

October 29, 1923: The secular Republic of Turkey is founded by Kemal Attatürk.

October 29, 1929: Black Tuesday, the Wall Street Crash leading to the Depression.

October 30, 1270: The eighth and final crusade is launched.

October 30, 1938: Orson Welles starts a panic in New York with his *War of the Worlds* radio program.

October 31, 1517: Martin Luther nails ninety-five theses for reform of the church on the door of the court church in Wittenberg, unleashing the Reformation.

October 31, 1984: Assassination of Indira Gandhi.

NOVEMBER

November 1885: First issue of *Watts' Literary Guide*, which is still in print today, now called the *New Humanist*.

November 1, 1755: Lisbon Earthquake, which provoked Voltaire's famous poem questioning God's apparent unconcern in the face of such suffering.

November 1, 1950: Pius XII announces the Assumption of Mary as infallible teaching, the only time papal infallibility has formally been used.

November 2, 1815: Birth of George Boole, English mathematician.

November 2, 1950: Death of George Bernard Shaw.

November 2, 2004: Dutch filmmaker Theo van Gogh murdered in Amsterdam by a Muslim fanatic.

November 3, 1394: Charles VI expels the Jews from France.

November 3, 1793: Olympe de Gouge, author of the *Declaration of the Rights of Woman*, is guillotined.

November 4, 1184: Pope Lucius III issues the decretal *Ad abolendum* to "make inquisition" for heresy.

November 4, 1646: Massachusetts enacts death penalty for all forms of heresy.

November 4, 1796: United States signs the Treaty of Tripoli, in which it declares it is in no sense a Christian nation.

November 4, 1869: The first issue of *Nature* appears.

November 5, 1892: Birth of J. B. S. Haldane, English geneticist.

November 5, 1906: Marie Curie becomes the first woman to lecture at the Sorbonne.

November 5, 1963: Viking origins in Newfoundland are discovered.

November 6, 1794: Thomas Paine is released from jail in France.

November 6, 1841: First issue of the *Oracle of Reason* is released, the first periodical dedicated to the promotion of atheism.

November 6, 1992: Richard Dawkins gives his "Religion as a Virus" address at Conway Hall, London.

November 6, 2003: Bush administration enacts a ban on partial-birth abortion, widely seen as a step toward a total ban.

November 7, 1637: Anne Hutchinson becomes the first American to be charged with heresy.

November 7, 1867: Birth of Marie Curie.

November 7, 1967: In New Zealand, theologian Lloyd Geering is acquitted of heresy at a Presbyterian show trial.

November 8, 392: Emperor Theodosius I imposes a complete ban on the worship of pagan gods.

November 8, 1895: William Röntgen discovers x-rays.

November 9, 1934: Birth of Carl Sagan.

November 9, 1989: The Berlin Wall is breached.

November 10, 1483: Birth of Martin Luther.

November 10, 2002: Declared by UNESCO as the World Science Day for Peace and Development.

November 11, 1867: Birth of Joseph McCabe.

November 11, 1997: The Universal Declaration on the Human Genome and Human Rights is adopted by UNESCO.

November 12, 1815: Birth of Elizabeth Cady Stanton.

November 12, 1921: In England J. W. Gott is sentenced to nine months hard labor for publishing two rationalist pamphlets.

November 13, 1791: French revolutionary government gives full citizenship to Jews, the first time they have had this right since 70 CE.

November 13, 1971: Mariner 9 enters the orbit of Mars, the first man-made object to do so.

November 14, 1856: Birth of J. M. Robertson.

November 14, 1889: Birth of Jawaharlal Nehru.

November 14, 1989: Death of Andrei Sakharov.

November 15, 1630: Death of Johannes Kepler.

November 15, 1902: Birth of Gora.

November 16, 1717: Birth of French encyclopedist, Jean le Rond d'Alembert.

November 16, 1946: UNESCO comes into operation.

November 17, 1858: Death of Robert Owen.

November 17, 1869: The Suez Canal is opened.

November 17, 1937: Birth of British comedian Peter Cook.

November 18, 1647: Birth of Pierre Bayle.

November 18, 1910: "Black Friday," arrest and detention of prominent Suffragettes in the United Kingdom.

November 18, 1978: Jim Jones's cult followers commit mass suicide in Guyana.

November 19, 1469: Birth of Guru Nanak, founder of the Sikh religion.

November 19, 1711: Birth of Russian Enlightenment figure Mikhail Lomonosov.

November 19, 1863: Abraham Lincoln delivers the Gettysburg Address.

November 20, 1906: Rev. Algernon Sidney Crapsey found guilty of heresy by New York Episcopal Church after becoming a rationalist.

November 20, 1945: Start of the Nuremberg war crimes trial, the first international trial of its kind in world history.

November 20, 1959: The UN adopts this day as Children's Rights Day.

November 21, 1694: Birth of Voltaire.

November 21, 2003: Dr. Younas Sheikh is released from jail in Pakistan.

November 22, 1819: Birth of Mary Ann Evans, "George Eliot."

November 22, 1963: Assassination of President Kennedy.

November 23, 1644: John Milton's *Areopagitica* is published, which becomes a rallying call for freedom of the press.

November 23, 1970: Pope Paul VI bans cardinals over eighty from voting for a pope.

November 24, 1632: Birth of Baruch Spinoza.

November 24, 1859: *The Origin of Species* is published.

November 24, 1970: Eric Idle's *Philosopher's Song* airs on television for the first time, on *Monty Python's Flying Circus.*

November 25, 1948: Cable television invented by Ed Parsons, an American inventor.

November 25, 2001: American scientists clone the first human embryo.

November 26, 1894: Birth of Norbert Weiner, founder of cybernetics.

November 26, 1966: The first tidal power station opens in France.

November 27, 1095: Pope Urban II preaches crusades against the Muslims.

November 28, 1820: Birth of Friedrich Engels.

November 28, 1967: Pulsars discovered by Jocelyn Bell, a graduate student at Cambridge University.

November 29, 1951: The United States carries out the first underground nuclear test.

November 30, 1835: Birth of Samuel Clemens, "Mark Twain."

November 30, 1874: Birth of Winston Churchill.

DECEMBER

December 1, 1959: Twelve nations sign the Antarctic Treaty.

December 1, 1964: Death of J. B. S. Haldane, English geneticist.

December 2, 1915: Albert Einstein's general theory of relativity is published.

December 2, 1942: First self-sustaining nuclear reaction started by human beings takes place in Chicago.

December 2, 1954: US Senate condemns Senator Joseph McCarthy for his witch hunt against supposed communists.

December 3, 1857: Birth of novelist Joseph Conrad.

December 3, 1893: Death of radical scientist John Tyndall.

December 3, 1984: Toxic gases from the Union Carbide factory in Bhopal, India, escape, killing and injuring tens of thousands of people.

December 4, 1131: Death of Omar Khayyam.

December 4, 1930: The Vatican approves the rhythm method of birth control.

December 5, 1901: Birth of Werner Heisenberg, discoverer of the Uncertainty Principle.

December 5, 1974: Last television screening of *Monty Python's Flying Circus*.

December 6, 334 BCE: Birth of Zeno the Stoic.

December 6, 1905: French Senate passes the bill for the separation of church and state.

December 6, 1956: Death of Dr. Ambedkar, campaigner for rights of untouchables in India.

December 6, 1992: Hindu fundamentalists destroy the Babri Masjid mosque in Ayodhya, sparking years of religious tension in India.

December 7, 1928: Birth of Noam Chomsky.

December 7, 1988: Mikhail Gorbachev gives a momentous speech to the UN, where he declares that the October Revolution belongs to history.

December 8, 1840: Henry Hetherington charged with blasphemy for distributing freethought pamphlets.

December 8, 1854: Pius IX enacts the Dogma of the Immaculate Conception.

December 8, 1864: Pius IX enacts the *Syllabus of Errors* which condemns most of the precepts of modernity.

December 8, 1864: Death of George Boole, English mathematician.

December 8, 1980: Assassination of John Lennon.

December 8, 1991: USSR is dissolved.

December 8, 1948: Draft of the Genocide Convention is adopted.

December 9, 1968: First use of a computer mouse.

December 9, 1996: Death of Mary Leakey, paleoanthropologist.

December 10, 1901: First Nobel Peace Prize awarded.

December 10, 1921: Albert Einstein presented Nobel Prize for physics.

December 10, 1948: Human Rights Day proclaimed at UN meeting in Paris.

December 10, 1979: Pope John Paul II acknowledges that the "Galileo question" should be reconsidered.

December 11, 1856: First issue of Charles Southwell's *Examiner*.

December 11, 1901: Guglielmo Marconi sends the first radio signal across the Atlantic Ocean.

December 12, 1863: Birth of Norwegian artist Edvard Munch.

December 12, 2000: US Supreme Court votes

5–4 to give George W. Bush victory over Al Gore.

December 13, 1545: Council of Trent opens, which sets the tone for the Counter-Reformation.

December 14, 1512: Hermann van Ryswyck burned at the stake for renouncing Christianity.

December 14, 1900: Max Planck gives first outline of quantum mechanics.

December 15, 1791: The Bill of Rights in United States is passed.

December 16, 1774: Boston Tea Party, where Boston citizens protest against a duty on tea they had not been consulted on.

December 16, 1917: Birth of Arthur C. Clarke.

December 16, 1951: Bertrand Russell outlines his "Liberal Decalogue" in the *New York Times*.

December 17: Date for the Roman Saturnalia festival.

December 17, 1538: Pope Paul III excommunicates Henry VIII.

December 18, 1829: Death of Jean-Baptiste de Lamarck, pre-Darwinian evolutionist.

December 18, 1912: Charles Dawson and Sir Arthur Smith Woodward reveal Piltdown Man to the Geological Society.

December 19, 1944: Birth of Richard Leakey, anthropologist and conservationist.

December 19, 1958: First radio message to Earth from space, from the American satellite Project Score.

December 20, 1860: South Carolina secedes from the Union over the issue of slavery, the first southern state to do so.

December 20, 1902: Birth of Sidney Hook.

December 20, 1952: Draft Convention of the Status of Women is passed at the United Nations.

December 20, 1996: Death of Carl Sagan.

December 21, 1620: The *Mayflower* lands at Plymouth, Massachusetts.

December 21, 1925: Birth of Paul Kurtz.

December 22, 1880: Death of George Eliot.

December 22, 1894: French soldier Alfred Dreyfus is convicted of treason in an example of hysterical anti-Semitism.

December 22, 1968: First live telecast from a manned spacecraft, from Apollo VIII.

December 23, 1954: Bertrand Russell broadcasts "Man's Peril," which acts as a catalyst to the creation of the antinuclear movement.

December 24, 1865: Ku Klux Klan is founded in Tennessee.

December 25: Birthday of Hercules, Mithras, Zas, Horus, Dionysus, Vishnu, Agni, and Tammuz.

December 25, 274 CE: Emperor Aurelian institutes this day as the birthday of the Unconquered Sun.

December 25, 336 CE: Declared by Christians in the West as the birthday of Jesus Christ. Adopted in Constantinople in 379 or 380 and in Alexandria by 432.

December 25, 1642: Birth of Isaac Newton.

December 25, 2000: Death of W. V. O. Quine.

December 26, 1791: Birth of Charles Babbage, inventor of the Analytical Machine, the precursor to the computer.

December 26, 1898: Marie Curie discovers radium.

December 27, 1831: Charles Darwin sets sail aboard the HMS *Beagle*.

December 27, 1908: Followers of Lee J. Spangler gather on top of South Mountain, near Nyack, New York, in specially made white dresses for the apocalypse Spangler had predicted.

December 28, 1706: Death of Pierre Bayle.

December 28, 1793: Thomas Paine is thrown in prison in France for opposing the killing of the deposed king.

December 28, 1945: US Congress officially endorses the Pledge of Allegiance.

December 29, 1889: Charles Bradlaugh addresses the Indian National Congress.

December 29, 1952: The first transistor hearing aid goes on sale.

December 30, 1924: Edwin Hubble announces the existence of other galaxies.

December 31, 1879: Thomas Edison demonstrates his electric light for the first time.

December 31, 1882: Death of French reformer Leon Gambetta.